About the cover

Edgar Degas, *The Cotton Exchange, New Orleans, 1873*

The cover image presents a portion of the larger painting that appears below. When they explore American histories, scholars consider many different aspects of America's past and connect them for a rich, fresh synthesis. This painting by the French artist Edgar Degas, whose aunt and uncle lived in Louisiana, appears to depict a thriving cotton business. However, the full picture includes a young man (Degas's brother René) reading *The Daily Picayune*, which reported the business's bankruptcy in 1873. Moreover, the painting does not show either the establishment in 1871 of the centralized New Orleans Cotton Exchange, which pushed out smaller competitors, or the laborers, including millions of newly freed African Americans, who produced the cotton sold by white entrepreneurs.

THE UNITED STATES

Elevation

Feet	Meters
Over 13,001	Over 3,001
6,561–13,000	2,001–3,000
3,281–6,560	1,001–2,000
1,641–3,280	501–1,000
661–1,640	201–500
0–660	0–200
Below sea level	Below sea level

CANADA

ATLANTIC OCEAN

PACIFIC OCEAN

Gulf of Mexico

MEXICO

BAHAMAS

CUBA

States and labels

MAINE — Augusta, Portland
N.H. — Concord, Manchester
VERMONT — Montpelier, Burlington
MASS. — Boston
R.I. — Providence
CONN. — Hartford, New Haven
NEW YORK — Albany, New York, Buffalo
Mt. Washington (6,288 ft.; 1,917 m)
Mt. Marcy
Lake Ontario
Lake Erie
Hudson River
NEW JERSEY — Trenton
DELAWARE — Dover
PENNSYLVANIA — Harrisburg, Philadelphia, Pittsburgh, Wheeling
MARYLAND — Baltimore, Annapolis
WASHINGTON, D.C.
Chesapeake Bay
Potomac River
VIRGINIA — Richmond, Norfolk
W. VA. — Charleston
NORTH CAROLINA — Raleigh, Charlotte
SOUTH CAROLINA — Columbia, Charleston
Mt. Mitchell (6,684 ft.; 2,037 m)
TIDEWATER
APPALACHIAN MTS.
GEORGIA — Atlanta
FLORIDA — Jacksonville, Orlando, Tallahassee, Miami
Lake Okeechobee
OHIO — Columbus, Cleveland, Cincinnati
Detroit
Lansing
MICHIGAN
Lake Huron
Lake Superior
Lake Michigan
INDIANA — Indianapolis
KENTUCKY — Frankfort, Louisville
Ohio River
Cumberland River
Tennessee River
TENNESSEE — Nashville, Knoxville, Memphis
ALABAMA — Montgomery, Birmingham
Alabama River
MISSISSIPPI — Jackson
GEORGIA
WISCONSIN — Madison, Milwaukee
Chicago
ILLINOIS — Springfield
CENTRAL LOWLAND
IOWA — Des Moines
MINNESOTA — St. Paul, Minneapolis
MISSOURI — Jefferson City, Kansas City, St. Louis
Missouri River
Mississippi River
LOUISIANA — Baton Rouge, New Orleans
ARKANSAS — Little Rock
Sioux Falls
NORTH DAKOTA — Bismarck
SOUTH DAKOTA — Pierre
BADLANDS
BLACK HILLS
NEBRASKA — Lincoln, Omaha
Platte River
KANSAS — Topeka, Wichita
GREAT PLAINS
OKLAHOMA — Oklahoma City, Tulsa
Arkansas River
Red River
TEXAS — Austin, Dallas, Fort Worth, San Antonio, Houston, Lubbock, El Paso
EDWARDS PLATEAU
LLANO ESTACADO
Pecos River
MONTANA — Helena, Billings
Yellowstone River
Snake River
WYOMING — Cheyenne
COLORADO — Denver, Colorado Springs
Mt. Elbert (14,433 ft.; 4,399 m)
Pikes Peak (14,110 ft.; 4,301 m)
GREAT DIVIDE BASIN
ROCKY MOUNTAINS
NEW MEXICO — Santa Fe, Albuquerque
Rio Grande
Colorado River
IDAHO — Boise
UTAH — Salt Lake City
Great Salt Lake
GREAT BASIN
NEVADA — Carson City, Las Vegas
ARIZONA — Phoenix, Tucson
MOJAVE DESERT
WASHINGTON — Olympia, Seattle, Spokane
Mt. Rainier (14,411 ft.; 4,392 m)
Mt. St. Helens (8,366 ft.; 2,550 m)
Columbia River
OREGON — Salem, Portland, Eugene
CASCADE RANGE
COAST RANGES
SIERRA NEVADA
Mt. Whitney (14,494 ft.; 4,418 m)
CALIFORNIA — Sacramento, San Francisco, Oakland, San Jose, Fresno, Los Angeles, San Diego
San Joaquin River
St. Lawrence River

Compass
N E S W (compass rose)

Scale
300 miles
300 kilometers
150

Puerto Rico inset
PUERTO RICO — San Juan
VIRGIN ISLANDS
ATLANTIC OCEAN
Caribbean Sea
100 miles
100 kilometers
50

Hawaii inset
HAWAII
Kauai, Niihau, Oahu — Honolulu, Molokai, Lanai, Maui, Kahoolawe, Hawaii
PACIFIC OCEAN
100 miles
100 kilometers
50

Alaska inset
ALASKA — Juneau, Anchorage
Mt. McKinley (20,320 ft.; 6,194 m)
BROOKS RANGE
ALASKA RANGE
ALEUTIAN ISLANDS
CANADA
RUSSIA
Yukon River
ARCTIC OCEAN
Gulf of Alaska
Bering Sea
500 miles
500 kilometers
250

Exploring American Histories

VALUE EDITION

VALUE EDITION

Exploring American Histories

A BRIEF SURVEY

Nancy A. Hewitt
Rutgers University

Steven F. Lawson
Rutgers University

Bedford/St. Martin's
Boston ◆ New York

To Mary and Charles Takacs, Florence and Hiram Hewitt,
Sarah and Abraham Parker, Lena and Ben Lawson,
who made our American histories possible.

For Bedford/St. Martin's

Publisher for History: Mary V. Dougherty
Senior Executive Editor for History: William J. Lombardo
Director of Development for History: Jane Knetzger
Associate Editor: Jennifer Jovin
Senior Production Editor: Christina M. Horn
Senior Production Supervisor: Lisa McDowell
Executive Marketing Manager: Sandra McGuire
Production Assistant: Erica Zhang
Indexer: Leoni Z. McVey
Cartography: Mapping Specialists, Ltd.
Photo Researcher: Naomi Kornhauser
Senior Art Director: Anna Palchik
Text Designer: Jerilyn Bockorick
Cover Designer: Billy Boardman
Cover Art: Edgar Degas (1834–1917), *The Cotton Exchange, New Orleans,* 1873 (oil on canvas).
 Musée des Beaux-Arts, Pau, France/Giraudon/The Bridgeman Art Library.
Composition: Cenveo Publisher Services
Printing and Binding: RR Donnelley and Sons

President, Bedford/St. Martin's: Denise B. Wydra
Director of Marketing: Karen R. Soeltz
Production Director: Susan W. Brown
Director of Rights and Permissions: Hilary Newman

Manufactured in the United States of America.

8   7   6   5   4   3
f   e   d   c   b   a

For information, write: Bedford/St. Martin's, 75 Arlington Street, Boston, MA 02116
 (617-399-4000)

ISBN 978-1-4576-5984-3 (Combined Edition)
ISBN 978-1-4576-5986-7 (Volume 1)
ISBN 978-1-4576-5985-0 (Volume 2)

Preface
Why This Book This Way

Our extensive experience teaching American history in a wide variety of classrooms led us to conclude that students learn history most effectively when they read historical narrative in conjunction with primary sources. Our conviction inspired us to pioneer a new kind of textbook that integrated a historical narrative with documents in a single book. With this Value Edition of *Exploring American Histories,* we've broken new ground again with **LaunchPad**, an interactive e-book and course space all-in-one that makes customizing and assigning the book and its resources easy and efficient. LaunchPad can be used on its own or in conjunction with this printed text, giving instructors and students the best of both worlds—the narrative text in an inexpensive, easy-to-read printed format as well as our highly acclaimed Document Projects and other resources and supplements delivered electronically, where their use and combination are limited only by the imagination of the instructor. LaunchPad is loaded with the full-color e-book plus LearningCurve, an adaptive learning tool; two Document Projects per chapter; additional primary sources; videos; chapter summative quizzes; and more. To learn more about the benefits of LearningCurve and LaunchPad, see the "Versions and Supplements" section on page xvii.

Many Histories in a Single Resource

For *Exploring American Histories,* we sought to reconceive the relationship of the textbook and the reader to create a mutually supportive set of course materials designed to help our students appreciate the diversity of America's history, to help instructors teach that primary sources are the building blocks of historical interpretation, and to encourage students to see that every past event can and should be considered from multiple perspectives.

The most innovative aspect of *Exploring American Histories,* and what makes it a true alternative, is that its format introduces a unique textbook structure organized around the broad theme of *diversity.* Diversity supports our presentation of an inclusive historical narrative, one that recognizes the American past as a series of interwoven stories made by a multiplicity of historical actors. We do this within a strong national framework that allows our readers to see how the various stories fit together and to understand why they matter. Our narrative is complemented by a wide variety of documents (discussed more fully below) that engage students with the diverse historical actors. In one of the chapter 1 Document Projects, we explore the first encounters between Spaniards and Native Americans in the sixteenth century, including Hernán Cortés's attempt to convert the Aztecs to Catholicism and the Aztec leaders' defense of their own religion and customs. In chapter 23, after reading reports and petitions from government officials and scientists and an eyewitness account of the aftermath of the atomic bombing, students can consider whether the United States should have detonated bombs in Hiroshima and Nagasaki.

The theme of diversity also allows us to foreground the role of individual agency as we push readers to consider the reasons behind historical change. Each chapter opens with a pair of **American Histories**, biographies that showcase individuals who experienced and influenced events in a particular period, and then returns to them throughout the chapter to strengthen the connections and highlight their place in the bigger picture. These biographies cover both well-known Americans—such as Daniel Shays, Frederick Douglass, Andrew Carnegie, and Eleanor Roosevelt—and those who never gained fame or fortune—such as the activist Amy Kirby Post, organizer Luisa Moreno, and World War II internee Fred Korematsu. Introducing such a broad range of biographical subjects illuminates the many ways that individuals shaped and were shaped by historical events. This strategy also works to make visible throughout the chapter the intersections where history from the top down meets history from the bottom up and to connect social and political histories with economic, cultural, and diplomatic developments. We work to show that events at the national level, shaped by elite political and economic leaders, have a direct impact on the lives of ordinary people; at the same time, we demonstrate that actions at the local level often have a significant influence on decisions made at the centers of national government and commerce. The discussions of the interrelationship among international, national, and local theaters and actors incorporate the pathbreaking scholarship of the last three decades, which has focused on gender, race, class, and ethnicity in North America and the United States, and on colonization, empire, and globalization in the larger world.

There is no one story about the past; there are many stories, and so we wanted to emphasize these plural *Histories* in the book's title. Indeed, on the last day of our own survey classes, we measure our success by how well our students can demonstrate that they understand this rich complexity that is central to the discipline, and whether they can put the multiple stories they have come to understand into the context of the larger whole. Instructors at all types of schools share our goal, and we hope that *Exploring American Histories* will help them enrich their students' understanding of events of the past.

Online Document Projects

To further demonstrate our theme of diversity and plural histories, we have selected a wide array of primary-source materials for the two Online Document Projects in each chapter. For each project, we supply distinctive pedagogy designed to help students make connections between the documents and the text's big themes. Each project is clearly cross-referenced within the narrative and is easily accessible in LaunchPad so that students can delve into certain topics after having read the broader historical context. Many of these projects incorporate multimedia sources such as audio and video files that until recently were unavailable to work with in class. With LaunchPad, teachers can choose which Document Projects they want to assign, add their own documents and questions, and rearrange the chapters to fit the way they teach the U.S. survey course.

Each Document Project includes five or six documents focused on a theme or topic central to that chapter. It is introduced by a brief overview and ends with interpretive questions that ask students to draw conclusions based on what they have learned in the chapter and read in the sources. The **Interpret the Evidence** and **Put It in Context** questions prompt students to analyze the documents, compare them to each other, and place them in a larger historical framework. **Multiple-choice questions** quiz students on the main ideas and themes of the documents and provide instant feedback.

Our choices of documents were influenced by the kinds of primary sources that exist. For some periods of American history and some topics, the available primary sources are limited and fragmentary. For other eras and issues, the sources are varied and abundant, indeed sometimes overwhelming, especially as we move into the twentieth century. In all time periods, some groups of Americans are far better represented in primary sources than are others. People who were wealthy, well educated, and politically powerful produced and preserved many sources about their lives. And their voices are well represented in this textbook. But we have also provided documents by American Indians, enslaved Africans, colonial women, rural residents, immigrants, working people, and young people. Moreover, the lives of those who left few sources of their own can often be illuminated by reading documents written by elites to see what information these documents yield, intentionally or unintentionally, about less well-documented groups.

We understand that the instructor's role is crucial in teaching students how to analyze primary-source materials and develop interpretations. Teachers can use the documents to encourage critical thinking and also to measure students' understanding and assess their progress. The integration of the documents with the narrative should prompt students to read more closely than they usually do, as they will see more clearly the direct connection between the two. We have organized the documents to give instructors the flexibility to use them in many different ways—as in-class discussion prompts, for take-home writing assignments, and even as the basis for exam questions—and also in different combinations, as the documents can be compared and contrasted with one another. The instructor's manual for *Exploring American Histories* provides a wealth of creative suggestions for using the documents program effectively (see the "Versions and Supplements" section on pages xviii–xix for more information on all the available instructor resources).

More Help for Students

We know that students often need help making sense of their reading. As instructors, all of us have had students complain that they cannot figure out what's important in the textbooks we assign. For many of our students, especially those just out of high school, their college history survey textbook is likely the most difficult book they have ever encountered. We understand the challenges that our students face, so in addition to the extensive document program, we have included the following pedagogical features designed to aid student learning:

- ◆ **Review and Relate** questions help students focus on main themes and concepts presented in each major section of the chapter.
- ◆ **Key terms** in boldface highlight important content. All terms are defined in a glossary at the end of the book.
- ◆ Clear **conclusions** help students summarize what they've read.
- ◆ A two-page **Chapter Review** lets students review key terms, important concepts, and notable events.

In addition, the book includes access to **LearningCurve**, an online adaptive learning tool that promotes engaged reading and focused review. Cross-references at the end of every chapter in the text prompt students to log in and rehearse their understanding of the material they have just read. Students move at their own pace and accumulate points as they go, giving the interaction a gamelike feel. Feedback for incorrect responses explains why the answer is incorrect and directs students back to the text to review before they attempt to answer the question again. The end result is that students understand the key elements of the text better and come to class better prepared. See the inside front cover for more details.

We imagine *Exploring American Histories* as a new kind of American history textbook, one that not only offers a strong, concise narrative but also challenges students to construct their own interpretations through primary-source analysis. We are thrilled that our hopes have come to fruition, and we believe that our textbook will provide a thought-provoking and highly useful foundation for every U.S. history survey course and will benefit students and faculty alike. The numerous opportunities provided for active learning will allow teachers to engage students in stimulating ways and help them experience the past in closer connection to the present. After all, active learning is the basis for active citizenship, and teaching the survey course is our chance as historians, whose work is highly specialized, to reach the greatest number of undergraduates. We hope not only to inspire the historical imaginations of those who will create the next generation of American histories but also to spur them to consider the issues of today in light of the stories of yesterday.

Acknowledgments

We wish to thank the talented scholars and teachers who were kind enough to give their time and knowledge to review the manuscript:

Benjamin Allen, *South Texas College*
Christine Anderson, *Xavier University*
Uzoamaka Melissa C. Anyiwo, *Curry College*
Anthony A. Ball, *Housatonic Community College*
Terry A. Barnhart, *Eastern Illinois University*
Edwin Benson, *North Harford High School*
Paul Berk, *Christian Brothers University*
Deborah L. Blackwell, *Texas A&M International University*
Thomas Born, *Blinn College*
Margaret Bramlett, *St. Andrews Episcopal High School*
Lauren K. Bristow, *Collin College*
Tsekani Browne, *Duquesne University*
Jon L. Brudvig, *Dickinson State University*
Dave Bush, *Shasta College*
Barbara Calluori, *Montclair State University*
Julia Schiavone Camacho, *The University of Texas at El Paso*
Jacqueline Glass Campbell, *Francis Marion University*
Amy E. Canfield, *Lewis-Clark State College*

Dominic Carrillo, *Grossmont College*
Mark R. Cheathem, *Cumberland University*
Laurel A. Clark, *University of Hartford*
Myles L. Clowers, *San Diego City College*
Hamilton Cravens, *Iowa State University*
Audrey Crawford, *Houston Community College*
John Crum, *University of Delaware*
Alex G. Cummins, *St. Johns River State College*
Susanne Deberry-Cole, *Morgan State University*
Julian J. DelGaudio, *Long Beach City College*
Patricia Norred Derr, *Kutztown University*
John Donoghue, *Loyola University Chicago*
Timothy Draper, *Waubonsee Community College*
David Dzurec, *University of Scranton*
Keith Edgerton, *Montana State University Billings*
Blake Ellis, *Lone Star College*
Christine Erickson, *Indiana University–Purdue University Fort Wayne*
Todd Estes, *Oakland University*
Gabrielle Everett, *Jefferson College*
Julie Fairchild, *Sinclair Community College*
Randy Finley, *Georgia Perimeter College*
Kirsten Fischer, *University of Minnesota*
Michelle Fishman-Cross, *College of Staten Island*
Jeffrey Forret, *Lamar University*
Kristen Foster, *Marquette University*
Susan Freeman, *Western Michigan University*
Nancy Gabin, *Purdue University*
Kevin Gannon, *Grand View University*
Benton Gates, *Indiana University–Purdue University Fort Wayne*
Bruce Geelhoed, *Ball State University*
Mark Gelfand, *Boston College*
Jason George, *The Bryn Mawr School*
Judith A. Giesberg, *Villanova University*
Sherry Ann Gray, *Mid-South Community College*
Patrick Griffin, *University of Notre Dame*
Aaron Gulyas, *Mott Community College*
Scott Gurman, *Northern Illinois University*
Melanie Gustafson, *University of Vermont*
Brian Hart, *Del Mar College*
Paul Hart, *Texas State University*
Paul Harvey, *University of Colorado Colorado Springs*
Woody Holton, *University of Richmond*
Vilja Hulden, *University of Arizona*
Colette A. Hyman, *Winona State University*
Brenda Jackson-Abernathy, *Belmont University*
Troy R. Johnson, *California State University Long Beach*
Shelli Jordan-Zirkle, *Shoreline Community College*

Jennifer Kelly, *The University of Texas at Austin*
Kelly Kennington, *Auburn University*
Andrew E. Kersten, *University of Wisconsin–Green Bay*
Janilyn M. Kocher, *Richland Community College*
Max Krochmal, *Duke University*
Peggy Lambert, *Lone Star College*
Jennifer R. Lang, *Delgado Community College*
John S. Leiby, *Paradise Valley Community College*
Mitchell Lerner, *The Ohio State University*
Matthew Loayza, *Minnesota State University, Mankato*
Gabriel J. Loiacono, *University of Wisconsin Oshkosh*
John F. Lyons, *Joliet Junior College*
Lorie Maltby, *Henderson Community College*
Christopher Manning, *Loyola University Chicago*
Marty D. Matthews, *North Carolina State University*
Eric Mayer, *Victor Valley College*
Suzanne K. McCormack, *Community College of Rhode Island*
David McDaniel, *Marquette University*
J. Kent McGaughy, *Houston Community College, Northwest*
Alan McPherson, *Howard University*
Sarah Hand Meacham, *Virginia Commonwealth University*
Brian Craig Miller, *Emporia State University*
Brett Mizelle, *California State University Long Beach*
Mark Moser, *The University of North Carolina at Greensboro*
Jennifer Murray, *Coastal Carolina University*
Peter C. Murray, *Methodist University*
Steven E. Nash, *East Tennessee State University*
Chris Newman, *Elgin Community College*
David Noon, *University of Alaska Southeast*
Richard H. Owens, *West Liberty University*
David J. Peavler, *Towson University*
Laura A. Perry, *University of Memphis*
Wesley Phelps, *University of St. Thomas*
Merline Pitre, *Texas Southern University*
Eunice G. Pollack, *University of North Texas*
Kimberly Porter, *University of North Dakota*
Cynthia Prescott, *University of North Dakota*
Gene Preuss, *University of Houston*
Sandra Pryor, *Old Dominion University*
Rhonda Ragsdale, *Lone Star College*
Michaela Reaves, *California Lutheran University*
Peggy Renner, *Glendale Community College*
Steven D. Reschly, *Truman State University*
Barney J. Rickman, *Valdosta State University*
Pamela Riney-Kehrberg, *Iowa State University*
Paul Ringel, *High Point University*

Timothy Roberts, *Western Illinois University*

Glenn Robins, *Georgia Southwestern State University*

Alicia E. Rodriquez, *California State University Bakersfield*

Mark Roehrs, *Lincoln Land Community College*

Patricia Roessner, *Marple Newtown High School*

John G. Roush, *St. Petersburg College*

James Russell, *St. Thomas Aquinas College*

Eric Schlereth, *The University of Texas at Dallas*

Ronald Schultz, *University of Wyoming*

Stanley K. Schultz, *University of Wisconsin–Madison*

Sharon Shackelford, *Erie Community College*

Donald R. Shaffer, *American Public University System*

David J. Silverman, *The George Washington University*

Andrea Smalley, *Northern Illinois University*

Molly Smith, *Friends School of Baltimore*

David L. Snead, *Liberty University*

David Snyder, *Delaware Valley College*

Jodie Steeley, *Merced College*

Bryan E. Stone, *Del Mar College*

Emily Straus, *SUNY Fredonia*

Jean Stuntz, *West Texas A&M University*

Nikki M. Taylor, *University of Cincinnati*

Heather Ann Thompson, *Temple University*

Timothy Thurber, *Virginia Commonwealth University*

T. J. Tomlin, *University of Northern Colorado*

Laura Trauth, *Community College of Baltimore County–Essex*

Russell M. Tremayne, *College of Southern Idaho*

Laura Tuennerman-Kaplan, *California University of Pennsylvania*

Vincent Vinikas, *The University of Arkansas at Little Rock*

David Voelker, *University of Wisconsin–Green Bay*

Ed Wehrle, *Eastern Illinois University*

Gregory Wilson, *University of Akron*

Maria Cristina Zaccarini, *Adelphi University*

Nancy Zens, *Central Oregon Community College*

Jean Hansen Zuckweiler, *University of Northern Colorado*

We also appreciate the help the following scholars and students gave us in pro-viding the information we needed at critical points in the writing of this text: Leslie Brown, Andrew Buchanan, Gillian Carroll, Susan J. Carroll, Paul Clemens, Dorothy Sue Cobble, Jane Coleman-Harbison, Alison Cronk, Elisabeth Eittreim, Phyllis Hunter, Tera Hunter, William Link, James Livingston, Julia Livingston, Gilda Morales, Vicki L. Ruiz, Susan Schrepfer, Bonnie Smith, Melissa Stein, Margaret Sumner, Jessica Unger, and Anne Valk. Jacqueline Castledine, Julia Sandy-Bailey, and Rob Heinrich worked closely with us in finding documents and creating the Document Projects.

We would particularly like to applaud the many hardworking and creative people at Bedford/St. Martin's who guided us through the labyrinthine process of writing a textbook from scratch. No one was more important to us than the indefatigable and unflappable Sara Wise, our developmental editor for the parent text. We are also deeply grateful to Patricia Rossi, who first persuaded us to undertake this project. Joan Feinberg had the vision that guided us through every page of this book. We could not have had a better team than Denise Wydra, Mary Dougherty, William Lombardo, Jane Knetzger, Christina Horn, Jennifer Jovin, Katherine Bates, Sandra McGuire, and Arrin Kaplan. They also enlisted Naomi Kornhauser, Charlotte Miller, Angela Morrison, Linda McLatchie, Heidi Hood, Shannon Hunt, John Reisbord, and Michelle McSweeney to provide invaluable service. Finally, we would like to thank our friends and family who supported and encouraged us while we were writing the parent textbook and who will undoubtedly continue to cheer us on through this and future editions.

Nancy A. Hewitt and Steven F. Lawson

Versions and Supplements

Adopters of the Value Edition of **Exploring American Histories** and their students have access to abundant resources, including documents, presentation and testing materials, volumes in the acclaimed Bedford Series in History and Culture, and much more. For more information on the offerings described below, visit the book's catalog site at bedfordstmartins.com/hewittlawsonvalue/catalog, or contact your local Bedford/St. Martin's sales representative.

Get the Right Version for Your Class

To accommodate different course lengths and course budgets, the Value Edition of *Exploring American Histories* is available in different formats, including e-books, which are available at a substantial discount.

- Combined edition (chapters 1–29): available in paperback and e-book formats
- Volume 1: To 1877 (chapters 1–14): available in paperback and e-book formats
- Volume 2: Since 1865 (chapters 14–29): available in paperback and e-book formats

Any of these volumes can be packaged with additional books for a discount. To get ISBNs for discount packages, see the online catalog at bedfordstmartins.com/hewitt lawsonvalue/catalog or contact your Bedford/St. Martin's representative.

NEW Assign LaunchPad—the Online, Interactive e-Book in a Course Space Enriched with Integrated Assets

The new standard in digital history, LaunchPad course tools are so intuitive to use that online, hybrid, and face-to-face courses can be set up in minutes. Even novices will find it easy to create assignments, track students' work, and access a wealth of relevant learning and teaching resources. It is the ideal learning environment for students to work with the text, maps, documents, and assessments. LaunchPad is loaded with the full interactive e-book plus LearningCurve, the Online Document Projects, additional primary sources, videos, chapter summative quizzes, and more. LaunchPad can be used as is or customized, and it easily integrates with course management systems. And with fast ways to build assignments, rearrange chapters, and add new pages, sections, or links, it lets teachers build the course materials they need and hold students accountable.

Let Students Choose Their e-Book Format. In addition to the LaunchPad e-book, students can purchase the downloadable *Bedford e-Book to Go for Exploring American Histories* from our Web site or find other PDF versions of the e-book at our publishing partners' sites: CourseSmart, Barnes & Noble NookStudy, Kno, CafeScribe, or Chegg.

NEW   Go Beyond the Printed Page with Bedford Integrated Media   As described in the preface and on the inside front cover, students purchasing new books receive access to LearningCurve and Online Document Projects for *Exploring American Histories.*

Assign LearningCurve so You Know What Your Students Know and They Come to Class Prepared. Assigning LearningCurve in place of reading quizzes is easy for instructors, and the reporting features help instructors track overall class trends and spot topics that are giving students trouble so they can adjust their lectures and class activities. This online learning tool is popular with students because it was designed to help them rehearse content at their own pace in a nonthreatening, gamelike environment. The feedback for wrong answers provides instructional coaching and sends students back to the book for review. Students answer as many questions as necessary to reach a target score, with repeated chances to revisit material they haven't mastered. When LearningCurve is assigned, students come to class better prepared.

Assign the Online Document Projects so Students Put Interpretation into Practice. This text comes with ready-made assignable document sets that highlight some of the major topics and themes discussed in the chapter narrative. Callouts to these assignments appear in each chapter and prompt students to go online to read and analyze the document set. Each project comes with an introduction that sets the specific context for the document set, and individual documents are accompanied by a brief headnote. In addition, multiple-choice questions help students analyze the sources by providing instant feedback, and each project culminates with **Interpret the Evidence** and **Put It in Context** questions that help students connect the sources to the broader historical narrative. With Online Document Projects, students draw their own conclusions about the past while practicing critical-thinking and synthesis skills.

Take Advantage of Instructor Resources

Bedford/St. Martin's has developed a rich array of teaching resources for this book and for this course. They range from lecture and presentation materials and assessment tools to course management options. Most can be downloaded or ordered at bedfordstmartins.com/hewittlawsonvalue/catalog.

Bedford Coursepack for Blackboard, Canvas, Desire2Learn, Angel, Sakai, or Moodle. We have free content to help you integrate our rich content into your course management system. Registered instructors can download coursepacks with no hassle and no strings attached. Content includes our most popular free resources and book-specific content for *Exploring American Histories*, Value Edition. Visit bedfordstmartins .com/coursepacks to see a demo, find your version, or download your coursepack.

Instructor's Resource Manual. The instructor's manual offers tools to both experienced and first-time instructors for preparing lectures and running discussions. It includes chapter-review material, teaching strategies, and a guide to chapter-specific supplements available for the text, plus suggestions on how to get the most out of LearningCurve.

Computerized Test Bank. The test bank includes a mix of carefully crafted multiple-choice, short-answer, and essay questions for each chapter. All questions appear in Microsoft Word format and in easy-to-use test bank software that allows instructors to add, edit, re-sequence, and print questions and answers. Instructors can also export questions into a variety of formats, including Blackboard, Desire2Learn, and Moodle.

The Bedford Lecture Kit:* PowerPoint Maps, Images, Lecture Outlines, and i>clicker Content.** Look good and save time with ***The Bedford Lecture Kit. These presentation materials are downloadable individually from the Instructor Resources tab at bedfordstmartins.com/hewittlawsonvalue/catalog and are available on ***The Bedford Lecture Kit* Instructor's Resource CD-ROM**. They provide ready-made and fully customizable PowerPoint multimedia presentations that include lecture outlines with embedded maps, figures, and selected images from the parent textbook and extra background for instructors. Also available are maps and selected images in JPEG and PowerPoint formats; content for i>clicker, a classroom response system, in Microsoft Word and PowerPoint formats; the Instructor's Resource Manual in Microsoft Word format; and outline maps in PDF format for quizzing or handing out. All files are suitable for copying onto transparency acetates.

***America in Motion:* Video Clips for U.S. History.** Set history in motion with *America in Motion,* an instructor DVD containing dozens of short digital movie files of events in twentieth-century American history. From the wreckage of the battleship *Maine,* to FDR's fireside chats, to Ronald Reagan speaking at the Brandenburg Gate, *America in Motion* engages students with dynamic scenes from key events and challenges them to think critically. All files are classroom-ready, edited for brevity, and easily integrated with PowerPoint or other presentation software for electronic lectures or assignments. An accompanying guide provides each clip's historical context, ideas for use, and suggested questions.

Videos and Multimedia. A wide assortment of videos and multimedia CD-ROMs on various topics in U.S. history is available to qualified adopters through your Bedford/St. Martin's sales representative.

Package and Save Your Students Money

For information on free packages and discounts up to 50%, visit bedfordstmartins.com/hewittlawsonvalue/catalog or contact your local Bedford/St. Martin's sales representative. The products that follow all qualify for discount packaging.

Bedford Digital Collections @ bedfordstmartins.com/bdc/catalog. This source collection provides a flexible and affordable online repository of discovery-oriented primary source projects and single primary sources that you can easily customize and link to from your course management system or Web site. Package discounts are available.

The Bedford Series in History and Culture. More than 150 titles in this highly praised series combine first-rate scholarship, historical narrative, and important primary documents for undergraduate courses. Each book is brief, inexpensive, and focused on a specific topic or period. For a complete list of titles, visit bedfordstmartins.com /history/series. Package discounts are available.

Rand McNally Historical Atlas of American History. This collection of more than 84 full-color maps illustrates key events and eras, from early exploration, settlement, expansion, and immigration to U.S. involvement in wars abroad and on U.S. soil. Introductory pages for each section include a brief overview, timelines, graphs, and photographs to quickly establish a historical context. Available for $5.00 when packaged with the print text.

Maps in Context: A Workbook for American History. Written by historical cartography expert Gerald A. Danzer (University of Illinois at Chicago), this skill-building workbook helps students comprehend essential connections between geographic literacy and historical understanding. Organized to correspond to the typical U.S. survey course, *Maps in Context* presents a wealth of map-centered projects and convenient pop quizzes that give students hands-on experience working with maps. Available free when packaged with the print text.

The Bedford Glossary for U.S. History. This handy supplement for the survey course gives students historically contextualized definitions for hundreds of terms—from *abolitionism* to *zoot suit*—that they will encounter in lectures, reading, and exams. Available free when packaged with the print text.

U.S. History Matters: A Student Guide to U.S. History Online. This resource, written by Kelly Schrum, Alan Gevinson, and the late Roy Rosenzweig (all of George Mason University), provides an illustrated and annotated guide to 250 of the most useful Web sites for student research in U.S. history as well as advice on evaluating and using Internet sources. This essential guide is based on the acclaimed "History Matters" Web site developed by the American Social History Project and the Center for History and New Media. Available free when packaged with the print text.

Trade Books. Titles published by sister companies Hill and Wang; Farrar, Straus and Giroux; Henry Holt and Company; St. Martin's Press; Picador; and Palgrave Macmillan are available at a 50% discount when packaged with Bedford/St. Martin's textbooks. For more information, visit bedfordstmartins.com/tradeup.

A Pocket Guide to Writing in History. This portable and affordable reference tool by Mary Lynn Rampolla, now also available as a searchable e-book, provides reading, writing, and research advice useful to students in all history courses. Concise yet comprehensive advice on approaching typical history assignments, developing critical-reading skills, writing effective history papers, conducting research, using and documenting sources, and avoiding plagiarism—enhanced with practical tips and examples throughout—has made this slim reference a best seller. Package discounts are available.

A Student's Guide to History. This complete guide to success in any history course provides the practical help students need to be effective. In addition to introducing students to the nature of the discipline, author Jules Benjamin teaches a wide range of skills from preparing for exams to approaching common writing assignments, and he explains the research and documentation process with plentiful examples. Package discounts are available.

Going to the Source: The Bedford Reader in American History. Developed by Victoria Bissell Brown and Timothy J. Shannon, this reader's strong pedagogical framework helps students learn how to ask fruitful questions in order to evaluate documents effectively and develop critical-reading skills. The reader's wide variety of chapter topics that complement the survey course and its rich diversity of sources—from personal letters to political cartoons—provoke students' interest as it teaches them the skills they need to successfully interrogate historical sources. Package discounts are available.

America Firsthand. With its distinctive focus on ordinary people, this primary documents reader, by Anthony Marcus, John M. Giggie, and David Burner, offers a remarkable range of perspectives on American history from those who lived it. Popular Points of View sections expose students to different perspectives on a specific event or topic, and Visual Portfolios invite analysis of the visual record. Package discounts are available.

Brief Contents

Contents

✔ e Access the interactive content online at **bedfordstmartins.com/hewittlawsonvalue.**

ONLINE DOCUMENT PROJECTS
* Civil War Letters
* Home Front Protest during the Civil War

ONLINE DOCUMENT PROJECTS
* Testing and Contesting Freedom
* Reconstruction in South Carolina

CHAPTER 16
American Industry in the Age of Organization
1877–1900   402

CHAPTER 17
Workers and Farmers in the Age
of Organization 1877–1900   431

CHAPTER 18

Cities, Immigrants, and the Nation 1880–1914   457

CHAPTER 19

Progressivism and the Search for Order
1900–1917   483

Maps, Figures, and Tables

Exploring American Histories

VALUE EDITION

1

✓ LearningCurve
bedfordstmartins.com/hewittlawsonvalue
After reading the chapter, use LearningCurve
to retain what you've read.

Mapping Global Frontiers

to 1585

AMERICAN HISTORIES

In 1519 a young Indian woman named Malintzin was thrust into the center of
dramatic events that transformed not only her world but also the world at
large. As a young girl, Malintzin, whose birth name is lost to history, lived in
the rural area of Coatzacoalcos on the frontier between the expanding
kingdom of the Mexica and the declining Mayan states of the Yucatán
peninsula. Raised in a noble household, Malintzin was fluent in Nahuatl, the
language of the Mexica.

In 1515 or 1516, when she was between the ages of eight and twelve,
Malintzin was taken by or given to Mexica merchants, perhaps as a peace
offering to stave off military attacks. She then entered a well-established
trade in slaves, consisting mostly of women and girls, who were sent
eastward to work in the expanding cotton fields. Malintzin was apparently
sold to a Chontal Mayan village along the Tabasco River near the Gulf of
Mexico. As a slave, Malintzin was among thousands of workers who planted,
watered, weeded, and harvested the cotton or beat and carded the raw fibers
into thread and spun and dyed the yarn. She may also have been forced into a
sexual relationship as the concubine of a landowner. Whatever her situation,
Malintzin learned the Mayan language during her captivity.

In 1517 Mayan villagers sighted Spanish adventurers along local rivers and
drove them off. But in 1519 the Spaniards returned. Well armed and sailing
huge boats, they traveled up the Tabasco River and attacked local villages. The
Maya's cotton armor and wooden arrows were no match for the invaders'

1

steel swords, guns, and horses. Forced to surrender, the Maya offered the Spaniards food, gold, and twenty enslaved women, including Malintzin. The Spanish leader, Hernán Cortés, baptized the enslaved women as Christians, though they neither understood nor consented to the ritual. He assigned each of them Christian names, including Marina, which was later changed to Malintzin. Cortés then divided the women among his senior officers, giving Malintzin to the highest-ranking noble.

Already fluent in Nahuatl and Mayan, Malintzin soon learned Spanish. Within a matter of months, she became the chief translator between the Spaniards and native peoples. As Cortés moved into territories ruled by the Mexica (whom the Spaniards called Aztecs), his success depended on his ability to understand Aztec ways of thinking and to convince subjugated groups to fight against their despotic rulers. Malintzin thus accompanied Cortés at every step, including his triumphant conquest of the Aztec capital in the fall of 1521.

At the same time that Malintzin played a key role in the conquest of the Aztecs, Martin Waldseemüller sought to map the frontiers along which these conflicts erupted. Born in present-day Germany in the early 1470s, Waldseemüller enrolled at the University of Fribourg in 1490, where he probably studied theology. He would gain fame, however, not as a cleric but as a cartographer, or mapmaker.

In 1507 Waldseemüller and Mathias Ringmann produced a map of the world, a small globe, and a Latin translation of the four voyages of the Italian explorer Amerigo Vespucci. The map and the globe, entitled *Universalis Cosmographia*, depicted the "known" world as well as the "new" worlds recently discovered by European explorers. The latter included an elongated

territory labeled America, set between the continents of Africa and Asia. A thousand copies of the map were produced, each consisting of twelve sections engraved on wood and covering some 36 square feet. The map offered a view of the world never before attempted.

Meeting of Hernán Cortés and Montezuma, from the Duran Codex, 1579. Biblioteca Nacional, Madrid, Spain/ Giraudon/The Bridgeman Art Library

In 1513 Waldseemüller and Ringmann published the world's first atlas, which included a Latin edition of the works of Ptolemy, the Greco-Egyptian mathematician and astronomer. Three years later, Waldseemüller produced an updated map of the world, the *Carta Marina*. Apparently in response to challenges regarding Vespucci's role in discovering new territories, he substituted the term *Terra Incognita* ("unknown land") for the region he had earlier labeled *America*. But the 1507 map had already circulated widely, and America became part of the European lexicon.

THE PERSONAL HISTORIES of Malintzin and Martin Waldseemüller were both shaped by the profound consequences of contact between the peoples of Europe and those of the Americas. Both Malintzin and Waldseemüller helped to map the frontiers of an increasingly global society.

 Online Document Project   **Mapping America**
bedfordstmartins.com/hewittlawsonvalue

It took much longer in the sixteenth century than today to travel from continent to continent and to communicate across such vast distances. Nonetheless, animals, plants, goods, ideas, and people began circulating regularly among Asia, Africa, Europe, and the Americas during the sixteenth century. Malintzin and Waldseemüller, in their very different ways, were part of these dramatic transformations.

Native Peoples in the Americas

It is likely that the first migrants to the Americas were northeast Asians who arrived some 13,000 to 15,000 years ago. By the time Malintzin participated in the Spanish conquest of the Aztecs in the early sixteenth century, the Americas probably had a population of 60 million to 70 million people. The Nahuatl- and Mayan-speaking groups whose lands bordered the Gulf of Mexico were among hundreds of native societies that covered this vast landmass. Most lived within a few hundred miles of the equator, while only about 6 million to 7 million people likely lived in present-day North America. Despite its isolation, the Americas, like other regions of the world, were home to diverse and dynamic societies, ranging from nomadic hunter-gatherers to large and sophisticated city-centered empires.

Native Peoples Develop Diverse Cultures

Much of what we know as the Americas was probably first settled by peoples from northeast Asia. Between about 16,000 and 14,000 B.C.E., the growth of glaciers during the Wisconsin period led to a dramatic drop in sea levels and created a land bridge in the Bering Straits, between present-day Siberia and Alaska. Early settlers probably traveled over this bridge, known as **Beringia**, following herds of mammoths, musk oxen, and woolly rhinoceroses.

While most of these groups settled along the coast or gradually pushed inland, others probably used boats, hugging the shore and landing at various points along the Pacific coastline. Whether on foot or by boat, most groups traveled southward, skirting melting glaciers and seeking better hunting grounds and more abundant plant life. The mammoths and other large game disappeared about 10,000 years ago, and many groups then depended on smaller game, fish, roots, berries, and other plant foods to survive. At the same time, migrations continued across the Bering Straits, with Inuit and Aleut peoples arriving in present-day Alaska about 5,000 years ago.

About 3,000 years ago, some communities in the Americas began establishing agricultural systems that encouraged more stable settlements, population growth, and the accumulation of possessions. In the Americas, horticulture—a form of agriculture in which people work small plots of land with simple tools—first developed in present-day Mexico. There men and women developed strains of maize (or Indian corn) with larger kernels and higher yields than those that grew in the wild. They also cultivated beans, squash, tomatoes, potatoes, and manioc (a root vegetable), providing rich sources of protein. The combination of beans, squash, and corn offered an especially nutritious diet while maintaining the fertility of the soil. Moreover, high yields produced surplus food that could be stored or traded to neighboring communities.

By 500 C.E., complex societies, rooted in intensive agriculture, began to thrive in the equatorial region. Between 500 and 1500 C.E., thousands of separate societies and cultures speaking hundreds of distinct languages developed in the Americas. Small bands of hunters and gatherers continued to thrive in deserts and forests while impressive civilizations marked by gigantic stone statuary, complex irrigation systems, and ornate gold and silver ornaments arose on swamplands and in the mountains.

The Aztecs, the Maya, and the Incas

Three significant civilizations had developed by the early sixteenth century: Aztec and Mayan societies in the equatorial region and the Inca society along the Pacific coast in present-day Peru. Technologically advanced and with knowledge of mathematics and astronomy, these societies were characterized by vast mineral wealth, large urban centers, highly ritualized religions, and complex political systems. Unlike their counterparts in Europe, Asia, and Africa, they did not develop the wheel to aid in transportation, nor did they have steel tools and weapons. Since most of their commerce was carried out over land or along rivers and coastlines, they did not build large boats. They also lacked horses, which had disappeared from the region thousands of years earlier. Still, the Aztecs, Maya, and Incas established grand cities and civilizations that rivaled those of the most sophisticated societies in the world.

Around 1325 C.E., the Aztecs, who called themselves Mexica, built their capital, Tenochtitlán, on the site of present-day Mexico City. As seminomadic warriors who had invaded and then settled in the region, the Aztecs drew on local residents' knowledge of irrigation and cultivation and adopted their written language. Aztec commoners, who tilled communally owned lands, were ruled over by priests and nobles. The nobles formed a warrior class and owned vast estates on which they employed both serfs and slaves captured from non-Aztec communities in the region. Priests promised fertility— for the land and its people—but demanded human sacrifices, including thousands of men and women from captured tribes. To sustain their society, Aztecs extended their trade networks into surrounding areas. Aztec artisans produced valuable trade goods like pottery, cloth, and leather goods that were exchanged for textiles, food items, and obsidian (the volcanic rock used to make sharp-edged tools) as well as bird feathers, tortoiseshells, and other luxury goods. As Malintzin's story illustrates, Aztecs also traded in slaves.

When Malintzin was sold to a Chontal Mayan village by Aztec merchants, she was being traded from one grand civilization to another. The **Maya** had slowly settled the Yucatán peninsula and the rain forests of present-day Guatemala between roughly 900 B.C.E. and 300 C.E. They established large cities that were home to skilled artisans and developed elaborate systems for irrigation and water storage. Farmers worked the fields and labored to build huge stone temples and palaces for rulers who claimed to be descended from the gods. Learned men developed mathematical calculations, hieroglyphic writing, and a calendar. Mayan astronomers also developed an amazingly accurate system for predicting eclipses of the sun and the moon.

Yet the Mayan civilization began to decline around 800 C.E. An economic crisis, likely the result of a drought and exacerbated by heavy taxation, probably drove peasant families into the interior. Many towns and religious sites were abandoned. Yet some communities survived the crisis and reemerged as thriving city-states. By the early sixteenth century, they traded with the Aztecs.

The **Incas** developed an equally impressive civilization in the Andes Mountains along the Pacific coast. The Inca empire, like the Aztec empire, was built on the accomplishments of earlier societies. At the height of their power, in the fifteenth century, the Incas controlled some sixteen million people spread over 350,000 square miles. They constructed an expansive system of roads and garrisons to ensure the flow of food, trade goods, and soldiers from their capital at Cuzco through the surrounding mountains and valleys. Pack trains of llamas hauled tribute from conquered tribes to provincial centers and then on to Cuzco.

The key to Inca success was the cultivation of fertile mountain valleys. Cuzco, some eleven thousand feet above sea level, lay in the center of the Inca empire, with the Huaylas and Titicaca valleys on either side. Here residents cut timber from dense forests and cultivated potatoes and other crops on terraces watered by an elaborate irrigation system. Some artisans crafted gold and silver from the rich mountains into jewelry and decorative items, while others excelled at stone carving, pottery, and weaving. Thousands of laborers constructed elaborate palaces and temples. And like the Aztecs, Inca priests sacrificed humans to the gods to stave off natural disasters and military defeat.

Native Cultures to the North

To the north of these grand civilizations, smaller societies with less elaborate cultures thrived. In present-day Arizona and New Mexico, the Mogollon and Hohokam established communities around 500 C.E. The Mogollon were expert potters while the Hohokam developed extensive irrigation systems. Farther north, in present-day Utah and Colorado, the ancient Pueblo people built adobe and masonry homes cut into cliffs around 750 C.E. The homes clustered around a sunken ceremonial room, the kiva. A century later, the center of this culture moved south to the San Juan River Basin, where the Pueblo constructed large buildings that housed the people and their rulers along with administrative offices, religious centers, and craft shops. When a prolonged drought settled on the region in the early twelfth century, many Pueblo moved back north into cliff dwellings that offered greater protection from invaders as well as from the heat and sun. By 1300 these areas, too, were gripped by drought, and the residents appear to have dispersed into smaller groups.

Farther north on the plains that stretched from present-day Colorado into Canada, hunting societies developed around herds of bison. A weighted spear-throwing device, called an *atlatl*, allowed hunters to capture smaller game, while nets, hooks, and snares allowed them to catch birds, fish, and small animals. For many such groups, hunting was supplemented by the gathering of berries, roots, and other edible plants. These Plains societies generally remained small and widely scattered since they needed a large expanse of territory to ensure their survival as they traveled to follow migrating animals or seasonal plant sources.

Hunting-gathering societies also emerged along the Pacific coast, but the abundance of fish, small game, and plant life there provided the resources to develop permanent settlements. The Chumash Indians, near present-day Santa Barbara, California, harvested resources from the land and the ocean. Women gathered acorns and pine nuts, while men fished along the coastal waters and in rivers and hunted deer and smaller animals. The Chumash, whose villages sometimes held a thousand inhabitants, participated in regional exchange networks up and down the coast. As many as 300,000 people may have lived along the Pacific in a diverse array of societies before the arrival of Europeans.

Even larger societies with more elaborate social, religious, and political systems developed near the Mississippi River. A group that came to be called the **Hopewell people** established a thriving culture there in the early centuries C.E. The river and its surrounding lands provided fertile fields and easy access to distant communities. Centered in present-day southern Ohio and western Illinois, the Hopewell constructed towns of four thousand to six thousand people. Artifacts from their burial sites reflect extensive trading networks that stretched from the Missouri River to Lake Superior, and from the Rocky Mountains to the Appalachian region and Florida.

Beginning around 500 C.E., the Hopewell culture gave birth to larger and more complex societies that flourished in the Mississippi River valley and to the south and east. As bows and arrows spread into the region, people hunted more game in the thick forests. But Mississippian groups also learned to cultivate corn. The development of corn as a staple crop allowed the population to expand dramatically, and more complex political and religious systems developed in which elite rulers gained greater control over the labor of farmers and hunters.

Mississippian peoples created massive earthworks sculpted in the shape of serpents, birds, and other creatures. Still visible in present-day north Georgia, eastern Oklahoma, and southern Ohio and at Cahokia Creek near modern East St. Louis, Illinois, some earthen sculptures stood over 70 feet high and stretched more than 1,300 feet in length. Mississippians also constructed huge temple mounds that could cover nearly 16 acres.

By about 1100 C.E., the community around Cahokia Creek had grown to some fifteen thousand inhabitants. Powerful chieftains extended their trade networks, conquered smaller villages, and created a centralized government. But the rulers proved too weak to maintain their control over numerous scattered towns. To the south, near present-day Tuscaloosa, Alabama, more than twenty flat-topped mounds formed an important ceremonial center in the thirteenth century. By 1400, however, the Mississippians began to lose power there as well. Over the next century, this once-flourishing culture declined, leaving behind vast temple mounds and stunning earthen sculptures.

REVIEW & RELATE

• Compare and contrast the Aztecs, Incas, and Maya. What similarities and differences do you note?

• How did the societies of North America differ from those of the equatorial zone and the Andes?

Europe Expands Its Reach

The complex societies that emerged in the Americas were made possible by an agricultural revolution that included the establishment of crop systems, the domestication of animals, and the development of tools. These developments had occurred 4000–3000 B.C.E. in the Fertile Crescent (see Map 1.1) in southwest Asia and in China. The increased productivity in these areas ensured population growth and allowed attention to science, trade, politics, religion, and the arts. Over millennia, knowledge from these civilizations made its way northward and westward into Europe, and at the height of the Roman empire in the early centuries C.E., Europe was part of dense global trade networks that connected the peoples of Europe, Africa, and Asia. With the decline of Roman power in western Europe, however, those connections broke down, and Europeans turned inward. It would take many centuries for European societies to recover. When they did, motivated by a desire to gain access to the riches of the East, they began to search for ways to regain their connections to the larger world.

The Mediterranean World

For several centuries before 1500, Islam proved one of the most dynamic cultural, political, and military forces in the world. By the ninth century, Islamic (also known as Muslim) regimes controlled most of southwest Asia and North Africa and conquered parts of the Iberian peninsula. The Muslims' greatest competitors were the Ottoman Turks, not European Catholics (Map 1.1). Still, in the eleventh and twelfth centuries, Catholic leaders launched several military and religious campaigns to reclaim the Holy Land for the church. Later known as the **Crusades**, these campaigns largely failed in establishing Christian settlements in the East and exacerbated conflicts with Greek Orthodox and Jewish communities. But they enhanced the roles of Italian merchants, who profited from both outfitting Crusaders and opening new trade routes to the East. Moreover, these campaigns inspired explorers and adventurers throughout Europe.

Medieval European elites were first introduced to goods and ideas from the East by merchant adventurers such as Marco Polo. He traveled to Cathay (his name for China) during the 1270s and published his *Travels* in 1292. Describing his adventures along the Silk Road, Polo introduced Europeans to "burning rocks" (coal), spices that preserved meat, and other wonders of the Far East.

Europeans also learned of successful civilizations in the Middle East, where inhabitants had managed to survive droughts and other ecological crises, largely

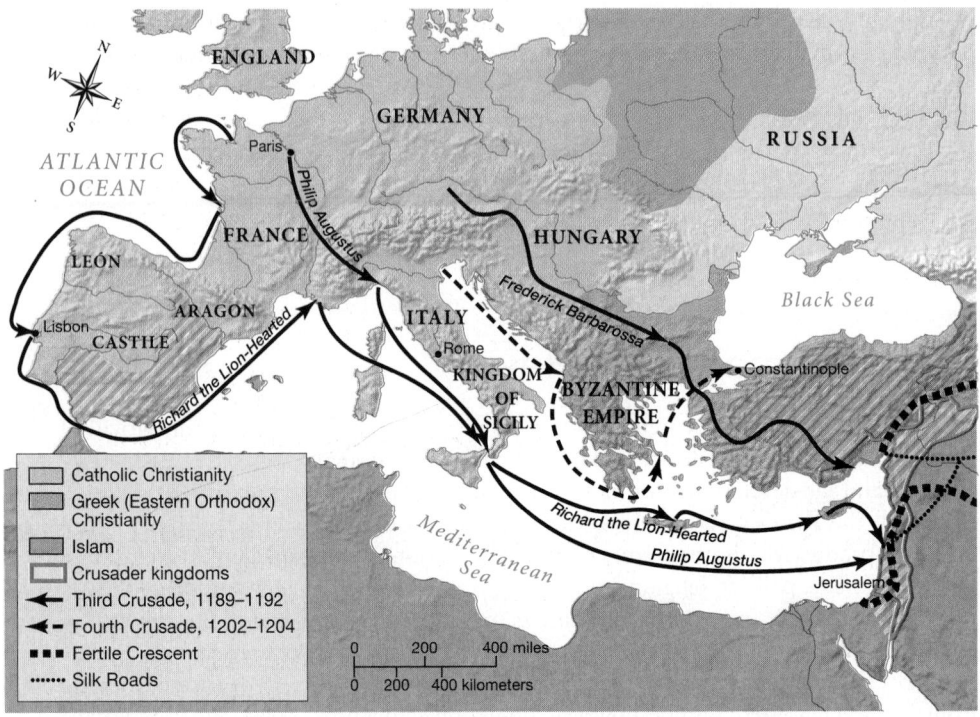

MAP 1.1

The Mediterranean World, c. 1150–1300 The Mediterranean Sea sat at the center of dynamic religious, political, and commercial networks. Crusaders traveled from Europe to Turkey, Arabia, and Persia, hoping to spread Christianity among Islamic peoples. In the thirteenth century, Marco Polo and other adventurers followed the Silk Road deeper into Asia, returning with goods, technologies, and diseases from the eastern Mediterranean, India, and China.

because of their productive economic systems. In the Mediterranean world, this productivity depended on technological advances in irrigation and navigation and on adequate labor in the form of slavery. Earlier European societies as well as the Aztecs, Incas, and Maya had put conquered peoples to work as slaves, but none compared to the vast network of slave-trading centers that fueled agricultural development in the Middle East. And it was the productivity of agriculture—developed centuries earlier than in Europe or America—that allowed societies along the southern Mediterranean, in northern Africa, and in southwest Asia to excel in astronomy, mathematics, architecture, and the arts.

Medieval European states proved far less adept at staving off human and environmental disasters than their counterparts to the south. Besieged by drought and disease as well as wars and peasant rebellions, rulers across the continent expended most of their resources on trying to sustain their population and protect their borders. Even launching trade with Asia led to disaster: In the 1340s, the bubonic plague was carried from Central Asia to Middle Eastern and European seaports by rats stowed away on ships. Sailors who contracted the disease at sea also spread the infection far and wide. From the 1340s to the early fifteenth century, the plague—later called the **Black Death**—periodically ravaged European cities and towns. During the initial outbreak between 1346 and 1350, about 36 million people—half of Europe's population—perished. At the same time, France and England engaged in a century-long war that added to the death and destruction.

By the early fifteenth century, the plague had retreated from much of Europe, and the climate had improved. Only then were European peoples able to benefit significantly from the riches of the East. Smaller populations led to an improved standard of living. Then rising birthrates and increased productivity, beginning in Italian city-states, fueled a resurgence of trade with other parts of the world. The profits from agriculture and commerce allowed the wealthy and powerful to begin investing in painting, sculpture, music, and literature and to pay jewelers, potters, and other craftsmen for their wares. Indeed, a cultural **Renaissance** (from the French word for "rebirth") flourished in the Italian city-states and then spread to France, Spain, the Low Countries, and central Europe.

The cultural rebirth went hand in hand with political unification as more powerful rulers extended their control over smaller city-states and principalities. In 1469, for example, the marriage of Isabella of Castile and Ferdinand II of Aragon led to the unification of Spain. By 1492 their combined forces expelled the last Muslim conquerors from the Iberian peninsula. Promoting Catholicism to create a more unified national identity, Isabella and Ferdinand also launched a brutal Inquisition against supposed heretics and executed or expelled Jews and Muslims. This reconquest of the Iberian peninsula fueled the revival of trade with North Africa, India, and other Asian lands.

Yet Italy controlled the most important routes through the Mediterranean, so leaders in Spain and Portugal sought alternate paths to riches. Their efforts were aided by explorers, missionaries, and merchants who traveled to Morocco, Turkey, India, and other distant lands. They brought back trade goods and knowledge of astronomy, shipbuilding, mapmaking, and navigation that allowed Iberians to venture farther south along the Atlantic coast of Africa and, eventually, west into the uncharted Atlantic Ocean.

Portugal Pursues Long-Distance Trade

Cut off from the Mediterranean by Italian city-states and Muslim forces in North Africa, Portugal looked toward the Atlantic. Motivated by dreams of wealth and a desire to challenge Muslim power, Portuguese rulers sought another route to India and the Far East. Although a tiny nation, Portugal benefited from the leadership of its young prince, Henry (1394–1460), who launched an effort to explore the African coast and find a passage to India via the Atlantic Ocean. Prince Henry—known as Henry the Navigator—gathered information from astronomers, geographers, mapmakers, and craftsmen in the Arab world and recruited Italian cartographers and navigators along with Portuguese scholars, sailors, and captains. He then launched a systematic campaign of exploration, observation, shipbuilding, and long-distance trade that revolutionized Europe and shaped developments in Africa and the Americas.

Prince Henry and his colleagues developed ships known as caravels—vessels with narrow hulls and triangular sails that were especially effective for navigating the coast of West Africa. His staff also created state-of-the-art maritime charts, maps, and astronomical tables; perfected navigational instruments; and mastered the complex wind and sea currents along the African coast. Soon Portugal was trading in gold, ivory, and slaves from West Africa. By the time Prince Henry died in 1460, his ships had ventured as far east as the Canary Islands and Cape Verde and as far south as Sierra Leone.

In 1482 Portugal built Elmina Castle, a trading post and fort on the Gold Coast (present-day Ghana). The castle served as a launching point for further expeditions and as protection against Spanish competitors. Five years later, a fleet led by Bartolomeu Dias rounded the Cape of Good Hope, on the southernmost tip of Africa, demonstrating the possibility of sailing directly from the Atlantic to the Indian Ocean. Vasco da Gama followed this route to India in 1497, returning to Portugal in 1499, his ships laden with cinnamon and pepper.

By the early sixteenth century, Portuguese traders wrested control of the India trade from Arab fleets. They established fortified trading posts at key locations on the Indian Ocean and extended their expeditions to Indonesia, China, and Japan. Within a decade, the Portuguese had become the leaders in international trade. Spain, England, France, and the Netherlands competed for a share of this newfound wealth by developing long-distance markets that brought spices, ivory, silks, cotton cloth, and other luxury goods to Europe.

Elmina Castle, 1603   This engraving by Johann Theodor de Bry depicts the fortress of São Jorge da Mina, known as Elmina Castle, on the African Gold Coast. Built in 1482 at the order of King John II of Portugal, the fort served as a supply base for Portuguese navigators and housed thousands of Africans bound for slavery in the Americas.   The Granger Collection, New York

With expanding populations and greater agricultural productivity, European nations developed more efficient systems of taxation, built larger military forces, and adapted gunpowder to new kinds of weapons. The surge in population provided the men to labor on merchant vessels, staff forts, and protect trade routes. More people began to settle in cities like London, Bristol, Amsterdam, and Venice, which became important commercial centers. Slowly, a form of capitalism based on market exchange, private ownership, and capital accumulation and reinvestment developed across much of Europe.

African slaves were among the most lucrative goods traded by European merchants. Slavery had been practiced in Europe and other parts of the world, including Africa, for centuries. But in most times and places, slaves were captives of war or individuals sold in payment for deaths or injuries to conquering enemies. Under such circumstances, slaves generally retained some legal rights, and bondage was rarely permanent and almost never inheritable. With the advent of large-scale European participation in the African slave trade, however, the system of bondage began to change, transforming Europe and Africa and eventually the Americas.

European Encounters with West Africa

In the 1440s, Portuguese ships began to trade along the West African (or Guinea) coast. The Portuguese established bases in port cities like Benin to collect trade goods, including slaves, for sale in Europe. The slave trade expanded with the building of Elmina Castle and by the early sixteenth century had increased significantly. Initially, Africans were viewed as "exotic" objects and were often put on display at courts or for popular entertainment. Increasingly, however, African slaves were put to work in households and shops or on large estates.

Still, Europeans were most familiar with North Africa, a region deeply influenced by Islam and characterized by large kingdoms, well-developed cities, and an extensive network of trading centers. In northeast Africa, including Egypt, city-states flourished, with ties to India, the Middle East, and China. In northwest Africa, Timbuktu linked North Africa to empires south of the Great Desert as well as to Europe. Here African slaves labored for wealthier Africans in a system of bound labor long familiar to Europeans.

As trade with western Africa increased, however, Europeans learned more about communities that lived by hunting and subsistence agriculture. By the mid-sixteenth century, European nations established competing forts along the African coast from the Gold Coast and Senegambia in the north to the Bight of Biafra and West Central Africa farther south. The men and women shipped from these forts to Europe generally came from communities that had been raided or conquered by more powerful groups. They arrived at the coast exhausted, hungry, dirty, and with few clothes. They worshipped gods unfamiliar to Europeans, and their cultural customs and social practices seemed strange and often frightening. Over time, it was the image of the captured West African slave that came to dominate European visions of the entire continent.

As traders from Portugal, Spain, Holland, and England brought back more stories and more African slaves, these negative portraits took deeper hold. Woodcuts and prints circulated in Europe that showed half-naked Africans who looked more like apes than humans. These images resonated with biblical stories like that of Ham, who sinned against his father, Noah. Noah then cursed Ham's son Canaan to a life of slavery. Increasingly, European Christians considered Africans the "sons of Ham," infidels rightly assigned by God to a life of bondage. This self-serving idea then justified the enslavement of black men, women, and children.

Of course, these images of West Africa failed to capture the diverse peoples who lived in the area's tropical rain forests, plains, and savannas. By the fourteenth century, agricultural productivity in the region fueled population growth and the rise of both city-states and trade networks. The Yoruba people developed walled towns ruled by obas, many of whom were women, who served as religious and political leaders. To the south lay the highly centralized kingdom of Benin. Its warrior king, Euware, had conquered some two hundred villages to create his kingdom and then used his power and wealth to promote trade and patronize the arts. Nearby the Igbo people rejected kingships in favor of title societies composed of wealthy men, women's associations tied to kinship, and hereditary organizations that created cohesion among competing groups. Despite their political and social differences, the Yoruba, Beni, and Igbo traded with one another and with more distant African kingdoms.

In addition to these powerful kingdoms, smaller societies based on farming or herding existed across western and central Africa. These communities were sometimes conquered by expanding kingdoms and their members sold as slaves within Africa. But once trade developed with Portugal, Spain, and other nations, these communities were increasingly raided to provide slaves for European markets. As the slave trade expanded in the sixteenth and seventeenth centuries, it destabilized large areas of western and central Africa, with smaller societies decimated by raids and even larger kingdoms damaged by the extensive commerce in human beings. As early as 1526, Afonso, the king of the Kongo people and a convert to Christianity, begged the Portuguese to end the slave trade: "Merchants are taking everyday our natives, sons of the land and the sons of our noblemen and vassals and our relatives."

Still, rulers of the most powerful African societies helped shape the slave trade. For instance, because women were more highly valued by Muslim traders in North Africa and Asia, African traders steered women to these profitable markets. At the same time, African societies organized along matrilineal lines—where goods and political power passed through the mother's line—often tried to protect women against enslavement. Other groups sought to limit the sale of men.

Ultimately, men, women, and children were captured by African as well as Portuguese, Spanish, Dutch, and English traders. Still, Europeans did not institute a system of perpetual slavery, in which enslavement was inherited from one generation to the next. Instead, Africans formed another class of bound labor, alongside peasants, indentured servants, criminals, and apprentices. Slavic-speaking workers imported from areas around the Black Sea were especially prominent on sugar plantations in the Mediterranean region. Indeed, the term *Slav* became the basis for the word *slave*. When the Ottoman Turks cut off access to Slavic laborers, Europeans increased their slave trade with Africa.

Distinctions among bound laborers on the basis of race had not yet fully developed. Thus affluent Europeans condemned pagan rituals, sexual licentiousness, and ignorance among both Slavic and African laborers. They also considered such traits common among their own peasants. When the English entered the African slave trade in the 1560s, via the privateer John Hawkins, they quickly put their own spin on such comparisons. In the sixteenth century, they viewed both Africans and the conquered Irish as "rude, beastly, ignorant, cruel, and unruly infidels."

- How and why did Europeans expand their connections with Africa and the Middle East in the fifteenth century?
- How did early European encounters with West Africans lay the foundation for later race-based slavery?

Worlds Collide

In the 1520s and 1530s, Spain and Portugal chartered traders to ship enslaved Africans to the Caribbean, Brazil, Mexico, and Peru. The success of this trade relied heavily on the efforts of European cartographers, who began to chart the coastlines, rivers, and inland territories of the Western Hemisphere described by explorers and adventurers. Their maps illustrated the growing connections among Europe, Africa, and the Americas even as they also reflected the continued dominance of the Mediterranean region, the Middle East, India, and China in European visions of the world. Yet that world was changing rapidly as Europeans introduced guns, horses, and new diseases to the Americas and came in contact with previously unknown flora and fauna. The resulting exchange of plants, animals, and germs transformed the two continents as well as the wider world.

Europeans Cross the Atlantic

The first Europeans to discover lands in the western Atlantic were Norsemen. In the early ninth century, Scandinavians colonized Ireland, and in the 870s they settled Iceland. A little more than a century later, seafarers led by Erik the Red reached Greenland. Sailing still farther west, Erik's son Leif led a party that discovered an area that they called Vinland, near the Gulf of St. Lawrence. The Norse established a small settlement there around 1000 C.E., and people from Greenland continued to visit Vinland for centuries. By 1450, however, the Greenland settlements had disappeared.

Nearly a half century after Norse settlers abandoned Greenland, a Genoese navigator named Christopher Columbus visited the Spanish court of Ferdinand and Isabella and proposed an **Enterprise of the Indies**. He planned to sail west across the Atlantic to Cipangu (Japan) and Cathay (China). Because Italian city-states controlled the Mediterranean and Portugal dominated the routes around Africa, Spain sought a third path to the rich Eastern trade. Columbus claimed he could find it.

Columbus's 1492 proposal was timely. Having just expelled the last Muslims from Granada and imposed Christian orthodoxy on a now-unified nation, the Spanish monarchs sought to expand their empire. Queen Isabella, ignoring the advice of two royal committees that had rejected Columbus's plan, decided to fund his initial venture. With her support, the Genoese captain headed off in three small ships with ninety men. They stopped briefly at the Canary Islands and then headed due west on September 6, 1492.

Columbus had calculated the distance to Cipangu based on Ptolemy's division of the world into 360 degrees of north-south lines of longitude. But in making his calculations, Columbus made a number of errors that led him to believe that it was possible to sail from Spain to Asia in about a month. The miscalculations nearly led to mutiny when Columbus's crew had not sighted land after more than four weeks at sea. Disaster was averted, however, when on October 12 a lookout spotted a small island. Columbus named the island San Salvador and made contact with local residents, whom he named Indians in the belief that he had found the East Indies. These "Indians" offered the newcomers food, drinks, and gifts. Columbus was impressed with their warm welcome and viewed their gold jewelry as a sign of greater riches in the region.

Although the native inhabitants and Columbus's men did not speak a common language, they communicated sufficiently to explore San Salvador as well as a larger island nearby, present-day Cuba. The crew then sailed on to an island they named Hispaniola. Nothing they saw resembled contemporary descriptions of China or the East Indies, but Columbus was convinced he had reached his destination. Leaving a small number of men behind, he sailed for Spain with samples of gold jewelry and tales of more wonders to come.

Columbus and his crew were welcomed as heroes when they returned to Spain in March 1493. Their discovery of islands seemingly unclaimed by any known power led the pope to confer Spanish sovereignty over all lands already claimed or to be claimed 100 leagues west of the Cape Verde Islands. A protest by Portugal soon led to a treaty that moved the line 270 leagues farther west, resulting ultimately in Portugal's control of Brazil and Spain's control of the rest of what would become known as South America.

Europeans Explore the Americas

Columbus made two more voyages to the Caribbean to claim land for Spain and sought to convince those who accompanied him to build houses, plant crops, and cut logs for forts. But the men had come for gold, and when the Indians stopped trading willingly, the Spaniards used force to claim their riches. Columbus sought to impose a more rigid discipline but failed. On his final voyage, he was forced to introduce a system of *encomiendas*, by which leading men received land and the labor of all Indians residing on it. Although he boasted to the Spanish crown that he had "placed under their Highnesses' sovereignty more land than there is in Africa and Europe," Columbus had lost the support of the Spanish authorities by the time he died in 1506. The islands he discovered were quickly dissolving into chaos as traders and adventurers fought with Indians and one another over the spoils of conquest. By then, no one believed that he had discovered a route to China, and few people understood the revolutionary importance of the lands he had found.

Nonetheless, Columbus's voyages inspired others to head across the Atlantic (Map 1.2). In 1497 another Genoese navigator, John Cabot (or Caboto), sailing under the English flag, headed into the northern Atlantic in a tiny ship with only eighteen men. He reached an island off Cape Breton, where he discovered good cod fishing but met no local inhabitants. Over the next several years, Cabot and his son Sebastian made more trips to North American shores, but England failed to follow up on their discoveries.

More important at the time, Portuguese and Spanish mariners continued to explore the western edges of the Caribbean. Amerigo Vespucci, a Florentine merchant, joined one such voyage in 1499. It was Vespucci's account of his journey that led Martin Waldseemüller to identify the new continent he charted on his 1507 *Universalis Cosmographia* as "America." Meanwhile, Spanish explorers subdued tribes like the Arawak and Taino in the Caribbean and headed toward the mainland. In 1513 Vasco Nuñez de Balboa

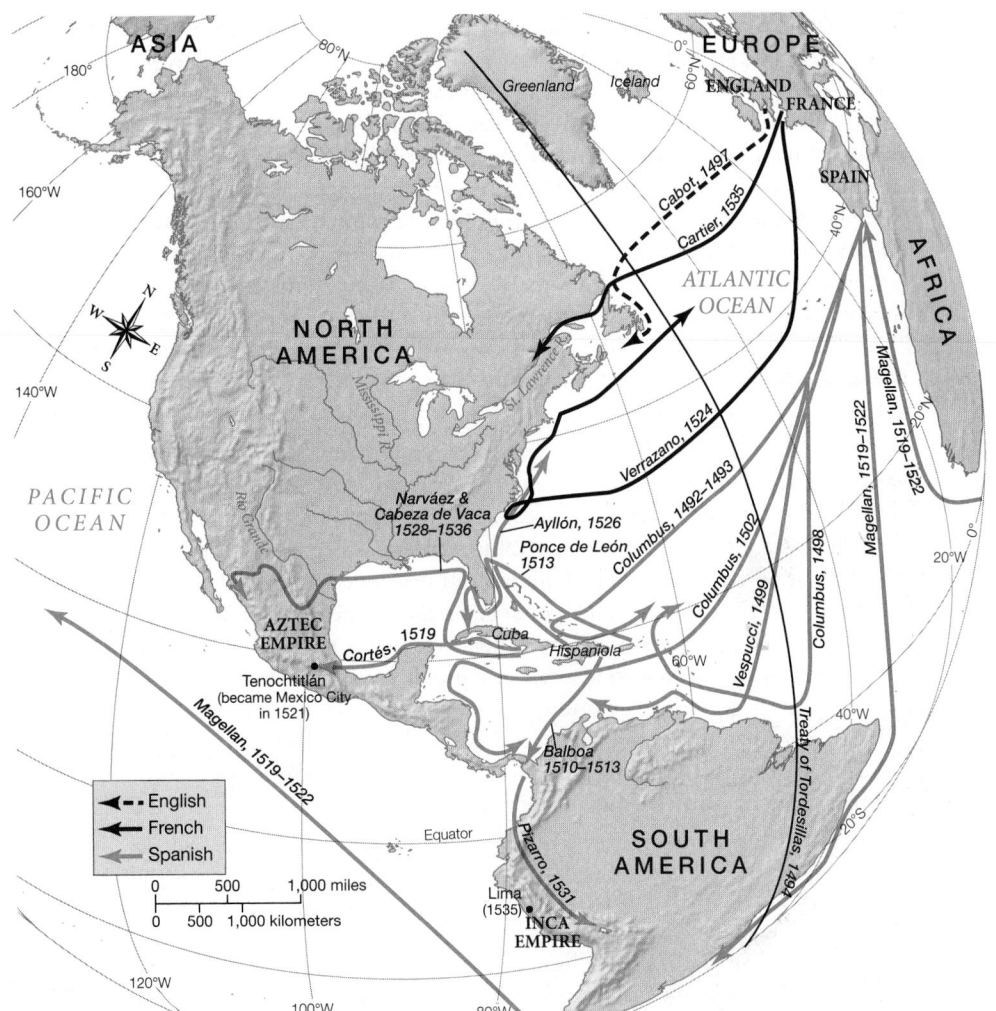

MAP 1.2

European Explorations in the Americas, 1492–1536   Early explorers, funded by Spain, sought trade routes to Asia or gold, silver, and other riches in the Americas. The success of these voyages encouraged adventurous Spaniards to travel throughout the West Indies and across South America and southern North America. It also inspired the first expeditions by the French and the English, who sought treasures farther north.

traveled across the Isthmus of Darien (now Panama) and became the first European to see the Pacific Ocean. That same year, Juan Ponce de León launched a search for gold and slaves along a peninsula to the north. Although he did not find riches there, he named the region Florida, meaning "flowery land," and claimed it for Spain.

Ferdinand Magellan launched an even more impressive expedition in August 1519 when he, with the support of Charles V of Spain, sought a passageway through South

America to Asia. In the first fifteen months, Magellan faced bad weather, disappointments, hostile Indians, and open mutiny. But he managed to maintain his authority, and in October 1520 his crew discovered a strait at the southernmost tip of South America that connected the Atlantic and Pacific Oceans. Ill with scurvy and near starvation, the crew reached Guam and then the Philippines in March 1521. Magellan died there a month later, but one of his five ships and eighteen of the original crew finally made it back to Seville in September 1522, having successfully circumnavigated the globe. Despite the enormous loss of life and equipment, Magellan's lone ship was loaded with valuable spices, his venture allowed Spain to claim the Philippine Islands, and his journals provided cartographers with vast amounts of knowledge about the world's oceans and landmasses.

Mapmaking and Printing

Waldseemüller's 1507 map reflected the expanding contacts among Europe, Africa, and the Americas. Over the following decades, as ships from Europe sailed back and forth across the Atlantic, cartographers charted newly discovered islands, traced coastlines and bays, and situated each new piece of data in relation to lands already known.

The dissemination of geographical knowledge was greatly facilitated by advances in information technology. The Chinese had developed a form of printing with wood blocks in the tenth century, and woodcut pictures appeared in Europe in the fifteenth century. In the 1440s, German craftsmen invented a form of movable metal type in which each letter was created in a separate mold. This allowed printers to rearrange the type for each page and create multiple copies of a single manuscript more quickly and more cheaply than ever before. Between 1452 and 1455, Johannes Gutenberg, a German goldsmith, printed some 180 copies of the Bible with movable type. Although this was not the first book printed using the new system, Gutenberg's Bible marked a revolutionary change in the production and circulation of written texts.

Innovations in printing helped publicize Portuguese and Spanish explorations, the travels of European adventurers, and the atlases created by Waldseemüller and other cartographers. Italian craftsmen contributed by manufacturing paper that was thinner and cheaper than traditional vellum and parchment. Books were still expensive, and they could be read only by the small minority of Europeans who were literate. Still, mechanical printing rapidly increased the speed with which knowledge was circulated, allowing a German mapmaker like Waldseemüller to read the journals of the Italian mariner Vespucci. Of course, not everything that was printed was accurate, but the ability to exchange ideas encouraged their expression and ensured the flow of information among scholars and rulers across Europe.

The peoples of the Americas had their own ways of charting land, waterways, and boundary lines and for circulating information. The Maya, for instance, developed a system of glyphs—images that represented prefixes, suffixes, numbers, people, or words. Scribes carved glyphs into large flat stones, or *stela*, providing local residents with histories of important events. In settled farming villages, this system communicated information to a large portion of the population. But it could not serve, as printed pages did, to disseminate ideas more widely. Similarly, the extant maps created by the Maya, Aztecs, and other native groups tended to focus on specific locales. Still, we know that these groups traded across long distances, so they must have had some means of tracing rivers, mountains, and villages beyond their own communities.

The Columbian Exchange

Even as maps documented Europeans' expanded knowledge of the Americas, they could not capture the experience of contact between peoples separated for centuries by the Atlantic Ocean. Most important, the Spaniards were aided in their conquest of the Americas as much by germs as by maps, guns, or horses. Because native peoples in the Western Hemisphere had had almost no contact with the rest of the world for millennia, they lacked immunity to most germs carried by Europeans. Disease along with warfare first eradicated the Arawak and Taino on Hispaniola, wiping out some 300,000 people. In the Inca empire, the population plummeted from about 9 million in 1530 to less than half a million by 1630. Among the Aztecs, the Maya, and their neighbors, the population collapsed from some 40 million people around 1500 to about 3 million a century and a half later. The germs spread northward as well, leading to catastrophic epidemics among the Pueblo peoples of the Southwest and the Mississippian cultures of the Southeast.

These demographic disasters—far more devastating even than the bubonic plague in Europe—were part of what historians call the Columbian exchange. But this exchange also involved animals, plants, and seeds and affected Africa and Asia as well as Europe and the Americas. The transfer of flora and fauna and the spread of diseases transformed the economies and environments of all four continents. Initially, however, it was the catastrophic decline in Indian populations that ensured the victory of Spain and other European powers over American populations, facilitating their subsequent exploitation of American land, labor, and resources.

The diseases that swept across the Americas came from Africa as well as Europe. Indeed, it was Africans' partial immunity to malaria and yellow fever that made them so attractive to European traders seeking laborers for Caribbean islands after the native population was decimated. African coconuts and bananas had already been introduced to Europe, while European traders had provided their African counterparts with iron and pigs. Asia also participated in the exchange, introducing Europe and Africa not only to the bubonic plague but also to sugar, rice, tea, and highly coveted spices.

America provided Europeans with high-yielding, nutrient-rich foods like maize and potatoes, as well as new indulgences like tobacco and cacao. The conquered Inca and Aztec empires also provided vast quantities of gold and silver, making Spain the treasure-house of Europe and ensuring its dominance on the continent for several decades. Sugar was first developed in the East Indies, but once it took root in the West Indies, it, too, became a source of enormous profits and, when mixed with cacao, created an addictive drink known as chocolate.

In exchange for products that America offered to Europe and Africa, these continents sent rice, wheat, rye, lemons, and oranges as well as horses, cattle, pigs, chickens, and honeybees to the Western Hemisphere (Map 1.3). The grain crops transformed the American landscape, particularly in North America, where wheat became a major food source. Cattle and pigs, meanwhile, changed native diets, while horses inspired new methods of farming, transportation, and warfare throughout the Americas.

The Columbian exchange benefited Europe far more than the Americas. Initially, it also benefited Africa, providing new crops with high yields and rich nutrients. Ultimately, however, the spread of sugar and rice to the West Indies and European cravings for tobacco and cacao increased the demand for labor, which could not be met by

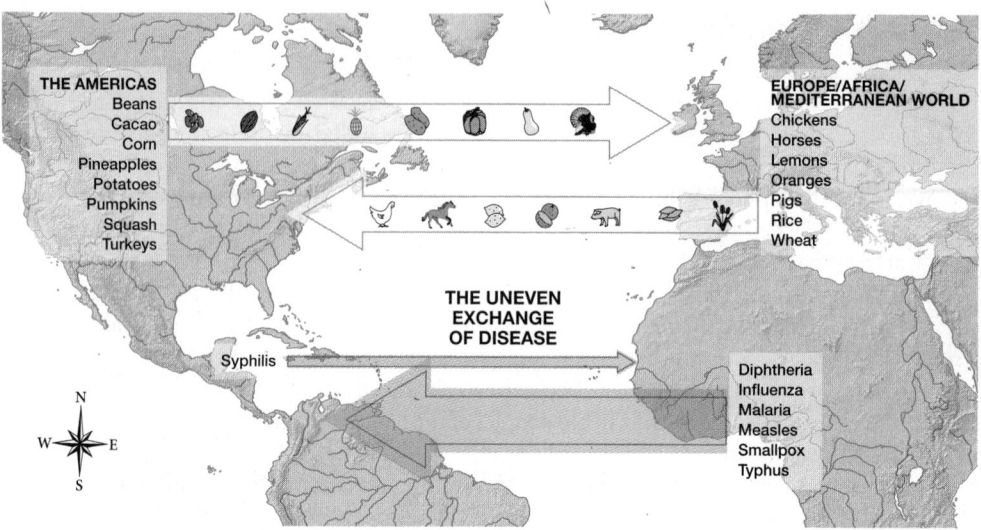

THE AMERICAS
Beans
Cacao
Corn
Pineapples
Potatoes
Pumpkins
Squash
Turkeys

EUROPE/AFRICA/
MEDITERRANEAN WORLD
Chickens
Horses
Lemons
Oranges
Pigs
Rice
Wheat

THE UNEVEN
EXCHANGE
OF DISEASE

Syphilis

N
W   E
S

Diphtheria
Influenza
Malaria
Measles
Smallpox
Typhus

MAP 1.3

The Columbian Exchange, 16th Century   When Europeans made contact with Africa and the Americas, they initiated an exchange of plants, animals, and germs that transformed all three continents. The contact among these previously isolated ecosystems caused dramatic transformations in food, labor, and mortality. American crops changed eating habits across Europe, while foreign grains and domesticated animals thrived in the Americas even as diseases devastated native populations.

the declining population of Indians. This situation ensured the expansion of the African slave trade. The consequences of the Columbian exchange were thus monumental for the peoples of all three continents.

REVIEW & RELATE

• What were the short-term consequences in both Europe and the Americas of Columbus's voyages?

• How did the Columbian exchange transform both the Americas and Europe?

Europeans Make Claims to North America

With the help of native translators, warriors, and laborers, Spanish soldiers called **conquistadors** conquered some of the richest and most populous lands in South America in the early sixteenth century. Others then headed north, hoping to find gold in the southern regions of North America or develop new routes to Asia. At the same time, rulers of other European nations, jealous of Spanish wealth, began to fund expeditions to North America. However, both France and England were ruled by weak monarchs and divided both religiously and politically. Consequently, their early efforts met with little success. By the late sixteenth century, Spanish supremacy in the Americas and the wealth acquired there transformed the European economy. But conquest also raised critical questions about Spanish responsibilities to God and humanity.

Spaniards Conquer Indian Empires

Although rulers in Spain supposedly set the agenda for American ventures, it was difficult to control the campaigns of their emissaries at such a distance. The Spanish crown held the power to grant successful leaders vast amounts of land and Indian labor, expanding the encomienda system introduced by Columbus. But the leaders themselves then divided up their prizes to reward those who served under them, giving them in effect an authority that they sometimes lacked in law. This dynamic helped make Cortés's conquest of the Aztecs possible.

Diego de Velásquez, a Spanish nobleman appointed the governor of Cuba, granted Cortés the right to explore and trade along the coast of South America. He gave him no authority, however, to attack native peoples in the region or claim land for himself. But seeing the possibility for gaining great riches, Cortés forged alliances with local rulers willing to join the attack against the Aztec chief, Montezuma. From the perspective of local Indian communities, Cortés's presence offered an opportunity to strike back against the brutal Aztec regime.

Despite their assumption of cultural superiority, many Spaniards who accompanied Cortés were astonished by Aztec cities, canals, and temples, which rivaled those in Europe. Bernal Díaz, a young foot soldier, marveled, "These great towns and cues [pyramid-like temples] and buildings rising from the water, all made of stone, seemed like an enchanted vision. . . . Indeed, some of our soldiers asked if it were not all a dream." Seeing these architectural wonders may have given some soldiers pause about trying to conquer the Indian kingdom. But when Montezuma presented Cortés with large quantities of precious objects, including gold-encrusted jewelry, as a peace offering, he alerted Spaniards to the vast wealth awaiting them in the Aztec capital.

When Cortés and his men marched to Tenochtitlán in 1519, Montezuma was indecisive in his response. After an early effort to ambush the Spaniards failed, the Aztec leader allowed Cortés to march his men into the capital city, where the Spanish conquistador took Montezuma hostage. In response, Aztec warriors attacked the Spaniards, but Cortés and his men managed to fight their way out of Tenochtitlán. They suffered heavy losses and might have been crushed by their Aztec foes but for the alliances they had made among native groups in the surrounding area. Given time to regroup, the remaining Spanish soldiers and their allies attacked the Aztecs with superior steel weapons, horses, and attack dogs and gained a final victory.

The Spanish victory was also aided by the germs that soldiers carried with them. The invaders unintentionally introduced smallpox to the local population, which led to a staggering epidemic. It swept through Tenochtitlán in 1521, killing thousands and leaving Montezuma's army dramatically weakened. This human catastrophe as much as military resources and strategies allowed Cortés to conquer the capital. He then claimed the entire region as New Spain, asserting Spanish authority over the native groups that had allied with him. The Spanish conquistador then settled in Tenochtitlán while his men constructed the new capital of Mexico City around him.

As news of Cortés's victory spread, other Spanish conquistadors sought gold and glory in the Americas. Most important, in 1524 Francisco Pizarro, with only 168 men and 67 horses, conquered the vast Inca empire in present-day Peru. Once again, the Spaniards were aided by the spread of European diseases and conflicts among peoples subjected to Inca rule. This victory ensured Spanish access to vast supplies of silver in Potosí (in present-day Bolivia) and the surrounding mountains. Spain was now in control of the most densely populated regions of South America, areas that also contained the greatest mineral wealth.

 Online Document Project
Spanish and Indian Encounters in the Americas, 1520–1555
bedfordstmartins.com/hewittlawsonvalue

Spanish Adventurers Head North

In 1526, following Pizarro's conquest of the Incas, a company of Spanish women and men traveled from the West Indies as far north as the Santee River in present-day South Carolina. They planned to settle in the region and then search for gold and other valuables. The effort failed, but two years later Pánfilo de Narváez—one of the survivors—led four hundred soldiers from Cuba to Florida's Tampa Bay. Seeking precious metals, the party instead confronted hunger, disease, and hostile Indians. The ragtag group continued to journey along the Gulf coast, until only four men, led by Álvar Núñez Cabeza de Vaca, made their way from Galveston Bay back to Mexico City.

A decade later, in 1539, a survivor of Narváez's ill-fated venture—a North African named Esteban—led a party of Spaniards from Mexico back north. Lured by tales of Seven Golden Cities, the party instead encountered Zuñi Indians, who attacked the Spaniards and killed Esteban. Still, the men who returned to Mexico passed on stories about an extensive system of pueblos, where many Spaniards believed mountains of gold were hidden. Hoping to find fame and fortune, Francisco Vásquez de Coronado launched a grand expedition northward in 1540. Angered when they discovered that the fabled "Seven Cities are seven little villages," Coronado and his men terrorized the region, burning towns and stealing food and other goods before returning to Mexico.

Hernando de Soto headed a fourth effort to find wealth in North America. He had first sailed to America in 1514 and participated in conquests around present-day Panama. There he achieved a reputation for brutality and gained wealth through the Indian slave trade and by looting native treasures. Then in 1539 de Soto received royal authority to explore Florida, and that spring he established a village near Tampa Bay with more than six hundred Spanish, Indian, and African men, a few women, and more than two hundred horses. A few months later, de Soto and the bulk of his company traveled up the west Florida coast with Juan Ortiz. Ortiz, a member of the Narváez expedition, was an especially useful guide and interpreter. That winter, the expedition traveled into present-day Georgia and the Carolinas in an unsuccessful search for riches (Map 1.4).

On their return trip, de Soto's men engaged in a brutal battle with local Indians led by Chief Tuskaloosa. Although the Spaniards claimed victory, they lost a significant number of men and horses and most of their equipment. Fearing that

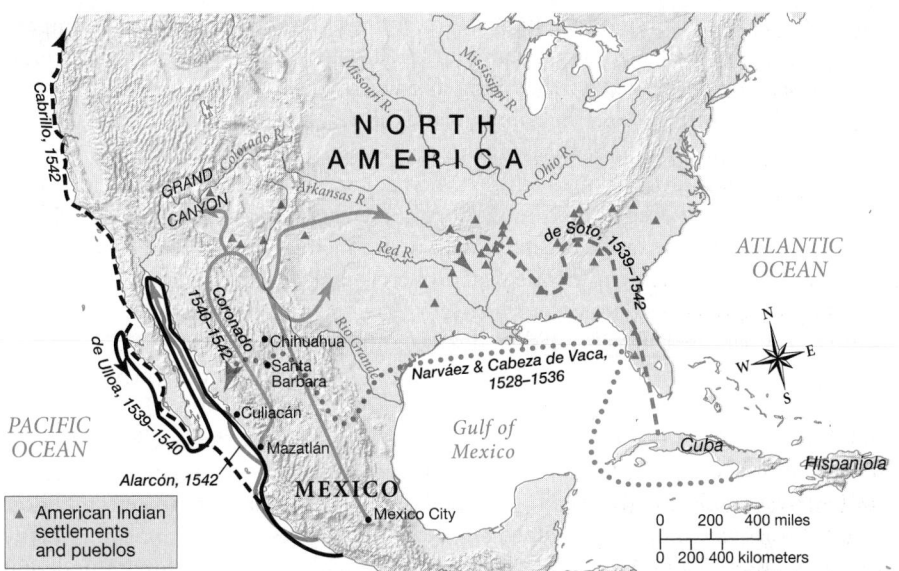

MAP 1.4

Spanish Explorations in North America, 1528–1542   Spanish explorers in North America hoped to find gold and other treasures. Instead, they encountered difficult terrain and native peoples hostile to Spanish intrusions. Many Spaniards died on these expeditions, and they failed to discover new sources of wealth. But they laid the foundations for Spanish settlements in Florida, northern Mexico, and California, in part by devastating local Indian populations.

word of the disaster would reach Spain, de Soto steered his men away from supply ships in the Gulf of Mexico and headed back north. The group continued through parts of present-day Tennessee, Arkansas, Oklahoma, and Texas, and in May 1541 they became the first Europeans to report seeing the vast Mississippi River. By the winter of 1542, the expedition had lost more men and supplies to Indians, and de Soto had died. The remaining members finally returned to Spanish territory in the summer of 1543.

The lengthy journey of de Soto and his men brought European diseases into new areas, leading to epidemics and the depopulation of once-substantial native communities. At the same time, the Spaniards left horses and pigs behind, creating new sources of food and transportation for native peoples. Although most Spaniards considered de Soto's journey a failure, the Spanish crown claimed vast new territories. Two decades later, in 1565, Pedro Menéndez de Avilés established a mission settlement on the northeast coast of Florida, named St. Augustine. It became the first permanent European settlement in North America and served as a model for missions later founded by Spaniards in Santa Fe, New Mexico, and in California.

Europeans Compete in North America

Spain's early ventures in North America helped inspire French and English explorers to establish their own footholds on the continent. The French entered the race for empire in 1524, when an Italian navigator named Giovanni da Verrazano led a French company along the coast of North America. Landing initially near Cape Fear on the Carolina coast, the expedition headed north, sailing into what would become New York harbor. Verrazano then continued north, claiming lands all along the coast for France.

A decade later, in 1534, the Frenchman Jacques Cartier sailed to the Gulf of St. Lawrence and traded for furs with the Micmac Indians. In two subsequent expeditions, Cartier pushed deeper into the territory known as Canada. Although he failed to discover precious metals or the elusive passage to the Pacific Ocean, Cartier's adventures inspired a French nobleman, the Sieur de Roberval, and several hundred followers to attempt a permanent settlement at Quebec in 1542. But the project was abandoned within a year because of harsh weather, disease, and high mortality.

English interest in North America was ignited by Spanish and French challenges to claims Cabot had made along the North Atlantic coast in the 1490s. To secure these rights, the English needed to colonize the disputed lands. Since the English crown did not have funds to support settlement, the earliest ventures were financed by minor noblemen who hoped to gain both wealth and the crown's favor. But early efforts failed. In 1583 inadequate financing doomed Sir Humphrey Gilbert's effort to plant a colony in Newfoundland, and inadequate supplies along with the harsh climate undercut Sir Ferdinando Gorge's settlement on the Maine coast the next year.

The most promising effort to secure an English foothold in North America was organized by Sir Walter Raleigh, a half-brother of Humphrey Gilbert. Claiming all the land north of Florida for England, Raleigh called the vast territory Virginia (after Elizabeth I, "the Virgin Queen"). Although he did not set foot in North America himself, in 1585 Raleigh sent a group of soldiers to found a colony on Roanoke Island, off the coast of present-day North Carolina. The colony would establish England's claims and serve as a launching point for raids against Spanish ships laden with valuables. This venture lasted less than a year before the company returned to England. But in 1587 Raleigh tried again to colonize the area, sending a group of 117 men, women, and children to Roanoke. When supply ships came to fortify the settlement in 1590, no trace of the English settlers remained.

By 1590, then, nearly a century after Columbus's initial voyage, only Spain had established permanent colonies in the Americas, mostly in the West Indies, Mexico, and South America. St. Augustine remained the only European outpost in North America. The French and the English, despite numerous efforts, had not sustained a single ongoing settlement by the end of the sixteenth century. Yet neither nation gave up hope of benefiting from the wealth of the Americas.

Spain Seeks Dominion in Europe and the Americas

The continued desire of European nations to gain colonies in the Americas resulted from the enormous wealth garnered by Spanish conquests. That wealth transformed economies throughout Europe. Between 1500 and 1650, Spanish ships carried home more than 180 tons of gold and 16,000 tons of silver from Mexico and Potosí. About one-fifth of this amount was taken by the Spanish crown for taxes; the rest was spent on goods imported from the Americas, Asia, or other European nations. Very little of this wealth was invested in improving conditions at home. Instead, the elite displayed their wealth in ostentatious ways: elaborate silver candelabras, dresses drenched in jewels, and lavish tapestries imported from Asia. Meanwhile the rapid infusion of gold and silver fueled inflation, making it harder for ordinary people to afford the necessities of life.

In one area, however, employment for the poor expanded rapidly. King Philip II, who ruled Spain from 1556 to 1598, used American gold and silver to fund a variety of military campaigns, ensuring an endless demand for soldiers and sailors. The king, a devout Catholic, claimed to be doing God's work as Spain conquered Italy and Portugal, including the latter's colonies in Africa, and tightened its grip on the Netherlands, which had been acquired by Spain through marriage in the early sixteenth century. In response, the English aristocrat Sir Walter Raleigh warned, "It is his [Philip's] Indian Gold that . . . endangereth and disturbeth all the nations of Europe."

Despite the obvious material benefits, the Spaniards were not blind to the enormous human costs of colonization, and the conquest of the Americas inspired heated debates within Spain. Roman Catholic bishops and priests, royal officials, and colonial leaders disagreed vehemently about whether Spanish conquerors could simply acquire riches from foreign lands or were required to Christianize those they conquered for the glory of God. While Catholic leaders believed that the conversion of native peoples was critical to Spanish success in the Americas, most royal officials and colonial agents viewed the extraction of precious metals as far more important. They argued that cheap labor was essential to creating wealth. Yet brutal conditions led to the death of huge numbers of Indians, and many church officials insisted that such conditions made it nearly impossible to gain new converts to Catholicism.

By 1550, tales of the widespread torture and enslavement of Indians convinced the Spanish king Carlos V to gather a group of theologians, jurists, and philosophers at Valladolid to discuss the moral and legal implications of conquest. From Mexico, Hernán Cortés sent the king a message, insisting that there was no need to consider the natives' views since they "must obey the royal orders of Your Majesty, whatever their nature." But not all the participants at Valladolid agreed. Bartolomé de Las Casas, a former conquistador and Dominican friar, spent many years preaching to Indians in America. He asked, "And so what man of sound mind will approve a war against men who are harmless, ignorant, gentle, temperate, unarmed, and destitute of every human defense?" Las Casas reasoned that even if Spain defeated the Indians, the souls of those killed would be lost to God, while among the survivors "hatred and loathing of the Christian religion" would prevail. He even suggested replacing Indian labor with African labor, apparently less concerned with the souls of black people.

Juan Ginés de Sepúlveda, the royal historian, attacked Las Casas's arguments. Although he had never set foot in America, he read reports of cannibalism and other violations of "natural law" among native peoples. Since the Indians were savages, the civilized Spaniards were obligated to "destroy barbarism and educate these people to a more humane and virtuous life." If they refused such help, Spanish rule "can be imposed upon them by force of arms." Like Ginés de Sepúlveda, Theodor de Bry never visited the Americas, yet his depictions of the region shaped European impressions. Although Ginés de Sepúlveda spoke for the majority at Valladolid, Las Casas and his supporters continued to press their case as Spain expanded its reach into North America.

Theodor de Bry, Engraving of the Black Legend, 1598 In the late 1500s, the engraver Theodor de Bry and his sons began creating a series of copperplate illustrations depicting the exploration of the Americas. Because de Bry had never visited the New World, his illustrations came from descriptions and pictures by explorers. He got a number of cultural facts wrong, but his scenes were detailed and graphic and enormously popular. This illustration depicts Spanish cruelty against Indians. Beinecke Rare Book and Manuscript Library, Yale University

At the same time, American riches increasingly flowed beyond Spain's borders. The Netherlands was a key beneficiary of this wealth, becoming a center for Spanish ship-building and trade. Still, the Dutch were never completely under Spanish control, and they traded independently with their European neighbors. Thus gold, silver, and other items made their way to France, England, and elsewhere. Goods also followed older routes across the Mediterranean to the Ottoman empire, where traders could make huge profits on exotic items from the Americas. Thus, while some Europeans suffered under Spanish power, others benefited from the riches brought to the continent. By the late sixteenth century, the desire for a greater share of those riches revitalized imperial dreams among the French and English as well as the Dutch.

REVIEW & RELATE

• What motives were behind the Spanish conquest and colonization of the Americas?

• What were the consequences in Europe of Spain's acquisition of an American empire?

Conclusion: A New America

When Spanish explorers happened upon the Americas, they brought Europeans into contact with native peoples who had inhabited the two continents for thousands of years. But these explorations and the conquests that followed did transform North and South America in dramatic ways. Martin Waldseemüller died in 1521 or 1522, so he was not able to incorporate into his maps the coastlines, waterways, and mountains reported by Magellan, Balboa, Cortés, Coronado, de Soto, Cartier, and other European adventurers. He would no doubt have been amazed to see the increasingly detailed maps that cartographers created of the elongated continent he first named America.

While mapmakers benefited from Europeans pushing deeper and deeper into the Americas, native residents were rarely asked if they wanted the plants, animals, goods, and germs offered by these invaders. Even Europeans seeking permanent settlements and peaceful trade relations with the Indians brought diseases that devastated local populations along with plants and animals that transformed their landscape, diet, and traditional ways of life.

Malintzin saw these changes firsthand. She watched as disease ravaged not only rural villages but even the capital city of Tenochtitlán. She encountered horses, pigs, attack dogs, and other European animals. She ate the foods and wore the clothes that her Spanish captors provided. Malintzin accompanied Cortés and his men as they conquered the Aztecs, and she watched as more Spaniards, including the first women, settled in New Spain. In 1522 she gave birth to Cortés's son; two years later, she served as interpreter when he ventured north from Mexico City to conquer more territory. In 1526 or 1527, however, she married a Spanish soldier, Juan Jaramillo, and settled in Mexico City. She soon had a daughter, Maria, and in 1528 Jaramillo and "his wife, doña Marina" were granted lands for an orchard and a farm. We do not know how long Malintzin lived or what she thought of her life as the wife of a Spanish gentleman. But her children would grow up in a world that was very different from the one in which their mother was raised. In the century to come, the contacts and conflicts between native peoples and Europeans escalated, especially in North America. So, too, did conflicts among European nations seeking to gain control of North American lands.

Chapter Review

MAKE IT STICK

LearningCurve **bedfordstmartins.com/hewittlawsonvalue**
After reading the chapter, use LearningCurve to retain what you've read.

IDENTIFY KEY TERMS

Identify and explain the significance of each term below.

Beringia (p. 3)
horticulture (p. 4)
Aztecs (p. 4)
Maya (p. 5)
Incas (p. 5)
Hopewell people (p. 6)
Crusades (p. 7)

Black Death (p. 9)
Renaissance (p. 9)
Enterprise of the Indies (p. 13)
encomiendas (p. 14)
Columbian exchange (p. 17)
conquistadors (p. 18)

REVIEW & RELATE

Answer the focus questions from each section of the chapter.

1. Compare and contrast the Aztecs, Incas, and Maya. What similarities and differences do you note?

2. How did the societies of North America differ from those of the equatorial zone and the Andes?

3. How and why did Europeans expand their connections with Africa and the Middle East in the fifteenth century?

4. How did early European encounters with West Africans lay the foundation for later race-based slavery?

5. What were the short-term consequences in both Europe and the Americas of Columbus's voyages?

6. How did the Columbian exchange transform both the Americas and Europe?

7. What motives were behind the Spanish conquest and colonization of the Americas?

8. What were the consequences in Europe of Spain's acquisition of an American empire?

ONLINE DOCUMENT PROJECTS

◆ **Mapping America**
◆ **Spanish and Indian Encounters in the Americas, 1520–1555**

After reading the primary sources in these document sets, answer the **Interpret the Evidence** questions to help you analyze each of the documents, and then answer the **Put It in Context** question(s) to help you relate the documents to the topics and themes you read about in the chapter.

bedfordstmartins.com/hewittlawsonvalue

TIMELINE OF EVENTS

13,000–11,000 B.C.E.	First northeast Asians migrate to the Americas	**1469**	Marriage of Isabella of Castile and Ferdinand II of Aragon leads to unification of Spain
1000 B.C.E.	Agriculture develops in some parts of the Americas	**1482**	Portugal builds Elmina Castle on the Gold Coast of West Africa
900 B.C.E.–300 C.E.	Maya settle Yucatán peninsula		
500 C.E.	Mogollon and Hohokam communities established in present-day Arizona and New Mexico	**1487**	Bartolomeu Dias rounds the Cape of Good Hope
		1492	Isabella and Ferdinand expel last Muslim conquerors from the Iberian peninsula
500–1400	Mississippian people establish complex societies centered on towns and massive earthworks		Columbus launches Enterprise of the Indies
800	Mayan civilization begins to decline	**1497**	Vasco da Gama reaches India by sailing around Africa
1000	Norse establish small settlement in North America	**1507**	Martin Waldseemüller and Mathias Ringmann publish *Universalis Cosmographia*
1292	Marco Polo publishes his *Travels*		
1325	Aztecs build Tenochtitlán	**1519**	Malintzin captured by Spaniards
1340s	Bubonic plague arrives in Europe from Asia	**1519–1521**	Spanish and Indian army led by Cortés conquers the Aztecs
1400–1500	Inca empire reaches the height of its power	**1519–1522**	Fleet led by Ferdinand Magellan circumnavigates the globe sailing west
1440s	Portuguese begin to trade along the coast of West Africa	**1524**	Francisco Pizarro conquers the Incas
1452–1455	Johannes Gutenberg uses movable type to produce 180 copies of the Bible	**1587**	English colony of Roanoke established in North America

✓ LearningCurve
bedfordstmartins.com/hewittlawsonvalue
After reading the chapter, use LearningCurve
to retain what you've read.

Colonization and Conflicts

1550–1680

AMERICAN HISTORIES

Born in 1580 to a yeoman farm family in Lincolnshire, the adventurer John Smith left England as a young man "to learne the life of a Souldier." After fighting and traveling in Europe, the Mediterranean, and North Africa for several years, Captain Smith returned to England around 1605. There he joined the Virginia Company, whose investors planned to establish a private settlement on mainland North America. In December 1606, Captain Smith sailed with a contingent of 104 men, arriving in Chesapeake Bay the following April. The group founded Jamestown, named in honor of King James I. In doing so, they claimed the land for themselves and their country. However, whatever abstract claims Captain Smith and his comrades believed they were making to the region, their settlement was located in an area already controlled by a powerful leader, Chief Powhatan, who headed a confederation of local tribes.

In December 1607, when Powhatan's younger brother discovered Smith and two of his Jamestown comrades in the chief's territory, the Indians executed the two comrades but eventually released Smith. It is likely that before sending him back to Jamestown, Powhatan performed an adoption ceremony in an effort to bring Smith and the English under his authority. A typical ceremony would have involved Powhatan sending out one of his daughters—in this case, Pocahontas, who was about twelve years old—to indicate that the captive was spared. But Smith either did not understand or refused to accept his new status. He later claimed that Pocahontas saved him out of love. At the time, however, he simply returned to Jamestown and urged the residents to build fortifications to enhance their strength and security.

The following fall, the colonists elected Smith president of the Jamestown council. Holding the power of a colonial governor, he argued that intimidating the Indians was the way to win Powhatan's respect. He also demanded that the English labor on farms and fortifications six hours a day. Many colonists resisted. Like Smith himself, most of the men were adventurers; they had little skill—and even less interest—in farming. They came to America not to settle down but to gain wealth and glory. Despite improvements in conditions in the colony under Smith's regime, the Virginia Company soon replaced him with a new set of leaders. In October 1609, angry and bitter, Smith returned to England.

Captain Smith criticized Virginia Company policies on a number of fronts, publishing his views in 1612, which brought him widespread attention. Smith then set out to map the northern Atlantic coast, and in 1616 he published a tract that emphasized the similarity of the area's climate and terrain to the British Isles, calling it New England. He argued that colonies there could be made commercially viable but that success depended on recruiting settlers with the necessary skills and offering them land and a say in the colony's management.

English men and women settled New England in the 1620s, but they did not invite Smith to join them. The first colonists to the region sought religious sanctuary, not commercial success or military dominance. Yet they, too, suffered schisms in their ranks. Anne Hutchinson, a forty-five-year-old wife and mother, was at the center of one such division. Also born in Lincolnshire, England, in 1591, about a decade after Smith, Anne was well educated by her father, a minister in the Church of England. In 1612 she married William Hutchinson, a merchant, and over the next twenty years she gave birth to thirteen children. The Hutchinsons began attending Puritan sermons and by 1630 had embraced the new faith. Four years later, they followed the Reverend John Cotton to Massachusetts Bay.

The Reverend Cotton was soon urging Anne Hutchinson to use her exceptional knowledge of the Bible to hold prayer meetings in her home on Sundays for pregnant and nursing women who could not attend regular services. Hutchinson, like Cotton, preached a covenant of grace, by which individuals must rely solely on God's grace and could play no part in their own salvation. By contrast, mainstream Puritan leaders claimed that a man or woman could cooperate with God's grace by leading a saintly life and performing good works.

Hutchinson began challenging Puritan ministers who opposed a pure covenant of grace, charging that they posed a threat to their congregations. She soon attracted a loyal following that included men as well as women. The growing size of her Sunday meetings helped convince Puritan leaders to call the first synod of their Congregational Church in August 1637. The synod denounced Hutchinson's views and condemned her Sunday meetings. When she refused to recant, she was put on trial. Standing alone to face a panel of forty-nine powerful men in November 1637, Hutchinson defended herself against charges that she presumed to teach men and failed to honor the ministers of the colony. Unmoved by her defense, the Puritan judges convicted her of heresy and banished her from Massachusetts Bay. Hutchinson, her husband, and their six youngest children, along with dozens of followers, then settled in the recently established colony of Rhode Island.

THE AMERICAN HISTORIES of John Smith and Anne Hutchinson illustrate the diversity of motives that drew English men and women to North America in the seventeenth century. Smith led a group of soldiers and adventurers seeking wealth and glory, both for themselves and for their king. In many ways, their efforts to colonize Virginia were an extension of a larger competition between European states. The roots of Hutchinson's journey to North America can be traced to the Protestant Reformation of the sixteenth century, a massive religious upheaval that divided Europe into rival religious factions. The Puritan faith that was so central to her life was an outgrowth

of the Reformation. Yet as different as these two people and their motives were, both worked to further English settlement in North America even as they generated conflict within their own communities. At the same time, those communities confronted the needs and desires of diverse native peoples as well as the colonial aspirations of other Europeans. These contending forces reshaped the landscape of North America between 1550 and 1680.

English captain Bartholomew Gosnold trading with Indians, Virginia, 1634.
© British Library/HIP/Art Resource, NY

Religious and Imperial Transformations

The Puritans were part of a relatively new religious movement known as **Protestantism** that had emerged around 1520. Protestants challenged Catholic policies and practices but did not form a single church of their own. Instead, a number of theologians, including Martin Luther and John Calvin, formed distinct denominations in various regions of Europe, especially the German states, Switzerland, France, England, and the Netherlands. Catholics sought to counter their claims by revitalizing their faith and reasserting control. These religious conflicts shaped developments in North America as groups with competing visions worked to claim lands and sometimes souls.

The Protestant Reformation

Critiques of the Catholic Church multiplied in the early sixteenth century, driven by papal involvement in conflicts among monarchs and corruption among church officials. But the most vocal critics focused on immorality, ignorance, and absenteeism among clergy. These anticlerical views appeared in popular songs and printed images as well as in learned texts by theologians such as Martin Luther.

Luther, a professor of theology in Germany, believed that faith alone led to salvation, which could be granted only by God. He challenged the claims of Pope Leo X and his bishop in Germany that individuals could achieve salvation by buying indulgences, which were documents that absolved the buyer of sin. The church profited enormously from these sales, but they suggested that God's grace could be purchased. In 1517 Luther wrote an extended argument against indulgences and sent it to the local bishop. Although intended for learned clerics and academics, his writings soon gained a wider audience.

Luther's followers, who protested Catholic practices, became known as Protestants. His teachings circulated widely through sermons and printed texts, and his claim that ordinary people should read and reflect on the Scriptures appealed to the literate middle classes. Meanwhile his attacks on indulgences and corruption attracted those who resented the church's wealth and priests' lack of attention to their flock. In Switzerland, John Calvin developed a version of Protestantism in which civil magistrates and reformed ministers ruled over a Christian society. According to Calvinist beliefs, God was all-knowing and absolutely sovereign, while man was weak and sinful. Calvin argued that God had decided at the beginning of time who was saved and who was damned. Calvin's idea, known as predestination, energized Protestants who understood salvation as a gift from an all-knowing God in which human "works" played no part.

The Protestant Reformation quickly spread through central and northern Europe. England, too, came under the influence of Protestantism in the 1530s, although for different reasons. When the pope refused to annul the marriage of King Henry VIII and Catherine of Aragon, Henry denounced papal authority and established the **Church of England**, or Anglicanism, with himself as "defender of the faith." Despite the king's conversion to Protestantism, the Church of England retained many Catholic practices.

In countries like Spain and France with strong central governments and powerful ties to the Catholic Church, a strong Catholic Counter-Reformation largely quashed Protestantism. At the same time, Catholic leaders initiated reforms to counter their critics. In 1545 Pope Paul II called together a commission of cardinals, known as the Council of Trent (1545–1563), to address contentious issues such as corrupt bishops and priests, indulgences, and other financial abuses. The council initiated reforms, such as the founding of seminaries to train priests and the return of monastic orders to their spiritual foundations.

Religious upheavals in Europe contributed significantly to empire building in North America. Protestant and Catholic leaders urged followers to spread their faith across the Atlantic, while religious minorities sought a safe haven in North America. Just as important, political struggles erupted between Catholic and Protestant rulers in Europe following the Reformation. The politicization of religious divisions resulted in peasant unrest, economic crises, and military conflicts that pushed (or forced) people to seek new opportunities in the Americas. Thus in a variety of ways, religious transformations in Europe fueled the construction of empires in America.

Spain's Global Empire Declines

As religious conflicts escalated in Europe, the Spaniards in America continued to push north from Florida and Mexico in hopes of expanding their empire. At times, they confronted Protestants seeking to gain a foothold in the New World. For example, French Protestants, known as Huguenots, settled in Florida in the 1550s. By 1565, Spanish soldiers had constructed a fort at St. Augustine and massacred some three hundred Huguenots. The fort's main purpose, however, was to limit raids on Spanish ships by French and English privateers seeking to enrich themselves and their monarchs.

Yet as a result of the Council of Trent and the Catholic Counter-Reformation, Spain increasingly emphasized its religious mission. Thus Spanish authorities decided in 1573 that missionaries rather than soldiers should direct all new settlements. Franciscan priests began founding missions on the margins of Pueblo villages north of Mexico. They named the area Nuevo México (New Mexico), and many learned Indian languages. Over the following decades, as many as twenty thousand Pueblos officially converted to Catholicism, although many still retained traditional beliefs and practices. Thus they continued to practice religious ceremonies at sacred shrines known as kivas. Missionaries periodically destroyed the shrines and flogged Pueblo ceremonial leaders, but to no avail.

At the same time, the Franciscans tried to force the Pueblo people to adopt European ways. They insisted that men rather than women farm the land and that the Pueblos speak, cook, and dress like the Spaniards. Yet the missionaries largely ignored Spanish laws intended to protect Indians from coerced labor. Indeed, the Franciscans forced the Pueblos to build churches, provide the missions with food, and carry their goods to market. Wealthy landowners who followed the missionaries into New Mexico also demanded tribute in the form of goods and labor.

Then in 1598 Juan de Oñate, a member of a wealthy mining family, established a trading post and fort in the upper Rio Grande valley. The 500 soldiers who accompanied him seized corn and clothing from Pueblo villages and murdered or raped those who resisted. When the Spanish force was confronted by Indians at the Acoma pueblo, 11 soldiers were killed. The Spanish retaliated, slaughtering 500 men and 300 women and children. But fearing reprisals from outraged Indians, most Spanish settlers withdrew from the region.

In 1610 the Spanish returned, founded Santa Fe, and established a network of missions and estates owned by *encomenderos*, Spanish elites granted land and the right to exploit local Indian labor. The Pueblo people largely accepted the new situation. In part, they feared military reprisals if they challenged Spanish authorities. But they were also faced with droughts and disease, as well as raids by hostile Apache and Navajo tribes. The Pueblos hoped to gain protection from Spanish soldiers and priests. Yet their faith in the Franciscans' spiritual power soon began to fade when conditions did not improve. Although Spain maintained a firm hold on Florida and its colonies in the West Indies, it began focusing most of its efforts on staving off growing resistance among the Pueblo people. Thus as other European powers expanded their reach into North America, the Spaniards were left with few resources to protect their eastern frontier.

France Enters the Race for Empire

In the late sixteenth century, French, Dutch, and English investors became increasingly interested in gaining a foothold in North America. But until Catholic Spain's grip on the Atlantic world was broken, other nations could not hope to compete for an American empire. It was the Protestant Reformation that helped shape the alliances that shattered Spain's American monopoly. As head of the Church of England, King Henry VIII and then his daughter Queen Elizabeth I sought closer political and commercial ties with Protestant nations like the Netherlands. At the same time, the queen assented to, and benefited from, Francis Drake's raids on Spanish ships. She rewarded him with a knight-hood for services to the crown. In 1588 King Philip II of Spain decided to punish England for its attacks against Spanish shipping and intervention in the Netherlands and sent a massive armada to spearhead the invasion of England. Instead, the English, aided by Dutch ships that were smaller and more mobile, defeated the armada and ensured that other nations could compete for riches and colonies in North America.

Although French rulers shared Spain's Catholic faith, the two nations were rivals, and the defeat of the armada provided them as well as the Dutch and English with greater access to North American colonies. Moreover, once in North America, the French adopted attitudes and policies that were significantly different from those of Spain. This was due in part to their greater interest in trade than in conquest. They needed to develop alliances with local inhabitants who could supply them with fish and furs to be sold in Europe. The French had fished the North Atlantic since the mid-sixteenth century, but in the 1580s they built stations along the Newfoundland coast for drying codfish. French traders then established relations with local Indians and eagerly exchanged iron kettles, which the native peoples desired, for beaver skins, which were highly prized in Europe.

By the early seventeenth century, France's King Henry IV sought to profit more directly from the resources in North America. With the Edict of Nantes (1598), the king ended decades of religious wars by granting political rights and limited toleration to French Protestants, the Huguenots. Now he could focus on developing the increas-ingly lucrative trade in American fish and furs. Samuel de Champlain, an experienced soldier and sailor, founded the first permanent French settlement in North America in 1608 at Quebec. Accompanied by several dozen of his men, Champlain joined a Huron raid on the Iroquois, who resided south of the Great Lakes. Using guns, which had rarely been seen in the region, the French helped ensure a Huron victory and a power-ful ally for the French. But the battle also fueled lasting bitterness among the Iroquois.

Trade relations flourished between the French and their Indian allies, but relatively few French men and even fewer French women settled in North America in the seven-teenth century. Government policies discouraged mass migration, and peasants were also concerned by reports of short growing seasons and severe winters in Canada. Cardinal Richelieu, the king's powerful chief minister, urged priests and nuns to migrate to New France and establish missions among the Indians, but he barred Huguenots from emigrating, which further limited colonization. Thus into the 1630s, French settlements in North America consisted largely of fishermen, fur traders, and Catholic missionaries.

Fur traders were critical to sustaining the French presence and warding off encroachment by the English. They journeyed along lakes and rivers throughout eastern Canada, aided by the Huron tribe. Some Frenchmen took Indian wives, who provided them with both domestic labor and kinship ties to powerful trading partners. These marriages also helped forge a middle ground in the Great Lakes region as French traders pushed westward and gained new Indian allies among the Ojibwe and Dakota tribes. The middle ground was a space in which shared economic interest motivated a remarkable degree of cultural exchange and mutual adaptation. Some French learned native languages and recognized the incredible value of canoes to their trade. They also came to appreciate Indian women's importance in gathering and preparing food, scraping beaver pelts, and weaving. At the same time, Indian communities adopted iron cooking pots and needles and European cloth. Jesuit missionaries, who entered New France in 1625, frowned on these marriages and the cultural exchanges they fostered. Nonetheless, they followed the path set out by fur traders and established missions among the Hurons and later the Ojibwes.

In their ongoing search for new sources of furs, the French established a fortified trading post at Montreal in 1643, and over the next three decades they continued to push farther west. However, in extending the fur trade beyond the St. Lawrence River valley, the French left their Huron allies open to attacks from the Iroquois. The Iroquois suffered from the same diseases that decimated other tribes, and they also wanted to keep the Huron tribe from trading their high-quality furs to the Dutch. With guns supplied by Dutch merchants, the Iroquois could fend off economic competition and secure captives to restore their population. The result was a series of devastating assaults on Huron villages in which dozens of Jesuits died alongside the Indians they had converted.

The ongoing wars among native rivals limited the ability of France to capitalize on its North American colonies. Indeed, the only hope of maintaining profits from the fur trade was to continue to move westward. But in doing so, the French carried European diseases into new areas, ignited warfare among more native groups, and stretched their always small population of settlers ever thinner. Still, French explorers, traders, and priests extended their reach across Canada and by 1681 moved southward along the Mississippi to a territory they named Louisiana in honor of King Louis XIV. There they would find themselves face-to-face with Spanish adventurers heading east from New Mexico.

The conflicts between commerce and conversion so evident in Spanish America were far less severe in New France. Not only did French traders rely on Indian allies, but French missionaries also sought to build on native beliefs and to learn their language and customs. Although the Jesuits assumed that their own religious beliefs and cultural values were superior to those of the Indians, they did seek to engage Indians on their own terms. Thus one French Jesuit employed the Huron belief that "our souls have desires which are inborn and concealed" to explain Christian doctrines of sin and salvation to potential converts. Still, French traders and missionaries carried deadly germs, and Catholics sought conversion, not mutual adaptation. Thus while Indians clearly benefited from their alliances with the French in the short term, the long-term costs were devastating.

The Dutch Expand into North America

The Dutch, who eagerly embraced the Protestant Reformation at home, made no pretense of bringing religion to Indians in America. From the beginning, their goals were primarily economic. As Spain's shipbuilding center, the Netherlands benefited from the wealth pouring in from South America. The affluent merchant class that emerged among the Dutch promoted the arts, and artists like Salomon van Ruysdael and Johannes Vermeer in turn captured the importance of trade in their work. But the Dutch also embraced Calvinism and sought to separate themselves from Catholic Spain. In 1581 the Netherlands declared its independence from King Philip II, although Spain refused to recognize the new status for several decades. Still, by 1600 the Netherlands was both a Protestant haven and the trading hub of Europe. Indeed, the Dutch East India Company controlled trade routes to much of Asia and parts of Africa.

With the technology and skills developed under Spanish control, the Dutch decided to acquire their own American colonies. In 1609 the Dutch established a trading center on the Hudson River in present-day New York, where they could trade with Iroquois to the west as well as with Indians who gathered beaver skins along Lake Champlain and farther north. The small number of Dutch traders developed especially friendly relations with the powerful Mohawk nation, and in 1614 the trading post was relocated to Fort Orange, near present-day Albany.

In 1624, to fend off French and English raids on ships sent downriver from Fort Orange, the Dutch established New Amsterdam on Manhattan Island, which they purchased from the Lenape Indians. The new settlement was organized by the Dutch West Indies Company, which had been chartered three years earlier. New Amsterdam was the centerpiece of the larger New Netherland colony and attracted a diverse community of traders, fishermen, and farmers. It was noted for its representative government and religious toleration, which ensured that religious differences did not get in the way of making money.

The European settlers of New Netherland may have gotten along with one another, but the same could not be said for the settlers and the local Indian populations. Tensions increased as Dutch colonists carved out farms north of New Amsterdam where larger communities of Algonquian Indians lived and where European pigs and cattle foraged in Indian cornfields. Algonquians in turn killed and ate Dutch livestock. In 1639 conflict escalated when Governor William Kieft demanded an annual tribute in wampum or grain. Local Algonquians resisted, raiding Dutch farms on the frontier and killing at least two colonists. Then in 1643 Kieft launched a surprise attack on an Indian encampment on Manhattan Island, murdering eighty people, mostly women and children. Outraged Algonquians burned and looted homes north of the city, killed livestock, and murdered settlers. For two decades, sporadic warfare continued, but eventually the Algonquians were defeated.

At the same time, the Dutch eagerly traded for furs with Mohawk Indians along the upper Hudson River. The Mohawks were a powerful tribe that had the backing of the even more powerful Iroquois Confederacy. Their ties to Indian nations farther west allowed them to provide beaver skins to Dutch traders long after beavers had died out in the Hudson valley. Still, the Mohawk people did not deceive themselves. As one chief proclaimed in 1659, "The Dutch say we are brothers and that we are joined together with chains, but that lasts only so long as we have beavers."

Meanwhile reports of atrocities by both Indians and the Dutch circulated in the Netherlands. These damaged New Amsterdam's reputation and slowed migration dramatically. Exhausted by the unrelenting conflicts, the Dutch surrendered New Amsterdam to the English without a fight when the latter sent a convoy to oust their former allies in 1664.

REVIEW & RELATE

- How did the Protestant Reformation shape the course of European expansion in the Americas?
- How did the French and Dutch colonies in North America differ from the Spanish empire to the south?

The English Seek an Empire

The English, like the French and the Dutch, entered the race for an American empire late. England's failed efforts to colonize North America in the sixteenth century had left them without a permanent settlement until the founding of **Jamestown** on the Chesapeake River in 1607. In the 1620s, the English also established settlements in the West Indies, which quickly became the economic engine of English colonization. Expansion into these areas demanded new modes of labor to ensure a return on investment. Beginning in the mid-sixteenth century, large numbers of European indentured servants and growing numbers of African men and women crossed the Atlantic, some voluntarily, many involuntarily.

The English Establish Jamestown

England's success in colonizing North America depended in part on a new economic model in which investors sold shares in joint-stock companies and sought royal support for their venture. In 1606 a group of London merchants formed the Virginia Company, and King James I granted them the right to settle a vast area of North America, from present-day New York to North Carolina. The proprietors promised to "propagate the *Christian* religion" among native inhabitants in the region, but they were far more interested in turning a profit.

Most of the men that the Virginia Company recruited as colonists were, like John Smith, adventurers who hoped to get rich through the discovery of precious metals. Arriving on the coast of North America in April 1607 after a four-month voyage, the weary colonists established Jamestown on a site they chose for its easy defense. Although bothered by the settlement's mosquito-infested environment, the colonists focused their energies on the search for gold and silver.

The Englishmen also made contact with the Indian chief Powhatan, who presided over a confederation of some 14,000 Algonquian-speaking Indians from 25 to 30 tribes. The **Powhatan Confederacy** was far more powerful than its English neighbors, and, indeed, for the first two years the settlers depended on the Indians to survive. Although the Jamestown settlers were often hungry, few of them engaged in farming. Moreover, the nearby water was tainted by salt from the ocean, and diseases that festered in the low lying area ensured a high death toll. Nine months after arriving in Virginia, only 38 of the original 105 settlers remained alive.

Despite the Englishmen's aggressive posture and inability to feed themselves, Powhatan initially assisted the settlers in hopes they could provide him with English cloth, iron hatchets, and even guns. His capture and subsequent release of John Smith in 1607 suggests his interest in developing trade relations with the newcomers even as he sought to subordinate them. But leaders like Captain Smith considered Powhatan and his warriors a threat rather than an asset. Although Jamestown residents could not afford to engage in open hostilities with local natives, they did raid villages for corn and other food, making Powhatan increasingly wary. The settlers' decision to construct a fort under Smith's direction only increased the Indians' concern.

Meanwhile the Virginia Company devised a new plan to stave off the collapse of its colony. It started selling seven-year joint-stock options to raise funds and recruited new settlers to produce staple crops—grapes, sugar, cotton, or tobacco—for export since the search for precious metals had failed. Interested individuals who could not afford to invest cash could sign on for service in Virginia. After seven years, these colonists would receive a hundred acres of land. In June 1609, a new contingent of colonists attracted by this plan—five hundred men and a hundred women—sailed for Jamestown.

The new arrivals, however, had not brought enough supplies to sustain the colony through the winter. Powhatan did offer some aid, but a severe dry spell meant that the Indians, too, suffered from shortages in the winter of 1609–1610. A "starving time" settled on Jamestown. By the spring of 1610, seven of every eight settlers who had arrived in Jamestown since 1607 were dead. One colonist noted that settlers "were destroyed by cruell diseases, as Swellings, Fluxes, [and] Burning Fevers," though most "died of mere famine."

That June, the sixty survivors decided to abandon Jamestown and sail for home. But in the harbor, they met three English ships loaded with supplies and three hundred more settlers. Fresh supplies and a larger population inspired the English to take a much more confrontational approach. Jamestown's new leaders adopted an aggressive military posture, attacking native villages, burning crops, killing many Indians, and taking others captive. They believed that such brutality would horrify neighboring tribes and convince them to obey English demands for food and labor.

Tobacco Fuels Growth in Virginia

It was not, however, military aggression but the discovery of a viable cash crop that saved the colony. Orinoco tobacco, a sweet-flavored leaf grown in the West Indies and South America, sold well in England and Europe. One Virginia colonist, John Rolfe, began to experiment with its growth in 1612. Within two years, it was clear that Orinoco tobacco prospered in Virginia soil. Production of the leaf soared as eager investors poured seeds, supplies, and labor into Jamestown. Exports multiplied rapidly, from 2,000 pounds in 1615 to 40,000 five years later and an incredible 1.5 million pounds by 1629. Although high taxes and overproduction led to declining prices in the 1630s, tobacco remained the most profitable cash crop on mainland North America throughout the seventeenth century.

Tobacco cultivation transformed relations between the English and the Indians. Farmers could increase their profits only by obtaining more land and more laborers. The Virginia Company sought to supply the laborers by offering those who could pay their own way land for themselves and their families. Those who could not afford passage could labor for landowners for seven years and then gain their independence and perhaps land of their own. Yet the land the Virginia Company so generously offered would-be colonists was, in most cases, already settled by members of the Powhatan Confederacy. Thus the rapid increase in tobacco cultivation intensified competition for land between colonists and Indians.

As circumstances began to change, Powhatan tried one last time to create an alliance between his confederacy and the English settlers. In 1614 he agreed to allow his daughter Pocahontas to marry John Rolfe. Pocahontas converted to Christianity, took the name Rebecca, and two years later traveled to England with Rolfe and their infant son. Rebecca was treated royally, but she fell ill and died in 1617. After her death, Rolfe returned to Virginia and continued to develop successful strains of tobacco. Soon after his return, Powhatan died, and his younger brother Opechancanough took over as chief.

In 1619 the English crown granted Virginia the right to establish a local governing body, the **House of Burgesses**. Its members could make laws and levy taxes, although the English governor or the company council in London held veto power.

At the same time, the Virginia Company resolved to recruit more female settlers as a way to increase the colony's population so that it "may spread into generations." Other young women and men arrived as **indentured servants**, working in the fields and homes of more affluent Englishmen for a set period of time, often seven years, in exchange for the price of passage to America.

Matoaks als Rebecka daughter to the mighty Prince Powhatan Emperour of Attanoughkomouck als virginia converted and baptized in the Christian faith, and wife to the worl. Mr. Joh. Rolff.

Simon van de Passe, Engraving of Pocahontas, 1616   Simon van de Passe created this portrait of Pocahontas during her visit to England in 1616. The engraving was commissioned by the Virginia Company as a way to market settlement in Jamestown. It was the only depiction of Pocahontas drawn from life because she died in London the following year. This engraving was copied, though not always accurately, many times during the eighteenth and nineteenth centuries.   Library of Congress

The first boatload of twenty Africans also arrived in Jamestown aboard a Dutch ship in 1619, bound as indentured servants to farmers desperate for labor.

Although the English colony still hugged the Atlantic coast, its expansion increased conflict with native inhabitants. In March 1622, after repeated English incursions on land cleared and farmed by Indians, Chief Opechancanough mobilized area tribes for a surprise attack on English settlements. The Indians killed nearly a third of the colonists. In retaliation, Englishmen assaulted native villages, killed inhabitants, burned cornfields, and sold captives into slavery.

Announcing victory in 1623, the English claimed they owned the land "by right of Warre." But hostilities continued for nearly a decade. In 1624, in the midst of the crisis, King James annulled the Virginia Company charter and took control of the colony. He appointed the governor and a small advisory council, required that legislation passed by the House of Burgesses be ratified by the Privy Council, and demanded that property owners pay taxes to support the Church of England. These regulations became the model for royal colonies throughout North America. Still, royal proclamations could not halt Indian opposition. In 1644 Opechancanough launched a second uprising against the English, in which some five hundred colonists were killed. However, after two years of bitter warfare, the Powhatan chief was finally captured and then killed. With the English population now too large to eradicate, the Chesapeake Indians finally submitted to English authority in 1646, paying tribute to remain on lands they had lived on for generations.

Expansion, Rebellion, and the Emergence of Slavery

By the 1630s, despite continued conflicts with Indians, Virginia was well on its way to commercial success. The most successful tobacco planters utilized indentured servants, including some Africans as well as thousands of English and Irish immigrants. Between 1640 and 1670, some 40,000 to 50,000 of these migrants settled in Virginia and neighboring Maryland (Map 2.1). Maryland was founded in 1632 when King Charles I, the successor to James I, granted most of the territory north of Chesapeake Bay and the title of Lord Baltimore to Cecilius Calvert. Calvert was among the minority of English who remained a Catholic, and he planned to create Maryland as a refuge for his persecuted coworshippers. Appointing his brother Leonard Calvert as governor, he carefully prepared for the first settlement. The Calverts recruited skilled artisans and farmers (mainly Protestant) as well as wealthy merchants and aristocrats (mostly Catholic) to establish St. Mary's City on the mouth of the Potomac River. Although conflict continued to fester between the Catholic elite and the Protestant majority, Governor Calvert convinced the Maryland assembly to pass the Act of Religious Toleration in 1649, granting religious freedom to all Christians.

Taken together, Maryland and Virginia formed the Chesapeake region of the English empire. Both colonies relied on tobacco to produce the wealth that fueled their growth, and both introduced African labor to complement the supply of white indentured servants. This proved especially important from 1650 on, as improved economic conditions in England meant fewer English men and women were willing to gamble on a better life in North America. Although the number of African laborers remained small until late in the century, there was a growing effort on the part of colonial leaders to increase their control over this segment of the workforce. Thus in 1660 the House of Burgesses passed an act that allowed African laborers to be enslaved. In 1664 Maryland followed suit. A slow if unsteady march toward full-blown racial slavery had begun.

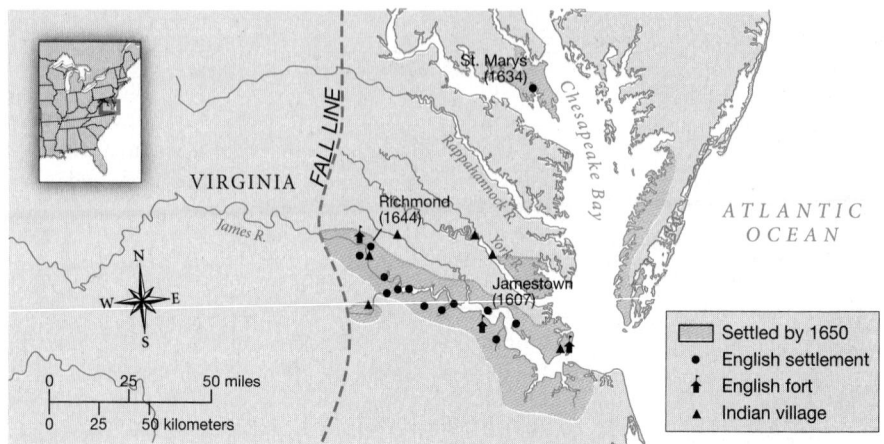

MAP 2.1

The Growth of English Settlement in the Chesapeake, c. 1650   With the success of tobacco, English plantations and forts spread along the James River and north to St. Mary's. By 1650 most Chesapeake Indian tribes had been vanquished or forced to move north and west. While the fall line, which marked the limit of navigable waterways, kept English settlements close to the Atlantic coast, it also ensured easy shipment of goods.

In legalizing human bondage, Virginia legislators followed a model established in Barbados, where the booming sugar industry spurred the development of plantation slavery. By 1660 Barbados had become the first English colony with a black majority population. Twenty years later, there were seventeen slaves for every white indentured servant on Barbados. The growth of slavery on the island depended almost wholly on imports from Africa since slaves there died faster than they could reproduce themselves. In the context of high death rates, brutal working conditions, and massive imports, Barbados systematized its slave code, defining enslaved Africans as chattel—that is, as mere property more akin to livestock than to human beings. Slaves existed to enrich their masters, and masters could do with them as they liked.

While African slaves would, in time, become a crucial component of the Chesapeake labor force, indentured servants made up the majority of bound workers in Virginia and Maryland for most of the seventeenth century. They labored under harsh conditions, and punishment for even minor infractions could be severe. Servants had holes bored in their tongues for complaining against their masters; they were beaten, whipped, and branded for a variety of "crimes"; and female servants who became pregnant had two years added to their contracts. Some white servants made common cause with black laborers who worked side by side with them on tobacco plantations. They ran away together, stole goods from their masters, and planned uprisings and rebellions.

By the 1660s and 1670s, the population of former servants who had become free formed a growing and increasingly unhappy class. Most were struggling economically, working as common laborers or tenants on large estates. Those who managed to move west and claim land on the frontier were confronted by hostile Indians like the Susquehannock. Virginia governor Sir William Berkeley had little patience with the complaints of these colonists. The labor demands of wealthy tobacco planters needed to be met, and frontier settlers' call for an aggressive Indian policy would hurt the profitable deerskin trade with the Algonquian Indians. Adopting a defensive strategy, Berkeley maintained a system of nine forts along the frontier that was supported by taxes, providing another aggravation for poorer colonists.

In late 1675, conflict erupted when frontier settlers attacked not the Susquehannock nation but rather Indian communities allied with the English since 1646. An even larger force of Virginia militiamen then surrounded a Susquehannock village and murdered five chiefs who tried to negotiate for peace. Susquehannock warriors retaliated with deadly raids on frontier farms. Despite the outbreak of open warfare, Governor Berkeley still refused to send troops, so disgruntled farmers turned to Nathaniel Bacon. Bacon, only twenty-nine years old and a newcomer to Virginia, came from a wealthy family and was related to Berkeley by marriage. But he defied the governor's authority and called up an army to attack all of the region's Indians, whether Susquehannocks or English allies. **Bacon's Rebellion** had begun. Frontier farmers formed an important part of Bacon's coalition. But affluent planters who had been left out of Berkeley's inner circle also joined Bacon in hopes of gaining access to power and profits. And bound laborers, black and white, assumed that anyone who opposed the governor was on their side.

In the summer of 1676, Governor Berkeley declared Bacon guilty of treason. Rather than waiting to be captured, Bacon led his army toward Jamestown. Berkeley then arranged a hastily called election to undercut the rebellion. Even though Berkeley had rescinded the right of men without property to vote, Bacon's supporters won control of the House of Burgesses, and Bacon won new adherents. These included "news wives," lower-class women who spread information (and rumors) about oppressive conditions, thereby aiding the rebels. As Bacon and his followers marched across Virginia, his men plundered the plantations of Berkeley supporters and captured Berkeley's estate at Green Spring. In September they reached Jamestown after the governor and his administration fled across Chesapeake Bay. The rebels burned the capital to the ground, victory seemingly theirs.

Only a month later, however, Bacon died of dysentery, and the movement he formed unraveled. Governor Berkeley, with the aid of armed ships from England, quickly reclaimed power. Outraged by the rebellion, he hanged twenty-three rebel leaders and incited his followers to plunder the estates of planters who had supported Bacon. But he could not undo the damage to Indian relations on the Virginia frontier. Bacon's army had killed or enslaved hundreds of once-friendly Indians and left behind a tragic and bitter legacy.

An even more important consequence of the rebellion was that wealthy planters and investors realized the depth of frustration among poor white men and women who were willing to make common cause with their black counterparts. Having regained power, the planter elite worked to crush any such interracial alliance. They promised most white rebels who put down arms the right to return home peacefully, and most complied. Virginia legislators then began to improve the conditions and rights of poorer white settlers while imposing new restrictions on blacks. At nearly the same time, in an effort to meet the growing demand for labor in the West Indies and the Chesapeake, King Charles II chartered the Royal African Company in 1672 to carry enslaved women and men from Africa to North America.

The English Compete for West Indies Possessions

While tobacco held great promise in Virginia, investors were eager to find other lucrative exports. Some turned their sights on the West Indies, where the English, the French, and the Dutch had all established bases on small islands during the sixteenth century. In the 1620s, the English developed more permanent settlements on St. Christopher, Barbados, and Nevis. Barbados quickly became the most attractive of these West Indies colonies. English migrants settled Barbados in growing numbers, clearing land and bringing in indentured servants from England, Ireland, and Scotland to cultivate tobacco and cotton and raise livestock.

The Dutch and the French also began establishing more permanent settlements in the West Indies. The Dutch colonized St. Martin and Curaçao, while the French settled Guadalupe, Martinique, and later Saint Domingue. The Dutch, however, profited mainly from carrying trade goods for other nations, while the French faced significant resistance from Carib Indians who resided on their island colonies. Thus neither developed their West Indies outposts to the same extent as the English. But even the English faced economic stagnation on Barbados as tobacco prices fell in the 1630s.

A few forward-looking planters were already considering another avenue to wealth: sugarcane. English and European consumers absorbed as much of the sweet gold as the market could provide, but producing sugar required expensive equipment and technical know-how as well as a large number of laborers. In addition, the sugar that was sent from America needed further refinement in Europe before being sold to consumers. The Dutch had learned the secrets of sugar cultivation from the Portuguese in Brazil, and they built the best refineries in Europe. But their small West Indies colonies could not supply sufficient raw material. By 1640 they decided to form a partnership with English planters, offering them the knowledge and financing to establish sugar plantations and mills on Barbados. That decision would reshape the economic and political landscape of North America and intensify competition for both land and labor.

REVIEW & RELATE

- How did the Virginia colony change and evolve between 1607 and the 1670s?
- How did the growth of the English colonies on the mainland and in the West Indies shape conflicts in Virginia and demands for labor throughout North America?

Pilgrims and Puritans Settle New England

Along with merchants, planters, and indentured servants, religious dissenters also traveled to North America. Critics of the Church of England formed a number of congregations in the early seventeenth century, and some sought refuge in New England. One such group, the Pilgrims (also known as Separatists), landed on the Massachusetts coast in 1620 and established a permanent settlement at Plymouth. Their goal was to establish a religious community wholly separate from the Anglican Church. The Puritans, who hoped to purify rather than separate from the Church of England, arrived a decade later with plans to develop their own colony. Over the next two decades, New England colonists prospered, but they also confronted internal dissent and conflicts with local Indians.

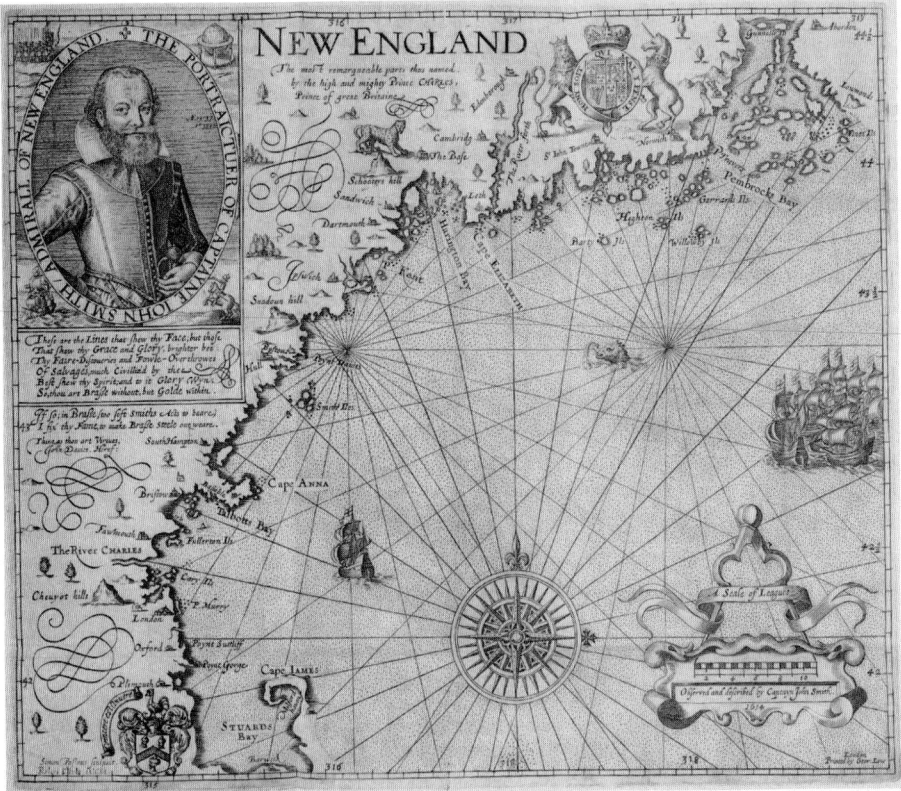

Map of New England in 1614 This engraving by the Dutchman Simon van de Passe in 1616 is based on a map drawn by the English explorer John Smith two years earlier. After leaving Jamestown, Smith, who is pictured in the upper left corner, sailed along the Atlantic coast of North America, a region he named New England.   Beinecke Rare Book and Manuscript Library, Yale University

Pilgrims Arrive in Massachusetts

In the 1610s, to raise capital, the Virginia Company began offering legal charters to groups of private investors, who were promised their own tract of land in the Virginia colony with minimal oversight by the governor or the company council. One such charter was purchased by a group of English Pilgrims who wanted to form a separate church and community in a land untainted by Catholicism, Anglicanism, or European cosmopolitanism. Thirty-five Pilgrims from Leiden in the Dutch Republic and several dozen from England signed on to the venture and set sail on the *Mayflower* from Plymouth, England, in September 1620.

Battered by storms, the ship veered off course, landing at Cape Cod in present-day Massachusetts in early December. With winter closing in, the exhausted passengers decided to disembark. Before leaving the ship, the settlers, led by William Bradford, signed a solemn pact, which they considered necessary because they were settling in a region where they had no legal authority. The Pilgrims agreed to "combine ourselves together into a civill body politick." The **Mayflower Compact** was the first written constitution adopted in North America. It followed the Separatist model of a self-governing religious congregation.

After several forays along the coast, the Pilgrims located an uninhabited village surrounded by cornfields where they established their new home, Plymouth. Uncertain of native intentions, the Pilgrims were unsettled by sightings of Indians near their hastily built fort. They did not realize that a smallpox epidemic in the area only two years earlier had killed nearly 90 percent of the local Wampanoag population, leaving them too weak to launch an assault on the Pilgrims. Indeed, fevers and other diseases proved far more deadly to the settlers than did Indians. By the spring of 1621, only half of the 102 Pilgrims remained alive.

Desperate to find food, the survivors were stunned when two English-speaking Indians—Samoset and Squanto—appeared at Plymouth that March. Both had been captured as young boys by English explorers, and they now negotiated a fragile peace between the Pilgrims and Massasoit, chief of the Wampanoag tribe. Although concerned by the power of English guns, Massasoit hoped to create an alliance that would assist him against his traditional native enemies. The Wampanoags supplied the English with seeds, fishing gear, and other goods that allowed them to take advantage of the short growing season and the abundant fish and wildlife in the region. The surviving Pilgrims soon regained their health.

In the summer of 1621, reinforcements arrived from England, and the next year the Pilgrims received a charter granting them rights to Plymouth Plantation and a degree of self-government. The region's cold climate turned out to be a boon as well, minimizing the spread of disease. These developments encouraged the Pilgrims to take a more aggressive stance toward Indians, like the Massachusetts tribe, who posed a threat to them. In 1623 Captain Miles Standish led an attack on a Massachusetts village after kidnapping and killing the chief and his younger brother. The survivors fled north and west, alerting other Indians to the Pilgrims' presence. Although Separatist leaders in Leiden were appalled that their brethren were assaulting rather than converting Indians, Standish's strategy ensured that Massasoit, the colonists' Wampanoag ally, was now the most powerful chief in the region.

The Puritan Migration

As the Pilgrims gradually expanded their colony during the 1620s, a new group of English dissenters, the **Puritans**, made plans to develop their own settlement. As religious dissenters, Puritans faced persecution in England. However, persecution was only one reason the Puritans chose to leave England. They believed that their country's church and government had grown corrupt and was being chastened by an all-powerful God. During the early seventeenth century, the English population boomed but harvests failed, the poor suffered from famine and rising prices, the number of beggars multiplied, and crime and taxes rose. The enclosure movement, in which landlords fenced in fields and hired a few laborers and tenants to replace a large number of peasant farmers, increased the number of landless vagrants. At the same time, the English cloth industry nearly collapsed under the weight of competition from abroad. In the Puritans' view, all of these problems were divine punishments for the nation's sins.

Thus, from the Puritans' perspective, New England was a safe haven from God's wrath. Puritan lawyer John Winthrop claimed that God offered New England as "a refuge for manye, whom he meant to save out of the general destruction." Consequently, under his leadership a group of affluent Puritans sought and received a royal charter for the Massachusetts Bay Company. To the Puritans, however, New England was more than just a place of safety. Unlike the Pilgrims, they believed that England and the Anglican Church could be redeemed. By prospering spiritually and materially in America, they could establish a model "City upon a Hill" that would then inspire reform among residents of the mother country.

About one-third of English Puritans chose to leave their homeland for North America. They were better supplied, more prosperous, and more numerous than either their Pilgrim or Jamestown predecessors. Arriving in an armada of seventeen ships, the settlers included ministers, merchants, craftsmen, and farmers. Many Puritans sailed with entire families in tow, ensuring the rapid growth of the colony. Having seen the risks of settling in unhealthy or unknown locales, they studied John Smith's map of the New England coast to select the best site for their community.

The first Puritan settlers arrived on the coast north of Plymouth in 1630 and named their community Boston, after the port city in England from which they had departed. Once established, they relocated the Massachusetts Bay Company's capital and records to New England, thereby converting their commercial charter into the founding document of a self-governing colony. They instituted a new kind of polity in which all adult males participated in the election of a governor (John Winthrop), deputy governor, and legislature. Although the Puritans suffered a difficult first winter, they quickly recovered and soon cultivated sufficient crops to feed themselves and a steady stream of new migrants. During the 1630s, some eighteen thousand Puritans migrated to New England, fourteen thousand of those to Massachusetts. Even without a cash crop like tobacco or sugar, the Puritan colony flourished.

Eager to take advantage of the abundant land, the close-knit community spread quickly beyond its original boundaries. The legislature, known as the General Court, was thus forced early on to develop policies for establishing townships with governing bodies that supported a local church and school. By the time the migration of Puritans slowed around 1640, the settlers had turned their colony into a thriving commercial center. They shipped codfish, lumber, wheat, rye, oats, pork, cheese, and other agricultural products to England in exchange for cloth, iron pots, and other manufactured goods and to the West Indies for rum and molasses. This trade, along with the healthy climate, relatively egalitarian distribution of property, and more equal ratio of women to men, ensured a stable and prosperous colony.

Puritans also sought friendly relations with some local natives; in their case it was with the neighboring Massachusetts tribe, who were longtime enemies of the Pilgrims' allies, the Wampanoags. Many Puritans hoped that their Indian neighbors could be converted to Christianity. Such efforts were made easier by the death of many of the Massachusetts tribe's religious leaders in the Pilgrim attack of 1623. Puritan missionaries taught their pupils how to read the Bible, and a few students attended Harvard College, founded in 1636. In an effort to wean converts from their traditional customs and beliefs, missionary John Eliot created "praying towns." There Christian Indians could live among others who shared their faith while being protected from English settlers seeking to exploit them. Yet most "praying Indians" continued to embrace traditional rituals and beliefs alongside Christian practices.

The Puritan Worldview

Opposed to the lavish rituals and hierarchy of the Church of England and believing that few Anglicans truly felt the grace of God, Puritans set out to establish a simpler form of worship. They focused on their inner lives and on the purity of their church and community. Puritans followed Calvin, believing in an all-knowing God who had seen his flock wander away from his most basic teachings. The true Word of God was presented in the Bible, not in the Anglican Book of Common Prayer or hymns written by modern composers. The biblically sanctioned church was a congregation formed by a group of believers who made a covenant with God. Only a small minority of people, known as Saints, were granted God's grace, and Puritans believed (or at least hoped) that their churches were filled with Saints.

Saints were granted God's grace even though all humans since the fall of Adam were deserving of perpetual damnation. Whether one was a Saint and thereby saved was predetermined by and known only to God. Yet Puritans believed that those who were chosen led a godly life. Visible signs included individuals' passionate response to the preaching of God's Word, their sense of doubt and despair over their own soul, and that wonderful sense of reassurance that came with God's "saving grace." Saints were also expected to be virtuous, neighborly, benevolent, and successful.

Puritans, like most Christians at the time, believed that signs of God's hand in the world were everywhere. They appeared in natural phenomena like comets, eclipses, and deformed births as well as in "remarkable providences" that eased believers' way. Thus when a smallpox epidemic killed several thousand Massachusetts Indians in 1633–1634, a Puritan town council observed: "Without this remarkable and terrible stroke of God upon the native, we would with much more difficulty have found room, and at a far greater charge have obtained and purchased land." Clearly God was shining his light on the Puritans, rather than on the Massachusetts.

Shared religious beliefs helped forge a unified community where faith guided civil as well as spiritual decisions. Most political leaders were devout Puritans. Indeed, ministers often served as members of the General Court or presided over town meetings. Puritan leaders determined who got land, how much, and where; they also served as judge and jury for those accused of crimes or sins. Their leadership was largely successful. Even if colonists differed over who should get the most fertile strip of land, they agreed on basic principles. Still, almost from the beginning, certain Puritans challenged some of the community's fundamental beliefs, and in the process, the community itself.

Dissenters Challenge Puritan Authority

In the early 1630s, Roger Williams, a Salem minister, criticized Puritan leaders for not being sufficiently pure in their rejection of the Church of England and the English monarchy. He preached that not all the Puritan leaders were Saints and that some were bound for damnation. Despite admonitions from the Massachusetts Bay authorities, Williams continued to rail against what he saw as deviations from the one true faith. By 1635 he was forced out of Salem and moved south with his followers to found Providence in the area that became Rhode Island. Believing that there were very few Saints in the world, Williams and his followers accepted that one must live among those who were not saved. Thus unlike Massachusetts Bay, Williams welcomed Quakers, Baptists, and Jews to the community, and his followers insisted on a strict separation of church and state. Williams also forged alliances with the Narragansetts, the most powerful Indian nation in the region, trading with them and securing land for a growing number of English settlers.

A year later, Anne Hutchinson and her followers joined Williams's Rhode Island colony. When put on trial in November 1637, Hutchinson was initially accused of sedition, or trying to overthrow the government by challenging colonial leaders, such as Governor John Winthrop, who were devout Puritans. An eloquent orator, Hutchinson ultimately claimed that her authority to challenge the Puritan leadership came from "an immediate revelation" from God, "the voice of his own spirit to my soul." Since Puritans believed that God spoke only through the intermediary of properly appointed male ministers, her claim was condemned as heretical.

Hutchinson was seen as a threat not only because of her religious beliefs but also because she was a woman. The Reverend Hugh Peter, for example, reprimanded her at trial: "You have stept out of your place, you have rather bine a Husband than a Wife and a preacher than a Hearer; and a Magistrate than a Subject." Thus the accusations against her were rooted as much in her challenge to gender hierarchies as to Puritan authority, although her accusers no doubt viewed these as synonymous.

Wars in Old and New England

As Anne Hutchinson and Roger Williams confronted the religious hierarchy, Puritans and Pilgrims faced another serious threat from the Pequot nation. Among the most powerful tribes in New England, the Pequots had been allies of the English for several years. Yet some Puritans feared that the Pequots, who opposed the colonists' continued expansion, "would cause all the Indians in the country to join to root out all the English." Using the death of two Englishmen in 1636 to justify a military expedition against the Pequots, the colonists went on the attack. The Narragansetts, whom Roger Williams had befriended, fought with the English in the **Pequot War**. After months of bloody conflict, the English and their Indian allies launched a brutal attack on a Pequot fort in May 1637 that left some four hundred men, women, and children dead. The English saw the victory as a sign of God's grace, and the Narragansetts saw it as the defeat of a powerful rival.

Puritans in England were soon engaged in armed conflict as well, but this time against other Englishmen. Differences over issues of religion, taxation, and royal authority had strained relations between Parliament and the crown for decades, as James I (r. 1603–1625) and his son Charles I (r. 1625–1649) sought to consolidate their own power at Parliament's expense. In 1642 the relationship between Parliament and King Charles I broke down completely, and the country descended into civil war. Oliver Cromwell, a Puritan, emerged as the leader of the Protestant parliamentary forces, and after several years of fighting, he claimed victory. Charles I was executed, Parliament established a republican commonwealth, and bishops and elaborate rituals were banished from the Church of England. Cromwell ruled England as a military dictator until his death in 1658. By then, much of England had tired of religious conflict and Puritan rule, so Charles I's son, Charles II (r. 1660–1685), was invited to return from exile on the continent and restore the monarchy and the Church of England. In 1660, when Charles II acceded to the throne, the Puritans recognized that their only hope for building a godly republic lay in North America.

During the civil war of the 1640s, English settlements had quickly spread throughout Connecticut, Massachusetts, and Rhode Island, as well as into Maine and what became New Hampshire. The English king and Parliament, embroiled in war, paid little attention to events in North America, allowing these New England colonies to develop with little oversight. In 1664, after the restoration of the monarchy, the English wrested control of New Amsterdam from the Dutch and renamed it New York. Although it would be another decade before they fully subordinated the Dutch to their rule, by 1674 the English could claim dominance—in population, trade, and politics—over the other European powers vying for empires along the northern Atlantic coast.

The spread of English control was, however, still contested by various Indian groups. In New England, only 15,000 to 16,000 native people remained by 1670, a loss of about 80 percent over fifty years. Meanwhile the English population soared from a few hundred to more than 50,000, with settlers expanding into new territories and encroaching on native hunting grounds. In 1671 the English demanded that the Wampanoags, who had been their allies since the 1620s, surrender their guns and be ruled by English law. Instead, many Indians hid their weapons and, over the next several years, raided frontier farms and killed several settlers. English authorities responded by hanging three Wampanoag men.

By 1675 the Wampanoag chief Metacom, called King Philip by the English, came to believe that Europeans had to be forced out of New England if Indians were going to survive. As conflict escalated between the English and the Wampanoags, Metacom gained the support of the Narragansett and Nipmuck Indians. Together warriors from the three tribes attacked white settlements throughout the region. Armed with hundreds of guns as well as more traditional knives, hatchets, and arrows, Indians terrorized frontier communities. They burned fields, killed male settlers, and took women and children captive.

Initially, the English were convinced they could win an easy victory over their Indian foes, but the war dragged on and became increasingly brutal on both sides. Some 1,000 English settlers were killed and dozens were taken captive during the war. Eighteen New England towns were destroyed, almost 1,200 homes were burned, and 8,000 cattle were slaughtered. Metacom's forces attacked Plymouth and Providence and marched within twenty miles of Boston. The English meanwhile made an alliance with Mohawks, Pequots, Mohegans, and praying Indians (mostly Christian Wampanoags) in the region, who ambushed Narragansett forces. The English also attacked enemy villages, killing hundreds of Indians and selling hundreds more into slavery in the West Indies, including Metacom's wife and son. Indian losses were catastrophic on both sides of the conflict, as food shortages and disease combined with military deaths to kill as many as 4,500 men, women, and children. About a quarter of the remaining Indian population of New England died in 1675–1676.

The war, called **King Philip's War** by the English, finally ended when Wampanoag, Narragansett, and Nipmuck forces ran short of guns and powder and the Mohawks ambushed and killed Metacom.

 Online Document Project   King Philip's War
bedfordstmartins.com/hewittlawsonvalue

The remaining Algonquian-speaking Indians moved north and gradually intermarried with tribes allied with the French. As the carnage of the war spilled into New York,

Iroquois leaders and colonists met at Albany in 1677. There they formed an alliance, the Covenant Chain, in hopes of forestalling future conflict so that they could continue their profitable fur trade. In the following decades, furs and land would continue to define the complex relations between Indians and Europeans across the northern regions of North America.

REVIEW & RELATE

- How did the Puritans' religious views shape New England's development?
- Why did conflict between New England settlers and the region's Indians escalate over the course of the seventeenth century?

Conclusion: European Empires in North America

When John Smith died in 1631, the English were just beginning to establish colonies in North America. Despite Smith's love of adventure, he realized early on that a successful empire in Virginia required a different approach than the Spanish had taken in Mexico and Peru. North American colonies demanded permanent settlement, long-term investment, and hard work. Liberal land policies, self-government, and trade formed the touchstones of colonies along the north Atlantic coast.

Yet as European colonists found different ways to prosper in Virginia, Massachusetts Bay, Quebec, and New Amsterdam, they faced daunting choices.

 Online Document Project
Comparing Virginia and Massachusetts Bay Colonies
bedfordstmartins.com/hewittlawsonvalue

Most important, should they create alliances with local Indians for sustenance and trade, or should they seek to dominate them and take what they needed? Smith, Miles Standish, and many other early settlers supported an aggressive policy, much like that of Spain. In Virginia this policy ended persistent threats from the Powhatan Confederacy by the 1640s. But many Europeans, especially in New England, New Amsterdam, and Canada, advocated a different approach. Some, like French Jesuit priests and Puritan missionaries, focused on the spiritual and material benefits of conversion. Far more argued that building alliances was the most effective means of advancing trade and gaining land, furs, and other goods valued by Europeans.

Throughout the early and mid-seventeenth century, English, Dutch, and French colonists profited from trade relations and military alliances with Indian nations. Nonetheless, European demands for land fueled repeated conflicts with tribes like the Pequots in the 1630s and the Wampanoags and Narragansetts in the 1670s. The exhaustion of furs along the Atlantic coast only increased the vulnerability of those Indians who could no longer provide this valuable trade item. Already devastated by European-borne diseases, their very survival was at stake. Indians in New Amsterdam as well as

New England resisted the loss of their land and livelihood, often with violence. It was such violence that led to the death of Anne Hutchinson. In 1642 she and her six youngest children moved to the outskirts of New Netherland after the death of her husband. They lived on an isolated farm on what is now Pelham Bay in the Bronx. A year later, Anne and all but one of her children were massacred by Indians outraged by Dutch governor William Kieft's 1643 slaughter of peaceful Indians on Manhattan Island.

Still, as European settlements reached deeper into North America in the late seventeenth century and early eighteenth century, their prosperity continued to depend on trade goods and land that were often in Indian hands. At the same time, a growing demand for labor led wealthier settlers to seek an increased supply of indentured servants from Europe and enslaved workers from Africa. Over the next half century, relations between wealthy and poor settlers, between whites and blacks, between settlers and Indians, and among the European nations that vied for empire would only grow more complicated.

Chapter Review

MAKE IT STICK

 LearningCurve **bedfordstmartins.com/hewittlawsonvalue**
After reading the chapter, use LearningCurve to retain what you've read.

IDENTIFY KEY TERMS

Identify and explain the significance of each term below.

Protestantism (p. 31)

Church of England (p. 31)

Jamestown (p. 36)

Powhatan Confederacy (p. 36)

House of Burgesses (p. 38)

indentured servants (p. 38)

Bacon's Rebellion (p. 41)

Pilgrims (p. 43)

Mayflower Compact (p. 44)

Puritans (p. 44)

Pequot War (p. 47)

King Philip's War (p. 48)

REVIEW & RELATE

Answer the focus questions from each section of the chapter.

1. How did the Protestant Reformation shape the course of European expansion in the Americas?

2. How did the French and Dutch colonies in North America differ from the Spanish empire to the south?

3. How did the Virginia colony change and evolve between 1607 and the 1670s?

4. How did the growth of the English colonies on the mainland and in the West Indies shape conflicts in Virginia and demands for labor throughout North America?

5. How did the Puritans' religious views shape New England's development?

6. Why did conflict between New England settlers and the region's Indians escalate over the course of the seventeenth century?

ONLINE DOCUMENT PROJECTS

◆ **King Philip's War**
◆ **Comparing Virginia and Massachusetts Bay Colonies**

After reading the primary sources in these document sets, answer the **Interpret the Evidence** questions to help you analyze each of the documents, and then answer the **Put It in Context** question(s) to help you relate the documents to the topics and themes you read about in the chapter.

bedfordstmartins.com/hewittlawsonvalue

TIMELINE OF EVENTS

1517	• Martin Luther denounces indulgences, sparking the Protestant Reformation
1530s	• England breaks with the Roman Catholic Church
1545–1563	• Council of Trent (Catholic Church)
1598	• Acoma pueblo uprising in New Mexico
	• Edict of Nantes (France)
1607	• Jamestown founded under leadership of Captain John Smith
1608	• First permanent French settlement in North America founded at Quebec
1609	• Dutch traders establish a settlement on the Hudson River
1612	• John Rolfe experiments with tobacco cultivation in Virginia
1619	• House of Burgesses established in Virginia
	• First Africans arrive in Virginia

1620	• Pilgrims found Plymouth settlement in Massachusetts
1624	• Dutch establish New Amsterdam on Manhattan Island
1630	• Puritans found Massachusetts Bay colony
1632	• Maryland founded
1635	• Roger Williams moves with followers to Rhode Island
1636–1637	• Pequot War
1637	• Anne Hutchinson banished from Massachusetts Bay colony
1642–1649	• English civil war
1660	• Monarchy restored in England
1660–1664	• House of Burgesses passes acts that allow enslavement of African laborers
1664	• Dutch surrender New Amsterdam to the English
1675–1676	• King Philip's War
1676	• Bacon's Rebellion

LearningCurve
✓ bedfordstmartins.com/hewittlawsonvalue
After reading the chapter, use LearningCurve
to retain what you've read.

3

Global Changes Reshape Colonial America

1680–1750

AMERICAN HISTORIES

In 1729, at age thirty, William Moraley Jr. signed an indenture to serve a five-year term as a "bound servant" in the "American Plantations." This was not what his parents had imagined for him. The only child of a journeyman watchmaker and his wife, Moraley received a good education and was offered a clerkship with a London lawyer. But Moraley preferred London's pleasures to legal training. At age nineteen, out of money, he was forced to return home and become an apprentice watchmaker for his father. Moraley's apprenticeship went no better than his clerkship, and in 1725, fed up with his son's lack of enterprise, Moraley's father rewrote his will, leaving him just 20 shillings. When Moraley's father died unexpectedly, his wife gave her son 20 pounds, and in 1728 Moraley headed back to London.

But London was in the midst of a prolonged economic crisis, and Moraley failed to find work. By May 1729, he was imprisoned for debt. Three months later, he sold his labor for five years in return for passage to America. Moraley sailed for Philadelphia in September and was indentured in January to a Quaker clockmaker in Burlington, New Jersey. Eventually, he tired of this situation as well, and he ran away. But when he was caught, he was not punished by having his contract extended, as happened to most fugitive servants. Instead, he was released before his indenture was up, after serving only three years.

Moraley spent the next twenty months traveling the northern colonies, but found no steady employment. Hounded by creditors, he boarded a ship in Philadelphia bound for Ireland. He returned to his mother's home, penniless and unemployed. In 1743, hoping to cash in on popular interest in adventure tales, he published an account of his travels. In the book, entitled *The Infortunate, the Voyage and Adventures of William Moraley, an Indentured Servant,* he offered a poor man's view of eighteenth-century North America. Like so much else in Moraley's life, the book was not a success.

In 1738, while Moraley was back in England trying to carve out a career as a writer, sixteen-year-old Eliza Lucas, the eldest daughter of a career British military officer, arrived in South Carolina. Her father, Colonel George Lucas, had inherited a 600-acre plantation, called Wappoo, six miles south of Charles Town (later Charleston), and moved his family there in hopes that the climate would improve his wife's health. Eliza had been born on Antigua, where her father served with the British army and owned a sugar plantation. Although the move north did not benefit his wife, it created an unusual opportunity for his daughter, who was left in charge of the estate when Colonel Lucas was called back to Antigua in May 1739.

For the next five years, Eliza Lucas managed Wappoo and two other Carolina plantations owned by her father. Rising each day at 5 a.m., she checked on the fields and the enslaved laborers who worked them, balanced the books, nursed her mother, taught her younger sister to read, and wrote to her younger brothers at school in England. In a large bound book, she kept the accounts; copies of her letters to family, friends, commercial agents, and fellow planters; and information on legal affairs.

She also embarked on plans to improve her family estates. With her father's enthusiastic support, Lucas began experimenting with new crops, particularly indigo. The indigo plant, which was first imported to Europe from India in the seventeenth century, produced a blue dye popular for coloring textiles. When her experiments proved successful, Lucas encouraged other planters to follow her lead, and with financial aid from the colonial legislature and Parliament, indigo became a profitable export from South Carolina, second only to rice.

THE AMERICAN HISTORIES of William Moraley and Eliza Lucas were shaped by a profound shift in global trading patterns that resulted in the circulation of labor and goods among Asia, Africa, Europe, and the Americas. Between 1680 and 1750, indentured servants, enslaved Africans, planters, soldiers, merchants, and artisans traveled along these new trade networks. So, too, did sugar, rum, tobacco, indigo, cloth, and a host of other items. As England, France, and Spain expanded their empires, colonists developed new crops for export and increased the demand for manufactured goods from home. Yet the vibrant, increasingly global economy was

English cartoon of industrious American colonists, mid-18th century. © Pictorial Press Ltd./Alamy

fraught with peril. Economic crises, the uncertainties of maritime navigation, and outbreaks of war caused constant disruptions. For some, the opportunities offered by colonization outweighed the dangers; for others, fortune was less kind, and the results were disappointing, even disastrous.

Europeans Expand Their Claims

Beginning with the restoration of Charles II to the throne in 1660, English monarchs began granting North American land and commercial rights to men who were loyal to the crown. Shaped in part by rebellions at home and abroad, the policies of English monarchs aimed to expand England's imperial reach at the lowest possible cost. France and Spain also expanded their empires in North America, frequently coming into conflict with each other in the late seventeenth and early eighteenth centuries. At the same time, American Indians challenged various European efforts to displace them from their homelands. A Pueblo rebellion against Spanish authorities in New Mexico provided other Indian nations with access to guns and horses. In Florida, Indian-Spanish conflicts allowed England to gain native allies.

English Colonies Grow and Multiply

To repay the men who helped him return to power, Charles II granted them land and commercial rights in North America (see chapter 2). The king rewarded his most important allies with positions on the newly formed Councils for Trade and Plantations. Many of the appointees also gained other benefits: partnerships in the Royal African

Company, vast lands along the South Atlantic coast, or charters for territory in Canada. In addition, he gave his brother James, the Duke of York, control over all the lands between the Delaware and Connecticut Rivers, once known as New Netherland, but now known as New York. He then conveyed the adjacent lands to investors who established the colonies of East and West Jersey. Finally, Charles II repaid debts to Admiral Sir William Penn by granting his son huge tracts of land in the Middle Atlantic region. Six years later, William Penn Jr. left the Church of England and joined the Society of Friends, or Quakers. This radical Protestant sect was severely persecuted in England, so the twenty-two-year-old Penn turned his holdings into a Quaker refuge named Pennsylvania.

Between 1660 and 1685, Penn and other English gentlemen were established as the proprietors of a string of **proprietary colonies** from Carolina to New York. These powerful aristocrats could govern largely as they wished as long as they conformed broadly to English traditions. Most envisioned a manorial system in which they and other gentry presided over workers producing goods for export. In practice, however, local conditions dictated what was possible, and by the 1680s a range of labor relationships had emerged. Following Bacon's Rebellion in Virginia (see chapter 2), small farmers and laborers in northern Carolina rose up and forced proprietors there to offer land at reasonable prices and a semblance of self-government. In the southern part of Carolina, however, English West Indian planters dominated. They created a mainland version of Barbados by introducing enslaved Africans as laborers, carving plantations out of coastal swamps, and trading with the West Indies.

William Penn provided a more progressive model of colonial rule. He established friendly relations with the local Lenni-Lenape Indians and drew up a Frame of Government in 1681 that recognized religious freedom for all Christians. It also allowed all property-owning men to vote and hold office. Under Penn's leadership, Pennsylvania attracted thousands of middling farm families, most of them Quakers, as well as artisans and merchants. By the time Charles II died in 1685, Pennsylvania was the most successful of his proprietary colonies.

Charles's death marked an abrupt shift in crown-colony relations. Charles's successor, James II, instituted a more authoritarian regime both at home and abroad. He consolidated the colonies in the Northeast and established tighter controls. His royal officials banned town meetings, challenged land titles granted under the original colonial charters, and imposed new taxes. Fortunately for the colonists, the Catholic James II alienated his subjects in England as well as in the colonies, inspiring a bloodless coup in 1688. His Protestant daughter Mary and her husband William of Orange (r. 1689–1702) then ascended the throne, introducing more democratic systems of governance in England and the colonies. This so-called **Glorious Revolution** inspired John Locke to write his famous treatise justifying the changes made by William and Mary. Locke challenged the divine right of monarchs and insisted that government depended on the consent of the governed.

Eager to restore political order and create a commercially profitable empire, William and Mary established the new colony of Massachusetts (which included Plymouth, Massachusetts Bay, and Maine) and restored town meetings and an elected assembly. But the 1692 charter also granted the English crown the right to appoint a royal governor and officials to enforce customs regulations. It ensured religious freedom to members of the Church of England and allowed all male property owners (not just

TABLE 3.1   **English Colonies Established in North America, 1607–1750**

Colony	Date	Original Colony Type	Religion	Status in 1750	Economic Activity
Virginia	1624	Proprietary	Church of England	Royal	Tobacco, wheat
Massachusetts	1630	Proprietary	Congregationalist	Royal	Fishing, mixed farming, shipbuilding materials, shipping
Maryland	1632	Royal	Catholic	Royal	Tobacco, wheat
Carolina	1663	Proprietary	Church of England	Royal	
North	1691				Shipbuilding materials, farming
South	1691				Rice, indigo
New Jersey	1664	Proprietary	Church of England	Royal	Wheat
New York	1664	Proprietary	Church of England	Royal	Furs, naval stores, mixed farming, shipping
Pennsylvania	1681	Proprietary	Quaker	Proprietary	Wheat
Delaware	1704	Proprietary	Lutheran/Quaker	Proprietary	Furs, farming, shipping
Georgia	1732	Trustees	Church of England	Royal	Rice
New Hampshire (separated from Massachusetts)	1741	Royal	Congregationalist	Royal	Mixed farming, lumber, shipbuilding materials

Puritans) to be elected to the assembly. In Maryland, too, the crown imposed a royal governor and replaced the Catholic Church with the Church of England as the established religion. And in New York, wealthy English merchants won the backing of the newly appointed royal governor, who instituted a representative assembly and supported a merchant-dominated Board of Aldermen. Thus, taken as a whole, William and Mary's policies asserted royal authority at the same time that they sought to create a partnership between England and colonial elites by allowing colonists to retain long-standing local governmental institutions (Table 3.1).

In the early eighteenth century, England's North American colonies took the form that they would retain until the revolution in 1776. In 1702 East and West Jersey united into the colony of New Jersey. Delaware separated from Pennsylvania in 1704. By 1710 North Carolina became fully independent of South Carolina, forming its own assembly and receiving its own charter. Finally, in 1732, the colony of Georgia was established as a buffer between Spanish Florida and the increasingly lucrative plantations of South

Carolina. At the same time, settlers pushed back the frontier in all directions. Wealthy Englishmen like Robert Livingston bought up land on the upper Hudson River and joined Dutch *patroons* who had earlier established vast estates in the region. Meanwhile families in Massachusetts carved out farms and villages on the New Hampshire and Maine frontier, while migrants and immigrants pushed the boundaries of Pennsylvania, Virginia, and the Carolinas westward.

France Seeks Lands and Control

When James II became king of England, he modeled himself after Louis XIV of France. Like Louis, James saw himself as ruling by divine right and with absolute power, but the French king was far more successful in establishing and sustaining his authority. During his long reign from 1661 to 1715, Louis XIV dominated European affairs and oversaw an expansion of North American possessions. Still, in 1680 New France comprised only ten thousand inhabitants, and one potential source of settlers—Protestant Huguenots—was denied the right to emigrate.

The French government thus extended the boundaries of its North American colonies more through exploration and trade than through settlement. In 1682 French adventurers and their Indian allies journeyed down the lower Mississippi River. Led by René-Robert Cavelier, Sieur de La Salle, the party traveled to the Gulf of Mexico and claimed all the land drained by its tributaries for Louis XIV. The new territory of Louisiana (named for the king) promised great wealth, but its development stalled when La Salle failed in his attempt to establish a colony.

Still eager for a southern outlet for furs, the French did not give up. After several more attempts at colonization in the early eighteenth century, French settlers maintained a toehold along Louisiana's Gulf coast. Most important, Pierre LeMoyne d'Iberville, a Canadian military officer, and his brother established forts at Biloxi and Mobile bays, where they traded with local Choctaw Indians. They recruited settlers from Canada and France, and the small outpost survived despite conflicts among settlers, pressure from the English, a wave of epidemics, and a lack of supplies from France. Still, Louisiana counted only three hundred French settlers by 1715.

Continuing to promote commercial relations with diverse Indian nations, the French built a string of missions and forts along the upper Mississippi and Illinois Rivers. These outposts in the continent's interior allowed France to challenge both English and Spanish claims to North America. And extensive trade with a range of Indian nations ensured that French power was far greater than the small number of French settlers would suggest.

The Pueblo Revolt and Spain's Fragile Empire

As New France pushed westward and southward, Spain continued to oversee an empire that was spread dangerously thin on its northern reaches. In New Mexico, tensions between Spanish missionaries and *encomenderos* and the Pueblo nation had simmered for decades (see chapter 2). Relations worsened in the 1670s when a drought led to famine among many area Indians and brought a revival of Indian rituals that the Spaniards viewed as a threat to Christianity. In addition, Spanish forces failed to protect the Pueblos against devastating raids by Apache and Navajo warriors. Finally, Catholic prayers proved unable to stop Pueblo deaths in a 1671 epidemic. When some of the Pueblos returned to their traditional priests, Spanish officials hanged three Indian leaders for idolatry and whipped and incarcerated forty-three others. Among those punished was Popé, a militant Pueblo who upon his release began planning a broad-based revolt.

On August 10, 1680, seventeen thousand Pueblo Indians initiated a coordinated assault on numerous Spanish missions and forts. They destroyed buildings and farms, burned crops and houses, and smeared excrement on Christian altars. The Spaniards retreated to Mexico without launching any significant counterattack.

Yet the Spaniards returned in the 1690s and reconquered parts of New Mexico, aided by growing internal conflict among the Pueblos and fierce Apache raids. The governor general of New Spain worked hard to subdue the province and in 1696 crushed the rebels and opened new lands for settlement. Meanwhile Franciscan missionaries established better relations with the Pueblos by allowing them to retain more indigenous practices and built new missions in the region.

Yet despite the Spanish reconquest, in the long run the **Pueblo revolt** limited Spanish expansion by strengthening other indigenous peoples in the region. In the aftermath of the revolt, some Pueblo refugees moved north and taught the Navajos how to grow corn, raise sheep, and ride horses. Through the Navajos, the Ute and Comanche peoples also gained access to horses. By the 1730s, the Comanches, who had become a fully equestrian society, launched mounted bison hunts and traded over vast areas. One key trading center formed at Taos in northern New Mexico, where Spanish control was weak. There Comanches sold captives as slaves and gained more horses, metal tools, and guns. Thus the Pueblos provided other Indian nations with the means to support larger populations, wider commercial networks, and more warriors. These nations would continue to contest Spanish rule.

At the same time, Spain sought to reinforce its claims to Texas (named after the Tejas Indians) in response to French settlements in the lower Mississippi valley. Thus, in the early eighteenth century, Spanish missions and forts appeared along the route from San Juan Batista to the border of present-day Louisiana. Although small and scattered, these outposts were meant to ensure Spain's claim to Texas. But the presence of large and powerful Indian nations, including the Caddo and the Apache, forced Spanish residents to accept many native customs in order to maintain their presence in the region.

Spain also faced challenges to its authority in Florida, where Indians resisted the spread of cattle ranching in the 1670s. Authorities imposed harsh punishments on those killing cows or raiding herds and forced hundreds of Indians to construct a stone fortress, San Marcos, at St. Augustine. Meanwhile the English wooed Florida natives by exchanging European goods for deerskins. Some Indians then moved their settlements north to the Carolina border. The growing tensions along this Anglo-Spanish border would turn violent when Europe itself erupted into war.

REVIEW & RELATE

• What role did the crown play in the expansion of the English North American colonies in the second half of the seventeenth century?

• How did the development of the Spanish and French colonies in the late seventeenth century differ from that of the English colonies?

European Wars and American Consequences

Developments in North America in the late seventeenth and early eighteenth centuries were driven as much by events in Europe as by those in the colonies. From 1689 until 1713, Europe was in an almost constant state of war, with continental conflicts spilling over into colonial possessions in North America. The result was increased tensions between colonists of different nationalities, Indians and colonists, and colonists and their home countries.

Colonial Conflicts and Indian Alliances

France was at the center of much of the European warfare of the period. Louis XIV hoped to expand France's borders and gain supremacy in Europe. To this end, he built a powerful professional army under state authority. By 1689 more than 300,000 well-trained troops had been outfitted with standardized uniforms and weapons. Having gained victories in the Spanish Netherlands, Flanders, Strasbourg, and Lorraine, the French army seemed invincible.

In the 1690s, France and England fought their first sustained war in North America, **King William's War** (1689–1697). The war began over conflicting French and English interests on the European continent, but it soon spread to the American frontier when English and Iroquois forces attacked French and Huron settlements around Montreal and northern New York. English and Iroquois forces captured Fort Royal in Acadia (present-day Nova Scotia), while the French destroyed Schenectady, New York, and attacked settlers in Maine and New Hampshire.

Although neither side had gained significant territory when peace was declared in 1697, the war had important consequences. Many colonists serving in the English army died of battle wounds, smallpox, and inadequate rations. Those who survived resented their treatment and the unnecessary deaths of so many comrades. The Iroquois fared even worse. Their fur trade was devastated, and hundreds of Mohawks and Oneidas were forced to flee from France's Indian allies along the eastern Great Lakes. "French Indians" and Iroquois continued to attack each other after the peace settlement, but in 1701 the Iroquois agreed to end the raids and remain neutral in all future European conflicts. Wary of further European entanglements, Iroquois leaders focused on rebuilding their tattered confederacy.

A second protracted conflict, known as the **War of the Spanish Succession** (1702–1713) or Queen Anne's War, had even more devastating effects on North America. The conflict erupted in Europe when Charles II of Spain died without an heir, launching a contest for the Spanish kingdom and its colonies. France and Spain squared off against England, the Netherlands, Austria, and Prussia. In North America, however, it was England alone that faced France and Spain, with each nation hoping to gain additional territory. Both sides recruited Indian allies.

After more than a decade of savage fighting, Queen Anne's War ended in 1713 with the Treaty of Utrecht, which sought to secure a prolonged peace by balancing the interests of the great powers in Europe and their colonial possessions. Yet England benefited the most in North America even as it consolidated power at home by incorporating Scotland into Great Britain through the 1707 Act of Union. Just six years later, France surrendered Newfoundland, Nova Scotia, and the Hudson Bay Territory to England, while Spain granted England control of St. Kitts in the West Indies, Gibraltar, and Minorca as well as the right to sell African slaves in its American colonies. Yet neither the treaty nor Britain's consolidation forestalled further conflict. Indeed, Spain, France, and Britain all strengthened fortifications along their North American borders (Map 3.1).

Indians Resist European Encroachment

The European conflicts in North America put incredible pressure on Indian peoples to choose sides. It was increasingly difficult for native peoples in colonized areas to remain autonomous, yet Indian nations were not simply pawns of European powers.

MAP 3.1

European Empires in North America, 1715–1750   France, Great Britain, and Spain competed with one another and with numerous Indian nations for control of vast areas of North America. Although European wars repeatedly spilled over into North America in the early to mid-eighteenth century, this map shows the general outlines of the empires claimed by each European nation in this period and the key forts established to maintain those claims.

Some sought European allies against their native enemies, and most improved their situation by gaining cloth, metal tools, guns, or horses from their European trading partners. However, many Indian nations suffered growing internal conflicts as war, trade, and colonial expansion increased the power of male warriors. In societies like the Cherokee and Iroquois, in which older women had long held significant economic and political authority, the rising power of young men threatened traditional gender and generational relations. In addition, struggles between the English and the French often fostered conflict among Indian peoples, reinforcing grievances that existed before European settlement.

The tensions among Indians escalated during the late seventeenth century as southern tribes like the Tuscarora, Yamasee, Creek, Cherokee, Caddo, and Choctaw gained European goods, including guns. As deer disappeared from the Carolinas and the lower Mississippi valley, the most precious commodity for trade became Indian captives sold as slaves. Indians had always taken captives in war, but some of those captives had been adopted into the victorious nation. Now, however, war was almost constant in some areas, and captives were more valuable for sale as slaves than as adopted tribesmen. Moreover, slave raiding occurred outside formal conflicts, intensifying hostilities across the southern region.

Still, during the 1710s, some southern Indians tried to develop a pan-Indian alliance similar to that forged by New England Indians in the 1670s (see chapter 2). First, a group of Tuscarora warriors, hoping to gain support from other tribes, launched an attack on North Carolina settlements in September 1711. Over the next several months, hundreds of settlers were killed and hundreds more fled. However, South Carolina colonists came to the aid of their North Carolina countrymen and persuaded Indian allies among the Yamasee, Catawba, and Cherokee nations to join forces against the Tuscaroras. Although some of these allies had traditionally been enemies, they now cooperated. Meanwhile political leaders in North Carolina convinced a competing group of Tuscaroras to ally with the colonists. By 1713 the war was largely over, and in 1715 the Tuscaroras signed a peace treaty and forfeited their lands. Many then migrated north and were accepted as the sixth nation of the Iroquois Confederacy.

The end of the war did not mean peace in the Carolinas, however. For the next two years, fierce battles erupted between a Yamasee-led coalition and the South Carolina militia. The Yamasee people remained deeply in debt to British merchants even as the trade in deerskins and slaves moved farther west. They thus secured allies among the Creeks and launched an all-out effort to force the British out. The Yamasee War marked the Indians' most serious challenge to European dominance. Indeed, it was even bloodier than King Philip's War. The British gained victory only after the Cherokees switched their allegiance to the colonists in early 1716 and thus ended the possibility of a major Creek offensive. The final Indian nations withdrew from the conflict in 1717, and a fragile peace followed.

The Yamasee War did not oust the British, but it did transform the political landscape of native North America. In its aftermath, the Creek and Catawba tribes emerged as powerful new confederations, the Cherokees became the major trading partner of the British, and the Yamasee nation was seriously weakened. And as the Cherokees allied with the British, the Creek and the Caddo tribes strengthened their alliance with the French. Meanwhile many Yamasees migrated to Spanish Florida, joining the Seminole nation.

Despite the British victory, colonists on the Carolina frontier faced raids on their settlements for decades to come. In the 1720s and 1730s, settlers in the Middle Atlantic colonies also experienced fierce resistance to their westward expansion. And attacks on New Englanders along the Canadian frontier periodically disrupted settlement there. Still, many Indian tribes were pushed out of their homelands. As they resettled in new regions, they alternately allied and fought with native peoples already living there. At the same time, the trade in Indian slaves expanded in the west as the French and the Spanish competed for economic partners and military allies.

Global Conflicts on the Southern Frontier

Indians were not the only people to have their world shaken by war. By 1720 years of warfare and upheaval had transformed the mind-set of many colonists, from New England to the Carolinas. Although most considered themselves loyal British subjects, many believed that British proprietors remained largely unconcerned with the colonies' welfare. Others resented the British army's treatment of colonial militia and Parliament's unwillingness to aid settlers against Indian attacks. Moreover, the growing numbers of settlers who arrived from other parts of Europe had little investment in British authority.

The impact of Britain's ongoing conflicts with Spain during the 1730s and 1740s on southern colonists illustrates this development. Following the Yamasee War, South Carolina became a royal colony, and its profitable rice and indigo plantations spread southward. Then, in 1732, Parliament established Georgia (named after King George II) on lands north of Florida as a buffer between Carolina colonists and their longtime Spanish foes. The colony was initiated by social reformers like James Oglethorpe who hoped to provide small farms for Britain's poor. Initially slavery was outlawed, and land grants usually consisted of 50 to 100 acres.

Despite the noble intentions of Georgia's founders, Spanish authorities were furious at this expansion of British territorial claims. Thus in August 1739, a Spanish naval ship captured an English ship captain who was trading illegally in the Spanish West Indies and severed his ear. In response, Great Britain attacked St. Augustine and Cartagena (in present-day Colombia), but its troops were repulsed. In 1742 Spain sent troops into Georgia, but Oglethorpe's militia pushed back the attack. By then, the American war had become part of a more general European conflict. Once again France and Spain joined forces while Great Britain supported Germany in Europe. When the war ended in 1748, Britain had ensured the future of Georgia and reaffirmed its military superiority. Once again, however, victory had come at the cost of the lives of many colonial settlers and soldiers, a fact that was not lost on the colonists, some of whom began to wonder if their interests and those of the British government were truly the same.

Southern Indians were also caught up in ongoing disputes among Europeans. While both French and Spanish forces attacked the British along the Atlantic coast, they sought to outflank each other in the lower Mississippi River valley and Texas. With the French relying on Caddo, Choctaw, and other Indian allies for trade goods and defense, the Spaniards needed to expand their alliances beyond the Tejas. Initially, however, Apache raids on Spanish missions led Spanish settlers to sell captured Apache women and children into slavery in Mexico. In 1749, however, Father Santa Ana convinced a Spanish general to send two Apache women and a man back to their village with a peace proposal. Shortly afterward, in an elaborate ceremony at the mission, the two sides literally buried their differences in a large pit and negotiated peace.

The British meanwhile became increasingly dependent on European immigrants to defend colonial frontiers against the French, Spaniards, and Indians. Certainly many Anglo-Americans moved westward as coastal areas became overcrowded, but frontier regions also attracted immigrants from Scotland and Germany who sought refuge and economic opportunity in the colonies. Many headed to the Virginia and Carolina frontier and to Georgia in the 1730s and 1740s. Meanwhile South Carolina officials recruited Swiss, German, and French Huguenot as well as Scots-Irish immigrants in the 1740s to settle along the Pee Dee River and other inland waterways. Small communities of Jews settled in Charleston as well. Gradually many of these immigrants moved south into Georgia, seeking more and cheaper land. Thus when Spanish, French, or Indian forces attacked the British colonial frontier, they were as likely to face Scots-Irish and German immigrants as Englishmen.

REVIEW & RELATE

- How did the European wars of the late seventeenth and early eighteenth centuries impact relations between colonists and England?
- How and why were Indians pulled into the wars between European powers fought in North America?

The Benefits and Costs of Empire

The combined forces of global trade and international warfare altered the political and economic calculations of imperial powers. This was especially true for British North America, where colonists settled as families and created towns that provided key markets for Britain's commercial expansion. Over the course of the eighteenth century, British colonists became increasingly avid consumers of products from around the world. Meanwhile the king and Parliament, determined to reap the benefits of their costly empire, sought greater control over these far-flung commercial networks.

Colonial Traders Join Global Networks

In the late seventeenth and early eighteenth centuries, trade became truly global. Not only did goods from China, India, the Middle East, Africa, and North America gain currency in England and the rest of Europe, but the tastes of European consumers also helped shape goods produced in other parts of the world. For instance, wealthy Englishmen had long desired fine porcelain from China, and by the early eighteenth century the Chinese were making teapots and bowls specifically for that market. The trade in cloth, tea, and sugar was similarly influenced by European tastes. The exploitation of African laborers contributed significantly to this global commerce. They were a crucial item of trade in their own right, and their labor in the Americas ensured steady supplies of sugar, rice, tobacco, indigo, and other goods for the world market.

By the early eighteenth century, both the volume and the diversity of goods multiplied. Silk, calico, porcelain, olive oil, wine, and other goods were carried from the East to Europe and the American colonies, while cod, mackerel, shingles, pine boards, barrel staves, rum, sugar, rice, and indigo filled ships returning west. A healthy trade also grew up within North America as New England fishermen, New York and Charleston merchants, and Caribbean planters met one another's needs. Salted cod and mackerel flowed to the Caribbean, and rum, molasses, and slaves flowed back to the mainland. This commerce required ships, barrels, docks, warehouses, and wharves, all of which ensured a lively trade in lumber, tar, pitch, and rosin. The volume of trade originating in British North America was impressive. Between April and December 1720, for example, some 425 ships sailed in and out of Boston harbor alone (Map 3.2).

The flow of information was critical to the flow of goods and credit. By the early eighteenth century, coffeehouses flourished in port cities around the Atlantic, providing access to the latest news. Merchants, ship captains, and traders met in person to discuss new ventures and to keep apprised of recent developments. British and American periodicals reported on parliamentary legislation, commodity prices in India and Great Britain, the state of trading houses in China, the outbreak of disease in foreign ports, and stock ventures in London. Thus colonists from Boston to Charleston could follow the South Seas Bubble in 1720, when shares in the British South Seas Company rose to astronomical heights and then collapsed. William Moraley's father was among the thousands of British investors who lost a great deal of money in this venture. But colonists could also track the rising price of wheat.

Imperial Policies Focus on Profits

In the midst of this growing international trade, European sovereigns worked to ensure that colonial possessions benefited their own treasuries. In the late seventeenth century, both Louis XIV and his English rivals embraced a system known as **mercantilism**, which centered on the maintenance of a favorable balance of trade, with more gold and silver flowing into the home country than flowed out. In France, finance minister Jean-Baptiste Colbert honed the system. Beginning in the 1660s, he taxed foreign imports while removing all barriers to trade within French territories. Colonies like New France provided valuable raw materials—furs, fish, lumber—that could be used to produce manufactured items for sale to foreign nations and to colonists.

While France's mercantile system was limited by the size of its empire, England benefited more fully from such policies. The English crown had access to a far wider array of natural resources and a larger market for its manufactured goods. As early as 1660, Parliament passed a Navigation Act that required merchants to conduct trade with the colonies only in English-owned ships. In addition, certain items imported from foreign ports—salt, wine, and oil, for instance—had to be carried in English ships or in ships with predominantly English crews. Finally, a list of "enumerated articles"—from tobacco and cotton to sugar and indigo—had to be shipped from the colonies to England before being re-exported to foreign ports. Thus the crown benefited directly or indirectly from nearly all commerce conducted by its colonies. But colonies, too, often benefited, as when Parliament helped subsidize the development of indigo in South Carolina.

 Online Document Project   The Production of Indigo
bedfordstmartins.com/hewittlawsonvalue

In 1663 Parliament expanded its imperial reach by requiring that goods sent from Europe to English colonies also pass through its ports. And a decade later, ship

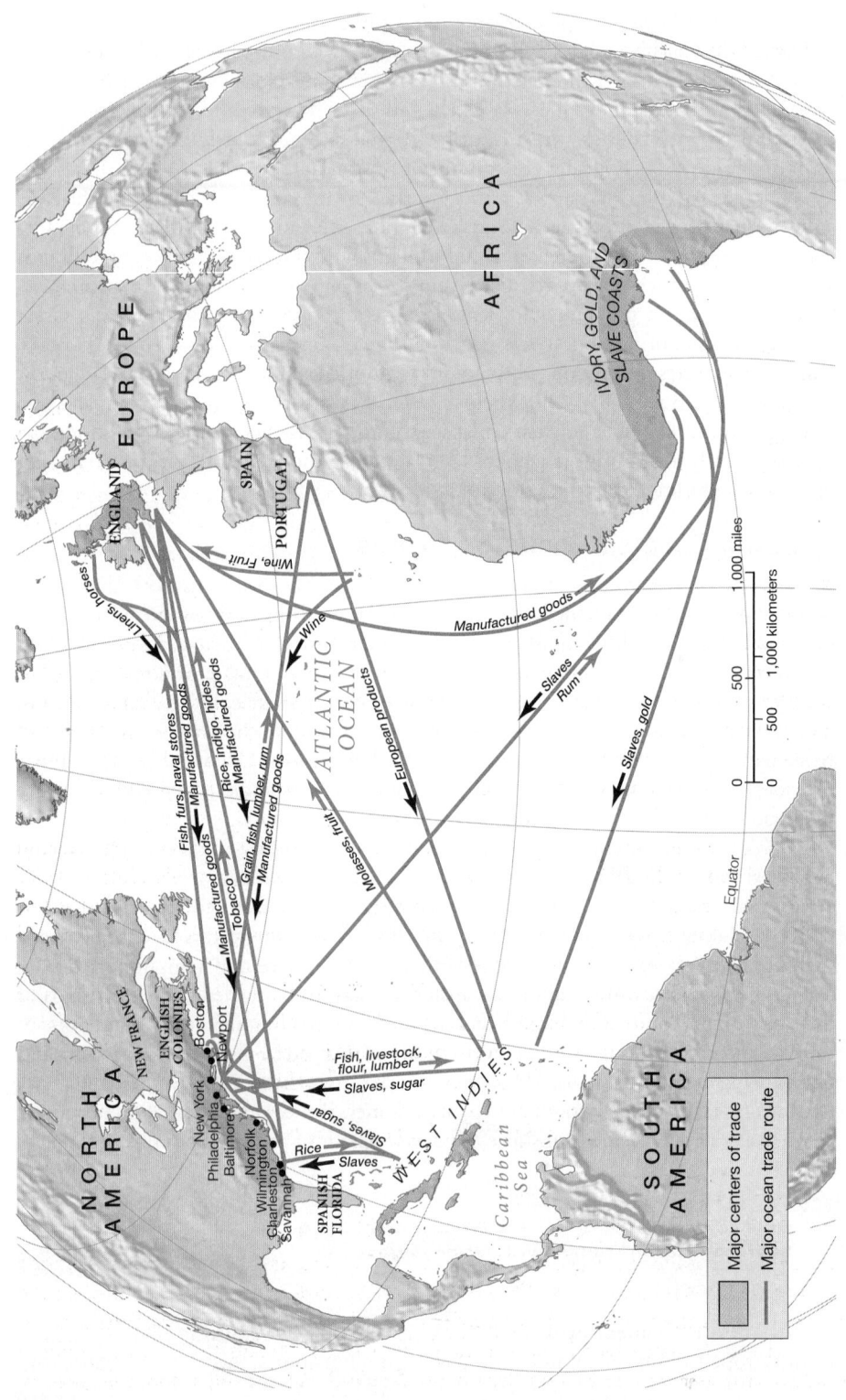

< **MAP 3.2**

North Atlantic Trade in the 18th Century   North Atlantic trade provided various parts of the British empire with raw materials, manufactured goods, and labor. Many ships traveled between only two regions because they were equipped to carry particular kinds of goods—slaves, grains, or manufactured goods. Ultimately, however, people and goods were exchanged among four key points: the West Indies, mainland North America, West Africa, and Great Britain.

captains had to pay a duty or post bond before carrying enumerated articles between colonial ports. Despite the Great Plague of 1665 and the London fire of 1666, England's overseas colonies fueled an economic upsurge. Indeed, when London was rebuilt after the fire, its wide boulevards, massive mercantile houses, crowded wharves, and bustling coffee shops marked it as the hub of an expanding commercial empire. Beginning in 1673, England sent customs officials to the colonies to enforce the various parliamentary acts. And by 1680, London, Bristol, and Liverpool all thrived as barrels of sugar, cases of indigo, and stacks of deerskin were unloaded and bolts of dyed cloth and cartons of felt hats were put on board for the return voyage. At the same time, the transformation of New Amsterdam into New York allowed England to incorporate the diverse commercial ventures that thrived in the Dutch colony into its imperial network.

Parliament then sought to quash nascent manufacturing in the colonies by prohibiting the sale of products such as American-made textiles (1699), hats (1732), and iron goods (1750). In addition, Parliament worked to restrict trade among the North American colonies. Settlers in the British West Indies had begun selling surplus fish, flour, and meat arriving from the mainland to their French neighbors. Meanwhile mainland colonists bought growing quantities of molasses, which they made into rum, from those same French islands at a much lower price than British West Indians could offer. Fearing French planters would dominate the sugar and molasses trade, Parliament passed the 1733 Molasses Act, which allowed mainland merchants to export fish and agricultural goods directly to the French West Indies but required them to pay a high import tariff on French molasses. The law might have crippled the American distilling industry, but mainland colonists instead began smuggling cheap French molasses into their ports and bribing customs officials to look the other way.

Despite the increasing regulation, American colonists could own British ships and transport goods produced in the colonies. Indeed, by the mid-eighteenth century, North American merchants oversaw 75 percent of the trade in manufactures sent from Bristol and London to the colonies and 95 percent of the trade with the West Indies. Ironically, then, a system established to benefit Great Britain ended up creating a mercantile elite in British North America. Most of those merchants traded in goods, but some traded in human cargo.

The Atlantic Slave Trade

Parliament chartered the Royal African Company in 1672, and England slowly expanded its role in the slave trade as the Dutch commercial empire waned. In 1713, when the British gained the right to sell slaves to Spanish colonies, that nation became a major player in the horrific trade in human cargo. Between 1700 and 1808, some 3 million captive Africans were carried on British and Anglo-American ships, about 40 percent

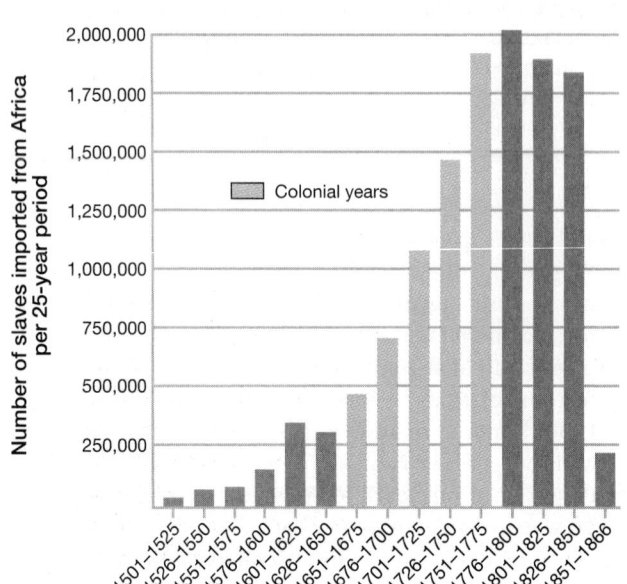

The Rise and Decline of the Slave Trade

FIGURE 3.1
The Slave Trade in Numbers, 1501–1866   Extraordinary numbers of Africans were shipped as slaves to other parts of the world from the sixteenth to the nineteenth century. These shipments increased dramatically during North America's colonial era (1601–1775). Although the slave trade transformed mainland North America, the vast majority of enslaved Africans were sent to Brazil and the West Indies.

Source: Trans-Atlantic Slave Trade Database, http://www.slavevoyages.org/tast/assessment/estimates.faces.

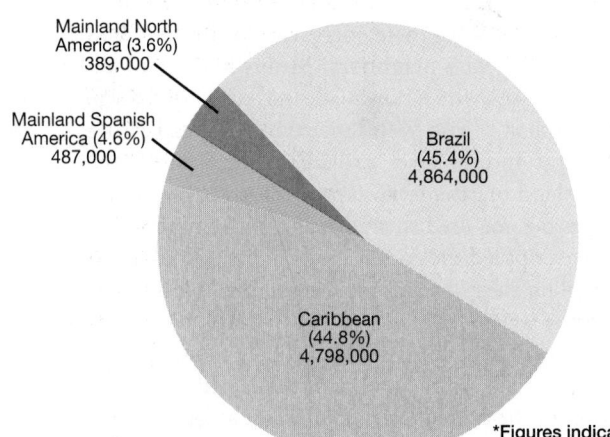

The Destinations of Slaves*

Mainland North America (3.6%)
389,000

Mainland Spanish America (4.6%)
487,000

Brazil (45.4%)
4,864,000

Caribbean (44.8%)
4,798,000

*Figures indicate numbers of slaves disembarked. Percentages are approximate and do not add up to 100%.

of the total of those sold in the Americas in this period (Figure 3.1). Half a million Africans died on the voyage across the Atlantic. Huge numbers also died in Africa, while being marched to the coast or held in forts waiting to be forced aboard ships. Yet despite this astounding death rate, the slave trade yielded enormous profits and had far-reaching consequences: The Africans that British traders bought and sold transformed labor systems in the colonies, fueled international trade, and enriched merchants, planters, and their families and partners.

European traders worked closely with African merchants to gain their human cargo. Where once they had traded textiles and alcohol for gold and ivory, Europeans now traded muskets, metalware, and linen for men, women, and children. Originally many of those sold into slavery were war captives. But by the time British and Anglo-American merchants became central to this notorious trade, their contacts in Africa were procuring labor in any way they could. The cargo included war captives, servants, and people snatched in raids specifically to secure slaves. Over time, African traders moved farther inland to fill the demand, devastating large areas of West Africa, particularly the Congo-Angola region, which supplied some 40 percent of all Atlantic slaves.

The trip across the Atlantic, known as the **Middle Passage**, was a brutal and often deadly experience for Africans. Exhausted and undernourished by the time they boarded the large oceangoing vessels, the captives were placed in dark and crowded holds. Most had been poked and prodded by slave traders, and some had been branded to ensure that a trader received the exact individuals he had purchased. Once in the hold, they might wait for weeks before the ship finally set sail. By that time, the foul-smelling and crowded hold became a nightmare of disease and despair. There was never sufficient food or fresh water for the captives, and women especially were subject to sexual abuse and rape by crew members. Many captives could not communicate with each other since they spoke different languages, and none of them knew exactly where they were going or what would happen when they arrived.

Those who survived the voyage were likely to find themselves in the slave markets of Barbados or Jamaica, where they were put on display for potential buyers. Once purchased, the slaves went through a period of **seasoning** as they regained their strength, became accustomed to their new environment, and learned commands in a new language. In this period of acculturation, enslaved laborers also confronted strange foods, new diseases, and unfamiliar tasks. Most were also given new names. Some did not survive seasoning, falling prey to malnutrition and disease or committing suicide. Others adapted to the new circumstances and adopted enough European or British ways to carry on even as they sought means to resist the shocking and oppressive conditions.

More than half of the slaves imported to the Lower South entered the mainland at Charleston, South Carolina. Beginning around 1700, enslaved Africans were shipped directly to Charleston rather than transshipped from the West Indies. Successful planters like Eliza Lucas likely had first choice of the new arrivals, sending agents to the wharves to buy Africans.

Seaport Cities and Consumer Cultures

The same trade in human cargo that brought misery to millions of Africans provided traders, investors, and plantation owners with huge profits that helped turn America's seaport cities into centers of culture and consumption. When Eliza Lucas arrived in Charleston in 1738, she noted that "the Metropolis is a neat pretty place. The inhabitants [are] polite and live in a very gentile [genteel] manner." Throughout British North America, seaports, with their elegant homes, fine shops, and lively social seasons, captured the most dynamic aspects of colonial life. Although cities like New York, Boston, Philadelphia, Baltimore, and Charleston contained less than 10 percent of the colonial population, they served as focal points of economic, political, social, and cultural activity.

Many affluent urban families shed the religious strictures or financial constraints that shaped the lives of their colonial forebearers and created a consumer revolution in

Charleston, 1739 This 1739 engraving offers a view of Charleston harbor from the Battery, where heavy rocks fortified the banks of the Cooper River and artillery later was placed in the American Civil War. Some of the ships in this scene carried slaves and consumer goods that made Charleston one of the great commercial centers in the South.   The Granger Collection, New York

North America. Changing patterns of consumption challenged traditional definitions of status. Less tied to birth and family pedigree, status in the colonies became more closely linked to financial success and a genteel lifestyle. Successful men of humble origins and even those of Dutch, Scottish, French, and Jewish heritage might join the British-dominated colonial gentry.

Of those who made the leap in the early eighteenth century, Benjamin Franklin was the most notable. He might have taken the path of the "infortunate" William Moraley Jr., but Franklin was apprenticed to his brother, a printer, an occupation that matched his interest in books, reading, and politics. At age sixteen, Franklin published (anonymously) his first essays in his brother's paper, the *New England Courant.* Two years later, a family dispute led Franklin to try his luck in New York and then Philadelphia. His fortunes were fragile, but hard work, a quick wit, good luck, and political connections led to success. In 1729 Franklin purchased the *Pennsylvania Gazette* and became the colony's official printer.

While Franklin worried about the concentration of wealth in too few hands, most colonial elites happily displayed their profits. Thus in the early eighteenth century, leading merchants in Boston, Salem, New York, and Philadelphia emulated British styles and built fine two- and three-story brick homes that had separate rooms for sleeping, eating, and entertaining guests. Mercantile elites also redesigned the urban landscape in the early eighteenth century. They donated money for brick churches and stately town halls. They constructed new roads, wharves, and warehouses to facilitate trade, and they invested in bowling greens and public gardens that beckoned affluent families on a Sunday afternoon.

Many Anglo-American elites used their knowledge of London fashions to reassert their British identity. Tea drinking was especially important in this regard, and families who could afford the finest furnishings and the time for extended social rituals made teatime a daily event. Yet the tea served at the home of Boston merchant Anthony Stoddard was imported from East Asia; the cups, saucers, and teapot were from China; and a handsome bowl held sugar from the West Indies. Stoddard decorated his home with heavily lacquered "japanned" boxes, French-patterned wallpaper, Indian calico bedding, and Italian silk curtains—all of which demonstrated that he was a successful merchant as well as a fashionable British citizen.

The spread of international commerce created a lively cultural life and great affluence in colonial cities. But it also created deep divisions between rich and poor. Wealthy merchants and professionals congregated in urban areas along with a middling group of artisans and shopkeepers and a growing class of unskilled laborers, widows, orphans, the elderly, the disabled, and the unemployed. The frequent wars of the late seventeenth and early eighteenth centuries contributed to these divisions by boosting the profits of merchants, shipbuilders, and artisans. They also improved the wages of seamen temporarily. But in their aftermath, rising prices, falling wages, and a lack of jobs led to the concentration of wealth in fewer hands.

> **REVIEW & RELATE**

- What place did North American colonists occupy in the eighteenth-century global trade network?
- How did the British government seek to maintain control over the colonial economy and ensure that its colonies served Britain's economic and political interests?

Labor in North America

What brought the poor and the wealthy together was the demand for labor. Labor was sorely needed in the colonies, but this did not mean that it was easy to find steady, high-paying employment. Many would-be laborers had few skills and faced fierce competition from other workers for limited, seasonal manual labor. Moreover, a majority of immigrants, both European and African, arrived in America with significant limits on their freedom.

Finding Work in the Colonies

The demand for labor did not necessarily help free laborers find work. Many employers preferred indentured servants, apprentices, or others who came cheap and were bound by contract. Others employed criminals or purchased slaves, who would provide years of service for a set price. Free laborers who sought a decent wage and steady employment needed to match their desire to work with skills that were in demand.

When William Moraley ended his indenture and sought work, he discovered that far fewer colonists than Englishmen owned timepieces, leaving him without a useful trade. So he tramped the countryside, selling his labor when he could, but found no consistent employment. Returning to New York and Philadelphia, William begged lodging from friends, considered marrying an elderly widow, was imprisoned for minor offenses, and accepted Quaker charity. But he fell ever deeper in debt. Thousands of other men and women, most without Moraley's education or skills, also found themselves at the mercy of unrelenting economic forces.

Many poor men and women found jobs building homes, loading ships, or spinning yarn. But they were usually employed for only a few months a year. The rest of the time they scrounged for bread and beer, begged in the streets, or stole what they needed. Most lived in ramshackle buildings filled with cramped and unsanitary rooms.

Freezing in winter and sweltering in summer, these quarters served as breeding grounds for smallpox, scarlet fever, and other diseases. Children born into such squalid circumstances were lucky to survive their first year. Those who survived could watch ships sail into port and earn a few pence running errands for captains or sailors, but they would never have access to the bounteous goods intended for those who lived in stately mansions.

By the early eighteenth century, older systems of labor, like indentured servitude, began to decline in many areas. In some parts of the North and across the South, white servants were gradually replaced by African slaves. At the same time, farm families who could not usefully employ all their children began to bind out sons and daughters to more prosperous neighbors. Apprentices, too, competed for positions. Unlike most servants, apprentices contracted to learn a trade. They trained under the supervision of a craftsman, who gained cheap labor by promising to teach a young man (and most apprentices were men) his trade. But master craftsmen limited the number of apprentices they accepted to maintain the value of their skills.

Another category of laborers emerged in the 1720s. A population explosion in Europe and the rising price of wheat and other items convinced many people to seek passage to America. Shipping agents offered them loans that were repaid when the immigrants found a colonial employer who would redeem (that is, repay) the original loan. In turn, these **redemptioners** labored for the employer for a set number of years, though they could live independently with their own family. The redemption system was popular in the Middle Atlantic colonies, especially among German immigrants who hoped to establish farms on the Pennsylvania frontier. While many succeeded, their circumstances could be extremely difficult.

Large numbers of convicts, too, entered the British colonies in the eighteenth century. Jailers in charge of Britain's overcrowded prisons offered inmates the option of transportation to the colonies. Hundreds were thus bound out each year to American employers. The combination of indentured servants, redemptioners, apprentices, and convicts ensured that as late as 1750 the majority of white workers—men and women—were bound to some sort of contract.

Sometimes white urban workers also competed with slaves, especially in the northern colonies. Africans and African Americans formed only a small percentage of the northern population, just 5 percent from Pennsylvania to New Hampshire in 1750. In the colony of New York, however, blacks formed about 14 percent of inhabitants. While some enslaved blacks worked on agricultural estates in the Hudson River valley and New Jersey, even more labored as household servants, dockworkers, seamen, and blacksmiths in New York City alongside British colonists and European immigrants (Figure 3.2). Considered a status symbol by many wealthy merchants, urban slaves were usually discouraged from marrying or bearing large numbers of children. However, some masters allowed their slaves to marry and set up independent households or to hire themselves out to other employers, as long as their wages were paid to their owners.

Coping with Economic Distress

White workers who were bound by contracts might have felt common cause with slaves, but most recognized that eventually they would be free. Despite the challenges faced by white workers who migrated to British North America in the early eighteenth century,

FIGURE 3.2

African Populations in the British West Indies, Northern Colonies, and Southern Colonies, 1650–1750 In 1650 the African population in the British West Indies already far exceeded that in mainland North America. Over the next century, the number of Africans and African Americans increased significantly on the mainland. But the growth was far greater in the southern than in the northern colonies, reaching 40 percent in the Chesapeake and Lower South colonies by the mid-eighteenth century.

Source: From *Time on the Cross: The Economics of American Negro Slavery* by Robert William Fogel and Stanley L. Engerman. Copyright © 1974 by Robert William Fogel and Stanley L. Engerman. Used by permission of W. W. Norton & Company, Inc.

many still improved their lives. Most servants, apprentices, redemptioners, and convicts hoped one day to purchase land, open a shop, or earn a decent wage. Yet gaining freedom did not promise economic success.

Several challenges confronted those looking to succeed. First, white women and men who gained their freedom from indentures or other contracts had to compete for jobs with a steady supply of redemptioners, convicts, and apprentices as well as other free laborers. Second, by the early eighteenth century, many areas along the Atlantic coast faced a land shortage that threatened the fortunes even of long-settled families. Finally, a population boom in Britain's North American colonies produced growing numbers of young people seeking land and employment. Thus many free laborers migrated from town to town and from country to city seeking work. They hoped to find farmers who needed extra hands for planting and harvesting or ship captains and contractors who would hire them to load or unload cargo or assist in the construction of homes and churches. The Royal Army and Navy also periodically sought colonial recruits, though mostly in times of war. Women meanwhile hoped for employment spinning yarn or working as cooks, laundresses, or nursemaids.

Seasonal and temporary demands for labor created a corps of transient workers. Many New England towns developed systems to "warn out" those who were not official residents. Modeled after the British system, warning-out was meant to ensure that strangers did not become public dependents. Still, being warned did not mean immediate removal. Sometimes transients were simply warned that they were not eligible for poor relief. At other times, constables returned them to an earlier place of residence. In many ways, warning-out served as an early registration system, allowing authorities to encourage the flow of labor, keep residents under surveillance, and protect the town's coffers. But it rarely aided those in need of work.

Residents who were eligible for public assistance might be given food and clothing or boarded with a local family. Many towns began appointing Overseers of the Poor to deal with the growing problem of poverty. By 1750 every seaport city had constructed an almshouse that sheltered residents without other means of support. In 1723 the Bridewell prison was added to Boston Almshouse, built in 1696. Then in 1739 a work-house was opened on the same site to employ the "able-bodied" poor in hopes that profits from it would help fund the almshouse and prison. Overseers in each city believed that a workhouse would "simultaneously correct the idle poor and instill in them a habit of industry by obliging them to work to earn their keep." Still, these efforts at relief fell far short of the need, especially in hard economic times.

Rural Americans Face Changing Conditions

While seaport cities and larger towns fostered a growing cohort of individuals who lived outside traditional households, families remained the central unit of economic organization in rural areas, where the vast majority of Americans lived. Yet even farms were affected by the transatlantic circulation of goods and people.

In areas along the Atlantic coast, rural families were drawn into commercial networks in a variety of ways. Towns and cities needed large supplies of vegetables, meat, butter, barley, wheat, and yarn. Farm families sold produce or homemade goods to residents and bought sugar, tea, and other imported items that diversified their diet. Few rural families purchased ornamental or luxury items, but cloth or cheese bought in town saved hours of labor at home. Just as important, coastal communities like Salem, Massachusetts, and Wilmington, Delaware, that were once largely rural became thriving commercial centers in the late seventeenth century.

In New England, the land available for farming shrank as the population soared. In the original Puritan colonies, the population rose from 100,000 in 1700 to 400,000 in 1750, and many parents were unable to provide their children with sufficient land for profitable farms. The result was increased migration to the frontier, where families were more dependent on their own labor and a small circle of neighbors. And even this option was not accessible to all. Before 1700, servants who survived their indenture had a good chance of securing land, but by the mid-eighteenth century only two of every ten were likely to become landowners.

In the Middle Atlantic region, the population surged from 50,000 in 1700 to 250,000 in 1750. The increase was due in part to the rapid rise in wheat prices, which leaped by more than 50 percent in Europe. Hoping to take advantage of this boon, Anglo-Americans, Germans, Scots-Irish, and other non-English groups flooded into western Pennsylvania, New York's Mohawk River valley, and the Shenandoah Valley of Virginia in the early eighteenth century. By the 1740s, German families had created self-contained communities in these areas. They worshipped in German churches, read German newspapers, and preserved German traditions. Meanwhile Scots-Irish immigrants, most of them Presbyterians, established churches and communities in New Jersey, central Pennsylvania, and western Maryland and Virginia (Map 3.3).

In the South, immigrants could acquire land more easily, but their chances for economic autonomy were increasingly influenced by the spread of slavery. As hundreds and then thousands of Africans were imported into the Carolinas in the 1720s and 1730s, economic and political power became more entrenched in the hands of planters and merchants. Increasingly, they controlled the markets, wrote the laws, and set the terms by which white as well as black families lived. Farms along inland waterways and

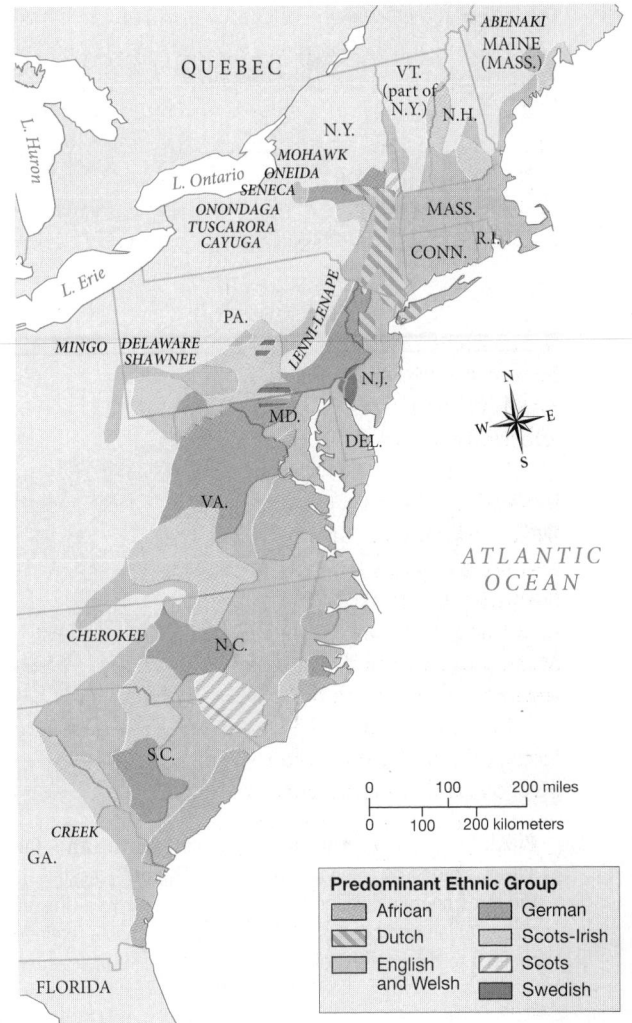

MAP 3.3

Ethnic and Racial Diversity in British North America, 1750 By 1750 British North America was a far more diverse region than it had been fifty years earlier. In 1700 the English dominated most regions, while the Dutch controlled towns and estates in the Hudson River valley. By 1750, however, growing numbers of African Americans, German and Scots-Irish immigrants, and smaller communities of other ethnic groups predominated in various regions.

on the frontier were crucial in providing food and other items for urban residents and for planters with large labor forces. But farm families depended on commercial and planter elites to market their goods and help defend their communities against hostile Indians or Spaniards.

Slavery Takes Hold in the South

The rise of slavery reshaped the South in numerous ways. The shift from white indentured servants to black slaves began in Virginia after 1676 (see chapter 2) and soon spread across the Chesapeake. The Carolinas, meanwhile, developed as a slave society from the start. Slavery in turn allowed for the expanded cultivation of cash crops like tobacco, rice, and indigo, which promised high profits for planters as well as merchants. But these developments also made southern elites more dependent on the global

Black Slaves Working on a Tobacco Plantation   This eighteenth-century engraving shows slaves laboring on a tobacco plantation. The bare-chested slaves have brought tobacco leaves from the fields and are packing them in barrels while well-dressed whites oversee their work. The head of the Indian displayed in the banner at the top is a reminder of the people who introduced tobacco to the English colonists.   Peter Newark American Pictures/The Bridgeman Art Library

market and limited opportunities for poorer whites and all blacks. They also ensured that Indians and many whites were pushed farther west as planters sought more land for their ventures.

In the 1660s, the Virginia Assembly passed a series of laws that made slavery a status inherited through the mother, denied that the status could be changed by converting to Christianity, and granted masters the right to kill slaves who resisted their authority (see chapter 2). In 1680 the Assembly made it illegal for "any negro or other slave to carry or arme himself with any club, staffe, gunn, sword, or any other weapon of defence or offence." Nor could slaves leave their master's premises without a certificate of permission. Those who disobeyed were whipped or branded. Increasingly harsh laws in Virginia and Maryland, modeled on those in Barbados, coincided with a rise in the number of slaves imported to the colony. The statutes also ensured the decline of the free black population in the Chesapeake. In 1668 one-third of all Africans and African Americans in Virginia and Maryland were still free, but the numbers dwindled year by year. Once the Royal African Company started supplying the Chesapeake with slaves directly from Africa in the 1680s, the pace of change quickened. By 1750, 150,000 blacks resided in the Chesapeake, and only about 5 percent remained free.

e Online Document Project   **The Atlantic Slave Trade**
bedfordstmartins.com/hewittlawsonvalue

Direct importation from Africa had other negative consequences on slave life. Far more men than women were imported, skewing the sex ratio in a population that was just beginning to form families and communities. Women like men performed heavy field work, and few bore more than one or two children. When these conditions sparked resistance by the enslaved, fearful whites imposed even stricter regulations. In 1705 the Virginia Assembly passed an omnibus "Negro Act" that incorporated earlier provisions and made absolutely clear the special legal status of the enslaved. For instance, while mistreated white servants could sue in court, black slaves could not. And a slave who ran away and was captured could be tortured and dismembered in hopes of "terrifying others from the like practices."

While slavery in the Carolinas was influenced by developments in the Chesapeake, it was shaped even more directly by practices in the British West Indies. Many wealthy families from Barbados, Antigua, and other sugar islands—including that of Colonel Lucas—established plantations in the Carolinas. At first, they brought slaves from the West Indies to oversee cattle and pigs and assist in the slaughter of livestock and curing of meat for shipment back to the West Indies. Some of the slaves grew rice, using techniques learned in West Africa, to supplement their diet. Owners soon realized that rice might prove very profitable. Although not widely eaten in Europe, rice could provide cheap and nutritious food for sailors, orphans, convicts, and peasants. Relying initially on Africans' knowledge, planters began cultivating rice for export.

The need for African rice-growing skills and the fear of attacks by Spaniards and Indians led Carolina owners to grant slaves rights unheard of in the Chesapeake or the West Indies. Initially slaves were allowed to carry guns and serve in the militia. For those who nonetheless ran for freedom, Spanish and Indian territories offered refuge. Still, most stayed, depending for support on bonds they had developed in the West Indies. The frequent absence of owners also offered Carolina slaves greater autonomy.

As rice cultivation expanded, however, slavery in the Carolinas turned more brutal. The Assembly enacted harsher and harsher slave codes to ensure control of the growing labor force. No longer could slaves carry guns, join militias, meet in groups, or travel without a pass. As planters began to import more slaves directly from Africa, sex ratios, already male dominated, became even more heavily skewed. In addition, older community networks from the West Indies were disrupted. Military patrols by whites were initiated to enforce laws and labor practices. Some plantations along the Carolina coast turned into virtual labor camps, where thousands of slaves worked under harsh conditions with no hope of improvement.

By 1720 blacks outnumbered whites in the Carolinas, and fears of slave rebellions inspired South Carolina officials to impose even harsher laws and more brutal enforcement measures. When indigo joined rice as a cash crop in the 1740s, the demand for slave labor increased further. Although far fewer slaves—about 40,000 by 1750—resided in South Carolina than in the Chesapeake, they constituted more than 60 percent of the colony's total population.

Africans Resist Their Enslavement

Enslaved laborers in British North America resisted their subjugation in a variety of ways. They sought to retain customs, foods, belief systems, and languages from their homelands. They tried to incorporate work patterns passed down from one generation to the next into new environments. They challenged masters and overseers by refusing to work, breaking tools, feigning illness, and other means of disputing whites' authority. Some ran for freedom, others fought back in the face of punishment, and still others used arson, poison, or other means to defy owners. A few planned revolts.

The consequences for resisting were severe, from whipping, mutilation, and branding to summary execution. Because whites were so fearful of rebellion, they often punished people falsely accused of planning revolts. Yet some slaves did plot ways to rise up against their owners or whites in general. Southern whites, living amid large numbers of blacks, were most deeply concerned about resistance and rebellion. But even in the North, whites did not doubt slaves' desire for freedom. As more slaves were imported directly from Africa, both the fear and the reality of rebellion increased.

In New York City in 1712, several dozen enslaved Africans and Indians set fire to a building. When whites rushed to the scene, the insurgents attacked them with clubs, pistols, axes, and staves, killing 8 and injuring many more. The rebels were soon defeated by the militia, however. Authorities executed 18 insurgents, burning several at the stake as a warning to others, while 6 of those imprisoned committed suicide. In 1741 a series of suspicious fires in the city led to accusations against a white couple who owned an alehouse where blacks gathered to drink. To protect herself from prosecution, an Irish indentured servant testified that she had overheard discussions of an elaborate plot involving black and white conspirators. Frightened of any hint that poor whites and blacks might make common cause, authorities immediately arrested suspects and eventually executed 34 people, including 4 whites. They also banished 72 blacks from the city. Among those executed was Cuffee, a slave who claimed that "a great many people have too much, and others too little."

The most serious slave revolt, however, erupted in South Carolina, just a few miles from Wappoo, the Lucas plantation. A group of recently imported Africans led the Stono rebellion in 1739. On Sunday, September 9, a group of enslaved men stole weapons from a country store and killed the owners. They then marched south, along the Stono River, beating drums and recruiting others to join them. Torching plantations and killing whites along the route, they had gathered more than fifty insurgents when armed whites overtook them. In the ensuing battle, dozens of rebels died. The militia, along with Indians hired to assist them, killed another twenty over the next two days and then captured a group of forty, who were executed without trial.

This revolt reverberated widely in a colony where blacks outnumbered whites nearly two to one, direct importation from Africa was at an all-time high, and Spanish authorities in Florida promised freedom to runaway slaves. In 1738 the Spanish governor formed a black militia company, and he allowed thirty-eight fugitive families to settle north of

St. Augustine and build Fort Mose for their protection. When warfare erupted between Spain and Britain over commercial rivalries in 1739, Carolina slaves may have seen their chance to gain freedom en masse. But as with other rebellions, this one failed, and the price of failure was death.

REVIEW & RELATE

- What were the sources of economic inequality in North America in the early eighteenth century?
- Under what kinds of contracts and conditions did poor people, both white and black, work?

Conclusion: Changing Fortunes in British North America

Global commerce, international wars, and immigration reshaped the economy and geography of North America between 1680 and 1750. Many colonists thrived, initiating a consumer revolution that transformed daily life and ensured the growth of seaport cities. Others found greater opportunities by pushing inland and establishing farms and communities along new frontiers. But many failed to benefit from either land or trade. White workers caught in a downward economic spiral, enslaved Africans, and Indians on the wrong side of a war—all became victims of international trade and imperial conflicts.

The development of manufacturing in England shaped the lives of working people on both sides of the Atlantic Ocean. William Moraley Jr., for example, lived out his life in Newcastle-upon-Tyne, making and repairing watches at a time when cheap watches were being turned out in large numbers. While master craftsmen and shop owners could make a good living, those with less skill and fewer funds commanded far lower wages. When Moraley died in January 1762, his only claim to fame was his "adventures" in the American colonies. Yet the nascent industrial revolution had far more positive effects for some colonists. The mechanization of cloth production in England demanded vast amounts of raw material from the English countryside and the colonies. It ensured, for example, the profitability of indigo. This crop benefited many South Carolina planters, including Eliza Lucas and—after her marriage in 1744—her husband, Charles Pinckney, a successful planter himself. Still, profits from indigo could be gained only through the labor of hundreds of slaves.

Eliza Pinckney's sons became important leaders in the colony, and despite their English education and the benefits they gained through British trade, both developed a strong belief in the rights of the colonies to control their own destinies. Like many American colonists, they were spurred by the consumer revolution, geographical expansion, growing religious and ethnic diversity, and conflicts with Indian and European enemies to develop a mind-set that differed significantly from their counterparts back home. As the fortunes of colonists rose or fell with the changing dynamics of global trade and as they grappled with the claims of Indians and the growth of slavery, some reimagined their relationships not only to production and consumption, agriculture and commerce, but also to the religious and political beliefs that had sustained them for generations.

Chapter Review

MAKE IT STICK

 LearningCurve **bedfordstmartins.com/hewittlawsonvalue**
After reading the chapter, use LearningCurve to retain what you've read.

IDENTIFY KEY TERMS

Identify and explain the significance of each term below.

proprietary colonies (p. 56)
Glorious Revolution (p. 56)
Pueblo revolt (p. 59)
King William's War (p. 60)
War of the Spanish Succession (p. 60)

mercantilism (p. 65)
Middle Passage (p. 69)
seasoning (p. 69)
redemptioners (p. 72)
Stono rebellion (p. 78)

REVIEW & RELATE

Answer the focus questions from each section of the chapter.

1. What role did the crown play in the expansion of the English North American colonies in the second half of the seventeenth century?

2. How did the development of the Spanish and French colonies in the late seventeenth century differ from that of the English colonies?

3. How did the European wars of the late seventeenth and early eighteenth centuries impact relations between colonists and England?

4. How and why were Indians pulled into the wars between European powers fought in North America?

5. What place did North American colonists occupy in the eighteenth-century global trade network?

6. How did the British government seek to maintain control over the colonial economy and ensure that its colonies served Britain's economic and political interests?

7. What were the sources of economic inequality in North America in the early eighteenth century?

8. Under what kinds of contracts and conditions did poor people, both white and black, work?

ONLINE DOCUMENT PROJECTS

◆ **The Production of Indigo**
◆ **The Atlantic Slave Trade**

After reading the primary sources in these document sets, answer the **Interpret the Evidence** questions to help you analyze each of the documents, and then answer the **Put It in Context** question(s) to help you relate the documents to the topics and themes you read about in the chapter.

bedfordstmartins.com/hewittlawsonvalue

TIMELINE OF EVENTS

1660
- Monarchy restored in England
- Parliament passes first of a series of Navigation Acts to regulate colonial commerce

1660–1685
- Charles II rewards his most important allies with proprietorships in North America

1672
- Royal African Company chartered

1680
- Pueblo revolt against Spanish rule in New Mexico

1688
- Glorious Revolution

1689–1697
- King William's War

1692
- New colony of Massachusetts established

1700–1750
- New England colonial population increases from 100,000 to 400,000
- Middle Atlantic colonial population increases from 50,000 to 250,000

1700–1808
- British and Anglo-American ships transport 3 million African slaves to the Americas

1702
- East and West Jersey unite into colony of New Jersey

1702–1713
- War of the Spanish Succession

1704
- Delaware separates from Pennsylvania

1705
- Virginia passes "Negro Act" consolidating and tightening earlier slave laws

1710
- North Carolina becomes fully independent of South Carolina

1711–1715
- Tuscaroras lead pan-Indian war against settlers in the Carolinas

1715–1717
- Yamasee War

1729
- Benjamin Franklin becomes Pennsylvania's official printer

1732
- Colony of Georgia established

1739
- Eliza Lucas takes charge of her father's South Carolina estates
- Stono rebellion

1743
- William Moraley publishes an account of his time in America

1749
- Spanish settlers in Texas make peace with the Apaches

4

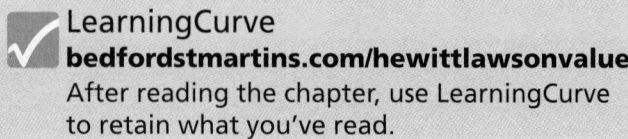

LearningCurve
bedfordstmartins.com/hewittlawsonvalue
After reading the chapter, use LearningCurve
to retain what you've read.

Religious Strife and Social Upheavals

1680–1750

AMERICAN HISTORIES

In the 1730s Gilbert Tennent, a leading preacher in the American colonies, outraged more traditional ministers with his evangelical zeal. The son of a Scots-Irish clergyman, Gilbert Tennent was born in Vinecash, Ireland, in 1703 and at age fifteen moved with his family to Philadelphia. After receiving an M.A. from Yale College in 1725, Gilbert was ordained a Presbyterian minister in New Brunswick, New Jersey, with little indication of the role he would play in a major denominational schism.

Tennent entered the ministry at a critical moment, when leaders of a number of denominations had become convinced that the colonies were descending into spiritual apathy. Tennent dedicated himself to sparking a rebirth of Christian commitment, and by the mid-1730s the pastor had gained fame as a revival preacher. At the end of the decade, he journeyed through the middle colonies with Englishman George Whitefield, an Anglican preacher known for igniting powerful revivals. Then in the fall of 1740, following the death of his wife, Tennent launched his own evangelical "awakenings."

Revivals inspired thousands of religious conversions across denominations, but they also fueled conflicts within established churches. Presbyterians in Britain and America disagreed about whether only those who had had a powerful, personal conversion experience were qualified to be ministers. Tennent made his opinion clear by denouncing unconverted ministers in his sermons, a position that led to his expulsion from the Presbyterian Church in 1741. But many local churches sought converted preachers, and four years later a group of ejected pastors formed a rival synod that trained its own evangelical ministers. During these upheavals, Tennent married a widow with children and became pastor of the New Building of Philadelphia, a church founded by Whitefield supporters. But he proved too moderate for many of the more enthusiastic congregants, who left to join the Baptist Church.

While ministers debated the proper means of saving sinners, ordinary women and men searched their souls. In Pomfret, Connecticut, Sarah Grosvenor certainly feared for hers in the summer of 1742 when the unmarried nineteen-year-old realized she was pregnant. Her situation was complicated by her status in the community. She was the daughter of Leicester Grosvenor, an important local landowner and town official, and Sarah's family regularly attended Pomfret's Congregational church.

The pew next to Sarah and her family was occupied by Nathaniel Sessions and his sons, including the twenty-six-year-old Amasa, who had impregnated Sarah. Many other young women became pregnant out of wedlock in the 1740s, but families accepted the fact as long as the couple married before the child was born. In Sarah's case, however, Amasa refused to marry her and suggested instead that she have an abortion.

For centuries, women had sought to end unwanted pregnancies by using herbal potions. Although Sarah was reluctant to follow this path, Amasa insisted. When the herbs failed to induce a miscarriage, he introduced Sarah to John Hallowell, a doctor who claimed he could remove the fetus with forceps, a recently developed instrument to aid in delivery. After admitting her agonizing situation to her older sister Zerviah and her cousin Hannah, Sarah allowed Hallowell to proceed. He finally induced a miscarriage, but Sarah soon grew feverish, suffered convulsions, and died ten days later.

Apparently Sarah's and Amasa's parents were unaware of the events leading to her demise. Then in 1745, a powerful religious revival swept through the region, and Zerviah and Hannah suffered great spiritual anguish. We are not sure whether they finally

The New Dutch Reformed Church, New York City, 1731.   Private Collection/ Peter Newark American Pictures/The Bridgeman Art Library

confessed their part in the affair, but that year officials finally brought charges against Sessions and Hallowell for Sarah's death. At the resulting trial, Zerviah and Hannah testified about their roles and those of Sessions and Hallowell. Still, their spiritual anguish did not lead to earthly justice. Hallowell was found guilty but escaped punishment by fleeing to Rhode Island. Sessions was acquitted and remained in Pomfret, where he married and became a prosperous farmer.

THE AMERICAN HISTORIES of Gilbert Tennent and Sarah Grosvenor were shaped by powerful religious forces—later called the Great Awakening—that swept through the colonies in the early eighteenth century. Those forces are best understood in the context of larger economic and political changes. Many young people became more independent of their parents and developed tighter bonds with siblings, cousins, and neighbors their own age. Towns and cities developed clearer hierarchies by class and status, which could protect wealthier individuals from being punished for their misdeeds. A double standard of sexual behavior became more entrenched as well, with women subject to greater scrutiny than men for their sexual behavior. Of course, most young women did not meet the fate of Sarah Grosvenor. Still, pastors like Gilbert Tennent feared precisely such consequences if the colonies—growing ever larger and more diverse—did not reclaim their religious foundations.

An Ungodly Society?

The upheavals that marked the lives of Gilbert Tennent and Sarah Grosvenor were shaped in part by economic and political changes that began several decades earlier. As American colonists became more engaged in international and domestic commerce, spiritual commitments appeared to wane. In New England, Congregational ministers condemned the apparent triumph of worldly ambition over religiosity. Nonetheless, some ministers saw economic success as a reward for godly behavior even as they worried that wealth and power opened the door to sin. In the late seventeenth century, these anxieties deepened when accusations of witchcraft erupted across southern New England.

The Rise of Religious Anxieties

In 1686 the Puritan minister Samuel Sewell railed against the behavior of Boston mercantile elites, many of whom spent more time at the counting house than the house of worship. Citing examples of their depravity in his diary, including drunkenness and cursing, he claimed that such "high-handed wickedness has hardly been heard of before." Sewell was outraged as well by popular practices such as donning powdered wigs in place of God-given hair, wearing scarlet and gold jackets rather than simple black cloth, and offering toasts rather than prayers.

While Sewell spoke for many Puritans concerned with the consequences of commercial success, other religious leaders tried to meld old and new. The Reverend Cotton Mather bemoaned the declining number of colonists who participated in public fast days and their greater interest in the latest fashions than in the state of their souls. Yet he was attracted by the luxuries available to colonists and hoped to make his son "a more finished Gentleman." Mather was also fascinated by new scientific endeavors and supported inoculations for smallpox, which others viewed as challenging God's power.

Certainly news of the Glorious Revolution in England (1688) offered Puritans hope of regaining their customary authority (see chapter 3). But the outbreak of King William's War in 1689 quickly ended any notion of an easy return to peace and prosperity. Instead, continued conflicts and renewed fears of Indian attacks on rural settlements heightened the sense that Satan was at work in the region. Soon, accusations of witchcraft joined outcries against other forms of ungodly behavior.

Cries of Witchcraft

Belief in witchcraft had been widespread in Europe and England for centuries. It was part of a general belief in supernatural causes for events that could not otherwise be explained—severe storms, a suspicious fire, a rash of deaths among livestock. God sent signs through nature, but so, too, did Satan. Thus people searched babies for deformities, scheduled important events using astrological charts, and feared eclipses of the sun. When a community began to suspect witchcraft, they often pointed to individuals who challenged cultural norms. Women who were quarrelsome, eccentric, or poor were especially easy to imagine as cavorting with evil spirits and invisible demons.

Witchcraft accusations tended to be most common in times of change and uncertainty. Over the course of the seventeenth century, colonists had begun to spread into new areas seeking more land and greater economic opportunities. But expansion brought with it confrontations with Indians, exposure to new dangers, and greater vulnerability to a harsh and unforgiving environment. As the stress of expansion mounted, witchcraft accusations emerged. Some 160 individuals, mostly women, were accused of witchcraft in Massachusetts and Connecticut between 1647 and 1692, although only 15 were put to death. They were linked to ruined crops, sickened neighbors, and the death of cattle. Many of the accused were poor, childless, or disgruntled women, but widows who inherited property also came under suspicion, especially if they fought for control against male relatives and neighbors.

The social and economic complexities of witchcraft accusations are well illustrated by the most famous of American witch-hunts, the Salem witch trials of the early 1690s. In 1692 Salem confronted conflicts between long-settled farmers and newer mercantile families, political uncertainties following the Glorious Revolution, ongoing fear of threats from Indians, and local quarrels over the choice of a new minister. These tensions were brought to a head when the Reverend Samuel Parris's daughter and niece learned voodoo lore and exotic dances from the household's West Indian slave, Tituba. The daughters and servants of neighboring families also became entranced by Tituba's tales and began to tell fortunes, speak in gibberish, and contort their bodies into painful positions. When the girls were questioned about their strange behavior, they pointed not only to Tituba but also to other people in the community. They first accused an elderly female pauper and a homeless widow of bewitching them, but soon they singled out respectable churchwomen as well as a minister, a wealthy merchant, and a four-year-old child.

Within weeks, more than one hundred individuals, 80 percent of them women, stood accused of witchcraft. When the new governor, William Phips, took office in May 1692, he set up a special court to handle the cases and appointed eight Puritan leaders, including Samuel Sewell, to preside. Twenty-seven of the accused came to trial, and twenty were found guilty based on testimony from the girls and on **spectral evidence**—whereby the girls were seen writhing, shaking, and crying out in pain when they came in contact with invisible spirits sent by the accused. Nineteen people were hanged, and one was pressed to death with stones.

But when accusations reached into prominent Salem and Boston families, Governor Phips stepped in. He ended the proceedings and released the remaining suspects. In the following months, leading ministers and colonial officials condemned the use of spectral evidence, and some of the young accusers recanted their testimony. Witch-hunts in North America were small affairs compared to those in Europe, rarely occurred outside New England, and died out by 1700. Yet for those caught up in the trials, the consequences were severe.

The Salem trials illuminate far more than beliefs in witchcraft, however. The trials pitted the daughters and servants of prosperous farmers against the wives and widows of recently arrived merchants. The accusers included young women like nineteen-year-old Mercy Lewis, who was bound out as a servant when her parents were killed by Indians. Fear of attack from hostile Indians, hostile officials in England, or hostile neighbors fostered anxieties in Salem, as it did in many colonial communities. Other anxieties also haunted the accusers. A shortage of land led many New England men to seek their fortune farther west, leaving young women with few eligible bachelors to choose from. Marriage prospects were affected as well by battles over inheritance. Thomas Putnam Jr., who housed three of the accusers, was in the midst of one such battle, which left his three sisters—the accusers' aunts—in limbo as they awaited legacies that could enhance their marriage prospects. As young women in Salem forged tight bonds in the face of such uncertainties, they turned their anger not against men, but instead against older women, including respectable "goodwives" like Abigail Faulkner.

REVIEW & RELATE

• What factors led to a rise in tensions within colonial communities in the early 1700s?

• How did social, economic, and political tensions contribute to an increase in accusations of witchcraft?

Family and Household Dynamics

Concerns about marriage, property, and inheritance were not limited to Salem or to New England. As the American colonies became more populous and the numbers of women and men more balanced, husbands gained greater control over the behavior of household members, and the legal and economic rewards available to most women declined. Colonial women with wealth, education, or special skills like midwifery or beer brewing might hold some power in their household and community. But those saddled with abusive husbands or masters quickly discovered that their rights and resources were severely limited.

Women's Changing Status

In most early American colonies, the scarcity of women and workers ensured that many white women gained economic and legal leverage. In the first decades of settlement in the Chesapeake, where women were in especially short supply and mortality was high, young women who arrived as indentured servants and completed their term might marry older men of property. If the husbands died first, widows often took control of the estate and passed on the property to their children. Even in New England, where the numbers of men and women were more balanced from the beginning, the crucial labor of wives in the early years of settlement was sometimes recognized by their control of family property after a husband's death.

By the late seventeenth century, however, as the sex ratio in the Chesapeake evened out, women lost the opportunity to marry "above their class" (Table 4.1). And across the colonies, widows lost control of family estates. Even though women still performed vital labor, the spread of indentured servitude and slavery lessened the recognition of their contributions, while in urban areas the rise of commerce highlighted their role as consumers rather than as producers. As a result, most wives and daughters of white settlers were assigned primarily domestic roles. While domestic chores involved hard physical labor, many women welcomed the change from the more arduous tasks performed by their mothers and grandmothers. Yet they also found their legal and economic rights restricted to those accorded their female counterparts in Great Britain.

According to English common law, a wife's status was defined as *feme covert*, which meant that she was legally covered over by (or hidden behind) her husband. The husband controlled his wife's labor, the house in which she lived, the property she brought into the marriage, and any wages she earned. He was also the legal guardian of their children, and through the instrument of a will he could continue to control the household after his death. In many ways, a wife's legal status was that of a child, with her husband acting in this context as her father.

With the growth and diversity of colonial towns and cities, the **patriarchal family**—a model in which fathers have absolute authority over wives, children, and servants—came to be seen as a crucial bulwark against disorder. Families with wealth were especially eager to control the behavior of their sons and daughters as they sought to build commercial and political alliances. The refusal of Amasa Sessions to marry Sarah Grosvenor, for instance, may have resulted from his belief that his father expected a better match. Although a few women escaped the worst strictures of patriarchal households, most were expected to comply with the wishes of their fathers and then their husbands. Even as widows, many found their finances and daily life shaped by a husband's will and its implementation by male executors.

TABLE 4.1   **Sex Ratios in the White Population for Selected Colonies, 1624–1755**

Date	Colony	White Male Population	White Female Population	Females per 100 Males
1624–1625	Virginia	873	222	25
1660	Maryland	c. 600	c. 190	32
1704	Maryland	11,026	7,136	65
1698	New York	5,066	4,677	92
1726	New Jersey	15,737	14,124	90
1755	Rhode Island	17,860	17,979	101

Working Families

For most colonial women and men, daily rounds of labor shaped their lives more powerfully than legal statutes or inheritance rights. Whatever their official status, husbands and wives depended on each other to support the family. By the early eighteenth century, many colonial writers promoted the idea of marriage as a partnership, even if the wife remained the junior partner. In 1712 Benjamin Wadsworth published his advice for *The Well-Ordered Family,* in which he urged couples to "delight in each other's company," "be helpful to each other," and "bear one another's burdens."

This concept of marriage as a partnership took practical form in communities across the colonies. In towns, the wives of artisans often learned aspects of their husband's craft and assisted their husbands in a variety of ways. Given the overlap between homes and workplaces in the eighteenth century, women often cared for apprentices, journeymen, and laborers as well as their own children. Husbands meanwhile labored alongside their subordinates and represented their family's interests to the larger community. Both spouses were expected to provide models of godliness and to encourage prayer and regular church attendance among household members.

On farms, where the vast majority of colonists lived, women and men played crucial if distinct roles. In general, wives and daughters labored inside the home as well as in the surrounding yard with its kitchen garden, milk house, chicken coop, dairy, or washhouse. Husbands and sons worked the fields, kept the livestock, and managed the orchards. However, we should not imagine such farm families as self-sufficient units. Many families supplemented their own labor with that of servants, slaves, or hired field hands. And surplus crops—from corn to apples to eggs—and manufactured goods, such as cloth, sausage, or nails, were exchanged with neighbors or sold at market, creating a linked economic community of small producers.

Indeed, in the late seventeenth and early eighteenth centuries, many farm families in long-settled areas participated in a household mode of production. Men lent each other tools and draft animals and shared grazing land, while women gathered together to spin, sew, and quilt. Individuals with special skills like midwifery or blacksmithing assisted neighbors, adding farm produce or credit to the family ledger. Surplus corn, wheat, beef, or wool might be exchanged for sugar and tea from traveling salesmen or for an extra hand from neighbors during the harvest. One woman's cheese might be bartered for another woman's jam. A family that owned the necessary equipment might brew barley and malt into beer, while a neighbor with a loom would turn yarn into cloth. The system of exchange, managed largely through barter, allowed individual households to function even as they became more specialized in what they produced.

Reproduction and Women's Roles

Maintaining a farm required the work of both women and men, which made marriage an economic as well as a social and religious institution. In the early eighteenth century, more than 90 percent of white women married. And as mortality declined in the South and remained low in the North, most wives spent the first twenty years of marriage bearing and rearing children. By 1700 a New England wife who married at age twenty and survived to forty-five bore an average of eight children, most of whom lived to adulthood. In the Chesapeake, where mortality rates remained higher and the sex ratio still favored men, marriage and birth rates were slightly lower and infant mortality higher. Still, by the 1720s, southern white women nearly matched the reproductive rates of their northern counterparts.

Fertility rates among enslaved Africans and African Americans were much lower than those among whites in the early eighteenth century, and fewer infants survived to adulthood. It was not until the 1740s that the majority of slaves were born in the colonies rather than imported. But slowly some slave owners began to realize that encouraging reproduction made good economic sense. Still, enslaved women, most of whom worked in the fields, gained only minimal relief from their labors during pregnancy. Female slaves who lived in seaport cities were more likely to work in homes or shops, a healthier environment than the fields. But owners in already-crowded urban households often discouraged marriage and childbearing.

Immigrants from Scotland, Ireland, and Europe, many of whom lived in the Middle Atlantic colonies, often bore large numbers of children. Quakers, German Mennonites, Scots-Irish Presbyterians, and other groups flowed into New Jersey, Pennsylvania, and Delaware. Some settled in New York City and Philadelphia, but even more spread into rural areas, filling the interior of New Jersey and populating the Pennsylvania frontier. As they pushed westward, growing families replicated the experiences of early colonists, depending on their own resources and those of their immediate neighbors to carve farms and communities out of the wilderness.

Wherever they settled, mothers combined childbearing and child rearing with a great deal of other work. While some affluent families could afford wet nurses and nannies, most colonial women fended for themselves or hired temporary help for particular tasks. Mothers with babies on hip and children under foot hauled water, fed chickens, collected eggs, picked vegetables, prepared meals, spun thread, and manufactured soap and candles. Children were at constant risk of disease and injury, but physicians were rare in many rural areas. Still, farm families were spared from the overcrowding, raw sewage, and foul water that marked most urban neighborhoods.

Colonists feared the deaths of mothers as well as of infants. In 1700 roughly one out of thirty births ended in the mother's death. Women who bore six to eight children thus faced death on a regular basis. Many prayed intensely before and during labor,

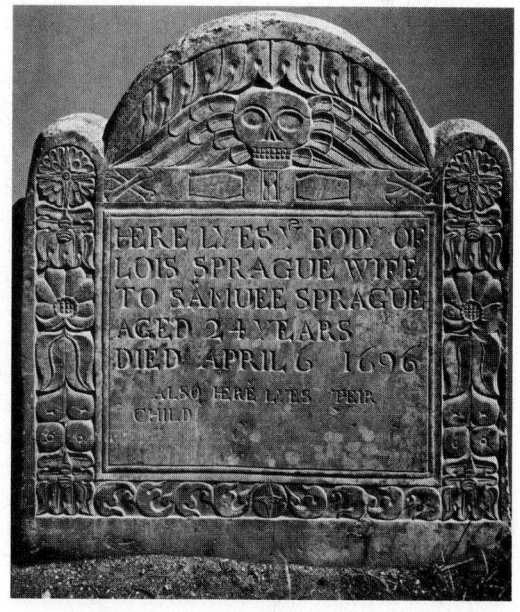

The Perils of Maternal Health
Women often died in childbirth in the late seventeenth century. In this instance, neither mother nor newborn survived. Lois Sprague, twenty-four years old, and her unnamed infant died on April 6, 1696. The skull with wings at the top of the gravestone was a typical symbol of death and heavenly ascension. Courtesy American Antiquarian Society

hoping to survive the ordeal. One minister urged pregnant women to prepare their souls, claiming, "For ought you to know your Death has entered into you."

When a mother died when her children were still young, her husband was likely to remarry soon afterward in order to maintain the family and his farm or business. Even though fathers held legal guardianship over their children, there was little doubt that child rearing, especially for young children and for daughters, was women's work. Many husbands acknowledged this role, prayed for their wife while in labor, and sought to ease her domestic burdens near the end of a pregnancy. But some women received only hostility and abuse from their husbands. In these cases, wives and mothers had few means to protect their children or themselves.

The Limits of Patriarchal Order

Sermons against fornication; ads for runaway spouses, servants, and slaves; reports of domestic violence; poems about domineering wives; petitions for divorce; and legal suits charging rape, seduction, or breach of contract—all of these make clear that ideals of patriarchal authority did not always match the reality. It is impossible to quantify precisely the frequency with which women experienced or resisted abuse at the hands of men. Still, a variety of evidence points to increasing tensions in the early eighteenth century around issues of control—by husbands over wives, fathers over children, and men over women.

Women's claims about men's misbehavior were often demeaned as gossip, but gossip could be an important weapon for those who had little chance of legal redress. In colonial communities, credit and thus trust were central to networks of exchange, so damaging a man's reputation could be a serious matter. Still, gossip was not as powerful as legal sanctions. Thus in cases in which a woman bore an illegitimate child, suffered physical and sexual abuse, or was left penniless by a husband who drank and gambled, she or her family might seek assistance from the courts.

Divorce was as rare in the colonies as it was in England. In New England, colonial law allowed for divorce, but few were granted and almost none to women before 1750. In other colonies, divorce could be obtained only by an act of the colonial assembly and was therefore confined to the wealthy and powerful. If a divorce was granted, the wife usually received "maintenance," an allowance that provided her with funds to feed and clothe herself. Yet without independent financial resources, she nearly always had to live with relatives. Custody of any children was awarded to the father because he had the economic means to support them, although infants or young girls might be assigned to live with the mother. Some couples were granted a separation of bed and board, which meant they lived apart but could not remarry. Here, too, the wife remained dependent on her estranged husband or on family members for economic support. A quicker and cheaper means of ending an unsatisfactory marriage was to abandon one's spouse. Again wives were at a disadvantage since they had few means to support themselves or their children. Colonial divorce petitions citing desertion and newspaper ads for runaway spouses suggest that husbands fled in at least two-thirds of such cases.

In the rare instances when women did obtain a divorce, they had to bring multiple charges against their husband. Domestic violence, adultery, or abandonment alone was insufficient to gain redress. Indeed, ministers and relatives were likely to counsel abused wives to change their behavior or suffer in silence since by Scripture and law a wife was subject to her husband's will. Even evidence of brutal assaults on a wife rarely led to legal redress. Because husbands had the legal right to "correct" their wives and children and because physical punishment was widely accepted, it was difficult to distinguish between "correction" and abuse.

Single women also faced barriers in seeking legal redress. By the late seventeenth century, church and civil courts in New England gave up on coercing sexually active couples to marry. Judges, however, continued to hear complaints of seduction or breach of contract brought by the fathers of single women who were pregnant but unmarried. Had Sarah Grosvenor survived the abortion, her family could have sued Amasa Sessions on the grounds that he gained "carnal knowledge" of her through "promises of marriage." If the plaintiffs won, the result was no longer marriage, however, but financial support for the child. In 1730 the Court of Common Pleas in Concord, Massachusetts, heard testimony from Susanna Holding that a local farmer, Joseph Bright, who was accused of fathering her illegitimate child, had "ruined her Reputation and Fortunes." When Bright protested his innocence, Holding found townsmen to testify that the farmer, "in his courting of her . . . had designed to make her his Wife." In this case, the abandoned mother mobilized members of the community, including men, to uphold popular understandings of patriarchal responsibilities. Without such support, women were less likely to win their case. Still, towns were eager to make errant men support their offspring so that the children did not become a public burden. And at least in Connecticut, a growing number of women initiated civil suits from 1740 on, demanding that men face their financial and moral obligations.

Women who were raped faced even greater legal obstacles than those who were seduced and abandoned. In most colonies, rape was a capital crime, punishable by death, and all-male juries were reluctant to find men guilty. In addition, men were assumed to be the aggressor in sexual encounters. Although bawdy women were certainly a part of colonial lore, it was assumed that most women needed persuading to engage in sex. Precisely when persuasion turned to coercion was less clear. Unlikely to win and fearing humiliation in court, few women charged men with rape. Yet more did so than the records might show since judges and justices of the peace sometimes downgraded rape charges to simple assault or fornication, that is, sex outside of marriage (Table 4.2).

White women from respectable families had the best chance of gaining support from local authorities, courts, and neighbors when faced with seduction, breach of contract, or rape. Yet such support depended on young people confiding in their elders. By the mid-eighteenth century, however, children were seeking more control over their sexual behavior and marriage prospects, and certain behaviors—for example, sons settling in towns distant from the parental home, younger daughters marrying before their older sisters, and single women finding themselves pregnant—increased noticeably. In part, these trends were natural consequences of colonial growth and mobility. The bonds that once held families and communities together began to loosen. But in the process, young women's chances of protecting themselves against errant men diminished. Just as important, even when they faced desperate situations, young women like Sarah Grosvenor increasingly turned to sisters and friends rather than fathers or ministers.

If women in respectable families found it difficult to redress abuse from suitors or husbands, the poor and those who labored as servants or slaves had even fewer options. Slaves in particular had little hope of prevailing against brutal owners. Even servants

TABLE 4.2   Sexual Coercion Cases Downgraded in Chester County, Pennsylvania, 1731–1739

Date	Defendant/Victim	Charge on Indictment in Testimony	Charge in Docket
1731	Lawrence MacGinnis/Alice Yarnal	Assault with attempt to rape	None
1731	Thomas Culling/Martha Claypool	Assault with attempt to rape	Assault
1734	Abraham Richardson/Mary Smith	Attempted rape	Assault
1734	Thomas Beckett/Mindwell Fulfourd	Theft (testimony of attempted rape)	Theft
1734	Unknown/Christeen Pauper	(Fornication charge against Christeen)	None
1735	Daniel Patterson/Hannah Tanner	Violent assault to ravish	Assault
1736	James White/Hannah McCradle	Attempted rape/adultery	Assault
1737	Robert Mills/Catherine Parry	Rape	None
1738	John West/Isabella Gibson	Attempt to ravish/assault	Fornication
1739	Thomas Halladay/Mary Mouks	Assault with intent to ravish	None

Source: *Rape and Sexual Power in Early America* by Sharon Block. Data from Chester County Quarter Sessions Docket Books and File Papers, 1730–1739. Copyright © 2006 by the University of North Carolina Press. Published for the Omohundro Institute of Early American History and Culture. Used by permission of the publisher. www.uncpress.unc.edu.

faced tremendous obstacles in obtaining legal independence from masters or mistresses who beat or sexually assaulted them. Colonial judges and juries generally refused to declare a man who was wealthy enough to support servants guilty of criminal acts against them. Moreover, female servants and slaves were regularly depicted in popular culture as lusty and immoral, making it even less likely that they would gain the sympathy of white male judges or juries. Thus for most servants and slaves, running away was their sole hope for escape from abuse; however, if they were caught, their situation would likely worsen. Even poor whites who lived independently had little chance of addressing issues of domestic violence, seduction, or rape through the courts. For unhappy couples beyond the help or reach of the law, abandonment was no doubt the most likely option. And as the colonies grew and diversified, leaving a wife and children or an abusive husband or master behind may have become a bit easier than it was in the small and isolated communities of earlier periods.

REVIEW & RELATE

• Why and how did the legal and economic status of colonial women decline between 1650 and 1750?

• How did patriarchal ideals of family and community shape life and work in colonial America? What happened when men failed to live up to those ideals?

Diversity and Competition in Colonial Society

As the English colonies in North America expanded, divisions increased between established families living in long-settled regions—whether on rural farmsteads or in urban homesteads—and the growing population of women and men with few resources. Although most colonists still hoped to own their own land and establish themselves as farmers, artisans, or shopkeepers, fewer were likely to succeed than in the past. By 1760 half of all white men in North America were propertyless. This growing class cleavage was accompanied by increasing racial, national, and religious diversity.

Population Growth and Economic Competition

After 1700, the population grew rapidly across the colonies. In 1700 about 250,000 people lived in England's North American colonies. By 1725 that number had doubled, and fifty years later it had reached 2.5 million. Much of the increase was due to natural reproduction, but in addition nearly 250,000 immigrants and Africans arrived in the colonies between 1700 and 1750.

Because more women and children arrived than in earlier decades, higher birthrates and a more youthful population resulted. At the same time, most North American colonists enjoyed a better diet than their counterparts in Europe and had access to more abundant timber, furs, fish, and other resources. Thus colonists in the eighteenth century began living longer, with more adults surviving to watch their children and grandchildren grow up.

As the population soared, the chance for individuals to obtain land or start a business of their own diminished. Even those with land did not always thrive: Farmers living in New England where the soil was exhausted or in swampy frontier regions or in areas already claimed by Indian, French, or Spanish settlers found that owning land did not automatically lead to prosperity. In the South Carolina backcountry, a visitor in the mid-eighteenth century noted that many residents "have nought but a Gourd to drink out of, nor a Plate, Knive or Spoon, a Glass, Cup, or anything." In the Carolinas and along the Hudson River, many farmers rented land from large landowners, thus ensuring limited profits even in years of relative abundance.

In prosperous parts of Middle Atlantic colonies like Pennsylvania, many landless laborers abandoned rural life and searched for urban opportunities. They moved to Philadelphia or other towns and cities in the region, seeking jobs as dockworkers, street vendors, or servants, or as apprentices in one of the skilled trades. But newcomers found the job market flooded and the chances for advancement growing slim (Figure 4.1).

In the South, too, divisions between rich and poor became more pronounced in the early decades of the eighteenth century. Tobacco was the most valuable product in the Chesapeake, and the largest tobacco planters lived in relative luxury. Families with extensive landholdings and large numbers of slaves grew rich. They developed mercantile contacts in seaport cities on the Atlantic coast and in the Caribbean and imported luxury goods from Europe. They also began training some of their slaves as domestic workers to relieve wives and daughters of the strain of household labor.

The profits from tobacco allowed a larger percentage of southern than northern whites to own land. In 1750 two-thirds of white families farmed their own land in Virginia, and an even higher percentage did so in the Carolinas. Yet small farmers became increasingly dependent on large landowners, who controlled markets, political

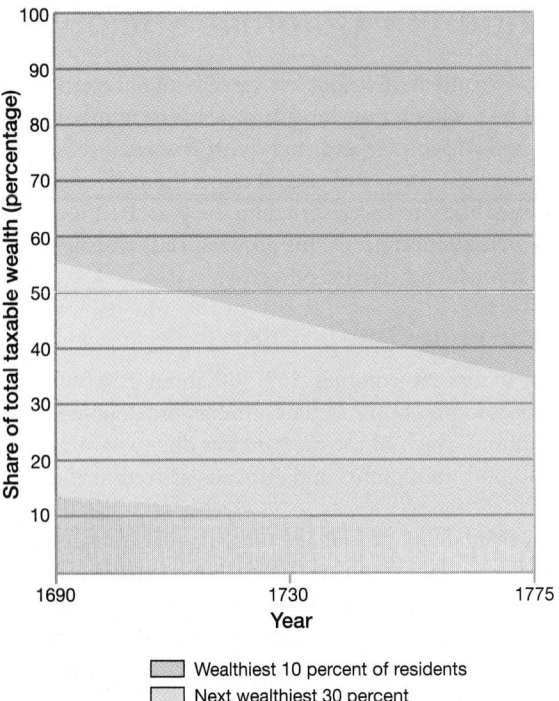

FIGURE 4.1

Wealth Inequality in Northern Cities, 1690–1775 During the eighteenth century, the wealth of merchants rose much faster than that of artisans and laborers. By 1750 the wealthiest 10 percent of the taxable residents of major northern cities owned 60 percent of the taxable wealth, while the poorest 60 percent owned less than 10 percent. This gap between rich and poor only increased over the next quarter century.

Source: Gary B. Nash, *The Urban Crucible: Social Change, Political Consciousness, and the Origins of the American Revolution* (Cambridge, MA: Harvard University Press, 1979).

Wealthiest 10 percent of residents
Next wealthiest 30 percent
Poorest 60 percent

authority, and the courts. Many artisans, too, depended on wealthy planters for their livelihood, working either for them directly or for the shipping companies and merchants that relied on plantation orders. And the growing number of tenant farmers relied completely on large landowners for their sustenance.

Some southerners fared far worse. One-fifth of all white southerners owned little more than the clothes on their backs in the mid-eighteenth century. Thus those with small plots of land could easily imagine what their future would be if they suffered a bad season, a fall in tobacco prices, or the death of a father or husband. At the same time, free blacks in the South found their opportunities for landownership and economic independence increasingly curtailed, while enslaved blacks had little hope of gaining their freedom and held no property of their own.

Increasing Diversity

Population growth and economic divisions were accompanied by increased diversity in the North American colonies. Indentured servants arrived from Ireland and Scotland as well as England. Africans were imported in growing numbers and entered a more highly structured system of slavery, whether laboring on southern farms, on northern estates, or in seaport cities. In addition, free families and redemptioners from Ireland, Scotland, the German states, and Sweden came in ever-larger numbers and developed their own communities and cultural institutions. There were also more colonists who had spent time in the Caribbean before settling on the mainland, and the frontiers of

British North America were filled with American Indians and French and Spanish settlers as well as European immigrants.

As the booming population increased the demand for land in the colonies, diverse groups of colonists pushed westward to find territory that either was not claimed by others or could be purchased. In Pennsylvania in the early eighteenth century, Moravian and Scots-Irish immigrants settled in areas like Shamokin that were dotted with Iroquois, Algonquian, and Siouan towns, negotiating with Indians to obtain farmland. At the same time, Delaware and Shawnee groups moved into Pennsylvania from New Jersey and the Ohio River valley and negotiated with colonists and the colonial government to establish communities for themselves. All along the Pennsylvania frontier, the lines between Indian and immigrant settlements blurred, and neither Indian chiefs nor colonial authorities seemed able to demarcate clear boundaries. Still, many communities prospered in the region, with white settlers exchanging European and colonial trade goods for access to Indian-controlled orchards, waterways, and lands (Map 4.1).

In the 1720s and 1730s, however, a flood of Scots-Irish settlers arrived in Pennsylvania when bad harvests and high rents caused them to flee oppressive conditions back home. The new immigrants overwhelmed native communities that

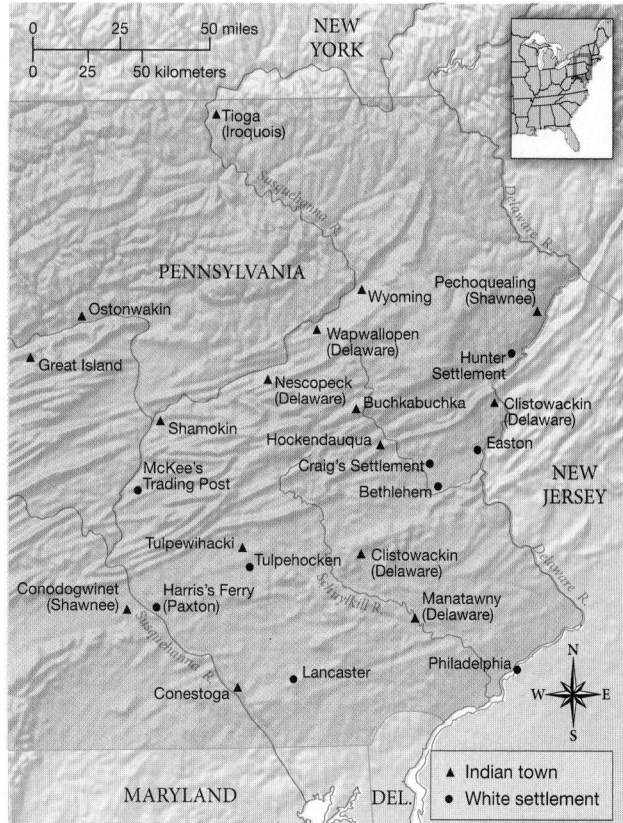

MAP 4.1

Frontier Settlements and Indian Towns in Pennsylvania, 1700–1740 German and Scots-Irish immigrants to Pennsylvania mingled with Indian settlements in the early eighteenth century as Delaware and Shawnee groups pushed east from New Jersey. In the 1720s and 1730s, however, European migration escalated dramatically in the fertile river valleys. In response, once-independent Indian tribes joined the Delaware and Shawnee nations to strengthen their position against the influx of colonists.

Source: *At the Crossroads: Indians & Empires on a Mid-Atlantic Frontier, 1700–1763* by Jane T. Merritt. Published for the Omohundro Institute of Early American History and Culture. Copyright © 2003 by the University of North Carolina Press. Used by permission of the publisher. www.uncpress.unc.edu

had welcomed earlier settlers. The death of William Penn in 1718 exacerbated the situation as his sons and closest advisers struggled to gain political and economic control over the colony, but this did not halt the flow of white settlers into the region. Indeed, as Indians were pushed to the margins, more diverse groups of European settlers moved into frontier territories.

Expansion and Conflict

As more and more colonists sought economic opportunities on the frontier, conflicts erupted regularly between earlier British and newer immigrant settlers as well as among immigrant groups. In Pennsylvania, Dutch, Scots-Irish, and German colonists took each other to court, sued land surveyors, and even burned down cabins built by their immigrant foes. For longtime British settlers, such acts only reinforced their sense that recent immigrants were a threat to their society. In 1728 James Logan, William Penn's longtime secretary, complained that the "Palatines [Germans] crowd in upon us and the Irish yet faster." For Logan, these difficulties were exacerbated by what he considered the "idle," "worthless," and "indigent" habits of Scots-Irish and other recent arrivals.

Despite their disparagement of others, Anglo-Americans hardly set high standards themselves, especially when negotiating with Indians. Even in Pennsylvania, where William Penn had established a reputation for (relatively) fair dealing, the desire for Indian land led to dishonesty and trickery. Colonial leaders' success in prying more territory from Indians, however, also resulted from conflicts within the Iroquois Confederacy. Hoping to assert their authority over the independent-minded Delaware Indians, Iroquois chiefs negotiated with Pennsylvania officials in the 1720s, claiming they held rights to much of the Pennsylvania territory. Colonial authorities then produced a questionable treaty supposedly drafted by Penn in 1686 to claim that large portions of that territory had already been ceded to settlers. James Logan "discovered" a copy of the treaty deed that allowed the English to control an area that could be walked off in a day and a half. The Iroquois finally agreed to this **Walking Purchase**, giving Pennsylvania officials the leverage they needed to persuade the Delawares to allow them to walk off the boundaries. By the time the Delawares acquiesced in the fall of 1737, Pennsylvania surveyors had already marked off the "shortest and best course," which allowed them to extend the boundaries by at least thirty miles beyond those set in the original, and questionable, treaty.

While extending colonial boundaries provided more land for hungry settlers, the rapid expansion of the colonial population ensured that conflicts would continue to erupt. Indian and British authorities repeatedly argued over treaty rights, boundary lines, and the power to cede or purchase land. Meanwhile migrants and immigrants on the Anglo-American frontier claimed land simply by taking control of it, building houses, and planting crops. This led to conflicts with local Indian communities that still considered the territory their own, with English officials who demanded legal contracts and deeds, and among immigrants who settled in the same area.

Immigrants also introduced greater religious diversity into the British colonies. But in Pennsylvania, several religious groups sought friendly relations with local Indians in order to secure land and trade goods. Some early immigrants, such as William Penn's Quakers, accepted Indian land claims and tried to pursue honest and fair negotiations. German Moravians who settled in eastern Pennsylvania in the 1740s also developed good trade relations with area tribes, shared in burial rituals, and acquiesced when the local Iroquois chief demanded the services of a blacksmith to make and repair guns. Meanwhile Scots-Irish Presbyterians settled along the western frontier and established alliances with Delaware and Shawnee groups there. These alliances were rooted less in religious principles, however, than in the hope of profiting from the fur trade when area Indians pursued new commercial partners after their former French allies became too demanding.

As tensions escalated between English and French authorities in the region, conflicts intensified among the various immigrant and religious communities and with Indians. Although colonists had disagreed many times before over policies toward native people, the dramatically different visions of Indian-settler relations rooted in distinct religious traditions magnified these differences and made it more difficult to find common ground. Growing religious diversity also created sharper boundaries within and between colonial communities. German Moravians and Scots-Irish Presbyterians in Pennsylvania established churches and schools separate from their Quaker neighbors, while Puritan New Englanders remained suspicious of Quakers as well as other Protestant sects. Moravians and other German sects also flourished in Georgia and the Carolinas, and nearly all sought to isolate themselves from the influences of other religious and ethnic groups.

Some religious groups were isolated as much by force as by choice. While most early Irish immigrants were Protestant, by the early eighteenth century more Irish Catholics began to arrive. Then in 1745 some forty thousand Scots who had supported the Catholic monarchs in England prior to the Glorious Revolution (see chapter 3) were shipped to the Carolinas after a failed rebellion. As traitors to the crown, they were doubly marginalized. But even long-settled Catholics, like those in Maryland, were looked on with suspicion by many Protestants. Jewish families also multiplied, founding the first American synagogues in Newport, Rhode Island; Savannah; Charleston; and Philadelphia. Although only a few hundred Jewish families resided in the colonies by 1750, they formed small but enduring communities in a number of seaport cities, where they developed a variety of mercantile ventures and practiced their faith.

Africans, too, brought new ideas and practices to North America. Transported by force to an unknown land, they may have found religious faith particularly important. Enslaved blacks included some Catholics from regions long held by the Portuguese and a few thousand Muslims, but many Africans embraced religions that were largely unknown to their Anglo-American masters. Even those planters who allowed Protestants to minister to their slaves discovered that many Africans and African Americans retained beliefs and rituals handed down across generations.

As religious affiliations in the colonies multiplied, they reinforced existing concerns about spiritual decline. Moreover, spiritual differences often exacerbated cleavages rooted in nationality and class. And they heightened concerns among many well-established families over the future of British culture and institutions in North America.

REVIEW & RELATE

- How and why did economic inequality in the colonies increase in the first half of the eighteenth century?
- How did population growth and increasing diversity contribute to conflict among and anxieties about the various groups inhabiting British North America?

Religious Awakenings

Whether rooted in fears that worldly concerns were overshadowing spiritual devotion or that growing religious diversity was undermining the power of the church, Protestant ministers lamented the state of faith in eighteenth-century America. Many church leaders in Britain and the rest of Europe shared their fears. Ministers eager to address this crisis of faith—identified in the colonies as **New Light clergy**—worked together to re-energize the faithful and were initially welcomed, or at least tolerated, by more traditional **Old Light clergy**. But by the 1740s, fears that revivalists had gone too far led to a backlash. Still, for a time, the religious awakenings of the early eighteenth century created a powerful sense of common cause among Protestant colonists of different faiths, nationalities, and classes and promised a rebirth of commitment to both spiritual values and the larger society.

The Roots of the Great Awakening

The European religious landscape had grown remarkably more diverse in the two hundred years following the Reformation as Presbyterians, Lutherans, Methodists, Baptists, Quakers, and a variety of smaller sects competed for followers. Another current also had an impact: By the eighteenth century, the **Enlightenment**, a cultural movement that emphasized rational and scientific thinking over traditional religion and superstition, had taken root, particularly among elites. As North American colonies attracted settlers from new denominations and as more and more colonists were influenced by Enlightenment thought, the colonists as a whole became more accepting of religious diversity.

There were, however, countervailing forces. The German **Pietists** in particular challenged Enlightenment ideas that had influenced many Congregational and Anglican leaders in Europe and the colonies. Pietists not only decried the power of established churches but also urged individuals to follow their heart rather than their head in spiritual matters. Only by restoring intensity and emotion to worship, they believed, could spiritual life be revived. Persecuted in Germany, Pietists migrated to Great Britain and North America, where their ideas influenced Scots-Irish Presbyterians, French Huguenots, and members of the Church of England. John Wesley, the founder of Methodism and a professor of theology at Oxford University, taught Pietist ideas to his students. George Whitefield was inspired by Wesley. Like the German Pietists whose ideas he embraced, Whitefield believed that the North American colonies offered an important opportunity to implement these ideas.

But not all colonists waited for Whitefield or the German Pietists to rethink their religious commitments. By 1700 both laymen and ministers voiced growing concern with the state of colonial religion. Preachers educated in England or at the few colleges established in the colonies, like Harvard College (1636) and the College of William and Mary (1693), often emphasized learned discourse over passion. At the same time, there were too few clergy to meet the demands of the rapidly growing population in North America. Many rural parishes covered vast areas, and residents grew discouraged at the lack of ministerial attention. Meanwhile urban churches increasingly reflected the class divisions of the larger society. In many meetinghouses, wealthier members paid substantial rents to seat their families in the front pews. Small farmers and shopkeepers rented the cheaper pews in the middle of the church, while the poorest congregants—

including landless laborers, servants, and slaves—sat on free benches at the very back or in the gallery. Educated clergy might impress the richest parishioners with their learned sermons, but they did little to move the spirits of the congregation at large.

In 1719 the Reverend Theodorus Freylinghuysen, a Dutch Reformed minister in New Brunswick, New Jersey, began emphasizing parishioners' emotional investment in Christ. The Reverend William Tennent arrived in neighboring Pennsylvania with his family about the same time. He despaired that Presbyterian ministers were too few in number to reach the growing population and, like Freylinghuysen, feared that their approach was too didactic and cold. Tennent soon established his own academy—one room in a log cabin—to train his four sons and other young men for the ministry. Though disparaged by Presbyterian authorities, the school attracted devout students. A decade later, in 1734–1735, Jonathan Edwards, a Congregational minister in Northampton, Massachusetts, made clear the value of religious appeals that emphasized emotion over logic. Proclaiming that "our people do not so much need to have their heads stored [with knowledge] as to have their hearts touched," he initiated a local revival that reached hundreds of colonists.

Like Edwards, William Tennent's son Gilbert urged colonists to embrace "a true living faith in Jesus Christ." Assigned a church in New Brunswick in 1726, Tennent met Freylinghuysen, who viewed conversion as a three-step process: Individuals must be convinced of their sinful nature, experience a spiritual rebirth, and then behave piously as evidence of their conversion. Tennent embraced these measures, believing they could lance the "boil" of an unsaved heart and apply the "balsam" of grace and righteousness. Then in 1739 Tennent met Whitefield, who launched a wave of revivals that revitalized and transformed religion across the colonies.

An Outburst of Revivals

Whitefield was perfectly situated to initiate the series of revivals that scholars later called the **Great Awakening**. Gifted with a powerful voice, he understood that the expanding networks of communication and travel—developed to promote commerce—could also be used to promote religion. Advertising in newspapers and broadsides and traveling by ship, coach, and horseback, Whitefield made seven trips to the North American colonies during his career, beginning in 1738. He reached audiences from Georgia to New England to the Pennsylvania backcountry and inspired ministers in the colonies to extend his efforts.

In 1739 Whitefield launched a fifteen-month preaching tour that reached tens of thousands of colonists. Like Edwards, Freylinghuysen, and Tennent, he asked individuals to invest less in material goods and more in spiritual devotion.

 Online Document Project   Awakening Religious Tensions
bedfordstmartins.com/hewittlawsonvalue

If they admitted their depraved and sinful state and truly repented, God would hear their prayers. The droughts and locusts that plagued farmers and the epidemics and fires that threatened city folk were signs of God's anger at the moral decay that marked colonial life. Whitefield danced across the platform, shouted and raged, and gestured dramatically, drawing huge crowds everywhere he went. And he went everywhere, preaching on 350 separate occasions in 1739–1740. He attracted 20,000 people to individual events, at a time when the entire city of Boston counted just 17,000 residents.

Whitefield encouraged local ministers like Tennent to join him in his efforts to revitalize Protestantism. Less concerned with denominational affiliation than with core beliefs and passionate preaching, Whitefield hailed his fellow revivalists as "burning and shining lights" and embraced the vitality (and disruption) that followed in their wake. New Light ministers carried on Whitefield's work throughout the 1740s, honing their methods and appeal. They denounced urbane and educated clergy, used extemporane-ous oratorical styles and outdoor venues to attract crowds, and invited colonists from all walks of life to build a common Christian community. Some became itinerant preachers, preferring the freedom to carry their message throughout the colonies to the security of a traditional pulpit.

New Light clergy brought young people to religion by the thousands. In addition, thousands of colonists who were already church members were "born again," recommitting themselves to their faith. Poor parishioners who felt little connection to preaching when they sat on the back benches eagerly joined the crowds at outdoor revivals, where they could stand as close to the pulpit as a rich merchant. Indeed, Tennent appealed especially to poor and single women and girls when he preached with Whitefield in Boston. Enthu-siastic parishioners from a wide range of denominations formed new churches. Some, like the New Building of Philadelphia, sought interdenominational communion, but most expanded the reach of particular denominations, whether Presbyterian, Congregational, Methodist, Baptist, or Anglican.

Religious Dissension

Initially, the Great Awakening drew support from large numbers of ministers because it increased religious enthusiasm and church attendance throughout the colonies. After decades of decline, religion once again took center stage. But the early embrace by Old Light clergy diminished as revivals spread farther afield, as critiques of educated clergy became more pointed, and as New Light clergy began carrying parts of older congrega-tions into new churches. A growing number of ministers and other colonial leaders began to fear that revivalists were providing lower-class whites, free blacks, and even women and slaves with compelling critiques of those in power. As the Great Awakening peaked in 1742, a backlash developed among more settled ministers and their congregations.

Itinerant preachers traveling across the South seemed especially threatening as they invited blacks and whites to attend revivals together and proclaimed their equality before God. Although it was rare that New Light clergy directly attacked slavery—indeed, many preached that worldly status was irrelevant to salvation—they implicitly challenged racial hierarchies. New Light preachers also gained more adherents among African Americans and American Indians than had earlier clergy by emphasizing communal singing and emotional expressions of the spirit, both of which echoed traditional African and Indian practices. Combined with their recruitment of young, poor, and female converts, such a broad appeal came to seem more dangerous than beneficial.

In the North, too, Old Light ministers and local officials began to question New Light techniques and influences. One of the most radical New Light preachers, James Davenport, attracted huge crowds when he preached in Boston in the early 1740s. Drawing thousands of colonists to Boston Common day after day, Davenport declared that the people "should drink rat poison rather than listen to corrupt, unconverted clergy." Claiming that Davenport's followers were "idle or ignorant Persons, [and] those of the Lowest Rank," Boston officials finally called a grand jury into session to silence him "on the charge of having said that Boston's ministers were leading the people blindfold to hell."

Although Davenport was unusual in directly linking corrupt clergy to a corrupt social order, he suggested to authorities the dangers of allowing revivalists to go unanswered. The extremes to which a few revivalists went also disturbed some New Light ministers, including Tennent, who eventually sought to reunite the Presbyterian Church he had helped to divide. From the beginning, he had celebrated Christian love and fellowship. In 1757 Tennent wrote a sacramental sermon entitled "Love to Christ" that emphasized pietistic communion. He then worked earnestly to reunite the New York and Philadelphia synods, and his efforts succeeded a year later.

Not all churches reconciled their differences so easily, however. Revivals continued throughout the 1740s, as the awakening in Pomfret, Connecticut, indicates. Yet over time, they lessened in intensity as churches and parishioners settled back into a more ordered religious life. Moreover, the central tenets of revivalist preaching—criticisms of educated clergy, itinerancy, and extemporaneous preaching—worked against the movement's institutionalization. The Great Awakening echoed across the colonies for at least another generation, but its influence was felt more often in attitudes and practices than in institutions.

For example, when, in 1750, King George II threatened to appoint an Anglican bishop for the North American colonies, many North American ministers, both Old Light and New, resisted the appointment. Most colonists had become used to religious diversity and toleration, at least for Protestants, and had little desire to add church officials to the existing hierarchies of colonial authorities. In various ways, revivalists also highlighted the democratic tendencies in the Bible, particularly in the New Testament. Thus even as they proclaimed God's wrath against sinners, they also preached that a lack of wealth and power did not diminish a person in God's eyes. Indeed, it was often the well educated, the wealthy, and the powerful who had the most to fear from the righteous. And revivalists honed a style of passionate and popular preaching that would shape American religion and politics for centuries to come. This mode of communication had immediate application as colonists mobilized to resist what they saw as tyrannical actions by colonial officials and others in authority.

(**REVIEW & RELATE**)

• What groups were most attracted to the religious revivals of the early eighteenth century? Why?

• What were the legacies of the Great Awakening for American religious and social life?

Political Awakenings

The effects of eighteenth-century religious awakenings rippled out from churches and revivals to influence social and political relations. In various areas of life, colonists began to question the right of those in power to impose their will on the community as a whole. Similar issues had surfaced before the revivals, but New Light clergy gave greater weight to political and social challenges, allowing colonists to view their resistance to traditional authorities as part of their larger effort to create a better and more just world.

Changing Political Relations

The settlements of the seventeenth century could be regulated with a small number of officials, and in most colonies male settlers agreed on who should rule. However, with geographical expansion, population growth, and commercial development, colonial officials—whether appointed by the crown or selected by local residents—found themselves confronted with a more complex, and more contentious, situation. Most officials were educated men who held property and had family ties to other colonial elites. Although they made decisions locally, ultimate political authority—or sovereignty—rested with the king and Parliament. The crown appointed governors, judges, and other royal officials and approved those elected locally. The king and Parliament held veto power over colonial legislation and made all decisions about war and peace. Finally, they set policy for the colonies in such critical areas as taxes and duties and military service.

While ultimate political sovereignty rested with authorities in England, the king and Parliament were too distant to have a hand in the daily workings of colonial life. Even royal officials appointed to carry out official policies often discovered that what sounded good in London was not practicable in North America. Another factor that weakened the power of royal officials was the tradition of town meetings and representative bodies, like the Virginia House of Burgesses, that had emerged within the colonies, giving colonists a stake in their own governance. Officials in England and the colonies assumed that most people would defer to those in authority, and they minimized resistance by holding public elections in which freemen cast ballots by voice vote. Not surprisingly, those with wealth and power, who often treated voters with food and drink on election days, continued to win office.

Still, evidence throughout the colonial period indicates that deference to authority was not always sufficient to maintain order. Roger Williams and Anne Hutchinson,

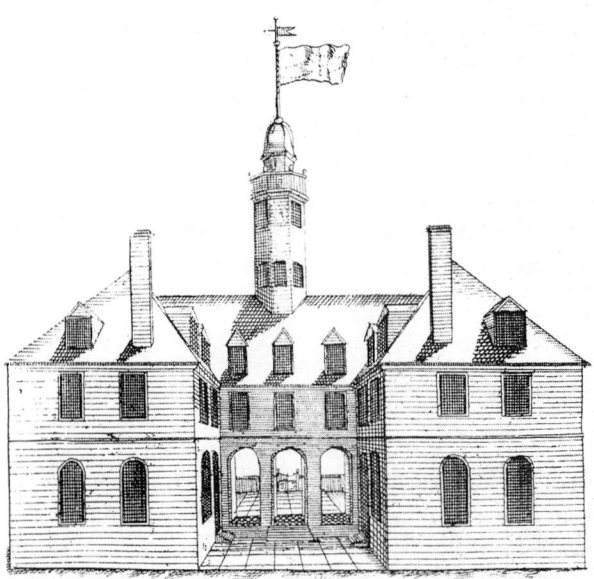

Virginia House of Burgesses This engraving depicts the Virginia House of Burgesses as it looked around 1740. Established in 1619, this legislature was the oldest institution of self-government in British North America. White men over the age of seventeen who owned land could vote for its members. After 1699, the House of Burgesses met in Williamsburg, where it remained throughout the colonial period. The Granger Collection, New York

Bacon's Rebellion, the Stono rebellion, the Salem witchcraft trials, and the radical preaching of James Davenport make clear that not everyone willingly supported their supposed superiors. These episodes of dissent and protest were widely scattered across time and place. But as the ideas disseminated by New Light clergy converged with changing political relations, resistance to established authority became more frequent and more collective.

Dissent and Protest

Protests against colonial elites multiplied from the 1730s on. The issues and methods varied, but they indicate a growing sense of political and economic autonomy among North American colonists. Some protests focused on royal officials like governors and Royal Navy captains; others focused on local authorities, merchants, or large landowners. Whatever the target of resistance, protests demonstrated colonists' belief that they had rights that were worth protecting, even against those who held legitimate authority. Just as importantly, dissenters included the poor, women, and African Americans as well as property-owning white men.

Access to reasonably priced food, especially bread, inspired regular protests in the eighteenth century. During the 1730s, the price of bread—a critical staple in colonial diets—rose despite falling wheat prices and a recession in seaport cities. Bread rioters attacked grain warehouses, bakeries, and shops, demanding more bread at lower prices. Like similar protests in Europe, these riots were often successful in the short run, though eventually prices began to rise again. They were often led by women, who were responsible for putting bread on the table; thus when grievances involved domestic or consumer issues, women felt they had the right to make their voices heard.

Public markets were another site where struggles over food led to collective protests. In 1737, for instance, Boston officials decided to construct a public market and charge fees to farmers who sold their goods there. Small farmers, who were used to selling produce from the roadside for free, clashed with officials and with larger merchants over the venture. Many Boston residents supported the protesters because the market fees would lessen competition and raise prices for consumers. When petitions to city officials had no effect, opponents demolished the market building and stalls in the middle of the night. Local authorities could find no witnesses to the crime. Like bread riots, the success of this protest was short-lived. Officials built another market; nonetheless, the protest had demonstrated the collective power of those with limited resources.

 Online Document Project **A New Commercial Culture in Boston**
bedfordstmartins.com/hewittlawsonvalue

Access to land was also a critical issue in the colonies. Beginning in the 1740s, protests erupted on estates in New Jersey and along the Hudson River in New York over the leasing policies of landlords as well as the amount of land controlled by speculators. When tenants and squatters petitioned colonial officials and received no response, they took collective action. They formed groups, targeted specific landlords, and then burned barns, attacked livestock, and emptied houses and farm buildings of furniture and tools. Eventually, they established regional committees to hear grievances and formed "popular" militia companies and courts to mete out justice to those who refused to renegotiate rental agreements and prices. When landlords and colonial officials called out local militia to arrest the perpetrators, they failed to consider that militia members were often the same poor men whose protests they ignored.

In seaport cities, a frequent source of conflict was the impressment of colonial men who were forcibly drafted into service in the Royal Navy. British officials, caught up in nearly continuous warfare in Europe, periodically raided portside communities in order to fill their complement of sailors. Not only sailors but also dockworkers and men drinking at taverns along the shore might find themselves suddenly inducted into military service. Facing high mortality rates, bad food, rampant disease, and harsh discipline on navy ships, these impressed men were unwilling to wait while colonial officials complained to the British government about the labor shortages that impressment caused. Instead, they fought back. In 1747 in Boston, a general impressment led to three days of rioting. An observer noted that "Negros, servants, and hundreds of seamen seized a naval lieutenant, assaulted a sheriff, and put his deputy in stocks, surrounded the governor's house, and stormed the Town House (city hall)." Such riots did not end the system of impressment, but they showed that colonists would battle those who sought to deprive them of their liberty.

The religious upheavals and economic uncertainties of the 1730s and 1740s led colonists to challenge colonial and British officials with greater frequency than in earlier decades. But most protests also accentuated class lines as the poor, small farmers, and craftsmen fought against merchants, landowners, and local officials. Still, the resistance to impressment proved that colonists could mobilize across economic differences when British policies affected diverse groups of colonial subjects.

Transforming Urban Politics

The development of cross-class alliances in the 1730s and 1740s was also visible in the more formal arena of colonial politics. Beginning in the 1730s, some affluent political leaders in cities like New York and Philadelphia began to seek support from a wider constituency. In most cases, it was conflicts among the elite that led to these appeals to the "popular" will. In 1731, for instance, a new royal charter confirmed New York City's existence as a "corporation" and stipulated the rights of freemen (residents who could vote in local elections after paying a small fee) and freeholders (individuals, whether residents or not, who held property worth £40 and could vote on that basis). A large number of artisans, shopkeepers, and laborers acquired the necessary means to vote, and shopkeepers and master craftsmen now sat alongside wealthier men on the Common Council. Yet most laboring men did not participate actively in elections until 1733, when local elites led by Lewis Morris sought to mobilize the mass of voters against royal officials, like Governor William Cosby, appointed in London.

Morris, a wealthy man and a judge, joined other colonial elites in believing that the royal officials recently appointed to govern New York were tied to ministerial corruption in England. Morris thus presented himself as the voice of the common man when he ran against a candidate approved by Cosby. On election day, hundreds of his supporters marched across the town green of Eastchester behind "two Trumpeters and 3 Violines." His opponent also mustered followers on horseback, escorted by royal officials, including the "high sheriff." But the voters chose Morris. The Morrisites then helped launch a newspaper, published by John Peter Zenger, a printer, to mobilize laborers, shopkeepers, and artisans on their behalf.

In his *New-York Weekly Journal,* Zenger leaped into the political fray, accusing Governor Cosby and his cronies of corruption, incompetence, election fraud, and tyranny. The vitriolic attacks led to Zenger's indictment for seditious libel and his imprisonment in November 1734. At the time, libel related only to whether published material undermined government authority, not whether it was true or false. But Zenger's lead attorney, Andrew Hamilton of Philadelphia, argued that truth must be recognized as a defense against charges of libel. Appealing to a jury of Zenger's peers, Hamilton proclaimed, "It is not the cause of a poor printer, nor of New York alone, which you are now trying. . . . It is the best cause. It is the cause of liberty." In response, jurors ignored the law as written and acquitted Zenger. A pamphlet about the case, authored by one of his lawyers and printed by Zenger in 1736, gained a wide readership in Britain and America.

Although the decision in the Zenger case did not lead to a change in British libel laws, it did signal the willingness of colonial juries to side with fellow colonists against king and Parliament, at least when it came to their right to censure public officials. Building on their success, Morris and his followers continued to gain popular support. In 1737 his son, Lewis Morris Jr., was appointed speaker of the new Assembly, and the Assembly appointed Zenger as its official printer. But soon after this victory, the group fell into disarray when royal officials offered political prizes to a few of their leaders. Indeed, the elder Morris accepted appointment as royal governor of New Jersey, after which he switched allegiances and became an advocate of executive authority. Nonetheless, the political movement he led had aroused ordinary freemen to participate in elections, and newspapers and pamphlets now readily attacked corrupt officials and threats to the rightful liberties of British colonists.

Even as freemen gained a greater voice in urban politics, they could challenge the power of economic and political leaders only when the elite were divided. Moreover, the rewards they gained sometimes served to reinforce class divisions. Thus many city workers had benefited when the elder Morris used his influence to ensure the building of the city's first permanent almshouse in 1736. The two-year project employed large numbers of artisans and laborers in a period of economic contraction. Once built, however, the almshouse became a symbol of the growing gap between rich and poor in the city and in the colonies more generally. Its existence was also used by future city councils as a justification to eliminate other forms of relief, leaving the poor in worse shape than before.

REVIEW & RELATE

- How did ordinary colonists, both men and women, black and white, express their political opinions and preferences in the first half of the eighteenth century?
- How did politics bring colonists together across economic lines in the first half of the eighteenth century? How did politics highlight and reinforce class divisions?

Conclusion: A Divided Society

By 1750 religious and political awakenings had transformed colonists' sense of their relation to spiritual and secular authorities. Both Gilbert Tennent and Sarah Grosvenor were caught up in these transitions. Like most colonists, they did not conceive of themselves as part of a united body politic but rather identified most deeply with their family, town, or church. Indeed, most colonists thought of themselves as English, or Scots-Irish, or German, rather than American. At best, they claimed identity as residents of Massachusetts, New Jersey, or South Carolina rather than British North America. By 1750 the diversity and divisions among colonists were greater than ever as class, racial, religious, and regional differences multiplied across the colonies. Still, by mid-century, religious leaders had gained renewed respect, colonial assemblies had wrested more autonomy from royal hands, freemen participated more avidly in political contests and debates, printers and lawyers insisted on the rights and liberties of colonists, and local communities defended those rights in a variety of ways. When military conflicts brought British officials into more direct contact with their colonial subjects in the following decade, they sought to check these trends, with dramatic consequences.

Chapter Review

MAKE IT STICK

 LearningCurve **bedfordstmartins.com/hewittlawsonvalue**
After reading the chapter, use LearningCurve to retain what you've read.

IDENTIFY KEY TERMS

Identify and explain the significance of each term below.

spectral evidence (p. 86)
patriarchal family (p. 87)
Walking Purchase (p. 96)
New Light clergy (p. 98)
Old Light clergy (p. 98)

Enlightenment (p. 98)
Pietists (p. 98)
Great Awakening (p. 99)
impressment (p. 104)

REVIEW & RELATE

Answer the focus questions from each section of the chapter.

1. What factors led to a rise in tensions within colonial communities in the early 1700s?

2. How did social, economic, and political tensions contribute to an increase in accusations of witchcraft?

3. Why and how did the legal and economic status of colonial women decline between 1650 and 1750?

4. How did patriarchal ideals of family and community shape life and work in colonial America? What happened when men failed to live up to those ideals?

5. How and why did economic inequality in the colonies increase in the first half of the eighteenth century?

6. How did population growth and increasing diversity contribute to conflict among and anxieties about the various groups inhabiting British North America?

7. What groups were most attracted to the religious revivals of the early eighteenth century? Why?

8. What were the legacies of the Great Awakening for American religious and social life?

9. How did ordinary colonists, both men and women, black and white, express their political opinions and preferences in the first half of the eighteenth century?

10. How did politics bring colonists together across economic lines in the first half of the eighteenth century? How did politics highlight and reinforce class divisions?

ONLINE DOCUMENT PROJECTS

- **Awakening Religious Tensions**
- **A New Commercial Culture in Boston**

After reading the primary sources in these document sets, answer the **Interpret the Evidence** questions to help you analyze each of the documents, and then answer the **Put It in Context** question(s) to help you relate the documents to the topics and themes you read about in the chapter.

bedfordstmartins.com/hewittlawsonvalue

TIMELINE OF EVENTS

1636	• Harvard College established
1647–1692	• Some 160 individuals tried for witchcraft in Massachusetts and Connecticut
1688	• Glorious Revolution
1692	• Salem witch trials
1693	• College of William and Mary established
1700–1750	• 250,000 immigrants and Africans arrive in the colonies
1700–1775	• Population of British North America grows from 250,000 to 2.5 million
1712	• Benjamin Wadsworth publishes *The Well-Ordered Family*
1720–1740	• Large numbers of Scots-Irish arrive in Pennsylvania
1734	• John Peter Zenger acquitted of libel in New York City
1736	• First permanent almshouse built in New York City

1737	• Delaware Indians acquiesce to Walking Purchase
	• Protest against public market in Boston
1739	• George Whitefield launches fifteen-month preaching tour of the colonies
1741	• Gilbert Tennent expelled from the Presbyterian Church
1742	• Sarah Grosvenor dies as a result of a botched abortion
1745	• 40,000 Scottish Catholics shipped to the Carolinas after a failed rebellion
1747	• Impressment leads to three days of rioting in Boston
1750	• American colonists resist appointment of an Anglican bishop for the North American colonies
1757	• George Tennent initiates effort to reunite the Presbyterian Church

5

✓ LearningCurve
bedfordstmartins.com/hewittlawsonvalue
After reading the chapter, use LearningCurve
to retain what you've read.

Wars and Empires

1750–1774

AMERICAN HISTORIES

Although best known as the founding father of the United States, George
Washington grew to adulthood as a loyal British subject. He was born in 1732
to a prosperous farm family in eastern Virginia. When George's father died in
1743, he became the ward of his half-brother Lawrence and moved to
Lawrence's Mount Vernon estate. Lawrence's father-in-law, William Fairfax,
was an agent for Lord Fairfax, one of the chief proprietors of the colony.
When George was sixteen, William hired him as an assistant to a party
surveying Lord Fairfax's land on Virginia's western frontier.

Although less well educated and less well positioned than the sons of
Virginia's largest planters, George shared their ambitions. As a surveyor, he
journeyed west, coming into contact with Indians, both friendly and hostile,
as well as other colonists seeking land. George himself began investing in
western properties. But when Lawrence Washington died in 1752, twenty-
year-old George suddenly became head of a large estate. He gradually
expanded Mount Vernon's boundaries and increased its profitability, in part by
adding to Mount Vernon's enslaved workforce. He now had the resources to
speculate more heavily in western lands.

George was soon appointed an officer in the Virginia militia, and in the
fall of 1753 Virginia's governor sent him to warn the French stationed near
Lake Erie against encroaching on British territory in the Ohio River valley.
The French commander rebuffed Washington and within six months gained
control of a British post near present-day Pittsburgh, Pennsylvania, and

named it Fort Duquesne. With help from Indians hostile to the French, Lieutenant Colonel Washington launched a surprise attack on Fort Duquesne in May 1754. The initial attack was successful and led the governors of Virginia and North Carolina to send in more troops under the command of the newly promoted Colonel Washington. The French then responded with a much larger force that repelled the British troops, and Washington was forced to surrender.

Colonel Washington gained valuable experience through both successful surveying expeditions and failed military ventures. As a landowner in Virginia and on the western frontier, he had also gained property to defend. Washington's fortunes and his family increased when he married the wealthy widow Martha Dandridge Custis in 1759 and became stepfather to her two children. An increasingly successful planter, Washington sought to extend Britain's North American empire westward as a way to create opportunities for an expanding population as well as a protective buffer against European and Indian foes.

Like Washington, Herman Husband hoped to improve his lot through hard work and the opportunities offered by the frontier. Born to a modest farm family in Maryland in 1724, he was swept up by the Great Awakening in the early 1740s. He became a New Light Presbyterian but later joined the Society of Friends, or Quakers. In 1754, as Washington headed to the Ohio valley, Husband explored prospects on the North Carolina frontier and decided to settle with his family at Sandy Creek.

Husband proved a successful farmer, but he denounced wealthy landowners and speculators who made it difficult for small farmers to obtain sufficient land. He also challenged established leaders in the Quaker meeting and was among a number of worshippers disowned from the Cane Creek Friends Meeting in 1764. Disputes within radical Protestant congregations were not unusual in this period as members with deep religious convictions chose the liberty of their individual conscience over church authority.

In 1766 a number of Quaker and Baptist farmers joined Husband in organizing the Sandy Creek Association. The group hoped to increase farmers' political clout as a way to combat corruption among local officials. The association disbanded after two years, but its ideas lived on in a group called the Regulation, which brought together frontier farmers who sought to "regulate" government abuse. Husband quickly emerged as one of the organization's chief spokesmen. The Regulators first tried to achieve reform through legal means. They petitioned the North Carolina Assembly and Royal Governor William Tryon, demanding legislative reforms and suing local officials for extorting labor, land, or money from poorer residents.

Husband wrote pamphlets articulating the demands of the Regulators and wielding religious principles to justify resistance to existing laws and customs. In certain ways, his ideas echoed those of colonial leaders like Governor Tryon, who had launched protests in 1765 against British efforts to impose taxes on the colonies. Tryon, however, viewed the Regulators as political foes who threatened the colony's peace and order. In 1768 he had Husband and other Regulators arrested, which confirmed the Regulators' belief that they could not receive fair treatment at the hands of colonial officials. They then turned to extralegal methods to assert their rights, such as taking over courthouses so that legal proceedings against debt-ridden farmers could not proceed. This led the Regulators into open conflict with colonial officials.

THE AMERICAN HISTORIES of Washington and Husband were shaped by both opportunities and conflicts. Mid-eighteenth-century colonial America offered greater opportunities for social advancement and personal expression than anywhere in Europe, but the efforts of individuals to take advantage of these opportunities often led to tension and discord. The conflicts on the frontiers of Virginia, Pennsylvania, and North Carolina foreshadowed a broader struggle for land and power within the American colonies. Religious and economic as well as political discord intensified in the mid-eighteenth century as conflicts within the colonies increasingly occurred alongside challenges to British authority. Individual men and women made difficult choices about where their loyalties lay. Whatever their grievances, most worked hard to reform systems they considered unfair or abusive before resorting to more radical means of instituting change. Some, such as Washington, became revered leaders. Others, like Husband, gained local support but were viewed by those in authority as extremists who threatened to subvert the religious, economic, and political order.

Join, or Die Benjamin Franklin created the first political cartoon in American history to accompany an editorial he wrote in the *Pennsylvania Gazette* in 1754. Franklin's cartoon urged the mainland British colonies to unite politically during the French and Indian War. Legend had it that a snake could come back to life if its severed sections were attached before dusk. Library of Congress

A War for Empire, 1754–1763

The war that erupted in the Ohio valley in 1754 sparked an enormous shift in political and economic relations in colonial North America. What began as a small-scale, regional conflict expanded into a brutal and lengthy global war. Known as the French and Indian War in North America and the Seven Years' War in Great Britain and Europe, the conflict led to a dramatic expansion of British territory in North America, but also to increasing demands from American colonists for more control over their own lives.

The Opening Battles

Even before Washington and his troops were defeated in July 1754, the British sought to protect the colonies against threats from the French and the Indians. To limit such threats, the British were especially interested in cementing an alliance with the powerful Iroquois Confederacy, composed of six northeastern tribes. Thus the British invited an official delegation from the Iroquois to a meeting in June 1754 in Albany, New York, with representatives from the New England colonies, New York, Pennsylvania, and Maryland. Benjamin Franklin of Philadelphia had drawn up a Plan of Union that would establish a council of representatives from the various colonial assemblies to debate issues of frontier defense, trade, and territorial expansion and to recommend terms mutually agreeable to colonists and Indians. Their deliberations were to be overseen by a president-general appointed and supported by the British crown.

The Albany Congress created new bonds among a small circle of colonial leaders, but it failed to establish a firmer alliance with the Iroquois or resolve problems of colonial governance. The British government worried that the proposed council would prove too powerful, undermining the authority of the royal government. At the same time, the individual colonies were unwilling to give up any of their autonomy in military, trade, and political matters to some centralized body. Moreover, excluded from Franklin's Plan of Union, the Iroquois delegates at the Albany Congress broke off talks with the British in early July. The Iroquois became more suspicious and resentful when colonial land agents and fur traders used the Albany meeting as an opportunity to make side deals with individual Indian leaders.

Yet if war was going to erupt between the British and the French, the Iroquois and other Indian tribes could not afford to have the outcome decided by imperial powers alone. For most Indians, contests among European nations for land and power offered them the best chance of survival in the eighteenth century. They gained leverage as long as various imperial powers needed their trade items, military support, and political alliances. This leverage would be far more limited if one European nation controlled most of North America.

The various Indian tribes adopted different strategies. The Delaware, Huron, Miami, and Shawnee nations, for example, allied themselves with the French, hoping that a French victory would stop the far more numerous British colonists from invading their settlements in the Ohio valley. Members of the Iroquois Confederacy, on the other hand, tried to play one power against the other, hoping to win concessions from the British in return for their military support. The Creek, Choctaw, and Cherokee nations also sought to perpetuate the existing stalemate among European powers by bargaining alternately with the British in Georgia and the Carolinas, the French in Louisiana, and the Spaniards in Florida.

Faced with incursions into their lands, some Indian tribes launched preemptive attacks on colonial settlements. Along the northern border of Massachusetts, for example, in present-day New Hampshire, Abenaki Indians attacked British settlements in August 1754, taking settlers captive and marching them north to Canada. There they traded them to the French, who later held the colonists for ransom or exchanged them for their own prisoners of war with the British.

The British government soon decided it had to send additional troops to defend its American colonies against attacks from Indians and intrusions from the French. General Edward Braddock and two regiments arrived in 1755 to expel the French from Fort Duquesne. At the same time, colonial militia units were sent to battle the French and their Indian allies along the New York and New England frontiers. Colonel Washington joined Braddock as his personal aide-de-camp. Within months, however, Braddock's forces were ambushed, bludgeoned by French and Indian forces, and Braddock was killed. Washington was appointed commander of the Virginia troops, but with limited forces and meager financial support from the Virginia legislature, he had little hope of victory.

Other British forces fared little better during the next three years. Despite having far fewer colonists in North America than the British, the French had established extensive trade networks that helped them sustain a protracted war with support from numerous Indian nations. They also benefited from the help of European and Canadian soldiers as well as Irish conscripts who happily fought their British conquerors. Alternating guerrilla tactics with conventional warfare, the French captured several important forts, built a new one on Lake Champlain, and moved troops deep into British territory. The ineffectiveness of the British and colonial armies also encouraged Indian tribes along the New England and Appalachian frontiers to reclaim land from colonists. Bloody raids devastated many outlying settlements, leading to the death and capture of hundreds of Britain's colonial subjects.

A Shift to Global War

As the British faced defeat after defeat in North America, European nations began to contest imperial claims elsewhere in the world. In 1756 France and Great Britain officially declared war against each other. Eventually Austria, Russia, Sweden, most of the German states, and Spain allied with France, while Portugal and Prussia sided with Great Britain. Naval warfare erupted in the Mediterranean Sea and the Atlantic and Indian Oceans. Battles were also fought in Europe, the West Indies, India, and the Philippines. By the end of 1757, Britain and its allies had been defeated in nearly every part of the globe. The war appeared to be nearing its end, with France in control.

Then in the summer of 1757, William Pitt took charge of the British war effort and transformed the political and military landscape. A man of formidable talents and grand vision, Pitt redirected British efforts toward victory in North America, while Prussian forces held the line in Europe. Pouring more soldiers and arms into the North American campaign along with young and ambitious officers, Pitt energized colonial and British troops.

By the summer of 1758, the tide began to turn. In July, British generals recaptured the fort at Louisbourg on Cape Breton Island, a key to France's defense of Canada. Then British troops with George Washington's aid seized Fort Duquesne, which was renamed Pittsburgh. Other British forces captured Fort Frontenac along the St. Lawrence River, while Prussia defeated French, Austrian, and Russian forces in Europe and Britain gained key victories in India (Map 5.1). In 1759 General Jeffrey Amherst captured Forts

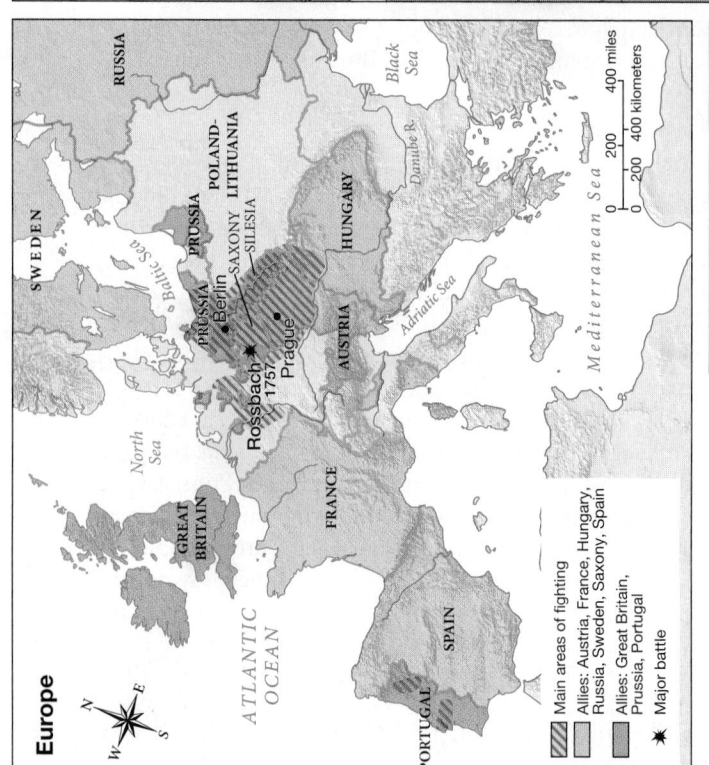

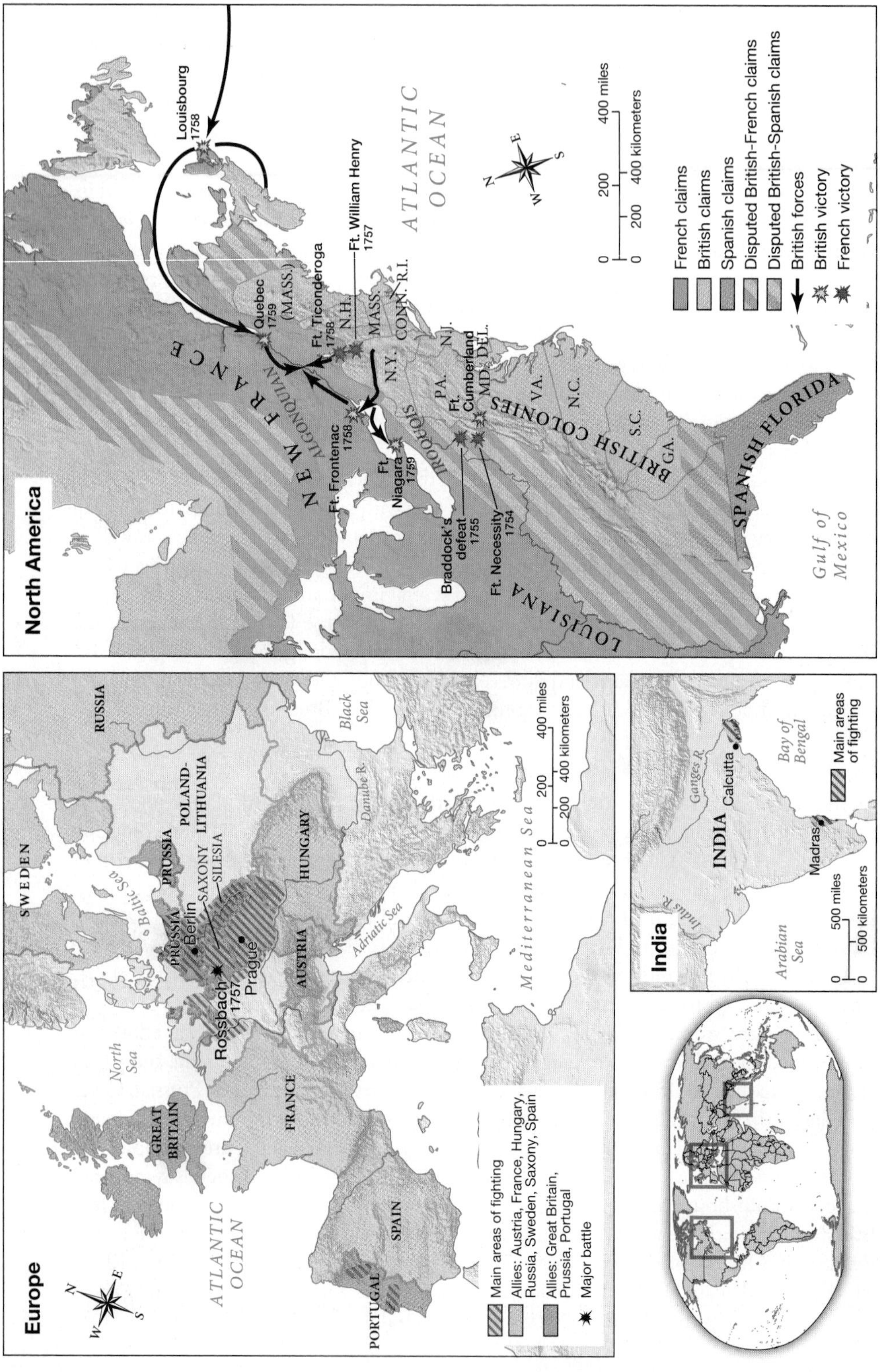

North America

Louisbourg 1758

ATLANTIC OCEAN

Ft. William Henry 1757

Quebec 1759 (MASS.)

Ft. Ticonderoga 1758

N.H.

MASS.

CONN. R.I.

N.Y.

N.J.

PA.

Ft. Cumberland

MD. DEL.

VA.

N.C.

S.C.

GA.

NEW FRANCE

ALGONQUIAN

IROQUOIS

Ft. Frontenac 1758

Ft. Niagara 1759

Braddock's defeat 1755

Ft. Necessity 1754

BRITISH COLONIES

SPANISH FLORIDA

LOUISIANA

Gulf of Mexico

N E W S

200   400 miles

200   400 kilometers

French claims
British claims
Spanish claims
Disputed British-French claims
Disputed British-Spanish claims
British forces
British victory
French victory

Europe

N E W S

ATLANTIC OCEAN

GREAT BRITAIN

SWEDEN

RUSSIA

North Sea

Baltic Sea

PRUSSIA

POLAND-LITHUANIA

SAXONY

SILESIA

Berlin

Prague

Rossbach 1757

HUNGARY

AUSTRIA

FRANCE

SPAIN

PORTUGAL

Black Sea

Danube R.

Adriatic Sea

Mediterranean Sea

200   400 miles

200   400 kilometers

Main areas of fighting
Allies: Austria, France, Hungary, Russia, Sweden, Saxony, Spain
Allies: Great Britain, Prussia, Portugal
★ Major battle

India

Bay of Bengal

Ganges R.

Indus R.

Calcutta

Madras

INDIA

Arabian Sea

Main areas of fighting

500 miles

500 kilometers

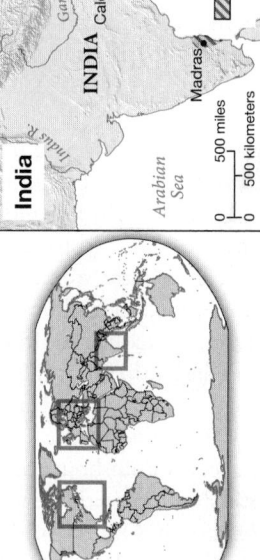

< **MAP 5.1**

The French and Indian War, 1754–1763   Clashes between colonial militia units and French and Indian forces erupted in North America in 1754. The conflict helped launch a wider war that engulfed Europe as well as the West Indies and India. In the aftermath of this first global war, Britain gained control of present-day Canada and India, but France retained its West Indies colonies.

Ticonderoga and Crown Point on Lake Champlain. Then General James Wolfe, with only four thousand men, attacked a much larger French force in Quebec. Despite heavy casualties, including Wolfe himself, the British won Quebec and control of Canada.

The Costs of Victory

Despite Wolfe's dramatic victory, the war dragged on in North America, Europe, India, and the West Indies for three more years. By then, however, King George III had tired of Pitt's grand, and expensive, strategy and dismissed him. He then opened peace negotiations with France and agreed to give up a number of conquered territories in order to finalize the **Peace of Paris** in 1763. Other countries were ready to negotiate as well. To regain control of Cuba and the Philippines, Spain ceded Florida to Great Britain. Meanwhile France rewarded Spain for its support by granting it Louisiana and all French lands west of the Mississippi River. Despite these concessions, the British empire reigned supreme, regaining control of India as well as North America east of the Mississippi, all of Canada, and a number of Caribbean islands.

The wars that erupted between 1754 and 1763 reshaped European empires, transformed patterns of global trade, and initially seemed to tighten bonds between North American residents and the mother country. English colonists in North America as well as their Scottish, Irish, German, and Dutch neighbors celebrated the British victory. Yet the Peace of Paris did not resolve many of the problems that had plagued the colonies before the war, and it created new ones as well.

The incredible cost of the war raised particularly difficult problems. Over the course of the war, the national debt of Great Britain had more than doubled. At the same time, as the North American colonies grew and conflicts erupted along their frontiers, the costs of administering these colonies increased fivefold. With an empire that stretched around the globe, the British crown and Parliament were forced to consider how to pay off war debts, raise funds to administer old and new territories, and keep sufficient currency in circulation for expanding international trade. Just as important, the Peace of Paris ignored the claims of the Iroquois, Shawnee, Creek, and other Indian tribes to the territories that France and Spain turned over to Great Britain. Nor did the treaty settle contested claims among the colonies themselves over lands in the Ohio valley and elsewhere along British North America's new frontiers.

Battles and Boundaries on the Frontier

The sweeping character of the British victory encouraged thousands of colonists to move farther west, into lands once controlled by France. This exacerbated tensions on the southern and western frontiers of British North America, tensions that escalated in the final years of the war and continued long after the Peace of Paris was signed.

In late 1759, for example, the Cherokee nation, reacting to repeated incursions on their hunting grounds, dissolved their long-term trade agreement with South Carolina. Cherokee warriors attacked backcountry farms and homes, leading to counterattacks by British troops. The fighting continued into 1761, when Cherokees on the Virginia frontier launched raids on colonists there. General Jeffrey Amherst then sent 2,800 troops to invade Cherokee territory and end the conflict. The soldiers sacked fifteen villages; killed men, women, and children; and burned acres of fields.

Although British raids diminished the Cherokees' ability to mount a substantial attack, sporadic assaults on frontier settlements continued for years. These conflicts fueled resentments among backcountry settlers against political leaders in more settled regions of the colonies who rarely provided sufficient funds or soldiers for frontier defense. The raids also intensified hostility toward Indians.

A more serious conflict erupted in the Ohio valley when Indians there realized the consequences of Britain's victory in Quebec. As the British took over French forts along the Great Lakes and in the Ohio valley in 1760, they immediately antagonized local Indian groups by hunting and fishing on tribal lands and depriving villages of much-needed food. British traders also defrauded Indians on numerous occasions and ignored traditional obligations of gift giving. They refused to provide kettles, gunpowder, or weapons to the Indians and thereby caused near starvation among many tribes that depended on hunting and trade.

The harsh realities of the British regime led some Indians to seek a return to ways of life that preceded the arrival of white men. An Indian visionary named Neolin, known to the British as the Delaware Prophet, preached that Indians had been corrupted by contact with Europeans and urged them to purify themselves by returning to their ancient traditions, abandoning white ways, and reclaiming their lands. Neolin was a prophet, not a warrior, but his message inspired others, including an Ottawa leader named Pontiac.

When news arrived in early 1763 that France was about to cede all of its North American lands to Britain and Spain, Pontiac convened a council of more than four hundred Ottawa, Potawatomi, and Huron leaders near Fort Detroit. Drawing on Neolin's vision, he mobilized support to drive out the British. In May 1763, Pontiac's forces laid siege to Detroit and soon gained the support of eighteen Indian nations. They then attacked Fort Pitt and other British frontier outposts and attacked white settlements along the Virginia and Pennsylvania frontier.

Accounts of violent encounters with Indians on the frontier circulated throughout the colonies and sparked resentment among local colonists as well as British troops. Many colonists did not bother to distinguish between friendly and hostile Indians, and General Amherst claimed that all Indians deserved extermination "for the good of mankind." A group of men from Paxton Creek, Pennsylvania, agreed. In December 1763, they raided families of peaceful, Christian Conestoga Indians near Lancaster, killing thirty. Protests from eastern colonists infuriated the Paxton Boys, who then marched on Philadelphia demanding protection from "savages" on the frontier.

Although violence on the frontier slowly subsided, neither side had achieved victory. Without French support, Pontiac and his followers ran out of guns and ammunition and had to retreat. About the same time, Benjamin Franklin negotiated a truce between the Paxton Boys and the Pennsylvania authorities, but it did not settle the fundamental issues over protection of western settlers. These conflicts convinced the British that the government could not endure further costly frontier clashes. So in October 1763, the crown issued a proclamation forbidding colonial settlement west of a line running down the Appalachian Mountains to create a buffer between Indians and colonists (Map 5.2).

The **Proclamation Line of 1763** denied colonists the right to settle west of the Appalachian Mountains. Instituted just months after the Peace of Paris was signed, the Proclamation Line frustrated colonists who sought the economic benefits won by a long

MAP 5.2

British Conflicts with Indians, 1758–1763, and the Proclamation Line   The entrance of British troops into former French territory in the Ohio River valley following the French and Indian War fueled conflicts with Indian nations. Colonists in Pennsylvania and the Carolinas also battled with Indians, including tribes who were allies or remained neutral during the war. Parliament established the Proclamation Line to limit westward expansion and thereby diminish such hostilities.

and bloody war. Small farmers, backcountry settlers, and squatters had hoped to improve their lot by acquiring rich farmlands, and wealthy land speculators like Washington had staked claims to property no longer threatened by the French or their Indian allies. Now both groups were told to stay put.

Conflicts over Land and Labor Escalate

Conflicts among colonists and with Britain were not confined to frontier regions. Land riots directed against the leasing policies of landlords and the greed of speculators had plagued New York's Hudson valley and New Jersey before the war, and these struggles continued into the 1760s. New clashes also occurred in the Carolinas as pioneer settlers like Herman Husband clashed with landlords and speculators there.

Even before the French and Indian War ended, the owners of large estates along the Hudson River in New York State raised rents and reduced the rights of tenants. These enormous estates had been granted in two periods. In 1629 the Dutch government established a patroon system by which men who provided fifty adult settlers to New Amsterdam were granted vast estates. Then in the early 1680s, the newly installed English governor Thomas Dongan granted lands to a select group of Englishmen. Some of these estates encompassed nearly 400 square miles, far larger than the island of Manhattan. In the early eighteenth century, the titles to some of these estates were challenged by small landowners and tenants, but even where legitimate titles existed, tenants declared a moral right to own the land they had long farmed. The manors and estates of the Hudson valley, they claimed, were more appropriate to a feudal government than to an enlightened empire.

Farmers in neighboring New Hampshire were drawn into battles over land when the king's Privy Council in London decided in 1764 that the Green Mountains belonged to New York rather than New Hampshire. Landlords along the Hudson River hoped to expand eastward into this region, but the farmers already living there claimed they had bought the land in good faith and deserved to keep it.

Following the Privy Council's decision, groups of farmers in New Hampshire waged guerrilla warfare against New York authorities, large landowners, and New York farmers who now claimed land that others had already cleared and settled. These Green Mountain Boys, led by Ethan Allen, refused to recognize New York authorities as legitimate in the region and established their own local governments and popular courts.

Inspired by the Green Mountain Boys and earlier uprisings in New Jersey, tenants in the Hudson valley banded together in 1765–1766. Under the leadership of William Prendergast, a group of tenants calling themselves Levellers refused to pay rent and instead claimed freehold title to the land they farmed. New York tenants petitioned the colonial assembly and sought redress in a variety of ways. But landowners refused to negotiate, and Prendergast concluded that "there was no law for poor men."

In many ways, the beliefs of Allen, Prendergast, and their followers echoed those of Herman Husband and the North Carolina **Regulators**. All of these groups developed visible, well-organized networks of supporters, targeted specific landlords, sought redress first through colonial courts and assemblies, and then established popular militias and other institutions to govern themselves and to challenge those in authority. These challenges included attacks on property: Burning barns, attacking livestock, and pulling down fences were common practices among irate farmers.

Conflicts in North Carolina escalated when the colonial assembly, dominated by the eastern slaveholding elite, passed a measure to build a stately mansion for Governor Tryon with public funds. Outraged frontier farmers, many already in debt and paying high taxes, withheld their taxes, took over courthouses, and harassed corrupt local officials. By the spring of 1771, faced with what he viewed as open rebellion on his western frontier, Governor Tryon recruited a thousand militiamen to confront the Regulators. In May, armed conflict erupted. The Regulators were defeated, and half a dozen leaders were publicly hanged. Herman Husband managed to escape and headed to the Pennsylvania frontier to establish a new homestead for his family. There, too, he met frontier farmers angered by their lack of political representation, economic opportunity, and protection from Indians.

(REVIEW & RELATE)

- How did the French and Indian War and the subsequent peace treaty affect relations between Britain and its North American subjects?
- How did the French and Indian War and the increasing power of large landowners contribute to conflict between average colonists and colonial elites?

Postwar British Policies and Colonial Unity

Throughout the 1750s and 1760s, ordinary colonists challenged the authority of economic and political elites to impose their will on local communities and individual residents. Before and during the French and Indian War, most of these challenges involved conflicts among colonists themselves. Yet in the decade following the war, from 1764 to 1774, common grievances against Britain united colonists on the frontier and along the eastern seaboard, allowing them to launch effective protests against the British government. British policies, like the Proclamation Line of 1763, inspired widespread dissent as poor farmers, large landowners, and speculators sought to expand westward. A second policy, impressment, by which the Royal Navy forced young colonial men into military service, also aroused anger across regions and classes. At the same time, the Great Awakening, for all the upheaval it had engendered, provided colonists with shared ideas about moral principles and new techniques for mass communication. Finally, Britain's efforts to repay its war debts by taxing colonists and its plan to continue quartering troops in North America led colonists to forge intercolonial protest movements.

Common Grievances

Like the Proclamation Line, which denied all colonists the right to settle beyond the Appalachian Mountains, the policy of impressment affected port city residents of all classes. British agents, desperate for seamen during the extended European wars of the eighteenth century, periodically impressed sailors and other poor men from British ports around the world, including seaboard cities in North America, and from merchant ships at sea. Impressment had been employed for decades by the time of the French and Indian War. Increasingly, however, merchants and other well-to-do American colonists joined common folk in demanding an end to this practice.

Seamen and dockworkers had good reason to fight off impressment agents. Men in the Royal Navy faced low wages, bad food, harsh punishment, rampant disease, and high mortality. As the practice escalated with each new war, the efforts of British naval officers and impressment agents to capture new "recruits" met violent resistance, especially in the North American colonies. At times, whole communities joined in the battle—relatives and friends, blacks and whites, women and men.

In 1757, in the midst of the French and Indian War, some 3,000 British soldiers cordoned off New York City and visited "the Taverns and other houses, where sailors usually resorted." According to printer Hugh Gaines, "All kinds of Tradesmen and Negroes" were hauled in by British press gangs. Local residents rioted along the docks the next day, but of the 800 men picked up the night before, some 400 were "retained in the service." With impressment robbing colonial seaports of much-needed laborers, some merchants and colonial officials began to petition Parliament for redress. But Parliament, seeing no reason why the British in America should avoid the fate of their counterparts in Great Britain, ignored the petitions.

In the aftermath of the French and Indian War, more serious impressment riots erupted in Boston, New York City, and Newport, Rhode Island. Increasingly, poor colonial seamen and dockworkers made common cause with owners of merchant ships and mercantile houses in protesting British policy. Colonial officials—mayors, governors, and custom agents—were caught in the middle. Some insisted on upholding the Royal Navy's right of impressment; others tried to placate both naval officers and local residents; and still others resisted what they saw as an oppressive imposition on the rights of colonists. Both those who resisted British authority and those who sought a compromise had to gain the support of the lower and middling classes to succeed.

Employers and politicians who opposed impressment gained an important advantage if they could direct the anger of colonists away from themselves and toward British officials and policies. The decision of British officials to continue quartering troops in the colonies gave local leaders another opportunity to join forces with ordinary colonists. Colonial towns and cities were required to quarter (that is, house and support) British troops even after the Peace of Paris was signed. While the troops were intended to protect the colonies against disgruntled Indians and French on their borders, they also provided reinforcements for impressment agents and surveillance over other illegal activities like smuggling and domestic manufacturing. Thus a range of issues and policies began to bind colonists together through common grievances against the British Parliament.

Forging Ties across the Colonies

The ties forged between poorer and wealthier colonists over issues of westward expansion, impressment, and quartering grew stronger in the 1760s, but they tended to be localized in seaport cities or in specific areas of the frontier. Creating bonds across the colonies required considerably more effort in a period when communication and transportation beyond local areas were limited. The Albany Congress of 1754 had been one of the first attempts to develop intercolonial bonds, but it had not been very successful. Means had to be found to disseminate information and create a sense of common purpose if the colonists were going to persuade Parliament to take their complaints seriously. One important model for such intercolonial communication was the Great Awakening.

By the 1750s, the Great Awakening seemed to be marked more by dissension than by unity as new denominations continued to split from traditional churches. For example, in the Sandy Creek region of North Carolina, home to Herman Husband, radical Protestants formed the Separate Baptists (named for their separation from traditional Baptists) in order to proclaim a message of absolute spiritual equality. From the late 1750s through the 1770s, Separate Baptists converted thousands of small farmers, poor whites, and enslaved women and men and established churches throughout Virginia, Georgia, and the Carolinas.

Methodists, Dunkards, Moravians, and Quakers joined Separate Baptists in offering southern residents religious experiences that highlighted spiritual equality. Appealing to blacks and whites, women and men, they challenged the social order, especially in frontier regions that were beyond the reach of many established institutions. Some dissenting preachers invited slaves and free blacks to attend their services alongside local white farmers and laborers. Slaveholders and other elite southerners considered such practices outrageous and a challenge to the political as well as the social order.

Most women and men who converted to Separate Baptism, Methodism, or other forms of radical Protestantism did not link their religious conversion directly to politics. Those who did, including many Regulators, suggested that religion was a force for division rather than unity in the colonies. But as more and more ordinary colonists and colonial leaders voiced their anger at offensive British policies, evangelical techniques used to rouse the masses to salvation became important for mobilizing colonists to protest.

Thus even though the Great Awakening had spent its religious passion in most parts of North America by the 1760s, the techniques of mass communication and critiques of opulence and corruption it initiated provided emotional and practical ways of forging ties among widely dispersed colonists. Many evangelical preachers had condemned the lavish lifestyles of colonial elites and the spiritual corruption of local officials who failed to consider the needs of their less well-to-do neighbors. Now in the context of conflicts with Great Britain, colonial leaders could turn such rhetoric against new targets of resentment by painting Parliament and British officials as aristocrats with little faith and less compassion.

During the Great Awakening, preachers also honed techniques of popular appeal that proved useful in uniting colonists to voice opposition to British policies. The public sermons and mass rallies meant to inspire loyalty to a greater moral cause could all be translated into forms applicable to political protest. These techniques challenged established forms of authority, which certainly gave pause to some colonial leaders. Nonetheless, casting aside deference to king and Parliament was necessary if colonists were going to gain rights within the British empire that met the needs of elites and laborers alike. The efforts of Great Britain to assert greater control over its North American colonies provided colonial dissidents an opportunity to test out these new ways to forge intercolonial ties.

Great Britain Seeks Greater Control

Until the French and Indian War, British officials and their colonial subjects coexisted in relative harmony. Economic growth led Britain to ignore much of the smuggling and domestic manufacturing that took place in the colonies. Although the system of mercantilism (see chapter 3) assumed that the colonies supplied raw materials and the mother country manufactured goods, a bit of manufacturing for local needs did not significantly disrupt British industry. Similarly, although the king and Parliament held ultimate political sovereignty, or final authority, over the American colonies, it was easier to allow some local government control over decisions, given the communication challenges created by distance.

This pattern of **benign** (or "salutary") **neglect** led some American colonists to view themselves as more independent of British control than they really were. Impressment offers a good example. The Royal Navy had the right to impress men when needed, yet even in the midst of the French and Indian War, American colonists viewed impressment as an unwarranted infringement on their rights as British subjects. Many colonists had also begun to see smuggling, domestic manufacturing, and local self-governance as rights rather than privileges. Thus when British officials decided to assert greater control, many colonists protested.

To King George III and to Parliament, asserting control over the colonies was both right and necessary. In 1763 King George appointed George Grenville to lead the British government. As prime minister and chancellor of the Exchequer, Grenville faced an economic depression in England, rebellious farmers opposed to a new tax on domestic cider, and growing numbers of unemployed soldiers returning from the war. He believed that regaining political and economic control in the colonies abroad could help resolve these crises at home.

Eighteenth-century wars, especially the French and Indian War, cost a fortune. British subjects in England paid taxes to help offset the nation's debts, even though few of them benefited as directly from the British victory as did their counterparts in the American colonies. The colonies would cost the British treasury more if the crown could not control colonists' movement into Indian territories, limit smuggling and domestic manufacturing, and house British troops in the colonies cheaply. With more British troops and officials stationed in or visiting the colonies during the French and Indian War, they had greater opportunities to observe colonial life. Many of these observers voiced concern about the extent of criminality in the colonies and the rebellious spirit that existed among many servants, seamen, frontiersmen, tenants, and even women and slaves. Others feared that the religious enthusiasm of the Great Awakening had nurtured disdain for established authority among the colonists. Clearly it was time to impose a true imperial order.

To establish order, Parliament launched a three-prong program. First, it sought stricter enforcement of existing laws and established a Board of Trade to centralize policies and ensure their implementation. The **Navigation Acts**, which prohibited smuggling, established guidelines for legal commerce, and set duties on trade items, were the most important laws to be enforced. Second, Parliament extended wartime policies into peacetime. For example, the Quartering Act of 1765 ensured that British troops would remain in the colonies to enforce imperial policy. Colonial governments were expected to support them by allowing them to use vacant buildings and providing them with food and supplies.

The third part of Grenville's colonial program was the most important. It called for the passage of new laws to raise funds and reestablish the sovereignty of British rule. The first revenue act passed by Parliament was the American Duties Act of 1764, known as the **Sugar Act**. It imposed an **import duty**, or tax, on sugar, coffee, wines, and other luxury items. The act also reduced the import tax on foreign molasses but insisted that the duty be collected, a shock to the many colonial merchants and rum distillers who relied on cheap molasses smuggled in from the French and Spanish Caribbean. The crackdown on smuggling increased the power of customs officers and established the first vice-admiralty courts in North America to ensure that the Sugar Act raised money for the crown. That same year, Parliament passed the Currency Act, which prohibited colonial assemblies from printing paper money or bills of credit. Taken together, these provisions meant that colonists would pay more money into the British treasury even as the supply of money (and illegal goods) diminished in the colonies.

Some colonial leaders protested the Sugar Act through speeches, pamphlets, and petitions, and Massachusetts established a **committee of correspondence** to circulate concerns to leaders in other colonies. However, dissent remained disorganized and ineffective. Nonetheless, the passage of the Sugar and Currency Acts caused anxiety among many colonists, which was heightened by passage of the Quartering Act the next year. Colonial responses to these developments marked the first steps in an escalating conflict between British officials and their colonial subjects.

REVIEW & RELATE

- How did Britain's postwar policies lead to the emergence of unified colonial protests?
- Why did British policymakers believe they were justified in seeking to gain greater control over Britain's North American colonies?

Resistance to Britain Intensifies

Over the next decade, between 1764 and 1774, the British Parliament sought to extend its political and economic control over the American colonies, and the colonists periodically resisted. With each instance of resistance, Parliament demanded further submission to royal authority. With each demand for submission, colonists responded with greater assertions of their rights and autonomy. Yet no one—neither colonists nor British officials—could have imagined in 1764, or even in 1774, that a revolution was in the making.

The Stamp Act Inspires Coordinated Resistance

Grenville decided that his next step would be to impose a stamp tax on the colonies similar to that long used in England. The stamp tax required that a revenue stamp be affixed to all transactions involving paper items, from newspapers and contracts to playing cards and diplomas. Grenville announced his plans in 1764, a full year before Parliament enacted the **Stamp Act** in the spring of 1765. The tax was to be collected by colonists appointed for the purpose, and the money was to be spent within the colonies at the direction of Parliament for "defending, protecting and securing the colonies." To Grenville and a majority in Parliament, the Stamp Act seemed completely fair. After all, Englishmen paid on average 26 shillings in tax annually, while Bostonians averaged just 1 shilling. Moreover, the act was purposely written to benefit the American colonies.

The colonists viewed it in a more threatening light. The Stamp Act differed from earlier parliamentary laws in three important ways. First, by the time of its passage, the colonies were experiencing rising unemployment, falling wages, and a downturn in trade.

All of these developments were exacerbated by the Sugar, Currency, and Quartering Acts passed by Parliament the previous year. Indeed, in cities like Boston, British soldiers often competed with colonists for scarce jobs in order to supplement their low wages. Second, critics viewed the Stamp Act as an attempt to control the *internal* affairs of the colonies. It was not an indirect tax on trade, paid by importers and exporters, but a direct tax on daily business: getting a marriage certificate, selling land, and publishing or buying a newspaper or an almanac. Third, such a direct intervention in the economic affairs of the colonies unleashed the concerns of leading colonial officials, merchants, lawyers, shopkeepers, and ministers that Parliament was taxing colonists who had no representation in its debates and decisions. Their arguments resonated with ordinary women and men, who were affected far more by the stamp tax than by an import duty on sugar, molasses, or wine.

By announcing the Stamp Act a year before its passage, Grenville assured that colonists had plenty of time to organize their opposition. In New York City, Boston, and other cities, merchants, traders, and artisans formed groups dedicated to the repeal of the Stamp Act. Soon Sons of Liberty, Daughters of Liberty, Sons of Neptune, Vox Populi, and similar organizations emerged to challenge the imposition of the Stamp Act. Even before the act was implemented, angry mobs throughout the colonies attacked stamp distributors. Some were beaten, others tarred and feathered, and all were forced to take an oath never to sell stamps again.

Colonists lodged more formal protests with the British government as well. The Virginia House of Burgesses, led by Patrick Henry, acted first. It passed five resolutions, which it sent to Parliament, denouncing taxation without representation. The Virginia Resolves were reprinted in many colonial newspapers and repeated by orators to eager audiences in Massachusetts and elsewhere. At the same time, the Massachusetts House adopted a circular letter—a written protest circulated to the other colonial assemblies—calling for a congress to be held in New York City in October 1765 to consider the threat posed by the Stamp Act.

In the meantime, popular protests multiplied. The protests turned violent in Boston, where Sons of Liberty leaders like Samuel Adams organized mass demonstrations. Adams modeled his oratory on that of itinerant preachers, but with a political twist. Sons of Liberty also spread anti-British sentiment through newspapers and handbills that they posted on trees and buildings throughout the city and in surrounding towns. At dawn on August 14, 1765, the Boston Sons of Liberty hung an effigy of stamp distributor Andrew Oliver on a tree and called for his resignation. A mock funeral procession, joined by farmers, artisans, apprentices, and the poor, marched to Boston Common. The crowd, led by twenty-seven-year-old Ebenezer Mackintosh—a shoemaker, a veteran of the French and Indian War, and a popular working-class leader—carried the fake corpse to the Boston stamp office and destroyed the building. Demonstrators saved pieces of lumber, "stamped" them, and set them on fire outside Oliver's house. Oliver, wisely, had already left town.

Oliver's brother-in-law, Lieutenant Governor Thomas Hutchinson, arrived at the scene and tried to quiet the crowd, but he only angered them further. They soon destroyed Oliver's stable house, coach, and carriage, which the crowd saw as signs of aristocratic opulence. Twelve days later, demonstrators attacked the homes of Judge William Story, customs officer Benjamin Hallowell, and Lieutenant Governor Hutchinson.

The battle against the Stamp Act unfolded across the colonies with riots, beatings, and resignations reported from Newport, Rhode Island, to New Brunswick, New Jersey, to Charles Town (later Charleston), South Carolina. In Charleston, slave trader and stamp agent Henry Laurens was attacked by white artisans who hanged him in effigy and then by white workers and finally by slaves who harassed him with chants of "Liberty! Liberty!!" On November 1, 1765, when the Stamp Act officially took effect, not a single stamp agent remained in his post in the colonies.

Protesters carefully chose their targets: stamp agents, sheriffs, judges, and colonial officials. Even when violence erupted, it remained focused, with most crowds destroying stamps and stamp offices first and then turning to the private property of Stamp Act supporters. These protests made a mockery of notions of deference toward British rule. But they also revealed growing autonomy on the part of middling- and working-class colonists who attacked men of wealth and power, sometimes choosing artisans rather than wealthier men as their leaders. However, this was not primarily a class conflict because many wealthier colonists made common cause with artisans, small farmers, and the poor. Indeed, colonial elites considered themselves the leaders, inspiring popular uprisings through the power of their political arguments and oratorical skills, although they refused to support actions they considered too radical. For example, when Levellers in the Hudson valley proclaimed themselves Sons of Liberty and sought assistance from Stamp Act rebels in New York City, the merchants, judges, and large landowners who led the protests there refused to help them.

It was these more affluent protesters who dominated the Stamp Act Congress in New York City in October 1765, which brought together twenty-seven delegates from nine colonies. The delegates petitioned Parliament to repeal the Stamp Act, arguing that taxation without representation was tyranny and that such laws "have a manifest Tendency to subvert the Rights and Liberties of the Colonists." Delegates then urged colonists to boycott British goods and refuse to pay the stamp tax. Yet they still proclaimed their loyalty to king and country.

The question of representation became a mainstay of colonial protests. Whereas the British accepted the notion of "virtual representation," by which members of Parliament gave voice to the views of particular classes and interests, the North American colonies had developed a system of representation based on locality. According to colonial leaders, only members of Parliament elected by colonists could represent their interests.

Even as delegates at the Stamp Act Congress declared themselves disaffected but loyal British subjects, they participated in the process of developing a common identity in the American colonies. Christopher Gadsden of South Carolina expressed the feeling most directly. "We should stand upon the broad common ground of natural rights," he argued. "There should be no New England man, no New-Yorker, known on the continent, but all of us Americans."

Eventually the British Parliament was forced to respond to colonial protests and even more to rising complaints from English merchants and traders whose business had been damaged by the colonists' boycott. Parliament repealed the Stamp Act in March 1766, and King George III granted his approval a month later. When news reached the colonies in May, crowds celebrated in the streets, church bells rang, and fireworks and muskets saluted the victory. Colonists now looked forward to a new and better relationship between themselves and the British government.

From the colonists' perspective, the crisis triggered by the passage of the Stamp Act demonstrated the limits of parliamentary control. Colonists had organized effectively

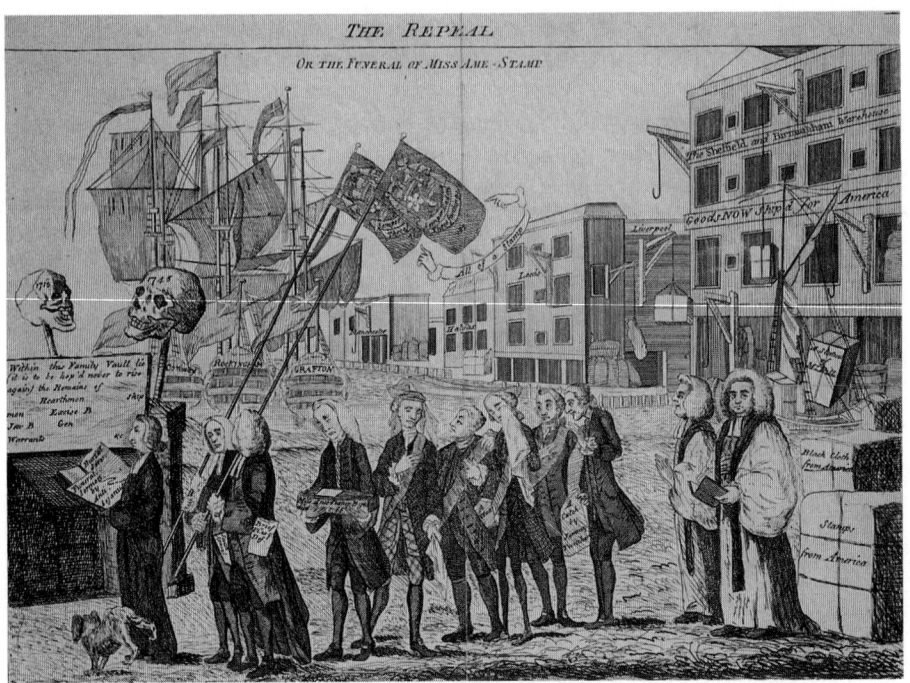

The Repeal, 1766   The announcement of the Stamp Act in 1764 ignited widespread protests throughout the colonies. Colonial governments petitioned Parliament for its repeal, crowds attacked stamp agents and distributors, broadsides and newspapers denounced "taxation without representation," and boycotts and mass demonstrations were organized in major cities, some of which turned violent. The cartoon celebrates the repeal of the Stamp Act by depicting a funeral for the act led by its supporters.   Library of Congress

and forced Parliament to repeal the hated legislation. Protests had raged across the colonies and attracted support from a wide range of colonists, including young and old, men and women, merchants, lawyers, artisans, and farmers. Individual leaders, like Patrick Henry of Virginia and Samuel Adams of Massachusetts, became more widely known through their fiery oratory and their success in appealing to the masses. The Stamp Act agitation also demonstrated the growing influence of ordinary citizens who led parades and demonstrations and joined in attacks on stamp agents and the homes of British officials. And the protests revealed the growing power of the written word and printed images in disseminating ideas among colonists. Broadsides, political cartoons, handbills, newspapers, and pamphlets circulated widely, reinforcing discussions and proclamations at taverns, rallies, demonstrations, and more formal political assemblies.

For all the success of the Stamp Act protests, American colonists still could not imagine in 1765 that protest would ever lead to open revolt against British sovereignty. More well-to-do colonists were concerned that a revolution against British authority might fuel a dual revolution in which small farmers, tenants, servants, slaves, and laborers would rise up against their political and economic superiors in the colonies. Even most middling- and working-class protesters believed that the best solution to the colonies' problems was to gain greater economic and political rights within the British empire, not to break from it. After all, Great Britain was the most powerful nation in the world, and the colonies could only benefit from their place in its far-reaching empire.

The Townshend Act and the Boston Massacre

The repeal of the Stamp Act in March 1766 led directly to Parliament's passage of the Declaratory Act. That act declared that Parliament had the authority to pass any law "to bind the colonies and peoples of North America" closer to Britain. No new tax or policy was established; Parliament simply wanted to proclaim Great Britain's political supremacy in the aftermath of the successful stamp tax protests.

Following this direct assertion of British sovereignty, relative harmony prevailed in the colonies for more than a year. Having rid themselves of the burden of parliamentary taxation, colonists were content to abide by less offensive restrictions on smuggling, domestic manufacturing, and similar matters. Then in June 1767, a new chancellor of the Exchequer, Charles Townshend, rose to power in England. He persuaded Parliament to return to the model offered by the earlier Sugar Act. The Townshend Act, like the Sugar Act, instituted an import tax on a range of items sent to the colonies, including glass, lead, paint, paper, and tea.

Now, however, even an indirect tax led to immediate protests and calls for a boycott of the items subject to the tax. In February 1768, Samuel Adams wrote a circular letter reminding colonists of the importance of the boycott, and the Massachusetts Assembly disseminated it to other colonial assemblies. In response, Parliament posted two more British army regiments in Boston and New York City to enforce the law, including the Townshend Act. Angry colonists did not retreat when confronted by this show of military force. Instead, a group of outspoken colonial leaders demanded that colonists refuse to import goods of any kind from Britain.

This boycott depended especially on the support of women, who were often in charge of the day-to-day purchase of household items that appeared on the boycott list. Women were expected to boycott a wide array of British goods—gloves, hats, shoes, cloth, sugar, and tea among them. Single women and widows who supported themselves as shopkeepers were expected to join male merchants and store owners in refusing to sell British goods. To make up for the boycotted goods, wives, mothers, and daughters produced homespun shirts and dresses and brewed herbal teas to replace British products.

Despite the hardships, many colonial women embraced the boycott. Twenty-two-year-old Charity Clarke voiced the feelings of many colonists when she wrote to a friend in England, "If you English folks won't give us the liberty we ask . . . I will try to gather a number of ladies armed with spinning wheels [along with men] who shall learn to weave & keep sheep, and will retire beyond the reach of arbitrary power." Women organized spinning bees in which dozens of participants produced yards and yards of homespun cloth. By 1770 wearing homespun came to symbolize women's commitment to the colonial cause.

Refusing to drink tea offered another way for women to show their support of protests against parliamentary taxation. In February 1770, more than "300 Mistresses of Families, in which number the Ladies of the Highest Rank and Influence," signed a petition in Boston and pledged to abstain from drinking tea, and dozens of women from less prosperous families signed their own boycott agreement.

Boston women's refusal to drink tea and their participation in spinning bees were part of a highly publicized effort to make their city the center of opposition to the Townshend Act. Printed propaganda, demonstrations, rallies, and broadsides announced to the world that Bostonians rejected Parliament's right to impose its will, or at least its taxes, on the American colonies. Throughout the winter of 1769–1770, boys and young men confronted British soldiers stationed in Boston. Although they were angry over Parliament's taxation policies, Boston men also considered the soldiers, who moonlighted for extra pay, as economic competitors. The taunts and tension soon escalated into violence.

By March 1770, 1,700 British troops were stationed in Boston, a city of 18,000 people. On the evening of March 5, boys began throwing snowballs and insults at the lone soldier guarding the Boston Customs House. An angry crowd began milling about, now joined by a group of sailors led by Crispus Attucks, an ex-slave of mixed African and Indian ancestry. The nervous guard called for help, and Captain Thomas Preston arrived at the scene with seven British soldiers. He appealed to the "gentlemen" present to disperse the crowd. Instead, the harangues of the crowd continued, and snowballs, stones, and other projectiles flew in greater numbers. Then a gun fired, and soon more shooting erupted. Eleven men in the crowd were hit, and four were "killed on the Spot," including Crispus Attucks.

Despite confusion about who, if anyone, gave the order to fire, colonists expressed outrage at the shooting of ordinary men on the streets of Boston. Samuel Adams and other Sons of Liberty, though horrified by the turn of events, recognized the incredible potential for anti-British propaganda. Adams organized a mass funeral for those killed, and thousands watched the caskets being paraded through the city. Newspaper editors and broadsides printed by the Sons of Liberty labeled the shooting a "massacre." When the accused soldiers were tried in Boston for the so-called Boston Massacre and the jury acquitted six of the eight of any crime, colonial leaders became more convinced that British rule had become tyrannical and that such tyranny must be opposed.

 Online Document Project   The Boston Massacre
bedfordstmartins.com/hewittlawsonvalue

To ensure that colonists throughout North America learned about the Boston Massacre, committees of correspondence formed once again to spread the news. These committees became important pipelines for sending information about plans and protests across the colonies, connecting seaport cities with one another and with like-minded colonists in the countryside. They also circulated an engraving by Bostonian Paul Revere that suggested the soldiers purposely shot at a peaceful crowd.

In the aftermath of the shootings, public pressure increased on Parliament to repeal the Townshend duties. Merchants in England and North America pleaded with Parliament to reconsider policies that had resulted in economic losses on both sides of the Atlantic. In response, Parliament repealed all of the Townshend duties except the import tax on tea. Parliament retained the tea tax to prove its political authority to do so.

Continuing Conflicts at Home

As colonists in Boston and other seaport cities rallied to protest British taxation, other residents of the thirteen colonies continued to challenge authorities closer to home. In the same years as the Stamp Act and Townshend Act protests, tenants in New Jersey and the Hudson valley continued their campaign for economic justice. So, too, did Herman

Husband and the Sandy Creek Association. Governor Tryon of North Carolina had been among those who claimed that Parliament had abused its power in taxing the colonies, but he did not recognize such abuses in his own colony. Instead, he viewed the Regulators, formed during the campaign against the Townshend Act, as traitors. The Regulators, however, insisted that they were simply trying to protect farmers and laborers from deceitful speculators, corrupt politicians, and greedy employers. A year after the Boston Massacre, Governor Tryon sent troops to quell what he viewed as open rebellion on the Carolina frontier. The Regulators amassed two thousand farmers to defend themselves, although Husband, a pacifist, was not among them. But when twenty Regulators were killed and more than a hundred wounded at the Battle of Alamance Creek in May 1771, he surely knew many of the fallen. Six Regulators were hanged a month later in front of Governor Tryon, local officials, and hundreds of neighboring farm families. Although North Carolina Regulators did not proclaim this the Alamance Massacre, many local residents harbored deep resentments against colonial officials for what they viewed as the slaughter of honest, hardworking men. Herman Husband fled the Carolina frontier and headed north.

Resentments against colonial leaders were not confined to North Carolina. An independent Regulator movement emerged in South Carolina in 1767. Far more effective than their North Carolina counterparts, South Carolina Regulators seized control of the western regions of the colony, took up arms, and established their own system of frontier justice. By 1769 the South Carolina Assembly negotiated a settlement with the Regulators, establishing new parishes in the colony's interior that ensured greater representation for frontier areas and extending colonial political institutions, such as courts and sheriffs, to the region.

Tea and Widening Resistance

For a brief period after the Boston Massacre, conflicts within the colonies generally overshadowed protests against British policies. During this period, the tea tax was collected, the increased funds ensured that British officials in the colonies were less dependent on local assemblies to carry out their duties, and general prosperity seemed to lessen the antagonism between colonists and royal authorities. In May 1773, however, all that changed. That month Parliament passed a new act that granted the East India Company a monopoly on shipping and selling tea in the colonies. Although this did not add any new tax or raise the price of tea, it did fuel a new round of protests.

Founded in the early seventeenth century, the East India Company had been one of the major trading companies in the British empire and a symbol of British commercial supremacy for more than 150 years. By the 1770s, however, it was on the verge of economic collapse and asked for a monopoly on the tea trade and the right to sell tea through its own agents rather than through independent shopkeepers and merchants in the colonies. Many members of Parliament had invested in the East India Company, so their decision to grant it a monopoly on tea involved financial as well as political considerations. Still, the decision was not seen as especially controversial since East India Company tea sold by company agents cost less, even with the tax, than smuggled Dutch or French tea.

Samuel Adams, Patrick Henry, Christopher Gadsden, and other radicals had continued to view the tea tax as an illegal imposition on colonists and refused to pay it as a matter of principle. They had established committees of correspondence to keep up the pressure for a colony-wide boycott, and Adams published and circulated "Rights of the Colonies," a pamphlet that listed a range of grievances against British policies. Their concerns became the basis for a new round of protests when Parliament granted the East India Company its monopoly. By eliminating colonial merchants from the profits to be made on tea and implementing a monopoly for a single favored company, Parliament pushed merchants into joining with radicals to demand redress.

Committees of correspondence quickly organized another colony-wide boycott. In some cities, like Charleston, South Carolina, tea was unloaded from East India Company ships but never sold. In others, like New York, the ships were turned back at the port. Only in Boston, however, did violence erupt as ships loaded with tea, and protected by British troops, sat anchored in the harbor. On the night of December 16, 1773, the Sons of Liberty organized a "tea party." After a massive rally against British policy, a group of about fifty men disguised as Indians boarded the British ships and dumped forty-five tons of tea into the sea.

Although hundreds of spectators knew who had boarded the ship, witnesses refused to provide names or other information to British officials investigating the incident. The Boston Tea Party was a direct challenge to British authority and resulted in massive destruction of valuable property.

Parliament responded immediately with a show of force. The **Coercive Acts**, passed in 1774, closed the port of Boston until residents paid for the tea, moved Massachusetts court cases against royal officials back to England, and revoked the colony's charter in order to strengthen the authority of royal officials and weaken that of the colonial assembly. The British government also approved a new Quartering Act, which forced Boston residents to accommodate more soldiers in their own homes or build more barracks.

The royal government passed the Coercive Acts to punish Massachusetts and to discourage similar protests in other colonies. Instead, the legislation, which colonists called the **Intolerable Acts**, spurred a militant reaction. Committees of correspondence spread news of the fate of Boston and the entire colony of Massachusetts. Colonial leaders, who increasingly identified themselves as patriots, soon formed committees of safety—armed groups of colonists who gathered weapons and munitions and vowed to protect themselves against British encroachments on their rights and institutions. Other colonies sent support, both political and material, to Massachusetts and instituted a boycott of British goods. All ranks of people—merchants, laborers, farmers, housewives—throughout the colonies joined the boycott.

At the same time, a group of patriots meeting in Williamsburg, Virginia, in the spring of 1774 called for colonies to send representatives to a **Continental Congress** to meet in Philadelphia the following September to discuss relations between the North American colonies and Great Britain.

By passing the Coercive Acts, Parliament had hoped to dampen the long-smoldering conflict with the colonies. Instead, it flared even brighter, with radical leaders committing themselves to the use of violence, moderate merchants and shopkeepers making common cause with radicals, and ordinary women and men embracing a boycott of all British goods.

The Continental Congress and Colonial Unity

When the Continental Congress convened in Philadelphia's Carpenter Hall in September 1774, fifty-six delegates represented every colony but Georgia. Many of these men—and they were all men—had met before. Some had worked together in the Stamp Act Congress in 1765; others had joined forces in the intervening years on committees of correspondence or in petitions to Parliament. Still, the representatives disagreed on many fronts.

First Continental Congress   This 1783 French engraving depicts the meeting of the First Continental Congress, held in Philadelphia in September 1774. Fifty-six delegates attended from every colony but Georgia. After spending most of the first day debating whether to start the meeting off with a prayer, the congress got down to the business of petitioning King George III to remedy the colonists' grievances.   The Granger Collection, New York

Some were radicals like Samuel Adams, Patrick Henry, and Christopher Gadsden. Others held moderate views, including George Washington of Virginia and John Dickinson of Pennsylvania. And a few, like John Jay of New York, voiced more conservative positions.

Despite their differences, all the delegates agreed that the colonies must resist further parliamentary encroachments on their liberties.

Online Document Project   **Defining Liberty, Defining America**
bedfordstmartins.com/hewittlawsonvalue

They did not talk of independence, but rather of reestablishing the freedoms that colonists had enjoyed in an earlier period: freedom from British taxes and from the presence of British troops and the right to control local economic and political affairs. Washington voiced the sentiments of many. Although opposed to the idea of independence, he echoed John Locke by refusing to submit "to the loss of those valuable rights and privileges, which are essential to the happiness of every free State, and without which life, liberty, and property are rendered totally insecure."

To demonstrate their unified resistance to the Coercive Acts, delegates called on colonists to continue the boycott of British goods and to end all colonial exports to Great Britain. Committees were established in all of the colonies to coordinate and enforce these actions. Delegates also insisted that Americans were "entitled to a free and exclusive power of legislation in their several provincial legislatures." By 1774 a growing number of colonists supported these measures and the ideas on which they were based.

The delegates at the Continental Congress could not address all the colonists' grievances, and most had no interest in challenging race and class relations within the colonies themselves. Nonetheless, it was a significant event because the congress drew power away from individual colonies—most notably Massachusetts—and local organizations like the Sons of Liberty and placed the emphasis instead on colony-wide plans and actions. To some extent, the delegates shifted leadership of colonial protests away from more radical artisans, like Ebenezer Mackintosh, and put planning back in the hands of men of wealth and standing. Moreover, even as they denounced Parliament, many representatives felt a special loyalty to the king and sought his intervention to rectify relations between the mother country and the colonies.

REVIEW & RELATE

• How and why did colonial resistance to British policies escalate in the decade following the conclusion of the French and Indian War?

• How did internal social and economic divisions shape the colonial response to British policies?

Conclusion: Liberty within Empire

From the Sugar Act in 1764 to the Continental Congress in 1774, colonists reacted strongly to parliamentary efforts to impose greater control over the colonies. Their protests grew increasingly effective as colonists developed organizations, systems of communication, and arguments to buttress their position. Residents of seacoast cities like Boston and New York City developed especially visible and effective challenges, in large part because they generally had the most to lose if Britain implemented new economic, military, and legislative policies.

In frontier areas, such as the southern backcountry, the Hudson valley, and northern New England, complaints against British tyranny vied with those against colonial land speculators and officials throughout the 1760s and 1770s. Still, few of these agitators questioned the right of white colonists to claim Indian lands or enslave African labor. In this sense, at least, most frontier settlers made common cause with more elite colonists who challenged British authority, including the many planters and large landowners who attended the Continental Congress.

One other tie bound the colonists together in 1774. No matter how radical the rhetoric, the aim continued to be resistance to particular policies, not independence from the British empire. Colonists sought greater liberty within the empire, focusing on parliamentary policies concerning taxation, troops, and local political control. Only on rare occasions did a colonist question the fundamental framework of imperial governance, and even then, the questions did not lead to a radical reformulation of economic or political relations. And despite some colonists' opposition to certain parliamentary acts, many others supported British policies. While royal officials and many of their well-to-do neighbors were horrified by the new spirit of lawlessness that had erupted in the colonies, the majority of colonists did not participate in the Sons or Daughters of Liberty, the colonial congresses, or the petition campaigns. Small farmers and back-country settlers were often far removed from centers of protest activity, while poor families in seaport cities who purchased few items to begin with had little interest in boycotts of British goods. Finally, some colonists still hesitated to consider open revolt against British rule for fear of a revolution from below. The activities of land rioters, Regulators, evangelical preachers, female petitioners, and African American converts to Christianity reminded more well-established settlers that the colonies harbored their own tensions and conflicts.

The fates of George Washington and Herman Husband suggest the uncertainties that still plagued the colonies and individual colonists in 1774. As Washington returned to his Virginia estate from the Continental Congress, he began to devote more time to military affairs. He took command of the volunteer militia companies in the colonies and chaired the committee on safety in his home county. Although still opposed to rebellion, he was nonetheless preparing for it. Herman Husband, on the other hand, had already watched his rebellion against oppressive government fail at the Battle of Alamance Creek. When the Continental Congress met in Philadelphia, he was living on the Pennsylvania frontier, trying to reestablish his farm and family there. Whether ruled by Great Britain or eastern colonial elites, he was most concerned with the rights of poor and working people. Yet he and Washington would have agreed with the great British parliamentarian Edmund Burke, who, on hearing of events in the American colonies in 1774, lamented, "Clouds, indeed, and darkness, rest upon the future."

Chapter Review

MAKE IT STICK

 LearningCurve bedfordstmartins.com/hewittlawsonvalue
After reading the chapter, use LearningCurve to retain what you've read.

IDENTIFY KEY TERMS

Identify and explain the significance of each term below.

Albany Congress (p. 112)

Peace of Paris (p. 115)

Proclamation Line of 1763 (p. 117)

Regulators (p. 118)

benign neglect (p. 122)

Navigation Acts (p. 122)

Sugar Act (p. 122)

import duty (p. 122)

committee of correspondence (p. 123)

Stamp Act (p. 123)

Sons of Liberty (p. 124)

Townshend Act (p. 127)

Boston Massacre (p. 128)

Coercive Acts (Intolerable Acts) (p. 130)

Continental Congress (p. 130)

REVIEW & RELATE

Answer the focus questions from each section of the chapter.

1. How did the French and Indian War and the subsequent peace treaty affect relations between Britain and its North American subjects?

2. How did the French and Indian War and the increasing power of large landowners contribute to conflict between average colonists and colonial elites?

3. How did Britain's postwar policies lead to the emergence of unified colonial protests?

4. Why did British policymakers believe they were justified in seeking to gain greater control over Britain's North American colonies?

5. How and why did colonial resistance to British policies escalate in the decade following the conclusion of the French and Indian War?

6. How did internal social and economic divisions shape the colonial response to British policies?

ONLINE DOCUMENT PROJECTS

◆ **The Boston Massacre**
◆ **Defining Liberty, Defining America**

After reading the primary sources in these document sets, answer the **Interpret the Evidence** questions to help you analyze each of the documents, and then answer the **Put It in Context** question(s) to help you relate the documents to the topics and themes you read about in the chapter.

bedfordstmartins.com/hewittlawsonvalue

TIMELINE OF EVENTS

1754–1763	• French and Indian War
1754	• George Washington launches surprise attack on Fort Duquesne
	• Albany Congress convenes
1757	• William Pitt takes charge of British war effort
May 1763	• Pontiac launches pan-Indian revolt to drive out British
June 1763	• Peace of Paris
October 1763	• British establish Proclamation Line of 1763
December 1763	• Paxton Boys attack Conestoga Indians
1764	• Green Mountain Boys resist New York authorities
	• Sugar Act passed
1765	• Stamp Act passed
	• Stamp Act Congress convenes
1766	• Sandy Creek Association formed
	• Stamp Act repealed and Declaratory Act passed
1767	• Townshend Act passed
1770	• Boston Massacre
1771	• Battle of Alamance Creek, North Carolina
1773	• Boston Tea Party
1774	• Coercive Acts passed
	• Continental Congress convenes in Philadelphia

6

LearningCurve
✓ bedfordstmartins.com/hewittlawsonvalue
After reading the chapter, use LearningCurve
to retain what you've read.

Revolutions

1775–1783

AMERICAN HISTORIES

On November 30, 1774, Thomas Paine arrived in Philadelphia aboard a ship
from London. At age thirty-seven, Paine had failed at several occupations
and two marriages. But he was an impassioned writer. A pamphlet he wrote
caught the eye of Benjamin Franklin, who helped him secure a job on *The
Pennsylvania Magazine* just as tensions between the colonies and Great
Britain neared open conflict.

Born in 1737, Paine was raised in an English market town by parents who
owned a small grocery store and made whalebone corsets. The Paines
managed to send him to school for a few years before his father introduced
him to the trade of corset-making. Over the next dozen years, Paine also
worked as a seaman, a preacher, a teacher, and an excise (or tax) collector.
He drank heavily and beat both his wives. Yet despite his personal vices,
Paine tried to improve himself and the lot of other British workers. He taught
working-class children how to read and write and attended lectures on
science and politics in London. As an excise collector in 1762, he wrote a
pamphlet that argued for better pay and working conditions for tax
collectors. He was fired from his job, but Franklin convinced Paine to try his
luck in Philadelphia.

Paine quickly gained in-depth political knowledge of the conflicts between
the colonies and Great Britain and gained patrons among Philadelphia's
economic and political elite. When armed conflict with British troops erupted
in April 1775, colonial debates over whether to declare independence

intensified. Pamphlets were a popular means of influencing these debates, and Paine hoped to write one that would tip the balance in favor of independence. In January 1776, his pamphlet *Common Sense* did just that.

An instant success, *Common Sense* provided a rationale for independence and an emotional plea for creating a new democratic republic. Paine urged colonists not only to separate from England but also to establish a political structure that would ensure liberty and equality for all Americans: "A government of our own is our natural right," he concluded. "'Tis time to part."

When *Common Sense* was published in 1776, sixteen-year-old Deborah Sampson was working as a servant to Jeremiah and Susanna Thomas in Marlborough, Massachusetts. Indentured at the age of ten, she looked after the Thomases' five sons and worked hard in both the house and the fields. Jeremiah Thomas thought education was above the lot of servant girls, but Sampson insisted on reading whatever books she could find. However, her commitment to American independence likely developed less from reading and more from the fighting that raged in Massachusetts and drew male servants and the Thomas sons into the Continental Army in the 1770s.

When Deborah Sampson's term of service ended in 1778, she sought work as a weaver and then a teacher. In March 1782, she disguised herself as a man and enlisted in the Continental Army, which was then desperate for recruits. Her height and muscular frame allowed her to fool local recruiters, and she accepted the bounty paid to those who enlisted. But Deborah never reported for duty, and when her charade was discovered, she was forced to return the money.

In May 1782, Sampson enlisted a second time under the name Robert Shurtliff. To explain the absence of facial hair, she told the recruiter that she was only seventeen years old. For the next year, Sampson, disguised as Shurtliff, marched, fought, and lived with her Massachusetts regiment. Her ability to carry off the deception was helped by lax standards of hygiene: Soldiers rarely undressed fully to bathe, and most slept in their uniforms.

Even after the formal end of the war in March 1783, Sampson/Shurtliff continued to serve in the Continental Army. In the fall of 1783, she was sent to Philadelphia to help quash a mutiny by Continental soldiers angered over the army's failure to provide back pay. While there, Sampson/Shurtliff fell ill with a raging fever, and a doctor at a local army hospital discovered that "he" was a woman. He reported the news to General John Paterson, and Sampson was honorably discharged, having served the army faithfully for more than a year.

AS THE AMERICAN HISTORIES of Thomas Paine and Deborah Sampson demonstrate, the American Revolution transformed individual lives as well as the political life of the nation. Paine had failed financially and personally in England but gained

Slaves destroy a statue of King George III in New York City on July 9, 1776.   Library of Congress

fame in the colonies through his skills as a patriot pamphleteer. Sampson, who was forced into an early independence by her troubled family, excelled as a soldier. Still, while the American Revolution offered opportunities for some colonists, it promised hardship for others. Most Americans had to choose sides long before it was clear whether the colonists could defeat Great Britain, and the long years of conflict (1775–1783) took a toll on families and communities across the thirteen colonies. Over the course of a long and difficult war, could the patriots attract enough Tom Paines and Deborah Sampsons to secure independence and establish a new nation?

The Question of Independence

The Continental Congress that met to protest the Coercive Acts (see chapter 5) adjourned in October 1774, but delegates reconvened in May 1775. During the intervening months, patriot leaders honed their arguments for resisting British tyranny, and committees of correspondence circulated the latest news and debates. While leading patriots began to advocate resistance in the strongest possible terms, the eruption of armed clashes between British soldiers and local farmers fueled the argument for independence. It also led the Continental Congress to establish a Continental Army in June 1775. A year later, in July 1776, as the fighting continued, the congress finally declared independence.

Armed Conflict Erupts

As debates over independence intensified, the Sons of Liberty and other patriot groups not only spread propaganda against the British but also gathered and stored weapons and organized and trained local militia companies. Female patriots continued the boycott of British goods but began to manufacture bandages and bullets as well. Some northern colonists freed enslaved African Americans who agreed to enlist in the militia. Others kept close watch on the movements of British troops.

On April 18, 1775, Boston patriots observed British soldiers boarding boats in the harbor. The British were headed to Lexington, intending to confiscate guns and ammunition hidden there and in neighboring Concord and perhaps arrest patriot leaders. Hoping to warn his fellow patriots of the approaching soldiers, Paul Revere beat them to Lexington but was stopped on the road to Concord by the British. By that time, however, a network of riders was spreading the alarm. One of them alerted Concord residents of the impending danger.

Early in the morning of April 19, the first shots rang out on the village green of Lexington. After a brief exchange between British soldiers and local militiamen—known as minutemen for the speed with which they assembled—eight colonists lay dead. The British troops then moved on to Concord, where they uncovered and burned colonial supplies. However, patriots in nearby towns had now been alerted. Borrowing guerrilla tactics from American Indians, colonists hid behind trees, walls, and barns and battered the British soldiers as they marched back to Boston, killing 73 and wounding 200.

Word of the conflict traveled quickly. Outraged Bostonians attacked British troops and forced them to retreat to ships in the harbor. The victory was short-lived, however, and the British soon regained control of Boston. But colonial forces entrenched themselves on hills just north of the city. Then in May, Ethan Allen and his Green Mountain Boys from Vermont joined militias from Connecticut and Massachusetts to capture the British garrison at Fort Ticonderoga, New York. The battle for North America had begun.

When the Second Continental Congress convened in Philadelphia on May 10, 1775, the most critical question for delegates like Pennsylvania patriot John Dickinson was how to ensure time for discussion and negotiation. Armed conflict had erupted, but did that mean that independence should, or must, follow? Other delegates insisted that independence was the only appropriate response to armed attacks on colonial residents. Patrick Henry of Virginia declared, "Gentlemen may cry 'peace, peace' but there is no peace. The war is actually begun!"

Less than a month later, on June 16, British forces under General Sir William Howe attacked patriot fortifications on Breed's Hill and Bunker Hill, north of the city. The British won the day when patriots ran out of ammunition. But the redcoats—so called because of their bright red uniforms—suffered more than 1,000 casualties, while only half that number of patriots were killed or wounded. This costly victory allowed the British to maintain control of Boston for nine more months, but the heavy losses emboldened patriot militiamen.

Building a Continental Army

The Battle of Bunker Hill convinced the congress to establish an army for the defense of the colonies and appoint forty-three-year-old Brigadier General George Washington as commander in chief. More comfortable leading troops than debating politics, Washington gave up his seat at the Continental Congress and on June 23 headed to Cambridge, Massachusetts, to take command of ten companies of frontier marksmen along with militia companies already engaged in battle.

Since the Continental Congress had not yet proclaimed itself a national government, Washington depended largely on the willingness of local militia companies to accept his command and of individual colonies to supply soldiers, arms, and ammunition. Throughout the summer of 1775, Washington wrote dozens of letters to patriot political leaders, including delegates at the Continental Congress, detailing the army's urgent need for men, supplies, and discipline. He sought to remove incompetent officers and improve order among the troops, who spent too much time drinking, gambling, visiting prostitutes, and fighting with militiamen from other locales.

As he sought to forge a disciplined army, Washington and his officers developed a twofold military strategy. Concerned about British forces and their Indian allies in Canada and New York, they sought to drive the British out of Boston and to secure the colonies from attack by enemy forces farther north. In November 1775, American troops under General Richard Montgomery captured Montreal. However, the difficult trek in cold weather decimated the patriot reinforcements led by General Benedict Arnold, and American troops failed to dislodge the British from Quebec. Smallpox ravaged many of the survivors.

Despite the disastrous outcome of the invasion of Canada, the Continental Army secured important victories in the winter of 1775–1776. To improve Washington's position in eastern Massachusetts, General Henry Knox retrieved weapons captured at Fort Ticonderoga. In March, Washington positioned the forty-three cannons on Dorchester Heights and surprised the British with a bombardment that drove them from Boston. General Howe was forced to retreat with his troops to Nova Scotia.

Reasons for Caution and for Action

As the British retreated from Boston, the war had already spread into Virginia. In the spring of 1775, local militias had forced Lord Dunmore, Virginia's royal governor, to take refuge on British ships in Norfolk harbor. Dunmore encouraged white servants and black slaves to join him there, and thousands did so. When Dunmore led his army back into Virginia in November 1775, hundreds of black men fought with British troops at the Battle of Great Bridge. Once he reclaimed the governor's mansion in Williamsburg, Dunmore issued an official proclamation that declared "all indent[ur]ed Servants, Negroes or others (appertaining to Rebels)" to be free if they were "able and willing to bear Arms" for the British.

Dunmore's Proclamation, which offered freedom to slaves willing to fight for the crown, heightened concerns among patriot leaders about the consequences of declaring independence. Although they wanted liberty for themselves, most did not want to disrupt the plantation economy or the existing social hierarchy. Could the colonies throw off the shackles of British tyranny without loosening other bonds at the same time? Given these concerns, many delegates at the Continental Congress, which included large planters, successful merchants, and professional men, hesitated to act.

Moreover, some still hoped for a negotiated settlement. But the king and Parliament refused to compromise in any way with colonies that they considered to be in rebellion. Instead, in December 1775, the king prohibited any negotiation or trade with the colonies, adding further weight to the claims of radicals that independence was a necessity. The January 1776 publication of Tom Paine's *Common Sense*, which sold more than 120,000 copies in three months, helped turn the tide toward independence as well.

Paine rooted his arguments both in biblical stories familiar to American readers and in newer scientific analogies, such as Isaac Newton's theory of gravity. It was Paine's ability to wield both religious and scientific ideas—appealing to the spirit and the intellect—that made *Common Sense* attractive to diverse groups of colonists. Within weeks of its publication, George Washington wrote to a friend that "the sound Doctrine and unanswerable reasoning containd [in] Common Sense" would convince colonists of the "Propriety of a Separation." Farmers and artisans also applauded *Common Sense*, debating its claims at taverns and coffeehouses, which had become increasingly popular venues for political discussion in the 1760s and 1770s.

By the spring of 1776, a growing number of patriots believed that independence was necessary. Colonies began to take control of their legislatures and instruct their delegates to the Continental Congress to support independence. The congress also sent an agent to France to request economic and military assistance for the patriot cause. And in May, the congress advised colonies that had not yet done so to establish independent governments.

Declaring Independence

Taken together, the spread of armed conflict and the rationale offered in *Common Sense* convinced patriots that the time to declare independence was at hand. In early June 1776, Richard Henry Lee of Virginia introduced a motion to the Continental Congress, resolving that "these United Colonies are, and of right ought to be, Free and Independent States." A heated debate followed in which Lee and John Adams argued passionately for independence. Eventually, even more cautious delegates, like Robert Livingston of New York, were convinced. Livingston concluded that "they should yield to the torrent if they hoped to direct it." He then joined Adams, Thomas Jefferson, Benjamin Franklin, and Roger Sherman on a committee to draft a formal statement justifying independence.

The thirty-three-year-old Jefferson took the lead in preparing the declaration. Building on ideas expressed by Paine, Adams, Lee, and George Mason, he drew on language used in the dozens of local "declarations" written earlier by town meetings, county officials, and colonial assemblies. The Virginia Declaration of Rights drafted by Mason in May 1776, for example, claimed that "all men are born equally free and independent, and have certain inherent natural Rights." Central to many of these documents was the contract theory of government proposed by the seventeenth-century British philosopher John Locke. He argued that sovereignty resided in the people, who submitted voluntarily to laws and authorities in exchange for protection of their life, liberty, and property. The people could therefore reconstitute or overthrow a government that abused its powers. Jefferson summarized this argument and then listed the abuses and crimes perpetrated by King George III against the colonies, which justified patriots' decision to break their contract with British authorities.

Once prepared, the **Declaration of Independence** was then debated and revised. In the final version, all references to slavery were removed. But delegates agreed to list among the abuses suffered by the colonies the fact that the king "excited domestic insurrections amongst us," referring to the threat posed by Dunmore to the institution of slavery. On July 2, 1776, delegates from twelve colonies approved the Declaration, with only New York abstaining. Independence was publicly proclaimed on July 4 when the Declaration was published as a broadside to be circulated throughout the colonies, although such an act was tantamount to treason.

> **REVIEW & RELATE**
>
> • What challenges did Washington face when he was given command of the Continental Army?
> • How and why did proponents of independence prevail in the debates that preceded the publication of the Declaration of Independence?

Choosing Sides

Probably no more than half of American colonists actively supported the patriots. Perhaps a fifth actively supported the British, including many merchants and most officials appointed by the king and Parliament. The rest tried to stay neutral or were largely indifferent unless the war came to their doorstep. Both patriots and loyalists included men and women from all classes and races and from both rural and urban areas.

Recruiting Supporters

Men who took up arms against the British before independence was declared and the women who supported them clearly demonstrated their commitment to the patriot cause. In some colonies, patriots had organized local committees, courts, and assemblies to assume governance should British officials lose their authority. White servants and enslaved blacks in Virginia who fled to British ships or marched with Lord Dunmore made their loyalties known as well. Some Indians, too, declared their allegiance early in the conflict. In May 1775, Guy Johnson, the British superintendent for Indian affairs for the northern colonies, left Albany, New York, and sought refuge in Canada. He was accompanied by 120 British loyalists and 90 Mohawk warriors. The latter were led by the mission-educated chief of the Mohawks, Joseph Brant (Thayendanegea), who had translated the Anglican prayer book into Mohawk and who had fought with the British in the French and Indian War.

The Continental Congress, like Johnson, recognized the importance of Indians to the outcome of any colonial war. It appointed commissioners from the "United Colonies" to meet with representatives of the six nations of the Iroquois Confederacy in August 1775. While Brant's group of Mohawk warriors had already committed to supporting the British, some Oneida Indians, influenced by missionary and patriot sympathizer Samuel Kirkland, wanted to support the colonies. Others, however, urged neutrality, at least for the moment.

Once independence was declared, there was far more pressure on all groups to choose sides. The stance of political and military leaders and soldiers was clear. But to win against Great Britain required the support of a large portion of the civilian population as well. As battle lines shifted back and forth across New England, the Middle Atlantic region, and the South, many civilians caught up in the fighting were faced with difficult choices.

Many colonists who remained loyal to the king found safe haven in cities like New York, Newport, and Charleston, which remained under British control throughout much of the war. **Loyalist** men were welcomed as reinforcements to the British army. Still, those who made their loyalist sympathies clear risked a good deal. When British troops were forced out of cities or towns they had temporarily occupied, many loyalists faced harsh reprisals. Patriots had no qualms about invading the homes of loyalists, punishing women and children, and destroying or confiscating property. Grace Galloway was denounced by former friends and evicted from her Philadelphia home after her loyalist husband, Joseph, fled to New York City in 1777.

Many loyalists were members of the economic and political elite, but others came from ordinary backgrounds.

 Online Document Project   **Loyalists in the American Revolution**
bedfordstmartins.com/hewittlawsonvalue

Tenants, small farmers, and slaves joined the loyalist cause in defiance of their landlords, their owners, and wealthy planters. The Hudson valley was home to many poorer loyalists, whose sympathy for the British was heightened by the patriot commitments of their wealthy landlords. When the fighting moved south, many former Regulators (see chapter 5) also supported the British as a result of their hostility to patriot leaders among North Carolina's eastern elite.

Perhaps most importantly, the majority of Indian nations ultimately sided with the British. The Mohawk, Seneca, and Cayuga nations in the North and the Cherokee and Creek nations in the South were among Great Britain's leading allies. Although British efforts to limit colonial migration, such as the Proclamation Line of 1763, had failed, most Indian nations still believed that a British victory offered the only hope of ending further encroachments on their territory.

Choosing Neutrality

Early in the war, many Indian nations proclaimed their neutrality. The Delaware and Shawnee nations, caught between British and American forces in the Ohio River valley, were especially eager to stay out of the fighting. The Shawnee chief Cornstalk worked tirelessly to maintain his nation's neutrality, but American soldiers killed him under a flag of truce in 1777. Eventually the Shawnees, like the Delawares, chose to ally with the British side after patriot forces refused to accept their claims of neutrality.

Colonists who sought to remain neutral during the war also faced hostility and danger. Some 80,000 Quakers, Mennonites, Amish, Shakers, and Moravians considered war immoral and embraced neutrality. These men refused to bear arms, hire substitutes, or pay taxes to new state governments. The largest number of religious pacifists lived in Pennsylvania. Despite Quakerism's deep roots there, pacifists were treated as suspect by both patriots and loyalists.

In June 1778, Pennsylvania authorities jailed nine Mennonite farmers who refused to take an oath of allegiance to the revolutionary government. Their worldly goods were sold by the state, leaving their wives and children destitute. Quakers were routinely fined and imprisoned for refusing to support the patriot cause and harassed by British authorities in the areas they controlled. At the same time, Quaker meetings regularly disciplined members who offered aid to either side, disowning more than 1,700 members during the Revolution. Betsy Ross was among those disciplined when her husband joined the patriot forces and she sewed flags for the Continental Army.

Committing to Independence

After July 4, 1776, the decision to support independence took on new meaning. If the United States failed to win the war, all those who actively supported the cause could be considered traitors. The families of Continental soldiers faced especially difficult decisions as the conflict spread across the colonies and soldiers moved farther and farther from home. Men too old or too young to fight proved their patriotism by gathering arms and ammunition and patrolling local communities.

Meanwhile some female patriots accompanied their husbands or fiancés as camp followers, providing food, laundry, sewing, and other material resources to needy soldiers. Most patriot women remained at home, however, and demonstrated their commitment to independence by raising funds, gathering information, and sending clothes, bedding, and other goods to soldiers at the front. The Continental Army was desperately short of supplies from the beginning of the war. Northern women were urged to increase cloth production, while farm women in the South were asked to plant crops to feed the soldiers. The response was overwhelming. Women in Hartford, Connecticut, produced 1,000 coats and vests and 1,600 shirts in 1776 alone. Mary Fraier of Chester County, Pennsylvania, was one of many women who collected clothing door-to-door and then washed and mended it before delivering it to troops stationed nearby. Other women opened their homes to soldiers wounded in battle or ill with fevers, dysentery, and other diseases.

Some African American women also became ardent patriots. Phillis Wheatley of Boston, whose owners taught her to read and write, published a collection of poems in 1776 and sent a copy to General Washington. She urged readers to recognize Africans as children of God:

> Remember Christians, Negroes, black as Cain,
> May be refin'd, and join th' angelic train

Rewarded with freedom by her master, Wheatley was among a small number of blacks who actively supported the patriot cause. Of course, the majority of black Americans labored as slaves in the South. While some joined the British in hopes of gaining their freedom, most were not free to choose sides.

REVIEW & RELATE

- How did colonists choose sides during the Revolutionary War? What factors influenced their decisions?
- Why did so many Indian tribes try to stay neutral during the conflict? Why was it so difficult for Indians to remain neutral?

Fighting for Independence

After July 4, 1776, battles between British and colonial troops intensified, and the patriots suffered a series of military defeats that must have made some wonder about the wisdom of undertaking a revolution. It was more than five months after independence was declared before patriots celebrated a military victory against the British. In 1777, however, the tide turned for the Continental Army, although British forces remained formidable. A year later, it was clear that victory would not be easily won and that each side needed support from women on the home front as well as men on the battlefront.

British Troops Gain Early Victories

In the summer of 1776, when General Washington tried to lead his army out of Boston to confront British troops en route to New York City, many soldiers deserted and returned home. They believed that New York men should defend New York. Among the soldiers who remained with Washington, many were landless laborers whose wives and sisters followed the troops as their only means of support. Although Washington deemed these "camp followers" undesirable, the few hundred women provided critical services to ordinary soldiers. Ultimately, Washington arrived in New York with 19,000 men, many of whom were poorly armed and poorly trained and some of whom were coerced into service by local committees of safety.

The ragtag Continental force faced a formidable foe with a powerful navy and a far larger and better-trained army. Throughout the summer, British ships sailed into New York harbor or anchored off the coast of Long Island. General Howe, hoping to overwhelm the colonists, ordered 10,000 troops to march into the city in the weeks immediately after the Declaration of Independence was signed. But the Continental Congress rejected Howe's offer of peace and a royal pardon.

So Howe prepared to take control of New York City by force and then march up the Hudson valley, isolating New York and New England from the rest of the rebellious colonies. He was aided by some 8,000 Hessian mercenaries (German soldiers being paid to fight for the British) and naval reinforcements under the command of Admiral Richard Howe. On August 27, 1776, British forces clashed with a far smaller contingent of Continentals on Long Island. More than 1,500 patriots were killed or wounded in the fierce fighting, diminishing the army's strength even further.

By November, the British had captured Fort Lee in New Jersey and attacked the Continental Army at Fort Washington, north of New York City. The large community of loyalists in the New York/New Jersey region served as ready hosts for General Howe and his officers, and ordinary redcoats survived by looting the stores, farms, and homes of patriots. Meanwhile Washington led his weary troops and camp followers into Pennsylvania, while the Continental Congress, fearing a British attack on Philadelphia, fled to Baltimore.

Although General Howe might have ended the patriot threat right then by a more aggressive campaign, he was interested primarily in wearing down the Continental Army so that the colonies would plead for peace. Neither he nor Washington engaged in full-scale frontal assaults. Washington did not have the troops or arms to do so, but he also hoped that the British would accept American independence once they saw the enormous effort it would take to defeat the colonies.

The British Burn New York City, 1776   This print by François Xavier Haberman shows several buildings along a New York City street set ablaze by the British troops of General William Howe on September 19, 1776. It also depicts citizens being beaten by redcoats while African slaves engage in looting. The British promised slaves their freedom if they opposed the patriots.   Library of Congress

Patriots Prevail in New Jersey

The Continental Army had not gained a single military victory between July 1776, when the colonies declared independence, and December. Fortunately for Washington, Howe followed the European tradition of waiting out the winter months and returning to combat after the spring thaw. This tactic gave the patriots the opportunity to regroup, repair weapons and wagons, and recruit soldiers. Yet Washington was not eager to face the cold and discomfort of the winter with troops discouraged by repeated defeats and retreats.

Camped in eastern Pennsylvania, Washington discovered that General Howe had sent Hessian troops to occupy the city of Trenton, New Jersey, just across the Delaware River. On Christmas Eve, Washington crossed the river with some 2,500 soldiers and attacked Trenton. The Continentals quickly routed the surprised Hessians. Then they marched on Princeton, where they battled three regiments of regular British troops, defeating them on January 3, 1777. The British army retreated from New Jersey, settling back into New York City, and the Continental Congress returned to Philadelphia. By January 1777, it seemed clear to both sides that the conflict would indeed be harder, more costly, and more deadly than anyone had imagined in the spring of 1775.

A Critical Year of Warfare

The British and Continental armies emerged from their winter camps in the spring of 1777. The British forces, including regular army units, American loyalists, Indian allies, Hessians, and naval men-of-war, were concentrated largely in New York City and Canada. The Continental forces, numbering fewer than 5,000 men, were entrenched near Morristown, New Jersey, far from the patriot centers of New England and from the coastal areas controlled by the British army and navy. Although the Continental Congress had returned to Philadelphia, it feared that the British would seek to capture the city and split the United States in two.

General Howe also believed that the key to victory was capturing Philadelphia, and he hoped that success there might lead the patriots to surrender. Washington's force was too small to defeat Howe's army, but it delayed his advance on the capital city by attacks along the way. En route, Howe learned that he was still expected to reinforce General John Burgoyne's soldiers, who were advancing south from Canada. Too late to redirect his efforts, Howe continued to Philadelphia and captured it in September 1777. Meanwhile Burgoyne and his 7,200 troops had regained control of Fort Ticonderoga on July 7. He continued south along the Hudson valley, but by late July his forces stalled as they waited for supplies from Canada and reinforcements from Howe and General Barry St. Leger.

In July, St. Leger had marched east through New York State while Joseph Brant and his sister Molly Brant, a powerful Indian leader in her own right, gathered a force of Mohawk, Seneca, and Cayuga warriors to support the British forces. But on August 6, they suffered a stunning defeat. At Oriskany, New York, a band of German American farmers led by General Nicholas Herkimer held off the British advance, allowing General Arnold to reach nearby Fort Stanwix with reinforcements. On August 23, the British and Indian troops were forced to retreat to Canada (Map 6.1).

General Howe's reinforcements never materialized, and Burgoyne now faced a brutal onslaught from patriot militiamen. Vermont's Green Mountain Boys, Continental soldiers under the command of Generals Horatio Gates and Benedict Arnold, and their

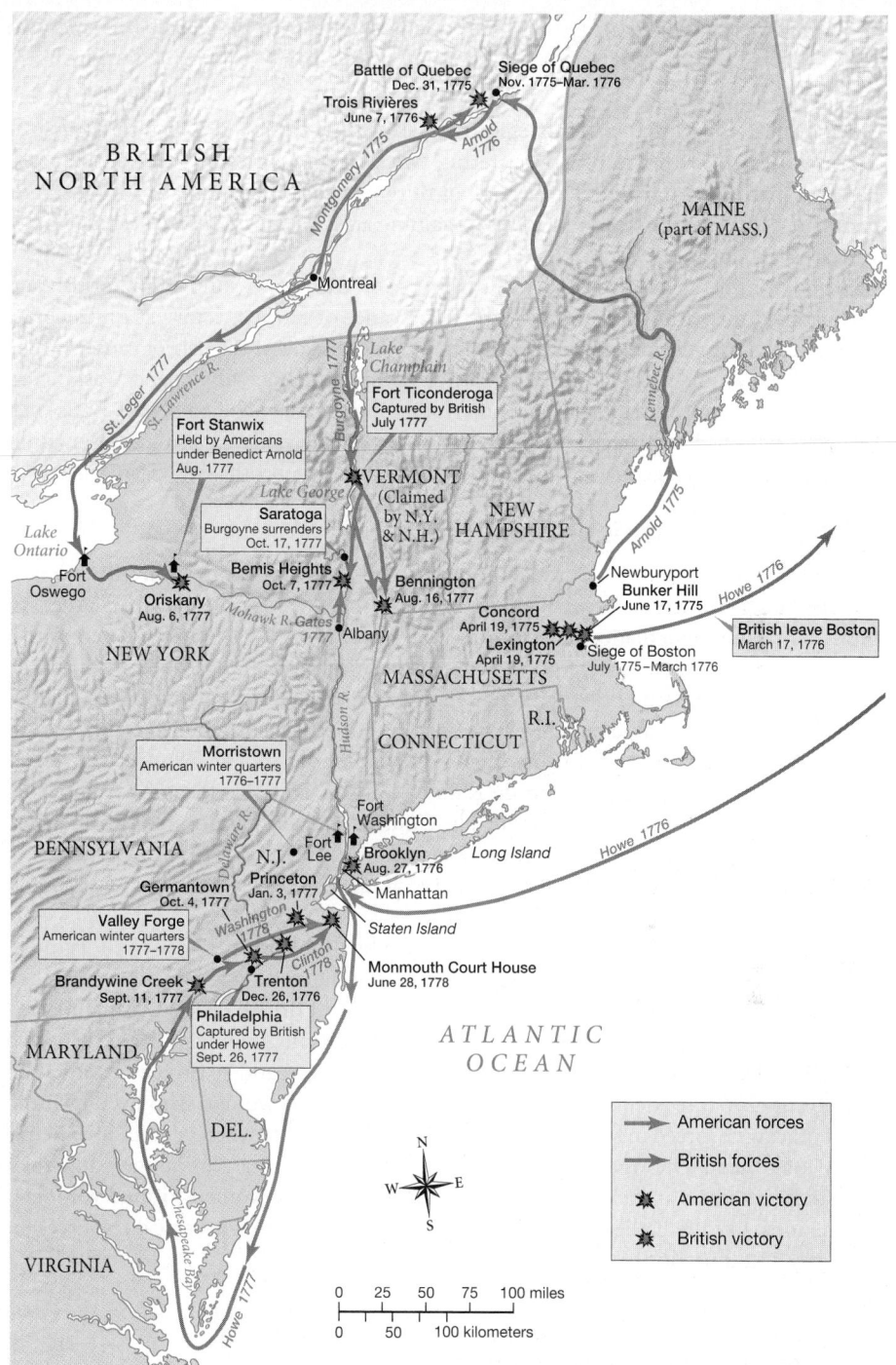

MAP 6.1
The War in the North, 1775–1778 After early battles in Massachusetts, patriots invaded Canada but failed to capture Quebec. The British army captured New York City in 1776 and Philadelphia in 1777, but New Jersey remained a battle zone through 1778. Meanwhile General Burgoyne secured Canada for Britain and then headed south, but his forces were defeated by patriots at the crucial Battle of Saratoga.

Oneida allies also poured into the region. In September, patriots defeated the British at Freeman's Farm, with the British suffering twice the casualties of the Continentals. Fighting intensified in early October, when Burgoyne lost a second battle at Freeman's Farm. Ten days later, he surrendered his remaining army of 5,800 men to General Gates at nearby Saratoga, New York.

The Continental Army's victory in the **Battle of Saratoga** stunned the British and strengthened the patriots. It undercut the significance of Howe's victory at Philadelphia and indicated the general's misunderstanding of the character of the patriot cause and the nature of the war he was fighting. The patriot victory gave hope to General Washington as his troops dug in at Valley Forge for another long winter and to members of the Continental Congress who had temporarily retreated to York, Pennsylvania. It also gave Benjamin Franklin greater leverage to convince French officials to support the American cause.

Patriots Gain Critical Assistance

Despite significant victories in the fall of 1777, the following winter proved especially difficult for Continental forces. The quarters at **Valley Forge** were again marked by bitter cold, poor food, inadequate clothing, and scarce supplies. Discipline deteriorated, and many recent recruits were poorly trained. Critical assistance arrived through the voluntary efforts of Baron Friedrich von Steuben, a Prussian officer recruited by Benjamin Franklin, who took charge of drilling soldiers. Other officers experienced in European warfare also joined the patriot cause during the winter of 1777–1778: the Marquis de Lafayette of France, Johann Baron de Kalb of Bavaria, and Thaddeus Kosciusko and Casimir Count Pulaski, both of Poland. The Continental Army continued to be plagued by problems of recruitment, discipline, wages, and supplies. But the contributions of Steuben, Lafayette, and other foreign volunteers, along with the leadership of Washington and his officers, sustained the military effort.

Patriots on the home front were also plagued by problems in 1777–1778. Families living in battlefield areas were especially vulnerable to the shifting fortunes of war. When British troops captured Philadelphia in the fall of 1777, a British officer commandeered the house of Elizabeth Drinker, a well-to-do Quaker matron. An angry Drinker reported that the officer moved in with "3 Horses 2 Cows 2 Sheep and 3 Turkeys" along with "3 Servants 2 White Men and one Negro Boy." Meanwhile women who lived far from the conflict were forced to fend for themselves as soldiers moved wherever the Continental Army took them. The wives of political leaders also faced long years alone while their husbands remained at their posts. To hasten the end, many women formed voluntary associations, like the Ladies Association of Philadelphia, to provide critical resources for the army and thus aid the patriot cause.

 Online Document Project   **Women in the Revolution**
   bedfordstmartins.com/hewittlawsonvalue

While most women worked tirelessly on the home front, some cast their fate with the army. Camp followers continued to provide critical services to the military, including cooking, washing, sewing, and nursing. They suffered along with the troops in the face of scarce supplies and harsh weather and depended like the soldiers on food, clothing, and bedding supplied by female volunteers in Philadelphia, Boston, Baltimore, and other cities.

Women with sufficient courage and resources served as spies and couriers for British and Continental forces. Lydia Darragh, a wealthy Philadelphian, eavesdropped on conversations among the British officers who occupied her house and then carried detailed notes to Washington hidden in the folds of her dress. Some women, like Nancy Hart Morgan of Georgia, took more direct action. Morgan protected her backcountry home from half a dozen British soldiers by lulling them into a sense of security at dinner, hiding their guns, and shooting two before neighbors came to hang the rest.

Some patriot women took up arms on the battlefield. A few, such as Margaret Corbin, accompanied their husbands to the front lines and were thrust into battle. When her husband was killed in battle at Fort Washington in November 1776, Corbin took his place loading and firing cannons until the fort fell to the British. In addition, a small number of women, like Deborah Sampson, disguised themselves as men and enlisted as soldiers.

Surviving on the Home Front

Whether black or white, enslaved or free, women and children faced hardship, uncertainty, loneliness, and fear as a result of the war. Even those who did not directly engage enemy troops took on enormous burdens during the conflict. Farm wives had to take on the tasks of plowing or planting in addition to their normal domestic duties. In cities, women worked ceaselessly to find sufficient food, wood, candles, and cloth to maintain themselves and their children. One desperate wife, Mary Donnelly, wrote, "[I was] afraid to open my Eyes on the Daylight [lest] I should hear my infant cry for Bread and not have it in my power to relieve him."

As the war spread, women watched as Continental and British forces slaughtered cattle and hogs for food, stole corn and other crops or burned them to keep the enemy from obtaining supplies, looted houses and shops, and kidnapped or liberated slaves and servants. Some home invasions turned savage. Both patriot and loyalist papers in New York, Philadelphia, and Charleston reported cases of rape.

Despite the desperate circumstances, most women knew they had to act on their own behalf to survive. Faced with merchants who hoarded goods in hopes of making greater profits when prices rose, housewives raided stores and warehouses and took coffee, sugar, and other items they needed. Others learned as much as they could about family finances so that they could submit reports to local officials if their houses, farms, or businesses were damaged or looted. Growing numbers of women banded together to assist one another, to help more impoverished families, and to supply troops badly in need of clothes, food, bandages, and bullets.

(**REVIEW & RELATE**)

- How did the patriot forces fare in 1776? How and why did the tide of war turn in 1777?
- What role did colonial women and foreign men play in the conflict in the early years of the war?

Governing in Revolutionary Times

Amid the constant upheavals of war, patriot leaders established governments to replace those abolished by declaring independence. At the national level, responsibilities ranged from coordinating and funding military operations to developing diplomatic relations with foreign countries and Indian nations. At the state level, constitutions had to be drafted and approved, laws enforced, and military needs assessed and met. Whether state or national, new governments had to assure their followers that they were not simply replacing old forms of oppression with new ones. Yet few states moved to eliminate the most oppressive institution in the nation, slavery.

Colonies Become States

For most of the war, the Continental Congress acted in lieu of a national government while the delegates worked to devise a more permanent structure. But the congress had little authority of its own and depended mainly on states for funds and manpower. Delegates did draft the **Articles of Confederation** in 1777 and submitted them to the states for approval. Eight of the thirteen states ratified the plan for a national government by mid-1778. But nearly three more years passed before the last state, Maryland, approved the Articles. The lack of a central government meant that state governments played a critical role throughout the war.

Even before the Continental Congress declared American independence, some colonies had forced royal officials to flee and established new state governments. Some states abided by the regulations in their colonial charters or by English common law. Others, including Delaware, South Carolina, Virginia, New Jersey, and Pennsylvania, created new governments based on a written constitution. Because the earliest constitutions were written in the midst of war, they were often completed in haste, sometimes by legislative bodies without any specific authorization and without popular approval of the final document.

These constitutions reflected the fear of centralized power that emerged from the struggle against British tyranny. In Pennsylvania, radical patriots influenced by Tom Paine developed one of the most democratic constitutions, enhancing the power of voters and legislators and limiting the power of the executive branch. The constitution established only one legislative house, elected by popular vote, and the governor was replaced by an executive council. Those elected to the legislature could not serve for more than four in any seven years to discourage the formation of a political aristocracy in the state. Although Pennsylvania's constitution was among the most radical, all states limited centralized power in some way.

Finally, most states, building on the model offered by Virginia, included in their constitutions a bill of rights that ensured citizens freedom of the press, freedom of elections, speedy trials by one's peers, humane punishments, and the right to form militias. Some state constitutions expanded these rights to include freedom of speech and assembly, the right to petition and to bear arms, and equal protection of the laws. The New Jersey constitution, written in 1776, enfranchised all free inhabitants who met the property qualifications, thereby allowing some single or widowed women and free blacks to vote in local and state elections. This surprising decision was apparently made with little debate or dissent.

Patriots Divide over Slavery

Although state constitutions were revolutionary in many respects, few of them addressed the issue of slavery. Only Vermont abolished slavery in its 1777 constitution. Legislators in Pennsylvania approved a gradual abolition law by which slaves born after 1780 could claim their freedom at age twenty-eight. In Massachusetts, two slaves sued for their freedom in county courts in 1780–1781. Quock Walker, who had been promised his freedom by a former master, sued his current master to gain manumission (release from slavery). About the same time, an enslaved woman, Mumbet, who was the widow of a Revolutionary soldier, initiated a similar case. Mumbet won her case and changed her name to Elizabeth Freeman. When Walker's owner appealed the local court's decision to free his slave, the Massachusetts Supreme Court cited the Mumbet case and ruled that slavery conflicted with the state constitution, which declared "all men . . . free and equal." Walker, too, was freed.

In southern states, however, slaves had little recourse to the law. No state south of Pennsylvania abolished the institution of slavery. And southerners held about 400,000 of the nation's 450,000 slaves. In states such as Virginia, the Carolinas, and Georgia, life for enslaved women and men grew increasingly harsh during the war. Because British forces promised freedom to blacks who fought with them, slave owners and patriot armies in the South did everything possible to ensure that African Americans did not make it behind British lines. The thousands who did manage to flee to British-controlled areas were often left to defend themselves when the redcoats retreated. There were exceptions. Lord Dunmore took a few thousand blacks with him when he fled Virginia in 1776, and British forces under General Sir Henry Clinton carried some 20,000 African Americans aboard ships retreating from Charleston and Savannah in 1781.

Despite the uncertain prospects for African Americans, the American Revolution dealt a blow to the institution of slavery. For many blacks, Revolutionary ideals required the end of slavery. Northern free black communities grew rapidly during and after the war, especially in seaport cities like New York, Philadelphia, and Boston where labor was in high demand. In the South, too, thousands of slaves gained freedom during the war, either by joining the British or by fleeing in the midst of battlefield chaos. As many as one-quarter of South Carolina's slaves had emancipated themselves by the end of the Revolution. Yet as the Continental Congress worked toward developing a framework for a national government, few delegates considered slavery or its abolition a significant issue.

Elizabeth "Mumbet" Freeman
This portrait of Elizabeth "Mumbet" Freeman was painted on ivory by Susan Anne Ridley Sedgwick in 1811 when Freeman was sixty-nine. The first slave to be freed in Massachusetts as a result of a court case, she later worked as a domestic servant for her attorney, Theodore Sedgwick, Susan Ridley Sedgwick's father-in-law.
© Massachusetts Historical Society, Boston/The Bridgeman Art Library

France Allies with the Patriots

The Continental Congress considered an alliance with France far more critical to patriot success than the issue of slavery. French financial and military support could aid the patriots immensely, and France's traditional rivalry with Great Britain made an alliance plausible.

For France, defeat of the British would mean increased trade with North America and redressing the balance of power in Europe, where Great Britain had gained the upper hand since France's defeat in the French and Indian War. Indeed, in 1775 the French government had secretly provided funds to smuggle military supplies to the colonies. In December 1776, the Continental Congress sent Benjamin Franklin to Paris to serve as an unofficial liaison for the newly independent United States. Franklin was enormously successful, securing supplies and becoming a favorite among the French aristocracy and ordinary citizens alike.

But the French were initially unwilling to forge a formal compact with the upstart patriots. Only when the Continental Army defeated General Burgoyne at Saratoga in October 1777 did King Louis XVI agree to an official alliance. By February 1778, Franklin had secured an agreement that approved trading rights between the United States and all French possessions. France then recognized the United States as an independent nation, relinquished French territorial claims on mainland North America, and sent troops to reinforce the Continental Army. In return, the United States promised to defend French holdings in the Caribbean. A year later, Spain allied itself with France to protect its own North American holdings.

British leaders, infuriated by the alliance, declared war on France. Yet doing so ensured that military conflicts would spread well beyond North America as French forces attacked British outposts in Gibraltar, the Bay of Bengal, Senegal in West Africa, and Grenada in the West Indies. British military expenditures skyrocketed from £4 million in 1775 to £20 million in 1782. Meanwhile, in addition to their attacks on British outposts, the French supplied the United States with military officers, weapons, funds, and critical naval resources. Spain contributed by capturing British forts in West Florida and using New Orleans as a base for privateering expeditions against British ships.

Faced with this new alliance, Britain's prime minister, Lord North (1771–1782), decided to concentrate British forces in New York City. This tactic forced the British army to abandon Philadelphia and return the city to patriot control in the summer of 1778. For the remainder of the war, New York City provided the sole British stronghold in the North, serving as a supply center and prisoner-of-war camp. At the same time, the American cause gained the support of the French navy, a critical addition given the limited state of American naval forces.

Raising Armies and Funds

The French alliance did create one unintended problem for the Continental Army. When Americans heard that France was sending troops, fewer men volunteered for military service, even when bounties were offered. Others took the bounty and then failed to report for duty. Local officials had the authority to draft men into the army or to accept substitutes for draftees. By the late 1770s, some draftees forced enslaved men to take their place; others hired landless laborers, the handicapped, or the mentally unfit as substitutes.

As the war spread south and west in 1778–1779, Continental forces were stretched thin, and enlistments faltered further. Soldiers faced injuries, disease, and shortages of food and ammunition. Soldiers also risked capture by the British, one of the worst fates to befall a Continental. Most patriot prisoners were held in jails in New York City or on ships in the harbor under abusive, unsanitary conditions. Colonel Ethan Allen, a captive for two and a half years, described the filthy accommodations, inadequate water, and horrid stench of the British prisons and noted the "hellish delight and triumph of the tories . . . exulting over the dead bodies of their murdered countrymen." A few brave women like Elizabeth Burgin carried food and other supplies to patriot prisoners of war. Altogether, between 8,000 and 11,500 patriots died in British prisons in New York— more than died in battle.

The Continental Congress could do little to aid prisoners or their families, given the financial problems it faced. With no authority to impose taxes on American citizens, the congress had to find other ways to meet its financial responsibilities. It borrowed money from wealthy patriots, accepted loans from France and the Netherlands, and printed money of its own—some $200 million by 1780. However, money printed by the states was still used far more widely than were Continental dollars. "Continentals" depreciated so quickly that by late 1780 it took one hundred continentals to buy one silver dollar's worth of goods.

The situation in Philadelphia, the seat of national government, demonstrated the difficulties caused by inflation. In January 1779, housewives, sailors, and artisans gathered on the cold streets to protest high prices and low wages. Although officials tried to regulate prices, riots erupted and flour merchants were especially targeted by mobs of women and young people. By October, Philadelphia militiamen joined the protests, marching on the house of James Wilson, a Philadelphia lawyer who sided with merchants accused of hoarding goods. Hours of rioting followed, and eventually fifteen militiamen were arrested and fined. But in the following days, city officials distributed much-needed food to the poor. The Fort Wilson riot echoed events in towns and cities across the young nation.

The congress finally improved its financial standing slightly by using a $6 million loan from France to back certificates issued to wealthy patriots. Meanwhile states raised money through taxes to provide funds for government operations, backing for its paper money, and other expenses. Most residents found such taxes incredibly burdensome given wartime inflation, and even the most patriotic began to protest further efforts to squeeze money out of them. Thus the financial status of the new nation remained precarious.

Indian Affairs and Land Claims

The congress also sought to settle land claims in the western regions of the nation and build alliances with additional Indian nations. The two issues were intertwined, and both were difficult to resolve. Most Indian nations had long-standing complaints against colonists who intruded on their lands, and many patriot leaders made it clear that independence would mean further expansion into western lands.

In the late 1770s, British forces and their Indian allies fought bitter battles against patriot militias and Continental forces all along the frontier. Each side destroyed property, ruined crops, and killed civilians. In the summer and fall of 1778, Indian and American civilians suffered through a series of brutal attacks in Wyoming, Pennsylvania; Onoquaga, New York (Brant's home community); and Cherry Valley, New York. Patriots and Indians also battled along the Virginia frontier after pioneer and militia leader Daniel Boone established a fort there in 1775.

In the South, 6,000 patriot troops laid waste to Cherokee villages in the Appalachian Mountains in retaliation for the killing of white intruders along the Watauga River by a renegade Cherokee warrior, Dragging Canoe. Yet a cousin of Dragging Canoe, Nancy Ward (Nanye-hi), who had married a white trader, remained sympathetic to the patriot cause. During the Revolution, she warned patriots of pending attacks by pro-British Cherokee warriors in 1776 and 1780, allowing the patriots to launch their own attacks. Ward apparently believed that white settlement was inevitable and that winning the friendship of patriots was the best way to ensure the survival of the Cherokee nation. Hers, however, was a minority voice among frontier Indians.

Much western land had already been claimed by individual states like Virginia, Massachusetts, Connecticut, New York, and Georgia. States with western claims hoped to use the lands to reward soldiers and expand their settlements. Maryland spoke for states without such claims, arguing that if such lands were "wrested from the common enemy by the blood and treasure of the thirteen States," they should be considered "common property, subject to be parcelled out by Congress into free and independent governments." In 1780 New York State finally ceded its western claims to the Continental Congress, and Connecticut and Massachusetts followed suit.

With land disputes settled, Maryland ratified the Articles of Confederation in March 1781, and a new national government was finally formed. But the congress's guarantee that western lands would be "disposed of for the common benefit of the United States" ensured continued conflicts with Indians.

REVIEW & RELATE

• What values and concerns shaped state governments during the Revolutionary War?

• What issues and challenges did the Continental Congress face even after the French joined the patriot side?

Winning the War and the Peace

From 1778 to 1781, the battlefront in the Revolution moved south and west. As conflicts with Britain and its Indian allies intensified along the western frontier, British troops reinforced by African American fugitives fought patriots in the Carolinas and Georgia. In the final years of the war, the patriots' ability to achieve victory rested on a combination of superb strategy, alliances with France and Spain, and the continued material support of affluent men and women. However, even after Britain's surrender in October 1781, the war dragged on while peace terms were negotiated. The celebrations of victory following the signing of a peace treaty were tempered by protests among Continental soldiers demanding back pay and by the realization of the new nation's looming problems.

Fighting in the West

While the congress debated the fate of western land claims, battles continued in the Ohio and Mississippi River valleys. British commanders at Fort Michilimackinac on Lake Huron recruited Sioux, Chippewa, and Sauk warriors to attack Spanish forces along the Mississippi, while soldiers at Fort Detroit armed Ottawa, Fox, and Miami warriors to assault American settlers flooding into the Ohio River valley. British forces from Fort Detroit also moved deeper into this region, establishing a post at Vincennes on the Wabash River.

The response to these British forays was effective, if not well coordinated. In 1778 a young patriot surveyor, George Rogers Clark of Virginia, organized a patriot expedition to counter Indian raids in the west and to reinforce Spanish and French allies in the upper Mississippi valley. He fought successfully against British and Indian forces at Kaskaskia and Cahokia on the Mississippi River. Then Clark marched his troops through the bitter February cold and launched a surprise attack on British forces at Vincennes. Although Detroit remained in British hands, Spanish troops defeated British-allied Indian forces that attacked St. Louis, giving the patriots greater control in the Ohio valley (Map 6.2).

In the summer of 1779, General John Sullivan led 4,000 patriot troops on a campaign to wipe out Mohawk, Seneca, Cayuga, and Onondaga villages in central and western New York. He succeeded in ending most attacks by Britain's Iroquois allies and disrupting the supplies being sent by British forces at Fort Niagara. Patriot attacks in Ohio also continued. In one of the worst atrocities fomented by patriots, Pennsylvania militiamen massacred more than one hundred Delaware men, women, and children near present-day Canton, Ohio, even though the Delawares had converted to Christianity and declared their neutrality.

Battles between Indian nations and American settlers did not end with the American Revolution. For the moment, however, patriot militia units and Continental forces supported by French and Spanish allies had defeated British and Indian efforts to control the Mississippi and Ohio River valleys.

War Rages in the South

Meanwhile British troops sought to regain control of southern states from Georgia to Virginia. British troops captured Savannah, Georgia, in 1778 and soon extended their control over the entire state. When General Clinton was called north in late 1778 to lead British troops against Washington's Continentals in New Jersey, he left the southern campaign in the hands of Lord Charles Cornwallis.

In May 1780, General Cornwallis reclaimed Charleston, South Carolina, and accepted the surrender of 5,000 Continental soldiers, the largest surrender of patriot troops during the war. He then evicted patriots from the city, purged them from the state government, gained military control of the state, and imposed loyalty oaths on all Carolinians able to fight. To aid his efforts, local loyalists organized militias to battle patriots in the interior. Banastre Tarleton led one especially vicious company of loyalists who slaughtered civilians and murdered many who surrendered. In retaliation, planter and merchant Thomas Sumter organized 800 men who showed a similar disregard for regular army procedures, raiding largely defenseless loyalist settlements near Hanging Rock, South Carolina, in August 1780.

Conflicts between patriots and loyalists raged across the South until the war's end (see Map 6.2). As retaliatory violence erupted in the interior of South Carolina, General Gates marched his Continental troops south to join 2,000 militiamen from Virginia and North Carolina. But his troops were exhausted and short of food, and on August 16 Cornwallis won a smashing victory against the combined patriot forces at Camden,

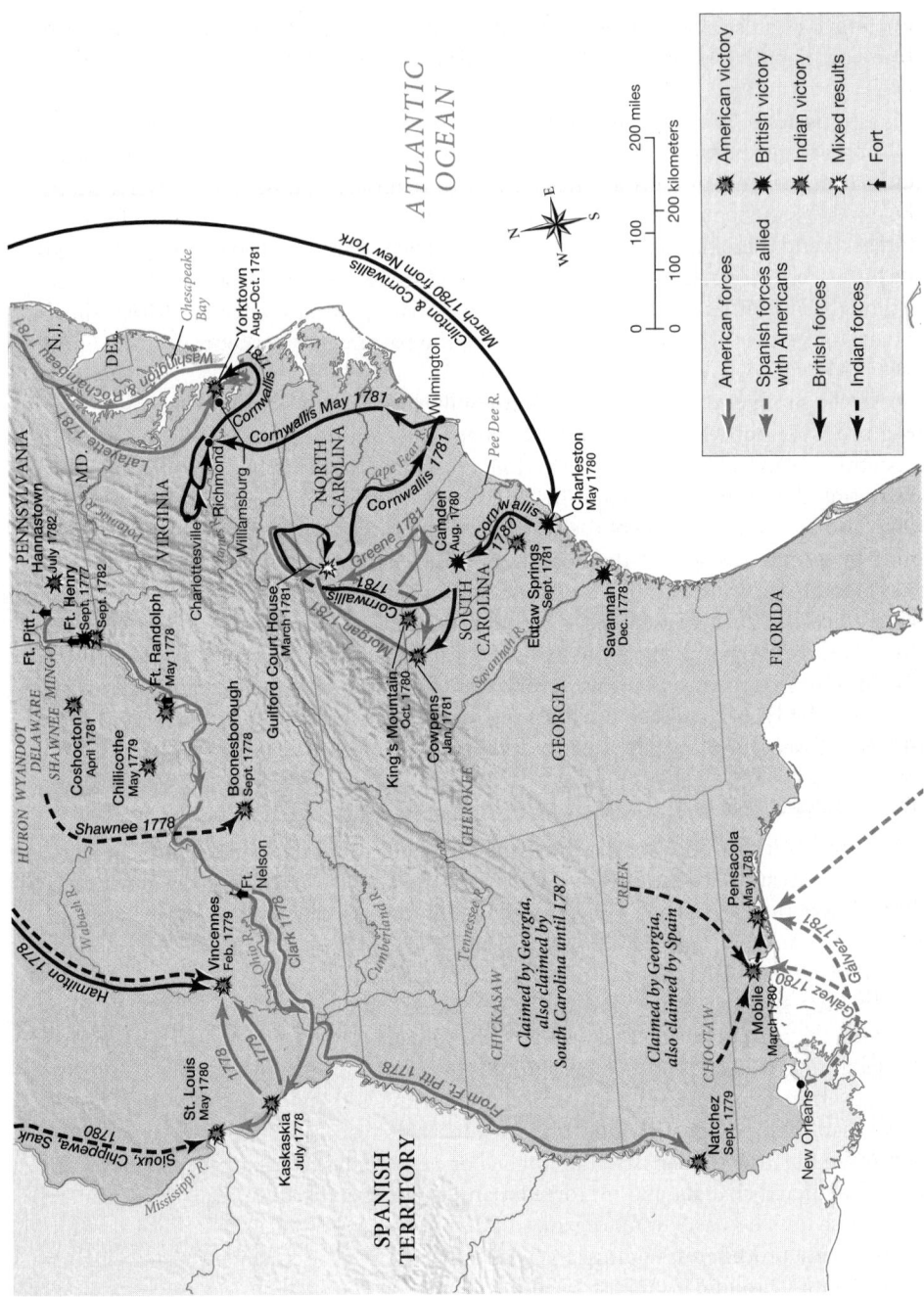

MAP 6.2

The War in the West and the South, 1777–1782   Between 1780 and 1781, major battles between Continental and British troops took place in Virginia and the Carolinas, and the British general Cornwallis finally surrendered at Yorktown, Virginia, in October 1781. But patriot forces also battled British troops and their Indian allies from 1777 to 1782 in the Ohio River valley, the lower Mississippi River, and the Gulf coast.

South Carolina. Soon after news of Gates's defeat reached General Washington, he heard that Benedict Arnold, commander at West Point, had defected to the British. Indeed, he had been passing information to the British for some time.

Suddenly, British chances for victory seemed more hopeful. Clinton had moved the bulk of northern troops into New York City and could send units south from there to bolster Cornwallis. Cornwallis was in control of Georgia and South Carolina, and local loyalists were eager to gain control of the southern countryside. Meanwhile Continental soldiers in the North mutinied in early 1780 over terms of enlistment and pay. Patriot morale was low, funds were scarce, and civilians were growing weary of the war.

Yet somehow the patriots prevailed. A combination of luck, strong leadership, and French support turned the tide. In October 1780, when Continental hopes looked especially bleak, a group of 800 frontier sharpshooters routed Major Patrick Ferguson's loyalist troops at King's Mountain in South Carolina. The victory kept Cornwallis from advancing into North Carolina and gave the Continentals a chance to regroup.

Shortly after the battle at King's Mountain, Washington sent General Nathanael Greene of Rhode Island to replace Gates as head of southern operations. Taking advice from local militia leaders like Daniel Morgan and Francis Marion, Greene divided his limited force into even smaller units. Marion and Morgan each led 300 Continental soldiers into the South Carolina backcountry, picking up hundreds of local militiamen along the way. At the village of Cowpens, Morgan drew Tarleton's much larger force into a circle of sharpshooters backed by Continentals and an armed cavalry. While Tarleton escaped, 100 of his men died and 800 were captured.

Cornwallis, enraged at the patriot victory, pursued Continental forces as they retreated. But Cornwallis's troops had outrun their cannons, and Greene circled back and attacked them at Guilford Court House. Although Cornwallis eventually forced the Continentals to withdraw from the battlefield, his troops suffered enormous losses. In August 1781, frustrated at the ease with which patriot forces still found local support in the South, he hunkered down in Yorktown on the Virginia coast and waited for Clinton to send reinforcements from New York.

Washington now coordinated strategy with his French allies. Comte de Rochambeau marched his 5,000 troops south from Rhode Island to Virginia as General Lafayette led his troops south along Virginia's eastern shore. At the same time, French naval ships headed north from the West Indies. One unit cut off a British fleet trying to resupply Cornwallis by sea. Another joined up with American privateers to bombard Cornwallis's forces. By mid-October, British supplies had run out, and it was clear that Clinton was not going to send reinforcements. On October 19, 1781, the British army admitted defeat.

An Uncertain Peace

The Continental Army had managed the impossible. It had defeated the British army and won the colonies' independence. Yet even with the surrender at **Yorktown**, the war continued in fits and starts. Peace negotiations in Paris dragged on as French, Spanish, British, and American representatives sought to settle a host of issues. Meanwhile British forces challenged Continental troops in and around New York City even as American recruiters found it nearly impossible to find new enlistments.

Some Continental soldiers continued to fight, but others focused on the long-festering issue of overdue wages. When the congress decided in June 1783 to discharge the remaining troops without providing back pay, a near mutiny erupted in Pennsylvania. Nearly 300 soldiers marched on the congress in Philadelphia. Washington sent troops, including Deborah Sampson/Robert Shurtliff, to put down the mutiny, and bloodshed was avoided when the Pennsylvania soldiers agreed to accept half pay and certificates for the remainder. Despite this compromise, the issue of back pay would continue to plague the nation over the next decade.

Meanwhile patriot representatives in Paris—Benjamin Franklin, John Adams, and John Jay—continued to negotiate peace terms. Rising antiwar sentiment on the British home front, especially after the surrender at Yorktown, forced the government's hand. But the Comte de Vergennes, the French foreign minister, opposed the Americans' republican principles and refused to consider the American delegates as his political equals. Given the importance of the French to the American victory, the congress had instructed its delegates to defer to French wishes. This blocked the American representatives from signing a separate peace with the British.

Eventually, however, U.S. delegates finalized a treaty that secured substantial benefits for the young nation. The United States gained control of all lands south of Canada and north of Louisiana and Florida stretching to the Mississippi River. In addition, the treaty recognized the United States to be "free Sovereign and independent states." Spain signed a separate treaty with Great Britain in which it regained control of Florida. Despite their role in the war, none of the Indian nations that occupied the lands under negotiation were consulted.

When the **Treaty of Paris** was finally signed on September 2, 1783, thousands of British troops and their supporters left the colonies for Canada, the West Indies, or England. British soldiers on the western frontier were supposed to be withdrawn at the same time, but they remained for many years and continued to foment hostilities between Indians in the region and U.S. settlers along the frontier.

The evacuation of the British also entailed the exodus of thousands of African Americans who had fought against the patriots. At the end of the war, British officials granted certificates of manumission to more than 1,300 men, 900 women, and 700 children. The largest number of these freed blacks settled in Nova Scotia, where they received small allotments of land from the British. Most, however, lacked the money, tools, or livestock to make such homesteads profitable. Despite these obstacles, some created a small Afro-Canadian community in Nova Scotia, while others migrated to areas considered more hospitable to black residents, such as Sierra Leone. Although thousands gained their freedom by taking up arms for the British, few were well rewarded for their efforts.

A Surprising Victory

Americans had managed to defeat one of the most powerful military forces in the world. That victory resulted from the convergence of many circumstances. Certainly Americans benefited from fighting on their own soil. Their knowledge of the land and its resources as well as earlier experiences fighting against Indians and the French helped prepare them for battles against the British.

Just as important, British troops and officers were far removed from centers of decision making and supplies. Even supplies housed in Canada could not be easily transported the relatively short distance into New York. British commanders were often hesitant to make decisions independently, but awaiting instructions from England proved costly on several occasions, especially since strategists in London often had little sense of conditions on the ground in America.

Both sides depended on outsiders for assistance, but here, too, Americans gained the advantage. While the British army certainly outnumbered its Continental adversary, it relied heavily on German mercenaries, Indian allies, and freed blacks to bolster its regular troops. In victory, such "foreign" forces were relatively reliable, but in defeat, many of them chose to look out for their own interests. The patriots meanwhile marched with French and Spanish armies well prepared to challenge British troops and motivated to gain advantages for France and Spain if Britain was defeated.

Perhaps most importantly, a British victory was nearly impossible without conquering the American colonies one by one. Because a large percentage of colonists supported the patriot cause, British troops had to contend not only with Continental soldiers but also with an aroused citizenry fighting for its independence.

REVIEW & RELATE

- How and why did the Americans win the Revolutionary War?
- What uncertainties and challenges did the new nation face in the immediate aftermath of victory?

Conclusion: Legacies of the Revolution

After the approval of the Declaration of Independence, Thomas Hutchinson, the British official who had gained fame during the Stamp Act upheavals in Boston, charged that patriot leaders had "sought independence from the beginning." But the gradual and almost reluctant move from resistance to revolution in the American colonies suggests otherwise. When faced with threats from British troops, a sufficient number of colonists took up arms to create the reality of war, and this surge of hostilities finally gave the advantage to those political leaders urging independence.

The victory over Great Britain won that independence but left the United States confronting difficult problems. Most soldiers simply wanted to return home and reestablish their former lives. But the government's inability to pay back wages and the huge debt the nation owed to private citizens and state and foreign governments hinted at difficult economic times ahead.

Like many soldiers, Deborah Sampson embraced a conventional life after the war. But times were hard. A decade after she was discharged, Massachusetts finally granted her a small pension for her wartime service. In 1804 Paul Revere successfully appealed to the U.S. Congress to grant her a federal pension. When Sampson died in 1827, a special congressional act awarded her children additional money. Many men also waited years to receive compensation for their wartime service while they struggled to reestablish farms and businesses and pay off the debts that accrued while they were fighting for independence.

Political leaders tried to address the concerns of former soldiers and ordinary citizens while they developed a governmental structure to manage an expansive and diverse nation. Within a few years of achieving independence, financial distress among small farmers and tensions with Indians on the western frontier intensified concerns about the ability of the confederation government to secure order and prosperity. In response, some patriots demanded a new political compact to strengthen the national government. But others feared that such a change would simply replicate British tyranny.

Leading revolutionaries engaged in heated debates over the best means to unify and stabilize the United States in the decade following the Revolution. However, some key leaders lived abroad in this period. Although Thomas Paine was awarded land and money by Pennsylvania and the U.S. Congress, in 1791 he moved to France, where he wrote pamphlets advocating revolution there. His increasingly radical political views and attacks on organized religion led many Americans to malign the former hero. He returned to the United States in 1802, but his death in New York City in 1809 was mentioned only briefly in most newspapers. Other patriot leaders remained celebrated figures, but Thomas Jefferson, Benjamin Franklin, and John Adams all spent significant amounts of time in England and France as ambassadors for the young nation. There they played key roles in building ties to European powers, thus ensuring U.S. security.

The legacies of the Revolution seemed far from clear in the decade following the American victory. As problems escalated, Americans were challenged to reimagine their political future while holding on to the republican impulses that drove them to revolution.

Chapter Review

IDENTIFY KEY TERMS

Identify and explain the significance of each term below.

Second Continental Congress (p. 139)

Dunmore's Proclamation (p. 140)

Common Sense (p. 140)

Declaration of Independence (p. 141)

loyalist (p. 142)

Battle of Saratoga (p. 148)

Valley Forge (p. 148)

Articles of Confederation (p. 150)

Yorktown (p. 157)

Treaty of Paris (p. 158)

REVIEW & RELATE

Answer the focus questions from each section of the chapter.

1. What challenges did Washington face when he was given command of the Continental Army?

2. How and why did proponents of independence prevail in the debates that preceded the publication of the Declaration of Independence?

3. How did colonists choose sides during the Revolutionary War? What factors influenced their decisions?

4. Why did so many Indian tribes try to stay neutral during the conflict? Why was it so difficult for Indians to remain neutral?

5. How did the patriot forces fare in 1776? How and why did the tide of war turn in 1777?

6. What role did colonial women and foreign men play in the conflict in the early years of the war?

7. What values and concerns shaped state governments during the Revolutionary War?

8. What issues and challenges did the Continental Congress face even after the French joined the patriot side?

9. How and why did the Americans win the Revolutionary War?

10. What uncertainties and challenges did the new nation face in the immediate aftermath of victory?

ONLINE DOCUMENT PROJECTS

◆ **Women in the Revolution**
◆ **Loyalists in the American Revolution**

After reading the primary sources in these document sets, answer the **Interpret the Evidence** questions to help you analyze each of the documents, and then answer the **Put It in Context** question(s) to help you relate the documents to the topics and themes you read about in the chapter.

bedfordstmartins.com/hewittlawsonvalue

TIMELINE OF EVENTS

April 19, 1775	• Battles of Lexington and Concord	**December 1776–January 1777**	• Patriot victories at Trenton and Princeton, New Jersey
June 1775	• Continental Congress establishes Continental Army	**October 1777**	• Patriot victory at Saratoga
June 16, 1775	• Battle of Bunker Hill	**Winter 1777–1778**	• Continental Army encamps at Valley Forge, Pennsylvania
August 1775	• Representatives of the Continental Congress meet with representatives of the six nations of the Iroquois Confederacy	**1778**	• Articles of Confederation ratified by eight states
		February 1778	• France enters into formal alliance with the United States
November 1775	• Dunmore issues his proclamation	**Summer 1779**	• Patriot forces wipe out Iroquois Confederacy villages on New York frontier
1776	• New Jersey constitution enfranchises all free inhabitants, including women and free blacks, who meet property qualifications	**1780–1781**	• Quock Walker and Elizabeth "Mumbet" Freeman successfully sue for their freedom in Massachusetts
January 1776	• Thomas Paine publishes *Common Sense*	**March 1781**	• Articles of Confederation ratified
July 4, 1776	• Continental Congress publicly declares independence	**October 19, 1781**	• British surrender at Yorktown, Virginia
July 1776–mid-December 1776	• British forces defeat Continental Army and force retreat	**May 1782**	• Deborah Sampson enlists in Continental Army under the name Robert Shurtliff
		September 2, 1783	• Treaty of Paris signed

7

Political Cultures

1783–1800

AMERICAN HISTORIES

Like many young farmers in Massachusetts, Daniel Shays enlisted in a local militia company in the early 1770s. Born to Irish parents in Hopkinton, Massachusetts, in 1747 and one of six children, Daniel received little formal education. In 1772 he married, had a child, and settled into farming. But in April 1775, he, his father, and his brother grabbed muskets and raced toward Concord to meet the British forces. By June, he was among the patriots defending Breed's Hill and Bunker Hill.

After distinguished service in the Continental Army, Shays resigned from service in 1780 and purchased a farm in Pelham, Massachusetts. He hoped to return to a normal life, but in the years following the Revolution, the nation entered a period of economic turmoil. Farmers in western Massachusetts, many deeply in debt, were especially hard hit. Debtors, including former soldiers and their families, lost their land, tools, livestock, clothes, and furniture, and many were also imprisoned. Although Shays managed to keep his farm, many of his neighbors faced eviction. Shays was chosen to represent his town at county conventions that petitioned the state government for economic relief. However, the Massachusetts legislature, sitting in Boston, largely ignored their concerns.

Angered by the legislature's failure to act, armed groups of farmers attacked courthouses throughout western Massachusetts in 1786. Although Shays was reluctant to lead the movement, he soon headed the largest contingent of farmer-soldiers, a band that eventually numbered more than a thousand men. After a series of small skirmishes against local militias, Massachusetts governor James Bowdoin moved to quash the rebellion. In January 1787, Shays and his men headed to the federal arsenal at Springfield, Massachusetts, to seize guns and ammunition. The farmers were routed by state militia and pursued by the governor's army. Many rebel leaders were captured; others, including Shays, escaped to Vermont and later New York State. Four were convicted and two were hanged before Bowdoin granted amnesty to the rest of the rebels, in hopes of avoiding further conflict.

This uprising, known as Shays's Rebellion, fueled grave concern on the part of many state and national leaders. They feared that the U.S. government was too weak to put down such insurgencies and advocated amending or replacing the Articles of Confederation to create a new political structure that would strengthen federal power. Among those outraged by the rebels was Alexander Hamilton, a young New York politician with an admirable record of military service. Hamilton was born illegitimate and impoverished in the British West Indies. Orphaned at eleven, he was apprenticed to a firm of merchants, where his gift for commerce and finance quickly became clear. The firm sent him for schooling to the American colonies, where he was drawn into the activities of radical patriots. Hamilton joined the Continental Army in 1776 and gained a reputation as courageous, even reckless, in the pursuit of military glory.

During the war, Hamilton fell in love with Elizabeth Schuyler, who came from a wealthy New York family, and they married in December 1780. After the American victory, Hamilton used military and marital contacts to establish himself as a lawyer and financier in New York City. In 1786 he focused his efforts on improving the state of the nation's finances. He was elected to the New York State legislature that spring and by fall was serving as a delegate to a convention on interstate commerce held in Annapolis, Maryland. Hamilton was among a small group of delegates who sought to strengthen the central government. They pushed through a resolution calling for a second convention "to render the constitution of the Federal Government adequate to the exigencies of the Union."

Although the initial response to the call was lukewarm, the eruption of Shays's Rebellion and the federal government's financial problems soon convinced many in the congress and the states that change was required. Although Hamilton played only a small role in the 1787 convention in Philadelphia, he worked tirelessly for ratification of the Constitution drafted there. Once the new federal government was established, in the fall of 1789 Hamilton accepted appointment to the job he most deeply desired, secretary of the treasury.

Farmer plowing near Moravian settlement of Salem, North Carolina, 1787. The Granger Collection, New York

AS ALEXANDER HAMILTON took charge of the nation's economic policy, Daniel Shays retreated to a modest living on the frontiers of New York State. Despite the suppression of Shays's Rebellion, the grievances that fueled the uprising persisted, and other problems confronted the new nation as well. Moreover, Hamilton's efforts to stabilize and strengthen the national economy, although deemed successful by many political and economic elites, sparked controversy and conflicts in the years ahead. As the American histories of Daniel Shays and Alexander Hamilton demonstrate, Americans may have come together to win the Revolutionary War, but not all Americans shared a common vision of the independent nation that military victory made possible.

Postwar Problems

The United States faced serious financial instability in its formative years. Other issues also threatened the emerging nation. Indians, with support from British allies, continued to launch raids against frontier settlements. Western migrants fueled these conflicts and forced the confederation government to take a more active role in governing its frontier territories. Meanwhile Spain closed the port of New Orleans to U.S. trade as states struggled to regulate commerce within the nation and abroad. Another threat to American trade arose off the coast of North Africa, where Barbary pirates attacked U.S. merchant ships. Issues of trade and piracy required diplomacy with European powers, but diplomatic relations were plagued with uncertainty given America's outstanding war debts and the relative weakness of the confederation government.

Officers Threaten Mutiny

As the American Revolution ground to an end, issues of military pay and government finances sparked conflict. Uprisings by ordinary soldiers were common but successfully put down. Threats by Continental officers, however, posed a greater problem. In March 1783, some five hundred officers were still encamped at Newburgh, New York. Many officers came from wealthy families and had served without pay during the war. In 1780 they had extracted a promise from the Continental Congress for half pay for life but had received no compensation since.

Some confederation leaders were sympathetic to the officers' plight and hoped to use pressure from this formidable group to enhance the powers of the congress. Hamilton was among the leaders pressing state governments to grant the confederation congress a new duty of 5 percent on imported goods. The federal government would thereby gain an independent source of revenue by which it could begin paying off its debts and ensure the loyalty of wealthy Americans who had helped finance the war. Perhaps the actions of the officers at Newburgh could convince states like New York to agree to the collection of this import duty.

Quietly encouraged by these supporters, dissident officers circulated petitions that included veiled threats of a military takeover. When the officers met on March 15, however, they were confronted by General George Washington, who urged the officers to respect civilian control of the government and to allow the fragile U.S. government time to prove itself. Most of the Newburgh officers quickly retreated from the "infamous propositions" circulated earlier. At the same time, congressional leaders, fearing a mutiny, promised the officers full pay for five years. Within weeks, news arrived that a peace treaty was near completion in Paris, and over the next three months the officers headed home.

Indians, Land, and the Northwest Ordinance

One anonymous petitioner at Newburgh suggested that the officers move as a group to "some unsettled country" and let the confederation fend for itself. In reality, no such unsettled country existed beyond the thirteen states. Numerous Indian nations and American settlers claimed control of these western lands, and more American settlers were arriving all the time. In 1784 some two hundred Indian leaders from the Iroquois, Shawnee, Creek, Cherokee, and other nations gathered in St. Louis, where they complained to the Spanish governor that the Americans were "extending themselves like a plague of locusts."

Despite the continued presence of British and Spanish troops in the Ohio River valley, the United States hoped to convince Indian nations—both friendly and hostile—that it controlled the territory. The confederation congress sought to strengthen these claims by signing treaties with the vanquished nations. In the fall of 1784, U.S. commissioners met with Iroquois delegates at Fort Stanwix, New York, and demanded land cessions that covered all of western New York and Pennsylvania as well as areas farther west. They backed up their demands with the threat of force. Although the six Indian nations in the council later refused to ratify the treaty, the U.S. government acted as though the treaty was valid. With a similar mix of negotiation and coercion, U.S. commissioners signed treaties at Fort McIntosh, Pennsylvania (1785), and Fort Finney, Ohio (1786), and claimed lands held by the Wyandots, Delawares, Shawnees, and others.

As more and more eastern Indians were pushed into the Ohio River valley, they crowded onto lands already claimed by other nations. Initially, these migrations increased conflict among Indians, but eventually some leaders used this forced intimacy to launch pan-Indian movements against further American encroachment on their land.

Indians and U.S. political leaders did share one concern over western lands: the vast numbers of squatters, mainly white men and women, who moved onto land to which they had no legal claim. In the fall of 1784, George Washington traveled with family members and slaves to survey nearly thirty thousand acres of western territory he had been granted as a reward for military service. He found much of the land occupied by squatters who refused to purchase their homesteads or pay rent to Washington. Unable to impose his will on the squatters, he became more deeply concerned about the weaknesses of the confederation government.

Washington feared that the federal government was not strong enough to protect his and others' property rights. Indeed, the confederation congress struggled just to convince the remaining states with western land claims to cede that territory to federal control. Slowly, however, between 1783 and 1785, the congress convinced the two remaining states with the largest western land claims, Virginia and Massachusetts, to relinquish all territory north of the Ohio River (Map 7.1).

MAP 7.1

Cessions of Western Land, 1782–1802 Beginning with the congress established under the Articles of Confederation, political leaders sought to resolve competing state claims to western territory based on colonial charters. The confederation congress and, after ratification of the Constitution, the U.S. Congress gradually persuaded all states to cede their claims and create a "national domain," part of which was then organized as the Northwest Territory.

To regulate this vast territory, Thomas Jefferson drafted the **Northwest Land Ordinance** in 1785. It provided that the territory be surveyed and divided into adjoining townships of thirty-six sections, each 1 square mile (640 acres) in area. He hoped to carve fourteen small states out of the region to enhance the representation of western farmers and to ensure the continued dominance of agrarian views in the national government. The congress revised his proposal, however, stipulating that only three to five states be created from the vast territory.

The population of the territory grew rapidly, with speculators buying up huge tracts of land and selling smaller parcels to eager settlers. In response, congressional leaders modified the original Northwest Ordinance in 1787 and clarified the process by which territories could become states. The congress appointed territorial officials and guaranteed residents the basic rights of U.S. citizens. After a territory's population reached 5,000, residents could choose an assembly, but the territorial governor retained the power to veto all legislation. When a prospective state reached a population of 60,000, it could apply for admission to the United States on an equal basis with the existing states. Thus the congress established an orderly system by which territories became states in the Union.

The 1787 ordinance also addressed concerns about race and political power in the region, though with mixed results. It encouraged fair treatment of Indian nations, although it did not include any means of enforcing such treatment and failed to resolve Indian land claims. It abolished slavery throughout the territory, but the law included a clause that mandated the return of fugitive slaves to their owners to forestall a flood of fugitives into the Northwest Territory. By restricting the number of states established in the territory, the ordinance also sought to limit the future clout of western settlers in the federal government.

Meanwhile, ownership of the region south of the Ohio River and west of the original thirteen states remained in dispute. By 1785 thirty thousand Americans had settled in Kentucky, and thousands more streamed into Tennessee. Spanish officials claimed rights to this land and signed treaties with Creek, Choctaw, and Chickasaw tribes in the area. Supplied with weapons by Spanish traders, these Indians along with Cherokees harassed Anglo-American settlers in the lower Mississippi valley. The region would remain an arena of conflict for decades to come.

Depression and Debt

Disputes over western lands were deeply intertwined with the economic difficulties that plagued the new nation. Victory in the Revolution was followed by years of economic depression and mushrooming debt. The war had fueled the demand for domestic goods and ensured high employment. However, after the peace settlement, both the demand and the jobs declined. In addition, international trade was slow to recover from a decade of disruption. Meanwhile, the nation was saddled with a huge war debt. Individuals, the states, and the federal government each viewed western lands as a solution to their problems. Farm families could move west and start over on "unclaimed" land; states could distribute land in lieu of cash payments to veterans or creditors; and the congress could sell land to fund its debts. Yet there was never enough land to meet these conflicting needs, nor did the United States hold secure title to the territory.

Some national leaders, including Hamilton, focused on other ways of repaying the war debt. Fearing that wealthy creditors would lose faith in the new nation if it could not repay its debts, they wanted to grant the federal government the right to collect a percentage of import duties as a way to increase its revenue. Meanwhile, legislators in a number of states, including Massachusetts, passed hard-money laws that required debts to be repaid in gold or silver rather than in paper currency. Creditors—mainly well-to-do merchants and professionals—favored hard-money measures to ensure repayment in full. Artisans and small farmers, including many veterans who had borrowed paper money during the war, were now asked to repay loans in hard currency as the money supply shrank. Taxes, too, were rising as states sought to cover the interest on wartime bonds held by affluent investors.

Failures of American diplomacy weakened the nation's economy further. In 1783 the British Parliament denied the United States the right to trade with the British West Indies, and New England merchants lost lucrative markets for fish, grain, and lumber. The following year, Spain, unhappy with Americans' insistence on pushing into disputed western territories, prohibited U.S. ships from accessing the port of New Orleans. This embargo closed off a primary trade route for western settlers. Spain and Great Britain also threatened U.S. sovereignty by conspiring with American citizens on the frontier and promising them protection from Indians. At the same time, British troops that had refused to abandon forts in the western United States urged Indians to harass frontier settlers.

The United States fared better in its relations with France and Holland. Both nations granted American ships the right to trade with their West Indies colonies. Yet the continuation of America's wartime alliance with France also ensured continued conflicts with Great Britain.

REVIEW & RELATE

- What challenges did the new nation face in the immediate aftermath of the Revolutionary War?
- How and why did the conflict between America and Great Britain continue after the war ended?

On the Political Margins

In the aftermath of the Revolution, the United States was forced to the political margins in international affairs. At the same time, as the new Republic moved from war to peace to nationhood, some groups within the nation were marginalized as well. Small farmers were among those who suffered in the postwar period, but they were not alone. Church leaders who had enjoyed government support in the colonial period now had to compete for members and funds. African Americans, whose hopes for freedom had been raised by the Revolution, continued to fight for full-fledged citizenship and an end to slavery. Women, too, faced challenges as they sought to claim a greater voice in the nation.

Separating Church and State

Government support of churches largely ended with the establishment of the United States. Anglican churches had long benefited from British support and collected taxes to support their ministry during the Revolution. Then in 1786 the Virginia Assembly approved the Statute of Religious Freedom, which was drafted earlier by Thomas Jefferson and made church attendance and support voluntary and eliminated many Anglican privileges. Other states soon followed suit, affecting all churches that had previously counted on government support.

Most states did require that officeholders be Christians, or even Protestants. But by the 1780s, that designation included a wide array of denominations. Especially in frontier areas, Baptists and Methodists, the latter of which broke off from the Anglican Church in 1784, gained thousands of converts. The Society of Friends, or Quakers, and the Presbyterians also gained new adherents in this period, while Catholics and Jews experienced greater tolerance than in the colonial era. In fact, in 1790 the Vatican appointed John Carroll the first Roman Catholic bishop of the United States. As a result of this diversity, no single religious voice or perspective dominated in the new nation. Instead, all denominations competed for members, money, and political influence.

Many Protestant churches were also challenged from within by free blacks who sought a greater role in church governance. In 1794 Richard Allen, a preacher who had been born a slave, led a small group of Philadelphia blacks who founded the first African American church in the United States. The Bethel African-American Methodist Church initially remained within the larger Methodist fold. By the early 1800s, however, Allen's church would serve as the basis for the first independent black denomination, the African Methodist Episcopal Church.

African Americans Struggle for Rights

Black churches provided one arena in which African Americans could demonstrate their independence. It was no accident that the Bethel African-American Methodist Church was founded in Philadelphia, which attracted large numbers of free blacks after passage of the state's gradual emancipation law in 1780. Although the northern states with the largest enslaved populations—New York and New Jersey—did not pass such laws until 1799 and 1804, the size of the free black population increased throughout the region.

Many of these free blacks were migrants from the South, where tens of thousands of enslaved women and men gained their freedom during or immediately following the Revolution (see chapter 6). A few slave owners took Revolutionary ideals to heart and emancipated their slaves following the war. Many others emancipated slaves in their wills. In addition, several states prohibited the importation of slaves from Africa during or immediately following the Revolution, including Delaware, Pennsylvania, Virginia, and Maryland. Despite these emancipations and prohibitions, the number of individuals enslaved in the United States in 1800 was far greater than in 1776, and the enslaved population continued to grow rapidly thereafter. Now, however, slavery was increasingly confined to the South. As northern states passed gradual abolition laws, southern states moved in the opposite direction, making it more difficult for owners to free their slaves and for free blacks to remain in the South.

The limits on emancipation in the South nurtured the growth of free black communities in the North, especially in seaport cities like Philadelphia, New York, Boston, and New Bedford, Massachusetts. In these areas, most African Americans focused on establishing families, finding jobs, and securing the freedom of relatives still enslaved. Others, like Richard Allen, sought to build black communities by establishing churches, schools, and voluntary societies and demanding a political voice. Some northern states, such as New Jersey, granted property-owning blacks the right to vote. Others, such as Pennsylvania, did not specifically exclude them. Records suggest that few black men participated in elections in the early Republic, yet many petitioned state and local governments—in the North and the South—to provide African American communities with schooling, burial grounds, and other forms of assistance.

Although blacks gained little support from most white Americans, they did have some allies. The Society of Friends, the only religious denomination to oppose slavery in the colonial period, became more adamant in its stance in the post-Revolutionary period. Many affluent Quakers finally freed their slaves and withdrew from the slave trade. Anthony Benezet, a Quaker writer and educator, advocated tirelessly for the abolition of slavery within the Society of Friends and directed the Negro School in Philadelphia, which he had founded in 1770.

Women Seek Wider Roles

Quaker women as well as men testified against slavery in the 1780s, writing statements on the topic in separate women's meetings. Although few other women experienced such spiritual autonomy, many gained a new sense of economic and political independence during the Revolution. Once peace was achieved, should they demand rights based on their wartime service or create new roles for themselves in the new Republic? Differences of age, wealth, region, race, and religion shaped women's responses to these questions.

The most famous Revolutionary claim for women's rights was penned by Abigail Adams in 1776 when she warned her husband, John, that "if particular care and attention is not paid to the Ladies we are determined to foment a Rebellion [sic], and will not hold ourselves bound by any Laws in which we have no voice, or Representation." Adams and other elite women sought a more public voice following the Revolution as well. Only in New Jersey could women—widowed or single, property-owning women—vote, and many cast ballots in state and local elections by the early nineteenth century.

The vast majority of women, however, could shape political decisions only by influencing their husbands, sons, and brothers. Fortunately, many leaders of the early Republic viewed virtuous wives and mothers as necessary to the development of a strong nation. In 1787 Benjamin Rush, a signer of the Declaration of Independence, published his *Essay on Female Education*. He believed that women could best shape political ideas and relations by "instructing their sons in principles of liberty and government" and rewarding husbands engaged in public service with "approbation and applause." To prepare young women for this enhanced domestic role, Rush suggested educating them in literature, music, composition, geography, history, and bookkeeping.

A more radical approach to women's education was presented by Judith Sargent Murray. Murray argued that "girls should be enabled to procure for themselves the necessaries of life; independence should be placed within their grasp." In addition to such practical instruction, Murray also advocated an education for girls that included science, mathematics, Latin, and Greek. She argued that at age two, boys and girls were intellectually equal. But from then on, "the one is taught to aspire, and the other is early confined and limited." A few American women in the late eighteenth century did receive broad educations, and some ran successful businesses; wrote plays, poems, and histories; and established urban salons where women and men discussed the issues of the day. In 1789 Massachusetts became the first state to institute free elementary education for all children, and female academies also multiplied in this period. Still, most girls' education was focused on preparing them for domesticity, and most women wielded what influence they had as an extension of their domestic responsibilities.

While women's influence was praised in the post-Revolutionary era, state laws rarely expanded women's rights. All states limited women's economic autonomy, although a few allowed married women to enter into business. Divorce was also legalized in many states but was still available only to the wealthy and well connected. Meanwhile women were excluded from juries and legal training and with rare exceptions from voting rights.

African American and Indian women lived under even more severe restraints than white women did. By the 1790s, the number of enslaved women began to increase rapidly once again. Even black women who gained their freedom could find jobs only as domestic servants or agricultural workers. Indian women also faced a difficult future. Years of warfare had enhanced men's role as warriors and diplomats while restricting women's political influence. Furthermore, American officials and missionaries encouraged Indians to embrace gender roles that mirrored those of Anglo-American culture by giving men hoes and women spinning wheels. When forced to move farther west, Indian women also lost political and economic authority that was linked to their traditional control over land, crops, and households.

Indebted Farmers Fuel Political Crises

Although many Americans struggled economically in the 1780s, ordinary men did gain a greater voice in politics. Under constitutions written during the Revolution, most state governments broadened the electorate, allowing men with less property (or in some cases no property) to vote and hold office. They also increased representation from western areas. Although most elected officials still came from the wealthier classes, many felt some responsibility to address the claims of the less fortunate.

Still, the economic interests of poor farmers and of wealthy merchants and landowners diverged sharply. As conflicts between rich and poor, debtors and creditors, escalated between 1783 and 1787, state governments came down firmly on the side of those with money. When petitions and elections failed, impoverished workers and farmers mounted protests. In New Hampshire, debt-ridden farmers marched on the original state capital at Exeter to demand reform. They were confronted by cavalry units, who quickly seized and imprisoned their leaders.

In addition to rebellions by farmers and debtors, many political and economic leaders were worried about the continued efforts of Great Britain and Spain to undercut U.S. sovereignty, ongoing struggles with Indian nations, and attacks on private property by squatters. When James Madison and Alexander Hamilton attended the 1785 convention in Annapolis to address problems related to interstate commerce, they discovered that their concerns about the weakness of the confederation were shared by many large landowners, planters, and merchants. Despite these concerns, state legislatures were reluctant to give up the powers conferred on them under the Articles.

Shays's Rebellion, the 1786 armed uprising by disgruntled, indebted farmers in western Massachusetts, turned the tide by crystallizing fears among prominent patriots about the limits of the confederation model. On December 26, 1786, Washington wrote Henry Knox to express his concerns about the rebellion and other upheavals along the frontier: "If the powers [of the central government] are inadequate, amend or alter them; but do not let us sink into the lowest states of humiliation and contempt." Hamilton, too, believed that Shays's Rebellion marked "almost the last stage of national humiliation." Speaking of the confederation government, he claimed that this "frail and toddering edifice seems ready to fall upon our heads and crush us beneath its ruins."

(REVIEW & RELATE)

- How did America's experience of the Revolutionary War change the lives of African Americans and women?

- What do uprisings by farmers and debtors tell us about social and economic divisions in the early Republic?

Reframing the American Government

The delegates who met in Philadelphia in 1787 did not agree on the best way to reform the government. Some delegates, like James Monroe of Virginia, hoped to strengthen the existing government by amending the Articles of Confederation. Others joined with Madison and Hamilton, who argued for nothing less than a new structure for governing the United States. Once representatives agreed to draft a new constitution, they still disagreed over questions of representation, the relations between state and national governments, and the limits of popular democracy.

Even after the ratification of the Constitution and the election of George Washington as president, there was much to do. The Senate, House of Representatives, and Supreme Court had to be organized. The president had to select administrators to help him implement policies and programs. A system for levying, collecting, and distributing funds had to be put in place, and a host of economic problems had to be addressed. Foreign powers and Indian nations needed to be assured that treaties would be honored and diplomatic relations

James Madison James Madison of Virginia was one of the framers of the Constitution and one of the authors of *The Federalist Papers*, which supported its ratification. This striking portrait of Madison was drawn around 1796–1797 by the artist James Sharples. Courtesy of Independence National Historical Park

reestablished. A bill of rights, demanded in so many ratifying conventions, had to be drafted and approved. Finally, both proponents and opponents of the Constitution had to be convinced that the U.S. government could respond to the varied needs of its citizens.

The Philadelphia Convention of 1787

The fifty-five delegates who attended the Philadelphia convention were composed of white, educated men of property, mainly lawyers, merchants, and planters. Although many delegates had played important roles in the Revolution, only eight had signed the Declaration of Independence two decades earlier. The elite status of the delegates and the paucity of leading patriots raised concern among those who saw the convention as a threat to the rights of states and of citizens. Whatever changes they imagined, all the delegates realized that discussions about restructuring the U.S. government could alarm many Americans, and thus they agreed to meet in secret until they had concluded their business.

On May 25, the convention opened, and delegates quickly turned to the key question: Was the convention going to revise the Articles of Confederation or draft an entirely new framework of governance? The majority of men came to Philadelphia with the intention of amending the Articles. However, a core group of federalists, who sought a more powerful central government, met in the weeks before the convention and drafted a plan to replace the Articles. This **Virginia Plan** proposed a strong centralized state, including a bicameral (two-house) legislature in which representation was to be based on population. Members of the two houses would select the national executive and the national judiciary. The new Congress would retain all the powers held by the confederation, and it would gain the power to settle disputes between states and veto legislation passed by an individual state. According to the Virginia Plan, Congress would not have the power to tax citizens or to regulate interstate or international commerce. Although most delegates opposed the Virginia Plan, it launched discussions in which strengthening the central government was assumed to be the goal.

Discussions of the Virginia Plan raised another issue that nearly paralyzed the convention: the question of representation. Heated debates pitted large states against small states even though political interests were not necessarily determined by size. Yet delegates held on to size as the critical issue in determining representation. In mid-June, William Patterson of New Jersey introduced a "small-state" plan in which Congress would consist of only one house, with each state having equal representation. Although Patterson's congressional plan was doomed to failure, he also articulated ideas of constitutional supremacy and judicial review that became key elements in the American legal system.

With few signs of compromise, the convention finally appointed a special committee of one delegate from each state to hammer out the problem of representation. Their report broke the logjam. Members of the House of Representatives were to be elected by voters in each state; members of the Senate would be appointed by state legislatures. Representation in the House would be determined by population—counted every ten years in a national census—and each state, regardless of size, would have equal representation in the Senate. The Senate could approve treaties and presidential appointments, try cases of impeachment, and initiate certain kinds of legislation. The House, however, had the singular authority to introduce all funding bills.

Included within this compromise was one of the few considerations of slavery at the Philadelphia convention. With little apparent debate, the committee decided that representation in the House of Representatives was to be based on an enumeration of the entire free population and three-fifths of "all other persons," that is, slaves. If delegates had moral scruples about this **three-fifths compromise**, most found them outweighed by the urgency of settling the troublesome question of representation.

Still, slavery was on the minds of delegates. In the same week that the Philadelphia convention tacitly accepted the institution of slavery, the confederation congress meeting in New York City outlawed slavery in the Northwest Territory. It was perhaps news of that decision that inspired representatives from Georgia and South Carolina to insist that the Constitution protect the slave trade. Delegates in Philadelphia agreed that "the migration or importation of such persons as any of the states now existing shall think proper to admit" would not be interfered with for twenty years. At the same time, northern delegates insisted that the three-fifths formula be used in assessing taxation as well as representation, ensuring that the South paid for the increased size of its congressional delegation with increased taxes.

Two other issues provoked considerable debate in the following weeks: the balance of power between states and the central government, and the degree of popular participation in selecting national leaders. The delegates supported federalism, a system in which states and the central government share power. But the new Constitution increased the powers of the central government significantly over those granted by the Articles of Confederation. The new Congress was granted the right to raise revenue by levying and collecting taxes and tariffs and coining money; to raise armies; to regulate interstate commerce; to settle disputes between the states; to establish uniform rules for the naturalization of immigrants; and to make treaties with foreign nations and Indians. But Congress could veto state laws only when those laws challenged "the supreme law of the land," and states retained all rights that were not specifically granted to the federal government.

One of the important powers retained by the states was the right to determine who was eligible to vote, but delegates in Philadelphia decided how much influence eligible voters would have in national elections. Members of the House of Representatives were to be elected directly by popular vote for two-year terms. Senators—two from each state—were to be selected by state legislatures for a term of six years. Voters were also involved only indirectly in the selection of the president. The president would be selected for a four-year term by an electoral college, members of which were appointed by state legislatures and equal to the whole number of senators and representatives to which the state was entitled. Finally, the federal judicial system was to be wholly removed from popular influence. Justices on the Supreme Court were to be appointed by the president and approved by the Senate. Once approved, they served for life to protect their judgments from the pressure of popular opinion.

With the final debates concluded, delegates agreed that approval by nine states, rather than all thirteen, would make the Constitution the law of the land. Some delegates sought formal reassurance that the powers granted the federal government would not be abused and urged inclusion of a bill of rights, modeled on the Virginia Declaration of Rights. But weary men eager to finish their business voted down the proposal. On September 17, 1787, the Constitution was approved and sent to the states for ratification.

Americans Battle over Ratification

Although the confederation congress neither approved nor rejected the Constitution, it did circulate the document to state legislatures and asked them to call conventions to consider ratification. At the same time, printers published thousands of copies of the Constitution in newspapers and as broadsides. Soon Americans were proclaiming their opinions from pulpits, papers, and other public platforms. In homes, churches, and taverns, ordinary citizens debated the wisdom of abolishing the confederation and establishing a stronger central government.

 Online Document Project   **Debating the Constitution**
bedfordstmartins.com/hewittlawsonvalue

There were many opinions on the Constitution, but the states were not allowed to modify the document, only to accept or reject it in whole. Fairly quickly then, two sides emerged. The **Federalists**, who supported ratification, came mainly from urban and commercial backgrounds and lived in towns and cities along the Atlantic coast. They viewed a stronger central government as essential to the economic and political stability of the nation. Their opponents, who were generally more rural, less wealthy, and more likely to live in interior or frontier regions, opposed increasing the powers of the central government. Known more for what they stood against than what they stood for, opponents were labeled **Antifederalists**.

The pro-Constitution position was most fully expressed in a series of eighty-five editorials that appeared in New York newspapers in 1787–1788 and were published collectively as *The Federalist Papers*. Written by James Madison, John Jay, and Alexander Hamilton, these brilliant essays articulated broad principles embraced by most supporters of the Constitution. Most notably, in *Federalist* No. 10, Madison countered the common wisdom that small units of government were most effective in representing the interests of their citizens and avoiding factionalism. Recognizing that factions were inevitable, he argued that in a large political body, groups with competing interests had to collaborate and compromise in order to rule. This check on the "tyranny of the majority" protected the rights and freedoms of all. Although these editorials did not have a profound impact on delegates during the ratification process, they had a major influence in shaping the government that emerged after ratification.

Antifederalists continued to view a large and powerful central government as leading to tyranny, invoking the actions of the British king and Parliament to illustrate their point. Small farmers worried that a strong central government filled with merchants, lawyers, and planters might place the interests of creditors above those of ordinary (and indebted) Americans. Some wealthy patriots, like Mercy Otis Warren of Boston, feared that the Constitution would hand over power to a few individuals who remained isolated from the "true interests of the people." Finally, many Americans were concerned about the absence of a bill of rights.

Federalists worked in each state to soften their critics by persuasive arguments, flattering hospitality, and timely compromises regarding a bill of rights. They also gained strength from a few states that ratified the Constitution quickly. By January 1788, Delaware, Pennsylvania, New Jersey, Georgia, and Connecticut had all approved the

Constitution. Federalists also gained the support of the most influential newspapers, which were based in eastern cities and tied to commercial interests.

Despite the Federalists' successes, the contest in many states became heated. In Massachusetts, Antifederalists, including some leaders of Shays's Rebellion, gained the majority among convention delegates. Many were deeply opposed to the centralization of power established by the Constitution. Federalists worked hard to overcome the objections of their opponents, drafting a bill of rights to be proposed for adoption following the Constitution's ratification. Finally, on February 6, the Massachusetts delegates voted 187 to 168 in favor of ratification. Maryland and South Carolina followed in April and May. A month later, New Hampshire Federalists won a close vote, making it the ninth state to ratify the Constitution.

Two of the most populous and powerful states, New York and Virginia, had not yet ratified. Passionate debates erupted in both states. Finally, after promising that a bill of rights would be added quickly, Virginia Federalists won the day by a few votes. A month later, New York also approved the Constitution by a narrow margin. The divided nature of the votes, and the fact that two states (North Carolina and Rhode Island) had still not ratified, meant that the new government would have to prove itself quickly (Table 7.1).

Organizing the Federal Government

Most political leaders hoped that the partisanship of the Federalist/Antifederalist struggle would fade away with the ratification of the Constitution. The electoral college's unanimous decision to name George Washington the first president helped calm some of this political turmoil. John Adams was selected as vice president. On April 30, 1789, Washington and Adams were sworn in at the nation's capital in New York City.

TABLE 7.1 **Votes of State Ratifying Conventions**

State	Date	For	Against
Delaware	December 1787	30	0
Pennsylvania	December 1787	46	23
New Jersey	December 1787	38	0
Georgia	January 1788	26	0
Connecticut	January 1788	128	40
Massachusetts	February 1788	187	168
Maryland	April 1788	63	11
South Carolina	May 1788	149	73
New Hampshire	June 1788	57	47
Virginia	June 1788	89	79
New York	July 1788	30	27
North Carolina	November 1788	194	77
Rhode Island	May 1790	34	32

Washington quickly established four departments—State, War, Treasury, and Justice—to bring order to his administration. Thomas Jefferson was named secretary of state; Henry Knox, secretary of war; Alexander Hamilton, secretary of the treasury; and Edmund Randolph, attorney general, head of the Department of Justice. These men had been major figures in the Revolution and helped draft the Constitution.

Congress was also busy in the spring of 1789. The Constitution called for a Supreme Court, but it offered little guidance on its practical organization. The Judiciary Act of 1789 established a Supreme Court composed of six justices along with thirteen district courts and three circuit courts to hear cases appealed from the states. Congress also worked quickly to establish a bill of rights. Representative James Madison gathered more than two hundred resolutions passed by state ratifying conventions and honed them down to twelve amendments, which Congress approved and submitted to the states for ratification. In 1791 ten of the amendments were ratified by the necessary three-fourths of the states, and these became the **Bill of Rights**. It guaranteed the rights of individuals and states in the face of a more powerful central government, including freedom of speech, the press, religion, and the right to petition.

Hamilton Forges an Economic Agenda

Even as the new government was being organized, its leaders recognized that without a stable economy, the best political structure could falter. Thus Washington's appointment of Alexander Hamilton as secretary of the treasury was especially significant. In formulating the nation's economic policy, Hamilton's main goal was to establish the nation's credit. This would strengthen the United States in the eyes of the world and tie wealthy Americans more firmly to the federal government.

Hamilton formulated a policy that involved funding the national debt at face value and assuming the remaining state debts as part of the national debt. To pay for this policy, he planned to raise revenue through government bonds, an excise tax on goods traded within the United States, and tariffs on imported goods. Hamilton also called for the establishment of a central bank to carry out the financial operations of the United States. His ideas were bold and controversial, but he had the support of Washington and key Federalists in Congress. Hamilton also had the charm and intellectual ability to persuade skeptics of the utility of his proposals and the wisdom to compromise when necessary. In three major reports to Congress—on public credit and a national bank in 1790 and on manufactures in 1791—he laid out a system of state-assisted economic development.

Hamilton's proposal to repay at face value the millions of dollars in securities issued by the confederation to foreign and domestic creditors was particularly controversial. Thousands of soldiers, farmers, artisans, and shop owners had been paid with these securities during the war, but most had long ago sold them for a fraction of their value to speculators. Thus speculators would make enormous profits if the securities were paid off at face value. Madison argued that the original owners of the securities should be rewarded in some way. Others, such as Patrick Henry, claimed that Hamilton's policy was intended "to erect, and concentrate, and perpetuate a large monied interest" that would prove "fatal to the existence of American liberty." Despite the passion of his opponents, Hamilton won the day.

The federal government's assumption of the remaining state war debts also faced fierce opposition, especially from southern states like Virginia that had already paid off their debt. Hamilton again won his case, though this time by agreeing to "redeem" (that is, reimburse) the money spent by states that had repaid their debts. In addition, Hamilton and his supporters had to agree to move the nation's capital from Philadelphia to a more central location along the Potomac River.

Funding the national debt, assuming the remaining state debts, and reimbursing states for debts already paid would cost $75.6 million (about $1.5 billion today). Rather than paying off the entire debt, Hamilton proposed the establishment of a Bank of the United States, funded by $10 million in stock to be sold to private stockholders and the national government. The bank would serve as a repository for income generated by taxes and tariffs and would grant loans and sell bills of credit to merchants and investors, thereby creating a permanent national debt. This, he argued, would bind investors to the United States, turning the national debt into a "national blessing."

Not everyone agreed with Hamilton's plans. Jefferson and Madison argued vehemently against the Bank of the United States, noting that there was no constitutional sanction for a federal bank. The secretary of the treasury fought back, arguing that Congress had the right to make "all Laws which shall be necessary and proper" for carrying out the provisions of the Constitution. Once again, Hamilton prevailed. Congress chartered the bank for a period of twenty years, and Washington signed the legislation into law.

The final piece of Hamilton's plan focused on raising revenue. Congress quickly passed tariffs on a range of imported goods. Tariffs generated some $4 million to $5 million annually for the federal government. Excise taxes placed on the consumption of wine, tea, coffee, and distilled spirits and on the sale of whiskey generated another $1 million each year. Some congressmen viewed these tariffs as a way to protect new industries in the United States, such as the furniture, tobacco, upholstery, hatmaking, and shoemaking industries. Hamilton was most concerned with generating income for the Treasury, but he also supported industrial development.

Hamilton's financial policies proved enormously successful in stabilizing the American economy, repaying outstanding debts, and tying men of wealth to the new government. The federal bank functioned effectively to collect and distribute the nation's resources. Commerce flourished, revenues rose, and confidence revived among foreign and domestic investors. Hamilton's support for "infant industries," expressed in his 1791 *Report on Manufactures*, also proved prescient even as farmers remained the backbone of the economy for decades to come.

REVIEW & RELATE

- What issues attracted the most intense debate during the drafting and ratification of the Constitution? Why?
- What role did Hamilton imagine the federal government playing in the American economy? Why were his proposals controversial?

Years of Crisis, 1792–1796

By 1792 Hamilton had succeeded in implementing his plan for U.S. economic development. Yet as Washington began his second term in the spring of 1793, signs of strain appeared throughout the nation. The French Revolution, which had begun to dissolve into chaos and terror, posed challenges to foreign trade and diplomacy. Reduced prices for western land fueled migration to the frontier, intensified conflicts between Indians and white settlers, and increased hostilities between the United States and Great Britain. Finally, the excise tax on whiskey inspired discontent among frontier farmers. This cluster of crises reinforced disagreements among Federalists, splitting them into warring factions during Washington's second term.

Foreign Trade and Foreign Wars

Jefferson and Madison led the faction opposed to Hamilton's policies. Their supporters were mainly southern Federalists who envisioned the country's future rooted in agriculture, not the commerce and industry supported by Hamilton and his allies. Jefferson agreed with the Scottish economist Adam Smith that an international division of labor could best provide for the world's people. Americans could supply Europe with food and raw materials in exchange for clothes and other items manufactured in Europe. When wars in Europe, including a revolution in France, disrupted European agriculture in the 1790s, Jefferson's views were reinforced.

The French Revolution (1789–1799) had broader implications for U.S. politics than simply increasing the profits from American wheat. The efforts of French revolutionaries to overthrow the monarchy, end feudal practices, and institute a republic gained enthusiastic support from many Americans, especially the followers of Jefferson and Madison. They formed Republican societies, modeled on the Sons of Liberty, to keep tabs on Federalist encroachments on American rights. Many members adopted the French term *citizen* when addressing each other. Moreover, the strong presence of workers and farmers among France's revolutionary forces sparked further critiques of the "monied power" that drove Federalist policies.

In late 1792, as French revolutionary leaders began executing thousands of priests, aristocrats, and members of the royal family in the Reign of Terror, wealthy Federalists grew more anxious. The beheading of King Louis XVI horrified them, as did the revolution's condemnation of Christianity. When France declared war against Prussia, Austria, and finally Great Britain, merchants worried about the impact on trade, and Hamilton feared a loss of valuable revenue from tariffs. In response, Congress passed the **Neutrality Act** in 1793, prohibiting ships of belligerent nations—including France or Great Britain—from using American ports. This act overrode a 1778 treaty, signed in the midst of the American Revolution, in which the United States had agreed to defend France in any war with Britain.

The immediate effect of the Neutrality Act was positive for American merchants. They eagerly increased trade with colonies in the British and French West Indies, and U.S. ships captured much of the lucrative sugar trade. Employment rose, and a building boom transformed seacoast cities as affluent residents hired carpenters, masons, and other craftsmen to construct fashionable homes in the "Federal" style. At the same time, farmers in the Chesapeake and Middle Atlantic regions benefited from European demand for grain, and the price of American wheat soared.

Yet these benefits did not bring about a political reconciliation. Instead, tensions escalated in the spring of 1793 when the French diplomat Edmond Genêt visited the United States. Republican clubs poured out to hear Citizen Genêt speak, and their members donated generously to support the French Revolution. Thousands of young Americans enlisted as volunteers on privateering vessels that harassed British and Spanish shipping in the Caribbean. At the same time, the British navy began stopping U.S. ships carrying French sugar and seized more than 250 vessels. American merchants were outraged and demanded that the government intervene to protect the "free trade" guaranteed by the Neutrality Act.

President Washington sent John Jay to England to negotiate a settlement with the British. In the meantime, Genêt's popularity began to fade as he sought to pull the United States into the war. Pro-British Federalists were more adamant than Republicans in their disapproval, arguing that Genêt was seeking to provoke conflict. Finally, in August 1793, just as yellow fever erupted in the nation's capital, Washington demanded Genêt's recall to France. Jay returned from England in 1794 with a treaty negotiated with the British, although many congressmen thought he had given away too much and were hesitant to ratify it. The treaty, for instance, did not include an agreement by the British to stop impressing American seamen.

The Whiskey Rebellion

Despite these foreign crises, it was the effect of Federalist policies on the American frontier that crystallized Republican opposition and led to the development of a Democratic-Republican Party. In the early 1790s, Republican societies from Maine to Georgia had demanded the removal of British and Spanish troops from frontier areas, while frontier farmers lashed out at Federalist enforcement of the so-called whiskey tax. Many farmers on the frontier grew corn and turned it into whiskey to make it easier to transport and more profitable to sell. The whiskey tax hurt these farmers, who considered themselves "industrious citizens" and "friends of liberty." Hundreds of them in Pennsylvania, North Carolina, and Kentucky petitioned the federal government for relief.

Much like their counterparts in Massachusetts in the 1780s, western Pennsylvania farmers rallied in 1792 and 1793 to protest the tax and those who enforced it. Former North Carolina Regulator Herman Husband was one of the most outspoken critics of the excise tax (see chapter 5). They burned sheriffs in effigy, marched on courthouses, assaulted tax collectors, and petitioned the federal government. Washington and his advisers failed to respond, paralyzed by a yellow fever epidemic in Philadelphia that ground government operations to a halt. By 1794 an all-out rebellion erupted, with protesters adopting slogans from Stamp Act protests, Shays's Rebellion, and even the French Revolution.

President Washington and his advisers worried that the rebellion could spread and feared that uprisings by white settlers might encourage Indians to rise up as well. Furthermore, Spanish and British soldiers were eager to foment trouble along the frontier, and the Whiskey Rebellion might spark intervention by either Spain or Great Britain. Federalists suspected that pro-French immigrants from Scotland and Ireland were behind the insurgency.

When Shays's Rebellion had erupted in 1787, the confederation government had had no power to intervene. Now, however, the United States could raise an army to quash such insurgencies. In August 1794, Washington federalized militias from four states, calling up nearly thirteen thousand soldiers. The president asked Hamilton, author of the whiskey tax, to accompany the troops into battle. The army that marched into western Pennsylvania in September vastly outnumbered the "whiskey rebels" and easily suppressed the uprising. Having gained victory, only two of the leaders were tried and convicted, and they were later pardoned by Washington.

Online Document Project **The Whiskey Rebellion**
bedfordstmartins.com/hewittlawsonvalue

Washington proved that the Constitution provided the necessary powers to put down internal threats. Yet in doing so, the administration horrified many Americans who viewed the force used against the farmers as excessive. Jefferson, who had resigned as secretary of state in 1793, joined Madison in his outrage at the government's action. Despite a strong aversion to partisan politics among leaders of the Revolutionary generation, the divisions inspired by Hamilton's policies convinced Jefferson and Madison to launch an opposition party known as the Democratic-Republican Party.

Further Conflicts on the Frontier

In one area, Federalists and Democratic-Republicans voiced common concerns: the continued threats to U.S. sovereignty by Indian, British, and Spanish forces. In 1790 Congress had passed the Indian Trade and Intercourse Act to regulate Indian-white relations on the frontier and to ensure fair and equitable dealings. However, the act was widely ignored. Traders regularly cheated Indians, settlers launched private expeditions to claim Indian lands illegally, and government agents approved sham treaties. Federal troops sent to the Northwest Territory to enforce the law ended up fighting against the Indians.

The government's failure to stem the flood of settlers into the Ohio and Mississippi River valleys proved costly. In 1790 Little Turtle, a war chief of the Miami nation, gathered a large force of Shawnee, Delaware, Ottawa, Chippewa, Sauk, Fox, and other Indians. This pan-Indian alliance successfully attacked federal troops in the Ohio valley that fall. A year later, the allied Indian warriors defeated a large force under General Arthur St. Clair, governor of the Northwest Territory (Map 7.2). The stunning defeat shocked Americans, who continued to blame British forces encamped in forts on U.S. soil for encouraging Little Turtle and his warriors. In the meantime, Spanish authorities negotiated with Creeks and Cherokees to attack U.S. settlements on the southern frontier.

Washington decided to deal with problems in the Northwest Territory first, sending 2,000 men under the command of General Anthony Wayne into the Ohio frontier. In the spring of 1794, Wayne's troops built Fort Defiance in the heart of Ohio territory. Augmented by several hundred mounted Kentucky riflemen, Wayne's forces then attacked some 1,500 to 2,000 Indians gathered at a nearby British fort. In the Battle of Fallen Timbers, the pan-Indian forces, led by Little Turtle, suffered a bitter defeat. A year later, the warring Indians in the Northwest Territory signed the Treaty of Greenville, granting the United States vast tracts of land.

Amid this turmoil, in November 1794 the Senate finally approved the **Jay Treaty** with Great Britain, which required the withdrawal of British forces from U.S. soil by 1796. But it also required Americans to make "full and complete compensation" to British firms for debts outstanding at the time of the American Revolution and limited U.S. trade with the British West Indies. Before Jay's controversial treaty took effect, Spain agreed to negotiate an end to hostilities on the southern frontier of the United States. Envoy Thomas Pinckney, a South Carolina planter, negotiated the treaty, which recognized the thirty-first parallel as the boundary between U.S. and Spanish territory

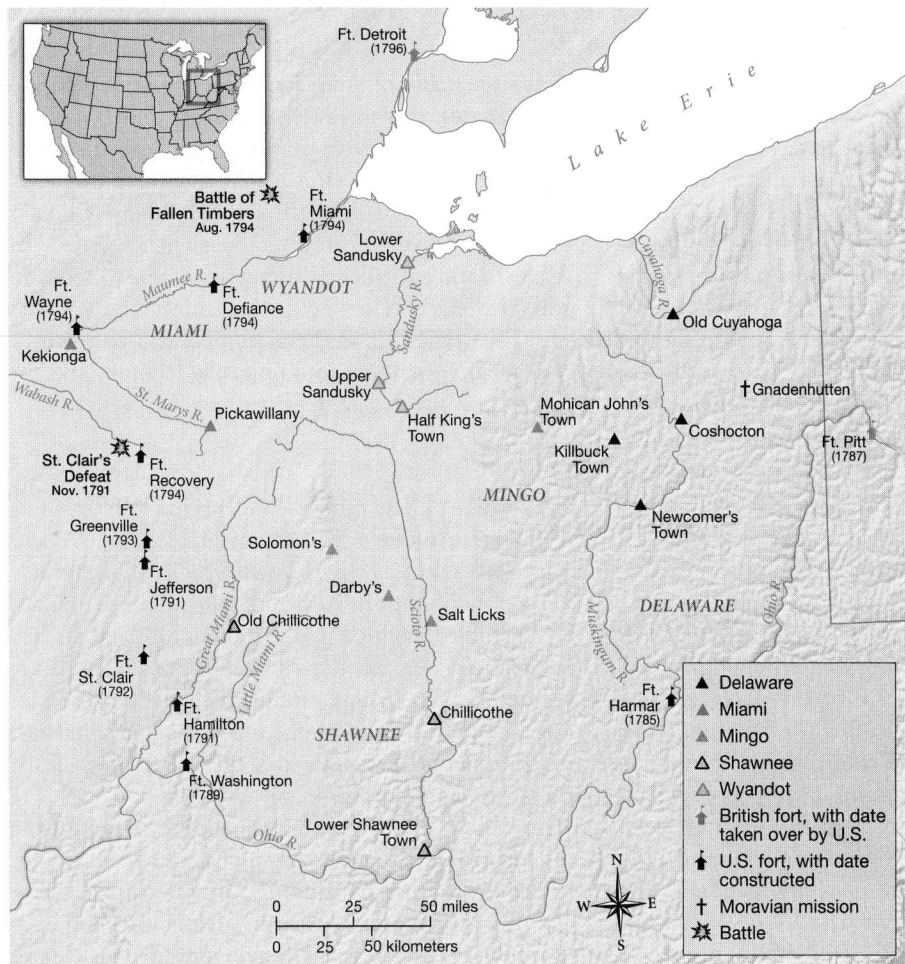

MAP 7.2
American Indians in the Ohio River Valley, c. 1785–1795   In the early to mid-eighteenth century, despite periodic conflicts, Indian tribes in the Ohio River valley forged trade and diplomatic relations with various colonial powers. But once the United States established the Northwest Territory in 1785, conflicts between Indians and U.S. settlers and soldiers escalated dramatically. As tribes forged pan-Indian alliances, the United States constructed numerous forts in the region.

in the South and opened the Mississippi River and the port of New Orleans to U.S. shipping. The Pinckney Treaty, ratified in 1796, advanced the interests of the South, while the Jay Treaty promoted those of the North.

> **REVIEW & RELATE**

- How did events overseas shape domestic American politics in the 1790s?
- What common concerns underlay the Whiskey Rebellion and Shays's Rebellion? How did the U.S. government deal differently with each?

The First Party System

In 1796 executive power was placed in the hands of politicians who represented opposing factions in the national government: John Adams (a Federalist) became president and Thomas Jefferson (a Democratic-Republican) vice president. The two disagreed fundamentally on a wide range of issues, and events soon heightened these divisions. Foreign crises once again fueled political antagonisms as fear of war with Britain or France intensified. In response to the increasingly passionate debates over foreign policy, Federalists in Congress passed two acts in 1798 relating to aliens (immigrants) and to sedition (activities that promote civil disorder). Instead of resolving tensions, however, these laws exacerbated opposition to Federalist rule. By 1800, as the nation's fourth presidential election approached, partisan debates had crystallized into opposing factions, and the Democratic-Republicans threatened to oust the Federalists from power.

The Adams Presidency

The election of 1796 was the first to be contested by candidates identified with opposing factions. After private consultations among party leaders, Federalists supported John Adams for president and Thomas Pinckney for vice president. Though less well organized, Democratic-Republicans chose Thomas Jefferson and Aaron Burr of New York to represent their interests. When the electoral college was established, political parties did not exist and, in fact, were seen as promoting conflict. Thus electors were asked to choose the best individuals to serve, regardless of their views. In 1796 they picked Adams for president and Jefferson for vice president, perhaps hoping to lessen partisan divisions by forcing men of different views to work together. Instead, the effects of an administration divided against itself were nearly disastrous, and opposing interests became even more thoroughly entrenched.

Adams and Jefferson had disagreed on almost every major policy issue during Washington's administration. Not surprisingly, the new president rarely took advice from his vice president, who continued to lead the opposition. At the same time, Adams retained most of Washington's appointees, who repeatedly sought advice from Hamilton, which further undercut Adams's authority. Worse still, the new president had poor political instincts and faced numerous challenges.

At first, foreign disputes enhanced the authority of the Adams administration. The Federalists remained pro-British, and French seizures of U.S. ships threatened to provoke war. In 1798 Adams tried to negotiate compensation for the losses suffered by merchants. When an American delegation arrived in Paris, however, three French agents demanded a bribe to initiate talks.

The Democratic-Republicans in Congress believed that Adams was exaggerating the issue to undermine U.S.-French relations. Adams then made public secret correspondence from the French agents, whose names were listed only as X, Y, and Z. Americans, including Democratic-Republicans, expressed outrage at this French insult to U.S. integrity, which became known as the **XYZ affair**. Congress quickly approved an embargo act that prohibited trade with France and permitted privateering against French ships. In May 1798, Congress allocated funds to build up the navy and defend the American coastline against attack. For the next two years, the United States fought an undeclared war with France.

Despite widespread support for his handling of the XYZ affair, Adams feared dissent from opponents at home and abroad. Consequently, the Federalist majority in Congress passed a series of security acts in 1798. The Alien Act allowed the president to order the imprisonment or deportation of noncitizens and was directed primarily at Irish and Scottish dissenters who criticized the government's pro-British policies. Congress also approved the Naturalization Act, which raised the residency requirement for citizenship from five to fourteen years. Finally, Federalists pushed through the Sedition Act, which outlawed "false, scandalous, or malicious statements against President or Congress" and penalized those who incited hatred of the government.

The First Amendment states that Congress "shall make no law . . . abridging the freedom of speech, or of the press." However, as a Federalist newspaper explained, in the current situation, "All who are against us are at war." No opposition to Federalist policies would be tolerated. Over the next several months, nearly two dozen Democratic-Republican editors and legislators were arrested for sedition, and some were fined and imprisoned.

Democratic-Republicans were, understandably, infuriated by the **Alien and Sedition Acts**. They considered the attack on immigrants an attempt to limit the votes of farmers, artisans, and frontiersmen, who formed the core of their supporters. The Sedition Act also challenged the party since it was Republican critics who faced arrest. Jefferson and Madison encouraged states to pass resolutions that would counter this violation of the Bill of Rights. Accepting resolutions drafted by Jefferson and Madison, legislators in Virginia and Kentucky declared the Alien and Sedition Acts "void and of no force." Virginia went even further, claiming that states had a right to nullify any powers exercised by the federal government that were not explicitly granted to it.

Although the Alien and Sedition Acts curbed dissent in the short run, they reinforced popular concerns about the power wielded by the Federalists. Combined with the on-going war with France, continuing disputes over taxes, and relentless partisan attacks and denunciations in the press, these acts set the stage for the presidential election of 1800.

The Election of 1800 The election of 1800 marked the first transfer of political power in the United States from one party to another. The Democratic-Republican candidate for president, Thomas Jefferson, defeated the Federalist Party incumbent, John Adams. On March 4, 1801, the *Columbian Centinel*, a Federalist newspaper in Boston, viewed Jefferson's inauguration as the end of the peace, prosperity, and honor achieved under the Federalists. The Granger Collection, New York

Monumental Inscription.

" *That life is long which answers Life's great end.*"

YESTERDAY EXPIRED,
Deeply regretted by MILLIONS of grateful Americans,
And by all GOOD MEN,
The FEDERAL ADMINISTRATION
Of the
GOVERNMENT of the *United States* :
Animated by
A WASHINGTON, an ADAMS ;—a
HAMILTON, KNOX, PICKERING, WOL-
COTT, M'HENRY, MARSHALL,
STODDERT and DEXTER.
Æt. 12 years.

Its death was occasioned by the
Secret Arts. and Open Violence
Of Foreign and Domestic Demagogues :
Notwithstanding its whole Life
Was devoted to the Performance of every Duty
to promote
The UNION, CREDIT, PEACE, PROSPER-
ITY, HONOR, and
FELICITY OF ITS COUNTRY.

At its birth it found
The Union of the States dissolving like a Rope of snow ;
It hath left it
Stronger than the Threefold cord.

It found the United States
Bankrupts in Estate and Reputation ;
It hath left them
Unbounded in Credit ; and respected throughout
the World.

The Election of 1800

By 1800 Adams had negotiated a peaceful settlement of U.S. conflicts with France, considering it one of the greatest achievements of his administration. However, other Federalists, including Hamilton, disagreed, continuing to seek open warfare and an all-out victory. Thus the Federalists faced the election of 1800 deeply divided. Democratic-Republicans meanwhile, although more loosely organized than the Federalists, united behind Jefferson. They portrayed the Federalists as the "new British," tyrants who abused their power and violated the rights guaranteed ordinary citizens.

For the first time, congressional caucuses selected candidates for each party. The Federalists agreed on Adams and Charles Cotesworth Pinckney of South Carolina. The Democratic-Republicans again chose Jefferson and Burr as their candidates. The campaign quickly escalated into a series of bitter accusations, with advocates for each side denouncing the other.

In the first highly contested presidential election, the different methods states used to record voters' preferences gained more attention. Only five states determined members of the electoral college by popular vote. In the rest of the states, legislatures appointed electors. In some states, voters orally declared their preference for president; in other states, voters submitted paper ballots. In addition, because the idea of party tickets was new, the members of the electoral college were not prepared for the situation they faced in January 1801, when Jefferson and Burr received exactly the same number of votes. After considerable political maneuvering, Jefferson, the intended presidential candidate, emerged victorious.

Jefferson labeled his election a revolution achieved not "by the sword" but by "the suffrage of the people." The election of 1800 was hardly a popular revolution, given the restrictions on suffrage (of some 5.3 million Americans, only about 550,000 could vote) and the limited participation of voters in selecting the electoral college. Still, partisan factions had been transformed into opposing parties, and the United States had managed a peaceful transition from one party in power to another, which was a development few other nations could claim in 1800.

REVIEW & RELATE

• What were the main issues dividing the Federalists and the Democratic-Republicans?

• What do the Alien and Sedition Acts tell us about attitudes toward political partisanship in late-eighteenth-century America?

Conclusion: A Young Nation Comes of Age

In the 1780s and 1790s, the United States faced numerous obstacles to securing its place as a nation. Financial hardship, massive debts, hostile Indians, and shifting European alliances and conflicts had to be addressed by a federal government that, under the Articles of Confederation, was relatively weak. Yet despite these challenges, the confederation congress did initiate diplomatic relations with European and Indian nations and successfully organized the vast Northwest Territory. Nonetheless, by 1787 concerns about national security, fueled by rebellious farmers and frontier conflicts, led to the drafting of a new constitution. After a fierce battle in many states, the Constitution was ratified, and the federal government's power to raise money, raise armies, and regulate interstate commerce was enhanced.

George Washington served as the first American president, and his administration implemented policies that enhanced U.S. power at home and abroad. Most important, Secretary of the Treasury Alexander Hamilton implemented a series of measures to stabilize the American economy, pay off Revolutionary War debts, and promote trade and industry. Yet these policies also aroused opposition among political leaders like Jefferson and Madison, who viewed agriculture as the foundation of the American nation. And specific acts like the whiskey tax also fueled antagonism among ordinary farmers and frontiersmen. Although the Federalists continued to support Hamilton's economic policies and pro-British diplomacy, they faced growing opposition from agrarian and pro-French Democratic-Republicans.

In 1798 the Federalist-controlled Congress passed the Alien and Sedition Acts, further unifying Democratic-Republicans. By 1800 the Democratic-Republicans had created an opposition party that was less solid in its structure than the Federalists but sufficiently powerful to win control of Congress and the presidency. This peaceful transition in power boded well for the young United States.

Despite political setbacks, the Federalist legacy remained powerful. Many of Hamilton's policies would continue to shape national economic growth, and the Federalists retained their political power in the Northeast for years to come. Hamilton himself retreated from public service following Jefferson's election. Marginalized by the defeat of the Federalists and tainted after admitting to an adulterous affair, he focused on his law practice. Yet he could not stay entirely clear of politics. In 1804 Aaron Burr was passed over as the vice presidential candidate by the Democratic-Republicans and decided to seek the governorship of New York instead. Hamilton worked tirelessly to defeat Burr, and when the vice president lost, he challenged his nemesis to a duel. On July 11, 1804, Burr fatally shot Hamilton. Even in death, though, Hamilton retained his stature as the architect of the nation's first economic policy.

Meanwhile Democratic-Republicans, many of whom were small farmers and frontiersmen, often fared worse than their Federalist counterparts, at least economically, even after Jefferson's election. We do not know whether Daniel Shays voted in 1800, but he likely supported Jefferson. The rebellion Shays led in 1787 had helped convince many political leaders of the need for a new constitution, yet his role in creating the new nation was largely forgotten. Indeed, Shays, like many ordinary Continental soldiers, spent the rest of his life in relative obscurity. Having moved with his family to eastern New York in 1788, he finally received a federal military pension in 1818, just seven years before he died.

Shays's pension was granted by a U.S. Congress still controlled by Democratic-Republicans. The Democratic-Republican Party would not be seriously challenged for national power until 1824, giving it nearly a quarter century to implement its vision of the United States. Yet developing a vision in opposition to that of the Federalists proved far easier than implementing that vision once the Democratic-Republicans—a heterogeneous group—held the power of the central government in their own hands.

Chapter Review

MAKE IT STICK

 LearningCurve **bedfordstmartins.com/hewittlawsonvalue**
After reading the chapter, use LearningCurve to retain what you've read.

IDENTIFY KEY TERMS

Identify and explain the significance of each term below.

Northwest Land Ordinance
  (1785 and 1787) (p. 168)
Shays's Rebellion (p. 172)
Virginia Plan (p. 174)
three-fifths compromise (p. 175)
Federalists (p. 176)
Antifederalists (p. 176)
Bill of Rights (p. 178)

Neutrality Act (p. 180)
Democratic-Republican Party (p. 181)
Whiskey Rebellion (p. 181)
Jay Treaty (p. 182)
Pinckney Treaty (p. 183)
XYZ affair (p. 184)
Alien and Sedition Acts (p. 185)

REVIEW & RELATE

Answer the focus questions from each section of the chapter.

1. What challenges did the new nation face in the immediate aftermath of the Revolutionary War?

2. How and why did the conflict between America and Great Britain continue after the war ended?

3. How did America's experience of the Revolutionary War change the lives of African Americans and women?

4. What do uprisings by farmers and debtors tell us about social and economic divisions in the early Republic?

5. What issues attracted the most intense debate during the drafting and ratification of the Constitution? Why?

6. What role did Hamilton imagine the federal government playing in the American economy? Why were his proposals controversial?

7. How did events overseas shape domestic American politics in the 1790s?

8. What common concerns underlay the Whiskey Rebellion and Shays's Rebellion? How did the U.S. government deal differently with each?

9. What were the main issues dividing the Federalists and the Democratic-Republicans?

10. What do the Alien and Sedition Acts tell us about attitudes toward political partisanship in late-eighteenth-century America?

ONLINE DOCUMENT PROJECTS

◆ **The Whiskey Rebellion**
◆ **Debating the Constitution**

After reading the primary sources in these document sets, answer the **Interpret the Evidence** questions to help you analyze each of the documents, and then answer the **Put It in Context** question(s) to help you relate the documents to the topics and themes you read about in the chapter.

bedfordstmartins.com/hewittlawsonvalue

TIMELINE OF EVENTS

1780–1804	• Northern states pass gradual emancipation laws
March 1783	• Officers encamped at Newburgh, New York, threaten to mutiny
1784	• U.S. commissioners meet with Iroquois delegates at Fort Stanwix, New York
1785	• Northwest Land Ordinance passed
	• Annapolis Convention
1786–1787	• Shays's Rebellion
1787	• Constitutional Convention in Philadelphia
	• Northwest Land Ordinance revised
June 1788	• U.S. Constitution ratified
1789	• Alexander Hamilton named secretary of the treasury
	• Judiciary Act of 1789 passed

1789–1799	• French Revolution
1790–1794	• Little Turtle leads pan-Indian alliance against American settlements in the Ohio valley
1791	• Bill of Rights ratified
1793	• Neutrality Act passed
July–October 1793	• Yellow fever epidemic paralyzes Philadelphia
1794	• Whiskey Rebellion
	• Bethel African-American Methodist Church in Philadelphia founded
1796	• Jay Treaty and Pinckney Treaty ratified
	• Democratic-Republicans and Federalists contest presidential election
1798	• Alien and Sedition Acts passed

8

LearningCurve
✓ **bedfordstmartins.com/hewittlawsonvalue**
After reading the chapter, use LearningCurve
to retain what you've read.

New Frontiers

1790–1820

AMERICAN HISTORIES

When Parker Cleaveland graduated from Harvard University in 1799, his well-to-do family might have expected him to pursue a career in medicine, law, or the ministry. Instead, he turned to teaching. In 1805 Cleaveland secured a position in Brunswick, Maine, a territory that was then part of the state of Massachusetts, as the first professor of mathematics and natural philosophy at Bowdoin College.

In 1806 he married Martha Bush, who joined him on the Maine frontier. The Cleavelands emerged as leading citizens of Brunswick, a community of some three thousand residents. Most local families supported themselves in the lumbering or shipbuilding trades, but the recently opened college attracted middle-class professionals, whose intellectual interests and consumption habits transformed Brunswick into a more cosmopolitan town.

Over the next twenty years, the Cleavelands raised eight children, boarded and fed dozens of students, entertained faculty and visiting scholars, and corresponded with professors at other institutions. The busy couple served as a model of new ideals of companionate marriage, in which husbands and wives shared interests, friendship, and affection. They also instilled republican virtue and scientific principles in their charges. While Parker taught the students math and science, Martha trained them in manners and morals.

Professor Cleaveland believed in using scientific research to benefit society. Thus when local workers asked him to identify colored rocks found in the river, Parker began studying geology and chemistry. In 1816 he published his

Elementary Treatise on Mineralogy and Geology, which served as a text for college students and a handbook for travelers interested in the topic. He also lectured throughout New England, displaying mineral samples and performing chemical experiments.

The Cleavelands viewed Bowdoin College and the surrounding community as a laboratory in which distinctly American values and ideas could be taught and sustained. So, too, did the residents of other college towns. Although less than 1 percent of men in the United States and no women attended universities at the time, frontier colleges were considered important vehicles for bringing republican virtue—especially the desire to act for the public good rather than for personal gain—to the far reaches of the young nation. Yet these colleges were also enmeshed in the country's racial history. Several were constructed with the aid of slave labor, and all were built on land purchased or confiscated from Indians. In Maine, the Penobscot nation lost considerable territory to whites following the American Revolution, much of it under the direction of Massachusetts governor John Bowdoin II, the college's namesake. Moreover, the Indians' displacement continued as the success of colleges like Bowdoin attracted more white families to frontier regions.

The purchase of the Louisiana Territory by President Thomas Jefferson in 1803 marked out a new American frontier and ensured further encroachments on native lands. This vast territory covered 828,000 square miles and stretched from the Mississippi River to the Rocky Mountains and from New Orleans to present-day Montana. The area was home to tens of thousands of Indian inhabitants.

In the late 1780s, a baby girl, later named Sacagawea, was born to a family of Shoshone Indians who lived in an area later included in the Louisiana Purchase. In 1800 she was on a berry-picking expedition when her group was attacked by a Hidatsa raiding party that killed several Shoshones and took a number of women and children captive. Sacagawea

Portrait of Meriwether Lewis, 1815.
Private Collection/The Bridgeman Art Library

and her fellow captives were marched some five hundred miles to a Hidatsa-Mandan village near present-day Bismarck, North Dakota. Eventually Sacagawea was sold to a French fur trader, Toussaint Charbonneau, along with another young Shoshone woman, and both became his wives.

In November 1804, an expedition led by Meriwether Lewis and William Clark set up winter camp near the village where Sacagawea lived. Lewis and Clark had been hired by the U.S. government to lead an exploring party through the newly acquired Louisiana Territory. Both Charbonneau, who spoke French and Hidatsa, and Sacagawea joined the expedition as interpreters in April 1805.

The only woman in the party, Sacagawea traveled with her infant son strapped to her back. Her presence was crucial, as Clark noted in his journal: "The Wife of Chabono our interpreter we find reconsiles all the Indians, as to our friendly intentions. A woman with a party of men is a token of peace."

BOTH CLEAVELAND AND SACAGAWEA forged new identities on the frontiers of the United States. Yet while Cleaveland gained fame as "the father of American mineralogy," Sacagawea was rarely mentioned in accounts of the journey over the following decades. The American histories of both Sacagawea and Cleaveland were shaped by the efforts of political leaders and ordinary citizens to extend the boundaries of the emerging nation. Their different fates make clear that the young United States was marked by stark racial, class, and gender divisions—divisions that were more often deepened than bridged by the nation's expansion westward.

Creating an American Identity

In his inaugural address in March 1801, President Thomas Jefferson noted that the United States was "kindly separated by nature and a wide ocean from the exterminating havoc of one quarter of the globe," that is, Europe. He believed that the distance allowed Americans to develop their own unique culture and institutions. Jefferson also viewed the nation's extensive frontiers as a boon to its development, providing room for "our descendants to the thousandth and thousandth generation."

For many Americans, education offered one means of ensuring a distinctive national identity. Public schools could train American children in republican values, while the wealthiest among them could attend private academies and colleges. Written works such as newspapers, sermons, books, and magazines helped forge a common identity among the nation's far-flung citizens. Even the presence of Indians and Africans contributed to art and literature that were uniquely American. In addition, the construction of a new capital city to house the federal government offered a potent symbol of nationhood.

Yet these developments also illuminated underlying conflicts that defined the young nation. The decision to move the U.S. capital south from Philadelphia was prompted by concerns among southern politicians about the power of northern economic and political elites. The very construction of the capital, in which enslaved and free workers labored side by side, highlighted racial and class differences in the nation. Educational opportunities differed by race and class as well as by sex. The question thus remained: Could a singular notion of American identity be forged in a country where differences of race, class, and sex loomed so large?

Education for a New Nation

The desire to create a specifically American culture began as soon as the Revolution ended. In 1783 Noah Webster, a schoolmaster, declared that "America must be as independent in *literature* as in *Politics*, as famous for *arts* as for *arms*." To this end, the twenty-five-year-old Webster published the *American Spelling Book*, which by 1810 had become the second best-selling book in the United States (the Bible was the first). In 1828 Webster produced his *American Dictionary of the English Language*.

Webster's books were widely used in the nation's expanding network of schools and academies and led to more standardized spelling and pronunciation of commonly used words. Before the Revolution, public education for children, which focused on basic reading and writing skills, was widely available in New England and the Middle Atlantic region. In the South, only those who could afford private schooling—perhaps a quarter of the boys and 10 percent of the girls—received any formal instruction. Few young people enrolled in high school in any part of the colonies, and far fewer attended college. Following the Revolution, state and national leaders proposed ambitious plans for public education. In 1789 Massachusetts became the first state to institute free public elementary education for all children, and private academies and boarding schools proliferated throughout the nation.

Before 1790, the American colonies boasted nine colleges that provided further education for young men, including Harvard, Yale, King's College (Columbia), Queen's College (Rutgers), and the College of William and Mary. After independence, many Americans worried that these institutions were tainted by British and aristocratic influences. Situated in urban centers or crowded college towns, they were also criticized as centers of vice where youth might be corrupted by "scenes of dissipation and amusement." New colleges based on republican ideals needed to be founded.

Frontier towns offered opportunities for colleges to enrich the community and benefit the nation. Located in isolated villages, these colleges assured parents that students would focus on education. The young nation benefited as well, albeit at the expense of Indians and their lands. The founders of Franklin College in Athens, Georgia, encouraged white settlement in the state's interior, an area still largely populated by Creeks and Cherokees. And frontier colleges provided opportunities for ethnic and religious groups outside the Anglo-American mainstream—like Scots-Irish Presbyterians—to cement their place in American society.

Frontier colleges were organized as community institutions in which extended families—composed of administrators and faculty, their wives and children, servants and slaves, and students—played the central role. The familial character of these colleges—and their lower tuition fees—was also attractive to parents. Women were viewed as exemplars of virtue in the new nation, and the wives of professors were thus especially important in maintaining a refined atmosphere. They held salons where students could learn proper deportment and social skills. They also served as maternal figures for young adults living away from home. In some towns, students in local female academies joined college men on field trips and picnics to cultivate proper relations between the sexes.

Literary and Cultural Developments

While frontier colleges expanded educational and cultural opportunities, older universities also contributed to the development of a national identity. A group known as the Hartford Wits, most of them graduates of Yale, gave birth to a new literary tradition. This circle of poets, playwrights, and essayists expressed distinctly American (though largely Federalist) perspectives. Members of the Hartford Wits published paeans to democracy, satires about Shays's Rebellion, and plays about specifically American dilemmas, such as the proper role of the central government in a republican nation.

The young nation also produced a number of novelists. Advances in printing and the production of paper increased the circulation of novels, a literary genre developed in Britain and continental Europe at the turn of the eighteenth century. At the same time, improvements in girls' education produced a growing audience among women, who were thought to be the genre's most avid readers. Novelists like Susanna Rowson and Charles Brockden Brown sought to educate readers about virtuous action by placing ordinary women and men in moments of high drama that tested their moral character. They also emphasized new marital ideals, by which husbands and wives became partners and companions in building a home and family.

Among the most important American literary figures to emerge in the early nineteenth century was Washington Irving. While living in Europe in the 1810s, he wrote a series of short stories and essays, including "The Legend of Sleepy Hollow" and "Rip Van Winkle," that were published in his *Sketchbook* in 1820. These popular folktales drew on the Dutch culture of the Hudson valley region in New York and often poked fun at more celebratory tales of early American history. But Irving also wrote serious essays. One challenged colonial accounts of Indian-English conflicts, which he argued ignored courageous actions by Indians while applauding atrocities committed by whites.

While Irving achieved fame by making fun of romanticized versions of American history, books that glorified the nation's past were also enormously popular. Among the most influential were a three-volume *History of the Revolution* (1805) written by Mercy Otis Warren and the *Life of Washington* (1806), a celebratory if somewhat fanciful biography by an Anglican clergyman, Mason "Parson" Weems. The influence of American authors increased as residents in both urban and rural areas purchased growing numbers of books. By 1820–1821, for instance, an astonishing 80 percent of households of middling wealth in Chester County, Pennsylvania, owned books.

Artists, too, devoted considerable attention to historical themes. Charles Willson Peale painted Revolutionary generals while serving in the Continental Army and became best known for his portraits of George Washington. Samuel Jennings offered a more radical perspective on the nation's character when he presented *Liberty Displaying the Arts and Sciences* (1792) to the Philadelphia Library Company. Many of the library's directors opposed slavery, and Jennings portrayed Lady Liberty offering a book to a group of attentive African Americans. Engravings, which were less expensive than paintings, circulated widely, and many also highlighted national symbols like flags, eagles, and Lady Liberty.

Engravings of nature were especially popular. Books like Cleaveland's *Elementary Treatise on Mineralogy and Geology* included plates that illustrated rocks and geological formations. William Bartram's *Travels* (1791), based on his journey through the southeastern United States and Florida, illustrated plants and animals, such as the alligator, previously unknown to Anglo-American scientists.

In the 1780s, Benjamin Franklin helped found the American Philosophical Society in Philadelphia to promote American literature and science. Like-minded gentlemen in Boston and Salem established the American Academy of Arts and Sciences. Colleges like Bowdoin, Franklin, and Dickinson advanced scientific research in frontier regions, while the University of Pennsylvania in Philadelphia established the nation's first medical school. As in the arts, American scientists built on developments in continental Europe and Great Britain, but the young nation prided itself on contributing its own expertise.

 Online Document Project
Literary and Cultural Developments in the Early United States
bedfordstmartins.com/hewittlawsonvalue

The Racial Limits of American Culture

One subject that received significant attention from writers and scientists in the United States was the American Indian. White Americans in the late eighteenth century often wielded native names and symbols as they worked to create a distinct national identity. In long-settled regions along the Atlantic seaboard, where Indian nations no longer posed a significant threat, some Americans followed in the tradition of the Boston Tea Party, dressing as Indians to protest economic and political tyranny. Antirent rioters in the Hudson valley, participants in the Whiskey Rebellion, and squatters in the backcountry of Maine disguised themselves as Indians before attacking landlords, tax collectors, and land speculators. More well-to-do whites also embraced Indian names, costumes, and symbols. Tammany societies, for example, which were named after a mythical Delaware chief called Tammend, promoted patriotism and republicanism in the late eighteenth century and attracted large numbers of skilled artisans, lawyers, and merchants.

Poets, too, focused on American Indians. In his 1787 poem "Indian Burying Ground," Philip Freneau offered a sentimental portrait that highlighted the lost heritage of a nearly extinct native culture in New England. The theme of lost cultures and heroic (if still savage) Indians became even more pronounced in American poetry in the following decades.

Such sentimental portraits of American Indians were less popular along the nation's frontier, where Indians still posed a threat. Even a woman like Sacagawea, who aided the efforts of Lewis and Clark, did not become the object of literary or artistic efforts for several generations. Sympathetic depictions of Africans and African Americans by white artists and authors appeared with even less frequency. Most were produced in the North and were intended, like Jennings's *Liberty*, for the rare patrons who opposed slavery. Typical images of blacks and Indians were far more demeaning. Especially when describing Indians in frontier regions, authors, artists, politicians, and soldiers tended to focus on their savagery, their duplicity, or both. Most images of Africans and African

Americans highlighted their innate inferiority and exaggerated their perceived physical and intellectual differences from white Americans.

Whether their depiction was realistic, sentimental, or derogatory, Africans, African Americans, and American Indians were almost always presented to the American public through the eyes of whites. Few blacks or Indians had access to English-language schools, books, or newspapers, and few whites were willing to publish or purchase works by those who did. Educated African Americans like the Reverend Richard Allen of Philadelphia or the Reverend Thomas Paul of Boston generally wrote for black audiences or corresponded privately with sympathetic whites. Similarly, cultural leaders among American Indians worked mainly within their own nation either to maintain traditional languages and customs or to introduce their people to Anglo-American ideas and beliefs.

White Americans who demanded improved education generally ignored or excluded blacks and Indians. Most southern planters had little desire to teach their slaves to read and write. Even in the North, states did not generally incorporate black children into their plans for public education. It was African Americans in cities with large free black populations who established the most long-lived schools for their race. The Reverend Allen opened a Sunday school for children in 1795 at his African Methodist Church, and other free blacks formed literary and debating societies for young people and adults. Still, only a small percentage of African Americans received an education equivalent to that available to whites in the new Republic.

U.S. political leaders were more interested in the education of American Indians, but government officials never proposed any systematic method of providing them with schools. Instead, various religious groups sent missionaries to the Seneca, Cherokee, and other tribes. A few of the most successful students were then sent to American colleges to be trained as ministers or teachers for their own people. However, just as with African Americans, only a small percentage of American Indians were taught to read or write in English, and whites made almost no efforts to teach Indians the languages and histories of their own nations.

The divergent approaches that whites took to Indian and African American education demonstrated broader assumptions about the two groups rooted in geographical expansion and slave labor. Most white Americans believed that Indians were untamed and uncivilized, but not innately different from Europeans. Africans and African Americans, on the other hand, were assumed to be inferior, and most whites believed that no amount of education could make blacks their intellectual or moral equals. As U.S. frontiers expanded, white Americans considered ways to "civilize" Indians and incorporate them into the nation. But the requirements of slavery made it much more difficult for whites to imagine African Americans as anything more than lowly laborers, despite free blacks who clearly demonstrated otherwise.

 Online Document Project   Race Relations in the Early Republic
bedfordstmartins.com/hewittlawsonvalue

Emigration and Colonization

Some African Americans did question the benefits of remaining in the United States. In the late 1780s, the Newport African Union Society in Rhode Island developed a plan to establish a community for American blacks in Africa. Many whites, too, viewed the settlement of blacks in Africa as the only way to solve the nation's racial dilemma. William

Thornton, a Quaker physician who had inherited his father's sugar plantation in the West Indies, joined a group in London who tried to establish a free black commonwealth on the west coast of Africa. He traveled to the United States to promote what he called colonization. But when Thornton presented his plans to the Free African Society in Philadelphia in 1787, local leaders opposed the effort.

Over the next three decades, the idea of emigration (as blacks viewed it) or colonization (as whites saw it) received widespread attention. Those who opposed slavery hoped to persuade slave owners to free or sell their human property on the condition that they be shipped to Africa. Others assumed that free blacks could find opportunities for economic, religious, and political leadership in Africa that did not exist in the United States. Still others simply wanted to rid the nation of its race problem by ridding it of blacks. In 1817 a group of southern slave owners and northern merchants formed the **American Colonization Society (ACS)** to carry "civilization" and Christianity to the African continent and establish colonies of freed slaves and free-born American blacks there. Although some African Americans supported this scheme, northern free blacks generally opposed it, viewing colonization as an effort originating "more immediately from prejudice than philanthropy."

Ultimately the plans of the ACS proved impractical. Particularly as cotton production expanded from the 1790s on, few slave owners were willing to emancipate their workers. Indeed, even in the supposedly enlightened communities where higher education flourished, slavery was widely accepted. In southern colleges, in particular, slaves cleared land, constructed buildings, cleaned rooms, did laundry, and prepared meals.

Building a National Capital

The construction of Washington City, the nation's new capital, depended on the labor of slaves as well. The capital was situated along the Potomac River in an area surrounded by farms and plantations. More than 300,000 slaves lived in Virginia and Maryland, the states that provided the land for the federal district, and the commissioners appointed to oversee the city's construction held almost 100 slaves themselves. Between 1792 and 1809, dozens of enslaved men were hired out by their owners, who were paid $50 to $70 annually for their slaves' labor on the city. Most enslaved men cleared land, built roads, and constructed the White House and the Capitol. Some performed skilled labor as carpenters and sawyers (who cut trees and lumber) or as assistants to stonemasons and surveyors. A few enslaved women were hired as cooks, nurses, and washerwomen.

Free blacks also participated in the development of Washington, working in many of the same positions as slaves did. One of the most noteworthy African Americans involved in the project was Benjamin Banneker, a self-taught clock maker, astronomer, and surveyor. He was hired as an assistant to the surveyor, Major Andrew Ellicott, in 1791, helping to plot the 100-square-mile area on which the capital was to be built.

African Americans worked alongside whites, including many Irish immigrants, whose wages were kept in check by the availability of slave labor. Most workers, regardless of race, faced poor housing, sparse meals, and limited medical care as well as malarial fevers. Despite these obstacles, in less than a decade, a system of roads was laid out and cleared, the Executive Mansion was built, and the north wing of the Capitol was completed.

Although Washington City was considered a symbol of the nation, it was experts from abroad who created the U.S. capital. The streets were laid out according to plans developed

The United States Capitol   This watercolor by William Russell Birch presents a view of the Capitol in Washington, D.C., before it was burned down by the British during the War of 1812. Birch had emigrated from England in 1794 and lived in Philadelphia. As this painting suggests, neither the Capitol nor the city was as yet a vibrant center of republican achievements.   Library of Congress

by the French engineer Pierre L'Enfant, the Executive Mansion was designed by the Irish-born James Hoban, and the Capitol building was envisioned by the West Indian physician turned architect (and colonizationist) William Thornton. The Capitol's construction was directed by the English architect Benjamin Latrobe, and African Americans and immigrants made up the majority of the labor force. What was perhaps most "American" about the nation's capital were the diverse races and nationalities that designed and built it.

Washington's founders envisioned the city as a beacon to the world, proclaiming the advantages of republican principles. But its location on a slow-moving river and its clay soil left the area hot, humid, and dusty in the summer and muddy and damp in the winter and spring. When John Adams and his administration moved to Washington in June 1800, they considered themselves on the frontiers of civilization. The mile-long road from the Capitol to the Executive Mansion was filled with tree stumps and was nearly impossible to navigate in a carriage. On rainy days, when roads proved impassable, officials walked or rode horses to work. That November, when Abigail Adams moved into the Executive Mansion, she complained that the roof leaked, the huge house was hard to heat, and firewood was difficult to obtain. Abigail Adams was not alone in criticizing the capital city. Although the founders considered it "an experiment in republican simplicity," most residents painted Washington in harsh tones. New Hampshire representative Ebenezer

Matroon wrote a friend, "If I wished to punish a culprit, I would send him to do penance in this place . . . this swamp—this lonesome dreary swamp, secluded from every delightful or pleasing thing." Others described the city as a "fever-stricken morass."

Despite the drawbacks, the new capital played an important role in the social and political world of American elites, drawing wealthy and influential Americans to this center of federal power. From January through March, the height of the social season, the wives of congressmen, judges, and other officials created a lively schedule of teas, parties, and balls in the new capital city. When Thomas Jefferson became president, he opened the White House to visitors on a regular basis, a style that seemed appropriate for the man who had drafted the Declaration of Independence. This, too, helped reshape the Washington social scene. Yet for all his republican principles, Jefferson moved into the Executive Mansion with a retinue of slaves.

In decades to come, Washington City would become Washington, D.C., a city with broad boulevards decorated with beautiful monuments to the American political experiment. And the Executive Mansion would become the White House, a proud symbol of republican government. Still, Washington was characterized by wide disparities in wealth, status, and power, which were especially visible when Jefferson occupied the Executive Mansion and slaves labored in its kitchen, laundry, and yard. Moreover, President Jefferson's efforts to incorporate new territories into the United States only exacerbated these divisions by providing more economic opportunities for planters, investors, and white farmers while ensuring the expansion of slavery and the decimation of American Indians.

(REVIEW & RELATE)

● How did developments in education, literature, and the arts contribute to the emergence of a distinctly American identity?

● What place did blacks and American Indians inhabit in the predominant white view of American society and culture?

Extending U.S. Borders

Thomas Jefferson, like other leading Democratic-Republicans, favored limited government, imagining a nation made up of small, independent farmers who had little need and less desire for an expansive federal government (see chapter 7). Initially, the president was successful in imposing his vision on the young government. By the middle of his first term, however, developments in international affairs converged with Supreme Court rulings to expand federal power. Jefferson contributed directly to this expansion by purchasing the Louisiana Territory from France. In turn, the development of this vast territory raised new questions about the place of Indians and African Americans in a republican society.

A New Administration Faces Challenges

In 1801 Democratic-Republicans worked quickly to implement their vision of limited federal power. Holding the majority in Congress, they repealed the hated whiskey tax and let the Alien and Sedition Acts expire. The Senate also approved

Jefferson's appointment of Albert Gallatin, who served as a lawyer for the whiskey rebels, as secretary of the treasury. The president significantly reduced government expenditures, and he and Gallatin immediately set about slashing the national debt, cutting it nearly in half by the end of Jefferson's second term. Democratic-Republicans also worked to curb the powers granted to the Bank of the United States and the federal court system.

Soon, however, international upheavals forced Jefferson to make fuller use of his presidential powers. The U.S. government had paid tribute to the Barbary States of North Africa during the 1790s to gain protection for American merchant ships. The new president opposed this practice and in 1801 refused to continue the payments. The Barbary pirates quickly resumed attacks on American ships, and Jefferson was forced to send the U.S. navy and Marine Corps to retaliate. Although the combined American and Arab mercenary force did not achieve their objective of capturing Tripoli, the Ottoman viceroy agreed to negotiate a new agreement with the United States. Seeking to avoid all-out war, Congress accepted a treaty with the Barbary States that reduced the tribute payment.

Jefferson had also followed the developing crisis in the West Indies during the 1790s. In 1791 slaves on the sugar-rich island of Saint Domingue launched a revolt against French rule. The **Haitian Revolution** escalated into a complicated conflict in which free people of color, white slave owners, and slaves formed competing alliances with British and Spanish forces as well as with leaders of the French Revolution. Finally, in December 1799, Toussaint L'Ouverture, a former slave and military leader, claimed the presidency of the new Republic of Haiti. But Napoleon Bonaparte seized power in France that same year and sent thousands of troops to reclaim the island. Although Toussaint was shipped off to France, where he died in prison, other Haitian rebels continued the fight. As the struggle intensified, thousands of Haitian refugees, black and white, fled to the United States. However, by November 1803, prolonged fighting, yellow fever, and the loss of sixty thousand soldiers forced Napoleon to admit defeat. Haiti became the first independent black-led nation in the Americas.

Incorporating the Louisiana Territory

Thomas Jefferson had enthusiastically supported the American and French revolutions, but he was not sympathetic to an independent black nation. Nonetheless, in France's defeat he saw an opportunity to gain navigation rights on the Mississippi River, which the French controlled. This was a matter of crucial concern to Americans living west of the Appalachian Mountains. Jefferson sent fellow Virginian James Monroe to France to offer Napoleon $2 million to ensure Americans the right of navigation and deposit (that is, offloading cargo from ships) on the Mississippi. To Jefferson's surprise, Napoleon offered instead to sell the entire **Louisiana Territory** for $15 million.

The president agonized over the constitutionality of such a purchase. Since the Constitution contained no provisions for buying land from foreign nations, a strict interpretation would not allow the purchase. In the end, though, the opportunity proved too tempting, and in late 1803 the president finally agreed to buy the Louisiana Territory based on a loose interpretation of the Constitution. Because the acquisition of the vast territory proved enormously popular among both politicians and ordinary Americans, few cared that it expanded presidential and congressional powers.

Congress soon appropriated funds for an exploratory expedition known as the **Corps of Discovery** to map the terrain. This effort, which Sacagawea and her husband joined, was led by Captain Meriwether Lewis, who had served as Jefferson's personal secretary, and William Clark, an army officer. Beginning on May 14, 1804, Lewis, Clark, and three dozen men traveled thousands of miles up the Missouri River, through the northern plains, over the Rocky Mountains, and beyond the Louisiana Territory to the Pacific coast. Members of the expedition meticulously recorded observations about local plants and animals as well as Indian residents, providing valuable evidence for young scientists like Parker Cleaveland and fascinating information for ordinary Americans.

Sacagawea was the only Indian to travel as a permanent member of the expedition, but other native women and men assisted the Corps when it journeyed near their villages. They provided food and lodging for the travelers, hauled baggage up steep mountain trails, and offered food, horses, and other trade items. The one African American on the expedition, a slave named York, also helped negotiate trade with local Indians. York recognized his value as a trader, hunter, and scout and asked Clark for his freedom when the expedition ended in 1806. York did eventually become a free man, but it is not clear whether it was by Clark's choice or because York escaped.

Other expeditions followed Lewis and Clark's successful venture. In 1806 Lieutenant Zebulon Pike led a group to explore the southern portion of the Louisiana Territory (Map 8.1). After traveling from St. Louis to the Rocky Mountains, the expedition traveled into Mexican territory. In early 1807, Pike and his men were captured by Mexican forces. They were returned to the United States at the Louisiana border that July. Pike had learned a great deal about lands that would eventually become part of the United States and about Mexican desires to overthrow Spanish rule, information that proved valuable over the next two decades.

Early in this series of expeditions, in November 1804, Jefferson stood for reelection, winning an easy victory. His popularity among farmers, already high, increased when Congress passed an act that reduced the minimum allotment for federal land sales from 320 to 160 acres. This act allowed more farmers to purchase land on their own rather than via speculators. Yet by the time of his second inauguration in March 1805, the president's vision of limiting the powers of the federal government had been shattered by his own actions and those of the Supreme Court.

The Supreme Court Extends Its Reach

The Supreme Court, the last bastion of Federalist power, extended its reach during Jefferson's presidency. In 1801, just before the Federalist-dominated Congress turned over power to the Democratic-Republicans, it passed a new **Judiciary Act**. The act created six additional circuit courts and sixteen new judgeships, which President Adams filled with Federalist "midnight appointments" before he left office. Jefferson accused the Federalists of having "retired into the judiciary" and worried that "from that battery all the works of Republicanism are to be beaten down and destroyed." Meanwhile John Marshall, who sat as the chief justice of the Supreme Court (1801–1835), insisted that the powers of the Court must be equal to and balance those of the executive and legislative branches.

One of the first cases to test the Court's authority involved a dispute over President Adams's midnight appointments. Jefferson's newly appointed secretary of state, James Madison, refused to deliver the appointment papers to several of these appointees,

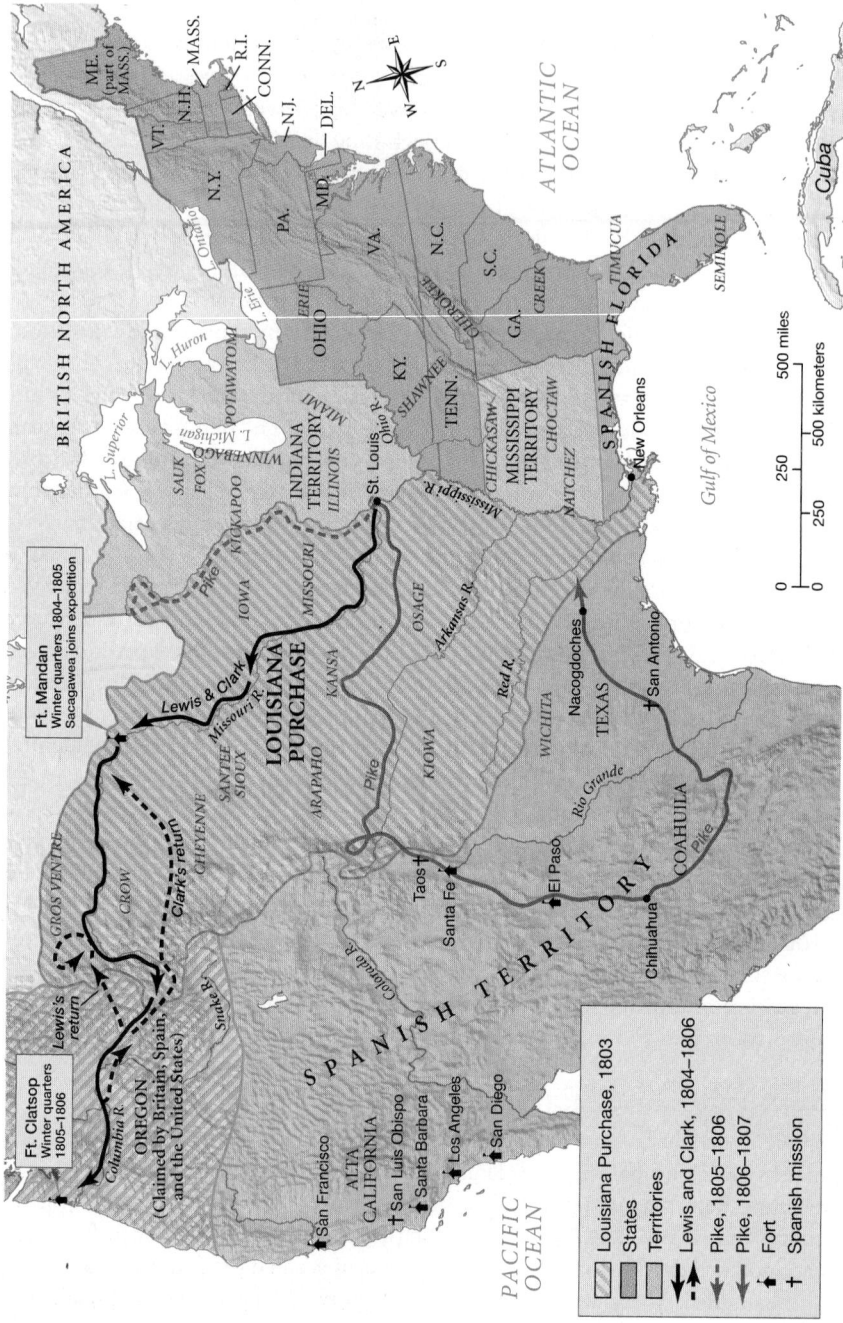

MAP 8.1

Lewis and Clark and Zebulon Pike Expeditions, 1804–1807   The expeditions led by Meriwether Lewis, William Clark, and Zebulon Pike illustrate the vast regions explored in just four years after the purchase of the Louisiana Territory by the United States. Lewis and Clark as well as Pike journeyed through and beyond the borders of that territory, gathering important information about Indian nations, plants, animals, and the natural terrain throughout the West.

including William Marbury. Marbury and three others sued Madison to receive their commissions. In *Marbury v. Madison* (1803), the Supreme Court ruled that it was not empowered to force the executive branch to give Marbury his commission. But in his decision, Chief Justice Marshall declared that the Supreme Court did have the duty "to say what the law is." He thus asserted a fundamental constitutional point: that the Supreme Court had the authority to decide what federal laws were constitutional. The following year, the Court also claimed the right to rule on the constitutionality of state laws. In doing so, the Court rejected the view of Democratic-Republicans who claimed that state legislatures had the power to repudiate federal law.

Over the next dozen years, the Supreme Court continued to assert Federalist principles. In 1810, to strengthen its claims for judicial review, the nation's highest court insisted that it was the proper and sole arena for determining matters of constitutional interpretation. In another case, *McCulloch v. Maryland* (1819), the Federalist-dominated Court reinforced its loose interpretation of the Constitution's implied powers clause. This clause gave the federal government the right to "make all laws which shall be necessary and proper" for carrying out the explicit powers granted to it by the Constitution. Federalists had used this clause to establish the first national bank. Despite Democratic-Republicans' early opposition to a national bank, Congress chartered the Second Bank of the United States in 1816. Its branch banks issued notes that circulated widely in local business communities. Legislators in Maryland, believing that these banks had gained excessive power, approved a tax on their operations. Marshall's Court ruled that the establishment of the bank was "necessary and proper" for the functioning of the national government and rejected Maryland's right to tax the branch bank, claiming that "the power to tax involves the power to destroy."

By 1820 the Supreme Court, under the forceful direction of John Marshall, had established the power of judicial review—the authority of the nation's highest court to rule on cases involving states as well as the nation. From the Court's perspective, the judiciary was as important an institution in framing and preserving a national agenda as Congress or the president.

Democratic-Republicans Expand Federal Powers

Although Democratic-Republicans generally opposed Marshall's rulings, they, too, continued to expand federal power. Once again, international developments drove the Jefferson administration's political agenda. By 1805 the security of the United States was threatened by continued conflicts between France and Great Britain. Both sought alliances with the young nation, and both ignored U.S. claims of neutrality. Indeed, each nation sought to punish Americans for trading with the other. Britain began stopping American ships carrying sugar and molasses from the French West Indies on the pretense of searching them for British deserters. Between 1802 and 1811, the Royal Navy impressed (forced into service) more than eight thousand sailors taken from such ships, including many American citizens. Remembering similar abuses during the colonial period, Americans demanded action. Yet the United States was in no position to launch a war against Great Britain. France claimed a similar right to stop American ships if they continued to trade with Great Britain.

Unable to convince foreign powers to recognize U.S. neutrality, Jefferson and Madison pushed for congressional passage of an embargo that they hoped would, like colonial boycotts, force Great Britain's hand. In 1807 Congress passed the **Embargo Act**, which prohibited U.S. ships from leaving their home ports until Britain and France repealed their restrictions on American trade. Although the act kept the United States out of war, it had a devastating impact on national commerce.

New England merchants immediately voiced their outrage. Some merchants began sending items to Europe via Canada. In response, Congress passed the Force Act, granting extraordinary powers to customs officials to end such smuggling. The economic pain spread well beyond the merchant class. Young professionals like Parker Cleaveland were affected by the embargo-fueled recession; he was forced to sell his home to the Bowdoin trustees and become their tenant in 1807. Farmers and planters also suffered the embargo's effects, as did urban workers, especially in port cities where sailors and dockworkers faced escalating unemployment. The recession raised deep concerns about the expansion of federal power. Congress and the president had not simply regulated international trade; they had brought it to a halt.

In Jefferson's first inaugural address, he acknowledged that "it will rarely fall to the lot of imperfect man to retire from this station [the presidency] with the reputation and the favor which bring him into it." Not only had Jefferson failed to contain the powers of the federal government, but the Embargo Act also threatened the livelihood of those who had once seen him as their champion. At the end of his second term, a Philadelphia seaman wrote to him, claiming that because of the Embargo Act he had lost what little he owned and threatening to "throttle his honored neck."

Despite such sentiments, many Americans still viewed Jefferson favorably. He had devoted his adult life to the creation of the American Republic, and he had purchased the Louisiana Territory, opening up vast lands to American exploration and development. This geographical boon had encouraged inventors and artisans to pursue ideas that would help the young nation take full advantage of its resources and recover from its current economic plight.

REVIEW & RELATE

- How did Jefferson and the Democratic-Republicans contribute to the expansion of the role of the federal government in American life?

- How did the conflict between France and Great Britain in the late eighteenth and early nineteenth centuries lead to domestic problems in the United States?

Remaking the U.S. Economy

As the United States expanded geographically, technological ingenuity became a highly valued commodity. The spread of U.S. settlements into new territories necessitated improved forms of transportation and increased the need for muskets and other weapons to protect the nation's frontier. The growing population also fueled improvements in agriculture and manufacturing to meet demands for clothing, food, and farm equipment. Continued conflicts with Great Britain and France also highlighted the need to develop the nation's natural resources and technological capabilities. Still, the daily lives of most Americans changed only slowly. And some workers, especially enslaved women and men, found that technological advances just added to their burdens.

The U.S. Population Grows and Migrates

Although Democratic-Republicans initially hoped to limit the powers of the national government, the rapid growth of the United States pulled in the opposite direction. An increased population, combined with the exhaustion of farmland along the eastern seaboard, fueled migration to the west as well as the growth of cities. By 1820 one-quarter of non-Indian Americans lived west of the Appalachian Mountains. These developments heightened conflicts with Indians and over slavery, but they also encouraged advances in transportation and communication and improvements in agriculture and manufacturing.

Sacagawea must have realized that the expedition she accompanied was a harbinger of white expansion, but many Indians only gradually came to realize that the few dozen men who joined Lewis and Clark heralded the arrival of hundreds and then thousands of migrants from the East. As white Americans encroached farther and farther on lands long settled by native peoples, Indian tribes in the eastern United States and the midsection of the nation were forced westward. As early as 1800, groups like the Shoshones, who originally inhabited the Great Plains, had been forced into the Rocky Mountains by Indians moving into the plains from the Mississippi and Ohio valleys (Map 8.2).

At the same time, although the vast majority of Americans continued to live in rural areas, a growing number moved to cities (defined as places with 8,000 or more inhabitants). New York City and Philadelphia both counted more than 100,000 residents by 1810. In New York, immigrants, most of them Irish, made up about 10 percent of the population in 1820 and twice that percentage five years later. During this time, the number of African Americans in New York City increased to more than 10,000. New cities began to emerge along the nation's frontier as well. After the United States acquired the Louisiana Territory, New Orleans grew rapidly, and western migration fueled the development of Cincinnati. Even smaller frontier towns served important functions for migrants traveling west. Trading posts appeared across the Mississippi valley, which eased the migration of thousands headed farther west. They served as sites of exchange between Indians and white Americans and created the foundations for later cities (Table 8.1).

Most Americans who headed west hoped to benefit from the increasingly liberal terms offered by the federal government for purchasing land. Yeomen farmers sought sufficient acreage to support their families and grow some additional crops for sale. They were eager to settle in western sections of the original thirteen states, in the Ohio River valley, or in newly opened territories along the Missouri and Kansas Rivers. In the South, small farmers had to compete with slave-owning planters who headed west in the early nineteenth century. Migrants to the Mississippi valley also had to contend with a sizable population of long-settled Spanish residents and French planters who had taken refuge from Saint Domingue with their slaves, as well as Chickasaw and Creek Indians in the South and Shawnee, Chippewa, Sauk, and Fox Indians farther north.

The development of roads and turnpikes hastened the movement of people and the transportation of goods. Frontier farmers required methods to get their produce to eastern markets quickly and cheaply. Before completion of the Lancaster Turnpike in Pennsylvania, it cost as much to carry wheat and other items overland the sixty-two miles to Philadelphia as it did to ship them by sea from Philadelphia to London. Those

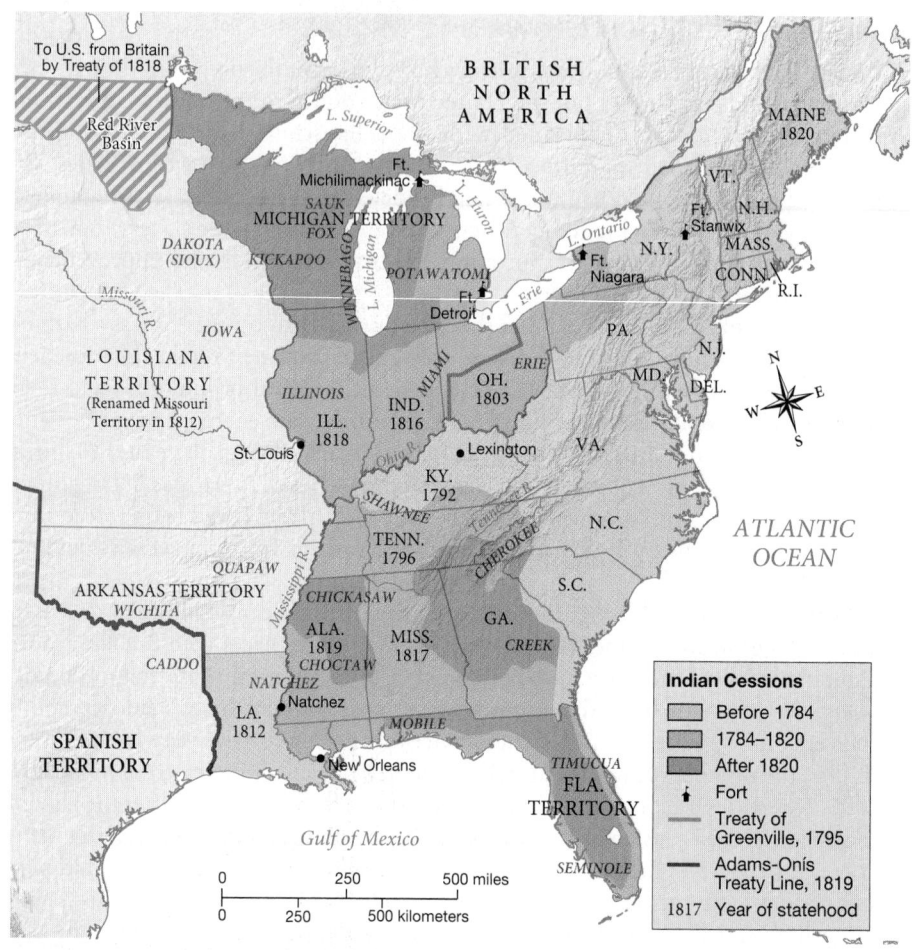

MAP 8.2

Indian Land Cessions, 1790–1820   With the ratification of the Constitution, the federal government gained greater control over Indian relations, including land cessions. At the same time, large numbers of white settlers poured into regions west of the Appalachian Mountains. The U.S. government gained most Indian land by purchase or treaty, but these agreements were often the consequence of military victories by the U.S. army.

who lived farther west faced even greater challenges. With the admission of Kentucky (1792), Tennessee (1796), and Ohio (1803) to the Union, demands for congressional assistance in building transportation routes grew louder. By 1819 five more states were admitted along the Mississippi River, from Louisiana to Illinois.

During Jefferson's administration, Albert Gallatin urged Congress to fund internal improvements—that is, roads and canals—to enhance the economic development of the nation. Legislatures chartered and sometimes helped fund improved transportation in their own states, but Gallatin focused on transportation across regions. He advocated a "great turnpike road" along the Atlantic seaboard from Maine to Georgia as well as

TABLE 8.1　Prices at George Davenport's Trading Post, Rock Island, Illinois, c. 1820

Item	Price	Item	Price
Ax	$6.00	Large copper kettle	$30.00
Beaver trap	$8.00	Lead	$0.20 per pound
Black silk handkerchief	$2.00	Lead shot for guns	$1.00 per 5 pounds
Breechcloth	$3.00	Medium copper kettle	$10.00
Bridles	$2.00–$10.00	Muskrat spear	$2.00
Chain for staking down traps	$0.75 per 6 feet	Muskrat trap	$5.00
		Muslin or calico shirt	$3.00
Combs	$1.00 per pair	Ordinary butcher knife	$0.50
File (for sharpening axes)	$2.00	Sheet iron kettle	$10.00
		Small copper kettle	$3.00
Flannel	$1.00 per yard	Spurs	$6.00 per pair
Flannel mantle	$3.00	Tin kettle	$14.00
Gunflints	$1.00 per 15	Tomahawk	$1.50
Hand-size mirrors	$0.25	Trade gun	$20.00–$25.00
Heavy wool cloth	$10.00 per yard	Wool blanket	$4.00
Hoe	$2.00	Wool mantle (short cloak or shawl)	$4.00
Horn of gunpowder	$1.50		
Horses	$35.00–$50.00		

Source: Will Leinicke, Marion Lardner, and Ferrel Anderson, *Two Nations, One Land* (Rock Island, IL: Citizens to Preserve Black Hawk Park, 1981).

roads to connect the four main rivers that flowed from the Appalachians to the Atlantic Ocean. In 1815 Congress approved funds for one such project, the **National Road** from western Maryland through southwestern Pennsylvania to Wheeling, West Virginia. This so-called Cumberland Road was completed in 1818, and in the following decades it was extended into Ohio and Illinois.

Carrying people and goods by water was even faster and cheaper than transporting them over land, but rivers ran mainly north and south. In addition, although loads could be delivered quickly downstream, the return voyage was long and slow. While politicians advocated the construction of canals along east-west routes to link river systems, inventors and mechanics focused on building boats powered by steam to overcome the problems of sending goods upriver.

Oliver Evans, a machinist in Philadelphia, developed a steam-powered gristmill—to produce flour from grain—in 1788. Then in 1804 he invented a high-pressure steam engine attached to a dredge that cleaned the silt around the docks in Philadelphia harbor. He had insufficient funds, however, to pursue work on a steam-powered boat.

In New York State, Robert Fulton sought to improve on Evans's efforts, using the low-pressure steam engine developed in England. Fulton had moved to Paris in the early nineteenth century to train as a painter. While there, he met the wealthy ambassador Robert Livingston, who helped negotiate the Louisiana Purchase. Livingston convinced Fulton to focus on engineering and provided funds for him to do so. In 1807 Fulton launched the first successful steamboat, the *Clermont*, which traveled up the Hudson River from New York City to Albany in only thirty-two hours. The powerful Mississippi River proved a greater challenge, but by combining Evans's high-pressure steam engine with a flat-bottom hull that avoided the river's sandbars, mechanics who worked along the frontier improved Fulton's original design and launched the steamboat era in the West.

Technology Reshapes Agriculture and Industry

Advances in agricultural and industrial technology paralleled the development of roads and steamboats. Here, too, a single invention spurred others, inducing a **multiplier effect** that inspired additional dramatic changes during the decades following the Revolution. Two inventions—the cotton gin and the spinning machine—were especially notable in transforming southern agriculture and northern industry, transformations that were deeply intertwined.

American developments were also closely tied to the earlier rise of industry in Great Britain. By the 1770s, British manufacturers had built spinning mills in which steam-powered machines spun raw cotton into yarn. Importing cotton from Britain's colonies, British manufacturers thrived. Eager to maintain their monopoly on industrial technology, the British made it illegal for engineers to emigrate. They could not, however, keep everyone who worked in a cotton mill from leaving the country. At age fourteen, Samuel Slater was hired as an apprentice in an English mill that used a yarn-spinning machine designed by Richard Arkwright. Slater was promoted to supervisor of the factory, but at age twenty-one he sought greater opportunities in America. While working in New York City, he learned that Moses Brown, a wealthy Rhode Island merchant, was seeking help in developing a machine like Arkwright's. Funded by Rhode Island investors and assisted by local craftsmen, Slater designed and built a spinning mill in Pawtucket.

The mill opened in December 1790 and began producing yarn, which was then woven into cloth in private shops and homes. By 1815 a series of cotton mills, most built to look like New England meetinghouses in order to limit hostility from local farmers, dotted the Pawtucket River. These factories promised a steady income for workers in the mills, most of whom were the wives and children of farmers, and ensured employment for weavers in the countryside. They also increased the demand for cotton in New England just as British manufacturers sought new sources of the crop as well.

Ensuring a steady supply of cotton, however, required another technological innovation, this one created by Eli Whitney. After graduating from Yale at age twenty-seven, Whitney agreed to serve as a private tutor for a planter family in South Carolina. On the ship carrying him to his new position, Whitney met Catherine Greene, widow of the Revolutionary War general Nathanael Greene. He ended up staying on her Mulberry Plantation near Savannah, Georgia, where local planters complained to him about the difficulty of making a profit on cotton in the area. Long-staple cotton, grown in the Sea Islands, yielded enormous profits, but the soil in most of the South could sustain only the short-staple variety, which required hours of intensive labor to separate its sticky green seeds from the cotton fiber.

In 1793, in as little as ten days, Eli Whitney built a machine that could ease the labor of deseeding short-staple cotton. His **cotton gin** consisted of a wooden box with a mesh screen, rollers, brushes, and wire hooks. The cotton boll was drawn through the mesh, where wire hooks caught the seeds and the rotating brushes then swept the cotton lint into a tray. Whitney's gin could clean as much cotton fiber in one hour as several workers could clean in a day. Recognizing the gin's value, Whitney received a U.S. patent, but because the machine was easy to duplicate, he never profited from his invention.

Fortunately, Whitney had other ideas that proved more profitable. In June 1798, amid U.S. fears of a war with France, the U.S. government granted him an extraordinary contract to produce 4,000 rifles in eighteen months. Rifles were then produced individually by highly trained artisans, but the inventor claimed he could devise a machine to manufacture guns in large quantities. By January 1801, having produced only 500 rifles, Whitney met with national political leaders to reassure them that success was near. Adapting the plan of Honoré Blanc, a French mechanic who devised a musket with interchangeable parts, Whitney demonstrated the potential for using machines to produce various parts of a musket, which could then be assembled in mass quantities. With Jefferson's enthusiastic support, the federal government extended Whitney's contract, and by 1809 his New Haven factory was turning out 7,500 guns annually.

Whitney's factory became a model for the **American system of manufacturing**, in which water-powered machinery and the division of production into many small tasks allowed less skilled workers to produce mass quantities of a particular item, like guns or shoes. Whitney viewed this system as a boon to men and women who were unable or unwilling to obtain apprenticeships in skilled crafts. In factories, they could be trained quickly to do a particular task and thereby support themselves or supplement family earnings from farming.

The factories developed by Whitney and Slater became training grounds for younger mechanics and inventors who devised improvements in machinery or set out to solve new technological puzzles. Their efforts also transformed the lives of generations of workers—enslaved and free—who planted and picked the cotton, spun the yarn, wove the cloth, and sewed the clothes that cotton gins and spinning mills made possible.

The Cotton Gin Invented by Eli Whitney in 1793, the cotton gin, which separated cotton fibers from seed, transformed American industry and agriculture. As presented in this engraving, which was likely part of the patent application, Whitney's invention was a relatively simple device that had an enormous impact on the South and the nation at large. Culver Pictures/ The Art Archive at Art Resource, NY

Transforming Household Production

Slater and Whitney were among the most influential American inventors, but both required the assistance and collaboration of other inventors, machinists, and artisans to implement their ideas. The achievement of these enterprising individuals was seen by many Americans as part of a larger spirit of inventiveness and technological ingenuity that marked the United States as a young nation. That spirit led to a cascade of inventions between 1790 and 1820.

Cotton gins and steam engines, steamboats and interchangeable parts, gristmills and spinning mills—each of these items and processes was improved upon over time and led to myriad other inventions. For instance, in 1811 Francis Cabot invented a power loom for weaving, a necessary step once spinning mills began producing more yarn than hand weavers could use. Similarly, Jethro Wood perfected the cast-iron plow in 1819, ensuring that western farmers could provide adequate food for the small but rising population of city dwellers and factory workers.

Despite these rapid technological advances, the changes that occurred in the early nineteenth century were more evolutionary than revolutionary. Most political leaders and social commentators viewed gradual improvement as a blessing. For many Americans, the ideal situation consisted of either small mills scattered through the countryside or household enterprises that could supply neighbors with finer cloth, wool cards, or other items that improved home production.

The importance of domestic manufacturing increased after passage of the Embargo Act as imports of cloth and other items fell dramatically. Small factories, like those along the Pawtucket River, increased their output, and so did ordinary housewives. Blacksmiths, carpenters, and wheelwrights busily repaired and improved the spindles, looms, and other equipment that allowed family members to produce more and better cloth from wool, flax, and cotton. New ideas about companionate marriage, which emphasized affection and mutual obligations between spouses, may have encouraged husbands and wives to work more closely in these domestic enterprises. While husbands generally carried out the heavier or more skilled parts of home manufacturing, like weaving, wives spun yarn and sewed together sections of cloth into finished goods.

At the same time, daughters, neighbors, and servants remained critical to the production of household items. In Hallowell, Maine, in the early nineteenth century, the midwife Martha Ballard worked alongside her daughters and a niece, producing the goods necessary to survive on the northern frontier, even as she supplemented her husband's income as a surveyor. In more populated areas, older forms of mutuality continued alongside newer patterns of companionate marriage. Neighbors shared tools and equipment while those with specialized skills assisted neighbors—threading a loom, for instance—in exchange for items they needed. Yet young couples who joined in these activities no doubt imagined themselves embarking on more egalitarian marriages than those of their parents. If they ended up living on the southern frontier, however, they might well discover that traditional patterns of hierarchical marriage prevailed there, shaping both household production and social life.

In wealthy households, whatever the contours of marriage, servants and slaves took on a greater share of domestic labor by the late eighteenth and early nineteenth centuries. Most female servants in the North were young and unmarried. Some arrived with children in tow or became pregnant while on the job, a mark of the rising rate of out-of-wedlock births following the Revolution. Planters' wives in the South had fewer worries in this regard because if household slaves became pregnant, their children added to the slave owner's labor supply. And on larger plantations, owners increasingly assigned a few enslaved women to spin, cook, wash clothes, make candles, and wait on table. Plantation mistresses also hired the wives of small farmers and landless laborers to turn cotton into yarn, weave yarn into cloth, and sew clothing for slaves and children. While mistresses in both regions continued to engage in household production, they also expanded their roles as domestic managers.

Still, at the turn of the nineteenth century, most people continued to live on family farms; to produce or trade locally for food, clothing, and other basic needs; and to use techniques handed down for generations to produce candles and soap, prepare meals, and deliver babies. Yet by 1820, their lives, like those of wealthier Americans, were transformed by the expanding market economy. More and more families sewed clothes with machine-spun thread made from cotton ginned in the American South, worked their fields with cast-iron plows, and varied their diet by adding items shipped from other regions by steamboats.

Technology, Cotton, and Slaves

Some of the most dramatic technological changes occurred in agriculture, and none was more significant than the cotton gin, which led to the vast expansion of agricultural production in the South. This in turn fueled regional specialization, ensuring that residents in one area of the nation—the North, South, or West—depended on those in other areas. Southern planters relied on a growing demand for cotton from northern merchants and manufacturers. At the same time, planters, merchants, manufacturers, and factory workers became more dependent on western farmers to produce the grain and livestock needed to feed the nation.

As cotton gins spread across the South, any thoughts of abolishing slavery in the region disappeared. Instead, cotton and slavery expanded into the interior of many southern states as well as into the lower Mississippi valley. Cotton was not the only crop produced in the South—in Louisiana, planters made their fortunes on sugar and in South Carolina on rice—but it quickly became the most important. In 1790 southern farms and plantations produced about 3,000 bales of cotton, each weighing about 300 pounds. By 1820, with the aid of the cotton gin, the South produced more than 330,000 bales annually (Table 8.2). For southern blacks, increased production meant increased burdens. Because seeds could be separated from raw cotton with much greater efficiency, farmers could plant vastly larger quantities of the crop. On small farms, the work was still performed primarily by family members, neighbors, or hired hands. But planters could purchase additional slaves, particularly as cotton prices rose in the early nineteenth century.

The dramatic increase in the amount of cotton planted and harvested each year was paralleled by

TABLE 8.2 Growth of Cotton Production in the United States, 1790–1830

Year	Production in Bales
1790	3,135
1795	16,719
1800	73,145
1805	146,290
1810	177,638
1815	208,986
1820	334,378
1825	532,915
1830	731,452

Source: Lewis Cecil Gray, *History of Agriculture in the Southern United States to 1860*, vol. 2 (Gloucester, MA: Peter Smith, 1958).

a jump in the size of the slave population. Thus even as northern states began to abolish the institution and the international slave trade ended (in 1808), southern planters significantly increased the number of slaves they held. Some smuggled in women and men from Africa and the Caribbean. Most planters, however, depended on enslaved women to bear more children, increasing the size of their labor force through natural reproduction. In addition, planters in the Deep South—from Georgia and the Carolinas west to Louisiana—began buying slaves from farmers in Maryland and Virginia, where cotton and slavery were less profitable.

In 1790 there were fewer than 700,000 slaves in the United States. By 1820 there were nearly 1.5 million. Still, because of the increased competition for field hands to plant, maintain, and harvest the cotton crop, the price of slaves increased, roughly doubling between 1795 and 1805. The dramatic growth of slave markets in Charleston and New Orleans was one measure of the continued importance of the slave trade as cotton lands moved west.

In the early nineteenth century, most white southerners believed that there was enough land to go around. And the rising price of cotton allowed small farmers to imagine they would someday be planters. Some southern Indians also placed their hopes in cotton. Cherokee and Creek Indians cultivated the crop, even purchasing black slaves to increase production. Some Indian villages now welcomed ministers to their communities, hoping that embracing Protestantism and "American" culture might allow them to retain their current lands. Yet other native residents foresaw the increased pressure for land that cotton cultivation produced and organized to defend themselves from whites invading their territory. Regardless of the policies adopted by Indians, cotton and slavery expanded rapidly into Cherokee- and Creek-controlled lands in the interior of Georgia and South Carolina. And the admission of the states of Louisiana, Mississippi, and Alabama between 1812 and 1819 marked the rapid spread of southern agriculture farther westward.

Enslaved men and women played critical roles in the South's geographical expansion. Without their labor, neither cotton nor sugar could have become mainstays of the South's economy. Because clearing new cotton fields and planting and harvesting sugarcane involved heavy labor, most planters selected young slave men and women to move west, breaking apart families in the process. Some slaves resisted their removal to new plantations. If forced to go, they could still use their role in the labor process to limit owners' control. Slaves worked slowly, broke tools, and feigned illness or injury. Enslaved women and men hid out temporarily as a respite from brutal work regimes or harsh punishments. Others ran to areas controlled by Indians, hoping for better treatment, or to regions where slavery was no longer legal.

Still, given the power and resources wielded by whites, most slaves had to find ways to improve their lives within the system of bondage. The end of the international slave trade helped blacks in this regard since planters then had to depend more on natural reproduction to increase their labor supply. To ensure that slaves lived longer and healthier lives, planters were forced to provide sturdier housing, better clothing, and increased food allotments. Some slaves gained leverage to fish, hunt, or maintain small gardens in order to improve their diet. With the birth of more children, southern blacks also developed more extensive kinship networks, ensuring that family members could care for children if their parents were compelled to move west. Enslavement was still brutal, but slaves made small gains that improved their chances of survival.

Southern slaves also established their own religious ceremonies, often held in the woods or swamps at night. African Americans were swept up as well in the religious revivals that burned across the southern frontier beginning in the 1790s. Itinerant preachers, or circuit riders, held camp meetings that tapped into deep emotional wells of spirituality. Baptist and Methodist clergy drew free and enslaved blacks as well as white frontier families to their gatherings. They encouraged physical displays of spiritual rebirth, from trembling and quaking to calling out and dancing, offering release from the oppressive burdens of daily life for poor whites and blacks alike.

Evangelical religion, combined with revolutionary ideals promoted in the United States and Haiti, proved a potent mix, and planters rarely lost sight of the potential dangers this posed to the system of bondage. Outright rebellions occurred only rarely, yet the successful revolt of blacks in Haiti reminded slaves and owners alike that uprisings were possible. In 1800 Gabriel, an enslaved blacksmith in Richmond, Virginia, plotted such a rebellion. His supporters rallied around the demand for "Death or Liberty." Gabriel's plan to kill all whites except those who opposed slavery failed when informants betrayed him to local authorities. Nonetheless, news of the plot traveled across the South and terrified white residents, reminding them that the promise of new frontiers could not be separated from the dangers embedded in the nation's oppressive racial history.

REVIEW & RELATE

- How did new inventions and infrastructure improvements contribute to the development of the American economy?
- Why did slavery expand rapidly and become more deeply entrenched in southern society in the early nineteenth century?

Conclusion: New Frontiers and New Challenges

The geographical and economic expansion that marked the period from 1790 to 1820 inspired scientific and technological advances as well as literary and artistic paeans to a distinctly American identity. For young, ambitious men like Parker Cleaveland, Eli Whitney, Washington Irving, and Meriwether Lewis, the frontiers that opened in education, science, literature, and exploration offered opportunities for fame and financial success. Though his name is unfamiliar today, Cleaveland was offered prestigious professorships as well as the presidency of Bowdoin College during the early decades of the nineteenth century. He chose, however, to live out his life as a professor of mathematics, chemistry, and mineralogy in Brunswick, Maine, where he died in 1858.

Of course, not all white men had the luxury of a college education or the resources to invest in commercial enterprises or technological improvements. Many sought opportunities on the frontier, hoping to find fertile land, abundant wildlife, or opportunities for trade. In some cases, they and their families faced Indians angered by the constant encroachment of white Americans on their lands. In other cases, land speculators and planters bought up western lands, raising prices and pushing the frontier farther west.

The same developments that provided opportunities for enterprising white men also transformed the lives of white women. Those of elite or middling status benefited from improved educational opportunities and new ideals that highlighted mothers' role in raising children and marriage based on companionship and mutual responsibilities. Yet these changes occurred gradually and unevenly, and many men expected their wives to fulfill all their traditional household obligations while also providing their husband with greater affection and attention. At the same time, domesticity itself changed as the market economy allowed some women to purchase goods they had once produced at home. Such changes increased expectations regarding the quality of domestic life, even though many women still had to supply most of their needs through intensive household labor.

Transformations in white society introduced even more difficult challenges for African Americans. While blacks in the North had greater hopes of gaining their freedom, most remained enslaved until the 1820s or later. Southern slaves faced far worse prospects. As cotton cultivation expanded into new territories, many slaves were forced to move west and to labor on bigger farms and plantations. There they honed means of survival and resistance that became even more crucial in the decades ahead.

At the same time, all along the expanding U.S. frontier, American Indians faced continued pressure to embrace white culture, leave their lands, or both. In 1810 Sacagawea, Charbonneau, and their son Baptiste apparently traveled to St. Louis at the invitation of William Clark, who offered to pay for Baptiste's education. The next spring, Charbonneau and his wife returned to their village, leaving Baptiste in Clark's care. It is not clear whether Sacagawea ever saw her son again, but William Clark penned the phrase "Se car ja we au Dead" on the cover of his cash book for 1825–1828, suggesting that she died during those years. By then, the Shoshone and Hidatsa nations where she was raised had begun to face the onslaught of white settlement. They, along with Indians living in older areas like Georgia, the Carolinas, and Tennessee, resisted the claims of the United States on their ancestral lands and struggled to control the embattled frontier.

Thus even as the young nation conquered new frontiers in education, technology, and the arts, it was forced to defend itself against attacks both internal and external. In the 1810s and 1820s, new conflicts erupted over slavery and against Indians. But the United States also faced its first major economic crisis, while Great Britain and France challenged American sovereignty. New frontiers created new opportunities but also intensified older challenges and conflicts.

Chapter Review

IDENTIFY KEY TERMS

Identify and explain the significance of each term below.

American Colonization Society (ACS) (p. 197)

Haitian Revolution (p. 200)

Louisiana Territory (p. 200)

Corps of Discovery (p. 201)

Judiciary Act of 1801 (p. 201)

Marbury v. Madison (p. 203)

McCulloch v. Maryland (p. 203)

Embargo Act (p. 203)

National Road (p. 207)

multiplier effect (p. 208)

cotton gin (p. 209)

American system of manufacturing (p. 209)

REVIEW & RELATE

Answer the focus questions from each section of the chapter.

1. How did developments in education, literature, and the arts contribute to the emergence of a distinctly American identity?

2. What place did blacks and American Indians inhabit in the predominant white view of American society and culture?

3. How did Jefferson and the Democratic-Republicans contribute to the expansion of the role of the federal government in American life?

4. How did the conflict between France and Great Britain in the late eighteenth and early nineteenth centuries lead to domestic problems in the United States?

5. How did new inventions and infrastructure improvements contribute to the development of the American economy?

6. Why did slavery expand rapidly and become more deeply entrenched in southern society in the early nineteenth century?

ONLINE DOCUMENT PROJECTS

◆ **Race Relations in the Early Republic**
◆ **Literary and Cultural Developments in the Early United States**

After reading the primary sources in these document sets, answer the **Interpret the Evidence** questions to help you analyze each of the documents, and then answer the **Put It in Context** question(s) to help you relate the documents to the topics and themes you read about in the chapter.

bedfordstmartins.com/hewittlawsonvalue

TIMELINE OF EVENTS

1789
• Massachusetts institutes free public elementary education for all children

1790
• Spinning mill designed and built by Samuel Slater opens

1790–1820
• Cotton production in the South increases from 3,000 to 330,000 bales annually

• U.S. slave population more than doubles from 700,000 to 1.5 million

1791–1803
• Free and enslaved blacks revolt against French rule in Saint Domingue

1792–1809
• New capital of Washington City constructed

1793
• Eli Whitney invents cotton gin

1801
• Federalists pass new Judiciary Act

• Jefferson sends U.S. force to challenge Barbary pirates

1803
• United States purchases Louisiana Territory from France

• Haiti established as the first independent black-led nation in the Americas

• *Marbury v. Madison*

1804–1806
• Corps of Discovery explores Louisiana Territory

April 1805
• Sacagawea joins Corps of Discovery

1807
• Robert Fulton launches first successful steamboat

• Embargo Act passed

1810
• Population of both New York and Philadelphia exceeds 100,000

1816
• Parker Cleaveland publishes *Elementary Treatise on Mineralogy and Geology*

1817
• American Colonization Society founded

1819
• *McCulloch v. Maryland*

1820
• One-quarter of non-Indian Americans live west of the Appalachian Mountains

• Washington Irving publishes *Sketchbook*

1828
• Noah Webster publishes *American Dictionary of the English Language*

✓ LearningCurve
bedfordstmartins.com/hewittlawsonvalue
After reading the chapter, use LearningCurve
to retain what you've read.

Defending and Redefining the Nation

1809–1832

AMERICAN HISTORIES

Dolley Payne, a future First Lady, was raised on a Virginia plantation. But her Quaker parents, moved by the Society of Friends' growing antislavery sentiment, decided to free their slaves. In 1783, when Dolley was fifteen, the Paynes moved to Philadelphia. There, Dolley's father suffered heavy economic losses, and Dolley lost her first husband and her younger son to yellow fever. In 1794 the young widow met and married Virginia congressman James Madison. The two made a perfect political couple. James was brilliant but reserved, while Dolley, witty and charming, loved entertaining. When the newly elected president Thomas Jefferson appointed James secretary of state in 1801, the couple moved to Washington.

Since Jefferson and his vice president, Aaron Burr, were widowers, Dolley Madison served as hostess for White House affairs. When James Madison succeeded Jefferson as president in 1809, he, too, depended on his wife's social skills and networks. Dolley held lively informal receptions to which she invited Federalists, Democratic-Republicans, diplomats, cabinet officers, and their wives. These social events helped bridge the ideological differences that continued to divide Congress and proved crucial in creating a unified front when Congress declared war on Great Britain in 1812.

During the War of 1812, British forces attacked Washington City and burned the Executive Mansion. With the president away, his wife was left to secure important state papers, emerging as a symbol of national courage at a critical moment in the war. When peace came the following year, Dolley Madison quickly reestablished a busy social calendar to help mend conflicts that had erupted during the war.

In 1817, at the end of the president's second term, the Madisons left Washington for Virginia just as a young Scots-Cherokee trader named John Ross entered the political arena. Born in 1790 in the Cherokee nation, John (also known as Guwisguwi) was the son of a Scottish trader and his wife, who was both Cherokee and Scottish. John Ross was raised in an Anglo-Indian world in eastern Tennessee where he played with Cherokee children and attended tribal ceremonies and festivals but was educated by private tutors and in Protestant missionary schools. At age twenty, Ross was appointed as a U.S. Indian agent among the Cherokees and during the War of 1812 served as an adjutant (or administrative assistant) in a Cherokee regiment.

After the war, Ross focused on business ventures in Tennessee, including the establishment of a plantation. He also became increasingly involved in Cherokee political affairs, using his bilingual skills and Protestant training to represent Indian interests to government officials. In 1819 Ross was elected president of the Cherokee legislature. In the 1820s, he moved to Georgia, near the Cherokee capital of New Echota, where he served as president of the Cherokee constitutional convention in 1827. Having overseen the first written constitution produced by an Indian nation, Ross was then elected principal chief in 1828. Over the next decade, he battled to retain the Cherokee homeland in Georgia, North Carolina, and Tennessee against the pressures of white planters and politicians.

Portrait presumed to be Tecumseh by an unknown artist. The Granger Collection, New York

AMERICAN POLITICS IN the early nineteenth century was a white man's world, but, as the American histories of Dolley Madison and John Ross demonstrate, it was possible for some of those on the political margins to influence national developments. Both Madison and Ross sought to defend and expand the democratic ideals that defined the young nation. The First Lady helped forge social networks and nurture a nascent political culture in Washington that included women as well as men. At the same time, she struggled with the issue of slavery on her husband's Montpelier plantation. Ross encouraged the Cherokee people to embrace Anglo-American religion, language, and political ideals in the hopes of providing them with a path to inclusion in the United States. Yet ultimately, given the nation's economic growth, he could not overcome the power of white planters and politicians to wrest territory from even the most Americanized Indians. Although Ross most directly confronted the limits of American democracy, Dolley Madison also grappled with the dilemmas posed to the nation's democratic ideals by the expansion of slavery and the limits of citizenship.

Conflicts at Home and Abroad

When Thomas Jefferson completed his second term as president in March 1809, he was succeeded by his friend and ally James Madison. Madison was the principal author of the Constitution; coauthor of *The Federalist Papers*, which ensured its ratification; and secretary of state in Jefferson's administration. Like Jefferson, he sought to end foreign interference in American affairs and to resolve conflicts between Indians and white residents on the nation's frontier. Congress itself was divided over how best to address these problems. By 1815 the United States had weathered a series of domestic and foreign crises, including another war with Britain, but American sovereignty remained fragile. At the same time, even though Madison (like Jefferson) believed in a national government with limited powers, he found himself expanding federal authority.

Tensions at Sea and on the Frontier

When President Madison took office, Great Britain and France remained embroiled in the Napoleonic Wars in Europe and refused to modify their policies toward American shipping or to recognize U.S. neutrality. American ships were subject to seizure by both nations, and British authorities continued to impress "deserters" into the Royal Navy. In response, the new president convinced Congress to pass the **Non-Intercourse Act** in 1809, which allowed Americans to trade with every nation except France and Britain. When that act failed to satisfy the warring nations or improve the economy, Congress approved a bill that opened trade with both Great Britain and France but allowed the president to reimpose an embargo on one nation if the other lifted its restrictions. When Napoleon promised to lift all restrictions on U.S. shipping, Madison stalled, giving British officials time to match France's policy. Britain refused.

In the midst of these crises, Madison also faced difficulties in the Northwest Territory. In 1794 General "Mad Anthony" Wayne had won a decisive victory against a multitribe coalition led by the Shawnees at the Battle of Fallen Timbers. But this victory inspired two forceful native leaders to create a pan-Indian alliance in the Ohio River valley. The Shawnee prophet Tenskwatawa and his half-brother Tecumseh, a warrior, encouraged native peoples to resist white encroachments on their territory and to give up all aspects of white society and culture, including clothing, liquor, and other popular trade goods. They imagined an Indian nation that stretched from the Canadian border to the Gulf of Mexico.

Although powerful Creek and Choctaw nations in the lower Mississippi valley refused to join the alliance, bands of Indians in the upper Midwest, frustrated with continuing white encroachments, rallied around the brothers. In 1808 Tenskwatawa and Tecumseh established Prophet Town along the Tippecanoe River in Indiana Territory. The next year, William Henry Harrison, the territorial governor, plied several Indian leaders with liquor and persuaded them to sign a treaty selling three million acres of land to the United States for only $7,600. Tecumseh was enraged by Harrison's methods and dismissed the treaty, claiming the land belonged to all the Indians together.

In November 1811, fearing the growing power of the Shawnee leaders, President Madison ordered Harrison to attack Prophet Town. With more troops and superior weapons, the U.S. army defeated the Shawnees, and soldiers then burned Prophet Town to the ground. The rout damaged Tenskwatawa's stature as a prophet, and he and his supporters fled to Canada. Skirmishes continued between Indians and U.S. troops along the Canadian border, but federal officials now returned their attention to conflicts with Great Britain.

War Erupts with Britain

Convinced that British officials in Canada fueled Indian resistance, supporters of war with Great Britain demanded an end to British intervention on the western frontier. They were even more concerned about British interference with transatlantic trade. Yet merchants in the Northeast, who depended on trade with Great Britain and the British West Indies, feared the commercial disruptions that war entailed. Once staunch supporters of expanding the power of the national government, New England Federalists now adamantly opposed a declaration of war.

For months, Madison avoided taking a clear stand for or against war. On June 1, 1812, however, having exhausted diplomatic efforts and seeing no end to these conflicts as long as the Napoleonic Wars raged across Europe, Madison sent a secret message to Congress outlining American grievances against Great Britain. Within weeks, Congress declared war by a sharply divided vote of 79 to 49 in the House of Representatives and 19 to 13 in the Senate.

Supporters claimed that a victory over Great Britain would end threats to U.S. sovereignty and raise Americans' stature in Europe, but the nation was ill prepared to launch a major offensive against such an imposing foe. Cuts in federal spending and falling tax revenues over the previous decade had diminished military resources. Democratic-Republicans had also failed to renew the charter of the Bank of the United States when it expired in 1811, so the nation lacked a vital source of credit. Nonetheless, many in Congress believed that Britain would be too distracted and overcommitted by the ongoing conflict with France to attack North America.

Meanwhile U.S. commanders devised plans to attack Canada. The most enthusiastic advocates of war imagined that the United States could defeat Britain and gain control of all of North America. Initially, however, the U.S. army and navy proved no match for Great Britain and its Indian allies. Tecumseh, who was appointed a brigadier general in the British army, helped capture Detroit. Joint British and Indian forces also launched successful attacks on Fort Dearborn, Fort Mackinac, and other points along the U.S.-Canadian border.

Even as U.S. forces faced defeat after defeat in the summer and fall of 1812, American voters reelected James Madison as president. His narrow victory demonstrated the geographical divisions caused by the war. Madison won most of the western and southern states, where the war was most popular, and was defeated in New England and New York, where Federalist opponents held sway.

After a year of fighting, U.S. forces—with the aid of crucial naval victories on the Great Lakes—finally drove the British back into Canada (Map 9.1). Tecumseh was killed

MAP 9.1

The War of 1812 Most conflicts in this war occurred in the Great Lakes region or around Washington, D.C. Yet two of the most significant victories were achieved by General Andrew Jackson in the South. At Horseshoe Bend, his troops defeated Creek allies of the British, and at New Orleans they beat British forces two weeks after a peace agreement was signed in Europe.

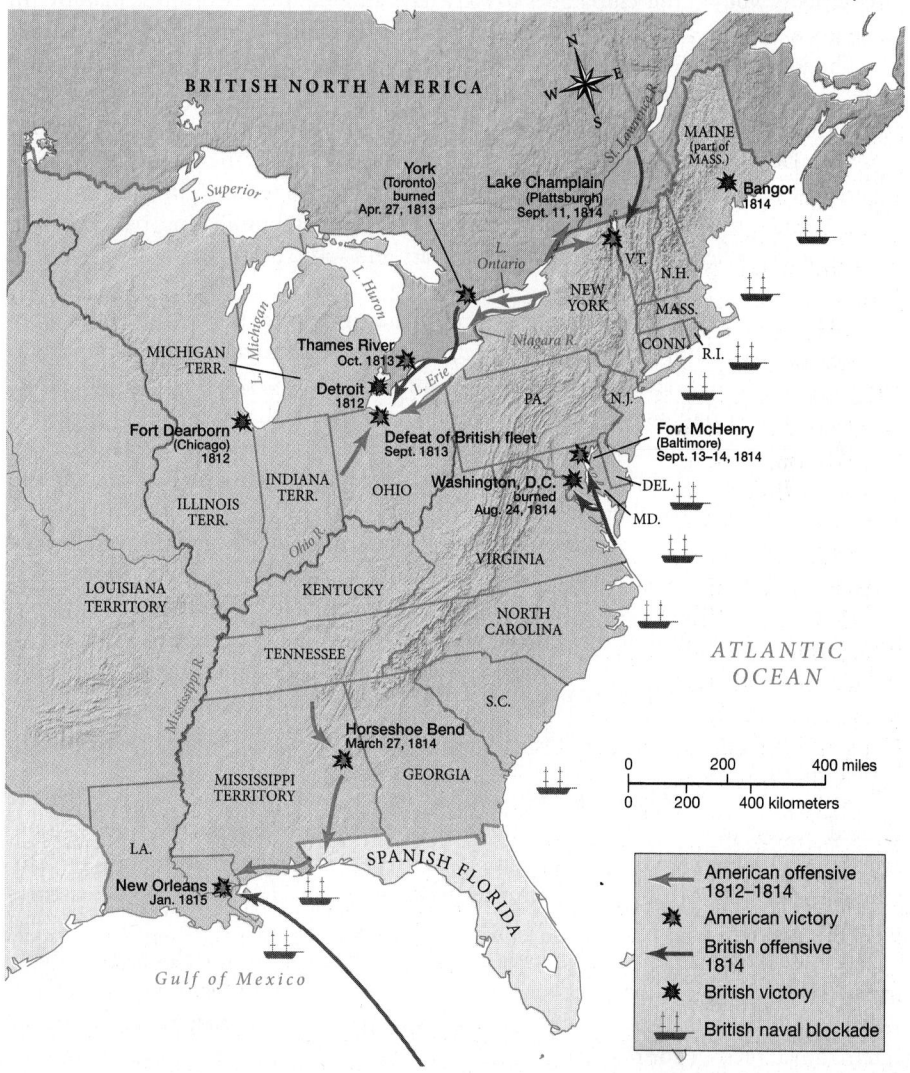

in Canada at the Battle of the Thames, and U.S. forces burned York (present-day Toronto). Yet just as U.S. prospects in the war improved, New England Federalists demanded retreat. In the fall of 1813, state legislatures in New England withdrew their support for any invasions of "foreign British soil," and Federalists in Congress sought to block appropriations for the war and challenge the deployment of local militia units into the U.S. army.

New England Federalists did not have sufficient power to change national policy, but they called a meeting at Hartford, Connecticut, in 1814 to consider their options. Some participants at the **Hartford Convention** called for New England's secession from the United States. Most, however, supported amendments to the U.S. Constitution that would limit presidents to a single term and ensure that presidents were elected from diverse states (so that Virginia planters could not dominate the executive branch). Other amendments would limit embargoes to sixty days and require a two-thirds majority in Congress to declare war, prohibit trade, or admit new states.

The ideas debated at Hartford gained increased attention as British forces once again launched attacks into the United States and British warships blockaded U.S. ports. In August 1814, the British sailed up the Chesapeake. As American troops retreated, Dolley Madison and a family slave, Peter Jennings, gathered up government papers and valuable belongings before fleeing the city. The redcoats then burned and sacked Washington City. The invasion of the U.S. capital was humiliating, but American troops quickly rallied to defeat the British in Maryland and expel them from Washington and New York.

Meanwhile news arrived from the South that in March 1814 militiamen from Tennessee led by Andrew Jackson had defeated a force of Creek Indians, important allies of the British. Cherokee warriors (and adjutant John Ross), longtime foes of the Creeks, joined the fight as well. At the Battle of Horseshoe Bend, in present-day Alabama, the combined U.S.-Cherokee forces slaughtered some eight hundred Creek warriors. Jackson then demanded punitive terms, and in the resulting treaty the Creek nation lost two-thirds of its tribal domain.

Despite sporadic U.S. victories, America was no closer to winning the war. In June 1814, the British finally defeated Napoleon, ending the war in Europe. And in December of that year, the British fleet landed thousands of seasoned troops at New Orleans, threatening U.S. control of that crucial port city. But exhausted from twenty years of European warfare, the British were losing steam as well. As a result, representatives of the two countries met in Ghent, Belgium, to negotiate a peace settlement. On Christmas Eve 1814, the Treaty of Ghent was signed, returning to each nation the lands it controlled before the war.

Although the war had officially ended, it took time for the news to reach the United States. In January 1815, American troops under General Andrew Jackson attacked and routed the British army at New Orleans. The victory cheered Americans, who did not know that peace had already been achieved, and Jackson became a national hero.

Although the War of 1812 achieved no official territorial gains, Jackson's late victory in the Battle of New Orleans made it appear that American forces had vanquished Great Britain. The war did represent an important defense of U.S. sovereignty and garnered international prestige for the young nation. In addition, Indians on the western frontier lost a powerful ally when British representatives at Ghent failed to act as advocates for their allies. Thus, in practical terms, the U.S. government gained greater control over vast expanses of land in the Ohio and Mississippi River valleys held by these Indian nations.

REVIEW & RELATE

• How were conflicts with Indians in the West connected to ongoing tensions between the United States and Great Britain on land and at sea?

• What were the long-term consequences of the War of 1812?

Expanding the Economy and the Nation

By further expanding federal powers, the War of 1812 reinforced political changes that had been under way for more than a decade. At the Hartford Convention, Federalists who had once advocated broad national powers called for restrictions on federal authority. By contrast, the Democratic-Republicans, who gained support in 1800 by demanding restraints on federal power, now applauded its expansion. Indeed, Democratic-Republicans in Congress sought to use federal authority to settle boundary disputes in the West, make investments in transportation, and reestablish a national bank. Increasingly, many ordinary Americans viewed such federal assistance as critical to the continued development of industry and agriculture.

Governments Fuel Economic Growth

At the nation's founding, Alexander Hamilton led a coalition that advocated the use of federal power to fuel commercial development. Over the following decade, this coalition's efforts to expand federal authority in the interest of commerce and industry inspired opposition within Federalist ranks. In 1800 Thomas Jefferson captured the presidency by advocating a reduction in federal powers and a renewed emphasis on the needs of small farmers and working men. Once in power, however, Jefferson and his Democratic-Republican supporters faced a series of economic and political developments that led many of them to embrace Hamilton's loose interpretation of the U.S. Constitution and support federal efforts to aid economic growth (see chapter 8). In the 1810s, for example, Democratic-Republican representative Henry Clay of Kentucky sketched out a plan called the **American System**, which combined federally funded internal improvements to aid farmers with federal tariffs to protect U.S. manufacturing and a national bank to oversee economic development.

Western expansion helped fuel the demand for federally funded internal improvements. The non-Indian population west of the Appalachian Mountains more than doubled between 1810 and 1820, from 1,080,000 to 2,234,000. The new residents included veterans of the War of 1812, many of whom received 160-acre parcels of land between the Illinois and Mississippi Rivers. They and their families established farms, shops, and communities throughout the territory. Four frontier states were admitted to the Union in just four years: Indiana (1816), Mississippi (1817), Illinois (1818), and Alabama (1819).

Population growth and commercial expansion moved hand in hand. In 1811 the first steamboat traveled down the Mississippi from the Ohio River to New Orleans; over the next decade, steamboat traffic expanded, and freight charges dropped precipitously. This development helped western and southern residents but hurt trade on overland routes between northeastern seaports and the Ohio River valley. The Cumberland Road, a federally funded highway linking Maryland and Ohio, reestablished this connection, and Congress passed bills to fund more ambitious federal transportation projects. But President Madison vetoed much of this legislation, believing that it overstepped even a loose interpretation of the Constitution.

Congress also developed new trade routes by negotiating treaties with Indian nations. For instance, an ancient trail from Missouri to Santa Fe, a town in northern Mexico, cut across territory claimed by the Osage Indians. White traders began using the trail in 1821, and four years later Congress approved a treaty with the Osage nation to guarantee right of way for U.S. merchants. In the following decade, the Santa Fe Trail became a critical route for commerce between the United States and Mexico.

East of the Appalachian Mountains, most internal improvement projects were funded by individual states. The most significant of these was New York's **Erie Canal**, a 363-mile waterway stretching from the Mohawk River to Buffalo that was completed in 1825. Tolls on the Erie Canal quickly repaid the tremendous cost of its construction. Freight charges and shipping times plunged. In 1820 transporting a ton of grain by land from Buffalo to New York City cost $100 and took 20 days; in 1825 shipping a ton of grain by canal between those two cities cost only $9 and took 6 days. And by linking western farmers to the Hudson River, the Erie Canal ensured that New York City became the nation's premier seaport (Map 9.2).

The Erie Canal's success inspired hundreds of similar projects in other states. Canals carried manufactured goods from New England and the Middle Atlantic states to rural households in the Ohio River valley. Western farmers, in turn, shipped hogs, hemp, flour, whiskey, and other farm products back east. Just as important, canals linked smaller cities within Pennsylvania and Ohio, facilitating the rise of commercial and manufacturing centers like Harrisburg, Pittsburgh, Cincinnati, and Toledo. Canals also allowed vast quantities of coal to be transported out of the Allegheny Mountains, fueling industrial development throughout the Northeast.

Americans Expand the Nation's Borders

In 1816, in the midst of the nation's economic resurgence, James Monroe, a Democratic-Republican from Virginia, won an easy victory in the presidential election over Rufus King, a New York Federalist. Monroe, who had served as secretary of state under Madison, hoped to use improved relations with Great Britain to resolve Indian problems on the frontier. Believing that hostile Indians would "lose their terror" once the British no longer encouraged them, he sent John Quincy Adams to London to negotiate treaties that limited U.S. and British naval forces on the Great Lakes, set the U.S.-Canadian border at the forty-ninth parallel, and provided for joint British-U.S. occupation of the Oregon Territory. In 1817 and 1818, the Senate approved these treaties, which further limited Indian rights and power in the North.

President Monroe harbored grave concerns about the nation's southern boundary as well. He sought to limit Spain's power in North America and stop Seminole Indians in western Florida and Alabama from claiming lands ceded to the United States by the defeated Creeks. Shifting from diplomacy to military force, in 1817 the president sent General Andrew Jackson and his Tennessee militia to force the Seminoles back into Florida. Nonetheless, he ordered Jackson to avoid direct conflict with Spanish forces for fear of igniting another war. But in the spring of 1818, having chased the Seminoles

MAP 9.2

Roads and Canals to 1837 During the 1820s and 1830s, state and local governments as well as private companies built roads and canals to foster migration and commercial development. The Erie Canal, completed in 1825, was the most significant of these projects. But many other states, particularly in the Northeast and the old Northwest, sought to duplicate that canal's success over the following decade.

deep into Florida, Jackson attacked two Spanish forts, hanged two Seminole chiefs, and executed two British citizens allied with local Indians.

Jackson's attacks spurred outrage among Spanish and British officials and many members of Congress. Indeed, the threat of conflict with Britain, Spain, and hostile

Indians prompted President Monroe to establish the nation's first peacetime army in 1818. In the end, however, the British chose to ignore the execution of citizens engaged in "unauthorized" activities, while Spain decided to sell the Florida Territory to the United States rather than fight to retain it. In the Adams-Onís Treaty (1819), negotiated by John Quincy Adams, Spain ceded all its lands east of the Mississippi to the United States along with ancient claims to the Oregon Territory.

Success in acquiring Florida encouraged the administration to look for other opportunities to limit European influence in the Western Hemisphere. By 1822 Argentina, Chile, Peru, Colombia, and Mexico had all overthrown Spanish rule. In March of that year, President Monroe recognized the independence of these southern neighbors, and Congress quickly established diplomatic relations with the new nations. Yet Monroe also secretly attempted to survey Mexican lands in hopes of gaining more territory for the United States. The following year, President Monroe added a codicil to a treaty with Russia that claimed that the Western Hemisphere was part of the U.S. sphere of influence. Although the United States did not have sufficient power to enforce what later became known as the **Monroe Doctrine**, it had quietly declared its intention to challenge Europeans for authority in the Atlantic world.

By the late 1820s, U.S. residents were moving to and trading with newly independent Mexican territories. Southern whites began occupying Mexican lands in east Texas, while midwestern traders traveled the Santa Fe Trail. Meanwhile New England manufacturers and merchants had begun shipping their wares via clipper ships to another Mexican territory, Alta California, whose residents eagerly purchased U.S.-made shoes, cloth, and tools.

Some Americans looked even farther afield. U.S. merchants had begun trading with China in the late eighteenth century, and by the early nineteenth century, ships from eastern ports carried otter pelts and other merchandise across the Pacific, returning with Chinese porcelains and silks. In the 1810s and 1820s, the Alta California and China trades converged, expanding the reach of U.S. merchants and the demand for U.S. manufactured goods. The desire to expand trade also led some Americans to look to the Pacific, especially Hawaii and Samoa, for additional markets and land.

Extended trade routes along with wartime disruptions of European imports fueled the expansion of U.S. manufacturing. By 1813 the area around Providence, Rhode Island, boasted seventy-six spinning mills with more than 51,000 spindles. Two years later, Philadelphia claimed pride of place as the nation's top industrial city, turning out glass, chemicals, metalwork, leather goods, and dozens of other products. Workers in factories, artisans' shops, and homes as well as in prisons and poorhouses contributed to an economic boom that seemed boundless.

Regional Economic Development

Clay's American System was intended to bind the various regions of the United States together. Yet even as roads, rivers, canals, and steamboats helped unify a growing nation, they also reinforced the development of regional economies. Although regional ties remained fluid, between 1815 and 1830 increasingly distinct economies developed that promoted the rise of particular labor systems and political priorities.

In the South, for instance, the defeat of the Creek nation, vast Indian land cessions, and the acquisition of Florida ensured the growth of cotton cultivation, which had been initiated by the invention of the cotton gin (see chapter 8). Although the foreign slave trade had ended in 1808, planters extended slavery into new lands to produce cash crops like cotton, sugar, and rice. They used profits from these goods to buy food from the West and shoes and cloth from the North. Small farmers, too, sought to benefit from rising cotton prices, planting as much of their land in cotton as they could. Because continuous cultivation drained nutrients from the soil, planters and small farmers constantly sought more fertile fields, leading to further pressure on those Indians who still controlled large areas of rich southern soil.

When James and Dolley Madison returned to Montpelier in 1817, they experienced the new possibilities and problems of southern agriculture. Plantation homes in long-settled areas like the Virginia piedmont became more fashionable as they incorporated luxury goods imported from China and Europe. The Madisons entertained hundreds of guests, hosted dinners and dances, and provided beds and meals for three dozen people at a time. But soil exhaustion in the region limited the profits from tobacco and made a shift to cotton impossible. While some Virginia planters made money by selling slaves to other planters farther south, James Madison refused to break up slave families who had worked the plantation for decades. With no desire to leave for lands farther west, he and Dolley were forced to reduce their standard of living.

Other white Americans, however, benefited from the expansion of southern agriculture. Of course, many cotton farmers made substantial profits in the 1810s. So did western farmers, who shipped vast quantities of food and other farm products to the South. Towns like Cincinnati, located across the Ohio River from Kentucky, sprang up as regional centers of commerce. In 1811 Cincinnati settlers still confronted Indians along the nearby White Water River. Eight years later, the booming town was incorporated as a city with nearly ten thousand residents.

Americans living in the Northeast increased their commercial connections with the South as well. Northern merchants became more deeply engaged in the southern cotton trade, opening warehouses in port cities like Savannah and Charleston and

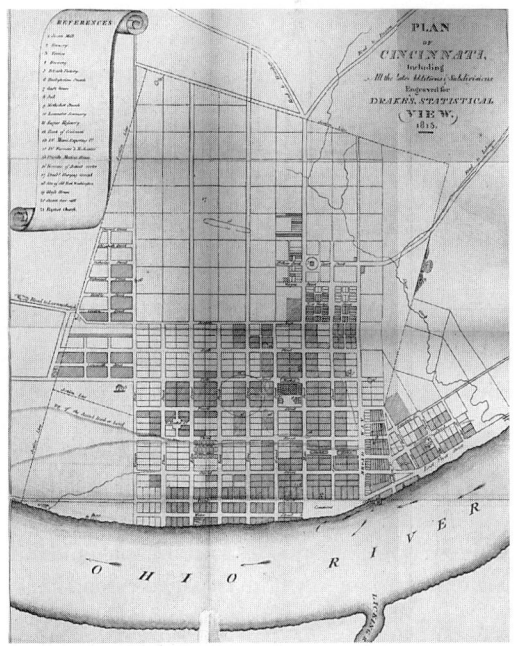

Plan of Cincinnati, 1815 This map, drawn four years before Cincinnati was incorporated as a city, illustrates the importance of the Ohio River to the city's development. Nestled along the riverbank, the village of Cincinnati was laid out in a grid pattern. The map lists a steam mill; two breweries; ferries; a potash factory, sugar refinery, and sawmill; churches; banks; and other important locations. Courtesy Archives & Rare Books Library, University of Cincinnati

sending cotton factors, or agents, into the countryside to broker deals with planters. Meanwhile the southern cotton boom fueled industrial expansion. Indeed, factory owners in New England shipped growing amounts of yarn, thread, and cloth along with shoes, tools, and leather goods to the South. As merchants in New England and New York focused on the cotton trade, those in Philadelphia and Pittsburgh built ties to western farmers, exchanging manufactured goods for agricultural products across the Appalachian Mountains.

REVIEW & RELATE

- What role did government play in early-nineteenth-century economic development?
- How and why did economic development contribute to regional differences and shape regional ties?

Economic and Political Crises

As America's regions developed distinct economies in the 1810s, they became more, not less, dependent on each other. Western farmers needed manufactured goods from the North; northern manufacturers needed raw cotton from the South; southern planters needed food crops from the West. The growth in trade required the expansion of commercial institutions such as banks, which forged economic links across the United States. This economic integration stimulated the economy, but interdependence also made the nation more vulnerable when financial crises hit. The panic of 1819, the nation's first severe recession, brought economic growth to an abrupt halt. At the same time, when Missouri applied for statehood in 1819, it set off the first serious national debate over slavery.

The Panic of 1819

The **panic of 1819** resulted primarily from irresponsible banking practices in the United States and was deepened by the declining overseas demand for American goods, especially cotton. Beginning in 1816, American banks, including the Second Bank of the United States (BUS), loaned out huge sums to settlers seeking land on the frontier and to merchants and manufacturers expanding their businesses. Many of these loans were not backed by sufficient collateral. Banks, meanwhile, issued notes without adequate hard currency as European governments, fearful of growing turmoil in South America, hoarded gold and silver. State and local banks and their clients were betting on continued economic growth to ensure repayment. Western banks were especially reckless in offering discounted loans. Then, as agricultural production in Europe revived with the end of the Napoleonic Wars, the demand for American foodstuffs dropped sharply. Farm income plummeted by roughly one-third in the late 1810s.

In 1818 the directors of the Second Bank, fearing a continued expansion of the money supply, tightened the credit it provided to branch banks. This sudden effort to curtail credit led to economic panic. Some branch banks failed immediately. Others survived by calling in loans to companies and individuals, who in turn demanded repayment from those to whom they had extended credit. The chain of indebtedness pushed more people to the brink of economic ruin just as factory owners cut their workforce and merchants limited orders for new goods. Both individuals and enterprises faced bankruptcy and foreclosures on mortgages. In New York State, property values fell from a total of $315 million in 1818 to $256 million in 1820. In Richmond, Virginia, property values fell by half during the panic.

Bankruptcies, foreclosures, unemployment, and poverty spread like a plague across the country. Cotton farmers were especially hard hit by declining exports and falling prices. Planters who had gone into debt to purchase land in Alabama and Mississippi were unable to pay their mortgages. Many western residents, who had invested all they had in new farms, lost their land or simply stopped paying their mortgages. This put further strains on state banks, some of which simply collapsed, leaving the Second Bank holding mortgages on vast amounts of western territory. At the same time, public land sales plummeted from $13.6 million in 1818 to $1.3 million in 1821.

Many Americans viewed banks as the cause of the panic. Some states defied the Constitution and the Supreme Court by trying to tax BUS branches or printing state banknotes with no specie (gold or silver) to back them. Some Americans called for government relief, but there was no system to provide the kinds of assistance needed. Meanwhile Congress debated how to reignite the nation's economic engines. Northern manufacturers called for even higher tariffs to protect U.S. products from foreign competition, but southern planters argued that high tariffs raised the price of manufactured goods even as agricultural profits declined. And working men, small farmers, and frontier settlers feared that their economic needs were being ignored by politicians with ties to bankers, planters, manufacturers, and merchants.

By 1823 the panic had largely dissipated, but the prolonged economic crisis had shaken national confidence, and citizens became more skeptical of federal authority and more suspicious of banks. From 1819 until the Civil War, one of the greatest limitations on national expansion remained the cycle of economic expansion and contraction, which was tied ever more closely to unregulated national and international markets.

 Online Document Project　**The Panic of 1819**
bedfordstmartins.com/hewittlawsonvalue

Slavery in Missouri

The spread of slavery fueled a second national crisis. In February 1819, the Missouri Territory applied for statehood. New York congressman James Tallmadge Jr. proposed that it be admitted only if it banned further importation of slaves and passed a gradual emancipation law modeled on those in many northern states. With the support of southern congressmen, however, whites in the territory defeated Tallmadge's proposals. The northern majority in the House of Representatives then rejected Missouri's admission.

Southern politicians were outraged, claiming that since the Missouri Territory allowed slavery, so should the state of Missouri. Although the region bordered the Northwest Territory, where slavery was outlawed in 1787, it also bordered the slave states of Kentucky and Tennessee. With cotton production moving ever westward, southern congressmen wanted to ensure the availability of new lands. They also wanted to ensure the South's power in Congress. Because the northern population had grown more rapidly than that in the South, by 1819 northern politicians controlled the House of Representatives. The Senate, however, was evenly divided, with two senators representing each state: eleven slave and eleven free. If northerners could block the admission of slave states like Missouri while allowing the admission of free states, the balance of power in the Senate would tip in the North's favor. Thus southern senators blocked the admission of Maine, which sought to separate itself from Massachusetts and become a free state.

For southern planters, the decision on Missouri defined the future of slavery. With foreign trade in slaves outlawed, planters relied on natural increase and trading slaves from older to newer areas of cultivation to meet the demand for labor. Moreover, with free blacks packing the congressional galleries in Washington to listen to congressmen debate Missouri statehood, supporters of slavery worried that divisions among whites could fuel resistance to slavery and even open revolt. Two rebellions had occurred in recent memory. In 1811 some four hundred slaves in Louisiana had killed two whites and burned several plantations. Their advance on New Orleans was stopped only when U.S. troops killed more than sixty rebels. Even more immediately, several hundred fugitive slaves had joined forces with Seminole Indians in 1817, raiding Georgia plantations and establishing autonomous communities in central Florida. Andrew Jackson's 1818 attack halted their activities, but most of the fugitive blacks escaped deep into Florida.

MAP 9.3

The Missouri Compromise and Westward Expansion, 1820s   The debate over the Missouri Compromise occurred just as the United States began expanding farther westward. Within a few years of its adoption, the growth of U.S. settlements in eastern Texas and increased trade with a newly independent Mexico suggested the importance of drawing a clear boundary between slave and free states.

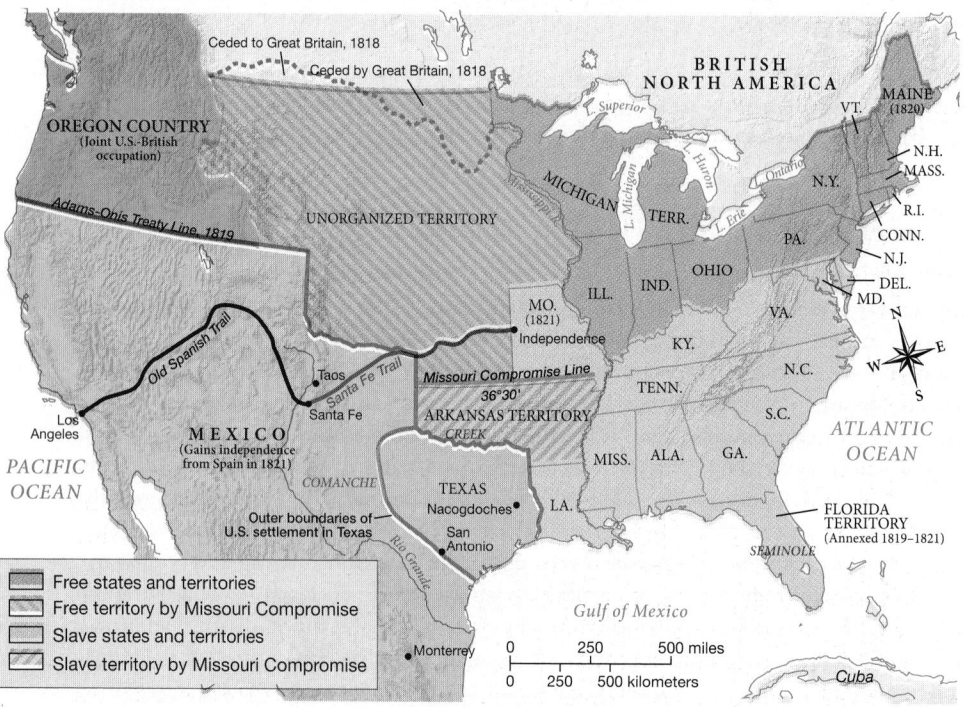

Free states and territories
Free territory by Missouri Compromise
Slave states and territories
Slave territory by Missouri Compromise

In 1820 Representative Henry Clay of Kentucky forged a compromise that resolved the immediate issues and promised a long-term solution. Maine was to be admitted as a free state and Missouri as a slave state, thereby maintaining the balance between North and South in the U.S. Senate (Map 9.3). At the same time, Congress agreed that the southern border of Missouri—latitude 36°30′—was to serve as the boundary between slave and free states throughout the Louisiana Territory.

The Missouri Compromise gained the support of a majority of representatives and senators and ended the crisis for the moment. Still, the debates made clear how quickly a disagreement over slavery could escalate into clashes that threatened the survival of the nation.

(REVIEW & RELATE)

• What were the political consequences of the panic of 1819?

• What regional divisions did the conflict over slavery in Missouri reveal?

Redefining American Democracy

With the frontier moving ever westward and the panic of 1819 shaking many Americans' faith in traditional political and economic leaders, the nation was ripe for change. Working men, small farmers, and frontier settlers, who had long been locked out of the electoral system by property qualifications and eastern elites, demanded the right to vote. They also looked for a different kind of candidate to champion their cause. Frontier heroes like Andrew Jackson, with few ties to banks, business, and eastern power brokers, appealed to this new constituency. The resulting political movement widened voting rights in the United States and brought more diverse groups of men into the electorate. Yet the new democratic movement advanced the interests only of white men. During the 1820s, African Americans lost political and civil rights in most northern and western states. Indians, too, fared poorly under the new political regime. While some white women gained greater access to political activities as a result of the expanded voting rights of fathers and husbands, they did not achieve independent political rights. Finally, during the 1820s and 1830s, ongoing conflicts over slavery, tariffs, and the rights of Indian nations transformed party alignments as a wave of new voters entered the political fray.

Expanding Voting Rights

Between 1788 and 1820, the U.S. presidency was dominated by Virginia elites and after 1800 by Democratic-Republicans. With little serious political opposition at the national level, few people bothered to vote in presidential elections. Far more people engaged in partisan and popular political activities at the state and local level. Many towns held public celebrations on the Fourth of July and election days, and politicians of every stripe invited women to participate. Female participants often sewed symbols of their partisan loyalties on their clothes and joined in parades and feasts organized by men.

This popular political activity stimulated interest in presidential elections following the panic of 1819, when, as Scottish traveler James Flint noted, "the faith of the people was shaken." Laboring men, who were especially vulnerable to economic downturns, demanded the right to vote as a means of forcing politicians to respond to their concerns.

In New York State, Martin Van Buren, a rising star in the Democratic-Republican Party, led the fight to eliminate property qualifications for voting. At the state constitutional convention of 1821, the committee on suffrage reflected his views, arguing that the only qualification for voting should be "the virtue and morality of the people." By the word *people*, Van Buren and the committee meant white men, but even this limited demand aroused heated opposition. A year earlier, attorney Daniel Webster had been elected to the Massachusetts constitutional convention, where he argued vociferously that "political power naturally and necessarily goes into the hands which hold the property."

Although many wealthy conservatives supported Webster's views, he lost the debate, and both Massachusetts and New York instituted universal white male suffrage. By 1825 most states along the Atlantic seaboard had lowered or eliminated property qualifications on white male voters. Meanwhile states along the frontier that had joined the Union in the 1810s established universal white male suffrage from the beginning. And by 1824 three-quarters of the states (18 of 24) allowed voters, rather than state legislatures, to elect members of the electoral college.

Yet as white men gained political rights in the 1820s, democracy did not spread to other groups. Indian nations were considered sovereign entities, so Indians voted in their own nations, not in U.S. elections. Women were excluded from voting because of their perceived dependence on men. New Jersey had granted single or widowed property-owning women the right to vote during the Revolution, but in 1807 the state legislature rescinded that right—along with suffrage for African American men—when small numbers of female and black voters proved they could make a difference in contested elections.

African American men faced challenges to their rights well beyond New Jersey. No southern legislature had ever granted blacks the right to vote, and in the 1820s northern states began to disfranchise African Americans. In many cases, expanded voting rights for white men went hand in hand with new restrictions on black men. In New York State, for example, the constitution of 1821, which eliminated property qualifications for white men, raised property qualifications for African American voters, disfranchising most African Americans in the state in the process.

When African American men protested their disfranchisement in northern states, some whites spoke out on their behalf. They claimed that denying rights to men who had in no way abused the privilege of voting set "an ominous and dangerous precedent." In response, opponents of black suffrage offered explicitly racist justifications. Some worried that blacks might eventually secure seats in state legislatures, on juries, and in Congress. Some argued that black voting would lead to interracial socializing, even marriage. However, the growing population of free blacks in northern cities posed the greatest threat. Once again, white politicians feared that black voters might hold the balance of power in close elections, forcing white civic leaders to accede to their demands. Gradually, racist arguments won the day, and by 1840, 93 percent of free blacks in the North were excluded from voting.

Racial Restrictions and Antiblack Violence

Restrictions on voting followed other constraints on African American men and women. As early as 1790, Congress limited naturalization (the process of becoming a citizen) to white aliens, or immigrants. It also excluded blacks from enrolling in federal militias. In 1820 Congress authorized city officials in Washington, D.C., to adopt a separate legal code governing free blacks and slaves. This federal legislation encouraged states to add their own restrictions, including segregation of public schools, public transportation, and public accommodations like churches and theaters. Such laws were passed in the North as well as in the South. Some northern legislatures even denied African Americans the right to settle in their state.

In addition, blacks faced mob and state-sanctioned violence across the country. In 1822 officials in Charleston, South Carolina, accused Denmark Vesey of following the revolutionary leader Toussaint L'Ouverture's lead and plotting a conspiracy to free the city's slaves. One of 1,500 free blacks residing in the city, Vesey had helped to organize churches, mutual aid societies, and other black institutions. Whites viewed these efforts as a threat to the future of slavery because such accomplishments challenged assumptions about black inferiority. Vesey may have organized a plan to free slaves in the city, but it is also possible that white officials concocted the plot in order to terrorize free blacks and slaves in the area and to shore up the power of ruling white elites. Despite scant evidence, Vesey and 34 of his alleged co-conspirators were found guilty and hanged. Another 18 were exiled outside the United States. The African Methodist Episcopal church where they supposedly planned the insurrection was torn down.

Northern blacks also suffered from violent attacks by whites. Assaults on individual African Americans often went unrecorded, but race riots received greater attention. For example, in 1829 white residents of Cincinnati attacked black neighborhoods, and more than half of the city's black residents fled. Many of them resettled in Ontario, Canada. They were soon joined by Philadelphia blacks who had been attacked by groups of white residents in 1832. Such attacks continued in northern cities throughout the 1830s.

Political Realignments

Restrictions on black political and civil rights converged with the decline of the Federalists in the North. Federalist majorities in New York State had approved the gradual abolition law of 1799. In 1821 New York Federalists advocated equal rights for black and white voters as long as property qualifications limited suffrage to respectable citizens. But Federalists were losing power by this time, and the concerns of African Americans were low on the Democratic-Republican agenda.

Struggles among Democratic-Republicans in the 1820s turned to a large extent on the same issue that had earlier divided them from Federalists: the limits of federal power. After nearly a quarter century in power, many Democratic-Republicans embraced a more expansive view of federal authority and a looser interpretation of the U.S. Constitution. Yet others in the party argued forcefully for a return to Jeffersonian principles of limited federal power and a strict construction of the Constitution. At the same time, rising young politicians—like Martin Van Buren and Andrew Jackson—and newly enfranchised voters sought to seize control of the party from its longtime leaders.

The election of 1824 brought these conflicts to a head, splitting the Democratic-Republicans into rival factions that by 1828 had coalesced into two distinct entities: the **Democrats** and the **National Republicans**. Unable to agree on a single presidential candidate in 1824, the Democratic-Republican congressional caucus fractured into four camps backing separate candidates: John Quincy Adams, Andrew Jackson, Henry Clay, and Secretary of the Treasury William Crawford. John C. Calhoun, Monroe's secretary of war, eventually threw his support behind Jackson and sought the vice presidency.

As the race developed, Adams and Jackson emerged as the two strongest candidates. John Quincy Adams's stature rested on his diplomatic achievements and the reputation of his father, former president John Adams. Like Clay, he favored internal improvements and protective tariffs that would bolster northern industry and commerce. Jackson, on the other hand, relied largely on his fame as a war hero and Indian fighter to inspire popular support. Like Crawford, he advocated limited federal power.

As a candidate who appealed to ordinary voters, Jackson held a decided edge. Jackson, outgoing and boisterous, claimed to support "good old Jeffersonian Democratic republican principles" and organized a campaign that took his case to the people. Emphasizing his humble origins, he appealed to small farmers and northern workers who hoped to emulate his success as a self-made man. Just as important, Jackson gained the support of Van Buren, who also wanted to expand the political clout of the "common [white] man" and limit the reach of a central government that was becoming too powerful.

The four presidential candidates created a truly competitive race. With more white men eligible to vote and more states allowing voters to choose members of the electoral college, turnout at the polls increased to more than a quarter of eligible voters. Jackson won the popular vote by carrying Pennsylvania, New Jersey, the Carolinas, and much of the West and led in the electoral college with 99 electors. But with no candidate gaining an absolute majority in the electoral college, the Constitution called for the House of Representatives to choose the president from the three leading contenders—Jackson, Adams, and Crawford. Clay, who came in fourth, asked his supporters to back Adams, ensuring his election. Once in office, President Adams appointed Clay his secretary of state. Jackson claimed that the two had engineered a "corrupt bargain" that denied the will of the people. Yet the decisions of Clay and Adams involved a logical alliance between two candidates who agreed on the need to increase federal investment in internal improvements, raise tariffs, and expand the powers of the BUS.

But when President Adams sought to implement his agenda, he ran into vigorous opposition in Congress led by Van Buren. Calhoun, who had been elected vice president, also opposed his policies. Van Buren argued against federal funding for internal improvements since New York State had financed the Erie Canal with its own monies. Calhoun, meanwhile, joined other southern politicians in opposing any expansion of federal power for fear it would then be used to restrict the spread of slavery.

The most serious battle in Congress, however, involved tariffs. The tariff of 1816 had excluded most cheap English cotton cloth from the United States, thereby allowing New England textile manufacturers to gain control of the domestic market. In 1824 the tariff was extended to more expensive cotton and woolen cloth and to iron goods. During the presidential campaign, Adams and Clay appealed to northern voters by advocating even higher duties on these items. When Adams introduced tariff legislation that extended duties to raw materials like wool, hemp, and molasses, he gained support from both Jackson and Van Buren, who considered these tariffs beneficial to farmers on the frontier. Despite the opposition of Vice President Calhoun and congressmen from older southern states, the tariff of 1828 was approved, raising duties on imports to an average of 62 percent.

The tariff of 1828, however, was Adams's only notable legislative victory. His foreign policy was also stymied by a hostile Congress. Moreover, Jackson's supporters gained a majority in the midterm elections of 1826, intensifying conflicts among Democratic-Republicans. Adams thus entered the 1828 election campaign with little to show in the way of domestic or foreign achievements, and Jackson and his supporters took full advantage of the president's political vulnerability.

The Presidential Election of 1828

The election of 1828 tested the power of the two major factions in the Democratic-Republican Party. President Adams followed the traditional approach of "standing" for office. He told supporters, "If my country wants my services, she must ask for them." Jackson and his supporters, who deeply distrusted established political leaders, chose instead to "run" for office. They took their case directly to the voters, introducing innovative techniques to create enthusiasm among the electorate.

Van Buren managed the first truly national political campaign in U.S. history, seeking to re-create the original Democratic-Republican coalition among farmers, northern artisans, and southern planters while adding a sizable constituency of frontier voters. He was aided in the effort by Calhoun, who again ran for vice president and supported the Tennessee war hero despite their disagreement over tariffs. Jackson's supporters organized state party conventions to nominate him for president rather than relying on the congressional caucus. They established local Jackson committees in critical states such as Virginia and New York. They organized newspaper campaigns and developed a logo, the hickory leaf, based on the candidate's nickname "Old Hickory."

Jackson traveled the country to build loyalty to himself as well as to his party. His Tennessee background, rise to great wealth, and reputation as an Indian fighter ensured his popularity among southern and western voters. He also reassured southerners that he advocated "judicious" duties on imports, suggesting that he might try to lower the rates imposed in 1828. At the same time, his support of the tariff of 1828 and his military credentials created enthusiasm among northern working men and frontier farmers.

President Adams's supporters demeaned the "dissolute" and "rowdy" men who poured out for Jackson rallies, and they also launched personal attacks on the candidate. Dragging politicians' private lives into public view was nothing new, but opposition papers focused their venom this time on the candidate's wife, Rachel. They questioned the timing of her divorce from her first husband and remarriage to Jackson, suggesting she was an adulterer and a bigamist. Rachel Jackson felt humiliated, but her husband refused to be intimidated by scandal.

Adams distanced himself from his own campaign. He sought to demonstrate his statesmanlike gentility by letting others speak for him. This strategy worked well when only men of wealth and property could vote. But with an enlarged electorate and an astonishing turnout of more than 50 percent of eligible voters, Adams's approach failed and Jackson became president. Jackson won handily in the South and the West and carried most of the Middle Atlantic states as well as New York. Adams dominated only in New England (Figure 9.1).

The election of 1828 formalized a new party alignment. During the campaign, Jackson and his supporters referred to themselves as "the Democracy" and forged a new national Democratic Party. In response, Adams's supporters called themselves National Republicans. The competition between Democrats and National Republicans heightened interest in national politics among ordinary voters and ensured that the innovative techniques introduced by Jackson would be widely adopted in future campaigns.

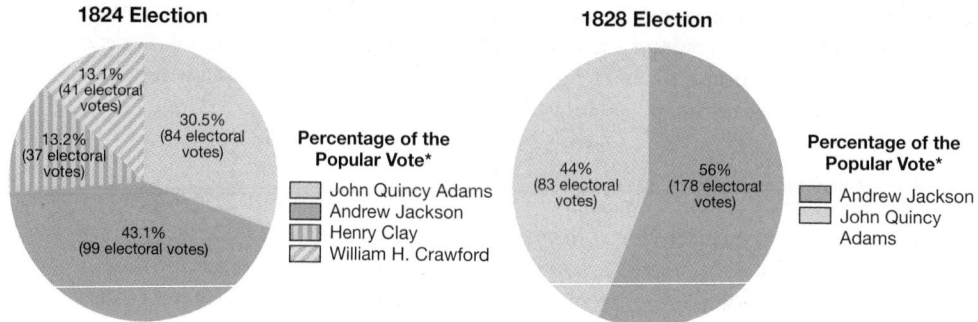

1824 Election

13.1%
(41 electoral votes)

30.5%
(84 electoral votes)

13.2%
(37 electoral votes)

43.1%
(99 electoral votes)

Percentage of the Popular Vote*

John Quincy Adams
Andrew Jackson
Henry Clay
William H. Crawford

1828 Election

44%
(83 electoral votes)

56%
(178 electoral votes)

Percentage of the Popular Vote*

Andrew Jackson
John Quincy Adams

*Popular vote percentages are approximate.

FIGURE 9.1

The Elections of 1824 and 1828   Andrew Jackson lost the 1824 election to John Quincy Adams when the decision was thrown into the House of Representatives. In 1828 Jackson launched the first popular campaign for president, mobilizing working-class white men who were newly enfranchised. Three times as many men—more than one million voters—cast ballots in 1828 than in 1824, ensuring Jackson's election as president.

Online Document Project   **The Election of 1828**
bedfordstmartins.com/hewittlawsonvalue

REVIEW & RELATE

• How and why did the composition of the electorate change in the 1820s?
• How did Jackson's 1828 campaign represent a significant departure from earlier patterns in American politics?

Jacksonian Democracy in Action

Many ordinary Americans held high expectations for Jackson's presidency, and Jackson hoped to make government more responsive to the "common man." But the president's notion of democracy, while inclusive of white men regardless of wealth or property, did not extend to Indians or African Americans. During his presidency, Indian nations would actively resist his efforts to take more of their land, and blacks would continue to resist their enslavement. Of more immediate importance, since President Jackson had to take clear positions on tariffs and other controversial issues, he could not please all of his constituents. He also confronted experienced adversaries like Clay, Webster, and John Quincy Adams, who was elected to the House of Representatives from Massachusetts in 1830. The president thus faced considerable difficulty in translating popular support into public policy.

A Democratic Spirit?

On March 4, 1829, crowds of ordinary citizens came to see their hero's inauguration. Jackson's wife Rachel had died less than three months earlier, leaving her husband devastated. Now Jackson, dressed in a plain black suit, walked alone to the Capitol as vast throngs of supporters waved and cheered. Wealthy planters were jammed shoulder to shoulder with frontier farmers and working men and women. Local African Americans also turned out for the spectacle. A somber Jackson read a brief inaugural address, took the oath of office, and then rode his horse through the crowds to the White House.

The size and enthusiasm of the crowds soon shattered the decorum of the inauguration. Author Margaret Bayard Smith reported mobs "scrambling, fighting, [and] romping" through the White House reception. Jackson was nearly crushed to death by "rabble" eager to shake his hand. Tubs of punch laced with rum, brandy, and champagne were finally placed on the lawn to draw the crowds outdoors.

Nonetheless, Jackson and his supporters viewed the event as a symbol of a new democratic spirit. Others were less optimistic. Bayard Smith warned against putting too much faith in "the people," who "have been found in all ages and countries where they get power in their hands, that of all tyrants, they are the most ferocious, cruel, and despotic." She and other conservative political leaders also saw echoes of the French Revolution in the unruly behavior of the masses. Supreme Court justice Joseph Story, too, feared "the reign of King 'Mob.'"

Tensions between the president and the capital's traditional leaders intensified in the first months of his administration. Jackson's appointment of Tennessee senator John Eaton as secretary of war added to the rancor. Eaton had had an affair with a woman thought to be of questionable character and later married her. When Jackson announced his plans to appoint Eaton to his cabinet, congressional leaders urged him to reconsider. When the president appointed Eaton anyway, the wives of Washington's leading politicians snubbed Mrs. Eaton and refused to accept her social calls. This time Jackson was outmaneuvered in what became known as the **Petticoat Affair**, and Eaton was eventually forced from office.

From the days of Dolley Madison, political wives had wielded considerable influence in Washington. In 1831 they pressured Eaton to resign. But the Petticoat Affair also led Jackson's entire cabinet to resign, after which his legislative agenda stalled in Congress and National Republicans regained the momentum lost after Adams's defeat. The Eaton appointment had reinforced concerns that the president used his authority to reward his friends. So, too, did his reliance on an informal group of advisers, known as the Kitchen Cabinet, rather than his official cabinet. While his administration opened up government posts to a wider range of individuals, ensuring more democratic access, he often selected appointees based on personal ties. The resulting **spoils system**—introduced by Jackson and continued by future administrations—assigned federal posts as gifts for partisan loyalty rather than as jobs that required experience or expertise.

Confrontations over Tariffs and the Bank

The Democratic Party that emerged in the late 1820s was built on an unstable foundation. The coalition that formed around Jackson included northern workers who benefited from high tariffs as well as southern farmers and planters who did not. It brought together western voters who sought federal support for internal improvements and strict constructionists who believed that such expenditures were unconstitutional. Weakened by conflicts over appointments, Jackson had to decide which factions to reward. In 1830 Congress passed four internal improvement bills with strong support from National

Republicans. Jackson vetoed each one, claiming that the "voice of the people" demanded careful spending. These vetoes worried his frontier supporters but pleased his southern constituency.

Southern congressmen, however, were more interested in his stand on tariffs. The tariff of 1828 still enraged many southern planters and politicians, but most believed that once Jackson reached the White House, he would reverse course and reduce this "Tariff of Abominations." Instead, he avoided the issue, and southern agriculture continued to suffer. Agricultural productivity in Virginia, South Carolina, and other states of the Old South was declining from soil exhaustion, while prices for staples like cotton and rice had not fully recovered after the panic of 1819. At the same time, higher duties on manufactured items meant that southerners had to pay more for the goods they bought.

Even as Calhoun campaigned with Jackson in 1828, the South Carolinian developed a philosophical argument to negate the effects of high tariffs on his state. Like opponents of the War of 1812, Calhoun drew on states' rights doctrines outlined in the Kentucky and Virginia Resolutions of 1798 (see chapter 7). In *The South Carolina Exposition and Protest*, published anonymously in 1828, Calhoun argued that states should have the ultimate power to determine the constitutionality of laws passed by Congress. When Jackson, after taking office, realized that his vice president advocated **nullification**—the right of individual states to declare individual laws void within their borders—it further damaged their relationship, which was already frayed by the Eaton affair.

When Congress debated the tariff issue in 1830, South Carolina senator Robert Hayne defended nullification. He claimed that the North intended to crush the South economically and that only the right of states to nullify federal legislation could protect southern society. In response, Daniel Webster denounced nullification and the states' rights doctrine on which it was built. At a banquet held after the Hayne-Webster debate, Jackson further antagonized southern political leaders by supporting Webster's position.

Matters worsened in 1832 when northern and western congressmen ignored their southern counterparts and confirmed the high duties set four years earlier. Jackson signed the 1832 tariff into law. In response, South Carolina held a special convention that approved an Ordinance of Nullification. It stated that duties on imports would not be collected in the state after February 1, 1833, and threatened secession if federal authorities tried to collect them. Many of the state's residents believed armed conflict was at hand, and some planters raised regiments to secure their property and defend what they viewed as the state's rights.

The tariff crisis thus escalated in the fall of 1832 just as Jackson faced reelection. The tariff debates had angered many southerners, and Calhoun refused to run again as his vice president. Fortunately for Jackson, however, opponents in Congress had provided him with another issue that could unite his supporters and highlight his commitment to the common man: the renewal of the BUS charter.

Clay and Webster persuaded Nicholas Biddle, head of the BUS, to request an early recharter of the bank. Jackson's opponents in Congress knew they had the votes to pass a new charter in the summer of 1832, and they hoped Jackson would veto the bill and thereby split the Democratic Party just before the fall elections. The Second Bank was a political quagmire. Although a private institution, it was chartered, or granted the right to operate, by the federal government, which owned 20 percent of its stock. The bank had stabilized the economy during the 1820s by regularly demanding specie (gold or silver) payments from state-chartered banks. This kept those banks from issuing too much paper money and thereby prevented inflation and higher prices. The Second Bank's tight-money policies also kept banks from expanding too rapidly in the western states. Bankers, merchants, and entrepreneurs in eastern cities as well as most planters applauded the bank's efforts, but its tight-money policies aroused hostility among the wider public. When state-chartered banks closed because of lack of specie, ordinary Americans were often stuck with worthless paper money. Tight-money policies also made it more difficult for individuals to get credit to purchase land, homes, or farm equipment.

As the president's opponents had hoped, Congress approved the new charter, and Jackson vetoed it. Yet rather than dividing the Democrats, Jackson's veto gained enormous support from voters across the country. In justifying his action, the president cast the Second Bank as a "monster" that was "dangerous to the liberties of the people"— particularly farmers, mechanics, and laborers—and promoted "the advancement of the few." Finally, Jackson noted that wealthy Britons owned substantial shares of the bank's stock and that national pride demanded ending the Second Bank's reign over the U.S. economy. Jackson rode the enthusiasm for his bank veto to reelection over National Republican candidate Henry Clay. Within a year, the Second Bank was dead, deprived of government deposits by Jackson.

Soon after his reelection, however, the president faced a grave political crisis related to the tariff issue. Jackson now supported lower tariffs, but he was adamant in his opposition to nullification. In early 1833, he persuaded Congress to pass a Force Bill, which gave him authority to use the military to enforce national laws in South Carolina. At the same time, Jackson made clear that he would work with Congress to reduce tariffs, allowing South Carolina to rescind its nullification ordinance without losing face. Open conflict was averted, but the question of nullification was not resolved.

Contesting Indian Removal

On another long-standing issue—the acquisition of Indian land—Jackson gained the support of white southerners and most frontier settlers. Yet not all Americans agreed with his effort to remove or exterminate Indians. In the 1820s, nations like the Cherokee that sought to maintain their homelands gained the support of Protestant missionaries who hoped to "civilize" Indians by converting them to Christianity and "American" ways. In 1819 Congress had granted these groups federal funds to establish schools and churches to help acculturate and convert Indian men and women. Presidents James Monroe and John Quincy Adams supported the rights of Indians to maintain their sovereignty if they embraced missionary goals. Jackson was much less supportive of efforts to incorporate Indians into the United States and sided with political leaders who sought to force eastern Indians to accept homelands west of the Mississippi River.

In 1825, three years before Jackson was elected president, Creek Indians in Georgia and Alabama were forcibly removed to Unorganized Territory (previously part of Arkansas Territory and later called Indian Territory) based on a fraudulent treaty. Jackson supported this policy. When he became president, politicians and settlers in Georgia, Florida, the Carolinas, and Illinois demanded federal assistance to force Indian communities out of their states.

The largest Indian nations vehemently protested their removal. The Cherokees, who had fought against the Creeks alongside Jackson at Horseshoe Bend, adopted a republican form of government in 1827 based on the U.S. Constitution. John Ross served as the president of the Cherokee constitutional convention, and a year later he was chosen principal chief in the first constitutional election. He and the other chiefs then declared themselves a sovereign nation within the borders of the United States. The Georgia legislature rejected the Cherokee claims of independence and argued that Indians were simply guests of the state. When Ross appealed to Jackson to recognize Cherokee sovereignty, the president refused. Instead, Jackson proclaimed that Georgia, like other states, was "sovereign over the people within its borders." At his urging, Congress passed the **Indian Removal Act** in 1830, by which the Cherokee and other Indian nations would be forced to exchange ancient claims on lands in the Southeast for a "clear title forever" on territory west of the Mississippi River. Still, the majority of Cherokees refused to accept these terms and worked assiduously to maintain control of their existing territory.

As the dispute between the Cherokee nation and Georgia unfolded, Jackson made clear his intention to implement the Indian Removal Act. In 1832 he sent federal troops into western Illinois to force Sauk and Fox peoples to move farther west. Instead, whole villages, led by Chief Black Hawk, fled to the Wisconsin Territory. Black Hawk and a thousand warriors confronted U.S. troops at Bad Axe, but the Sauk and Fox warriors were decimated in a brutal daylong battle. The survivors were forced to move west.

Cherokee Phoenix   As U.S. officials pressured the Cherokee nation to relocate west of the Mississippi River, Cherokee leaders sought to convince them that the tribe had become Americanized. Elias Boudinot, whose Cherokee name was Galagina Uwatie, attended Christian mission schools and married a white woman. In 1828 he published the bilingual *Phoenix* to build internal unity and gather support against Cherokee removal.   Library of Congress

Meanwhile the Seminole Indians, who had fought against Jackson when he invaded Florida in 1818, prepared for another pitched battle to protect their territory, while John Ross pursued legal means to resist removal through state and federal courts. The contest for Indian lands would continue well past Jackson's presidency, but the president's desire to force indigenous nations westward would ultimately prevail.

REVIEW & RELATE

- What did President Jackson's response to the Eaton affair and Indian removal reveal about his vision of democracy?
- To what extent did Jackson's policies favor the South? Which policies benefited or antagonized which groups of southerners?

Conclusion: The Nation Faces New Challenges

From the 1810s through the early 1830s, the United States was buffeted by a series of crises. The War of 1812 threatened the stability of the nation, not only due to attacks on its recently constructed capital city but also because New Englanders so deeply opposed the conflict that some considered seceding from the Union. The panic of 1819 then threw the nation into economic turmoil and led to demands for expanded voting rights for white men. It also heightened disputes over banks and tariffs as residents of various regions and classes sought to ensure their own financial security. The admission of Missouri similarly intensified debates over slavery as white southerners saw themselves losing out in population growth and political representation to the North. At the same time, the western expansion that allowed territories like Missouri to claim statehood also escalated struggles over Indian rights. By the 1820s, those struggles involved a diverse array of Indian nations as well as deep differences among white Americans over the future of native peoples who had embraced Christianity and other forms of "civilization."

In navigating these difficult issues, some Americans sought to find a middle ground. Dolley Madison worked to overcome partisan divisions through social networking. After the death of her husband, James, in 1836, she returned to Washington, where her house on Lafayette Street became a center of social activity for politicians, ambassadors, and their wives. Although her son's mismanagement of Montpelier forced her to sell the beloved estate, Dolley secured her old age when Congress purchased President James Madison's papers from her. Similarly, John Ross wielded his biracial heritage to seek rights for Indians within a white-dominated world. He served as both a lobbyist for Cherokee interests in Washington and an advocate of acculturation to Anglo-American ways among the Cherokee. Still, congressional passage of the Indian Removal Act in 1830 challenged Ross's efforts to maintain his tribe's sovereignty and homeland. When Henry Clay was reelected to the U.S. Senate in November 1831, he spoke out against Cherokee removal. But Clay was more widely known for helping to forge key compromises on the admission of Missouri and on tariffs. In each case, he hoped to bring a deeply divided Congress together and provide time for the nation's political leaders to develop more permanent solutions.

Yet despite the efforts of Madison, Ross, Clay, and others, differences often led to division in the 1820s and 1830s. Indeed, Henry Clay provided the final push that ensured John Quincy Adams's selection as president in 1824. In the aftermath of that election, two distinct political parties emerged out of the once-united Democratic-Republicans: the Democrats and the National Republicans. In the context of the political, military, and economic upheaval that marked the early Republic, it is not surprising that a charismatic but divisive figure like Andrew Jackson emerged to lead the new Democratic Party. Transforming the process of political campaigning, he gave voice to the "common man," but he also introduced the spoils system to government, smashed the Second Bank of the United States, and forced thousands of Indians off their lands. The extermination and removal of Indians then fostered the geographical expansion of American settlements southward and westward, ensuring the growth of slavery.

Dolley Madison, who lived into the late 1840s, and John Ross, who survived the Civil War, observed the continuing conflicts created by geographical expansion and partisan agendas. Madison remained a beloved figure in Washington, escorted through the Executive Mansion by President James K. Polk in February 1849, just months before her death. Ross, however, faced much more difficult circumstances as the Cherokee nation divided over whether to accept removal. Ross fought to delay removal as long as possible but eventually oversaw the forced march west of thousands of Cherokees. In their new homes, Cherokees continued to fight each other and the U.S. government. Indeed, Ross died in 1866 in Washington, D.C., while trying to negotiate a new treaty with the federal government.

Despite the dramatically different backgrounds and careers of Madison and Ross, both worked to bridge differences in the young nation, and both defended it against attack. Both harbored democratic ideals of a nation that could incorporate women as well as men, Indians as well as whites. Ultimately, however, neither had the power to overcome the partisan rivalries and economic crises that shaped the young nation or to halt the rising tensions over Indian lands and slave labor that would continue to plague Americans in the decades to come.

Chapter Review

MAKE IT STICK

LearningCurve **bedfordstmartins.com/hewittlawsonvalue**
After reading the chapter, use LearningCurve to retain what you've read.

IDENTIFY KEY TERMS

Identify and explain the significance of each term below.

Non-Intercourse Act (p. 219)
Hartford Convention (p. 222)
American System (p. 223)
Erie Canal (p. 224)
Monroe Doctrine (p. 226)
panic of 1819 (p. 228)
Missouri Compromise (p. 231)

Democrats and National Republicans
 (p. 233)
Petticoat Affair (p. 237)
spoils system (p. 237)
nullification (p. 238)
Indian Removal Act (p. 240)

REVIEW & RELATE

Answer the focus questions from each section of the chapter.

1. How were conflicts with Indians in the West connected to ongoing tensions between the United States and Great Britain on land and at sea?

2. What were the long-term consequences of the War of 1812?

3. What role did government play in early-nineteenth-century economic development?

4. How and why did economic development contribute to regional differences and shape regional ties?

5. What were the political consequences of the panic of 1819?

6. What regional divisions did the conflict over slavery in Missouri reveal?

7. How and why did the composition of the electorate change in the 1820s?

8. How did Jackson's 1828 campaign represent a significant departure from earlier patterns in American politics?

9. What did President Jackson's response to the Eaton affair and Indian removal reveal about his vision of democracy?

10. To what extent did Jackson's policies favor the South? Which policies benefited or antagonized which groups of southerners?

ONLINE DOCUMENT PROJECTS

◆ **The Panic of 1819**
◆ **The Election of 1828**

After reading the primary sources in these document sets, answer the **Interpret the Evidence** questions to help you analyze each of the documents, and then answer the **Put It in Context** question(s) to help you relate the documents to the topics and themes you read about in the chapter.

bedfordstmartins.com/hewittlawsonvalue

TIMELINE OF EVENTS

1809	• Non-Intercourse Act passed
1811	• First steamboat travels down the Mississippi to New Orleans
	• William Henry Harrison defeats Shawnees at Prophet Town
June 1812	• War of 1812 begins
1814	• Hartford Convention
March 1814	• Battle of Horseshoe Bend
August 1814	• British burn Washington City
December 1814	• Treaty of Ghent
1815	• Battle of New Orleans
1817–1818	• Andrew Jackson fights Spanish and Seminole forces in Florida
1818	• Great Britain and U.S. agree to joint occupation of Oregon Territory
1819	• Spain cedes Florida to U.S.; establishes boundary between U.S. and Spanish territory through the Adams-Onís Treaty

	• Panic of 1819 sparks severe recession that lasts until 1823
1820	• Missouri Compromise
1821	• White traders begin using Santa Fe Trail
1822	• Denmark Vesey accused of organizing a slave uprising
1823	• Monroe Doctrine articulated
1825	• Erie Canal completed
1828	• Tariff of 1828 passed
	• John Ross elected principal chief of the Cherokee nation
1829	• Petticoat Affair
1830	• Indian Removal Act passed
1832	• South Carolina passes Ordinance of Nullification
1833	• Force Bill passed

10

LearningCurve
bedfordstmartins.com/hewittlawsonvalue
After reading the chapter, use LearningCurve
to retain what you've read.

Slavery Expands South and West

1830–1850

AMERICAN HISTORIES

Although James Henry Hammond became one of the richest plantation owners in South Carolina, he began life more modestly. Born in 1807 near Newberry, South Carolina, he was the only one of six siblings to earn a college degree. Certain that a legal career would lead to wealth and power, James opened a law practice in Columbia, the state capital, in 1828. Two years later, bored by his profession, he established a newspaper, the *Southern Times*. Writing bold editorials that supported nullification of the "Tariff of Abominations," Hammond quickly gained attention and acclaim.

While launching his journalistic career, James courted Catherine Fitzsimmons, the daughter of a wealthy, politically connected family. When they married in June 1831, James became master of Silver Bluff, a 7,500-acre plantation worked by 147 slaves. Giving up his editorial career to focus on managing the estate, he quickly gained prominence as an agricultural reformer and was elected to the U.S. House of Representatives in 1834.

Hammond's political career was erratic. In 1836 he led a campaign that resulted in congressional passage of the so-called gag rule, ensuring that antislavery petitions would be tabled rather than read on the floor of the House. Soon afterward, he took ill and resigned from Congress, but he returned to politics in 1842 as governor of South Carolina. His ambitions were stymied once more, however, when Catherine discovered that James had made sexual advances on his four nieces, aged thirteen to sixteen. Fearing public exposure, Hammond withdrew from politics, but he soon joined southern intellectuals in arguing that slavery was a positive good rather than a necessary evil.

This proslavery argument intensified in the late 1840s as northern reformers sought to halt the spread of slavery into newly acquired lands in the West. In the early nineteenth century, a thriving trade in enslaved workers had developed between the Upper South and more fertile areas in the Lower South. It bolstered the economy in both regions but also highlighted the brutalities of bondage. With westward expansion, this internal trade in slaves burgeoned.

Solomon Northrup was among tens of thousands of African Americans who endured the ravages of the internal slave trade. Unlike the vast majority, however, Northrup was born free in Minerva, New York, in 1808. His father, Mintus, had been born into slavery but was freed by his owner's will. Once free, Mintus acquired sufficient property to qualify to vote, an impressive achievement for a former slave.

After his marriage to Anne Hampton at the age of twenty-one, Solomon found employment transporting goods along the region's waterways. He was also hired as a fiddle player for local dances, while Anne worked as a cook in neighborhood taverns. In 1834 the couple moved to Saratoga Springs, a tourist haven that provided more job opportunities. There they raised their three children until tragedy struck.

In March 1841, Solomon met two white circus performers who hired him to play fiddle for them on tour. They paid his wages up front and told him to obtain documents proving his free status. After reaching Washington, D.C., however, Northrup was drugged, chained, and sold to James Birch, a notorious slave trader. Northrup was resold in New Orleans to William Ford, whom he later described as a "kind, noble, candid Christian man" who was nonetheless blind "to the inherent wrong at the bottom of the system of Slavery." Ford gave Northrup a new name, Platt, and put him to work as a raftsman while Northrup tried unsuccessfully to get word to his wife.

In 1842 Ford sold "Platt" to a neighbor, John Tibeats, who whipped and abused his workers. When Tibeats attacked his newly acquired slave with an ax, Northrup fought back and fled to Ford's house. His former owner shielded him from Tibeats's wrath and arranged his sale to Edwin Epps, who owned a large cotton plantation. For the next ten years, Northrup worked the fields and played the fiddle at local dances.

Finally, in 1852 Samuel Bass, a Canadian carpenter who openly acknowledged his antislavery views, came to work on Epps's house. Northrup persuaded Bass to send a letter to his wife in Saratoga Springs. Anne Northrup, astonished to hear from her husband after more than a decade, took the letter to lawyer Henry Northrup, the son of Mintus's former owner. After months of legal efforts, Henry traveled to Louisiana and, with the help of a local judge, freed Solomon Northrup in January 1853.

South Carolina Plantation   This wood engraving from the mid-nineteenth century depicts a planter's residence on the Cumbee River, South Carolina. When cotton prices began to rise after 1843, leading planters invested more of their profits in fancy houses and luxurious furnishings. They bought expensive clothing and jewelry for their wives and daughters and traveled abroad with their families.   The Granger Collection, New York

THE AMERICAN HISTORIES of Solomon Northrup and James Henry Hammond were both intertwined in the struggle over slavery. By 1850 slave labor had become central to the South's and the nation's economic success, even as slave ownership became concentrated in the hands of a smaller proportion of wealthy white families. The concentration of more slaves on each plantation created a stronger sense of community and a truly African American culture, although it did not negate the brutality of the institution. At the same time, the volatility of the cotton market fueled economic instability, which planters claimed could be resolved only by cultivating more cotton. In response, sympathetic administrations in Washington forcibly removed Indians from the Southeast, supported independence for Texas, and proclaimed war on Mexico. But these policies led to growing conflicts with western Indian nations and heightened political conflicts over slavery and the nation's future.

Planters Expand the Slave System

The cotton gin, developed in the 1790s, ensured the growth of southern agriculture into the 1840s (see chapter 8). As the cotton kingdom spread west, planters forged a distinctive culture around the institution of slavery. But slavery limited the development of cities, technology, and educational institutions, leaving the South increasingly dependent on the North and West for food, industrial goods, commercial resources, books and magazines, and even higher education. In addition, westward expansion extended the trade in slaves within the South, shattering black families. Still, southern planters viewed themselves as national leaders, both the repository of traditional American values and the engine of economic progress.

A Plantation Society Develops in the South

Plantation slavery existed throughout the Americas in the early nineteenth century. British, French, Dutch, Portuguese, and Spanish colonies in the West Indies and South America all housed large numbers of slaves and extensive plantations. In the U.S. South, however, the volatile cotton market and a scarcity of fertile land kept most plantations relatively small before 1830. But from the early 1840s on, territorial expansion and profits from cotton, as well as from rice and sugar, fueled a period of conspicuous consumption. Successful southern planters now built grand houses and purchased a variety of luxury goods.

As plantations grew, especially in states like South Carolina and Mississippi where slaves outnumbered whites, a wealthy aristocracy sought to ensure productivity by employing harsh methods of discipline. Masters whipped slaves for a variety of offenses, from not picking enough cotton to breaking tools or running away. Although James Henry Hammond imagined himself a progressive master, he used the whip liberally, hoping thereby to ensure that his estate generated sufficient profits to purchase fancy furnishings, trips to Europe, fashionable clothing, and fine jewelry.

Increased attention to comfort and luxury helped make the heavy workload of plantation mistresses tolerable. Although mistresses were idealized for their beauty, piety, and grace, they took on considerable managerial responsibilities. They directed the domestic slaves as well as the feeding, clothing, and medical care of the entire labor force. They were expected to organize and preside over lavish social events, host relatives and friends for extended stays, and direct the plantation in their husband's absence. When James was traveling, Catherine Hammond struggled to manage the estate while caring for their seven children.

Of course, plantation mistresses were relieved of the most arduous labor by enslaved women, who cooked, cleaned, and washed for the family, cared for the children, and even nursed the babies. Wealthy white women benefited from the best education, the greatest access to music and literature, and the finest clothes and furnishings to be had in the region. Yet the pedestal on which plantation mistresses stood was shaky, built on a patriarchal system in which husbands and fathers held substantial power. For example, most wives were forced to ignore the sexual relations that husbands initiated with female slaves. As Mary Boykin Chesnut explained in her diary, "Every lady tells you who is the father of all the Mulatto children in everybody's household, but those in her own, she seems to think drop from the clouds or pretends to think so." In 1850, when Catherine Hammond discovered James's sexual relations with an enslaved mother and daughter, she moved to Charleston with her two youngest daughters. Most wives, however, stayed put, and some took out their anger and frustration on slave women already victimized by their husbands. Moreover, some mistresses owned slaves themselves, traded them on the slave market, and gave them as gifts or bequests to family members and friends.

Not all slaveholders were wealthy planters like the Hammonds, with fifty or more slaves and extensive landholdings. Far more planters in the 1830s and 1840s owned between twenty and fifty slaves, and an even larger number of farmers owned just three to six slaves. These small planters and farmers could not afford to emulate the lives of the largest slave owners. Still, as Hammond wrote a friend in 1847, "The planters here are essentially what the nobility are in other countries. They stand at the head of society & politics."

Urban Life in the Slave South

The insistence on the supremacy of slave owners had broad repercussions. The richest men in the South invested in slaves, land, and household goods, with little left to develop industry, technology, or urban institutions. The largest factory in the South, the Tredegar Iron Works in Richmond, Virginia, was constructed in 1833, and by 1850 it employed several hundred free and enslaved African Americans. Most southern industrialists, however, like South Carolina textile manufacturer William Gregg, employed poor white women and children. But neither Tredegar nor a scattering of textile mills fundamentally reshaped the region's economy.

The South also fell behind in urban development. The main exception was port cities, which boasted fine shops, a growing professional class, and ready access to national and international news. Yet even in Baltimore, Charleston, and Savannah, commerce was often directed by northern agents, especially cotton brokers. In addition, nearly one-third of southern whites had no access to cash and instead bartered goods and services, further restricting the urban economy. In the South, only Baltimore and New Orleans reached a population of 100,000 by 1850.

Despite their relative scarcity, southern cities attracted many free blacks, providing them with the best hope of finding employment and distancing themselves from hostile planters. The growing demand for cheap domestic labor in urban areas and planters' greater willingness to emancipate less valuable single female slaves meant that free black women generally outnumbered men in southern cities. These women worked mainly as washerwomen, cooks, and general domestics, while free black men labored as skilled artisans, dockworkers, or sailors in southern seaports. In these jobs, free blacks competed with slaves and with growing numbers of Irish, German, and Jewish immigrants who flocked to southern cities in the 1840s and 1850s. The presence of immigrants and free blacks and the reputation of ports as escape hatches for runaway slaves ensured that cities remained suspect in the South.

The scarcity of cities and industry also curtailed the development of transportation. State governments and private citizens invested little in roads, canals, and railroads. Most small farmers traded goods locally, and planters used the South's extensive river system to ship goods to commercial hubs. Where rivers did not meet this need, rail lines were sometimes built. However, only Virginia and Maryland, with their proximity to the nation's capital, developed extensive rail networks.

The Consequences of Slavery's Expansion

Outside the South, industry and agriculture increasingly benefited from technological innovation. Indeed, the booming textile industry in New England fueled the demand for cotton and drove up prices during the 1840s and 1850s. Planters, however, continued to rely on intensive manual labor. Even reform-minded planters focused on fertilizer and crop rotation rather than machines to enhance productivity. The limited use of new technologies—such as iron plows or seed drills—resulted from a lack of investment capital and planters' attitudes toward African American laborers. Believing them to be inherently lazy, ignorant, and untrustworthy, planters refused to purchase expensive equipment that might be broken or purposely sabotaged. Instead, they relied on continually expanding the acreage under cultivation.

One result of these practices was that a declining percentage of white Southerners came to control vast estates with large numbers of enslaved laborers. Between 1830 and 1850, the absolute number of both slaves and owners grew. But slave owners became a smaller proportion of all white Southerners because the white population grew faster than the number of slave owners. At the same time, distinctions among wealthy planters, small slaveholders, and whites who owned no slaves also increased.

The concern with productivity and profits and the concentration of more slaves on large plantations did have some benefits for black women and men. The end of the international slave trade in 1808 forced planters to rely more heavily on natural reproduction to increase their labor force. Thus many planters thought more carefully about how they treated their slaves, who were increasingly viewed as "valuable property." It was no longer good business to work slaves to death, cripple them with severe whippings, or cut off fingers, ears, or other body parts.

Nonetheless, owners continued to whip slaves with regularity and made paltry investments in diet and health care for enslaved workers. Most slaves lived in small houses with dirt floors and minimal furniture and were given three or four suits of clothes a year despite laboring six days a week. They ate a diet high in calories, especially fats and carbohydrates, but with little meat, fish, fresh vegetables, or fruits. The high mortality rate among slave infants and children—more than twice that of white children to age five—reflected the limits of planters' care.

The spread of slavery into Mississippi, Louisiana, Alabama, Missouri, and Texas affected both white and black families, though again not equally. The younger sons of wealthy planters were often forced to move to the frontier, and their families generally lived in rough quarters on isolated plantations. Such moves were far more difficult for slaves, however. Between 1830 and 1850, more than 440,000 slaves were forced to move from the Upper South to the Lower South (Map 10.1). On the southern frontier, they endured especially harsh conditions as they carved out new cotton fields and rice paddies or planted and harvested sugarcane. Many of these frontier slaves had been torn away from their families and communities.

By the 1830s, slave markets blossomed in Richmond, Charleston, Savannah, Natchez, New Orleans, and Washington, D.C. Solomon Northrup described one in Washington, D.C., in 1841 where a woman named Eliza watched as her son Randall was "won" by a planter from Baton Rouge. She promised "to be the most faithful slave that ever lived" if he would also buy her and her daughter. The slave trader threatened the desperate mother with a hundred lashes, but neither his threats nor her tears could change the outcome. As slavery spread westward, such scenes were repeated thousands of times.

Online Document Project   **Life in Slavery**
bedfordstmartins.com/hewittlawsonvalue

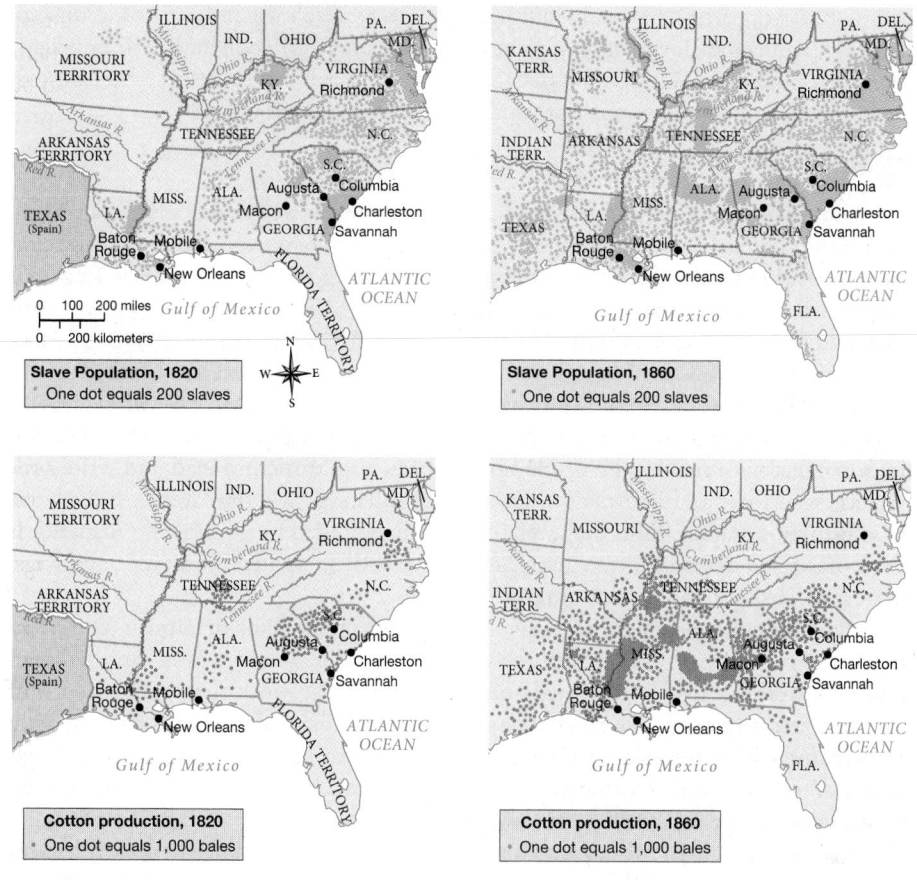

MAP 10.1

The Spread of Slavery and Cotton, 1820–1860   While tobacco, rice, and sugar remained important crops in a few states, cotton became the South's and the nation's major export. The need to find more fertile fields led planters to migrate to Alabama, Mississippi, and Louisiana. As a result of cotton's success, the number of enslaved people increased dramatically, the internal slave trade expanded, and labor demands intensified.

> **REVIEW & RELATE**

- What role did the planter elite play in southern society and politics?
- What were the consequences of the dominant position of slave-based plantation agriculture in the southern economy?

Slave Society and Culture

Because slave labor formed the backbone of the southern economy, enslaved workers gained some leverage against owners and overseers. But these women and men did not simply define themselves in relation to whites. They also developed relationships and identities within the slave quarters. By maintaining aspects of African culture, creating strong kinship networks, and embracing religion, southern blacks found ways to lighten their bondage. Many also found small ways to resist their enslavement on an everyday basis. Others resisted more openly, and a small number organized rebellions against their masters.

Slaves Fuel the Southern Economy

The labor of enslaved blacks drove the nation's economy as well as the South's. In 1820 the South produced some 500,000 bales of cotton, much of it exported to England. By 1850 the region produced nearly 3 million bales, feeding textile mills in New England and abroad. A decade later, cotton accounted for nearly two-thirds of the U.S. export trade and added nearly $200 million a year to the American economy.

Carpenters, blacksmiths, and other skilled slaves were sometimes hired out and allowed to keep a small amount of the money they earned. They traveled to nearby households, compared their circumstances to those on other plantations, and sometimes made contact with free blacks. Some skilled slaves also learned to read and write and had access to tools and knowledge denied to field hands. And they were less likely to be sold to slave traders. Still, they were constantly hounded by whites who demanded travel passes and deference, were more acutely aware of alternatives to slavery, and were often suspected of involvement in rebellions.

Household slaves sometimes received old clothes and bedding or leftover food from their owners. Yet they were under the constant surveillance of whites, and women especially were vulnerable to sexual abuse. Moreover, the work they performed was physically demanding. Enslaved women chopped wood, hauled water, baked food, and washed clothes. Fugitive slave James Curry recalled that his mother, a cook in North Carolina, rose early each morning to milk fourteen cows, bake bread, and churn butter. She was responsible for meals for her owners and the slaves. In summer, she cooked her last meal around eight o'clock, after which she milked the cows again. Then she returned to her quarters, put her children to bed, and often fell asleep while mending clothes.

Field hands often left their youngest children in the care of cooks and washerwomen. But once slaves reached the age of eleven or twelve, they were put to work full-time. Although field labor was defined by its relentless pace and drudgery, it also brought together large numbers of slaves for the entire day and thus helped forge bonds among laborers on the same plantation. Songs provided a rhythm for their work and offered slaves the chance to communicate their frustrations or their hopes.

Field labor was generally organized by task or by gang. Under the task system, typical on rice plantations, a slave could return to his or her quarters once the day's task was completed. This left time for some slaves to cultivate gardens, fish for supper, make quilts, or repair furniture. In the gang system, widely used on cotton plantations, men and women worked in groups under the supervision of a driver and swept across fields hoeing, planting, or picking.

Developing an African American Culture

Amid hard work and harsh treatment, slaves created social bonds and a rich culture of their own. Thus blacks in America continued to employ African names, like Cuffee and Binah, generations after their enslavement. Even if masters gave them English names, they might use African names in the slave quarters to sustain family and community networks and memories. Some also retained elements of West African languages. Along the South Carolina and Georgia coast, enslaved workers spoke Gullah, a dialect that combined African words and speech patterns with English. Agricultural techniques, medical practices, forms of dress, folktales, songs and musical instruments, dances, and courtship rituals—all demonstrated the continued importance of West African and Caribbean culture to African Americans. This **syncretic culture**, which combined elements from Africa and the Caribbean with those from the United States, was disseminated as slaves hauled cotton to market, forged families across plantation boundaries, or were sold farther south. It was also handed down across generations through storytelling, music, rituals, and religious services.

Religious practices offer an important example of syncretic cultural forms. Africans from Muslim communities often continued to pray to Allah even if they were also required to attend Protestant churches. Black preachers who embraced Christianity developed rituals that combined African and American elements. In the early nineteenth century, slaves eagerly embraced the evangelical teachings offered by Baptist and Methodist preachers, which echoed some of the expressive spiritual forms in West Africa. By midcentury, African Americans made up one-third of Baptist and perhaps one-quarter of Methodist church membership. On Sunday mornings, slaves might listen to white ministers proclaim that slavery was God's will; that evening, they might gather in the woods to hear their own preachers tell of God's love and the possibilities of black liberation, at least in the hereafter. Slaves often incorporated drums, conch shells, dancing, or other West African elements into these worship services.

Although most black preachers were men, a few women gained a spiritual following in slave communities. Many female slaves embraced religion enthusiastically, hoping that Christian baptism might substitute for West African rituals that protected newborn babies. Enslaved women also called on church authorities to intervene when white owners or overseers or even enslaved men abused them. They also considered the church one means of sanctifying slave marriages that were not recognized legally.

Slaves also generally provided health care for their community. Most slave births were attended by black midwives, and African American healers often turned to herbal medicines, having discovered southern equivalents to cures used in West Africa. Forced to labor in the fields, gather branches and roots in the forest, and supplement their meager rations with local plants, slaves were far more attuned to the natural world than were their owners.

Resistance and Rebellion

Many owners worried that black preachers and West African folktales inspired blacks to resist enslavement. Fearing defiance, planters went to incredible lengths to control seemingly powerless slaves. Although they were largely successful in quelling open revolts, they were unable to eliminate more subtle forms of opposition, like slowing the pace of work, feigning illness, and damaging white-owned equipment, food, and clothing. Even slaves' ability to sustain a distinct African American culture was viewed by some planters as undermining the institution of bondage. More overt forms of resistance—such as truancy and running away, which disrupted work and lowered profits—also proved impossible to stamp out.

The forms of everyday resistance slaves employed varied in part on their location and resources. Skilled artisans, mostly men, could do more substantial damage because they used more expensive tools, but they were less able to protect themselves through pleas of ignorance. Field laborers could damage only hoes and a few cotton plants, but they could do so on a regular basis without exciting suspicion. House slaves could burn dinners, scorch shirts, break china and glassware, and even poison owners or burn down houses. Often considered the most loyal slaves, they were also among the most feared because of their intimate contact with white families. Single male slaves were the most likely to run away, planning their escape carefully to get as far as possible before their owners noticed they were missing. Women who fled plantations were more likely to hide out for short periods in the local area and return at night to get food and visit family. Eventually, isolation, hunger, or concern for children led most of these truants to return if slave patrols did not find them first.

Despite their rarity, efforts to organize slave uprisings, such as that planned by Gabriel (see chapter 8) and the one supposedly hatched by Denmark Vesey (see chapter 9) in the early nineteenth century, continued to haunt southern whites. Rebellions in the West Indies, especially the one in Saint Domingue, also echoed through the early nineteenth century. Then in 1831 a seemingly obedient slave named Nat Turner organized a revolt in rural Virginia that stunned whites across the South. Turner was a self-styled preacher and religious visionary who believed that God had

Nat Turner's Rebellion   This woodcut depicts the rebellion in the top panel and the capture of rebels below. It was published in 1831 by Samuel Warner, a New York publisher who based his lurid account on eyewitness testimony and the supposed confessions of participants. He linked the Turner rebellion to the Haitian Revolution and to suspected (though unproven) conspiracies elsewhere in the South.   Library of Congress

given him a mission. On the night of August 21, he and his followers killed their owners, the Travis family, and then headed to nearby plantations in Southampton County. The bloody insurrection led to the deaths of 57 white men, women, and children and liberated more than 50 slaves. But on August 22, outraged white militiamen burst on the scene and eventually captured the black rebels. Turner managed to hide out for two months but was eventually caught. Tried and convicted on November 5, he was hanged six days later. Virginia executed 55 other African Americans suspected of assisting Turner. White mobs also beat, tortured, or killed some 200 more blacks with no connection to the rebellion.

Nat Turner's rebellion instilled panic among white Southerners, who now worried they might be killed in their sleep by a seemingly submissive slave. News of the uprising traveled through slave communities as well, inspiring both pride and anxiety. The execution of Turner and his followers reminded African Americans how far whites would go to protect the institution of slavery.

REVIEW & RELATE

* How did enslaved African Americans create ties of family, community, and culture?
* How did enslaved African Americans resist efforts to control and exploit their labor?

Planters Tighten Control

Fears of rebellion led to stricter regulations of black life, and actual uprisings temporarily reinforced white solidarity. Yet yeomen farmers, poor whites, and middle-class professionals all voiced some doubts about the ways in which human bondage affected southern society. To unite these disparate groups, planters wielded their economic and political authority, highlighted bonds of kinship and religious fellowship, and promoted an ideology of white supremacy. Their efforts intensified as northern states and other nations began eradicating slavery.

Harsher Treatment for Southern Blacks

Slave revolts led many southern states to impose harsher controls; however, Nat Turner's rebellion led some white Virginians to question slavery itself. In December 1831, the state Assembly established a special committee to consider the crisis. Representatives from western counties, where slavery was never profitable, argued for the gradual abolition of slavery and the colonization of the state's black population in Africa. Hundreds of women in the region sent petitions to the Virginia legislature supporting these positions. But slaveholders from eastern districts claimed that even discussing emancipation might encourage blacks who observed the Assembly's debates to rebel.

Advocates of colonization gained significant support, but the state's leading intellectuals spoke out adamantly for the benefits of slavery. Professor Thomas Dew, president of the College of William and Mary, emphasized the advantages for planters and slaves alike. Dew claimed that slaveholders performed godly work in raising Africans from the status of brute beast to civilized Christian. Dew's proslavery argument turned the tide, and in the fall of 1832 the Virginia legislature rejected gradual emancipation and imposed new restrictions on slaves and free blacks.

From the 1820s to the 1840s, more stringent codes were passed across the South. Most southern legislatures prohibited owners from manumitting their slaves, made it illegal for whites to teach slaves to read or write, limited the size and number of independent black churches, abolished slaves' already-limited access to courts, outlawed slave marriage, banned antislavery literature as obscene, defined rape as a crime only against white women, and outlawed assemblies of more than three blacks without a white person present.

States also regulated the lives of free blacks. Some prohibited free blacks from residing within their borders, others required large bonds to ensure good behavior, and most forbade free blacks who left the state from returning. The homes of free blacks could be raided at any time on suspicion of possessing stolen goods or harboring runaways, and the children of free black women were subject to stringent apprenticeship laws that kept many in virtual slavery.

Planters, aided by state legislatures and local authorities, proved largely successful in controlling slaves, but there was a price to pay. Laws to regulate black life tended to restrict education, mobility, and urban development for southern whites as well. Such laws also characterized the region's primary labor force as savage, heathen, and lazy, hardly a basis for sustained economic development. And the regulations increased tensions between poorer whites, who were often responsible for enforcement, and wealthy whites, who benefited most clearly from their imposition.

White Southerners without Slaves

Yeomen farmers, independent landowners who did not own any slaves, had a complex relationship with the South's plantation economy. Many were related to slave owners, and they often depended on planters to ship their crops to market. Some hoped to rise into the ranks of slaveholders one day, and others made extra money by hiring themselves out to planters. Yet yeomen farmers also recognized that their economic interests often diverged from those of planters. As growing numbers gained the right to vote in the 1820s and 1830s, they voiced their concerns in county and state legislatures.

Most yeomen farmers believed in slavery, but they sometimes challenged planters' authority and assumptions. In the Virginia slavery debates, small farmers from western districts advocated gradual abolition. In other states, they advocated more liberal policies toward debtors and the protection of fishing rights. Yeomen farmers also questioned certain ideals embraced by elites. Although plantation mistresses considered manual labor beneath them, the wives and daughters of many small farmers had to work in the fields, haul water, chop wood, and perform other arduous tasks. Still, yeomen farmers' ability to diminish planter control was limited by the continued importance of cotton to the southern economy.

In their daily life, however, many small farmers depended more on friends and neighbors than on the planter class. Barn raisings, corn shuckings, quilting bees, and other collective endeavors offered them the chance to combine labor with sociability. Church services and church socials also brought communities together. Farmers lost such ties when they sought better land on the frontier. There, families struggled to establish new crops and new lives in relative isolation but hoped that fertile fields might offer the best chance to rise within the South's rigid class hierarchy.

One step below the yeomen farmers were the even larger numbers of white Southerners who owned no property at all. These poor whites depended on hunting and fishing in frontier areas, performing day labor on farms and plantations, or working on docks or as servants in southern cities. Poor whites competed with free blacks and slaves for employment and often harbored resentments as a result. Yet they also built alliances based on their shared economic plight. Poor immigrants from Ireland, Wales, and Scotland were especially hostile to American planters, who reminded them of English landlords.

Some poor whites remained in the same community for decades, establishing themselves on the margins of society. They attended church regularly, performed day labor for affluent families, and taught their children to defer to their betters. In Savannah and other southern cities, wealthy families organized benevolent associations and more affluent immigrants established mutual aid societies to help poorer members of their community in hard times. It was the most respectable among this downtrodden class who had the best chance of securing assistance.

Other poor whites moved frequently and survived by combining legal and illegal ventures. Some rejected laws and customs established by elites and joined forces with blacks or other poor whites. These men and women often had few ties to local communities, little religious training or education, and settled scores with violence. Although poor whites unnerved southern elites by flouting the law and sometimes befriending poor blacks, they could not mount any significant challenge to planter control.

Unlike poor whites, the South's small but growing middle class sought stability and respectability. These middle-class Southerners, who worked as doctors, lawyers, journalists, teachers, and shopkeepers, often looked to the North for models to emulate. Many were educated in northern schools and developed ties with their commercial or professional counterparts in northern cities. They were avid readers of newspapers, religious tracts, and literary periodicals published in the North. And like middle-class Northerners, southern businessmen often depended on their wives' social and financial skills to succeed.

Nonetheless, middle-class southern men shared many of the social attitudes and political priorities of slave owners. They participated alongside planters in benevolent associations, literary and temperance (antialcohol) societies, and agricultural reform organizations. Most middle-class Southerners also adamantly supported slavery and benefited from planters' demands for goods and services. In fact, some suggested that bound labor might be as useful to industry as it was to agriculture, and they sought to expand the institution further. Despite the emergence of a small middle class, however, the gap between rich and poor continued to expand in the South.

Planters Seek to Unify Southern Whites

Planters faced another challenge as nations in Europe and South America began to abolish slavery. Antislavery views, first expressed by a few Enlightenment thinkers and Quakers, gained growing support among evangelical Protestants in Great Britain and the United States and among political radicals in Europe. Slave rebellions in Saint Domingue (Haiti) and the British West Indies in the early nineteenth century intensified these efforts. In 1807 the British Parliament forbade the sale of slaves within its empire and in 1834 emancipated all those who remained enslaved. France followed suit in 1848. As Spanish colonies such as Mexico and Nicaragua gained their independence in the 1820s and 1830s, they, too, eradicated the institution. Meanwhile gradual abolition laws in the northern United States slowly eliminated slavery there. Although slavery continued in Brazil and in Spanish colonies such as Cuba and serfdom remained in Russia, international attitudes toward human bondage were shifting.

In response, planters wielded their political and economic power to forge tighter bonds among white Southerners. According to the three-fifths compromise in the U.S. Constitution, areas with large slave populations gained more representatives in Congress than those without. The pattern held for state elections, too. In addition, well-educated planters and their allies were the likeliest candidates for office and the most successful. Planters also used their resources to provide credit for those in need, offer seasonal employment for poorer whites, transport crops to market for yeomen farmers, and contribute food, clothing, and other goods in times of crisis. Few poorer whites could afford to antagonize these affluent benefactors.

Wealthy planters also emphasized ties of family and faith. James Hammond, for example, assisted his siblings and other family members financially throughout their lives. Many slave owners also worshipped alongside their less well-to-do neighbors, and both the pastor and the congregation benefited from maintaining good relations with the wealthiest congregants. Many church members, like many relatives and neighbors, genuinely admired and respected planter elites who looked out for them.

Still, planters did not take white solidarity for granted. From the 1830s on, they relied on the ideology of white supremacy to cement the belief that all whites, regardless of class or education, were superior to all blacks. Following on Thomas Dew, southern elites argued with growing vehemence that the moral and intellectual failings of blacks meant that slavery was not just a necessary evil but actually a positive good. At the same time, they insisted that blacks harbored deep animosity toward whites, which could be controlled only by regulating every aspect of their lives. Combining racial fear and racial pride, planters forged bonds with poor and middling whites to guarantee their continued dominance. They also sought support from officials in the nation's capital.

REVIEW & RELATE

- What groups made up white southern society? How did their interests overlap? How did they diverge?
- How and why did the planter elite seek to reinforce white solidarity?

Democrats Face Political and Economic Crises

Southern planters depended on federal power to expand and sustain the system of slavery. Although President Andrew Jackson disappointed slave owners on issues such as the tariff and states' rights, he stood with them on the policies of Indian removal and independence for Texas. Jackson's successor in the White House, Martin Van Buren, continued his predecessor's Indian policies and his support for the Republic of Texas. But Van Buren faced a more well-organized opposition in the Whig Party, which formed in the 1830s, while Texas rebels faced powerful resistance from Mexican and Comanche forces. Then in 1837 a prolonged and severe economic panic gripped the nation, creating an opportunity for the Whigs to end Democratic control of the federal government.

Continued Conflicts over Indian Lands

In 1830 Congress had passed the Indian Removal Act in hopes of settling the powerful Cherokee and Seminole tribes on land west of the Mississippi River. Not all Indian peoples went peacefully. As federal authorities forcibly removed the majority of Seminoles to Indian Territory between 1832 and 1835, a minority fought back. Jackson and his military commanders expected that this Second Seminole War would be short-lived. However, they misjudged the Seminoles' strength; the power of their charismatic leader, Osceola; and the resistance of African American fugitives living among the Seminoles. Hundreds of southern slaves had fled to Florida in the early nineteenth century seeking freedom. Some married Seminole women, while others were reenslaved by Seminole Indians. But the Seminoles treated slaves with more leniency than did southern whites, allowing them to live on small farms with their own families and enjoy many of the rights of full members of the tribe. Thus free and enslaved blacks fought fiercely against Seminole removal.

The war continued long after Jackson left the presidency. During the seven-year guerrilla war, 1,600 U.S. troops died and the government spent more than $30 million. U.S. military forces defeated the Seminoles in 1842 only by luring Osceola into an army camp with false promises of a peace settlement. Instead, officers took him captive, finally breaking the back of the resistance. Still, to end the conflict, the U.S. government had to allow fugitive slaves living among the Seminoles to accompany the tribe to Indian Territory.

Members of the Cherokee nation also resisted removal, but they fought their battles in the arena of public opinion and in the courts. Throughout the early nineteenth century, growing numbers of Cherokees had embraced "Americanization" programs offered by white missionaries, educators, and government agents. John Ross and other Indian leaders urged Cherokee people to accommodate to white ways, believing it was the best means to ensure the continued control of their own communities. When Georgia officials sought to impose new regulations on the Cherokees living within the state's borders, tribal leaders took them to court and sought to use evidence of their Christianity, domesticity, and republican government to maintain their rights.

In 1831 *Cherokee Nation v. Georgia* reached the Supreme Court, where Indian leaders demanded recognition as a separate nation as stipulated in the U.S. Constitution. Chief Justice John Marshall spoke for the majority when he ruled that all Indians in the United States were "domestic dependent nations" rather than fully sovereign governments. The Court thus denied a central part of the Cherokees' claim. Yet the following year, in *Worcester v. Georgia*, Marshall and the Court declared that the state of Georgia could not impose *state* laws on the Cherokees, for they had "territorial boundaries, within which their authority is exclusive," and that both their land and their rights were protected by the federal government.

President Jackson held a distinctly different view. He argued that only the removal of the Cherokees west of the Mississippi River could ensure their "physical comfort," "political advancement," and "moral improvement." Most southern whites agreed because they sought to expand cotton production into fertile Cherokee fields. But Protestant women and men in the North launched a massive petition campaign in 1830 supporting the Cherokees' right to their land. The Cherokees themselves forestalled action through Jackson's second term, but many federal and state officials continued to press for the tribe's removal.

In December 1835, U.S. officials convinced a small group of Cherokee men—without tribal sanction—to sign the **Treaty of New Echota**. It proposed the exchange of 100 million acres of Cherokee land in the Southeast for $68 million and 32 million acres in Indian Territory. Cherokee leaders, including John Ross, lobbied Congress to reject the treaty, but to no avail. In May 1836, Congress approved the treaty by a single vote and set the date for final removal two years later. Although most of the 17,000 Cherokees resisted this plan, they had few means left to defy the U.S. government (Map 10.2).

In May 1838, the U.S. army began to forcibly remove any Cherokee who had not yet resettled in Indian Territory. General Winfield Scott, assisted by 7,000 U.S. soldiers, forced some 15,000 Cherokees into forts and military camps that June. The Cherokees

---

MAP 10.2 .

Indian Removals and Relocations, 1820s–1850s In the 1820s and 1830s, the federal government used a variety of tactics, including military force, to expel Indian nations residing east of the Mississippi River. As these tribes resettled in the West, white migration along the Oregon and other trails began to increase. The result, by 1850, was the forced relocation of many western Indian nations as well.

spent the next several months without sufficient food, water, sanitation, or medicine. The situation went from bad to worse. In October, when the Cherokees began the march west, torrential rains were followed by snow. Although the U.S. army planned for a trip of less than three months, the journey actually took five months. As supplies ran short, many Indians, weakened by disease and hunger, died, including Ross's wife. The remaining Cherokees completed this Trail of Tears, as it became known, in March 1839. But thousands remained near starvation a year later.

The Battle for Texas

While whites in Georgia sought Cherokee land, those on the frontier looked toward Texas. Some Southerners had moved into Texas in the early nineteenth century, but the Adams-Onís Treaty of 1819 guaranteed Spanish control of the territory. Then in 1821 Mexicans overthrew Spanish rule and claimed Texas as part of the new Republic of Mexico. But Mexicans, like the Spaniards before them, faced serious competition from Comanche Indians, who controlled vast areas to the north and west and launched raids into Texas for horses and other livestock.

Eager to increase settlement in the area and to create a buffer against the Comanches, the Mexican government granted U.S. migrants some of the best land in eastern Texas. It hoped these settlers—many of whom brought slaves to cultivate cotton—would eventually spread into the interior, where Comanche raids had devastated Mexican communities. To entice more Southerners, the Mexican government negotiated a special exemption for U.S. planters when it outlawed slavery in 1829. But rather than spreading into the interior, U.S. farmers and planters stayed east of the Colorado River, out of reach of Comanche raiders and close to U.S. markets in Louisiana.

While the Mexican residents of Texas developed a vibrant Tejano culture that combined Catholicism, Spanish language and culture, and indigenous customs, U.S. settlers resisted acculturation. Instead, they continued to worship as Protestants, speak English, send their children to separate schools, and trade mainly with the United States. By 1835 the 27,000 white Southerners and their 3,000 slaves far outnumbered the 3,000 Mexicans living in eastern Texas.

Forming a majority of the east Texas population and eager to expand their plantations and trade networks, growing numbers of U.S. settlers demanded independence.

 Online Document Project   **Claiming Texas**
bedfordstmartins.com/hewittlawsonvalue

Then in 1836 Mexicans elected a strong nationalist leader, General Antonio López de Santa Anna, as president. He sought to rein in Tejanos angered over their vulnerability to Comanche attacks and to curb American settlers seeking further concessions. When Santa Anna appointed a military commander to rule Texas, independence-minded U.S. migrants organized a rebellion. On March 2, they declared eastern Texas an independent republic and adopted a constitution that legalized slavery. Some elite Tejanos, long neglected by authorities in Mexico City, sided with the rebels. The rebellion appeared to be short-lived, however. On March 6, 1836, General Santa Anna crushed settlers defending the Alamo in San Antonio. His troops killed all 250 men at the fort but freed the women and children. Soon thereafter, Santa Anna captured the U.S. settlement at Goliad.

Although Santa Anna's troops suffered more than 1,500 casualties, several times those of the rebel forces, the general was convinced that the uprising was over. But the U.S. government, despite its claims of neutrality, aided the rebels with funds and army officers. Newspapers in New Orleans and New York picked up the story of the Alamo and published dramatic accounts of the battle, describing the Mexican fighters as brutal butchers bent on saving Texas for the pope. These stories, though more fable than fact, increased popular support for the war at a time when many Americans were growing increasingly hostile to Catholic immigrants in the United States.

As hundreds of armed volunteers headed to Texas, General Sam Houston led rebel forces in a critical victory at San Jacinto in April 1836. While the Mexican government refused to recognize rebel claims, it did not try to regain the lost ground in east Texas. Few of the U.S. volunteers arrived in time to participate in the fighting, but some settled in the newly liberated region. Still, the failure of Santa Anna to recognize Texan independence kept the U.S. government from granting the territory statehood for fear it would lead to war with Mexico. Fortunately for the rebels, the Comanche nation did recognize the Republic of Texas and developed trade relations with residents to gain access to the vast U.S. market.

Meanwhile President Jackson worried that admitting a new slave state might split the national Democratic Party just before the fall elections. To limit debate on the issue, Congress passed a **gag rule** in March 1836 that tabled all antislavery petitions without being read. Nevertheless, thousands of women and men from Ohio to Massachusetts still flooded the House of Representatives with petitions opposing the annexation of Texas.

Van Buren and the Panic of 1837

With Jackson suffering from tuberculosis, the Democratic convention chose Vice President Martin Van Buren to run for president in 1836. The Whigs hoped to defeat Van Buren by bringing together diverse supporters: financiers and commercial farmers who advocated internal improvements and protective tariffs; merchants and manufacturers who favored a national bank; evangelical Protestants who objected to Jackson's Indian policy; and Southerners who were antagonized by the president's heavy-handed use of federal authority. But these disparate interests led the Whigs to nominate three different men for president, and this lack of unity allowed Democrats to fend off an increasingly powerful opposition. Although Van Buren won the popular vote by only a small margin (50.9 percent), he secured an easy majority in the electoral college.

Inaugurated on March 4, 1837, President Van Buren soon faced another crisis that threatened the Democrats' hold on power. The **panic of 1837** started in the South and was rooted in the changing fortunes of American cotton in Great Britain. During the 1830s, the British invested heavily in cotton plantations and brokerage firms, and southern planters used the funds to expand cotton production and improve shipping facilities. British banks also lent large sums to states such as New York to fund internal improvements. This infusion of British money into the U.S. economy fueled inflation, and in February 1837 rising prices prompted protests by farmers and workers. But worse problems lay ahead.

In late 1836, the Bank of England, faced with bad harvests and declining demand for textiles, had tightened credit to limit the flow of money out of the country. This forced British investors to call in their loans and drove up interest rates in the United States just as cotton prices started to fall. Some of the largest American cotton merchants were forced to declare bankruptcy. The banks where they held accounts then failed—ninety-eight of them in March and April 1837 alone.

The economic crisis hit the South hard. Cotton prices fell by nearly half in less than a year. Land values declined dramatically, many southern whites lost farms and homes, port cities came to a standstill, and cotton communities on the southern frontier collapsed. The damage soon radiated throughout the United States. Northern brokers, shippers, and merchants were devastated by losses in the cotton trade, and northern banks were hit by unpaid debts incurred for canals and other internal improvements. Entrepreneurs who borrowed money to expand their businesses defaulted in large numbers. Shopkeepers, artisans, and farmers in the North and Midwest suffered unemployment and foreclosures.

Many Americans, especially in the North and West, blamed Jackson's war against the Bank of the United States for precipitating the panic. They were also outraged at Van Buren's refusal to intervene in the crisis. Probably no federal policy could have resolved the problems created by the "credit bubble," which had been brought on by the ready availability of British money. Still, the president's apparent disinterest in the plight of the people inspired harsh criticisms from ordinary citizens as well as political opponents. Worse, despite brief signs of recovery in 1838, the depression deepened in 1839 and continued for four more years.

The Whigs Win the White House

Van Buren was clearly vulnerable as he faced reelection in 1840. Eager to exploit the Democrats' weakness, the Whig Party organized its first national convention that fall and united behind military hero William Henry Harrison (see chapter 9). Harrison was born to a wealthy planter family in Virginia, but the sixty-eight-year-old soldier was portrayed as a self-made man who lived in a simple log cabin in Indiana. His running mate, John Tyler, another Virginia gentleman and a onetime Democrat, joined the Whigs because

William Henry Harrison Campaign Poster, 1840 The 1840 presidential campaign pitted the incumbent Martin Van Buren against William Henry Harrison. Harrison, the Whig Party candidate, was portrayed as a man from humble origins even though he was the son of a wealthy Virginia planter. His campaign slogan "Tippecanoe and Tyler Too" highlighted his military background and leadership in the defeat of Tenskwatawa at the Battle of Tippecanoe. The campaign was a rousing success, and Harrison and his running mate, John Tyler, handily defeated Van Buren with 53 percent of the popular vote. Library of Congress

of his opposition to Jackson's stand on nullification. Whig leaders hoped he would attract southern voters. Taking their cue from the Democrats, the Whigs organized rallies, barbecues, parades, and mass meetings. They turned the tables on their foe by portraying Van Buren as an aristocrat who enjoyed fine wines and expensive clothes and Harrison as the hero of the common man. Reminding voters that Harrison had defeated Tenskwatawa at the Battle of Tippecanoe, the Whigs adopted the slogan "Tippecanoe and Tyler Too."

The Whigs also welcomed women into the campaign. By 1840 thousands of women had circulated petitions against Cherokee removal, organized temperance societies, promoted religious revivals, and joined charitable associations. They embodied the kind of moral force that the Whig Party claimed to represent. In October 1840, Whig senator Daniel Webster spoke to a gathering of 1,200 women. He praised women's moral virtues and asked audience members to encourage their brothers and husbands to vote for Harrison.

The Whig strategy paid off handsomely on election day when some 80 percent of eligible voters cast ballots. Harrison won easily, and the Whigs gained a majority in Congress. Yet the election's promise was shattered when "old Tippecanoe" died of pneumonia a month after his inauguration. Whigs in Congress now had to deal with John Tyler, whose sentiments were largely southern and Democratic. Frustrating Whig plans for reform with vetoes, Tyler allowed the Democratic Party to regroup and set the stage for close elections in 1844 and 1848.

REVIEW & RELATE

• How and why did Indian nations in the Southeast resist removal to the West while some Indians in the West forged ties with U.S. markets?

• What events and developments led to a Whig victory in the election of 1840?

The National Government Looks to the West

Despite the Whig victory in 1840, planters wielded considerable clout in Washington, D.C., because of the importance of cotton to the U.S. economy. In turn, Southerners needed federal support to expand into more fertile areas. The presidential election of 1844 turned on this issue, with Democratic candidate James K. Polk demanding continued expansion into Oregon and Mexico. Once Polk was in office, his claims were contested not only by Britain and Mexico but also by the Comanches, who controlled the southern plains. After the United States won vast Mexican territories in 1848, conflicts with Indians and debates over slavery only intensified.

Expanding to Oregon and Texas

Southerners eager to expand the plantation economy looked not only to the West for additional lands but also to Cuba and Nicaragua in the 1830s and 1840s. Although efforts to capture these areas failed, planters continued to press for expansion. Yet expansion was not merely a southern strategy. Northerners demanded that the United States renounce its joint occupation of the Oregon Country with Great Britain. And some northern politicians and businessmen believed that acquisition of lands in Hawaii and Samoa could benefit U.S. trade. In 1844 the Democratic Party built on these expansionist dreams to recapture the White House.

Initially, Democrats could not agree on a candidate, but they ultimately nominated a Tennessee congressman and governor, James K. Polk. The Whigs, unwilling to nominate Tyler for president, chose the well-known Kentucky senator Henry Clay. Polk ran on a platform that proclaimed the "Reoccupation of Oregon and the Annexation of Texas." Clay, meanwhile, remained uncommitted on the issue of Texas. This proved his undoing when the small but growing Liberty Party, adamantly opposed to slavery, denounced annexation. Liberty Party candidate James G. Birney captured just enough votes in New York State to throw the state and the election to Polk.

In February 1845, a month before Polk took office, Congress passed a joint resolution annexing the Republic of Texas. The day before Polk's inauguration, Florida was also admitted to statehood. That summer, John L. O'Sullivan, editor of the *Democratic Review*, captured the American mood by declaring that nothing must interfere with "the fulfillment of our manifest destiny to overspread the continent allotted by Providence for the free development of our yearly multiplying millions." This vision of manifest destiny—of the nation's God-given right to expand its borders—defined Polk's presidency.

With the Florida and Texas questions seemingly resolved, President Polk turned his attention to Oregon, which stretched from the forty-second parallel to latitude 54°40' and was jointly occupied by Great Britain and the United States. Residents of either nation could settle anywhere in the region, but most of the British lived north of the Columbia River, while most Americans settled to the south.

In 1842, three years before Polk took office, settlers' glowing reports of the mild climate and fertile soil around Puget Sound had inspired thousands of farmers and traders to migrate to Oregon. Americans flooded into the Willamette valley, and merchants involved in the China trade imagined a thriving U.S. trading post on the Oregon coast. Alarmed by this "Oregon fever," the British tried to confine Americans to areas south of the Columbia River. But American settlers demanded access to the entire territory, proclaiming "Fifty-four forty or fight!" As president, Polk encouraged migration into Oregon, but he was unwilling to risk war with Great Britain. Instead, diplomats negotiated a treaty in 1846 that extended the border with British Canada (the forty-ninth parallel) to the Pacific Ocean. Over the next two years, Congress admitted Iowa and Wisconsin to statehood, reassuring northern residents that expansion benefited all regions of the nation.

Many of the lands newly claimed by the U.S. government were home to vast numbers of Indians. Indeed, the West had become more crowded as the U.S. government forced eastern tribes to move west of the Mississippi (see Map 10.2). When the Cherokee and other southeastern tribes were removed to Indian Territory, for example, they confronted local tribes such as the Osage. Pushed into the Southwest, the Osages came into conflict with the Comanches, who had earlier fought the Apaches for control of the southern plains. Other Indian nations were pushed onto the northern plains from the Old Northwest. There the Sioux became the dominant tribe by the 1830s after seizing hunting grounds from the Omahas, Iowas, and Cheyennes, who resettled farther south and west.

The flood of U.S. migrants into Texas and the southern plains transformed relations among Indian nations as well as with Mexico. In the face of Spanish and then Mexican claims on their lands, for example, the Comanches forged alliances with former foes like the Wichitas and the Osages. The Comanches also developed commercial ties with tribes in Indian Territory and with Mexican and Anglo-American traders on the frontiers of their respective nations. In these ways, they hoped to benefit from the imperial ambitions of the United States and Mexico while strengthening bonds among Indians in the region.

Comanche expansion was especially problematic for Mexico once it achieved independence in 1821. The young nation did not have sufficient resources to sustain the level of gift giving that Spanish authorities used to maintain peace. As a result, Comanche warriors launched continual raids against Tejano settlements in Texas. But the Comanches also developed commercial relations with residents of New Mexico, who flaunted trade regulations promulgated in Mexico City in order to maintain peace with neighboring Indians. By 1846 Comanche trade and diplomatic relations with New Mexican settlements had seriously weakened the hold of Mexican authorities on their northern provinces.

Pursuing War with Mexico

At the same time, with Texas now a state, Mexico faced growing tensions with the United States. Conflicts centered on Texas's western border. Mexico insisted on the Nueces River as the boundary line, while Americans claimed all the land to the Rio Grande. In January 1846, Polk secretly sent emissary John Slidell to negotiate with Mexico, offering President José Herrera $30 million for New Mexico and California after securing the Rio Grande boundary. But Polk also sent U.S. troops under General Zachary Taylor across the Nueces River. Mexican officials refused to see Slidell and instead sent their own troops across the Rio Grande. Meanwhile U.S. naval commanders prepared to seize San Francisco Bay if war was declared. The Mexican government responded to these hostile overtures by sending more troops into the disputed Texas territory.

When fighting erupted near the Rio Grande in May 1846 (Map 10.3), Polk claimed that "American blood had been shed on American soil" and declared a state of war. Many Whigs in Congress protested, arguing that the president had provoked the conflict. Congressman Abraham Lincoln of Illinois demanded that Polk "show me the spot" where U.S. blood was shed. However, antiwar Whigs failed to convince the Democratic majority, and Congress voted to finance the war.

The South was solidly behind the war. As the Charleston, South Carolina, *Courier* declared: "Every battle fought in Mexico and every dollar spent there, but insures the acquisition of territory which must widen the field of Southern enterprise and power in the future." Most Northerners also supported the war. Although ardent opponents of slavery protested, most Americans considered westward expansion a boon (see Map 10.3).

Once the war began, battles erupted in a variety of locations. In May 1846, U.S. troops defeated Mexican forces in Palo Alto and Resaca de la Palma. A month later, the U.S. army captured Sonoma, California, with the aid of local settlers. John Frémont then led U.S. forces to Monterey, California, where the navy launched a successful attack and declared the territory part of the United States. That fall, U.S. troops gained important victories at Monterrey, Mexico, just west of the Rio Grande, and Tampico, along the Gulf coast.

Although the Mexican army outnumbered U.S. forces, it failed to capitalize on this advantage. In the northern provinces, Mexican soldiers were ill equipped for major battles, and in the heart of Mexico divisions among political and military leaders limited battlefield success. Still, Mexican soldiers and residents fought fiercely against the American invaders.

Despite major U.S. victories, Santa Anna, who reclaimed the presidency of Mexico during the war, refused to give up. In February 1847, his troops attacked General

MAP 10.3

The Mexican-American War, 1846–1848　Although a dispute over territory between the Nueces River and the Rio Grande initiated the Mexican-American War, most of the fighting occurred between the Rio Grande and Mexico City. In addition, U.S. forces in California launched battles to claim independence for that region even before gold was discovered there.

Taylor's forces at Buena Vista and nearly secured a victory. Polk then agreed to send General Winfield Scott to Veracruz with 14,000 soldiers. Capturing the port in March, Scott's army marched on to Mexico City. After a crushing defeat of Santa Anna at Cerro Gordo, the president-general was removed from power, and the new Mexican government sought peace.

With victory ensured, U.S. officials faced a difficult decision: How much Mexican territory should they claim? The U.S. army in central Mexico faced continued guerrilla attacks. Meanwhile Whigs and some northern Democrats denounced the war as a southern conspiracy to expand slavery. In this context, Polk agreed to limit U.S. claims to the northern regions of Mexico. Eager to unite the Democratic Party before the fall election, the president signed the **Treaty of Guadalupe Hidalgo** in February 1848, and the U.S. Senate ratified it in March. The treaty committed the United States to pay Mexico $15 million in return for control over Texas north and east of the Rio Grande plus California and the New Mexico territory.

Debates over Slavery Intensify

News of the U.S. victory traveled quickly across the United States. In the South, planters imagined slavery spreading into the lands acquired from Mexico. Northerners, too, applauded the expansion of U.S. territory but focused on California as a center for agriculture and commerce. Yet the acquisition of new territory only heightened sectional conflicts. Debates over slavery had erupted during the war, with a few northern Democrats joining Whigs in denouncing "the power of slavery" to "govern the country, its Constitutions and laws." In August 1846, Democratic congressman David Wilmot of Pennsylvania proposed outlawing slavery in all territory acquired from Mexico so that the South could not profit from the war. The **Wilmot Proviso** passed in the House, but in the Senate, Southerners and proslavery northern Democrats killed it.

The presidential election of 1848 opened with the unresolved question of whether to allow slavery in the territories acquired from Mexico. Polk, exhausted by the war effort and divisions among Democrats, refused to run for a second term. In his place, Democrats nominated Lewis Cass, a senator from Michigan and an ardent expansionist. He had suggested that the United States purchase Cuba from Spain in 1848 and advocated seizing all of Oregon and more of Mexico. Hoping to keep northern antislavery Democrats in the party, Cass campaigned for what he called "squatter sovereignty," by which residents in each territory would decide whether to make the region free or slave. This strategy put the slavery question on hold but satisfied almost no one.

The Whigs, too, hoped to avoid the slavery issue for fear of losing southern votes. They nominated Mexican-American War hero General Zachary Taylor, a Louisiana slaveholder with no political experience. The Whigs were pleased that he had not taken a stand on slavery in the western territories. But they sought to reassure their northern wing by nominating Millard Fillmore of Buffalo, New York, for vice president. As a member of Congress in the 1830s, he had opposed the annexation of Texas, and he had a reputation for fiscal responsibility and charitable endeavors.

The Liberty Party, disappointed in the Whig ticket, decided to run its own candidate for president. But leaders who hoped to expand their support reconstituted themselves as the Free-Soil Party. Its leaders focused on excluding slaves from the western territories rather than on the moral injustice of slavery. Still, Free-Soilers argued that slavery empowered "aristocratic men" and threatened the rights of "the great mass of the people." The party nominated former president Martin Van Buren and appealed to small farmers and urban workers who hoped to benefit from western expansion.

Once again, the presence of a third party affected the outcome of the election. While Whigs and Democrats tried to avoid the slavery issue, Free-Soilers demanded attention to it. By focusing on the exclusion of slavery in western territories rather than its abolition, the Free-Soil Party won more adherents in northern states. Indeed, Van Buren won enough northern Democrats so that Cass lost New York State and the 1848 election. Zachary Taylor and the Whigs won, but only by placing a southern slaveholder in the White House.

(REVIEW & RELATE)

- How did western expansion both benefit Americans and exacerbate conflicts among them?
- How did the Mexican-American War reshape national politics and intensify debates over slavery?

Conclusion: Geographical Expansion and Political Division

By the mid-nineteenth century, the United States stood at a crossroads. Most Americans considered expansion advantageous and critical to revitalizing the economy. Planters believed it was vital to slavery's success. While most white Northerners were willing to leave slavery alone where it already existed, many hoped to keep it out of newly acquired territories. The vast lands gained from Mexico in 1848 intensified these debates. Between 1830 and 1850, small but growing numbers of Northerners joined slaves, American Indians, and Mexicans in protesting U.S. expansion. Even some yeomen farmers and middle-class professionals in the South questioned whether extending slavery benefited the region economically and politically. But these challenges remained limited until 1848, when the fight over slavery in the territories fractured the Democratic Party, created a crisis for the Whigs, and inspired the growth of the Free-Soil Party.

Political realignments continued over the next decade, fueled by growing antislavery sentiment in the North and proslavery ideology in the South. In 1853 Solomon Northrup horrified thousands of antislavery readers with his book *Twelve Years a Slave*, which vividly described his life in bondage. Such writings alarmed planters like James Henry Hammond, who continued to believe that slavery was "the greatest of all the great blessings which Providence has bestowed upon our glorious region." Yet in insisting on the benefits of slave labor, the planter elite inspired further conflict with Northerners, whose lives were increasingly shaped by commercial and industrial developments and the expansion of free labor.

Chapter Review

MAKE IT STICK

LearningCurve **bedfordstmartins.com/hewittlawsonvalue**
After reading the chapter, use LearningCurve to retain what you've read.

IDENTIFY KEY TERMS

Identify and explain the significance of each term below.

syncretic culture (p. 253)
Nat Turner's rebellion (p. 255)
yeomen farmers (p. 256)
Whig Party (p. 258)
Second Seminole War (p. 259)
Treaty of New Echota (p. 260)
Trail of Tears (p. 261)

Tejanos (p. 261)
Alamo (p. 261)
gag rule (p. 262)
panic of 1837 (p. 262)
manifest destiny (p. 265)
Treaty of Guadalupe Hidalgo (p. 268)
Wilmot Proviso (p. 268)

REVIEW & RELATE

Answer the focus questions from each section of the chapter.

1. What role did the planter elite play in southern society and politics?
2. What were the consequences of the dominant position of slave-based plantation agriculture in the southern economy?
3. How did enslaved African Americans create ties of family, community, and culture?
4. How did enslaved African Americans resist efforts to control and exploit their labor?
5. What groups made up white southern society? How did their interests overlap? How did they diverge?
6. How and why did the planter elite seek to reinforce white solidarity?
7. How and why did Indian nations in the Southeast resist removal to the West while some Indians in the West forged ties with U.S. markets?
8. What events and developments led to a Whig victory in the election of 1840?
9. How did western expansion both benefit Americans and exacerbate conflicts among them?
10. How did the Mexican-American War reshape national politics and intensify debates over slavery?

ONLINE DOCUMENT PROJECTS

◆ **Claiming Texas**
◆ **Life in Slavery**

After reading the primary sources in these document sets, answer the **Interpret the Evidence** questions to help you analyze each of the documents, and then answer the **Put It in Context** question(s) to help you relate the documents to the topics and themes you read about in the chapter.

bedfordstmartins.com/hewittlawsonvalue

TIMELINE OF EVENTS

1820–1850	• Southern cotton production increases from about 500,000 bales to 3 million bales	**March 1836**	• James Hammond leads campaign that results in congressional gag rule
1821	• Mexico overthrows Spanish rule and encourages U.S. settlement in Texas	**1837**	• Panic of 1837 triggers recession
1830–1850	• 440,000 slaves from the Upper South sold to owners in the Lower South	**October 1838– March 1839**	• Trail of Tears
1831	• *Cherokee Nation v. Georgia*	**1840**	• Whigs win the presidency and gain control of Congress
August 1831	• Nat Turner leads slave uprising in Virginia	**1841**	• Solomon Northrup kidnapped and sold into slavery
December 1831	• Virginia's Assembly establishes special committee on slavery	**1845**	• U.S. annexes Texas
1832	• *Worcester v. Georgia*	**1846**	• U.S. settles dispute with Great Britain over Oregon
1833	• Tredegar Iron Works established	**May 1846– February 1848**	• Mexican-American War
1834	• Britain abolishes slavery	**August 1846**	• David Wilmot proposes Wilmot Proviso
1835–1842	• Second Seminole War	**March 1848**	• Treaty of Guadalupe Hidalgo
1836	• Treaty of New Echota	**1853**	• Solomon Northrup publishes *Twelve Years a Slave*
March 2, 1836	• U.S. settlers declare eastern Texas an independent republic		
March 6, 1836	• General Santa Anna crushes U.S. rebels at the Alamo		

11

LearningCurve
bedfordstmartins.com/hewittlawsonvalue
After reading the chapter, use LearningCurve
to retain what you've read.

Social and Cultural Ferment in the North

1820–1850

AMERICAN HISTORIES

Charles Grandison Finney, one of the greatest preachers of the nineteenth century, was born in 1792 and raised in rural New York State. As a young man, Finney studied the law. But in 1821, like many others of his generation, he experienced a powerful religious conversion. No longer interested in a legal career, he turned to the ministry instead.

After being ordained in the Presbyterian Church, Finney joined "New School" ministers who rejected the more conservative traditions of the Presbyterian Church and embraced a vigorous evangelicalism. In the early 1830s, while his wife, Lydia, remained at home with their growing family, the Reverend Finney traveled throughout New York State preaching about Christ's place in a changing America. He held massive revivals in cities along the Erie Canal, most notably in Rochester, and then moved on to New York City. He achieved his greatest success in places experiencing rapid economic development and an influx of migrants and immigrants, where the clash of cultures and classes fueled fears of moral decay. Spiritual renewal could rescue the young nation from sin and depravity.

Finney urged Christians to actively seek salvation. Once individuals reformed themselves, he said, they should work to abolish poverty, intemperance, prostitution, and slavery. He expected women to participate in revivals and good works but advised them to balance these efforts with their domestic responsibilities, an ideal modeled by his own wife.

In many ways, Amy Kirby Post fit Finney's ideal. She raised five children while devoting herself to spiritual and social reform. However, Amy Kirby was born into a large, close-knit Quaker family in the farming community of Jericho, New York. While most Quakers believed in quiet piety rather than evangelical revivals, their faith also provided solace in times of sorrow. In 1823, at age twenty-one, Amy became engaged to a fellow Quaker in central New York, where her sister Hannah lived with her husband, Isaac Post. But her fiancé died in June 1825 just before their wedding. Hannah took sick a year later, and Amy nursed her until her death in April 1827. She stayed on to care for Hannah's two young children and two years later married Isaac Post.

Amy experienced these personal upheavals in the midst of heated religious controversies among Quakers. In the 1820s, Elias Hicks claimed that the Society of Friends had abandoned its spiritual roots and become too much like a traditional church. His followers, called Hicksites, insisted that Friends should reduce their dependence on disciplinary rules, elders, and preachers and rely instead on the "Inner Light"—the spirit of God dwelling within each individual. When the Society of Friends divided into Hicksite and Orthodox branches in 1827, Amy Kirby and Isaac Post joined the Hicksites.

In 1836 Amy Post moved with her husband and four children to Rochester, New York. In a city marked by the spirit of Finney's revivals, Quakers emphasized quiet contemplation rather than fiery sermons and emotional conversions. But the Society of Friends allowed women to preach when moved by the spirit. Quaker women also held separate meetings to discipline female congregants, evaluate marriage proposals, and write testimonies on important religious issues.

Amy Post's spiritual journey was increasingly shaped by the rising tide of abolition. Committed to ending slavery, she joined non-Quakers in signing an 1837 antislavery petition. Five years later, she helped found the Western New York Anti-Slavery Society, which included Quakers and evangelicals, women and men, and blacks and whites. Post's growing commitment to abolition caused tensions in the Hicksite Meeting since some members opposed working in "worldly" organizations alongside non-Quakers. By 1848 Post and other radical Friends had withdrawn from the Hicksite Meeting and invited like-minded people to join them in the newly established Congregational Friends. Their meetings attracted abolitionists, advocates of Indian rights and women's rights, and peace activists, all causes Post embraced.

THE AMERICAN HISTORIES of Charles Finney and Amy Post were shaped by the dynamic religious, social, and economic developments in the early-nineteenth-century United States. Finney changed the face of American religion, aided by masses

Portrait of Jarena Lee, the first female preacher of the African Methodist Episcopal Church, 1844. Library of Congress

of evangelical Protestants. The rise of cities and the expansion of industry in the northern United States made problems like poverty, unemployment, alcohol abuse, crime, and prostitution more visible, drawing people to Finney's message. Other Americans brought their own religious traditions to bear on the problems of the day. Some, like Post, were so outraged by the moral stain of slavery that they burst traditional religious bonds and reconsidered what it meant to do God's work. For both Finney and Post, Rochester—the fastest-growing city in the nation between 1825 and 1835—exemplified the problems and the possibilities created by urban expansion and social change.

The Growth of Cities

Commercial and industrial development, immigration from Europe, and migration from rural areas led to the rapid growth of U.S. cities from 1820 on. Urbanization stimulated economic expansion but also created social upheaval. Cultural divisions intensified in urban areas where Catholics and Protestants, workers and the well-to-do, immigrants, African Americans, and native-born whites lived side by side. The emergence of a middle class of shopkeepers, professionals, and clerks might have bridged these divides, but most middle-class Americans highlighted their distinctiveness from both the wealthy few at the top and the mass of workers and the poor at the bottom.

The Lure of Urban Life

Across the North, urban populations boomed. As centers of national and international commerce, seaports like New York and Philadelphia gained the greatest population in the early to mid-nineteenth century. But boomtowns also emerged along inland waterways. Rochester, New York, first settled in 1812, was flooded by goods and people once the Erie Canal was completed in 1825. Between 1820 and 1850, the number of cities with 100,000 inhabitants grew from two to six. In the Northeast, some farm communities doubled or tripled in size and were incorporated into neighboring cities such as Philadelphia. By 1850, among the nation's ten most populous urban centers, only two—Baltimore and New Orleans—were located in the South.

Cities increased not only in size but also in the diversity of their residents. During the 1820s, some 150,000 European immigrants entered the United States; during the

1830s, nearly 600,000; and during the 1840s, more than 1,700,000. This surge of immigrants included more Irish and German settlers than ever before as well as large numbers of Scandinavians. Many settled along the eastern seaboard, but others added to the growth of frontier cities such as Cincinnati, St. Louis, and Chicago.

Irish families had settled in North America early on, most of them Scots-Irish Presbyterians. Then in the 1830s and 1840s, the Irish countryside was plagued by bad weather, a potato blight, and harsh economic policies imposed by the English government. In 1845–1846 a full-blown famine forced thousands of Irish farm families—most of them Catholic—to emigrate. Young Irish women emigrated in especially large numbers, working as seamstresses and domestics to help fund passage to the United States for other family members. Poor harvests, droughts, failed revolutions, and repressive landlords convinced large numbers of Germans and Scandinavians to flee their homelands as well. By 1850 the Irish made up about 40 percent of immigrants to the United States, and Germans nearly a quarter (Figure 11.1).

Commerce and industry attracted immigrants to northern cities. These newcomers provided an expanding pool of cheap labor that further fueled economic growth. Banks, mercantile houses, and dry goods stores multiplied. Industrial enterprises in cities such as New York and Philadelphia included mechanized factories as well as traditional workshops in which master craftsmen oversaw the labor of apprentices. Credit and insurance agencies were created to aid entrepreneurs in their ventures. The increase in business also drove the demand for ships, newspapers catering to merchants and businessmen, warehouses, and other trade necessities, which created a surge in jobs and attracted even more people.

Businesses that focused on leisure also flourished. In the 1830s, theater became affordable to working-class families, who attended comedies, musical revues, and morality

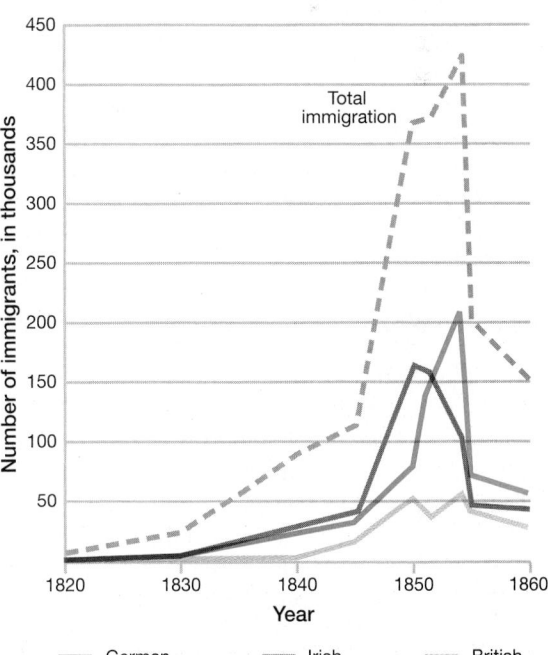

FIGURE 11.1

Immigration to the United States, 1820–1860 Famine, economic upheaval, and political persecution led masses of people from Ireland, Germany, and Britain to migrate to the United States from the 1820s through the 1850s. The vast majority settled in cities and factory towns in the North or on farms in the Midwest. An economic recession in the late 1850s finally slowed immigration, though only temporarily.

plays. They also joined middle- and upper-class audiences at productions of Shakespeare and nationalistic dramas in which strong and clever Americans triumphed over English aristocrats. Minstrel shows mocked self-important capitalists but also portrayed African Americans in crude caricatures. One of the most popular characters was Jim Crow, who appeared originally in an African American song. In the 1820s, he was incorporated into a song-and-dance routine by Thomas Rice, a white performer who blacked his face with burnt cork.

Museums, too, became a favorite destination for city dwellers. Many were modeled on P. T. Barnum's American Museum on lower Broadway in New York City. These museums were not staid venues for observing the fine arts or historical artifacts. Instead, they offered an abundance of exhibits and entertainment, including wax figures, archaeological antiquities, medical instruments, and insect collections, as well as fortune-tellers, bearded ladies, and snake charmers.

The lures of urban life were especially attractive to the young. Single men and women and newly married couples flocked to cities. By 1850 half the residents of New York City, Philadelphia, and other seaport cities were under sixteen years old. Young men sought work in construction, in the maritime trades, or in banks and commercial houses, while young women competed for jobs as seamstresses and domestic servants.

The Roots of Urban Disorder

In addition to stimulating economic growth by providing the labor that made industrial development possible, immigrants also transformed the urban landscape in the nineteenth century. They filled factories and workshops, crowded into houses and apartments, and built ethnic institutions, including synagogues and convents—visible indicators of the growing diversity of the American city.

Such marks of difference aroused growing concern among native-born Protestants. Crude stereotypes of immigrant groups appeared more frequently, and anti-Catholicism and anti-Semitism flourished in the 1830s and 1840s. Jews, who were long denied admission to skilled crafts and professions in Europe, had little choice but to pursue commercial ventures. Yet they were portrayed not as well-educated businessmen but as manipulative moneylenders. Similarly, many Irishmen enjoyed a beer with friends after laboring at difficult and low-paid jobs. But rather than being viewed as hardworking comrades, they were often pictured as habitual drunkards.

Rural Americans, seeking better jobs and new social experiences, added to urban diversity. Native-born white men often set out on their own, but most white women settled in cities under the supervision of a husband, a landlady, or an employer. African Americans, too, sought greater opportunities in urban areas. In the 1830s, more blacks joined Philadelphia's vibrant African American community, attracted by its churches, schools, and mutual aid and literary societies. New Bedford, Massachusetts, a thriving whaling center, provided employment for black men, including growing numbers of fugitive slaves, as well as for American Indians from the region. Although relative racial tolerance prevailed in New Bedford, in most urban areas racial minorities faced hostility and discrimination that limited their opportunities.

Even as cities promised better lives for many immigrants and migrants, they also posed dangers. Battles erupted between immigrant and native-born residents, Protestant and Catholic gangs, and white and black workers. Robberies, gambling, prostitution, and other criminal activities flourished. Diseases spread quickly through densely populated neighborhoods. When innovations in transportation made it possible for more affluent residents to distance themselves from crowded inner cities, they leaped at the chance. The first horse-drawn streetcar line was built in New York City in 1832, and as lines multiplied there and elsewhere, wealthy families moved to less crowded neighborhoods away from the urban center.

Violence increased as economic competition intensified in the 1840s. Native-born white workers and employers pushed Irish immigrants to the bottom of the economic ladder, where they competed with African Americans. Yet Irish workers insisted that their whiteness gave them a higher status than skilled blacks. When black temperance reformers organized a parade in Philadelphia in August 1842, white onlookers—mostly Irish laborers—attacked the marchers. Blacks fought back, and the conflict escalated into a riot.

Americans who lived in small towns and rural areas regularly read news of urban riots, murders, robberies, and vice. Improvements in printing created vastly more and cheaper newspapers. Tabloids wooed readers by publishing sensational stories of crime, sex, and scandal. Even more respectable newspapers carried stories about urban mayhem, and religious periodicals warned their parishioners against the city's moral temptations. After Congress funded construction of the first telegraph line in 1844 between Baltimore and Washington, D.C., news could travel even more quickly. In response to both a real increase in crime and a heightened perception of urban dangers, cities—beginning with Boston in 1845—replaced voluntary night watchmen with police forces. Fire companies, too, became established parts of city government, and city and county jails expanded with the population.

The New Middle Class

Members of the emerging middle class were among the most avid readers of the burgeoning numbers of newspapers and magazines. They included ambitious businessmen, successful shopkeepers, doctors, and lawyers as well as teachers, journalists, ministers, and other salaried employees. In Britain, the middle class emerged at the turn of the nineteenth century. In the United States, it was still a class in the making, rather than a stable entity, in the first half of the nineteenth century. At the top rungs, wealthy entrepreneurs and professionals adopted luxurious lifestyles. At the lower rungs, a growing cohort of salaried clerks and managers hoped that their hard work, honesty, and thrift would be rewarded with upward mobility.

Education, religious affiliation, and sobriety were important indicators of middle-class status. A well-read man who attended a well-established church and drank in strict moderation was marked as belonging to this new rank. A middle-class man was also expected to own a comfortable home, marry a pious woman, and raise well-behaved children. Entrance to the middle class required the efforts of wives as well as husbands, and so couples adopted new ideas about marriage and family. They believed that marital relationships should be based on affection and companionship rather than the husband's supreme authority. As partners for life, the husband focused on achieving financial security while the wife managed the household. The French traveler Alexis de Tocqueville captured this development in *Democracy in America* (1835). "In no country," he wrote, "has such constant care been taken . . . to trace two clearly distinct lines of action for the two sexes." The millions of women who toiled on farms and plantations or as mill workers and domestic servants certainly challenged this notion of **separate spheres** for men and women, but it captured the middle-class ideal.

The rise of the middle class inspired a flood of advice books, ladies' magazines, religious periodicals, and novels that advocated new ideals of womanhood, ideals that emphasized the centrality of child rearing and homemaking to women's identities. This cult of domesticity seemed to restrict wives to home and hearth, where they provided their husbands with respite from the cares and corruptions of the world. But wives were also expected to cement social and economic bonds by visiting the wives of business associates, serving in local charitable societies, and attending prayer circles. In carrying out these duties, the ideal woman bolstered her family's status by performing public as well as private roles.

Middle-class families also played a crucial role in the growing market economy. Although wives and daughters were not expected to work for wages, they were responsible for much of the family's consumption. They purchased factory-produced shoes and cloth, handcrafted clocks and cast-iron stoves, fine European crystal, and porcelain figures imported from China. Some middling housewives also bought basic goods once made at home, such as butter and candles. And middle-class children required books, pianos, and dancing lessons.

Although increasingly recognized for their ability to consume wisely, middle-class women still performed significant domestic labor. Only upper-middle-class women could afford servants. Most middle-class women, aided by daughters or temporary "help," cut and sewed garments, cultivated gardens, canned fruits and vegetables, plucked chickens, cooked meals, and washed and ironed clothes. As houses expanded in size and clothes became fancier, these chores continued to be laborious and time-consuming. But they were also increasingly invisible, focused inwardly on the family rather than outwardly as part of the market economy.

Middle-class men contributed to the consumer economy as well. Most directly, they created and invested in industrial and commercial ventures. But in carrying out their business and professional obligations, they supported new leisure pursuits. Many joined colleagues at restaurants, the theater, or sporting events. They also attended plays and lectures with their wives, visited museums, and took their children to the circus.

REVIEW & RELATE

• Why did American cities become larger and more diverse in the first half of the nineteenth century?

• What values and beliefs did the emerging American middle class embrace?

The Rise of Industry

Although the percentage of Americans employed in manufacturing never rose above 10 percent of the laboring population in the mid-nineteenth century, industrial enterprises in the Northeast transformed the nation's economy. In the 1830s and 1840s, factories grew considerably in size, and some investors, especially in textiles, constructed factory towns. Textile mills now relied heavily on the labor of girls and young women recruited from rural areas, while urban workshops hired varied groups of workers, including children, young women and men, and older adults. As industry expanded, however, working men's access to highly skilled jobs declined. The panic of 1837 exacerbated this trend and also increased tensions within the working class, especially among workers from different ethnic and racial backgrounds.

Factory Towns and Women Workers

In the late 1820s, investors and manufacturers joined forces to create factory towns in the New England countryside, the most famous of which was constructed in Lowell, Massachusetts, along the Merrimack River. Funded by the Boston Associates, a group of investors from eastern Massachusetts, the Lowell mills were based on an earlier experiment in nearby Waltham. In the Waltham system, every step of the production process was mechanized. The factories were far larger than earlier ones and were built as part of a planned community that included boardinghouses, government offices, and churches. Agents for the Waltham system traveled throughout New England to recruit the daughters of farm families as workers. They assured parents that their daughters would be watched over by managers and foremen as well as by landladies. The young women were required to attend church and observe curfews, and their labor was regulated by clocks and bells to ensure discipline and productivity.

Textile towns allowed young women to contribute to family finances while living in a well-ordered environment. Farm families needed more cash because of the growing market economy, and daughters could save money for the clothes and linens required for married life. Factory jobs also provided an alternative to marriage as young New England men moved west and left a surplus of women behind. The boardinghouses provided a relatively safe, all-female environment for the young workers, and sisters and neighbors often lived together. Despite constant regulation and supervision, many rural women viewed factory work as an adventure. They could send money home and still set aside a bit for themselves, and they could attend lectures and concerts, meet new people, and acquire a wider view of the world.

Initially, factory towns offered many benefits to young women and their families, but by the 1830s working conditions began to deteriorate. Factory owners cut wages, lengthened hours, and sped up machines, forcing women to produce more cloth in less time for lower pay. Many boardinghouses became overcrowded, and company officials regulated both rents and expenses, so higher prices for lodging did not necessarily mean better food or furnishings. Factory workers launched numerous strikes in the 1830s against longer hours, wage cuts, and speedups in factory production. The solidarity required to sustain these strikes was forged in boardinghouses and at church socials as well as on the factory floor.

Despite the mill workers' solidarity, it was not easy to overcome the economic power wielded by manufacturers. Working women's efforts at collective action were generally short-lived, lasting only as long as the strike itself. Then employees returned to their jobs until the next crisis hit. And as competition increasingly cut into profits, owners resisted mill workers' demands more vehemently. When the panic of 1837 intensified fears of job loss, women's organizing activities were doomed until the economy recovered.

Deskilling and the Response of Working Men

While the construction of factory towns expanded economic opportunities for young women, the gradual decline of time-honored crafts narrowed the prospects for working men. As craft workshops increased in size, they hired fewer skilled workers and more men who learned only a single aspect of production—cutting barrel staves or attaching soles to shoes. Like mill operatives, these workers performed distinct tasks, many of which were mechanized over the course of the nineteenth century. The final product was less distinctive than an item crafted by a skilled artisan, but it was also less expensive and available in mass quantities.

The shift from craft work to factory work threatened to undermine working men's skills, pay, and labor conditions. Soon masters hired foremen to regulate the workforce and installed bells and clocks to regulate the workday. Artisans were offended by the new regime, which treated them as wage-earning dependents rather than as independent craftsmen. As the process of **deskilling** transformed shoemaking, printing, bookbinding, tailoring, and other trades, laboring men fought to maintain their status.

Some workers formed mutual aid societies to provide assistance in times of illness, injury, or unemployment. Others participated in religious revivals or joined fraternal orders, such as the Masons and the Red Men, to find the camaraderie they once enjoyed at work. The expansion of voting rights in the 1820s offered another avenue for action. The first workingmen's political party was founded in Philadelphia in 1827, and soon white farmers, mechanics, and workingmen started joining forces throughout the North to advocate for principles of liberty and equality. Self-educated artisans like Thomas Skidmore of New York City argued for the redistribution of property and the abolition of inheritance to equalize wealth in the nation. However, most workingmen's parties focused on more practical proposals: government distribution of free land in the West, the abolition of compulsory militia service and imprisonment for debt, public funding for education, and the regulation of banks and corporations. Although the success of these parties at the polls was modest, by the 1830s Democrats and Whigs adopted many of their proposals.

Workingmen, like workingwomen, also formed unions to demand better wages and working conditions. In the 1820s and 1830s, skilled journeymen held mass meetings to protest employers' efforts to extend the workday from ten to eleven hours, merge smaller workshops into larger factories, and cut wages. In New York City in 1834, labor activists formed a citywide federation, the General Trades Union, which provided support for striking workers. The National Trades Union was established later that year, with delegates representing more than twenty-five thousand workers across the North. These organizations aided skilled workers but refused admission to women and unskilled men.

Broad labor organizations proved difficult to sustain because of differences in skill and ethnicity as well as in age and marital status among members. Even workingmen's parties, which recruited men across occupations and ages, refused to recruit laborers who could not vote—women, new immigrants, and most blacks. With the onset of the panic of 1837, the common plight of workers became clearer. But the economic crisis made unified action nearly impossible as individuals sought to hold on to what little they had by any means available.

The Panic of 1837 in the North

The panic of 1837 began in the South, but it hit northern cotton merchants hard (see chapter 10). Textile factories drastically cut production, metal foundries that supplied their machinery were wiped out, workers lost their jobs, and merchants and investors went broke. Those who kept their jobs saw their wages cut in half. As with the panic of

1819, hunger plagued urban residents while crops rotted in the Midwest because farmers could not afford to harvest them. In Rochester, the Posts were among hundreds who lost their homes to foreclosure. Petty crime, prostitution, and violence also rose as men and women struggled to make ends meet.

In Lowell and other textile towns, hours increased and wages fell. Just as important, the process of deskilling intensified. Factory owners considered mechanization one way to improve their economic situation. In the 1830s and 1840s, the sewing machine was invented and improved. When it came into widespread use in the 1850s, factories began to mass-produce inexpensive clothing, employing women who worked for low wages. Mechanical reapers, steam boilers, and the steam press transformed other occupations as manufacturers

Hat Manufacturing, 1850   This 1850 lithograph advertises Charles Oakford's hat factory in Philadelphia. Like many industries, hat making became increasingly mechanized in the 1840s. Here Oakford talks with a client in the center of the room, across from his steam-powered lathe, while workers stand at stations shaping and stacking hats. A boy packs the merchandise into a box ready for shipping.   © Philadelphia History Museum at the Atwater Kent/The Bridgeman Art Library

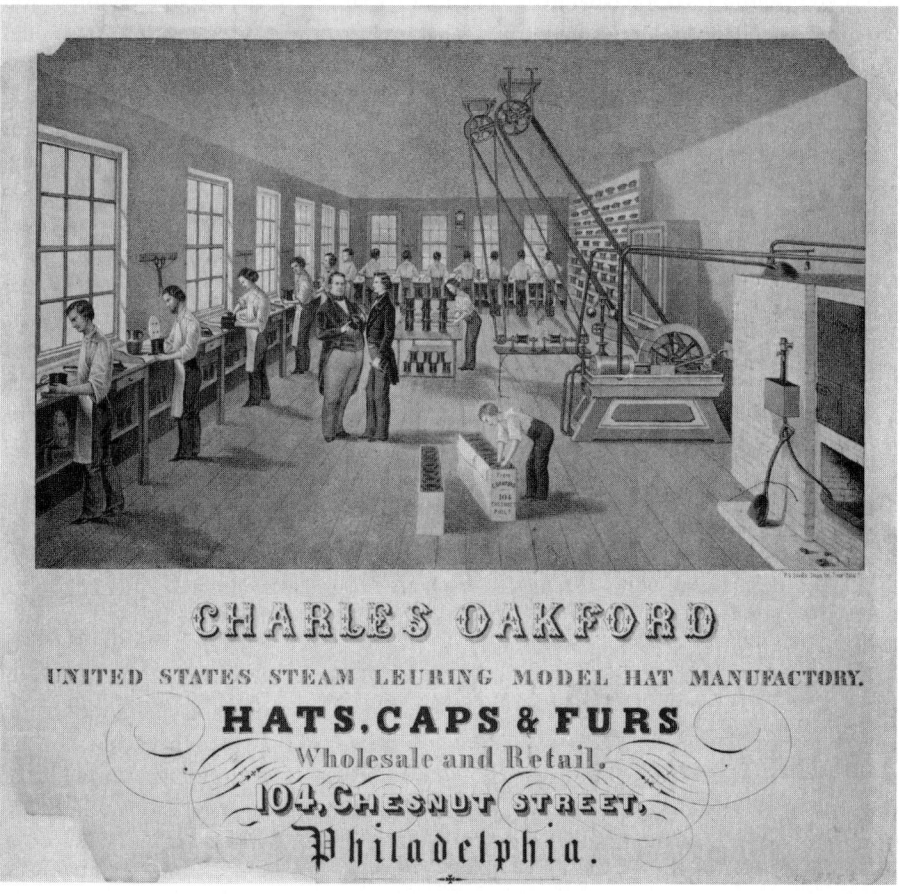

invested more of their resources in machines. At the same time, the rising tide of immigrants provided a ready supply of relatively cheap labor. Artisans tried to maintain their traditional skills and status, but in many trades they were fighting a losing battle.

By the early 1840s, when the panic subsided, new technologies did spur new jobs. Factories demanded more workers to handle new machines that ran at a faster pace. The ease of harvesting wheat inspired changes in flour milling that required engineers to design machines and mechanics to build and repair them. The steam press allowed publication of more newspapers and magazines, creating positions for editors, publishers, printers, engravers, reporters, and sales agents. Advertising became an occupation unto itself.

Following the panic, new labor organizations also emerged to address workers' changing circumstances. Many of these unions were made up of a particular trade or ethnic group, and almost all continued to address primarily the needs of skilled male workers. Textile operatives remained the one important group of organized female workers. In the 1840s, workingwomen joined with workingmen in New England to fight for a ten-hour day. Slowly, however, farmers' daughters abandoned the fight and left the mills as Irish immigrants flooded the labor market and agreed to accept lower pay and longer hours.

For most women in need, charitable organizations offered more support than unions did. Organizations like Philadelphia's Female Association for the Relief of Women and Children in Reduced Circumstances provided a critical safety net for many poor families since public monies for such purposes were limited. Although nearly every town and city provided some form of public assistance in this period, municipalities never had sufficient resources to meet the needs of growing populations, much less the extraordinary demands posed by hard times. Despite financial constraints, towns and cities continued to expand almshouses and workhouses, offer some financial assistance, and provide land and supplemental funds for private benevolent ventures like orphan asylums.

Rising Class and Cultural Tensions

By the 1840s, leaders of both public and private charitable endeavors linked relief to the moral character of those in need and generally measured that character by the standards of affluent Protestants. Upper-class Americans had long debated whether the poor would learn habits of industry and thrift if they were simply given aid without working for it. Concern over the "idle poor"—those who were physically able to work but did not—intensified as more and more immigrants joined the ranks of the needy. The debate was deeply gendered. Women and children were considered the worthiest recipients of aid, and middle- and upper-class women the appropriate dispensers of charity. Successful men, meanwhile, often linked poverty to weakness and considered giving pennies to a beggar an unmanly act that indulged the worst traits of the poor. They focused on building workhouses or expanding almshouses, though preferably at little expense to city residents.

The panic of 1837 convinced some benevolent leaders that public workhouses and almshouses offered the best hope for helping the poor. Alternatively, charitable societies sought to improve the environment in an effort to change the conditions that produced poverty. In the 1840s and 1850s, they built orphan asylums, schools, hospitals, and homes for working women to provide vulnerable residents with housing, education, domestic skills, and advice.

The "undeserving" poor faced grimmer choices. They received public assistance only through the workhouse or the local jail. Rowdy men who gambled away what little they earned, prostitutes who tempted respectable men into vice, and immigrants who preferred idle poverty to virtuous labor figured in newspaper articles, investigative reports, and novels. In fictional portrayals, naive girls were often the victims of immoral men or unfortunate circumstance. One of the first mass-produced books in the United States, Nathaniel Hawthorne's *The Scarlet Letter* (1850) was set in Puritan New England but addressed contemporary concerns about the seduction of innocents. It illustrated the social ostracism and poverty suffered by a woman who bore a child out of wedlock.

Other fictional tales placed the blame for fallen women on foreigners, especially Catholics. Such works drew vivid portraits of young nuns ravished by priests and then thrown out pregnant and penniless. These stories attracted tens of thousands of readers in the United States and heightened anti-Catholic sentiment, which periodically boiled over into attacks on Catholic homes, schools, churches, and convents.

Economic competition further intensified conflicts between immigrants and native-born Americans. By the 1840s, Americans who opposed immigration took the name **nativists** and launched public campaigns against foreigners, especially Irish Catholics. In May 1844, nativists clashed with Irishmen in Philadelphia after shots were fired from a firehouse. A dozen nativists and one Irishmen were killed the first day. The next night, nativists looted and burned Irish businesses and Catholic churches.

Most native-born workers distanced themselves from immigrants, but others believed that class solidarity was crucial to overcoming the power wielded by employers. Nevertheless, only highly skilled immigrants were likely to gain entrance to labor organizations. Although immigrants with sufficient resources to open businesses or establish themselves in professions might gain middle-class status, only pious immigrants from Protestant backgrounds were likely to be truly accepted into middle-class society.

REVIEW & RELATE

- How and why did American manufacturing change over the course of the first half of the nineteenth century?
- How did Northerners respond to the hard times that followed the panic of 1837? How did responses to the crisis vary by class, ethnicity, and religion?

Saving the Nation from Sin

Americans had established Bible societies, prayer circles, and urban missions as early as the 1810s. These efforts were infused with new energy as evangelical fires—lit by southern camp meetings in the early nineteenth century—swept across the North. Men and women of all classes and races embraced this **Second Great Awakening** to express deeply held beliefs and reclaim a sense of the nation's godly mission. Yet evangelical Protestantism was not the only religious tradition to thrive in the 1830s and 1840s. The Quaker and Unitarian faiths also grew in this period. Catholic churches and Jewish synagogues expanded along with immigration, and new religious groups—including Mormons and Millerites—attracted thousands of followers. At the same time, transcendentalists sought deeper engagements with nature as another path to spiritual renewal.

The Second Great Awakening

Although diverse religious traditions flourished in the United States, evangelical Protestantism proved the most powerful in the 1820s and 1830s. Evangelical churches hosted revivals, encouraged conversions, and organized prayer and missionary societies. This second wave of religious revivals began in Cane Ridge, Kentucky, in 1801, took root across the South, and then spread northward. Although revivals had diminished by the late 1830s, they erupted periodically through the 1850s and again during the Civil War. But it was the revivals of the 1830s that transformed Protestant churches and the social fabric of northern life.

Northern ministers like Charles Grandison Finney adopted techniques first wielded by southern Methodists and Baptists: plain speaking, powerful images, and mass meetings. But Finney molded these techniques for a more affluent audience and held his "camp meetings" in established churches. Northern evangelicals also insisted that religious fervor demanded social responsibility and that good works were a sign of salvation.

In the late 1820s, boomtown growth along the Erie Canal aroused deep concerns about the rising tide of sin. In September 1830, the Reverend Finney arrived in Rochester and began preaching in the city's Presbyterian churches. Arguing that "nothing is more calculated to beget a spirit of prayer, than to unite in social prayer with one who has the spirit himself," Finney led prayer meetings that lasted late into the night. Individual supplicants walked to special benches designated for anxious sinners, who were prayed over in public. Female parishioners played crucial roles, encouraging their husbands, sons, friends, and neighbors to submit to God.

Thousands of Rochester residents joined in the evangelical experience as Finney's powerful message spilled over into other denominations. But the significance of the Rochester revivals went far beyond a mere increase in church membership. Finney had converted "the great mass of the most influential people" in the city: merchants, lawyers, doctors, master craftsmen, and shopkeepers. Equally important, he proclaimed that if Christians were "united all over the world the Millennium [Christ's Second Coming] might be brought about in three months." Local preachers in Rochester and the surrounding towns took up his call, and converts committed themselves to preparing the world for Christ's arrival.

Lyman Beecher, a powerful Presbyterian minister in Boston, declared that the spiritual renewal of the early 1830s was the greatest revival of religion the world had ever seen. Middle-class and wealthy Americans were swept into Presbyterian, Congregational, and Episcopalian churches, while Baptists and Methodists ministered mainly to laboring women and men. Black Baptists and Methodists evangelized in their own communities, where independent black churches combined powerful preaching with haunting spirituals. In Philadelphia, African Americans built fifteen churches between 1799 and 1830. Over the next two decades, a few black women, such as Jarena Lee, joined men in evangelizing among African American Methodists and Baptists.

Tens of thousands of Christian converts both black and white embraced evangelicals' message of moral outreach. They formed Bible, missionary, and charitable societies; Sunday schools; and reform organizations. No movement gained greater impetus from the revivals than did **temperance**, which sought to moderate and then ban the sale and consumption of alcohol. In the 1820s, Americans fifteen years and older consumed six to seven gallons of distilled alcohol per person per year (about double the amount consumed today).

Middle-class evangelicals, who once accepted moderate drinking as healthful and proper, now insisted on eliminating alcohol consumption in the United States.

New Spirits Rising

Although enthusiasm for temperance and other reforms waned during the panic of 1837 and many churches lost members, the Second Great Awakening revived following the panic. Increasingly, however, evangelical ministers competed for souls with a variety of other religious groups. In the 1840s, diverse religious groups flourished, many of which supported good works and social reform. The Society of Friends, or Quakers, the first religious group to refuse fellowship to slaveholders, grew throughout the early and mid-nineteenth century. Having divided in 1827 and then again in 1848, the Society of Friends continued to grow. So, too, did its influence in reform movements as activists like Amy Post carried Quaker testimonies against alcohol, war, and slavery into the wider society. Unitarians also combined religious worship with social reform. Their primary difference from other Christians was their belief in a single unified higher spirit rather than the Trinity of the Father, the Son, and the Holy Spirit. First established in Boston in 1787, Unitarian societies spread across New England in the 1820s, emerging mainly out of Congregational churches. Opposed to evangelical revivalism, Unitarians nonetheless spread west and south in the 1830s and 1840s, attracting well-to-do merchants and manufacturers as well as small farmers, shopkeepers, and laborers. Dedicated to a rational approach to understanding the divine, Unitarian church members included prominent literary figures such as Ralph Waldo Emerson and Harvard luminaries such as William Ellery Channing.

Other churches grew as a result of immigration. Dozens of Catholic churches were established to meet the needs of many Irish and some German immigrants. With the rapid increase in the number of Catholic churches, more Irish priests were ordained in the United States, and women's religious orders also became increasingly Irish in the 1840s and 1850s. By 1860 the Irish numbered 1.6 million of the 2.2 million Catholics in the United States. Meanwhile synagogues, Hebrew schools, and Hebrew aid societies signaled the growing presence of Jews in the United States. They came chiefly from Germany, though Jews were far fewer in number than Catholics.

Entirely new religious groups also flourished in the 1840s. One of the most important was the Church of Jesus Christ of Latter-Day Saints, or Mormons, founded by Joseph Smith. Smith claimed that he began to receive visions from God at age fifteen and was directed to dig up gold plates inscribed with instructions for redeeming the Lost Tribes of Israel. *The Book of Mormon* (1830), supposedly based on these inscriptions, granted spiritual authority to the unlearned and mercy to the needy while it castigated the pride and wealth of those who oppressed the humble and the poor. At the same time, Smith founded the Church of Jesus Christ of Latter-Day Saints, which he led as the Prophet. Although seeking converts, the church did not admit African Americans to worship.

Smith founded not only a church but a theocracy (a community governed by religious leaders). In the mid-1830s, Mormons established a settlement at Nauvoo, Illinois, built homes and churches, and recruited followers from the eastern United States and from England. But after Smith received revelations sanctioning polygamy, local authorities arrested him and his brother, and a mob lynched them. Brigham Young, a successful missionary, took over as Prophet and in 1846 led 12,000 followers west, 5,000 of whom built a thriving theocracy near the Great Salt Lake, in what would become the Utah Territory in 1850.

New religious groups also formed by separating from established denominations, just as Unitarians had split from Congregationalists. William Miller, a prosperous farmer and Baptist preacher, led one such movement. He claimed that the Bible proved that the Second Coming of Jesus Christ would occur in 1843. Thousands of Americans read Millerite pamphlets and newsletters and attended sermons by Millerite preachers. When various dates for Christ's Second Coming passed without incident, however, Millerites developed competing interpretations for the failure and divided into distinct groups. The most influential group formed the Seventh-Day Adventist Church in the 1840s.

Transcendentalism

Another important movement for spiritual renewal was rooted in the transcendent power of nature. The founder of this transcendentalist school of thought was Ralph Waldo Emerson, a Unitarian pastor who gave up his post to travel and read. In 1836 he published an essay entitled "Nature" that expressed his newfound belief in a Universal Being. This Being existed as an ideal reality beyond the material world and was accessible through nature. The natural world Emerson described was distinctly American and offered hope that moral perfection could be achieved in the United States despite the corruptions of civil society and man-made governments. Emerson expressed his ideas in widely read essays and books and in popular lectures to packed houses.

From the 1830s on, Emerson's town of Concord, Massachusetts, served as a haven for writers, poets, intellectuals, and reformers who embraced his views. Many Unitarians and other liberal Protestants in the Boston area were drawn to **transcendentalism** as well. In 1840 Margaret Fuller, a close friend of Emerson, became the first editor of *The Dial*, a journal dedicated to transcendental thought. In 1844 she moved to New York City, where the editor Horace Greeley hired her as a critic at the *New York Tribune*. While in New York, she published her ideas about the conflict between women's assigned roles and their innate abilities in *Woman in the Nineteenth Century* (1845), which combined transcendental ideas with arguments for women's rights.

Henry David Thoreau also followed the transcendentalist path. He grew up in Concord and read "Nature" while a student at Harvard. In July 1845, Thoreau moved to a cabin near Walden Pond and launched an experiment in simple living. A year later, he was imprisoned overnight for refusing to pay his taxes as a protest against slavery and the Mexican-American War. In the anonymous *Civil Disobedience* (1846), he argued that individuals of conscience had the right to resist government policies they believed to be immoral. Five years later, Thoreau published *Walden*, which offered a classic statement of the interplay among a simple lifestyle, natural harmony, and social justice.

Emerson also urged Americans to break their cultural dependence on Europe, and American artists agreed. Led by Thomas Cole, members of the Hudson River School painted romanticized landscapes from New York's Catskill and Adirondack Mountains. The sweeping vistas tied the nation's power to its natural beauty. Western vistas inspired artistic efforts as well. George Catlin portrayed the dramatic scenery of western mountains, gorges, and waterfalls and offered moving portraits of Plains Indians, who, he feared, faced extinction. Other artists captured birds, plants, and animals distinctive to the West. Although relatively few Americans had yet visited the region, many hung copies of frontier paintings on their walls or marveled at them in books and magazines. Clearly the hand of God must be at work in such glorious landscapes.

REVIEW & RELATE

- What impact did the Second Great Awakening have in the North?
- What new religious organizations and viewpoints emerged in the first half of the nineteenth century, *outside* of Protestant evangelical denominations?

Organizing for Change

Both religious commitments and secular problems spurred social activism in the 1830s and 1840s. In cities, small towns, and rural communities, Northerners founded organizations, launched campaigns, and established institutions to better the world around them. Yet even those Americans who agreed that society needed to be reformed did not share a common sense of priorities or solutions. Moreover, while some activists worked to persuade Americans to follow their lead, others insisted that change would occur only if imposed by law.

Varieties of Reform

Middle-class Protestant women and men formed the core of many reform movements in the early to mid-nineteenth century. They had more time and money to devote to social reform than did their working-class counterparts and were less tied to traditional ways than were their wealthy neighbors. Nonetheless, workers and farmers, African Americans and immigrants, Catholics and Jews also participated in efforts to improve society. The array of causes reformers pursued was astonishing: charity to the poor and sick; establishing religious missions; prison reform, health reform, dress reform, and educational reform; eradicating prostitution; aid to orphans, the deaf, the blind, the mentally ill, and immigrants; the exclusion of immigrants; the rights of workers, of women, and of Indians; ending alcohol and tobacco abuse; abolishing capital punishment; racial justice; and the abolition of slavery.

Reformers used different techniques to pursue their goals. Since women could not vote, for example, they were excluded from direct political participation. Instead, they established charitable associations, distributed food and medicine, constructed asylums, circulated petitions, organized boycotts, arranged meetings and lectures, and published newspapers and pamphlets. Other groups with limited political rights—African Americans and immigrants, for instance—embraced similar modes of action. White men wielded these forms of activism but also organized political campaigns and lobbied legislators. The techniques employed were also affected by the goals of a particular movement. Moral suasion worked best with families, churches, and local communities, while legislation was more likely to succeed if the goal involved transforming people's behavior across a whole state or region.

Reformers often used a variety of tactics to support a single cause, and many changed their approach over time. For instance, reformers who sought to eradicate prostitution began by praying in front of urban brothels and attempting to rescue "fallen" women. They soon launched *The Advocate of Moral Reform*, a newspaper that published morality tales, advice to mothers, and the names of men who visited brothels. Moral reform societies in small towns and rural areas worked to alert young women and men to the dangers of city life. Those in cities opened Homes for Virtuous and Friendless Females in the 1840s to provide safe havens for vulnerable women. But moral reformers also started to petition state legislators to make punishments for men who hired prostitutes as harsh as those for prostitutes themselves.

The Temperance Movement

Many moral reformers also advocated temperance. Organized temperance work began in 1826 with the founding of the American Temperance Society, an all-male organization led by clergy and businessmen who focused on alcohol abuse among working-class men. Religious revivals then inspired the establishment of some 5,000 local chapters with more than 100,000 members. Over time, the temperance movement changed the goal from moderation to total abstinence, targeted middle-class and elite as well as working-class men, and welcomed women's support. Wives and mothers were expected to persuade family members to stop drinking, sign a temperance pledge, and commit their newly sober souls to God. To promote this work, women founded dozens of female temperance societies in the 1830s. African Americans, too, created their own temperance organizations.

Some white working men viewed temperance as a way to gain dignity and respect. For Protestants, in particular, embracing temperance distinguished them from Irish Catholic workers, who were caricatured as happy drunkards. Some working-class temperance advocates also criticized liquor dealers, whom they considered to be greedy capitalists overseeing "the vilest, meanest, most earth-cursing and hell-filling business ever followed."

Despite the rapid growth of temperance organizations, moral suasion failed to reduce alcohol consumption significantly. As a result, many temperance advocates turned to legal reform in the 1840s, hoping to legislate where they could not persuade. In 1851 Maine passed legislation that prohibited the sale of all alcoholic beverages. By 1855 twelve states had joined Maine in restricting the manufacture or sale of alcohol. Yet these stringent measures inspired a backlash. Hostile to the imposition of middle-class Protestant standards on the population at large, Irish workers in Maine organized the Portland Rum Riot in 1855. It led to the law's repeal the next year.

Legal strategies generally complemented rather than replaced moral arguments. Temperance advocates continued to publish short stories, magazine articles, sermons, and novels alerting Americans to the dangers of "demon rum." Working-class families were often the subjects of didactic tales written by and for the middle class. But laboring men and women had their own ideas about how to deal with alcohol abuse. Small groups of men who abused alcohol gathered together in the 1840s and formed Washingtonian societies—named in honor of the nation's founder—to help each other stop drinking. Martha Washington societies appeared shortly thereafter, composed not of female alcoholics but of the wives, mothers, and sisters of male alcoholics.

Temperance advocates thus used various strategies to limit alcohol abuse and its consequences. Over the course of the nineteenth century, these efforts gradually reduced the consumption of beer, wine, and spirits, although they did not eliminate the problem.

Utopian Communities

While most reformers reached out to the wider society to implement change, some activists withdrew into self-contained communities that they hoped would serve as models for other groups. The architects of these **utopian societies** turned to European intellectuals and reformers for inspiration as well as to American religious and republican ideals.

In the 1820s, Scottish and Welsh labor radicals such as Frances Wright, Robert Owen, and his son Robert Dale Owen established utopian communities in the United States. They believed that a young nation founded on republican principles would be particularly open to experiments in communal labor, gender equality, and (in Wright's case) racial justice. Their efforts ultimately failed, but they did arouse impassioned debate. After founding the community of New Harmony, Indiana, in 1828 with his father, Robert Dale Owen returned briefly to Europe. He then joined Wright in New York City, where they established a reform newspaper, reading room, and medical dispensary. Resettling in New Harmony in 1833, Owen continued to advocate for workers' rights, birth control, and the abolition of slavery. But he also embraced Jacksonian democracy and won election to the Indiana House of Representatives and then the U.S. Congress. Owen thus pursued both utopian communalism and political activism in the larger society.

Former Unitarian minister George Ripley also sought to bridge a critical divide— between physical and intellectual labor. He established a transcendentalist community at Brook Farm in Massachusetts in 1841. In 1845 the farm was reconfigured according to the principles of the French socialist Charles Fourier, who believed that cooperation across classes was necessary to temper the conflicts inherent in capitalist society. He developed a plan for communities, called phalanxes, where residents chose jobs based on their individual interests and were paid according to the contribution of each job to the community's well-being. Fourier also advocated equality for women. More than forty Fourierist phalanxes were founded in the northern United States during the 1840s.

A more uniquely American experiment, the Oneida community, was established in central New York by John Humphrey Noyes in 1848. He and his followers believed that Christ's Second Coming had already occurred and embraced the communalism of the early Christian church. But Noyes also advocated sexual freedom and developed a plan for "complex marriage" in which women were liberated from male domination and constant childbearing. Divorce and remarriage were permitted, children were raised communally, and a form of birth control was instituted. Despite the public outrage provoked by Oneida's sexual practices, the community recruited several hundred residents and thrived for more than three decades.

REVIEW & RELATE

- How did the temperance movement reflect the range of tactics and participants involved in reform during the 1830s and 1840s?
- What connections can you identify between utopian communities and mainstream reform movements in the first half of the nineteenth century?

Abolitionism Expands and Divides

For a small percentage of Northerners, slavery was the ultimate injustice. While most Northerners applauded themselves for ridding their region of the institution, antislavery advocates urged them to recognize the North's continued complicity in human bondage. After all, slaves labored under brutal conditions to provide cotton for New England factories, sugar and molasses for northern tables, and profits for urban traders. Free blacks were among the most vocal advocates of abolition. Yet their leadership became a source of conflict as more whites joined the movement in the 1830s. The place of the church, of women, and of politics in antislavery efforts also caused controversy. In addition, abolitionists disagreed over whether to focus on abolishing slavery in the South or simply preventing its extension into western territories. Although these debates often weakened individual organizations, they expanded the number and range of antislavery associations and campaigns.

The Beginnings of the Antislavery Movement

In the 1820s, African Americans and a few white Quaker allies led the fight to abolish slavery. They published pamphlets, lectured to small audiences, and helped runaway slaves escape. In 1829 David Walker wrote the most militant statement of black abolitionist sentiment, *Appeal . . . to the Colored Citizens*. The free son of an enslaved father, Walker left his North Carolina home for Boston in the 1820s. There he became an agent and a writer for *Freedom's Journal*, the country's first newspaper published by African Americans. In his *Appeal*, Walker criticized the false promises of African colonization and warned that slaves would claim their freedom by force if whites did not agree to emancipate them. Quaker abolitionists, such as Benjamin Lundy, the editor of the *Genius of Universal Emancipation*, admired Walker's courage but rejected his call for violence.

William Lloyd Garrison, a white Bostonian who worked on Lundy's Baltimore newspaper, was inspired by Walker's radical stance. In 1831 he returned to Boston and

The *Amistad* Revolt, 1839 This illustration depicts the mutiny of forty-nine African slaves led by Cinqué on board the Spanish ship *Amistad* off the coast of Cuba. After the rebels killed Captain Ramón Ferrer, they sailed to Long Island, New York. In subsequent judicial proceedings, the federal courts ruled that the slaves were entitled to their freedom, and they were returned to Africa.   Beinecke Rare Book and Manuscript Library, Yale University

Death of Capt. Ferrer, the Captain of the Amistad, July, 1839.

launched his own abolitionist newspaper, the *Liberator*, urging white antislavery activists to embrace the black perspective. White reformers, he claimed, worried more about the moral and practical problems that slavery posed for whites than about the wrongs it imposed on blacks. From blacks' perspective, Garrison claimed, the goal must be immediate, uncompensated emancipation.

The *Liberator* demanded that whites take an absolute stand against slavery where it existed and halt its spread. With the aid of like-minded reformers in Boston, Philadelphia, and New York City, Garrison organized the **American Anti-Slavery Society (AASS)** in 1833. By the end of the decade, the AASS boasted branches in dozens of towns and cities, from Boston to Salem, Ohio. Members supported lecturers and petition drives, criticized churches that refused to denounce slavery, and proclaimed that the U.S. Constitution was a proslavery document. Some Garrisonians also participated in the work of the **underground railroad**, a secret network of activists who assisted fugitives fleeing enslavement.

In 1835 Sarah and Angelina Grimké joined the AASS and soon began lecturing for the organization. Daughters of a prominent South Carolina planter, they had moved to Philadelphia and converted to Quakerism. As Southerners, their denunciations of slavery carried particular weight. Yet as women, their public presence aroused fierce opposition. In 1837 Congregationalist ministers in Massachusetts decried their presence in front of "promiscuous" audiences of men and women.

The Grimkés were not the first women to speak out against slavery. Maria Stewart, a free black widow, lectured in Boston in 1831–1832. She demanded that northern blacks take more responsibility for ending slavery in the South and for fighting racial discrimination everywhere. In 1833 free black and white Quaker women formed an interracial organization, the Philadelphia Female Anti-Slavery Society. The organization built on the earlier efforts of white Quakers and free blacks in Philadelphia to boycott slave-produced goods such as cotton and sugar.

The abolitionist movement and the AASS quickly expanded to the frontier, and by 1836 Ohio claimed more antislavery groups than any other state. That year, Ohio women initiated a petition to abolish slavery in the District of Columbia, which was circulated from Rhode Island to Illinois. The petition campaign inspired the first national meeting of women abolitionists, held in New York City in 1837. But in Ohio and the rest of the Midwest, female and male abolitionists worked side by side, claiming it was their Christian duty "to *unite* our efforts for the accomplishment of the holy object of our association."

Abolition Gains Ground and Enemies

The abolitionist movement shocked many Northerners, and in the late 1830s violence often erupted in response to antislavery agitation. Mobs threatened participants at the 1838 Antislavery Convention of American Women at Pennsylvania Hall in Philadelphia. After black and white women left the meeting arm in arm, the hall was burned to the ground. From 1834 to 1838, mobs routinely attacked antislavery meetings, lecturers, and presses as AASS agents crisscrossed the North recruiting followers and organizing local societies.

The massive petition campaigns in 1836 and 1837 generated both support and opposition. Thousands of women and men, including Amy Post and her husband Isaac, signed their names to petitions to ban slavery in the District of Columbia, end the internal slave trade, and oppose the annexation of Texas. While some evangelical women considered such efforts part of their Christian duty, evangelical ministers (including the Reverend Finney) condemned antislavery work as outside women's sphere. Many female evangelicals retreated in the face of clerical disapproval, but others continued their efforts alongside their nonevangelical sisters.

 Online Document Project
The Second Great Awakening and Women's Activism
bedfordstmartins.com/hewittlawsonvalue

Many politicians were also opposed to mass petitioning, whether by women or men, so in 1836 Congress passed the gag rule (see chapter 10).

But gag rules did not silence abolitionists. In the 1840s, fugitive slaves helped alert Northerners to the horrors of slavery. The most important of the fugitive abolitionists was Frederick Douglass, a Maryland-born slave who fled to New Bedford, Massachusetts, in 1838. He met Garrison in 1841, joined the AASS, and four years later published his life story, *Narrative of the Life of Frederick Douglass, as Told by Himself.* Having revealed his identity as a fugitive slave, Douglass sailed for England, where he launched a successful two-year lecture tour. He then returned to the United States; moved to Rochester, New York; and began publishing his own antislavery newspaper, the *North Star.* Amy Post befriended Douglass, and the Western New York Anti-Slavery Society raised funds and subscribers to support his work.

While eager to have fugitive slaves tell their dramatic stories, many abolitionist leaders did not match Post's vigorous support of African American activists asserting an independent voice. Although these abolitionists opposed slavery, they still believed that blacks were inferior to whites. Thus several affiliates of the AASS refused to accept black members. Those that did often faced resignations from members who opposed the innovation. Ultimately, the independent efforts of black activists such as Douglass helped to expand the antislavery movement even as they made clear the limits of white abolitionist ideals.

Conflicts also arose over the responsibility of churches to challenge slavery. The major Protestant denominations included southern as well as northern churches. If mainstream churches such as Presbyterians, Baptists, or Methodists refused communion to slave owners, their southern branches would certainly secede. Still, from the 1830s on, abolitionists pressured their churches to take Christian obligations seriously and denounce human bondage. Individual churches responded, but aside from the Society of Friends, larger denominations failed to follow suit.

In response, abolitionists urged individual Christians to break with churches that continued to accept slaveholders. Antislavery preachers and parishioners pushed the issue, and some worshippers "came out" from mainstream churches to form antislavery congregations. Union churches, composed of evangelical "come outers" from various denominations, were founded in New York State and New England. White Wesleyan Methodists and Free Will Baptists joined African American Methodists and Baptists in insisting that congregants oppose slavery in order to gain membership. Although these churches remained small, they served as constant reminders to mainstream denominations of their continued ties to slavery.

Abolitionism and Women's Rights

Women were increasingly active in the AASS and the "come outer" movement, but their growing participation aroused opposition even among abolitionists. By 1836–1837, female societies formed the backbone of antislavery petition campaigns. More women also joined the lecture circuit, including Abby Kelley, a fiery Quaker orator who demanded that women be granted an equal role in the movement. But when Garrison and his supporters appointed Kelley to the AASS business committee in the spring of 1839, they triggered a crisis. At the AASS annual convention that May, debates erupted over the propriety of women participating "in closed meetings with men." Of the 1,000 abolitionists in attendance, some 300 walked out in protest. The opposition came mainly from the evangelical wing of the movement and included Lewis Tappan, one of the chief financiers of the AASS. The dissidents soon formed a new organization, the American and Foreign Anti-Slavery Society, which excluded women from public lecturing and officeholding but encouraged them to support men's efforts.

The Garrisonians responded by expanding the roles of women in the AASS. In 1840 local chapters appointed a handful of female delegates, including Lucretia Mott, to the World Anti-Slavery Convention in London. The majority of men at the meeting, however, rejected the female delegates' credentials. Women were then forced to watch the proceedings from a separate section of the hall, confirming for some that women could be effective in campaigns against slavery only if they gained more rights for themselves.

Finally, in July 1848, a small circle of women, including Lucretia Mott and a young American she met in London, Elizabeth Cady Stanton, organized the first convention focused explicitly on women's rights. Held in Stanton's hometown of Seneca Falls, New York, the convention attracted three hundred women and men, including Garrisonian abolitionists, radical Quakers, and members of the antislavery Liberty Party. James Mott presided over part of the convention and Frederick Douglass spoke, but women dominated the proceedings. One hundred participants signed a **Declaration of Sentiments** that called for women's equality in everything from education and employment to legal rights and voting. Two weeks later, a second convention in Rochester, New York, took the radical action of electing a woman, Abigail Bush, to preside. Here, too, Douglass and other black abolitionists as well as local working women participated.

Although abolitionism provided much of the impetus for the women's rights movement, it was not the only influence. Strikes by seamstresses and mill workers in the 1830s and 1840s highlighted women's economic needs. Utopian communities experimented with gender equality, and temperance reformers focused attention on domestic violence against women and called for changes in divorce laws. A diverse coalition advocated for married women's property rights. Women's rights were also debated among the Seneca Indians in western New York. Like the Cherokees, Seneca women had lost traditional rights over land and tribal policy as their nation adopted more Anglo-American ways. In the summer of 1848, the creation of a written constitution threatened to enshrine these losses in writing. The Seneca constitution did strip women of their role in selecting chiefs but protected their right to vote on any decision to sell tribal lands. Earlier in 1848, revolutions had erupted against repressive regimes in France and elsewhere in Europe. Antislavery papers like the *North Star* covered developments in detail, including European women's demands for political and civil recognition. French rebels such as Jeanne Deroin and German revolutionaries such as Mathilde Anneke were especially noted for their advocacy of women's rights. The meetings in Seneca Falls and Rochester drew on these ideas and influences even as they attended primarily to the rights of white American women.

The Rise of Antislavery Parties

As women's rights conventions began calling for female suffrage, debates over the role of partisan politics in the antislavery campaign intensified. Keeping slavery out of western territories depended on the actions of Congress, as did abolishing slavery in the nation's capital and ending the internal slave trade. Moral suasion had seemingly done little to change minds in Congress or in the South. To force abolition onto the national political agenda, the **Liberty Party** was formed in 1840. Many Garrisonians were appalled at the idea of participating in what they considered a proslavery government, but the Liberty Party gained significant support among abolitionists in New York, the Middle Atlantic states, and the Midwest.

 Online Document Project   Debating Abolition
bedfordstmartins.com/hewittlawsonvalue

The Whigs and Democrats sought to avoid the antislavery issue in order to keep their southern and northern wings intact, but that strategy became much more difficult once the Liberty Party entered campaigns. In 1840 the party won less than 1 percent of the popular vote but organized large rallies that attracted men, women, and children. In sparsely settled regions like Illinois, Garrisonians even joined Liberty Party supporters to get out the antislavery message. In 1844 the party won a little more than 2 percent of the vote, but this time its presence in the race was enough to ensure a victory for James K. Polk over the Whig candidate, Henry Clay (see chapter 10).

When President Polk led the United States into war with Mexico, interest in an antislavery political party surged. In 1848 the Liberty Party gained the support of antislavery Whigs, also called Conscience Whigs; northern Democrats who opposed the extension of slavery into the territories; and African American leaders like Frederick Douglass, who broke with Garrison on the issue of electoral politics. Seeing a political opportunity, more practically minded political abolitionists founded the Free-Soil Party, which quickly subsumed the Liberty Party. Free-Soilers focused less on the moral wrongs of slavery than on the benefits of keeping western territories free for northern whites. The Free-Soil Party nominated Martin Van Buren, a former Democrat, for president in 1848 and won 10 percent of the popular vote. Once again, the result was to send a slaveholder to the White House—Zachary Taylor, who had led U.S. troops in the war with Mexico. Nonetheless, the Free-Soil Party had expanded beyond the Liberty Party, raising fears in the South and in the two major parties that the battle over slavery could no longer be contained.

REVIEW & RELATE

• How did the American Anti-Slavery Society differ from earlier abolitionist organizations?

• How did conflicts over gender and race shape the development of the abolitionist movement in the 1830s and 1840s?

Conclusion: From the North to the Nation

Charles Grandison Finney followed these developments from Oberlin College, where he served as president in the 1840s. Resistant to women's growing demands for rights and skeptical that politics could transform society, he continued to view individual conversions as the wellspring of change. As the nation expanded westward, he trained ministers to travel the frontier converting American Indians to Christianity and reminding Christian pioneers of their religious obligations. After the discovery of gold in California in 1848, religious leaders of every faith feared that the desire for material gain would once again lead Americans to neglect spiritual responsibilities.

Amy Post watched close friends leave for California with husbands struck by gold fever. Other friends and coworkers moved to Ohio, Michigan, and Kansas. Those who remained in Rochester became even more immersed in abolitionist campaigns but continued to clash over the best strategies for achieving their goals. Amy Post, like most Quakers, rejected participation in a government that accepted slavery and fomented war, causing a rift with Frederick Douglass. The disagreement caused her deep personal anguish, but the debates revitalized the movement, creating new opportunities for action.

Finney and Post were among tens of thousands of Northerners inspired by religious and reform movements between 1820 and 1850. Driven by urban and industrial development, immigration, and moral concerns, activists focused on a wide range of causes. But abolitionism carried the most powerful national implications. The addition of vast new territories at the end of the Mexican-American War in 1848 ensured that those concerns would become even more pressing in the decade ahead.

Chapter Review

MAKE IT STICK

 LearningCurve **bedfordstmartins.com/hewittlawsonvalue**
After reading the chapter, use LearningCurve to retain what you've read.

IDENTIFY KEY TERMS

Identify and explain the significance of each term below.

separate spheres (p. 278)
deskilling (p. 280)
nativists (p. 283)
Second Great Awakening (p. 283)
temperance (p. 284)
transcendentalism (p. 286)
utopian societies (p. 289)

Appeal . . . to the Colored Citizens (p. 290)
Liberator (p. 291)
American Anti-Slavery Society (AASS)
  (p. 291)
underground railroad (p. 291)
Declaration of Sentiments (p. 293)
Liberty Party (p. 294)

REVIEW & RELATE

Answer the focus questions from each section of the chapter.

1. Why did American cities become larger and more diverse in the first half of the nineteenth century?

2. What values and beliefs did the emerging American middle class embrace?

3. How and why did American manufacturing change over the course of the first half of the nineteenth century?

4. How did Northerners respond to the hard times that followed the panic of 1837? How did responses to the crisis vary by class, ethnicity, and religion?

5. What impact did the Second Great Awakening have in the North?

6. What new religious organizations and viewpoints emerged in the first half of the nineteenth century, *outside* of Protestant evangelical denominations?

7. How did the temperance movement reflect the range of tactics and participants involved in reform during the 1830s and 1840s?

8. What connections can you identify between utopian communities and mainstream reform movements in the first half of the nineteenth century?

9. How did the American Anti-Slavery Society differ from earlier abolitionist organizations?

10. How did conflicts over gender and race shape the development of the abolitionist movement in the 1830s and 1840s?

ONLINE DOCUMENT PROJECTS

◆ **The Second Great Awakening and Women's Activism**
◆ **Debating Abolition**

After reading the primary sources in these document sets, answer the **Interpret the Evidence** questions to help you analyze each of the documents, and then answer the **Put It in Context** question(s) to help you relate the documents to the topics and themes you read about in the chapter.

bedfordstmartins.com/hewittlawsonvalue

TIMELINE OF EVENTS

1820–1850 • Size, number, and diversity of northern cities grow; immigration surges	**1842** • Amy Post helps found the Western New York Anti-Slavery Society
1823 • Textile factory town built in Lowell, Massachusetts	**1843** • William Miller predicts Second Coming of Christ
1826 • American Temperance Society founded	**1844** • Congress funds construction of the first telegraph line
1827 • First workingmen's political party founded	**May 1844** • Anti-immigrant violence rocks Philadelphia
1829 • David Walker publishes *Appeal . . . to the Colored Citizens*	**1845** • Frederick Douglass publishes *Narrative of the Life of Frederick Douglass*
1830 • Joseph Smith publishes *The Book of Mormon*	• Margaret Fuller publishes *Woman in the Nineteenth Century*
September 1830 • Charles Grandison Finney brings Second Great Awakening to Rochester, New York	**1845–1846** • Irish potato famine
	1846 • Henry David Thoreau publishes *Civil Disobedience*
1833 • William Lloyd Garrison founds American Anti-Slavery Society (AASS)	**1848** • Free-Soil Party formed
	• Frederick Douglass publishes the *North Star*
1837–1842 • Panic of 1837	
1839 • American Anti-Slavery Society splits over the role of women in the society	**July 1848** • Seneca Falls Woman's Rights Convention
1840 • Liberty Party formed	**1851** • Maine prohibits the sale of alcoholic beverages
• World Anti-Slavery Convention, London	

✓ LearningCurve
bedfordstmartins.com/hewittlawsonvalue
After reading the chapter, use LearningCurve
to retain what you've read.

Imperial Ambitions and Sectional Crises

1848–1861

AMERICAN HISTORIES

John C. Frémont, a noted explorer and military leader and the first presidential nominee of the Republican Party, rose from humble beginnings. He was the illegitimate child of Anne Beverley Whiting Pryor of Savannah, Georgia, who abandoned her wealthy husband and ran off with a French immigrant, Jean Charles Fremon. As a young man, John changed his last name to Frémont, either reclaiming the original spelling or seeking to create a more aristocratic one. He attended the College of Charleston, where he excelled at mathematics, but was eventually expelled for neglecting his studies. Frémont was hired to teach aboard a navy ship in 1833 through the help of an influential South Carolina politician. He then obtained a surveying position to map new railroad lines and Cherokee lands in Georgia and was finally appointed a second lieutenant in the Corps of Topographical Engineers.

In 1840 Lieutenant Frémont traveled to Washington, D.C., to assist in publishing maps and reports from an expedition along the upper Mississippi River. The following year, the twenty-eight-year-old explorer eloped with Jessie Benton, the seventeen-year-old daughter of Missouri senator Thomas Hart Benton. Despite the scandal, Senator Benton supported his son-in-law's selection for a federally funded expedition to the West. In 1842 Frémont and his guide, Kit Carson, led twenty-three men along the emerging Oregon Trail. Two years later, John returned to Washington, where he and his wife Jessie wrote a vivid report on the Oregon Territory and California. Congress published the report, which inspired a wave of hopeful migrants to head west.

John Frémont shared many Americans' imperial ambitions, but his success was tainted by a quest for personal glory. On a federal mapping expedition in 1845, he left his post and headed to California. Arriving in the Sacramento valley in the winter of 1846, he stirred support among U.S. settlers for war with Mexico. His brash behavior nearly provoked a battle that would have wiped out his small company. Frémont then fled to the Oregon Territory, where he and Kit Carson became involved in conflicts with Modoc Indians. Then, as the nation moved closer to war with Mexico, Frémont returned to California, where he supported Anglo-American settlers' efforts to declare the region an independent republic. Although Frémont was denied the republic's governorship, he worked tirelessly for California's admission to the Union and served as one of the state's first senators. With his wife's encouragement, he also embraced abolition and in 1856 was nominated for president by the new Republican Party.

Dred Scott also traveled the frontier in the 1830s and 1840s, but not of his own free will. Born a slave in Southampton, Virginia, around 1800, he and his master, Peter Blow, moved west to Alabama in 1818 and then relocated to St. Louis, Missouri, in 1830. Three years later, short of funds, Blow sold Scott to Dr. John Emerson, an assistant surgeon in the U.S. army. In 1836 Emerson took Scott to Fort Snelling in the Wisconsin Territory, a free territory that offered glimpses of a different life. There Scott met Harriet Robinson, a young African American woman who was enslaved to the local Indian agent. Her master was also a justice of the peace and agreed to marry the couple in 1837 and transfer ownership of Harriet to Dr. Emerson. When Emerson was transferred back to St. Louis, the Scotts returned with him. After his death in 1843, the couple was hired out to local residents in St. Louis by Emerson's widow.

In April 1846, the Scotts initiated lawsuits in the Missouri courts seeking their freedom. The Missouri Supreme Court had ruled in earlier cases that slaves who resided for any time in free territory must be freed, and the Scotts had lived and married in Wisconsin. Dred Scott's former owners, the Blows, supported his suit, and in 1850 the Missouri Circuit Court ruled in the Scotts' favor. However, the Emerson family appealed the decision to the state Supreme Court, with Harriet's case to follow the outcome of her husband's. Two years later, that court ruled against all precedent and overturned the lower court's decision. Dred Scott then appealed to the U.S. Supreme Court, but it, too, ultimately ruled against the Scotts, leaving them enslaved.

THE AMERICAN HISTORIES of John Frémont and Dred Scott were shaped by the explosive combination of westward expansion and the growing regional division over the issue of slavery. Whereas Frémont joined expeditions to map and conquer the West, Scott followed the migrations of slave owners and soldiers. Both Frémont and Scott found

Wagon Train, 1860 This early photograph, taken in 1860, shows a train of covered wagons, oxen, and men on horseback setting out from Manhattan, Kansas.   Kansasmemory.org/Kansas State Historical Society

strength through marriage. Jessie Frémont served as her husband's confidante and coauthor, providing both practical and emotional support through nearly fifty years of marriage. Harriet Scott joined her husband in the prolonged litigation to win their freedom. Frémont also opposed slavery, but he focused on legislative means to end it. From their different positions, these two men reflected the dramatic changes that occurred as westward expansion pushed the issues of empire and slavery to the center of national debate.

Claiming the West

During the 1830s and 1840s, national debates over slavery intensified. The most important battles now centered on western territories gained through victory in the war with Mexico. Before 1848, government-sponsored expeditions had opened up vast new lands for American pioneers seeking opportunity. Eastern migrants, along with immigrants from Germany and Scandinavia, moved west in growing numbers. Then, following the Mexican-American War and the discovery of gold in California, tens of thousands of men rushed to the Pacific coast seeking riches. But the West was already home to a diverse population that included Indians, Mexicans, Mormons, and missionaries. Eager pioneers converged, and often clashed, with these groups.

Traveling the Overland Trail

In the 1830s, a few white families had ventured to the western frontier. Some traveled around the southern tip of South America by ship or across the Isthmus of Panama by boat and mule train. But a growing number followed overland trails to the far West. In

1836 Narcissa Whitman and Eliza Spaulding joined a group traveling to the Oregon Territory, the first white women to make the trip. They accompanied their husbands, both Presbyterian ministers, who hoped to convert the region's Indians. Their letters to friends and associates back east described the rich lands and needy souls in the Walla Walla valley and encouraged further migration.

The panic of 1837 also prompted Americans to head west as thousands of U.S. migrants and European immigrants sought new opportunities in the 1840s. They were drawn to Oregon, the Rocky Mountain region, and the eastern plains. The Utah Territory, not yet officially part of the United States, attracted large numbers of Mormons. Some pioneers opened trading posts in the West where Indians exchanged goods with Anglo-American settlers or with merchants back east. Small settlements developed around these posts and near the expanding system of forts that dotted the region.

For many pioneers, the journey on the Oregon Trail began at St. Louis. From there, they traveled by wagon train across the Great Plains and the Rocky Mountains to the Pacific coast. By 1860 some 350,000 Americans had made the journey, claimed land from the Mississippi to the Pacific, and transformed the United States into an expanding empire.

Because the trip to the West required funds for wagons and supplies, most pioneers were of middling status. The three- to six-month journey was also physically demanding, and most pioneers traveled with family members to help share the labor and provide support, though men outnumbered women and children, comprising some 60 percent of western migrants.

Early in the journey, women and men generally followed their customary roles: Men hunted, fished, and drove the wagons, while women cooked, washed, and watched the children. But traditional roles often broke down on the trail, and even conventional domestic tasks posed novel problems. Women had to cook unfamiliar food over open fires in all kinds of weather and with only a handful of pots and utensils. They washed laundry in rivers or streams, and on the plains they had to haul water for cooking or cleaning from great distances. Wood, too, was scarce on the plains, and women and children gathered buffalo dung (called "chips") for fuel. Men frequently had to gather food rather than hunt and fish, or they had to learn to catch strange (and sometimes dangerous) animals, such as jack rabbits and rattlesnakes. Few men were prepared for the arduous work of pulling wagons out of ditches or floating them across rivers with powerful currents. Nor were many of them expert in shoeing horses or fixing wagon wheels, tasks that were performed by skilled artisans at home.

Expectations changed dramatically when men took ill or died on the journey. Then wives drove the wagon, gathered or hunted for food, and learned to repair axles and other wagon parts. When large numbers of men were injured or ill, women might serve as scouts and guides or pick up guns to defend wagons under attack by Indians or wild animals. Yet despite the growing burdens on pioneer women, they gained little power over decision making. Moreover, the addition of men's jobs to women's responsibilities was rarely reciprocated. Few men cooked, did laundry, or cared for children on the trail. Single men generally paid women on the trail to perform such chores for them, and a husband who lost his wife on the journey generally relied on "neighbor" women as he would at home.

In one area, however, relative equality reigned. Men and women were equally suscep-tible to disease, injury, and death on the trail. Accidents, gunshot wounds, drowning, broken bones, and infections affected individuals on every wagon train. Some groups were struck as well by influenza, cholera, measles, mumps, or scarlet fever—all deadly in the early nineteenth century. In addition, about 20 percent of women on the overland trail became pregnant, which posed even greater dangers than at home given rough roads, a lack of water, the abundance of dirt, and the frequent absence of midwives and doctors. Some 20 percent of women lost children or spouses on the trip west, though most had little time to mourn. Wagon trains usually stopped only briefly to bury the dead, leaving a cross or a pile of stones to mark the grave, and then moved on. Overall, about one in ten to fifteen migrants died on the western journey, leaving some 65,000 graves along the trails west.

The Gold Rush

Despite the hazards, more and more Americans traveled the Oregon Trail, the Santa Fe Trail, and other paths to the Pacific coast. Initially only a few thousand Americans settled in California. Some were agents sent by New England merchants to purchase fine leather made from the hides of Spanish cattle raised in the area. Several of these agents married into families of elite Mexican ranchers, known as Californios, and adopted their culture, even converting to Catholicism.

However, the Anglo-American presence in California changed dramatically after 1848 when gold was discovered at Sutter's Mill in northeastern California. News of the discovery brought tens of thousands of new settlers from the eastern United States, South America, Europe, and Asia. In the gold rush, "forty-niners" raced to claim riches in the California mountains, and men vastly outnumbered women. Single men came with brothers, neighbors, or friends. Married men left wives and children behind, promising to send for them once they struck gold. Some 80,000 arrived in 1849 alone.

The rapid influx of gold seekers heightened tensions between newly arrived whites, local Indians, and Californios. Forty-niners confiscated land owned by Californios, shattered the fragile ecosystem in the California mountains, and forced Mexican and Indian men to labor for low wages or a promised share in uncertain profits. New conflicts erupted when foreign-born migrants joined the search for wealth. Forty-niners from the United States regularly stole from and assaulted foreign-born competitors—whether Asian, European, or South American. With the limited number of sheriffs and judges in the region, most criminals knew they were unlikely to be arrested, much less tried and convicted.

The gold rush also led to conflicts over gender roles as thousands of male migrants demanded food, shelter, laundry, and medical care. Some women in the region earned a good living by renting rooms, cooking meals, washing clothes, or working as prostitutes. But many faced heightened forms of exploitation. Indian and Mexican women were especially vulnerable to sexual harassment and rape, while Chinese women were imported specifically to provide sexual services for male miners.

Chinese men were also victims of abuse by whites, as evidenced by Chinese workers who were hired by a British mining company and then run off their claim by Anglo-American gold seekers. Yet some Chinese men used the skills traditionally assigned them in their homeland—cooking and washing clothes—to earn a far steadier income than prospecting for gold could provide. Other men also took advantage of the demand for goods and services. Levi Strauss, a twenty-four-year-old German Jewish immigrant, moved from New York to San Francisco to open a dry goods store in 1853. He was soon producing canvas and then denim pants that could withstand harsh weather and long wear. These blue jeans made Strauss far richer than any forty-niner seeking gold.

A Crowded Land

While U.S. promoters of migration continued to depict the West as an open territory waiting to be tamed and cultivated, it was in fact the site of competing imperial ambitions in the late 1840s. Despite granting statehood to Texas in 1845 and winning the war against Mexico in 1848, the United States had to compete with Comanche, Sioux, and other powerful Indian nations for control of the Great Plains (see chapter 10). As the U.S. government sought to secure land for railroads and forts and as American migrants and European immigrants carved out farms and villages, they had to contend with a range of Indian nations that refused to relinquish control (Map 12.1).

Although attacks on wagon trains were rare, Indians did threaten frontier settlements throughout the 1840s and 1850s. Settlers often retaliated, and U.S. army troops joined them in efforts to push Indians back from areas newly claimed by whites. Yet in many parts of the West, Indians were as powerful as whites, and they did not cede territory without a fight. For example, the Reverend Marcus Whitman and his wife Narcissa became victims of their success in promoting western settlement. In 1843 Marcus returned east and led one thousand Christian emigrants on a "Great Migration" to the Oregon Territory. The settlers were enthusiastic about their new homes, but the arrival of more whites proved disastrous for local Indians. The pioneers brought a deadly measles epidemic to the region, killing thousands of Cayuse and Nez Percé Indians. In 1847, convinced that whites brought disease but no useful medicine, a group of Cayuse Indians killed the Whitmans and ten other white settlers.

Yet violence against whites could not stop the flood of migrants into the Oregon Territory. Indeed, attacks by one Indian tribe were often used to justify assaults on any Indian tribe. For example, John Frémont and Kit Carson, whose party had been attacked by a group of Modoc Indians in Oregon in 1846, took their revenge by destroying a Klamath Indian village and killing men, women, and children there. The defeat of Mexico and the discovery of gold in California in 1848 only intensified these conflicts.

Although Indians and white Americans were the main players in many battles, Indian nations also competed with each other. In the southern plains, drought and disease exacerbated those conflicts in the late 1840s and dramatically changed the balance of power in the region. In 1845 the southern plains were struck by a dry spell, which lasted on and off until the mid-1860s. Three years later, smallpox ravaged Comanche villages, and then forty-niners heading to California introduced a virulent strain of cholera that killed prominent Comanche leaders as well as hundreds of their followers. In the late 1840s, the Comanches were the largest Indian nation, with about twenty thousand members; by the mid-1850s, less than half that number remained.

Yet the collapse of the Comanche empire was not simply the result of outside forces. As the Comanches expanded their trade networks and incorporated smaller Indian nations into their orbit, they overextended their reach. Most important, they allowed too many bison to be killed in order to meet the needs of their Indian allies and the demand for bison robes by Anglo-American and European traders. The Comanches also herded growing numbers of horses, which required expansive grazing lands and winter havens in the river valleys and pushed the bison onto more marginal lands. Opening up the Santa Fe Trail to commerce multiplied the problems by destroying vegetation, polluting springs, and thus damaging some of the last refuges for bison. The prolonged drought then completed the depopulation of the bison on the southern plains. Without

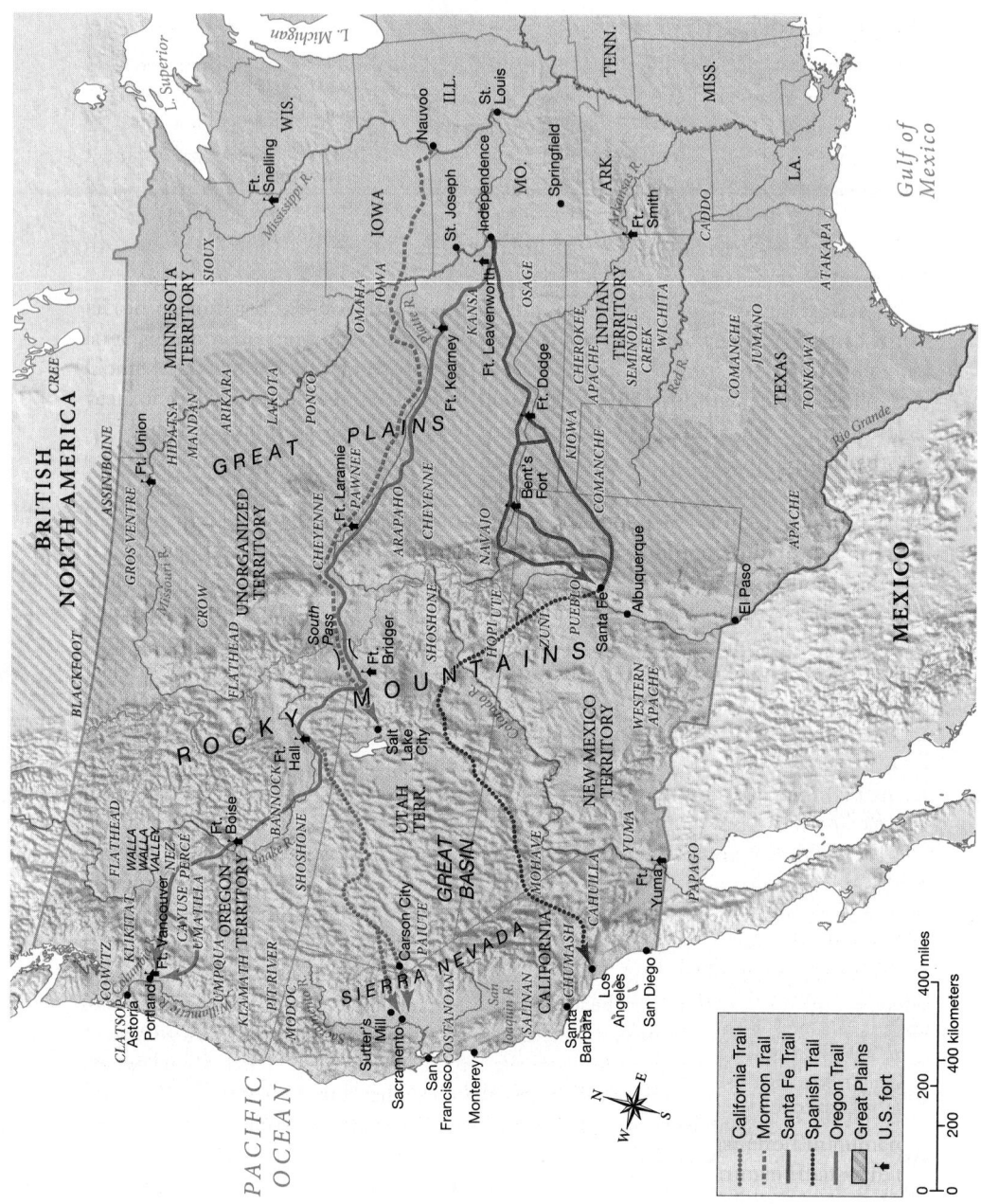

MAP 12.1

Western Trails and Indian Nations, c. 1850 As wagon trains and traders journeyed west in rapidly growing numbers during the 1830s and 1840s, the United States established forts along the most well-traveled routes. At the same time, Indians claimed or were forced into new areas through the pressure of Indian removals, white settlement, and the demands of hunting, trade, and agriculture.

bison, the Comanches lost one of their most critical trade items; by the late 1850s, they were left without the goods or leverage to sustain their commercial and political networks. As the Comanche empire collapsed, former Indian allies sought to advance their own interests. These two developments reignited Indian wars on the southern plains as tens of thousands of Anglo-Americans and European immigrants poured through the region.

African Americans also participated in these western struggles. Many were held as slaves by southeastern tribes forced into Indian Territory, while others were freed and married Seminole or Cherokee spouses. The Creeks proved harsh masters, prompting some slaves to escape north to free states or south to Mexican or Comanche territory. Yet as southern officers in the U.S. army moved to frontier outposts to secure American dominance, they carried more slaves into the region. Many, including Dr. Emerson, changed posts frequently, taking slaves like Dred Scott into western territories that were alternately slave and free. Still, it was white planters who brought the greatest numbers of African Americans into Texas, Missouri, and Kansas, pushing the frontier of slavery ever westward. At the same time, some free blacks joined the migration voluntarily in hopes of finding better economic opportunities and less overt racism on the frontier.

REVIEW & RELATE

• Why did Americans go west in the 1830s and 1840s, and what was the journey like?

• What groups competed for land and resources in the West? How did competition lead to violence?

Expansion and the Politics of Slavery

The place of African Americans and of slavery in the West aroused intense political debates as territories in the region began to seek statehood. Debates over the eradication of slavery and limits on its expansion had shaped the highly contested presidential election of 1848 (see chapters 10 and 11). After the Mexican-American War, the battle between proponents and opponents of slavery intensified and focused more specifically on its westward expansion. Each time a territory achieved the requirements for statehood, a new crisis erupted. To resolve these crises required strong presidential and congressional leadership, judicial moderation, and a spirit of compromise among the people as well as their representatives. None of these conditions prevailed. Instead, passage of the Fugitive Slave Act in 1850 aroused deeper hostilities, and President Franklin Pierce (1853–1857) encouraged further expansion but failed to address the crises that ensued.

California and the Compromise of 1850

In the winter of 1849, just before Zachary Taylor's March inauguration, California applied for admission to the Union as a free state. Some California political leaders opposed slavery on principle. Others wanted to "save" the state for whites by outlawing slavery, discouraging free blacks from migrating to the state, and restricting the rights of American Indian, Mexican, and Chinese residents. Yet the internal debates among Californians were not uppermost in the minds of those in Congress. Southerners were concerned about the impact of California's free-state status on the sectional balance in

Congress, while northern Whigs were shocked when President Taylor suggested that slavery should be allowed anywhere in the West.

Other debates percolated in Congress at the same time. Many Northerners were horrified by the spectacle of slavery and slave trading in the nation's capital and argued that it damaged America's international reputation. Southerners, meanwhile, complained that the Fugitive Slave Act of 1793 was being widely ignored in the North, as abolitionists aided runaways seeking freedom. A boundary dispute between Texas and New Mexico irritated western legislators, and Texas continued to claim that debts it accrued while an independent republic and during the Mexican-American War should be assumed by the federal government.

Senator Henry Clay of Kentucky, the Whig leader who had hammered out the Missouri Compromise in 1819–1820, again tried to resolve the many conflicts that stalled congressional action. He offered a compromise by which California would be admitted as a free state; the remaining land acquired from Mexico would be divided into two territories—New Mexico and Utah—and slavery there would be decided by popular sovereignty; the border dispute between New Mexico and Texas would be decided in favor of New Mexico, but the federal government would assume Texas's war debts; the slave trade (but not slavery) would be abolished in the District of Columbia; and a new and more effective fugitive slave law would be approved. Although Clay's compromise offered something to everyone, his colleagues did not immediately embrace it.

By March 1850, after months of debate, the sides remained sharply divided, with senators on both sides of the issue opposing the measure. John C. Calhoun, a proslavery senator from South Carolina, refused to support any compromise that allowed Congress to decide the fate of slavery in the western territories. Meanwhile William H. Seward, an antislavery Whig senator from New York, proclaimed that in all good conscience he could not support a compromise that forced Northerners to help hunt down fugitives from slavery. Daniel Webster, a Massachusetts Whig and an elder statesman, appealed to his fellow senators to support the compromise in order to preserve the Union, but Congress adjourned with the fate of California undecided.

Before the Senate reconvened in the fall of 1850, however, the political landscape changed in unexpected ways. Henry Clay retired in the spring of 1850, leaving the Capitol with his last great legislative effort unfinished. On March 31, Calhoun died; his absence from the Senate made compromise more likely. In July, President Taylor died unexpectedly, and his vice president, Millard Fillmore of Buffalo, New York, was elevated to the presidency. Fillmore then appointed Webster as secretary of state, removing him from the Senate as well.

In September 1850, with President Fillmore's support, a younger cohort of senators and representatives steered the **Compromise of 1850** through Congress, one clause at a time, thereby allowing legislators to support only those parts of the compromise they found palatable. In the end, all the provisions passed, and Fillmore quickly signed the bills into law. California entered the Union as a free state, and John C. Frémont entered Congress as one of that state's first two senators. The Compromise of 1850, like the Missouri Compromise thirty years earlier, fended off a sectional crisis, but it also signaled future problems. Would popular sovereignty prevail when later territories sought admission to the Union, and would Northerners abide by a fugitive slave law that called on them to aid directly in the capture of runaway slaves?

Rescue of Fugitive Slaves   This 1872 illustration portrays the dramatic rescue of the North Carolina slave Jane Johnson and her two children aboard a Philadelphia ferry in 1855 as they accompanied their owner on a trip through the free state of Pennsylvania. They were liberated by members of the Pennsylvania Anti-Slavery Society, led by the black abolitionist William Still, who boarded the boat and removed them to safety.   Photo Researchers, Inc.

The Fugitive Slave Act Inspires Northern Protest

The fugitive slave laws of 1793 and 1824 mandated that all states aid in apprehending and returning runaway slaves to their owners. The **Fugitive Slave Act of 1850** was different in two important respects. First, it eliminated jury trials for alleged fugitives. Second, the law required individual citizens, not just state officials, to help return runaways or else risk being fined or imprisoned. The act angered many Northerners who believed that the federal government had gone too far in protecting the rights of slaveholders and thereby aroused sympathy for the abolitionist cause.

Before 1850, the most well-known individuals aiding fugitives were free blacks such as David Ruggles in New York City; Jermaine Loguen in Syracuse, New York; and, after his own successful escape, Frederick Douglass in Rochester, New York. Their main allies in this work were white Quakers such as Amy and Isaac Post in Rochester; Thomas Garrett in Chester County, Pennsylvania; and Levi and Catherine Coffin in Newport, Indiana. The work was dangerous. Charles Turner Torrey, a white Congregationalist minister, may have aided as many as four hundred fugitives, but he was eventually caught and imprisoned. He died of tuberculosis in a Baltimore jail in 1846.

Following passage of the Fugitive Slave Act, the number of slave owners and hired slave catchers pursuing fugitives increased dramatically. But so, too, did the number of northern abolitionists helping blacks escape. Enslaved women and men followed various paths northward from rural plantations and southern cities. Once they crossed into free territory, most fugitives contacted free blacks or individuals known to be sympathetic to their cause. They then began the often slow progress along the underground railroad, from house to house or barn to barn, until they found safe haven. A small number of fortunate slaves were led north by fugitives like Harriet Tubman, who returned south repeatedly to free dozens of family members and other enslaved men and women. Fugitives followed disparate paths through the Midwest, Pennsylvania, New York, and New England, and there was little coordination among the "conductors" from one region or state to another. But the underground railroad was nonetheless an important resource for fugitives, some of whom sought refuge in Canada while others hoped to blend into free black communities in the United States.

Free blacks were endangered by the claim that slaves hid themselves in their midst. In Chester County, Pennsylvania, on the Maryland border, newspapers reported on at least a dozen free blacks who were kidnapped or arrested as runaways in the first three months of 1851. One provision of the Fugitive Slave Act encouraged such arrests: Commissioners were paid $10 for each slave sent back but only $5 if a slave was not returned. Without the right to a trial, a free black could easily be sent south as a fugitive. It was this fear that prompted hundreds of African Americans, both free and enslaved, to flee to Canada.

At the same time, a growing number of Northerners challenged the federal government's right to enforce the law. Blacks and whites organized protest meetings throughout the free states. At a meeting in Boston in 1851, abolitionist William Lloyd Garrison denounced the law: "We execrate it, we spit upon it, we trample it under our feet." Abolitionists also joined forces to rescue fugitives who had been arrested. In Syracuse, New York, in October 1851, Jermaine Loguen, Samuel Ward, and the Reverend Samuel J. May led a well-organized crowd as it broke into a Syracuse courthouse to rescue a fugitive slave known as Jerry. They successfully hid him from authorities and then spirited him to Canada. As such incidents increased across the North, Daniel Webster bemoaned the lack of respect for federal law, and President Fillmore lamented the rise of "mob rule." But northern abolitionists gained growing sympathy from their neighbors and became bolder in denouncing both the Fugitive Slave Act and "the bloodhound kidnappers" who sought to enforce it.

Meanwhile members of Congress continued to debate the law's effects. Senator Frémont was among the legislators who helped defeat a bill that would have imposed harsher penalties on those who assisted runaways. And Congress felt growing pressure to calm the situation, including from foreign officials who were horrified by the violence required to sustain slavery in the United States. Abolitionist speakers like Frederick Douglass, who spent six months denouncing the Fugitive Slave Act across Canada, Ireland, and England, intensified foreign concern over the law. Great Britain and France had already abolished slavery in their West Indian colonies and found it hard to support what they saw as extreme policies to keep the institution alive in the United States. Yet neither southern slaveholders nor northern abolitionists were willing to compromise any further.

Pierce Encourages U.S. Expansion

In the presidential election of 1852, the Whigs and the Democrats tried once again to appeal to voters across the North-South divide by running candidates who either skirted the critical issues of the day or held ambiguous views. The Democrats, who had great difficulty choosing a candidate, finally nominated Franklin Pierce. A successful New

Hampshire lawyer who opposed abolition, Pierce had served in Congress from 1833 to 1842 and in the U.S. army during the Mexican-American War. The Whigs rejected Vice President Millard Fillmore, who had angered many in the party by supporting popular sovereignty and vigorous enforcement of the Fugitive Slave Act. The Whig Party turned instead to another military leader, General Winfield Scott of Virginia, to head the ticket. General Scott had served with distinction in the war against Mexico, but he had not expressed any proslavery views. The Whigs thus hoped to gain southern support while maintaining their northern base. The Free-Soil Party, too, hoped to expand its appeal, given northern hostility to the Fugitive Slave Act. But Free-Soilers were unable to take advantage of the moment, nominating John P. Hale, a relatively unknown former Democratic senator from New Hampshire.

Franklin Pierce's eventual victory left the Whigs and the Free-Soilers in disarray. A third of southern Whigs threw their support to the Democrats, seeking a truly proslavery party. Many Democrats who had supported Free-Soilers in 1848, like Martin Van Buren, were driven to vote for Pierce by their enthusiasm over the admission of California as a free state. But despite the Democratic triumph, that party also remained fragile. The nation now faced some of its gravest challenges under a president with limited political experience and no firm base of support. His cabinet included men of widely differing views, part of an effort to appease the various factions of the Democratic Party. But when confronted with difficult decisions, Pierce often received contradictory advice and generally pursued his own expansionist vision.

Early in his administration, Pierce focused on expanding U.S. trade and extending the "civilizing" power of U.S. institutions to other parts of the world. Inspired by the promise of new markets, Pierce and his supporters sought to shift Americans' attention outward. Trade with China had declined in the 1840s, but the United States had begun commercial negotiations with Japan in 1846. These came to fruition in 1854, when U.S. emissary Commodore Matthew C. Perry obtained the first formal treaty with Japan that allowed for mutual trading. Within four years, Pierce and his agent, international trader Townsend Harris, succeeded in expanding commercial ties and enhancing diplomatic relations with Japan, in large part by ensuring U.S. support for the island nation against its traditional enemies in China, Russia, and Europe.

Although the president rejected Commodore Perry's offer to take military possession of Formosa and other territories near Japan, Pierce was willing to consider conquests in the Caribbean and Central America. For decades, U.S. politicians, particularly Southerners, had looked to gain control of Cuba, Mexico, and Nicaragua. A "Young America" movement within the Democratic Party imagined manifest destiny reaching southward as well as westward. In hopes of stirring up rebellious Cubans against Spanish rule, some Democrats joined with private adventurers to send three expeditions, known as *filibusters*, to invade Cuba under the leadership of Cuban exile General Narciso Lopez. In 1854 the capture of one of the filibustering ships led to an international incident. Spanish officials confiscated the ship, while Democrats eager to add Cuba to the United States urged Pierce to seek an apology and redress from Spain. But many northern Democrats rejected any effort to obtain another slave state, and Pierce was forced to withdraw even tacit federal approval for the filibusters.

Other politicians still pressured Spain to sell Cuba to the United States. These included Pierce's secretary of state, William Marcy, and the U.S. ambassador to Great Britain, James Buchanan, as well as the ministers to France and Spain. In October 1854, these ministers met in Ostend, Belgium, and sent a letter to Pierce: "If we possess the power, [the United States is justified] by every law, human and Divine" in taking Cuba by force. When this Ostend Manifesto was leaked to the press, Northerners were outraged. They viewed the whole episode as "a dirty plot" to gain more slave territory and forced Pierce to give up any plans to obtain Cuba. In 1855 a private adventurer named William Walker, who had organized four filibusters to Nicaragua, invaded that country and set himself up as ruler. He then invited southern planters to take up vast lands he had confiscated from local farmers and to reintroduce slavery in Nicaragua. Pierce and many Democrats endorsed his plan, but neighboring Hondurans forced Walker from power in 1857 and executed him by firing squad three years later. Although Pierce's expansionist dreams failed, his efforts heightened sectional tensions.

REVIEW & RELATE

- What steps did legislators take in the 1840s and early 1850s to resolve the issue of the expansion of slavery?
- How were slavery and American imperialist ambitions intertwined in the 1840s and 1850s?

Sectional Crises Intensify

The political crises that divided Americans in the 1850s infused cultural as well as political life, leading to a lively trade in antislavery literature. This cultural turmoil, combined with the weakness and fragmentation of the existing political parties, helped give rise to the Republican Party in 1854. Although it spoke almost solely for Northerners who opposed the continued expansion of slavery, the Republican Party soon absorbed enough Free-Soilers, Whigs, and northern Democrats to become a major political force. The events that drove these cultural and political developments included continued challenges to the Fugitive Slave Act, a battle over the admission of Kansas to the Union, and a Supreme Court ruling in the *Dred Scott* case.

Popularizing Antislavery Sentiment

The Fugitive Slave Act had forced Northerners to reconsider their role in sustaining the institution of slavery. In 1852, just months before Franklin Pierce was elected president, their concerns were heightened by the publication of the novel *Uncle Tom's Cabin* by Harriet Beecher Stowe. Stowe's father, Lyman Beecher, and brother Henry were among the nation's leading evangelical clergy, and her sister Catharine had opposed Cherokee removal and promoted women's education. Stowe was inspired to write *Uncle Tom's Cabin* by passage of the Fugitive Slave Act in 1850, and the story originally ran as a forty-installment serial in an abolitionist periodical, the *National Era*. Once published in book form, the novel sold more than 350,000 copies in a matter of months.

Uncle Tom's Cabin built on accounts by former slaves as well as tales gathered by abolitionist lecturers and writers. During the 1850s, tales of life in bondage received growing attention in the North in both abolitionist circles and the mainstream press. The autobiographies of Frederick Douglass (1845), Josiah Henson (1849), and Henry Bibb (1849) set the stage for Stowe's novel. So, too, did the expansion of the antislavery press, which by the 1850s included dozens of newspapers across the North, the Midwest, and eastern Canada. Antislavery poems and songs also circulated widely and were performed at abolitionist conventions and fund-raising fairs.

Still, nothing captured the public's attention as did *Uncle Tom's Cabin*. Read by millions in the United States and England and translated into French and German, the book reached a mass audience, far exceeding the reach of other abolitionist literature. Its sentimental portrait of saintly slaves and its vivid depiction of cruel masters and overseers offered white Northerners a way to identify with enslaved blacks. Although some African Americans were frustrated by its demeaning portraits of northern free blacks, they recognized that it helped to fuel anger at the Fugitive Slave Act and at efforts to expand slavery into new territories. Its success and its limitations also convinced other fugitives, including Harriet Jacobs, to publish their real-life stories.

In some cases, the real-life stories of fugitive slaves surpassed their fictional counterparts for emotional impact. In May 1854, abolitionists sought to free fugitive slave Anthony Burns from a Boston courthouse, where his master was attempting to reclaim him. They failed to secure his release, and Burns was soon marched to the docks to be shipped south. Twenty-two companies of state militia held back tens of thousands of Bostonians who lined the streets, hissing and shouting "Kidnappers!" at the soldiers and police. A year later, supporters purchased Burns's freedom from his master, but the incident raised anguished questions among local residents. In a city that was home to intellectual, religious, and antislavery leaders such as Ralph Waldo Emerson, the Reverend Theodore Parker, and William Lloyd Garrison, Bostonians wondered how they had come so far in aiding and abetting slavery.

The Kansas-Nebraska Act Stirs Dissent

Kansas provided the first test of the effects of *Uncle Tom's Cabin* on northern sentiments toward slavery's expansion. As white Americans slowly displaced Indian nations from their homelands, large and diverse groups of Indians settled in the northern half of the Louisiana Territory. This unorganized region had once been considered beyond the reach of white settlement, but Senator Stephen Douglas of Illinois was eager to have a transcontinental railroad run through his home state. He needed the federal government to gain control of land along the route he proposed, and therefore he argued for the establishment of a vast Nebraska Territory. But to support his plan, Douglas also needed to convince southern congressmen, who sought a route through their own region. Much of the unorganized territory lay too far north to support plantation slavery, but a small portion lay directly west of Missouri, the northernmost slave state. According to the Missouri Compromise, states lying above the southern border of Missouri were automatically free. To gain southern support, Douglas sought to reopen the question of slavery in the territories. Pointing to the Compromise of 1850, by which territories acquired from Mexico would decide the fate of slavery by popular sovereignty, he argued that the same standard should apply to all new territories.

In January 1854, Douglas introduced the **Kansas-Nebraska Act** to Congress. The act extinguished Indians' long-held treaty rights in the region and repealed the Missouri Compromise. Two new territories—Kansas and Nebraska—would be carved out of the unorganized lands, and each would determine whether to enter the nation as a slave or

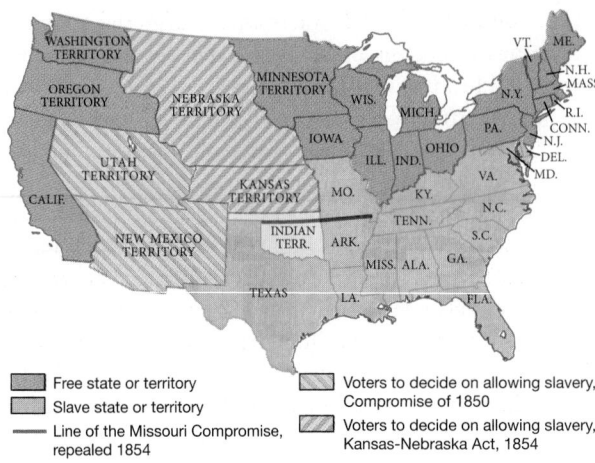

MAP 12.2
Kansas-Nebraska Territory From 1820 on, Congress attempted to limit sectional conflict. But the Missouri Compromise (1820) and the Compromise of 1850 failed to resolve disagreements over slavery's expansion. The creation of the Kansas and Nebraska territories in 1854 also heightened sectional conflict and ensured increased hostilities with Indians in the region.

Free state or territory
Slave state or territory
Line of the Missouri Compromise, repealed 1854
Voters to decide on allowing slavery, Compromise of 1850
Voters to decide on allowing slavery, Kansas-Nebraska Act, 1854

a free state by a referendum of eligible voters (Map 12.2). The act spurred intense opposition from most Whigs and some northern Democrats who wanted to retain the Missouri Compromise line. Months of fierce debate followed. Finally, on May 25, Douglas's proposed act passed by a comfortable majority when most Democrats followed the party line to vote yes. President Pierce quickly signed the bill into law.

Passage of the Kansas-Nebraska Act enraged many Northerners, who considered the dismantling of the Missouri Compromise a sign of the rising power of the South. They were infuriated that the South—or what some now called the Slave Power Conspiracy—had once again benefited from northern politicians' willingness to compromise. Although few of these opponents considered the impact of the law on Indians, the act also shattered treaty provisions that had protected the Arapaho, Cheyenne, Ponco, Pawnee, and Sioux nations. These Plains Indians lost half the land they had held by treaty as thousands of settlers swarmed into the newly organized territories. In the fall of 1855, conflicts between white settlers and Indians erupted across the southern and central plains. The U.S. army then sent six hundred troops to retaliate against a Sioux village, killing eighty-five residents of Blue Water in the Nebraska Territory and triggering continued violence throughout the region.

As tensions escalated across the nation, Americans faced the 1854 congressional elections. The Democrats, increasingly viewed as supporting the priorities of slaveholders, lost badly in the North. But the Whig Party also proved weak, having failed to stop the Slave Power from extending its leverage over federal policies. A third party, the American Party, was founded in the early 1850s and attracted native-born workers and Protestant farmers who were drawn to its anti-immigrant and anti-Catholic message (see chapter 11). Responding to these political realignments, another new party—the Republicans—was founded in the spring of 1854. Led by antislavery Whigs, the **Republican Party** slowly attracted former Free-Soilers to its ranks. Among its early members was a Whig politician from Illinois, Abraham Lincoln.

Born in Kentucky in 1809, Lincoln moved north to Illinois with his family and worked as a farmhand and surveyor. He also taught himself the rudiments of the law and was elected to the state legislature in 1834. In 1842 he married Mary Todd, the daughter of a wealthy banker, and established a lucrative law practice. Four years later, Lincoln was elected as a Whig to the House of Representatives. Serving his two-year term during the crisis over war with Mexico, he challenged Polk's claim that the first blood had been shed on U.S. soil (see chapter 11). After resuming his Springfield law practice, Lincoln joined the new Republican Party in 1856.

Although established only months before the fall 1854 elections, the Republican Party gained significant support in the Midwest, particularly in state and local campaigns. Meanwhile the American Party gained control of the Massachusetts legislature and nearly captured New York as well. These victories marked the demise of the Whigs as a national party. Although the American Party dissolved as a political force by 1856, the Republicans continued to gain strength. They replaced the Whig Party—which was built on a national constituency—with a party rooted solely in the North.

 Online Document Project
Sectional Politics and the Rise of the Republican Party
bedfordstmartins.com/hewittlawsonvalue

Like Free-Soilers, the Republicans argued that slavery should not be extended into new territories. But the Republicans also advocated a program of commercial and industrial development and internal improvements. With this platform, the party attracted a broader base than did earlier antislavery political coalitions. The Republican Party included both ardent abolitionists and men whose only concern was keeping western territories open to free white men. This latter group was more than willing to accept slavery where it already existed and to exclude black migrants, who might compete for jobs and land, from western states and territories.

Bleeding Kansas and the Election of 1856

The 1854 congressional elections exacerbated sectional tensions by bringing representatives from a strictly northern party—the Republicans—into Congress, where Democrats and Southerners, by virtue of their seniority, controlled most of the powerful committee assignments. But the conflicts over slavery reached far beyond the nation's capital. After passage of the Kansas-Nebraska Act, advocates and opponents of slavery poured into Kansas in anticipation of a vote on whether the state would enter the Union slave or free. Southerners flooded in from Missouri, while emigrant aid societies in the North funded antislavery settlers willing to relocate to Kansas.

As Kansas prepared to hold its referendum, settlers continued to arrive daily, making it difficult to determine who was eligible to vote. In 1855 Southerners installed a proslavery government at Shawnee Mission, while abolitionists established a stronghold in Lawrence. Violence erupted when proslavery settlers invaded Lawrence, killing one resident, demolishing newspaper offices, and plundering shops and homes. Fearing that the southern settlers who had come to Kansas were better armed than the antislavery Northerners in the territory, eastern abolitionists raised funds to ship rifles to Kansas. The Reverend Henry Ward Beecher of Brooklyn, a popular preacher and leading abolitionist, advocated armed self-defense. As cases of Sharps rifles arrived in Kansas, they came to be known as Beecher's Bibles.

Longtime abolitionist John Brown took more direct action. He joined four of his sons already living in Kansas and, with two friends, kidnapped five proslavery advocates from their homes along Pottawatomie Creek and hacked them to death. The so-called Pottawatomie Massacre infuriated southern settlers; in response, they drew up the Lecompton Constitution, which declared Kansas a slave state. President Pierce made his support of the proslavery government clear, but Congress remained divided. While Congress deliberated, armed battles continued. In the first six months of 1856, another two hundred settlers were killed in what became known as **Bleeding Kansas**.

Fighting also broke out on the floor of Congress. Republican senator Charles Sumner of Massachusetts delivered an impassioned speech against the continued expansion of what he termed the Slave Power. He launched scathing verbal attacks on planter politicians like South Carolina senator Andrew Butler, who supported the admission of Kansas as a slave state. Butler's nephew, Preston Brooks, a Democratic member of the House of Representatives, felt compelled to redress his family's honor. He assaulted Sumner in the Senate chamber, beating him senseless with a cane. Sumner, who never fully recovered from his injuries, was considered a martyr in the North. Meanwhile Brooks was feted across the state of South Carolina.

The presidential election of 1856 began amid an atmosphere poisoned by violence and recrimination. The Democratic Party nominated James Buchanan, a proslavery advocate and longtime party stalwart from Pennsylvania. The young Republican Party ticket was headed by John C. Frémont. The American Party, in its final presidential contest, selected former president Millard Fillmore as its candidate. The strength of nativism in politics was waning, however, and Fillmore won only the state of Maryland. Frémont attracted cheering throngs as he traveled across the nation. Large numbers of women turned out to see Jessie Frémont, the first national candidate's wife to play a significant role in a campaign. Frémont carried most of the North and the West, establishing the Republican Party's dominance in those regions. Buchanan, claiming that he alone could preserve the Union, captured the South along with Pennsylvania, Indiana, and Illinois. Although Buchanan won only 45.2 percent of the popular vote, he received a comfortable majority in the electoral college, securing his victory. But even as the nation was becoming increasingly divided along sectional lines, President Buchanan did little to resolve these differences.

The *Dred Scott* Decision

Just two days after Buchanan's inauguration, the Supreme Court finally announced its decision in the *Dred Scott* case. Led by Chief Justice Roger Taney, a proslavery Southerner, the majority ruled that a slave was not a citizen and therefore could not sue in court. Indeed, Taney claimed that black men had no rights that a white man was bound to respect. The ruling annulled Scott's suit and meant that he and his wife remained enslaved. But the ruling went further. The *Dred Scott* **decision** declared that Congress had no constitutional authority to exclude slavery from any territory, thereby nullifying the Missouri Compromise and any future effort to restrict slavery's expansion. Buchanan was happy to have the fate of slavery taken out of the hands of Congress, hoping it would alleviate sectional tensions. His hopes proved unfounded. Instead of quieting the debate over slavery, the ruling further outraged many Northerners, who were now convinced that a Slave Power conspiracy had taken hold of the federal government.

Dred and Harriet Scott   This illustration of Dred Scott and his wife Harriet appeared in the June 27, 1857, issue of *Frank Leslie's Illustrated Newspaper*, four months after the Supreme Court ruled that the Scotts were not legally entitled to their freedom. In the 1830s, Dred and Harriet had received permission from their owners to marry, and they had two children.   Library of Congress

In 1858, when Stephen Douglas faced reelection to the U.S. Senate, the Republican Party nominated Abraham Lincoln to oppose him. The candidates participated in seven debates in which they explained their positions on slavery in the wake of the *Dred Scott* decision. Pointing to the landmark ruling, Lincoln asked Douglas how he could favor popular sovereignty, which allowed residents to keep slavery out of a territory, and yet support the *Dred Scott* decision, which protected slavery in all territories. Douglas devised a clever response, known as the Freeport Doctrine. He claimed that if residents did not adopt local legislation to protect slaveholders' property, they could thereby exclude slavery for all practical purposes. At the same time, he accused Lincoln of advocating "negro equality," a position that went well beyond his opponent's views. Lincoln did support economic opportunity for free blacks, but not political or social equality. Still, the Republican candidate did declare that "this government cannot endure permanently half slave and half free. . . . It will become all one thing or all the other."

The Lincoln-Douglas debates attracted national attention, but the Illinois legislature selected the state's senator. Narrowly controlled by Democrats, it returned Douglas to Washington. Although the senator retained his seat, he was chastened by how far the Democratic Party had tilted toward the South. So when President Buchanan tried to push the Lecompton Constitution through Congress, legitimating the proslavery government in Kansas, Douglas opposed him. The two struggled over control of the party, with Douglas winning a symbolic victory in January 1861 when Kansas was admitted as a free state. By then, however, the Democratic Party had split into southern and northern wings, and the nation was on the verge of civil war.

REVIEW & RELATE

• What factors contributed to the spread of antislavery sentiment in the North beyond committed abolitionists?

• How did the violence in Kansas in the mid-1850s reflect and intensify the growing sectional divide within the nation?

From Sectional Crisis to War

During the 1850s, a profusion of abolitionist lectures, conventions, and literature increased antislavery sentiment in the North. Mainstream as well as antislavery newspapers now covered rescues of fugitives, the *Dred Scott* case, and the bloody crisis in Kansas. Republican candidates in state and local elections also kept concerns about slavery's expansion and southern power alive. Nothing, however, riveted the nation's attention as much as John Brown's raid on the federal arsenal at Harpers Ferry, Virginia, in 1859. A year later, Republican Abraham Lincoln captured the White House. In the wake of his election, South Carolina seceded from the Union, agreeing with the president-elect that the nation could no longer exist half slave and half free.

John Brown's Raid

John Brown was committed not only to the abolition of slavery but also to complete equality between whites and blacks. A friend to many abolitionist leaders, Brown held views quite similar to those of David Walker, whose 1829 *Appeal* (see chapter 11) warned that slaves would eventually rise up and claim their freedom by force of arms. By 1859, following the bloody battles in Kansas, Brown believed strongly that direct action was the only answer. Deeply religious, he saw himself as the instrument of God's plan to liberate the enslaved.

Brown focused his efforts on the federal arsenal in **Harpers Ferry, Virginia**. With 18 followers—including 5 African Americans and 13 whites, including 3 of his sons—Brown planned to capture the arsenal and distribute the arms stored there to slaves in the surrounding area. He hoped this action would ignite a rebellion that would take down the plantation system. He tried to convince Frederick Douglass to join the venture, but Douglass, who admired Brown, considered it a foolhardy plan. However, the passionate rebel Brown did manage to persuade a small circle of white abolitionists to bankroll the effort.

On the night of October 16, 1859, Brown and his men successfully kidnapped some leading townsmen and seized the arsenal. Local residents were stunned but managed to alert authorities, and state militia swarmed into Harpers Ferry. The next day, federal troops arrived, led by Colonel Robert E. Lee. The rebels had failed to consider how they would alert slaves to the arsenal's capture so that slaves could gain access to the town and the weapons. With state and federal troops flooding into Harpers Ferry, Brown and his men were soon under siege, trapped in the arsenal. Fourteen rebels were killed, including two of Brown's sons. On October 18, Brown and three others were captured.

As word of the daring raid spread, Brown was hailed as a hero by devoted abolition-ists and depicted as a madman by southern planters. Southern whites were sure he was part of a widespread conspiracy led by power-hungry abolitionists. Federal authorities moved quickly to quell slaveholders' fears and end the episode. Brown rejected his lawyer's advice to plead insanity, and a local jury found him guilty of murder, criminal conspiracy, and treason on October 31. He was hanged on December 2, 1859.

John Brown's execution unleashed a massive outpouring of grief, anger, and uncertainty across the North. Abolitionists organized parades, demonstrations, bonfires, and tributes to the newest abolitionist martyr. Even many Quakers and other pacifists viewed John Brown as a hero for giving his life in the cause of emancipation. But most northern politicians and editors condemned the raid as a rash act that could only intensify sectional tensions.

 Online Document Project   Visions of John Brown
bedfordstmartins.com/hewittlawsonvalue

Among southern whites, fear and panic greeted the raid on Harpers Ferry, and the execution of John Brown did little to quiet the outrage they felt at having their peculiar institution once again threatened with violence. Southern intellectuals had developed a sophisticated proslavery argument that they believed demonstrated the benefits of bondage for African Americans and its superiority to the northern system of wage labor. Yet neither that argument nor any federal law or Supreme Court decision seemed able to deter antislavery activism. Not surprisingly, Americans on both sides of the sectional divide considered the 1860 presidential election critical to the nation's future.

The Election of 1860

Brown's hanging set the tone for the 1860 presidential campaign. The Republicans met in Chicago in May 1860 and made clear that they sought national prominence by distancing themselves from the more radical wing of the abolitionist movement. The party platform condemned John Brown along with southern "Border Ruffians" who initiated the violence in Kansas. The platform accepted slavery where it already existed, but continued to advocate its exclusion from western territories. Finally, the party plat-form argued forcefully for internal improvements and protective tariffs. On the third ballot, Republicans nominated Abraham Lincoln as their candidate for president. Recognizing the impossibility of gaining significant votes in the South, the party focused instead on winning large majorities in the Northeast and Midwest.

The Democrats met in Charleston, South Carolina. Although Stephen Douglas was the leading candidate, he could not assuage southern delegates who were still angry that Kansas had been admitted as a free state. Mississippi senator Jefferson Davis then introduced a resolution to protect slavery in the territories, but Douglas's northern sup-porters rejected it. When President Buchanan came out against Douglas, the Democratic convention ended without choosing a candidate. Instead, various factions held their own conventions. A group of largely northern Democrats met in Baltimore and nomi-nated Douglas. Southern or "cotton" Democrats selected John Breckinridge, the current vice president and a Kentucky slaveholder, on a platform that included the extension of slavery and the annexation of Cuba. The Constitutional Union Party, composed mainly of former southern Whigs, advocated "no political principle other than the Constitution of the country, the union of the states, and the enforcement of the laws." Its members nominated Senator John Bell of Tennessee, a onetime Whig.

Although Lincoln won barely 40 percent of the popular vote, he carried a clear majority in the electoral college. With the admission of Minnesota and Oregon to the Union in 1858 and 1859, free states now outnumbered slave states eighteen to fifteen, and Lincoln won all but one of them. Moreover, free states in the Middle Atlantic and Midwest were among the most populous in the nation and therefore had a large number of electoral votes. Douglas ran second to Lincoln in the popular vote, but Bell and Breckinridge captured more electoral votes than Douglas did. Despite a deeply divided electorate, Lincoln became president (Map 12.3).

Although many abolitionists were wary of the Republicans' position on slavery, especially their willingness to leave slavery alone where it already existed, most were nonetheless relieved at Lincoln's victory and hoped he would become more sympathetic to their views once in office. Meanwhile, southern whites, especially those in the deep South, were furious that a Republican had won the White House without carrying a single southern state.

The Lower South Secedes

On December 20, 1860, six weeks after Lincoln's election, the legislature of South Carolina announced that because "a sectional party" had engineered "the election of a man to the high office of President of the United States whose opinions and purposes are hostile to slavery, [the people of South Carolina dissolve their union with] the other states of North America." The first southern state had seceded from the Union, and its leaders now worked to convince neighboring states to join them. In early 1861, Mississippi, Florida, Alabama, Georgia, Louisiana, and Texas followed suit. Representatives from these states met on February 8 in Montgomery, Alabama,

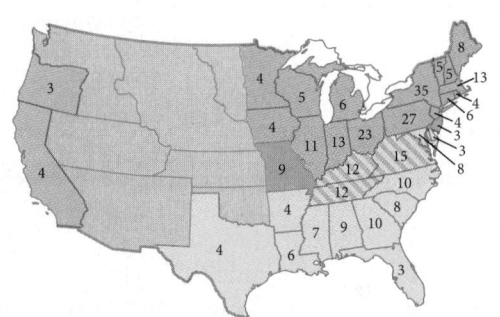

Candidate	Electoral Vote	Popular Vote	Percentage of Popular Vote
Abraham Lincoln (Republican)	180	1,866,452	39.9
John C. Breckinridge (Southern Democrat)	72	847,953	18.1
Stephen A. Douglas (Northern Democrat)	12	1,375,157	29.4
John Bell (Constitutional Union)	39	590,631	12.6

MAP 12.3

The Election of 1860 Four candidates vied for the presidency in 1860, and the voters split along clearly sectional lines. Although Stephen Douglas ran a vigorous campaign and gained votes in all regions of the country, he won a majority only in Missouri. Lincoln triumphed in the North and far West, and Breckinridge in most of the South.

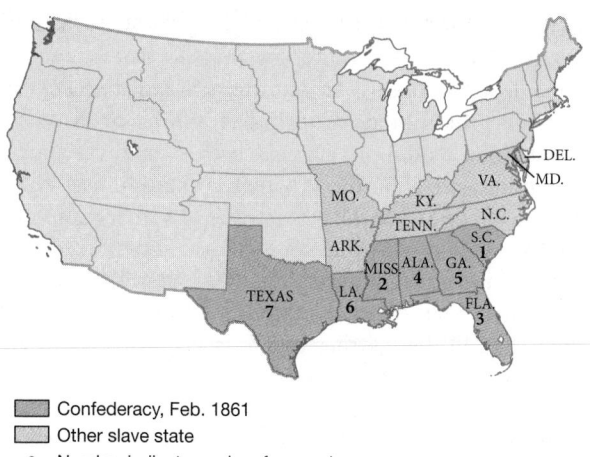

MAP 12.4
The Original Confederacy
Seven states in the Lower South seceded from the United States and formed the Confederate States of America in February 1861. While the original Confederacy was too limited in population and resources to defend itself against the U.S. government, its leaders hoped that other slave states would soon join them.

Confederacy, Feb. 1861
Other slave state
2   Number indicates order of secession

where they adopted a provisional constitution, elected Mississippi senator and slaveholder Jefferson Davis as their president, and established the **Confederate States of America** (Map 12.4).

Although President Buchanan was aware of developments in the South, he did nothing. His cabinet included three secessionists and two unionists, one of whom resigned in mid-December in frustration over Buchanan's failure to act. But Washington, D.C., was filled with southern sympathizers, who urged caution on an already timid president. Although some Northerners were shocked by the decision of South Carolina and its allies, many others supported their right to leave or believed they would return to the Union when they realized they could not survive economically on their own. Moreover, with Virginia, Maryland, and other Upper South slave states still part of the nation, the secession movement seemed both limited and unlikely to succeed.

Buchanan did urge Congress to find a compromise, and Kentucky senator John Crittenden proposed a plan that gained significant support. Indeed, Congress approved the first part of his plan, which called for a constitutional amendment to protect slavery from federal interference in any state where it already existed. But the second part of Crittenden's plan failed to pass after Republicans voiced their unanimous opposition. It would have extended the Missouri Compromise line (latitude 36°30′) to the California border and barred slavery north of that line. South of that line, however, slavery would be protected, including in any territories "acquired hereafter." Fearing that passage would encourage southern planters to once again seek territory in Cuba, Mexico, or Central America, Lincoln and the Republicans rejected the proposal. Despite the hopes of the Buchanan administration, it was becoming apparent that compromise was impossible. The Confederacy was not a fleeting disruption of the national order. It was the beginning of the Civil War.

REVIEW & RELATE

• How and why did John Brown's raid on Harpers Ferry move the country closer to civil war?

• Why did many in the South believe that the election of Abraham Lincoln was cause for secession?

Conclusion: The Coming of the Civil War

Dred Scott did not live to see Abraham Lincoln take the oath of office in March 1861. Following the Supreme Court's 1857 ruling, Scott was returned to Irene Emerson, who had married abolitionist Calvin Chaffee while awaiting the Supreme Court ruling. When that ruling was announced, Chaffee found himself the owner of the most well-known slave in America. He quickly returned Dred Scott and his family to his original owners, the Blow family. On May 26, 1857, the Blows freed the Scotts, so Dred Scott spent the last year and a half of his life as a free man. His wife Harriet and his daughters survived to see Lincoln inaugurated, the Confederacy defeated, and slavery abolished throughout the nation. Although they had to face a brutal civil war, they could take comfort from the fact that the *Dred Scott* case had helped to solidify northern support for both Lincoln and abolition.

John C. Frémont, like almost all slavery opponents, was outraged at the *Dred Scott* decision. He had helped to open the far West to settlement and bring California into the Union as a free state. Yet these achievements led to the demise of large numbers of Indians and fueled the battle over slavery. Despite the efforts of the Comanche and other Indian nations to fend off white encroachment, the U.S. government and eastern settlers claimed more and more territory in the 1840s and 1850s. By 1860, however, most white Americans thought less and less about Indian policy as they focused more and more on slavery.

Some Confederate planters imagined a nation that included Cuba, Nicaragua, and other slave territories. Meanwhile Northerners proved they would fight back. Those outraged by the Fugitive Slave Act had launched rescues of fugitives, and those appalled by Bleeding Kansas applauded John Brown's raid. These more militant activists were joined by thousands of more moderate Northerners who voted for Lincoln in the fall of 1860. By the time Abraham Lincoln took office in March 1861, the ever-widening political chasm brought the United States face-to-face with civil war.

Yet even as war erupted, the issue of slavery remained unresolved. When Frémont was appointed major general in charge of the Department of the West in 1861, he faced a chaotic situation as proslavery forces tried to wrest Missouri from Union control. In response to a Confederate military victory in August 1861 at Wilson's Creek in southwest Missouri, Frémont issued a limited emancipation proclamation, freeing the slaves of Missourians who supported the Confederacy. But the order flew in the face of Lincoln's efforts to keep Missouri from joining the Confederacy and was soon rescinded. Southern states had seceded and were willing to wage war to maintain slavery. Was the North willing to face prolonged battles and high casualties to reunite the nation and abolish human bondage once and for all?

Chapter Review

IDENTIFY KEY TERMS

Identify and explain the significance of each term below.

Oregon Trail (p. 301)

gold rush (p. 302)

Compromise of 1850 (p. 306)

Fugitive Slave Act of 1850 (p. 307)

Uncle Tom's Cabin (p. 310)

Kansas-Nebraska Act (p. 311)

Republican Party (p. 312)

Bleeding Kansas (p. 314)

Dred Scott **decision** (p. 314)

Harpers Ferry, Virginia (p. 316)

Confederate States of America (p. 319)

REVIEW & RELATE

Answer the focus questions from each section of the chapter.

1. Why did Americans go west in the 1830s and 1840s, and what was the journey like?

2. What groups competed for land and resources in the West? How did competition lead to violence?

3. What steps did legislators take in the 1840s and early 1850s to resolve the issue of the expansion of slavery?

4. How were slavery and American imperialist ambitions intertwined in the 1840s and 1850s?

5. What factors contributed to the spread of antislavery sentiment in the North beyond committed abolitionists?

6. How did the violence in Kansas in the mid-1850s reflect and intensify the growing sectional divide within the nation?

7. How and why did John Brown's raid on Harpers Ferry move the country closer to civil war?

8. Why did many in the South believe that the election of Abraham Lincoln was cause for secession?

ONLINE DOCUMENT PROJECTS

◆ **Visions of John Brown**
◆ **Sectional Politics and the Rise of the Republican Party**

After reading the primary sources in these document sets, answer the **Interpret the Evidence** questions to help you analyze each of the documents, and then answer the **Put It in Context** question(s) to help you relate the documents to the topics and themes you read about in the chapter.

bedfordstmartins.com/hewittlawsonvalue

TIMELINE OF EVENTS

1842	• John C. Frémont leads expedition along the Oregon Trail	**1854–1858**	• Period of violence in Bleeding Kansas
1843	• Marcus and Narcissa Whitman lead 1,000 Christian emigrants to the Oregon Territory	**1857**	• Supreme Court ruling in *Dred Scott* case
		1858	• Lincoln-Douglas debates
		October 16, 1859	• John Brown's raid on Harpers Ferry, Virginia
1845	• Texas granted statehood		
1846	• Dred Scott and his family sue for their freedom	**December 2, 1859**	• John Brown executed
1848	• Gold discovered at Sutter's Mill in California	**November 1860**	• Abraham Lincoln elected president
1850	• Compromise of 1850	**December 20, 1860**	• South Carolina secedes from the Union
	• Fugitive Slave Act passed	**January 1861**	• Mississippi, Florida, Alabama, Georgia, Louisiana, and Texas secede
1852	• Harriet Beecher Stowe publishes *Uncle Tom's Cabin*		
1854	• U.S.-Japanese treaty allows for mutual trading	**February 1861**	• Confederate States of America established
	• Republican Party founded	**March 1861**	• Lincoln inaugurated as president
May 1854	• Fugitive slave Anthony Burns returned to his owner		
	• Kansas-Nebraska Act passed		

13

LearningCurve
bedfordstmartins.com/hewittlawsonvalue
After reading the chapter, use LearningCurve
to retain what you've read.

Civil War
1861–1865

AMERICAN HISTORIES

Though born into slavery in 1818, by 1860 Frederick Douglass had become a
celebrated orator, editor, and abolitionist. He ensured his fame in 1845 with
publication of the *Narrative of the Life of Frederick Douglass*. In it, he
described his experiences of slavery in Maryland, his defiance against his
masters, and his eventual escape to New York in September 1838 with the
help of Anna Murray, a free black servant.

Frederick and Anna married in New York and then moved to New
Bedford, Massachusetts, and changed their last name to Douglass to
avoid capture. But in 1841 Frederick began lecturing for the American
Anti-Slavery Society, offering stirring accounts of his enslavement and
escape. By publishing his *Narrative* four years later, Douglass made his
capture even more likely, so in August 1845 he left for England, where
wildly enthusiastic audiences attended his lectures and supporters raised
funds to purchase his freedom. Douglass returned to Massachusetts in
1847, a truly free man.

A year later, Frederick moved to Rochester, New York, with Anna and their
five children to launch his abolitionist paper, the *North Star*. Over the next
decade, he became the most famous black abolitionist in the United States
and an outspoken advocate of women's rights. He also broke with the
Garrisonian branch of abolitionists by joining the Liberty Party and later the
Free-Soil and Republican parties. He was thus well placed when war erupted
in April 1861 to lobby President Lincoln to make emancipation a war aim and
enlist African Americans in the Union army.

Douglass embraced electoral politics and the use of military force to end
slavery. His greatest fear was that Lincoln was more committed to

323

reconstituting the Union than to abolishing slavery. But after the president issued the Emancipation Proclamation in January 1863, Douglass spoke enthusiastically on its behalf. At the same time, he continued to believe that military service was essential for black men to demonstrate their patriotism. His stirring editorial "Men of Color, to Arms" was turned into a recruiting poster, and he urged his own sons to join the Massachusetts Fifty-fourth Colored Infantry, one of the first African American regiments. But Douglass also protested discrimination against black troops and lobbied for federal protections of black civil rights.

Like Douglass, Rose O'Neal was born on a Maryland plantation, but she was white and free. Her father was likely John O'Neal, a planter who was slain by a slave in 1817, when Rose was four years old. In early adolescence, she moved to Washington, D.C., with her older sister. They lived with an aunt who ran a fashionable boardinghouse near Capitol Hill. The boarders included John C. Calhoun, whose states' rights views Rose eagerly embraced. Intrigued by the lively political debates that marked the Jacksonian era, she was also schooled in the social graces. Charming and beautiful, Rose was welcomed into elite social circles, including invitations from Dolley Madison. In 1835 she married Robert Greenhow, a cultivated Virginian who worked for the State Department.

Rose O'Neal Greenhow quickly became a favorite Washington hostess. Like Dolley Madison, she entertained congressmen, cabinet ministers, and foreign diplomats with a wide range of views. In the midst of this social and political whirl, Rose gave birth to four daughters. Yet she also remained deeply invested in her husband's career. She assisted Robert in the 1840s as he researched U.S. land claims in the Pacific Northwest. Ardent proslavery expansionists, the Greenhows supported efforts to acquire Cuba, and in 1850 they traveled to Mexico City to study California land claims. When Robert died in 1854, Rose moved into a smaller house in Washington but continued to entertain political leaders and sustained friendships with powerful men like President James Buchanan.

In May 1861, just as the Civil War commenced, a U.S. army captain about to join the Confederate cause recruited Greenhow to head an espionage ring in Washington, D.C. With her close ties to southern sympathizers working in government offices and her extensive social network, Greenhow gathered important intelligence on Union political and military plans. Although she initially avoided suspicion, by August Greenhow was investigated and placed under house arrest. When she continued to smuggle out letters, embarrassing Union officials, she was sent to the Old Capitol Prison in January 1862. Once again, Greenhow managed to transmit information and riled up the other prisoners. In June, she was exiled to Richmond, where Confederate president Jefferson Davis hailed her as a hero and awarded her $2,500.

Union family in camp of Thirty-first Pennsylvania Infantry near Washington, D.C., 1862. Library of Congress

THE AMERICAN HISTORIES of Frederick Douglass and Rose O'Neal Greenhow were shaped by the sectional conflict over slavery that culminated in the Civil War. Both were born on Maryland plantations, one as a slave and the other a daughter of slave owners. Both honed their innate talents, one as an orator and a writer, the other as a hostess and gatherer of intelligence. And both embraced the Civil War as the last best hope for national salvation, one on the side of union and emancipation, the other on the side of secession and slavery. They were among hundreds of thousands of Americans—men and women, black and white, North and South—who saw the war as a means to achieve their goals: a free nation, a haven for slavery, or a reunited country.

The Nation Goes to War

When Abraham Lincoln took office, seven states in the Lower South had already formed the Confederate States of America, and the threat of more secessions remained. Lincoln had promised not to interfere with slavery where it already existed, but many southern whites were unconvinced by such assurances. By seceding, the southern slaveholding class also proclaimed its unwillingness to become a permanent minority in the nation. Still, not all slave states were yet willing to cut their ties to the nation, and Northerners, too, disagreed about the consequences of secession and the appropriate response to it. Once fighting erupted, however, preparations for war became the primary focus in both the North and the South.

The South Embraces Secession

Confederate president Davis joined other planters in arguing that Lincoln's victory jeopardized the future of slavery and that secession was, therefore, a necessity. Advocates of secession contended that the federal government had failed to implement fully the Fugitive Slave Act and the *Dred Scott* decision. With Republicans in power, they were convinced that the administration would do even less to support southern interests. White Southerners also feared that a Republican administration might inspire a massive uprising of slaves. In the aftermath of John Brown's raid on Harpers Ferry, one southern newspaper warned that the region was "slumbering over a volcano, whose smoldering fires may, at any quiet starry midnight, blacken the social sky with the smoke of desolation and death." Secession would allow whites to maintain greater control over the South's black population.

Slaveholders were also anxious about the loyalty of white Southerners who did not own slaves. "I mistrust our own people more than I fear all of the efforts of the Abolitionists," claimed a South Carolina politician in 1859. He went on to argue that by denouncing social and economic inequality, Republicans might recruit nonslaveholders to their party and thereby create a "contest for slavery . . . in the South between people of the South." Secession would effectively isolate southern yeomen from potential Republican allies.

When Lincoln was inaugurated, legislators in the Upper South still hoped a compromise could be reached. Although many Northerners believed that the secessionists needed to be punished, Lincoln sought to bring the Confederates back into the Union without using military force. Yet he also sought to demonstrate Union strength to curtail further secessions. He focused on **Fort Sumter** in South Carolina's Charleston harbor, where a small Union garrison was running low on food and medicine. On April 8, 1861, Lincoln dispatched ships to the fort but promised to use force only if the Confederates blocked his peaceful effort to send supplies.

Lincoln's action presented the Confederate government with a choice. It could attack the Union vessels and bear responsibility for starting a war, or it could permit a "foreign power" to maintain a fort in its territory. President Davis and his advisers chose the aggressive course, demanding the unconditional surrender of Fort Sumter before supplies arrived. The commanding officer refused, and on April 12 Confederate guns opened fire. Two days later, Fort Sumter surrendered. On April 15, Lincoln called for 75,000 volunteers to put down the southern insurrection.

The declaration of war led whites in the Upper South to reconsider secession. Some small farmers and landless whites in the region were drawn to Republican promises of free labor and free soil and remained suspicious of the goals and power of secessionist planters. Moreover, their land sat in the direct path of military engagement. Yet the vast majority of southern whites, rich and poor, defined their liberty in relation to black bondage. They feared that Republicans would free the slaves and introduce racial amalgamation in the South.

Fearing more secessions, Lincoln used the powers of his office to keep the border states that allowed slavery—Maryland, Delaware, Missouri, and Kentucky—in the Union. He waived the right of habeas corpus (which protects citizens against arbitrary arrest and detention), jailed secessionists, arrested state legislators, and limited freedom of the press. Despite these measures, four more slave states—North Carolina, Virginia, Tennessee, and Arkansas—seceded. Of these, Virginia was by far the most significant. It was strategically located near the nation's capital. Richmond was also home to the South's largest iron manufacturer, which could produce weapons and munitions. By June 1861, the Confederacy had moved its capital to Richmond in recognition of Virginia's importance.

When the first seven states seceded, outrage and anxiety escalated in the North. Textile manufacturers feared the permanent loss of the southern cotton crop, and bankers worried whether Confederates would repay their loans. In northeastern cities, stock prices plummeted, banks shut their doors, factories laid off workers, and unsold goods piled up on docks. But the firing on Fort Sumter prompted many Northerners to line up behind Lincoln's call for war. Manufacturers and merchants, once intent upon maintaining economic links with the South, now rushed to support the president, while northern workers, including immigrants, responded to Lincoln's call for volunteers. They assumed that the Union, with its greater resources and manpower, could quickly set the nation right. New York editor Horace Greeley proclaimed, "Jeff Davis and Co. will be swingin' from the battlements at Washington at least by the 4th of July." A Philadelphia newspaper echoed, "This much-ado about nothing will end in a month." Greeley and his fellow journalists were sadly mistaken.

Both Sides Prepare for War

At the onset of the war, the Union held a decided advantage in resources and population. The Union states held more than 60 percent of the U.S. population, while the Confederate states held less than 40 percent. And the Confederacy included several million slaves who would not be armed for combat. The Union also outstripped the Confederacy in manufacturing and even led the South in agricultural production. The North's many miles of railroad track ensured greater ease in moving troops and supplies. And the Union could launch far more ships to blockade southern ports (Figure 13.1).

Yet Union forces were less prepared for war than were the Confederates, who had been organizing troops and gathering munitions for months. To match their efforts, Winfield Scott, general in chief of the U.S. army, told Lincoln he would need at least 300,000 men committed to serve for two or three years. But the president, who feared unnerving Northerners, asked for only 75,000 volunteers for three months. Recruits poured into state militias, and thousands more offered their services directly to the federal government. Yet rather than forming a powerful national army led by seasoned officers, Lincoln left recruitment, organization, and training largely to the states. The

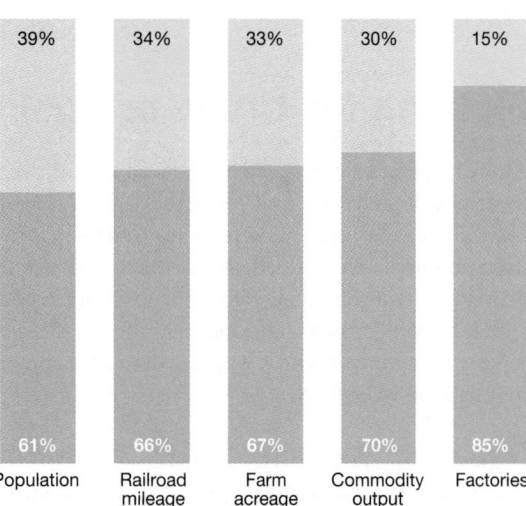

FIGURE 13.1
Economies of the North and South, 1860 This figure provides graphic testimony to the enormous advantages in resources the North held on the eve of the Civil War. Perhaps most surprisingly, the North led the South in farm acreage as well as factories and commodity output. Over four years of war, the North's significantly larger population would also prove crucial.

Source: Data from Stanley Engerman, "The Economic Impact of the Civil War," in *The Reinterpretation of American Economic History*, ed. Robert W. Fogel and Stanley Engerman (New York: Harper and Row).

39%	34%	33%	30%	15%
61%	66%	67%	70%	85%
Population	Railroad mileage	Farm acreage	Commodity output	Factories

☐ North ☐ South

result was disorganization and the appointment of new officers based more on political connections than on military expertise.

Confederate leaders also initially relied on state militia units and volunteers, but they prepared for a prolonged war from the start. Before the firing on Fort Sumter, President Davis signed up 100,000 volunteers for a year's service. The labor provided by slaves allowed a large proportion of white working-age men to volunteer for military service. And Southerners knew they were likely to be fighting mainly on home territory, where they had expert knowledge of the terrain. When the final four states joined the Confederacy, the southern army also gained important military leadership. It ultimately recruited 280 West Point graduates, including Robert E. Lee, Thomas "Stonewall" Jackson, James Longstreet, and others who had proved their mettle in the Mexican-American War.

The South's advantages were apparent in the first major battle of the war. But Confederate troops were also aided by information on Union plans sent by Rose Greenhow. Confederate forces were thus well prepared when 30,000 Union troops marched on northern Virginia on July 21, 1861. At the Battle of Bull Run (or Manassas), 22,000 Confederates repelled the Union attack. During the fighting, 800 men lost their lives, giving Americans their first taste of the carnage that lay ahead. Civilians from Washington who traveled to the battle site to view the combat had to flee for their lives to escape Confederate artillery.

Despite Union defeats at Bull Run and Wilson's Creek, Missouri, in August 1861, the Confederate army did not follow up with major strikes against Union forces. Meanwhile the Union navy began blockading the South's deepwater ports. When the armies settled into winter camps in 1861–1862, both sides recognized that the war was likely to be a long struggle demanding a far greater commitment of men and resources than anyone had imagined just months earlier.

REVIEW & RELATE

- What steps did Lincoln take to prevent war? Why were they ineffective?
- What advantages and disadvantages did each side have at the onset of the war?

Fighting for Union or against Slavery?

The Union and the Confederacy faced very different tasks in the war. The South had to defend its territory and force the federal government to halt military action. The North had to bring the Confederacy to its knees by invading the South and isolating it from potential allies abroad. While most northern leaders believed that the nation could be reunited without challenging the institution of slavery, enslaved Southerners immediately looked for ways to loosen their bonds. Meanwhile northern abolitionists worked to convince Lincoln and Congress that only emancipation could resolve the problems that had led to war.

Debating the Role of African Americans

The outbreak of war intensified debates over abolition. Some 225,000 African Americans lived in the free states, and many offered their services in the hopes that victory would lead to the emancipation of southern slaves. At a recruitment meeting in Cleveland,

African American leaders proclaimed, "Today, as in the times of '76, we are ready to go forth and do battle in the common cause of our country." But Secretary of War Simon Cameron had no intention of calling up black soldiers, and some local officials prohibited African American recruitment meetings.

Northern optimism about a quick victory contributed to the rejection of black soldiers. Union leaders also feared that whites would not enlist if they had to serve alongside blacks. In addition, Lincoln and his advisers were initially wary of letting a war to preserve the Union become a war against slavery, and they feared that any further threat to slavery might drive the four slave states that remained in the Union into the Confederacy. African Americans and their supporters nevertheless believed that the war opened a door to freedom and that continued pressure might convince Union leaders to change their minds. As activist Amy Post proclaimed, "The abolitionists surely have a job to do now in influencing and directing the bloody struggle, that it may end in Emancipation."

For their part, southern slaves quickly realized that the presence of Union troops made freedom a distinct possibility. Enslaved workers living near battle sites circulated information on Union troop movements. Then, as slaveholders in Virginia began to send male slaves to more distant plantations for fear of losing them, some slaves chose to flee. Those who could headed to Union camps, where they provided labor as well as knowledge of the local terrain and the location of Confederate forces. Slave owners, in turn, followed fugitives into Union camps and demanded their return. Some Union commanders denied slaves entrance or returned them to their masters, but a few Union officers saw the value of embracing these fugitives.

On the night of May 23, 1861, for example, three Virginia slaves paddled upriver to the Union outpost at Fort Monroe, requesting sanctuary from General Benjamin Butler. Butler was no abolitionist, but he realized that slaves were valuable assets to the Union cause and so offered them military protection. He claimed fugitive slaves as **contraband** of war: property forfeited by the act of rebellion. As news of Butler's decision spread, more runaways sought refuge at Fort Monroe. Within four days, another sixty-seven slaves had arrived at "Freedom Fort."

Lincoln endorsed Butler's policy as a legitimate tactic of war because it allowed the Union to strike at the institution of slavery without proclaiming a general emancipation that might prompt the border states with slaves to secede. Congress expanded Butler's policy. On August 6, 1861, it passed a confiscation act, proclaiming that any slave owner whose bondsmen were used by the Confederate army would lose all claim to those slaves. Although it was far from a clear-cut declaration of freedom, the act spurred the hopes of abolitionists.

Fighting for the Right to Fight

From the start, the Union army recruited a wide array of Americans. Indeed, nearly every ethnic and racial group served in Union ranks except African Americans. German and Irish immigrants; Catholic, Protestant, and Jewish Americans; native-born whites from the Northeast and Midwest; and Mexican American soldiers in the West all fought with the Union army. In an effort to eliminate this one exception, abolitionists had long argued that African Americans would make excellent soldiers, and Radical Republicans in Congress emphasized the military advantages of allowing black enlistment. As Massachusetts senator Charles Sumner explained, "You will observe that I propose no crusade for abolition. [Emancipation] is to be presented strictly as a measure of military necessity."

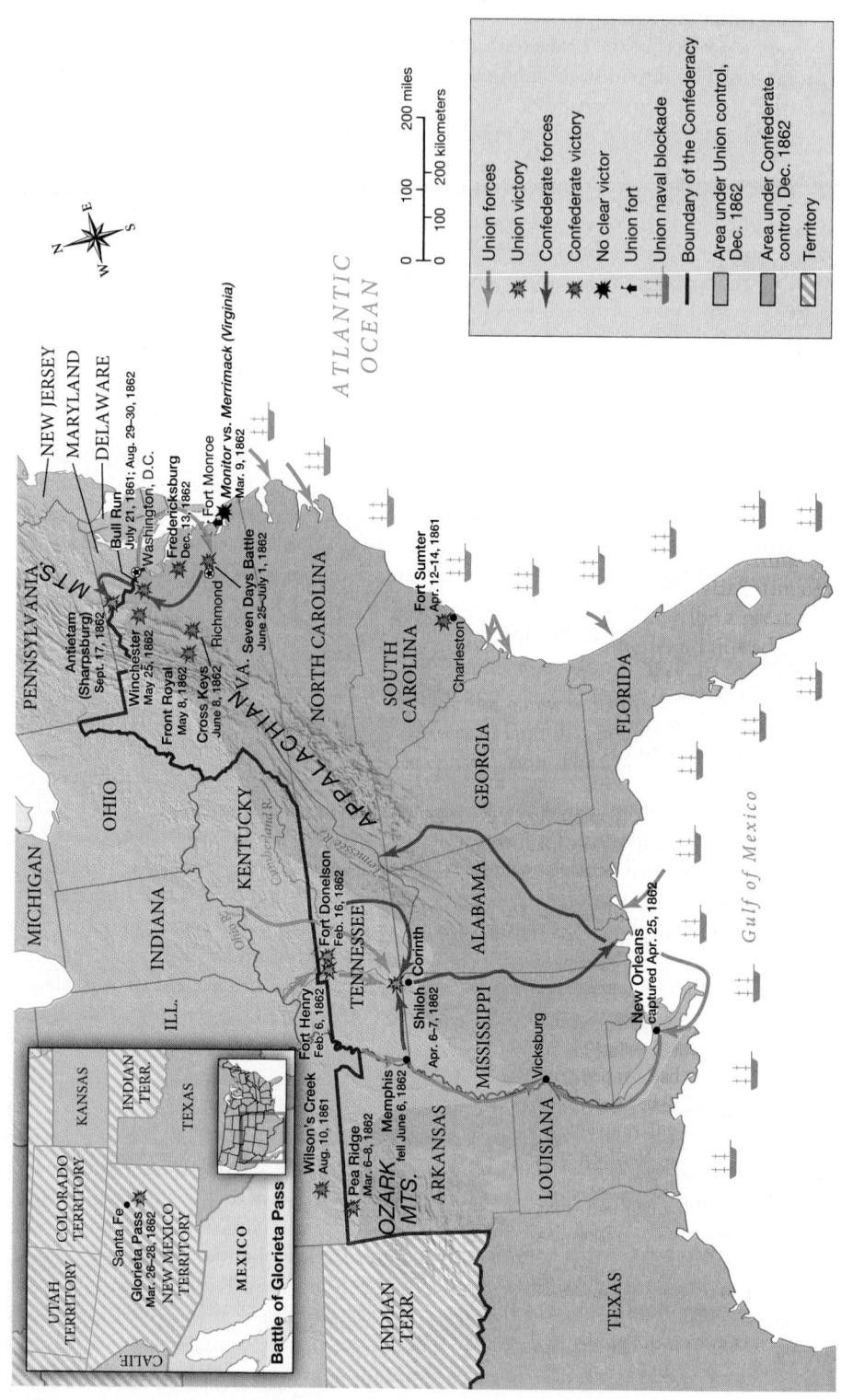

| Union forces |
| Union victory |
| Confederate forces |
| Confederate victory |
| No clear victor |
| Union fort |
| Union naval blockade |
| Boundary of the Confederacy |
| Area under Union control, Dec. 1862 |
| Area under Confederate control, Dec. 1862 |
| Territory |

0   100   200 miles
0   100   200 kilometers

ATLANTIC OCEAN

Gulf of Mexico

NEW JERSEY
MARYLAND
DELAWARE
PENNSYLVANIA
Bull Run
July 21, 1861; Aug. 29–30, 1862
Fredericksburg
Dec. 13, 1862
Washington, D.C.
Fort Monroe
Monitor vs. Merrimack (Virginia)
Mar. 9, 1862
Antietam (Sharpsburg)
Sept. 17, 1862
Winchester
May 25, 1862
Front Royal
May 8, 1862
Cross Keys
June 8, 1862
Richmond
Seven Days Battle
June 25–July 1, 1862
N.VA.
NORTH CAROLINA
SOUTH CAROLINA
Fort Sumter
Apr. 12–14, 1861
Charleston
GEORGIA
FLORIDA
OHIO
KENTUCKY
APPALACHIAN MTS.
Cumberland R.
Tennessee R.
Ohio R.
MICHIGAN
INDIANA
ILL.
Fort Donelson
Feb. 16, 1862
Fort Henry
Feb. 6, 1862
TENNESSEE
Corinth
Shiloh
Apr. 6–7, 1862
ALABAMA
MISSISSIPPI
Vicksburg
LOUISIANA
New Orleans
captured Apr. 25, 1862
Memphis
fell June 6, 1862
ARKANSAS
OZARK MTS.
Pea Ridge
Mar. 6–8, 1862
Wilson's Creek
Aug. 10, 1861
TEXAS
INDIAN TERR.

UTAH TERRITORY
COLORADO TERRITORY
KANSAS
INDIAN TERR.
TEXAS
NEW MEXICO TERRITORY
Santa Fe
Glorieta Pass
Mar. 26–28, 1862
MEXICO
CALIF.

Battle of Glorieta Pass

< MAP 13.1

Early Civil War Battles, 1861–1862   In 1861 and 1862, the Confederate army stunned Union forces with a series of dramatic victories in Virginia and Missouri. However, the Union army won a crucial victory at Antietam (Sharpsburg); gained control of Confederate territory in Tennessee, Arkansas, and Mississippi; fended off Confederate efforts to gain New Mexico Territory; and established a successful naval blockade of Confederate ports.

Meanwhile American Indians fought on both sides. The Comanches negotiated with both Union and Confederate agents while raiding the Texas frontier for horses and cattle. The Confederacy gained the greatest support from slaveholding Indians who had earlier been removed from the Southeast. The Cherokee general Stand Watie led a pan-Indian force that battled alongside white Confederate troops on the western frontier. However, most members of the Cherokee and other southeastern tribes, along with Osage, Delaware, and Seneca Indians, sided with the Union. Ely Parker, a Seneca sachem and engineer, rose to become a lieutenant colonel in the Union army, serving with General Ulysses S. Grant.

While some Indian regiments were rejected by state officials, African Americans were barred from enlisting by federal authority. In 1862, however, a series of military defeats helped transform northern attitudes. Although Union forces gained ground along the southern Mississippi River, they lost important battles farther north. In the spring of 1862, Confederate troops led by Stonewall Jackson won a series of stunning victories against three Union armies in Virginia's Shenandoah Valley. That June and July, General Robert E. Lee fought General George B. McClellan to a standstill in the Seven Days Battle near Richmond. Then in August, Lee, Jackson, and General James Longstreet joined forces to defeat Union troops at the Second Battle of Bull Run (Map 13.1).

As the war turned against the North, the North turned against slavery. In April 1862, Congress approved a measure to abolish slavery in the District of Columbia, symbolizing a significant shift in Union sentiment. During that bloody summer, Congress passed a second confiscation act, declaring that the slaves of anyone who supported the Confederacy should be "forever free of their servitude, and not again held as slaves." Finally, Congress passed a militia act that allowed "persons of African descent" to be employed in "any military or naval service for which they may be found competent." Lincoln quickly signed these acts into law.

Yet support for the 1862 militia act also built on Union victories. In April 1862, a Union blockade led to the capture of New Orleans, while the **Battle of Shiloh** in Tennessee provided the army entrée to the Mississippi valley. There Union troops came face-to-face with slavery. Few of these soldiers were abolitionists, but many were shocked by what they saw. At some captured plantations, soldiers discovered instruments used to torture slaves. One Union soldier reported he had seen "enough of the horror of slavery to make one an Abolitionist forever." Local blacks also provided valuable intelligence to Union officers.

The rising death toll also increased support for African American enlistment. The Battle of Shiloh was the bloodiest battle in American history up to that point. Earlier battles had resulted in a few hundred or even a few thousand casualties, but Shiloh raised the carnage to a new level. General Grant marveled, "I saw an open field . . . so covered with dead that it would have been possible to walk across the clearing, in any direction, stepping only on dead bodies without a foot touching the ground." As the war continued, such deadly battles became routine. The Union army would need every available man to sustain its effort against the Confederates.

Amid the roller coaster of victory and defeat, African Americans gave practical force to the 1862 militia act. In October 1862, a group of African American soldiers in the First Kansas Colored Volunteers repulsed Confederates at a battle in Missouri. Early the next year, another black regiment—the Massachusetts Fifty-fourth—attracted recruits from across the North. Frederick Douglass helped recruit a hundred men from New York State, including his three sons—Charles, Lewis, and Frederick Jr. In the South, Colonel Thomas Wentworth Higginson and other abolitionist officers organized former slaves into units like the First South Carolina Volunteers. By late 1863, tens of thousands of African American soldiers were serving with distinction and contributing to key northern victories.

Union Politicians Consider Emancipation

By the fall of 1862, African Americans and abolitionists had gained widespread support for emancipation as a necessary goal of the war. In making a final decision, Lincoln and his cabinet had to consider numerous factors. Embracing abolition as a war aim would likely prevent international recognition of southern independence, a significant advantage; but it might also arouse deep animosity in the slaveholding border states and drive them from the Union.

International recognition was critical to the Confederacy. Support from European nations might persuade the North to accept southern independence. More immediately, recognition would ensure markets for southern agriculture and access to manufactured goods and war materiel. Confederate officials were especially focused on Britain, the leading market for cotton and a potentially important supplier of industrial products. President Davis considered sending Rose Greenhow to England to promote the Confederate cause among British textile workers and government officials, who were concerned about disruptions to their economy caused by the Union blockade.

Fearing that the British might capitulate to Confederate pressure, abolitionist lecturers toured Britain, reminding residents of their early leadership in the antislavery cause. The abolitionists recognized that the Union's formal commitment to emancipation could give the North an edge in the battle for public opinion and prevent diplomatic recognition of the Confederacy. By the summer of 1862, Lincoln agreed. But he wanted to proclaim emancipation as a sign of Union strength, not weakness, so he waited for a victory before making a formal announcement.

A series of Union defeats in the summer of 1862 had allowed Lee to march his army into Union territory in Maryland. On September 17, Longstreet joined Lee in a fierce battle along Antietam Creek as Union troops brought the Confederate advance to a standstill near the town of Sharpsburg. Union forces suffered more than 12,000 casualties and the Confederates more than 10,000, the bloodiest single day in U.S. warfare. Yet because Lee and his army were forced to retreat, Lincoln claimed Antietam as a great victory. Five days later, the president announced his preliminary **Emancipation Proclamation** to the assembled cabinet. He held firm despite a bloody defeat at Fredericksburg, Virginia, that December, when Confederate troops inflicted nearly 13,000 Union casualties while suffering only 5,000 of their own.

On January 1, 1863, Lincoln signed the final edict, proclaiming that slaves in areas still in rebellion were "forever free" and inviting them to enlist in the Union army. In many ways, the proclamation was a conservative document, applying only to slaves largely beyond the reach of federal power. Its provisions exempted from emancipation the 450,000 slaves in the loyal border states, 275,000 slaves in Union-occupied Tennessee, and tens of thousands more in Louisiana and Virginia. The proclamation also justified the abolition of southern slavery on military, not moral, grounds.

Despite its limits, the Emancipation Proclamation prompted joyous "Watch Meetings" as abolitionists and free blacks met to give thanks as the edict took effect. At black churches across the North, crowds sang "Glory Hallelujah," "John Brown's Body," and "Marching On." If the Union proved victorious, the Emancipation Proclamation promised a total transformation of southern society.

REVIEW & RELATE

- What arguments did each side make in the debate over African American enlistment in the Union army?
- How and why did the Civil War become a war to end slavery?

War Transforms the North and the South

For soldiers caught in the midst of battle, for civilians caught between warring armies, and for ordinary families seeking to survive the upheaval, political pronouncements did little to alleviate the dangers they faced. The extraordinary death tolls in Civil War battles shocked Americans on both sides. On the home front, the war created labor shortages and severe inflation in both the North and the South. It initially disrupted industrial and agricultural production as men were called to service, but the North recovered fairly quickly by building on its prewar industrial base and technological know-how. In the South, manufacturing increased, with some enslaved laborers pressed into service as industrial workers. But pulling slaves away from agricultural work only created more problems on plantations, which were already suffering labor shortages. These changing circumstances required women to take on new responsibilities on the home front and the battlefront. But the dramatic transformations also inspired dissent and protest as rising death tolls and rising prices made the costs of war ever clearer.

Life and Death on the Battlefield

Few soldiers entered the conflict knowing what to expect. A young private wrote home that his idea of combat had been that the soldiers "would all be in line, all standing in a nice level field fighting, a number of ladies taking care of the wounded, etc., etc., but it isn't so."

 Online Document Project　Civil War Letters
bedfordstmartins.com/hewittlawsonvalue

Even where traditional forms of engagement did occur, improved weaponry turned them into scenes of carnage. Although individual soldiers could fire only a few times a minute, their Enfield and Springfield rifles were murderously effective at a quarter-mile distance. New conical bullets that expanded to fit the grooves of rifles proved far more accurate and more deadly than older round bullets. Minié balls that exploded on impact also increased fatalities. By mid-1863, the rival armies relied on heavy fortifications, elaborate trenches, and distant mortar and artillery fire when they could, but the casualties continued to rise, especially since the trenches proved to be a breeding ground for disease.

The hardships and discomforts of war extended beyond combat itself. As General Lee complained before the fighting at Antietam, many soldiers went into battle in ragged uniforms and without shoes. In the First Battle of Bull Run, a Georgia major reported that more than one hundred of his men were barefoot, "many of whom left bloody foot-prints among the thorns and briars through which they rushed." Rations, too, ran short. Food was dispensed sporadically and was often spoiled. Many Union troops survived primarily on an unleavened biscuit called hardtack as well as small amounts of meat and beans and enormous quantities of coffee. At least their diet improved over the course of the war as the Union supply system grew more efficient. Confederate troops, however, subsisted increasingly on cornmeal and fatty meat. As early as 1862, Confederate soldiers were gathering food from the haversacks of Union dead.

"There is more dies by sickness than gets killed," a recruit from New York complained in 1861. Indeed, for every soldier who died as a result of combat, three died of disease. Measles, dysentery, typhoid, and malaria killed thousands who drank contaminated water, ate tainted food, and were exposed to the elements. Prisoner-of-war camps were especially deadly locales. Debilitating fevers in a camp near Danville, Virginia, spread to the town, killing civilians as well as soldiers. In the fall of 1862, yellow fever and malaria killed nearly five hundred in Wilmington, Delaware, as infected soldiers built fortifications along the beaches.

African American troops fared worst of all. The death rate from disease for black Union soldiers was nearly three times greater than that for white Union soldiers, reflecting their generally poorer health upon enlistment, the hard labor they performed, and the minimal medical care they received in the field. Those who began their army careers in contraband camps fared even worse, with a camp near Nashville losing a quarter of its residents to death in just three months in 1864.

Even for white soldiers, medical assistance was primitive. Antibiotics did not exist, antiseptics were still unknown, and a perennial shortage of anesthetics meant that amputations were frequently conducted without it. Union soldiers did gain some access to better medical care from the **U.S. Sanitary Commission**, which was established by the federal government in June 1861 to improve and coordinate the medical care of Union soldiers. Nonetheless, a commentator accurately described most field hospitals as "dirty dens of butchery and horror."

The need to bury the dead after battle was also a gruesome task. Early in the war, officers and enlisted men tried to recover and bury individual remains, but this practice proved unfeasible given the vast numbers killed. Instead, mass graves provided the final resting place for many soldiers on both sides. As the horrors of battle sank in and enlisted men discovered the inadequacies of food, sanitation, and medical care, large numbers of soldiers deserted. As the number of volunteers declined and the number of deserters rose, both the Confederate and the Union governments were eventually forced to institute conscription laws to draft men into service.

The Northern Economy Booms

As the war dragged on, the North's economic advantages became more apparent. The Union could provide more arms, food, and clothing to its troops and more of the necessities of life for families back home. Indeed, the Civil War quickened the industrial development of the North that had begun in the early nineteenth century. By 1860 manufacturing establishments in the region outnumbered those in the South six to one, with 1.3 million industrial workers in the North compared with only 110,000 in the South. Northern factories flourished as they turned out weapons, ammunition, blankets, clothing, and shoes, and shipyards built the fleets that blockaded southern ports.

Initially, the effects of the war on northern industry were little short of disastrous. Raw cotton for textiles was no longer available, southern planters stopped ordering shoes, and trade fell off precipitously in seaport cities. By 1863, however, the economic picture had improved dramatically. Coal mining and iron production boomed in Pennsylvania. In New England, woolen manufacturing replaced cotton, and the shoe industry thrived on orders from the army. Merchants dealing in war materiel made particularly handsome profits.

The economic boom was linked to a vast expansion in the federal government's activities. Direct orders from the War Office for blankets, firearms, boots, and other goods fueled the industrial surge. The government also granted large contracts to northern railroads to carry troops and supplies. With southern Democrats out of federal office, Congress increased the protection of northern industries by passing a steep tariff on imported manufactured goods. The government also hired thousands of "sewing women," who worked under contract in their homes (often in crowded tenements) to make uniforms for Union soldiers. Other women joined the federal labor force as clerical workers, who sustained the expanding bureaucracy by handling the increasing amounts of government-generated paperwork.

That paperwork multiplied exponentially when the federal government created a national currency and a national banking system. Before the Civil War, private banks (chartered by the states) issued their own banknotes, which were used in most economic transactions. During the war, Congress revolutionized this system, giving the federal government the power to create currency, issue federal charters to banks, and take on national debt (which totaled $2 billion by the war's end). The government used its new powers to flood the nation with treasury bills, commonly called **greenbacks**. The federal budget mushroomed as well—from $63 million in 1860 to nearly $1.3 billion in 1865. By the end of the war, the federal bureaucracy had grown to be the nation's largest single employer.

These federal initiatives provided a tremendous stimulus to industry, and northern manufacturers greeted them, on the whole, with enthusiasm. But they faced one daunting problem: a shortage of labor. Over half a million workers left their jobs to serve in the Union army, and others were hired by the expanding federal bureaucracy. Manufacturers dealt with the labor shortage primarily by mechanizing more tasks and by increasing the employment of native-born women and children and recently arrived immigrants. Mechanization advanced quickly in the clothing and shoe industries, allowing more jobs to be filled by unskilled or semiskilled workers. Industrialists also formed organizations such as the Boston Foreign Emigrant Aid Society to encourage European migration, which had fallen off sharply in the first two years of the war. By 1863 the number of immigrants—mostly Irish, German, and British—had reached pre-1860 levels and continued to increase. Combining the lower wages paid to women and immigrants with production speedups, manufacturers improved their profits while advancing the Union cause.

Urbanization and Industrialization in the South

Although Southerners had gone to war to protect an essentially rural lifestyle, several factors encouraged the growth of industry and cities during the war. The creation of a large governmental and military bureaucracy brought thousands of Southerners to the Confederate capital of Richmond. Refugees merely trickled into cities during the early years of the war, but by 1863 they were flooding Atlanta, Savannah, and Mobile.

Industrialization also contributed to urban growth. Military necessity spurred southern industrialization. At the beginning of the war, the South contained only 15 percent of the factories in the United States. But unable to buy industrial goods from the North and limited in its trade with Europe, the South was forced to industrialize. By January 1863, the huge Tredegar Iron Works in Richmond employed more than 2,500 men, black and white. A factory to produce cannons opened in Selma, Alabama, where more than 10,000 people worked in war industries. According to a local newspaper, clothing and shoe factories had "sprung up almost like magic" in Natchez and Jackson, Mississippi. War widows and orphans, enslaved blacks, and white men too old or injured to fight were recruited for industrial labor in many cities.

The vast expansion of the South's cities and industry enhanced class consciousness during the war. When Virginia legislators introduced a bill in the fall of 1863 to control food prices, Richmond workers hailed it by voicing their resentment toward the rich. "From the fact that he consumes all and produces nothing," they proclaimed, "we know that without [our] labor and production the man with money could not exist." Workers also criticized lavish balls hosted by the wives of wealthy industrialists, planters, and politicians during the war. Women like Mary Boykin Chesnut, a planter's wife, insisted that such events were necessary to maintain morale and demonstrate that the South was far from defeated. But the *Richmond Enquirer* captured the views of the laboring class, arguing that these events were "shameful displays of indifference to national calamity . . . a mockery of the misery and desolation that covers the land."

Women Aid the War Effort

Women of all classes contributed to the Union and Confederate war effort in numerous ways. Thousands filled jobs in agriculture, industry, and the government that were traditionally held by men. Others sought to assist the war effort more directly, by serving as nurses, spies, couriers, or soldiers; gathering supplies; and lobbying to influence government policies. Although Rose Greenhow and a few other women were recruited as spies early in the conflict, most military and political officials initially opposed women's direct engagement in the war. Yet so many women organized relief efforts early on that the federal government organized the U.S. Sanitary Commission to coordinate their efforts. By 1862 tens of thousands of women had volunteered funds and assistance through hundreds of local chapters across the North and Midwest. They hosted fund-raising fairs, coordinated sewing and knitting circles, rolled bandages, and sent supplies to the front lines. With critical shortages of medical staff, some female nurses and doctors eventually gained acceptance in northern hospitals and field camps. Led by such memorable figures as Clara Barton, Mary Ann "Mother" Bickerdyke, and Dr. Mary Walker, northern women almost entirely replaced men as military nurses by the end of the war.

In the South, too, much of the medical care was performed by women. But without a government-sanctioned body to coordinate efforts and lobby for resources, women were left largely to their own devices, and nursing was never recognized as a legitimate profession for them. As a result, a Confederate soldier's chances of dying from wounds or disease were even greater than those of his Union counterpart. Nonetheless, southern women worked tirelessly to supply soldiers with clothes, blankets, munitions, and food. But this work, too, was often performed locally and by individuals rather than as part of a coordinated Confederate effort. For example, Ann Cobb, the wife of a Georgia officer, went door-to-door among neighbors to gather provisions for her husband's eighty-man unit.

Some Union and Confederate women played even more unusual roles in the war. A few dozen women joined Greenhow in gathering information for military and political authorities. One of the most effective on the Union side was the former fugitive Harriet Tubman. She worked as a spy in South Carolina from 1862 to 1864 and regularly secured military intelligence from slaves living behind Confederate lines. Even more women served as couriers, carrying messages across battle lines to alert officers of critical changes in military orders or in the opponent's position. In addition, at least four hundred women disguised themselves as men and fought as soldiers; the identities of many were discovered only after they were wounded in battle.

Finally, abolitionist women sought to influence federal wartime policies. Following the Emancipation Proclamation, Elizabeth Cady Stanton, Susan B. Anthony, and Lucy Stone founded the **Women's National Loyal League** and launched a massive petition drive to broaden Lincoln's policy. Collecting 260,000 signatures,

Dr. Mary E. Walker   Dr. Mary E. Walker received her medical degree from Syracuse Medical College and became the first female army surgeon. Wearing bloomers (pants under a skirt), she assisted soldiers and civilians in numerous battlefield areas. Captured by Confederate troops in 1864, Walker soon returned to Union ranks. She was the first woman awarded the Medal of Honor for military service.   Library of Congress

two-thirds of them from women, the League demanded a congressional act "emancipating all persons of African descent" everywhere in the nation.

Dissent and Protest in the Midst of War

While the Women's National Loyal League lobbied Congress for universal emancipation, other Northerners wondered whether defeating the Confederacy was worth the cost. Families were hard hit as wages fell and prices rose, and many Northerners cared more about the safe return of their husbands and sons than the fate of slavery. As the war dragged on, these concerns led to a rising tide of dissent and protest.

 Online Document Project   Home Front Protest during the Civil War
bedfordstmartins.com/hewittlawsonvalue

Despite the expanding economy, northern farmers and workers suffered tremendously during the war. Women, children, and old men took over much of the field labor in the Midwest, trying to feed their families and produce sufficient surplus to supply the army and pay their mortgages and other expenses. In the East, too, inflation eroded the earnings of factory workers, servants, and day laborers. As federal greenbacks flooded the market and military production took priority over consumer goods, prices climbed about 20 percent faster than wages. While industrialists garnered huge profits, railroad stocks leaped to unheard-of prices, and government contractors made huge gains, ordinary workers suffered. A group of Cincinnati seamstresses complained to President Lincoln in 1864 about employers "who fatten on their contracts by grinding immense profits out of the labor of their operatives." Although Republicans pledged to protect the rights of workers, employers successfully lobbied a number of state legislatures to pass laws prohibiting strikes. The federal government, too, proved a better friend to business than to labor. When workers at the Parrott arms factory in Cold Spring, New York, struck for higher wages in 1864, the government sent in troops, declared martial law, and arrested the strike leaders.

Discontent intensified when the Republican Congress passed a draft law in March 1863. The **Enrollment Act** provided for draftees to be selected by an impartial lottery, but a loophole allowed a person with $300 to pay the government in place of serving or to hire another man as a substitute. Many workers deeply resented the draft law's profound inequality. Some also opposed the emancipation of slaves who, they assumed, would compete for scarce jobs once the war ended.

Dissent turned to violence in July 1863 when the new draft law went into effect. Riots broke out in cities across the North. In New York City, where inflation caused tremendous suffering and a large immigrant population solidly supported the Democratic machine, implementation of the draft triggered four days of the worst rioting Americans had ever seen. Women and men—many of them Irish and German immigrants—attacked Protestant missionaries, Republican draft officials, and wealthy businessmen. Homes in wealthy neighborhoods were looted, but the free black community became the rioters' main target. Rioters lynched at least a dozen African Americans and looted and burned the city's Colored Orphan Asylum. The violence ended only when Union troops put down the riot by force. By then, more than one hundred New Yorkers lay dead.

A more prolonged battle raged in Missouri, where Confederate sympathizers never reconciled themselves to living in a Union state. From the beginning of this "inner civil war," prosouthern residents formed militias and staged guerrilla attacks on Union supporters. The militias, with the tacit support of Confederate officials, claimed thousands of lives and forced the Union army to station troops in the area. The militia members hoped that Midwesterners, weary of the conflicts, would elect peace Democrats and end the war.

Northern Democrats saw the widening unrest as a political opportunity. Although some Democratic leaders supported the war effort, many others—whom opponents called **Copperheads**, after the poisonous snake—rallied behind Ohio politician Clement L. Vallandigham in opposing the war. Presenting themselves as the "peace party," these Democrats enjoyed considerable success in eastern cities where inflation was rampant and immigrant workers were caught between low wages and military service. The party was also strong in parts of the Midwest where sympathy for the southern cause and antipathy to African Americans ran deep.

In the South, too, some whites expressed growing dissatisfaction with the war. In April 1862, Jefferson Davis had signed the first conscription act in U.S. history, inciting widespread opposition. The concept of a national draft undermined the southern tradition of states' rights. As in the North, men could hire a substitute if they had enough money, and an October 1862 law exempted men owning twenty or more slaves from military service. Although the exemption was supposedly a response to growing unruliness among slaves in the absence of masters, in practice it meant that large planters, many of whom served in the Confederate legislature, had exempted themselves from fighting. As one Alabama farmer fumed, "All they want is to get you pumpt up and go to fight for their infernal negroes, and after you do their fighting you may kiss their hine parts for all they care."

Small farmers were also hard hit by policies that allowed the Confederate army to take whatever supplies it needed. The army's forced acquisition of farm produce intensified food shortages that had been building since early in the war. The southern economy was rooted in cash crops rather than foodstuffs. Quantities of grain and livestock were produced in South Carolina, central Virginia, and central Tennessee, but by 1863 the latter two areas had fallen under Union control. The Union blockade of port cities and the lack of an extensive railroad or canal system in the South limited the distribution of what food was available. Hungry residents of the Shenandoah Valley discovered that despite military victories there, food shortages worsened as Confederate troops ravaged the countryside.

Food shortages drove up prices on basic items like bread and corn, while the Union blockade and the focus on military needs dramatically increased the price of other consumer goods. As the Confederate government issued more and more treasury notes to finance the war, inflation soared 2,600 percent in less than three years. Food riots, often led by women, broke out in cities across the South, including the Confederate capital of Richmond.

Conscription, food shortages, and inflation took their toll on support for the Confederacy. The devastation of the war itself added to these grievances. Most battles were fought in the Upper South or along the Confederacy's western frontier, where small farmers saw their crops, animals, and fields destroyed. A phrase that had seemed cynical in 1862—"A rich man's war and a poor man's fight"—became the rallying cry of the southern peace movement in 1864. The Washington Constitutional Union, a secret peace society with a large following among farmers, elected several members to the Confederate Congress. Another secret organization centered in North Carolina took more drastic measures, providing Union forces with information on southern troop movements and encouraging desertion by Confederates. In mountainous regions of the South, draft evaders and deserters formed guerrilla groups that attacked draft officials and actively impeded the war effort. In western North Carolina, some women hid deserters, raided grain depots, and burned the property of Confederate officials.

When slaveholders led the South out of the Union in 1861, they had assumed the loyalty of yeomen farmers, the deference of southern ladies, and the privileges of the southern way of life. Far from preserving social harmony and social order, however, the war undermined ties between elite and poor Southerners, between planters and small farmers, and between women and men. Although most white Southerners still supported the Confederacy in 1864 and internal dissent alone did not lead to defeat, it did weaken the ties that bound soldiers to their posts in the final two years of the war.

REVIEW & RELATE

• What were the short- and long-term economic effects of the war on the North?

• How did the war change the southern economy? What social tensions did the war create in the South?

The Tide of War Turns

In the spring of 1863, Lee's army defeated a Union force twice its size at Chancellorsville, Virginia, setting the stage for a Confederate thrust into Pennsylvania. Yet Lee's decision to go on the offensive ultimately proved the Confederacy's undoing. Even as draft riots erupted across the North in July 1863, the Union won two decisive military victories: at Gettysburg, Pennsylvania, and Vicksburg, Mississippi. These victories improved northern morale while devastating Confederate hopes. At the same time, the flood of African Americans, including former slaves, into the Union army transformed the very meaning of the war. In late 1864 and early 1865, the momentum favored the Union, and the South was forced to consider prospects for peace.

Key Victories for the Union

In mid-1863, Confederate commanders believed the tide was turning in their favor. Following victories at Fredericksburg and Chancellorsville, General Lee launched an invasion of northern territory. While the Union army maneuvered to protect Washington, D.C., from Lee's advance, General Joseph Hooker resigned as head of the Union army. When Lincoln appointed George A. Meade as the new Union commander, the general immediately faced a major engagement at **Gettysburg**, Pennsylvania. If Confederates won a victory there, European countries might finally recognize the southern nation and force the North to accept peace.

Neither Lee nor Meade set out to launch a battle in this small Pennsylvania town. But Lee was afraid of outrunning his supply lines, and Meade wanted to keep Confederates from gaining control of the roads that crossed at Gettysburg. So on July 1, fighting commenced, with Lee pushing Union forces to the south of town. The Union vanguard managed to hold the ground along Cemetery Ridge until more troops arrived the following day. Although Confederate troops suffered heavy losses on July 2, Lee believed that Union forces were spread thin and ordered General George Pickett to launch a frontal assault on July 3 (Map 13.2). But Pickett's men were mowed down as they crossed an open field. The battle was a disaster for the South: More than 4,700 Confederates were killed, including a large number of officers; another 18,000 were wounded, captured, or missing. Although the Union suffered similar casualties, it had more men to lose, and it could claim victory.

As a grieving Lee retreated to Virginia, the South suffered another devastating defeat. Troops under General Ulysses S. Grant had been pounding Vicksburg, Mississippi, for months. In May 1863, Grant sent his men in a wide arc around the city and attacked from the east, setting the stage for a six-week siege. Although civilians refused to leave and even hid out in caves to outlast the Union barrage, Confederate troops were forced to surrender the city on July 4. This victory was even more important strategically than Gettysburg (Map 13.2). Combined with a victory five days later at Port Hudson, Louisiana, the Union army now controlled the entire Mississippi valley, the richest

---

MAP 13.2
Battles of Gettysburg and Vicksburg, 1863   The three-day battle in Gettysburg and the six-week siege of Vicksburg led to critical victories for the Union. Together, these victories forced General Lee's troops back into Confederate territory and gave the Union control of the Mississippi River. Still, the war was far from over. Confederate troops controlled the southern heartland, and Northerners wearied of the ever-increasing casualties.

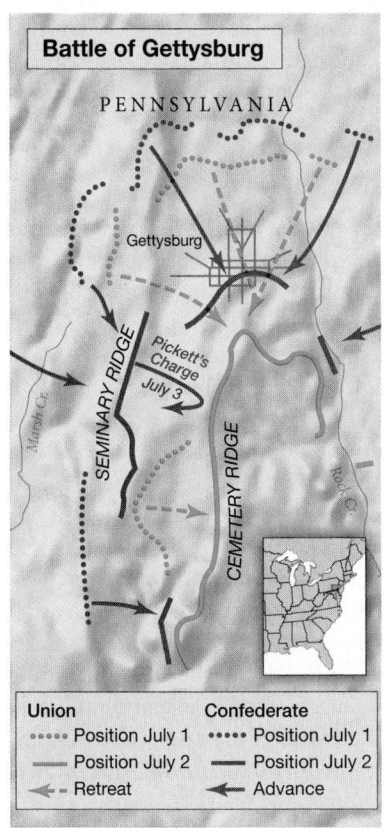

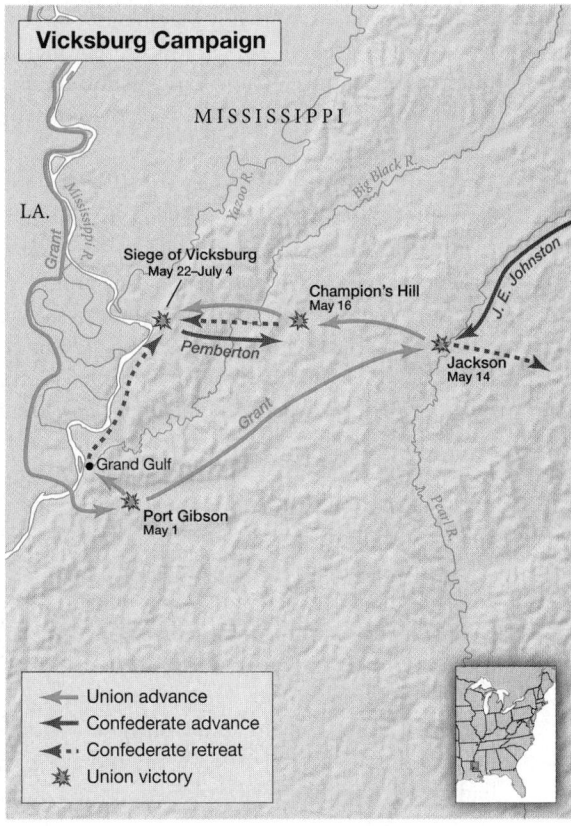

plantation region in the South. This series of victories also effectively cut off the Confederacy from Louisiana, Arkansas, and Texas, ensuring Union control of the West. In November 1863, Grant's troops achieved a major victory at Chattanooga, opening up much of the South's remaining territory to invasion. Thousands of slaves deserted their plantations, and many joined the Union war effort.

As 1864 dawned, the Union had twice as many forces in the field as the Confederacy, whose soldiers were suffering from low morale, high mortality, and dwindling supplies. Although some difficult battles still lay ahead, the war of attrition (in which the larger, better-supplied Union forces slowly wore down their Confederate opponents) had begun to pay dividends.

The changing Union fortunes increased support for Lincoln and his congressional allies. Union victories and the Emancipation Proclamation also convinced Great Britain not to recognize the Confederacy as an independent nation. And the heroics of African American soldiers, who in 1863 engaged in direct and often brutal combat against southern troops, encouraged wider support for emancipation. Republicans, who now fully embraced abolition as a war aim, were nearly assured the presidency and a congressional majority in the 1864 elections.

Northern Democrats still campaigned for peace and the readmission of Confederate states with slavery intact. They nominated George B. McClellan, the onetime Union commander, as their candidate for president. McClellan attracted working-class and immigrant voters who traditionally supported the Democrats and who bore the heaviest burdens of the war. But Democratic hopes for victory in November were crushed when Union general William Tecumseh Sherman captured Atlanta, Georgia, just two months before the election. Lincoln and the Republicans won easily, giving the party a clear mandate to continue the war to its conclusion.

African Americans Contribute to Victory

Lincoln's election secured the eventual downfall of slavery. Yet neither the president nor Congress eradicated human bondage on their own. From the fall of 1862 on, African Americans enlisted in the Union army and helped ensure that nothing short of universal emancipation would be the outcome of the war. By the spring of 1865, nearly 200,000 African Americans were serving in the Union army and navy. Private Thomas Long, a former slave serving with the First South Carolina Volunteers, explained the connection between African American enlistment and emancipation: "If we hadn't become sojers, all might have gone back as it was before; our freedom might have slipped through de two houses of Congress and President Linkum's four years might have passed by and notin' been done for us. But now tings can neber go back, because we have showed our energy and our courage and our naturally manhood."

In the border states, which were exempt from the Emancipation Proclamation, enslaved men were adamant about enlisting since those who served in the Union army were granted their freedom. Because of this provision, slaveholders in the border states did everything in their power to prevent their slaves from joining the army, including assault and even murder. Despite these efforts, between 25 and 60 percent of military-age enslaved men in the four border states joined the Union army and quickly distinguished themselves in battle. By the end of the war, approximately 37,000 black soldiers had given their lives for freedom and the Union.

Yet despite their courage and commitment, black soldiers felt the sting of racism. They were segregated in camps, given the most menial jobs, and often treated as inferiors by white recruits and officers. Many blacks, for instance, were assigned the gruesome and exhausting task of burying the dead after grueling battles in which they had fought alongside whites. Particularly galling was the Union policy of paying black soldiers less than whites were paid. African American soldiers openly protested this discrimination even after a black sergeant who voiced his views was charged with mutiny and executed by firing squad in February 1864. An African American corporal wrote to Lincoln, describing the blood black troops had shed for the Union and asking, "We have done a Soldier's Duty. Why can't we have a Soldier's pay?" The War Department finally equalized wages in June 1864.

One of African American soldiers' primary concerns was to liberate slaves as Union armies moved deeper into the South. During 1863 and 1864, thousands more slaves headed for Union lines, joining the "contraband" who had escaped earlier in the war. Even those forced to remain on plantations realized that Union troops and freedom were headed their way. In areas close to Union lines, they talked openly of the advancing army. "Now they gradually threw off the mask," a slave remembered of this moment, "and were not afraid to let it be known that the 'freedom' in their songs meant freedom of the body in this world."

The Final Battles and the Promise of Peace

In the spring of 1864, the war entered its final stage. That March, Lincoln placed General Grant in charge of all Union forces, and he embarked on a strategy of **total war**, including attacks against civilian as well as military targets. Grant was willing to accept huge casualties in order to achieve victory. Over the next year, he led his troops overland through western Virginia in an effort to take Richmond. At the same time, he ordered General Sherman to head south through Georgia, destroying the remnants of the plantation system.

Grant's troops headed toward Richmond, where Lee's army controlled strong defensive positions. The Confederates won narrow victories in May 1864 at the Battles of the Wilderness and Spotsylvania Court House. In June, 7,000 Union soldiers were killed in one hour during a frontal assault at Cold Harbor, Virginia, where Confederates once again turned back the Union army. But Grant continued to push forward. Although Lee lost fewer men (31,000 casualties at Cold Harbor versus 55,000 for the Union), his army was melting away with each so-called victory.

The battles took a terrible toll on soldiers on both sides. Union troops and civilians called Grant "the butcher" for his seeming lack of regard for human life. Grant, however, was not deterred. He laid siege to Petersburg in June 1864, where both sides lived in trenches and tunnels for months on end. That August, Sherman also laid siege to Atlanta, but on September 2 he ordered his troops out of the trenches, swept around the city, and destroyed the roads and rails that connected it to the rest of the Confederacy. When General John B. Hood and his southern troops abandoned their posts, Sherman telegraphed Lincoln: "Atlanta is ours, and fairly won." The victory cut the South in two.

Sherman then led his troops on a 300-mile march to the Atlantic coast and north through the Carolinas. Embracing the strategy of total war, his troops cut a path of destruction 50 miles wide during their "March to the Sea," destroying crops, livestock,

Richmond in Ruins, April 1865 This photograph captures the devastation the war brought to the Richmond and Petersburg Railroad Depot after General Grant drove General Lee's troops out of the Confederate capital in April 1865. This defining moment marked the end of the Civil War and the defeat of the South. During the next decade, the North and South struggled over reconfiguring the Union. Library of Congress

and houses before they reached Savannah in late December. Nearly 18,000 enslaved men, women, and children left the ruined plantations and sought to join Sherman's victorious troops. To the fleeing slaves' dismay, soldiers refused to take them along. Worse, some Union soldiers abused African American men, raped black women, or stole their few possessions. Angry Confederates captured many of those who were turned away, killing some and reenslaving others.

Sherman's callous actions caused a scandal in Washington. In January 1865, Lincoln dispatched Secretary of War Edwin Stanton to Georgia to investigate the charges. At an extraordinary meeting in Savannah, Stanton and Sherman met with black ministers to hear their complaints and to ask what newly emancipated African Americans wanted. The ministers spoke movingly of the war lifting "the yoke of bondage." Freed blacks, they argued, "could reap the fruit of their own labor" and, if given land, "take care of ourselves, and assist the Government in maintaining our freedom." In response, Sherman issued **Field Order Number 15**, setting aside more than 400,000 acres of captured

Confederate land to be divided into small plots for former slaves. Although Sherman's order proved highly controversial, it suggested that the Civil War might, in the end, be a revolutionary force for change.

As defeat loomed, even Confederate leaders began to talk of emancipating the slaves. Jefferson Davis called for recruiting slaves into the army, with their payment to include freedom for themselves and their families. The Confederate Congress passed such a law in early 1865, but it was too late to make any difference. Still, the very idea suggested that the Civil War had turned southern society upside down.

In early April 1865, with Sherman heading toward Raleigh, North Carolina, Grant captured Petersburg and then drove Lee and his forces out of Richmond. In one of the war's most dramatic moments, seasoned African American troops led the final assault on the city and were among the first Union soldiers to enter the Confederate capital. On April 9, after a brief engagement at Appomattox Court House, Virginia, Lee surrendered to Grant with fewer than 30,000 soldiers remaining under his command. Within hours, his troops began heading home. Although Confederate soldiers continued to engage Union forces in North Carolina and west of the Mississippi, the Civil War, for all intents and purposes, had come to an end.

The legal abolition of slavery was initiated in Washington a few months before Lee's surrender. Following on the petitions submitted by the Women's National Loyal League, Congress passed the **Thirteenth Amendment** to the U.S. Constitution on January 31, 1865, prohibiting slavery and involuntary servitude anywhere in the United States. Although it still required approval by three-quarters of the states, wartime experiences made ratification likely. Some states and cities had already enacted laws to ease racial inequities. Ohio, California, and Illinois repealed statutes barring blacks from testifying in court and serving on juries. San Francisco, Cincinnati, Cleveland, and New York City desegregated their streetcars. In May 1865, Massachusetts passed the first comprehensive public-accommodations law in U.S. history, ensuring equal treatment in theaters, stores, schools, and other social spaces. With the final surrender of the Confederacy, many Northerners were hopeful that the nation reunited would be stronger and more just.

REVIEW & RELATE

- What role did African Americans play in the defeat of the South?
- How did the Union win the war? How did attitudes toward African Americans change in the final year of the war?

Conclusion: An Uncertain Future

Jubilation in the North did not last long. On April 14, less than a week after Lee's surrender, Abraham Lincoln was shot at Ford's Theatre by a Confederate fanatic named John Wilkes Booth. The president died the next day, leading to an outpouring of grief across the North and leaving the entire nation in shock.

Lincoln left behind an incredible legacy. He had led the Union to victory in a devastating civil war, promulgated the Emancipation Proclamation, and resolved the conflict between competing systems based on slavery and free labor. More than 600,000

Americans died in the war, but nearly 4 million Americans who had been born enslaved were now free. At the same time, northern and southern women had entered the labor force and the public arena in numbers never before imagined. Soldiers returned to their families, jobs, and communities with experiences and knowledge, but also with physical and emotional wounds that transformed their lives. And the federal government had extended its reach into more and more areas of daily life. The war had dramatically accelerated the pace of economic, political, and social change, transforming American society both during the war and afterward.

Still, the legacies of the war were far from certain in 1865. Defeated Southerners looked for heroes, and most considered Confederate generals the greatest representatives of the "Lost Cause." They honored Lee and his officers with statues, portraits, poems, and parades. Confederate women worked endlessly to preserve the memory of both military leaders and ordinary soldiers. They formed memorial associations to decorate cemeteries and promoted a southern perspective on the war in schools and history books. They also joined in paying tribute to heroines like Rose O'Neal Greenhow. Greenhow had traveled to England and France in 1863, promoting Confederate bond issues and publishing a book about her imprisonment under "abolition rule." On her return in August 1864, the British vessel she was on was pursued by federal ships blockading the harbor. Fearing capture, Greenhow insisted that she be rowed ashore carrying a bag of gold coins, the profits from her book. But the boat overturned in high seas, and Greenhow drowned. She was buried with full military honors in Wilmington, North Carolina.

Victorious Northerners had far more reason to celebrate, but they knew that much still needed to be done. Frederick Douglass was thrilled that slavery had been abolished, but he argued vehemently that "the work of Abolitionists is not done." He was deeply committed to the enfranchisement of African American men as the means to secure the rights of former slaves, for he had no illusions about the lengths to which many whites would go to protect their traditional privileges. Although Douglass considered the Republican Party the best hope for reconstructing the nation, not everyone shared his agenda. Some white abolitionists argued that their work was done; some women's rights advocates thought they were as entitled to voting rights as were black men; some militant blacks viewed the Republican Party as too moderate. Moreover, many northern whites were exhausted by four years of war and hoped to leave the problems of slavery and secession behind. Others wanted to rebuild the South quickly in order to ensure the nation's economic recovery. These competing visions—between Northerners and Southerners and within each group—would shape the promises of peace in ways few could imagine at the end of the war.

Chapter Review

MAKE IT STICK

 LearningCurve bedfordstmartins.com/hewittlawsonvalue
After reading the chapter, use LearningCurve to retain what you've read.

IDENTIFY KEY TERMS

Identify and explain the significance of each term below.

Fort Sumter (p. 326)
contraband (p. 329)
Battle of Shiloh (p. 331)
Emancipation Proclamation (p. 332)
U.S. Sanitary Commission (p. 334)
greenbacks (p. 335)
Women's National Loyal League (p. 337)

Enrollment Act (p. 338)
Copperheads (p. 339)
Gettysburg (p. 340)
total war (p. 343)
Field Order Number 15 (p. 344)
Thirteenth Amendment (p. 345)

REVIEW & RELATE

Answer the focus questions from each section of the chapter.

1. What steps did Lincoln take to prevent war? Why were they ineffective?
2. What advantages and disadvantages did each side have at the onset of the war?
3. What arguments did each side make in the debate over African American enlistment in the Union army?
4. How and why did the Civil War become a war to end slavery?
5. What were the short- and long-term economic effects of the war on the North?
6. How did the war change the southern economy? What social tensions did the war create in the South?
7. What role did African Americans play in the defeat of the South?
8. How did the Union win the war? How did attitudes toward African Americans change in the final year of the war?

ONLINE DOCUMENT PROJECTS

◆ **Civil War Letters**
◆ **Home Front Protest during the Civil War**

After reading the primary sources in these document sets, answer the **Interpret the Evidence** questions to help you analyze each of the documents, and then answer the **Put It in Context** question(s) to help you relate the documents to the topics and themes you read about in the chapter.
bedfordstmartins.com/hewittlawsonvalue

TIMELINE OF EVENTS

1845	• Frederick Douglass publishes *Narrative of the Life of Frederick Douglass*
April 14, 1861	• Fort Sumter surrenders to Confederate forces
May 23, 1861	• General Benjamin Butler declares escaped slaves "contraband"
June 1861	• U.S. Sanitary Commission established
July 21, 1861	• First Battle of Bull Run (Manassas)
August 6, 1861	• Confiscation Act passed
April 1862	• Slavery abolished in the District of Columbia • Battle of Shiloh • Jefferson Davis signs conscription act
June 1862	• Rose O'Neal Greenhow exiled to the South
September 1862	• Battle of Antietam • Lincoln issues preliminary Emancipation Proclamation
January 1, 1863	• Lincoln signs Emancipation Proclamation
March 1863	• Enrollment Act passed in North
July 1863	• Draft riots in New York City • Battle of Gettysburg • Battle of Vicksburg
September 2, 1864	• Atlanta falls; Sherman begins "March to the Sea"
1865	• 200,000 African Americans serving in the Union army and navy
January 1865	• Sherman issues Field Order Number 15
January 31, 1865	• Congress passes Thirteenth Amendment
April 9, 1865	• General Lee surrenders to General Grant at Appomattox Court House
April 14, 1865	• Assassination of President Abraham Lincoln

14

✓ LearningCurve
bedfordstmartins.com/hewittlawsonvalue
After reading the chapter, use LearningCurve
to retain what you've read.

Emancipations and Reconstructions

1863–1877

AMERICAN HISTORIES

Jefferson Franklin Long spent his life improving himself and his race. Born a slave in Alabama in 1836, Long showed great resourcefulness in taking advantage of the limited opportunities available to him under slavery. His master, a tailor who moved his family to Georgia, taught him the trade, but Long taught himself to read and write. When the Civil War ended, he opened a tailor shop in Macon, Georgia. The measure of financial security he earned allowed him to turn his attention to politics and participate in the Republican Party. Elected as Georgia's first black congressman in 1870, Long was committed to fighting for the political rights of freed slaves. In his first appearance on the House floor, he spoke out against a bill that would allow former Confederate officials to return to Congress. He questioned their loyalty to the Union from which they had recently rebelled and noted that many belonged to secret societies, such as the Ku Klux Klan, that intimidated black citizens. Despite his pleas, the measure passed, and Long decided not to run for reelection.

By the mid-1880s, Long had become disillusioned with the ability of black Georgians to achieve their objectives within the electoral system. Instead, he counseled African Americans to turn to institution building as the best hope for social and economic advancement. Advocating "Christianity, morality, education, and industry," Long helped found the Union Brotherhood Lodge, a black mutual aid society, with branches throughout central Georgia, that provided social and economic services for its members. He died in 1901, during a time of political disfranchisement and racial segregation that swept through

Georgia and the rest of the South. In fact, after Long, Georgia would not elect another black congressman for a hundred years.

Jefferson Long and Andrew Johnson shared many characteristics, but their views on race led them to support decidedly different programs following the Civil War. Whereas Long fought for the right of self-determination for African Americans, Johnson believed that whites alone could decide what was best for freedmen. Born in 1808 in Raleigh, North Carolina, Andrew Johnson grew up in poverty. At the age of thirteen or fourteen, Johnson became a tailor's apprentice, but he ran away before completing his contract. Johnson settled in Tennessee in 1826 and, like Long, opened a tailor shop. The following year, he married Eliza McCardle, who taught him how to write. He began to prosper, purchasing his own home, farm, and a small number of slaves.

As he made his mark in Greenville, Tennessee, Johnson moved into politics, following fellow Tennessean Andrew Jackson into the Democratic Party. Success followed success as he advanced to higher political positions, and by the time the Civil War broke out, he was a U.S. senator. During his early political career, Johnson, a social and political outsider, championed the rights of workers and small farmers against the power of the southern aristocracy.

At the onset of the Civil War, Johnson remained loyal to the Union even when Tennessee seceded in 1861. As a reward for his loyalty, President Abraham Lincoln appointed Johnson as military governor of Tennessee. In 1864 the Republican Lincoln chose the Democrat Johnson to run with him as vice president, thereby constructing a successful unity ticket. Less than six weeks after their inauguration in March 1865, Johnson became president upon Lincoln's assassination.

Fate placed Reconstruction in the hands of Andrew Johnson. After four years, the brutal Civil War between the rebellious southern states that seceded from the Union and the northern states that fought to preserve the nation had come to a close. Yet the hard work of reunion remained. Toward this end, President Johnson oversaw the reestablishment of state legislatures in the former Confederate states. These reconstituted governments agreed to the abolition of slavery, but they passed measures that restricted black civil and political rights. Johnson accepted these results and considered the southern states as having fulfilled their obligations for rejoining the Union. Most Northerners reached a different conclusion. Having won the bloody war, they suspected that they were now losing the peace to Johnson and the defeated South.

THE AMERICAN HISTORIES of Andrew Johnson and Jefferson Long intersected in Reconstruction, the hard-fought battle to determine the fate of the postwar South and the meaning of freedom for newly emancipated African Americans. Would the end of slavery be little more than a legal technicality, as Johnson and many other white Southerners hoped, or would Long's vision of a deeper economic and racial transformation prevail? From 1865 to 1877, the period of Reconstruction, Americans of all races and from all regions participated in the resolution of this question.

Prelude to Reconstruction

Even before Andrew Johnson became president in 1865 and emancipation freed Jefferson Long, Reconstruction had begun on a small scale. During the Civil War, blacks remaining in Union-occupied areas, such as the Sea Islands, located off the coast of South Carolina, had some experience with freedom. When Union troops arrived and most southern whites fled, the slaves chose to stay on the land. Some farmed for themselves, but most were employed by northern whites who moved south to demonstrate the profitability of newly freed black labor. The return of former plantation owners after the war generated conflicts. Rather than work for whites, freedpeople preferred to establish their own farms; but if forced to work for whites, they insisted on negotiating their wages instead of simply accepting what whites offered. Wives and mothers often refused to labor for whites at all in favor of caring for their own families. These conflicts reflected the priorities that would shape the actions of freedpeople across the South in the immediate aftermath of the war. For freedom to be meaningful, it had to include economic independence, the power to make family decisions, and the right to have some control over community issues.

African Americans Embrace Emancipation

When U.S. troops arrived in Richmond, Virginia, in April 1865, it signaled to the city's enslaved African American population that the war was over and that freedom was, finally, theirs. African American men, women, and children took to the streets and crowded into churches to celebrate. They gathered to dance, sing, pray, and shout. Four days after Union troops arrived, 1,500 African Americans, including a large number of soldiers, packed First African Baptist, the largest of the city's black churches. During the singing of the hymn "Jesus My All to Heaven Is Gone," they raised their voices at the line "This is the way I long have sought." Elsewhere in Virginia, black

Jack and Abby Landlord, freed slaves from Savannah, Georgia, 1875. Culver Pictures/The Art Archive at Art Resource, NY

schoolchildren sang "Glory Hallelujah," and house slaves snuck out of the dinner service to shout for joy in the slave quarters. As the news of the Confederacy's defeat spread, newly freed African Americans across the South experienced similar emotions. However, the news did not reach some isolated plantations in Georgia, Louisiana, South Carolina, and Texas for months. David Harris, a South Carolina planter, claimed that he did not hear about the emancipation edict until June 1865. He did not mention it to the slaves on his plantation until August, when Union troops stationed nearby made it impossible for him to keep it from his workers any longer. Whenever they discovered their freedom, blacks recalled the moment vividly. Many years later, Houston H. Holloway, a Georgia slave who had been sold three times before he was twenty years old, recalled the day of emancipation. "I felt like a bird out a cage," he reported. "Amen. Amen, Amen. I could hardly ask to feel any better than I did that day."

For southern whites, however, the end of the war brought fear, humiliation, and uncertainty. From their point of view, the jubilation of their former slaves was salt in their wounds. In many areas, blacks celebrated their release from bondage under the protection of Union soldiers. When the army moved out, freedwomen and freedmen suffered deeply for their enthusiasm. When troops departed the area surrounding Columbia, South Carolina, for example, a plantation owner and his wife vented their anger and frustration on a former slave. The girl had assisted Union soldiers in finding silverware, money, and jewelry hidden by her master and mistress. Her former owners hanged the newly emancipated slave. Other whites beat, whipped, raped, slashed, and shot blacks who they felt had been too joyous in their freedom or too helpful to the Yankee invaders. As one North Carolina freedman testified, the Yankees "tol' us we were free," but once the army left, the planters "would get cruel to the slaves if they acted like they were free."

Newly freed slaves also faced less visible dangers. During the 1860s, disease swept through the South and through the contraband camps that housed many former slaves; widespread malnutrition and poor housing heightened the problem. A smallpox epidemic that spread south from Washington, D.C., killed more than sixty thousand freedpeople.

Despite the danger of acting free, southern blacks eagerly pursued emancipation. They moved; they married; they attended school; they demanded wages; they refused to work for whites; they gathered up their families; they created black churches and civic associations; they held political meetings. Sometimes, black women and men acted on their own, pooling their resources to advance their freedom. At other times, they called on government agencies for assistance and support. The most important of these agencies was the newly formed Bureau of Refugees, Freedmen, and Abandoned Lands, popularly known as the Freedmen's Bureau. Created by Congress in 1865 and signed into law by President Lincoln, the bureau provided ex-slaves with economic and legal resources. Private organizations—particularly northern missionary and educational associations, most staffed by former abolitionists, free blacks, and evangelical Christians— also aided African Americans in their efforts to give meaning to freedom.

Reuniting Families Torn Apart by Slavery

The first priority for many newly freed blacks was to reunite families torn apart by slavery. Men and women traveled across the South to find spouses, children, parents, siblings, aunts, and uncles. Well into the 1870s and 1880s, parents ran advertisements in newly established black newspapers, providing what information they knew about their children's whereabouts and asking for assistance in finding them. They sought help in their quests from government officials, ministers, and other African Americans. Milly Johnson wrote to the Freedmen's Bureau in March 1867, after failing to locate the five children she had lost under slavery. In the end, she was able to locate three of her children, but any chance of discovering the whereabouts of the other two was lost when the records of the slave trader who purchased them burned during the war. Although such difficulties were common, thousands of slave children were reunited with their parents in the aftermath of the Civil War.

Husbands and wives, or those who considered themselves as such despite the absence of legal marriage under slavery, also searched for each other. Those who lived on nearby plantations could now live together for the first time. Those whose husband or wife had been sold to distant plantation owners had a more difficult time. They wrote (or had letters written on their behalf) to relatives and friends who had been sold with their mate; sought assistance from government officials, churches, and even their former masters; and traveled to areas where they thought their spouse might reside.

Many such searches were complicated by long years of separation and the lack of any legal standing for slave marriages. In 1866 Philip Grey, a Virginia freedman, located his wife, Willie Ann, and their daughter Maria, who had been sold away to Kentucky years before. Willie Ann was eager to reunite with her husband, but in the years since being sold, she had remarried and borne three children. Her second husband had joined the Union army and was killed in battle. When Willie Ann wrote to Philip in April 1866, explaining her new circumstances, she concluded: "If you love me you will love my children and you will have to promise me that you will provide for them all as well as if they were your own. . . . I know that I have lived with you and loved you then and love you still." Other spouses finally located their partner, only to discover that the husband or wife was happily married to someone else and refused to acknowledge the earlier relationship.

Despite these complications, most former slaves who found their spouse sought to legalize their relationship. Ministers, army chaplains, Freedmen's Bureau agents, and teachers were flooded with requests to perform marriage ceremonies. In one case, a Superintendent for Marriages for the Freedmen's Bureau in northern Virginia reported that he gave out seventy-nine marriage certificates on a single day in May 1866. In another, four couples went right from the fields to a local schoolhouse, still dressed in their work clothes, where the parson married them.

Of course, some former slaves hoped that freedom would allow them to leave an unhappy relationship. Having never been married under the law, couples could simply separate and move on. Complications arose, however, if they had children. In Lake City, Florida, in 1866, a Freedmen's Bureau agent asked for advice from his superiors on how to deal with Madison Day and Maria Richards. They refused to legalize the relationship forced on them under slavery, but both sought custody of their three children, the oldest only six years old. As with white couples in the mid-nineteenth century, the father eventually was granted custody on the assumption that he had the best chance of providing for the family financially.

Free to Learn

Reuniting families was only one of the many ways that southern blacks proclaimed their freedom. Learning to read and write was another. The desire to learn was all but universal. Writing of freedpeople during Reconstruction, Booker T. Washington, an educator and a former slave, noted, "It was a whole race trying to go to school. Few were too young, and none too old, to make the attempt to learn." A newly liberated father in Mississippi proclaimed, "If I nebber does nothing more while I live, I shall give my children a chance to go to school, for I considers education [the] next best ting to liberty."

A variety of organizations opened schools for former slaves during the 1860s and 1870s. By 1870 nearly a quarter million blacks were attending one of the 4,300 schools established by the Freedmen's Bureau. Black and white churches and missionary societies also launched schools. Even before the war ended, the American Missionary Association called on its northern members to take the freedpeople "by the hand, to guide, counsel and instruct them in their new life." This and similar organizations sent hundreds of teachers, black and white, women and men, into the South to open schools in former plantation areas. Their attitudes were often paternalistic and the schools were segregated, but the institutions they established offered important educational resources for African Americans.

The demand for education was so great that almost any kind of building was pressed into service as a schoolhouse. A mule stable in Helena, Arkansas; a billiard room on the Sea Islands; a courthouse in Lawrence, Kansas; and a former cotton shed on a St. Simon Island plantation all attracted eager students. In New Orleans, local blacks converted a former slave pen into a school and named it after the famous activist, orator, and ex-slave Frederick Douglass.

Parents worked hard to keep their children in school during the day. Children, as they gained the rudiments of education, passed on their knowledge to mothers, fathers, and older siblings whose work responsibilities prevented them from attending school. Still, many freedpeople, having worked all day in fields, homes, or shops, then walked long distances in order to get a bit of education for themselves. In New Bern, North Carolina, where many blacks labored until eight o'clock at night, a teacher reported that they still insisted on spending at least an hour "in earnest application to study."

Freedmen and freedwomen sought education for a variety of reasons. Some, like the Mississippi father noted above, viewed it as a sign of liberation. Others knew that they must be able to read the labor contracts they signed if they were ever to be free of exploitation by whites. Some men and women were eager to correspond with relatives far away, others to read the Bible. Growing numbers hoped to participate in politics, particularly the public meetings organized by freedpeople in cities across the South following the end of the war. These gatherings met to set an agenda for the future, and nearly everyone demanded that state legislatures immediately establish public schools for African Americans. Most black delegates agreed with A. H. Ransier of South Carolina, who proclaimed that "in proportion to the education of the people so is their progress in civilization."

Despite the enthusiasm of blacks and the efforts of the federal government and private agencies, schooling remained severely limited throughout the South. A shortage of teachers and of funding kept enrollments low among blacks and whites alike. The isolation of black farm families and the difficulties in eking out a living limited the resources available for education. Only about a quarter of African Americans were literate by 1880.

Black Churches Take a Leadership Role

One of the constant concerns freedpeople expressed as they sought education was the desire to read the Bible and other religious material. Forced under slavery to listen to white preachers who claimed that God had placed Africans and their descendants in bondage, blacks sought to interpret the Bible for themselves. Like many other churches, the African Methodist Episcopal Church, based in Philadelphia, sent missionaries and educators into the South. These church leaders were eager to open seminaries, such as Shaw University in Raleigh, North Carolina, to train southern black men for the ministry.

From the moment of emancipation, freedpeople gathered at churches to celebrate community events. Black Methodist and Baptist congregations spread rapidly across the South following the Civil War. In these churches, African Americans were no longer forced to sit in the back benches listening to white preachers claim that the Bible legitimated slavery. They were no longer punished by white church leaders for moral infractions defined by white masters. Now blacks filled the pews, hired black preachers, selected their own boards of deacons and elders, and invested community resources in purchasing land, building houses of worship, and furnishing them. Churches were the largest structures available to freedpeople in many communities and thus were used for a variety of purposes by a host of community organizations. They often served as schools, with hymnals and Bibles used to teach reading. Churches also hosted picnics, dances, weddings, funerals, festivals, and other events that brought blacks together to celebrate their new sense of freedom, family, and community. Church leaders, especially ministers, often served as arbiters of community standards of morality.

One of the most important functions of black churches in the years immediately following the Civil War was as sites for political organizing. Some black ministers worried that political concerns would overwhelm spiritual devotions. Others agreed with the Reverend Charles H. Pearce of Florida, who declared, "A man in this State cannot do his whole duty as a minister except he looks out for the political interests of his people." Whatever the views of ministers, black churches were among the few places where African Americans could express their political views free from white interference.

> **REVIEW & RELATE**
>
> - What were freedpeople's highest priorities in the years immediately following the Civil War? Why?
> - How did freedpeople define freedom? What steps did they take to make freedom real for themselves and their children?

National Reconstructions

Presidents Abraham Lincoln and Andrew Johnson viewed Reconstruction as a process of national reconciliation. They sketched out terms by which the former Confederate states could reclaim their political representation in the nation without much difficulty. Southern whites, too, sought to return to the Union quickly and with as little change as possible. Congressional Republicans, however, had a more thoroughgoing reconstruction in mind. Like many African Americans, Republican congressional leaders expected the South to extend constitutional rights to the freedmen and to provide them with the political and economic resources to sustain their freedom. Over the next decade, these competing visions of Reconstruction played out in a hard-fought and tumultuous battle over the social, economic, and political implications of the South's defeat and of the abolition of slavery.

Abraham Lincoln Plans for Reunion

In December 1863, President Lincoln issued the **Proclamation of Amnesty and Reconstruction**. He believed that the southern states could not have constitutionally seceded from the Union and therefore only had to meet minimum standards before they regained their political and constitutional rights. Lincoln declared that defeated southern states would have to accept the abolition of slavery and that new governments could be formed when 10 percent of those eligible to vote in 1860 (which in practice meant white southern men but not blacks) swore an oath of allegiance to the United States. Lincoln's plan granted amnesty to all but the highest-ranking Confederate officials, and the restored voters in each state would elect members to a constitutional convention and representatives to take their seats in Congress. In the next year and a half, Arkansas, Louisiana, and Tennessee reestablished their governments under Lincoln's "Ten Percent Plan."

Republicans in Congress had other ideas. They argued that the Confederates had broken their contract with the Union when they seceded and should be treated as "conquered provinces" subject to congressional supervision. In 1864 Congress passed the Wade-Davis bill, which established much higher barriers for readmission to the Union than did Lincoln's plan. For instance, the Wade-Davis bill substituted 50 percent of voters for the president's 10 percent requirement. Lincoln put a stop to this harsher proposal by using a pocket veto—refusing to sign it within ten days of Congress's adjournment.

Although Lincoln and his fellow Republicans in Congress disagreed about many aspects of postwar policy, Lincoln was flexible, and his actions mirrored his desire both to heal the Union and to help southern blacks. For example, the president supported the **Thirteenth Amendment**, abolishing slavery, which passed Congress in January 1865 and was sent to the states for ratification. In March 1865, Lincoln signed the law to create the Freedmen's Bureau. That same month, the president also expressed his sincere wish for reconciliation between the North and the South. "With malice toward none, with charity for all," Lincoln declared in his second inaugural address, "let us strive on to finish the work . . . to bind up the nation's wounds." Lincoln would not, however, have the opportunity to shape Reconstruction with his balanced approach. When he was assassinated in April 1865, it fell to Andrew Johnson, a very different sort of politician, to lead the country through the process of national reintegration.

Andrew Johnson and Presidential Reconstruction

The nation needed a president who could transmit northern desires to the South with clarity and conviction and ensure that they were carried out. Instead, the nation got a president who substituted his own aims for those of the North, refused to engage in meaningful compromise even with sympathetic opponents, misled the South into believing that he could achieve restoration quickly, and subjected himself to political humiliation. Like his mentor, Andrew Jackson, Andrew Johnson was a staunch Union man. He proved his loyalty by serving diligently as military governor of Union-occupied Tennessee from 1862 to 1864. In the 1864 election, Lincoln chose Johnson, a Democrat, as his running mate in a thinly veiled effort to attract border-state voters. The vice presidency was normally an inconsequential role, so it mattered little to Lincoln that Johnson, a southern Democrat, was out of step with many Republican Party positions.

As president, however, Johnson's views took on profound importance. Born into rural poverty, Johnson had no sympathy for the southern aristocracy. Johnson had been a slave owner himself for a time, so his political opposition to slavery was not rooted in moral convictions. Instead, it sprang from the belief that slavery gave plantation owners inordinate power and wealth, which came at the expense of the majority of white Southerners who owned no slaves. He saw emancipation as a means to "break down an odious and dangerous [planter] aristocracy," not to empower blacks. Consequently, he was unconcerned with the fate of African Americans in the postwar South. He saw no reason to punish the South or its leaders because he believed that the end of slavery would doom the southern aristocracy. He hoped to bring the South back into the Union as quickly as possible and then let Southerners take care of their own affairs.

Johnson's views, combined with a lack of political savvy and skill, left him unable to work constructively with congressional Republicans, even the moderates who constituted the majority, such as Senators Lyman Trumbull of Illinois, William Pitt Fessenden of Maine, and John Sherman of Ohio. Moderate Republicans shared the prevalent belief of their time that whites and blacks were not equal, but they argued that the federal government needed to protect newly emancipated slaves. Senator Trumbull warned that without national legislation, ex-slaves would "be tyrannized over, abused, and virtually reenslaved." They expected southern states, where 90 percent of African Americans lived, to extend basic civil rights to the freedpeople, including equal protection and due process of law, and the right to work and hold property.

Nearly all Republicans shared these positions. The Radical wing of the party, however, wanted to go still further. Led by Senator Charles Sumner of Massachusetts and Congressman Thaddeus Stevens of Pennsylvania, this small but influential group advocated suffrage, or voting rights, for African American men as well as the redistribution of southern plantation lands to freed slaves. Stevens called on the federal government to provide freedpeople "a homestead of forty acres of land," which would give them some measure of economic independence. Nonetheless, whatever disagreements the Radicals had with the moderates, all Republicans believed that Congress should have a strong voice in determining the fate of the former Confederate states. From May to December 1865, with Congress out of session, they waited to see what Johnson's restoration plan would produce, ready to assert themselves if his policies deviated too much from their own.

At first, it seemed as if Johnson would proceed as they hoped. He appointed provisional governors to convene new state constitutional conventions and urged these conventions to ratify the Thirteenth Amendment abolishing slavery, revoke the states' ordinances of secession, and refuse to pay Confederate war debts, which the victorious North did not consider legitimate because repayment would benefit southern bondholders who financed the rebellion. He also allowed the majority of white Southerners to obtain amnesty and a pardon by swearing their loyalty to the U.S. Constitution, but he required those who had held more than $20,000 of taxable property—the members of the southern aristocracy—to petition him for a special pardon to restore their rights. Republicans expected him to be harsh in dealing with his former political foes. Instead, Johnson relished the reversal of roles that put members of the southern elite at his mercy. As the once prominent petitioners paraded before him, the president granted almost all of their requests for pardons.

By the time Congress convened in December 1865, Johnson was satisfied that the southern states had fulfilled his requirements for restoration. Moderate and Radical Republicans disagreed, seeing few signs of change or contrition in the South. As a result of Johnson's liberal pardon policy, many former leaders of the Confederacy won election to state constitutional conventions and to Congress. Indeed, Georgians elected Confederate vice president Alexander H. Stephens to the U.S. Senate. In addition, although most of the reconstituted state governments ratified the Thirteenth Amendment, South Carolina and Mississippi refused to repudiate the Confederate debt, and Mississippi rejected the Thirteenth Amendment.

Far from providing freedpeople with basic civil rights protection, the southern states passed a variety of **black codes** intended to reduce blacks to a condition as close to slavery as possible. Some laws prohibited blacks from bearing arms; others outlawed intermarriage and excluded blacks from serving on juries. Many of these laws were designed to ensure that white landowners had a supply of black labor now that slavery had ended. The codes made it difficult for blacks to leave plantations unless they proved they could support themselves. Many southern whites contended that they were acting no differently than their northern counterparts who used vagrancy laws to maintain control over workers.

Northerners viewed this situation with alarm. In their eyes, the postwar South looked very similar to the Old South, with a few cosmetic adjustments. If the black codes prevailed, one Republican proclaimed, "then I demand to know of what practical

Mourning at Stonewall Jackson's Gravesite, 1866 Many Northerners were concerned that the defeat of the Confederacy did not lessen white Southerners' devotion to the "Lost Cause" of a society based on the domination of African Americans. Women, who led the efforts to memorialize Confederate soldiers, are shown at the gravesite of General Stonewall Jackson in Lexington, Virginia.   Virginia Military Institute Archives

value is the amendment abolishing slavery?" Others wondered what their wartime sacrifices had been for if the South admitted no mistakes, was led by the same people, and continued to oppress its black inhabitants. The *Chicago Tribune* declared that Northerners would not allow the black codes to "disgrace one foot of soil in which the bones of our soldiers sleep and over which the flag of freedom waves."

 Online Document Project   Testing and Contesting Freedom
bedfordstmartins.com/hewittlawsonvalue

Johnson and Congressional Resistance

Faced with growing opposition in the North, Johnson stubbornly held his ground. He insisted that the southern states had followed his plan and were entitled to resume their representation in Congress. Republicans objected, and in December 1865 they barred the admission of southern lawmakers, an action that Johnson denounced as illegitimate. Up to this point, it was still possible for Johnson and Congress to work together, if Johnson had been willing to compromise. He was not. Instead, Johnson pushed moderates into the Radical camp with a series of legislative vetoes that challenged the fundamental tenets of Republican policies toward African Americans and the South. In January 1866, the president refused to sign a bill passed by Congress to extend the life of the Freedmen's Bureau for another two years. A few months later, he vetoed the Civil Rights Act, which Congress had passed to protect freedpeople in the South from the restrictions placed on them by the black codes. These bills represented a consensus among moderate and Radical Republicans on the government's responsibility toward former slaves.

Johnson justified his vetoes on both constitutional and personal grounds. Along with Democrats, he contended that so long as Congress refused to admit southern representatives, it could not legally pass laws affecting the South. The chief executive also condemned the Freedmen's Bureau bill because it infringed on the rights of states to handle their internal affairs concerning education and economic matters. Johnson's vetoes exposed his racism and his lifelong belief that the evil of slavery lay in the harm it did to poor white Southerners, not to enslaved blacks. Johnson argued that these congressional bills discriminated against whites, who would receive no benefits under them, and put whites at a disadvantage with blacks who received government assistance. Johnson's private secretary recorded in his diary, "The president has at times exhibited a morbid distress and feeling against the Negroes," including those like Jefferson Long, who spoke out for their full civil rights.

Johnson's actions united moderates and Radicals against him. In April 1866, Congress repassed both the Freedmen's Bureau extension and Civil Rights Act over the president's vetoes. In June, lawmakers adopted the **Fourteenth Amendment**, which incorporated many of the provisions of the Civil Rights Act, and submitted it to the states for ratification (see Appendix). Reflecting its confrontational dealings with the president, Congress wanted to ensure more permanent protection for African Americans than simple legislation could provide. Lawmakers also wanted to act quickly, as the situation in the South seemed to be deteriorating rapidly. The previous month, a race riot had broken out in Memphis, Tennessee. For a day and a half, white mobs, egged on by local police, went on a rampage, during which they terrorized black residents of the city and burned their houses and churches. "The late riots in our city," the editor of a Memphis newspaper asserted, "have satisfied all of one thing, that the *southern man* will not be ruled by the *negro*."

The Fourteenth Amendment defined citizenship to include African Americans, thereby nullifying the ruling in the *Dred Scott* case of 1857, which declared that blacks were not citizens. It extended equal protection and due process of law to all persons and not only citizens. The amendment repudiated Confederate debts, which some state governments had refused to do, and it barred Confederate officeholders from holding elective office unless Congress removed this provision by a two-thirds vote. Although most Republicans were upset with Johnson's behavior, at this point they were not willing to embrace the Radical position entirely. Rather than granting the right to vote to black males at least twenty-one years of age, the Fourteenth Amendment gave the states the option of excluding blacks and accepting a reduction in congressional representation if they did so.

Johnson remained inflexible. Instead of counseling the southern states to accept the Fourteenth Amendment, which would have sped up their readmission to the Union, he encouraged them to reject it. Ironically, Johnson's home state of Tennessee ratified the amendment, but the other states refused. In the fall of 1866, Johnson decided to take his case directly to northern voters before the midterm congressional elections. Campaigning for candidates who shared his views, he embarked on a swing through the Midwest. Clearly out of touch with northern public opinion, Johnson attacked Republican lawmakers and engaged in shouting matches with audiences. On election day, Republicans increased their majorities in Congress and now controlled two-thirds of the seats, providing them with greater power to override presidential vetoes.

Congressional Reconstruction

When the Fortieth Congress convened in 1867, Republican lawmakers charted a new course for Reconstruction. With moderates and Radicals united against the president, Congress intended to force the former Confederate states not only to protect the basic civil rights of African Americans but also to grant them the vote. Moderates now agreed with Radicals that unless blacks had access to the ballot, they would not be able to sustain their freedom. Extending the suffrage to African Americans also aided the fortunes of the Republican Party in the South by adding significant numbers of new black voters. By the end of March, Congress enacted three Military Reconstruction Acts. Together they divided ten southern states into five military districts, each under the supervision of a Union general and his troops (Map 14.1). The male voters of each state, regardless of race, were to elect delegates to a constitutional convention; only former Confederate officials were disfranchised. The conventions were required to draft constitutions that guaranteed black suffrage and ratified the Fourteenth Amendment. Within a year, North Carolina, South Carolina, Florida, Alabama, Louisiana, and Arkansas had fulfilled these obligations and reentered the Union.

Having ensured congressional Reconstruction in the South, Republican lawmakers turned their attention to disciplining the president. Johnson continued to resist congressional policy and used his power as commander in chief to order generals in the military districts to soften the intent of congressional Reconstruction. In response, Congress passed the Command of the Army Act in 1867, which required the president to issue all orders to army commanders in the field through the General of the Army in Washington, D.C., Ulysses S. Grant. The Radicals had won over Grant and knew they could count on him to carry out their policies. Even more threatening to presidential power, Congress

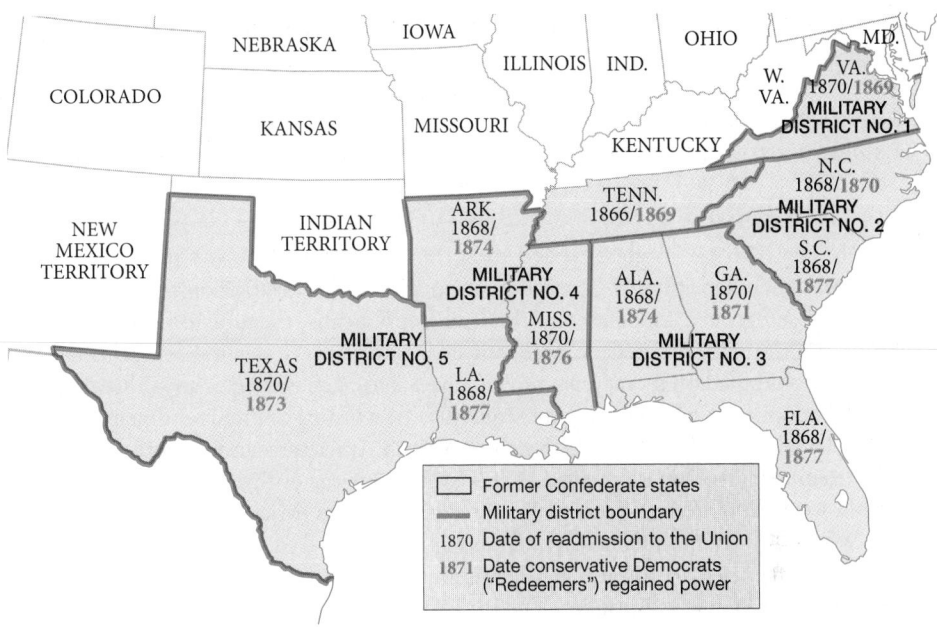

MAP 14.1

Reconstruction in the South   In 1867 Congress enacted legislation dividing the former Confederate states into five military districts. All the states were readmitted to the Union by 1870, and white, conservative Democrats (Redeemers) had replaced Republicans in most states by 1875. Only in Florida, Louisiana, and South Carolina did federal troops remain until 1877.

passed the **Tenure of Office Act**, which prevented Johnson from firing cabinet officers sympathetic to congressional Reconstruction. This measure barred the chief executive from removing from office any appointee that the Senate had ratified previously without returning to the Senate for approval.

Johnson sincerely believed that the Tenure of Office Act violated his presidential prerogative to remove subordinates he considered disloyal or incompetent. He may have had a legitimate constitutional point. However, the quick-tempered Johnson chose to confront the Radical Republicans directly rather than find a way to maneuver around a congressional showdown. In February 1868, Johnson fired Secretary of War Edwin Stanton, a Lincoln appointee and a Radical sympathizer, without Senate approval. In response, congressional Radicals prepared articles of impeachment on eleven counts of misconduct, including willful violation of the Tenure of Office Act.

In late February, the House voted 126 to 47 to impeach Johnson, the first president ever to be impeached, or charged with unlawful activity. The case then went to trial in the Senate, where the chief justice of the Supreme Court presided and a two-thirds vote was necessary for conviction and removal from office. After a six-week hearing, the Senate fell one vote short of convicting Johnson. Most crucial for Johnson's fate were the votes of seven moderate Republicans who refused to find the president guilty of violating his oath to uphold the Constitution, convinced that Johnson's actions were insufficient to merit the enormously significant step of removing a president from office. Although Johnson narrowly remained in office, Congress effectively ended his power to shape Reconstruction policy.

Not only did the Republicans restrain Johnson but they also won the presidency in 1868. Ulysses S. Grant, the popular Civil War Union general, ran against Horatio Seymour, the Democratic governor of New York. Although an ally of the Radical Republicans, Grant called for reconciliation with the South. He easily defeated Seymour, winning nearly 53 percent of the popular vote and 73 percent of the electoral vote.

The Struggle for Universal Suffrage

In February 1869, Congress passed the Fifteenth Amendment to protect black suffrage, which had initially been guaranteed by the Military Reconstruction Acts. A compromise between moderate and Radical Republicans, the amendment prohibited voting discrimination based on race, but it did not deny states the power to impose qualifications based on literacy, payment of taxes, moral character, or any other standard that did not directly relate to race. Subsequently, the wording of the amendment provided loopholes for white leaders to disfranchise African Americans and any other "undesirable" elements. The amendment did, however, cover the entire nation, including the North, where several states, such as Connecticut, Kansas, Michigan, New York, Ohio, and Wisconsin, still excluded blacks from voting.

The Fifteenth Amendment sparked serious conflicts not only within the South but also among old abolitionist allies. The American Anti-Slavery Society disbanded with abolition, but many members believed that important work still remained to be done to guarantee the rights of freedpeople. They formed the American Equal Rights Association immediately following the war. Members of this group divided over the Fifteenth Amendment.

Women's rights advocates, such as Elizabeth Cady Stanton and Susan B. Anthony, had earlier objected to the Fourteenth Amendment because it inserted the word *male* into the Constitution for the first time when describing citizens. Although they had been ardent abolitionists before the war, Stanton and Anthony worried that postwar policies intended to enhance the rights of southern black men would further limit the rights of women. Some African American activists also voiced concern. At a meeting of the Equal Rights Association in 1867, Sojourner Truth noted, "There is quite a stir about colored men getting their rights, but not a word about colored women."

The Fifteenth Amendment ignored women. At the 1869 meeting of the Equal Rights Association, differences over supporting the measure erupted into open conflict. Stanton and Anthony denounced suffrage for black men only, and Stanton now supported her position on racial grounds. She claimed that the "dregs of China, Germany, England, Ireland, and Africa" were degrading the U.S. polity and argued that white, educated women should certainly have the same rights as immigrant and African American men. Black and white supporters of the Fifteenth Amendment, including Frances Ellen Watkins Harper, Wendell Phillips, Abby Kelley, and Frederick Douglass, denounced Stanton's bigotry. Believing that southern black men urgently needed suffrage to protect their newly won freedom, they argued that the ratification of black men's suffrage would speed progress toward the achievement of suffrage for black and white women.

This conflict led to the formation of competing organizations committed to women's suffrage. The National Woman Suffrage Association, established by Stanton and Anthony, allowed only women as members and opposed ratification of the Fifteenth Amendment. The American Woman Suffrage Association, which attracted the support of women and men, white and black, supported ratification. Less than a year later, in the spring of 1870, the Fifteenth Amendment was ratified and went into effect. However, the amendment did not grant the vote to either white or black women. As a result, women suffragists turned to the Fourteenth Amendment to achieve their goal. In 1875 Virginia Minor, who had been denied the ballot in Missouri, argued that the right to vote was one of the "privileges and immunities" granted to all citizens under the Fourteenth Amendment. In *Minor v. Happersatt*, the Supreme Court ruled against her.

REVIEW & RELATE

• What was President Johnson's plan for reconstruction? How were his views out of step with those of most Republicans?

• What characterized congressional Reconstruction? What priorities were reflected in congressional Reconstruction legislation?

Remaking the South

With President Johnson's power effectively curtailed, reconstruction of the South moved quickly. However, despite the fears of southern whites and their supporters in the North, the results were neither extreme nor revolutionary. Although African Americans for the first time participated extensively in electoral politics and made unprecedented gains, whites retained control of the majority of the region's wealth and political power. In contrast to revolutions and civil wars in other countries, only one rebel was executed for war crimes (the commandant of Andersonville Prison in Georgia); only one high-ranking official went to prison (Jefferson Davis); no official was forced into exile, though some fled voluntarily; very little land was confiscated and redistributed; and most rebels regained voting rights and the ability to hold office within seven years after the end of the rebellion.

Whites Reconstruct the South

During the first years of congressional Reconstruction, two groups of whites occupied the majority of elective offices in the South. A significant number of native-born Southerners joined Republicans in forming postwar constitutions and governments. Before the war, some had belonged to the Whig Party and opposed secession from the Union. Many mountain dwellers in Alabama, Georgia, North Carolina, and Tennessee had demonstrated a fiercely independent strain and had remained loyal to the Union. As a white resident of the Georgia mountains commented, "Now is the time for every man to come out and speak his principles publickly and vote for liberty as we have been in bondage long enough." Small merchants and farmers who detested large plantation owners also threw their lot in with the Republicans. Even a few ex-Confederates, such as General James A. Longstreet, decided that the South must change and allied with the Republicans. The majority of whites who continued to support the Democratic Party viewed these whites as traitors. They showed their distaste by calling them **scalawags**, an unflattering term meaning "scoundrels."

At the same time, northern whites came south to support Republican Reconstruction. They had varied reasons for making the journey, but most considered the South a new frontier to be conquered culturally, politically, and economically. Some had served in the

Union army during the war, liked what they saw of the region, and decided to settle there. Some came to help provide education and assist the freedpeople in adjusting to a new way of life. As a relatively underdeveloped area, the South also beckoned fortune seekers and adventurers who saw in the South an opportunity to get rich building railroads, establishing factories, and selling consumer goods. Southern Democrats denounced such northern interlopers as **carpetbaggers**, suggesting that they invaded the region with all their possessions in a satchel, seeking to plunder it and then leave. This characterization applied to some, but it did not accurately describe the motivations of most transplanted Northerners. While they did seek economic opportunity, they were acting as Americans always had in settling new frontiers and pursuing dreams of success. In dismissing them as carpetbaggers, their political enemies employed a double standard because they did not apply this demeaning label to those who traveled west—from both the North and the South—in search of economic opportunity at the expense of Indians and Mexicans settled there. Much of the negative feelings directed toward carpetbaggers resulted primarily from their attempts to ally with African Americans in reshaping the South.

Black Political Participation and Economic Opportunities

As much as the majority of southern whites detested scalawags and carpetbaggers, the primary targets of white hostility were African Americans who attempted to exercise their hard-won freedom. Blacks constituted a majority of voters in five states—Alabama, Florida, South Carolina, Mississippi, and Louisiana—while in Georgia, North Carolina, Texas, and Virginia they fell short of a majority. They did not use their ballots to impose black rule on the South as many white Southerners feared. Only in South Carolina did African Americans control the state legislature, and in no state did they manage to elect a governor. Nevertheless, for the first time in American history, blacks won a wide variety of elected positions. More than six hundred blacks served in state legislatures; another sixteen, including Jefferson F. Long, held seats in the U.S. House of Representatives; and two from Mississippi were chosen to serve in the U.S. Senate.

Officeholding alone does not indicate the enthusiasm that former slaves had for politics. African Americans considered politics a community responsibility, and in addition to casting ballots, they held rallies and mass meetings to discuss issues and choose candidates. Although they could not vote, women attended these gatherings and helped influence their outcome. Covering a Republican convention in Richmond in October 1867, held in the African First Baptist Church, the *New York Times* reported that "the entire colored population of Richmond" attended. Freedpeople also formed associations to promote education, economic advancement, and social welfare programs, all of which they saw as deeply intertwined with politics. These included organizations like Richmond's Mutual Benefit Society, a group formed by single mothers, and the Independent Order of St. Luke, a mutual aid society for black women and men. African American women led both.

The efforts of southern blacks to bolster their freedom included building alliances with sympathetic whites. The resulting interracial political coalitions produced considerable reform in the South. These coalitions created a public school system where none had existed before the war; provided funds for social services, such as poor relief and state hospitals; upgraded prisons; and rebuilt the South's transportation system by supporting railroads and construction projects. Moreover, the state constitutions that the Republicans wrote brought a greater measure of political democracy and equality to the South by extending the right to vote to poor white men as well as black men. Some states allowed married women greater control over their property and liberalized the criminal justice system. In effect, these Reconstruction governments brought the South into the nineteenth century.

Obtaining political representation was one way in which African Americans defined freedom. Economic independence constituted a second. Without government-sponsored land redistribution, however, the options for southern blacks remained limited. Lacking capital to start farms, they entered into various forms of tenant contracts with large landowners. **Sharecropping** proved the most common arrangement. Blacks and poor whites became sharecroppers for much the same economic reasons. They received tools and supplies from landowners and farmed their own plots of land on the plantation. In exchange, sharecroppers turned over a portion of their harvest to the owner and kept some for themselves. Crop divisions varied but were usually explained in detail on written agreements. To make this system profitable, sharecroppers concentrated on producing staple crops such as cotton and tobacco that they could sell for cash.

The benefits of sharecropping proved more valuable to black farmers in theory than in practice. To tide them over during the growing season, croppers had to purchase household provisions on credit from a local merchant, who was often also the farmers' landlord. At the mercy of store owners who kept the books and charged high interest rates, tenants usually found themselves in considerable debt at the end of the year. To satisfy the debt, merchants devised a crop lien system in which tenants pledged a portion of their yearly crop to satisfy what they owed. Most indebted tenants found themselves bound to the landlord because falling prices in agricultural staples during this period meant that they did not receive sufficient return on their produce to get out of debt. For many African Americans, sharecropping turned into a form of virtual slavery.

The picture for black farmers was not all bleak, however. About 20 percent of black farmers managed to buy their own land. Through careful management and extremely hard work, black families planted gardens for household consumption and raised chickens for eggs and food. Despite its pitfalls, sharecropping provided a limited measure of labor independence and allowed some blacks to accumulate small amounts of cash.

Following the war's devastation, many of the South's white, small farmers known as yeomen also fell into sharecropping. Yet planters, too, had changed. Many sons of planters abandoned farming and became lawyers, bankers, and merchants. Despite these changes, one thing remained the same: White elites ruled over blacks and poor whites, and they kept these two economically exploited groups from uniting by fanning the flames of racial prejudice.

Economic hardship and racial bigotry drove many blacks to leave the South. In 1879 former slaves pooled their resources to create land companies and purchase property in Kansas on which to settle. They created black towns that attracted some 25,000 African American migrants from the South, known as **Exodusters**. Kansas was ruled by the Republican Party and had been home to the great antislavery martyr John Brown. As one hopeful freedman from Louisiana wrote to the Kansas governor in 1879, "I am anxious to reach your state . . . because of the sacredness of her soil washed in the blood of humanitarians for the cause of black freedom." Exodusters did not find the Promised Land, however, as poor-quality land and unpredictable weather made farming on the Great Plains a hard and often unrewarding experience. Nevertheless, for many African

American migrants, the chance to own their own land and escape the oppression of the South was worth the hardships. In 1880 the census counted 40,000 blacks living in Kansas.

White Resistance to Congressional Reconstruction

Despite the Republican record of accomplishment during Reconstruction, white Southerners did not accept its legitimacy. They accused interracial governments of conducting a spending spree that raised taxes and encouraged corruption. Indeed, taxes did rise significantly, but mainly because of the need to provide new educational and social services. Corruption, where building projects and railroad construction were concerned, was common during this time. Still, it is unfair to single out Reconstruction governments and especially black legislators as inherently depraved, as their Democratic opponents did. Economic scandals were part of American life after the Civil War. As enormous business opportunities arose and the pent-up energies that had gone into battles over slavery exploded into desires to accumulate wealth, many business leaders and politicians made unlawful deals to enrich themselves.

Most Reconstruction governments had only limited opportunities to transform the South. By the end of 1870, civilian rule had returned to all of the former Confederate states, and they had reentered the Union. Republican rule did not continue past 1870

Exodusters   This photograph of two black couples standing on their homestead was taken around 1880 in Nicodemus, Kansas. These settlers, known as Exodusters, had migrated to northwest Kansas following the end of Reconstruction. They sought economic opportunity free from the racial repression sweeping the South.   Library of Congress

in Virginia, North Carolina, and Tennessee and did not extend beyond 1871 in Georgia and 1873 in Texas. In 1874 Democrats deposed Republicans in Arkansas and Alabama; two years later, Democrats triumphed in Mississippi. In only three states—Louisiana, Florida, and South Carolina—did Reconstruction last until 1877.

 Online Document Project   Reconstruction in South Carolina
bedfordstmartins.com/hewittlawsonvalue

The Democrats who replaced Republicans trumpeted their victories as bringing "redemption" to the South. Of course, these so-called Redeemers were referring to the white South. For black Republicans and their white allies, redemption meant defeat, not resurrection. Democratic victories came at the ballot boxes, but violence, intimidation, and fraud usually paved the way. It was not enough for Democrats to attack Republican policies. They also used racist appeals to divide poor whites from blacks and backed them up with force. In 1865 in Pulaski, Tennessee, General Nathan Bedford Forrest organized Confederate veterans into a social club called the Knights of the Ku Klux Klan (KKK). The name came from the Greek word *kuklos*, meaning "circle." Spreading throughout the South, the KKK did not function as an ordinary social association; its followers donned robes and masks to hide their identities and terrify their victims. Ku Kluxers wielded rifles and guns and rode on horseback to the homes and churches of black and white Republicans to keep them from voting. When threats did not work, they murdered their victims. In 1871, for example, 150 African Americans were killed in Jackson County in the Florida Panhandle. A black clergyman lamented, "That is where Satan has his seat." Here and elsewhere, many of the individuals targeted had managed to buy property, gain political leadership, or in other ways defy white stereotypes of African American inferiority. Local rifle clubs, hunting groups, and other white supremacist organizations joined the Klan in waging a reign of terror. During the 1875 election in Mississippi, which toppled the Republican government, armed terrorists killed hundreds of Republicans and scared many more away from the polls.

To combat the terror unleashed by the Klan and its allies, Congress passed three Force Acts in 1870 and 1871. These measures empowered the president to dispatch officials into the South to supervise elections and prevent voting interference. Directed specifically at the KKK, one law barred secret organizations from using force to violate equal protection of the laws. In 1872 Congress established a joint committee to probe Klan tactics, and its investigations produced thirteen volumes of vivid testimony about the horrors perpetrated by the Klan. Elias Hill, a freedman from South Carolina who had become a Baptist preacher and teacher, was one of those who appeared before Congress. He and his brother lived next door to each other. The Klansmen went first to his brother's house, where, as Hill testified, they "broke open the door and attacked his wife, and I heard her screaming and mourning [moaning]. . . . At last I heard them have [rape] her in the yard. She was crying and the Ku-Klux were whipping her to make her tell where I lived." When Klansmen finally discovered Elias Hill, they dragged him out of his house, accused him of preaching against the Klan, beat and whipped him, and threatened to kill him. On the basis of such testimony, the federal government prosecuted some 3,000 Klansmen. Only 600 were convicted, however. As the Klan disbanded in the wake of federal prosecutions, other vigilante organizations arose to take its place.

REVIEW & RELATE

• What role did black people play in remaking southern society during Reconstruction?

• How did southern whites fight back against Reconstruction? What role did terrorism and political violence play in this effort?

The Unmaking of Reconstruction

The violence, intimidation, and fraud perpetrated by Redeemers against black and white Republicans in the South does not fully explain the unmaking of Reconstruction. Although Republicans in Congress enacted legislation combating the KKK and racial discrimination in public facilities, by the early 1870s white Northerners had grown weary of the struggle to protect the rights of freedpeople. In the minds of many, white Northerners had done more than enough for black Southerners, and it was time to focus on other issues. Growing economic problems intensified this feeling. More and more northern whites came to believe that any debt owed to black people for northern complicity in the sin of slavery had been wiped out by the blood shed during the Civil War. By the early 1870s, burying and memorializing the Civil War dead emerged as a common concern among white Americans, in both the North and the South. White America was once again united, if only in the shared belief that it was time to move on, consigning the issues of slavery and civil rights to history.

The Republican Retreat

Most northern whites shared the racial views of their counterparts in the South. Although they had supported protection of black civil rights and suffrage, they still believed that African Americans were inferior to whites, and social integration was no more tolerable to them than it was to white Southerners. They began to sympathize with racist complaints voiced from the South that blacks were not capable of governing honestly and effectively.

In 1872 a group calling themselves **Liberal Republicans** challenged the reelection of President Grant, the Civil War general who had won the presidency on the Republican ticket in 1868. Financial scandals had racked the Grant administration. This high-level corruption reflected the get-rich-quick schemes connected to economic speculation and development following the Civil War. Outraged by these misdeeds and the rising level of immoral behavior in government and business, Liberal Republicans nominated Horace Greeley, editor of the *New York Tribune*, to run against Grant. They linked government corruption to the expansion of federal power that accompanied Reconstruction, and called for the removal of troops from the South and amnesty for former Confederates. They also campaigned for civil service reform in order to establish a merit system for government employment and for abolition of the "spoils system"—in which the party in power rewarded loyal supporters with political appointments—that had been in place since the administration of Andrew Jackson.

The Democratic Party believed that Liberal Republicans offered the best chance to defeat Grant, and it endorsed Greeley. Despite the scandals that surrounded him, Grant remained popular. Moreover, the main body of Republicans "waved the bloody shirt," reminding northern voters that a ballot cast for the opposition tarnished the memory of brave Union soldiers who had died during the war. With the newly created national cemeteries, particularly the one established in Arlington, Virginia, providing a vivid reminder of the hundreds of thousands of soldiers killed, the "bloody shirt" remained a potent symbol. The president won reelection with an even greater margin than he had four years earlier. Nevertheless, the attacks against Grant foreshadowed the Republican retreat on Reconstruction. Among the Democrats sniping at Grant was Andrew Johnson. Johnson had returned to Tennessee, and in 1874 the state legislature chose the former president to serve in the U.S. Senate. He continued to speak out against the presence of federal troops in the South until his death in 1875.

Congressional and Judicial Retreat

By the time Grant began his second term, Congress was already considering bills to restore officeholding rights to former Confederates who had not yet sworn allegiance to the Union. Black representatives, such as Georgia congressman Jefferson Long, as well as some white lawmakers, remained opposed to such measures, but in 1872 Congress removed the penalties placed on former Confederates by the Fourteenth Amendment and permitted nearly all rebel leaders the right to vote and hold office. Two years later, for the first time since the start of the Civil War, the Democrats gained a majority in the House of Representatives and prepared to remove the remaining troops from the South.

Economic concerns increasingly replaced racial considerations as the top priority for northern Republican leaders. Northerners and Southerners began calling more loudly for national unity and reconciliation. In 1873 a financial panic resulting from the collapse of the Northern Pacific Railroad triggered a severe economic depression lasting late into the decade. Tens of thousands of unemployed workers across the country worried more about finding jobs than they did about blacks in the South. Businessmen, too, were plagued with widespread bankruptcy. As workers looked to labor unions for support, business leaders looked to the federal government for assistance. When strikes erupted across the country in 1877, most notably the Great Railway Strike, employers asked the U.S. government to remove troops from the South and dispatch them against strikers in the North and the West.

While Northerners sought a way to extricate themselves from Reconstruction, the Supreme Court weakened enforcement of the civil rights acts. In 1873 the *Slaughterhouse* cases defined the rights that African Americans were entitled to under the Fourteenth Amendment very narrowly. Reflecting the shift from moral to economic concerns, the justices interpreted the amendment as extending greater protection to corporations in conducting business than that extended to blacks. As a result, blacks had to depend on southern state governments to protect their civil rights, the same state authorities that had deprived them of their rights in the first place. In *United States v. Cruikshank* (1876), the high court narrowed the Fourteenth Amendment further, ruling that it protected blacks against abuses only by state officials and agencies, not by private groups such as the Ku Klux Klan. Seven years later, the Court struck down the Civil Rights Act of 1875, which had extended "full and equal treatment" in public accommodations for persons of all races.

The Presidential Compromise of 1876

The presidential election of 1876 set in motion events that officially brought Reconstruction to an end. The Republicans nominated Rutherford B. Hayes, a Civil War officer and governor of Ohio. A supporter of civil service reform, Hayes was chosen, in part, because he was untainted by the corruption that plagued the Grant administration. The Democrats selected their own crusader against bribery and graft, Governor Samuel J. Tilden of New York, who had prosecuted political corruption in New York City.

The outcome of the election depended on twenty disputed electoral votes, nineteen from the South and one from Oregon. Tilden won 51 percent of the popular vote, but Reconstruction political battles in Florida, Louisiana, and South Carolina put the election up for grabs. In each of these states, the outgoing Republican administration certified Hayes as the winner, while the incoming Democratic regime declared for Tilden.

The Constitution assigns Congress the task of counting and certifying the electoral votes submitted by the states. Normally, this is merely a formality, but 1876 was different. Democrats controlled the House, Republicans controlled the Senate, and neither branch would budge on which votes to count. Hayes needed all twenty for victory; Tilden needed only one. To break the logjam, Congress created a fifteen-member **Joint Electoral Commission**, composed of seven Democrats, seven Republicans, and one independent (five members of the House, five U.S. senators, and five Supreme Court justices). As it turned out, the independent commissioner, Justice David Davis, resigned, and his replacement, Justice Joseph P. Bradley, voted with the Republicans to count all twenty votes for Hayes, making him president (Map 14.2).

Still, Congress had to ratify this count, and disgruntled southern Democrats in the Senate threatened a filibuster—unlimited debate—to block certification of Hayes. With the March 4, 1877, date for the presidential inauguration creeping perilously close and no winner officially declared, behind-the-scenes negotiations finally helped settle the controversy. A series of meetings between Hayes supporters and southern Democrats led to a bargain. According to the agreement, Democrats would support Hayes in exchange for the president appointing a Southerner to his cabinet, withdrawing the last federal troops from the South, and endorsing construction of a transcontinental railroad through the South. This **compromise of 1877** averted a crisis over presidential succession, underscored increased southern Democratic influence within Congress, and marked the end to strong federal protection for African Americans in the South.

REVIEW & RELATE

• Why did northern interest in Reconstruction wane in the 1870s?

• What common values and beliefs among white Americans were reflected in the compromise of 1877?

Conclusion: The Legacies of Reconstruction

Reconstruction was, in many ways, profoundly limited. African Americans did not receive the landownership that would have provided them with the economic independence to bolster their freedom from the racist assaults of white Southerners. The civil and political rights that the federal government conferred did not withstand Redeemers' efforts to disfranchise and deprive the freedpeople of equal rights. The Republican Party shifted its priorities elsewhere, and Democrats gained enough political power nationally to short-circuit federal intervention, while numerous problems remained unresolved in the South. Northern support for racial equality did not run very deep, so white Northerners, who shared many of the prejudices of white Southerners,

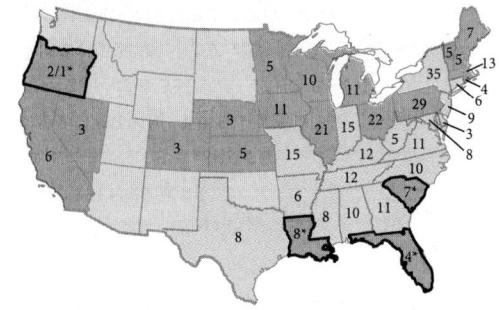

MAP 14.2

The Election of 1876 The presidential election of 1876 got swept up in Reconstruction politics. Democrats defeated Republicans in Florida, Louisiana, and South Carolina, but both parties claimed the electoral votes for their candidates. A federal electoral commission set up to investigate the twenty disputed votes, including one from Oregon, awarded the votes and the election to the Republican, Rutherford B. Hayes.

Candidate	Electoral Vote	Popular Vote	Percentage of Popular Vote
Rutherford B. Hayes (Republican)	185*	4,036,298	47.9**
Samuel J. Tilden (Democrat)	184	4,288,590	51.0
——— Disputed electoral outcome			

*20 electoral votes were disputed.
**Percentages do not total 100 because some popular votes went to other parties.

were happy to extricate themselves from further intervention in southern racial matters. Nor was there sufficient support to give women, white and black, the right to vote. Finally, federal courts, with growing concerns over economic rather than social issues, sanctioned Northerners' retreat by providing constitutional legitimacy for abandoning black Southerners and rejecting women's suffrage in court decisions that narrowed the interpretation of the Fourteenth and Fifteenth Amendments.

Despite all of this, Reconstruction did transform the country. As a result of Reconstruction, slavery was abolished, and the legal basis for freedom was enshrined in the Constitution. Indeed, blacks exercised a measure of political and economic freedom during Reconstruction that never entirely disappeared over the decades to come. In many areas, freedpeople, as exemplified by Congressman Jefferson Franklin Long among many others, asserted what they could never have during slavery—control over their lives, their churches, their labor, and their families. What they could not practice during their own time because of racial discrimination, their descendants would one day revive through the promises codified in the Fourteenth and Fifteenth Amendments.

African Americans transformed not only themselves; they transformed the nation. The Constitution became much more democratic and egalitarian through inclusion of the Reconstruction amendments. Reconstruction lawmakers took an important step toward making the United States the "more perfect union" that the nation's Founders had pledged to create. Reconstruction established a model for expanding the power of the federal government to resolve domestic crises that lay beyond the abilities of states and ordinary citizens. It remained a powerful legacy for those elected officials in the future who dared to invoke it. And Reconstruction transformed the South to its everlasting benefit. It modernized state constitutions, expanded educational and social welfare systems, and unleashed the repressed potential for industrialization and economic development that the preservation of slavery had restrained. Ironically, Reconstruction did as much for white Southerners as it did for black Southerners in liberating them from the past.

Chapter Review

MAKE IT STICK

 LearningCurve **bedfordstmartins.com/hewittlawsonvalue**
After reading the chapter, use LearningCurve to retain what you've read.

IDENTIFY KEY TERMS

Identify and explain the significance of each term below.

Freedmen's Bureau (p. 352)
Proclamation of Amnesty and
    Reconstruction (p. 356)
Thirteenth Amendment (p. 356)
black codes (p. 358)
Fourteenth Amendment (p. 359)
Tenure of Office Act (p. 361)
Fifteenth Amendment (p. 362)
American Equal Rights Association (p. 362)
National Woman Suffrage Association
    (p. 362)

American Woman Suffrage Association
    (p. 362)
scalawags (p. 363)
carpetbaggers (p. 364)
sharecropping (p. 365)
Exodusters (p. 365)
Redeemers (p. 367)
Knights of the Ku Klux Klan (KKK) (p. 367)
Liberal Republicans (p. 368)
Joint Electoral Commission (p. 370)
compromise of 1877 (p. 370)

REVIEW & RELATE

Answer the focus questions from each section of the chapter.

1. What were freedpeople's highest priorities in the years immediately following the Civil War? Why?

2. How did freedpeople define freedom? What steps did they take to make freedom real for themselves and their children?

3. What was President Johnson's plan for reconstruction? How were his views out of step with those of most Republicans?

4. What characterized congressional Reconstruction? What priorities were reflected in congressional Reconstruction legislation?

5. What role did black people play in remaking southern society during Reconstruction?

6. How did southern whites fight back against Reconstruction? What role did terrorism and political violence play in this effort?

7. Why did northern interest in Reconstruction wane in the 1870s?

8. What common values and beliefs among white Americans were reflected in the compromise of 1877?

ONLINE DOCUMENT PROJECTS

◆ **Testing and Contesting Freedom**
◆ **Reconstruction in South Carolina**

After reading the primary sources in these document sets, answer the **Interpret the Evidence** questions to help you analyze each of the documents, and then answer the **Put It in Context** question(s) to help you relate the documents to the topics and themes you read about in the chapter.

bedfordstmartins.com/hewittlawsonvalue

TIMELINE OF EVENTS

1863
- Lincoln issues Proclamation of Amnesty and Reconstruction

1865
- Ku Klux Klan formed
- Freedmen's Bureau established
- Congress passes Thirteenth Amendment

April 1865
- Lincoln assassinated; Andrew Johnson becomes president

May–December 1865
- Presidential Reconstruction under Andrew Johnson

1866
- Congress passes extension of Freedmen's Bureau and Civil Rights Act over Johnson's presidential veto
- Congress passes Fourteenth Amendment

1867
- Military Reconstruction Acts divide the South into military districts
- Congress passes Command of the Army and Tenure of Office Acts

1868
- Andrew Johnson impeached

1869
- Congress passes Fifteenth Amendment
- Women's suffrage movement splits over support of Fifteenth Amendment

1870
- 250,000 blacks attend schools established by the Freedmen's Bureau
- Civilian rule reestablished in all former Confederate states

1870–1871
- Jefferson Long serves as a Republican congressman from Georgia

1870–1872
- Congress takes steps to curb KKK violence in the South

1872
- Liberal Republicans challenge reelection of President Grant

1873
- Financial panic sparks depression lasting until the late 1870s

1873–1883
- Supreme Court limits rights of African Americans

1875
- Congress passes Civil Rights Act outlawing discrimination in public accommodations, which the Supreme Court rules unconstitutional in 1883

1877
- Republicans and southern Democrats reach compromise resulting in the election of Rutherford B. Hayes as president and the end of Reconstruction

1879
- Black Exodusters migrate from South to Kansas

Frontier Encounters

1865–1896

AMERICAN HISTORIES

As an adult, Phoebe Ann Moses embodied the excitement and adventure of
the mythical American West. Her childhood, however, was one of poverty
and hardship. Born in 1860, Phoebe Ann grew up east of the Mississippi,
seventy miles north of Cincinnati, Ohio. One of seven surviving children,
she was sent to an orphanage at the age of nine, after her father died and
her mother could not care for all her children. After working for a farm
family, she ran away at the age of twelve and found a new home with a
recently remarried widow. Over the next four years, Phoebe Ann learned to
ride and hunt and became an expert shot with a rifle. At fifteen, she
entered a shooting contest and defeated a professional marksman, Frank
Butler. The competition sparked a romance, and the two married in 1876.
Phoebe Ann changed her professional name to "Annie Oakley," and she and
Butler went on tour throughout the Midwest in an act that featured
precision shooting.

In 1884 Oakley and Butler met William F. "Buffalo Bill" Cody in New
Orleans. Cody had been a buffalo hunter on the Great Plains and an army
scout during the Indian wars of the 1870s. In 1883, as the western frontier
began to recede and the U.S. government relocated Native Americans who
lived there, Cody attempted to recapture and reinvent the frontier
experience by staging "Wild West" shows. A year later, he hired Oakley, with
Butler serving as her manager. For the next fifteen years, the diminutive
Oakley was the star of the show. Wearing a fringed skirt, an embroidered
blouse, and a broad felt hat emblazoned with a star, she stood atop her
horse and shot the lights out of a revolving wheel of lit candles and took

dead aim at other targets tossed in the air. Oakley toured Europe and fascinated heads of state and audiences alike with her version of "western authenticity." Fans at home and overseas displayed great nostalgia for a fast-diminishing era. When the census of 1890 reported that no open land was left to settle and thus no western frontier was left to conquer, Oakley's popularity soared. She continued performing in Wild West shows until her death in 1926.

While Annie Oakley portrayed the Wild West, Geronimo had lived it. Born to a Chiricahua Apache family in what was then northern Mexico (present-day Arizona and New Mexico), Geronimo led Apaches in a constant struggle against Spain, Mexico, and the United States. Driven to the hills of Arizona and New Mexico by Spanish conquistadors centuries before Geronimo was born, Apaches raided settlements to support themselves. In 1851 a band of Mexicans raided an Apache camp, murdering Geronimo's mother, wife, and three children. After fighting Mexicans, Geronimo clashed with U.S. troops and evaded capture until 1877, when an Indian agent arrested him in New Mexico. Sent to a reservation, Geronimo escaped and for eight years engaged in daring raids against his foes. In 1886 two Chiricahua scouts recruited by General Nelson Miles led the military to Geronimo. Against an army of five thousand soldiers, the Apache warrior, with a band of eighteen fighters and some women and children, finally surrendered and was eventually relocated by the U.S. government to Fort Sill, Oklahoma.

The once-elusive warrior decided to take advantage of his legendary reputation. With Buffalo Bill cashing in on America's fascination with the mythic West and "savage" Indians, Geronimo, like Annie Oakley, exploited this appeal. He sold photos of himself and pieces of his clothing; he appeared at the 1904 World's Fair in St. Louis, selling bows and arrows and autographs; and in 1905 he rode in President Theodore Roosevelt's inaugural parade as an example of a "tamed" Indian. Although he converted to Christianity, Geronimo, ever the rebel, was later expelled from his church for gambling. Crass commercialism and religious conversion aside, Geronimo never gave up the idea of returning to his birthplace. As long as the U.S. government prohibited him from going back to his ancestral lands in the Southwest, he considered himself a "prisoner of war." And so he remained until his death in 1909.

AS PROFOUNDLY DIFFERENT as Annie Oakley's and Geronimo's individual histories were, they both contributed to the creation of a shared story, the myth of the American West. The West has great fascination in American culture. Stories about the frontier have romanticized both cowboys and Indians. These stories have also glorified individualism, self-help, and American ingenuity and minimized cooperation, organization, and the role of foreign influence in developing the West. As the American histories of Annie Oakley and Geronimo make clear, reality presents a more complicated picture of a diverse region initially inhabited by native peoples who were pushed aside by the arrival of white settlers and immigrants. In the areas known as the Great Plains and the far West, women took on new roles, and new cities emerged to accommodate the influx of miners, ranchers, and farmers.

Opening the West

The lands west of the Mississippi were not hospitable to farmers and other adventurers lured by the appeal of cheap land and a fresh start. These pioneers faced many challenges with rugged determination; however, they could not have settled the West on their own. Federal policy and foreign investment played a large role in encouraging and financing the development of the West. Railroads were essential in transforming the region (Map 15.1).

The Great Plains

In the mid-nineteenth century, the western frontier lay in the **Great Plains**. This region spreads through present-day North and South Dakota, Nebraska, Kansas, Oklahoma, Texas, Montana, Wyoming, Colorado, New Mexico, Idaho, Utah, Arizona, and Nevada. Lying on both sides of the Rocky Mountains, the Great Plains plateau was a semiarid territory with an average yearly rainfall of twenty inches, enough to sustain short grasslands but not many trees. Bison, pronghorn antelope, jack rabbits, and prairie dogs roamed over great distances to nourish themselves on the sparse vegetation that grew in this delicate ecosystem. Grasshoppers and locusts periodically swarmed into the area. Indian hunters in the very dry central and southern plains—Apache, Arapaho,

Cheyenne, Comanche, Kiowa—opened up these lands to human habitation and survived by hunting and cultivating the grasslands.

Prospects for sedentary farmers in this dry region did not appear promising. In 1878 geologist John Wesley Powell issued a report that questioned whether the land beyond the easternmost portion of the Great Plains could support small farming. Lack of rainfall, he argued, would make it difficult or even impossible

Lone Wolf and his wife Etla, Kiowa Indians, c. 1860.   Library of Congress

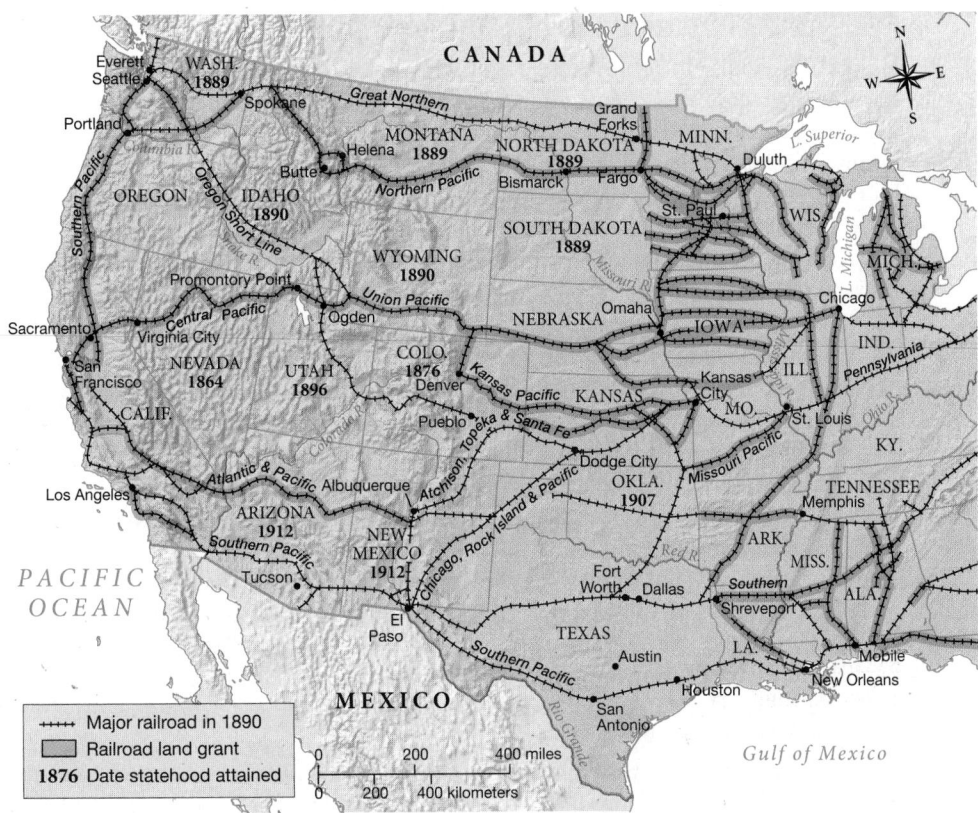

MAP 15.1

The American West, 1860–1900   Railroads played a key role in the expansion and settlement of the American West. The network of railroads running throughout the West opened the way for extensive migration from the East and for the development of a national market. None of this would have been possible without the land grants provided to the railroads by the U.S. government.

for homesteaders to support themselves on family farms of 160 acres. Instead, he recommended that for the plains to prove economically sustainable, settlers would have to work much larger stretches of land, around 2,560 acres (4 square miles). This would provide ample room to raise livestock under dry conditions.

Powell's words of caution did little to diminish Americans' conviction, dating back to Thomas Jefferson, that small farmers would populate the territories brought under U.S. jurisdiction and renew democratic values as they ventured forth. Charles Dana Wilber, a booster of settlement in Nebraska, summed up the view of those who saw no barriers to the expansion of small farmers in the plains. Rejecting the idea that either a Divine Creator or nature had determined that these lands should remain a "perpetual desert," Wilber asserted that "in reality there is no desert anywhere except by man's permission or neglect." Along with millions of others, he had great faith in Americans' ability to turn the Great Plains into a place where Jefferson's republican vision could take root and prosper.

Federal Policy and Foreign Investment

Despite the popular association of the West with individual initiative and self-sufficiency, the federal government played a huge role in facilitating the settlement of the West. National lawmakers enacted legislation offering free or cheap land to settlers and to mining, lumber, and railroad companies. The U.S. government also provided subsidies for transporting mail and military supplies, recruited soldiers to subdue the Indians who stood in the way of expansion, and appointed officials to govern the territories.

Along with federal policy, foreign investment helped fuel development of the West. Lacking sufficient funds of its own, the United States turned to Europe to finance the sale of public bonds and private securities. European financial houses held a majority ownership in the United States Mortgage Company and the Equitable Trust Company of New York, both of which bought and sold mortgages. European firms also invested in American mines, with the British leading the way. In 1872 an Englishman wrote that mines in Nevada were "more British than American." The development of the western cattle range—the symbol of the American frontier and the heroic cowboy—was also funded by overseas financiers. At the height of the cattle boom in the 1880s, British firms supplied some $45 million to underwrite ranch operations.

The largest share of money that flowed from Europe to the United States came with the expansion of the railroads, the most important ingredient in opening the West (Figure 15.1). The economist Joseph Schumpeter concluded that it was "primarily English (and other European) capital which took the responsibility for a great part of the $2 billion which are said to have been expended on American railroads from 1867 to 1873."

The **transcontinental railroad** became the gateway to the West. In 1862 the Republican-led Congress appropriated vast areas of land that railroad companies could use to lay their tracks or sell to raise funds for construction. The Central Pacific Company

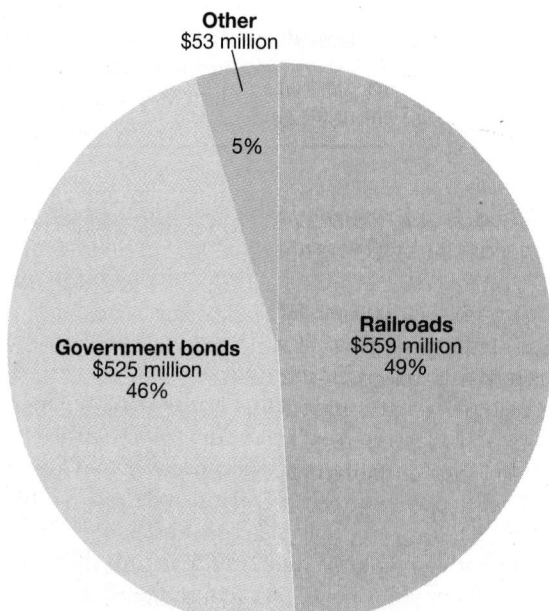

Other
$53 million

5%

Government bonds
$525 million
46%

Railroads
$559 million
49%

FIGURE 15.1

British Foreign Investment in the United States, 1876

British investment was an important source of funding for westward expansion following the Civil War. Nearly half of all British loans went toward financing railroad construction, which required large capital expenditures. The British also invested heavily in government bonds and to a lesser extent in cattle ranching and mining enterprises.

Source: Data from Mina Wilkins, *The History of Foreign Investment in the United States to 1914* (Cambridge, MA: Harvard University Press, 1989), 164.

built from west to east, starting in Sacramento, California. The construction project attracted thousands of Chinese railroad workers, boosting the sparse population of the western territory. From the opposite direction, the Union Pacific Company began laying track in Council Bluffs, Iowa, and hired primarily Irish workers. In May 1869, the Central Pacific and Union Pacific crews met at Promontory Point, Utah, amid great celebration. Workmen from the two companies drove a golden spike to complete the connection. For many Americans recovering from four years of brutal civil war and still embroiled in southern reconstruction (see chapter 14), the completion of the transcontinental railroad renewed their faith in the nation's ingenuity and destiny. A wagon train had once taken six to eight weeks to travel across the West. That trip could now be completed by rail in seven days. The railroad allowed both people and goods to move faster and in greater numbers than before. The West was now open not just to rugged pioneers but to anyone who could afford a railroad ticket.

The building of the railroads fostered corruption. Union Pacific promoters created a fake construction company called the Crédit Mobilier, which they used to funnel government bond and contract money into their own pockets. They also bribed congressmen to avoid investigation into their sordid dealings. Despite these efforts, in 1872 Congress exposed these wrongdoings.

REVIEW & RELATE

- What role did the federal government play in opening the West to settlement and economic exploitation?
- Explain the determination of Americans to settle in land west of the Mississippi River despite the challenges the region presented.

Conquest of the Frontier

American pioneers may have thought they were moving into a wilderness, but the West was home to large numbers of American Indians. Before pioneers and entrepreneurs could go west to pursue their economic dreams, the U.S. government would have to remove this unwelcome obstacle to American expansion. Through treaties—most of which Americans broke—and war, white Americans conquered the Indian tribes inhabiting the Great Plains during the nineteenth century. After the native population was largely subdued, those who wanted to reform Indian policy focused on carving up tribal lands and forcing Indians to assimilate into American society.

Indian Civilizations

Long before white settlers appeared, the frontier was already home to diverse peoples. The many native groups who inhabited the West spoke distinct languages, engaged in different economic activities, and competed with one another for power and resources. The descendants of Spanish conquistadors had also lived in the Southwest and California since the late sixteenth century, pushing the boundaries of the Spanish empire northward from Mexico. Indeed, Spaniards established the city of Santa Fe as the territorial capital of New Mexico years before the English landed at Jamestown, Virginia, in 1607. The United States then acquired the New Mexican and California territories as spoils of the Mexican-American War in 1848.

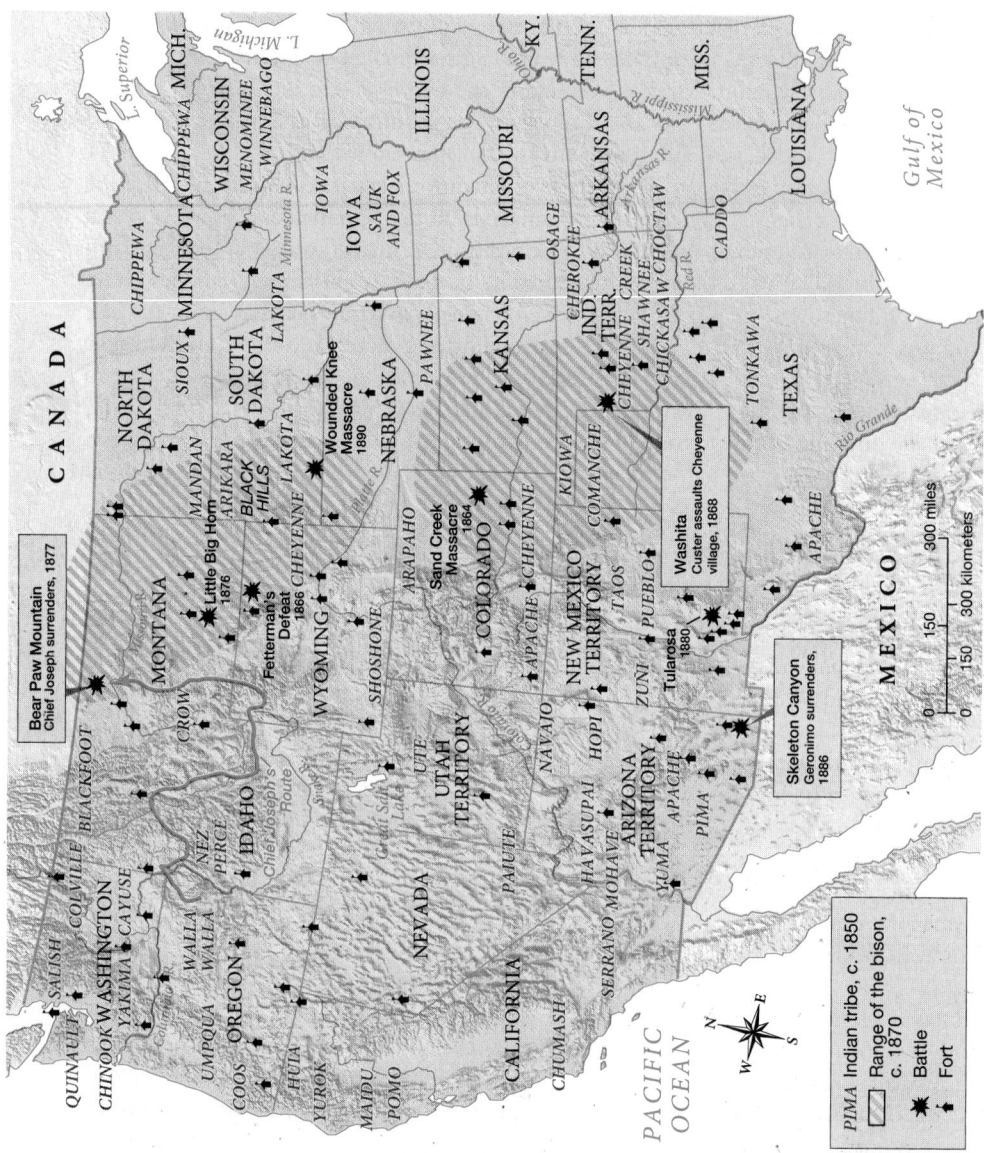

MAP 15.2

The Indian Frontier, 1870 Western migration posed a threat to the dozens of Indian tribes and the immense herds of bison in the region. The tribes had signed treaties with the U.S. government recognizing the right to live on their lands. The presence of U.S. forts did not protect the Indians from settlers who invaded their territories.

By the end of the Civil War, around 350,000 Indians were living west of the Mississippi. They constituted the surviving remnants of the 1 million people who had occupied the land for thousands of years before Europeans set foot in America. Nez Percé, Ute, and Shoshone Indians lived in the Northwest and the Rocky Mountain region; Lakota, Cheyenne, Blackfoot, Crow, and Arapaho tribes occupied the vast expanse of the central and northern plains; and Apaches, Comanches, Kiowas, Navajos, and Pueblos made up the bulk of the population in the Southwest. Some of the tribes, such as the Cherokee, Creek, and Shawnee, had been forcibly removed from the East during Andrew Jackson's presidency in the 1830s. The tribes each adapted in unique ways to the geography and climate of their home territories, spoke their own language, and had their own history and traditions. Some were hunters, others farmers; some nomadic, others sedentary. In New Mexico, the Apaches, including Geronimo, were expert horsemen and fierce warriors, while the Pueblo Indians built homes out of adobe and developed a flourishing system of agriculture. The lives of all Indian peoples were affected by the arrival of Europeans, but the consequences of cross-cultural contact varied considerably depending on the history and circumstances of each tribe (Map 15.2).

Given the rich assortment of Indian tribes, it is difficult to generalize about Indian culture and society. Pueblo Indians cultivated the land through methods of irrigation that foreshadowed modern practices. The Pawnees periodically set fire to the land to improve game hunting and the growth of vegetation. Indians on the southern plains gradually became enmeshed in the market economy for bison robes, which they sold to American traders. Indians were not pacifists, and they engaged in warfare with their enemies in disputes over hunting grounds, horses, and honor. However, the introduction of guns by European and American traders had transformed Indian warfare into a much more deadly affair than had existed previously. And by the mid-nineteenth century, some tribes had become so deeply engaged in the commercial fur trade with whites that they had depleted their own hunting grounds.

Native Americans had their own approach toward nature and the land they inhabited. Most tribes did not accept private ownership of land, as white pioneers did. Indians recognized the concept of private property in ownership of their horses, weapons, tools, and shelters, but they viewed the land as the common domain of their tribe, for use by all members. "The White man knows how to make everything," the Hunkpapa Lakota chieftain Sitting Bull remarked, "but he does not know how to distribute it." This communitarian outlook also reflected native attitudes toward the environment. They considered human beings not as superior to the rest of nature's creations, but rather as part of an interconnected world of animals, plants, and natural elements. Chief Joseph, leader of the Nez Percé Indians, explained to whites who tried to encroach on his land: "The country was made without lines of demarcation, and it's no man's business to divide it. . . . I see whites all over the country gaining wealth, and see their desire to give us lands that are worthless. . . . The earth and myself are of one mind. The measure of the land and the measure of our bodies are the same." According to this view, all plants and animals were part of a larger spirit world, which flowed from the power of the sun, the sky, and the earth.

The bison played a central role in Indian religion and society. By the mid-nineteenth century, approximately thirty million bison (commonly known as buffalo) grazed on the Great Plains. Before acquiring guns, Indians used a variety of means to hunt their prey, including bows and arrows and spears. Some rode their horses to chase bison and stampede them over cliffs. The meat from the buffalo provided food; its hide provided material to construct tepees and make blankets and clothes; bones were crafted into tools, knives, and weapons; even bison dung served a purpose—after it dried and hardened, "buffalo chips" became an excellent source of fuel. It is therefore not surprising that the Plains Indians dressed up in colorful outfits, painted their bodies, and danced to the almighty power of the buffalo and the spiritual presence within it.

Indian hunting societies contained gender distinctions, primarily around the use of horses to pursue bison. The task of riding horses to hunt bison became men's work; women waited for the hunters to return and then prepared the buffalo hides. Nevertheless, women refused to think of their role as passive: They saw themselves as sharing in the work of providing food, shelter, and clothing for the members of their tribe. Similarly, the religious belief that the spiritual world touched every aspect of the material world gave women an opportunity to experience this transcendent power without the mediation of male leaders, including the revered medicine men.

Changing Federal Policy toward Indians

The U.S. government started out by treating western Indians as autonomous nations, thereby recognizing their stewardship over the land they occupied. In 1851 the **Treaty of Fort Laramie** confined tribes on the northern plains to designated areas in an attempt to keep white settlers from encroaching on their land. A treaty two years later applied these terms to tribes on the southern plains. Indians kept their part of the agreement, but white miners racing to strike it rich did not. They roamed through Indian hunting grounds in search of ore and faced little government enforcement of the existing treaties. In fact, the U.S. military made matters considerably worse. On November 29, 1864, a peaceful band of 700 Cheyennes and Arapahos under the leadership of Chief Black Kettle gathered at Sand Creek, Colorado, supposedly under guarantees of U.S. protection. Instead, Colonel John M. Chivington and his troops launched an attack, despite a white flag of surrender hoisted by the Indians, and brutally scalped and killed some 270 Indians, mainly women and children. A congressional investigation later determined that the victims "were mutilated in the most horrible manner." Although there was considerable public outcry over the incident, as evidenced by the congressional investigation, the government did nothing to increase enforcement of its treaty obligations. In almost all disputes between white settlers and Indians, the government sided with the whites, regardless of the Indians' legal rights.

The duplicity of the U.S. government was not without consequences. The Sand Creek massacre unleashed Indian wars throughout the central plains, where the Lakota Sioux led the resistance from 1865 to 1868. In 1866 they killed eighty soldiers under the command of Captain William J. Fetterman in Wyoming. After two years of fierce fighting, both sides signed a second Treaty of Fort Laramie, which gave northern tribes control over the "Great Reservation" set aside in parts of present-day Montana, Wyoming, North Dakota, and South Dakota. Another treaty placed the southern tribes in a reservation carved out of western Oklahoma.

One of the tribes that wound up in Oklahoma was the Nez Percé. Originally settled in the corner where Washington, Oregon, and Idaho meet, the tribe was forced to sign a treaty ceding most of its land to the United States and to relocate onto a reservation. In 1877 Chief Joseph led the Nez Percé out of the Pacific Northwest, directing his people in an excruciating but daring march of 1,400 miles over mountains into Montana and Wyoming as federal troops pursued them. Intending to flee to Canada, the Nez Percé were finally intercepted in the mountains of northern Montana, just thirty miles from the border. Exhausted by the incredible journey, they surrendered. Subsequently, the government relocated these northwestern Indians to the southwestern territory of Oklahoma. In 1879 Chief Joseph pleaded with lawmakers in Congress to return his people to their home and urged the U.S. government to live up to the original intent of the treaties. His words carried some weight, and the Nez Percé returned under armed escort to a reservation in Washington.

The treaties did not produce a lasting peace. Though most of the tribes relocated onto reservations, some refused. The Apache chief Victorio explained why he would not resettle his people on a reservation. "We prefer to die in our own land under the tall cool pines," he declared. "We will leave our bones with those of our people. It is better to die fighting than to starve." General William Tecumseh Sherman, commander of the military forces against the Indians, issued orders to "push his measures for the utter destruction and subjugation of all who are outside the reservations in a hostile attitude." He went on to propose that the army "shall prosecute the war with vindictive earnestness against all hostile Indians till they are obliterated or beg for mercy." In November 1868, Lieutenant Colonel George Armstrong Custer took Sherman at his word and assaulted a Cheyenne village, killing more than one hundred Indians. Nearly a decade later, in 1876, the Indians, this time Lakota Sioux, exacted revenge by killing Custer and his troops at the **Battle of the Little Big Horn** in Montana. Yet this proved to be the final victory for the Lakota nation, as the army mounted an extensive and fierce offensive against them that shattered their resistance.

Among the troops that battled the Indians were African Americans. Known as "**buffalo soldiers**," a name given to them by the Indians but whose origin is unclear, they represented a cross section of the postwar black population looking for new opportunities that were now available after their emancipation. One enlisted man recalled: "I got tired of looking mules in the face from sunrise to sunset. Thought there must be a better livin' in this world." Some blacks enlisted to learn how to read and write; others sought to avoid unpleasant situations back home. Cooks, waiters, painters, bakers, teamsters, and farmers signed up for a five-year stint in the army at $13 a month. A few gained more glory than money. In May 1880, Sergeant George Jordan of the Ninth Cavalry led troops under his command to fend off Apache raids in Tularosa, New Mexico, for which he was awarded the Congressional Medal of Honor.

Indian Defeat

By the late 1870s, Indians had largely succumbed to U.S. military supremacy. The tribes, as their many victories demonstrated, contained agile horsemen and skilled warriors, but the U.S. army was backed by the power of an increasingly industrial economy. Telegraph lines and railroads provided logistical advantages in the swift deployment of U.S. troops and the ability of the central command to communicate with field officers. Although Indians had acquired firearms over the years from American traders as well as from defeated enemies on the battlefield, the army boasted an essentially unlimited supply of superior weapons. The diversity of Indians and historic rivalries among tribes also made it difficult for them to unite against their common enemy. The federal government exploited these divisions by hiring Indians to serve as army scouts against their traditional tribal foes.

In addition to federal efforts to subdue Indians, other disasters devastated native peoples in the second half of the nineteenth century. Even before the Civil War, many Indians had died of diseases such as smallpox, cholera, scarlet fever, and measles, for which they lacked the immunity that Europeans and white Americans had acquired. Moreover, Indian policy was fundamentally flawed by cultural misunderstanding. Even the most sensitive white administrators of Indian affairs considered Indians a degraded race, in accordance with the scientific thinking of the time. At most, whites believed that Indians could be lifted to a higher level of civilization, which in practice meant a withering away of their traditional culture and heritage.

 Online Document Project   **American Indians and Whites on the Frontier**
bedfordstmartins.com/hewittlawsonvalue

The wholesale destruction of the bison was the final blow to Indian independence. As railroads pushed their tracks beyond the Mississippi, they cleared bison from their path by sending in professional hunters with high-powered rifles to shoot the animals. Buffalo Bill Cody built his reputation by working as a crack sharpshooter for the Kansas Pacific Railroad. At the same time, buffalo products such as shoes, coats, and hats became fashionable in the East. By the mid-1880s, hunters had killed more than thirteen million bison. As a result of the relentless move of white Americans westward and conspicuous consumption back east, bison herds were almost annihilated.

Faced with decimation of the bison, broken treaties, and their opponents' superior military technology, Native Americans' capacity to wage war collapsed. Indians had little choice but to settle on shrinking reservations that the government established for them. The absence of war, however, did not necessarily bring them security. In the late 1870s, gold discoveries in the Black Hills of North Dakota ignited another furious rush by miners who swooped into the sacred lands supposedly guaranteed to the Lakota people. Rather than honoring its treaties, the U.S. government forced the tribes to relinquish still more land. Government officials continued to encourage western expansion by white settlers despite previous agreements with the Indians. General Custer's Seventh Cavalry was part of the military force trying to push Indians out of this mining region, when it was annihilated at the Little Big Horn in 1876. Elsewhere, Congress opened up a portion of western Oklahoma to white homesteaders in 1889. Although this land had not been assigned to specific tribes relocated in Indian Territory, more than eighty thousand Indians from various tribes lived there. This government-sanctioned land rush only added to the pressure from homesteaders and others to acquire more land at the expense of the Indians. A decade later, Congress officially ended Indian control of Indian Territory.

Reforming Indian Policy

As reservations continued to shrink under expansionist assault and government acquiescence, a movement arose to reform Indian policy. Largely centered in the East where few Indians lived, reformers came to believe that the future welfare of Indians lay not in sovereignty but in assimilation. In 1881 Helen Hunt Jackson published *A Century of Dishonor*, her exposé of the unjust treatment the Indians had received, including broken promises and fraudulent activities by government agents. Roused by this depiction of the Indians' plight, groups such as the Women's National Indian Association joined with ministers and philanthropists to advocate the transformation of native peoples into full-fledged Americans.

From today's vantage point, these well-intentioned reformers could be viewed as contributing to the demise of the Indians by trying to eradicate their cultural heritage. Judged by the standards of their own time, however, they truly wanted to save the Indians from the brutality and corrupt behavior they had endured, and they honestly believed they were acting in the Indians' best interests. The most advanced thinking among anthropologists at the time offered an approach that supported assimilation as the only alternative to extinction. The influential Lewis Morgan, author of *Ancient Society* (1877), concluded that all cultures evolved through three stages: savagery, barbarism, and civilization. Indians occupied the lower rungs, but reformers argued that by adopting white values they could become civilized. In effect, this would mean the cultural extermination of the Indians, but reformers such as Richard Henry Pratt, the founder of the Carlisle Indian School, stressed salvation as their motive. "Do not feed America to the Indian, which is tribalizing and not an Americanizing process," he wrote, "but feed the Indian to America, and America will do the assimilating and annihilate the problem."

Reformers such as Pratt faced opposition from white Americans who doubted that Indian assimilation was possible. For many Americans, secure in their sense of their own superiority, the decline and eventual extinction of the Indian peoples was an inevitable consequence of what they saw as Indians' innate inferiority. For example, a Wyoming newspaper predicted: "The same inscrutable Arbiter that decreed the downfall of Rome has pronounced the doom of extinction upon the red men of America." And it warned: "To pretend to defer this by mawkish sentimentalism . . . is unworthy of the age."

Reformers found their legislative spokesman in Senator Henry Dawes of Massachusetts. As legislative director of the Boston Indian Citizenship Association, Dawes shared Christian reformers' belief that becoming a true American would save both the Indians and the soul of the nation. "Soon I trust," Dawes remarked, "we will wipe out the disgrace of our past treatment and lift the [Indian] up into citizenship and manhood and cooperation with us to the glory of the country." A Republican who had served in Congress since the Civil War, Dawes had the same paternalistic attitude toward Indians as he had toward freed slaves. He believed that if both degraded groups worked hard and practiced thrift and individual initiative in the spirit of Dawes's New England Puritan forebears, they would succeed. The key for Dawes was private ownership of land.

Passed in 1887, the **Dawes Act** ended tribal rule and divided Indian lands into 160-acre parcels. The act allocated one parcel to each family head. The government held the lands in trust for the Indians for twenty-five years; at the end of this period, the Indians would receive American citizenship. In return, the Indians had to abandon their religious and cultural rites and practices, including storytelling and the use of medicine men. Whatever lands remained after this reallocation—and the amount was considerable—would be sold on the open market, and the profits from the sales would be placed in an educational fund for Indians.

Unfortunately, like most of the policies it replaced, the Dawes Act proved detrimental to Native Americans. Indian families received inferior farmlands and inadequate tools to cultivate them, while speculators reaped profits from the sale of the "excess" Indian lands. A little more than a decade after the Dawes Act went into effect, Indians controlled 77 million acres of land, down sharply from the 155 million acres they held in 1881. Additional legislation in 1891 forced Indian parents to send their children to boarding schools or else face arrest. At these educational institutions, Indian children were given "American" names, had their long hair cut, and wore uniforms in place of their native dress. The program for boys provided manual and vocational training and that for girls taught domestic skills, so that they could emulate the gender roles in middle-class American families. However, this schooling offered few skills of use in an economic world undergoing industrial transformation. The students "found themselves in a twilight world," one historian claimed. "They were not equipped or allowed to enter American society as equals, yet they had been subjected to sufficient change as to make returning to the reservations difficult and sometimes traumatic."

Indian Assimilation and Resistance

Not all Indians conformed to the government's attempt at forced acculturation. Some refused to abandon their traditional social practices, and others rejected the white man's version of private property and civilization. Many displayed more complicated approaches to survival in a world that continued to view Indians with prejudice. Geronimo and Sitting Bull participated in pageants and Wild West shows but refused to disavow their heritage. Ohiyesa, a Lakota also known as Charles Eastman, went to boarding school, graduated from Dartmouth College, and earned a medical degree from Boston University. He supported passage of the Dawes Act, believed in the virtues of an American education, and worked for the Bureau of Indian Affairs. At the same time, he spoke out against government corruption and fraud perpetrated against Indians. Reviewing his life in his later years, Eastman/Ohiyesa reflected: "I am an Indian and while I have learned much from civilization . . . I have never lost my Indian sense of right and justice."

Disaster loomed for those who resisted assimilation and held on too tightly to the old ways. In 1888 the prophet Wovoka, a member of the Paiute tribe in western Nevada, had a vision that Indians would one day regain control of the world and that whites would disappear. He believed that the Creator had provided him with a **Ghost Dance** that would make this happen. The dance spread to thousands of Lakota Sioux in the northern plains. Seeing the Ghost Dance as a sign of renewed Indian resistance, the army attempted to put a stop to the revival. On December 29, 1890, the Seventh Cavalry, Custer's old regiment, chased three hundred ghost dancers to Wounded Knee Creek on the Pine Ridge Reservation in present-day South Dakota. In a confrontation with the Lakota leader Big Foot, a gunshot accidentally rang out during a struggle with one of his followers. The cavalry then turned the full force of their weaponry on the Indians. When the hail of bullets ceased, about 250 Native Americans, many of them women and children, lay dead.

The message of the massacre at Wounded Knee was clear for those who raised their voices against Americanization. As Black Elk, a spiritual leader of the Oglala Lakota tribe, asserted: "A people's dream died there. . . . There is no center any longer, and the sacred tree is dead." It may not have been the policy of the U.S. government to exterminate the Indians as a people, but it was certainly U.S. policy to destroy Indian culture and society once and for all.

> **REVIEW & RELATE**
>
> • How and why did federal Indian policy change during the nineteenth century?
>
> • Describe some of the ways that Indian peoples responded to federal policies. Which response do you think offered their greatest chance for survival?

The Mining Frontier

Among the settlers pouring into Indian Territory in the Rocky Mountains were miners in search of gold and silver. These prospectors envisioned instant riches that would come from a lucky strike. The vast majority found only backbreaking work, danger, and frustration. Miners continued to face hardship and danger as industrial mining operations took over from individual prospectors, despite the efforts of some miners to fight for better wages and working conditions. By 1900 the mining rush had peaked, and many of the boomtowns that had cropped up around the mining industry had emptied out.

The Business of Mining

The discovery of gold in California in 1848 had set this mining frenzy in motion. Over the next thirty years, successive waves of gold and silver strikes in Colorado, Nevada, Washington, Idaho, Montana, and the Dakotas lured individual prospectors with shovels and wash pans. One of the biggest finds came with the Comstock Lode in the Sierra Nevada. All told, miners extracted around $350 million worth of silver from this source. Two of those who came to share in the wealth were Samuel Clemens and his brother Orion. Writing from Carson City, Nevada, Samuel described his new surroundings to his family: "The country is fabulously rich in gold, silver, copper, lead . . . thieves, murderers, desperadoes, ladies . . . lawyers, Christians, Indians, Chinamen, Spaniards, gamblers, sharpers, coyotes . . . poets, preachers, and jackass rabbits." He did not find his fortune in Nevada and soon turned his attention to writing, finally achieving success as the author called Mark Twain.

Like Twain, many of those who flocked to the Comstock Lode and other mining frontiers were men. Nearly half were foreign-born, many of them coming from Mexico or China. Using pans and shovels, prospectors could find only the ore that lay near the surface of the earth and water. Once these initial discoveries were played out, individual prospectors could not afford to buy the equipment needed to dig out the vast deposits of gold and silver buried deep in the earth. As a result, western mining operations became big businesses run by men with the financial resources necessary to purchase industrial mining equipment.

When mining became an industry, prospectors became wageworkers. In Virginia City, Nevada, miners labored for $4 a day, which was a decent wage for the time, but one that barely covered the monthly expenses of life in a mining boomtown. Moreover, the work was extremely dangerous. Mine shafts extended down more than a thousand feet, and working temperatures regularly exceeded 100 degrees Fahrenheit. Noxious fumes, fires, and floods of scalding water flowing through the shafts posed a constant threat. Between 1863 and 1880, at least three hundred miners died on the job, and accidents were a daily occurrence, leaving many men disabled and out of work with no compensation.

Struggling with low pay and dangerous work conditions, western miners sought to organize. In the mid-1860s, unions formed in the Comstock Lode areas of Virginia City and Gold Hill, Nevada. Although these unions had some success, they also provoked a violent backlash from mining companies determined to resist union demands. Companies hired private police forces to help break strikes. Such forces were often assisted by state militias deployed by elected officials with close ties to the companies. For example, in 1892 the governor of Idaho crushed an unruly strike by calling up the National Guard, a confrontation that resulted in the deaths of seven strikers. A year later, mine workers formed one of the most militant labor organizations in the nation, the Western Federation of Miners. Within a decade, it had attracted fifty thousand members. However, union solidarity did not extend to all races and ethnicities. The union was made up of members from Irish, English, Italian, Slavic, and Greek backgrounds but excluded Chinese, Mexican, and Indian workers from its ranks.

Life in the Mining Towns

Men worked the mines, but women flocked to the area as well. In Storey County, Nevada, the heart of the Comstock Lode, the 1875 census showed that women made up about half the population. Most employed women worked long hours as domestics in boardinghouses, hotels, and private homes. Prostitution, which was legal, accounted for the single largest segment of the female workforce. Most prostitutes were between the ages of nineteen and twenty-four, and they entered this occupation because few other well-paying jobs were available to them. The demand for their services remained high among the large population of unmarried men. Yet prostitutes faced constant danger, and many were victims of physical abuse, robbery, and murder.

Boomtowns like Virginia City sported a wild assortment of miners. They sought relief in taverns, brothels, and opium dens. In Butte, Montana, miners frequented bars with such colorful names as "Bucket of Blood," "The Cesspool," and "Graveyard." They boarded in houses run by characters nicknamed "Mag the Rag," "Take-Five Annie," "Ellen the Elephant," and "The Racehorse." A folk tune described Butte's annual gala event, the "Hopheads' [drug addicts'] Ball":

> All the junkies were invited
> Yes every gink [skinny man] and muff [prostitute]
> Not a single one was slighted
> If they were on the stuff [opium].
> Invitations were presented
> To every hustler and her man.
> They even sent up invites
> To the hopheads in the can [jail].

As early as the 1880s, gold and silver discoveries had played out in the Comstock Lode. Boomtowns, which had sprung up almost overnight, now became ghost towns as gold and silver deposits dwindled. Even more substantial places like Virginia City, Nevada, experienced a severe decline as the veins of ore ran out. One revealing sign of the city's plummeting fortunes was the drop in the number of prostitutes, which declined by more than half by 1880. The mining frontier then shifted from gold and silver to copper, lead, and zinc, centered in Montana and Idaho. As with the early prospectors in California and Nevada, these miners eventually became wageworkers for giant consolidated mining companies. By the end of the nineteenth century, the Amalgamated Copper Company and the American Smelting and Refining Company dominated the industry.

Mining towns that survived, like Butte, became only slightly less rowdy places, but they did settle into more complex patterns of urban living. Though the population remained predominantly young and male, the young men were increasingly likely to get married and raise families. Residents lived in neighborhoods divided by class and ethnicity. For example, in Butte the west side of town became home to the middle and upper classes. Mine workers lived on the east side in homes subdivided into apartments and in boardinghouses. "The houses were almost skin to skin," one resident described the area, "and boy, there were kids all over in the neighborhood." The Irish lived in one section; Finns, Swedes, Serbs, Croatians, and Slovenes in other sections. Each group formed its own social, fraternal, and religious organizations to relieve the harsh conditions of overcrowding, poor sanitation, and discrimination. Residents of the east side relied on one another for support and frowned on those who deviated from their code of solidarity. "They didn't try to outdo the other one," one neighborhood woman remarked. "If you did, you got into trouble. . . . If they thought you were a little richer than they were, they wouldn't associate with you." Although western mining towns retained distinctive qualities, in their social and ethnic divisions they came to resemble older cities east of the Mississippi River.

REVIEW & RELATE

- How and why did the nature of mining in the West change during the second half of the nineteenth century?
- How did miners and residents of mining towns reshape the frontier landscape?

Ranching and Farming Frontiers

Ranchers and farmers heading west also faced harsh realities. Cowboys worked long hours in tough but boring conditions on the open range. Farmers endured great hardships in trying to raise crops in an often inhospitable climate. Women played a critical role as pioneers, often setting out to acquire their own land or helping to run the family farm. Falling crop prices, however, led to soaring debt and forced many farmers into bankruptcy and off their land. Despite difficult physical and economic conditions, many of these women and men showed grit and determination not only in surviving but in improving their lives as well.

The Life of the Cowboy

There is no greater symbol of the frontier West than the cowboy. As portrayed in novels and film, the cowboy hero was the essence of manhood, an independent figure who fought for justice and defended the honor and virtue of women. Never the aggressor, he fought to protect law-abiding residents of frontier communities. Having helped tame some wild western town, the cowboy rode off into the sunset in search of new frontiers to challenge him.

This romantic image excited generations of American readers and later movie and television audiences. In reality, cowboys' lives were much more mundane. Cowpunchers worked for paltry monthly wages, put in long days herding cattle, and spent part of the night guarding them on the open range. Their major task was to make the 1,500-mile Long Drive along the Chisholm Trail. Beginning in the late 1860s, cowboys moved cattle from ranches in Texas through Oklahoma to rail depots in Kansas towns such as

Abilene and Dodge City; from there, cattle were shipped by train eastward to slaughterhouses in Chicago. Life along the trail was monotonous, and riders had to contend with bad weather, dangerous work, and disease.

Numbering around forty thousand and averaging twenty-four years of age, the cowboys who rode through the Great Plains from Texas to Kansas came from diverse backgrounds. The majority, about 66 percent, were white, predominantly southerners who had fought for the South during the Civil War. Most of the rest were divided evenly between Mexicans, who had first tended cattle during Spanish rule in the Southwest, and African Americans, some of whom were former slaves and others Union veterans of the Civil War.

Besides experiencing rugged life on the range, black and Mexican cowboys faced racial discrimination. Jim Perry, an African American who rode for the three-million-acre XIT Ranch in Texas for more than twenty years, complained: "If it weren't for my damned old black face I'd have been boss of one of these divisions long ago." Mexican *vaqueros*, or cowboys, earned one-third to one-half the wages of whites, whereas blacks were usually paid on a par with whites. Because the cattle kingdoms first flourished during Reconstruction, racial discrimination and segregation carried over into the Southwest. On one drive along the route to Kansas, a white boss insisted that a black cowboy eat and sleep separately from whites and shot at him when he refused to heed this order. Another white trail driver admitted that blacks "were usually called on to do the hardest work around the outfit." Nevertheless, the close proximity in which cowboys worked and the need for cooperation to overcome the pitfalls of the Long Drive made it difficult to enforce rigid racial divisions on the open range.

Large ranchers benefited the most from the cowboys' grueling work. Spaniards had originally imported cattle into the Southwest, and by the late nineteenth century some 5 million Texas longhorn steers grazed in the area. Cattle that could be purchased in Texas for $3 to $7 fetched a price of $30 to $40 in Kansas. The extension of railroads across the West opened up a quickly growing market for beef in the East. The development of refrigerated railroad cars guaranteed that slaughtered meat could reach eastern consumers without spoiling. With money to be made, the cattle industry rose to meet the demand. Fewer than 40 ranchers owned more than 20 million acres of land. One ranch in Texas spanned 200 miles and stocked 150,000 steers annually. Easterners and Europeans joined the boom and invested money in giant ranches. By the mid-1880s, approximately 7.5 million head of cattle roamed the western ranges, and large cattle ranchers became rich. Cattle ranching had become fully integrated into the national commercial economy.

Then the bubble burst. Ranchers who were already raising more cattle than the market could handle increasingly faced competition from cattle producers in Canada and Argentina. Prices spiraled downward. Another source of competition came from homesteaders who moved into the plains and fenced in their farms with barbed wire, thereby reducing the size of the open range. Yet the greatest disaster occurred from 1885 to 1887. Two frigid winters, together with a torrid summer drought, destroyed 90 percent of the cattle on the northern plains of the Dakotas, Montana, Colorado, and Wyoming. Under these conditions, outside capital to support ranching diminished, and many of the great cattle barons went into bankruptcy. This economic collapse consolidated the remaining cattle industry into even fewer hands. Some of those forced out of business turned to raising sheep, which require less water and grass than cattle to survive. The cowboy, never more than a hired hand, became a laborer for large corporations.

Farmers Head West

The federal government played a major role in opening up the Great Plains to the farmers who eventually clashed with cattlemen. The Republican Party of Abraham Lincoln had opposed the expansion of slavery in order to promote the virtues of free soil and free labor for white men and their families. During the Civil War, preoccupation with battlefield losses did not stop the Republican-controlled Congress from passing the **Homestead Act**. As an incentive for western migration, the act established procedures for distributing 160-acre lots to western settlers, on condition that they develop and farm their land. What most would-be settlers did not know, however, was that lots of 160 acres were not suitable to conditions on the Great Plains. As geologist John Wesley Powell would demonstrate, the intensive techniques needed to farm 160-acre plots simply would not work in the harsh, dry climate of the Great Plains.

Reality did not deter pioneers and adventurers. In fact, weather conditions in the region temporarily fooled them. The decade after 1878 witnessed an exceptional amount of rainfall west of the Mississippi. Though not precisely predictable, this cycle of abundance and drought had been going on for millennia. One settler, convinced that Providence was smiling on Americans, remarked about the sudden burst of rain: "The Lord knowed we needed more land an' He's gone and changed the climate." In addition, innovation and technology bolstered dreams of success. Farmers planted heartier strains of wheat imported from Russia that survived the fluctuations of dry and wet and hot and cold weather. Machines produced by industrial laborers in northern factories to the east allowed farmers to plow tough land and harvest its yield. Steel-tipped plows, threshers, combines, and harvesters expanded production greatly, and windmills and pumping equipment provided sources of power and access to scarce water.

The people who accepted the challenge of carving out a new life were a diverse lot. The Great Plains attracted a large number of immigrants from Europe, some two million by 1900. Minnesota and the Dakotas welcomed communities of settlers from Sweden and Norway. Nebraska housed a considerable population of Germans, Swedes, Danes, and Czechs. About one-third of the people who migrated to the northern plains came directly from a foreign country. Many of the rest, both native-born and foreign-born, had lived in towns and villages along the Mississippi River before they decided to seek new opportunities farther west.

Railroads and land companies lured settlers to the plains with tales of the fabulous possibilities that awaited their arrival. The federal government had given railroads generous grants of public land on which to build their tracks as well as parcels surrounding the tracks that they could sell off to raise revenue for construction. Western railroads advertised in both the United States and Europe, proclaiming that migrants to the plains would find "the garden spot of the world." The land "will grow anything that any other country will grow, and with less work," the Rock Island Railroad announced, "because it rains here more than any other place, and at just the right time."

Having lured prospective settlers with exaggerated claims, railroads offered bargain rates to transport them to their new homes. Families and friends often journeyed together and rented an entire car on the train, known as "the immigrant car," in which they loaded their possessions, supplies, and even livestock. Often migrants came to the end of the rail line before reaching their destination. They completed the trip by wagon or stagecoach.

Commercial advertising alone did not account for the desire to journey westward. Settlers who had made the trip successfully wrote to relatives and neighbors back east and in the old country about the chance to start fresh. Linda Slaughter, the wife of an army doctor in the Dakotas, gushed: "The farms which have been opened in the vicinity of Bismarck have proven highly productive, the soil being kept moist by frequent rains. Vegetables of all kinds are grown with but little trouble." Descriptions of abundance, combined with a spirit of adventure, inspired Lucy Goldthorpe to claim a homestead near Epping in the Dakota Territory. "Even if you hadn't inherited a bit of restlessness and a pioneering spirit from your ancestors," she asserted, "it would have been difficult to ward off the excitement of the boom which, like the atmosphere, involved every conversation."

Those who took the chance shared a faith in the future and a willingness to work hard and endure misfortune. They found their optimism and spirits sorely tested. Despite the company of family members and friends, settlers faced a lonely existence on the vast expanse of the plains. Homesteads were spread out, and a feeling of isolation became a routine part of daily life.

With few trees around, early settlers constructed sod houses. These structures let in little light but a good deal of moisture, keeping them gloomy and damp. A Nebraskan who lived in this type of house jokingly remarked: "There was running water in our

Women Homesteaders in Nebraska   The Chrisman sisters—Lizzie, Lutie, Jennie Ruth, and Hattie—are shown outside their sod house in 1886. They are among the thousands of homesteaders who moved west in the late nineteenth century and built homes from the only natural resource the Great Plains had in abundance: sod.   AP Photo

sod house. It ran through the roof." Bugs, insects, and rodents, like the rain, often found their way inside to make living in such shelters even more uncomfortable.

If these dwellings were bleak, the climate posed even greater challenges. The plains did experience an unusual amount of rainfall in the late 1870s and early 1880s, but severe drought quickly followed. A plague of grasshoppers ravaged the northern plains in the late 1870s, destroying fruit trees and plants. Intense heat in the summer alternated with frigid temperatures in the winter. The Norwegian American writer O. E. Rolvaag, in *Giants in the Earth* (1927), his epic novel about Norwegian settlement in the Great Plains, described the extreme hardships that accompanied the fierce weather: "Blizzards from out of the northwest raged, swooped down and stirred up a greyish-white fury, impenetrable to human eyes. As soon as these monsters tired, storms from the northeast were sure to come, bringing more snow."

Women Homesteaders

The women of the family were responsible for making these houses more bearable. Mothers and daughters were in charge of household duties, cooking the meals, canning fruits and vegetables, and washing and ironing clothing. Despite the drudgery of this work, women contributed significantly to the economic well-being of the family by occasionally taking in boarders and selling milk, butter, and eggs.

In addition, a surprisingly large number of single women staked out homestead claims by themselves. Some were young, unmarried women seeking, like their male counterparts, economic opportunity. Others were widows attempting to take care of their children after their husband's death. One such widow, Anne Furnberg, settled a homestead in the Dakota Territory in 1871. Born in Norway, she had lived with her husband and son in Minnesota. After her husband's death, the thirty-four-year-old Furnberg moved with her son near Fargo and eventually settled on eighty acres of land. She farmed, raised chickens and a cow, and sold butter and eggs in town. The majority of women who settled in the Dakotas were between the ages of twenty-one and twenty-five, most had never been married, and a majority were native-born children of immigrant parents. A sample of nine counties in the Dakotas shows that more than 4,400 women became landowners. Nora Pfundheler, a single woman, explained her motivation: "Well I was 21 and had no prospects of doing anything. The land was there, so I took it."

Once families settled in and towns began to develop, women, married and single, directed some of their energies to moral reform and extending democracy on the frontier. Because of loneliness and grueling work, some men turned to alcohol for relief. Law enforcement in newly established communities was often no match for the saloons that catered to a raucous and drunken crowd. In their roles as wives, mothers, and sisters, many women tried to remove the source of alcohol-induced violence that disrupted both family relationships and public decorum. In Kansas in the late 1870s, women flocked to the state's Woman's Christian Temperance Union, founded by Amanda M. Way. Although they did not yet have the vote, in 1880 these women vigorously campaigned for a constitutional amendment that banned the sale of liquor.

Temperance women also threw their weight behind the issue of women's suffrage. In 1884 Kansas women established the statewide Equal Suffrage Association, which delivered to the state legislature a petition with seven thousand signatures in support of women's suffrage. Their attempt failed, but in 1887 women won the right to vote and run for office in all Kansas municipal elections. By the end of the nineteenth century, fifteen women had held city offices throughout the state. Julia Robinson, who campaigned for women's suffrage in Kansas, recalled the positive role that some men played: "My father had always said his family of girls had just as much right to help the government as if we were boys, and mother and he had always taught us to expect Woman Suffrage in our day." Kansas did not grant equal voting rights in state and national elections until 1912, but women obtained full suffrage before then in many western states.

 Online Document Project   Women in the West
bedfordstmartins.com/hewittlawsonvalue

Farming on the Great Plains

Surviving loneliness, drudgery, and the weather still did not guarantee financial success for homesteaders. In fact, the economic realities of farming on the plains proved formidable. Despite the image of yeomen farmers—individuals engaged in subsistence farming with the aid of wives and children—most agriculture was geared to commercial transactions. Few farmers were independent or self-reliant. Farmers depended on barter and short-term credit. They borrowed from banks to purchase the additional land necessary to make agriculture economically feasible in the semiarid climate. They also needed loans to buy machinery to help increase production and to sustain their families while they waited for the harvest.

Instead of raising crops solely for their own use, farmers concentrated on the cash crops of corn and wheat. The price of these commodities depended on the impersonal economic forces of an international market that connected American farmers to growers and consumers throughout the world. When supply expanded and demand remained relatively stable during the 1880s and 1890s, prices fell. This deflation made it more difficult for farmers to pay back their loans, and banks moved to foreclose. Corn growers had a hedge against falling prices. By withholding some of their corn from market, they could feed it to their hogs, fatten them up, and sell them at higher prices. The reduction in the supply of corn caused prices to rise until it was worth selling corn again.

This "corn-hog cycle," however, did not benefit wheat growers. When prices plummeted, they had little choice but to raise more wheat in the hope that increased volume would yield more income. Instead, the expansion in supply, coming as it did from so many farmers, merely depressed prices further, leaving wheat farmers with debts they could not repay. Under these circumstances, almost half of the homesteaders in the Great Plains picked up and moved either to another farm or to a nearby city. Large operators bought up the farms they left behind and ran them like big businesses. As had been the case in mining and ranching, western agriculture was increasingly commercialized and consolidated over the course of the second half of the nineteenth century.

The federal government unwittingly aided this process of commercialization and consolidation, to the benefit of large companies. The government sought to make bigger plots of land available in regions where small farming had proven impractical. The Desert Land Act (1877) offered 640 acres to settlers who would irrigate the land, but it brought small relief for farmers because the land was too dry. These properties soon fell out of the hands of homesteaders and into those of cattle ranchers. The Timber and Stone Act (1878) allowed homesteaders to buy 160 acres of forestland at $2.50 an acre. Lumber companies hired "dummy entrymen" to file claims and then quickly transferred the titles and added the parcels to their growing tracts of woodland.

REVIEW & RELATE

- How did market forces contribute to the boom and bust of the cattle ranching industry?
- How did women homesteaders on the Great Plains in the late nineteenth century respond to frontier challenges?

Pushing Farther West

Some pioneers settled on the Great Plains or moved west for reasons beyond purely economic motives. The Mormons, for example, settled in Utah to find a religious home. The West Coast states of Washington, Oregon, and especially California, with their abundant resources and favorable climates, beckoned adventurers to travel beyond the Rockies and settle along the Pacific Ocean. The far West attracted many white settlers and foreign immigrants—especially Chinese—who encountered Spaniards and Mexicans already inhabiting the region. This encounter among diverse cultural groups sparked clashes that produced more oppression than opportunity for nonwhites.

Mormons Head West

Unlike miners, cowboys, and farmers, Mormons sought refuge in the West for religious reasons. By 1870 the migration of Mormons (members of the Church of Jesus Christ of Latter-Day Saints) into the Utah Territory had attracted more than 85,000 settlers, most notably in Salt Lake City. Originally traveling to Utah under the leadership of Brigham Young in the late 1840s, Mormons had come under attack from opponents of their religion and the federal government for several reasons. Most important, Mormons believed in polygamy (the practice of having more than one wife at a time), which violated traditional Christian standards of morality. Far from seeing the practice as immoral, Mormon doctrine held polygamy as a blessing that would guarantee both husbands and wives an exalted place in the afterlife. Non-Mormons denounced polygamy as a form of involuntary servitude, similar to African American slavery. In reality, only a small minority of Mormon men had multiple wives, and most of these polygamists had only two wives.

Mormons also departed from the mainstream American belief in private property. The church considered farming a communal enterprise. To this end, church elders divided land among their followers, so that, as Brigham Young explained, "each person perform[ed] his several duties for the good of the whole more than for individual aggrandizement." Mormon communities also displayed a tolerant attitude toward the Native American tribes they encountered, learning their languages in order to convert rather than destroy them.

In the 1870s, the federal government took increased measures to control Mormon practices. In *Reynolds v. United States* (1879), the Supreme Court upheld the criminal conviction of a polygamist Mormon man. Previously in 1862 and 1874, Congress had banned plural marriages in the Utah Territory, and the justices ruled that despite their religious convictions, Mormons possessed no constitutional right to violate federal law. Congress went further in 1882 by passing the Edmunds Act, which disfranchised men engaging in polygamy. In 1887 Congress aimed to slash the economic power of the church by limiting Mormon assets to $50,000 and seizing the rest for the federal Treasury. A few years later, under this considerable pressure, the Mormons officially abandoned polygamy.

Related to the attack on polygamy was the question of women's suffrage. In 1870 voters in Utah endorsed a referendum granting women the right to vote, which enfranchised more than seventeen thousand women. Emmeline B. Wells, a Mormon woman who defended both women's rights and polygamy, argued that women "should be recognized as . . . responsible being[s]," capable of choosing plural marriage of their own free will. Opponents of enfranchisement contended that as long as polygamy existed, extending the vote to "enslaved" Mormon women would only perpetuate the practice because they would vote the way their husbands did. This point of view prevailed, and the Edmunds-Tucker Act (1887) rescinded the right to vote for women in the territory. Only with the rejection of polygamy did Congress accept statehood for Utah in 1896. The following year, the state extended the ballot to women.

Californios

As with the nation's other frontiers, migrants to the West Coast did not find uninhabited territory. Besides Indians, the largest group that lived in California consisted of Spaniards and Mexicans. Since the eighteenth century, these *Californios* had established themselves as farmers and ranchers. The 1848 Treaty of Guadalupe Hidalgo, which ended the Mexican-American War, supposedly guaranteed the property rights of Californios and granted them U.S. citizenship, but reality proved different. Mexican American miners had to pay a "foreign miners tax," and Californio landowners lost their holdings to squatters, settlers, and local officials. Anglo politicians argued that the descendants of the original owners of Spanish land grants did not use them efficiently, and clever lawyers used the courts to deprive Californios of much of their property. By the end of the nineteenth century, about two-thirds of all land originally owned by Spanish-speaking residents had fallen into the hands of Euro-American settlers. By this time, many of these once proud and wealthy Californios had been forced into poverty and the low-wage labor force. The loss of land was matched by a diminished role in the region's government, as economic decline, ethnic bias, and the continuing influx of white migrants combined to greatly reduce the political influence of the Californio population.

Spaniards and Mexicans living in the Southwest met the same fate as the Californios. Although they battled to keep their landholdings, they did not receive the first-class citizenship promised by the Treaty of Guadalupe Hidalgo. When Anglo cattle ranchers began forcing Mexican Americans off their land near Las Vegas, New Mexico, a rancher named Juan Jose Herrera assembled a band of masked night riders known as *Las Gorras Blancas* (The White Caps). In 1889 and 1890, as many as seven hundred White Caps burned Anglo fences, haystacks, barns, and homes. They also set fire to thousands of railroad ties when the Atchison, Topeka, and Santa Fe Railroad refused to increase wages for Hispanic workers. In the end, however, Spanish-speaking inhabitants could not prevent the growing number of whites from pouring onto their lands and isolating them politically, economically, and culturally.

The Chinese in the Far West

California and the far West also attracted a large number of Chinese immigrants. Migration to California and the West Coast was part of a larger movement in the nineteenth century out of Asia that brought impoverished Chinese to Australia, Hawaii, Latin America, and the United States. The Chinese migrated for several reasons in the decades after 1840. Internal conflicts in China sent them in search of refuge. Economic dislocation related to the British Opium Wars (1839–1842 and 1856–1860), along with bloody family feuds and a decade of peasant rebellion from 1854 to 1864, propelled migration. Faced with unemployment and starvation, the Chinese sought economic opportunity overseas. One man recounted the hardships that drove him to emigrate: "Sometimes we went hungry for days. My mother and [I] would go over the harvested rice fields of the peasants to pick the grains they dropped. . . . We had only salt and water to eat with the rice."

Chinese immigrants were attracted first by the 1848 gold rush and then by jobs building the transcontinental railroad. By 1880 the Chinese population had grown to 200,000, most of whom lived in the West. San Francisco became the center of the transplanted Chinese population, which congregated in the city's Chinatown. Under the leadership of a handful of businessmen, Chinese residents found jobs, lodging, meals, and social, cultural, and recreational outlets. Most of those who came were young unmarried men who intended to earn enough money to return to China and start anew. The relatively few women who immigrated came as servants or prostitutes.

For many Chinese, the West proved unwelcoming. When California's economy slumped in the mid-1870s, many whites looked to the Chinese as scapegoats. White workingmen believed that the plentiful supply of Chinese laborers in the mines and railroads undercut their demands for higher wages. They contended that Chinese would work for less because they were racially inferior people who lived degraded lives. Anti-Chinese clubs mushroomed in California during the 1870s, and they soon became a substantial political force in the state. The Workingmen's Party advocated laws that restricted Chinese labor, and it initiated boycotts of goods made by Chinese people. Vigilantes attacked Chinese in the streets and set fire to factories that employed Asians. The Workingmen's Party and the Democratic Party joined forces in 1879 to craft a new state constitution that blatantly discriminated against Chinese residents. In many ways, these laws resembled the Jim Crow laws passed in the South that deprived African Americans of their freedom following Reconstruction (discussed in chapter 16).

Pressured by anti-Chinese sentiment on the West Coast, the U.S. government enacted drastic legislation to prevent any further influx of Chinese. The **Chinese Exclusion Act** of 1882 banned Chinese immigration into the United States and prohibited those Chinese already in the country from becoming naturalized American citizens. As a result, the Chinese remained a predominantly male, aging, and isolated population until World War II. The exclusion act, however, did not stop anti-Chinese assaults. In the mid-1880s, white mobs drove Chinese out of Eureka, California; Seattle and Tacoma, Washington; and Rock Springs, Wyoming.

Rock Springs Massacre   This engraving depicts the Rock Springs massacre in Wyoming. On September 3, 1885, a mob of white coal miners killed at least 28 Chinese miners, injured 15, and burned 75 homes of Chinese residents. The violence came after years of anti-Chinese sentiment in the western United States. White miners blamed the Chinese for working for lower wages and taking their jobs.   The Granger Collection, New York

REVIEW & RELATE

- What migrant groups were attracted to the far West? What drew them there?
- Explain the rising hostility to the Chinese and other minority groups in the late-nineteenth-century far West.

Conclusion: The Ambiguous Legacy of the Frontier

The legacy of the pioneering generation of Americans has proven mixed. Men and women pioneers left their old lives behind and boldly pushed into uncharted territory to reinvent themselves. They encountered numerous obstacles posed by difficult terrain, forbidding climate, and unfamiliar inhabitants of the land they sought to harness. They built their homes, tilled the soil to raise crops, and mined the earth to remove the metals it contained. They developed cities that would one day rival those back east: San Francisco, Los Angeles, Seattle, and Denver. These pioneers served as the advance guard of America's expanding national and international commercial markets. As producers of staple crops and livestock and consumers of manufactured goods, they contributed to the expansion of America's factories, railroads, and telegraph communication system. The nation would memorialize their spirit as a model of individualism and self-reliance.

In fact, settlement of the West required more than individual initiative and self-determination. Without the direct involvement of the federal government, settlers would not have received free or inexpensive homesteads and military protection to clear native inhabitants out of their way. Without territorial governors and judges appointed by Washington to preside over new settlements, there would have been even less law, order, and justice than appeared in the rough-and-tumble environment that attracted outlaws, con artists, and speculators. Railroads, mining, and cattle ventures all relied heavily on foreign investors. Moreover, all the individualism and self-reliance that pioneers brought would not have saved them from the harsh conditions and disasters they faced without banding together as a community and pitching in to create institutions that helped them collectively. Despite their desire to achieve success, various pioneers—farmers, prospectors, cowboys—mostly found it difficult to make it on their own and began working for larger farming, mining, and ranching enterprises, with many of them becoming wageworkers. And for an experience that has been portrayed as a predominantly male phenomenon, settlement of the West depended largely on women.

Pioneers did not fully understand the land and people they encountered. More from ignorance than design, settlers engaged in agricultural, mining, and ranching practices that depleted fragile grasses, eroded hillsides, and polluted rivers and streams with runoff wastes. The settlement of the West nearly wiped out the bison and left Native Americans psychologically demoralized, culturally endangered, and economically impoverished. Some Indians willingly adopted white ways, but most of them fiercely resisted acculturation. Other nonwhite minorities in the West, such as Mexicans and Chinese, experienced less extreme treatment, but they suffered nonetheless.

Panoramic landscape paintings often depicted glorious scenes of the Wild West, but the truth was more nuanced. Annie Oakley pleased audiences with daring exploits that glorified a West she had not experienced. Geronimo surrendered and spent the rest of his life exiled from his native lands. He, too, tried to follow the path of Oakley, but his public appearances could not hide the devastation that he and other Native Americans had experienced. The western frontier represented both opportunity and loss.

Chapter Review

MAKE IT STICK

 LearningCurve **bedfordstmartins.com/hewittlawsonvalue**
After reading the chapter, use LearningCurve to retain what you've read.

IDENTIFY KEY TERMS

Identify and explain the significance of each term below.

Great Plains (p. 376)
transcontinental railroad (p. 378)
Treaty of Fort Laramie (p. 382)
Battle of the Little Big Horn (p. 383)
buffalo soldiers (p. 383)
Dawes Act (p. 385)
Ghost Dance (p. 386)

Comstock Lode (p. 387)
Long Drive (p. 389)
Homestead Act (p. 391)
Mormons (p. 395)
Californios (p. 396)
Chinese Exclusion Act
   (p. 397)

REVIEW & RELATE

Answer the focus questions from each section of the chapter.

1. What role did the federal government play in opening the West to settlement and economic exploitation?

2. Explain the determination of Americans to settle in land west of the Mississippi River despite the challenges the region presented.

3. How and why did federal Indian policy change during the nineteenth century?

4. Describe some of the ways that Indian peoples responded to federal policies. Which response do you think offered their greatest chance for survival?

5. How and why did the nature of mining in the West change during the second half of the nineteenth century?

6. How did miners and residents of mining towns reshape the frontier landscape?

7. How did market forces contribute to the boom and bust of the cattle ranching industry?

8. How did women homesteaders on the Great Plains in the late nineteenth century respond to frontier challenges?

9. What migrant groups were attracted to the far West? What drew them there?

10. Explain the rising hostility to the Chinese and other minority groups in the late-nineteenth-century far West.

ONLINE DOCUMENT PROJECTS

◆ **American Indians and Whites on the Frontier**
◆ **Women in the West**

After reading the primary sources in these document sets, answer the **Interpret the Evidence** questions to help you analyze each of the documents, and then answer the **Put It in Context** question(s) to help you relate the documents to the topics and themes you read about in the chapter.

bedfordstmartins.com/hewittlawsonvalue

TIMELINE OF EVENTS

1848	• Gold discovered in California
1851	• First Treaty of Fort Laramie
1862	• Homestead Act passed
1864	• Sand Creek massacre
1865–1868	• Lakota Sioux lead Indian resistance
Late 1860s	• Large-scale cattle drives begin
1868	• Second Treaty of Fort Laramie
1869	• Transcontinental railroad completed
1870s	• Gold discovered in Black Hills of North Dakota
1876	• Battle of the Little Big Horn
1877	• Desert Land Act
1878	• John Wesley Powell questions suitability of Great Plains for small-scale farming
	• Timber and Stone Act
1881	• Helen Hunt Jackson publishes *Century of Dishonor*
1882	• Edmunds Act passed
	• Chinese Exclusion Act passed
1884	• Annie Oakley joins William Cody's Wild West show
1885–1887	• Cattle industry collapses
1886	• Geronimo captured
1887	• Dawes Act passed
	• Kansas women win right to vote and run for office in municipal elections
1889–1890	• Mexican American White Caps attack Anglo property
1890	• Massacre at Wounded Knee
1893	• Western Federation of Miners formed

16

LearningCurve
bedfordstmartins.com/hewittlawsonvalue
After reading the chapter, use LearningCurve
to retain what you've read.

American Industry in the Age of Organization

1877–1900

AMERICAN HISTORIES

In 1848 Will and Margaret Carnegie left Scotland and sailed to America, hoping to find a better life for themselves and their two children. Once settled in Pittsburgh, Pennsylvania, the family went to work, including thirteen-year-old Andrew, who found a job in a textile mill. For $1.25 per week, he dipped spools into an oil bath and fired the factory furnace—tasks that left him nauseated by the smell of oil and frightened by the boiler. Nevertheless, like the hero of the rags-to-riches stories that were so popular in his era, Andrew Carnegie persevered, rising from poverty to great wealth through a series of jobs and clever investments. As a teenager, he worked as a messenger in a telegraph office and was soon promoted to telegraph operator. A superintendent of the Pennsylvania Railroad Company noticed Andrew's aptitude and made him his personal assistant and telegrapher. While in this position, Carnegie learned about the fast-developing railroad industry and purchased stock in a sleeping car company; the returns from that investment tripled his annual salary. Carnegie then became a railroad superintendent in western Pennsylvania, and by the time he was thirty-five, he had earned handsome returns on his investments in various industrial companies, as well as from oil investments he made just as that industry was emerging.

Andrew Carnegie eventually founded the greatest steel company in the world and became one of the wealthiest men of his time. In an era before personal and corporate income taxes, Carnegie earned hundreds of millions of dollars. He also became one of the era's greatest philanthropists, fulfilling his sense of community obligation by giving away a great deal of his fortune.

John Sherman also believed in public service, but for him it would come through politics. Sherman was born in Lancaster, Ohio, in 1823, a quarter of a century before the Carnegies set sail for the United States. Sherman became a lawyer like his father, an Ohio Supreme Court judge, and in 1844 he set up a practice with his older brother, William Tecumseh Sherman, the future Civil War general and Indian fighter (see chapter 15). Like Carnegie, Sherman made shrewd investments that made him a wealthy man, although not on the same scale as Carnegie.

Sherman decided to enter politics and in 1854 won election from Ohio to the House of Representatives as a member of the newly created Republican Party. He rose up the leadership ranks as Republicans came to national power with the election of Abraham Lincoln to the presidency in 1860. From 1861 to 1896, Sherman held a variety of major political positions, including U.S. senator from Ohio and secretary of the treasury under President Rutherford B. Hayes. After his term as treasury secretary ended, he returned to the Senate and wielded power as one of the top Republican Party leaders. Sherman, who had joined the Radical Republicans during Reconstruction (see chapter 14), did not hesitate to move with the Republican Party as its interests shifted from racial equality to promoting business and industry. With his background as chair of the Senate Finance Committee and as secretary of the treasury, Sherman was the most respected Republican of his time in dealing with monetary and financial affairs. Marcus Alonzo Hanna, a wealthy industrialist, considered the Ohio senator "our main dependence in the Senate for the protection of our business interests." Like Hanna, Sherman believed that government should serve business. His most famous accomplishment, the Sherman Antitrust Act, which authorized the government to break up organizations that restrained competition, embodied this belief. It enacted limited reforms without harming powerful business interests.

WHILE THE AMERICAN HISTORIES of Andrew Carnegie and John Sherman began very differently, both men played a prominent role in developing the government-business partnership that was crucial to the rapid industrialization of the United States. Carnegie's organization and management skills helped shape the formation of large-scale business. At the same time, Sherman and his fellow lawmakers provided support for that enterprise, using the power of government to reduce risks for businessmen and to increase incentives for economic expansion. In the view of men like Carnegie and Sherman, government's primary purpose was, in fact, to advance the agenda and interests of the business community—an agenda they were certain was in the best interests of the country as a whole.

The emphasis Carnegie and Sherman placed on the government-business alliance was, in part, a reaction to the extreme economic volatility of the late nineteenth century. The economy experienced painful depressions in the 1870s, 1880s, and 1890s, each accompanied by business failures and mass unemployment. Though recovery came in every instance and industrial output continued to soar, these financial fluctuations left businessmen ever more intent on stabilizing profits, wages, and prices. When faced with harsh economic realities and swift change, businessmen chose organization, cooperation, and government support as strategies to deal with the challenges they confronted.

America Industrializes

In this Age of Organization between 1870 and 1900, the United States grew into a global industrial power. Transcontinental railroads spurred this breathtaking transformation, linking regional markets into a national market for manufactured goods; at the same time, railroads themselves served as a massive new market for raw materials, new technologies, and, perhaps most important, steel. Building on advantages developed over the course of the nineteenth century, the Northeast and the Midwest led the way in the new economy, while efforts to industrialize the South met with uneven success. Men like Andrew Carnegie became both the heroes and the villains of their age. They engaged in ruthless practices that would lead some to label the new industrialists "robber barons," but they also created ingenious systems of industrial organization and corporate management that altered the economic landscape of the country and changed the place of the United States in the world.

The New Industrial Economy

The industrial revolution of the late nineteenth century originated in Europe. Great Britain was the world's first industrial power, but by the 1870s Germany had emerged as a major challenger for industrial dominance, increasing its steel production at a rapid rate and leading the way in the chemical and electrical industries. The dynamic economic growth stimulated by industrial competition quickly crossed the Atlantic. Eager and ambitious American entrepreneurs and engineers soon began applying the latest industrial innovations to U.S. enterprises.

Industrialization transformed the American economy. As industrialization took hold, the U.S. gross domestic product, the output of all goods and services produced annually, quadrupled—from $9 billion in 1860 to $37 billion in 1890. During this same period, the number of Americans employed by industry doubled, as American workers moved from farms to factories and immigrants flooded in from overseas to fill newly created industrial jobs. Moreover, the nature of industry itself changed, as small factories catering to local markets were displaced by large-scale firms producing for national and international markets. The midwestern cities of Chicago, Cincinnati, and St. Louis joined Boston, New York, and Philadelphia as centers of factory production, while the exploitation of

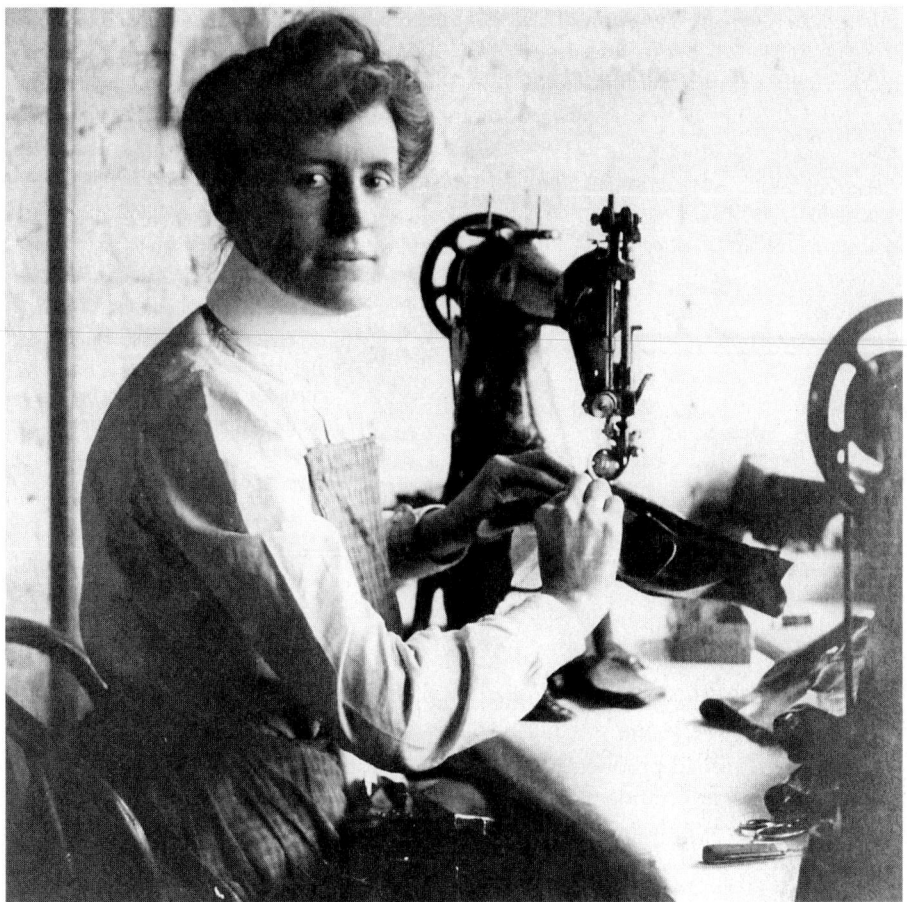

Shoe-factory worker in Lynn, Massachusetts, 1895.   The Granger Collection, New York

the natural resources in the West took on an increasingly industrial character. Trains, telegraphs, and telephones connected the country in ways never before possible. In 1889 the respected economist David A. Wells marveled at what had occurred over the past two decades: "An almost total revolution has taken place, and is yet in progress, in every branch and in every relation of the world's industrial and commercial system."

Wells did not exaggerate. From 1870 to 1913, the United States experienced an extraordinary rate of growth in industrial output: In 1870 American industries turned out 23.3 percent of the world's manufacturing production; by 1913 this figure had jumped to 35.8 percent. In fact, U.S. output in 1913 almost equaled the combined total for Europe's three leading industrial powers: Germany, the United Kingdom, and France. Of these European countries, only Germany experienced a slight rise in output from 1870 to 1913 (2.5 percent), while Britain's output dropped a precipitous 17.8 percent and France's declined 3.9 percent. By the end of the nineteenth century, the United States was surging ahead of northern Europe as the manufacturing center of the world.

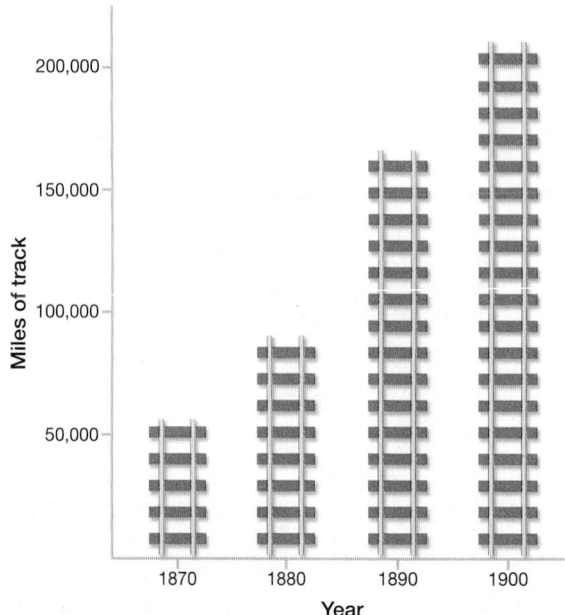

FIGURE 16.1

Expansion of the Railroad System, 1870–1900 The great expansion of the railroads in the late nineteenth century fueled the industrial revolution and the growth of big business. Connecting the nation from East Coast to West Coast, transcontinental railroads created a national market for natural resources and manufactured goods. The biggest surge in railroad construction occurred west of the Mississippi River and in the South.

At the heart of the American industrial transformation was the railroad. Large-scale business enterprises would not have developed without a national market for raw materials and finished products. A consolidated system of railroads crisscrossing the nation facilitated the creation of such a market (Figure 16.1). In addition, railroads were direct consumers of industrial products, stimulating the growth of a number of industries through their consumption of steel, wood, coal, glass, rubber, brass, and iron. For example, late-nineteenth-century railroads purchased more than 90 percent of the steel produced in U.S. factories. Finally, railroads contributed to economic growth by increasing the speed and efficiency with which products and materials were transported. One observer guessed that in 1890 if the country had to rely only on roads and waterways instead of trains to ship agricultural and industrial goods, the nation would have lost approximately $560 million, or 5 percent, of its gross national product.

Before railroads could create a national market, they had to overcome several critical problems. In 1877 railroad lines dotted the country in haphazard fashion. They primarily served local markets and remained unconnected at key points. This lack of coordination stemmed mainly from the fact that each railroad had its own track gauge (the width between the tracks), making shared track use impossible and long-distance travel extremely difficult.

The consolidation of railroads solved many of these problems. In 1886 railroad companies finally agreed to adopt a standard gauge. Railroads also standardized time zones, thus eliminating confusion in train schedules. During the 1870s, towns and cities each set their own time zone, a practice that created discrepancies among them. In 1882 the time in New York City and in Boston varied by 11 minutes and 45 seconds. The following year, railroads agreed to coordinate times and divided the country into four standard time zones. Most cities soon cooperated, but not until 1918 did the federal government legislate the standard time zones that the railroads had first adopted.

Innovation and Inventions

As important as railroads were, they were not the only engine of industrialization. American technological innovation created new industries, while expanding the efficiency and productivity of old ones. Inventor Thomas Alva Edison began his career by devising ways to improve the telegraph and expand its uses. In 1866 a transatlantic telegraph cable connected the United States and Europe, allowing businessmen on both sides of the ocean to pursue profitable commercial ventures. New inventions also allowed business offices to run more smoothly: Typewriters were invented in 1868, carbon paper in 1872, adding machines in 1891, and mimeograph machines in 1892. As businesses grew, they needed more space for their operations. The construction of towering skyscrapers in the 1880s in cities such as Chicago and New York was made possible by two innovations: structural steel, which had the strength to support tall buildings; and elevators, equipped with a safety device invented by Elisha Graves Otis in the 1850s.

Among the thousands of patents filed each year, Alexander Graham Bell's telephone revolutionized communications. By 1880 fifty-five cities offered local service and catered to a total of 50,000 subscribers, most of them business customers. A decade later, long-distance service connected New York, Boston, and Chicago, and by 1900 around 1.5 million telephones were in operation. Bell profited handsomely from his invention, created his own firm, and in 1885 established the giant American Telephone and Telegraph Company (AT&T).

Perhaps the greatest technological innovations that advanced industrial development in the late nineteenth century came in steel manufacturing. In 1859 Henry Bessemer, a British inventor, designed a furnace that burned the impurities out of melted iron and converted it into steel. The open-hearth process, devised by another Englishman, William Siemens, further improved the quality of steel by removing additional impurities from the iron. Railroads replaced iron rails with steel because it was lighter, stronger, and more durable than iron. Steel became the major building block of industry, furnishing girders and cables to construct manufacturing plants and office structures. As production became cheaper and more efficient, steel output soared from 13,000 tons in 1860 to 28 million tons in the first decade of the twentieth century.

Factory machinery needed constant lubrication, and the growing petroleum industry made this possible. A new drilling technique devised in 1859 tapped into pools of petroleum located deep below the earth's surface. In the post–Civil War era, new distilling techniques transformed this thick, smelly liquid into lubricating oil for factory machinery. This process of "cracking" crude oil also generated lucrative by-products for the home, such as kerosene and paraffin for heating and lighting. Robert A. Chesebrough discovered that a sticky oil residue could soothe cuts and burns, and in 1870 he began manufacturing a product he would soon trademark as Vaseline Petroleum Jelly. After 1900, the development of the gasoline-powered, internal combustion engine for automobiles opened up an even richer market for the oil industry.

Railroads also benefited from innovations in technology. Improvements included air brakes and automatic coupling devices to attach train cars to each other. Elijah McCoy, a trained engineer and the son of former slaves, was forced because of racial discrimination to work at menial railroad jobs shoveling coal and lubricating train parts every few miles to keep the gears from overheating. This grueling experience encouraged him to invent and patent an automatic lubricating device to improve efficiency.

Early innovations resulted from the genius of individual inventors, but by the late nineteenth century technological progress was increasingly an organized, collaborative effort. Thomas Edison and his team served as the model. In 1876 Edison set up a research laboratory in Menlo Park, New Jersey. Housed in a two-story, white frame building, Edison's "invention factory" was staffed by a team of inventors and craftsmen. Edison believed that "genius was 1 percent inspiration and 99 percent perspiration," and he devoted nearly every waking hour, often ignoring his family, to coordinating the invention process. In 1887 Edison opened another laboratory, ten times bigger than the one at Menlo Park, in nearby Orange, New Jersey. These facilities pioneered the research laboratories that would become a standard feature of American industrial development in the twentieth century.

Edison expected his research factories to produce "a minor invention every ten days and a big thing every six months or so." Edison and his crew largely succeeded. During his lifetime, Edison filed 1,093 U.S. patents; although he has received most of the credit, a good number of his inventions were the result of collaborative research. Out of his laboratory flowed inventions that revolutionized American business and culture. The phonograph and motion pictures changed the way people spent their leisure time. The electric lightbulb illuminated people's homes and made them safer by eliminating the need for candles and gas lamps, which were fire hazards. It also brightened city streets, making them available for outdoor evening activities, and lit up factories so that they could operate all night long.

Like his contemporaries who were building America's huge industrial empires, Edison cashed in on his workers' inventions. He joined forces with the Wall Street banker J. P. Morgan to finance the Edison Electric Illuminating Company, which in 1882 provided lighting to customers in New York City. Goods produced by electric equipment jumped in value from $1.9 million in 1879 to $21.8 million in 1890. In 1892, Morgan helped Edison merge his companies with several competitors and reorganized them as the General Electric Corporation, which became the industry leader.

Building a New South

Although the largely rural South lagged behind the North and the Midwest in manufacturing, industrial expansion did not bypass the region. Well aware of global economic trends and eager for the South to achieve its economic potential, southern business leaders and newspaper editors, especially the *Atlanta Constitution*'s editor Henry Grady, saw industrial development as the key to the creation of a **New South**. Attributing the Confederate defeat in the Civil War to the North's superior manufacturing output and railroad supply lines, New South proponents hoped to modernize their economy in a similar fashion. One of those boosters was Richard H. Edmonds, the Virginia-born editor of the *Manufacturers' Record*. He extolled the virtues of the "real South" of the 1880s, characterized by "the music of progress—the whirr of the spindle, the buzz of the saw, the roar of the furnace, the throb of the locomotive." The South of Edmonds's vision would move beyond the regional separatism of the past and become fully integrated into the national economy.

Railroads were the key to achieving such economic integration, so after the Civil War new railroad tracks were laid throughout the South. Not only did this expanded railroad system create direct connections between the North and the South, but it also facilitated the growth of the southern textile industry. Seeking to take advantage of plentiful cotton, cheap labor, and the improved transportation system, investors built textile mills throughout the South, especially in the Carolinas and Georgia. Victims of falling prices and saddled with debt, sharecroppers and tenant farmers moved into mill towns in search of better employment. Mill owners preferred to hire girls and young women, who worked for low wages, to spin cotton and weave it on the looms. To do so, however, owners had to employ their entire family, for mothers and fathers would not let their daughters relocate without their supervision. Whatever attraction the mills offered applied only to whites. The pattern of white supremacy emerging in the post-Reconstruction South kept African Americans out of all but the most menial jobs.

Blacks contributed greatly to the construction of railroads in the New South, but they did not do so as free men. Convicts, most of whom were African American, performed the exhausting work of laying tracks through hills and swamps. Southern states used the **convict lease** system, in which blacks, usually imprisoned for minor offenses, were hired out to private companies to serve their time or pay off their fine. The convict lease system brought additional income to the state and supplied cheap labor to the railroads and planters, but it left African American convict laborers impoverished and virtually enslaved.

 Online Document Project   **Labor and Race in the New South**
bedfordstmartins.com/hewittlawsonvalue

The South attracted a number of industries besides textile manufacturing. In the 1880s, James B. Duke established a cigarette manufacturing empire in Durham, North Carolina. Nearby tobacco fields provided the raw material that black workers prepared for white workers, who then rolled the cigarettes by machine. Acres of timber pines in the Carolinas, Florida, and Alabama sustained a lucrative lumber industry, one of the few to employ whites and blacks equally. Rich supplies of coal and iron in Alabama fostered the growth of the steel industry in Birmingham, which produced more than a million tons of steel at the turn of the twentieth century (Map 16.1).

Despite this frenzy of industrial activity, the New South in many ways resembled the Old South. Southern entrepreneurs still depended on northern investors to supply much of the capital for investment. Investors were attracted by the low wages that prevailed in the South, but low wages also meant that southern workers remained poor and, in many cases, unable to buy the manufactured goods produced by industry. Efforts to diversify agriculture beyond tobacco and cotton were constrained by a sharecropping system based on small, inefficient plots. In fact, even though industrialization did make considerable headway in the South, the economy remained overwhelmingly agricultural. This suited many white southerners who wanted to hold on to the individualistic, agrarian values they associated with the Old South. In this way, they sought to remain distinct from what they considered the acquisitive North. Yoked to old ideologies and a system of forced labor, modernization in the South could go only so far.

Industrial Consolidation

In both the North and the South, nineteenth-century industrialists strove to minimize or eliminate competition. To gain competitive advantages and increase profits, industrial entrepreneurs concentrated on reducing production costs, charging lower

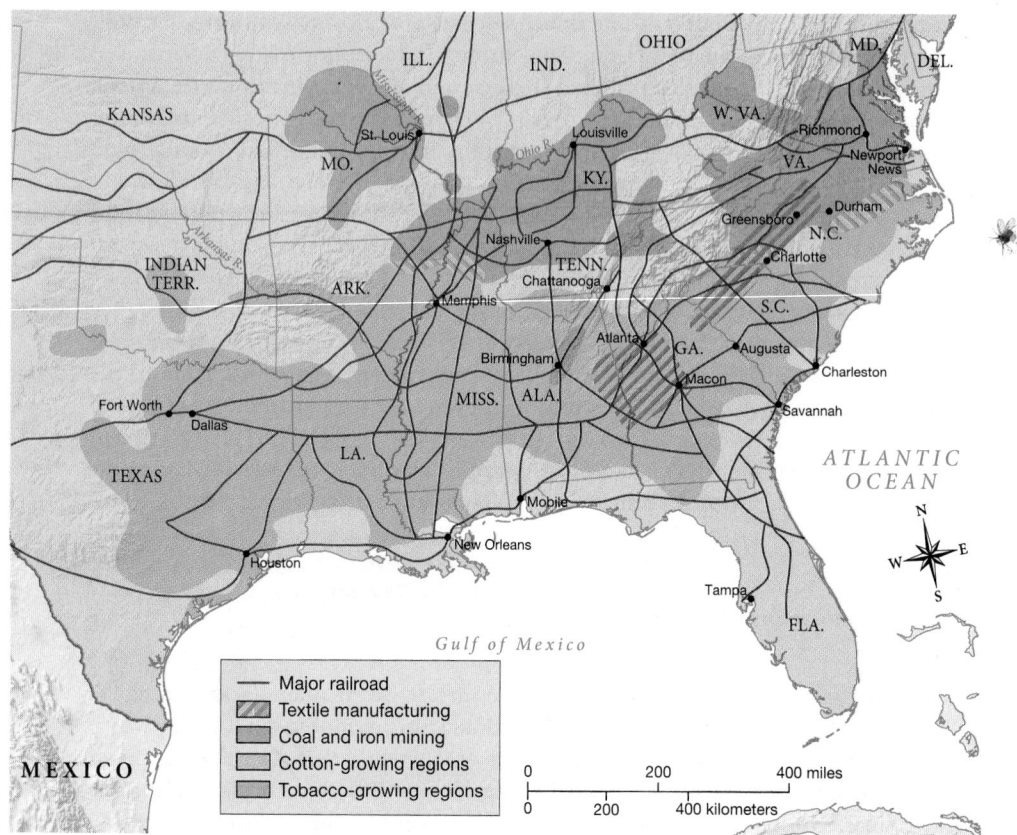

MAP 16.1

The New South, 1900   Although the South remained largely agricultural by 1900, it had made great strides toward building industries in the region. This so-called New South boasted an extensive railway network that provided a national market for its raw materials and manufactured goods, including coal, iron, steel, and textiles. Still, the southern economy in 1900 depended primarily on raising cotton and tobacco.

prices, and outselling the competition. Successful firms could then acquire rival companies that could no longer afford to compete, creating an industrial empire in the process.

Building such industrial empires was not easy, however, and posed creative challenges for business ventures. Heavy investment in machinery resulted in very high fixed costs (or overhead) that did not change much over time. Because overhead costs remained stable, manufacturers could reduce the per-unit cost of production by increasing the output of a product—what economists call "economy of scale." Manufacturers thus aimed to raise the volume of production and find ways to cut variable costs—for labor and materials, for example. Shaving off even a few pennies from the cost of making each unit could save millions of dollars on the total cost of production. Through such savings, a factory owner could sell his product more cheaply than his competitors and gain a larger share of the market.

A major organizational technique for reducing costs and underselling the competition was **vertical integration**. "Captains of industry," as their admirers called them, did not just build a business; they created a system—a network of firms, each contributing to the final product. Men like Andrew Carnegie controlled the various phases of production from top to bottom (vertical), extracting the raw materials, transporting them to the factories, manufacturing the finished products, and shipping them to market. In 1881, when Carnegie combined his operations with those of Henry Clay Frick of Pennsylvania, he gained not only a talented factory manager but also access to Frick's coal business. By using vertical integration, Carnegie eliminated middlemen and guaranteed regular and cheap access to supplies. He also avoided duplications in machinery, lowered inventories, and gained increased flexibility by shifting segments of the labor force to areas where they were most needed. This integrated system demanded close and careful management of the overall operation, which Carnegie provided. He manufactured steel with improved efficiency and cut costs. His credo became "Watch the costs and the profits will take care of themselves."

Businessmen also employed another type of integration—**horizontal integration**. This approach focused on gaining greater control over the market by acquiring firms that sold the same products. John D. Rockefeller, the founder of the mammoth Standard Oil Company, specialized in this technique. In the mid-1870s, he brought a number of key oil refiners into an alliance with Standard Oil to control four-fifths of the industry. At the same time, the oil baron ruthlessly drove out or bought up marginal firms that could not afford to compete with him. One such competitor testified to a congressional committee in 1879 about how Standard Oil had squeezed him out: "[Rockefeller] said that he had facilities for freighting and that the coal-oil business belonged to them; and any concern that would start in that business, they had sufficient money to lay aside a fund and wipe them out."

Horizontal integration was also a major feature in the telegraph industry. By 1861 Western Union had strung 76,000 miles of telegraph line throughout the nation. Founded in 1851, the company had thrived during the Civil War by obtaining most of the federal government's telegraph business. The firm had 12,600 offices housed in railroad depots throughout the country and strung its lines adjacent to the railroads. In the eight years before Cornelius Vanderbilt bought Western Union in 1869, the value of its stock jumped from $3 million to $41 million. Seeing an opportunity to make money, Wall Street tycoon Jay Gould set out to acquire Western Union. In the mid-1870s, Gould, who had obtained control over the Union Pacific Railway, financed companies to compete with the giant telegraph outfit. Gould did not succeed until 1881, when he engineered a takeover of Western Union by combining it with his American Union Telegraph Company. Gould made a profit of $30 million on the deal. On February 15, the day after the agreement, the *New York Herald Tribune* reported: "The country finds itself this morning at the feet of a telegraphic monopoly," a business that controlled the market and destroyed competition.

Bankers played a huge role in engineering industrial consolidation. No one did it more skillfully than John Pierpont Morgan. In the 1850s, Morgan started his career working for a prominent American-owned banking firm in London, and in 1861 he created his own investment company in New York City. Unlike the United States, Great Britain had a surplus of capital that bankers sought to invest abroad. Morgan played the central role in channeling funds from Britain to support the construction of major

American railroads. During the 1880s and 1890s, Morgan orchestrated the refinancing of several ailing railroads, including the Baltimore & Ohio and the Southern Railroad. To maintain control over these enterprises, the Wall Street financier placed his allies on their boards of directors and selected the companies' chief operating officers. Morgan then turned his talents for organization to the steel industry. In 1901 he was instrumental in merging Carnegie's company with several competitors in which he had a financial interest. United States Steel, Morgan's creation, became the world's largest industrial corporation, worth $1.4 billion. By the end of the first decade of the twentieth century, Morgan's investment house held more than 340 directorships in 112 corporations, amounting to more than $22 billion in assets, the equivalent of $608 billion in 2012, all at a time when there was no income tax.

The Growth of Corporations

With economic consolidation came the expansion of **corporations**. Before the age of large-scale enterprise, the predominant form of business ownership was the partnership. Unlike partnerships, corporations provided investors with "limited liability." This meant that if the corporation went bankrupt, shareholders could not lose more than they had invested. Limited liability encouraged investment by keeping the shareholders' investment in the corporation separate from their other assets. In addition, corporations provided "perpetual life." Partnerships dissolved on the death of a partner, whereas corporations continued to function despite the death of any single owner. This form of ownership brought stability and order to financing, building, and perpetuating what was otherwise a highly volatile and complex business endeavor.

Capitalists devised new corporate structures to gain greater control over their industries. Rockefeller's Standard Oil Company led the way by creating the trust, a monopoly formed through consolidation. To evade state laws against monopolies, Rockefeller created a petroleum trust. He combined other oil firms across the country with Standard Oil and placed their owners on a nine-member board of trustees that ran the company. Subsequently, Rockefeller fashioned another method of bringing rival businesses together. Through a holding company, he obtained stock in a number of other oil companies and held them under his control.

The movement to create trusts, Rockefeller boasted, "was the origin of the whole system of modern economic administration." Statistics backed up his assessment. Between 1880 and 1905, more than three hundred mergers occurred in 80 percent of the nation's manufacturing firms. Great wealth became heavily concentrated in the hands of a relatively small number of businessmen. Around two thousand businesses, a tiny fraction of the total number, dominated 40 percent of the nation's economy.

In their drive to consolidate economic power and shield themselves from risk, corporate titans generally had the courts on their side. In *Santa Clara County v. Southern Pacific Railroad Company* (1886), the Supreme Court decided that under the Fourteenth Amendment, which originally dealt with the issue of federal protection of African Americans' civil rights, a corporation was considered a "person." In effect, this ruling gave corporations the same right of due process that the framers of the amendment had meant to give to former slaves. In the 1890s, a majority of the Supreme Court embraced this interpretation. The right of due process shielded corporations from prohibitive government regulation of the workplace, including the passage of legislation reducing the number of hours in the workday.

Yet trusts did not go unopposed. In 1890 Congress passed Senator Sherman's Antitrust Act, which outlawed monopolies that prevented free competition in interstate commerce. The bill passed easily with bipartisan support because it merely codified legal principles that already existed. Sherman and his colleagues never intended to stifle large corporations, which through efficient business practices came to dominate the market. Rather, the lawmakers attempted to limit underhanded actions that destroyed competition. The judicial system further bailed out corporate leaders. In *United States v. E.C. Knight Company* (1895), a case against the "sugar trust," the Supreme Court rendered the Sherman Act virtually toothless by ruling that manufacturing was a local activity within a state and that, even if it was a monopoly, it was not subject to congressional regulation. This ruling left most trusts in the manufacturing sector beyond the jurisdiction of the Sherman Antitrust Act.

The introduction of managerial specialists, already present in European firms, proved the most critical innovation for integrating industry. With many operations controlled under one roof, large-scale businesses required a corps of experts to oversee and coordinate the various steps of production. Comptrollers and accountants pored over financial records to keep track of every penny spent and dollar earned. Traffic managers directed the movement of raw materials into plants and finished products out for distribution. Marketing executives were in charge of advertising goods and finding new markets. Efficiency experts sought to cut labor costs and make the production process operate more smoothly. Frederick W. Taylor, a Philadelphia engineer and businessman, developed the principles of scientific management. Based on his concept of reducing manual labor to its simplest components and eliminating independent action on the part of workers, managers introduced time-and-motion studies. Using a stopwatch, they calculated how to break down a job into simple tasks that could be performed in the least amount of time. From this perspective, workers were no different from the machines they operated.

Another vital factor in creating large-scale industry was the establishment of retail outlets that could sell the enormous volume of goods pouring out of factories. As consumer goods became less expensive, retail outlets sprang up to serve the growing market for household items, including watches, jewelry, sewing machines, cameras, and an assortment of rugs and furniture. Customers could shop at department stores—such as Macy's in New York City, Filene's in Boston, Marshall Field's in Chicago, Nordstrom's in Seattle, Gump's in San Francisco, Nieman Marcus in Dallas, Jacome's in Tucson, Rich's in Atlanta, and Burdine's in Miami—where they were waited on by a growing army of salesclerks. Or they could buy the cheaper items in Frank W. Woolworth's five and ten cent stores, which opened in towns and cities nationwide. Chain supermarkets—such as the Great Atlantic and Pacific Tea Company (A&P), founded in 1869—sold fruits and vegetables packed in tin cans. They also sold foods from the meatpacking firms of Gustavus Swift and Philip Armour, which shipped them on refrigerated railroad cars. Mail-order catalogs allowed Americans in all parts of the country to buy consumer goods without leaving their home. The catalogs of Montgomery Ward (established in 1872) and Sears, Roebuck (founded in 1886) offered tens of thousands of items. Rural free delivery (RFD), instituted by the U.S. Post Office in 1891, made it even easier for farmers and others living in the countryside to obtain these catalogs and buy their merchandise without having to travel miles to the nearest post office. By the end of the nineteenth century, the industrial economy had left its mark on almost all aspects of life in almost every corner of America.

REVIEW & RELATE

- What were the key factors behind the acceleration of industrial development in late-nineteenth-century America?
- How did industrialization change the way American businessmen thought about their companies and the people who worked for them?

Free Markets and Rugged Individuals

American industrialization developed as rapidly as it did in large part because it was reinforced by traditional ideas and values. The notion that hard work and diligence would result in success meant that individuals felt justified, even duty-bound, to strive to achieve upward mobility and accumulate wealth. Churches, schools, intellectuals, and popular writers combined to buttress this doctrine of success. Those who succeeded believed that they had done so because they were more talented, industrious, and resourceful than others. Thus prosperous businessmen regarded competition and the free market as essential to the health of an economic world they saw based on merit. Yet these same businessmen also created trusts that destroyed competition, and they depended on the government for resources and protection. This obvious contradiction, along with the profoundly unequal distribution of wealth that characterized the late-nineteenth-century economy, generated a good deal of criticism of business tycoons and their beliefs.

The Doctrine of Success

Those at the top of the new industrial order justified their great wealth in a manner that most Americans could understand. The ideas of the Scottish economist Adam Smith, in *The Wealth of Nations* (1776), had gained popularity during the American Revolution. Advocating **laissez-faire** ("let things alone"), Smith contended that an "Invisible Hand," guided by natural law, guaranteed the greatest economic success if the government let individuals pursue their own self-interest unhindered by outside and artificial influences. In the late nineteenth century, businessmen and their conservative allies on the Supreme Court used Smith's doctrines to argue against restrictive government regulation. They equated their right to own and manage property with the personal liberty protected by the Fourteenth Amendment. Thus the Declaration of Independence, with its defense of "life, liberty, and the pursuit of happiness," and the Constitution, which enshrined citizens' political freedom, became instruments to guarantee unfettered economic opportunity and safeguard private property.

The view that success depended on individual initiative was reinforced in schools and churches. The McGuffey Readers, widely used to educate children, taught moral lessons of hard work, individual initiative, reliability, and thrift. The popular dime novels of Horatio Alger portrayed the story of young men, such as Ragged Dick, who rose through pluck and luck from "rags to riches." Americans could also hear success stories in houses of worship. Russell Conwell, pastor of the Grace Baptist Church in Philadelphia, delivered a widely printed sermon entitled "Acres of Diamonds," which equated godliness with riches and argued that ordinary people had an obligation to strive for material wealth. "I say that you ought to get rich, and it is your duty to get rich," Conwell declared, "because to make money honestly is to preach the gospel."

Conwell followed his own advice and became wealthy from the fees he earned delivering his popular sermon.

If economic success was a matter of personal merit, it followed that economic failure was as well. The British philosopher Herbert Spencer proposed a theory of social evolution based on this premise in his book *Social Statics* (1851). Imagining a future utopia, Spencer wrote, "Man was not created with an instinct for his own degradation, but from the lower he has risen to the higher forms. Nor is there any conceivable end to his march to perfection." In his view, those at the top of the economic ladder were closer to perfection than were those at the bottom. Any effort to aid the unfortunate would only slow the march of progress for society as a whole. Spencer's book proved extremely popular, selling nearly 400,000 copies in the United States by 1900. In recalling how Spencer's ideas influenced him, Carnegie wrote, "I remember that light came as in a flood and all was clear." Publication of Charles Darwin's landmark *On the Origin of Species* (1859) appeared to provide some scientific legitimacy for Spencer's view. The British naturalist argued that plants, animals, and humans progressed or declined because of their ability or inability to adapt favorably to the environment and transmit these characteristics to future generations. The connection between the two men's ideas has led some to label Spencer and his supporters "Social Darwinists." However, few defenders of laissez-faire principles in the late nineteenth century had actually read Darwin or referred to themselves as Social Darwinists, a term that came into widespread use only in the twentieth century.

Doctrines of success gained favor because they helped Americans explain the rapid economic changes that were disrupting their lives. Although most ordinary people would not climb out of poverty to middle-class respectability, let alone affluence, they clung to ideas that promised hope. After all, if a man like Carnegie could rise from poverty to become a multimillionaire, why not them? It mattered little that most of those who achieved extraordinary wealth did not emerge from the working class but rather came from the middle class. Ideas such as Spencer's that linked success with progress provided a way for those who did not do well to understand their failure and blame themselves for their own inadequacies. At the same time, the notion that economic success derived from personal merit legitimized the fabulous wealth of those who did rise to the top.

Capitalists such as Carnegie found a way to soften both the message of extreme competition and its impact on the American public. Denying that the government should help the poor, they proclaimed that men of wealth had a duty to furnish some assistance. In his famous essay **"The Gospel of Wealth"** (1889), Carnegie declared that "a man who died rich died disgraced." He argued that the rich should act as stewards of the wealth they earned. As trustees, they should administer their surplus income for the benefit of the community. Carnegie distinguished between charity (direct handouts to individuals), which he deplored, and philanthropy (building institutions that would raise educational and cultural standards), which he advocated. For example, Carnegie, Rockefeller, and railroad tycoons Leland Stanford and Cornelius Vanderbilt all gave endowments (and their names) to universities to provide education for those who worked hard to achieve it. Russell Conwell also gave away his fortune to various philanthropic enterprises, most notably the founding of Temple University in Philadelphia, which opened its doors to poor men seeking a higher education. Carnegie was particularly generous in funding libraries (he provided the buildings but not the books) because they allowed people to gain knowledge through their own efforts.

Capitalists may have sung the praises of individualism and laissez-faire, but their actions contradicted their words. Successful industrialists in the late nineteenth century sought to destroy competition, not perpetuate it. Their efforts over the course of several decades produced giant corporations that measured the worth of individuals by calculating their value to the organization. As John D. Rockefeller, the master of consolidation, proclaimed, "The day of individual competition in large affairs is past and gone."

 Online Document Project   Debates about Laissez-Faire
bedfordstmartins.com/hewittlawsonvalue

Nor did capitalists strictly oppose government involvement. Although industrialists did not want the federal government to take any action that *retarded* their economic efforts, they did favor the use of the government's power to *promote* their enterprises and to stimulate entrepreneurial energies. Thus manufacturers pushed for congressional passage of high tariffs to protect goods from foreign competition and to foster development of the national marketplace. Industrialists demanded that federal and state governments dispatch troops when labor strikes threatened their businesses. They persuaded Washington to provide land grants for railroad construction and to send the army to clear Native Americans and bison from their tracks. They argued for state and federal courts to interpret constitutional and statutory law in a way that shielded property rights against attacks from workers. In large measure, capitalists succeeded not in spite of governmental support but because of it.

Challenges to Laissez-Faire

Proponents of government restraint and unbridled individualism did not go unchallenged. Critics of laissez-faire created an alternative ideology for those who sought to organize workers and expand the role of government as ways of restricting capitalists' power over labor and ordinary citizens.

Lester Frank Ward attacked laissez-faire in his book *Dynamic Sociology* (1883). A largely self-taught man who worked as a civil servant for the federal government, Ward did not disparage individualism but viewed the main function of society as "the organization of happiness." Contradicting Herbert Spencer, Ward maintained that societies progressed when government directly intervened to help citizens—even the unfortunate. Indeed, society could initiate "the systematic realization of its own interests, in the same manner that an intelligent and keen-sighted individual pursues his life-purposes." Rejecting laissez-faire, Ward argued that what people "really need is more government in its primary sense, greater protection from the rapacity of the favored few."

Some academics supported Ward's ideas. Most notably, economist Richard T. Ely applied Christian ethics to his scholarly assessment of capital and labor. He condemned the railroads for dragging "their slimy length over our country, and every turn in their progress is marked by a progeny of evils." In his book *The Labor Movement* (1886), Ely suggested that the ultimate solution for social ills resulting from industrialization lay in "the union of capital and labor in the same hands, in grand, wide-reaching, co-operative enterprises."

Two popular writers, Henry George and Edward Bellamy, added to the critique of materialism and greed. In *Progress and Poverty* (1879), George lamented: "Amid the greatest accumulations of wealth, men die of starvation." He blamed the problem on rent, which he viewed as an unjustifiable payment on the increase in the value of land, what he called "unearned increment." His remedy was to have government confiscate rent earned on land by levying a single tax on landownership. Though he advocated government intervention, he did not envision an enduring role for the state once it had imposed the single tax. By contrast, Bellamy imagined a powerful central government. In his novel *Looking Backward, 2000–1887* (1888), Bellamy scorned the "imbecility of private enterprise" and attacked industrialists who "maim and slaughter workers by thousands." In his view, the federal government should take over large-scale firms, administer them as workers' collectives, and redistribute wealth equally among all citizens.

Neither Bellamy, George, Ward, nor Ely endorsed the militant socialism of Karl Marx. The German philosopher predicted that capitalism would be overthrown and replaced by a revolutionary movement of industrial workers that would control the means of economic production and establish an egalitarian society. Although his ideas gained popularity among European labor leaders, they were not widely accepted in the United States during this period. George referred to Marx as "the prince of muddleheads." George and other critics believed that the American political system could be reformed without resorting to the extreme solution of a socialist revolution. They favored a cooperative commonwealth of capital and labor, with the government acting as an umpire between the two.

REVIEW & RELATE

- In the late nineteenth century, how did many Americans explain individual economic success and failure?
- How did the business community view the role of government in the economy at the end of the nineteenth century?

Society and Culture in the Gilded Age

Wealthy people in the late nineteenth century used their fortunes to support lavish, indulgent lifestyles. For many of them, especially those with recent wealth, opulence rather than good taste was the standard of adornment. This tendency inspired writer Mark Twain and his collaborator Charles Dudley Warner to describe this era of wealth creation and vast inequality as the **Gilded Age**.

Twain and Warner had the very wealthy in mind when they coined the phrase, but others further down the social ladder found ways to participate in the culture of consumption. The rapidly expanding middle class enjoyed modest homes furnished with mass-produced consumer goods. Women played the central role in running the household, as most wives remained at home to raise children. Women and men often spent their free time attending meetings and other events sponsored by the many social, cultural, and political organizations that flourished during this era. Such prosperity was, however, largely limited to whites. For the majority of African Americans still living in the South, life proved much harder. In response to black aspirations for social and economic advancement, white politicians imposed a rigid system of racial segregation on the South. Although whites championed the cause of individual upward mobility, they restricted opportunities to achieve success to whites only.

Wealthy and Middle-Class Pleasures

In Chicago's Gold Coast, Boston's Back Bay, Philadelphia's Rittenhouse Square, San Francisco's Nob Hill, Denver's Quality Hill, and Cincinnati's Hilltop, urban elites lived lives of incredible material opulence. J. P. Morgan and John D. Rockefeller built lavish homes in New York City. William Vanderbilt constructed luxurious mansions along Fifth Avenue in Manhattan. High-rise apartment buildings also catered to the wealthy. Overlooking Central Park, the nine-story Dakota Apartments boasted fifty-eight suites, a banquet hall, and a wine cellar. Famous architects designed some of the finest of these stately homes, which their millionaire residents furnished with an eclectic mix of priceless art objects and furniture in a jumble of diverse styles. The rich and famous established private social clubs, sent their children to exclusive prep schools and colleges, and worshipped in the most fashionable churches.

Second homes, usually for use in the summer, were no less expensively constructed and decorated. Besides residences in Manhattan and Newport, Rhode Island, the Vanderbilts constructed a "home away from home" in the mountains of Asheville, North Carolina. The Biltmore, as they named it, contained 250 rooms, 40 master bedrooms, and an indoor swimming pool. Edward Julius Berwind of Philadelphia, who made his fortune in coal, constructed a magnificent summer residence in Newport. Modeled after a mid-eighteenth-century French chateau, The Elms cost $1.4 million (approximately $38.6 million in 2012) and was furnished with an assortment of Renaissance ceramics and French and Venetian paintings.

The wealthy also built and frequented opera houses, concert halls, museums, and historical societies as testimonies to their taste and sophistication. For example, the Vanderbilts, Rockefellers, Goulds, and Morgans financed the completion of the Metropolitan Opera House in New York City in 1883. When the facility opened, a local newspaper commented about the well-heeled audience: "The Goulds and the Vanderbilts and people of that ilk perfumed the air with the odor of crisp greenbacks." Upper-class women often traveled abroad to visit the great European cities and ancient Mediterranean sites.

Industrialization and the rise of corporate capitalism also brought an array of **white-collar workers** in managerial, clerical, and technical positions. These workers formed a new, expanded middle class and joined the businesspeople, doctors, lawyers, teachers, and clergy who constituted the old middle class. More than three million white-collar workers were employed in 1910, nearly three times as many as in 1870.

Middle-class families decorated their residences with comfortable, mass-produced furniture, musical instruments, family photographs, books, periodicals, and a variety of memorabilia collected in their leisure time. They could relax in their parlors and browse through mass-circulation magazines like *Ladies' Home Journal* and *The Delineator*, a fashion and arts journal. They might also read a wide variety of popular newspapers that competed with one another with sensationalist stories. Or they could read some of the era's outpouring of fiction, including romances, dime novels, westerns, humor, and social realism, an art form that depicted working-class life.

In the face of rapid economic changes, middle-class women and men joined a variety of social and professional organizations that were arising to deal with the problems accompanying industrialization (Table 16.1). During the 1880s, charitable organizations such as the American Red Cross were established to provide disaster relief. In 1892 the General Federation of Women's Clubs was founded to improve women's educational

TABLE 16.1   An Age of Organizations, 1876–1896

Category	Year of Founding	Organization
Charitable	1881	American Red Cross
	1887	Charity Organization Society
	1889	Educational Alliance
	1893	National Council of Jewish Women
Sports/Fraternal	1876	National League of Baseball
	1882	Knights of Columbus
	1888	National Council of Women
	1892	General Federation of Women's Clubs
	1896	National Association of Colored Women
Professional	1883	Modern Language Association
	1884	American Historical Association
	1885	American Economic Association
	1888	American Mathematical Society

and cultural lives. Four years later, the National Association of Colored Women organized to help relieve suffering among the black poor, defend black women, and promote the interests of the black race. Many scholarly organizations were formed during this decade, including the American Historical Association, the Modern Language Association, and the American Mathematical Society.

During these swiftly changing times, adults became increasingly concerned about the nation's youth and sought to create organizations that catered to young people. Formed before the Civil War in England and expanded to the United States, the Young Men's Christian Association (YMCA) grew briskly during the 1880s as it erected buildings where young men could socialize, build moral character, and engage in healthy physical exercise. The Young Women's Christian Association (YWCA) provided similar opportunities for women. African Americans also participated in "Y" activities through the creation of racially separate branches.

Changing Gender Roles

Middle-class wives generally remained at home, caring for the house and children, often with the aid of a servant. Whereas in the past farmers and artisans had worked from the home, now most men and women accepted as natural the separation of the workplace and the home caused by industrialization and urbanization. Although the birthrate and marriage rates among the middle class dropped during the late nineteenth century, wives were still expected to care for their husbands and family first to fulfill their feminine duties.

Even though daughters increasingly attended colleges reserved for women, such as Smith, Radcliffe, Wellesley, and Mount Holyoke, their families viewed education as a means of providing refinement rather than a career. One physician aptly summed up the prevailing view that women could only use their brains "but little and in trivial matters" and should concentrate on serving as "the companion or ornamental appendage to man."

Middle-class women were now confronted with the new consumer culture. Department stores, chain stores, ready-made clothes, and packaged goods, from Jell-O and Kellogg's Corn Flakes to cake mixes, competed for the money and loyalty of female consumers. Hairdressers, cosmetic companies, and department stores offered a growing and ever-changing assortment of styles, even as they also provided new jobs to those unable to afford the latest fashions without a weekly paycheck. The expanding array of consumer goods did not, however, decrease women's domestic workload. They had more furniture to dust, fancier meals to prepare, changing fashions to keep up with, higher standards of cleanliness to maintain, and more time to devote to entertaining. Yet the availability of mass-produced goods to assist the housewife in her chores made her role as consumer highly visible, while making her role as worker nearly invisible.

For the more socially and economically independent young women—those who attended college or beauty and secretarial schools—new worlds of leisure opened up.

Shopping in a Department Store   In cities around the country, department stores offered a variety of items appealing to middle-class consumers, especially women. In this photograph from 1893, shoppers interested in purchasing gloves receive personal attention from well-dressed salesclerks behind the counter of Rike's Department Store in Dayton, Ohio.   © Bettmann/CORBIS

Bicycling, tennis, and croquet became popular sports for women in the late nineteenth century. So, too, did playing basketball, both in colleges and through industrial leagues. Indeed, women's colleges made sports a requirement, to offset the stress of intellectual life and produce a more well-rounded woman. Young women who sought an air of sophistication dressed according to the image of the Gibson Girl, the creation of illustrator Charles Dana Gibson. In the 1890s, the Gibson Girl became the model for the energetic, athletic "new woman," with her upswept hair, fancy hats, long skirts, flowing blouses, and disposable income.

Middle-class men enjoyed their leisure by joining fraternal organizations. Writing in the *North American Review* in 1897, W. G. Harwood commented that the late nineteenth century was the "Golden Age of Fraternity." Five and a half million men (of some 19 million adult men in the United States) joined fraternal orders, such as the Odd Fellows, Masons, Knights of Pythias, and Elks. These groups offered middle-class men a network of business contacts and gave them a chance to enjoy a communal, masculine social environment otherwise lacking in their lives.

In fact, historians have referred to a "crisis of masculinity" afflicting a segment of middle- and upper-class men in the late nineteenth and early twentieth centuries. Middle-class occupations whittled away the sense of autonomy that men had experienced in an earlier era when they worked for themselves. The emergence of corporate capitalism had swelled the ranks of the middle class with organization men, who held salaried jobs in managerial departments. At the same time, the push for women's rights, especially the right to vote, and women's increasing involvement in civic associations threatened to reduce absolute male control over the public sphere.

Responding to this gender crisis, middle-class men sought ways to exert their masculinity and keep from becoming frail and effeminate. Psychologists like G. Stanley Hall warned that unless men returned to a primitive state of manhood, they risked becoming feminized and spiritually paralyzed. To avoid this, they should build up their bodies and engage in strenuous activities to improve their physical fitness. Edgar Rice Burroughs's *Tarzan of the Apes* (1912) extolled primitive manhood and contrasted its natural virtues with the vices of becoming overcivilized.

Men turned to sports to cultivate their masculinity. Besides playing baseball and football, they could attend various sporting events. Baseball became the national pastime, and men could root for their home team and establish a community with the thousands of male spectators who filled up newly constructed ballparks. These fields of dirt and grass were situated amid urban businesses, apartment buildings, and traffic and served as a metaphor for the preservation of an older, pastoral life alongside the hubbub of modern technology. Baseball, which had started as a game played by elites in New York City in the 1840s, soon became a commercially popular sport. It spread across the country as baseball clubs in different cities competed with each other. The sport came into its own with the creation of the professional National League in 1876 and the introduction of the World Series in 1903 between the winners of the National League and the American League pennant races.

Boxing also became a popular spectator sport in the late nineteenth century. Bareknuckle fighting—without the protection of gloves—epitomized the craze to display pure masculinity. A boxing match lasted until one of the fighters was knocked out, leaving both fighters bloody and battered.

During the late nineteenth century, middle-class women and men also had increased opportunities to engage in different forms of sociability and sexuality. Gay men and lesbians could find safe havens in New York City's Greenwich Village and Chicago's North Side for their own entertainment. Although treated by medical experts as sexual "inverts" who might be cured by an infusion of "normal" heterosocial contact, gays and lesbians began to emerge from the shadows of Victorian-era sexual constraints around the turn of the twentieth century. "Boston marriages" constituted another form of relationship between women. The term apparently came from Henry James's book *The Bostonians* (1886), which described a female couple living together in a monogamous, long-term relationship. This conjugal-style association appealed to financially independent women who did not want to get married. Many of these relationships were sexual, but some were not. In either case, they offered women of a certain class an alternative to traditional, heterosexual marriage.

Black America and Jim Crow

While wealthy and middle-class whites experimented with new forms of social behavior, African Americans faced greater challenges to preserving their freedom and dignity. In the South, where the overwhelming majority of blacks lived, post-Reconstruction southern governments adopted various techniques to keep blacks from voting. To circumvent the Fifteenth Amendment, southern states devised suffrage qualifications that they claimed were racially neutral, and the Supreme Court ruled in their favor. They instituted the poll tax, a tax that each person had to pay in order to cast a ballot. Poll taxes fell hardest on the poor, a disproportionate number of whom were African American. Disfranchisement reached its peak in the 1890s, as white southern governments managed to deny the vote to most of the black electorate (Map 16.2). Literacy tests officially barred the uneducated of both races, but they were administered in a manner that discriminated against blacks while allowing illiterate whites to satisfy the requirement. Many literacy tests contained a loophole called a "grandfather clause." Under this exception, men whose father or grandfather had voted in 1860—a time when white men but not black men, most of whom were slaves, could vote in the South—were excused from taking the test.

In the 1890s, white southerners also imposed legally sanctioned racial segregation on the region's black citizens. Commonly known as **Jim Crow** laws (named for a character in a minstrel show, where whites performed in blackface), these new statutes denied African Americans equal access to public facilities and ensured that blacks lived apart from whites. In 1883, when the Supreme Court struck down the 1875 Civil Rights Act (see chapter 14), it gave southern states the freedom to adopt measures confining blacks to separate schools, public accommodations, seats on transportation, beds in hospitals, and sections of graveyards. In 1896 the Supreme Court sanctioned Jim Crow, constructing the constitutional rationale for legally keeping the races apart. In *Plessy v. Ferguson*, the high court ruled that a Louisiana law providing for "equal but separate" accommodations for "whites" and "coloreds" on railroad cars did not violate the equal protection clause of the Fourteenth Amendment. In its decision, the Court concluded that civil rights laws could not change racial destiny. "If one race be inferior to the other socially," the justices explained, "the Constitution of the United States cannot put them on the same plane." In practice, however, white southerners obeyed the "separate" part of the equation but never provided equal services. If blacks tried to overstep the bounds of Jim Crow in any way that whites found unacceptable,

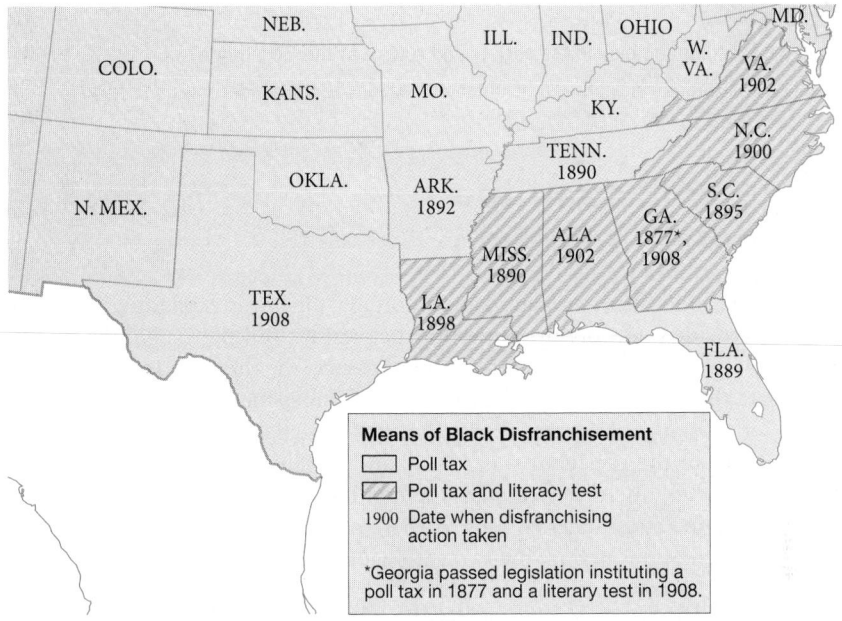

MAP 16.2

Black Disfranchisement in the South, 1889–1908   After Reconstruction, black voters posed a threat to the ruling Democrats by occasionally joining with third-party insurgents. To repel these challenges, Democratic Party leaders made racial appeals to divide poor whites and blacks. Chiefly in the 1890s and early twentieth century, white leaders succeeded in disfranchising black voters (and some poor whites), mainly by adopting poll tax and literacy requirements.

they risked their lives. Between 1884 and 1900, nearly 1,700 blacks were lynched in the South. Victims were often subjected to brutal forms of torture before they were hanged or shot.

In everyday life, African Americans carried on as best they could. Segregation provided many African Americans with opportunities to build their own businesses, control their own churches, develop their own schools staffed by black teachers, and form their own civic associations and fraternal organizations. Segregation, though harsh and unequal, did foster a sense of black community, promoted a rising middle class, and created social networks that enhanced racial pride. Founded in 1898, the North Carolina Life Insurance Company, one of the leading black-owned and black-operated businesses, employed many African Americans in managerial and sales positions. Burial societies ensured that their members received a proper funeral when they died. As with whites, black men joined lodges such as the Colored Masons and the Colored Odd Fellows, while women participated in the YWCA and the National Association of Colored Women. A small percentage of southern blacks resisted Jim Crow by migrating to the North, where blacks still exercised the right to vote, more jobs were open to them, and segregation was less strictly enforced.

REVIEW & RELATE

• What role did consumption play in the society and culture of the Gilded Age?

• How did industrialization contribute to heightened anxieties about gender roles and race?

National Politics in the Era of Industrialization

Politicians such as John Sherman played an important role in the expanding industrial economy that provided new opportunities for the wealthy and the expanding middle class. For growing companies and corporations to succeed, they needed a favorable political climate that would support their interests. Businessmen frequently looked to Washington for assistance at a time when politicians were held in low repute. During this era, the office of the president was a weak and largely administrative post, and corporate leaders were unconcerned with the quality of the mind and character of presidents, legislators, and judges so long as these officials furthered their economic objectives. For much of this period, the two national political parties battled to a stand-off, which resulted in congressional gridlock with little accomplished. Yet spurred by fierce partisan competition, political participation grew among the electorate.

Why Great Men Did Not Become President

James Bryce, a British observer of American politics, devoted a chapter of his book *The American Commonwealth* (1888) to "why great men are not chosen presidents." He acknowledged that the office of president "is raised far above all other offices [and] offers too great a stimulation to ambition." Yet he believed that the White House at-tracted mediocre occupants because the president functioned mainly as an executor. The stature of the office had shrunk following the impeachment of Andrew Johnson and the reassertion of congressional power during Reconstruction (see chapter 14). Presidents considered themselves mainly as the nation's top administrator. They did not see their roles as formulating policy or intervening on behalf of legislative objectives. Presidents had only a small White House staff to assist them, which reflected the mea-ger demands placed on their office, especially in times of peace, which prevailed until 1898. The Civil Service Act of 1883 had reduced even further the political patronage the president had at his disposal. With the office held in such low regard, Bryce asserted, "most of the ablest men for thought, planning, and execution in America, go into the business of developing the national resources of the country." During the Age of Organization, great men became corporate leaders, not presidents.

Perhaps aware that they could expect little in the way of assistance or imagination from national leaders, voters refused to give either Democrats or Republicans solid support. No president between Ulysses S. Grant and William McKinley won back-to-back elections or received a majority of the popular vote. The only two-time winner, the Democrat Grover Cleveland, lost his bid for reelection in 1888 before triumphing again in 1892. Republicans scored victories in four out of six presidential contests from 1876 to 1896, but the vote tallies were extremely close.

Nevertheless, the presidency attracted accomplished individuals. Rutherford B. Hayes (1877–1881), James A. Garfield (1881), and Benjamin Harrison (1889–1893) all had served ably in the Union army as commanding officers during the Civil War and had prior political experience. The nation greatly mourned Garfield following his assassination in 1881 by Charles Guiteau, a disgruntled applicant for federal patronage. Upon Garfield's death, Chester A. Arthur (1881–1885) became president. He had served as a quartermaster general during the Civil War, had a reputation as sympathetic to African American civil rights, and had run the New York City Customs House effectively. Grover Cleveland (1885–1889, 1893–1897) first served as mayor of Buffalo and then as governor of New York. All of these men, as even Bryce admitted, worked hard, possessed common sense, and were honest. However, they were uninspiring individuals who lacked qualities of leadership that would arouse others to action.

Congressional Inaction

Character alone did not diminish the power of the president. More important was the structure of Congress, which prevented the president from providing vigorous leadership. Throughout most of this period, Congress remained narrowly divided. Majorities continually shifted from one party to the other. For all but two terms, Democrats controlled the House of Representatives, while Republicans held the majority in the Senate. Divided government meant that during his term in office no late-nineteenth-century president had a majority of his party in both houses of Congress. Turnover among congressmen in the House of Representatives, who were elected every two years, was quite high, and there was little power of incumbency. For example, of the twenty-one congressmen from Ohio elected in 1882, only ten had served in the previous session, and only four of the ten won reelection two years later. The Senate, however, provided more continuity and allowed senators, with six-year terms of office, to amass greater power than congressmen could, as evidenced by John Sherman serving six terms in the upper chamber.

For all the power that Congress wielded, it failed to govern effectively or efficiently. Contemporary observers lamented the dismal state of affairs in the nation's capital. A cabinet officer in 1869 complained: "You can't use tact with a Congressman! A Congressman is a hog! You must take a stick and hit him on the snout!"

Although both the House and the Senate contained men of great talent, fine speaking ability, and clever legislative minds, the rules of each body turned orderly procedure into chaos. In the House, measures did not receive adequate attention on the floor because the Speaker did not have the power to control the flow of systematic debate. Committee chairmen held a tight rein over the introduction and consideration of legislation and competed with one another for influence in the chamber. Congressmen showed little decorum as they conducted business on the House floor. Representatives chatted with each other, their voices drowning out the speakers at the podium, or they ignored the business at hand and instead answered correspondence and read newspapers.

The Senate, though more manageable in size and more stable in membership (only one-third of its membership stood for reelection every two years), did not function much more smoothly. Despite party affiliations, senators thought very highly of their own judgments and very little of the value of party unity. The position of majority leader, someone who could impose discipline on his colleagues and design a coherent legislative agenda, had not yet been created. An exasperated Woodrow Wilson, who favored the British system of parliamentary government, attributed the problem to the failure to place trust in somebody "to assume final responsibility and blame." Wilson, the author of *Congressional Government* (1885) and a future president, concluded: "Our government is defective as it parcels out power and confuses responsibility." Under these circumstances, neither the president nor Congress governed efficiently or responsibly.

An Energized and Entertained Electorate

Despite all the difficulties of the legislative process, political candidates eagerly pursued office and conducted extremely heated campaigns. The electorate considered politics a form of entertainment. Political parties did not stand for clearly stated issues or offer innovative solutions; instead, campaigns took on the qualities of carefully staged performances. Candidates crafted their oratory to arouse the passions and prejudices of their audiences, and their managers handed out buttons, badges, and ceramic and glass plates stamped with the candidates' faces and slogans.

Partisanship helped fuel high political participation. During this period, voter turnout in presidential elections was much higher than at any time in the twentieth century. Region, as well as historical and cultural allegiances, replaced ideology as the key to party affiliation. The wrenching experience of the Civil War had cemented voting loyalties for many Americans. After Reconstruction, white southerners tended to vote Democratic; northerners and newly enfranchised southern blacks generally voted Republican. However, geographic region alone did not shape political loyalties; a sizable contingent of Democratic voters remained in the North, and southern whites and blacks periodically abandoned both the Democratic and Republican parties to vote for third parties.

Religion played an important role in shaping party loyalties during this period of intense partisanship. The Democratic Party tended to attract Protestants of certain sects, such as German Lutherans and Episcopalians, as well as Catholics. These faiths emphasized religious ritual and the acceptance of personal sin. They believed that the government should not interfere in matters of morality, which should remain the province of Christian supervision on Earth and divine judgment in the hereafter. By contrast, other Protestant denominations, such as Baptists, Congregationalists, Methodists, and Presbyterians, highlighted the importance of individual will and believed that the law

1892 Presidential Campaign Plate   Before radio, television, and the Internet, political parties advertised candidates in a variety of colorful ways, including banners, buttons, ribbons, and ceramic and glass plates. Voters, who turned out in record numbers during the late nineteenth century, coveted these items. This plate shows the 1892 Democratic presidential ticket of Grover Cleveland and Adlai Stevenson, who lost the election.   Collection of Steven F. Lawson

could be shaped to eradicate ignorance and vice. These Protestants were more likely to cast their ballots for Republicans, except in the South, where regional loyalty to the Democratic Party trumped religious affiliation.

Some people went to the polls because they fiercely disliked members of the opposition party. Northern white workers in New York City or Cincinnati, Ohio, for example, might vote against the Republican Party because they viewed it as the party of African Americans. Other voters cast their ballots against Democrats because they identified them as the party of Irish Catholics, intemperance, and secession.

Although political parties commanded fierce loyalties, the parties remained divided internally. For example, the Republicans pitted "Stalwarts" against "Half Breeds." Led by Senators Roscoe Conkling and Chester Arthur of New York, Zachariah Chandler of Michigan, and John Logan of Illinois, the Stalwarts presented themselves as the "Old Guard" of the Republican Party, what they called the "Grand Old Party" (GOP). The Half Breeds, a snide name given to them by the Stalwarts, tended to be younger Republicans and were represented by Senators James G. Blaine, John Sherman, and James A. Garfield of Ohio and George Frisbie Hoar of Massachusetts. This faction claimed to be more open to new ideas and less wedded to the old causes that the Republican Party promoted, such as racial equality. In the end, however, the differences between the two groups had less to do with ideas than with which faction would have greater power within the Republican Party.

Overall, the continuing strength of party loyalties produced equilibrium as voters cast their ballots primarily along strict party lines. The outcome of presidential elections depended on key "undecided" districts in several states in the Midwest and in New York and nearby states, which swung the balance of power in the electoral college. Indeed, from 1876 to 1896 all winning candidates for president and vice president came from Ohio, Indiana, Illinois, New York, and New Jersey.

REVIEW & RELATE

• What accounted for the inefficiency and ineffectiveness of the federal government in the late nineteenth century?

• How would you explain the high rates of voter turnout and political participation in an era of uninspiring politicians and governmental inaction?

Conclusion: Industry in the Age of Organization

From 1877 to 1900, American businessmen demonstrated a zeal for organization. Prompted by new technology that opened up national markets of commerce and communication, business entrepreneurs created large-scale corporations that promoted industrial expansion. Borrowing from European investors and importing and improving on European technology, by 1900 U.S. industrialists had surpassed their overseas counterparts.

Capitalists made great fortunes and lived luxurious lifestyles, emulating the fashions of European elites. Most corporate leaders did not rise from poverty but instead came from the upper middle class and had access to education and connections. Those like Andrew Carnegie, who rose from rags to riches, were the exceptions. The wealthy explained their success as the result of individual effort and hard work. This idea was reinforced in schoolbooks such as the McGuffey Readers, the novels of Horatio Alger, and religious sermons, like those of Russell Conwell.

Although most working Americans did not achieve much wealth in the Age of Organization, they had faith in the possibility of improving their economic position. Members of the middle class lived less extravagantly than did the wealthy; nonetheless, they enjoyed the comforts of the growing consumer economy. Although Jim Crow restricted the black middle class and a heightened sense of masculinity inhibited opportunities available to white women, both groups managed to carve out ways to lift themselves economically and socially.

In gaining success, the wealthy exchanged individualism for organization, competition for consolidation, and laissez-faire for government support. Without pro-business policies from Washington lawmakers and favorable decisions from the Supreme Court, big business would not have developed as rapidly as it did in this era. To prosper, corporations needed sympathetic politicians—whether to furnish free land for railroad expansion, enact tariffs to protect manufacturers, or protect private property. Even when a public outcry led to the regulation of trusts, the pro-business senator John Sherman shaped the legislation so as to minimize damage to corporate interests. In general, national politicians avoided engaging in fierce ideological conflicts, but they, too, organized. The political parties they fashioned encouraged a high level of political participation among voters.

It remained for those who did not share in the glittering wealth of the Gilded Age to find ways to resist corporate domination. The next chapter explores the efforts of workers and farmers to remedy the economic, social, and political ills that accompanied industrialization.

Chapter Review

IDENTIFY KEY TERMS

Identify and explain the significance of each term below.

New South (p. 408)

convict lease (p. 409)

vertical integration (p. 411)

horizontal integration (p. 411)

corporation (p. 412)

Sherman Antitrust Act (p. 413)

laissez-faire (p. 414)

"The Gospel of Wealth" (p. 415)

Gilded Age (p. 417)

white-collar workers (p. 418)

Jim Crow (p. 422)

Plessy v. Ferguson (p. 422)

REVIEW & RELATE

Answer the focus questions from each section of the chapter.

1. What were the key factors behind the acceleration of industrial development in late-nineteenth-century America?

2. How did industrialization change the way American businessmen thought about their companies and the people who worked for them?

3. In the late nineteenth century, how did many Americans explain individual economic success and failure?

4. How did the business community view the role of government in the economy at the end of the nineteenth century?

5. What role did consumption play in the society and culture of the Gilded Age?

6. How did industrialization contribute to heightened anxieties about gender roles and race?

7. What accounted for the inefficiency and ineffectiveness of the federal government in the late nineteenth century?

8. How would you explain the high rates of voter turnout and political participation in an era of uninspiring politicians and governmental inaction?

ONLINE DOCUMENT PROJECTS

◆ **Debates about Laissez-Faire**
◆ **Labor and Race in the New South**

After reading the primary sources in these document sets, answer the **Interpret the Evidence** questions to help you analyze each of the documents, and then answer the **Put It in Context** question(s) to help you relate the documents to the topics and themes you read about in the chapter.

bedfordstmartins.com/hewittlawsonvalue

TIMELINE OF EVENTS

1859
- Charles Darwin publishes *On the Origin of Species*
- Henry Bessemer improves steel production process

1860–1890
- U.S. gross domestic product quadruples

1866
- Transatlantic telegraph cable completed

1868
- Typewriter invented

1870–1900
- U.S. becomes a global industrial power

1870–1910
- Number of U.S. white-collar workers triples

1870s
- John D. Rockefeller takes control of oil refining business

1872
- Montgomery Ward established

1876
- Thomas Edison establishes research laboratory in Menlo Park, New Jersey

1881
- James Garfield assassinated

1883
- Civil Service Act passed

1884–1900
- 1,700 blacks lynched in the South

1885
- Alexander Graham Bell founds American Telephone and Telegraph

1886
- U.S. railroads adopt standard gauge
- *Santa Clara County v. Southern Pacific Railroad Company*

1889
- Andrew Carnegie publishes "The Gospel of Wealth"

1890
- Sherman Antitrust Act passed

1890s
- African Americans disfranchised in the South

1891
- Rural free delivery (RFD) begins

1895
- *United States v. E.C. Knight Company*

1896
- *Plessy v. Ferguson*

1901
- United States Steel established

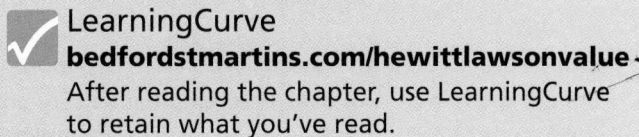

LearningCurve
bedfordstmartins.com/hewittlawsonvalue
After reading the chapter, use LearningCurve
to retain what you've read.

Workers and Farmers in the Age of Organization

1877–1900

AMERICAN HISTORIES

John McLuckie worked at the Edgar Thompson Steel Works, Andrew Carnegie's plant in Homestead, Pennsylvania. A former miner, McLuckie earned $65 a month as an assistant steel roller. In this town of some eleven thousand residents, where nearly everyone worked for Carnegie, the popular McLuckie was twice elected mayor and headed the Amalgamated Association of Iron and Steel Workers, one of the largest unions in the country. Although McLuckie earned a relatively decent income for that time, steelworkers and other industrial laborers had little power over the terms and conditions under which they worked. Visiting fraternal lodges and saloons, where steelworkers congregated after grueling twelve-hour shifts, he spread the message of standing up to corporate leaders. "The constitution of this country," McLuckie declared, "guarantees all men the right to live, but in order to live we must keep up a continuous struggle."

In 1892 McLuckie faced the fight of his life when he battled with Carnegie and his plant manager, Henry Clay Frick, over wages and working conditions at the Homestead plant. Like Carnegie, the owners of a host of industries— including railroads, petroleum, textiles, cigarettes, communications, and electric power—had created giant organizations that produced great wealth but also reshaped the working conditions of ordinary Americans. Toward the

431

end of the nineteenth century, workers who labored for these industrial giants sought greater control over their employment by organizing unions to increase their power to negotiate with their employers. The events that unfolded in Homestead in 1892 revealed that workers were vastly outmatched in their struggle with management.

Mary Elizabeth Clyens was the daughter of Irish Catholic parents who came to the United States as part of the great wave of Irish immigration that began in the 1840s. The sixth of eight children, Mary was raised in western Pennsylvania but moved to Kansas in 1870 to teach at a Catholic girls' school. There she met and married Charles L. Lease, a pharmacist turned farmer. The couple, however, could not support themselves and their four children through farming, and in 1883 the Leases moved to Wichita, where Charles returned to his original profession. In Wichita, Mary found a much wider scope to express her interests and beliefs than she had on the farm. She joined a variety of organizations and worked in support of Irish independence, women's suffrage, and movements to advance the cause of industrial workers and farmers exploited by big business, railroads, and banks.

Lease entered state and national politics through the Populist Party, which formed in 1890 to challenge the power of large corporations and their political allies, promote the interests of small farmers, and create an alliance between farmers and industrial workers. A mesmerizing speaker, she urged her audiences, according to reporters, to "raise less corn and more hell." In her book *The Problem of Civilization Solved* (1895), Lease offered a variety of remedies for late-nineteenth-century America's economic and political ills, including nationalizing railroad and telegraph lines, increasing the currency supply, and expanding popular democracy. She briefly served as president of the Kansas State Board of Charities when the Populists came to power in 1893, but her tendency to "raise hell" with elected officials in her party led to her removal from office. Following the collapse of the Populist Party in 1896, Lease and her family moved to New York City. She worked as a journalist, divorced her husband, and remained active as a speaker for educational reform and birth control until her death in 1931.

THE AMERICAN HISTORIES of John McLuckie and Mary Elizabeth Lease were linked by the economic and political forces that shaped the lives of both factory workers and farmers in industrialized America. Even though the culture of rural America was quite different from that of the nation's industrial towns and cities, farmers and workers faced many of the same problems. Over the course of the late nineteenth century, both groups had seen control over the nature and terms of their work pass from the individual worker or farmer to large corporations and financial institutions. Both groups felt marginalized, dependent, and devalued. McLuckie and Lease were part of a larger effort by laborers and farmers to fight for their own interests against the concentrated economic and political power of big business and to regain control of their lives and their work.

Working People Organize

Industrialists were not the only ones who built organizations to promote their economic interests. Like their employers, working men and women also saw the benefits of organizing to increase their political and economic leverage. Determined to secure decent wages and working conditions, workers joined labor unions, formed political parties, and engaged in a variety of collective actions, including strikes. However, because workers' organizations were beset by internal conflicts over occupational status, race, ethnicity, and gender and were no match for the powerful alliance between corporations and

Striking coal miners' wives protest the arrival of Pinkerton detectives in Buchtel, Ohio, 1884.   The Granger Collection, New York

the federal government, they failed to become a lasting national political force. Workers fared better in their own communities, where family, neighbors, and local businesses were more likely to come to their aid.

The Industrialization of Labor

The industrialization of the United States described in chapter 16 transformed the work-place, bringing together large numbers of laborers under difficult conditions. In 1870 few factories employed 500 or more workers. Thirty years later, more than 1,500 companies had workforces of this size, including General Electric, International Harvester, Pullman Palace Car Company, and U.S. Steel. Just after the Civil War, manufacturing employed 5.3 million workers; thirty years later, the figure soared to more than 15.1 million. Most of these new industrial workers came from two main sources. First, farmers like the Leases who could not make a decent living from the soil moved to nearby cities in search of factory jobs. Although mostly white, this group also included blacks who sought to escape the oppressive conditions of sharecropping. Between 1870 and 1890, some 80,000 African Americans journeyed from the rural South to cities in the South and the North to search for employment. Second, the economic opportunities in America drew millions of immigrants from Europe over the course of the nineteenth century. Immigrant workers initially came from northern Europe, mainly from England, Ireland, Germany, and Scandinavia. However, by the end of the nineteenth century, the number of immigrants from southern and eastern European countries, such as Austria-Hungary, Greece, Italy, and Russia, had surpassed those coming from northern Europe.

Inside factories, **unskilled workers**, those with no particular skill or expertise, encountered a system undergoing critical changes, as small-scale manufacturing gave way to larger and more mechanized operations. Immigrants, who made up the bulk of unskilled laborers, had to adjust both to a new country and to unfamiliar, unpleasant, and often dangerous industrial work. A traveler from Hungary who visited a steel mill in Pittsburgh that employed many Hungarian immigrants compared the factories to penitentiaries. "In making a tour of these prisons," he wrote, "wherever the heat is most insupportable, the flames most choking, there we are certain to find compatriots bent and wasted with toil." Nor were any government benefits—such as workers' compensation or unemployment insurance—available to industrial laborers who were hurt in accidents or laid off from their jobs.

Skilled workers, who had particular training or abilities and were more difficult to replace, were not immune to the changes brought about by industrialization and the creation of large-scale business enterprises. In the early days of manufacturing, skilled laborers operated as independent craftsmen. They provided their own tools, worked at their own pace, and controlled their production output. This approach to work enhanced their sense of personal dignity, reflected their notion of themselves as free citizens, and distinguished them from the mass of unskilled laborers. Mechanization, however, undercut their autonomy by dictating both the nature and the speed of production through practices of scientific management (see chapter 16). Instead of producing goods, skilled workers increasingly applied their craft to servicing machinery and keeping it running smoothly. One example of workers' resistance to this loss of independence on the shop floor occurred in Lowell, Massachusetts. Responding to a new regulation requiring all employees to report to their jobs in work clothes at the opening bell and to remain there with the door locked until the closing bell, a machinist promptly packed his tools, quit, and told his boss that he had not "been brought up under a system of slavery." While owners reaped the benefits of the mechanization and regimentation of the industrial workplace, many skilled workers saw such "improvements" as a threat to their freedom.

Still, most workers did not oppose the technology that increased their productivity and resulted in higher wages. Compared to their mid-nineteenth-century counterparts, industrial laborers now made up a larger share of the general population, earned more money, and worked fewer hours. During the 1870s and 1880s, the average industrial worker's real wages (actual buying power) increased by 20 percent. At the same time, the average workday declined from ten and a half hours to ten hours. From 1870 to 1890, the general price index dropped 30 percent, allowing consumers to benefit from lower prices.

Yet workers were far from content, and the lives of industrial workers remained extremely difficult. Although workers as a group saw improvements in wages and hours, they did not earn enough income to support their families adequately. Also, there were widespread disparities based on job status, race, ethnicity, sex, and region. Skilled workers earned more than unskilled workers. Whites were paid more than African Americans, who were mainly shut out of better jobs. Immigrants from northern Europe, who had settled in the United States before southern Europeans, tended to hold higher-paying skilled positions. Southern factory workers, whether in textiles, steel, or armaments, earned less than their northern counterparts. And women, an increasingly important component of the industrial workforce, earned less than men. On average, women earned only 25 percent of what men did.

Between 1870 and 1900, the number of female wageworkers grew by 66 percent, accounting for about one-quarter of all nonfarm laborers. The majority of employed women, including those working in factories, were single and between the ages of sixteen and twenty-four. Overall, only 5 percent of married women worked outside the home, although 30 percent of African American wives were employed. Women workers were concentrated in several areas. White and black women continued to serve as maids and domestics. Others took over jobs that were once occupied by men. They became teachers, nurses, clerical workers, telephone operators, and department store salesclerks. Although these jobs were initially seen as opening up new opportunities for women, they soon became identified as "women's work," which meant lower pay and less potential for professional advancement. Other women toiled in manufacturing jobs requiring fine eye-hand coordination, such as cigar rolling and work in the needle trades and textile industry.

Women also turned their homes into workplaces. In crowded apartments, they sewed furs onto garments, made straw hats, prepared artificial flowers, and fashioned jewelry. Earnings from piecework (work that pays at a set rate per unit) were even lower than factory wages, but they allowed married women with young children to contribute to the family income. When sufficient space was available, families rented rooms to boarders, and women provided meals and housekeeping for the lodgers. Some female workers found other ways to balance work with the needs and constraints of family life. To gain greater autonomy in their work, black laundresses began cleaning clothes in their own homes, rather than their white employers' homes, so that they could control their own work hours. In 1881 black washerwomen in Atlanta conducted a two-week strike to secure higher fees from white customers.

Manufacturing also employed many child workers. By 1900 about 10 percent of girls and 20 percent of boys between the ages of ten and fifteen worked, and at least

1.7 million children under the age of sixteen held jobs. Employers often exposed children to dangerous and unsanitary conditions. Although some children got fresh air working as newsboys, shining shoes, and collecting junk, most worked long, hard hours breathing in dust and fumes as they labored in textile mills, tobacco plants, print shops, and coal mines. In Indiana, young boys worked the night shift in dark, windowless glass factories. One of the adults working in a Rhode Island textile mill lamented: "Poor, puny weak little children are kept at work the entire year without intermission or even a month for schooling." Children under the age of ten, known as "breaker boys," climbed onto filthy coal heaps and picked out unprocessed material. Working up to twelve-hour days, these children received less than a dollar a day.

Women and children worked because the average male head of household could not support his family on his own pay, despite the increase in real wages. As Carroll D. Wright, director of the Massachusetts Bureau of the Statistics of Labor, reported in 1882, "A family of workers can always live well, but the man with a family of small children to support, unless his wife works also, has a small chance of living properly." For example, in 1883 in Joliet, Illinois, a railroad brakeman tried to support his wife and eight children on $360 a year. They rented a three-room house for $5 per month and ate mainly bread and potatoes. A state investigator described the way they lived: "Clothes ragged, children half dressed and dirty. They all sleep in one room regardless of sex. The house is devoid of furniture, and the entire concern is as wretched as could be imagined." Although not all laborers lived in such squalor, many wageworkers barely lived at subsistence level.

Although the average number of working hours dropped during this era, many laborers put in more than 10 hours a day on the job. In 1890 bakers worked more than 65 hours a week, steelworkers more than 66, and canners 77. In the steel industry, blast-furnace operators toiled 12 hours a day, 7 days a week. They received a day off every 2 weeks, but only if they worked a 24-hour shift. Given the long hours and back-breaking work, it is not surprising that accidents were a regular feature of industrial life. Each year tens of thousands were injured on the job, and thousands died as a result of mine cave-ins, train wrecks, explosions in industrial plants, and fires at textile mills and garment factories. Railroad employment was especially unsafe—accidents ended the careers of one in six workers.

Agricultural refugees who flocked to cotton mills in the South also faced dangerous working conditions. Working twelve-hour days breathing the lint-filled air from the processed cotton posed health hazards, especially for the very young and the elderly. Textile workers also had to place their hands into heavy machinery to disentangle threads, making them extremely vulnerable to serious injury. Wages scarcely covered necessities, and on many occasions families did not know where their next meal was coming from. North Carolina textile worker J. W. Mehaffry complained that the mill owners "were slave drivers" who "work their employees, women, and children from 6 a.m. to 7 p.m. with a half hour for lunch." The company supplied houses, but the occupants had "very little furniture, just a couple of beds. Just enough to get by on is about all we had." Their meals usually consisted of potatoes, cornbread, and dried beans cooked in fat. This diet, without dairy products and fresh meat, led to outbreaks of pellagra, a debilitating disease caused by niacin (vitamin B3) deficiency.

Although wages and working hours improved slightly for some workers, employers kept the largest share of the increased profits that resulted from industrialization. In 1877 John D. Rockefeller collected dividends at the rate of at least $720 an hour, roughly double what his average employee earned in a year. Despite some success stories, prospects for upward mobility for most American workers remained limited. Unskilled workers might climb up the economic ladder during their lifetime, but usually not more than one rung. A manual worker might rise into the ranks of the semiskilled but would not make it into the middle class. And to achieve even this small upward mobility required putting the entire family to work and engaging in rigorous economizing, what one historian called "ruthless underconsumption." The Horatio Alger "rags to riches" stories (see chapter 16) proved a myth for nearly all workers. Despite their best efforts, most Americans remained part of the working class.

Organizing Unions

Faced with improving but inadequate wages and hazardous working conditions, industrial laborers sought to counter the concentrated power of corporate capitalists by joining forces. They attempted to organize unions—groups of workers seeking rights and benefits from their employers through their collective efforts. Union organizing was prompted by attitudes that were common among employers. Most employers were convinced that they and their employees shared identical interests, and they believed that they were morally and financially entitled to establish policies on their workers' behalf. They refused to engage in negotiations with labor unions (a process known as collective bargaining) and rejected unions as illegitimate organizations. Although owners appreciated the advantages of companies banding together to eliminate competition or to lobby for favorable regulations, similar collective efforts by workers struck them as unfair, even immoral. It was up to the men who supplied the money and the machines—rather than the workers—to determine what was a fair wage and what were satisfactory working conditions. In 1877 William H. Vanderbilt, the son of transportation tycoon Cornelius Vanderbilt, explained this way of thinking: "Our men feel that although I . . . may have my millions and they the rewards of their daily toil, still we are about equal in the end. If they suffer, I suffer, and if I suffer they cannot escape." Needless to say, many workers disagreed. One of labor's central demands was the institution of the eight-hour workday. The idea came from Great Britain, which had industrialized earlier in the nineteenth century. In 1817 the British socialist Robert Owen had summarized this demand as "Eight hours labor, Eight hours recreation, Eight hours rest." This goal had not yet been achieved in Britain or the rest of industrial Europe when American labor activists picked it up in the 1860s, spreading the message through parades and rallies sponsored by Eight-Hour Leagues.

A growing number of working people failed to see the relationship between employer and employee as mutually beneficial. Increasingly, they considered labor unions to be the best vehicle for communication and negotiation between workers and owners. Though not the first national workers' organization, the Noble Order of the Knights of Labor, founded by Uriah Stephens in 1869, initiated the most extensive and successful campaign after the Civil War to unite workers and challenge the power of corporate capitalists. "There is no mutuality of interests . . . [between] capital and labor," the Massachusetts chapter of the Knights proclaimed. "It is the iron heel of a soulless monopoly, crushing the manhood out of sovereign citizens." In fact, the essential premise of the Knights was that *all* workers shared common interests that were very different from those of owners. Thus the union excluded only those it believed preyed on citizens both economically and morally—lawyers, bankers, saloonkeepers, and professional gamblers.

The Knights did not enjoy immediate success. Their participation in the Great Railroad Strike of 1877 (see chapter 14) drew some attention to the union, but the Knights did not really begin to flourish until Terence V. Powderly replaced Stephens as Grand Master of the organization in 1879. Powderly advocated the eight-hour workday, the abolition of child labor, and equal pay for women. Under his leadership, the Knights accepted African Americans, immigrants, and women as members, though they excluded Chinese immigrant workers, as did other labor unions. As a result, the Knights experienced a surge in membership from 9,000 in 1879 to nearly a million in 1885 (including John McLuckie), about 10 percent of the industrial workforce.

Rapid growth proved to be a mixed blessing. As membership grew, Powderly and the national organization exercised less and less control over local chapters. In fact, local chapters often defied the central organization by engaging in strikes, a labor tactic Powderly had officially disavowed. Nonetheless, with Powderly standing mainly on the sidelines, members of the Knights struck successfully against the Union Pacific Railroad and the Missouri Pacific Railroad in 1885. The following year, on May 1, 1886, local assemblies of the Knights joined a nationwide strike to press for an eight-hour workday, again without Powderly's approval. However, this strike was soon overshadowed by events in Chicago that would prove to be the undoing of the Knights (Figure 17.1).

For months before the general strike, the McCormick Harvester plant in Chicago had been at the center of an often violent conflict over wages and work conditions. On May 3, 1886, police killed two strikers in a clash between union members and strikebreakers who tried to cross the picket lines. In response, a group of anarchists led by the German-born activist August Spies called for a rally in **Haymarket Square** to protest police violence. Consisting mainly of foreign-born radicals, anarchists believed that government represented the interests of capitalists and stifled freedom for workers.

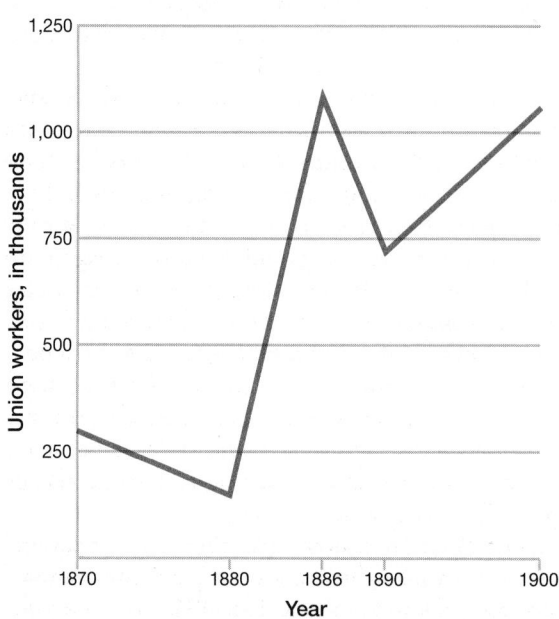

FIGURE 17.1
Union Membership, 1870–1900   Union membership fluctuated widely in the late nineteenth century. After reaching a low point in 1880, the number of union members rebounded after organizing by the Knights of Labor. Membership plummeted in the years after the Haymarket Square incident of 1886 but soared again in the 1890s through the efforts of the American Federation of Labor and western miners.

Source: Data from Richard B. Freeman, "Spurts in Union Growth: Defining Moments and Social Processes" (working paper 6012, National Bureau of Economic Research, Cambridge, MA, 1997).

Anarchists differed among themselves, but they generally advocated tearing down government authority, restoring personal freedom, and forming worker communes to replace capitalism. To achieve their goals, anarchists like Spies advocated the violent overthrow of government.

The Haymarket rally began at 8:30 in the evening of May 4 and attracted no more than 1,500 people, who listened to a series of speeches as rain fell. By 10:30 p.m., when the crowd had dwindled to some 300 people, 180 policemen decided to break it up. As police moved into the square, someone set off a bomb. The police fired back, and when the smoke cleared, seven policemen and four protesters lay dead. Most of the fatalities and injuries resulted not from the bomb but from the police crossfire after the explosion. A subsequent trial convicted eight anarchists of murder, though there was no evidence that any of them had planted a bomb or used weapons; four of them, including August Spies, were executed. Although Powderly and other union leaders denounced the anarchists and the bombing, the incident greatly tarnished the labor movement. Capitalists and their allies in the press attacked labor unionists as radicals prone to violence and denounced strikes as un-American. Following the Haymarket incident, the membership rolls of the Knights plunged to below 500,000. By the mid-1890s, the Knights had fewer than 20,000 members.

As the fortunes of the Knights of Labor faded, the **American Federation of Labor (AFL)** grew in prominence, offering an alternative vision of unionization. Instead of one giant industrial union that included all workers, skilled and unskilled, the AFL organized only skilled craftsmen—the labor elite—into trade unions. In 1886 Samuel Gompers, a British-born cigar maker, became president of the AFL. Gompers considered trade unions "the business organizations of the wage earners to attend to the business of the wage earners" and favored the use of strikes. No social reformer, the AFL president concentrated on obtaining better wages and hours for workers so that they could share in the prosperity generated by industrial capitalism. By 1900 the AFL had around a million members. It achieved these numbers by recruiting the most independent, highest-paid, and least replaceable segment of the labor force—white male skilled workers. Unlike the Knights, the AFL had little or no place for women and African Americans in its ranks.

As impressive as the AFL's achievement was, the union movement as a whole experienced only limited success in the late nineteenth century. Only about one in fifteen industrial workers belonged to a union in 1900. Union membership was low for a variety of reasons. First, the political and economic power of corporations and the prospects of retaliation made the decision to sign up for union membership a risky venture. Second, the diversity of workers made organizing a difficult task. Foreign-born laborers came from many countries and were divided by language, religion, ethnicity, and history. Moreover, European immigrants quickly adopted native-born whites' racial prejudices against African Americans. Third, despite severe limitations in social mobility, American workers generally retained their faith in the benefits of the capitalist system. The pervasive doctrine of success defined workers not as laborers locked into the lower class but as businessmen on the rise, each with the potential to become a Rockefeller or a Carnegie. Finally, the government used its legal and military authority to side with employers and suppress militant workers.

Southern workers were the most resistant to union organizing. The agricultural background of mill workers left them with a heightened sense of individualism and isolation. In addition, their continued connection to family and friends in the countryside offered a potential escape route from industrial labor. Finally, employers' willingness to use racial tensions to divide working-class blacks and whites prevented them from joining together to further their common economic interests.

Clashes between Workers and Owners

Despite the difficulties of organizing workers, labor challenged some of the nation's largest industries in the late nineteenth century. Faced with owners' refusal to recognize or negotiate with unions, workers marshaled their greatest source of power: withholding their labor and going on strike. Employers in turn had powerful weapons at their command to break strikes. They could recruit strikebreakers and mobilize private and public security forces to protect their businesses. That workers went on strike against such odds testified to their desperation and courage.

Workers in the United States were not alone in their efforts to combat industrial exploitation. In England, laborers organized for better wages and working conditions. In 1888 in London, young women who worked as matchmakers staged a walkout to protest the exorbitant fines that employers imposed on them for arriving even one minute late to work. With community support, they won their demands. From 1888 to 1890, the number of strikes throughout Europe grew from 188 to 289. In 1890 thousands of workers in Budapest, Hungary, rose up to protest unsafe working conditions. European workers also campaigned for the right to vote, which, unlike white male American workers, they were denied on economic grounds.

In the United States in the 1890s, labor mounted several highly publicized strikes. Perhaps the most famous was the 1892 Homestead strike. Steelworkers at Carnegie's Homestead, Pennsylvania, factory lived seven miles east of Pittsburgh and, like John McLuckie, played an active role in local politics and civic affairs. Residents generally believed that Andrew Carnegie's corporation paid decent wages that allowed them to support their families and buy their own homes. In 1892 craftsmen earned $180 a month, and they appeared to have Carnegie's respect. Others, like McLuckie, earned less than half that amount, and unskilled workers made even less.

In 1892, with steel prices falling, Carnegie decided to replace some of his skilled craftsmen with machinery, cut wages, save on labor costs, and bust McLuckie's union, the Amalgamated Association of Iron and Steel Workers, with which he had voluntarily negotiated in the past. Knowing that his actions would provoke a strike and seeking to avoid the negative publicity that would result, Carnegie left the country and went to Scotland, leaving his plant manager, Henry Clay Frick, in charge.

Fiercely anti-union, Frick prepared for the strike by building a three-mile, fifteen-foot-high fence, capped with barbed wire and equipped with searchlights, around three sides of the Homestead factory. A hated symbol of the manager's hostility, the fence became known as "Fort Frick." Along the fourth side of the factory flowed the Monongahela River. Frick had no intention of negotiating seriously with the union on a new contract, and on July 1 he ordered a lockout. Only employees who rejected the union and accepted lower wages could return to work. The small town rallied around the workers, and the union members won a temporary victory. On July 6, barge-loads of armed Pinkerton detectives, hired by Frick to protect the plant, set sail toward the factory entrance alongside the Monongahela. McLuckie, the head of the Amalgamated, denounced the Pinkertons as "a band of cutthroats, thieves, and murderers in the employ of unscrupulous capital for the oppression of honest labor." From the shore, union men shot at the barges and set fire to a boat they pushed toward the Pinkertons. When the smoke cleared, the Pinkertons surrendered and hastily retreated onshore as women and men chased after them.

This triumph proved costly for the union. The battle left nine strikers and three Pinkerton detectives dead. Although community officials were on the workers' side, Frick convinced the governor of Pennsylvania to send in state troops to protect the factory and the strikebreakers. On July 23, Alexander Berkman, an anarchist who had no connection with the union, entered Frick's office and shot the steel executive in the neck, leaving him wounded but alive. The resulting unfavorable publicity, together with the state's prosecution of the union, broke the strike. Subsequently, steel companies blacklisted the union leaders for life, and McLuckie fled Pennsylvania and wound up nearly penniless in Arizona. Ever the philanthropist, when Carnegie heard of McLuckie's plight in 1900, he tried to give his former adversary some money anonymously. The proud and still defiant McLuckie declined the offer, but a friend of Carnegie's arranged for an Arizona railroad to hire him as a machinery-repair superintendent.

Like Andrew Carnegie, George Pullman considered himself an enlightened employer who took good care of the men who worked in his luxury sleeping railcar factory outside Chicago. However, also like the steel titan, Pullman placed profits over personnel. In 1893 a severe economic depression prompted Pullman to cut wages without correspondingly reducing the rents that his employees paid for living in company houses. This dual blow to worker income and purchasing power led to a fierce strike the following year. The Pullman workers belonged to the American Railway Union, headed by Eugene V. Debs, who believed that labor organizing was an integral part of a worker's rights of political and economic citizenship. After George Pullman refused to negotiate, the union voted to go on strike.

In the end, the Pullman strike was broken not by the Pullman company but by the federal government. The railroad managers association persuaded President Grover Cleveland's attorney general, Richard Olney, a former railroad lawyer, that strikers were interfering with delivery of the U.S. mail transported by train. Cleveland ordered federal troops to get the railroads operating, but the workers still refused to capitulate. Olney then obtained an injunction (a court order) from the federal courts to restrain Debs and other union leaders from continuing the strike. The government used the Sherman Antitrust Act to punish unions for conspiring to restrain trade, something it had rarely done with respect to large corporations. Refusing to comply, Debs and other union officials were charged with contempt, convicted under the Sherman Antitrust Act, and sent to jail. The strike collapsed.

 Online Document Project   The Pullman Strike of 1894
bedfordstmartins.com/hewittlawsonvalue

Debs remained unrepentant. After serving his jail sentence, he became even more radical. In 1901 he helped establish the Socialist Party of America. German exiles who came to the United States following revolutions in Europe in 1848 had brought with them the revolutionary ideas of the German philosopher Karl Marx. Marx argued that capital and labor were engaged in a class struggle that would end in a victory for the proletariat, the abolition of private property, and socialist rule. This revolution would come about through the violent overthrow of capitalist government and its replacement by communism. Marxist ideas attracted a small following in the United States, mainly among the foreign-born population. By contrast, other types of European socialists, including the German Social Democratic Party, which Marx denounced, appealed for working-class support by advocating the creation of a more just and humane economic system through the ballot box, not by violent revolution. Debs, born and raised in Terre Haute, Indiana, favored this nonviolent, democratic brand of socialism and managed to attract a broader base of supporters by articulating socialist doctrines in the language of cooperation and citizenship that many Americans shared. Debsian socialism appealed not only to industrial workers but also to dispossessed farmers and miners in the Southwest and Midwest.

Western miners had a history of labor activism, and by the 1890s they were ready to listen to radical ideas. Shortly after the Homestead strike ended in 1892, silver miners in Coeur d'Alene, Idaho, walked out after owners slashed their wages by 15 percent. Employers refused to recognize any union, obtained an injunction against the strike, imported strikebreakers to run the mines, and persuaded Idaho's governor to impose martial law, in which the military took over the normal operation of civilian affairs. The work stoppage lasted four months, resulting in the arrest of six hundred strikers, including their leader, Ed Boyce. Although the workers lost, the following year they succeeded in forming the Western Federation of Miners, a radical union that continued their fight.

The **Industrial Workers of the World (IWW)**, which emerged largely through the efforts of the Western Federation of Miners, sought to raise wages, improve working conditions, and gain union recognition for the most exploited segments of American labor. The IWW, or "Wobblies" as they were popularly known, offered an alternative to Samuel Gompers's American Federation of Labor by attempting to unite all skilled and unskilled workers in an effort to overthrow capitalism. The Wobblies favored strikes and direct-action protests rather than collective bargaining or mediation. At their rallies and strikes, they often encountered government force and corporation-inspired mob violence. Nevertheless, the IWW had substantial appeal among lumberjacks in the Northwest, dockworkers in port cities, miners in the West, farmers in the Great Plains, and textile workers in the Northeast. Of their 150 strikes, the most successful ones involved miners in Goldfield, Nevada (1906–1907); textile workers in Lawrence, Massachusetts (1912); and silk workers in Paterson, New Jersey (1913).

Even though industrialists usually had state and federal governments as well as the media on their side, workers continued to press for their rights. Workers used strikes as a last resort when business owners refused to negotiate or recognize their demands to organize themselves into unions. Although most late-nineteenth-century strikes failed, striking unionists nonetheless called for collective bargaining, higher wages, shorter hours, and improved working conditions—an agenda that unions and their political allies would build on in the future.

Working-Class Leisure in Industrial America

Despite the economic hardships and political repression that industrial laborers faced in the late nineteenth century, workers carved out recreational spaces over which they had control and that offered relief from their backbreaking toil. Time clocks, often ·

viewed as an annoying part of scientific management, nevertheless clearly emphasized the difference between working and nonworking hours. For many, Sunday became a day of rest that took on a secular flavor.

Working-class leisure patterns varied by gender, race, and region. Women did not generally attend spectator sporting events, such as baseball and boxing matches, which catered to men. Nor did they find themselves comfortable in union halls and saloons, where men found solace in drink. Working-class wives preferred to gather to prepare for births, weddings, and funerals or to assist neighbors who lost their homes because of fire, death, or greedy landlords.

Once employed, working-class daughters found a greater measure of independence and free time by living in rooming houses on their own. Women's wages were only a small fraction of men's earnings, so working women rarely made enough money to support a regular social life along with paying for rent, food, and clothes. Still, they found ways to enjoy their free time. Some single women went out in groups, hoping to meet men who would pay for drinks, food, or a vaudeville show. Others dated so that they knew they would be taken care of for the evening. Some of the men who "treated" on a date assumed a right to sexual favors in return, and some of these women then expected men to provide them with housing and gifts in exchange for an ongoing sexual relationship. Thus emotional and economic relationships became intertwined in complicated ways.

Around the turn of the twentieth century, dance halls flourished as one of the mainstays of working-class communities throughout the nation. Huge dance palaces that held three thousand to five thousand people were built in the entertainment districts of most large cities. They made their money by offering music with lengthy intermissions for the sale of drinks and refreshments. Women and men also attended cabarets, some of which were racially integrated. In so-called red-light districts of the city, prostitutes earned money entertaining their clients with a variety of sexual pleasures.

Not all forms of leisure were strictly segregated along class lines. A number of forms of cheap entertainment appealed not only to working-class women and men but also to their middle-class counterparts. By the turn of the twentieth century, most large American cities featured amusement parks. Brooklyn's Coney Island stood out as the most spectacular of these sprawling playgrounds of fun and excitement. In 1884 the world's first roller coaster was built at Coney Island, providing thrills to those brave enough to ride it. Chicago residents could enjoy the Ferris wheel, which appeared at the 1893 World's Columbian Exposition. Designed by George Ferris, who operated a firm specializing in structural steel, the wheel rose 250 feet in the air, was propelled by two 1,000-horsepower steam engines, and accommodated 1,440 riders at a time.

Vaudeville houses—with their minstrel shows (whites in blackface) and comedians, singers, and dancers—brought howls of laughter to working-class audiences. Nickelodeons charged five cents to watch short films. Live theater generally attracted more wealthy patrons; however, the Yiddish theater, which flourished on New York's Lower East Side, and other immigrant-oriented stage productions appealed mainly to working-class audiences.

Southern workers also enjoyed music in their leisure time. Cheap banjoes and fiddles were mass-produced by the end of the nineteenth century. Pianos also became readily available, and one mountain boy, on hearing a piano for the first time, commented that it was the "beautifullest thing he had ever heard."

Trocadero Music Hall, 1893   The Trocadero Music Hall in Chicago opened in 1893 to attract people attending the city's upcoming World's Fair. It provided a mix of classical music and exotic European variety acts, as shown above, but drew really huge audiences with the appearance of Eugene Sandow, a body builder who exhibited feats of great physical strength.   Library of Congress

Itinerant musicians entertained audiences throughout the South. Lumber camps, which employed mainly African American men, offered a popular destination for these musicians. Each camp contained a "barrelhouse," also called a "honky tonk" or a "juke joint." Besides showcasing music, the barrelhouse also gave workers the opportunity to "shoot craps, dice, drink whiskey, dance, every modern devilment you can do," as one musician who played there recalled. From the Mississippi delta emerged a new form of music—the blues. W. C. Handy, "the father of the blues," discovered this music in his travels through the delta, where he observed that southern blacks "sang about everything. Trains, steamboats, steam whistles, sledge hammers, fast women, mean bosses, stubborn mules." They performed these songs of woe accompanying themselves with anything that would make a "musical sound or rhythmical effect, anything from a harmonica to a washboard." Meanwhile in New Orleans, an amalgam of black musical forms evolved into jazz. Musicians such as "Jelly Roll" Morton experimented with a variety of sounds, putting together African and Caribbean rhythms with European music, mixing pianos with clarinets, trumpets, and drums. Blues and jazz spread throughout the South, appearing in juke joints in Atlanta and Memphis, where men and women danced the night away.

In mountain valley mill towns, southern white residents preferred "old time" music, but with a twist. Originally enjoyed by British settlers, traditional ballads and folk songs concerned the deeds of kings and princes; rural southerners modified the lyrics to extol the exploits of outlaws and adventurers. Country music, which combined romantic ballads and folk tunes to the accompaniment of guitars, banjoes, and organs, emerged as a distinct brand of music by the twentieth century. As with African Americans, in the late nineteenth century working-class and rural whites found new and exciting types of music to entertain them in their leisure. Religious music also appealed to both white and black audiences and drew crowds to evangelical revivals held in tents on acres of grass fields.

Mill workers also amused themselves by engaging in social, recreational, and religious activities. Women visited each other and exchanged confidences, gossip, advice on child rearing, and folk remedies. Men from various factories organized baseball teams that competed in leagues with one another. Managers of a mill in Charlotte, North Carolina, admitted that they "frequently hired men better known for their batting averages than their work records."

REVIEW & RELATE

- How did industrialization change the American workplace? What challenges did it create for American workers?
- How did workers resist the concentrated power of industrial capitalists in the late nineteenth century, and why did such efforts have only limited success?

Farmers Organize

Like industrial workers, farmers experienced severe economic hardships and a loss of political power in the face of rapid industrialization. The introduction of new machinery such as the combine harvester, introduced in 1878, led to substantial increases in the productivity of American farms. Soaring production, however, led to a decline in agricultural prices in the late nineteenth century, a trend that was accelerated by increased agricultural production around the world. Faced with an economic crisis caused by falling prices and escalating debt, farmers fought back, creating new organizations to champion their collective economic and political interests.

Farmers Unite

From the end of the Civil War to the mid-1890s, increased production of wheat and cotton, two of the most important American crops, led to a precipitous drop in the price these crops fetched on the open market. Falling prices created a debt crisis for many farmers. Most American farmers were independent businessmen who borrowed money to pay for land, seed, and equipment. When their crops were harvested and sold, they repaid their debts with the proceeds. As prices fell, farmers increased production in an effort to cover their debts. This tactic led to a greater supply of farm produce in the marketplace and even lower prices. Unable to pay back loans, many farmers lost their property in foreclosures to the banks that held their mortgages and furnished them credit.

To make matters worse, farmers lived isolated lives. Spread out across vast acres of rural territory, farmers had few social and cultural diversions to enliven the long, hard days they worked from sunup to sundown. As the farm economy declined, more and more of their children left the monotony of rural America behind and headed for cities in search of new opportunities and a better life.

Early efforts to organize farmers were motivated by a desire to counteract the isolation of rural life by creating new forms of social interaction and cultural engagement. In 1867, Oliver H. Kelly, who worked as a clerk in the Department of Agriculture, founded the Patrons of Husbandry to brighten the lonely existence of rural Americans through educational and social activities, including lectures, agricultural fairs, and picnics. Known as **Grangers** (from the French word for "granary"), the association grew rapidly in the early 1870s, especially in the Midwest and the South. Between 1872 and 1874, approximately fourteen thousand new Grange chapters were established.

In addition to helping to alleviate rural isolation, Grangers formed farm cooperatives to sell their crops at higher prices and pool their purchasing power to buy finished goods at wholesale prices. The Grangers' interest in promoting the collective economic interests of farmers led to their increasing involvement in politics. Rather than forming a separate political party, Grangers endorsed candidates who favored their cause. Perhaps

Granger Movement, 1876   As the farmer's central placement in this lithograph implies, farmers were the heart of the Granger movement. The title is a variation on the movement's motto, "I Pay for All." A farmer with a plough and two horses stands at the center of the scene providing food for all, while other occupational types positioned around him echo a similar refrain based on their profession. Note the attitude toward the broker implied by the label "I Fleece You All."   Library of Congress

their most important objective was the regulation of shipping and grain storage prices. In many areas, individual railroads had monopolies on both of these services and, as a result, were able to charge farmers higher-than-usual rates to store and ship their crops. By electing sympathetic state legislators, Grangers managed to obtain regulations that placed a ceiling on the prices railroads and grain elevators could charge. The Supreme Court temporarily upheld these victories in *Munn v. Illinois* (1877) by affirming the constitutionality of state regulation of private property that benefited the public interest. In 1886, however, in *Wabash v. Illinois* the Supreme Court reversed itself and struck down these state regulatory laws as hindering the free flow of interstate commerce.

Another apparent victory for regulation came in 1887 when Congress passed the Interstate Commerce Act, establishing the **Interstate Commerce Commission (ICC)** to regulate railroads. Although big businessmen could not prevent occasional government regulation, they managed to render it largely ineffective. Large railroad lines found it easier to influence decisions of the ICC than those of agencies at the state level, which were more inclined to support local farmers and other shippers. In time, railroad advocates came to dominate the ICC and enforced the law in favor of the railway lines rather than the shippers. Implementation of the Sherman Antitrust Act (see chapter 16) also favored big business. From the standpoint of most late-nineteenth-century capitalists, national regulations often turned out to be more of a help than a hindrance.

By the late 1880s, the Grangers had abandoned electoral politics and once again devoted themselves strictly to social and cultural activities. A number of factors explain the Grangers' return to their original mission. First, prices began to rise for some crops, particularly corn, relieving the economic pressure on midwestern farmers. Second, the passage of regulatory legislation in a number of states convinced some Grangers that their political goals had been achieved. Finally, a lack of marketing and business experience led to the collapse of many agricultural collectives.

The withdrawal of the Grangers from politics did not, however, signal the end of efforts by farmers to form organizations to advance their economic interests. While farmers in the midwestern corn belt experienced some political success and an economic upturn, farmers farther west in the Great Plains and in the Lower South fell more deeply into debt, as the price of wheat and cotton on the international market continued to drop. In both of these regions, farmers organized **Farmers' Alliances**. In the 1880s, Milton George formed the Northwestern Farmers' Alliance. At the same time, Dr. Charles W. Macune organized the much larger Southern Farmers' Alliance, which boasted more than 4 million members. Southern black farmers, excluded from the Southern Farmers' Alliance by prevailing white supremacist sentiment, created a parallel Colored Farmers' Alliance, which attracted approximately a quarter of a million supporters. The Alliances formed a network of recruiters to sign up new members. No recruiter was more effective than Mary Elizabeth Lease, who excited farm audiences with her forceful and colorful rhetoric, delivering 160 speeches in the summer of 1890 alone. Not only did Lease urge farmers and workers to unite against capitalist exploitation, but she also agitated for women's rights and voiced her determination "to place the mothers of this nation on an equality with the fathers."

The Southern Farmers' Alliance advocated a sophisticated plan to solve the farmers' problem of mounting debt. Macune devised a proposal for a **subtreasury system**. Under this plan, the federal government would locate offices near warehouses in which farmers could store nonperishable commodities. In return, farmers would receive federal loans for 80 percent of the current market value of their produce. In theory, temporarily taking crops off the market would decrease supply and, assuming demand remained stable, lead to increased prices. Once prices rose, farmers would return to the warehouses, redeem their crops, sell them at the higher price, repay the government loan, and leave with a profit. Of the many recommendations proposed by the Alliances, the subtreasury system came closest to suggesting a realistic solution to the problem of chronic farm debt.

The first step toward creating a nationwide farmers' organization came in 1889, when the Northwestern and Southern Farmers' Alliances agreed to merge. Alliance leaders, including Lease, saw workers as fellow victims of industrialization, and they invited the Knights of Labor to join them. They also attempted to lower prevailing racial barriers by bringing the Colored Farmers' Alliance into the coalition. The following year, the National Farmers' Alliance and Industrial Union held its convention in Ocala, Florida. The group adopted resolutions endorsing the subtreasury system, as well as recommendations that would promote the economic welfare of farmers and extend political democracy to "the plain people." These proposals included tariff reduction, government ownership of banks and railroads, a constitutional amendment creating direct election of U.S. senators, adoption of the secret ballot, and provisions for state and local referenda to allow voters to initiate and decide public issues.

Finally, the Alliance pressed the government to increase the money supply by expanding the amount of silver coinage in circulation. In the Alliance's view, such a move would have two positive, and related, consequences. First, the resulting inflation would lead to higher prices for agricultural commodities, putting more money in farmers' pockets. Second, the real value of farmers' debts would decrease, since the debts were contracted in pre-inflation dollars and would be paid back with inflated currency. Naturally, the eastern bankers who supplied farmers with credit opposed such a policy. In fact, in 1873 Congress, under the leadership of Senator John Sherman, had halted the purchase of silver by the Treasury Department, a measure that helped reduce the money supply. Investment bankers, such as J. P. Morgan, opposed a bimetallic monetary standard that added silver to gold coinage. They believed that only the use of gold would preserve the faith that foreign investors had in U.S. currency. Under the Sherman Silver Purchase Act (1890), the government resumed buying silver, but the act placed limits on its purchase and did not guarantee the creation of silver coinage by the Treasury. In the past, some members of the Alliance, including Lease, had favored expanding the money supply with greenbacks (paper money). However, to attract support from western silver miners, Alliance delegates emphasized the free and unlimited coinage of silver. Alliance supporters met with bitter disappointment, though, as neither the Republican nor the Democratic Party embraced their demands. Rebuffed, farmers took an independent course and became more directly involved in national politics through the formation of the Populist Party.

Populists Rise Up

In 1892 the National Farmers' Alliance moved into the electoral arena as a third political party. The People's Party of America, known as the Populists, held its first nominating convention in Omaha, Nebraska, in 1892. In addition to incorporating the Alliance's Ocala planks into their platform, they adopted recommendations to broaden the party's appeal to industrial workers. Populists endorsed a graduated income tax, which would impose higher tax rates on higher income levels. They also favored the eight-hour workday, a ban on using Pinkerton "mercenaries" in labor disputes, and immigration restriction, which stemmed from the unions' desire to keep unskilled workers from glutting the market and depressing wages. Reflecting the influence of women such as Mary Lease, the party endorsed women's suffrage. Although African Americans contributed to the founding of the Populists, the party did not offer specific proposals to prohibit racial discrimination or segregation. Rather, the party focused on remedies to relieve the economic plight of impoverished white and black farmers in general.

 Online Document Project   **The Meanings of Populism**
bedfordstmartins.com/hewittlawsonvalue

In 1892 the Populists nominated for president former Union Civil War general James B. Weaver. Although Weaver came in third behind the Democratic victor, Grover Cleveland, and the Republican incumbent, Benjamin Harrison, he managed to win more than one million popular votes and 22 electoral votes. For a third party competing for the presidency for the first time, this was a noteworthy accomplishment.

At the state level, Populists performed even better. They elected 10 congressional representatives, 5 U.S. senators, 3 governors, and 1,500 state legislators. Two years later, the party made even greater strides by increasing its total vote by 42 percent and achieving its greatest strength in the South. This electoral momentum positioned the Populists to make an even stronger run in the next presidential election. The economic depression that began in 1893 and the political discontent it generated further enhanced Populist chances for success.

REVIEW & RELATE

- Why was life so difficult for American farmers in the late nineteenth century?
- What were the similarities and differences between farmers' and industrial workers' efforts to organize in the late nineteenth century?

The Depression of the 1890s

When the Philadelphia and Reading Railroad went bankrupt in early 1893, it set off a chain reaction that pushed one-quarter of American railroads into insolvency. As a result, on May 5, 1893, "Black Friday," the stock market collapsed in a panic, triggering the depression of 1893. Making this situation worse, England and the rest of industrial Europe had experienced an economic downturn several years earlier. As a result, in the early 1890s foreign investors began selling off their American stocks, leading to a flow of gold coin out of the country and further damage to the banking system. Hundreds of banks failed, which hurt the business people and farmers who relied on a steady flow of bank credit to keep their enterprises afloat. By the end of 1894, some 3 million people, nearly 12 percent of the American workforce, remained unemployed. Tens of thousands of homeless people wandered the streets of major American cities. The depression became the chief political issue of the mid-1890s and resulted in a realignment of power between the two major parties. Rather than capitalizing on depression discontent, however, the Populist Party split apart and collapsed.

Depression Politics

President Grover Cleveland's handling of the depression only made a bad situation worse. Railroad executive James J. Hill warned the president, "Business is at a standstill and the people are becoming thoroughly aroused. Their feeling is finding expression about as it did during the War of the Rebellion [Civil War]." With talk of civil war in the air, the Cleveland administration faced protest marches and labor strife. In the spring of 1894, Jacob Coxey, a wealthy businessman and Populist reformer from Ohio, and his associate, Carl Browne, led a march on Washington, D.C., demanding that Cleveland and Congress initiate a federal public works program to provide jobs for the unemployed. Coxey had previously supported the Greenback Party, which advocated inflating the money supply with paper currency to stimulate the economy and help those in distress. Though highly critical of the favored few who dominated the federal government, Coxey had faith that if "the people . . . come in a body like this, peaceably to discuss their grievances and demanding immediate relief, Congress . . . will heed them and do it quickly." For him, "relief" meant both creating jobs and increasing the money supply. After traveling for a month from Ohio, Coxey led a parade of some five hundred unemployed people into the nation's capital. Attracting thousands of spectators, **Coxey's army** attempted to mount their protest on the grounds of the Capitol building. In response, police broke up the demonstration and arrested Coxey for trespassing. Cleveland turned a deaf ear to Coxey's demands for federal relief and also disregarded protesters participating in nearly twenty other marches on Washington.

In the coming months, Cleveland's political stock plummeted further. He responded to the Pullman strike in the summer of 1894 by obtaining a federal injunction against the strikers and dispatching federal troops to Illinois when the workers disobeyed it. The president's action won him high praise from the railroads and conservative business interests, but it showed millions of American workers that the Cleveland administration did not have a solution for ending the suffering caused by the depression. From the outset of his term, the president had made his intentions about government assistance clear: "While the people should patriotically and cheerfully support their Government, its functions do not include the support of the people." In normal times, these words reflected the prevailing philosophy of self-help that most Americans shared, but in the midst of a severe depression they sounded heartless.

Making matters worse, Cleveland convinced Congress to repeal the Sherman Silver Purchase Act. This angered western miners, who relied on strong silver prices, along with farmers in the South and Great Plains who were swamped by mounting debt. At the same time, the removal of silver as a backing for currency caused private investors to withdraw their gold deposits from the U.S. Treasury. To keep the government financially solvent, Cleveland worked out an agreement with a syndicate led by J. P. Morgan to help sell government bonds, a deal that netted the businessmen a huge profit. In the midst of economic suffering, this deal looked like a corrupt bargain between government and the rich designed to ensure that the rich got richer as the poor got poorer.

In 1894 Congress also passed the Wilson-Gorman Act, which raised tariffs on imported goods. Intended to protect American businesses by keeping the price of imported goods high, it also deprived foreigners of the necessary income with which to buy American exports. This drop in exports did not help economic recovery. The Wilson-Gorman Act did include a provision that the Populists and other reformers endorsed: a progressive income tax of 2 percent on all annual earnings over $4,000. No federal income tax existed at this time, so even this mild levy elicited cries of "socialism" from conservative critics, who challenged the tax in the courts. They found a receptive audience in the Supreme Court. In *Pollack v. Farmers Loan and Trust* (1895), the justices, who had already struck down a number of attempts to regulate business, declared the income tax unconstitutional and denounced it as the opening wedge in "a war of the poor against the rich; a war constantly growing in intensity and bitterness."

With Cleveland's legislative program in shambles and his inability to solve the depression abundantly clear, the Democrats suffered a crushing blow at the polls. In the congressional elections of 1894, the party lost an astonishing 120 seats in the House. This defeat offered a preview of the political shakeup that loomed ahead.

Political Realignment in the Election of 1896

The presidential election of 1896 marked a turning point in the political history of the nation, one that would shape national politics for the next thirty-six years. Democrats nominated William Jennings Bryan of Nebraska, a farmers' advocate who favored silver coinage. When he vowed that he would not see Republicans "crucify mankind on a cross of gold," the Populists endorsed him as well. Bryan was the first major party nominee for the White House since 1868 who did not come from Ohio, Indiana, or New York.

Republicans nominated William McKinley, the governor of Ohio and a supporter of the gold standard and high tariffs on manufactured and other goods. While Bryan barnstormed around the country, McKinley remained at his home in Canton, Ohio, to conduct his campaign from his front porch. His campaign manager, Marcus Alonzo Hanna, an ally of Ohio senator John Sherman, raised an unprecedented amount of money, about $16 million, mainly from wealthy industrialists who feared that the free and unlimited coinage of silver would debase the U.S. currency. Hanna saturated the country with pamphlets, leaflets, and posters, many of them written in the native languages of immigrant groups. He also hired a platoon of speakers to fan out across the country denouncing Bryan's free silver cause as financial madness. Republican Theodore Roosevelt, who would later become president himself, remarked that Hanna advertised McKinley "as if he were patent medicine." By contrast, Bryan raised about $1 million and had to travel around the country making personal appearances, in part to compensate for his campaign's lack of funds.

The outcome of the election transformed the Republicans into the majority party in the United States. McKinley won 51 percent of the popular vote and 61 percent of the electoral vote, making him the first president since Grant in 1872 to win a majority of the popular vote. More important than this specific contest, however, was that the election proved critical in realigning the two parties. Voting patterns shifted with the 1896 election, giving Republicans the edge in party affiliation among the electorate not only in this contest but also in presidential elections over the next three decades (Map 17.1).

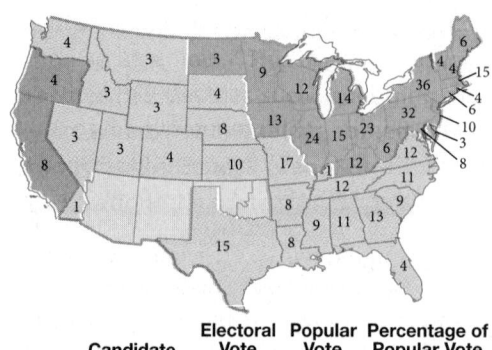

Candidate	Electoral Vote	Popular Vote	Percentage of Popular Vote
William McKinley (Republican)	271	7,102,246	51.1
William J. Bryan (Democrat)	176	6,492,559	47.7

MAP 17.1

The Election of 1896   William McKinley's election in 1896 resulted in a realignment of political power in the United States that lasted until 1932. Republicans became the nation's majority party by forging a coalition of big business and urban industrial workers from the Northeast and Midwest. Democratic strength was confined to the South and small towns and rural areas of the Great Plains and Mountain states.

What happened to produce this critical realignment in electoral power? The main ingredient was Republicans' success in fashioning a coalition that included both corporate capitalists and their workers. Although Bryan made sincere appeals for the votes of urban dwellers and industrial workers along class lines, they generally fell on deaf ears. Many of these voters took out their anger on Cleveland's Democratic Party and Bryan as its standard-bearer for failing to end the depression. In addition, Bryan, who hailed from Nebraska and reflected small-town agricultural America and its values, could not win over the swelling numbers of urban immigrants who considered Bryan's world alien to their experience. A great orator, Bryan nevertheless sounded anti-urban, and his defeat signaled the decline of rural America in presidential politics. His campaign was the last serious effort to win the White House with mostly farm and small-town votes.

The election of 1896 broke the political stalemate in the Age of Organization. The core of Republican backing came from industrial cities of the Northeast and Midwest. Republicans won support from their traditional constituencies of Union veterans, businessmen, and African Americans and added to it the votes of a large number of urban wageworkers. The campaign persuaded voters that the Democratic Party represented the party of depression and that Republicans stood for prosperity and progress. Another factor helping the Republicans was that in 1897 the depression finally ended, largely as a result of gold discoveries in Alaska, which helped increase the money supply, and foreign crop failures, which raised American farm prices. Democrats managed to hold on to the South as their solitary political base.

The Decline of the Populists

The year 1896 also marked the end of the Populists as a national force, as the party was torn apart by internal divisions over policy priorities and electoral strategy. Populist leaders such as Tom Watson of Georgia did not want the Populist Party to emphasize free silver above the rest of its reform program. Other northern Populists, who either had fought on the Union side during the Civil War or had close relatives who did, such as Mary Lease, could not bring themselves to join the Democrats, the party of the old Confederacy. Nevertheless, the Populist Party officially backed Bryan, but to retain its identity, the party nominated Watson for vice president on its own ticket. After McKinley's victory, the Populist Party collapsed.

Losing the presidential election alone did not account for the disintegration of the Populists. Several problems plagued the third party. The nation's recovery from the depression removed one of the Populists' prime sources of electoral attraction. Despite appealing to industrial workers, the Populists were unable to capture their support. The free silver plank attracted silver miners in Idaho and Colorado, but the majority of workers failed to identify with a party composed mainly of farmers. As consumers of agricultural products, industrial laborers did not see any benefit in raising farm prices. Populists also failed to create a stable, biracial coalition of dispossessed farmers. Most southern white Populists did not truly accept African Americans as equal partners, even though both groups had mutual economic interests. Southern white Populists framed their arguments around class as the central issue driving the exploitation of farmers and workers by wealthy planters and industrialists. However, in the end, they succumbed to racial prejudice.

To eliminate Populism's insurgent political threat, southern opponents found ways to disfranchise black and poor white voters. During the 1890s, southern states inserted into their constitutions voting requirements that virtually eliminated the black electorate and greatly diminished the white electorate. Seeking to circumvent the Fifteenth Amendment's prohibition against racial discrimination in the right to vote, conservative white lawmakers adopted regulations based on wealth and education because blacks were disproportionately poor and had lower literacy rates. They instituted poll taxes, which imposed a fee for voting, and literacy tests, which asked tricky questions designed to trip up would-be black voters (see chapter 16). In 1898 the Supreme Court upheld the constitutionality of these voter qualifications in *Williams v. Mississippi*. Recognizing the power of white supremacy, the Populists surrendered to its appeals.

Tom Watson provides a case in point. He started out by encouraging racial unity but then switched to divisive politics. In 1896 the Populist vice presidential candidate, who had assisted embattled black farmers in his home state of Georgia, called on citizens of both races to vote against the crushing power of corporations and railroads. By whipping up racial antagonism against blacks, his Democratic opponents appealed to the racial pride of poor whites to keep them from defecting to the Populists. Chastened by the outcome of the 1896 election and learning from the tactics of his political foes, Watson embarked on a vicious campaign to exclude blacks from voting. "What does civilization owe the Negro?" he bitterly asked. "Nothing! Nothing! NOTHING!!!" Only by disfranchising African Americans and maintaining white supremacy, Watson and other white reformers reasoned, would poor whites have the courage to vote against rich whites.

Nevertheless, even in defeat the Populists left an enduring legacy. Many of their political and economic reforms—direct election of senators, the graduated income tax, government regulation of business and banking, and a version of the subtreasury system (called the Commodity Credit Corporation, created in the 1930s)—became features of reform in the twentieth century. Populists also foreshadowed other attempts at creating farmer-labor parties in the 1920s and 1930s. Perhaps their greatest contribution, however, came in showing farmers that their old individualist ways would not succeed in the modern industrial era. Rather than re-creating an independent political party, most farmers looked to organized interest groups, such as the Farm Bureau, to lobby on behalf of their interests. Whatever their approach, farmers both reflected and contributed to the Age of Organization.

• How did the federal government respond to the depression of 1893?

• What were the long-term political consequences of the depression of 1893?

Conclusion: A Passion for Organization

From 1877 to 1900, industrial workers and farmers joined the march toward organization led by the likes of Carnegie, Rockefeller, and Morgan. These wealthy titans of industry and finance had created the large corporations that transformed the rhythms and meanings of factory labor and farm life. Working people such as John McLuckie met the challenges of the new industrial order by organizing unions. Lacking the power of giant companies, which was reinforced by the federal government, labor unions nevertheless carved out sufficient space for workers to join together in their own defense to resist absolute corporate rule. At the same time, farmers, perhaps the most individualistic workers, and their advocates, such as Mary Elizabeth Lease, created organizations that proposed some of the most forward-looking solutions to remedy the ills accompanying industrialization. Though the political fortunes of the Grangers and Populists declined, their message persisted: Resourceful and determined workers and farmers could, and should, join together to ensure survival not just of the fittest but of the neediest as well.

Under the pressure of increased turmoil surrounding industrialization and a brutal economic depression, the political system reached a crisis in the 1890s. Despite the historic shift in party loyalties brought about by the election of William McKinley, it remained to be seen whether political party realignment could furnish the necessary leadership to address the problems of workers and farmers. Industrialization had proven painful and disorienting for millions of Americans. The events of the 1890s convinced many Americans, including many in the middle class, that the hands-off approach to social and economic problems that had prevailed in the past was no longer acceptable. In cities and states across the country, men and women took up the cause of reform. They had to wait for national leaders to catch up to them.

Chapter Review

MAKE IT STICK

LearningCurve **bedfordstmartins.com/hewittlawsonvalue**
After reading the chapter, use LearningCurve to retain what you've read.

IDENTIFY KEY TERMS

Identify and explain the significance of each term below.

unskilled workers (p. 434)
skilled workers (p. 434)
unions (p. 437)
collective bargaining (p. 437)
Noble Order of the Knights of Labor
   (p. 437)
Haymarket Square (p. 438)
American Federation of Labor (AFL)
   (p. 439)
Homestead strike (p. 440)
Pullman strike (p. 441)

Industrial Workers of the World (IWW)
   (p. 442)
Grangers (p. 446)
Interstate Commerce Commission (ICC)
   (p. 447)
Farmers' Alliances (p. 447)
subtreasury system (p. 447)
Populists (p. 448)
depression of 1893 (p. 449)
Coxey's army (p. 450)

REVIEW & RELATE

Answer the focus questions from each section of the chapter.

1. How did industrialization change the American workplace? What challenges did it create for American workers?

2. How did workers resist the concentrated power of industrial capitalists in the late nineteenth century, and why did such efforts have only limited success?

3. Why was life so difficult for American farmers in the late nineteenth century?

4. What were the similarities and differences between farmers' and industrial workers' efforts to organize in the late nineteenth century?

5. How did the federal government respond to the depression of 1893?

6. What were the long-term political consequences of the depression of 1893?

ONLINE DOCUMENT PROJECTS

♦ **The Pullman Strike of 1894**
♦ **The Meanings of Populism**

After reading the primary sources in these document sets, answer the **Interpret the Evidence** questions to help you analyze each of the documents, and then answer the **Put It in Context** question(s) to help you relate the documents to the topics and themes you read about in the chapter.

bedfordstmartins.com/hewittlawsonvalue

TIMELINE OF EVENTS

1865–1895	• U.S. manufacturing jobs jump from 5.3 million to 15.1 million	**1890**	• Sherman Silver Purchase Act passed
1867	• Patrons of Husbandry (Grange) founded	**1890s**	• Southern states strip blacks of the right to vote
1869	• Noble Order of the Knights of Labor founded	**1892**	• Homestead steelworkers' strike • Populist Party established
1870–1900	• Number of female wageworkers increases by 66 percent	**1893**	• Depression triggered by stock market collapse
1877	• Great Railroad Strike	**1894**	• Pullman strike
1879	• Terence Powderly becomes leader of Knights of Labor		• Coxey's army marches to Washington
1880s	• Northwestern, Southern, and Colored Farmers' Alliances formed		• Sherman Silver Purchase Act repealed
1886	• Haymarket Square violence	**1896**	• Populists back William Jennings Bryan for president
	• American Federation of Labor founded	**1897**	• Depression ends
1887	• Interstate Commerce Act passed		• Populist Party declines
1889	• Northwestern and Southern Farmers' Alliances merge	**1901**	• Eugene Debs establishes Socialist Party of America

☑ LearningCurve
bedfordstmartins.com/hewittlawsonvalue
After reading the chapter, use LearningCurve
to retain what you've read.

Cities, Immigrants, and the Nation

1880–1914

AMERICAN HISTORIES

In the fall of 1905, Beryl Lassin faced a difficult choice. Living in the *shtetl* (a Jewish town) of Borrisnov in western Russia, Lassin had few if any opportunities as a young locksmith. Beryl and his wife, Lena, lived at a dangerous time in Russia. Jews were subject to periodic pogroms, state-sanctioned outbreaks of anti-Jewish violence carried out by local Christians. Beryl also faced a discriminatory military draft that required conscripted Jews to serve twenty-year terms in the army, far longer than their Christian countrymen. His wife's brother had already left Russia for the United States, and the couple decided that Beryl should follow his brother-in-law's example before the draft caught up with him. The couple couldn't afford two steamship tickets, so with the understanding that his wife would follow as soon as possible, Beryl set sail for America alone on the steamship *Zeeland*, which sailed from Antwerp, Belgium, on October 7, 1905. He was crammed into the steerage belowdecks with hundreds of other passengers, most of them fellow Jews. Ten days later, his ship chugged into New York harbor, where Beryl found a less than hospitable greeting. Disembarking at Ellis Island, the processing center for immigrants, he stood in long lines and underwent a strenuous medical examination, including a painful eye inspection, to ensure that he was fit to enter the country. He also had to prove that he had someplace to go, in his case the apartment of his brother-in-law on New York City's Lower East Side. With no money, Beryl boarded a ferry across the Hudson that took him to a new life in the United States.

Less than a year later, Lena joined her husband. Over the next decade, the couple had five children. Shortly after the youngest girl was born, Lena died of cancer. Her death threw the family into turmoil, as Beryl, now called Ben, had to place two of the three youngest children in the Hebrew Children's Home and the other in foster care. The children were reunited with their father when Ben remarried, but life was still difficult. Ben was injured at his job as a mechanic and did not work full-time again. To make ends meet, his three eldest boys dropped out of school and went to work. Still, like many other immigrants, Ben's family managed to leave the crowded Lower East Side, following a trail blazed by earlier Jewish immigrants to Harlem and then the Bronx. Ben preferred to speak in Yiddish and never learned to read English. Nor did he become an American citizen, and after World War I, as an alien, he had to register annually with the federal government. His children, however, were all citizens because they had been born in the United States.

On June 8, 1912, another immigrant followed a similar route that took her on a different journey. Seventeen years old and unmarried, Maria Vik decided to leave her home in the small village of Kiestyderocz, Hungary. As a Catholic, Maria did not experience the religious persecution that Beryl did. Like many other Hungarians who ventured to the United States at this time, Maria, the oldest daughter, left to help support her family back in the old country. She had an aunt living in the United States, and she came across with a Hungarian couple who escorted young women for domestic service in America. Her sea voyage began in Hamburg, Germany, aboard the ship *Amerika*, and unlike Beryl she had a cabin in second class.

Maria, too, landed at Ellis Island and passed the rigorous entry exams. Soon she boarded a train for Rochester in western New York. There she worked as a cook for a German physician, learned English, and led an active social life within the local Hungarian community. In Rochester, she met and fell in love with Karoly (Charles) Takacs, a cabinetmaker from Hungary, who, like Beryl Lassin, had come to avoid the military draft. Charles became a citizen in May 1916. By marrying him, Mary, as she was now called, became a citizen as well.

The couple moved forty-five miles west of Rochester to Middleport and purchased a small farm in a neighborhood filled with Hungarian immigrants. Because so many Hungarians lived in the area, Mary spoke mainly Hungarian and began to speak more English only when the oldest of her four children entered kindergarten.

The American histories of Beryl Lassin and Maria Vik Takacs took one to the urban bustle of New York City, the other to a quiet, rural village in western New York State. The Lassins, who rented walk-up apartments in five-story buildings and whose children had to drop out of school, did not fare as well economically as did the Takacses, who owned property and sent their three daughters to college. However, as different as their lives in America were, neither Beryl nor Maria regretted their choice to leave Europe for the United States. Like millions of other immigrants at the turn of the twentieth century, they had come to America to build better lives for themselves and their families, and both saw their children and grandchildren succeed in ways that they could have only dreamed of in their native countries. Indeed, Ben Lassin changed his surname to Lawson, and his son Murray married Ceil Puchowitzky (Parker), the daughter of another Russian-Jewish immigrant. Mary and Charles's daughter Irene married Robert Hewitt, whose family arrived from northern Europe in the nineteenth century. Murray's son, Steven F. Lawson, and Irene's daughter, Nancy A. Hewitt—the grandchildren of Beryl and Maria, respectively—became historians, got married, and wrote this textbook. The experiences of the Lawson and Hewitt families, like countless others, reflect the complicated ways that immigrants were transformed into Americans at the same time that the United States was forever changed by the new additions to its population.

THE LASSINS AND the Takacses were part of a flood of immigrants who entered the United States from 1880 to the outbreak of World War I in 1914. Unlike the majority of earlier immigrants, who had come from northern Europe, most of the more than 20 million people who arrived during this period came from southern and eastern Europe. They entered the United States mainly through seaports in the Northeast, but some came through ports in New Orleans, Louisiana, and Key West and Tampa, Florida, in the South; across the Texas and California borders from Mexico; and through ports in San Francisco and Seattle on the West Coast. Though many moved to small towns and rural villages, most remained in cities, which experienced enormous population growth as a result. In these large urban areas, impoverished immigrants entered the political mainstream of American life, welcomed by political bosses and their machines, who saw in them a chance to gain the allegiance of millions of new voters. At the same time, their coming upset many middle- and upper-class city dwellers who blamed these new arrivals for lowering the quality of urban life.

A New Wave of Immigrants

For more than three hundred years following the settlement of the North American colonies, the majority of white immigrants to America were northern European Protestants. Black Americans were brought forcibly from Africa, mainly by way of the West Indies and the Caribbean. Although African Americans originally followed their own religious practices, most eventually converted to Protestantism. By the end of the nineteenth

An Italian family on the ferry from Ellis Island to New York City, 1905.   Private Collection/Peter
Newark American Pictures/The Bridgeman Art Library

century, however, a new pattern of immigration had emerged, one that included much
greater ethnic and religious diversity. These new immigrants often encountered hostility from those whose ancestors had arrived generations earlier, and faced the difficult
challenge of retaining their cultural identities while becoming assimilated as Americans.

Immigrants Arrive from Many Lands

Immigration to the United States was part of a worldwide phenomenon. In addition to
the United States, European immigrants also journeyed to other countries in the Western
Hemisphere, especially Canada, Argentina, Brazil, and Cuba. Others left China, Japan,
and India and migrated to Southeast Asia and Hawaii. From England and Ireland,
migrants ventured to other parts of the British empire, including Australia, New Zealand,
and South Africa. As with those who came to the United States, these immigrants left
their homelands to find new job opportunities or to obtain land to start their own farms.
In countries like Australia, New Zealand, and South Africa, white settlers often pushed
aside native peoples—Aborigines in Australia, Maori in New Zealand, and blacks in
South Africa—to make communities for themselves. Whereas most immigrants chose

to relocate voluntarily, some made the move bound by labor contracts that limited their movement during the terms of the agreement. Chinese, Mexican, and Italian workers made up a large portion of this group.

The late nineteenth century saw a shift in the country of origin of immigrants to the United States: Instead of coming from northern and western Europe, many now came from southern and eastern European countries, most notably Italy, Greece, Austria-Hungary, Poland, and Russia. In 1882 around 789,000 immigrants entered the United States, 87 percent of whom came from northern and western Europe. By contrast, twenty-five years later in 1907, of the 1,285,000 newcomers who journeyed to America, 81 percent originated from southern and eastern Europe.

Most of those settling on American shores after 1880 were Catholic or Jewish and hardly knew a word of English. They tended to be even poorer than immigrants who had arrived before them, coming mainly from rural areas and lacking suitable skills for a rapidly expanding industrial society. In the words of one historian, who could easily have been describing Beryl Lassin's life: "Jewish poverty [in Russia] is a kind of marvel for . . . it has origins in fathers and grandfathers who have been wretchedly poor since time immemorial." Even after relocating to a new land and a new society, such immigrants struggled to break patterns of poverty that were, in many cases, centuries in the making.

Immigrants came from other parts of the world as well. From 1860 to 1924, some 450,000 Mexicans migrated to the U.S. Southwest. Many traveled to El Paso, Texas, near the Mexican border, and from there hopped aboard one of three railroad lines to jobs on farms and in mines, mills, and construction. Cubans, Spaniards, and Bahamians traveled to the Florida cities of Key West and Tampa, where they established and worked in cigar factories. Tampa grew from a tiny village of a few hundred people in 1880 to a city of 16,000 in 1900. Although Congress had excluded Chinese immigration after 1882, it did not close the door to migrants from Japan. Unlike the Chinese, the Japanese had not competed with white workers for jobs on railroad and other construction projects. Moreover, Japan had emerged as a major world power in the late nineteenth century and gained some grudging respect from American leaders by defeating Russia in the Russo-Japanese War of 1904–1905. Some 260,000 Japanese arrived in the United States during the first two decades of the twentieth century. Many of them first settled in Hawaii and then moved to the West Coast states of California, Oregon, and Washington, where they worked as farm laborers and gardeners and established businesses catering to a Japanese clientele. Nevertheless, like the Chinese before them, Japanese immigrants were considered part of an inferior "yellow race" and encountered discrimination in their West Coast settlements.

This wave of immigration changed the composition of the American population. By 1910 one-third of the population was foreign-born or had at least one parent who came from abroad. Foreigners and their children made up more than three-quarters of the population of New York City, Detroit, Chicago, Milwaukee, Cleveland, Minneapolis, and San Francisco. Immigration, though not as extensive in the South as in the North, also altered the character of southern cities. About one-third of the population of Tampa, Miami, and New Orleans consisted of foreigners and their descendants. The borderland states of Texas, New Mexico, Arizona, and southern California contained similar percentages of immigrants, most of whom came from Mexico.

These immigrants came to the United States largely for economic, political, and religious reasons. Nearly all were poor and expected to find ways to make money in America. U.S. railroads and steamship companies advertised in Europe and recruited passengers by emphasizing economic opportunities in the United States. Early immigrants wrote to relatives back home extolling the virtues of what they had found, perhaps exaggerating their success. However, for people barely making a living, or for those subject to religious discrimination and political repression, what did it matter if they arrived in America and the streets were not paved in gold, as legend had it? In fact, if many of the streets were not paved at all, at least the immigrants could get jobs paving them!

The importance of economic incentives in luring immigrants is underscored by the fact that millions returned to their home countries after they had earned sufficient money to establish a more comfortable lifestyle. Of the more than 27 million immigrants from 1875 to 1919, 11 million returned home (Table 18.1). One immigrant from Canton, China, accumulated a small fortune as a merchant on Mott Street, in New York City's Chinatown. According to residents of his hometown in China, "[Having] made his wealth among the barbarians this man had faithfully returned to pour it out among his tribesmen, and he is living in our village now very happy." Jews, Mexicans, Czechs, and Japanese had the lowest rates of return. Immigrant groups facing religious or political persecution in their homeland were the least likely to return. It is highly doubtful that a poor Jewish immigrant like Beryl Lassin would have received a warm welcome home in his native Russia, if he had been allowed to return at all.

Creating Immigrant Communities

Immigrants were processed at their port of entry, and the government played no role in their relocation in America. New arrivals were left to search out transplanted relatives and other countrymen on their own. In cities such as New York, Boston, and Chicago, immigrants occupied neighborhoods that took on the distinct ethnic characteristics of the groups that inhabited them. A cacophony of different languages echoed in the streets as new residents continued to communicate in their mother tongues. The neighborhoods of immigrant groups often were clustered together, so residents were as likely to learn phrases in their neighbors' languages as they were to learn English.

TABLE 18.1 Percentage of Immigrant Departures versus Arrivals, 1875–1914

Year	Arrivals	Departures	Percentage of Departures to Arrivals
1875–1879	956,000	431,000	45%
1880–1884	3,210,000	327,000	10%
1885–1889	2,341,000	638,000	27%
1890–1894	2,590,000	838,000	32%
1895–1899	1,493,000	766,000	51%
1900–1904	3,575,000	1,454,000	41%
1905–1909	5,533,000	2,653,000	48%
1910–1914	6,075,000	2,759,000	45%

The formation of **ghettos**—neighborhoods dominated by a single ethnic, racial, or class group—eased immigrants' transition into American society. Without government assistance or outside help, these communities assumed the burden of meeting some of the challenges that immigrants faced in adjusting to their new environment. Living within these ethnic enclaves made it easier for immigrants to find housing, hear about jobs, buy food, and seek help from those with whom they felt most comfortable. **Mutual aid societies** sprang up to provide social welfare benefits, including insurance payments and funeral rites. "A *landsman* died in the factory," a founder of one such Jewish association explained, and the worker was buried in an unmarked grave. When his Jewish neighbors heard about it, "his body [was] dug up, and the decision taken to start our organization with a cemetery." Group members established social centers where immigrants could play cards or dominoes, chat and gossip over tea or coffee, host dances and benefits, or just relax among people who shared a common heritage. In San Francisco's Chinatown, the largest Chinese community in California, such organizations usually consisted of people who had come from the same towns in China. These groups performed a variety of services, including finding jobs for their members, resolving disputes, campaigning against anti-Chinese discrimination, and sponsoring parades and other cultural activities. One society member explained: "We are strangers in a strange country. We must have an organization to control our country fellows and develop our friendship."

The same impulse to band together occurred in immigrant communities throughout the nation. On the West Coast, Japanese farmers joined *kenjinkai*, which not only provided social activities but also helped first-generation immigrants locate jobs and find housing. In Ybor City, Tampa's cigar-making section, mutual aid organizations rose to meet the needs of Spaniards, Cubans, Afro-Cubans, and Italians. El Centro Español sponsored dances catering to Spaniards, only to be outdone by the rival El Centro Asturiano, which constructed a building that contained a 1,200-seat theater with a 27-by-80-foot stage, "$4,000 worth of modern lighting fixtures, a *cantina*, and a well stocked *biblioteca* (library)." Cubans constructed their own palatial $60,000 clubhouse, El Círculo Cubano, with lovely stained-glass windows, a pharmacy, a theater, and a ballroom. Less splendid and more economical, La Unión Martí-Maceo became the home away from home for Tampa's Afro-Cubans. Besides the usual attractions, the club sponsored a baseball team that competed against other Latin teams. The establishment of such clubs and cultural centers speaks to the commitment of Tampa's immigrant groups to enhance their communities—a commitment backed up with significant financial expenditures.

Besides family and civic associations, churches and synagogues provided religious and social activities for ghetto dwellers. The number of Catholic churches nationwide more than tripled—from 3,000 in 1865 to 10,000 in 1900. Churches celebrated important landmarks in their parishioners' lives—births, baptisms, weddings, and deaths—in a far warmer and more personal manner than did clerks in city hall. Like mutual aid societies, churches offered food and clothing to those who were ill or unable to work and fielded sports teams to compete in recreational leagues. Immigrants altered the religious practices and rituals in their churches to meet their own needs and expectations, many times over the objections of their clergy. Various ethnic groups challenged the orthodox practices of the Catholic Church and insisted that their parishes adopt religious icons that they had worshipped in the old country. These included patron saints or protectresses from Old World towns, such as the Madonna del Carmine, whom Italian Catholics in New York's East Harlem celebrated with an annual festival that their priests considered a pagan ritual. Women played the predominant role in running these street festivities. German Catholics challenged Vatican policy by insisting that each ethnic group have its own priests and parishes. Some Catholics, like Mary Vik, who lived in rural areas that did not have a Catholic church in the vicinity, attended services with local Christians from other denominations.

Religious worship also varied among Jews. German Jews had arrived in the United States in an earlier wave of immigration than their eastern European coreligionists. By the early twentieth century, they had achieved some measure of economic success and founded Reform Judaism, with Cincinnati, Ohio, as its center. This brand of Judaism relaxed strict standards of worship, including absolute fidelity to kosher dietary laws, and allowed prayers to be said in English. By contrast, eastern European Jews, like Beryl Lassin, observed the traditional faith and went to *shul* (synagogue) on a regular basis, maintained a kosher diet, and prayed in Hebrew.

With few immigrants literate in English, foreign-language newspapers prolifer-ated to inform their readers of local, national, and international events. Between the mid-1880s and 1920, 3,500 new foreign-language newspapers came into exis-tence. These newspapers helped sustain ethnic solidarity in the New World as well as maintain ties to the Old World. Newcomers could learn about social and cultural activities in their communities and keep abreast of news from their homeland. German-language tabloids dominated the field and featured such dailies as the *New Yorker Staatszeitung,* the *St. Louis Anzeiger des Westens,* the *Cincinnati Volkesblatt,* and the *Wisconsin Banner.*

Like other communities with poor, unskilled populations, immigrant neighborhoods bred crime. Young men joined gangs based on ethnic heritage and battled with those of other immigrant groups to protect their turf. Adults formed underworld organiza-tions—some of them tied to international criminal syndicates, such as the Mafia—that trafficked in prostitution, gambling, robbery, and murder. Tongs (secret organizations) in New York City's and San Francisco's Chinatowns, which started out as mutual aid societies, peddled vice and controlled the opium trade, gambling, and prostitution in their communities. A survey of New York City police and municipal court records from 1898 concluded that Jews "are prominent in their commission of forgery, violation of corporation ordinance, as disorderly persons (failure to support wife or family), both grades of larceny, and of the lighter grade of assault."

Crime was not the only social problem that plagued immigrant communities. Newspapers and court records reported husbands abandoning their wife and children, engaging in drunken and disorderly conduct, or abusing their family. Boarders whom immigrant families took into their homes for economic reasons also posed problems. Cramped spaces created a lack of privacy, and male boarders sometimes attempted to assault the woman of the house while her husband and children were out to work or in school. Finally, generational conflicts within families began to develop as American-born children of immigrants questioned their parents' values. Daughters born in America sought to loosen the tight restraints imposed by their parents. If they worked outside the home, young women were expected to turn their wages over to their parents. A young Italian woman, however, displayed her independence after receiving her first paycheck. "I just went downtown first and I spent a lot, more than half of my money," she admitted. "I just went hog wild." Thus the social organizations and mutual aid societies that immigrant groups established were more than a simple expression of ethnic solidarity and pride. They were also a response to the very real problems that challenged the health and stability of immigrant communities.

Hostility toward Recent Immigrants

On October 28, 1886, the United States held a gala celebration for the opening of the Statue of Liberty in New York harbor, a short distance from Ellis Island. French sculptors Frédéric-Auguste Bartholdi and Alexandre-Gustave Eiffel had designed the 151-foot-tall monument, *Liberty Enlightening the World*, to appear at the Centennial Exposition in Philadelphia in 1876. Ten years overdue, the statue arrived in June 1885, but funds were still needed to finish construction of a base on which the sculpture would stand. Ordinary people dipped into their pockets for spare change, contributing to a campaign that raised $100,000 so that Lady Liberty could finally hold her uplifted torch for all to see. In 1903 the inspiring words of Emma Lazarus, a Jewish poet, were inscribed on the pedestal welcoming new generations of immigrants.

> Give me your tired, your poor,
> Your huddled masses yearning to breathe free,
> The wretched refuse of your teeming shore,
> Send these, the homeless, tempest-tossed to me,
> I lift my lamp beside the golden door!

Despite the welcoming inscription on the Statue of Liberty, many Americans whose families had arrived before the 1880s considered the influx of immigrants from southern and eastern Europe at best a necessary evil and at worst a menace. Industrialists counted on immigrants to provide the cheap labor that performed backbreaking work in their factories. Not surprisingly, existing industrial workers saw the newcomers as a threat to their economic livelihoods. In their view, the arrival of large numbers of immigrants could only result in greater competition for jobs and lower wages. Moreover, even though most immigrants came to America to find work and improve the lives of their families, a small portion antagonized and frightened capitalists and middle-class Americans with their radical calls for the reorganization of society and the overthrow of the government. Of course, the vast majority of immigrants were not radicals, but a large proportion of radicals were recent immigrants. During times of labor-management strife (see chapter 17), this fact made it easier for businessmen and their spokesmen in the press to advance the notion that anti-American radicalism was a chronic immigrant disease.

Anti-immigrant fears linked to ideas about race and ethnicity had a long history in the United States. In 1790 Congress passed a statute restricting citizenship to those deemed white:

> Any Alien being a free white person, who shall have resided within the limits and under the jurisdiction of the United States for the term of two years, may be admitted to become a citizen thereof on application to any common law Court of record in any one of the States wherein he shall have resided for the term of one year at least, and making proof to the satisfaction of such Court that he is a person of good character, and taking the oath or affirmation prescribed by law to support the Constitution of the United States.

This standard excluded American Indians, who were regarded as savages, and African Americans, most of whom were slaves at the time. In 1857 the Supreme Court ruled that even free blacks were not citizens. From the very beginning of the United States, largely Protestant lawmakers debated whether Catholics and Jews qualified as whites. Although lawmakers ultimately included Catholics and Jews within their definition of "white," over the next two centuries Americans viewed racial categories as not simply matters of skin color. Ethnicity (country or culture of origin) and religion became absorbed into and intertwined with racial categories. A sociological study of Homestead, Pennsylvania, published in 1910 broke down the community along the following constructed racial lines: "Slav, English-speaking European, native white, and colored." Russian Jewish immigrants such as Beryl Lassin were recorded as Hebrews rather than as Russians, suggesting that Jewishness was seen by Christian America as a racial identity.

Scores of races were presumed to exist based on perceived shades of skin color. In 1911 a congressional commission on immigration noted that Poles are "darker than the Lithuanians" and "lighter than the average Russian." These were not neutral judgments, however. Natural scientists and social scientists had given credence to the idea that some races and ethnic groups were superior and others were inferior. Based on Darwin's theory of evolution (see chapter 16), biologists and anthropologists constructed measures of racial hierarchies, placing descendants of northern Europeans with lighter complexions—Anglo-Saxons, Teutonics, and Nordics—at the top of the evolutionary scale. Those with darker skin were deemed inferior "races," with Africans and Native Americans at the bottom. Scholars attempting to make disciplines such as history more "scientific" accepted these racial classifications. At Johns Hopkins University, the leading center of academic training in the social sciences in the 1880s, historian Herbert Baxter Adams argued that the influx of southern European immigrants threatened the capacity for self-government developed in the United States by early settlers originating from Great Britain and Germany. The prevailing sentiment of this era reflected demeaning images of many immigrant groups: Irish as drunkards, Chicanos and Cubans as lazy, Italians as criminals, Hungarians as ignorant peasants, Jews as cheap and greedy, and Chinese as drug addicts. These characteristics resulted supposedly from inherited biological traits, rather than from extreme poverty or other environmental conditions.

Newer immigrants, marked as racially inferior, became a convenient target of hostility. Skilled craftsmen born in the United States viewed largely unskilled workers from abroad who would work for low wages as a threat to their attempts to form unions and keep wages high. Middle-class city dwellers blamed urban problems on the rising tide of foreigners. In addition, Protestant purists felt threatened by Catholics and Jews and believed these "races" incapable or unworthy of assimilation into what they considered to be the superior white, Anglo-Saxon, and Protestant culture. In 1890 social scientist Richard Mayo Smith wrote, "It is scarcely probable that by taking the dregs of Europe, we shall produce a people of high social intelligence and morality."

Nativism—the belief that foreigners pose a serious danger to one's native society and culture—arose as a reactionary response to immigration. New England elites, such as Massachusetts senator Henry Cabot Lodge and writer John Fiske, argued that southern European, Semitic, and Slavic races did not fit into the "community of race" that had founded the United States. In 1893 Lodge and fellow Harvard graduates established the Immigration Restriction League and lobbied for federal legislation that would exclude adult immigrants unable to read in their own language. In 1887 Henry F. Bowers of Clinton, Iowa, founded a similar organization, the American Protective Association, which claimed a total membership of 2.5 million at its peak. The group proposed restricting Catholic immigration, making English a prerequisite to American citizenship, and prohibiting Catholics from teaching in public schools or holding public offices. Obsessed with the supposed threat posed by Catholics, Bowers directed the expansion of the organization throughout the Midwest.

Proposals to restrict immigration, however, did nothing to deal with the millions of foreigners already in America. To preserve their status and power and increase the size of the native-born population, nativists embraced the idea of **eugenics**—a pseudoscience that advocated "biological engineering"—and supported the selective breeding of "desirable" races to counter the rapid population growth of "useless" races. Accordingly, eugenicists promoted the institutionalization of people deemed "unfit," sterilization of those considered mentally impaired, and the licensing and regulation of marriages to promote better breeding. In pushing for such measures, eugenicists believed that they were following the dictates of modern science and acting in a humane fashion to prevent those deemed unfit from causing further harm to themselves and to society. Alexander Graham Bell (see chapter 16), the inventor of the telephone, was one of the early champions of eugenics and immigration restriction.

Others took a less harsh approach. As had been the case with American Indians (see chapter 15), reformers stressed the need for immigrants to assimilate into the dominant culture, embrace the values of individualism and self-help, adopt American styles of dress and grooming, and exhibit loyalty to the U.S. government. They encouraged immigrant children to attend public schools, where they would learn to speak English and adopt American cultural rituals by celebrating holidays such as Thanksgiving and Columbus Day. In 1892 schools adopted the pledge of allegiance, written by Francis Bellamy, which recited American ideals of "liberty and justice for all" and affirmed loyalty to the nation and its flag. Educators encouraged adult immigrants to attend night classes to learn English. Ben Lassin tried this approach sporadically, but he did not prove to be an apt pupil. Like many immigrants, he made only limited progress toward assimilation.

The Assimilation Dilemma

If immigrants were not completely assimilated, neither did they remain the same people who had lived on the farms and in the villages of Europe, Asia, Mexico, and the Caribbean. Some sought to become full-fledged Americans, like Mary Vik, or at least see that their children did so. Writer Israel Zangwill, an English American Jew, portrayed this goal and furnished the enduring image of assimilation in his 1908 play *The Melting-Pot*. Zangwill portrayed people from distinct backgrounds entering the cauldron of American life, mixing together, and emerging as citizens identical to their native-born counterparts. This representation of the **melting pot** became the ideal as depicted in popular cartoons, ceremonies adopted by business corporations, and lessons presented in school classrooms.

However, the melting pot worked better as an ideal than as a mirror of reality. Immigrants during this period never fully lost the social, cultural, religious, and political identities they had brought with them. Even if all immigrants had sought full assimilation, which they did not, the anti-immigrant sentiment of many native-born Americans reinforced their status as strangers and aliens. The same year that Zangwill's play was published, Alfred P. Schultz, a New York physician, provided a dim view of the prospects of assimilation in his book *Race or Mongrel*. Schultz dismissed the melting pot theory that public schools could change the children of all races into Americans, which he found absurd.

Online Document Project   **"Melting Pot" or "Vegetable Soup"?**
bedfordstmartins.com/hewittlawsonvalue

Thus most immigrants faced the dilemma of assimilating while holding on to their heritage. Sociologist W. E. B. Du Bois summed up this predicament for one of the nation's earliest transported groups. In his monumental *The Souls of Black Folk* (1903), Du Bois wrote that African Americans felt a "two-ness," an identity carved out of their African heritage together with their lives as slaves and free people in America. This "double-consciousness . . . two souls, two thoughts, two unreconciled strivings" also applies to immigrants at the turn of the twentieth century. Immigrants who entered the country after 1880 were more like vegetable soup—an amalgam of distinct parts within a common broth—than a melting pot.

REVIEW & RELATE

• What challenges did new immigrants to the United States face?
• What steps did immigrants take to meet these challenges?

Becoming an Urban Nation

In the half century after the Civil War, the population of the United States quadrupled, but the urban population soared sevenfold. In 1870 one in five Americans lived in cities with a population of 8,000 or more. By 1900 one in three resided in cities of this size. In 1870 only Philadelphia and New York had populations over half a million. Twenty years later, in addition to these two cities, Chicago's population exceeded 1 million; St. Louis, Boston, and Baltimore had more than 500,000 residents; and Cleveland, Buffalo, San Francisco, and Cincinnati boasted populations over 250,000. Urbanization was not confined to the Northeast and Midwest. Denver's population jumped from 4,700 in 1870 to more than 107,000 in 1890. During that same period, Los Angeles grew nearly fivefold, from 11,000 to 50,000, and Birmingham leaped from 3,000 to 26,000. "We live in the age of great cities," the Reverend Samuel Lane Loomis, a Massachusetts schoolteacher, remarked in 1886. "Each successive year finds a stronger and more irresistible current sweeping in towards the centers of life." This phenomenal urban growth also brought remarkable physical changes to the cities, as tall buildings reached toward the skies, electric lights brightened the nighttime hours, and water and gas pipes, sewers, and subways snaked below the ground.

The New Industrial City

Urban growth in America was part of a long-term global phenomenon. Between 1820 and 1920, some 60 million people globally moved from rural to urban areas. Most of them migrated after the 1870s, and as noted earlier, millions journeyed from towns and villages in Europe to American cities. Yet the number of Europeans who migrated internally was greater than those who went overseas. As in the United States, Europeans moved from the countryside to urban areas in search of jobs. Many migrated to the city on a seasonal basis, seeking winter employment in cities and then returning to the countryside at harvest time. Whether as permanent or temporary urban residents, these migrants took jobs as bricklayers, factory workers, and cabdrivers.

Before the Civil War, commerce was the engine of growth for American cities. Ports like New York, Boston, New Orleans, and San Francisco became distribution centers for imported goods or items manufactured in small shops in the surrounding countryside. Cities in the interior of the country located on or near major bodies of water, such as Chicago, St. Louis, Cincinnati, and Detroit, served similar functions. As the extension of railroad transportation led to the development of large-scale industry (see chapter 16), these cities and others became industrial centers as well.

Industrialization contributed to rapid urbanization in several ways. It drew those living on farms, who either could not earn a satisfactory living or were bored by the isolation of rural areas, into the city in search of better-paying jobs and excitement. One rural dweller in Massachusetts complained: "The lack of pleasant, public entertainments in this town has much to do with our young people feeling discontented with country life." In 1891, a year after graduating from Kansas State University, the future newspaper editor William Allen White headed to Kansas City, enticed, as he put it, by the "marvels" of "the gilded metropolis." In addition, while the mechanization of farming increased efficiency, it also reduced the demand for farm labor. In 1896 one person could plant, tend, and harvest as much wheat as it had taken eighteen farmworkers to do sixty years before.

Industrial technology also made cities more attractive and livable places. Electricity extended nighttime entertainment and powered streetcars to convey people around town. Improved water and sewage systems provided more sanitary conditions, especially given the demands of the rapidly expanding population. Structural steel and electric elevators made it possible to construct taller and taller buildings, which gave cities such as Chicago and New York their distinctive skylines. Scientists and physicians made significant progress in the fight against the spread of contagious diseases, which had become serious problems in crowded cities.

 Online Document Project   **Class and Leisure in the American City**
bedfordstmartins.com/hewittlawsonvalue

Although immigrants increasingly accounted for the influx into the cities, before 1890 the rise in urban population came mainly from Americans on the move. In addition to young men like William Allen White, young women left the farm to seek their fortune. The female protagonist of Theodore Dreiser's novel *Sister Carrie* (1900) abandons small-town Wisconsin for the lure of Chicago. In real life, mechanization created many "Sister Carries" by making farm women less valuable in the fields. The possibility of purchasing mass-produced goods from mail-order houses such as Sears, Roebuck also left young women less essential as homemakers because they no longer had to sew their own clothes and could buy labor-saving appliances from catalogs.

Similar factors drove rural black women and men into cities. Plagued by the same poverty and debt that white sharecroppers and tenants in the South faced, blacks suffered from the added burden of racial oppression and violence in the post-Reconstruction period. From 1870 to 1890, the African American population of Nashville, Tennessee, soared from just over 16,000 to more than 29,000. In Atlanta, Georgia, the number of blacks jumped from slightly above 16,000 to around 28,000. Richmond, Virginia, and Montgomery, Alabama, followed suit, though the increase was not quite as high.

Economic opportunities were more limited for black migrants than for their white counterparts. African American migrants found work as cooks, janitors, and domestic servants. Work in cotton mills remained off-limits to blacks, but many found employment as manual laborers in manufacturing companies—including tobacco factories, which employed women and men; tanneries; and cottonseed oil firms—and as dockworkers. In 1882 the Richmond Chamber of Commerce applauded black workers as "easily taught" and "most valuable hand[s]." Although the overwhelming majority of blacks worked as unskilled laborers for very low wages, others opened small businesses such as funeral parlors, barbershops, and construction companies or went into professions such as medicine, law, banking, and education that catered to residents of segregated black neighborhoods. Despite considerable individual accomplishments, by the turn of the twentieth century most blacks in the urban South had few prospects for upward economic mobility.

In 1890, although 90 percent of African Americans lived in the South, a growing number were moving to northern cities to seek employment and greater freedom. Boll weevil infestations during the 1890s decimated cotton production and forced sharecroppers and tenants off farms. At the same time, blacks saw significant erosion of their political and civil rights in the last decade of the nineteenth century. Most black citizens in the South were denied the right to vote and experienced rigid, legally sanctioned racial segregation in all aspects of public life (see chapter 16). Between 1890 and 1914 approximately 485,000 African Americans left the South. By 1914 New York, Chicago, and Philadelphia each counted more than 100,000 African Americans among their population, and another twenty-nine northern cities contained black populations of 10,000 or more. An African American woman expressed her enthusiasm about the employment she found in Chicago, where she earned $3 a day working in a railroad yard. "The colored women like this work," she explained, because "we make more money . . . and we do not have to work as hard as at housework," which required working sixteen-hour days, six days a week.

Although many blacks found they preferred their new lives to the ones they had led in the South, the North did not turn out to be the promised land of freedom. Black newcomers encountered discrimination in housing and employment. Residential segregation confined African Americans to racial ghettos, such as the South Side of Chicago and New York City's Harlem. Black workers found it difficult to obtain skilled employment despite their qualifications, and women and men most often toiled as domestics, janitors, and part-time laborers.

Nevertheless, African Americans in northern cities built their own communities that preserved and reshaped their southern culture and offered a degree of insulation against the harshness of racial discrimination. A small black middle class appeared in Washington, D.C., Philadelphia, Chicago, and New York City consisting of teachers, attorneys, and small business people. In 1888 African Americans organized the Capital Savings Bank of Washington, D.C. Ten years later, two black real estate agents in New York City were worth more than $150,000 each, and one agent in Cleveland owned $100,000 in property. The rising black middle class provided leadership in the formation of mutual aid societies, lodges, and women's clubs. Newspapers such as the *Chicago Defender* and *Pittsburgh Courier* furnished local news to their subscribers and reported

African American Family, 1900 Despite the rigid racial segregation and oppression that African Americans faced in the late nineteenth century, some black families found ways to achieve economic success and upward mobility. With its piano and fine furniture, the home of this African American family reflects middle-class conventions of the period. The father is a graduate of Hampton Institute, a historically black university founded after the Civil War to educate freedpeople. Library of Congress

national and international events affecting people of color. As was the case in the South, the church was at the center of black life in northern cities. More than just religious institutions, churches furnished space for social activities and the dissemination of political information. The Baptist Church attracted the largest following among blacks throughout the country, followed by the African Methodist Episcopal (AME) Church. By the first decade of the twentieth century, more than two dozen churches had sprung up in Chicago alone. Whether housed in newly constructed buildings or in storefronts, black churches provided worshippers freedom from white control. They also allowed members of the northern black middle class to demonstrate what they considered to be respectability and refinement. This meant discouraging enthusiastic displays of "old-time religion," which celebrated more exuberant forms of worship. As the Reverend W. A. Blackwell of Chicago's AME Zion Church declared, "Singing, shouting, and talking [were] the most useless ways of proving Christianity." This conflict over modes of religious expression reflected a larger process that was under way in black communities at the turn of the twentieth century. As black urban communities in the North grew and developed, tensions and divisions emerged within the increasingly diverse black community, as a variety of groups competed to shape and define black culture and identity.

Cities Expand Upward and Outward

As the urban population increased, cities expanded both out and up. Before 1860, the dominant form of brick and stone construction prevented buildings from rising more than four or five stories. As late as 1880, church steeples usually remained the tallest structures in cities. However, as cities became much more populous, land values soared. During the 1870s and 1880s, one piece of property in Chicago rose in value from $160 to $800. In Denver, the value of a city block leaped from $6,500 to $205,000, and in New York City a lot that sold for $80 in 1840 fetched $8,000 forty years later. Steep prices prompted architects to make the most of small, expensive plots of land by finding ways to build taller structures. Architects began using cast-iron columns instead of the thick, heavy walls of brick that limited floor space. The resulting "cloudscrapers" raised the urban skyline to ten stories. The development of structural steel, which was stronger and more durable than iron, turned cloudscrapers into **skyscrapers**, which stretched some thirty stories into the air. With the development of the electric elevator and the radiator, which replaced fireplaces with hot water circulated through pipes, even taller skyscrapers came to loom over downtown business districts in major cities.

Cities also expanded horizontally, as new transportation technology made it possible for residents to move around a much larger urban landscape. In the mid-nineteenth century in cities such as Boston and Philadelphia, pedestrians could still walk from one end of the city to the other within an hour. If residents preferred to ride public conveyances, they could pay a fare and hop on board a horse-drawn railcar. These vehicles moved slowly and left tons of horse manure in the streets. To avoid such problems, in 1873 San Francisco, followed by Seattle and Chicago, installed a system of cable-driven trolley cars. Still, these trolleys proved slow and unreliable. By 1914, however, advances in transportation converted walking cities into riding cities.

Electricity provided the transportation breakthrough. In 1888 naval engineer Frank J. Sprague, who had once worked for inventor Thomas Edison, completed the first electric trolley line in Richmond, Virginia. Electric-powered streetcars traveled twice as fast as horses and left little mess on the streets. Subways could run underground without asphyxiating passengers and workmen with a steam engine's smoke and soot. Boston opened the first subway in 1897, followed by New York City in 1904.

Bridges spanning large rivers and waterways also helped extend the boundaries of the inner city. Railroad companies had originally worked out the details of constructing such bridges, but not until 1883 did they become the symbol of urban growth. In that year, the Brooklyn Bridge opened, connecting Manhattan with the city of Brooklyn. Designed and engineered by John Augustus Roebling, the bridge had taken thirteen years to complete and cost twenty men their lives. It stretched more than a mile across the East River and was broad enough for a footpath, two double carriage lanes, and two railroad lines. In addition, the bridge featured arches cut like giant cathedral windows. In looking up at its supporting cables, one observer marveled that they hung "like divine messages from above." During its first year in operation, more than 11 million people passed over the bridge; today, more than 51 million vehicles cross the bridge each year.

The electrification of public transportation and the construction of bridges made it feasible for some people to live considerable distances from their workplace. In the eighteenth and nineteenth centuries, middle- and upper-class merchants and professionals usually lived near their shops and offices in the heart of the city, surrounded by their employees. After 1880, the huge influx of immigration brought large numbers of impoverished workers to city centers. The resulting traffic congestion and overcrowded housing pushed wealthier residents to seek more open spaces in which to build houses. The new electric trolley lines allowed middle-class urbanites to move miles away from downtown areas. With an investment of $2,000 to $10,000, a considerable sum in those days, they built roomy homes filled with modern conveniences on leafy streets. In 1850 the Boston metropolis spread in a radius of two to three miles around the city and had a population of 200,000. In 1900 suburban Boston ringed the city in a ten-mile radius, with a population of more than 1 million. Increasingly, cities divided into two parts: an inner commercial and industrial core housing the working class, and outer communities occupied by a wealthier class of white, older-stock Americans.

How the Other Half Lived

As the middle and upper classes fled the industrial urban center for the suburbs, the working poor moved in to replace them. They lived in old factories and homes and in shanties and cellars. Because land values were higher in the city, the poorest people could least afford high rents. To make ends meet, families crowded into existing apartments, sometimes taking in boarders to help pay the rent. This led to increased population density and overcrowding in the urban areas where immigrants lived. On New York's Lower East Side, the population density was the highest in the world. In 1880, 47,000 people lived within the teeming area. Ten years later, the number had climbed to more than 57,000, a population density of 334,080 per square mile, about ten times the citywide average. Such overcrowding fostered communicable diseases and frustration, giving the area the nicknames "typhus ward" and "suicide ward."

Overcrowding combined with extreme poverty turned immigrant neighborhoods into slums, which were characterized by substandard housing. Impoverished immigrants typically lived in multiple-family apartment buildings called **tenements** (legally defined as containing more than three families). First constructed in 1850, these early dwellings often featured windowless rooms and little or no plumbing and heating. In 1879 a New York law reformed the building codes and required minimal plumbing facilities and that all bedrooms (but not all rooms) have a window. Constructed on narrow 25-by-100-foot lots, these five- and six-story buildings included four small apartments on a floor and had only two toilets off the hallway. Tenements stood right next to each other, with only an air shaft separating them. Although these dwellings marked some improvement in living conditions, they proved miserable places to live in—dark, damp, and foul smelling. In 1895 a federal government housing inspector observed that the air shafts provided "imperfect light and ventilation" and that "refuse matter or filth of one kind or another [was] very apt to accumulate at the bottom, giving rise to noxious odors." The air shafts also operated as a conduit for fires that moved swiftly from one tenement to another.

In fact, the density of late-nineteenth-century cities could turn individual fires into citywide disasters. The North Side of Chicago burned to the ground in 1871, and Boston and Baltimore suffered catastrophic fires as well. On April 18, 1906, an earthquake in San Francisco set the city ablaze, causing about 1,500 deaths and terrible destruction of businesses and homes. Such fires could, however, have long-term positive consequences. The great urban conflagrations encouraged construction of fireproof buildings made of brick and steel instead of wood. In addition, citizens organized fire watches and established municipal fire departments to replace volunteer companies. As an unintended side effect, fires provided cities with a chance to rebuild. Chicago's skyscrapers and its system of urban parks were built on land cleared by fire.

Besides furnishing grossly inadequate housing, tenements stood out as eyesores, "scabs" on the landscape, especially for those who had lived in cities before the new wave of immigration began. In 1890 Jacob Riis, a Danish immigrant, newspaperman, and photographer, illustrated the brutal conditions endured by tenement families such as Beryl Lassin's on New York's Lower East Side. "In the stifling July nights," he wrote in *How the Other Half Lives*, "when the big barracks are like fiery furnaces, their very walls giving out absorbed heat, men and women lie in restless, sweltering rows, panting for air and sleep." Under these circumstances, Riis lamented, an epidemic "is excessively fatal among the children of the poor, by reason of the practical impossibility of isolating the patient in a tenement." Despite their obvious problems, tenements soon spread to other cities such as Cleveland, Cincinnati, and Boston, and one block might have ten of these buildings, housing as many as four thousand people.

With all the misery they spawned as places to live, tenements also functioned as workplaces. Czech immigrants made cigars in their apartments from six in the morning until nine at night, seven days a week, for about 6 cents an hour. By putting an entire family to work, they could make $15 a week and pay their rent of $12 a month. Clothing contractors in particular saw these tenement **sweatshops** as a cheap way to produce their products. By jamming two or three sewing machines into an apartment and paying workers a fixed amount for each item they produced, contractors kept their costs down and avoided factory regulations. Riis observed men, women, and children "bending over their machines, or ironing clothes at the window, half-naked. Proprieties do not count on the East Side."

Even when immigrants left sweatshop apartments and went to work in factories, they continued to face exploitation. The Jewish and Italian clothing workers who toiled in the **Triangle Shirtwaist Company**, located in New York City's Greenwich Village, worked long hours for little pay. In 1911 a fire broke out on the eighth story of the factory and quickly spread to the ninth and tenth floors. The fire engines' ladders could not reach that high, and one of the exits on the ninth floor was locked to keep workers from stealing material. More than 140 people died in the blaze—some by jumping out the windows, but most by getting trapped behind the closed exit door.

Slums compounded the potential for disease, poor sanitation, fire, congestion, and crime. Living on poor diets, slum dwellers proved particularly vulnerable to epidemics. Cholera and typhoid—as well as an outbreak of yellow fever in Memphis in the 1870s and in Tampa in the 1870s and 1880s—killed tens of thousands. Tuberculosis was even deadlier. An epidemic that began in a slum neighborhood could easily spread into more affluent areas of the city. Children suffered the most. Almost one-quarter of the children born in American cities in 1890 did not live to celebrate their first birthday.

Contributing to the outbreak of disease was faulty sewage disposal, a problem that vexed city leaders. Until the invention of the modern indoor flush toilet in the early twentieth century, people relied on outdoor toilets, with as many as eight hundred people using a single facility. All too often, cities dumped human waste into rivers that also supplied drinking water. In 1881 the exasperated mayor of Cleveland called the

Cuyahoga River "an open sewer through the center of the city." Two years later, a group of Philadelphians complained that their water was "not only distasteful and unwholesome for drinking, but offensive for bathing purposes." At the same time, the great demand for water caused by the population explosion resulted in lower water pressure. Consequently, residents in the upper floors of tenements had to carry buckets of water from the lower floors. Until cities overcame their water and sanitation challenges, epidemics would continue to plague urban dwellers.

Urban crowding created other problems as well. Traffic moved slowly through densely populated cities. Pedestrians and commuters had to navigate around throngs of people walking on sidewalks and streets, peddlers selling out of pushcarts, and piles of garbage cluttering the walkways. Streets remained in poor shape. In 1889 the majority of Cleveland's 440 miles of streets consisted of sand and gravel. Chicago did not fare much better. In 1890 most road surfaces were covered with wooden blocks, and three-quarters of the city's more than 2,000 miles of streets remained unpaved. Rainstorms quickly made matters worse by turning foul-smelling, manure-filled streets into mud. Washington, D.C., solved much of the problem of clogged roads by covering them with asphalt. For the most part, only smaller cities like New Haven, Connecticut, could afford to pave the streets.

Poverty and overcrowding contributed to increased crime. The U.S. murder rate quadrupled between 1880 and 1900, at a time when the murder rates in most European cities were declining. In New York City, crime thrived in slums with the apt names of "Bandit's Roost" and "Hell's Kitchen," and groups of young hoodlums, such as the "Sewer Rats" and "Rock Gang," preyed on unsuspecting citizens. Poverty forced some of the poor to turn to theft or prostitution. One twenty-year-old prostitute, who supported her sickly mother and four brothers and sisters, lamented: "Let God Almighty judge who's to blame most, I that was driven, or them that drove me to the pass I'm in." Rising criminality led to the formation of urban police departments, though many law officers supplemented their incomes by collecting graft (illegal payments) for ignoring criminal activities.

REVIEW & RELATE

- What factors contributed to rapid urban growth in the late nineteenth century?
- How did the American cities of 1850 differ from those of 1900? What factors account for these differences?

Urban Politics at the Turn of the Century

The problems that booming cities faced in trying to absorb millions of immigrants proved formidable and at times seemed insurmountable. From a governmental standpoint, cities had limited authority over their own affairs. They were controlled by state legislatures and needed state approval to raise revenues and pass regulations. For the most part, there were no zoning laws to regulate housing construction. Private companies owned public utilities, and competition among them produced unnecessary duplication and waste. The government services that did exist operated on a segmented basis, with the emphasis on serving wealthier neighborhoods at the expense

Philadelphia, 1897   This photograph shows the hustle and bustle of Philadelphia, which along with other cities grew enormously in the late nineteenth century. Urban politicians had to grapple with the challenges posed by the incredible pace of change, including the rapid influx of immigrants. The presence in this scene of carts, a horse, and a streetcar shows a city in transition.   Library of Congress

of the city at large. Missing was a vision of the city as a whole, one that would view the distinct sections as part of a larger tapestry. Cities had become so large and complex that no one could stand back and see the entire picture.

Political Machines and City Bosses

City government in the late nineteenth century was fragmented. Mayors usually did not have much power, and decisions involving public policies such as housing, transportation, and municipal services often rested in the hands of private developers. For instance, by 1890 Chicago had eleven branches of government that were constantly at odds with one another. Bringing some order out of this chaos, the **political machine** functioned to give cities the centralized authority and services that they otherwise lacked. At the head

of the machine was the political **boss.** Although the boss himself (and they were all men) held some public office, his real authority came from leadership of the machine. These organizations maintained a tight network of loyalists throughout city wards (districts), each of which contained designated representatives responsible for catering to the needs of their constituents. Whether Democratic or Republican, political machines did not care about philosophical issues; they were concerned primarily with staying in power.

The strength of political machines rested in large measure on immigrants. The organization provided a kind of public welfare when private charity could not cope satisfactorily with the growing needs of the poor. Machines doled out turkeys on holidays, furnished a load of coal for the winter, provided jobs in public construction, arranged for shelter and meals if tenement houses burned down, and intervened with the police and the courts when a constituent got into trouble. Bosses sponsored baseball clubs, held barbecues and picnics, and attended christenings, bar mitzvahs, weddings, and funerals, sometimes all in a single day. George Washington Plunkitt, a boss in New York City's Tammany Hall machine, called it was a "strenuous life." For enterprising members of immigrant groups—and is proved especially true for the Irish during this period—the machine offered upward mobility out of poverty as they rose through its ranks.

The poor were not the only group that benefited from connections to political machines. The machine and its functionaries helped businessmen maneuver through the maze of contradictory and overlapping co regulating building and licenses that impeded their routine course of activities. In addition to assisting legitimate business - men, the machine facilitated the underworld commerce of vice, prostitution, and gambling by acting as an arbiter to keep this le within established boundaries—all for a cut of the illegal profits.

In return for these services, the machine received the votes of grateful immigrants and a plentiful supply of funds from businessmen. When challenged by reformers or other political rivals, the machine readily engaged in corrupt election practices to maintain — its power. Mobilizing the "graveyard vote," bosses took names from tombstones to pad lists of registered voters. They also hired "repeaters" to vote more than once under phony names and did not flinch from dumping whole ballot boxes into the river or using hired thugs to scare opponents from the polls.

Bosses enriched themselves through graft and corruption. They secured protection money from both legitimate and illegitimate business interests in return for their services. Boss William Marcy Tweed, the head of Tammany Hall in the 1860s and 1870s, swindled New York City out of a fortune while supervising the construction of a lavish three-story courthouse in lower Manhattan. The original budget for the building was $250,000, but the city spent more than $13 million on the structure, making out checks to Tweed's phony associates "T. C. Cash" and "Philip F. Dummey." The building remained unfinished in 1873, when Tweed was convicted on fraud charges and went to jail. In later years, Tammany Hall's Plunkitt distinguished this kind of "dishonest graft" from the kind of "honest graft" that he practiced. If he received inside information about a future sale of city property, Plunkitt reasoned, why shouldn't he get a head start, buy it at a low price, and then sell it at a higher figure? As he delighted in saying, "I seen my opportunities and I took 'em." What could be more American?

Yet the services of political machines came at a high cost. Corruption and graft led to higher taxes on middle-class residents. Moreover, the image of the political boss as a modern-day Robin Hood who stole from the rich and gave to the poor is greatly exaggerated. Much of the proceeds of machine activities went into the private coffers of machine bosses and other functionaries and did not go to worthy public ventures. Traffic in vice might have run more smoothly under the coordination of the machine, but the safety and health of city residents hardly improved. Most importantly, although immigrants and the poor did benefit from an informal system of social welfare, the machine had no interest in resolving the underlying causes of their problems. As the dominant urban political party organization, the machine cared little about issues such as good housing, job safety, and sufficient wages. The British observer James Bryce, who toured America in the late 1880s and admired much of what he saw, nevertheless judged the machine-controlled municipal governments to be the one conspicuous failure of the United State." It remained for others to provide alternative approaches to relieving the plight of the urban poor.

Urban Reformers

The men and women who criticized political bosses and machines—and the corruption and vice they fostered—usually came from the ranks of the upper middle class and the wealthy. Their solution to the urban crisis typically centered around toppling the political machine and replacing it with a civil service that would allow government to function on the basis of merit rather than influence peddling and cronyism. Both locally and nationally, they pushed for civic reform. In 1883 Congress responded to this demand by passing the **Pendleton Civil Service Reform Act**, which required federal jobs to be awarded on the basis of merit, as determined by competitive examinations, rather than through political connections. As for the immigrants who supported machine politics, these reformers preferred to deal with them from afar and expected that through proper education they might change their lifestyles and adopt American ways.

Another group of Americans from upper- and middle-class backgrounds put aside whatever prejudices they might have held about working-class immigrants and dealt directly with newcomers to try to solve various social problems. These reformers—mostly young people, and many of them men and college graduates—took up residence in **settlement houses** located in urban slums. Settlement houses offered a variety of services to community residents, including day care for children; cooking, sewing, and secretarial classes; neighborhood playgrounds; counseling sessions; and meeting rooms for labor unions. Settlement house organizers, pioneers of the social work profession, understood that immigrants gravitated to the political machine or congregated in the local tavern not because they were inherently immoral but because these institutions helped mitigate their suffering and, in some cases, offered concrete paths to advancement. Although settlement house workers wanted to Americanize immigrants, they also understood immigrants' need to hold on to remnants of their original culture.

By 1900 approximately one hundred settlement houses had been established in major American cities. Jane Addams, who founded Hull House in Chicago, contended that "the dependence of classes on each other is reciprocal" and insisted that "the things which make men alike are finer and better than the things that keep them apart." Other settlement houses reflecting a similar philosophy included the South End House in Boston, directed by Robert A. Woods, and the Henry Street Settlement in New York City, founded by Lillian Wald. Addams and Wald, as well as other social workers, preferred a hands-on approach. They actively mobilized neighborhood residents to engage in politics and to vote for candidates who understood their problems and would campaign for improved garbage collection, housing inspection, better schools, and other community improvements.

Religiously inspired reform provided similar support for slum dwellers. In contrast to clergy such as Russell Conwell (see chapter 16), who emphasized cash more than Christ, some Protestant ministers began to argue that immigrants' problems resulted not from chronic racial or ethnic failings but from their difficult environment. One of the best-known figures among this group was Washington Gladden, a minister who had lived in Springfield and Columbus, Ohio. Originally a defender of laissez-faire, by the mid-1880s Gladden had come to believe that unregulated private enterprise was "ineq-uitable." He compared financial speculators to vampires "sucking the life-blood of our commerce." In books and from the pulpit, Gladden preached Christianity as a "social gospel," which included support for civil service reform, antimonopoly regulation, in-come tax legislation, factory inspection laws, and workers' right to strike.

Despite the efforts of social gospel advocates and the charitable organizations that arose to help relieve human misery, such as the Salvation Army, private attempts to combat the various urban ills, however well-meaning, proved insufficient. The problems were structural, not personal, and one group or even several operating together did not have the resources or power to make urban institutions more efficient, equitable, and humane. As Jane Addams noted, "Private beneficence is totally inadequate to deal with the vast numbers of the city's disinherited." If reformers were to succeed in tackling the most significant social problems and make lasting changes in American society and politics, they would have to enlist state and federal governments.

REVIEW & RELATE

• What role did political machines play in late-nineteenth-century cities?

• Who led the opposition to machine control of city politics, and what solutions and alternatives did they offer?

Conclusion: A Nation of Cities

Immigrants from southern and eastern Europe who came to the United States between the 1880s and 1914 survived numerous hardships as they strove to create a better life for their families. Like industrialists, workers, and farmers, they organized to advance collective interests. Immigrants joined together in neighborhood groups—houses of worship, fraternal organizations, burial societies, political machines, and settlement houses—to promote their own welfare. Some achieved success and returned to their homelands to live in relative splendor. Most of those who remained in the United States, like Mary Vik and Ben Lassin, struggled to earn a living but managed to pave the way for their children and grandchildren to obtain better education and jobs. Mary's grand-daughter, Nancy A. Hewitt, earned a Ph.D. in history from the University of Pennsylvania, and Ben's grandson, Steven F. Lawson, earned a doctorate in history from Columbia University. They became university professors and in writing this book have tried to preserve their grandparents' legacy.

Immigrants were not the only group on the move in the late nineteenth century. African Americans migrated in search of political freedom and economic opportunity. They relocated from the rural South to the urban South and North, where they continued to encounter discrimination. Yet cities gave them more leeway to develop their own political, economic, cultural, and social institutions than they had before. Although they encountered segregation, African Americans in the North were allowed to vote, a tool they would use to gain equality in the future. Because of long-standing patterns of racism, supported by law, African Americans would struggle much longer than did white immigrants to obtain equality and justice.

Few public institutions attempted to aid immigrants or racial minorities as they made the difficult transition to urban and industrial life. Yet immigrants did participate in urban politics through the efforts of political bosses and their machines who sought immigrant votes. In return, political machines provided immigrants with rudimentary social and political services that they could rarely find anywhere else. Political machines, however, bred corruption, along with higher taxes to fund their extravagances. Dishonest government prompted middle- and upper-class urban dwellers to take up reform in order to sweep the political bosses out of office and diminish the power of their immigrant supporters, as we will see in the next chapter.

Chapter Review

MAKE IT STICK

LearningCurve bedfordstmartins.com/hewittlawsonvalue
After reading the chapter, use LearningCurve to retain what you've read.

IDENTIFY KEY TERMS

Identify and explain the significance of each term below.

ghettos (p. 463)

mutual aid societies (p. 463)

nativism (p. 466)

eugenics (p. 467)

melting pot (p. 467)

skyscrapers (p. 472)

tenements (p. 473)

sweatshops (p. 474)

Triangle Shirtwaist Company (p. 474)

political machine (p. 476)

boss (p. 477)

Pendleton Civil Service Reform Act
  (p. 478)

settlement houses (p. 478)

REVIEW & RELATE

Answer the focus questions from each section of the chapter.

1. What challenges did new immigrants to the United States face?

2. What steps did immigrants take to meet these challenges?

3. What factors contributed to rapid urban growth in the late nineteenth century?

4. How did the American cities of 1850 differ from those of 1900? What factors account for these differences?

5. What role did political machines play in late-nineteenth-century cities?

6. Who led the opposition to machine control of city politics, and what solutions and alternatives did they offer?

ONLINE DOCUMENT PROJECTS

◆ "Melting Pot" or "Vegetable Soup"?
◆ Class and Leisure in the American City

After reading the primary sources in these document sets, answer the **Interpret the Evidence** questions to help you analyze each of the documents, and then answer the **Put It in Context** question(s) to help you relate the documents to the topics and themes you read about in the chapter.

bedfordstmartins.com/hewittlawsonvalue

TIMELINE OF EVENTS

1880–1914	• Period of significant immigration to United States	**1892**	• U.S. schools adopt pledge of allegiance
1882	• Chinese Exclusion Act passed	**1893**	• Immigration Restriction League founded
1883	• Pendleton Civil Service Reform Act requires that federal jobs be awarded on the basis of merit	**1897**	• Boston opens first subway system in the United States
	• Brooklyn Bridge opens	**1903**	• W. E. B. Du Bois publishes *The Souls of Black Folk*
1886	• Statue of Liberty opens in New York City	**1906**	• San Francisco earthquake
1887	• American Protective Association formed to restrict immigration	**1908**	• Israel Zangwill publishes *The Melting-Pot*
		1911	• Triangle Shirtwaist Company fire in New York City

LearningCurve
bedfordstmartins.com/hewittlawsonvalue
After reading the chapter, use LearningCurve
to retain what you've read.

Progressivism and the Search for Order

1900–1917

AMERICAN HISTORIES

Gifford Pinchot grew up on a lavish Connecticut estate catered to by tutors and governesses and vacationing in rural areas, where Gifford learned to hunt, fish, and enjoy the splendor of nature. Yet Pinchot rejected a life of leisure and gentility. Like other affluent young men and women of his time, Pinchot sought to make his mark through public service, in his case by working to conserve and protect America's natural resources. In 1885, following his father's advice, Gifford entered Yale University to study forestry. However, the university did not offer a forestry program, reflecting the predominant view that the nation's natural resources were, for all practical purposes, unlimited. Pinchot cobbled together courses in various scientific fields at Yale, but he knew that after graduating his only option for further study was to travel to Europe, where forests were treated as crops that needed care and replenishing.

By the time Pinchot returned in 1890, many Americans had begun to see the need to conserve the nation's forests, waterways, and oil and mineral deposits and to protect its wild spaces. Drawing on his training as a scientist and his experiences in Europe, Pinchot advocated the use of natural resources by sportsmen and businesses under carefully regulated governmental authority. Appointed to head the Federal Division of Forestry in 1898, Pinchot found a vigorous ally in the White House when Theodore Roosevelt took office in 1901 after William McKinley's assassination. In 1907 Pinchot began to speak of the need for *conservation*, which he defined as "the use of the natural resources now existing on this continent for the benefit of the people who live here now." This use of resources included responsible business practices in industries such as logging and mining.

Not all environmentalists agreed. In contrast to Pinchot, author and nature photographer Geneva (Gene) Stratton-Porter focused her energies on *preservation*, the protection of public land from any private development and the creation of national parks. Born in 1863 in Wabash County, Indiana, Stratton-Porter spent her childhood on a farm roaming through fields, watching birds, and observing "nature's rhythms." After marrying in 1886, Stratton-Porter took up photography and hiked into the wilderness of Indiana to take pictures of wild birds.

Stratton-Porter built a reputation as a nature photographer. She also published a series of novels and children's books that revealed her vision of the harmony between human beings and nature. She urged readers to preserve the environment for plant life and wildlife so that men and women could lead a truly fulfilling existence on Earth and not destroy God's creation. Of all the preservationists, Stratton-Porter reached the widest audience. Five of her books sold more than a million copies, and several were made into movies.

THE AMERICAN HISTORIES of Gifford Pinchot and Gene Stratton-Porter reveal the efforts of just two of the many individuals who searched for ways to control the damaging impact of modernization on the United States. From roughly 1900 to 1917, many Americans sought to bring some order out of the chaos accompanying rapid industrialization and urbanization. Despite the magnitude of the issues they targeted, those who believed in the need to combat the problems of industrial America possessed an optimistic faith—sometimes derived from religious principles, sometimes from a secular outlook—that they could relieve the stresses and strains that modern life brought. Such people were not bound together by a single, rigid ideology. Instead, they were united by faith in the notion that if people joined together and applied human intelligence to the task of improving the nation, progress was inevitable. So widespread was this hopeful conviction that we call this period the Progressive Era.

In pursuit of progress and stability, reformers tried to control the behavior of groups they considered a threat to the social order. Equating difference with disorder, many progressives tried to impose white middle-class standards of behavior on immigrant populations. Some sought to eliminate the "problem" altogether by curtailing further immigration from southern and eastern Europe. Many white progressives, particularly in the South, supported segregation and disfranchisement, which limited opportunities for African Americans. At the same time, however, black progressives and their white allies created organizations dedicated to securing racial equality.

The women's suffrage organization headquarters of Ohio, 1912. Schlesinger Library, Radcliffe Institute, Harvard University/ The Bridgeman Art Library

The Roots of Progressivism

At the turn of the twentieth century, many Americans believed that the nation was in dire need of reform. Two decades of westward expansion, industrialization, urbanization, and skyrocketing immigration had transformed the country in unsettling and, in the minds of many, dangerous ways. In the aftermath of the social and economic turmoil that accompanied the depression of the 1890s, many members of the middle and upper classes were convinced that unless they took remedial measures, the country would collapse under the weight of class conflict. Progressives advocated governmental intervention, yet they sought change without radically altering capitalism or the democratic political system. A progressive newspaper editor explained in 1912: "The world moves and we have to move with it. So with all that is going on with politics today. . . . It is evolution, and not revolution."

Progressive Origins

Progressives contended that old ways of governing and doing business did not address modern conditions. In one sense, they inherited the legacy of the Populist movement of the 1890s. Progressives attacked laissez-faire capitalism, and by regulating monopolies they aimed to limit the power of corporate trusts, which they saw as a threat to economic and political democracy. Like the Populists, progressive reformers advocated instituting an income tax as well as a variety of initiatives designed to give citizens a greater say in government. However, progressives differed from Populists in fundamental ways. Perhaps most important, progressives were interested primarily in urban and industrial America, while the Populist movement had emerged in direct response to the problems that plagued rural America in the late nineteenth century.

Progressives were heirs to the intellectual critics of the late nineteenth century who challenged laissez-faire and rejected Herbert Spencer's doctrine of the "survival of the fittest" (see chapter 16). **Pragmatism** greatly influenced progressives. Identified with

Harvard psychologist and philosopher William James and philosopher John Dewey, pragmatists contended that the meaning of truth did not reside in some absolute doctrine but could only be discovered through experience. Ideas had to be measured by their practical consequences. From these critics, progressives derived a healthy skepticism toward rigid dogma and instead relied on human experience to guide social action.

Reformers also drew inspiration from the religious ideals of the **social gospel** (see chapter 18). In *Christianity and the Social Crisis* (1907), the Protestant clergyman Walter Rauschenbusch of Rochester, New York, urged Christians to embrace the teachings of Jesus on the ethical obligations for social justice and to put these teachings into action by working among the urban poor. Progressive leaders such as Theodore Roosevelt and Gifford Pinchot combined the moral fervor of the social gospel with the rationalism of the gospel of scientific efficiency.

Pragmatism and the social gospel appealed to members of the new middle class. Before the Civil War, the middle class had consisted largely of ministers, lawyers, physicians, and small proprietors. The growth of large-scale businesses during the second half of the nineteenth century expanded the middle class, which now included men whose professions grew out of industrialization, such as engineering, corporate management, and social work. The new middle class established organizations to promote their own professional goals and further the public interest. One of the most powerful groups, the American Medical Association (AMA), had originally formed in 1847 but grew rapidly at the turn of the century. The AMA raised qualifications to increase the level of education required to practice medicine, thus limiting access to the profession. Progressivism drew many of its most devoted adherents from this new middle class.

Muckrakers

The growing desire for reform at the turn of the century received a boost from investigative journalists known as **muckrakers**. Popular magazines such as *McClure's* and *Collier's* sought to increase their readership by publishing exposés of corruption in government and the shady operations of big business. Filled with details uncovered through intensive research, these articles had a sensationalist appeal that both informed and aroused their mainly middle-class readers. In 1902 journalist Ida Tarbell lambasted the ruthless and dishonest business practices of the Rockefeller family's Standard Oil Company, the model of corporate greed. Lincoln Steffens wrote about machine bosses' shameful rule in cities such as Chicago, Cincinnati, Cleveland, Minneapolis, New York, St. Louis, and Philadelphia. Ida B. Wells, a Memphis journalist, wrote scathing articles and pamphlets condemning the lynching of African Americans. Other muckrakers exposed fraudulent practices in insurance companies, child labor, drug abuse, and prostitution.

Ironically, President Theodore Roosevelt coined the term *muckraker* in 1906 not as a compliment but as a sign of disgust for journalists he thought were more interested in making sensationalist charges than in carefully documenting their stories. He compared them to the character in John Bunyan's novel *Pilgrim's Progress* who was so absorbed in looking at the filth (muck) on the ground that he did not see a beautiful gift offered to him. Roosevelt feared that if muckraking became too sensational and unrestrained, it would threaten moderate reform and encourage more radical alternatives. Yet muckrakers did succeed in raising middle-class awareness and generated wide support for the political reforms that Roosevelt and other progressives proposed.

REVIEW & RELATE

- What late-nineteenth-century trends and developments influenced the progressives?
- Why did the progressives focus on urban and industrial America?

Humanitarian Reform

Humanitarian reformers focused on the plight of urban immigrants, African Americans, and the underprivileged. They tried mainly to improve housing and working conditions for impoverished city dwellers. Their motives were not always purely altruistic. Unless living standards improved, many reformers reasoned, immigrants and racial minorities would contaminate the cities' middle-class inhabitants with communicable diseases, escalating crime, and threats to traditional cultural norms. These reformers also supported suffrage for women, whose votes, they believed, would help purify electoral politics and elect candidates committed to social and moral reform.

Female Progressives and the Poor

Women played the leading role in efforts to improve the lives of the impoverished. Jane Addams, the daughter of a wealthy businessman, had toured Europe after graduating from a women's college in Illinois. The Toynbee Hall settlement house in London impressed her for its work in helping poor residents of the area. In 1889 Addams, after returning home to Chicago, and her friend Ellen Starr established **Hull House** as a center for social reform in the northwest neighborhood of the city. Hull House inspired a generation of young women to work directly in immigrant communities. Many were college-educated, professionally trained women who were shut out of jobs in male-dominated professions. Staffed mainly by women, settlement houses became all-purpose urban support centers. Not only did they provide recreational facilities, social activities, and educational classes for neighborhood residents, but they also became launching pads for campaigns aimed at improving living and working conditions for the urban poor. Calling on women to take up **civic housekeeping**, Addams maintained that women could protect their individual households from the chaos of industrialization and urbanization only by attacking the sources of that chaos in the community at large.

Settlement house and social workers occupied the front lines of humanitarian reform, but they found considerable support from women's clubs. Formed after the Civil War, these local groups provided protected spaces for middle-class women to meet, share ideas, and work on common projects. In 1890 these local associations were brought together under the umbrella of the General Federation of Women's Clubs, which by the end of the nineteenth century counted 495 chapters and 160,000 members. By 1900 these clubs—which had initially been devoted to discussions of religion, culture, and science—began to help the needy and lobby for social justice legislation. "Since men are more or less closely absorbed in business," one club woman remarked about this civic awakening, "it has come to pass that the initiative in civic matters has devolved largely upon women." Starting out in towns and cities, club women carried their message to state and federal governments and campaigned for legislation that would establish social welfare programs for working women and their children.

In an age of strict racial segregation, African American women formed their own clubs to undertake reform activities. They sponsored day care centers, kindergartens, and work and home training projects. The activities of black club women, like those of white club women, reflected a class bias, and they tried to lift up poorer blacks to ideals of middle-class womanhood. In doing so, they challenged white supremacist notions that black women and men were incapable of raising healthy and strong families. By 1916 the National Association of Colored Women, whose motto was "lifting as we climb," boasted 1,000 clubs and 50,000 members.

White working-class women also organized, but because of employment discrimination there were few, if any, black female industrial workers to join them. Building on the settlement house movement and together with middle-class and wealthy women, working-class women founded the National Women's Trade Union League (WTUL) in 1903. The WTUL was dedicated to securing higher wages and improved working conditions, and its slogan, "The Eight-Hour Day: A Living Wage; to Guard the Home," expressed its objectives. The WTUL recognized that many women needed to earn an income to help support their families, and it backed protective legislation based on women's specific needs.

Believing women to be physically weaker than men, most female reformers advocated special legislation to protect women in the workplace. They campaigned for state laws prescribing the maximum number of hours women could work, and they succeeded in 1908 when they won a landmark victory in the Supreme Court in *Muller v. Oregon*, which upheld an Oregon law establishing a ten-hour workday for women. These reformers also convinced lawmakers in forty states to establish pensions for mothers and widows. In 1912 their focus shifted to the federal government with the founding of the Children's Bureau in the Department of Commerce and Labor. Headed by Julia Lathrop, an Addams disciple from Illinois, the bureau attracted female reformers, collected sociological data, and devised a variety of publicly funded social welfare measures. In 1916 Congress enacted a law banning child labor under the age of fourteen (it was declared unconstitutional in 1918). In 1921 Congress passed the Shepherd-Towner Act, which allowed nurses to offer maternal and infant health care information to mothers.

Not all women believed in the idea of protective legislation for women. In 1898 Charlotte Perkins Gilman published *Women and Economics*, in which she argued against the notion that women were ideally suited for domesticity. She contended that women's accepted relationship to men was unnatural. "We are the only animal species in which the female depends on the male for food," Gilman wrote, "the only animal species in which the sex relation is also the economic relation." Emphasizing the need for economic independence, Gilman advocated the establishment of communal kitchens that would free women from household chores and allow them to compete on equal terms with men in the workplace. Emma Goldman, an anarchist critic of capitalism and middle-class sexual morality, also spoke out against the kind of marriage that made women "keep their mouths shut and their wombs open." She endorsed "free love," in which women and men enjoyed sex equally. These and a growing number of other women did not consider themselves reformers so much as radicals, and even feminists—women who aspire to reach their full potential and gain access to the same opportunities as men.

Fighting for Women's Suffrage

Until 1910, women did not have the right to vote, except in a handful of western states (see chapter 15). The passage of the Fourteenth and Fifteenth Amendments had disappointed many campaigners for women's suffrage. Although the amendments extended citizenship to African Americans and protected the voting rights of black men, they left women, both white and black, ineligible to vote. The Fourteenth Amendment had underscored this distinction by specifically referring to "male inhabitants" in its provision dealing with voting for national officials (see chapter 14). Following Reconstruction, the two major organizations campaigning for women's suffrage at the state and national levels—Susan B. Anthony and Elizabeth Cady Stanton's National Woman Suffrage Association and Lucy Stone and Julia Ward Howe's American Woman Suffrage Association—failed to achieve major victories. In 1890 the two groups combined to form the National American Woman Suffrage Association, and by 1918 women could vote in fifteen states and the territory of Alaska (Map 19.1).

Suffragists included a broad coalition of supporters and based their campaign on a variety of arguments. Reformers such as Jane Addams stressed that suffrage for women would be an extension of "civic housekeeping." They attributed corruption in politics to the absence of women's maternal influence. In this way, mainstream suffragists couched their arguments within traditional conceptions of women as family nurturers. They claimed that men should not fear women's desire to vote; rather, they should see it as an expansion of traditional household duties into the public sphere. By contrast, suffragists such as Alice Paul rejected arguments stressing women's domesticity and their inherent difference from men. Paul, who had earned a Ph.D. from the University of Pennsylvania and two law degrees, asserted that women deserved the vote on the basis of their equality with men as citizens. She founded the National Woman's Party and in 1923 proposed that Congress adopt an Equal Rights Amendment to provide full legal equality to women.

Traditionalists, both male and female, fought against women's suffrage. They believed that women were best suited by nature to devote themselves to their families and leave the rough-and-tumble world of politics to men. Suffrage opponents insisted that extending the right to vote to women would destroy the home, lead to the moral degeneracy of children, and tear down the social fabric of the country.

Campaigns for women's suffrage did not apply to all women. White suffragists in the South often manipulated racial prejudice to support female enfranchisement. In the

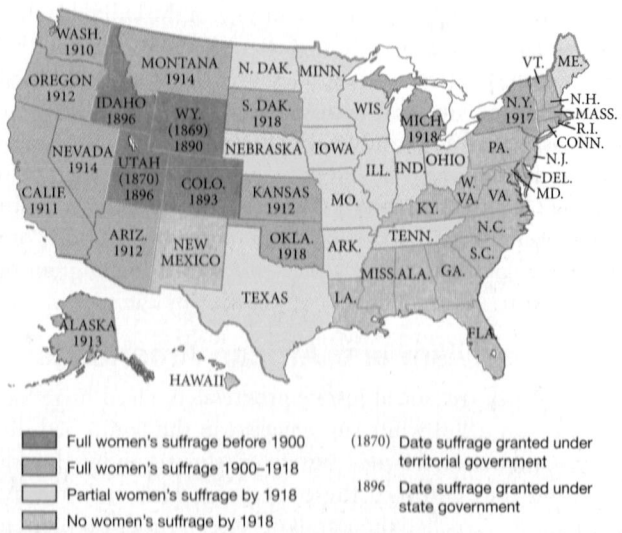

MAP 19.1

Women's Suffrage

Western states and territories were the first to approve women's suffrage. Yet even as western states enfranchised women, most placed restrictions on or excluded African American, American Indian, Mexican American, and Asian American women. States granting partial suffrage allowed women to vote only in certain contests, such as municipal or school board, primary, or presidential elections.

Full women's suffrage before 1900
Full women's suffrage 1900–1918
Partial women's suffrage by 1918
No women's suffrage by 1918

(1870) Date suffrage granted under territorial government
1896 Date suffrage granted under state government

wake of the Populist Party's efforts to recruit black voters in the 1890s, most of the former Confederate states rewrote their constitutions or enacted statutes removing African Americans from the voter rolls through the use of poll taxes, literacy tests, and grandfather clause requirements (see chapter 17). Although they did not constitute a majority, outspoken white suffragists such as Rebecca Latimer Felton from Georgia, Belle Kearney from Mississippi, and Kate Gordon from Louisiana used white supremacist arguments to make a case for white women gaining the vote. As long as even a fraction of black men voted and the Fifteenth Amendment continued to exist, they contended that allowing southern white women to vote would preserve white supremacy by offsetting black men's votes. These arguments also had a class component. Poll taxes and literacy tests disfranchised poor, uneducated whites. Extending the vote to white women would benefit mainly those in the middle class who had some education and enough family income to satisfy restrictive literacy test and poll tax requirements.

Many middle-class women outside the South used similar reasoning, but they targeted newly arrived immigrants instead of African Americans. Many Protestant women and men viewed Catholics and Jews from southern and eastern Europe as racially inferior and spiritually dangerous. They blamed such immigrants for the ills of the cities in which they congregated, and some suffragists believed that the vote of middle-class Protestant women would help clean up the mess the immigrants created. One supporter proclaimed that suffragists "had always recognized the usefulness of woman suffrage as a counterbalance to the foreign vote."

African American women challenged these racist arguments and mounted their own drive for female suffrage. If "white women needed the vote to acquire advantages and protection of their rights," Adella Hunt Logan of Tuskegee, Alabama, remarked, "then Black women needed the vote even more so." African American women had an additional incentive to press for enfranchisement. As the target of white sexual predators during slavery and its aftermath, some black women saw the vote as a way to address this problem. Although they did not gain much support from the National American Woman Suffrage Association, by 1916 African American women worked through the National Association of Colored Women and formed suffrage clubs throughout the nation.

The campaign for women's suffrage in the United States was part of an international movement. Victories in New Zealand (1893), Australia (1902), and Norway (1913) spurred on American suffragists. In the 1910s, radical American activists found inspiration in the militant tactics employed by some in the British suffrage movement. Activists such as Alice Paul conducted wide-ranging demonstrations in Washington, D.C., including chaining themselves to the gates of the White House. Although mainstream suffrage leaders denounced these new tactics, they gained much-needed publicity for the movement, which in turn aided the lobbying efforts of more moderate activists. In 1919 Congress passed the Nineteenth Amendment granting women the vote. The following year, the amendment was ratified by the states.

Progressivism and African Americans

As with suffrage, social justice progressives faced huge barriers in the fight for racial equality. By 1900 white supremacists in the South had disfranchised almost all black voters and imposed a rigid system of segregation in education and all aspects of public life, and they enforced these measures with violence. From 1880 to 1900, white supremacists lynched thousands of African Americans, often because of perceived violations of racial norms. Antiblack violence also took the form of race riots that erupted in southern cities such as Wilmington, North Carolina, and Tampa, Florida, in 1898 and Atlanta in 1906. Farther north, in Springfield, Illinois, a riot broke out in 1908 when the local sheriff tried to protect two black prisoners, one accused of raping a white woman and the other charged with murdering a white man, from a would-be lynch mob. This confrontation triggered two days of white violence against blacks, some of whom fought back, leaving twenty-four businesses and forty homes destroyed and seven people (two blacks and five whites) dead.

As the situation for African Americans deteriorated, black leaders responded in several ways. Booker T. Washington espoused an approach that his critics called accommodation but that he defended as practical. Born a slave and emancipated at age nine, Washington attended Hampton Institute in his home state of Virginia. Run by sympathetic whites, the school considered moral training its top priority. In their view, because slavery had hindered black advancement, African Americans would first have to build up their character and accept the virtues of abstinence, thrift, and industriousness before seeking a more intellectual education. In 1881 Washington founded **Tuskegee Institute** in Alabama, which he modeled on Hampton. In 1895 white business and civic leaders invited Washington to deliver an address at a cotton exposition held in Atlanta. The black educator received an enthusiastic reception for his message urging African Americans to remain in the South, accept racial segregation, concentrate on moral and economic development, and avoid politics. At the same time, he called on white leaders to fulfill their part of the bargain by protecting blacks from the growing violence directed at them.

White leaders in both the South and the North embraced Washington, and he became the most powerful African American of his generation. He secured philanthropic contributions from white benefactors for Tuskegee and other schools he favored. He had considerable influence over leading black newspapers and in 1900 organized the National Negro Business League. Although he discouraged public protests against segregation, he emphasized racial pride and solidarity among African Americans. "We are a nation within a nation," he commented, and "[we must] see to it that in every wise and legitimate way our people are taught to patronize racial enterprises." Yet Washington was a complex figure, who secretly financed and supported court challenges to electoral disfranchisement, railroad segregation, jury discrimination, and peonage (forced labor to repay debt).

Washington's enormous power did not discourage opposing views among African Americans. Ida B. Wells, like Washington, had been born a slave. In 1878, at age sixteen, Wells lost her parents in a yellow fever epidemic that swept through her hometown in Mississippi. To support her five siblings, she took a job in Memphis as a teacher. Six years later, Wells sued the Chesapeake & Ohio Railroad for moving her from the first-class "Ladies Coach" to the segregated smoking car because she was black. She won her case in the lower court, but her victory was reversed by the Tennessee Supreme Court. Undeterred, she began writing for the *Free Speech* newspaper, in which she owned a one-third interest. When her articles exposing injustices in the Memphis school system got her fired from teaching, she took up journalism full-time.

Unlike Washington, Wells believed that black leaders had to speak out vigorously against racial inequality and lynching. From 1885 to 1900, approximately 2,500 people were lynched, most of them southern blacks. One lynching took place in Memphis on March 9, 1892, when three black men were murdered by a white mob. The victims had operated a grocery store that had become the target of hostility from white competitors, who forcibly tried to put it out of business. In response, the black businessmen resisted an assault by armed whites and shot three of them in self-defense. Wells applauded the black store owners' actions. As she wrote, "When the white man . . . knows he runs as great a risk of biting the dust every time his Afro-American victim does, he will have greater respect for Afro-American life." Subsequently arrested for their armed resistance, the three men were snatched from jail and lynched.

In response to Wells's articles about the Memphis lynching, a white mob burned down her newspaper's building. She fled to Chicago, where she continued to investigate the issue of lynching. In a report she published, she refuted the myth that the rape of white women by black men was the leading cause of lynching and asserted that evidence of such crimes was scarce. She concluded that racists used this brand of extralegal violence to ensure that African Americans would not challenge white supremacy. Wells took her campaign throughout the North and to Europe, where she gave lectures condemning lynching. She also joined the drive for women's suffrage, which she hoped would give black women a chance to use their votes to help combat racial injustice.

W. E. B. Du Bois also rejected Washington's accommodationist stance and urged blacks to demand first-class citizenship. In contrast to Washington and Wells, Du Bois had not experienced slavery. His ancestors were free blacks, and he grew up in Great Barrington, Massachusetts. Educated at Fisk University, a black institution, he transferred to Harvard and earned a Ph.D. in history. In 1899 he published *The Philadelphia Negro*, the first scientific study of the plight of blacks in urban America—a scholarly counterpart to the emerging investigative literature that fueled progressive reform. Du Bois agreed with Washington about advocating self-help as a means for advancement, but he did not believe this effort would succeed without a proper education and equal voting rights. In *The Souls of Black Folk* (1903), Du Bois argued that African Americans needed a liberal arts education, in the tradition of Fisk and Harvard, rather than the manual training and industrial arts curriculum at Tuskegee. Du Bois contended that a classical, humanistic education would produce a cadre of leaders, the "Talented Tenth," who would guide African Americans to the next stage of their development. Rather than forgoing immediate political rights, as Washington advocated, African American leaders should demand the universal right to vote. Only then, Du Bois contended, would African Americans gain equality, self-respect, and dignity as a race.

Du Bois was an intellectual who put his ideas into action. In 1905 he spearheaded the creation of the Niagara Movement, a group that first met on the Canadian side of Niagara Falls because participants could not find accommodations open to blacks in Buffalo, New York. The all-black organization demanded the vote and equal access to public facilities for African Americans. By 1909 internal squabbling and a shortage of funds had crippled the group. That same year, however, Du Bois became involved in the creation of an organization that would shape the fight for racial equality throughout the twentieth century: the **National Association for the Advancement of Colored People (NAACP)**. In addition to Du Bois, Ida B. Wells, and veterans of the Niagara Movement, white activists played leading roles in forming the organization. They included Jane Addams; Mary White Ovington, a settlement house worker in Brooklyn; and William English Walling, a social worker, socialist, and cofounder of the Women's Trade Union League. The descendants of white abolitionists also contributed significantly to the birth of the group. Of the fifty-two white signers of the document calling for the creation of the NAACP, fifteen were former abolitionists or their descendants. Beginning in 1910, the NAACP initiated court cases challenging racially discriminatory voting practices and other forms of bias in housing and criminal justice. Its first victory came in 1915, when its lawyers convinced the Supreme Court to strike down the grandfather clause that discriminated against black voters (*Guinn v. United States*).

African Americans also pursued social justice initiatives outside the realm of politics. Southern blacks remained committed to securing a quality education for their children after whites failed to live up to their responsibilities under *Plessy v. Ferguson*. Governor James K. Vardaman of Mississippi, who served from 1904 to 1908, expressed the prevailing racist sentiment: "Education only spoils a good field hand and makes a shyster lawyer or a fourth-rate teacher. It is money thrown away." Black schools remained inferior to white schools, and African Americans did not receive a fair return from their tax dollars; in fact, a large portion of their payments helped subsidize white schools. To raise money for books, buildings, and teacher salaries, blacks voluntarily taxed themselves in addition to the property taxes they were required to pay the county to support schools. Du Bois calculated that black Mississippians paid 113 percent of the costs of their own schools through double taxation.

Black women played a prominent role in promoting education. For example, Charlotte Hawkins Brown, born in North Carolina and educated in Massachusetts, returned to her home state in 1901 and set up the Palmer Memorial Institute outside of Greensboro. In these endeavors, black educators received financial assistance from northern philanthropists, white club women interested in moral uplift of the black race, and religious missionaries seeking converts in the South. By 1910 more than 1.5 million black children went to school in the South, most of them taught by the region's 28,560 black teachers. Thirty-four black colleges existed, and more than 2,000 African Americans held college degrees.

REVIEW & RELATE

• What role did women play in the early-twentieth-century fight for social justice?

• How did social reformers challenge discrimination against women and minorities?

Morality and Social Control

In many cases, progressive initiatives crossed over from social reform into social control. Convinced that the "immorality" of the poor was the cause of social disorder, some reformers sought to impose middle-class standards of behavior and morality on the lower classes. As with other forms of progressivism, progressives interested in social control were driven by a variety of motives. However, regardless of their motives, efforts to prohibit alcohol, fight prostitution, and combat juvenile delinquency often involved attempts to repress and control the poor. Some social control progressives went even further in their effort to impose their own morality, calling for restrictions on immigration, particularly from southern and eastern Europe and Asia. Anti-immigration advocates viewed cultural and religious differences as a threat and sought to prevent such people from becoming part of American society in the first place.

Prohibition

Prohibition campaigns began long before the Civil War but scored few important successes until after 1865. In 1869 anti-alcohol forces established the Prohibition Party, and in 1881 Kansas became the first state whose constitution banned the consumption of alcohol. Women spearheaded the prohibition movement by forming the **Woman's Christian Temperance Union (WCTU)** in 1874. Frances Willard headed the group from 1879 until her death in 1898. Willard held a broad view of temperance reform that grew from religious, moral, and social justice convictions. Under her direction, the WCTU and its nationwide chapters supported women's suffrage, laws to end child labor, and labor unions. Willard built the temperance movement around the need to protect the home. Husbands and fathers who drank excessively were also likely to abuse their wives and children and to drain the family finances. Prohibiting the consumption of alcohol would, therefore, help combat these evils. At the same time, the quality of family and public life would be improved if women received the right to vote and young children completed their education without having to go to work. Although Willard died before progressive reform had gained momentum, she influenced activists such as Jane Addams. However, with her death, WCTU leaders withdrew from supporting broad social reforms and concentrated instead on the single issue of temperance.

At the turn of the twentieth century, the Anti-Saloon League (ASL) became the dominant force in the prohibition movement. Established in 1893, the league grew out of evangelical Protestantism, with Baptists and Methodists leading the way. The group had particular appeal in the rural South, where Protestant fundamentalism flourished. Between 1906 and 1917, twenty-one states, mostly in the South and West, banned liquor sales. However, concern over alcohol was not confined to the South. Middle-class progressives in northern cities, who identified much of urban decay with the influx of immigrants, saw the tavern as a breeding ground for immoral activities. In 1913 the ASL convinced Congress to pass the Webb-Kenyon Act, which banned the transportation of alcoholic beverages into dry states. After the United States entered World War I in 1917, reformers argued that prohibition would help win the war by conserving grain used to make liquor and by saving soldiers from intoxication. The Eighteenth Amendment, ratified in 1919, made prohibition the law of the land.

The Crusade against Vice

Alarmed by the expansion in the number of brothels and "streetwalkers" that accompanied the growth of cities, progressives sought to eliminate prostitution. Some framed the issue in terms of public health, linking prostitution to the spread of sexually transmitted diseases. Others presented the crusade as an effort to protect female virtue. In 1907 the muckraking *McClure's Magazine*, reporting on the spread of prostitution in Chicago, contended that many of the women were victims of "white slavery" and had been forced into prostitution against their will. Such reformers were generally interested only in white women, who, unlike African American and Asian women in similar circumstances, were considered sexual innocents coerced into prostitution. Still others claimed that prostitutes themselves were to blame, seeing women who sold their sexual favors as inherently immoral.

Reformers offered two different approaches to the problem. Taking the moralistic solution, Representative James R. Mann of Chicago steered through Congress the White Slave Trade Act in 1910, banning the transportation of women across state lines for immoral purposes. This legislation became known as the Mann Act after its sponsor. By contrast, the American Social Hygiene Association, founded in 1914, subsidized scientific research into sexually transmitted diseases, funded investigations to gather more information, and drafted model ordinances for cities to curb prostitution. By 1915 every state had laws making sexual solicitation a crime. The United States' entry into World War I further helped curtail prostitution; brothels near military bases were closed because reformers argued that soldiers' health was at risk.

Prosecutors used the Mann Act to enforce codes of traditional racial as well as sexual behavior. In 1910 Jack Johnson, an African American boxer, defeated the white heavyweight champion, Jim Jeffries. Black Americans took great pride in his triumph, while his victory upset some white men who were obsessed with preserving their racial dominance and masculine integrity. Johnson's relationships with white women further angered some whites, who eventually succeeded in bringing down the outspoken, black champion by prosecuting him on morals charges in 1913.

Moral crusaders also sought to eliminate the use and sale of narcotics. By 1900 approximately 250,000 people in the United States were addicted to opium, morphine, or cocaine—far fewer, however, than those who abused alcohol. Patent medicines, such as "Mrs. Winslow's Soothing Syrup," a remedy for crying babies, contained diluted amounts of opium, and cocaine was an ingredient in Coca-Cola until 1903. On the West Coast, immigration opponents associated opium smoking with the Chinese and tried to eliminate its use as part of their wider anti-Asian campaign. In alliance with the American Medical Association, which had a professional stake in the issue, reformers convinced Congress to pass the Harrison Narcotics Control Act of 1914, prohibiting the sale of narcotics except by a doctor's prescription.

Progressives also tried to combat juvenile delinquency. Led by women, these reformers lobbied for a juvenile court system that focused on reha-bilitation rather than punishment for youthful offenders. Judge Ben Lindsay of Denver, Colorado, removed delinquents from dysfunctional

The Crusade against White Slavery Published by Clifford B. Roe and B. S. Steadwell in 1911, *The Great War on White Slavery* campaigned against prostitution and the criminals who lured impoverished young women into what they called "the human stockyards . . . for girls." As an assistant state's attorney in Chicago, Roe prosecuted more than 150 cases against sex traffickers. He exemplified progressivism's moral reform impulse.
© Mary Evans Picture Library/The Image Works

homes and made them wards of the state. Despite progressives' sincerity, many youthful offenders doubted their intentions. Young women often appeared before a magistrate because their parents did not like their choice of friends, their sexual conduct, or their frequenting dance halls and saloons. These activities, which violated middle-class social norms, had now become criminalized, even if in a less coercive and punitive manner than that applied to adults.

Immigration Restriction

Moral reformers tended to perceive immigrants as innately predisposed to vice. As a result, some reformers sought to restrict immigration. Anti-immigrant sentiment often reflected racial and religious bigotry, as reformers concentrated on preventing Catholics, Jews, and all non-Europeans from entering the United States. Social scientists validated these prejudices by categorizing darker-skinned immigrants as inferior races. The harshest treatment was reserved for Asians. In 1882 Congress passed the Chinese Exclusion Act (see chapter 15), and in 1908 President Theodore Roosevelt entered into an executive agreement with Japan that reduced Japanese immigration to the United States. For many Californians, this agreement was not strict enough. In 1913 the state legislature passed a statute barring Japanese immigrants from buying land, a law that twelve other states subsequently enacted.

In 1917 reformers succeeded in further restricting immigration. Congress passed legislation to ban illiterates who could not read English or their native language from entering the country. The act also denied entry to other undesirables: "alcoholics," "feeble-minded persons," "epileptics," "people mentally or physically defective," "professional beggars," "anarchists," and "polygamists." In barring those considered unfit to enter the country, lawmakers intended to keep out those who could not support themselves and might become a public ward of the state and, in the case of anarchists and polygamists, people who threatened the nation's political and religious values.

 Online Document Project **Progressivism and Social Control** **bedfordstmartins.com/hewittlawsonvalue**

REVIEW & RELATE

• What practices and behaviors of the poor did social control progressives find most alarming? Why?

• What role did anti-immigrant sentiment play in motivating and shaping progressives' social control initiatives?

Good Government Progressivism

In an effort to diminish the power of corrupt urban political machines and unregulated corporations, progressives pushed for good government reforms, promoting initiatives they claimed would produce greater efficiency, openness, and accountability in government. Many of the progressives' proposed reforms appeared, at least on the surface, to give citizens more direct say in their government; however, a closer look reveals a more complicated picture.

Municipal and State Reform

Cities were at the forefront of government reform during the Progressive Era. Antiquated systems of municipal rule failed to keep up with the problems ushered in by immigration and accelerated urban growth. Political machines distributed city services to meet skyrocketing demands within a system bloated by corruption and graft (see chapter 18). Upper-middle-class businessmen and professionals fed up with wasteful and inefficient political machines sought to institute new forms of government that functioned more rationally and cost less.

The adoption of the commission form of government was a hallmark of urban reform. The idea originally came from the South in response to a hurricane in 1900 that destroyed the Texas Gulf coast city of Galveston and disabled its local government. Municipal leaders faced the crisis by establishing a commission composed of five men to operate the government. They replaced the old form of a mayor and city council with elected commissioners, each of whom ran a municipal department as if it were a business. By 1917 the commission form of government had spread to more than four hundred cities throughout the country. Governments with a mayor and city council also began to appoint city managers, who functioned as chief operating officers, to foster businesslike efficiency. The head of the National Cash Register Company, who helped bring the city manager system to Dayton, Ohio, praised it for resembling "a great business enterprise whose stockholders are the people."

To help overturn political machines, reformers adopted direct primaries so that voters could select candidates rather than allowing a handful of politicians to decide elections behind closed doors. Urban bosses had thrived on decentralized ward elections. To reverse the influence of immigrants clustered in ghettos who supported their own ethnic candidates and to topple the machines that catered to them, municipal reformers replaced district elections with citywide "at-large" elections. Ethnic enclaves lost not only their ward representatives but also a good deal of their influence because citywide election campaigns were expensive, shifting power to those who could afford to run. Good government progressives equated efficiency and honesty with democracy; however, rather than extending democracy to immigrant groups and racial minorities, these changes had the opposite effect. Working- and lower-class residents of cities still retained the right to vote, but their power was diluted.

In the South, where fewer immigrants lived, white supremacists employed these tactics to build on steps taken in the late nineteenth century to disfranchise African Americans. Southern lawmakers diminished whatever black political power remained by adopting at-large elections and commission governments. Throughout the South, direct primary contests (or "white primaries") were closed to blacks.

If urban progressivism fell short of putting democratic ideals into practice, it did produce a number of mayors who carried out genuine reforms. As Frederic C. Howe, a key adviser to Cleveland mayor Tom L. Johnson, observed, "The challenge of the city has become one of decent human existence." Elected in 1901, Johnson implemented measures to assess taxes more equitably, regulate utility companies, and reduce public transportation fares. Samuel "Golden Rule" Jones, who served as Toledo's mayor from 1897 to 1903, supported social justice measures by establishing an eight-hour workday for municipal employees, granting them paid vacations, and prohibiting child labor. Under Mayor Hazen Pingree, who served from 1889 to 1896, Detroit constructed additional schools and recreational facilities and put the unemployed to work on municipal projects during economic hard times.

Progressives also took action at the state level. Robert M. La Follette, Republican governor of Wisconsin from 1901 to 1906, led the way by initiating a range of reforms to improve the performance of state government and increase its accountability to constituents. During his tenure as governor, La Follette dismantled the statewide political machine by instituting direct party primaries, an expanded civil service, a law forbidding direct corporate contributions to political parties, a strengthened railroad regulatory commission, and a graduated income tax. In 1906 La Follette entered the U.S. Senate, where he battled for further reform.

Governors in other states picked up and expanded La Follette's progressive agenda. In New York, Governor Charles Evans Hughes implemented measures to regulate insurance companies and public utilities. In New Jersey, Governor Woodrow Wilson sought reforms similar to those in Wisconsin. On the West Coast, California's reform governor Hiram Johnson challenged the powerful Southern Pacific Railroad. In 1913 three-quarters of the states ratified the Seventeenth Amendment, which mandated that U.S. senators would be elected by popular vote, instead of being chosen by state legislatures. This constituted another effort to remove the influence of money from politics.

Conservation and Preservation of the Environment

The penchant for efficiency that characterized good government progressivism also shaped progressive efforts to conserve natural resources. As chief forester in the Department of Agriculture, Gifford Pinchot emphasized the efficient use of resources and sought ways to reconcile the public interest with private profit motives. His approach often won support from large lumber companies, which had a long-term interest in sustainable forests. Large companies also saw conservation as a way to drive their smaller competitors out of business, as large companies could better afford the additional costs associated with managing healthy forests.

This gospel of efficiency faced a stiff test in California. After the devastating earthquake of 1906, San Francisco officials, coping with water and power shortages, asked the federal government to approve construction of a hydroelectric dam and reservoir in **Hetch Hetchy valley**, located in Yosemite National Park. The pragmatic Pinchot supported the project because he saw it as the best use of the land for the greatest number of people. The famed naturalist John Muir, who had spearheaded the establishment of Yosemite, strongly disagreed. He campaigned to save Hetch Hetchy from "ravaging commercialism" and warned against choosing economic gains over spiritual values. "Dam Hetch Hetchy!" Muir exclaimed. "As well dam for water-tanks the people's cathedrals and churches, for no holier temple has ever been consecrated by the heart of man." After a bruising seven-year battle, Pinchot (by this time a private citizen) triumphed. Still, this incursion into a national park, the first since the system was initiated in 1872 with Yellowstone National Park, helped spur the development of environmentalism as a political movement.

Besides the clash with preservationists, the Hetch Hetchy Dam project reveals another aspect of the progressive conservation movement. Like progressives who focused on urban and political issues, progressive conservationists had a racial bias. Conservationists such as Pinchot may have seen themselves as acting in the public interest, but their definition of "the public" did not include all Americans. In planning for the Hetch Hetchy Dam, progressives did not consult with the Mono Lake Paiutes who lived in Yosemite and who were most directly affected by the project. Conservation was meant to serve the interests of white San Franciscans and not those of the Indian inhabitants of Yosemite.

REVIEW & RELATE

• Who gained and who lost political influence as a result of progressive reforms?

• How did a commitment to greater efficiency shape progressives' political and environmental initiatives?

Presidential Progressivism

The problems created by industrialization and the growth of big business were national in scope. No municipal or state government had the authority, power, and finances to address issues that transcended political boundaries and affected people throughout the country. Recognizing this fact, prominent progressives sought national leadership positions. Two of the three early-twentieth-century presidents, Theodore Roosevelt and Woodrow Wilson, instituted progressive reforms during their terms. In the process, they reinvigorated the presidency, an office that had declined in power and importance during the late nineteenth century.

Theodore Roosevelt and the Square Deal

Born into a moderately wealthy New York family, Theodore Roosevelt graduated from Harvard in 1880 and entered government service. Appointed by William McKinley as assistant secretary of the navy in 1897, Roosevelt left his post the following year to form a regiment of soldiers—the "Rough Riders"—and fought in Cuba against Spanish forces. In 1898 voters in New York sent the popular war hero to Albany as the new Republican governor. Elected as William McKinley's vice president in 1900, Roosevelt became president after McKinley's assassination a year later.

Roosevelt brought an activist style to the presidency. Rather than seeing himself as merely administering the nation's business, he considered his office a **bully pulpit**—a platform from which to promote his programs and from which he could rally public opinion. To this end, he used his energetic and extroverted personality to establish an unprecedented rapport with the American people, providing newspaper reporters with a limitless supply of colorful stories about his life and exploits.

For all his exuberance and energy, President Roosevelt pursued a moderate domestic course. Like his progressive colleagues, he opposed ideological extremism in any form. Rather than promoting any particular cause, Roosevelt believed that as head of state he could serve as an impartial arbiter among competing factions and determine what was best for the public. Reform was, in his view, the best defense against revolution.

As president, Roosevelt sought to provide economic and political stability, what he referred to as a "Square Deal." He insisted that "a republic such as ours can exist only by virtue of the orderly liberty which comes through the equal domination of the law over all men alike." The coal strike that began in Pennsylvania in 1902 gave Roosevelt an opportunity to play the role of impartial mediator and defender of the public good.

Miners had gone on strike for an eight-hour workday, a pay increase of 20 percent, and recognition of their union. Roosevelt sympathized with the plight of the workers, but he was more concerned that a prolonged strike would choke the supply of heating fuel to consumers as winter approached. Union representatives agreed to have the president create a panel to settle the dispute, but George F. Baer, president of the Reading Railroad, which also owned the mines, pledged that he would never agree to the workers' demands. Disturbed by what he considered the owners' "arrogant stupidity," Roosevelt threatened to dispatch federal troops to take over and run the mines. When the owners backed down, the president established a commission that hammered out a compromise giving the strikers a 10 percent wage hike and a reduction of the workday to nine hours, but not union recognition.

At the same time, Roosevelt used his executive authority to tackle the problems caused by giant business trusts. In February 1902, the president instructed the Justice Department to sue the Northern Securities Company under the Sherman Antitrust Act (see chapter 16), a law that had rarely been used against big business since its passage in 1890. Northern Securities held monopoly control of the northernmost transcontinental railway lines. The powerful financier behind Northern Securities, J. P. Morgan, believed that he could do business with Roosevelt as he had with previous presidents. "Send your man to my man and they can fix it up," Morgan informed Roosevelt. However, the president's man at the Justice Department responded: "We don't want to fix it up, we want to stop it." In 1904 the Supreme Court ordered that the Northern Securities Company be dissolved, ruling that the firm had restricted competition. With this victory, Roosevelt affirmed the federal government's power to regulate business trusts that violated the public interest. Overall, Roosevelt initiated twenty-five suits under the Sherman Antitrust Act, including litigation against the tobacco and beef trusts and the Standard Oil Company, actions that earned him the title of "trustbuster."

Roosevelt distinguished between "good" trusts, which acted responsibly, and "bad" trusts, which abused their power and hurt consumers. Railroads had earned an especially bad reputation with the public for charging higher rates to small shippers and those in remote regions while granting rebates to favored customers, such as Standard Oil. In 1903 Roosevelt helped persuade Congress to pass the Elkins Act, which outlawed railroad rebates. Three years later, the president increased the power of the Interstate Commerce Commission to set maximum railroad freight rates. In 1903 Roosevelt also secured passage of legislation that established the Department of Commerce and Labor. Within this cabinet agency, the Bureau of Corporations gathered information about large companies in an effort to promote fair business practices.

Soaring in popularity, Roosevelt ran for president in 1904 and easily defeated the Democratic nominee, Judge Alton B. Parker. During the next four years, the president applied antitrust laws even more vigorously than before. He steered through Congress various reforms concerning the railroads, such as the Hepburn Act (1906), which standardized shipping rates, and took a strong stand for conservation of public lands. Roosevelt charted a middle course between preservationists and conservationists. He reserved 150 million acres of timberland as part of the national forests, an action that delighted the preservationists. At the same time, he authorized the expenditure of more than $80 million in federal funds to construct dams, reservoirs, canals, and other conservation projects, largely in the West.

Not all reform came from Roosevelt's initiative. Congress passed two notable consumer laws in 1906 that reflected the multiple and sometimes contradictory forces that shaped progressivism. That year, Upton Sinclair published *The Jungle*, a muckraking novel that portrayed the impoverished lives of immigrant workers in Packingtown (Chicago) and the deplorable working conditions they endured. Outraged readers responded to the vivid description of the shoddy and filthy ways the meatpacking industry slaughtered animals and prepared beef for sale. The book revealed in grisly detail how the meat cut up for sausage "would be dosed with borax and glycerine, and dumped into hoppers, and made over again for home consumption." The largest and most efficient meatpacking firms had financial reasons to support reform as well. They were losing money because European importers refused to purchase tainted meat. Congress responded by passing the Meat Inspection Act, which benefited consumers and provided a way for large corporations to eliminate competition from smaller, marginal firms that could not afford to raise standards to meet the new federal meat-processing requirements.

In 1906 Congress also passed the Pure Food and Drug Act, which prohibited the sale of adulterated and fraudulently labeled food and drugs. The impetus for this law came from consumer groups, medical professionals, and government scientists. Dr. Harvey Wiley, a chemist in the Department of Agriculture, drove efforts for reform from within the government. He considered it part of his professional duty to eliminate harmful products (Table 19.1).

TABLE 19.1   National Progressive Legislation

1903	Department of Commerce and Labor established to promote fair business practices
1906	Pure Food and Drug Act
	Meat Inspection Act; Hepburn Act
1910	White Slave Trade Act
1913	Underwood Act reduces tariffs to benefit farmers
	Sixteenth Amendment (graduated income tax)
	Seventeenth Amendment (election of senators by popular vote)
	Federal Reserve System
1914	Harrison Narcotics Control Act
	Federal Trade Commission
	Clayton Antitrust Act
1916	Adamson Act provides eight-hour workday for railroad workers
	Keating-Owen Act outlaws child labor in firms engaged in interstate commerce
	Workmen's Compensation Act
1919	Eighteenth Amendment (prohibition)
1920	Nineteenth Amendment (women's suffrage)

Roosevelt initially gave African Americans reason to believe that they, too, would get a square deal. In October 1901, at the outset of his first term, Roosevelt invited Booker T. Washington to a dinner at the White House. White supremacists in the South denounced the social gathering as a "damnable outrage." Though Roosevelt dismissed this criticism, he never invited another black guest. Also in his first term, Roosevelt supported the appointment of a few black Republicans to federal posts in the South. When segregationist whites chased Minnie Cox from her job as postmistress of Indianola, Mississippi, Roosevelt refused to accept her resignation and closed the post office.

Nevertheless, Roosevelt lacked a commitment to black equality and espoused the racist ideas of eugenics then in fashion (see chapter 18). He deplored the declining birthrate of native-born white Americans compared with that of eastern and southern European newcomers and African Americans, whom he considered inferior stock. He argued that unless Anglo-Saxon women produced more children, whites would end up committing "race suicide." "If the women flinch from breeding," Roosevelt worried, "the . . . death of the race takes place even quicker." Roosevelt never wavered in his belief in the superiority of the white race over people of color.

Once he won reelection in 1904, Roosevelt had less political incentive to defy the white South. He stopped cooperating with southern black officeholders and maneuvered to build the Republican Party in the region with all-white support. However, his most reprehensible action involved an incident that occurred in Brownsville, Texas, in 1906. White residents of the town charged that black soldiers stationed at Fort Brown shot up the main street, killing one man and wounding another. Roosevelt ordered that unless the perpetrators stepped forward, the entire regiment would receive dishonorable discharges without a court-martial. Roosevelt never doubted the guilt of the black soldiers, and when no one admitted responsibility, he summarily dismissed 167 men from the military. Although the president spoke out against the brutality of lynching blacks in the South, he participated in this mass "legal lynching" of African American soldiers.

Taft Retreats from Progressivism

When Roosevelt decided not to seek another term as president in 1908, choosing instead to back William Howard Taft as his successor, he thought he was leaving his reform legacy in capable hands. A Roosevelt loyalist and an Ohio native, Taft had compiled a distinguished record as a federal judge, solicitor general of the United States, governor of the Philippines, and secretary of war. Taft easily defeated the Democratic candidate, William Jennings Bryan, who was running for the presidency for the third and final time.

Taft's presidency did not proceed as Roosevelt and his progressive followers had hoped. Taft did not have the charisma or energy of his predecessor and appeared to move in slow motion compared with Roosevelt. More important, the new president, in contrast to Roosevelt, had a narrower view of the scope of his office and its power to shape public opinion. Taft proved a weak leader and frequently took stands opposite to those of progressives. After convening a special session of Congress in March 1909 to support lower tariffs, a progressive issue, the president retreated in the face of conservative Republican opposition in the Senate. That year, when lawmakers passed the Payne-Aldrich tariff, which raised duties on imports, Taft signed it into law, thereby alienating key progressive legislators such as Senator Robert M. La Follette. The president also remained aloof from the fight by House insurgents to curb the dictatorial powers of Speaker Joseph Cannon, a foe of reform.

The situation deteriorated even further in the field of conservation, which was close to Roosevelt's heart. When Pinchot criticized Taft's secretary of the interior, Richard Ballinger, for returning restricted Alaskan coal mines to private mining companies in 1910, Taft fired Pinchot. Taft did not oppose conservation—he transferred more land from private to public control than did Roosevelt—but his dismissal of Pinchot angered conservationists.

Even more harmful to Taft's political fortunes, Roosevelt turned against his hand-picked successor. After returning from a hunting safari in Africa and a speaking tour of Europe in 1910, Roosevelt became increasingly troubled by Taft's missteps. The loss of the House of Representatives to the Democrats in the 1910 elections highlighted the split among Republicans that had developed under Taft. A year later, relations between the ex-president and the incumbent further deteriorated when Roosevelt attacked Taft for filing antitrust litigation against U.S. Steel for a deal that the Roosevelt administration had approved in 1907. Ironically, Roosevelt, known as a trustbuster, believed that filing more lawsuits under the Sherman Antitrust Act yielded diminishing returns, whereas Taft, the conservative, initiated more antitrust litigation than did Roosevelt.

The Election of 1912

Convinced that only he could heal the party breach, Roosevelt announced that he would run for the 1912 Republican presidential nomination. However, despite Roosevelt's widespread popularity among rank-and-file Republicans, Taft still controlled the party machinery and the majority of convention delegates. Losing to Taft on the first ballot, an embittered but optimistic Roosevelt formed a third party to sponsor his run for the presidency. Roosevelt excitedly told thousands of supporters gathered in Chicago, including Jane Addams and Gifford Pinchot, that he felt "as strong as a bull moose," which became the nickname for Roosevelt's new **Progressive Party**.

In accepting the nomination of his new party, Roosevelt articulated the philosophy of **New Nationalism**. He argued that the federal government should use its considerable power to fight against the forces of special privilege and for social justice for the majority of Americans. To this end, the Progressive Party platform advocated income and inheritance taxes, an eight-hour workday, the abolition of child labor, workers' compensation, fewer restrictions on labor unions, and women's suffrage. This last plank mobilized the efforts of women throughout the country who, like Jane Addams, supported the party that she said "pledged itself to the protection of children, to the care of the aged, to the relief of overworked girls, to the safeguarding of burdened men."

Roosevelt was not the only progressive candidate in the contest. The Democrats nominated Woodrow Wilson, the reform governor of New Jersey. The son of a Presbyterian minister, Wilson had the moral conviction of a pastor who knew what was best for his flock. As an alternative to Roosevelt's New Nationalism, Wilson offered his **New Freedom**. As a Democrat and a southerner (he was born in Virginia), Wilson had a more limited view of government than did the Republican Roosevelt. Wilson envisioned a society of small businesses, with the government's role confined to ensuring open competition among businesses and freedom for individuals to make the best use of their opportunities. Unlike Roosevelt's New Nationalism, Wilson's New Freedom did not embrace social reform and rejected federal action in support of women's suffrage and the elimination of child labor.

If voters considered either Roosevelt's or Wilson's brand of reform too mainstream, they could cast their ballots for Eugene V. Debs, the Socialist Party candidate who had been imprisoned for his leadership in the Pullman strike (see chapter 17). He favored overthrowing capitalism through peaceful, democratic methods and replacing it with government ownership of business and industry for the benefit of the working class.

The Republican Party split decided the outcome of the election. The final results gave Roosevelt 27 percent of the popular vote and Taft 23 percent. Together they had a majority, but because they were divided, Wilson became president, with 42 percent of the popular vote and 435 electoral votes. Finishing fourth, Debs did not win any electoral votes, but he garnered around a million popular votes (6 percent). Counting the votes for Wilson, Roosevelt, and Debs, the American electorate overwhelmingly cast their ballots for reform.

Online Document Project
The New Nationalism, the New Freedom, and the Election of 1912
bedfordstmartins.com/hewittlawsonvalue

Woodrow Wilson and the New Freedom Agenda

Once in office, Wilson hurried to fulfill his New Freedom agenda. Even though he differed from Roosevelt about the scope of federal intervention, both men believed in a strong presidency. An admirer of the British parliamentary system, Wilson viewed the president as an active and strong leader whose job was to provide his party with a legislative program. The 1912 elections had given the Democrats control over Congress, and Wilson expected his party to support his New Freedom measures.

Tariff reduction came first. The Underwood Act of 1913 reduced import duties, a measure that appealed to southern and midwestern farmers who sought lower prices on the manufactured goods they bought that were subject to the tariff. The law also incorporated a reform that progressives had adopted from the Populists: the graduated income tax (tax rates that increase at higher levels of income). The ratification of the Sixteenth Amendment in 1913 provided the legal basis for the income tax after the Supreme Court had previously declared such a levy unconstitutional. The graduated income tax was meant to advance the cause of social justice by moderating income inequality. The need to recover revenues lost from lower tariffs provided an additional practical impetus for imposing the tax. Because the law exempted people earning less than $4,000 a year from paying the income tax, more than 90 percent of Americans owed no tax. Those with incomes exceeding this amount paid rates ranging from 1 percent to 6 percent on $500,000 or more.

Also in 1913, Wilson pressed Congress to consider banking reform. As chronic debtors who had to borrow against next year's crops, farmers favored a system supervised by the government that afforded them an ample supply of credit at low interest rates. Eastern bankers wanted reforms that would stabilize a system plagued by cyclical financial panics, the most recent in 1907, while keeping the banking system under the

Woodrow Wilson and William Howard Taft   This photograph shows Woodrow Wilson (left) on inauguration day in 1913 with his predecessor, William Howard Taft. Taft, a Republican, had disappointed progressives, especially Theodore Roosevelt, during his one term in office. Wilson, a Democrat, would expand progressive reforms from 1913 to 1917. Not considered a jovial man, Wilson is seen here enjoying himself as he takes office.   Library of Congress

private control of bankers. The resulting compromise created the Federal Reserve System. The act established twelve regional banks. These banks lent cash reserves to member banks in their districts at a "rediscount rate," a rate that could be adjusted according to the fluctuating demand for credit. Federal Reserve notes (paper money insured by the government) also became the medium of exchange and the foundation for a uniform currency. The Federal Reserve Board, appointed by the president and headquartered in Washington, D.C., supervised the system. Nevertheless, as with other progressive agencies, the experts selected to oversee the new banking system came from within the banking industry itself. Although farmers won a more rational and flexible credit supply, Wall Street bankers retained considerable power over the operation of the Federal Reserve System.

Next, President Wilson took two steps designed to help resolve the problem of economic concentration. First, in 1914 he persuaded Congress to create the Federal Trade Commission. Although the agency replaced Roosevelt's Bureau of Corporations, it pursued basically the same approach that Roosevelt had favored. The commission had the power to investigate corporate activities and prohibit "unfair" practices (which the law left undefined). Wilson's second measure directly attacked monopolies. Enacted in 1914, the Clayton Antitrust Law strengthened the Sherman Antitrust

Act by banning certain corporate operations, such as price discrimination and over-lapping membership on company boards, which undermined economic competition. The statute also exempted labor unions from prosecution under antitrust legislation, reversing the policy initiated by the federal government in the wake of the Pullman strike (see chapter 17).

By the end of his second year in office, Wilson had achieved most of his New Freedom objectives. Political considerations, however, soon forced him to widen his progressive agenda and support measures he had previously rejected. With the Republican Party once again united after the electoral fiasco of 1912, Democrats lost a substantial number of seats in the 1914 congressional elections, though they still maintained a majority. Fearful for his prospects for reelection in 1916, Wilson resumed the campaign for progressive legislation. Wilson appealed to Roosevelt's constituency by supporting New Nationalism social justice measures. In 1916 he signed into law the Adamson Act, which provided an eight-hour workday and overtime pay for railroad workers; the Keating-Owen Act, outlawing child labor in firms that engaged in interstate commerce; and the Workmen's Compensation Act, which provided insurance for federal employees in case of injury. In supporting programs that required greater intervention by the federal government, Wilson had placed political expediency ahead of his professed principles. He would later show a similar flexibility when he lent his support to a women's suffrage amendment, a cause he had long opposed.

Despite facing a challenge from a united Republican Party led by progressive Charles Evans Hughes, a former governor of New York, Wilson won the 1916 election with slightly less than 50 percent of the vote. Wilson's reelection owed little to the support of African Americans. W. E. B. Du Bois, who backed Wilson in 1912 for pledging to "assist in advancing the interest of [the black] race," had become disillusioned with the president. Born in the South and with deep southern roots, Wilson surrounded himself with white appointees from the South, some of whom told racist jokes at cabinet meetings. Despite black protests, Wilson held a screening in the White House of the film *Birth of a Nation*, which glorified the Ku Klux Klan and denigrated African Americans. Making the situation worse, Wilson introduced racial segregation into government offices and dining facilities in the nation's capital, and blacks lost jobs in post offices and other federal agencies throughout the South. In Wilson's view, segregation and discrimination were in the "best interests" of African Americans.

Still, President Wilson achieved much of the progressive agenda—more, in fact, than he had intended to when he first came to office. By the beginning of his second term, the federal government had further extended regulation over the activities of corporations and banks. Big business and finance still wielded substantial power and maintained considerable leeway in conducting their own affairs, but Wilson had steered the government on a course that also benefited ordinary citizens, including passage of social justice measures he had originally opposed.

REVIEW & RELATE

- How did the progressive agenda shape presidential politics in the first two decades of the twentieth century?
- How and why did the role of the president in national politics change under Roosevelt, Taft, and Wilson?

Conclusion: The Progressive Legacy

By the end of the Progressive Era, Americans had come to expect more from their government. They were more confident that their food and medicine were safe, that children would not have to sacrifice their health and education by going to work, that women laborers would not be exploited, and that political officials would be more responsive to their wishes. As a result of the efforts of environmentalists as different as Gifford Pinchot and Gene Stratton-Porter, the nation expanded its efforts both to conserve and to preserve its natural resources. These and other reforms accomplished what Theodore Roosevelt, Woodrow Wilson, and their fellow progressives wanted: to bring order out of chaos.

In challenging laissez-faire and championing governmental intervention, progressives did not intend to stamp out individualism or competition. These values were too embedded in the American political tradition, a system that held the allegiance of most reformers. Rather, progressives sought to balance individualism with social justice and social control. Despite cloaking many of their political reforms in democratic garb, middle- and upper-class progressives generally were more interested in augmenting their ability to advance their own agenda than in expanding opportunities for political participation for all Americans. Confident that they spoke for the "interests of the people," progressives had little doubt that increasing their own political power would be good for the nation as a whole.

Progressivism was not for whites only, but racial boundaries shaped the progressive movement. Blacks were active participants in progressivism, whether through extending educational opportunities, working in settlement houses, campaigning for women's suffrage, or establishing the NAACP. Nevertheless, racism was also a characteristic of progressivism. White southern reformers generally favored disfranchisement and segregation. Northern whites did not prove much more sympathetic, as Theodore Roosevelt's handling of the Brownsville incident shows. The southern-born Woodrow Wilson provided even more ample evidence of the racist dimensions of progressivism. Immigrants also found themselves unwelcome targets of moral outrage as progressives forced these newcomers to conform to middle-class standards of social behavior. Crusades for temperance, physical hygiene, and moral reform all shared a desire to mold people deemed inferior into proper citizens, uncontaminated by chronic vice and corruption.

Progressivism was not monolithic and included a range of disparate and overlapping efforts to reorder political, social, moral, and physical environments. Except for the brief existence of the Progressive Party in 1912, reformers did not have a tightly knit organization or a fixed agenda. Leaders were more likely to come from the middle class, but support came from the rich as well as the poor, depending on the issue. Of course, many Americans did not embrace progressive principles, as conservative opponents continued to hold power and to fight against reform. Nevertheless, by 1920 a combination of voluntary changes and government intervention had cleared the way to regulate corporations, increase governmental efficiency, and promote social justice. Progressives succeeded in ameliorating conditions that might have produced violent revolution and more disorder. In time, they would bring their ideas to reordering international affairs.

Chapter Review

MAKE IT STICK

 LearningCurve **bedfordstmartins.com/hewittlawsonvalue**
After reading the chapter, use LearningCurve to retain what you've read.

IDENTIFY KEY TERMS

Identify and explain the significance of each term below.

pragmatism (p. 485)
social gospel (p. 486)
muckrakers (p. 486)
Hull House (p. 487)
civic housekeeping (p. 487)
suffragists (p. 489)
Tuskegee Institute (p. 491)
National Association for the Advancement
 of Colored People (NAACP) (p. 492)

Woman's Christian Temperance Union
 (WCTU) (p. 494)
Hetch Hetchy valley (p. 498)
bully pulpit (p. 499)
Progressive Party (p. 503)
New Nationalism (p. 503)
New Freedom (p. 503)

REVIEW & RELATE

Answer the focus questions from each section of the chapter.

1. What late-nineteenth-century trends and developments influenced the progressives?

2. Why did the progressives focus on urban and industrial America?

3. What role did women play in the early-twentieth-century fight for social justice?

4. How did social reformers challenge discrimination against women and minorities?

5. What practices and behaviors of the poor did social control progressives find most alarming? Why?

6. What role did anti-immigrant sentiment play in motivating and shaping progressives' social control initiatives?

7. Who gained and who lost political influence as a result of progressive reforms?

8. How did a commitment to greater efficiency shape progressives' political and environmental initiatives?

9. How did the progressive agenda shape presidential politics in the first two decades of the twentieth century?

10. How and why did the role of the president in national politics change under Roosevelt, Taft, and Wilson?

ONLINE DOCUMENT PROJECTS
◆ **Progressivism and Social Control**
◆ **The New Nationalism, the New Freedom, and the Election of 1912**

After reading the primary sources in these document sets, answer the **Interpret the Evidence** questions to help you analyze each of the documents, and then answer the **Put It in Context** question(s) to help you relate the documents to the topics and themes you read about in the chapter.

bedfordstmartins.com/hewittlawsonvalue

TIMELINE OF EVENTS

1874 • Woman's Christian Temperance Union (WCTU) founded

1889 • Jane Addams and Ellen Starr establish Hull House

1890 • National American Woman Suffrage Association formed

1895 • Booker T. Washington delivers Atlanta address

1900 • First commission form of government established in Galveston, Texas

1902 • President Roosevelt settles coal strike

1903 • National Women's Trade Union League founded

1906 • Meat Inspection Act and Pure Food and Drug Act passed

1908 • Race riot in Springfield, Illinois

1909 • National Association for the Advancement of Colored People (NAACP) founded

1910 • Gifford Pinchot is fired by President Taft

1912 • Roosevelt forms Progressive Party
• Children's Bureau of the Department of Commerce and Labor established

1913 • Sixteenth Amendment instituting a graduated income tax ratified
• Federal Reserve System created

1914 • Harrison Narcotics Control Act passed
• Federal Trade Commission created
• Passage of Clayton Antitrust Act to benefit labor unions

1916 • Keating-Owen Act outlaws child labor
• Workmen's Compensation Act provides disability insurance

1919 • Eighteenth Amendment establishing prohibition ratified

1920 • Nineteenth Amendment granting women the right to vote ratified

20

LearningCurve
✓ bedfordstmartins.com/hewittlawsonvalue
After reading the chapter, use LearningCurve
to retain what you've read.

Empire and Wars

1898–1918

AMERICAN HISTORIES

Alfred Thayer Mahan came from a military family. Born in 1840, he grew up in West Point, New York, where his father served as dean of the faculty at the U.S. Military Academy. Seeking to emerge from his father's shadow, Alfred attended the U.S. Naval Academy, from which he graduated and received his commission in 1861, just as the Civil War was getting under way. His wartime experience convinced him that the navy, with its plodding, antiquated wooden vessels, needed a dramatic overhaul.

After the war, Mahan continued his naval career. Rather than making his mark on the high seas, Captain Mahan built his reputation as a military historian and strategist at the U.S. Naval War College. In 1890 he published *The Influence of Sea Power upon History*, in which he argued that the great imperial powers in modern history—Spain, the Netherlands, Great Britain, and France—had succeeded because they possessed strong navies and merchant marines. In his view, sea power had allowed these nations to defeat their enemies, conquer territories, and establish colonies from which they extracted raw materials and opened markets for finished goods. Appearing at a time when European nations were embarking on a new round of empire building, this book and subsequent writings had an enormous influence on American imperialists, including Theodore Roosevelt. Mahan's work reinforced the belief of men like Roosevelt that the long-term prospects of the United States depended on the acquisition of strategic outposts in Asia and the Caribbean that could guarantee American access to overseas markets.

As the economic and strategic importance of the Caribbean grew in the minds of imperial strategists such as Mahan and Roosevelt, the Cuban freedom fighter José Martí developed a very different vision of the region's future. Born in 1853 to Spanish immigrants who had migrated to Cuba for economic reasons, Martí got involved in the fight for Cuban independence from Spain as a teenager. In 1869, at age seventeen, he was arrested for protest activities during a revolutionary uprising against Spain. Sentenced to six years of hard labor, Martí was released after six months and was forced into exile. He returned to Cuba in 1878, only to be arrested and deported again the following year.

Martí settled in the United States, where, along with other Cuban exiles, he continued to promote Cuban independence and the establishment of a democratic republic. He conceived of the idea of *Cuba Libre* (Free Cuba) not just as a struggle for political independence but also as a social revolution that would erase unfair distinctions based on race and class. "Our goal," Martí declared in 1892, "is not so much a mere political change as a good, sound, and just and equitable system." Martí united disparate elements in expatriate communities in the United States and the Caribbean under the banner of a single Cuban Revolutionary Party.

When Cubans once again rebelled against Spain in 1895, Martí returned to Cuba to fight alongside his comrades. On May 19, 1895, only three months after he had returned to Cuba, Martí died in battle. Cuba ultimately won its independence from Spain, but Martí's vision of *Cuba Libre* was only partially realized. In 1898 the United States intervened on the side of the Cuban rebels, guaranteeing their victory, but not their freedom. America entered the war to gain control over Cuba, not to help Cubans take control of their own country.

THE AMERICAN HISTORIES of Alfred Thayer Mahan and José Martí embodied disparate understandings of America's relationship with the rest of the world. Up until the late nineteenth century, most Americans associated colonialism with the European powers and saw overseas expansion as incompatible with American values of independence and self-determination. In this context, they shared Martí's point of view. The American imperialism espoused by Mahan and others, therefore, represented a reversal of traditional American attitudes. Supporters of American imperialism saw the acquisition and control of overseas territories, by force if necessary, as essential to the protection of American interests. This perspective would come to dominate American foreign policy in the early twentieth century. Theodore Roosevelt and Woodrow Wilson, progressive presidents who sanctioned increased federal regulation of economic and moral matters within the United States, also supported vigorous intervention in world affairs. Although Roosevelt and Wilson differed in style and approach, in foreign affairs they asserted America's right to use its power to secure order and thwart revolution wherever American interests were seen to be threatened. Having become a major power on the world stage in the early twentieth century, the United States chose to enter World War I, in which rival European alliances battled for imperial domination. The end of the war heightened America's critical role in world affairs but brought neither lasting peace nor the dissolution of empire.

Red Cross poster, 1917.   Library of Congress

The Awakening of Imperialism

The United States became a modern imperial power relatively late. In the decades following the Civil War, the U.S. government concentrated most of its energies on settling the western territories, pushing Native Americans aside, and extracting the region's resources. Unlike Europe, the United States possessed a sparsely inhabited frontier that would furnish land for its growing population, as well as raw materials and markets for its industries. By the end of the nineteenth century, however, sweeping economic, cultural, and social changes led many Americans to conclude that the time had come for the country to assert its power beyond its borders. Convinced of the argument for empire advanced by Mahan and other imperialists, American officials embraced an expansionist foreign policy. In a burst of overseas expansion from 1898 to 1904, the United States acquired Guam, Hawaii, the Philippines, and Puerto Rico; established a protectorate in Cuba; and exercised force to build a canal through Panama. These gains paved the way for subsequent U.S. intervention in Haiti, the Dominican Republic, and Nicaragua.

The Economics of Expansion

The industrialization of America and the growth of corporate capitalism stimulated imperialist desires in the late nineteenth century. Throughout its early history, the United States had sought overseas markets for exports, particularly its agricultural products. However, the importance of exports to the American economy increased dramatically in the second half of the nineteenth century, as industrialization gained momentum. In 1870 American exports totaled $500 million. By 1905 the value of American exports had increased sixfold to $1.5 billion (Figure 20.1). John D. Rockefeller's Standard Oil Company led the way in selling products to European and Asian markets, and firms such as Coca-Cola, Kodak, and McCormick earned profits by exporting soft drinks, cameras, and farm machinery, respectively.

The bulk of American exports went to the developed markets of Europe and Canada, which had the greatest purchasing power. Although the less economically advanced

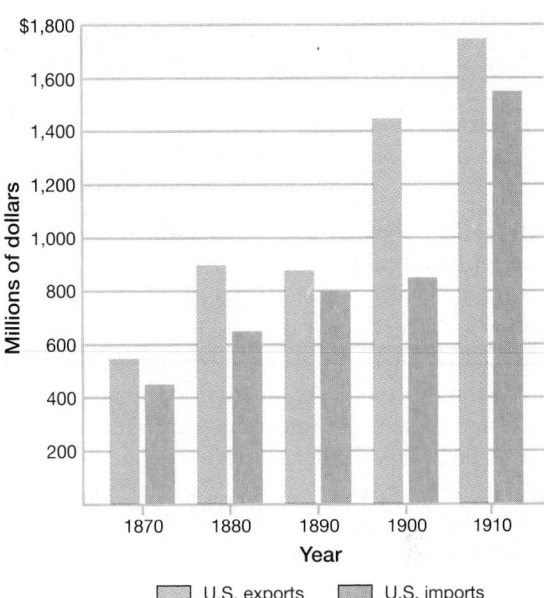

FIGURE 20.1

U.S. Exports and Imports, 1870–1910   As American industrial power increased at the end of the nineteenth century, exports increased dramatically. Between 1870 and 1910, U.S. exports more than tripled. Imports rose as well but were restrained by protective tariffs.

nations of Latin America and Asia did not have the same ability to buy American products, businessmen still considered these regions—especially China, with a population of millions of potential consumers—as future markets for American industries.

The desire to expand foreign markets remained a steady feature of American business interests. The fear that the domestic market for manufactured goods was shrinking gave this expansionist hunger greater urgency. The fluctuating business cycle of boom and bust that characterized the economy in the 1870s and 1880s reached its peak in the depression of the 1890s, the most severe economic downturn up to that point in American history. The social unrest that accompanied this depression, including protest marches and strikes (see chapter 17), worried business and political leaders about the stability of the country. The way to sustain prosperity and contain radicalism, many businessmen agreed, was to find foreign markets for goods that poured out of factories but could not be absorbed at home. Senator William Frye of Maine argued, "We must have the market [of China] or we shall have revolution."

Similar commercial ambitions led many Americans to see Hawaii as an imperial prize. Interest in the islands dated back to the early nineteenth century. American missionaries first visited the Hawaiian Islands in 1820. As missionaries tried to convert native islanders to Christianity, American businessmen sought to establish plantations on the islands, especially to grow sugarcane, as the market for sugar had grown rapidly during the 1870s and 1880s. In exchange for duty-free access to the U.S. sugar market, white Hawaiians signed an agreement in 1887 that granted the United States exclusive rights to a naval base at Pearl Harbor in Honolulu.

The growing influence of white sugar planters on the islands alarmed native Hawaiians. In 1891 Queen Liliuokalani, a strong nationalist leader who voiced the slogan "Hawaii for the Hawaiians," sought to increase the power of the indigenous peoples she governed, at the expense of the sugar growers. In 1893 white plantation owners, with the cooperation of the American ambassador to Hawaii and 150 U.S. marines, overthrew the queen's government. Once in command of the government, they entered into a treaty of annexation with the United States. However, President Grover Cleveland opposed annexation and withdrew the treaty. Nevertheless, planters remained in power and waited for a suitable opportunity to seek annexation.

Cultural Justifications for Imperialism

Imperialists linked overseas expansion to practical, economic considerations, but race was also a key component in their arguments for empire. Drawing on Herbert Spencer's concept of "survival of the fittest," many Americans and western Europeans declared themselves superior to nonwhite peoples of Latin America, Asia, and Africa. Buttressing their arguments with racist studies claiming to demonstrate scientifically the "racial" superiority of white Protestants, imperialists claimed a "natural right" of conquest and world domination (see chapter 19).

Imperialists added an ethical dimension to this ideology by contending that "higher civilizations" had a duty to uplift inferior nations. In *Our Country* (1885), the Congregationalist minister Josiah Strong proclaimed the superiority of the Anglo-Saxon, or white northern European, race and the responsibility of the United States to spread the "blessings" of its Christian way of life throughout the world. Secular intellectuals, such as historian John Fiske, praised the English race for settling the United States and predicted that "its language . . . its religion . . . its political habits, and . . . the blood of its people" would become "predominant" in the less civilized parts of the globe.

As in Hawaii, Christian missionaries served as foot soldiers for the advancing American commercial empire. In fact, there was often a clear connection between religious and commercial interests. For example, in 1895 industrialists John D. Rockefeller Jr. and Cyrus McCormick created the World Student Christian Federation, which dispatched more than five thousand young missionaries throughout the world, many of them women. Likewise, it was no coincidence that China, an enormous potential market for American products, became a magnet for American missionary activity. By 1920 missionaries in China were operating schools, hospitals, orphanages, leper colonies, churches, and seminaries, seeking to convert the "backward" Chinese to Christianity and the American way of life. Many Americans hoped that, under missionary supervision, the Chinese would become consumers of both American ideas and American products.

Gender and Empire

Gender anxieties provided an additional motivation for American imperialism. In the late nineteenth century, with the Civil War long over, many Americans worried that the rising generation of American men lacked opportunities to test and strengthen their manhood. For example, in 1897 Mississippi congressman John Sharp Williams lamented the waning of "the dominant spirit which controlled in this Republic [from 1776 to 1865] . . . one of honor, glory, chivalry, and patriotism." Such gender anxieties were not limited to elites. The depression of the 1890s hit working-class men hard, causing them to question their self-worth as they lost the ability to support their families. In this context, the poem "The White Man's Burden," written by the British writer and poet Rudyard Kipling in 1899, touched a nerve with American men. In the poem, Kipling urges white men to take up the "burden" of bringing civilization to non-Western peoples. By embracing the imperialist project, they would regain their manly honor.

The growing presence of women as political activists in campaigns for suffrage and moral, humanitarian, and governmental reforms was particularly troubling to male identity. Some men warned that dire consequences would result if women succeeded in feminizing politics. Alfred Thayer Mahan believed that women's suffrage would undermine the nation's military security because women lacked the will to use physical force. He asserted that giving the vote to women would destroy the "constant practice of the past ages by which to men are assigned the outdoor rough action of life and to women that indoor sphere which we call the family." As Mahan's comment shows, calling American men to action was often paired with a call for American women to leave the public arena and return to the home.

American males could reassert their manhood by adopting a militant spirit. An English verse from 1878 described this attitude: "We don't want to fight, yet by Jingo! If we do, we've got the ships, we've got the men, and got the money too." Known as **jingoists**, war enthusiasts such as Theodore Roosevelt could not contain their desire to find a war in which to prove their masculinity. "You and your generation have had your chance from 1861 to 1865," Roosevelt exclaimed to a Civil War veteran. "Now let us of this generation have ours!" Captain Mahan concurred. "No greater danger could befall civilization than the disappearance of the warlike spirit (I dare say *war*) among civilized men," he asserted. "There are too many barbarians still in the world." Mahan and Roosevelt echoed the British jingoists' pride in naval power. The Naval Act of 1890 authorized funding for construction of three battleships to join the two existing ones. These warships would provide the foundation for a revitalized navy capable of safeguarding American interests in the Atlantic and Pacific Oceans. Ten years later, the U.S. fleet had grown to seventeen battleships and six armored cruisers, making it the third most powerful navy in the world, up from twelfth place in 1880. Having built a powerful navy, the United States would soon find opportunities to use it.

REVIEW & RELATE

- What role did economic developments play in prompting calls for an American empire? What role did social and cultural developments play?
- Why did the United States embark on building an empire in the 1890s and not decades earlier?

The War with Spain

The United States went to war with Spain in 1898 not to defend itself from attack but because American policymakers decided that Cuban independence from Spain was in America's national interest. American leaders had long coveted Cuba for its economic resources and strategic location in the Caribbean. When the Cubans revolted against Spain in the mid-1890s, the United States seized its chance. Victory over Spain, however, brought America much more than control over Cuba. In the peace negotiations following the war, the United States acquired a significant portion of Spain's overseas empire, turning the United States into a major imperial power.

Cuba Libre

The Cuban War for Independence began in 1895 around the concept of *Cubanidad*—pride of nation. José Martí envisioned that this war of national liberation from Spain would provide land to impoverished peasants and offer genuine racial equality for the large Afro-Cuban population that had been liberated from slavery less than a decade earlier, in 1886. Black Cubans, such as Antonio Maceo, flocked to the revolutionary cause and constituted a significant portion of the senior ranks in the rebel army.

The insurgents fought a brilliant guerrilla war. Facing some 200,000 Spanish troops, 50,000 rebels ground them down in a war of attrition. The Cuban insurgents burned crops, laid siege to land, and cut railroad lines to keep the Spaniards from using these vital resources. Within eighteen months, the rebellion had spread across the island and garnered the support of all segments of the Cuban population. The Spanish government's brutal attempts to crack down on the rebels only stiffened their resistance. By the end of 1897, the Spanish government recognized that the war was going poorly and offered the rebels a series of reforms that would give the island home rule within the empire but not independence. Sensing victory, the insurgents held out for total separation to realize their vision of **Cuba Libre**, an independent Cuba with greater social and racial equality.

The revolutionaries had every reason to feel confident as they wore down Spanish troops. First, they had help from the climate. One-quarter of Spanish soldiers had contracted yellow fever, malaria, and other tropical illnesses and remained confined to hospitals. The chief military commander of the rebel forces, General Maximo Gómez, bragged that his three best generals were "*Junio, Julio,* and *Agosto,*" referring to the months of June, July, and August, which ushered in the rainy season and increased the spread of disease. Second, mounting a successful counterinsurgency would have required far more troops than Spain could spare. Its forces were spread too thin around the globe to keep the empire intact. In addition to Cuba, Spain stationed some 200,000 troops in Puerto Rico, the Philippines, and Africa. Finally, antiwar sentiment was mounting in Spain, and on January 12, 1898, Spanish troops mutinied in Havana. Speaking for many, a former president of Spain asserted: "Spain is exhausted. She must withdraw her troops and recognize Cuban independence before it is too late." U.S. Secretary of State John Sherman concurred: "Spain will lose Cuba. . . . She cannot continue the struggle."

The War of 1898

With the Cuban insurgents on the verge of victory, American policymakers, including President William McKinley, came to favor military intervention as a way to increase American control of postwar Cuba. By intervening before the Cubans won on their own, the United States staked its claim for determining the postwar relationship between the two countries and protecting its vital interests in the Caribbean, including the private property rights of American landowners in Cuba.

The American press, however, helped build support for American intervention not by focusing on economic interests and geopolitics but by framing the war as a matter of American honor. Most Americans followed the war through newspaper accounts. William Randolph Hearst's *New York Journal* competed with Joseph Pulitzer's *New York World* to see which could provide the most lurid coverage of Spanish atrocities. The two newspapers sent correspondents to Cuba to cover every grisly story they could find—and to make up stories, if necessary. Known disparagingly as **yellow journalism**, these sensationalist newspaper accounts aroused jingoistic outrage against Spain.

On February 9, 1898, the *Journal* printed a letter that had come into Hearst's possession. Under the headline "Worst Insult to the United States in History," the newspaper quoted a private letter from Enrique Depuy de Lôme, the Spanish minister in Washington, scorning President McKinley as a "weak" politician who pandered to "the crowd" to win public favor. Nearly a week later, on February 15, the battleship *Maine*, anchored in Havana harbor, exploded, killing 266 American sailors. American newspapers blamed Spain. The *World* shouted the rallying cry "Remember the *Maine*! To hell with Spain!" Assistant Secretary of the Navy Theodore Roosevelt seconded this sentiment by denouncing the explosion as a Spanish "act of treachery." Why the Spaniards would choose to blow up the *Maine* and provoke war with the United States while already losing to Cuba remained unanswered, but the incident was enough to turn American opinion toward war.

On April 11, 1898, McKinley asked Congress to declare war against Spain. The declaration included an amendment proposed by Senator Henry M. Teller of Colorado declaring that Cuba "ought to be free and independent." Yet the document left enough room for American maneuvering to satisfy the imperial ambitions of the McKinley administration. In endorsing independence, the war proclamation asserted the right of the United States to remain involved in Cuban affairs until it had achieved "pacification." On April 21, the United States officially went to war with Spain.

In going to war, McKinley embarked on an imperialistic course that had been building since the early 1890s. The president signaled the broader expansionist concerns behind the war when, shortly after it began, he successfully steered a Hawaiian annexation treaty through Congress. Businessmen joined imperialists in seizing the moment to create a commercial empire that would catch up to their European rivals.

It was fortunate for the United States that the Cuban insurgents had seriously weakened Spanish forces before the Americans arrived. The U.S. army, consisting of fewer than 30,000 men, lacked sufficient strength to conquer Cuba on its own, and McKinley had to mobilize some 200,000 National Guard troops and assorted volunteers. Theodore Roosevelt resigned from his post as assistant secretary of the navy and organized his own regiment, called "Rough Riders." American forces faced several problems: They lacked battle experience; supplies were inadequate; their uniforms were not suited for the hot, humid climate of a Cuban summer; and the soldiers did not have immunity from tropical diseases.

African American soldiers, who made up about one-quarter of the troops, encountered additional difficulties. As more and more black troops arrived in southern ports for deployment to Cuba, they faced increasingly hostile crowds, angered at the presence of armed African American men in uniform. In Tampa, Florida, where troops gathered from all over the country to be transported to Cuba, racial tensions exploded on the afternoon of June 8. Intoxicated white soldiers from Ohio grabbed a two-year-old black boy from his mother and used him for target practice, shooting a bullet through his shirtsleeve. In retaliation, African American soldiers stormed into the streets and exchanged gunfire with whites, leaving three whites and twenty-seven black soldiers wounded. Reporting the story of this "riot," the *Atlanta Constitution* denounced the "wild and demonic conduct of the [N]egro regulars," completely ignoring the behavior of the white troops that had prompted the fracas. Undaunted, black troops went on to distinguish themselves on Cuban battlefields.

Despite military inexperience, logistical problems, and racial tensions, the United States quickly defeated the weakened Spanish military, and the war was over four months after it began. During the war, 460 Americans died in combat, far fewer than the more than 5,000 who lost their lives to disease. It was not surprising, then, that Secretary of State John Hay referred to the hostilities as "a splendid little war." The subsequent peace treaty ended Spanish rule in Cuba, ceded Puerto Rico and the Pacific island of Guam to the United States, and recognized American occupation of the Philippines until the two countries could arrange a final settlement. As a result of the territorial gains in the war, American foreign-policy strategists could now begin to construct the empire that Mahan had envisioned.

A Not-So-Free Cuba

Although Congress had adopted the **Teller Amendment** in 1898 pledging Cuba's independence from Spain, President McKinley and his supporters insisted that Cuban self-rule would come only after pacification. Racial prejudice and cultural chauvinism blinded Americans to the contributions Cubans had made to defeat Spain. When white commanding officers arrived in Cuba, they expressed shock at the large number of blacks in the Cuban military, many of whom held leadership positions. One U.S. officer reported to the *New York Times*: "The typical Cuban I encountered was a treacherous, lying, cowardly, thieving, worthless half-breed mongrel, born of a mongrel spawn of [Spain], crossed upon the fetches of darkest Africa and aboriginal America." José Martí may have been fighting for racial equality, but the U.S. government certainly was not.

Because U.S. officials presumed that Cuba was unfit for immediate freedom, the island remained under U.S. military occupation until 1902. The highlight of Cuba's transition to self-rule came with the adoption of a governing document based on the U.S. Constitution. However, the Cuban constitution came with strings attached. In March 1901, Congress passed the **Platt Amendment**, introduced by Senator Orville Platt of Connecticut, which limited Cuban sovereignty. The amendment prohibited the Cuban government from signing treaties with other nations without U.S. consent, permitted the United States to intervene in Cuba to preserve independence and remove threats to economic stability, and leased Guantánamo Bay to the United States as a naval base, an arrangement that continues to this day. American officials pressured Cuban leaders to incorporate the Platt Amendment into their constitution. When U.S. occupation ended in 1902, Cuba was not fully independent. Instead, the United States established Cuba as a protectorate, paving the way for economic exploitation of the island and the return of American troops to safeguard investments.

The Philippine War

Even before invading Cuba, the United States had won a significant battle against Spain on the other side of the world. At the outset of the war, the U.S. Pacific Fleet, under the command of Commodore George Dewey, attacked Spanish forces in their colony of the Philippines. Dewey defeated the Spanish flotilla in Manila Bay on May 1, 1898, killing nearly four hundred Spanish sailors, while eight Americans suffered only minor injuries. Two and a half months later, American troops followed up with an invasion of Manila, and Spanish forces promptly surrendered (Map 20.1).

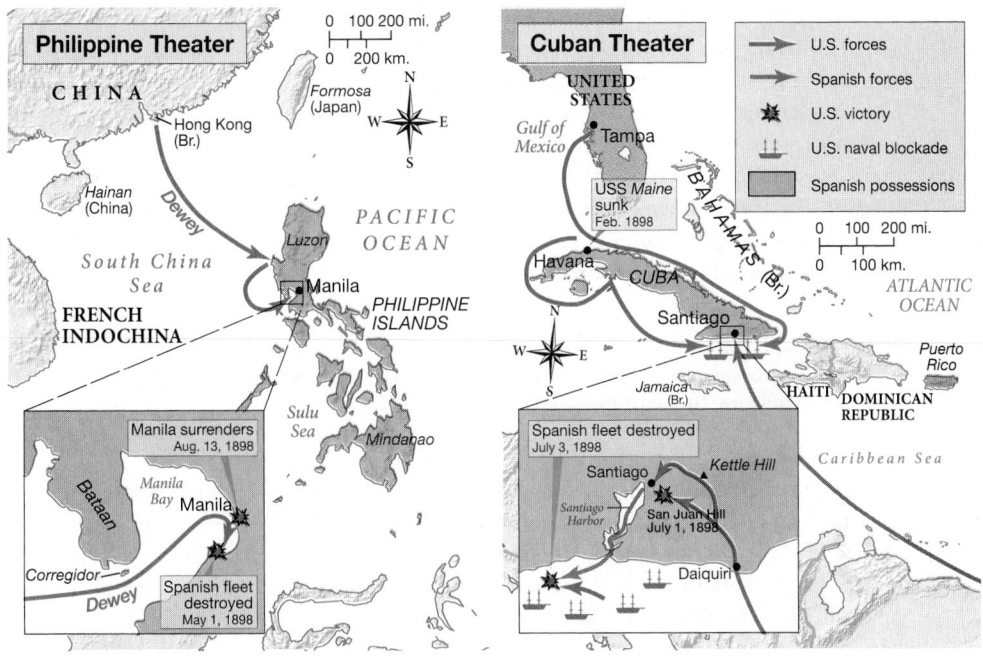

MAP 20.1
The War of 1898   The United States and Spain fought the War of 1898 on two fronts—the Philippines and Cuba. Naval forces led by Admiral George Dewey made the difference in the U.S. victory by first defeating the Spaniards in Manila Bay and then off the coast of Cuba. In Cuba, rebels had seriously weakened the Spanish military before U.S. ground troops secured victory.

While pacifying Cuba, the U.S. government had to decide what to do with the Philippines. Imperialists viewed American control of the islands as an important step forward in the quest for entry into the China market. The Philippines could serve as a naval station for the merchant marine and the navy to safeguard potential trade with the Asian mainland. Moreover, President McKinley believed that if the United States did not act, another European power would take Spain's place, something he thought would be "bad business and deplorable."

With this in mind, McKinley decided to annex the Philippines. As with Cuba, McKinley and many other Americans believed that nonwhite Filipinos were not yet capable of self-government. Indiana senator Albert Beveridge commented: "We must never forget that in dealing with the Filipinos we deal with children." McKinley agreed and set out "to educate the Filipinos, and uplift and Christianize them." As was often the case with imperialism, assumptions of racial and cultural superiority provided a handy justification for the pursuit of economic and strategic advantage.

The president's plans, however, ran into vigorous opposition. Anti-imperialist lawmakers took a strong stand against annexing the Philippines. Despite the jingoist fervor surrounding the War of 1898, opponents of imperialism constituted a vocal group. Their cause drew support from such prominent Americans as industrialist Andrew Carnegie, social reformer Jane Addams, writer Mark Twain, and labor organizer Samuel

Gompers, all of whom joined the **Anti-Imperialist League**, founded in November 1898. Some argued that the United States would violate its anticolonialist heritage by acquiring the islands. Union leaders feared that annexation would prompt the migration of cheap laborers into the country and undercut wages. Others worried about the financial costs of supporting military forces across the Pacific. Most anti-imperialists had racial reasons for rejecting the treaty. Like imperialists, they considered Asians to be inferior to Europeans. In fact, many anti-imperialists held an even dimmer view of the capabilities of people of color than did their opponents, rejecting the notion that Filipinos could be "civilized" under American tutelage.

 Online Document Project   Imperialism versus Anti-Imperialism
bedfordstmartins.com/hewittlawsonvalue

Despite this opposition, the imperialists won out. Approval of the treaty annexing the Philippines in 1898 marked the beginning of problems for the United States. As in Cuba, rebellion had preceded American occupation. At first, the rebels welcomed the Americans as liberators, but once it became clear that American rule would simply replace Spanish rule, the mood changed. Led by Emilio Aguinaldo, insurgent forces fought back against the 70,000 troops sent by this latest colonial power. "Either independence or death!" became the battle cry of Aguinaldo's rebel army. The rebels adopted guerrilla tactics and resorted to terrorist assaults against the U.S. army.

U.S. forces responded in kind, adopting harsh methods to suppress the uprising. General Jacob H. Smithy ordered his troops to "kill and burn, and the more you kill and burn, the better you will please me." Racist sentiments inflamed passions against the dark-skinned Filipino insurgents. One American soldier wrote home saying that "he wanted to blow every nigger into nigger heaven." American counterinsurgency efforts, which indiscriminately targeted combatants and civilians alike, alienated the native population. An estimated 200,000 Filipino civilians died between 1899 and 1902.

The Americans' taste for war and sacrifice quickly waned. Nearly 5,000 Americans died in the Philippine war, far more combat deaths than in Cuba. With casualties mounting and reports growing of combat-related atrocities, antiwar sentiment spread in the United States. Dissenters turned imperialist arguments of manly American honor upside down. Reports of battlefield horrors inflicted on Filipino civilians prompted Senator George L. Wellington of Maryland to complain that the army had "step by step departed from the broad highway of honorable warfare . . . and [had] adopted methods of barbarism and savagery such as the wild natives of the unconquered Philippine Islands could not approach." For many Americans, the "splendid little war" had turned into a sordid affair. Anti-imperialists claimed that the war had done nothing to affirm American manhood; rather, they charged, the United States acted as a bully, taking the position of "a strong man" fighting against "a weak and puny child."

Despite growing casualties on the battlefield and antiwar sentiment at home, the conflict ended with an American military victory. In March 1901, U.S. forces captured Aguinaldo and broke the back of the rebellion. Exhausted, the Filipino leader asked his comrades to lay down their arms. In July 1901, President McKinley appointed Judge William Howard Taft of Ohio as the first civilian governor to oversee the government of the Philippines. For the next forty-five years, except for a brief period of Japanese rule during World War II, the United States remained in control of the islands.

REVIEW & RELATE

• Why did the United States go to war with Spain in 1898?

• In what ways did the War of 1898 mark a turning point in the relationship between the United States and the rest of the world?

Extending U.S. Imperialism, 1899–1913

The War of 1898 turned the United States into an imperial nation. Once the war was over, and with its newly acquired empire in place, the United States sought to extend its influence, competing with its European rivals for even greater global power. President Theodore Roosevelt and his successors achieved Captain Mahan's dream of building a Central American canal and wielded American military and financial might in the Caribbean with little restraint. At the same time, the United States took a more active role in Asian affairs.

Theodore Roosevelt and "Big Stick" Diplomacy

After President McKinley was assassinated in 1901, Vice President Theodore Roosevelt succeeded him as president. As in domestic matters, Roosevelt believed in using power to protect American commercial and strategic interests as well as to preserve international order and stability. In his view, the United States required a strong military and the political will to use it. "It is contemptible for a nation, as for an individual," Roosevelt instructed Congress, "[to] proclaim its purposes, or to take positions which are ridiculous if unsupported by potential force, and then to refuse to provide this force." This Progressive Era interventionist, inspired by Captain Mahan's writings, welcomed his nation's new role as a major world power. From this point on, the United States would play the role of an international policeman, using force if necessary to keep the peace.

As the most important part of his international agenda, Roosevelt sought to demonstrate American might and preserve order in the Caribbean and Central and South America. The building of the Panama Canal provides a case in point. Mahan considered a canal across Central America as vital because it would provide faster access to Asian markets and improve the U.S. navy's ability to patrol two oceans effectively. The United States took a step toward realizing Mahan's goal in 1901, when it signed the Hay-Pauncefote Treaty with Britain, granting the United States the right to construct a canal connecting the Atlantic and Pacific Oceans. After first considering Nicaragua, Roosevelt settled on Panama as the prime location. A French company had already begun construction at this site and had completed two-fifths of the operation; however, when it ran out of money, it sold its holdings to the United States for the bargain price of $40 million.

Before the United States could resume building, it had to negotiate with the South American country of Colombia, which controlled Panama. Secretary of State Hay and Colombian representatives reached an agreement highly favorable to the Americans, which the Colombian government refused to ratify. When Colombia held out for a higher price, Roosevelt accused the Colombians of being "utterly incapable of keeping order" in Panama and declared that transit across Panama was vital to world commerce. In 1903 the president supported a pro-American uprising by sending warships into the harbor of Panama City, an action that prevented the Colombians from quashing the insurrection. Roosevelt quickly recognized the new government of Panama and signed a treaty with it granting the United States the right to build the canal and exercise "power and authority" over it. In 1914, under American control, the Panama Canal opened to sea traffic.

With the United States controlling Cuba, the Panama Canal, and Puerto Rico, President Roosevelt intended to deter any threats to America's power in the region. The economic instability of Central American and Caribbean nations provided Roosevelt with the opportunity to brandish what he called a "big stick" to keep these countries in check and prevent intervention by European powers also interested in the area. (The term comes from a proverb Roosevelt was fond of quoting: "Speak softly and carry a big stick.") Referring to neighboring countries to the south, the president grumbled: "These wretched republics cause me a great deal of trouble." In 1904, when the government of the Dominican Republic was teetering on the edge of bankruptcy and threatened to default on $22 million in European loans, Roosevelt sprang into action. He announced U.S. opposition to any foreign intervention to reclaim debts, a position that echoed the principles of the Monroe Doctrine, which in 1823 proclaimed that the United States would not tolerate outside intervention in the Western Hemisphere. However, the president went even further and added his own corollary to the Monroe Doctrine by affirming the right of the United States to intervene in the internal affairs of any country in Latin America or the Caribbean that displayed "chronic wrong-doing" and could not preserve order and manage its own affairs. The **Roosevelt Corollary** proclaimed what Cubans and Panamanians already knew: The United States considered the region south of its border to be within its sphere of influence. Retaining nominal independence, the countries of Central America and the Caribbean had to behave according to U.S. wishes or face American military invasion.

Opening the Door in China

Roosevelt displayed American power in other parts of the world. His major concern was protecting the **Open Door** policy in China that his predecessor McKinley had engineered to secure naval access to the China market. By 1900 European powers already dominated foreign access to Chinese markets, leaving scant room for newcomers. When the United States sent 2,500 troops to China in August 1900 to help quell a nationalist uprising against foreign involvement known as the Boxer uprising, European competitors in return were compelled to allow the United States free trade access to China.

In 1904 the Russian invasion of the southern Chinese province of Manchuria prompted the Japanese to attack the Russian fleet. Roosevelt held mixed emotions about the Japanese. The president admired Japanese military prowess, but he worried that if Japan succeeded in driving the Russians out of the area, it would cause "a real shifting of equilibrium as far as the white races are concerned." To prevent that from happening, Roosevelt convened a peace conference in Portsmouth, New Hampshire, in 1905. Under the agreement reached at the conference, Japan received control over Korea and parts of Manchuria but pledged to support the United States' Open Door policy. In 1906,

Boxer Uprising In 1900 the Society of Righteous and Harmonious Fists, a Chinese militaristic and secret society known as the Boxers, attacked foreign diplomatic offices in Beijing to expel outsiders. This illustration from Hunan province portrays the Boxers killing foreigners and burning Christian books. The Boxers viewed Christian missionaries as cultural enemies. A coalition of multinational forces crushed the uprising. Kharbine-Tapabor/The Art Archive at Art Resource, NY

fresh from this achievement, the president sent sixteen American battleships on a trip around the globe in a show of force meant to demonstrate that the United States was serious about taking its place as a premier world power.

When Roosevelt's secretary of war, William Howard Taft, became president (1909–1913), he continued his predecessor's foreign policy with slight modification. Proclaiming that he would rather substitute "dollars for bullets," Taft encouraged private bankers to invest money in the Caribbean and Central America. Eager to embrace the president's policy of **dollar diplomacy**, the bankers doubled their investments in the region. Yet Taft did not rely on financial influence alone. He backed up American commercial investments by dispatching more than 2,000 U.S. troops to the region to guarantee economic stability. The president sought to extend his dollar diplomacy to China by trying to weaken Russia's and Japan's hold over Manchuria, but he succeeded only in drawing the two rivals closer together.

Taft's diplomacy also led to extensive intervention in Nicaragua. In 1909 American fruit and mining companies in Nicaragua helped install a regime sympathetic to their interests. When a group of rebels threatened this pro-American government, Taft invoked the Roosevelt Corollary and sent in American marines to police the country and deter further uprisings. They remained there for another twenty-five years. Under the U.S. occupation, American bankers took control of the country's customs houses and paid off debts owed to foreign investors, a move meant to forestall outside intervention in a nation that was now under American "protection."

REVIEW & RELATE

- How did the United States assert its influence and control over Latin America in the early twentieth century?
- How did U.S. policies in Latin America mirror U.S. policies in Asia?

Wilson and American Foreign Policy, 1912–1917

When Woodrow Wilson became president in 1913, he pledged to open a new chapter in America's relations with Latin America and the rest of the world. The United States would continue to support order, stability, and American access to overseas markets, but it would no longer "carry a big stick." Disdaining power politics and the use of force, Wilson vowed to place diplomacy and moral persuasion at the center of American foreign policy. Diplomacy, however, proved less effective than he had hoped. Despite Wilson's stated commitment to the peaceful resolution of international issues, during his presidency the American military intervened repeatedly in Latin American affairs, and American troops fought on European soil in the bloody global conflict that contemporaries called the Great War.

Diplomacy and War

Despite his stated preference for moral diplomacy, Wilson preserved the U.S. sphere of influence in the Caribbean using much the same methods as had Roosevelt and Taft. To protect American investments from political disturbances and economic crises, the president sent marines to Haiti in 1915, to the Dominican Republic in 1916, and to Cuba in 1917.

The most serious challenge to Wilson's diplomacy came in Mexico, where he found his ideals tempered by reality. The **Mexican revolution** in 1911 spawned a civil war among various insurgent factions. The resulting instability threatened U.S. interests in Mexico, particularly oil. When Mexicans refused to accept Wilson's demands to install leaders he considered "good men," Wilson withdrew diplomatic recognition from Mexico. In a disastrous attempt to influence Mexican politics, Wilson sent the U.S. navy to the port of Veracruz on April 22, 1914, leading to a bloody clash that killed 19 Americans and 126 Mexicans. The situation worsened after Wilson first supported and then turned against one of the rebel competitors for power in Mexico, General Francisco "Pancho" Villa. In response to this betrayal, Villa and 1,500 troops rode across the border and attacked the town of Columbus, New Mexico. In July 1916, Wilson ordered General John Pershing to send 10,000 army troops three hundred miles into Mexico in an attempt to capture Villa. The operation was a complete failure that only further angered Mexican leaders and confirmed their sense that Wilson had no respect for Mexican national sovereignty. In January 1917, Wilson ordered Pershing to withdraw his troops.

The president had little choice. At the same time as the situation in Mexico was deteriorating, a much more serious problem was developing in Europe. On June 28, 1914, an ardent Serbian nationalist, intending to strike a blow against Austria-Hungary, assassinated the Austrian archduke Franz Ferdinand in Sarajevo, the capital of the province of Bosnia. This terrorist attack plunged Europe into what would become a world war, fracturing the unsteady peace that had been maintained for the previous forty years. On August 4, 1914, the Central Powers—Germany, the Ottoman empire, and Austria-Hungary—officially declared war against the Allies—Great Britain, France, and Russia (Italy joined them in 1915).

As the most powerful neutral nation, the United States looked on from afar. For the first three years of the Great War, Wilson kept the United States neutral, though privately he believed that a British defeat would be "fatal to our form of Government and American ideals." Nevertheless, the president urged Americans to remain "in fact as well as in name impartial in thought as well as action." Peace activists sought to keep Wilson to his word. In 1915 women reformers and suffragists such as Jane Addams and Carrie Chapman Catt organized the Women's Peace Party to keep the United States out of war. One of its leaders, Lucia True Ames Mead, called replacing war with law "the most pressing reform before civilization to-day." Yet even Mead showed how difficult it was to keep a neutral mind. "There can be no peace," she exclaimed, "until the military domination of [Germany] is destroyed."

Wilson faced two key problems in keeping the country out of war. First, America had closer and more important economic ties with the Allies than with the Central Powers, a disparity that would only grow as the war went on. The Allies purchased more than $750 million in American goods in 1914, a figure that quadrupled over the next three years. By contrast, the Germans bought approximately $350 million worth of American products in 1914; by 1917 the figure had shrunk to $30 million. Moreover, when the Allies did not have the funds to pay for American goods, they sought loans from private bankers. Initially, the Wilson administration followed the wishes of Secretary of State William Jennings Bryan, who argued that providing these loans would violate "the true spirit of neutrality." In 1915, however, Wilson reversed course. Concerned that failure to keep up the prewar level of commerce with the Allies would hurt the country economically, the president authorized private loans. The gap in financial transactions with the rival war powers grew even wider; by 1917 American bankers had loaned the Allies $2.2 billion, compared with just $27 million to Germany.

The second problem facing Wilson arose from Great Britain's and Germany's differing war strategies. As the superior naval power, Britain established a blockade of the North Sea to quarantine Germany and starve it into submission. The British navy violated international law by mining the waters to bottle up the German fleet and keep foreign ships from supplying Germany with food and medicines. The blockade even ensnared U.S. ships, despite the fact that the United States, as a neutral nation, had the right to ship non-war items to Germany. However, Britain extended the list of prohibited items and hauled American vessels into British ports. Although Wilson protested this treatment, he did so weakly. He believed that the British could pay compensation for such violations of international law after the war.

Confronting a strangling blockade, Germany depended on the newly developed U-boat (*Unterseeboot*, or submarine) to counter the British navy. In February 1915, Germany declared a blockade of the British Isles and warned citizens of neutral nations to stay off British ships in the area. U-boats, which were lighter and sleeker than British battleships and merchant marine ships, relied on surprise. This strategy violated the rules of engagement under international maritime law, which required belligerent ships to allow civilians to leave passenger liners and cargo ships before firing. The British complicated the situation for the Germans by flying flags of neutral countries on merchant vessels and arming them with small "defensive" weapons. Therefore, if U-boats played by the rules and surfaced before inspecting merchant ships, they risked being blown out of the water by disguised enemy guns.

Under these circumstances, American neutrality could not last long. On May 15, 1915, catastrophe struck. Without surfacing and identifying itself, a German submarine off the Irish coast attacked the British luxury liner *Lusitania*, which had departed from New York City en route to England. Although the ship's stated objective was to provide passengers with relaxation, sumptuous dining, and dancing, its cargo contained a large supply of ammunition for British weapons. The U-boat's torpedoes rapidly sank the ship, killing 1,198 people, including 128 Americans.

Outraged Americans called on the president to respond; some, including Theodore Roosevelt, advocated the immediate use of military force. Despite his pro-British sentiments, Wilson resisted going to war. Instead, he held the Germans in "strict accountability" for their action. Appalled by the loss of human life, Wilson demanded that Germany refrain from further attacks against passenger liners and offer a financial settlement to the *Lusitania*'s survivors. Unwilling to risk war with the United States, the Germans consented.

Wilson had, however, only delayed America's entry into the war. By pursuing a policy of neutrality that treated the combatants unequally and by insisting that Americans had a right to travel on the ships of belligerent nations, the president diminished the chance that the United States would stay out of the war. Recognizing this situation, Secretary of State Bryan resigned following the *Lusitania* affair over what he considered the president's one-sided understanding of "strict accountability." Wilson quickly replaced him with a more pro-British secretary of state, Robert Lansing, who endorsed Wilson's expansion of the loan program to Britain.

Throughout 1916, Wilson pursued two separate but interrelated policies that embodied the ambivalence that he and the American people shared about the war. On the one hand, with Germany alternating between continued U-boat attacks and apologies, the president sought to build the country's military preparedness in the event of war. He signed into law the National Defense Act, which increased the size of the army, navy, and National Guard. On the other hand, Wilson stressed his desire to remain neutral and stay out of the war. With American public opinion divided on the Great War, Wilson chose to run for reelection as a peace candidate. The president sent his personal emissary, Colonel Edward House, to Europe to negotiate an armistice and end the fighting, without success. The Democrats adopted the slogan "He kept us out of war" and also emphasized the president's substantial record of progressive reform. Wilson won a narrow victory against Charles Evans Hughes, the former governor of New York, who wavered between advocating peace and criticizing Wilson for not sufficiently supporting the Allies.

Making the World Safe for Democracy

As 1917 dawned, the Great War headed toward its third bloody year. Neither side wanted a negotiated peace because each counted on victory to gain sufficient territory and financial compensation to justify the great sacrifices in human lives and materiel caused by the conflict. Nevertheless, Wilson tried to persuade the belligerents to abandon the battlefield for the bargaining table. On January 22, 1917, he declared that the world needed a "peace without victory," one based on self-determination, freedom of the seas, respect for international law, and the end of hostile alliances. It was a generous vision from a nation that had made few sacrifices.

Germany quickly rejected Wilson's proposal. America had never been truly neutral, and Germany's increasingly desperate leaders saw no reason to believe that the situation would change. In 1915 and again in 1916, to prevent the United States from entering the war, Germany had pledged to refrain from using its most potent weapon, the U-boat, against passenger ships and merchant ships. However, the Germans now chose to change course and resume unrestricted submarine warfare, calculating that they could defeat the Allies before the United States declared war and its troops could make a substantial difference. On February 1, 1917, Germany announced that it would attack all ships, including unarmed American merchant vessels that penetrated its blockade of Great Britain. In response, Wilson used his executive power to arm merchant ships, bringing the United States one step closer to war.

The country moved even closer to war after the **Zimmermann telegram** became public. On February 24, the British turned over to Wilson an intercepted message from Arthur Zimmermann, the German foreign minister, to the Mexican government. The decoded note revealed that Germany had offered Mexico an alliance in the event that the United States joined the Allies. If the Central Powers won, Mexico would receive the territory it had lost to the United States in the mid-nineteenth century—Texas, New Mexico, and Arizona. When U.S. newspapers broke the story several days later, it inflamed public opinion and provided the Wilson administration another reason to fear a German victory.

In late February and March, German U-boats sank several armed American merchant ships, and on April 2, 1917, President Wilson asked Congress to declare war against Germany and the other Central Powers. After four days of vigorous debate led by opponents of the war—including the first female elected representative, Jeanette P. Rankin from Montana—Congress voted to approve the war resolution. However, the United States underscored its historic commitment against "entangling alliances" by refusing to officially join the Allies, instead declaring itself an "Associated Power."

President Wilson had not reached his decision lightly. For three years, he resisted calls for war. His policies had tended to favor the Allies, but the president understood that going to war would have grave consequences. He knew that he would be sending thousands of American men to their deaths and that the "spirit of ruthless brutality [would] enter the very fiber of our national life." In the end, however, Wilson decided that only by going to war would he be able to ensure that the United States played a role in shaping the peace. For the president, the security of the nation rested on respect for law, human rights, and extension of free governments. "The world must be made safe for democracy," he informed Congress in his war message, and he had concluded that the only way to guarantee this outcome was by helping to defeat Germany.

Trench Warfare   Trench warfare was at the center of the fighting in World War I. Both sides constructed a network of trenches and dugout shelters, fortified by barbed wire, and fought from these trenches to wear the enemy down. In this photograph, members of the 369th Infantry, a segregated African American unit nicknamed the "Harlem Hellfighters," occupy trenches to repel a German offensive into France in 1918.   The Art Archive at Art Resource, NY

It would take a while for Americans to live up to the lyrics of George M. Cohan's patriotic song "Over There," which announced that "the Yanks [were] coming" to rescue the Allies from defeat. First, the United States needed a large army, which it created through the draft. The Selective Service Act of 1917 conscripted 3 million men by war's end. Mobilizing such a large force required substantial time, and American troops on the battlefield did not make much of an impact until 1918. Before then, the U.S. navy made the greatest contribution. American warships joined the British in escorting merchant vessels, combating German submarines, and laying mines in the North Sea. The United States also provided crucial funding and supplies to the Allies as their reserves became depleted.

U.S. troops finally began to make an impact in Europe in May 1918. Allied forces were exhausted and weary, and in November 1917 they had suffered a further blow when the Russian Revolution installed a Bolshevik (Communist) regime that negotiated a separate peace with the Central Powers. Fresh recruits from the United States helped shift the war toward Allied victory. From May through September, more than 1 million American troops under the command of General Pershing helped the Allies repel German offensives in northern France near the Belgian border. One momentous battle in the Argonne Forest lasted two months until the Allies broke through enemy lines and pushed toward Germany. Nearly 50,000 American troops died in the fierce fighting, and another 230,000 were injured. Like their European counterparts, who suffered a staggering 8 to 10 million casualties, Americans experienced the horrors of war magnified by new technology. Dug into filthy trenches, soldiers dodged rapid machine-gun fire, heavy artillery explosions, and poison gas shells. In the end, however, American troops succeeded in tipping the balance in favor of the Allies. On November 11, 1918, an exhausted Germany surrendered.

> **REVIEW & RELATE**
>
> • In what ways, if any, did President Wilson's approach to Latin American affairs differ from that of his predecessors?
> • Why did President Wilson find it so difficult to keep the United States out of World War I?

Fighting the War at Home

Modern global warfare required full mobilization at home. With U.S. ground forces entering the fray late in the war, most Americans felt the effects of mobilization far more dramatically on the home front than on the battlefront. In preparing to support the war effort, the country drew on recent experience. The progressives' passion for organization, expertise, efficiency, and moralistic control was harnessed to the effort of placing the economy on a wartime footing and rallying the American people behind the war. In the process, the government gained unprecedented control over American life. At the same time, the war effort also produced unforeseen economic and political opportunities.

Government by Commission

Progressives had relied on government commissions to regulate business practices as well as health and safety standards, and in July 1917 the Wilson administration followed suit by establishing the War Industries Board (WIB) to supervise the purchase of military supplies and to gear up private enterprise to meet demand. However, the WIB was largely ineffective until March 1918, when the president found the right man to lead it. He chose Wall Street financier Bernard Baruch, who recruited staff from business enterprises that the board regulated. Baruch prodded businesses into compliance mainly by offering lucrative contracts rather than by coercion. Working for a token $1 a year (but still on their company payrolls), the members of this agency helped reduce the chaos of mobilization. Ultimately, these businessmen created a government partnership with the corporate sector that would last beyond the war.

Labor also experienced significant gains through government regulation. Shortages of workers and an outbreak of strikes—more than four thousand in 1917—hampered the war effort. In April 1918, Wilson created the National War Labor Board (NWLB) to settle labor disputes. The agency consisted of representatives from unions, corporations, and the public. In exchange for obtaining a "no strike pledge" from organized labor, the NWLB supported an eight-hour workday with time-and-a-half pay for overtime, labor's right to collective bargaining, and equal pay for equal work by women.

The NWLB fell short of reaching this last goal, but the war employed more than a million women who had not held jobs before. As military and government services expanded, women found greater opportunities as telephone operators, nurses, and clerical workers. At the same time, the number of women employed as domestic servants declined. Women took over formerly male jobs driving streetcars, delivering ice, assembling airplane motors, operating drill presses, oiling railroad engines, and welding parts. Yet women's incomes continued to lag significantly behind those of men performing the same tasks.

Americans probably experienced the expanding scope of government intervention most directly through the efforts of three new agencies that regulated consumption and travel. Wilson appointed Herbert Hoover, a progressive mining engineer, to head the Food Administration. Hoover sought to increase the military and civilian food supply mainly through voluntary conservation measures. He generated a massive publicity campaign urging Americans to adopt "wheatless Mondays," "meatless Tuesdays," and "porkless Thursdays and Saturdays." Chicago housewives demonstrated their ingenuity in cooking leftovers, as evidenced by a sharp decline in the volume of raw garbage in the city. The government also mobilized schoolchildren to plant vegetable gardens to increase food production for the home front. Wilson considered children's work in the School Garden Army "just as real and patriotic an effort as the building of ships or the firing of cannon."

Consumers saved gas and oil under the prodding of the Fuel Administration. The agency encouraged fuel "holidays" along the line of Hoover's voluntary restrictions and created daylight saving time to conserve fuel by adding an extra hour of sunlight to the end of the workday. The Fuel Administration also offered higher prices to coal companies in order to increase productivity. Patterns of consumer travel changed under government regulation. The Railroad Administration acted more forcefully than most other agencies. Troop and supply shipments depended on the efficient operation of the railways. The administration controlled the railroads during the war, coordinating train schedules, overseeing terminals and regulating ticket prices, upgrading tracks, and raising workers' wages.

Winning Hearts and Minds

America's entry into the Great War did not immediately end the significant antiwar sentiment. Consequently, Wilson waged a campaign to rally support for his aims and to stimulate patriotic fervor. To generate enthusiasm and ensure loyalty, the president named Denver journalist George Creel to head the **Committee on Public Information (CPI)**, which focused on generating propaganda.

Online Document Project
The Committee on Public Information and Wartime Propaganda
bedfordstmartins.com/hewittlawsonvalue

Creel recruited a vast network of lecturers to speak throughout the country and spread patriotic messages. The committee coordinated rallies to sell bonds and raise money to fund the war. The CPI persuaded reporters to censor their war coverage, and most agreed in order to avoid government intervention. The agency helped produce films depicting the Allies as heroic saviors of humanity and the Central Powers as savage beasts. The CPI also distributed colorful and sometimes lurid posters emphasizing the depravity of the enemy and the nation's moral responsibility to defeat the Central Powers. All the talk of fighting for democracy encouraged groups with long-standing grievances because of their treatment at home to rally around the flag. W. E. B. Du Bois, one of the founders of the NAACP, backed Wilson's democratic aims in the hope that the war would lead to racial equality in the United States.

Propaganda did not, however, prove sufficient, and many Americans remained deeply divided about the war. To suppress dissent, Congress passed the Espionage Act in 1917 and the Sedition Act a year later. Both limited freedom of speech by criminalizing certain forms of expression. The **Espionage Act** prohibited antiwar activities, including interfering with the draft. It also banned the mailing of publications advocating forcible interference with any laws. The **Sedition Act** punished individuals who expressed beliefs disloyal or abusive to the American government, flag, or military uniform. Of the slightly more than two thousand prosecutions under these laws, only a handful concerned charges of actual sabotage or espionage. Most defendants brought to trial were critics who merely spoke out against the war. In 1918, for telling a crowd that the military draft was a form of slavery that turned inductees into "cannon fodder," the Socialist Party's Eugene V. Debs was tried, convicted, and sentenced to ten years under the Espionage Act. (President Warren G. Harding pardoned Debs in 1921.) The Justice Department also went after the Industrial Workers of the World (IWW), which continued to initiate labor strikes during the war. The government broke into the offices of the IWW, ransacked the Wobblies' files for evidence of disloyalty, and arrested more than 130 members, including their dynamic leader Big Bill Haywood, who subsequently fled to the Soviet Union to avoid jail.

Government efforts to promote national unity and punish those who did not conform prompted local communities to enforce "one hundred percent Americanism." Civic groups banned the playing of German music and operas from concert halls, and schools prohibited teaching the German language. Arbiters of culinary taste, prompted by patriotic enthusiasm, renamed foods with German origins—sauerkraut became "liberty cabbage," and hamburgers became "liberty sandwiches." Such sentiments were expressed in a more sinister fashion when mobs assaulted German Americans.

Prejudice toward German Americans was further inflamed by the formation of the **American Protective League (APL)**, a quasi-official association endorsed by the Justice Department. Consisting of 200,000 chapters throughout the country, the APL employed individuals to spy on German residents suspected of disloyal behavior. In cooperation with the Bureau of Investigation (later the FBI), APL members tried to uncover German spies, but most often they found little more than German immigrants who merely retained attachments to family and friends in their homeland. Gossip and rumor fueled many of the league's loyalty probes. In May 1918, the APL sent one of its agents to investigate the cook of a family living in Manhattan, because she allegedly had "a picture of the Kaiser in her room" and was "very pro-German and talks in favor of the Germans." The investigator found no photograph of the kaiser or any other evidence of suspicious behavior.

The repressive side of progressivism came to the fore in other ways as well. Anti-immigrant bias, shared by many reformers, flourished. The effort to conserve manpower and grain supplies bolstered the impulse to control standards of moral behavior, particularly those associated with immigrants, such as drinking. This anti-immigrant prejudice in part explains the ratification of the Eighteenth Amendment in 1919, prohibiting the sale of all alcoholic beverages. Yet not all the moral indignation unleashed by the war resulted in restriction of freedom. After considerable wartime protest and lobbying, women suffragists succeeded in securing the right to vote (see chapter 19).

Waging Peace

In January 1918, ten months before the war ended, President Wilson presented Congress with his plan for peace without rancor. Wilson centered his ideas around **Fourteen Points**, principles that he hoped would prevent future wars. Based on his assessment of the causes of the Great War, Wilson envisioned a generous peace treaty that included freedom of the seas, open diplomacy and the abolition of secret treaties, free trade, self-determination for colonial subjects, and a reduction in military spending. More important than any specific measure, Wilson's proposal hinged on the creation of the **League of Nations**, a body of large and small nations that would guarantee peaceful resolution of disputes and back up decisions through collective action, including the use of military force as a last resort.

Following the armistice that ended the war on November 11, 1918, Wilson personally took his message to the Paris Peace Conference, the postwar meeting of the victorious Allied nations that would set the terms of the peace. The first sitting president to travel overseas, Wilson was greeted in Paris by joyous crowds when he arrived leading the American delegation.

For nearly six months, Wilson tried to convince reluctant Allied leaders to accept the central components of his plan. Having exhausted themselves financially and having suffered the loss of a generation of young men, the Allies intended to scoop up the spoils of victory and make the Central Powers pay dearly. The European Allies intended to hold on to their respective colonies regardless of Wilson's call for self-determination, and as a nation that depended on a strong navy, Britain refused to limit its options by discussing freedom of the seas. Perhaps Georges Clemenceau, France's president, best expressed his colleagues' skepticism about Wilson's idealistic vision: "President Wilson and his Fourteen Points bore me. Even God Almighty has only ten!"

During the conference, Wilson was forced to compromise on a number of his principles in order to retain the cornerstone of his diplomacy—the establishment of the League of Nations. He abandoned his hope for peace without bitterness by agreeing to a "war guilt" clause that levied huge economic reparations on Germany for starting the war. He was willing to sacrifice some of his ideals because the league took on even greater importance in the wake of the Communist revolution in Russia. The president believed that capitalism, as regulated and reformed during the Progressive Era, would raise living conditions throughout the world as it had done in the United States, would prevent the spread of communism, and would benefit U.S. commerce by paving the way to free trade. Wilson needed the league to keep the peace so that war-ravaged and recovering nations had the opportunity to practice economic freedom and political democracy. In the end, the president won agreement for the establishment of his cherished League of Nations. The final treaty signed at the palace of Versailles, just outside Paris, authorized the league to combat aggression against any member nation through collective military action.

The Failure of Ratification

In July 1919, after enduring bruising battles in Paris, Wilson returned to Washington, D.C., only to face another wrenching struggle in the Senate over ratification of the Versailles treaty. The odds were stacked against Wilson from the start. The Republicans held a majority in the Senate, and Wilson needed the support of two-thirds of the

Senate to secure ratification. Moreover, Henry Cabot Lodge, the Republican chairman of the Senate Foreign Relations Committee, opposed Article X of the League of Nations covenant, which sanctioned collective security arrangements against military aggression. Lodge argued that such an alliance compromised the United States' independence in conducting its own foreign relations. The Massachusetts senator wanted the United States to preserve the possibility of unilateral action without being restrained by the league's policies. Lodge had at least thirty-nine senators behind him, more than enough to block ratification. Conceding the need to protect the country's national self-interest, the president agreed to modifications to the treaty so that the Monroe Doctrine and America's obligations in the Caribbean and Central America were kept intact. Lodge, who loathed Wilson, was not satisfied and insisted on adding fourteen "reservations" limiting compliance with the treaty, including strong language affirming Congress's right to declare war before agreeing to a League of Nations military action.

Wilson's stubbornness more than equaled Lodge's, and the president refused to compromise further over the league. Insisting that he was morally bound to honor the treaty he had negotiated in good faith, Wilson rejected additional changes demanded by Lodge and his supporters. Making matters worse, Wilson faced resistance from sixteen lawmakers dubbed "irreconcilables," who opposed the league under any circumstances. Mainly Republicans from the Midwest and West, they voiced the traditional American rejection of entangling alliances.

To break the logjam, the president attempted to rally public opinion behind him. In September 1919, he embarked on a nationwide speaking tour to carry his message directly to the American people. Over a three-week period, he traveled eight thousand miles by train, keeping a grueling schedule that exhausted him. After a stop in Pueblo, Colorado, on September 25, Wilson collapsed and canceled the rest of his trip. On October 2, Wilson suffered a massive stroke that nearly killed him. The effects of the stroke, which left him partially paralyzed, emotionally unstable, and mentally impaired, dimmed any remaining hopes of compromise. The full extent of his illness was kept from the public, and his wife, Edith, ran the White House for the next eighteen months.

On November 19, 1919, the Senate rejected the amended treaty. The following year, Wilson had one final chance to obtain ratification, but still he refused to accept reservations. He ignored leaders of his own party who were willing to vote for the Republican-sponsored amendments. "Let Lodge compromise," the president responded defiantly. In March 1920, treaty ratification failed one last time, falling just seven votes short of the required two-thirds majority. Had Wilson shown the same willingness to compromise that he had in Paris, the outcome might have been different. In the end, however, the United States never signed the Treaty of Versailles or joined the League of Nations, weakening the league and diminishing the prospects for long-term peace.

REVIEW & RELATE

- What steps did the U.S. government take to control the economy and public opinion during World War I?
- How did President Wilson's wartime policies and his efforts to shape the peace that followed reflect his progressive roots?

Conclusion: An American Empire

In the final decade of the nineteenth century, the United States transformed itself into an imperial power. Presidents McKinley and Roosevelt carried out the strategy outlined by Captain Alfred Thayer Mahan to enlarge the navy, construct a canal linking the Atlantic and Pacific Oceans, and acquire coaling stations and bases in the Pacific to service the fleet. U.S. officials disregarded the nationalistic aspirations of freedom fighters such as José Martí in Cuba and Emilio Aguinaldo in the Philippines in favor of the imperial spoils gained from winning the War of 1898. The United States justified intervention on moral grounds predicated on racist beliefs: As a fit and manly nation, the United States had the responsibility to uplift inferior peoples to "civilized" standards and make them capable of self-government. This justification quickly wore thin. To crush the rebellion in the Philippines, the military engaged in atrocities that called into question the honor and virtue of the United States. Once it achieved victory in the Philippines, the nation concentrated its efforts on maintaining territories primarily for commercial purposes. Within the few short years from 1898 to 1904, this commercial empire had fallen into place.

The progressive presidents, Roosevelt and Wilson, created and sustained an American empire. They disagreed significantly in approach—Roosevelt favoring force, Wilson preferring negotiations; Roosevelt a realist, Wilson a moralist—but in practice they shared a willingness to use military power to protect national interests. These two presidents helped construct the modern American state, an expanded federal government that officially sanctioned cooperation with responsible corporate leaders. This relationship reached its peak during World War I. In mobilizing the home front, the Wilson administration blurred the line between public and private business by expanding the reach of government over the economy and curtailed personal liberty.

In 1917, because of its heavy reliance on trade with foreign countries, especially in Europe, the United States confronted its first major international crisis of the twentieth century. Wilson reluctantly led the country into war to guarantee a world order in which reasonable nations attempted to resolve controversies through negotiation, not violence. The failure of the United States to join the League of Nations, for which the president was largely responsible, shattered that idealistic dream.

The United States retreated from joining an international body offering collective security, but it did not isolate itself from participation in the world. The country emerged from the war in excellent financial shape; it had become the leading foreign creditor, and its industrial capacity had greatly expanded. Tending its commercial empire in the Caribbean and Central America, the United States probed for new markets in Asia and the Middle East. It would take another two decades for policymakers to realize that the country's refusal to support a strong collective response to expansionist aggression posed serious dangers for American commerce and values.

Chapter Review

MAKE IT STICK

 LearningCurve bedfordstmartins.com/hewittlawsonvalue
After reading the chapter, use LearningCurve to retain what you've read.

IDENTIFY KEY TERMS

Identify and explain the significance of each term below.

jingoists (p. 515)
Cuba Libre (p. 516)
yellow journalism (p. 517)
Teller Amendment (p. 518)
Platt Amendment (p. 518)
Anti-Imperialist League (p. 520)
Roosevelt Corollary (p. 522)
Open Door (p. 522)
dollar diplomacy (p. 523)
Mexican revolution (p. 524)

Zimmermann telegram (p. 527)
War Industries Board (WIB) (p. 529)
National War Labor Board (NWLB) (p. 529)
Committee on Public Information (CPI)
(p. 530)
Espionage Act (p. 531)
Sedition Act (p. 531)
American Protective League (APL) (p. 531)
Fourteen Points (p. 532)
League of Nations (p. 532)

REVIEW & RELATE

Answer the focus questions from each section of the chapter.

1. What role did economic developments play in prompting calls for an American empire? What role did social and cultural developments play?

2. Why did the United States embark on building an empire in the 1890s and not decades earlier?

3. Why did the United States go to war with Spain in 1898?

4. In what ways did the War of 1898 mark a turning point in the relationship between the United States and the rest of the world?

5. How did the United States assert its influence and control over Latin America in the early twentieth century?

6. How did U.S. policies in Latin America mirror U.S. policies in Asia?

7. In what ways, if any, did President Wilson's approach to Latin American affairs differ from that of his predecessors?

8. Why did President Wilson find it so difficult to keep the United States out of World War I?

9. What steps did the U.S. government take to control the economy and public opinion during World War I?

10. How did President Wilson's wartime policies and his efforts to shape the peace that followed reflect his progressive roots?

ONLINE DOCUMENT PROJECTS

◆ **Imperialism versus Anti-Imperialism**
◆ **The Committee on Public Information and Wartime Propaganda**

After reading the primary sources in these document sets, answer the **Interpret the Evidence** questions to help you analyze each of the documents, and then answer the **Put It in Context** question(s) to help you relate the documents to the topics and themes you read about in the chapter.

bedfordstmartins.com/hewittlawsonvalue

TIMELINE OF EVENTS

1880–1900	• U.S. creates third most powerful navy in the world	**1914**	• Panama Canal opens under American control
1890	• Alfred Mahan publishes *The Influence of Sea Power upon History*		• World War I begins
		1915	• German submarine sinks the *Lusitania*
1893	• American plantation owners overthrow Queen Liliuokalani of Hawaii	**1916**	• Wilson sends U.S. troops into Mexico to capture Pancho Villa
1895	• Cuban War for Independence begins	**1917**	• Zimmermann telegram becomes public
1898	• U.S. battleship *Maine* explodes		• United States enters World War I
	• The War of 1898 begins		• Espionage Act passed
	• Anti-Imperialist League founded		• War Industries Board established
1899–1902	• Philippine-American War		• Committee on Public Information established
1901	• Platt Amendment passed	**1918**	• Sedition Act passed
1904	• Roosevelt Corollary announced		• National War Labor Board established
1909	• U.S. intervenes in Nicaragua on behalf of American fruit and mining companies		• Germany surrenders, ending World War I
		1919	• Wilson loses battle for ratification of Treaty of Versailles

21

✓ LearningCurve
bedfordstmartins.com/hewittlawsonvalue
After reading the chapter, use LearningCurve
to retain what you've read.

An Anxious Affluence

1919–1929

AMERICAN HISTORIES

David Curtis (D. C.) Stephenson's relentless pursuit of the American dream kept him constantly on the move. Born in 1891 to Texas sharecroppers, Stephenson moved with his family to the Oklahoma Territory in 1901. After quitting school at age sixteen, he drifted around the state for more than a decade, working for a string of newspapers and gaining a reputation as a heavy drinker and a ladies' man. In 1915 he married and appeared to settle down; however, he soon lost his newspaper job, abandoned his pregnant wife, and hit the road working for one newspaper after another in between binges of drunkenness. His wife divorced him, and in 1917 Stephenson joined the army to fight in World War I. He was stationed stateside, but his service was marked by a series of drunken brawls and sexual misadventures. Nevertheless, he rose to the rank of second lieutenant and received an honorable discharge in 1919.

Stephenson remarried and settled in Indiana, where he finally found financial and political success. In 1920 he joined the Ku Klux Klan (KKK), the Reconstruction-era organization that had reemerged in 1915 in Georgia. The newly revived Klan spread beyond the South, targeting African Americans, recent immigrants, Jews, and Catholics as enemies of traditional Protestant family values. Stephenson directed Klan operations in twenty-three states, building a profitable empire on fear and prejudice as well as get-rich-quick schemes that appealed to the spirit of American adventure. A few years later, however, his old pattern of self-destruction led to his arrest and conviction on rape and second-degree murder charges and the end of his Klan career.

Ossian Sweet also pursued the American dream. Like Stephenson, he rose from humble beginnings, but he had far more to overcome. The descendant

537

of slaves, Sweet was born in 1895 and grew up in the central Florida town of Bartow. Hoping to shield him from the violence that whites used to keep Bartow's blacks in their place, Sweet's parents sent him north when he was thirteen years old to get an education.

After attending Wilberforce University in Ohio and Howard Medical School in Washington, D.C., Sweet moved to Detroit in 1921 to open a medical practice in the city's ghetto known as "Black Bottom." He married, and in 1924 the Sweets decided to buy a house for their growing family, which now included an infant daughter, in a working-class neighborhood occupied exclusively by whites. Before the Sweets moved in, their white neighbors, with Klan backing, began organizing to keep them out.

When the Sweet family finally moved into their house on September 8, 1925, they encountered a hostile crowd in the street. Dr. Sweet had brought some backup with him, including two younger brothers and several friends. Armed in case the mob got out of hand, the Sweets and their defenders fired their weapons at the crowd after rocks smashed through the upstairs windows of the house. When the shooting stopped and the police restored calm, one white man lay dead and another wounded. Dr. Sweet, his wife Gladys, and the other nine occupants of his house went on trial on first-degree murder charges. The NAACP represented the eleven defendants and hired the famous criminal defense attorney Clarence Darrow. After two trials—the first ended in a hung jury—Darrow won an acquittal for his clients in 1926.

THE AMERICAN HISTORIES of Ossian Sweet and D. C. Stephenson illustrate the competing forces that shaped the 1920s. Both achieved a measure of financial success, but they did so in the post–World War I atmosphere of growing social friction and intense racial resentments. After serving in the war, many blacks and ethnic minorities had a greater sense of pride in themselves. When Sweet's parents decided to send him north to get an education, they were responding to the racial violence that plagued the South, but they were also demonstrating their belief that a better life was possible for their son. By contrast, Stephenson grew wealthy by tapping into the same racial tensions that shaped the Sweets' lives. Just as the census of 1890 had announced the end of the frontier, the census of 1920 indicated that the population of rural America had dwindled and that the majority of Americans now lived in cities with more than 2,500 people. Many who considered themselves "100 percent Americans," born and bred in small towns or living in sections of cities with homogeneous populations, believed that racial and ethnic minorities threatened their power. Although the general prosperity of the period masked the tensions lying beneath the surface, it did not eliminate them. As the experiences of D. C. Stephenson and Ossian Sweet show, the decade following the end of World War I opened up fresh avenues for economic prosperity as well as new sites for cultural clashes exacerbated by the tensions of modern America.

Three women strolling on Seventh Avenue in Harlem, 1927. The Granger Collection, New York

Postwar Turmoil

The return of peace in 1918 brought with it problems that would persist into the 1920s. Government efforts to suppress opposition to U.S. involvement in World War I fostered an atmosphere of repression that continued after the war ended, culminating in a wave of anti-Communist actions known as the Red scare. An influenza epidemic that killed hundreds of thousands of Americans and millions of people around the world heightened the climate of fear. Finally, the abrupt and painful transition away from a wartime economy produced inflation, labor unrest, and escalating racial tensions. The 1920s would come to be known as a decade of prosperity, but in the years immediately following the war the prospects for growth and stability seemed bleak.

The Supreme Court and Civil Liberties

On March 3, 1919, the Supreme Court invoked the Espionage Act to uphold the conviction of Charles Schenck, the general secretary of the Socialist Party, for mailing thousands of leaflets opposing the military draft. Delivering the Court's unanimous opinion, Justice Oliver Wendell Holmes argued that during wartime Congress has the authority to prohibit individuals from using words that create "a clear and present danger" to the safety of the country. Although the trial record failed to show that Schenck's leaflets had convinced any young men to resist conscription, the Court upheld his conviction under Holmes's doctrine.

Later in 1919, the Supreme Court demonstrated what a slippery slope the "clear and present danger" test presented for freedom of speech in a case that concerned what many American leaders believed posed a great threat to the nation: the spread of world-wide communism, the system of government that challenged capitalism. The success of the Bolshevik Revolution in Russia in 1917 and the subsequent creation of the Union of Soviet Socialist Republics terrified officials of capitalist countries in western Europe and the United States. Their concerns escalated in 1918, when Russia, until then an Allied power, signed a separate treaty with Germany and pulled out of the war (see chapter 20). In response, President Woodrow Wilson ordered U.S. troops to assist anti-Communist Russian forces fighting against the Bolshevik regime.

Wilson's actions generated vocal opposition from American supporters of the Russian Revolution. In New York City, a small group of anarchists and socialists welcomed the fall of capitalism in Russia and the prospects of a worker-controlled state that would promote economic democracy. Many of these activists were immigrants who had fled from Russia to avoid czarist repression against political dissidents and Jews. In August 1918, a handful of anarchists, including Jacob Abrams, dropped leaflets off a building on the Lower East Side urging workers to protest "barbaric [American] intervention" and calling on them to engage in "a general strike" until the United States removed its troops from Russia. The government prosecuted six defendants, five men and one woman, for violating the Espionage and Sedition Acts; the jury found all of them guilty. On November 10, 1919, in *Abrams v. United States*, the Supreme Court affirmed the trial verdict, finding the distribution of the incendiary leaflets in wartime illegal.

  Online Document Project   **The *Abrams* Case and the Red Scare**
    bedfordstmartins.com/hewittlawsonvalue

The Red Scare, 1919–1920

The conviction in the *Abrams* case reflected broader concern over the Red scare—the fear of Communist-inspired radicalism in the wake of the Russian Revolution. Though communism failed to gain a foothold in the United States, the actions of a tiny contingent of radicals kept the threat alive and played into the hands of ambitious politicians and business leaders who wanted to crush labor agitation, which they perceived as anti-American.

Immediate postwar economic problems further increased the anxiety of American citizens, reinforcing the position of officials who sought to restore order by suppressing radicals. Industries were slow to convert their plants from military to civilian production, and consumer goods therefore remained in short supply. The war had brought jobs and higher wages on the home front, and consumers who had been restrained by wartime rationing were eager to spend their savings. With demand greatly exceeding supply, however, prices soared by 77 percent, frustrating consumers. At the same time, farmers, who had benefited from wartime conditions, faced falling crop prices as European nations resumed agricultural production and the federal government ended price supports.

A series of widespread strikes launched by labor unions in 1919 contributed to the fear that the United States was under assault by sinister, radical forces. As skyrocketing inflation undercut wages and employers launched a new round of union-busting efforts, labor went on the offensive. In 1919 more than four million workers went on strike nationwide, including those in key industries such as steel, transportation, and ship-building. In September, striking Boston policemen left the city unguarded, resulting in widespread looting and violence. Massachusetts governor Calvin Coolidge sent in the National Guard to break the strike and restore order.

Public officials and newspapers decried the violence, but they also greatly exaggerated the peril. Communists and socialists did support some union activities; however, few of the millions of workers who struck for higher wages and better working conditions had ties to extremists or sought to overthrow capitalism. The major prewar radical organization, the Industrial Workers of the World, never recovered from the government harassment that had crippled it during World War I. Postwar Communist parties in the United States claimed fewer than seventy thousand followers. However, scattered acts of real violence allowed government and business leaders to stir up anxieties about the Communist threat. On May 1, 1919, radicals sent more than thirty incendiary devices through the mail to prominent Americans, though authorities defused them before the mail bombs reached their intended targets. The following month, bombs exploded in eight cities, including one at the doorstep of the home of A. Mitchell Palmer, the attorney general of the United States, who emerged shocked but uninjured.

After the attack on his home, Palmer launched a government crusade to root out and prosecute Communist extremists. Like many American officials, Palmer traced the source of radicalism to recent immigrants, mainly those from Russia and eastern and southern Europe. To track down what he called the "moral perverts and hysterical neurasthenic [neurotic] women who abound in communism," Palmer selected J. Edgar Hoover, a young Washington, D.C., lawyer, to head the General Intelligence Division in the Department of Justice. In November 1919, based on Hoover's research and undercover activities, government agents in twelve cities rounded up and arrested hundreds of foreigners, including the anarchist and feminist Emma Goldman. Goldman, along with some 250 people caught in the government dragnet, were soon deported to Russia. Over the next few months, the Palmer raids continued in more than thirty cities. Authorities seized approximately six thousand suspected radicals from their homes and community centers, took them to police stations, interrogated them without the benefit of legal counsel, and held them incommunicado without stipulating the charges against them. Of the thousands arrested, the government found reason to deport 556. The raids failed to uncover extensive plots to overthrow the U.S. government, nor did they lead to the arrest of the bombers.

Initially, most American citizens supported the Palmer raids, but their enthusiasm quickly waned. Many came to see the violations of civil liberties that accompanied the raids as a greater threat to the nation's traditions than the existence of a handful of American Communists. In 1920 a group of pacifists, progressives, and constitutional lawyers formed the American Civil Liberties Union (ACLU) to monitor government abridgments of the Bill of Rights. Although the Palmer raids ended, the Red scare manifested itself in different forms throughout the 1920s. After J. Edgar Hoover became director of the Bureau of Investigation (later renamed the Federal Bureau of Investigation) in 1921, he continued spying on suspected radicals, collecting information on a variety of Americans, and increasing his power over the next several decades.

Compounding the anxieties fueled by the Red scare, a medical crisis plunged Americans into panic. In late 1918, just as World War I was ending, an influenza epidemic struck the United States. Part of a worldwide contagion, the disease infected nearly 20 percent of the U.S. population and killed more than 675,000 people. Soldiers returning home from the war brought the flu virus with them. Infants and the elderly succumbed, as well as able-bodied young men and women. As the death toll mounted over the course of 1919, terror gripped the nation. Susanna Turner, a volunteer at an emergency hospital in Philadelphia, recalled: "The fear in the hearts of people just withered them. They were afraid to go out, afraid to do anything. If you asked a neighbor for help, they wouldn't do so because they weren't taking any chances. It was a horror-stricken time." A staggering 50 to 100 million people worldwide are estimated to have died from the flu before it subsided in 1920.

Racial Violence in the Postwar Era

Racial strife also heightened postwar anxieties. Drawn by the promise of wartime industrial jobs, more than 400,000 African Americans left the South beginning in 1917 and 1918 and headed north hoping to escape poverty and racial discrimination. (By 1930 another 800,000 blacks had left the South.) This exodus became known as the great migration. Black newspapers such as the *Chicago Defender* circulated throughout the South, offering glowing stories of the opportunities that adventurous blacks would find if they moved. Some 75,000 southern blacks heeded the call and relocated to Chicago. During World War I, many found work in steel mills, meatpacking, shipbuilding, and other heavy industries, but most were relegated to low-paying jobs. Still, as a carpenter earning $95 a month wrote from Chicago to a friend back in Hattiesburg, Mississippi: "I should have been here 20 years ago. I just begin to feel like a man." Most African American women remained employed as domestic workers, but more than 100,000 obtained manufacturing jobs.

For many blacks, however, the North was not the "promised land" they expected. Instead, they encountered bitter opposition from white migrants from the South competing for employment and scarce housing. As black and white veterans returned from the war, racial hostilities exploded. In 1919 race riots erupted in twenty-five cities throughout the country, including one in Washington, D.C., that left a deep impression on Ossian Sweet, who witnessed it firsthand.

The worst of these disturbances occurred in Chicago during what James Weldon Johnson, a poet and an NAACP official, called "Red Summer." On a hot July day, a black youth swimming at a Lake Michigan beach inadvertently crossed over into an area of water customarily reserved for whites. In response, white bathers shouted at the swimmer to return to the black section of the beach. To make their point more forcefully, they hurled stones at him. The black swimmer drowned, and word of the incident quickly spread through white and black neighborhoods in Chicago. For thirteen days, mobs of blacks and whites attacked each other, ransacked businesses, and torched homes. Over the course of the riots, at least 15 whites and 23 blacks died, 178 whites and 342 blacks were injured, and more than a thousand black families were left homeless. Against this background, D. C. Stephenson's Ku Klux Klan began to flourish in the North.

REVIEW & RELATE

• What factors combined to produce the turmoil of the immediate postwar period?

• What factors contributed to the rise in racial tensions that accompanied the transition from wartime to peacetime?

People of Plenty

Despite the turbulence of the immediate postwar period and the persistence of underlying social and racial tensions, the 1920s were a time of vigorous economic growth. Between 1922 and 1927, the economy grew by 7 percent a year, the largest peacetime rate up to that point. Over the decade, the gross domestic product (then called the gross national product), per capita income, and the average purchasing power of wage earners all soared. At the same time, unemployment rates remained low, as producers added new workers in an effort to keep up with increasing consumer demand. Aligning themselves with big business, government officials took an active role in stimulating economic growth. Their efforts shaped and accelerated economic developments that amounted to a second industrial revolution.

Government Promotion of the Economy

The general prosperity of the 1920s owed a great deal to backing by the federal government. Republicans controlled the presidency and Congress, and though they claimed to stand for principles of laissez-faire and opposed various economic and social reforms, they were willing to use governmental power to support large corporations and the wealthy.

Senator Warren G. Harding of Ohio, who was elected president in 1920, pledged to restore "normalcy" after World War I and the tumult of the Red scare. Summing up the Republican philosophy, Harding declared that he and his party wanted "less government in business and more business in government." Harding's cabinet appointments reflected this goal. Treasury Secretary Andrew Mellon, a banker and an aluminum company titan, believed that the government should stimulate economic growth by reducing taxes on the rich, raising tariffs to protect manufacturers from foreign competition, and trimming the budget. The Republican Congress enacted much of this agenda, reducing spending and lowering inheritance and corporate taxes. During the Harding administration, tax rates for the wealthy, which had skyrocketed during World War I, plummeted from 66 percent to 20 percent. Mellon believed that those on the lower rungs of the economic ladder would prosper once business people invested the extra money they received from tax breaks into expanding production. Supposedly, the wealth would trickle down through increased jobs and purchasing power. At the same time, Republicans turned Progressive Era regulatory agencies such as the Federal Trade Commission and the Federal Reserve Board into boosters for major corporations and financial institutions by weakening regulatory enforcement.

Secretary of Commerce Herbert Hoover had an even greater impact than Mellon in cementing the government-business partnership during the 1920s. A progressive who ably headed the Food Administration during World War I, Hoover believed that the federal government had a role to play in the economy and in lessening economic suffering. Rejecting government control of business activities, however, he insisted on voluntary cooperation between the public and private sectors. The secretary of commerce favored the creation of trade associations in which businesses would collaborate to stabilize production levels, prices, and wages. In turn, the Commerce Department would provide helpful data and information to improve productivity and trade.

Hoover's vision fit into a larger Republican effort to weaken unions by promoting voluntary business-sponsored worker welfare initiatives. For example, under the American Plan (the name itself implied that unions were "un-American"), some firms established health insurance and pension plans for their workers. As early as 1914, Henry Ford provided his autoworkers over twenty-two years old "a share in the profits of the house" equal to a minimum wage of $5 a day, and he cut the workday from nine hours to eight hours. Already under pressure from such tactics, unions were further damaged by a series of Supreme Court rulings that restricted strikes and overturned hard-won union victories such as child labor legislation and minimum wage laws. By 1929 union membership had dropped from approximately five million to three million, or about 10 percent of the industrial labor market.

Scandals during the presidency of Warren G. Harding diminished its luster but did not tarnish the shine of Republican economic policy. The Teapot Dome scandal grabbed the most headlines. In 1921 Interior Secretary Albert Fall collaborated with Navy Secretary Edwin Denby to transfer naval oil reserves to the Interior Department. Fall then parceled out these properties to private companies. As a result, Harry F. Sinclair's Mammoth Oil Company received a lease to develop the Teapot Dome section in Wyoming. In return for this handout, Sinclair delivered more than $300,000, much of it in cash, to Fall. In the wake of congressional hearings launched by Senator Thomas J. Walsh of Montana, one of the few progressives remaining in Congress, Fall and Sinclair were convicted on a number of criminal charges and sent to jail.

Harding's sudden death from a heart attack in August 1923 brought Vice President Calvin Coolidge to the presidency. The former Massachusetts governor, who had sent state troops to quell the Boston police strike in 1919, distanced himself from the scandals of his predecessor's administration but reaffirmed Harding's economic policies. "The chief business of the American people is business," President Coolidge remarked succinctly.

Americans Become Consumers

The 1920s marked a period of economic expansion and general prosperity. National income rose from approximately $63 billion to $88 billion and per capita income jumped from $641 to $847, an increase of 32 percent. The purchasing power of wage earners climbed approximately 20 percent.

This great spurt of economic growth in the 1920s resulted from the application of technological innovation and scientific management techniques to industrial production (Figure 21.1). Perhaps the greatest innovation came with the introduction of the assembly line. First used in the automobile industry before World War I, the assembly line moved the product to a worker who performed a specific task before sending it along to the next worker. This deceptively simple system, perfected by Henry Ford, saved enormous time and energy by emphasizing repetition, accuracy, and standardization. As a result, a new car rolled out of one of Ford's auto plants in less than a minute—earlier it had taken twelve and a half hours. Streamlined production lowered costs, which, in turn, allowed Ford to lower prices. The price of a new Model T dropped from $725 in 1910 to $290 in the early 1920s.

Besides the automobile, the second industrial revolution focused on the production of consumer-oriented goods previously considered luxuries. The electrification of urban homes created demand for a wealth of new laborsaving appliances; rural areas,

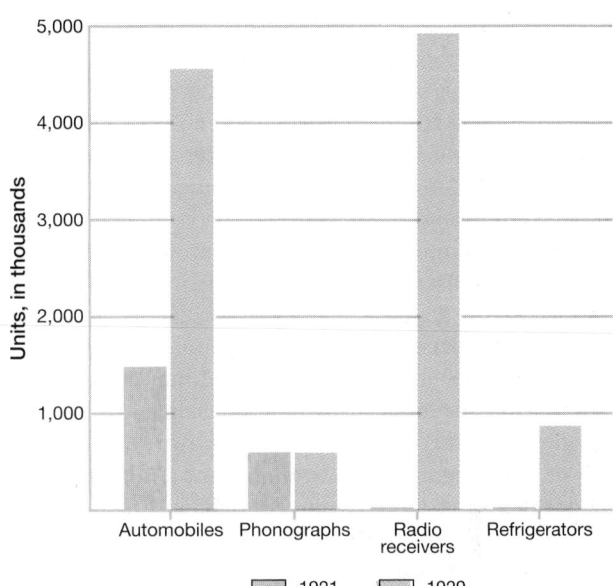

FIGURE 21.1
Production of Consumer Goods, 1921 and 1929 Rising per capita income, lower manufacturing costs, urban electrification, and advertising spurred the production of consumer goods in the 1920s. The most popular new items—automobiles and radios—brought Americans together through better transportation and communication.

most of which lacked electricity, did not benefit. Refrigerators, washing machines, toasters, and vacuum cleaners appealed to middle-class housewives whose husbands could afford to purchase them. Wristwatches replaced bulkier pocket watches. Radios became the chief source of home entertainment, and families gathered around the radio console to listen to music, news, and sports. Religious and political radio programs helped spread their particular faiths and ideologies, and those farmers equipped with electricity depended on the radio for weather reports and agricultural prices.

Although such household items changed the lives of many Americans, no single product had as profound an effect on American life in the 1920s as the automobile. Auto sales soared in the 1920s from 1.5 million to 5 million, making Henry Ford a multimillionaire and fueling the growth of related industries such as steel, rubber, petroleum, and glass. In 1929 Ford and his competitors at General Motors, Chevrolet, and Oldsmobile employed nearly 4 million workers, and around one in eight American workers toiled in factories connected to automobile production.

The automobile also changed day-to-day living patterns. Although most roads and highways consisted of dirt and contained rocks and ruts, enough were paved to extend the boundaries of suburbs farther from the city. By the end of the 1920s, around 17 percent of Americans lived in suburbia. Cars allowed families to travel to vacation destinations at greater distances from their homes. Even the roadside landscape changed to accommodate weary travelers, as gas stations, diners, and motels sprang up to serve them, and advertisers constructed billboards along the roads to remind them of what they needed. Each year, vacation resorts on the east and west coasts of Florida attracted thousands of tourists who drove south to enjoy the state's balmy climate and beautiful beaches. The use of automobile technology blended the conveniences of modern America with the primitiveness of the environment. Outdoor camping became the craze.

The automobile also provided new dating opportunities for young men and women. At the turn of the twentieth century, a young man courted a woman by going to her home and sitting with her on the sofa or out on the porch under the watchful eyes of her parents and family members. When the couple left the house, they might walk to a park and listen to a bandstand concert, again in the company of others. With the arrival of the automobile, couples could move from the couch in the parlor to the backseat of a car, away from adult supervision. Driving to a "lover's lane" in a Model T and drinking from a flask of prohibited alcohol, the young couple could explore new sexual terrain that had been denied them in the past (most likely "petting"—kissing and rubbing rather than intercourse).

Although Ford and his fellow manufacturers had succeeded in lowering prices for consumers, they still had to convince Americans to spend their hard-earned money to purchase their products. Turning for help to New York City's Madison Avenue, the location of the fledgling advertising industry, manufacturers nearly tripled their spending on advertising over the course of the 1920s. Firms pitched their products around price and quality, but they directed their efforts more than ever to the personal psychology of the consumer. Advertisers played on consumers' unexpressed fears, unfulfilled desires, hopes for success, and sexual fantasies. The producers of Listerine mouthwash transformed a product previously used to disinfect hospitals into one that fought the dreaded but made-up disease of halitosis (bad breath). Advertisers told people that they could measure success through consumption. Purchasing a General Electric (GE) all-steel refrigerator not only would preserve food longer but also would enhance the owners' reputation among their neighbors. "Happy to own it . . . proud to show it" headlined one ad explaining the virtues of GE's new product.

Although average wages and incomes rose during the 1920s, the majority of Americans did not have the disposable income to afford the bounty of new consumer goods. To resolve this problem, companies extended credit in dizzying amounts. By 1929 consumers purchased 60 percent of their cars and 80 percent of their radios and furniture on credit in the form of installment plans and owed a total of $3 billion. "Buy now and pay later" became the motto of corporate America. By putting a small amount down and making monthly payments with interest, people could obtain an assortment of consumer items they otherwise could not afford.

Perilous Prosperity

Prosperity in the 1920s was real enough, but behind the impressive financial indicators flashed warnings that profound danger loomed ahead. Perhaps most important, the boom was accompanied by growing income inequality. A majority of workers lived below the poverty line, and farmers plunged deeper into hard times. Corporate profits increased much faster than wages, resulting in a disproportionate share of the wealth going to the rich. The combined income of the top 1 percent of families was greater than that of the 42 percent at the bottom (Figure 21.2); 66 percent lived below the income level ($1,800 to $2,000 annually) necessary to maintain an adequate standard of living. In addition, less than 1 percent of families accumulated 34 percent of the nation's savings, while around 78 percent of families had no savings at all.

Income inequality was a critical problem because America's new mass-production economy depended on ever-increasing consumption, and higher income groups could

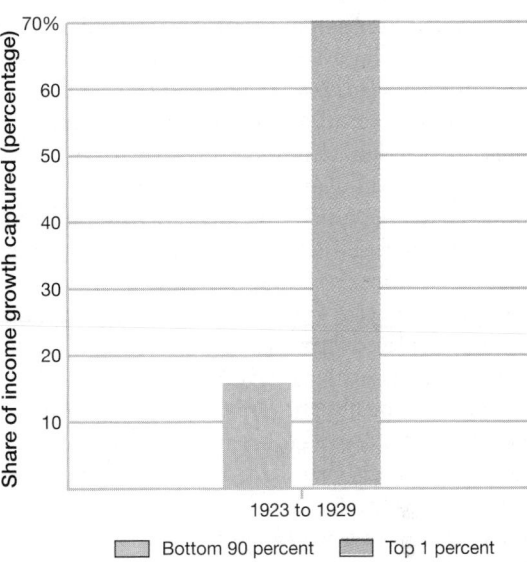

FIGURE 21.2

Income Inequality, 1923–1929 Although the U.S. economy expanded rapidly in the early 1920s, the accumulation of vast wealth among a small percentage of Americans created growing inequality. Although most Americans could purchase new consumer goods only by buying on credit, the richest 1 percent engaged in risky stock and real estate ventures to further enhance their wealth.

consume only so much, no matter how much of the nation's wealth they controlled. While the expansion of consumer credit helped hide this fundamental weakness, the low wages earned by most Americans drove down demand over time. Cutbacks in demand forced manufacturers to reduce production, thereby reducing jobs and increasing unemployment. In the days before unemployment insurance, this placed an increased burden on families to make ends meet and dragged down the demand for consumer goods even further. By 1926, as a result of lagging purchasing power, the growth of automobile sales had begun to slow, as did new housing construction—signs of an economy heading for trouble.

At the same time, the wealthy few used their disproportionate savings to speculate in the stock market and risky real estate ventures. To encourage investments, brokers promoted buying stocks on margin (credit) and required down payments of only a fraction of the market price. Without vigilant governmental oversight, banks and lending agencies extended credit without taking into account what would happen if a financial panic occurred and they were suddenly required to call in all of their loans. To make matters worse, the banking system operated on shaky financial grounds, combining savings facilities with speculative lending operations. With minimal interference from the Federal Trade Commission, business people frequently managed firms in a reckless way that created a high level of interdependence among them. For example, Samuel Insull, who owned a gas and electric utilities empire, was the chairman of the board of sixty-five companies, a director of eighty-five others, and the president of an additional seven corporations. This interlocking system of corporate ownership and control meant that the collapse of one company could bring down many others, while also imperiling the banking houses that had generously financed them.

Rampant real estate speculation in Florida foreshadowed these dangers, as private developers and the state government promoted tourism and land purchases. In many cases, investors bought properties sight unseen, as speculators and unscrupulous agents worked under the assumption that land values would continue to increase forever. However, severe storms in 1926 and 1928 abruptly halted the increase in land values. Land prices spiraled downward, speculators defaulted on bank loans, and financial institutions tottered.

Throughout the 1920s, fortunes plummeted for farmers as well. Despite the growing urbanization of the nation, farmers still made up one-third of the population. Declining world demand following the end of World War I, together with increased productivity because of the mechanization of agriculture, drove down farm prices and income. Between 1925 and 1929, falling wheat and cotton prices cut farm income in half. The collapse of farm prices had the most devastating effects on tenants and share-croppers who were forced off their lands through mortgage foreclosures. Around three million displaced farmers migrated to cities, where they had to compete with unskilled laborers for factory jobs and often found themselves among the ranks of the unemployed.

Internationally, the United States encountered serious economic obstacles. World War I had destroyed European economies, leaving them ill equipped to repay the $11 billion they had borrowed from the United States. Much of the Allied recovery, and hence the ability to repay debts, depended on obtaining the reparations imposed on Germany at the conclusion of World War I (see chapter 20). Germany, however, was in even worse shape than France and Britain and could not meet its obligations. Without a prosperous Europe, the American economy suffered. In 1924 the U.S. government sent Charles G. Dawes, a banker and soon to become Coolidge's vice president, to negotiate with Britain, France, and Germany to find a solution to their mutual problem. Under the terms of the eventual agreement, the United States provided loans to Germany to pay its reparations. In turn, Britain and France reduced the size of Germany's payments. The result was a series of circular payments. American banks loaned money to Germany, which used the money to pay reparations to Britain and France, which, in turn, used Germany's reparations payments to repay debts owed to American banks. What appeared a satisfactory resolution at the time ultimately proved a calamity. In undertaking this revolving-door solution, American bankers added to the cycle of spiraling credit and placed themselves at the mercy of unstable European economies. Compounding the problem, Republican administrations in the 1920s supported high tariffs on imports, reducing foreign manufacturers' revenues and therefore their nations' tax receipts, making it more difficult for these countries to pay off their debts.

REVIEW & RELATE

- Describe the relationship between business and government in the 1920s.
- Why was a high level of consumer spending so critical to 1920s prosperity, and why was the economic expansion of the 1920s ultimately unsustainable?

Challenges to Social Conventions

While most of the nation ignored growing evidence of the fragility of American prosperity, the social and cultural consequences of the second industrial revolution received considerable attention, as new, distinctly modern cultural patterns emerged. Advertising and credit, two of the mainstays of modern capitalism, sought to bypass the time-honored virtues of saving and living within one's means. Conventional sexual standards came under assault from the growth of the film and automobile industries, which influenced fashion styles and dating practices. In addition to moral and social behavior, traditional racial assumptions came under attack. African American writers and artists condemned the kind of racism Ossian Sweet experienced, drew on their rich racial legacies, and produced a cultural renaissance. Other blacks, led by the Jamaican immigrant Marcus Garvey, rejected the integrationist strategy of the NAACP in favor of black nationalism.

Breaking with the Old Morality

Challenges to the virtues of thrift and sacrifice were accompanied by a transformation of the moral codes of late-nineteenth-century America, especially those relating to sex. The entertainment industry played a large role in promoting relaxed attitudes toward sexual relations to a mass audience throughout the nation. The motion picture business, increasingly centered in Hollywood after 1920, attracted women and men to movie palaces where they could see swashbuckling heroes and glamorous heroines. In an era of silent movies, patrons in the nation's twenty thousand movie houses were enthralled not by the occasional dialogue printed on the screen but by the powerfully attractive images of the film stars.

Originally shown as short films for 5 cents in nickelodeons, the movies appealed to a national audience. Melodramas and comedies entertained the masses, and films such as D. W. Griffith's *Birth of a Nation* (1915) appealed to racial prejudices by glorifying the Ku Klux Klan. By the 1920s, films had expanded into feature-length pictures, Hollywood film studios had blossomed into major corporations, and movies were shown in ornate theaters in cities and towns across the country. The star system was born, and matinee idols such as Douglas Fairbanks, Charlie Chaplin, Clara Bow, and Mary Pickford influenced fashions and hairstyles. Female stars dressed as "flappers" and wooed audiences. Representing the liberated new woman, flappers wore short skirts, used ample makeup (formerly associated with prostitutes), smoked cigarettes in public, drank illegal alcoholic beverages, and gyrated to jazz tunes on the dance floor.

Americans could enjoy new entertainment opportunities and still remain faithful to traditional values. By 1929 approximately 40 percent of households owned a radio and could listen to stations affiliated with the two major broadcasting networks: the Columbia Broadcasting System (CBS) and the National Broadcasting Company (NBC). Shows such as *The General Motors Family* and *The Maxwell House Hour* blended product advertising with family entertainment. *Amos 'n' Andy* garnered large audiences by satirizing black working-class life, which, intentionally or not, reinforced racist stereotypes. In cities like New York and Chicago, immigrants could tune in to foreign-language radio programs aimed at non-English-speaking ethnic groups, which offered them an outlet for preserving their identity in the face of the increasing homogeneity fostered by the national consumer culture.

The most spirited challenge to both traditional values and the modern consumer culture came from a diverse group of intellectuals known as the Lost Generation. Gertrude Stein coined the term to describe the disillusionment that many of her fellow writers and artists felt after the ravages of World War I. Already concerned about the impact of mass culture and corporate capitalism on individualism and free thought, they focused their talents on criticizing what they saw as the hypocrisy of old values and the conformity ushered in by the new. In the novel *This Side of Paradise* (1920), F. Scott Fitzgerald complained that his generation had "grown up to find all Gods dead, all wars fought, all faith in man shaken." In a series of novels, including *Main Street* (1920), *Babbitt* (1922), and *Elmer Gantry* (1927), Sinclair Lewis ridiculed the narrow-mindedness of small-town life, the empty materialism of businessmen, and the insincerity of evangelical preachers. Journalist Henry Louis (H. L.) Mencken picked up these subjects in the pages of his magazine, *The American Mercury*. From his vantage point in Baltimore, Maryland, he lampooned the beliefs and behavior of Middle America and groused that its residents had turned democracy into "boobocracy," or government by boobs.

While radio audiences howled with laughter over the exploits of *Amos 'n' Andy*, scholars discredited conventional wisdom about race. Challenging studies that purported to demonstrate the intellectual superiority of whites over blacks, Columbia University anthropologist Franz Boas argued that any apparent intelligence gap between the races resulted from environmental factors and not heredity. His student Ruth Benedict further argued that the culture of so-called primitive tribes such as the Pueblo Indians, which emphasized cooperation and spiritual ideals, produced a less stressful and more emotionally connected lifestyle than that of more advanced societies. The ideas of Sigmund Freud, an Austrian psychoanalyst, shifted emphasis away from culture and race to individual consciousness. His disciples stressed the role of the unconscious mind and the power of the sex drive in shaping human behavior, beliefs that gained traction not only in university education but also in advertising appeals.

The African American Renaissance

The greatest challenge to conventional notions about race came from black Americans. The influx of southern black migrants to the North spurred by World War I and continuing into the 1920s created a black cultural renaissance, with New York City's Harlem and the South Side of Chicago leading the way. Black intellectuals joined their white counterparts in criticizing conventional social and cultural norms. Gathered in Harlem—with a population of more than 120,000 African Americans in 1920 and growing every day—a group of black writers paid homage to the New Negro, the second generation born after emancipation. These New Negro intellectuals refused to accept white supremacy. In militant voices, they expressed pride in their race, sought to perpetuate black racial identity, and demanded full citizenship and participation in American society. Intending to enrich the culture of the United States, black writers and poets drew on themes from African American life and history for inspiration in their literary works.

 Online Document Project   The New Negro and the Harlem Renaissance
bedfordstmartins.com/hewittlawsonvalue

These men and women made up the "Talented Tenth," the leaders of the black race whom W. E. B. Du Bois had spoken of in *The Souls of Black Folk* (1903). James Weldon Johnson, a writer and the chief executive of the NAACP, commented: "The final measure of the greatness of all peoples is the amount and standard of the literature and art they have produced." The poets, novelists, and artists of the Harlem Renaissance captured the imagination of blacks and whites alike. Many of these artists increasingly rejected white standards of taste as well as staid middle-class, black values. Writers Langston Hughes and Zora Neale Hurston in particular drew inspiration from the vernacular of African American folk life. In 1926 Hughes defiantly asserted: "We younger Negro artists who create now intend to express our dark-skinned selves without fear or shame. If white people are pleased, we are glad. If they are not, it doesn't matter."

Black music became a vibrant part of mainstream American popular culture in the 1920s. Traveling musicians such as Ferdinand "Jelly Roll" Morton, Louis Armstrong, Edward "Duke" Ellington, and singer Bessie Smith developed and popularized two of America's most original forms of music—jazz and the blues. Emerging from brothels and bars in the South, these unique compositions grew out of the everyday experiences of black life and expressed the thumping rhythms of work, pleasure, and pain. Such music did not remain confined to dance halls and clubs in black communities; it soon spread to white musicians and audiences for whom the hot beat of jazz rhythms meant emotional freedom and the expression of sexuality.

Marcus Garvey and Black Nationalism

In addition to providing a fertile ground for African American intellectuals, Harlem became the headquarters of the most significant alternative black political vision of the 1920s. In 1916 the Jamaican-born Marcus Mosiah Garvey settled in Harlem and became

Marcus Garvey Dressed in military regalia topped off with a plumed hat, the Jamaican immigrant Marcus Garvey embodied the spirit of black nationalism after World War I. His Universal Negro Improvement Association, headquartered in Harlem, attracted a sizable following in the United States, the Caribbean, Central America, Canada, and Africa. Garvey advocated black political and economic independence. NY Daily News via Getty Images

the leading exponent of black nationalism. In 1914 Garvey had set up the **Universal Negro Improvement Association (UNIA)** in Jamaica, an organization through which he promoted racial separation and pride. Unlike the leaders of the NAACP, who sought equal access to American institutions and cooperation with whites, Garvey favored a "Back to Africa" movement that would ultimately repatriate many black Americans to their ancestral homelands on the African continent. Together with the indigenous black African majority, transplanted African Americans would help overthrow colonial rule and use their power to assist black people throughout the world.

Garvey's appeal did not rely primarily on this utopian project. Instead, the UNIA concentrated on building the economic strength of black communities in the United States through self-help. In the pages of his newspaper, *Negro World*, Garvey promoted ventures such as his Black Star Line steamship company, established in 1919. After raising more than $200,000 in less than four months, the company acquired a fleet of three less-than-seaworthy ships on which it planned to transport passengers between the United States, the West Indies, and Africa. The UNIA's companies opened up blue-collar and white-collar jobs to black men and women that were generally unavailable to them in white-owned firms.

In addition to offering an outlet for dreams of economic advancement, Garvey tapped into the racial discontent of African Americans for whom living in the United States had proven so difficult. He denounced what he saw as the accommodationist efforts of the NAACP and declared, "To be a Negro is no disgrace, but an honor, and we of the UNIA do not want to become white." Indeed, he proclaimed "Black is Beautiful" and asserted that both God and Jesus were black. Ironically, the UNIA and D. C. Stephenson's Klan agreed on the necessity of racial segregation, though Garvey never accepted the premise that blacks were inferior. Garvey dressed in a military uniform with a saber dangling from his belt and a plumed hat atop his head. His appeals to black manhood were also accompanied by a celebration of black womanhood. He set up the Black Cross Nurses, and his wife, Amy Jacques Garvey, went beyond her husband's traditional notions of femininity to extol the accomplishments of black women in politics and culture. Garveyism became the first mass African American movement in U.S. history and was especially effective in recruiting working-class blacks. UNIA branches were established in thirty-eight states throughout the North and South and attracted some 500,000 members.

Given his ideas and outspokenness, Garvey soon made powerful enemies. Du Bois and fellow members of the NAACP despised him. The black socialist labor leader A. Philip Randolph, who saw the UNIA program as just another form of exploitative capitalism, labeled Garvey an "unquestioned fool and ignoramus." Yet Garvey's downfall came from his own business practices. Convicted in 1925 of mail fraud related to his Black Star Line, Garvey served two years in federal prison until President Coolidge commuted his term and had the Jamaican citizen deported. Garvey continued to carry on his activities from England, but without his presence the UNIA lost most of its following in the United States.

REVIEW & RELATE

• How did new forms of entertainment challenge traditional morality and traditional gender roles?

• Describe the black cultural and intellectual renaissance that flourished in the 1920s.

Culture Wars

Attacks on traditional cultural and racial values did not go uncontested. During this era when technological innovations overturned traditional economic values, when modes of social behavior were in a state of flux, and when white supremacy came under assault, it is not surprising that many segments of the population resisted these changes. Rallying around ethnic and racial purity, Protestant fundamentalism, and family values, defenders of an older America attempted to roll back the tide of modernity.

Nativists versus Immigrants

The 1920s experienced a surge in nativist (anti-immigrant) and racist thinking that in many ways reflected long-standing fears. The end of World War I brought a new wave of Catholic and Jewish emigration from eastern and southern Europe, triggering religious prejudice among Protestants. Just as immigrants had been linked to socialism and anarchism in the 1880s and 1890s, old-stock Americans associated these immigrants with immoral behavior and political radicalism and saw them as a threat to their traditional culture and values. Moreover, as in the late nineteenth century, native-born workers saw immigrants as a source of cheap labor that threatened their jobs and wages.

The **Sacco and Vanzetti case** provides the most dramatic evidence of this nativism. In 1920 a botched robbery at a shoe company in South Braintree, Massachusetts, resulted in the murder of the bookkeeper and guard. Police arrested Nicola Sacco, a shoemaker, and Bartolomeo Vanzetti, a fish peddler, and charged them with the crime. These two Italian immigrants shared radical political views as anarchists and World War I draft evaders. The subsequent trial revolved around their foreign birth and ideology more than the facts pertaining to their guilt or innocence. The presiding judge at the trial referred to the accused as "anarchistic bastards" and "damned dagos" (a derogatory term for "Italians"). Convicted and sentenced to death, Sacco and Vanzetti lost their appeals for a new trial. Criticism of the verdict came from all over the world. Workers in Mexico, Argentina, Uruguay, France, and Morocco organized vigils and held rallies in solidarity with the condemned men. The American minister to Venezuela reported that "practically all the lower classes regarded them as martyrs." Despite support from influential lawyers such as Harvard's Felix Frankfurter, the two men were executed in the electric chair in 1927.

The Sacco and Vanzetti case provides an extreme example of 1920s nativism, but the anti-immigrant views that contributed to the two men's conviction and execution were commonplace during the period and shared by Americans across the social spectrum. Many Americans, including Henry Ford, saw immigrants as a threat to cherished traditions. In his commitment to "One-Hundred Percent Americanism," Ford tried to preserve traditional values. He strongly supported prohibition and denounced the frenetic sounds and sexual overtones of Jazz Age music and dancing. Ford felt that immigrants were the cause of a decline in American morality. He contended that aliens did not understand "the principles which have made our [native] civilization," and he blamed the influx of foreigners for society's "marked deterioration" during the 1920s. He stirred up anti-immigrant prejudices mainly by targeting Jews. Believing that an international Jewish conspiracy was attempting to subvert non-Jewish societies, Ford serialized in his company newspaper the so-called *Protocols of the Elders of Zion*, an anti-Semitic tract concocted in czarist Russia to justify pogroms against Jews. Ford continued to publish it even after the document was proven a fake in 1921.

Ford joined other nativists in supporting legislation to restrict immigration. In 1924 Congress passed the **National Origins Act**, a quota system on future immigration. The measure limited entry by any foreign group to 2 percent of the number of people of that nationality who resided in the United States in 1890. The statute's authors were interested primarily in curbing immigration from eastern and southern Europe. They chose 1890 as the benchmark for immigration because most newcomers from those two regions entered the United States after that year. Quotas established for northern Europe, about 70 percent of the total, went unfilled, while those for southern and eastern Europe could not accommodate the vast number of people who sought admission. The law continued to bar East Asian immigration altogether.

With immigration of those considered "undesirable" severely if not completely curtailed, some nativist reformers shifted their attention to Americanization, which developed into one of the largest social and political movements in American history. Speaking about immigrants, educator E. P. Cubberly said, "Our task is to break up their groups and settlements, to assimilate and amalgamate these people as a part of our American race, to implant in their children the northern-European conception of righteousness, law and order, and popular government." Business corporations conducted Americanization and naturalization classes on factory floors. Schools, patriotic societies, fraternal organizations, women's groups, and labor unions launched citizenship classes. Even the U.S. Catholic hierarchy joined the effort by prohibiting the creation of new parishes based on nationality and increasingly requiring the use of English for confessions and sermons.

In the Southwest and on the West Coast, whites aimed their Americanization efforts at the growing population of Mexican Americans. Subject to segregated education, Mexican Americans were expected to speak English in their classes. "The opening of school," an Arizona teacher's journal noted, "will provide an opportunity for all the Mexican children . . . to study under separate tutelage until they have acquired a thorough mastery of the English language." Anglo school administrators and teachers generally believed that Mexican Americans were suited for farmwork and manual trades. For Mexican Americans, therefore, Americanization meant vocational training and preparation for low-status, low-wage jobs.

Despite attempts at Americanization, ethnic groups did not dissolve into a melting pot and lose their cultural identities. First-generation Americans—the children of immigrants—learned English, enjoyed American popular culture, and dressed in fashions of the day. Yet in cities around the country where immigrants had settled, ethnic enclaves remained intact and preserved the religious practices and social customs of their residents. Americanization may have watered down the "vegetable soup" of American diversity, but it did not completely eliminate the variety and distinctiveness of its flavors.

Resurrection of the Ku Klux Klan

Nativism received its most spectacular boost from the reemergence of the Ku Klux Klan in 1915. Originally an organization dedicated to terrorizing emancipated African Americans and their white Republican allies in the South during Reconstruction, the KKK branched out during the 1920s to the North and West. In addition to blacks, the new Klan targeted

Catholics and Jews, as well as anyone who was alleged to have violated community moral values. The organization consisted of a cross section of native-born Protestants primarily from the middle and working classes who sought to reverse a perceived decline in their social and economic power. Revived by W. J. Simmons, a former Methodist minister, the new Klan celebrated its founding at Stone Mountain, Georgia, near Atlanta. There, Klansmen bowed to the twin symbols of their cause, the American flag and a burning cross that represented their fiery determination to stand up for Christian morality and against all those considered "un-American." People flocked to the new KKK. By the mid-1920s, Klan membership totaled more than three million men and women. Tens of thousands of members outfitted in white sheets and pointed hoods openly paraded down Pennsylvania Avenue in Washington, D.C., the route of presidential inaugurations. Not confined to rural areas, the revived Klan counted a significant following in D. C. Stephenson's Indianapolis and Ossian Sweet's Detroit, as well as in Chicago, Denver, Portland, and Seattle. Rural dwellers who had moved into cities with large numbers of black migrants and recent immigrants found solace in Klan vows to preserve "Native, white, Protestant supremacy."

The phenomenal growth of the KKK in the 1920s probably resulted more from the desire to reestablish traditional values than from sheer hostility toward blacks. In the face of challenges to traditional values, a changing sexual morality, and the flaunting of prohibition, wives joined their husbands as devoted followers. Protestant women appreciated the Klan's message condemning abusive husbands and fathers and the group's affirmation of the status of white Protestant women as the embodiment of virtue. In the post-suffrage era, the Klan also provided its female members with an incentive to vote by encouraging them to counteract the influence of newly enfranchised Catholic, Jewish, Latina, and African American women.

Like the original Klan, its successor resorted to terror tactics. Acting under cover of darkness and concealed in robes and hoods, Klansmen burned crosses to scare their victims, many of whom they beat, kidnapped, tortured, and murdered. To gain greater legitimacy and to appeal to a wider audience, the Klan also participated in electoral politics. The KKK succeeded in electing governors in Georgia and Oregon, a U.S. senator from Texas, numerous state legislators, and other officials in California, Indiana, Michigan, Ohio, and Oklahoma. Politicians routinely joined the Klan to advance their careers, whether they shared its views or not. For example, Hugo Black, a Klansman from Alabama, won election as U.S. senator and was appointed to the Supreme Court, where he accumulated a distinguished record as a progressive jurist.

Fundamentalism versus Modernism

Protestant fundamentalists also fought to uphold traditional values against modern-day incursions. Around 1910, two wealthy Los Angeles churchgoers had subsidized and distributed a series of booklets called *The Fundamentals*, incorporating many statements about the literal truth of the Bible. With three million copies in circulation nationwide, the booklets informed readers that the Bible offered a true account of the genesis and development of humankind and the world and that its words had to be taken literally. After 1920, believers of this approach to interpreting the Bible became known as "fundamentalists." Their preachers spread the message of old-time religion through carnival-like revivals, and preachers used the new medium of radio to broadcast their sermons.

Fundamentalism divided many Protestant denominations, but its appeal was strongest in the Midwest and the South—the so-called Bible belt—where residents felt deeply threatened by the secular aspects of modern life that left their conventional religious teachings open to skepticism and scorn.

Nothing bothered fundamentalist Protestants as much as Charles Darwin's theory of evolution. In *On the Origin of Species* (1859), Darwin replaced the biblical story of creation with a scientific theory of the emergence and development of life that centered on evolution and natural selection. Fundamentalists rejected this explanation and repudiated the views of fellow Protestants who attempted to reconcile Darwinian evolution with God's Word by reading the Bible as a symbolic representation of what might have happened. Few people had actually read Darwin, and fundamentalists derided him by emphasizing the popular misconception that he had written that human beings had descended directly from apes (in fact, he maintained that simians and humans had a common ancestor). To combat any other interpretation but the biblical one, in 1925 lawmakers in Arkansas, Florida, Mississippi, Oklahoma, and Tennessee made it illegal to teach in public schools and colleges "any theory that denies the story of the Divine Creation of man as taught in the Bible."

Shortly after the anti-evolution law passed, the town of Dayton, Tennessee, decided to take advantage of it. Local business people and town boosters wanted to put their town on the map and attract new investment to the area. They recruited John Scopes, a general science high school teacher and part-time football coach. Scopes defied the law by lecturing from a biology textbook that presented Darwin's theory. At the same time, the interests of the town boosters converged with those of the ACLU, which wanted to challenge the restrictive state statute on the grounds of free speech and academic freedom and attract new members to the organization. Together, these two very different groups succeeded in turning an ordinary judicial hearing into the "trial of the century."

The resulting trial brought Dayton more fame, much of it negative, than the planners had bargained for. When court convened in July 1925, millions of people listened over the radio to the first trial ever broadcast. Reporters from all over the country descended on Dayton to keep their readers informed of the proceedings, while cynical journalists such as H. L. Mencken ridiculed Dayton and its residents.

Inside the courtroom, a monumental confrontation took place. Clarence Darrow headed the defense team. A controversial and colorful criminal lawyer from Chicago, who in a few months would defend Ossian Sweet, Darrow doubted the existence of God. On the other side, William Jennings Bryan, three-time Democratic candidate for president and secretary of state under Woodrow Wilson, assisted the prosecution. As a Protestant fundamentalist, Bryan believed that accepting scientific evolution would undermine the moral basis of politics and that communities should have the right to determine their children's school curriculum. A Seventh-Day Adventist minister summed up what the fundamentalists considered to be at stake: "[Darwin's theory] breeds corruption, lust, immorality, greed, and such acts of criminal depravity as drug addiction, war, and atrocious acts of genocide."

The presiding judge, John T. Raulston, set the tone for the trial by beginning each session with a prayer. He ruled that scientists could not take the stand to defend evolution because he considered their testimony "hearsay," given that they had not been present at the creation. The defense nearly collapsed until Darrow called the willing Bryan to the stand as "an expert on the Bible." The clash of these two titans provided excellent theater but changed few minds. The jury took only eight minutes to declare Scopes guilty. Two weeks after the trial, Bryan died in his sleep, still convinced that his views had prevailed. Scopes's conviction was overturned by an appeals court on a technicality. Yet fundamentalists remained as certain as ever in their beliefs, and anti-evolution laws stayed in force until the 1970s. The trial had not "settled" anything. Rather, it served to highlight a cultural division over the place of religion in American society that persists to the present day.

(REVIEW & RELATE)

• What was the connection between anti-immigrant sentiment and the defense of tradition during the 1920s?

• Who challenged the new morality associated with modernization? Why?

Politics and the Fading of Prosperity

These cultural clashes tore the Democratic Party apart, leaving Republicans in command of national politics. As it attracted a growing number of urban immigrants to its ranks alongside its customary base of white southerners, the Democratic Party tried to reconcile the tensions between traditional and modern America. Its failure to do so kept Republicans in power despite growing evidence of their inability to resolve serious economic problems. Although many progressives continued to press for reform, they were all but powerless to prevent the coming economic crisis.

The Battle for the Soul of the Democratic Party

The 1924 presidential election exposed the social and cultural fault lines within the Democratic Party. Since the end of Reconstruction and the "redemption" of the South by southern Democrats, the Republican Party had ceased to compete for office in the region. Southern Democrats, along with party supporters from the rural Midwest, shared strong fundamentalist religious beliefs and an enthusiasm for prohibition that usually placed them at odds with big-city northern Democrats. The urban wing of the party increasingly represented immigrant populations that rejected prohibition as contrary to their social practices and supported political machines, which many rural Democrats found odious and an indicator of cultural degradation. These distinctions, however, were not absolute—some rural dwellers opposed prohibition, and some urbanites supported temperance.

Delegates to the 1924 Democratic convention in New York City had trouble deciding on a party platform and a presidential candidate. When urban delegates from the Northeast attempted to insert a plank condemning D. C. Stephenson's Ku Klux Klan for its intolerance, they lost by a thin margin. Proponents of this measure owed their defeat to the sizable number of convention delegates who either belonged to the Klan or had been backed by it.

The selection of the presidential ticket proved even more divisive. Urban Democrats favored the nomination of New York governor Alfred E. Smith. Smith came from an Irish Catholic immigrant family, had grown up on New York City's Lower East Side, and was sponsored by the Tammany Hall machine. The epitome of everything that rural

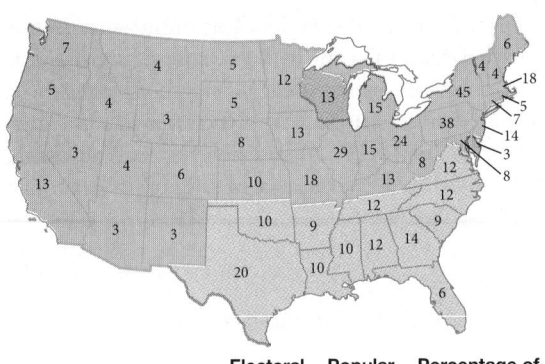

MAP 21.1
The Election of 1924

Republican Calvin Coolidge, who became president in August 1923 on the death of Warren Harding, continued Harding's policies of limited government regulation and corporate tax cuts. Coolidge easily defeated Democrat John Davis, whose strength was confined to the South. Running as the Progressive Party candidate, Senator Robert La Follette won 16 percent of the popular vote but carried only his home state of Wisconsin, with 13 electoral votes.

Candidate	Electoral Vote	Popular Vote	Percentage of Popular Vote
Calvin Coolidge (Republican)	382	15,725,016	54.0
John W. Davis (Democrat)	136	8,386,503	28.8
Robert M. La Follette (Progressive)	13	4,822,856	16.6

Democrats despised, Smith further angered opponents with his outspoken denunciation of prohibition. Prohibitionists fiercely opposed Smith, and he lost the nomination to John W. Davis, a West Virginia Protestant and a supporter of prohibition. The intense intraparty fighting left the Democrats deeply divided going into the general election. To no one's surprise, Davis lost to Calvin Coolidge in a landslide (Map 21.1).

In 1928, however, when the Democrats met in Houston, Texas, the delicate cultural equilibrium within the Democratic Party had shifted in favor of the urban forces. With Stephenson and the Klan discredited and no longer a force in Democratic politics, the delegates nominated Al Smith as their presidential candidate. To balance the ticket, they tapped for vice president Joseph G. Robinson, a senator from Arkansas, a Protestant, and a supporter of prohibition.

The Republicans selected Herbert Hoover, one of the most popular men in the United States. His biography read like a script of the American dream. Born in Iowa to a Quaker family, he became an orphan at the age of nine and moved to Oregon to live with relatives. After graduating from Stanford University in 1895, he began a career as a prosperous mining engineer and a successful businessman. Affectionately called "the Great Humanitarian" for his European relief efforts after World War I, Hoover served as secretary of commerce during the Harding and Coolidge administrations. His name became synonymous with the Republican prosperity of the 1920s. In accepting his party's nomination for president in 1928, Hoover optimistically declared: "We in America today are nearer to the final triumph over poverty than ever before in the history of the land." A Protestant supporter of prohibition from a small town, Hoover was everything Smith was not.

The outcome of the election proved predictable. Running on prosperity and pledging a "chicken in every pot and two cars in every garage," Hoover trounced Smith with 58 percent of the popular vote and more than 80 percent of the electoral vote. Despite the weakening economy, Smith lost usually reliable Democratic votes to religious and ethnic prejudices. The New Yorker prevailed only in Massachusetts, Rhode Island, and six southern states but failed to win his home state. A closer look at the election returns showed a significant party realignment under way. Smith succeeded in identifying the Democratic Party with urban, ethnic-minority voters and attracting them to the polls. Despite the landslide loss, he captured the twelve largest cities in the nation, all of which had gone Republican four years earlier. In another fifteen big cities, Smith did better than the Democrat ticket had done in the 1924 election, thereby encouraging the country's ethnic minorities to support the party of Thomas Jefferson and Woodrow Wilson. To break the Republicans' national dominance, the Democrats would need a candidate who appealed to both traditional and modern Americans. Smith's defeat, however, laid the foundation for future Democratic political success.

Where Have All the Progressives Gone?

The Democrats and Republicans were not the only parties that attracted voters in the 1920s. Some voters continued to cast their ballot for the Socialist Party. Others took the opportunity to voice their disapproval of Republican policies by voting for the remaining progressive candidates. Progressives did manage to hold on to seats in Congress,

Robert M. La Follette, 1924   Wisconsin senator Robert M. La Follette, running for president on the Progressive Party ticket in 1924, campaigns in Chicago with his son, Robert Jr., seated next to him. La Follette and his running mate, Senator Burton K. Wheeler of Montana, favored higher taxes for the wealthy, collective bargaining rights for factory workers, and limits on Supreme Court power.   Chicago History Museum, image DN-0077813/Photo: *Chicago Daily News*

and in 1921 they helped pass the Shepherd-Towner Act, which appropriated federal funds to establish maternal and child centers (see chapter 19). But their efforts to restrict the power of the Supreme Court, reduce tax cuts for the wealthy, nationalize railroads, and extend agricultural relief to farmers were rebuffed by conservative legislative majorities. In 1924 reformers nominated Senator Robert M. La Follette of Wisconsin to run for president on a revived Progressive Party ticket, but he came in a distant third and won only five million popular votes and the electoral votes of his home state. The Progressive Party collapsed soon after La Follette died in 1925.

Still, progressivism managed to stay alive on the local and state levels. Gifford Pinchot, a Roosevelt ally and a champion of conservation (see chapter 19), twice won election as governor of Pennsylvania starting in 1922. Social workers continued their efforts to alleviate urban poverty and lobby for government assistance to the poor. Even at the national level, women in the Children's Bureau maintained the progressive legacy by supporting assistance to families and devising social welfare proposals. Progressivism did not disappear during the 1920s, but it did fight an uphill and often losing battle during an age of conservative political ascendancy. Its weakness contributed to the government's failure to check the worst corporate and financial practices, a failure that would play a role in the nation's economic collapse.

Financial Crash

On October 29, 1929, a day that became known as **Black Tuesday**, stock market prices tumbled. Over the previous five years, the rising market, bolstered by optimistic buyers, earned huge profits for investors, and the value of stocks nearly doubled. In late October, panicked sellers sent stock prices into free fall, culminating in the selling of more than 16 million shares valued at $32 billion on October 29. Although only 2.5 percent of Americans owned stock, the stock market crash had an enormous impact on the economy and the rest of the world. Because so much of the stock boom depended on generous margin requirements (a down payment of only 5 to 10 percent), when investor-borrowers got caught short by falling prices, they could not repay the financial institutions that had extended them credit. Banks and lending agencies, with their interlocking management and overextension of credit, had difficulty withstanding the turmoil unleashed by the stock market crash.

The 1929 crash did not cause the decade-long Great Depression that followed. The seeds for the greatest economic catastrophe in American history had been planted earlier. The economy had endured a series of panics and depressions in the past, but nothing like what happened between 1929 and 1940. The causes stemmed from flaws in an economic system that produced a great disparity of wealth, inadequate consumption, overextension of credit both at home and abroad, and the government's unwillingness to relieve the plight of farmers. Republican administrations made matters worse by lowering taxes on the rich and raising tariffs to benefit manufacturers. The Federal Reserve Board exacerbated the situation by keeping interest rates high, thereby making it difficult for people to get loans and repay debts. The failure was not that of the United States alone; the depression affected capitalist nations throughout the world. The stock market collapse crushed whatever confidence the American public had that the unfettered law of supply and demand and laissez-faire economics could ensure prosperity.

- How did divisions within the Democratic Party contribute to Republican political dominance in the 1920s?
- What underlying economic weaknesses led to the Great Depression?

Conclusion: The Roaring Twenties

While the second industrial revolution spurred extraordinary prosperity, the 1920s ended in an unprecedented economic collapse. During the decade, industrialists produced and marketed wares in a manner that drew the mass of Americans into the economy as laborers and consumers. Automobiles, fueled by gasoline, traveled up and down streets and highways. Electricity powered household appliances and ran movie projectors in theaters throughout the nation. People living in California, Michigan, Florida, or New Jersey had similar opportunities to buy consumer products and partake in a mass culture made possible by movies and radio. Producing for a mass market, industrial giants like Henry Ford transformed the nature of work and pleasure. The assembly line revolutionized the pace of labor and turned it into a standardized routine. The automobile transformed dating patterns and opened up new opportunities for the exploration of romance and sex.

For most Americans earning very modest incomes, the fruits of the consumer revolution were beyond their reach. The image of the 1920s as an era of widespread prosperity is exaggerated. Most Americans lived at or below the poverty line and earned just enough money to acquire the bare necessities. They could live beyond their means through an ample supply of credit, but their poverty contrasted with the increasing concentration of wealth in the hands of the richest Americans. Businessmen like Henry Ford attempted to take care of their workers through higher wages and assorted benefits, but their paternalism depended on the continuation of good economic times. The stock market crash of 1929 and the ensuing Great Depression exposed the shortcomings of the corporate business world, inadequate oversight by the federal government, and an overreliance on the private sector to look after the nation's economic health.

The weaknesses of the economy, which appear clear in retrospect, were often hidden behind the clash over cultural differences. Guardians of traditional morality and values worried about the effects of more than fifty years of industrialization, immigration, and urbanization. Issues such as the enforcement of prohibition, the teaching of evolution in the schools, and whether a Catholic should be elected president dominated political discussion, while efforts to assist farmers and workers were unsuccessful. These battles marked a turning point in American history—the transition from a traditional, rural, Protestant society to an urban, ethnically and religiously diverse one. The widespread popularity of D. C. Stephenson's Ku Klux Klan throughout the South and the North demonstrated that the older America of white, northern European Protestants did not intend to relinquish political or cultural power without a struggle. At the same time, ethnic minorities represented by Al Smith had no intention of backing down. Neither did millions of African Americans, whether they joined the NAACP, as did Ossian Sweet, or supported Marcus Garvey's UNIA. During the next decade, Americans from all backgrounds would battle more than cultural threats; they would fight for their economic survival.

Chapter Review

MAKE IT STICK

 LearningCurve **bedfordstmartins.com/hewittlawsonvalue**
After reading the chapter, use LearningCurve to retain what you've read.

IDENTIFY KEY TERMS

Identify and explain the significance of each term below.

Red scare (p. 540)
Palmer raids (p. 541)
great migration (p. 542)
American Plan (p. 544)
Teapot Dome scandal (p. 544)
second industrial revolution (p. 544)
new woman (p. 549)

Lost Generation (p. 549)
New Negro (p. 550)
Universal Negro Improvement Association (UNIA) (p. 552)
Sacco and Vanzetti case (p. 553)
National Origins Act (p. 554)
Black Tuesday (p. 560)

REVIEW & RELATE

Answer the focus questions from each section of the chapter.

1. What factors combined to produce the turmoil of the immediate postwar period?

2. What factors contributed to the rise in racial tensions that accompanied the transition from wartime to peacetime?

3. Describe the relationship between business and government in the 1920s.

4. Why was a high level of consumer spending so critical to 1920s prosperity, and why was the economic expansion of the 1920s ultimately unsustainable?

5. How did new forms of entertainment challenge traditional morality and traditional gender roles?

6. Describe the black cultural and intellectual renaissance that flourished in the 1920s.

7. What was the connection between anti-immigrant sentiment and the defense of tradition during the 1920s?

8. Who challenged the new morality associated with modernization? Why?

9. How did divisions within the Democratic Party contribute to Republican political dominance in the 1920s?

10. What underlying economic weaknesses led to the Great Depression?

ONLINE DOCUMENT PROJECTS
♦ **The *Abrams* Case and the Red Scare**
♦ **The New Negro and the Harlem Renaissance**

After reading the primary sources in these document sets, answer the **Interpret the Evidence** questions to help you analyze each of the documents, and then answer the **Put It in Context** question(s) to help you relate the documents to the topics and themes you read about in the chapter.

bedfordstmartins.com/hewittlawsonvalue

TIMELINE OF EVENTS

1914	• Universal Negro Improvement Association (UNIA) formed
1915	• Ku Klux Klan revived
1917–1918	• 400,000 African Americans leave South as part of great migration
1917	• Russian Revolution begins
1918–1920	• Worldwide influenza epidemic
1919	• 4 million workers go on strike nationwide
	• Race riots erupt in twenty-five U.S. cities
	• Radicals mail incendiary devices to prominent Americans
	• Palmer raids begin
1920	• American Civil Liberties Union (ACLU) formed
	• David Curtis Stephenson joins the Ku Klux Klan
1920s	• Harlem Renaissance
1921	• J. Edgar Hoover becomes director of the Bureau of Investigation (later the FBI)
	• Teapot Dome scandal
1924	• National Origins Act passed
	• Charles Dawes negotiates with the Allies to reduce Germany's reparations payments
1925–1929	• U.S. farm income drops by 50 percent
1925	• Scopes trial
1926	• Ossian Sweet and family acquitted of first-degree murder charges
1927	• Sacco and Vanzetti executed
1928	• Democrat Al Smith loses presidential election but wins ten largest cities
1929	• Stock market crash sparks Great Depression

22

✓ LearningCurve
bedfordstmartins.com/hewittlawsonvalue
After reading the chapter, use LearningCurve
to retain what you've read.

Depression, Dissent, and the New Deal

1929–1940

AMERICAN HISTORIES

Anna Eleanor Roosevelt came from an old Dutch American family of wealthy merchants and bankers. In 1901, at the age of fifteen, she saw her uncle Theodore succeed William McKinley as president. Like other girls of her generation, Eleanor was expected to marry and become a "charming wife." Eleanor appeared well on her way toward doing so when she struck up a relationship with her distant cousin Franklin Delano Roosevelt, whom she married in 1905. Over a ten-year period, Eleanor gave birth to six children, further reinforcing her status as a traditional woman of her class.

Two events, however, set her life on a very different path than the one she had embarked on when she married Franklin. First, thirteen years into her marriage Eleanor discovered that her husband was having an affair with her social secretary, Lucy Mercer. She did not divorce him but made it clear that she would stay with him primarily as a mother to their children and a political partner. Second, in 1921 the thirty-nine-year-old Franklin contracted polio. Although he recovered, Franklin would never walk again or stand without the aid of braces. From this point on, Eleanor threw herself into public life, taking a more active role in her husband's political career and writing about personal and political issues for a range of publications.

After her husband won the presidency in 1932, Eleanor did not function as a typical First Lady. She played a very public role promoting her husband's agenda, and she also took advantage of her own extensive network of friends and acquaintances in labor unions, civil rights organizations, and women's groups to advance a variety of causes. In many ways more liberal than her husband, Eleanor was a fierce advocate for the rights of women, minorities, workers, and the poor. Behind the scenes, she pushed her husband to move further to the political left.

Eleanor Roosevelt's proximity to power provided her with a unique position from which to confront the problems of her day. She was not, however, alone in her desire to work for social and economic justice. Luisa Moreno provides a striking example of an activist whose American story bears little resemblance to that of Eleanor Roosevelt. A native of Guatemala, Moreno moved to Mexico and then New York City, where she led a difficult life. In the midst of the Great Depression, Moreno worked as a seamstress in a sweatshop to support her young child and unemployed husband. Like tens of thousands of people disillusioned with capitalism, in 1930 she joined the Communist Party but quit several years later.

In 1935 Moreno went to Florida to organize cigar workers for the American Federation of Labor (AFL). Despite numerous successes, she grew tired of the AFL's refusal to recruit unskilled workers and jumped to the Congress of Industrial Organizations (CIO), which formed in 1935. That same year, she began working for the United Cannery, Agricultural, Packing, and Allied Workers of America (UCAPAWA), an affiliate of the CIO. Encouraged by the federal government's establishment of the National Labor Relations Board in 1935 to safeguard union organizing, by 1943 Moreno and her colleagues in the UCAPAWA had won more than thirty elections recognizing their union among cannery workers.

Moreno also promoted the advancement of Latinos throughout the United States. In 1939 she helped create El Congreso de Pueblos de Habla Española (The Congress of Spanish-Speaking People). Besides championing equal access to jobs, education, housing, and health care, the organization pressed to end the segregation of Latinos in schools and public accommodations. Moreno was not nearly as well known as Eleanor Roosevelt, but she worked just as hard to fight poverty, exploitation, and racial bigotry on behalf of people whom President Franklin Roosevelt called "the forgotten Americans."

WHILE THE AMERICAN HISTORIES of Eleanor Roosevelt and Luisa Moreno were very different, both of their lives were shaped in fundamental ways by the same global catastrophe, the Great Depression. The economic crisis that erupted in 1929 made a bad situation worse for the majority of Americans. Even before the Great Depression, most Americans lived at or near the poverty level, surviving month to month. By 1933, millions of Americans had lost even this tenuous hold on economic security, as unemployment reached a record 25 percent, a figure that did not include those who had stopped looking for work. Succeeding President Herbert Hoover, Franklin

Children of Mexican cotton laborers, Casa Grande, Arizona, 1937. Library of Congress

Roosevelt initiated policies that departed profoundly from the reliance on private charity and voluntary efforts that had characterized Republican responses to economic problems throughout the 1920s. Proclaiming the establishment of a New Deal for America, Roosevelt expanded the power of the federal government in ways that previously had taken place only during wartime, and he forged a new political order in which the Democratic Party ruled for generations to come.

The Great Depression

Herbert Hoover had the unenviable task of assuming the presidency in 1929 as the economy crumbled. Given his long history of public service, he seemed the right man for the job. Hoover, however, was unwilling to make a fundamental break with the economic approaches of the past and proved unable to effectively communicate his genuine concern for the plight of the poor. Despite his sincere efforts, the depression deepened. Among the hardest hit were minority groups already suffering from discrimination. As unemployment rose and more and more farmers lost their land, many Americans, made desperate by their economic plight and angered by the inadequate response of their government, took to the streets in protest.

Hoover Faces the Depression

National prosperity was at its peak when the Republican Hoover entered the White House in March 1929. The nation had little reason to doubt him when he boasted in his inaugural address: "We in America today are nearer to the final triumph over poverty than ever before in the history of any land. The poorhouse is vanishing from among us." These words were still ringing in the public's ears when the stock market crashed later that year.

Hoover brought to the presidency a blend of traditional and progressive ideas. He believed that government and business should form voluntary partnerships to work toward common goals. Rejecting the principle of absolute laissez-faire, he nonetheless argued that the government should extend its influence lightly over the economy—to encourage and persuade sensible behavior, but not to impose itself on the private sector.

The Great Depression sorely tested Hoover's beliefs. Having placed his faith in cooperation rather than coercion, the president relied on voluntarism to get the nation through hard economic times. Hoover hoped that management and labor, through gentle persuasion, would hold steady on prices and wages and calmly wait until the worst of the depression passed. In the meantime, for those in dire need, the president turned to local communities and private charities. Hoover expected municipal and state governments to shoulder the burden of providing relief to the needy, just as they had during previous economic downturns.

Hoover's remedies failed to rally the country back to good economic health. Initially, business people responded positively to the president's request to maintain the status quo, but when the economy did not bounce back, they lost confidence and defected. Nor did local governments and private agencies have the funds to provide relief to all those who needed it. With tax revenues in decline, some 1,300 municipalities across the country had gone bankrupt by 1933. Chicago and other cities stopped paying their teachers. Benevolent societies and religious groups could handle short-term misfortunes, but they could not cope with the ongoing disaster of mass unemployment (Figure 22.1).

As confidence in recovery fell and the economy sank deeper into depression, President Hoover shifted direction. Without abandoning his belief in voluntarism, the president persuaded Congress to lower income tax rates and to allocate an unprecedented $423 million for federal public works projects. In 1929 the president signed into law the Agricultural Marketing Act, a measure aimed at raising prices for long-suffering farmers.

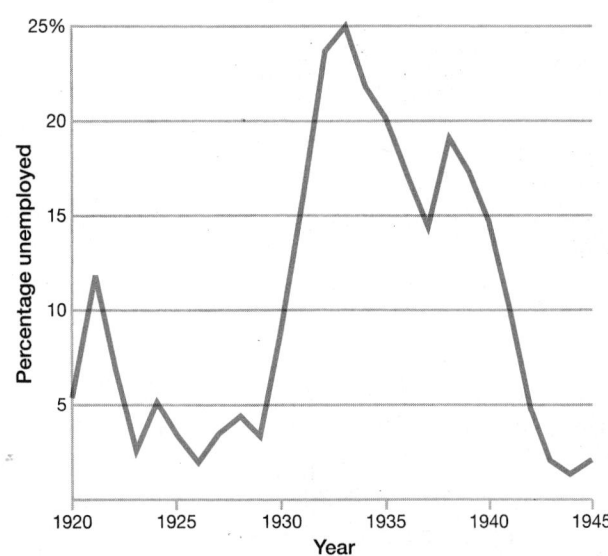

FIGURE 22.1

Unemployment, 1920–1945 Business prosperity and immigration restriction ensured low unemployment during most of the 1920s. When unemployment rose dramatically in the late 1920s, President Hoover failed to handle the crisis. During the 1930s, President Roosevelt's New Deal initiatives did lower unemployment to some extent. Still, only mobilizing the nation for war in 1941 created a significant increase in jobs.

In general, Hoover had the right idea, but he retreated from initiating greater spending because he feared government deficits more than unemployment. With federal accounting sheets showing a rising deficit, Hoover reversed course in 1932 and joined with Congress in sharply raising income, estate, and corporate taxes on the wealthy. This effectively slowed down investment and new production, throwing millions more American workers out of jobs. The Hawley-Smoot Act passed by Congress in 1930 made matters worse. In an effort to replenish revenues and protect American farmers and companies from foreign competition, the act increased tariffs on agricultural and industrial imports. However, other countries retaliated by lifting their import duties, which hurt American companies because it diminished demand for American exports.

In an exception to his aversion to spending, Hoover lobbied Congress to create the Reconstruction Finance Corporation (RFC) to supply loans to banks in danger of collapsing, financially strapped railroads, and troubled insurance companies. By injecting federal dollars into these critical enterprises, the president and lawmakers expected to produce dividends that would trickle down from the top of the economic structure to the bottom. Renewed investment supposedly would increase production, create jobs, raise the income of workers, and generate consumption and economic recovery. In 1932 Congress gave the RFC a budget of $1.5 billion to employ people in public works projects, a significant allocation for those individuals hardest hit by the depression.

This notable departure from Republican economic philosophy fell short of its goal. The RFC spent its budget too cautiously, and its funds reached primarily those institutions that could best afford to repay the loans, ignoring the companies in the greatest difficulty. Whatever the president's intentions, wealth never trickled down. Hoover was not indifferent to the plight of others so much as he was incapable of breaking away from his ideological preconceptions. He refused to support expenditures for direct relief (what today we call welfare) and hesitated to extend assistance for work relief because he believed that it would ruin individual initiative and character.

Hoover and the United States did not face the Great Depression alone; it was a worldwide calamity. By 1933 Germany, France, and Great Britain all faced mass unemployment. In Britain, one survey showed that around 20 percent of the population lacked sufficient food, clothing, and housing. As with American agriculture, European farmers had been suffering since the 1920s from falling prices and increased debt, and the depression further exacerbated this problem. In this climate of extreme social and economic unrest, authoritarian dictators came to power in a number of European countries, including Germany, Italy, Spain, and Portugal. Each claimed that his country's social and economic problems could be solved only by placing power in the hands of a single, all-powerful leader.

Hoovervilles and Dust Storms

The depression hit all areas of the United States hard. In large cities, families crowded into apartments with no gas or electricity and little food to put on the table. In Los Angeles, people cooked their meals over wood fires in backyards. An observer in Philadelphia reported a house containing a family of eleven. "They've got no shoes, no pants," he lamented. "In the house, no chairs. My God, you go in there, you cry, that's all." In many cities, the homeless constructed makeshift housing consisting of cartons, old newspapers, and cloth—shanties that journalists derisively dubbed **Hoovervilles**.

Thousands of hungry citizens wound up living under bridges in Portland, Oregon; in wrecked autos in city dumps in Brooklyn, New York, and Stockton, California; and in abandoned coal furnaces in Pittsburgh. In Chicago, a fight broke out among fifty men over scraps of food placed in the garbage outside of a restaurant.

Rural workers fared no better. Landlords in West Virginia and Kentucky evicted coal miners and their families from their homes in the dead of winter, forcing them to live in tents. Farmers in the Great Plains, who were already experiencing foreclosures, were little prepared for the even greater natural disaster that lay waste to their farms. In the early 1930s, dust storms swept through western Kansas, eastern Colorado, western Oklahoma, the Texas Panhandle, and eastern New Mexico, destroying crops and plant and animal life. The storms resulted from both climatological and human causes. A series of droughts had destroyed crops and turned the earth into sand, which gusts of wind deposited on everything that lay in their path. Though they did not realize it at the time, plains farmers, by focusing on growing wheat for income, had neglected planting trees and grasses that would have kept the earth from eroding and turning into dust. Instead, dust storms brought life to a grinding halt, blocking out the midday sun.

Online Document Project   **The Depression in Rural America**
bedfordstmartins.com/hewittlawsonvalue

As the storms continued through the 1930s, most residents—approximately 75 percent—remained on the plains and rode out the blizzards of dust. Millions, however, headed for California by train, automobiles, and trucks looking for relief from the plague of swirling dirt and hoping to find jobs in the state's fruit and vegetable fields. Although they came from several states besides Oklahoma, these migrants came to be known as "Okies," a derogatory term used by those who resented and looked down on the poverty-stricken newcomers to their communities. John Steinbeck's novel *The Grapes of Wrath* (1939) portrayed the plight of the fictional Joad family, as storms and a bank foreclosure destroyed their Oklahoma farm and sent them on the road to California. "[Route] 66 is the path of a people in flight," Steinbeck wrote, "refugees from dust and shrinking land, from the thunder of tractors and shrinking ownership, from the desert's slow northward invasion, from the twisting winds that howl up out of Texas, from the floods that bring no richness to the land and steal what little richness is there." By no means did all the migrants suffer the misfortunes of the Joads, and many of them succeeded in establishing new lives in the West.

Challenges for Minorities

Given the demographics of the workforce, the overwhelming majority of Americans who lost their jobs were white men; yet racial and ethnic minorities, including African Americans, Latinos, and Asian Americans, suffered disproportionate hardship. Racial discrimination had kept these groups from achieving economic and political equality, and the Great Depression added to their woes.

Traditionally the last hired and the first fired, blacks occupied the lowest rungs on the industrial and agricultural ladders. "The depression brought everybody down a peg or two," the African American poet Langston Hughes wryly commented. "And the

Negroes had but few pegs to fall." Despite the great migration to the North during and after World War I, three-quarters of the black population still lived in the South. They worked mostly as farmers, but 80 percent did not own their own land. Mainly share-croppers and tenant farmers, black southerners were mired in debt that they could not repay as crop prices plunged to record lows during the 1920s. As white landowners struggled to save their farms by introducing machinery to cut labor costs, they forced black sharecroppers off the land and into even greater poverty. Nor was the situation better for black workers employed at the lowest-paying jobs as janitors, menial laborers, maids, and laundresses. On average, African Americans earned $200 a year, less than one-quarter of the average wage of white factory workers.

The economic misfortune that African Americans experienced was compounded by the fact that they lived in a society rigidly constructed to preserve white supremacy. The 25 percent of blacks living in the North faced racial discrimination in employment, housing, and the criminal justice system, but at least they could express their opinions and desires by voting. In Chicago, the growing African American community elected a black congressman, the Republican Oscar DePriest. By contrast, black southerners remained segregated and disfranchised by law. The depression also exacerbated racial tensions, as whites and blacks competed for the shrinking number of jobs. Lynching, which had declined from fifty-nine murders of blacks in 1921 to seven in 1929, surged upward—in 1933 twenty-four blacks lost their lives to this form of terrorism.

Events in Scottsboro, Alabama, reflected the special misery African Americans faced during the Great Depression. Trouble erupted in 1931. Two young, unemployed white women, Ruby Bates and Victoria Price, snuck onto a freight train heading to Huntsville, Alabama. Before the train reached the Scottsboro depot, a fight broke out between black and white men on top of the freight car occupied by the two women. After the train pulled in to Scottsboro, the local sheriff arrested nine black youths between the ages of twelve and twenty. Charges of assault quickly escalated into rape, when the women told authorities that the black men in custody had molested them on board the train. The accused narrowly escaped a mob lynching when the governor sent in the National Guard to ensure that they stood trial.

Going to court, however, did not guarantee a fair trial. The court-appointed attorney was less than competent and had little time to prepare his clients' cases. It probably made little difference, as the all-white male jury swiftly convicted the accused; only the youngest defendant was not sentenced to death. The Communist Party, whose member-ship had increased as despair over the depression mounted, rushed to defend the youths, providing legal and financial assistance for them and their families. The Supreme Court spared the lives of the Scottsboro Nine by overturning their guilty verdicts in 1932 on the grounds that the defendants did not have adequate legal representation and again in 1935 because blacks had been systematically excluded from the jury pool. Although Ruby Bates had recanted her testimony and there was no physical evidence of rape, retrials in 1936 and 1937 produced the same guilty verdicts, but this time the defendants did not receive the death penalty—a minor victory considering the charges. State pros-ecutors dismissed charges against four of the accused, all of whom had already spent six years in jail. Despite international protests against this racist injustice, the last of the remaining five did not leave jail until 1950.

Racism also worsened the impact of the Great Depression on Spanish-speaking Americans. Mexicans and Mexican Americans made up the largest segment of the Latino population living in the United States at the outset of the depression. Concentrated in the Southwest and California, they worked in a variety of low-wage factory jobs and as migrant laborers in fruit and vegetable fields. The depression reduced the Mexican-born population living in the United States in two ways. The federal government began deporting unemployed workers back to Mexico, as many as 500,000, some of whom may have been American citizens. Many more returned to Mexico voluntarily when demand for labor in the United States dried up.

Those who remained endured growing hardships. Relief agencies refused to provide them with the same benefits as whites. Like African Americans, they encountered discrimination in public schools, in public accommodations, and at the ballot box. Conditions remained harshest for migrant workers toiling long hours for little pay and living in overcrowded and poorly constructed housing. Employers had little incentive to improve the situation because there were plenty of white migrant workers to fill their positions. The same held true in factories. Employers justified keeping pay low by claiming that Mexican workers would only spend pay raises on "tequila and worthless trinkets in the dime stores."

The transient nature of agricultural work and the legal vulnerability of Mexican laborers who were not citizens made it difficult for workers to organize, but Mexican American laborers engaged in dozens of strikes in California and Texas in the early 1930s. Most ended in defeat, but a few, such as a five-week strike of pecan shellers in San Antonio, Texas, led by Luisa Moreno, won better working conditions and higher wages. Despite these hard-fought victories, the condition of Latinos remained precarious.

On the West Coast, Asian Americans also remained economically and politically marginalized. Barred from entry into the United States after passage of the 1924 National Origins Act, the Japanese population remained steady. Japanese immigrants (*Issei*) eked out a living as small farmers, grocers, and gardeners, despite California laws preventing them from owning land. Many college-educated *Nisei* (U.S.-born children) found few professional opportunities available to them, and they often returned to work in family businesses. The depression magnified the problem. Like other racial and ethnic minorities, the Japanese found it harder to find even the lowest-wage jobs now that unemployed whites were willing to take them. As a result, about one-fifth of Japanese immigrants returned to Japan during the 1930s.

The Chinese suffered a similar fate. They remained isolated in ethnic communities along the West Coast. Discriminated against in schools and most occupations, many operated restaurants and laundries. Chinese immigrants had been barred from entering the United States since the Chinese Exclusion Act of 1882. Yet approximately 45 percent of people of Chinese ancestry had been born in the United States and thus were citizens. During the depression, those Chinese who did not obtain assistance through governmental relief turned instead to their own community organizations and to extended families to help them through the hard times.

Filipinos, who lived mainly on the Pacific coast and worked as low-wage agricultural workers, were subject to the same kind of racial animosity as other darker-skinned minorities, despite their colonial relationship with the United States. In 1934 anti-Filipino hostility reached its height when Congress passed the Tydings-McDuffie Act. The measure accomplished two aims at once: The act granted independence to the Philippines, and it restricted Filipino immigration into the United States.

Families under Strain

With millions of men unemployed, women faced increased family responsibilities. Stay-at-home wives had to care for their children and provide emotional support for out-of-work husbands who had lost their role as the family breadwinner. Despite the loss of income, homemakers continued their daily routines of shopping, cooking, cleaning, and child rearing.

Disproportionate male unemployment led to an increase in the importance of women's income. The depression hit male-dominated industries like steel mills and automakers the hardest. As a result, men were more likely to lose their jobs than women, who were concentrated in low-paying jobs like domestic service, nursing, and secretarial work. Although more women held on to their jobs, their often meager wages had to go further, since many now had to support unemployed fathers and husbands. During the 1930s, federal and local governments sought to increase male employment by passing laws to keep married women from holding civil service and teaching positions. Nonetheless, more and more married women entered the workplace, and by 1940 the proportion of women in the job force had grown by about 25 percent.

As had been the case in previous decades, a higher proportion of African American women than white women worked outside the home in the 1930s. By 1940 less than 40 percent of African American women held jobs, compared to about 25 percent of white women. Racial discrimination played a key role in establishing this pattern. Black men faced higher unemployment rates than did their white counterparts, and what work was available was often limited to the lowest-paying jobs. As a result, black women faced greater pressure to supplement family incomes. Still, unemployment rates for black women reached as high as 50 percent during the 1930s. During more prosperous times, they had worked in white homes as domestic servants, but the depression forced white families to cut back on household expenses. Many African American women lost some of their domestic jobs to white working-class women who could find work nowhere else.

Despite increased burdens, most American families remained intact and discovered ways to survive the economic crisis. They pared down household budgets, made do without telephones and new clothes, and held on to their automobiles for longer periods of time. What money they managed to save they often spent on movies. Comedies, gangster movies, fantasy tales, and uplifting films helped viewers forget their troubles, if only for a few hours. Radio remained the chief source of entertainment, and radio sales doubled in the 1930s as listeners tuned in to soap operas, comedy and adventure shows, news reports, and musical programs.

The Season of Discontent

As the depression deepened, angry citizens found a variety of ways to express their discontent. Farmers had suffered economic hardship longer than any other group. Even before 1929, they had seen prices spiral downward, but in the early 1930s agricultural income plummeted 60 percent, and one-third of farmers lost their land (Figure 22.2). Some farmers decided that the time had come for drastic action. In the summer of 1932, Milo Reno, an Iowa farmer, created the Farm Holiday Association to organize farmers in order to keep their produce from going to market and thereby raise prices. Strikers blocked roads and kept reluctant farmers in line by smashing their truck windshields and headlights and slashing their tires. When law enforcement officials arrested fifty-five demonstrators

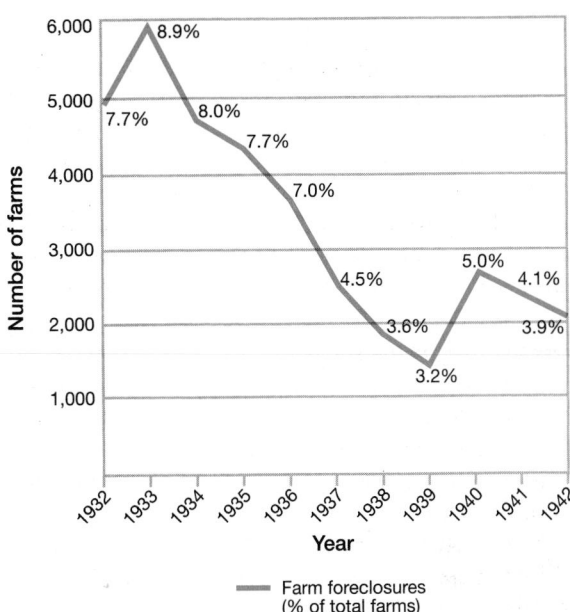

FIGURE 22.2

Farm Foreclosures, 1932–1942 A drop of 60 percent in prices led to a wave of farm foreclosures and rural protests in the early 1930s. From 1934 on, federal programs that promoted rural electrification, crop allotments, commodity loans, and mortgage credits allowed many farmers to retain their land. But tenant farmers and sharecroppers, particularly in the South, rarely benefited from these programs.

in Council Bluffs, thousands of farmers marched on the jail and forced their release. The boycott spread to Nebraska and Wisconsin, and the violence increased. Despite armed attempts to prevent foreclosures and the intentional destruction of vast quantities of farm produce, the Farm Holiday Association failed to achieve its goal of raising prices.

Disgruntled urban residents also resorted to protest. Although the Communist Party remained a tiny group of just over 10,000 members in 1932, it played a large role in organizing the dispossessed. In major cities such as New York, Communists set up unemployment councils and led marches and rallies demanding jobs and food. In Harlem, the party endorsed rent strikes by African American apartment residents against their landlords. Party members did not confine their activities to the urban Northeast. They also went south to defend the Scottsboro Nine and to organize industrial workers in the steel mills of Birmingham and sharecroppers in the surrounding rural areas of Alabama. On the West Coast, Communists played an active role in the motion picture business, unionized seamen and waterfront workers, and led strikes.

One of the most visible protests of the early 1930s centered on events at the Ford factory in Dearborn, Michigan. As the depression worsened after 1930, Henry Ford, who had initially pledged to keep employee wages steady, changed his mind and reduced wages. The paternalistic Ford declared that it was "a good thing the recovery is prolonged. Otherwise people wouldn't profit by the illness." His laborers thought otherwise. On March 7, 1932, spearheaded by Communists, three thousand autoworkers marched from Detroit to Ford's River Rouge plant in nearby Dearborn. When they reached the factory town, they faced policemen indiscriminately firing bullets and tear gas, which killed four demonstrators. The attack provoked great outrage. Around forty thousand mourners attended the funeral of the four protesters; sang the Communist anthem, the "Internationale"; and surrounded the caskets, which were draped in a red banner emblazoned with a picture of Bolshevik hero Vladimir Lenin.

Protests spread beyond Communist agitators. The federal government faced an uprising by some of the nation's most patriotic and loyal citizens—World War I veterans. Scheduled to receive a $1,000 bonus for their service, unemployed veterans could not wait until the payment date arrived in 1945. Instead, in the spring of 1932 a group of ex-soldiers from Portland, Oregon, set off on a march on Washington, D.C., to demand immediate payment of the bonus by the federal government. By the time they reached the nation's capital, the ranks of this **Bonus Army** had swelled to around twenty thousand veterans. They camped in the Anacostia Flats section of the city, constructed ramshackle shelters, and in many cases moved their families in with them. After intensive lobbying efforts, the House approved a bonus bill, but the Senate rejected it. Discouraged, many veterans abandoned the makeshift camps and returned home.

The rest of the Bonus Army remained in place until late July. The Hoover administration declined to negotiate with the demonstrators. When Hoover decided to clear the capital of the protesters, violence ensued. Rather than engaging in a measured and orderly removal, General Douglas MacArthur overstepped presidential orders and used excessive force to disperse the veterans and their families. The Third Cavalry, commanded by George S. Patton, torched tents and sent their residents fleeing from the city. The "Battle of Anacostia Flats" left more than one hundred marchers wounded and one dead.

In this one-sided battle, the biggest loser was President Hoover. Through four years of the country's worst depression, Hoover had lost touch with the American people. His cheerful words of encouragement fell increasingly on deaf ears. As workers, farmers, and veterans stirred in protest, Hoover appeared aloof, standoffish, and insensitive.

REVIEW & RELATE

• How did President Hoover respond to the problems and challenges created by the Great Depression?

• How did different segments of the American population experience the depression?

The New Deal

The nation was ready for a change, and on election day 1932, with hard times showing no sign of abating, Democratic presidential candidate Franklin Delano Roosevelt defeated Hoover easily. Roosevelt's sizable victory provided him with a mandate to take the country in a bold, new direction. However, few Americans, including Roosevelt himself, knew exactly what the new president meant to do or what his pledge of a New Deal would mean for the country.

Roosevelt Restores Confidence

As a presidential candidate, Roosevelt presented no clear, coherent policy. He did not spell out how his plans for the country would differ from Hoover's, but he did refer broadly to providing a "new deal" and bringing to the White House "persistent experimentation." He pledged to put more faith "in the forgotten man at the bottom of the economic pyramid." These flights of rhetoric, however, were balanced by the Democratic candidate's harsh denunciation of Hoover for excessive governmental

Franklin Delano Roosevelt Campaigning in Georgia   New York governor Franklin Roosevelt greets farmers in Georgia as he campaigns for president in 1932 as the Democratic candidate. Photographers were careful not to show that Roosevelt was unable to use his legs, which were paralyzed after he contracted polio in 1921. Roosevelt forged a coalition of farmers and urban workers and easily defeated the incumbent Hoover.   AP Photo

spending and failure to balance the budget. Roosevelt's appeal derived more from the genuine compassion he was able to convey than from the specificity of his promises. In this context, Eleanor Roosevelt's evident concern for people's suffering and her history of activism made Franklin Roosevelt even more attractive.

Instead of any fixed ideology, Roosevelt followed what one historian has called "pragmatic humanism." A seasoned politician who understood the need for flexibility, Roosevelt blended principle and practicality. "It is common sense," Roosevelt explained, "to take a method and try it. If it fails, admit it frankly and try another. But above all, try something." More than any president before him, FDR, as he became affectionately known, created an expectation among Americans that the federal government would take concrete action to improve their lives. A Colorado woman expressed her appreciation to Eleanor Roosevelt: "Your husband is *great*. He seems lovable even tho' he is a 'politician.'" A textile worker echoed this sentiment: "The president isn't going to forget us." The New Deal would take its twists and turns, but Roosevelt never lost the support of the majority of Americans.

Starting with his inaugural address, in which he declared that "the only thing we have to fear is fear itself," Roosevelt took on the task of rallying the American people and restoring their confidence in the future. Using the power of radio to communicate directly with the American people, Roosevelt delivered regular **fireside chats** in which he boosted morale and informed his audience of the steps the government was taking to help solve their problems. Not limited to rhetoric, Roosevelt's **New Deal** would provide relief, put millions of people to work, raise prices for farmers, extend conservation projects, revitalize America's financial system, and rescue capitalism.

Steps toward Recovery

In March 1933, President Roosevelt issued an executive order shutting down banks for several days to calm the panic that gripped many Americans in the wake of bank failures and the loss of their life's savings. Shortly after, Congress passed the administration's Emergency Banking Act, which subjected banks to Treasury Department inspection before they reopened, reorganized the banking system, and provided federal funds to bail out banks on the brink of closing. This assertion of federal power allowed solvent banks to reopen. Boosting confidence further, Congress passed the Glass-Steagall Act in June 1933. The measure created the Federal Deposit Insurance Corporation (FDIC), insuring personal savings accounts up to $5,000, and detached commercial banks from investment banks to avoid risky speculation. The president also sought tighter supervision of the stock market, whose collapse many blamed for sparking the Great Depression. By June 1934, Roosevelt had signed into law measures setting up the Securities and Exchange Commission (SEC) to regulate the stock market and ensure that corporations gave investors accurate information about their portfolios.

The regulation of banks and the stock exchange did not mean that Roosevelt was antibusiness. He affirmed his belief in a balanced budget and sought to avoid a $1 billion deficit by cutting government workers' salaries and lowering veterans' pensions. Roosevelt also tried to keep the budget under control by ending prohibition, which would allow the government to tax alcohol sales and eliminate the cost of enforcement. The Twenty-first Amendment, ratified in 1933, ended the more than decade-long experiment with temperance.

These initial measures restored confidence in the presidency and in the federal government's willingness and ability to redress some of the problems responsible for the economic crisis. Yet the Roosevelt administration had much more to accomplish before those hardest hit by the depression felt some relief. Roosevelt viewed the Great Depression as a crisis analogous to war and adapted many of the bureaus and commissions used during World War I to ensure productivity and mobilize popular support to fit the current economic emergency. Many former progressives lined up behind Roosevelt, including women reformers and social workers who had worked in government and private agencies during the 1920s to develop programs for mothers, children, and the poor. At his wife Eleanor's urging, Roosevelt appointed one of them, Frances Perkins, as the first woman to head a cabinet agency—the Department of Labor.

Rehabilitating agriculture and industry stood at the top of the New Deal's priority list. Farmers came first. In May 1933, Congress passed the **Agricultural Adjustment Act**, aimed at raising prices by reducing production. The Agricultural Adjustment Administration (AAA) paid farmers subsidies to produce less in the future, and for farmers who had already planted their crops (including corn, cotton, rice, tobacco, and wheat) and raised livestock, the agency paid them to plow under a portion of their harvest, slaughter hogs, and destroy dairy products. By 1935 the program succeeded in raising farm income by 50 percent. Large farmers remained the chief beneficiaries of the AAA because they could afford to cut back production. In doing so, especially in the South, they forced off the land sharecroppers who no longer had plots to farm. Even when sharecroppers managed to retain a parcel of their acreage, AAA subsidies went to the landowners, who did not always distribute the designated funds owed to the share-croppers. Though poor white farmers felt the sting of this injustice, the system of white supremacy existing in the South guaranteed that blacks suffered most.

After the Supreme Court voided the AAA in 1936 for imposing an unlawful tax on food processors in order to fund the subsidies, Congress enacted several pieces of legislation designed to limit production and provide aid to small farmers. The second AAA, passed in 1938, offered agricultural subsidies to reduce cultivation on the basis of conservation and soil erosion prevention, which overcame judicial objections. To deal with continuing rural poverty among sharecroppers and tenant farmers, Congress provided loans for displaced farmers.

The Roosevelt administration exhibited its boldest initiative in creating the **Tennessee Valley Authority (TVA)** in 1933 to bring low-cost electric power to rural areas and help redevelop the entire Tennessee River valley region through flood-control projects. In contrast to the AAA and other farm programs in which control stayed in private hands, the TVA owned and supervised the building and operation of public power plants, starting with the Muscle Shoals Dam in Alabama, which progressives had lobbied for since the 1920s. For farmers outside the Tennessee River valley, the Rural Electrification Administration helped them obtain cheap electric power starting in 1935, and for the first time tens of thousands of farmers experienced the modern conveniences that electricity brought (though most farmers would not get electric power until after World War II).

Roosevelt and Congress also acted to deal with the soil erosion problem behind the dust storms. In 1933, the Department of Interior established a Soil Erosion Service, and two years later Congress created a permanent Soil Conservation Service in the Department of Agriculture. Although these measures would prove beneficial in the long run, they did nothing to prevent even more severe storms from rolling through the Dust Bowl, as it was now known, in 1935 and 1936.

At the same time, Roosevelt concentrated on industrial recovery. He kept Hoover's RFC intact, but he went far beyond his predecessor in sanctioning government participation in the economy. In 1933 Congress passed the National Industrial Recovery Act, which established the **National Recovery Administration (NRA)**. This agency allowed business, labor, and the public (represented by government officials) to create codes to regulate production, prices, wages, hours, and collective bargaining. Designers of the NRA expected that if wages rose and prices remained stable, consumer purchasing power would climb, demand would grow, and businesses would put people back to work. For this plan to work, business people needed to keep prices steady by absorbing some of the costs of higher wages. The head of the NRA, Hugh S. Johnson, a veteran of the War Industries Board during World War I, engaged in a highly visible public relations campaign. Johnson argued that regulatory codes were good for everyone. Like rules for a fair fight, they would "eliminate eye-gouging and knee-groining and ear-chewing in business," Johnson proclaimed. Businesses and industries that joined the NRA displayed the symbol of a blue eagle to signal their participation, and officials whipped up patriotic fervor on its behalf.

However, the NRA did not function as planned, nor did it bring the desired recovery. Businesses did not exercise the necessary restraint to keep prices steady. Large manufacturers dominated the code-making committees, and because Roosevelt had suspended enforcement of the antitrust law, they could not resist taking collective action to force smaller firms out of business. The NRA legislation guaranteed labor the right to unionize, but the agency did not vigorously enforce collective bargaining. The government failed to intervene to redress the imbalance of power between labor and management because Roosevelt depended primarily on big business to generate economic improvement. Moreover, the NRA had created codes for too many businesses, and government officials could not properly oversee them all. In 1935 the Supreme Court delivered the final blow to the NRA by declaring it an unconstitutional delegation of legislative power to the president.

Direct Assistance and Relief

Economic recovery programs were important, but they took time to take effect, and many Americans needed immediate help. Thus relief efforts and direct job creation were critical parts of the New Deal. Created in the early months of Roosevelt's term, the Federal Emergency Relief Administration (FERA) provided cash grants to states to revive their bankrupt relief efforts. Unlike Hoover's RFC, the FERA did not expect states to repay the loans, but it left administration of the programs to state and local agencies. Roosevelt chose Harry Hopkins, the chief of New York's relief agency, to head the FERA and distribute its initial $500 million appropriation. On the job for two hours, Hopkins had already spent $5 million. He did not calculate whether a particular plan "would work out in the long run," because, as he remarked, "people don't eat in the long run—they eat every day."

Harold Ickes, secretary of the interior and director of the Public Works Administration (PWA), oversaw efforts to rebuild the nation's infrastructure. Funding architects, engineers, and skilled workers, the PWA built the Grand Coulee, Boulder, and Bonneville dams in the West; the Triborough Bridge in New York City; 70 percent of all new schools constructed between 1933 and 1939; and a variety of municipal buildings, sewage plants, port facilities, and hospitals.

Yet neither the FERA nor the PWA provided enough emergency relief to the millions who faced the winter of 1933–1934 without jobs or the money to heat their homes. In response, Hopkins persuaded Roosevelt to launch a temporary program to help needy Americans get through this difficult period. Both men favored "work relief"—giving people jobs rather than direct welfare payments whenever practical. The Civil Works Administration (CWA) lasted four months, but in that brief time it employed more than 4 million people on about 400,000 projects that built 500,000 miles of roads, 40,000 schools, 3,500 playgrounds, and 1,000 airports. Montana got its state capitol building renovated, Pittsburgh erected its Cathedral of Learning, Boston's unemployed teachers went back to their classes, writers and artists remained at their desks and canvases, singers toured the nation, and ninety-four Indians restocked the Kodiak Islands off the coast of Alaska with rabbits.

One of Roosevelt's most successful relief programs was the **Civilian Conservation Corps (CCC)**, created shortly after he entered the White House. The CCC recruited unmarried men between the ages of eighteen and twenty-five for a two-year stint.

It removed them from relief rolls and the glut of the job market and put them to work planting forests; cleaning up beaches, rivers, and parks; and building bridges and dams. To build discipline, the U.S. army ran the CCC, furnished uniforms, and set up military-style camps. Participants received $1 per day, and the government sent $25 of the $30 in monthly wages directly to their families, helping make this the most popular of all New Deal programs. The CCC employed around 2.5 million men and lasted until 1942.

New Deal Critics

Despite the unprecedented efforts of the Roosevelt administration to spark recovery, provide relief, and encourage reform between 1933 and 1935, the country remained in depression, and unemployment still hovered around 20 percent. A liberal but not a radical, Roosevelt found himself under attack from both the left and the right. On the right, conservatives questioned New Deal spending and the growth of big government. On the left, the president's critics argued that he had not done enough to topple wealthy corporate leaders from power and relieve the plight of the downtrodden.

 Online Document Project   **Franklin Roosevelt's New Deal and Its Critics**
bedfordstmartins.com/hewittlawsonvalue

The Great Depression and Hoover's inability to ameliorate its most damaging effects dealt a serious blow to the Republican Party and to the conservative opposition to federal government intervention with which it was identified. In 1934 officials of the Du Pont Corporation and General Motors formed the American Liberty League. The group, according to one of its founders, set out to educate the nation about "the value of encouraging people to work; encouraging people to get rich." From the point of view of the league's founders, the New Deal was little more than a vehicle for the spread of socialism and communism. The organization spent $1 million attacking what it considered to be Roosevelt's "dictatorial" policies and his assaults on free enterprise. The league, however, failed to attract support beyond a small group of northern industrialists, Wall Street bankers, and a few disaffected Democrats.

Roosevelt also faced criticism from the left. Communist Party membership reached its peak of around 75,000 in 1938, and though the party remained relatively small in numbers, it attracted intellectuals and artists whose voices could reach the larger public. The party's efforts to save the Scottsboro Nine boosted its appeal among African Americans. Party members also led unionizing drives in both the North and the South and displayed great talent and energy in organizing workers where resistance to unions was greatest. In the mid-1930s, the party followed the Soviet Union's antifascist foreign policy and joined with left-leaning, non-Communist groups, such as unions and civil rights organizations, to oppose the growing menace of fascism in Europe, particularly in Germany and Italy. By the end of the decade, however, the party had lost many members, as revelations about the tyrannical behavior of the Soviet dictator Joseph Stalin emerged and after the Soviet Union reversed its anti-Nazi foreign policy.

The greatest challenge to Roosevelt came from a trio of talented men who reflected diverse beliefs. Through charisma, organizational skills, or a combination of both, each of them created his own national campaign criticizing the New Deal. Francis Townsend, a retired California physician, proposed a "Cure for Depressions." In 1934 he formed the Old-Age Revolving Pensions Corporation, whose title summed up the doctor's idea. Townsend would have the government give all Americans over the age of sixty a monthly pension of $200 if they retired and spent the entire stipend each month. He promoted this scheme as a simple panacea for the ailing economy. Retirements would open up jobs for younger workers, and the income these workers received, along with the pension for the elderly, would pump ample funds into the economy to promote recovery. The government would fund the Townsend plan with a 2 percent "transaction" or sales tax. By 1936 Townsend Clubs had attracted about 3.5 million members throughout the country, and one-fifth of all adults in the United States signed a petition endorsing the Townsend plan.

While Townsend appealed mainly to the elderly, Charles E. Coughlin attracted Catholics and a lower-middle-class following. An outspoken priest from the Detroit suburb of Royal Oak, Michigan, Father Coughlin used his popular national radio broadcasts to talk about economic and political issues. Originally a Roosevelt supporter, by 1934 Coughlin had begun criticizing the New Deal for catering to greedy bankers. He spoke to millions of radio listeners about the evils of the Roosevelt administration, the godless Communists who had allegedly infested it, and international bankers—coded language referring to Jews—who supposedly manipulated it. In 1935 Coughlin's popularity reached its peak as he organized the National Union for Social Justice, which supported monetary inflation to help debt-ridden farmers and the nationalization of banks to control lending practices. As the decade wore on, his strident anti-Semitism and his growing fondness for fascist dictatorships abroad overshadowed his economic justice message, and Catholic officials ordered him to stop broadcasting.

Huey Pierce Long of Louisiana, known as "the Kingfish," posed the greatest political threat to Roosevelt. Unlike Townsend and Coughlin, Long had built and operated a successful political machine, first as governor and then as U.S. senator, taking on the special interests of oil and railroad corporations in his home state. Early on he had backed Roosevelt, but Long found the New Deal wanting. "Not a single thin dime of concentrated, bloated, pompous wealth, massed in the hands of a few people," Long claimed, "has been raked down to relieve the masses." In 1934 Long established the Share Our Wealth society, promising to make "every man a king" by presenting families with a $5,000 homestead and a guaranteed annual income of $2,000. To accomplish this, Long proposed levying heavy income and inheritance taxes on the wealthy. Although the financial calculations behind his bold plan did not add up, Share Our Wealth clubs counted some seven million members. The swaggering senator departed from most of his segregationist southern colleagues by appealing to a coalition of disgruntled farmers, industrial workers, and African Americans (as governor of Louisiana, he supported repeal of the poll tax). Before Long could help lead a third-party campaign for president, he was shot and killed in 1935.

REVIEW & RELATE

• What steps did Roosevelt take to stimulate economic recovery and provide relief to impoverished Americans during his first term in office?

• What criticisms did Roosevelt's opponents level against the New Deal?

The New Deal Moves to the Left

Facing criticism from within his own party about the pace and effectiveness of the New Deal, and with the 1936 election looming, Roosevelt moved to the left. He adopted harsher rhetoric against recalcitrant corporate leaders; beefed up economic and social programs for the unemployed, the elderly, and the infirm; and revived measures to redress the power imbalance between management and labor. In doing so, he fashioned a political coalition that would deliver a landslide victory in 1936 and allow the Democratic Party to dominate electoral politics for the next three decades.

Expanding Relief Measures

Even though the New Deal had helped millions of people, millions of others still felt left out, as the popularity of Townsend, Coughlin, and Long indicated. "We the people voted for you," a Columbus, Ohio, worker wrote the president in disgust, "but it is a different story now. You have faded out on the masses of hungry, idle people. . . . The very rich is the only one who has benefited from your new deal."

In 1935 the president seized the opportunity to win his way back into the hearts of the "forgotten Americans"—poor farmers, industrial workers, and marginalized minority groups. Although Roosevelt favored a balanced budget, political necessity forced him to embark on deficit spending to expand the New Deal. Federal government expenditures would now exceed tax revenues, but New Dealers argued that these outlays would stimulate job creation and economic growth, which ultimately would replenish government coffers. Based on the highly successful but short-lived Civil Works Administration, the **Works Progress Administration (WPA)** provided jobs for the unemployed with a far larger budget, starting out with $5 billion. To ensure that the money would be spent, Roosevelt appointed Harry Hopkins to head the agency. Although critics condemned the WPA for employing people on unproductive "make-work" jobs and jibed that its initials stood for "We Poke Around"—a criticism not entirely unfounded—overall the WPA did a great deal of good. The agency constructed or repaired more than 100,000 public buildings, 600 airports, 500,000 miles of roads, and 100,000 bridges. The WPA employed about 8.5 million workers during its eight years of operation.

The WPA also helped artists, writers, and musicians. Under its auspices, the Federal Writers Project, the Federal Art Project, the Federal Music Project, and the Federal Theater Project encouraged the production of cultural works and helped bring them to communities and audiences throughout the country. Actors staged plays, dancers performed ballets, and musicians held recitals outside the usual centers of high culture in New York, Boston, and Chicago. Writers Richard Wright, Ralph Ellison, Clifford Odets, Saul Bellow, John Cheever, Margaret Walker, and many others nourished both their works and their stomachs while employed by the WPA. Painters created elaborate murals on the walls of post offices and other government buildings. Historians and folklorists researched and prepared city and state guides and interviewed black ex-slaves whose narratives of the system of bondage would otherwise have been lost.

In addition to the WPA, the National Youth Administration (NYA) employed millions of young people. The NYA provided part-time work to 600,000 college undergraduates, 1.5 million high school students, and 2.6 million jobless youth who no longer attended school. Their work ranged from clerical assignments and repairing automobiles to building tuberculosis isolation units and renovating schools. Heading the NYA in Texas, the young Lyndon B. Johnson worked hard to expand educational and construction projects to unemployed whites and blacks. The Division of Negro Affairs, headed by the Florida educator Mary McLeod Bethune and the only minority group subsection in the NYA, ensured that African American youths would benefit from the programs sponsored by the agency.

Despite their many successes, these relief programs had a number of flaws. The WPA paid participants relatively low wages. The $660 in annual income earned by the average worker fell short of the $1,200 that a family needed to survive. In addition, the WPA limited participation to one family member. In most cases, this meant the male head of the household. As a result, women made up only about 14 percent of WPA workers, and even in the peak year of 1938, the WPA hired only 60 percent of eligible women. With the exception of the program for artists, most women hired by the WPA worked in lower-paying jobs than men.

Establishing Social Security

The elderly also required immediate relief and insurance in a country that lagged behind the rest of the industrialized world in helping its aged workforce. In August 1935, the president rectified this shortcoming and signed into law the **Social Security Act**. The measure provided that at age sixty-five, eligible workers would receive retirement payments funded by payroll taxes on employees and employers. The law also extended beyond the elderly by providing unemployment insurance for those temporarily laid off from work and welfare payments for the disabled who were permanently out of a job as well as for destitute, dependent children of single parents.

The Social Security program had significant limitations. The act excluded farm, domestic, and laundry workers, who were among the neediest Americans and were disproportionately African American. The reasons for these exclusions were largely political. The president needed southern Democrats to support this measure, and as a Mississippi newspaper observed: "The average Mississippian can't imagine himself chipping in to pay pensions for able bodied Negroes to sit around in idleness." The system of financing pensions also proved unfair. The payroll tax, which imposes the same fixed percentage on all incomes, is a regressive tax, one that falls hardest on those with lower incomes. The regressiveness of the tax proved to be an additional handicap for immediate economic recovery because the tax payments took purchasing power out of the hands of workers, whereas pension payments would not begin for several years. Social Security also disadvantaged working women, who on average earned less than men; nor did it take into account the unpaid labor of women who remained in the home to take care of their children.

Even with its flaws, Social Security revolutionized the expectations of American workers. It created a compact between the federal government and its citizens, and workers insisted that their political leaders fulfill their moral responsibilities to keep the system going. President Roosevelt recognized that the tax formula might not be economically sound, but he had a higher political objective in mind. He believed that payroll taxes would give contributors the right to collect their benefits and that "with those taxes in there, no damn politician can ever scrap my social security program." Social Security also helped create a larger middle-class constituency for Roosevelt and the Democratic Party.

Organized Labor Strikes Back

In 1935 Congress passed the **National Labor Relations Act**, also known as the Wagner Act for its leading sponsor, Senator Robert F. Wagner Sr. of New York. The law created the National Labor Relations Board (NLRB), which protected workers' right to organize labor unions without owner interference. During the 1930s, union membership rolls soared from fewer than 4 million workers to more than 10 million, including more than 800,000 women. At the outset of the depression, barely 6 percent of the labor force belonged to unions, compared with 33 percent in 1940.

Government efforts boosted this growth, but these spectacular gains were due primarily to workers' grassroots efforts set in motion by economic hard times. Workers in key industries—automobiles, steel, rubber, and textiles—took the lead. The number of striking workers during the first year of the Roosevelt administration soared from nearly 325,000 to more than 1.5 million. Organizers such as Luisa Moreno traveled the country to bring as many people as possible into the union movement. The most important development within the labor movement occurred in 1935, with the creation of the Congress of Industrial Organizations (CIO). After the American Federation of Labor (AFL), which consisted mainly of craft unions, rejected a proposal by John L. Lewis of the United Mine Workers to incorporate industrial workers under its umbrella, Lewis and representatives of seven other AFL unions defected and formed the CIO. Unlike the AFL, the new union sought to recruit a wide variety of workers without respect to race, gender, or region.

In 1937, two years after its founding, the CIO mounted a full-scale organizing campaign. More than 4.5 million workers participated in some 4,700 strikes, strangling mass-production industries. Unions found new ways to protest poor working conditions and arbitrary layoffs. Members of the United Auto Workers (UAW), a CIO affiliate, launched a **sit-down strike** against General Motors (GM) in Flint, Michigan, to win union recognition, higher wages, and better working conditions. Strikers refused to work but remained in the plants, shutting them down from the inside. Workers felt a new sense of power and confidence, a belief that they were more important than machines. "We learned we can take the plant," one striker gloated. "We already knew how to run them." When the company sent in local police forces to evict the strikers on January 11, 1937, the barricaded workers bombarded the police with spare machine parts and anything that was not bolted down. The community rallied around the strikers, and wives and daughters called "union maids" formed the Women's Emergency Brigade, which supplied sit-downers with food and water and kept up their morale. Neither the state nor the federal government interfered with the work stoppage, and after six weeks GM acknowledged defeat and recognized the UAW. Most of the other auto companies soon followed, though Henry Ford's was one of the last.

Despite some setbacks in 1937, especially in the steel industry, most strikes were settled in the union's favor, and by the end of the decade "big labor," as the AFL and CIO unions were known, had become a significant force in American politics and a leading backer of the New Deal. However, this big labor/big government alliance left out non-unionized industrial and agricultural workers, many of whom were African American or other minorities and lacked adequate bargaining power. Employers often passed on the burden of higher industrial wages to consumers in the form of higher prices.

A Half Deal for Minorities

President Roosevelt made significant gestures on behalf of African Americans. He appointed Mary McLeod Bethune and Robert Weaver to staff New Deal agencies and gathered an informal "Black Cabinet" in the nation's capital to advise him on matters pertaining to race. He also reversed the racial segregation policy his Democratic predecessor Woodrow Wilson had initiated in federal offices and facilities. The Roosevelt administration established the Civil Liberties Unit (later renamed Civil Rights Section) in the Department of Justice, which investigated racial discrimination. Eleanor Roosevelt acted as a visible symbol of the White House's concern with the plight of blacks, a role that culminated in her public support for the black singer Marian Anderson. In 1939 Eleanor Roosevelt quit the Daughters of the American Revolution, a women's organization, when it refused to allow Anderson to hold a concert in Constitution Hall in Washington, D.C. Instead, the First Lady brought Anderson to sing on the steps of the Lincoln Memorial before an integrated audience of 75,000 and to millions more on the radio.

Perhaps the greatest measure of Franklin Roosevelt's impact on African Americans came when large numbers of black voters switched from the Republican to the Democratic Party in 1936, a pattern that has lasted to the present day. "Go turn Lincoln's picture to the wall," a black observer wryly commented after the election. "That debt has been paid in full."

Yet overall the New Deal did little to break down racial inequality. President Roosevelt believed that the plight of African Americans would improve, along with all downtrodden Americans, as New Deal measures restored economic health. Black leaders disagreed. They argued that the NRA's initials stood for "Negroes Ruined Again" because the agency displaced black workers and approved lower wages for blacks than for whites. The AAA dislodged black sharecroppers, a problem later ameliorated somewhat by New Deal programs such as the Farm Security Administration. New Deal programs such as the CCC and those for building public housing maintained existing patterns of segregation. Both the Social Security Act and the Fair Labor Standards Act omitted from coverage jobs that black Americans were most likely to hold. When members of Congress did propose legislation to combat lynching and eliminate the poll tax on voting, Roosevelt offered only lukewarm support for fear of alienating his southern Democratic allies; consequently, these bills went down to defeat.

This pattern of halfway reform persisted for other minorities. Since the end of the Indian wars in 1890 (see chapter 15), Native Americans had lived in poverty, forced onto reservations that offered few economic opportunities and where whites carried out a relentless assault on their culture. By the early 1930s, American Indians earned an average income of less than $50 a year—compared with $800 for whites—and their unemployment rate was three times higher than that of white Americans. For the most part, they lived on lands that whites had given up on as unsuitable for farming or mining. The policy of assimilation established by the Dawes Act of 1887 had exacerbated the problem by depriving Indians of their cultural identities as well as their economic livelihoods. In 1934 the federal government reversed its course. Spurred on by John Collier, the commissioner of Indian affairs,

The Indian New Deal   John Collier, commissioner of Indian affairs under President Roosevelt, favored a New Deal for Native Americans. An advocate for Indian culture, Collier implemented reform legislation that replaced the policy of Indian assimilation with that of self-determination. In this 1935 photograph, Collier watches his boss, Secretary of the Interior Harold Ickes, sign the Flathead [Montana] Indian Constitution as tribal leaders look on.   © Bettmann/CORBIS

Congress passed the **Indian Reorganization Act (IRA)**, which terminated the Dawes Act, authorized self-government for those living on reservations, extended tribal landholdings, and pledged to uphold native customs and language.

Although the IRA brought economic and social improvements for Native Americans, many problems remained. Despite his considerable efforts, Collier approached Indian affairs from the top down. One historian remarked that Collier had "the zeal of a crusader who knew better than the Indians what was good for them." The Indian commissioner failed to appreciate the diversity of native tribes and administered laws that contradicted Native American political and economic practices. For example, the IRA required the tribes to operate by majority rule, whereas many of them reached decisions through consensus, which respected the views of the minority. Although 174 tribes accepted the IRA, 78 tribes, including the Seneca, Crow, and Navajo, rejected it.

Twilight of the New Deal

Roosevelt's shift to the left paid political dividends, and in 1936 the president won reelection by a landslide. His sweeping victory proved to be one of the rare critical elections that signified a fundamental political realignment. Democrats replaced Republicans as the majority party in the United States, overturning thirty-six years of Republican rule. While

Roosevelt had won convincingly in 1932, not until 1936 did the president put together a stable coalition that could sustain Democratic dominance for many years to come.

In 1936 Roosevelt trounced Alfred M. Landon, the Republican governor of Kansas, and Democrats increased their congressional majorities by staggering margins. The vote broke down along class lines. Roosevelt won the votes of 80 percent of union members, 81 percent of unskilled workers, and 84 percent of people on relief, compared with only 42 percent of high-income voters. Millions of new voters came out to the polls, and most of them supported Roosevelt's New Deal coalition of the poor, farmers, urban ethnic minorities, unionists, white southerners, and African Americans.

The euphoria of his triumph, however, proved short-lived. An overconfident Roosevelt soon reached beyond his electoral mandate and within two years found himself unable to extend the New Deal. In 1937 Roosevelt asked Congress to increase the size of the Supreme Court through a **court-packing plan**. He justified this as a matter of reform, claiming that the present nine-member Court could not handle its workload, much of it generated by the avalanche of New Deal legislation. Roosevelt attributed a good deal of the problem to the advanced age of six of the nine justices, who were over seventy years old. Under his proposal, the president would make one new appointment for each judge over the age of seventy who did not retire so long as the bench did not exceed fifteen members. In reality, Roosevelt schemed to "pack" the Court with supporters to prevent it from declaring New Deal legislation such as Social Security and the Wagner Act unconstitutional.

The plan backfired. Conservatives charged Roosevelt with seeking to destroy the separation of powers enshrined in the Constitution among the executive, legislative, and judicial branches. They portrayed the president as a "dictator," which, although a distorted characterization, touched a nerve in those concerned with the rise of tyrants in Germany and Italy. In the end, the president failed to expand the Supreme Court, but he preserved his legislative accomplishments. In a series of rulings, the chastened Supreme Court approved Social Security, the Wagner Act, and other New Deal legislation. Nevertheless, the political fallout from the court-packing fight damaged the president and his plans for further legislative reform.

Roosevelt's court-packing plan alienated many southern Democratic members of Congress who previously had sided with the president. Traditionally suspicious of the power of the federal government, southern lawmakers worried that Roosevelt was going too far toward centralizing power in Washington at the expense of states' rights. Southern Democrats formed a coalition with conservative northern Republicans who shared their concerns about the expansion of federal power and excessive spending on social welfare programs. Their antipathy toward labor unions, especially in the wake of the sit-down strikes, further bound them together. Although they held a minority of seats in Congress, this **conservative coalition** could block unwanted legislation by using the filibuster in the Senate (unlimited debate that could be shut down only with a two-thirds vote). The coalition could not defeat Roosevelt's **Fair Labor Standards Act** (1938), which established minimum wages at 40 cents an hour and maximum working hours at forty per week, but after 1938 these conservatives made sure that no other New Deal legislation passed.

Roosevelt also lost support because the recession of 1937 overlapped with the Supreme Court fight. When federal spending soared after passage of the WPA and other relief measures adopted in 1935, the president lost his economic nerve for deficit spending. He called for reduced spending, which increased unemployment and slowed economic recovery. At the same time, as the Social Security payroll tax took effect, it reduced the purchasing power of workers, thereby exacerbating the impact of reduced government spending. This "recession within the depression" further eroded congressional support for the New Deal.

The country was still deep in depression in 1939. Unemployment was at 17 percent, with more than 11 million people out of work. Most of those who were poor at the start of the Great Depression remained poor. Recovery came mainly to those who were temporarily impoverished as a result of the economic crisis. The distribution of wealth remained skewed toward the top. In 1933 the richest 5 percent of the population controlled 31 percent of disposable income; in 1939 the figure stood at 26 percent.

Against this backdrop of persistent difficult economic times, the president's popularity began to fade. In the midterm elections of 1938, Roosevelt campaigned against Democratic conservatives in an attempt to reinvigorate his New Deal coalition. His efforts failed to purge the conservatives he hoped to unseat and upset many ordinary citizens who associated the tactic with that used by European dictators who had recently risen to power. As the decade came to a close, Roosevelt turned his attention away from the New Deal and increasingly toward a new war in Europe that, like World War I twenty-five years earlier, threatened to engulf the entire world.

REVIEW & RELATE

- Why and how did the New Deal shift to the left in 1934 and 1935?
- Despite the president's landslide victory in 1936, why did the New Deal stall during Roosevelt's second term in office?

Conclusion: New Deal Liberalism

Franklin Roosevelt succeeded in expanding the scope of public authority. The New Deal brought unprecedented government involvement in the lives of people, whether rich or poor. Businesses were subject to increased regulation even as they retained control over hiring and firing, production, and pricing. The federal government grew considerably during the 1930s, jumping from 605,000 employees to more than 1 million, and turned citizens' attention from local and state authorities to officials in Washington, D.C. Yet the New Deal rescued the capitalist system, doing little to alter the fundamental structure of the American economy. It left corporations, the stock market, farms, and banks in the hands of private enterprise. Indeed, by the end of the 1930s large corporations had more power over markets than ever before. Income and wealth remained unequally distributed, nearly to the same extent as it had been before Roosevelt took office in 1933.

Roosevelt forged a middle path between reactionaries and revolutionaries at a time when the fascist tyrants Adolf Hitler and Benito Mussolini gained power in Germany and Italy respectively and Joseph Stalin ruthlessly consolidated his rule in the Communist Soviet Union. By contrast, the American president expanded democratic capitalism, bringing a broader cross section of society to the decision-making table. Big business no longer held unilateral authority but instead found its power balanced by big labor, big agriculture, and big government. Roosevelt's "broker state" of multiple competing interests provided for greater democracy than a government dominated exclusively by business elites. This system did not benefit those who remained unorganized and wielded little power, but marginalized groups—African Americans, Latinos, and Native Americans—did receive greater recognition and self-determination from the federal government. Moreover, in the coming decades these groups, too, would find ways to take advantage of the power of collective action and claim a place at the bargaining table.

President Roosevelt also solidified the institution of the presidency as the focal point for public leadership. His cheerfulness, hopefulness, and pragmatism rallied millions of individuals behind him. Even after Roosevelt died in 1945, the public retained its expectation that leadership came from the White House.

Through his programs and force of personality, Franklin Roosevelt convinced Americans that he cared about their welfare and that the federal government would not ignore their suffering. With his chin cocked upward, a fedora hat on his head, and a cigarette holder protruding from his smiling mouth, Roosevelt assured the depression-weary public that it had somewhere to turn for relief. He was not universally beloved: Millions of Americans despised him because they thought he was leading the country toward socialism, and he did not solve all the problems the country faced—it would take government spending for World War II to end the depression. Still, together with his wife Eleanor, Franklin Roosevelt conveyed a sense that the American people belonged to a single community, capable of banding together to solve the country's problems, no matter how serious they were or how intractable they might seem.

Chapter Review

MAKE IT STICK

 LearningCurve **bedfordstmartins.com/hewittlawsonvalue**
After reading the chapter, use LearningCurve to retain what you've read.

IDENTIFY KEY TERMS

Identify and explain the significance of each term below.

Hoovervilles (p. 568)
Scottsboro Nine (p. 570)
Bonus Army (p. 574)
fireside chats (p. 576)
New Deal (p. 576)
Agricultural Adjustment Act (p. 576)
Tennessee Valley Authority (TVA) (p. 577)
National Recovery Administration
　(NRA) (p. 577)
Civilian Conservation Corps (CCC) (p. 578)

Share Our Wealth (p. 580)
Works Progress Administration (WPA)
　(p. 581)
Social Security Act (p. 582)
National Labor Relations Act (p. 583)
sit-down strike (p. 583)
Indian Reorganization Act (IRA) (p. 585)
court-packing plan (p. 586)
conservative coalition (p. 586)
Fair Labor Standards Act (p. 586)

REVIEW & RELATE

Answer the focus questions from each section of the chapter.

1. How did President Hoover respond to the problems and challenges created by the Great Depression?

2. How did different segments of the American population experience the depression?

3. What steps did Roosevelt take to stimulate economic recovery and provide relief to impoverished Americans during his first term in office?

4. What criticisms did Roosevelt's opponents level against the New Deal?

5. Why and how did the New Deal shift to the left in 1934 and 1935?

6. Despite the president's landslide victory in 1936, why did the New Deal stall during Roosevelt's second term in office?

ONLINE DOCUMENT PROJECTS

◆ **The Depression in Rural America**
◆ **Franklin Roosevelt's New Deal and Its Critics**

After reading the primary sources in these document sets, answer the **Interpret the Evidence** questions to help you analyze each of the documents, and then answer the **Put It in Context** question(s) to help you relate the documents to the topics and themes you read about in the chapter.

bedfordstmartins.com/hewittlawsonvalue

TIMELINE OF EVENTS

1931
• Scottsboro Nine tried for rape

1932–1939
• Dust storms sweep through Great Plains

1932
• Creation of Reconstruction Finance Corporation

• River Rouge autoworkers' strike

• Milo Reno creates the Farm Holiday Association

• Bonus Army marches on Washington, D.C.

1933
• Roosevelt takes steps to stabilize banking and financial systems

• Agricultural Adjustment Act passed

• Federal Emergency Relief Administration (FERA) created

• Tennessee Valley Authority (TVA) created

• National Recovery Administration (NRA) created

• Civilian Conservation Corps (CCC) created

1934
• Indian Reorganization Act (IRA) passed

• Francis Townsend forms Old-Age Revolving Pensions Corporation

• Huey Long establishes Share Our Wealth movement

• Securities and Exchange Commission (SEC) established

1935
• Charles E. Coughlin organizes National Union for Social Justice

• Works Progress Administration (WPA) established

• Social Security Act passed

• National Labor Relations Act passed

• Congress of Industrial Organizations (CIO) founded

• Creation of the Soil Conservation Service

1937
• United Auto Workers conduct sit-down strikes against General Motors in Flint, Michigan

• Roosevelt proposes to increase the size of the Supreme Court

1938
• Fair Labor Standards Act passed

23

LearningCurve
bedfordstmartins.com/hewittlawsonvalue
After reading the chapter, use LearningCurve
to retain what you've read.

World War II

1933–1945

AMERICAN HISTORIES

One month after Japan attacked the U.S. naval base at Pearl Harbor on December 7, 1941, and the United States entered World War II, President Franklin Roosevelt approved a full-scale effort to develop an atomic bomb. As scientific director of this top-secret program, called the Manhattan Engineering District Project, physicist J. Robert Oppenheimer orchestrated the work of more than 3,000 scientists, technicians, and military personnel at the Los Alamos Laboratories near Santa Fe, New Mexico. The thirty-seven-year-old Oppenheimer, the son of German American Jews, had studied theoretical physics in England and Germany and then returned to the United States to teach physics. He was also interested and engaged in world events. When the Nazis began persecuting German Jews in the early 1930s, Oppenheimer helped Jews gain asylum in the United States.

On July 16, 1945, Oppenheimer and his team successfully tested their new weapon. The explosion, which had a force equal to more than 18,000 tons of TNT, lit up the predawn sky with a blast so powerful that it broke a window 125 miles away and so bright that a blind woman claimed she saw a flash of light. A mushroom cloud shot up 41,000 feet into the sky over ground zero, where a 1,200-foot-wide crater had formed. Oppenheimer understood that the world had been permanently transformed. Quoting from Hindu scriptures, he remembered thinking at the moment of the explosion, "I am become death, destroyer of worlds."

On August 6, 1945, Army Air Corps planes dropped an atomic bomb on the Japanese city of Hiroshima and three days later another one on Nagasaki, resulting in the deaths of more than 200,000 civilians. Profoundly shaken by the death and destruction his efforts had produced, Oppenheimer observed: "If atomic bombs are to be added to the arsenals of a warring world, or to the arsenals of nations preparing for war, then the time will come when mankind will curse the names of Los Alamos and Hiroshima."

While Oppenheimer and his team remained cloistered at Los Alamos, Fred Korematsu and some 112,000 Japanese Americans lived in internment camps, imprisoned for no other reason than their Japanese ancestry. Born in Oakland, California, in 1919 to Japanese immigrants, Fred and his three brothers grew up like many first-generation Americans. Fred's parents spoke Japanese at home and maintained the cultural traditions of their native land, while their sons learned English in public school, ate hamburgers, and played football and basketball like other children their age. After graduating from high school in 1938, Korematsu worked on the Oakland docks as a welder.

After the 1941 bombing of Pearl Harbor, residents on the West Coast turned their anger on the Japanese and Japanese Americans living among them. As assimilated as Fred Korematsu and many other Nisei (the U.S.-born children of Japanese immigrants) had become, white Americans doubted their loyalty and viewed them as a threat to national security. Korematsu could no longer get a haircut in a white-owned barbershop; the Boilermakers Union expelled him, and he lost his job as a welder; and he was not allowed to join the U.S. coast guard because of his race.

These indignities foreshadowed events to come. On March 21, 1942, President Roosevelt issued Executive Order 9066 authorizing military commanders on the West Coast to take any measures necessary to promote national security. Consequently, officials imposed a curfew on Japanese Americans, excluded them from designated areas, and prohibited them from traveling more than twenty-five miles from their homes. On May 9, the military ordered Korematsu's family to report to Tanforan Racetrack in San Mateo, from which they would be transported to internment camps throughout the West. Although the rest of his family complied with the order, Fred refused. He adopted the name "Clyde Sarah" and claimed to be of Spanish-Hawaiian ancestry. However, Korematsu's efforts to resist internment failed. Three weeks later, he was arrested and later transferred to the Topaz internment camp in south-central Utah. Found guilty of violating the original evacuation order, Korematsu received a sentence of five years of probation. When he appealed his conviction to the U.S. Supreme Court in 1944, the high court upheld the verdict. By the time the first atomic bomb exploded over Hiroshima, the government had closed down the internment camp where Fred Korematsu lived, and he had regained his freedom.

Woman working at the Republic Drill and Tool Company in Chicago, Illinois, 1942. Library of Congress

THE AMERICAN HISTORIES of both Fred Korematsu and J. Robert Oppenheimer were shaped by the profound changes brought about by war. Korematsu was subjected to the full force of anti-Japanese sentiment that followed the attack on Pearl Harbor, while Oppenheimer played a key role in developing a weapon that he feared would lead to the destruction of mankind. Both men experienced a mixture of hope and uneasiness as they looked ahead to the postwar world.

The war that these two men experienced in such different ways marked a critical point for the United States in the twentieth century. World War II finally ended the Great Depression, cementing the trend toward government intervention in the economy that had begun with the New Deal. With the war fought almost entirely on foreign soil, the United States converted its factories to wartime production and became the "arsenal of democracy," putting millions of Americans to work in the process, including African Americans, other minorities, and women. All Americans contributed to the war effort, whether they wanted to or not, through rationing and higher taxes. Overseas, soldiers fought fierce battles in Europe, Africa, and Asia. The combined military power of the Allies, led by the United States, Great Britain, and the Soviet Union, finally defeated the Axis nations of Germany, Italy, and Japan, but not until the fighting had killed 60 to 70 million people, more than half of whom were civilians, and ushered in the Atomic Age.

The Road toward War

The end of World War I did not bring peace and prosperity to Europe. The harsh peace terms imposed on the Central Powers in 1919 left the losers, especially Germany, deeply resentful. The war saddled both sides with a huge financial debt and produced economic instability, which contributed to the Great Depression. In the Far East, Japanese invasions of China and Southeast Asia threatened America's Open Door policy (see chapter 20). The failure of the United States to join the League of Nations dramatically reduced the organization's ability to maintain peace and stability. German expansionism in Europe in the late 1930s moved President Roosevelt and the nation toward war, but it took the Japanese attack on Pearl Harbor to bring the United States into the global conflict.

The Growing Crisis in Europe

Despite its failure to join the League of Nations, the United States did not withdraw from international affairs behind a wall of total isolationism in the 1920s. It participated in arms control negotiations; signed the Kellogg-Briand Pact, which outlawed war as an instrument of national policy but proved unenforceable; and expanded its foreign investments in Central and Latin America, Asia, the Middle East, and western Europe. In 1933 a new possibility for trade emerged when the Roosevelt administration extended diplomatic recognition to the Soviet Union (USSR).

Overall, the country did not retreat from foreign affairs so much as it refused to enter into collective security agreements that would restrain its freedom of action. To the extent that American leaders practiced isolationism, they did so mainly in the political sense of rejecting internationalist organizations such as the League of Nations and the World Court, institutions that might require military cooperation to implement their decisions.

The experience of World War I had reinforced this brand of political isolationism, which was reflected in an outpouring of antiwar sentiments in the late 1920s and early 1930s. Best-selling novels like Ernest Hemingway's *Farewell to Arms* (1929), Erich Maria Remarque's *All Quiet on the Western Front* (1929), and Dalton Trumbo's *Johnny Got His Gun* (1939) presented graphic depictions of the horror and futility of war. Beginning in 1934, Senate investigations chaired by Gerald Nye of North Dakota concluded that bankers and munitions makers—"merchants of death" as one contemporary writer labeled them—had conspired to push the United States into war in 1917. Nye's hearings appealed to popular antibusiness sentiment in depression-era America.

Following the Nye committee hearings, Congress passed a series of **Neutrality Acts**, each designed to make it more difficult for the United States to become entangled in European armed hostilities. In 1935 Congress prohibited the sale of munitions to either warring side and authorized the president to warn Americans against traveling on passenger liners of belligerent nations. The following year, lawmakers added private loans to the ban, and in 1937 they required belligerents to pay cash for nonmilitary purchases and ship them on their own vessels—so-called cash-and-carry provisions.

Events in Europe, however, made U.S. neutrality ever more difficult to maintain. After rising to power as chancellor of Germany in 1933, Adolf Hitler revived Germany's economic and military strength despite the Great Depression. Hitler installed National Socialism (Nazism) at home and established the empire of the Third Reich abroad. The *Führer* (Leader) whipped up patriotic fervor by scapegoating and persecuting Communists and Jews. To garner support for his actions, Hitler manipulated German feelings of humiliation for losing World War I and having been forced to sign the "war guilt" clause (see chapter 20) and pointed to the disastrous effects of the country's inflation-ridden economy. In 1936 Hitler sent troops to occupy the Rhineland between Germany and France in blatant violation of the Treaty of Versailles.

Hitler did not stop there. Citing the need for more *lebensraum* (space for living) for the Germanic people, he pushed for German expansion into eastern Europe. In March 1938, he forced Austria to unite with Germany. In September of that year, Hitler signed the Munich Accord with Great Britain and France, allowing Germany to annex the Sudetenland, the mainly German-speaking, western region of Czechoslovakia. Hitler still wanted more land and was convinced that his western European rivals would not stop him, so in March 1939 he sent German troops to invade and occupy the rest of Czechoslovakia. Hitler proved correct; Britain and France did nothing in response, in hopes that he would stop with Czechoslovakia—what critics of inaction called "appeasement."

Hitler's Italian ally, Benito Mussolini, joined him in war and conquest. In 1935 Italian troops invaded Ethiopia; deposed its leader, Emperor Haile Selassie; and occupied the small African nation. The following year, both Germany and Italy intervened in the Spanish civil war, providing military support for General Francisco Franco in his effort to overthrow the democratically elected, socialist republic of Spain. While the United States and Great Britain remained on the sidelines, only the Soviet Union officially assisted the Loyalist defenders of the Spanish republic. In violation of American law, private citizens, many of whom were Communists, volunteered to serve on the side of the Spanish Loyalists and fought on the battlefield as the Abraham Lincoln Brigade. Other sympathetic Americans, such as J. Robert Oppenheimer, feared the spread of dictatorships and provided financial assistance for the anti-Franco government. Despite these efforts, Franco's forces seized control of Spain in early 1939, another victory for Hitler and Mussolini.

The Challenge to Isolationism

As Europe drifted toward war, public opinion polls revealed that most Americans wanted to stay out of any European conflict. The president, however, thought it likely that the United States would eventually need to assist the Western democracies. Given the United States' economic dominance in the world and its dependence on international commerce, Roosevelt feared that Germany and Italy threatened a stable world order. Still, Roosevelt had to tread lightly in the face of the Neutrality Acts that Congress had passed between 1935 and 1937 and overwhelming public opposition to American involvement in Europe.

Germany's aggression in Europe eventually led to full-scale war. When Germany invaded Poland in September 1939, Britain and France declared war on Germany and Italy. Just before the invasion, the Soviet Union had signed a nonaggression agreement with Germany, which carved up Poland between the two nations and permitted the USSR to occupy the neighboring Baltic states of Latvia, Lithuania, and Estonia. Soviet leader Joseph Stalin had few illusions about Hitler's ultimate design on his own nation, but he concluded that by signing this pact he could secure his country's western borders and buy additional time. (In June 1941, the Germans broke the pact and invaded the Soviet Union.)

Roosevelt responded to the outbreak of war by reaffirming U.S. neutrality. Unlike Woodrow Wilson, however, he recognized that this position would be hard to maintain, asserting, "This nation will remain a neutral nation, but I cannot ask that every American remain neutral in thought as well," and "Even a neutral cannot be asked to close his mind or close his conscience." Despite his sympathy for the Allies, which most Americans had come to share, the president stated his hope that the United States could stay out of the war: "Let no man or woman thoughtlessly or falsely talk of Americans sending its armies to European fields."

With the United States on the sidelines, German forces marched toward victory. By the spring of 1940, German armies had launched a *blitzkrieg* (lightning war) across Europe, defeating and occupying Denmark, Norway, the Netherlands, Belgium, and

Luxembourg. The greatest shock occurred in June 1940 when France fell to the German onslaught and Nazi troops marched into Paris. Britain now stood virtually alone, and its position seemed tenuous. The British had barely succeeded in evacuating their forces from France by sea when the German Luftwaffe (air force) began a relentless bombing campaign on London and other targets in the Battle of Britain.

With German victories mounting, committed opponents of American involvement in foreign wars organized the **America First Committee**. Gerald Nye helped found the organization, which attracted New Deal critics such as Father Charles Coughlin and William Lemke; business leaders who opposed Roosevelt, such as Sears, Roebuck head Robert Wood; and aviation hero Charles A. Lindbergh, who admired what Hitler had accomplished in building up the Luftwaffe. America First tapped into the feeling of isolationism and concern among a diverse group of Americans who did not want to get dragged into another foreign war.

The surrender of France and the Battle of Britain drastically changed Americans' attitude toward entering the war. Before Germany invaded France, 82 percent of Americans thought that the United States should not aid the Allies. After France's defeat, in a complete turnaround, some 80 percent of Americans favored assisting Great Britain in some way, though most expected that this aid would lead to further U.S. involvement. However, four out of five Americans polled opposed immediate entry into the war. As a result, the politically astute Roosevelt portrayed all U.S. assistance to Britain as a way to prevent American military intervention by allowing Great Britain to defeat the Germans on its own.

From September 1940 to November 1941, the Roosevelt administration helped Britain in any way it could, short of going to war against Germany. On September 2, 1940, the president sent fifty obsolete destroyers to the British in return for leases on British naval bases in Newfoundland, Bermuda, and the British West Indies. These aging warships did not have much military value, but they provided a great morale boost to the British, who were being pounded by German air attacks. Two weeks later, on September 16, Roosevelt persuaded Congress to pass the Selective Service Act, the first peacetime military draft in U.S. history, which quickly registered more than 16 million men.

This political maneuvering came as Roosevelt campaigned for an unprecedented third term in 1940. He defeated the Republican Wendell Willkie, a Wall Street lawyer who shared Roosevelt's anti-isolationist views. However, both candidates accommodated voters' desire to stay out of the European war, and Roosevelt went so far as to promise American parents: "Your boys are not going to be sent into any foreign war."

Roosevelt's campaign promises did not halt the march toward war. Roosevelt succeeded in pushing Congress to pass the **Lend-Lease Act** in March 1941. With Britain running out of money and its shipping devastated by German submarines, this measure circumvented the cash-and-carry provisions of the Neutrality Acts. The United States would lend or lease equipment, but no one expected the recipients to return the used weapons and other commodities. As one critic of the act declared, "Lending war equipment is a good deal like chewing gum, you don't really want it back!" To protect British ships carrying American supplies, the president extended naval and air patrols in the North Atlantic. In response, German submarines began sinking U.S. ships. By May 1941, Germany and the United States were engaged in an undeclared naval war.

The United States Enters the War

Financially, militarily, and ideologically, the United States had aligned itself with Britain, and Roosevelt expected that the nation would soon be formally at war. After passage of the Lend-Lease Act, American and British military planners agreed that defeating Germany would become the top priority if the United States entered the war. In August 1941, Roosevelt and British prime minister Winston Churchill met in Newfoundland, where they signed the **Atlantic Charter**, a lofty statement of war aims that included principles of freedom of the seas, self-determination, free trade, and "freedom from fear and want"—ideals that laid the groundwork for the establishment of a postwar United Nations. At the same meeting, Roosevelt promised Churchill that the United States would protect British convoys in the North Atlantic as far as Iceland while the nation waited for a confrontation with Germany that would rally the American public in support of war. The president got what he wanted. After several attacks on American ships by German submarines in September and October, the president persuaded Congress to repeal the neutrality legislation of the 1930s and allow American ships to sail across the Atlantic to supply Great Britain. By December, the nation was close to open war with Germany.

The event that finally prompted the United States to enter the war, however, occurred not in the Atlantic but in the Pacific Ocean. For nearly a decade, U.S. relations with Japan had deteriorated over the issue of China's independence. American Christian missionaries had established their presence in China, and since the turn of the twentieth century the U.S. government had promoted the Open Door policy to protect its access to Chinese markets. The United States did little to challenge the Japanese invasion and occupation of Manchuria in 1931, but after Japanese armed forces moved farther into China in 1937, Roosevelt took action. The president skirted the Neutrality Acts by refusing to declare war, but he did supply arms to China. When a bombing raid by Japanese planes inadvertently sank the U.S. gunboat *Panay* in the Yangtze River and killed two sailors, Japan apologized, thereby temporarily reducing tensions between the two countries.

Yet relations between Japan and the United States did not substantially improve. In 1940 the Japanese government signed the Tripartite Pact with Germany and Italy, which created a mutual defense agreement among the Axis powers. That same year, Japanese troops invaded northern Indochina, and Roosevelt responded by embargoing sales of aviation fuel and scrap metal, products that Japan needed for war. This embargo did not deter the Japanese; in July, they occupied the remainder of Indochina to gain access to the region's natural resources. The Roosevelt administration retaliated by freezing Japanese assets and cutting off all trade with Japan. The two countries maneuvered to the edge of war.

On the quiet Sunday morning of December 7, 1941, Japan attacked the U.S. Pacific Fleet stationed at Pearl Harbor in Honolulu, Hawaii. This surprise air and naval assault killed more than 2,400 Americans and damaged eight battleships, three cruisers, three destroyers, and nearly two hundred airplanes. The bombing raid abruptly ended isolationism and rallied the American public behind President Roosevelt, who pronounced December 7 "a date which will live in infamy." The next day, Congress overwhelmingly voted to go to war with Japan, and on December 11 Germany and Italy declared war on the United States in response. In little more than a year after his reelection pledge to keep the country out of war, Roosevelt sent American men to fight overseas.

- How did American public opinion shape Roosevelt's foreign policy in the years preceding U.S. entry into World War II?
- What events in Europe and the Pacific ultimately brought the United States into World War II?

Global War

World War II pitted the "Grand Alliance" of Great Britain, the Soviet Union, the French government in exile, and the United States against the Axis powers of Germany, Japan, and Italy. The Allies consisted of the world's leading colonial power, Great Britain; the world's lone Communist nation, the Soviet Union; and the world's strongest capitalist country, the United States—ingredients for an uncomfortable alliance. From the outset, the United States deployed military forces to contain Japanese aggression, but its most immediate concern was to defeat Germany. Before battles in Europe, Asia, and four other continents concluded, more than 60 million people perished, including 405,000 Americans. Six million Jewish civilians died in the Holocaust, the Nazi regime's genocidal effort to eradicate Europe's Jewish population. The Soviet Union experienced the greatest losses—nearly 27 million soldiers and civilians, more than two-fifths of all those killed.

War in Europe

United against Hitler, the Grand Alliance divided over how quickly to mount a counterattack directly on Germany. The Soviet Union, which bore the brunt of the fighting in trying to repel the German army's invasion, demanded the speedy opening of a second front through France and into Germany to take the pressure off its forces. The British wanted to fight first in northern Africa and southern Europe, in part to remove Axis forces from territory that endangered their economic interests in the Mediterranean and the oil-rich Middle East and in part to buy time to rebuild their depleted fighting strength. President Roosevelt understood Soviet demands for immediately establishing a second front, but such a plan would involve fierce and bloody battles to attack the center of Axis strength. The president did not want to risk losing public support early in the war if the United States experienced heavy casualties. He approved his military advisers' plans for an invasion of France from England in 1943, but in the meantime he agreed with Churchill to fight the Germans and Italians on the periphery of Europe.

From a military standpoint, this circuitous approach proved successful. In October 1942, British forces in North Africa overpowered the Germans at El Alamein, pushing them out of Egypt and removing their threat to the Suez Canal. The following month, British and American troops landed in Algeria and Morocco, controlled by the pro-Nazi French government, and under the British general Bernard Montgomery and the American general George S. Patton they engaged the desert forces of the German general Erwin Rommel. After some early defeats, the combined strength of British and American ground, air, and naval forces drove the Germans out of Africa in May 1943.

These military victories failed to relieve political tensions among the Allies. Although the Soviets had managed to stop the German offensive against Stalingrad, the deepest penetration of enemy troops into their country, Stalin expected the second front to begin as promised in the spring of 1943. He was bitterly disappointed when Roosevelt, hoping to replenish military resources that had been lost in North Africa, postponed the cross–English Channel invasion of France until 1944. To Stalin, it appeared as if his allies were looking to gain a double triumph by letting the Communists and Nazis beat each other into submission. Churchill's strong anti-Communist beliefs fueled Stalin's suspicions.

Instead of opening a second front in France, British, American, and Canadian troops invaded Italy from its southern tip in July 1943. Their initial victories quickly led to the removal of Mussolini and his retreat to northern Italy, where he lived under German protection (Map 23.1). Not until June 4, 1944, did the Allies occupy Rome in central Italy and force the Germans to retreat.

To overcome Stalin's dissatisfaction with the postponement of opening the second front, President Roosevelt issued orders to give the Soviets unlimited access to Lend-Lease supplies to sustain their war efforts and to care for their citizens. In November 1943, the American president and the British prime minister met with the Soviet leader

MAP 23.1

World War II in Europe, 1941–1945   By late 1941, the Axis powers had brought most of Europe and the Mediterranean region under their control. But between 1942 and 1945, the Allied powers drove them back. Critical victories at Leningrad and Stalingrad, in North Africa, and on the beaches of Normandy forced the retreat, and then the defeat, of the Axis powers.

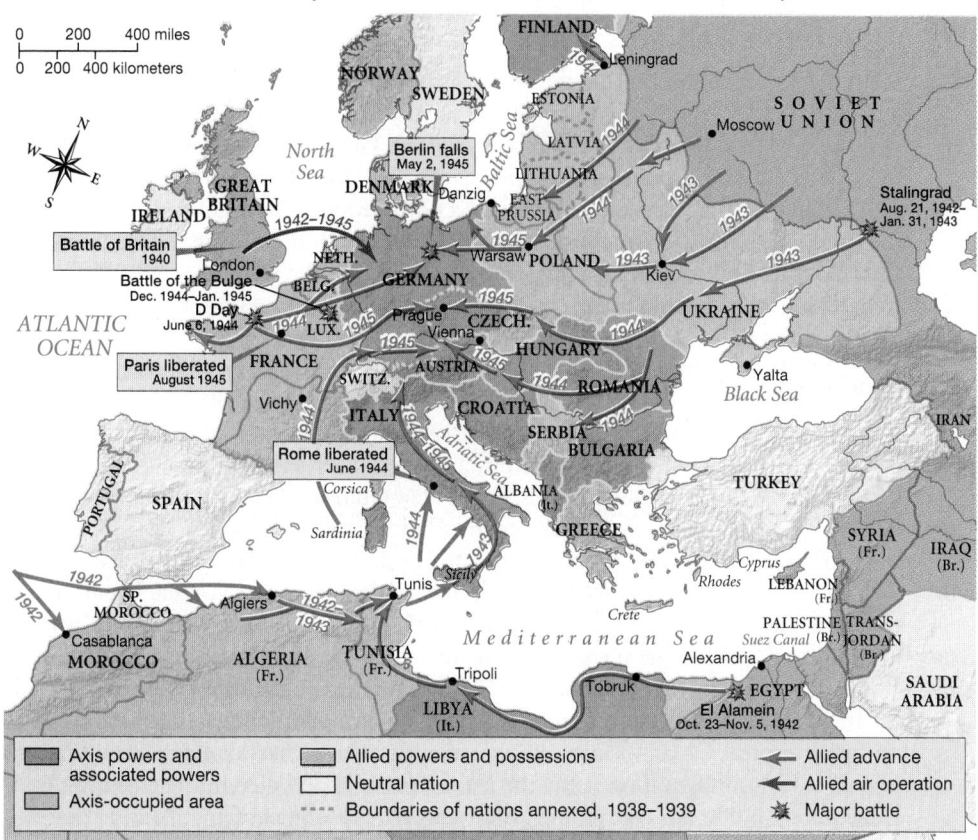

in Tehran, Iran. Roosevelt and Stalin seemed to get along well. Stalin agreed to deploy troops against Japan after the war in Europe ended, and Roosevelt agreed to open the second front within six months. Churchill joined Roosevelt and Stalin in supporting the creation of an international organization to ensure postwar peace.

This time the Americans and British kept their word, and the Allies finally embarked on the second-front invasion. Under the command of General Dwight D. Eisenhower, on June 6, 1944—called **D Day**—more than 1.5 million American, British, and Canadian troops crossed the English Channel in 4,000 boats and landed on the beaches of Normandy, France. Paratrooper landings behind German lines and naval bombardments supported this astonishing amphibious assault. Despite deadly machine-gun fire from German troops placed on higher ground, the Allied forces managed to establish a beachhead. The bravery and discipline of the troops, along with their superior numbers, overcame the Germans and opened the way for the Allies to liberate Paris in August 1944. By the end of the year, the Allies had regained control of the rest of France and most of Belgium.

Amid these Allied victories, Roosevelt won a fourth term against Republican challenger Thomas E. Dewey, governor of New York. He dumped from the campaign ticket his vice president, Henry A. Wallace, a liberal on economic and racial issues, and replaced him with Senator Harry S. Truman of Missouri, who was more acceptable to southern voters. Despite his declining health, Roosevelt won easily with 432 electoral votes and a margin of more than 3.5 million popular votes.

War in the Pacific

With the Soviet Union bearing the brunt of the fighting in eastern Europe, the United States shouldered the burden of fighting Japan. U.S. military commanders began a two-pronged counterattack in the Pacific in 1942. General Douglas MacArthur, whose troops had escaped from the Philippines as Japanese forces overran the islands in May 1942, planned to regroup in Australia, head north through New Guinea, and return to the Philippines. At the same time, Admiral Chester Nimitz directed the U.S. Pacific Fleet from Hawaii toward Japanese-occupied islands in the western Pacific. If all went well, MacArthur's ground troops and Nimitz's naval forces would combine with General Curtis LeMay's air forces to overwhelm Japan.

All went according to plan in 1942. Shortly after the Philippines fell to the Japanese, the Allies won a major victory in May in the Battle of the Coral Sea, off the northwest coast of Australia. The following month, the U.S. navy achieved an even greater victory when it defeated the Japanese in the Battle of Midway Island, northwest of Hawaii. In August, the fighting moved to the Solomon Islands, east of New Guinea, where U.S. forces waged fierce battles at Guadalcanal Island. After six months of heavy casualties on both sides, the Americans finally dislodged the Japanese. By late 1944, American, Australian, and New Zealand troops had put the Japanese on the defensive with further victories in the Mariana Islands, north of Guam, and the Marshall Islands, east of the Philippines, allowing General MacArthur to return to the island that the Japanese had forced him to abandon three years earlier.

In 1945 the United States mounted its final offensive against Japan. In preparation for an invasion of the Japanese home islands, American marines won important battles on Iwo Jima and Okinawa, two strategic islands off the coast of Japan. The fighting proved costly—on Iwo Jima alone, the Japanese fought and died nearly to the last man while killing 6,000 Americans and wounding 20,000 others, demonstrating that the

Japanese would ferociously defend their homeland against the American invasion planned for November. At the same time, the U.S. Army Air Corps conducted firebomb raids over Tokyo and other major cities, killing some 330,000 Japanese civilians. These attacks were conducted by newly developed B-29 bombers, which could fly more than 3,000 miles and could be dispatched from Pacific island bases captured by the U.S. military. The purpose of this strategic bombing was to destroy Japan's economic capability to sustain the war rather than to destroy their military forces. B-29s dropped bombs that set fire to Japanese buildings, which were constructed mainly of wood, and ignited firestorms that caused widespread destruction. At the same time, the navy blockaded Japan, further crippling its economy and reducing its supplies of food, medicine, and raw materials (Map 23.2). Still, the Japanese government refused to surrender and indicated its determination to resist by launching *kamikaze* attacks (suicidal airplane crashes) on American warships and airplanes.

MAP 23.2

World War II in the Pacific, 1941–1945　　After bombing Pearl Harbor on December 7, 1941, Japan captured the Philippines and wrenched control of Asian colonies from the British, French, and Dutch and then occupied eastern China. The Allied powers, led by U.S. forces, eventually defeated Japan by winning a series of hard-fought victories on Central Pacific islands and by bombing Hiroshima and Nagasaki.

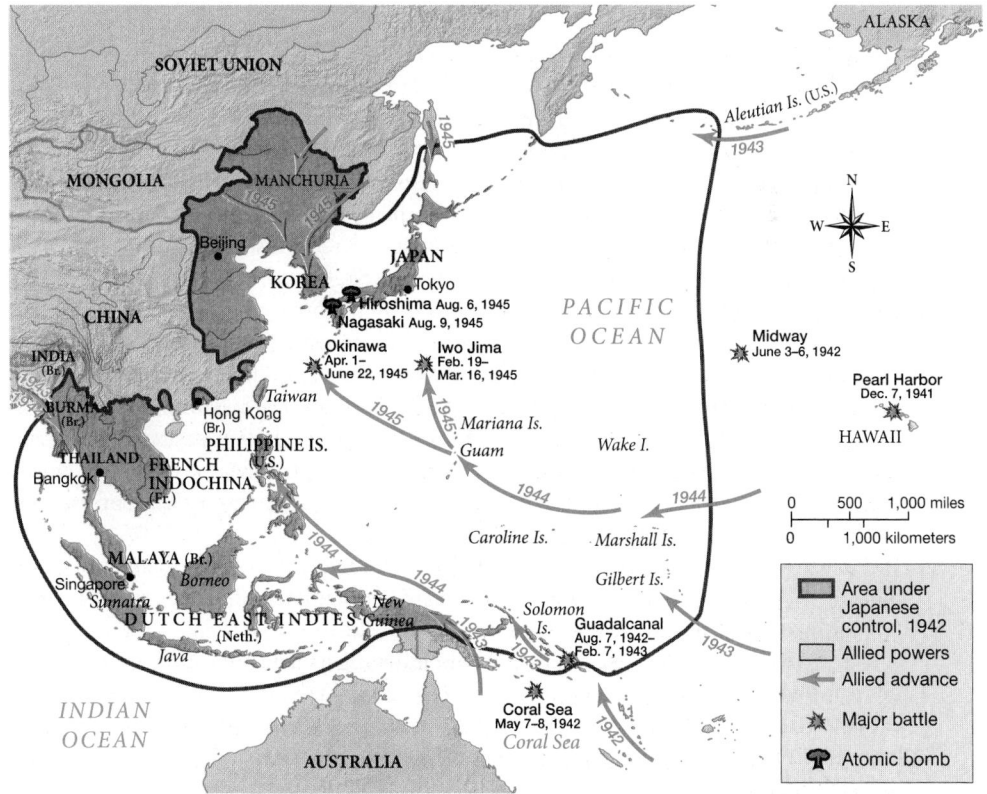

Ending the War

With victory in sight in both Europe and the Pacific, the Allies addressed problems of postwar relations. In February 1945, Roosevelt and Churchill met with Stalin in the resort city of Yalta in the Ukraine. There they clashed over the question of the postwar government of Poland and whether to recognize the claim of the Polish government in exile in London, which the United States and Great Britain supported, or that of the pro-Soviet government, which had spent the war in the USSR. The loosely worded Yalta Agreement that resulted from the conference called for the establishment of permanent governments in Poland and the rest of eastern Europe through free elections. Because the USSR considered Poland vital to its national security—it had been invaded from Europe through Poland twice in the past thirty years—the Soviets interpreted the Yalta accord differently than did the Americans and the British, a difference of opinion that soon degenerated into a serious rupture in relations among the parties known as the "Big Three."

Despite this controversy, the Allies left Yalta united over other issues. They renewed their commitment to establishing the United Nations, and the Soviets reaffirmed their intention to join the war against Japan three months after Germany's surrender. The Allies also reached a tentative agreement on postwar Germany. The United States, Great Britain, the Soviet Union, and France would parcel out the defeated country into four zones, each occupied by one of the powers. They would further subdivide Berlin into four sectors because the capital city fell within the Soviet occupation area. As with the accord over Poland, the agreement concerning Germany created tension after the war.

The Yalta Conference concluded just as the final assault against Germany was under way. The Germans had launched one last offensive in mid-December 1944. Mobilizing troops from remaining outposts in Belgium, they attacked Allied forces in what became known as the Battle of the Bulge because of the way that their assault looked when sketched on Allied maps. After an initial German drive into enemy lines, American and British fighting men recovered and sent the Germans retreating across the Rhine River and back into Germany. Pushing from the west, General Eisenhower stopped at the Elbe River, where he had agreed to meet up with Red Army troops who were charging from the east to Berlin. After an intense assault by the Soviets, the German capital of Berlin fell, and on April 25 Russian and American forces linked up in Torgau on the Elbe River. They achieved this triumph two weeks after Franklin Roosevelt died at the age of sixty-three from a cerebral hemorrhage. On April 30, 1945, with Berlin shattered, Hitler committed suicide in his bunker. A few days earlier, Italian antifascist partisans had captured and executed Mussolini in northern Italy. On May 2, German troops surrendered in Italy, and on May 7 the remnants of the German government formally surrendered. The war in Europe ended the next day.

With the war over in Europe, the United States made its final push against Japan. Since 1942, J. Robert Oppenheimer and his team of scientists and engineers had labored feverishly to construct an atomic bomb. Few people knew about this top-secret project, and Congress appropriated $2 billion without knowing its true purpose. Under Colonel Leslie Groves of the Army Corps of Engineers, the military supervised the Manhattan Project, which operated at five sites around the country. The need for tight security hampered the project because the military did not want scientists in different locations to confer with one another.

Vice President Harry S. Truman did not learn about the details of the Manhattan Project until Roosevelt's death in April 1945, and in July he found out about the first atomic test while en route to a conference in Potsdam, Germany, with Stalin and Churchill. He ordered the State Department to issue a vaguely worded ultimatum to the Japanese demanding their immediate surrender or else face annihilation, though the message did not state specifically by what means. When Japan indicated that it would surrender if the United States allowed the country to retain its emperor, Hirohito, the Truman administration refused and demanded unconditional surrender. As a further blow to Japan, Stalin was preparing to send the Soviet military to attack Japanese troops in Manchuria on August 8, which would seriously weaken Japan's ability to hold out.

On August 6, before the Soviets' planned invasion, the *Enola Gay*, an American B-29 Super Fortress bomber, dropped an atomic bomb on Hiroshima. The weapon immediately killed 80,000 civilians, and tens of thousands later died slowly from radiation poisoning. Three days later, on August 9, Japan still had not surrendered, and the Army Air Corps dropped another atomic bomb on Nagasaki, killing more than 100,000 civilians. Following these bombings and the advance of the Soviet army into Manchuria, Japan announced on August 14 that it would surrender; the formal surrender ceremony took place on September 2, 1945.

At the time, very few Americans questioned the decision to drop atomic bombs on Japan. Truman believed, probably correctly, that had Roosevelt been alive, he would have authorized use of the bombs. Newly on the job, Truman hesitated to reverse a decision already reached by his predecessor. He reasoned that his action would save American lives because the U.S. military would not have to launch a costly invasion of Japan's home islands. He also felt justified in giving the order because he sought retaliation for the surprise attack on Pearl Harbor and for Japanese atrocities against American soldiers, especially in the Philippines. With an invasion of Japan planned for November and projections for the loss of American lives ranging from hundreds of thousands to 2 million, the servicemen slated to fight there, as well as their relatives, friends, and neighbors, welcomed Truman's decision.

 Online Document Project   **The Decision to Drop the Atomic Bomb**
bedfordstmartins.com/hewittlawsonvalue

Evidence of the Holocaust

The end of the war revealed the full extent and horror of Germany's calculated and methodical slaughter of certain religious, ethnic, and political groups. As Allied troops liberated Germany and Poland, they saw for themselves the brutality of the Nazi concentration camps that Hitler had set up to execute or work to death 6 million Jews and another 5 million "undesirables"—Slavs, Poles, Gypsies, homosexuals, the physically and mentally disabled, and Communists. At Buchenwald and Dachau in Germany and at Auschwitz in Poland, the Allies encountered the skeletal remains of inmates tossed into mass graves, dead from starvation, illness, and executions. Crematoria on the premises contained the ashes of inmates first poisoned and then incinerated. Troops also freed the "living dead," those still alive but seriously ill and undernourished. One U.S.

soldier reported his initial impression of the inmates: "They were . . . all skin and bones. They were sick, starving, and dying."

These horrific discoveries shocked the public, but evidence of what was happening had appeared early in the war. Journalists like Varian Fry had outlined the Nazi atrocities against the Jews several years before. "Letters, reports, tables all fit together. They add up to the most appalling picture of mass murder in all human history," Fry wrote in the *New Republic* magazine in 1942. He called on Roosevelt and Churchill to speak out forcefully, urged the pope to excommunicate Catholics who participated in Nazi crimes, and proposed sending food to occupied countries to counter the Nazi claim that they were killing Jews and Poles because there was not enough food to go around.

The Roosevelt administration did little in response, despite receiving evidence of the Nazi death camps beginning in 1942. It chose not to send planes to bomb the concentration camps or the railroad lines leading to them, deeming it too risky militarily and too dangerous for the inmates. In a less defensible decision, the Roosevelt administration refused to relax immigration laws to allow Jews and other persecuted minorities to take refuge in the United States, and only 21,000 managed to find asylum. The State Department, which could have modified these policies, was staffed with anti-Semitic officials, and though President Roosevelt expressed sympathy for the plight of Hitler's victims, he believed that winning the war as quickly as possible was the best way to help them.

REVIEW & RELATE

• How did the Allies win the war in Europe and in the Pacific?

• How did tensions among the Allies shape both their military strategy and their postwar plans?

The Home-Front Economy

The global conflict had profound effects on the American home front. World War II ended the Great Depression, restored economic prosperity, and increased labor union membership. At the same time, it smoothed the way for a closer relationship between government and private defense contractors, later referred to as the **military-industrial complex**. The war extended U.S. influence in the world and offered new economic opportunities at home. Despite fierce and bloody military battles throughout the world, Americans kept up morale by rallying around family and community.

Managing the Wartime Economy

To mobilize for war, President Roosevelt increased federal spending to unprecedented levels. Federal government employment during the war expanded to an all-time high of 3.8 million workers, four times as many as during the New Deal, setting the foundation for a large, permanent Washington bureaucracy. War orders fueled economic growth, productivity, and employment. In 1939 the federal budget stood at $9 billion; by the end of the war, it had grown to more than $100 billion. The gross national product increased from $91 billion to $166 billion during the war (Figure 23.1), union membership rose from around 9 million to nearly 15 million, and unemployment dropped from 8 million to less than 1 million. The armed forces helped reduce unemployment

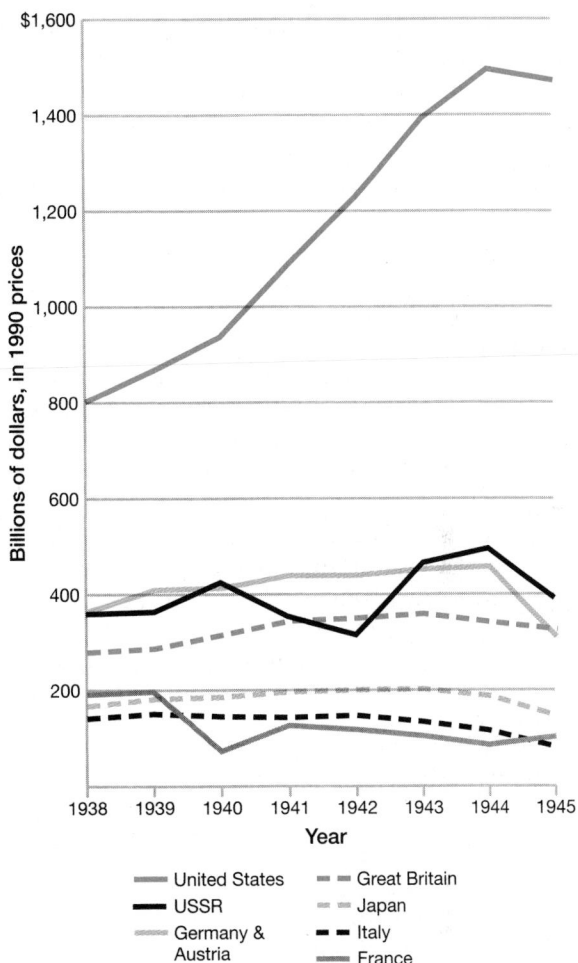

Source: Data from Mark Harrison, ed., *The Economics of World War II: Six Great Powers in International Comparison* (Cambridge: Cambridge University Press, 1998), 11.

FIGURE 23.1

Real Gross Domestic Product of the Great Powers, 1938–1945

Although World War II stalled or damaged the economic productivity of most of the warring nations, the U.S. economy grew dramatically between 1938 and 1944. With all the battles taking place outside the continental United States, the demand for food, weapons, ships, airplanes, gasoline, and other items by Great Britain and other Allied powers ensured increased employment, productivity, and profits for American workers.

significantly by enlisting 12 million men and women, 7 million of whom had been unemployed. Workers earned extra income for overtime work, but because of the rationing of consumer goods, Americans had to defer personal spending.

Prosperity was not limited to any one region. The industrial areas of the Northeast and Midwest once again boomed, as automobile factories converted to building tanks and other military vehicles, oil refineries processed gasoline to fuel them, steel and rubber companies manufactured parts to construct these vehicles and the weapons they carried, and textile and shoe plants furnished uniforms and boots for soldiers to wear. As farmers provided food for the nation and its allies, the index of farm production (which was 100 in 1939) jumped from 108 in 1940 to 126 in 1946. The economy diversified geographically. Fifteen million Americans—11 percent of the entire population—migrated between 1941 and 1945, and another 12 million left their homes and joined the armed forces. The war transformed the agricultural South into a budding industrial region. The federal government poured more than $4 billion in contracts into the South to operate military camps, contract with textile factories to clothe the military, and use its ports to build and launch warships. The availability of jobs in southern cities attracted sharecroppers and tenant farmers, black and white, away from the countryside and promoted urbanization while reducing the region's dependency on the plantation economy. In similar fashion, the West Coast prospered because it was the gateway to the Pacific war. The federal government established aircraft plants and shipbuilding yards in California, Oregon, and Washington, resulting in extraordinary population growth in Los Angeles, San Diego, San Francisco, Portland, and Seattle. Black and white migrants from Texas, Mississippi, and Louisiana headed west to take advantage of these opportunities.

Following the attack on Pearl Harbor, Congress passed the War Powers Act, which authorized the president to reorganize federal agencies any way he thought necessary to win the war. Roosevelt replaced the agencies he had created to combat the Great Depression with another outpouring of organizations to fight the Axis powers. In 1942 the president established the **War Production Board** to oversee the economy. The agency enticed business corporations to meet ever-increasing government orders by negotiating lucrative contracts that helped underwrite their costs, lower their taxes, and guarantee large profits. During the course of the war, corporate net profits nearly doubled. The government also suspended antitrust enforcement, giving private companies great leeway in running their enterprises. Much of the antibusiness hostility generated by the Great Depression evaporated as the Roosevelt administration recruited business executives to supervise government agencies for the token pay of $1 a year. Indeed, the close relationship between the federal government and business that emerged during the war produced the military-industrial complex—the government-business alliance that would have a vast influence on the future development of the economy.

In the first three years of the war, the United States increased military production by some 800 percent. American factories accounted for more than half of worldwide manufacturing output. On their best days, U.S. plants built a ship a day and an airplane every five minutes. By 1945 the United States had produced 86,000 tanks, nearly 300,000 airplanes, 15 million rifles and machine guns, and 6,500 ships.

Financing this enormous enterprise took considerable effort. The federal government spent more than $320 billion, ten times the cost of World War I. To pay for the war, the federal government sold $100 billion in bonds, only about half of what was needed. The rest came from increased income tax rates, which for the first time affected low- and middle-income workers who had paid little or no tax before. At the same time, the tax rate for the wealthy was boosted to 94 percent. In addition to paying higher taxes, American consumers shouldered the burden of inflation. Shortages in household and personal goods produced higher prices, which meant lower purchasing power. During the war, consumer prices jumped by 28 percent, despite the efforts of another federal agency, the Office of Price Administration, to stabilize them.

Building up the armed forces was the final ingredient in the mobilization for war. In 1940 about 250,000 soldiers were serving in the U.S. military, compared with Germany's 6 to 8 million troops. By 1945 American forces had grown to more than 12 million men and women through voluntary enlistments and a draft of men between the ages of eighteen and forty-five. The military reflected the diversity of the U.S. population. The sons of immigrants fought alongside the sons of older-stock Americans. Although the military tried to exclude homosexuals, they managed to join the fighting forces. Some 700,000 African Americans served in the armed forces, but civilian and military officials confined them to segregated units in the army, assigned them to menial work in the navy, and excluded them from the U.S. Marine Corps. The Army Air Corps created a segregated fighting unit trained at Tuskegee Institute in Alabama, and these Tuskegee airmen, like their counterparts among the ground forces, distinguished themselves in battle. Women could not fight in combat, but 140,000 joined the Women's Army Corps, and 100,000 joined the navy's WAVES (Women Accepted for Voluntary Emergency Service). In these and other service branches, women contributed mainly as nurses and performed transportation and clerical duties.

The concentration of power in the executive branch that accompanied the war effort, together with the president's expanded role in international diplomacy, fostered what historian Arthur Schlesinger Jr. termed "the imperial presidency." As commanders in chief, Roosevelt and his successors waged war and negotiated peace by controlling and manipulating the flow of information that reached Congress and the American public. Together with the burgeoning military-industrial complex, the imperial presidency redistributed power both within Washington and throughout the country at large.

Tuskegee Airmen　Twenty black pilots, among those known as the Tuskegee airmen, line up for a photograph, which they signed. The Army Air Corps created two segregated units of African American airmen, the 442nd Bombardment Group and the 99th Pursuit Squadron. The latter flew combat missions in Europe. The success of the Tuskegee airmen contributed to the postwar desegregation of the armed forces.　Courtesy National Park Service, Museum Management Program and Tuskegee Institute National Historic Site, TUAI 31, http://www.cr.nps.gov/museum/exhibits/tuskegee /lgimage/air28.htm

The government relied on corporate executives to manage wartime economic conversion, but without the sacrifice and dedication of American workers, their efforts would have failed. The demands for wartime production combined with the departure of millions of American workers to the military created a labor shortage that gave unions increased leverage. By 1945 the membership rolls of organized labor had grown from 9 million to nearly 14 million. In 1942 the Roosevelt administration established the **National War Labor Board**, which regulated wages, hours, and working conditions and authorized the government to take over plants that refused to abide by its decisions. Unions at first refrained from striking but later in the war organized strikes to protest the disparity between workers' wages and corporate profits. In 1943 Congress responded by passing the Smith-Connally Act, which prohibited walkouts in defense industries and set a thirty-day "cooling-off" period before unions could go out on strike.

New Opportunities for Women

World War II opened up new opportunities for women in the paid workforce. Between 1940 and the peak of wartime employment in 1944, the number of employed women rose more than 50 percent to 6 million. Given severe labor shortages caused by increased production and the exodus of male workers into the armed forces, for the first time in U.S. history married working women outnumbered single working women. At the start of the war, about half of women employees held poorly paid clerical, sales, and service jobs. Women in manufacturing labored mainly in low-wage textile and clothing factories. During the war, however, the overall number of women in manufacturing grew 141 percent; in industries producing directly for war purposes, the figure jumped by 463 percent. By contrast, the number of women in domestic service dropped by 20 percent. As women moved into defense-related jobs, their incomes also improved.

As impressive as these figures are, they do not tell the whole story. First, although married women entered the job market in record numbers, most of these workers were older and without young children. Women over the age of thirty-five accounted for 60 percent of those entering the workforce. The government did little to encourage young mothers to work, and few efforts were made to provide assistance for child care for those who did. One notable exception was the Kaiser Corporation shipyards, which operated child care facilities twenty-four hours a day. In contrast to this situation, in Great Britain child care programs were widely available. Second, openings for women in manufacturing jobs did not guarantee equality. Women received lower wages for work comparable to the work that men performed, and women did not have the same chances for advancement. Typical union benefits, such as seniority, hurt women, who were generally the most recent hires. In fact, some contracts stipulated that women's tenure in jobs previously held by men would last only for the duration of the war.

Gender stereotypes continued to dominate the workforce and society in general. Magazine covers with the image of "Rosie the Riveter," a woman with her sleeves rolled up and her biceps bulging, became a symbol for the recruitment of women, but reality proved different. The government, private employers, and mass media advertised for women workers by adapting traditional views of women to their new roles. One piece of literature suggested that an overhead crane operated "just like a gigantic clothes wringer" and that winding wire spools was very much like crocheting. Women who took war jobs were viewed not so much as war workers but as women temporarily occupying "men's jobs" during the emergency. As the war drew to a close, public relations campaigns shifted gears and encouraged the same women they had recently recruited to prepare to return home.

Everyday Life on the Home Front

Morale on the home front remained generally high during the war, as prosperity returned and American casualties proved relatively light compared with those of other Allied nations. As in World War I, the government set up an agency, the Office of War Information, to promote patriotism and urge Americans to contribute to the war effort any way they could. Schoolchildren collected scrap metal and rubber to donate to the production of military vehicles and weapons, and families planted "victory gardens" to grow vegetables for domestic consumption. Mothers and daughters helped staff USO (United Service Organizations) dances and recreational activities for soldiers headquartered in the United States. Americans also contributed to the war effort by adhering to restrictions on the consumption of consumer goods. Rationing cards restricted purchases of gasoline for cars and for food such as meat, butter, and sugar.

Hollywood kept the American public entertained, and movie attendance reached a record high of more than 100 million viewers. Films portrayed the heroism of soldiers on battlefields in Guadalcanal and Bataan. They celebrated the courage of Russian allies in propaganda epics such as *Mission to Moscow* (1943) and explored the depth of personal and political loyalties in classics such as *Casablanca* (1943). Hollywood stars signed up for the military, and some fought overseas; others, such as Ronald Reagan, made informational films and entertained the troops. A number of Hollywood celebrities, including the comedic actor Carole Lombard, helped raise funds in war bond drives. Others such as Betty Grable kept up servicemen's spirits by posing for photos that GIs pinned up in their lockers, tents, and equipment.

For many, life went on, but not quite in the same way. Around 15 million Americans moved during the war, with more than half of them relocating out of state. With husbands at war and wives at work, many children became "latchkey kids" who stayed home alone after school until their mothers or fathers returned from their jobs. With less parental supervision, juvenile delinquency rose, resulting in increased teenage arrests for robbery, vandalism, and loitering. Prostitution flourished around military installations, and with it came more cases of sexually transmitted diseases. High school graduation rates, especially for boys, fell sharply, but many of the dropouts found jobs to add to the family income and relieve the labor shortage. With the end of the Great Depression and with more young people working, marriage rates increased, and couples wed at a younger age. By 1945 the winding down of the war and the rapidly increasing number of marriages produced the first signs of a "baby boom." At the same time, the stresses of life during wartime, including long separations of husbands and wives, also resulted in higher divorce rates.

REVIEW & RELATE

- How did the war accelerate the trend that began during the New Deal toward increased government participation in the economy?
- How did the war affect life on the home front for the average American?

Fighting for Equality at Home

The war also had a significant impact on race relations. The fight to defeat Nazism, a doctrine based on racial prejudice and white supremacy, offered African Americans a chance to press for equal opportunity at home. By contrast, Japanese Americans experienced intensified discrimination and oppression as wartime anti-Japanese hysteria led to the internment of Japanese Americans, an erosion of their civil rights. They were freed toward the end of the war, but their incarceration left scars. Finally, Mexican Americans benefited from wartime jobs but continued to experience ethnic prejudice.

The Origins of the Civil Rights Movement

In 1941 A. Philip Randolph, the head of the Brotherhood of Sleeping Car Porters, applied his labor union experience to the struggle for civil rights. He announced that he planned to lead a 100,000-person march on Washington, D.C., in June 1941 to protest racial discrimination in government and war-related employment as well as segregation in the military. Although Randolph believed in an interracial alliance of working people, he insisted that participation in the march be open only to African Americans. He took this position because he wanted to show that blacks could lead their own movement and to prevent the presence of white Communists from diverting attention from the message. Inching the country toward war, but not yet engaged militarily, President Roosevelt wanted to avoid any embarrassment the proposed march would bring to the forces supporting democracy and freedom. With his wife Eleanor serving as go-between, Roosevelt agreed to meet with Randolph and worked out a compromise. Randolph called off the march, and in return, on June 25, 1941, the president issued Executive Order 8802, creating the **Fair Employment Practice Committee (FEPC)**. Roosevelt refused to order the desegregation of the military, but he set up a committee to investigate inequality in the armed forces. Although the FEPC helped African Americans gain a greater share of jobs in key industries than they had before, the effect was limited because the agency did not have enforcement power.

The march on Washington movement was emblematic of rising civil rights activity. Black leaders proclaimed their own "two-front war" with the symbol of the "Double V" to represent victory against racist enemies both abroad and at home. The National Association for the Advancement of Colored People continued its policy of fighting racial discrimination in the courts. In 1944 the organization won a significant victory in a case from Texas, *Smith v. Allwright*, which outlawed all-white Democratic primary elections in the traditionally one-party South. As a result of the decision, the percentage of African Americans registered to vote in the South doubled between 1944 and 1948. In 1942 early civil rights activists also founded the interracial Congress of Racial Equality (CORE) in Chicago. CORE protested directly against racial inequality in public accommodations. Its members, including the black pacifists Bayard Rustin and James Farmer, organized "sit-ins" at restaurants and bowling alleys that refused to serve African Americans. Students at Howard University in Washington, D.C., used the same tactics, with some success, to protest racial exclusion from restaurants and cafeterias in the nation's capital. Although these demonstrations did not get the national attention that postwar protests would, they constituted the prelude to the civil rights movement.

Population shifts on the home front during World War II exacerbated racial tensions, resulting in violence. As jobs opened up throughout the country at military installations and defense plants, hundreds of thousands of African Americans moved from the rural South to the urban South, the North, and the West. Cities could not handle this rapid influx of people and failed to provide sufficient housing to accommodate those who migrated in search of employment. Competition between white and black workers for scarce housing spilled over into tensions in crowded transportation and recreational facilities. In 1943 the stress caused by close wartime contact between the races exploded in more than 240 riots. The most serious one occurred in Detroit, where federal troops had to restore order after whites and blacks fought with each other following a dispute at a popular amusement park that killed thirty-four people.

Struggles for Mexican Americans

Immigration from Mexico increased significantly during the war. To address labor shortages in the Southwest and on the Pacific coast, in 1942 the United States negotiated an agreement with Mexico for contract laborers (*braceros*) to enter the country for a limited time to work as farm laborers and in factories. From the Southwest, Mexican migrants found their way to industrial cities of the Midwest and California. Most U.S. residents of Mexican ancestry were, however, American citizens. Like other Americans, they settled into jobs to help fight the war, while more than 300,000 Mexican Americans served in the armed forces.

The war heightened Mexican Americans' consciousness of their civil rights. As one Mexican American World War II veteran recalled: "We were Americans, not 'spics' or 'greasers.' Because when you fight for your country in a World War, against an alien philosophy, fascism, you are an American and proud to be in America." In southern California, Ignacio Lutero Lopez, the publisher of the newspaper *El Espectador* (The Spectator), campaigned against segregation in movie theaters, swimming pools, and other public accommodations. He organized boycotts against businesses that discriminated against or excluded Mexican Americans. Wartime organizing led to the creation of the Unity Leagues, a coalition of Mexican American business owners, college students, civic leaders, and GIs that pressed for racial equality. In Texas, Mexican Americans joined the League of United Latin American Citizens (LULAC), a largely middle-class group that challenged racial discrimination and segregation in public accommodations. Members of the organization emphasized the use of negotiations to redress their grievances, but when they ran into opposition, they resorted to economic boycotts and litigation. The war encouraged LULAC to expand its operations in Arizona and throughout the Southwest.

Mexican American citizens encountered hostility from recently transplanted whites and longtime residents. Tensions were greatest in Los Angeles. A small group of Mexican American teenagers joined gangs and identified themselves by wearing zoot suits—colorful, long, loose-fitting jackets with padded shoulders and baggy pants tapered at the bottom. Not all zoot-suiters were gang members, but many outside their communities failed to make this distinction. Dressed in wide-brimmed hats worn atop slicked-back hair, with pocket watches and chains dangling from their trousers, these young men offended white sensibilities of fashion and proper decorum. Sailors stationed at naval bases in southern California found their dress and swagger provocative. On the night of June 4, 1943, squads of seamen stationed in Long Beach invaded Mexican American

Zoot Suit Riots, 1943 This photograph shows two Latino youths after they were attacked by a group of sailors who slashed their clothing during the zoot suit riots in Los Angeles in June 1943. They are wearing the popular zoot suit style of wide shirt collars and baggy pants tapered at the bottom. Hulton Archive/ Getty Images

neighborhoods in East Los Angeles, indiscriminately attacked both zoot-suiters and those not dressed in this garb on the streets, and beat them up. The police sided with the sailors and arrested Mexican American youths who tried to fight back. After four days, the **zoot suit riots** ended as civilian and military authorities restored order. In response, the Los Angeles city council banned the wearing of zoot suits in public and made it a criminal offense.

The Ordeal of Japanese Americans

World War II marked a significant crossroads for the protection of civil liberties, the freedoms people have from government interference as enshrined in the Bill of Rights. In general, the federal government did not repress civil liberties as harshly as it had during World War I, primarily because opposition to World War II was not nearly as great. The chief potential for radical dissent came from the Communist Party, but after the Germans attacked the Soviet Union in June 1941, Communists and their sympathizers rallied behind the war effort and did whatever they could to stifle any protest that threatened the goal of defeating Germany. On the other side of the political spectrum, after the attack on Pearl Harbor conservative isolationists in the America First Movement quickly threw their support behind the war.

Of the three ethnic groups associated with the Axis enemy—Japanese, Germans, and Italians—Japanese Americans received by far the worst treatment from the civilian population and state and federal officials. Germans had experienced animosity and repression on the home front during World War I (see chapter 20), but like Italian immigrants they had generally assimilated into the wider population. When baseball was the national pastime during the 1930s and 1940s, Lou Gehrig, of German ancestry, and his Italian American teammate Joe DiMaggio of the New York Yankees reigned as popular heroes. At the same time, Fiorello La Guardia, an Italian American, had a large following as mayor of New York City. In addition, German Americans and Italian Americans had spread out across the country, while Japanese Americans remained concentrated in distinct geographical pockets along the West Coast. Although German Americans and Italian Americans experienced prejudice, they had come to be considered racially white, unlike Japanese Americans. Nevertheless, the government arrested about 1,500 Italians considered "enemy aliens" and placed around 250 of them in internment camps. It also arrested more than 11,000 Germans, some of them American citizens who were considered a danger.

 Online Document Project   **Anti-Japanese Prejudice during World War II**
bedfordstmartins.com/hewittlawsonvalue

The **internment**, or forced relocation and detainment, of Italians and Germans in the United States paled in comparison with that of the Japanese. Nearly all people of Japanese descent lived along the West Coast. Government officials relocated all of those living there—citizens and noncitizens alike—to camps in Arizona, Arkansas, California, Colorado, Idaho, Texas, Utah, and Wyoming. In Hawaii, the site of the Japanese attack on Pearl Harbor, the Japanese population, nearly one-third of the territory's population, was too large to transfer and instead lived under martial law. Only a thousand or so were interned. The few thousand Japanese Americans living elsewhere in the continental United States remained in their homes.

It did not matter that Fred Korematsu had been born in the United States, had a white girlfriend of Italian heritage, and counted whites among his best friends. His parents had come from Japan, and for much of the American public, his racial heritage meant that he was not a true American. As one American general put it early in the war, "A Jap's a Jap. It makes no difference whether he is an American citizen or not." Along with more than 100,000 people of Japanese descent, two-thirds of whom were American citizens, Korematsu spent most of the war in an internment camp. Unlike Nazi concentration camps, these facilities did not work inmates to death or execute them. Yet Japanese Americans lost their freedom and protection under the Bill of Rights and the Fourteenth Amendment. Distinguished American leaders—including President Roosevelt, California attorney general Earl Warren, and Supreme Court justice Hugo Black—convinced themselves that depriving Japanese Americans of their civil liberties did not result from racism. Despite scant evidence that Japanese Americans were disloyal or harbored spies or saboteurs, U.S. officials chose to believe that as a group they threatened national security. The government established a system that questioned German Americans and Italian Americans on an individual basis if their loyalty came under suspicion. By contrast, U.S. officials identified all Japanese Americans and Japanese resident aliens with the nation that had attacked Pearl Harbor, and incarcerated them. In this respect, the United States was not unique. Following the United States' lead, Canada interned its Japanese population, more than 75 percent of whom held Canadian citizenship.

For their part, Japanese Americans made the best they could out of this situation. They had been forced to dispose of their homes and sell their possessions and businesses quickly, either selling or renting them at very low prices or simply abandoning them.

They left their neighborhoods with only the possessions they could carry. They lived in wooden barracks divided into one-room apartments and shared communal toilets, showers, laundry, and dining facilities. The camps provided schools, recreational activities, and opportunities for religious worship, except for Shintoism, the official religion of Japan. Some internees attempted to farm, but the arid land on which the camps were located made this nearly impossible. Inmates who worked at jobs within the camp earned monthly wages of $12 to $19, far less than they would have received outside the camps.

Japanese Americans responded to their internment in a variety of ways. Many formed community groups, and some expressed their reactions to the emotional upheaval by writing of their experiences or displaying their feelings through artwork. Contradicting beliefs that their ancestry made them disloyal or not real Americans, some 18,000 men joined the army, and many fought gallantly in some of the war's fiercest battles on the European front with the 442nd Regiment, one of the most heavily decorated units in the military. Nisei soldiers were among the first, along with African American troops, to liberate Jews from German concentration camps. Others, like Korematsu, remained in the camps and challenged the legality of President Roosevelt's executive order, which had allowed military officials to exclude Japanese Americans from certain areas and evacuate them from their homes. Gordon Hirabayashi, a student at the University of Washington, had filed suit against the establishment of a curfew specifically targeted at Japanese Americans. In 1942 the Supreme Court rejected his appeal, as it did Korematsu's two years later. Finally, in December 1944, shortly after he won election to his fourth term as president, Roosevelt rescinded Executive Order 9066.

In contrast to the treatment of Japanese Americans, the status of Chinese Americans improved markedly during the war. With China under Japanese occupation, Congress repealed the Chinese Exclusion Act in 1943, making the Chinese the first Asians who could become naturalized citizens. Chinese American men also fought in integrated military units like their Filipino peers. For the first time, the war opened up jobs to Chinese American men and women outside their ethnic economy.

Despite the violation of the civil liberties of Japanese American citizens, the majority did not become embittered against the United States. Rather, most of the internees returned to their communities after the war and resumed their lives, still intent on pursuing the American dream from which they had been so harshly excluded; however, some 8,000 Japanese Americans renounced their U.S. citizenship and repatriated to Japan in 1945. After briefly moving to Detroit, Korematsu returned to San Leandro, California, with his wife and two children. Still, Korematsu had trouble finding regular employment because he had a criminal record for violating the exclusion order. Unlike most inmates of German concentration camps, Korematsu survived, but in the name of national security the government had established the precedent of incarcerating groups deemed "suspect." It took four decades for the U.S. government to admit its mistake and apologize, and in 1988 Congress awarded reparations of $20,000 to each of the 60,000 living internees. In 1998 President Bill Clinton awarded Korematsu the Presidential Medal of Freedom—the highest decoration a civilian can receive.

REVIEW & RELATE

• What new challenges and opportunities did the war present to minority groups?

• Why were Japanese Americans singled out as a particular threat to national security?

Conclusion: The Impact of World War II

Like Woodrow Wilson before World War I, Franklin Roosevelt initially charted a course of neutrality before the United States entered World War II. Yet Roosevelt believed that the rise of European dictatorships and their expansionist pursuits throughout the world threatened American national security. He saw signs of trouble early, but responding to antiwar sentiment from lawmakers and the American public, he maneuvered carefully to keep the nation from going to war. Like President Lincoln preceding the Confederate bombardment of Fort Sumter, Roosevelt waited for a blatant enemy attack before declaring war. The Japanese attack on Pearl Harbor in 1941 provided that justification.

On the domestic front, World War II accomplished what Franklin Roosevelt's New Deal could not. Prosperity and nearly full employment returned only after the nation's factories began supplying the Allies and the United States joined in the fight against the Axis powers. Mobilization for war also completed what the New Deal had begun: the tremendous growth and centralization of power in the federal government. Washington, D.C., became the chief source of authority to which Americans looked for solutions to problems concerning economic security and financial development. Most people looked to the future with optimism following sixteen years of depression and war.

The federal government showed that it would use its authority to expand equal rights for African Americans. The war swung national power against racial discrimination, and various civil rights victories during the war served as precursors to the civil rights movement of subsequent decades. The war also heightened Mexican Americans' consciousness of oppression and led them to organize for civil rights. In neither case, however, did the war erase white prejudice.

At the same time, the federal government did not hesitate to trample on the civil liberties of Japanese Americans. The president succumbed to wartime antagonism against Japanese immigrants and their children. However, the same did not happen to the white descendants of the other Axis nations. Yet like white and black Americans, the Nisei displayed their patriotism by distinguishing themselves as soldiers on the battlefields of Europe.

The war brought women into the workforce as never before, providing a measure of independence and distancing them from their traditional roles as wives and mothers. Nevertheless, the government and private employers made it clear that they expected most female workers to give up their jobs to returning servicemen and to become homemakers once the war ended.

Finally, the war thrust the United States onto the world stage as one of the world's two major superpowers alongside the Soviet Union. This position posed new challenges. In sole possession of the atomic bomb, the most powerful weapon on the planet, and fortified by a robust economy, the United States filled the international power vacuum created by the weakening and eventual collapse of the European colonial empires. The fragile alliance that had held together the United States and the Soviet Union shattered soon after the end of World War II. The Atomic Age, which J. Robert Oppenheimer helped usher in with a powerful weapon of mass destruction, and the government oppression that Korematsu endured in the name of national security did not disappear. Rather, they expanded in new directions and shaped the lives of all Americans for decades to come.

Chapter Review

MAKE IT STICK

 LearningCurve **bedfordstmartins.com/hewittlawsonvalue**
After reading the chapter, use LearningCurve to retain what you've read.

IDENTIFY KEY TERMS

Identify and explain the significance of each term below.

Neutrality Acts (p. 594)
America First Committee (p. 596)
Lend-Lease Act (p. 596)
Atlantic Charter (p. 597)
second front (p. 598)
D Day (p. 600)
Yalta Agreement (p. 602)
Manhattan Project (p. 602)

Enola Gay (p. 603)
military-industrial complex (p. 604)
War Production Board (p. 606)
National War Labor Board (p. 608)
Fair Employment Practice Committee
(FEPC) (p. 610)
zoot suit riots (p. 612)
internment (p. 613)

REVIEW & RELATE

Answer the focus questions from each section of the chapter.

1. How did American public opinion shape Roosevelt's foreign policy in the years preceding U.S. entry into World War II?

2. What events in Europe and the Pacific ultimately brought the United States into World War II?

3. How did the Allies win the war in Europe and in the Pacific?

4. How did tensions among the Allies shape both their military strategy and their postwar plans?

5. How did the war accelerate the trend that began during the New Deal toward increased government participation in the economy?

6. How did the war affect life on the home front for the average American?

7. What new challenges and opportunities did the war present to minority groups?

8. Why were Japanese Americans singled out as a particular threat to national security?

ONLINE DOCUMENT PROJECTS

◆ **The Decision to Drop the Atomic Bomb**
◆ **Anti-Japanese Prejudice during World War II**

After reading the primary sources in these document sets, answer the **Interpret the Evidence** questions to help you analyze each of the documents, and then answer the **Put It in Context** question(s) to help you relate the documents to the topics and themes you read about in the chapter.

bedfordstmartins.com/hewittlawsonvalue

TIMELINE OF EVENTS

1933	• United States extends diplomatic recognition to the Soviet Union
	• Adolf Hitler becomes chancellor of Germany
1935–1937	• Neutrality Acts passed
1938	• Germany annexes the Sudetenland
1939	• Germany occupies Czechoslovakia
	• Germany and Soviet Union invade Poland; World War II begins
1940	• Battle of Britain begins
	• Japan, Germany, and Italy sign Tripartite Pact
1941	• Lend-Lease Act passed
	• Fair Employment Practice Committee (FEPC) created
	• Roosevelt and Churchill sign Atlantic Charter
December 7, 1941	• Japan attacks U.S. naval base at Pearl Harbor
December 11, 1941	• Germany and Italy declare war on the United States

1942	• Congress of Racial Equality (CORE) established
	• War Production Board and National War Labor Board formed
	• Roosevelt approves Manhattan Project
	• Roosevelt issues order that leads to internment of Japanese Americans
1943	• Zoot suit riots
	• Race riots in Detroit and more than 240 cities
June 6, 1944	• D Day invasion begins
1945	• Final U.S. offensive against Japan, with victories at Iwo Jima and Okinawa
February 1945	• Yalta Conference
May 1945	• Germany surrenders
July 1945	• First successful atomic bomb test
August 1945	• U.S. drops atomic bombs on Hiroshima and Nagasaki
September 1945	• Japan formally surrenders

24

☑ LearningCurve
bedfordstmartins.com/hewittlawsonvalue
After reading the chapter, use LearningCurve
to retain what you've read.

The Opening of the Cold War

1945–1954

AMERICAN HISTORIES

Did one American's fears about Soviet intentions spark a decades-long conflict that threatened the world with nuclear destruction? Certainly no one person can be held responsible for the Cold War between the United States and the Soviet Union, but George Frost Kennan played a critical role in shaping the confrontation between these two superpowers. Kennan's views were based on extensive experience with the Soviets. A graduate of Princeton University, where he majored in history, and a career diplomat, Kennan served two tours of duty at the U.S. Embassy in Moscow. During the first, from 1933 to 1937, he witnessed the brutality of the Stalin regime, as countless "enemies of the state" were arrested, exiled, or executed in Stalin's purges. His experiences convinced him that there was little basis for a positive relationship between the United States and the Soviet Union.

Kennan's second tour of duty in Moscow, from 1944 to 1946, came at a critical juncture in U.S.-Soviet relations. As the war came to a close, tensions over the nature of the postwar world escalated, and by 1946 the wartime alliance had collapsed. Against this backdrop, Kennan sent an 8,000-word telegram to Secretary of State James F. Byrnes outlining a proposal for future U.S. strategy. Convinced that Stalin was committed to expanding communism throughout the world, Kennan advised President Harry S. Truman to adopt a policy of *containment*. In Kennan's view, all Soviet efforts at expansion should be met with firm resistance. At the same time, the United States should take an active role in rebuilding the economies of war-torn Western European countries, thereby reducing the appeal of communism to their populations. Kennan's concept of containment would become the basis for President Truman's foreign policy and would establish the initial strategic parameters of the Cold War.

Kennan, however, was not a rigid cold warrior. He soon insisted that his containment strategy had been misunderstood. As the Cold War intensified and expanded, Kennan argued that containment would work best through political and economic rather than military means. Increasingly, his views fell out of favor at the State Department, and Kennan left in 1950 in a disagreement with the Truman administration's growing militarization of the conflict with the Soviet Union.

Julius and Ethel Rosenberg were casualties of the Cold War that Kennan helped shape. Accused of passing military secrets to the Soviet Union, they were tried for espionage in an atmosphere of growing anti-Communist fervor. Ethel Greenglass and her future husband, Julius Rosenberg, both grew up in families that suffered economically during the Great Depression. During the 1930s, Ethel worked as a secretary in New York City and took part in labor union organizing. Like other young idealists of the period, she became disillusioned with capitalism and joined the Young Communist League. Julius attended the City College of New York, where he, too, joined the Young Communist League. Three years after they met in 1936, Julius and Ethel married and started a family.

During World War II, Julius worked for the Army Signal Corps as an engineer, but his political past came back to haunt him. In 1945 he lost his job after a security investigation revealed his Communist Party membership. Five years later, the federal government charged that during World War II the Rosenbergs had provided classified information about the construction of the atomic bomb to the Soviet Union, charges that the Rosenbergs denied.

A jury found them guilty on April 5, 1951, and the presiding judge sentenced them to death under the 1917 Espionage Act, which prohibited the transmission of information "relating to the national defense" to a foreign government. Despite an international campaign for clemency and after unsuccessful appeals to the Supreme Court, on June 19, 1953, the Rosenbergs became the only two American civilians executed for espionage during the Cold War. Though recent evidence has confirmed Julius Rosenberg's role as a spy, the case against Ethel remains inconclusive. Without the heightened Cold War climate that then existed in the country, it is likely that neither would have gone to the electric chair.

U.S. soldier in Korea, 1951. Time & Life Pictures/Getty Images

THE AMERICAN HISTORIES of both George Kennan and Julius and Ethel Rosenberg revolved around their views of communism and the Soviet Union. Kennan designed an approach to containing Soviet aggression based on his close dealings with Stalin—one that he believed would check Soviet expansion without precipitating another world war. The Rosenbergs believed in communism's promise of social and economic equality and saw the Soviet Union as a defense against Nazi aggression—views that led Julius into spying for the Soviets, a U.S. ally, during World War II. Kennan and the Rosenbergs were famous in their time and played prominent roles in the Cold War, but in at least one respect they were unexceptional. As the Cold War deepened over the course of the 1950s, the lives of all Americans would be profoundly shaped by the epic military and ideological battle between the superpowers.

The Origins of the Cold War, 1945–1947

The wartime partnership between the United States and the Soviet Union (USSR) was an alliance of necessity. Putting aside ideological differences and a history of mutual distrust, the two nations joined forces to combat Nazi aggression. As long as the Nazi threat existed, the alliance held, but as the war ended and attention turned to the postwar world, the allies became adversaries. The two nations did not engage directly in war, but they entered into a struggle for political, economic, and military superiority known as the Cold War. In general, most Cold War maneuvers did not take place on battlefields; rather they consisted of building military and economic alliances to establish spheres of influence, stopping short of "hot wars" (actual fighting) between the United States and the Soviet Union.

Mutual Misunderstandings

Guided by competing ideological and economic values, the United States and the Soviet Union pursued their national interests on the world stage in a manner that led to dangerous confrontations. After World War II, the United States came to believe that the Soviet Union desired world revolution to spread communism, a doctrine hostile to free market individualism. At the same time, the Soviet Union viewed the United States as seeking to make the world safe for capitalism, thereby reducing Soviet chances to obtain economic resources and rebuild its war-shattered economy. Thus each nation tended to see the other's actions in the most negative light possible and to see global developments as a zero-sum game, one in which every victory for one side was necessarily a defeat for the other.

Problems had already surfaced during World War II, but President Franklin D. Roosevelt and Joseph Stalin were able to keep tensions in check (see chapter 23). The president went a long way toward defusing Stalin's concerns at the Yalta Conference in 1945. Stalin viewed the Eastern European countries that the Soviets had liberated from the Germans, especially Poland, as a buffer to protect his nation from future attacks by Germany. He refused to allow hostile, anti-Communist governments to rule these countries and wanted to maintain a regional sphere of influence favorable to Soviet foreign policy objectives. Roosevelt understood Stalin's reasoning, and he recognized political realities: The Soviet military already occupied Eastern Europe, a state of affairs that increased Stalin's bargaining position. Still, while accepting Stalin's basic position, the president insisted that the Yalta Agreement include a guarantee of free elections in Eastern Europe. Roosevelt believed in spreading democracy and freedom, but he was also a realist, and the Yalta Agreement reflected his effort to strike a delicate balance.

By contrast, his successor, Harry S. Truman, took a much less nuanced approach to U.S.-Soviet relations. He believed that the Soviets threatened "a barbarian invasion of Europe," and he intended to deter it. Stalin's ruthless purges within the Soviet Union in the 1930s and 1940s, which led to the deaths of millions of his opponents, convinced Truman that the Soviet dictator was paranoid and extremely dangerous. President Truman did not expect the United States to achieve "100 percent of what we propose" in negotiations with the Russians, but "we should be able to get eighty-five percent." In his first meeting with Soviet foreign minister Vyacheslav Molotov in April 1945, Truman rebuked the Russians for failing to support free elections in Poland. Molotov, recoiling from the sharp tone of Truman's remarks, replied: "I have never been talked to like that in my life."

Despite this rough start, Truman did not immediately abandon the idea of cooperation with the Soviet Union. At the Potsdam Conference in Germany in July 1945, Truman and Stalin agreed on several issues (see chapter 23). The two leaders reaffirmed the concept of free elections in Eastern Europe; Soviet troop withdrawal from the oil fields of northern Iran, which bordered the USSR; and the partition of Germany into four Allied occupation zones. (Berlin was also divided into four occupation zones.) After Stalin assured Truman that he did not support the Communist revolution in China against the Western-backed government of Jiang Jieshi (Chiang Kai-shek), Truman wrote, "I can deal with Stalin. He is honest—but smart as hell."

Within six months of the war's end, the president had changed his mind, and relations between the two countries quickly soured. The United States was the only nation in the world with the atomic bomb, which it had used on Japan, and boasted the only economy reinvigorated by the war. As a result, the Truman administration believed that it held the upper hand against the Soviets and could gain most of what it wanted. With this in mind, the State Department offered the Soviets a $6 billion loan, which they needed to help rebuild their war-ravaged economy. But when the Soviets undermined free elections in Poland in 1946 and established a compliant government, the United States withdrew the offer. Soviet troops also remained in northern Iran, closing off the oil fields to potential capitalist enterprises. The failure to reach agreement over international control of atomic energy proved the last straw. Before reaching an accord, the United States wanted to make sure it would keep its atomic weapons, while the Soviets first wanted the United States to destroy its nuclear arsenal. Clearly, the former World

War II allies did not trust each other, and each suspected the other of trying to gain an atomic advantage.

Truman had significantly underestimated the strength of the Soviet position. The Soviets were well on their way toward building their own atomic weapons, negating the Americans' nuclear advantage. In the meantime, until the Russians obtained the bomb, they could rely on the power of their huge army—the largest in the world—poised in Eastern Europe. The Soviets could also ignore the enticement of U.S. economic aid by taking resources from East Germany and mobilizing the Russian people to rebuild their country's industry and military. Indeed, on February 9, 1946, Stalin delivered a tough speech to rally Russians to make sacrifices to enhance national security. By asserting that communism was "a better form of organization than any non-Soviet social system," he implied, according to George Kennan, that capitalist nations could not coexist with communism and that future wars were unavoidable unless communism triumphed over capitalism.

Whether Stalin meant this speech as an unofficial declaration of a third world war was not clear, but U.S. leaders interpreted it this way. A few days after Stalin spoke, Kennan sent his 8,000-word telegram from the U.S. Embassy in Moscow to Washington, blaming the Soviets for stirring up international tensions and confirming that Stalin could not be trusted. "Driven by a neurotic view of world affairs," Kennan maintained, "[the Soviet Union] would respond only to force." The following month, on March 15, former British prime minister Winston Churchill gave a speech in Truman's home state of Missouri, which the president read in advance and presumably approved. Declaring that "an iron curtain has descended across the Continent" of Europe, Churchill observed that "there is nothing [the Russians] admire so much as strength, and there is nothing for which they have less respect than for military weakness." This comment reaffirmed Truman's sentiments expressed the previous year: "Unless Russia is faced with an iron fist and strong language another war is in the making." The message was clear: Unyielding resistance to the Soviet Union was the only way to avoid another world war.

Not all Americans agreed with this view. Although some 60 percent of the public believed that cooperation with the Soviets was unlikely, a minority argued that a more amicable relationship was possible. Led by Roosevelt's former vice president Henry Wallace, who served as Truman's secretary of commerce, critics voiced concern about taking a "hard line" against the Soviet Union. Stalin was pursuing a policy of expansion, they agreed, but for limited reasons. Wallace claimed that the Soviets merely wanted to protect their borders by surrounding themselves with friendly countries, just as the United States had done by establishing spheres of influence in the Caribbean. Except for Poland and Romania, Stalin initially accepted an array of governments in Eastern Europe, allowing free elections in Czechoslovakia, Hungary, and, to a lesser extent, Bulgaria. Only as Cold War tensions escalated did the Soviets tighten control over all of Eastern Europe, snuffing out any semblance of democracy. Critics such as Wallace considered this outcome the result of a self-fulfilling prophecy; by misinterpreting Soviet motives, the Truman administration pushed Stalin to counter the American hard line with a hard line of his own.

The Truman Doctrine

By 1947 U.S.-Soviet relations had reached a new low. International arms control had proven futile, the United States had gone to the United Nations to pressure the Soviets to withdraw from Iran, and the rhetoric from both sides had become warlike. From the

American vantage point, Soviet actions to expand communism in Eastern Europe appeared to threaten democracies in Western Europe. By contrast, the Soviets viewed the United States as seeking to extend economic control over nations close to their borders and to weaken communism in the Soviet Union.

Events in Greece allowed Truman to take the offensive and apply Kennan's policy of containment. The Mediterranean Sea linked the United Kingdom (formerly Great Britain) to the Middle East, the Suez Canal, and its Asian colonies, and the British therefore considered it vitally important to keep Greece within its sphere of influence. During the war, Churchill and Stalin had agreed that after the war the United Kingdom (UK) would resume its oversight of Greece, while the Soviets would predominate in Eastern Europe. All did not go according to plan. In 1946 a civil war broke out in Greece between the right-wing monarchy, which the UK supported, and a coalition of insurgents consisting of members of the wartime anti-Nazi resistance, Communists, and non-Communist opponents of the repressive government. Under normal conditions, the British would have provided the necessary resources to prop up the Greek government. The United Kingdom, however, was exhausted by the war and in desperate financial shape, so it had no choice but to turn to the United States for help.

The Truman administration agreed to help the UK. Although the Greeks were fighting a civil war, the president and his advisers viewed the situation differently. They believed that the presence of Communists among the Greek rebels meant that Moscow was behind the insurgency. In fact, Stalin was not aiding the revolutionaries; the assistance came from the Communist leader of Yugoslavia, Josip Broz Tito, who acted independently of the Soviets and would soon break with them. Following Kennan's lead in advocating containment, Truman incorrectly believed that all Communists around the world were ultimately controlled by the Kremlin.

While Truman was convinced that the United States had to intervene in Greece to contain the spread of communism, he still had to convince the Republican-controlled Congress and the American people to go along. In 1946 the Republicans had run on a platform of lowering taxes and cutting government spending—positions that enjoyed considerable public support and were incompatible with appropriating huge sums to support the Greek government. In order to overcome potential opposition to its plans, the Truman administration exaggerated the danger of Communist control of Greece. Truman sent Undersecretary of State Dean Acheson to testify before a congressional committee that "like apples in a barrel infected by one rotten one, the corruption of Greece would infect Iran and all to the east." The administration's presentation of the issues to the American public was even more dramatic. On March 12, 1947, Truman gave a speech to a joint session of Congress that was broadcast over national radio to millions of listeners. He interpreted the civil war in Greece as a titanic struggle between freedom and totalitarianism that threatened the free world. "I believe," the president declared, "that it must be the policy of the United States to support free peoples who are resisting attempted subjugation by armed minorities or by outside pressures." Truman's rhetoric stretched the truth on many counts—the armed minorities to which the president referred had fought the Nazis; the Soviets did not supply the insurgents; the right-wing monarchy, propped up by the military, was hardly democratic; and the United Kingdom had long exerted "outside pressure." Truman achieved his goal of frightening both lawmakers and the public, and Congress appropriated $400 million in military aid to fortify the existing governments of Greece and neighboring Turkey.

The **Truman Doctrine**, which pledged to contain the expansion of communism, was the cornerstone of American foreign policy throughout the Cold War. The United States committed itself to shoring up governments, whether democratic or dictatorial, as long as they were avowedly anti-Communist. Americans believed that the rest of the world's nations wanted to be like the United States and therefore would not willingly accept communism, which they thought could be imposed only from the outside by the Soviet Union and never reasonably chosen from within.

Although Truman misread Soviet intentions with respect to Greece, Stalin's regime had given him cause for worry. Soviet actions that imposed communism in Poland, along with the USSR's refusal to withdraw troops from the Baltic states of Latvia, Lithuania, and Estonia, reinforced the president's concerns about Soviet expansionism and convinced many in the U.S. government that Stalin had no intention of abiding by his wartime agreements. Difficulties in negotiating with the Soviets about international control of atomic energy further worried American foreign-policy makers about Russian designs for obtaining the atomic bomb.

The Marshall Plan and Economic Containment

George Kennan's version of containment called for economic and political aid to check Communist expansion. In this context, to forestall Communist inroads and offer humanitarian assistance to Europeans facing homelessness and starvation, the Truman administration offered economic assistance to the war-torn continent. Secretary of State George Marshall recognized that if the United States did not offer help, European nations would face "economic, social, and political deterioration of a very grave character," which in turn might plunge the world and the United States, which depended heavily on European markets, into another Great Depression. In a June 1947 speech that drew heavily on Kennan's ideas, Marshall sketched out a plan to provide financial assistance to Europe. Although he invited any country, including the Soviet Union, that experienced "hunger, poverty, desperation, and chaos" to apply for aid, Marshall did not expect Stalin to ask for assistance. To do so would require the Soviets to supply information to the United States concerning the internal operations of their economy and to admit to the failure of communism.

Following up Marshall's speech, Truman asked Congress in December 1947 to authorize $17 billion for European recovery. With conservative-minded Republicans still in control of Congress, the president's spending request faced steep opposition. The Soviet Union inadvertently came to Truman's political rescue. Stalin interpreted the proposed **Marshall Plan** of economic assistance as a hostile attempt by the United States to gain influence in Eastern Europe. To forestall this possibility, in late February 1948 the Soviets extinguished the remaining democracy in Eastern Europe by engineering a Communist coup in Czechoslovakia. Congressional lawmakers viewed this action as further proof of Soviet aggression. In April 1948, they approved the Marshall Plan, providing $13 billion in economic assistance to sixteen European countries over the next five years.

REVIEW & RELATE

- Why did American policymakers believe that containing Communist expansion should be the foundation of American foreign policy?
- What role did mutual misunderstandings and mistrust play in the emergence of the Cold War?

The Cold War Hardens, 1948–1952

After 1947, the Cold War intensified. Both sides increased military spending and took measures to enhance their military presence around the world. Fueled by growing distrust, the Soviet Union and the United States engaged in inflammatory rhetoric that added to the danger that the conflict posed to world peace. In 1950 the United States, in cooperation with the United Nations, sent troops to South Korea to turn back an invasion from the Communist North. During the late 1940s and early 1950s, the president gained expanded power to initiate wars and increase spending for military and national security agencies.

Military Containment

The New Deal and World War II had increased the power of the president and his ability to manage economic and military crises. The Cold War further strengthened the presidency and shifted the balance of governmental power to the executive branch, creating what has been called the imperial presidency.

As the Cold War heated up, Congress granted the president enormous authority over foreign affairs and internal security. The National Security Act, passed in 1947, created the Department of Defense as a cabinet agency (replacing the Department of War), consolidated control of the various military services under its authority, and established the Joint Chiefs of Staff, composed of the heads of the army, navy, air force, and marines. To advise the president on military and foreign affairs, the act set up the National Security Council (NSC), a group presided over by the national security adviser. The NSC also consisted of the secretaries of state, defense, the army, the navy, and the air force and any others the president might choose to designate.

In addition to this panel, the National Security Act established the Central Intelligence Agency (CIA) as part of the executive branch. Because of the nation's poor experience analyzing intelligence prior to World War II, the CIA was given the responsibility of coordinating intelligence gathering and conducting espionage abroad to counter Soviet spying operations. Another new intelligence agency, the National Security Agency, created in 1949, monitored overseas communications through the latest technological devices. Together, these agencies enhanced the president's ability to conduct foreign affairs with little congressional oversight and out of public view.

By 1948 the Truman administration had decided that an economically healthy Germany, with its great industrial potential, provided the key to a prosperous Europe and consequently a depression-proof United States. Rebuilding postwar Germany would also fortify the eastern boundary of Europe against Soviet expansion. In mid-1948, the United States, United Kingdom, and France consolidated their occupation zones, created the Federal Republic of Germany (West Germany), and initiated economic reforms to stimulate a speedy recovery. This prompted the Soviet Union, which saw a strong Germany as a threat to its national security, to respond in a belligerent manner. Stalin closed the access roads from the border of West Germany to Berlin, located in the Soviet zone of East Germany, effectively cutting off the city from the West.

The Soviet blockade of West Berlin turned the Cold War even colder. Without provisions from the United States and its allies in West Germany, West Berliners could not survive. In an effort to break the blockade, Truman ordered a massive airlift known

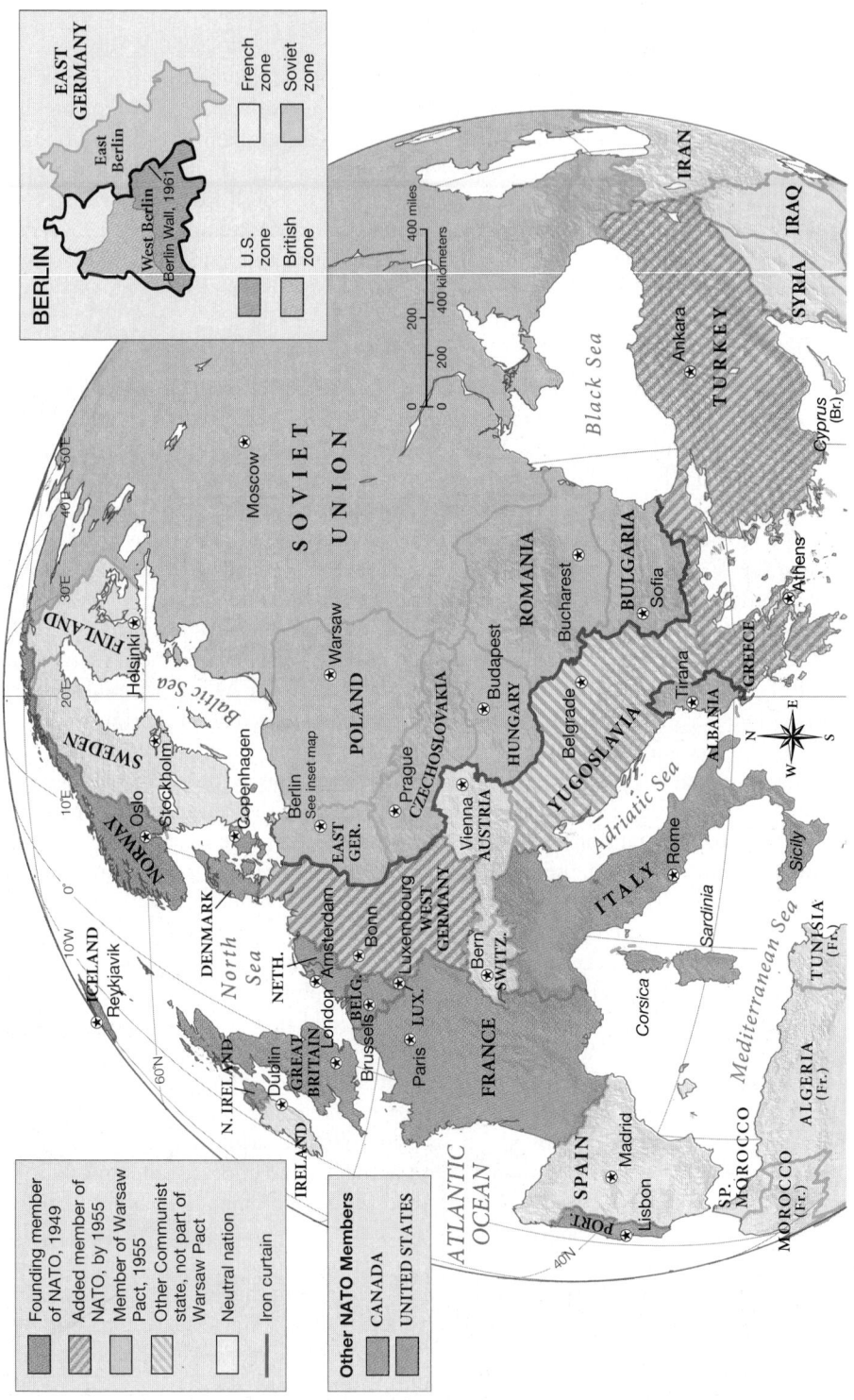

< **MAP 24.1**
The Cold War in Europe, 1945–1955   In 1946, the four major victorious wartime allies
divided Germany and Berlin into distinct sectors, leading to increasing conflict. Between 1949 and
1955, the descent of what Winston Churchill called the "iron curtain" of communism and the
creation of rival security pacts headed by the United States and the Soviet Union hardened these
postwar divisions into a prolonged Cold War.

as "Operation Vittles," during which American and British planes transported more
than 2.5 million tons of supplies to West Berlin. After nearly a year of these flights, the
Berlin airlift ended in the spring of 1949 when the Russians backed off and once again
allowed their adversaries to supply West Berlin on the ground.

Although the two superpowers narrowly avoided war over Berlin, their subsequent
actions kept the conflict alive. Both nations fashioned military alliances to keep the other
at bay. In April 1949, the United States joined eleven European countries in the **North
Atlantic Treaty Organization (NATO)**. A peacetime military alliance, NATO established a collective security pact in which an attack on one member was viewed as an
attack on all (Map 24.1). Pledging to defend Europe, Truman dispatched four army
divisions to Western Europe to show his resolve against Soviet aggression. In 1949 the
Russians followed suit by organizing the Council for Mutual Economic Assistance to
help their satellite nations rebuild and six years later by creating the Warsaw Pact military
alliance, the respective counterparts in Eastern Europe to the Marshall Plan and NATO.

Amid the growing militarization of the Cold War, 1949 brought two new shocks
to the United States and its allies. First, in September the Russians successfully tested an
atomic bomb. Second, Communist forces within China led by Mao Zedong and Zhou
Enlai succeeded in overthrowing the U.S.-backed government of Jiang Jieshi and creating the People's Republic of China. These two events convinced many in the United
States that the threat posed by communism was escalating rapidly.

In response, the National Security Council met to reevaluate U.S. strategy in fighting the Cold War. In April 1950, the NSC recommended to Truman that the United
States intensify its containment policy both abroad and at home. The document it
handed over to the president, entitled **NSC-68**, spelled out the need for action in ominous language. "The Soviet Union, unlike previous aspirants to hegemony," NSC-68
warned, "is animated by a new fanatic faith, antithetical to our own, and seeks to impose
its absolute authority over the rest of the world. It is in this context that this Republic
and its citizens . . . stand in their deepest peril." Having sketched out the dire threat
posed by Russia's acquisition of the atomic bomb, the NSC made specific recommendations to combat this new challenge. NSC-68 proposed that the United States develop
an even more powerful nuclear weapon, the hydrogen bomb; increase military spending;
and continue to negotiate NATO-style alliances around the globe. Departing from the
original guidelines for the CIA, the president's advisers proposed that the United States
engage in "covert means" to foment and support "unrest and revolt in selected strategic
[Soviet] satellite countries." At home, the government should prepare Americans for the
Communist danger by enhancing internal security and civil defense programs.

· Truman agreed with many of the principles behind NSC-68 but worried about the
cost of funding it. The problem remained a political one. Though the Democrats once
again controlled both houses of Congress, there was little sentiment to raise taxes and

slash the economic programs established during the New Deal. However, circumstances abruptly changed when, in June 1950, shortly after the president received the NSC report, Communist North Korea invaded U.S.-backed South Korea. In response to this attack, Truman took the opportunity to put into practice key recommendations of NSC-68.

The Korean War

Like Germany, Korea emerged from World War II divided between U.S. and Soviet spheres of influence. Above the 38th parallel, which divided the Korean peninsula, the Communist leader Kim Il Sung ruled North Korea with support from the Soviet Union. Below that latitude, the anti-Communist leader Syngman Rhee governed South Korea. The United States supported Rhee, but with American forces occupying Japan and the Philippines, in January 1950 Secretary of State Dean Acheson did not regard South Korea as part of the vital Asian "defense perimeter" that the United States guaranteed to protect from Communist aggression. Truman had already removed remaining American troops from the country the previous year. On June 25, 1950, an emboldened Kim Il Sung sent troops to invade South Korea, seeking to unite the country under his leadership.

In the aftermath of the invasion, Korea took on new importance to American policymakers. Drawing a parallel between the situation in Korea and the appeasement of the Nazis before World War II, Truman remarked that he had seen strong nations invade the weak before and that the failure of democracies to act only encouraged aggressors. If South Korea fell, the president believed, Communist leaders would be "emboldened to override nations closer to our own shores." Thus the Truman Doctrine was now applied to Asia as it had previously been applied to Europe. This time, however, American financial aid would not be enough. It would be up to the U.S. military to contain the Communist threat.

Truman did not seek a declaration of war from Congress. According to Acheson, consulting Congress would delay matters and "weaken and confuse [our] will." Instead, Truman chose a multinational course of action. With the Soviet Union boycotting the United Nations over its refusal to admit the Communist People's Republic of China, the United States obtained authorization from the UN Security Council to send a peacekeeping force to Korea. In the absence of a declaration of war, Truman, as commander in chief, sent American troops to enforce what he called a "police action." Fifteen other countries joined UN forces, but the United States supplied the bulk of the troops, as well as their commanding officer, General Douglas MacArthur. In reality, MacArthur reported to the president, not the United Nations.

Before MacArthur could mobilize his forces, the North Koreans had penetrated most of South Korea, except for the port of Pusan on the southwest coast of the peninsula. In a daring counterattack, on September 15, 1950, MacArthur dispatched land and sea forces to capture Inchon, northwest of Pusan on the opposite coast, to cut off North Korean supply lines. Joined by UN forces pushing out of Pusan, MacArthur's Eighth Army troops chased the enemy northward in retreat back over the 38th parallel.

Now Truman had to make a key decision. MacArthur wanted to invade North Korea, defeat the Communists, and unify the country under Syngman Rhee. Instead of sticking to his original goal of containing Communist aggression against South Korea, Truman succumbed to the lure of liberating all of Korea from the Communists. MacArthur received permission to proceed, and on October 9 his forces crossed the 38th parallel into North Korea. Within three weeks, UN troops marched through the country until they reached the Yalu River, which bordered China. With the U.S. military massed along their southern perimeter, the Chinese warned that they would send troops to repel the invaders if the Americans crossed the Yalu. Both General MacArthur and Secretary of State Acheson, based on faulty CIA intelligence, discounted this threat, figuring that the Chinese Communists did not want to fight another war so recently after winning their revolution. They were wrong. Truman approved MacArthur's plan to cross the Yalu, and on November 27, 1950, China sent more than 300,000 troops south into North Korea. This proved disastrous for the United States; within two months, Communist troops regained control of North Korea, allowing them once again to invade South Korea. On January 4, 1951, the South Korean capital of Seoul fell to Chinese and North Korean troops (Map 24.2).

MAP 24.2
The Korean War, 1950–1953 Considered a "police action" by the United Nations, the Korean War cost the lives of nearly 37,000 U.S. troops. Approximately one million Koreans were killed, wounded, or missing. Each side pushed deep into enemy territory, but neither could achieve victory. When hostilities ceased in 1953, a demilitarized zone near the original boundary line separated North and South Korea.

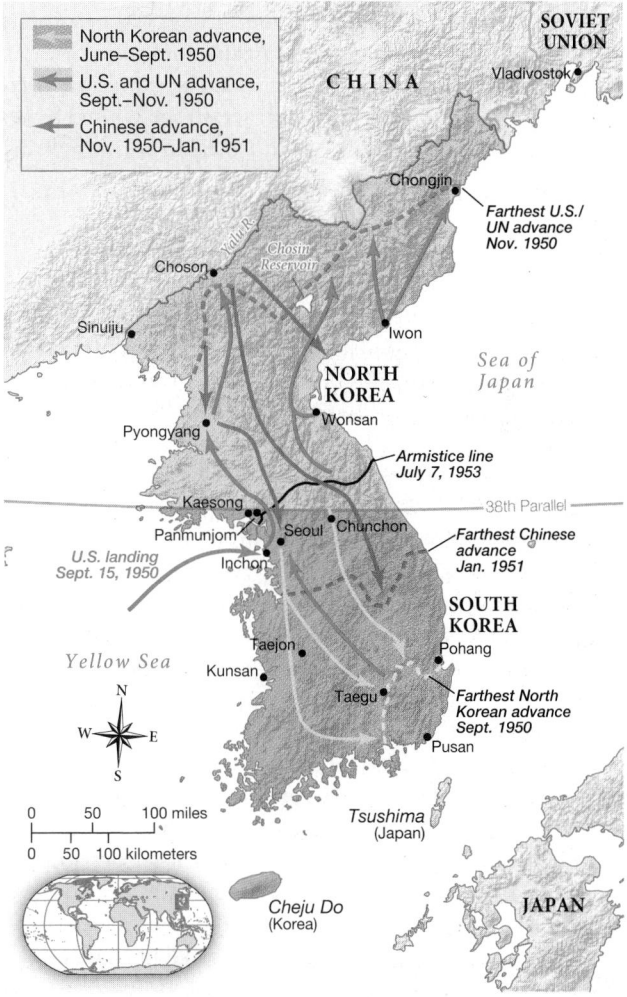

By the spring of 1951, the war had degenerated into a stalemate. UN forces succeeded in recapturing Seoul and repelling the Communists north of the 38th parallel. This time, with the American public anxious to end the war and with the presence of the Chinese promising an endless, bloody predicament, the president sought to replace combat with diplomacy. The American objective would be containment, not Korean unification.

Truman's change of heart infuriated General MacArthur, who was willing to risk an all-out war with China and to use nuclear weapons to win. After MacArthur spoke out publicly against Truman's policy by remarking, "There is no substitute for victory," the president removed him from command on April 11, 1951. However, even with the change in strategy and leadership, the war dragged on for two more years until July 1953, when a final armistice agreement was reached. By this time, Truman's term of office had ended.

The Korean War cost the United States 54,000 lives and $54 billion. This sacrifice of human lives and economic resources made the war unpopular among the American people. Few understood what good, if any, was accomplished. If American soldiers had to die and suffer, many Americans questioned why the Truman administration was satisfied with containment and not the expulsion of communism from Asia once and for all. When MacArthur returned to the United States, he was greeted as a hero, reflecting public dissatisfaction with a war in which fighting to a draw was represented as a victory.

The War and the Imperial Presidency

The Korean War boosted the imperial presidency by allowing the president to bypass Congress and the Constitution to initiate wars in the name of "police actions." The war allowed Truman to expand his powers as commander in chief and augmented the strength of the national security state over which he presided. As a result of the Korean conflict, the military draft became a regular feature of American life for young men over the next two decades. The expanded peacetime military was active around the globe, operating bases in Europe, Asia, and the Middle East. During the war, the military budget rose from $13.5 billion to $50 billion, strengthening the connection between economic growth and permanent mobilization to fight the Cold War. The war also permitted President Truman to reshape foreign policy along the lines sketched in NSC-68, including the extension of U.S. influence in Southeast Asia. Consequently, he authorized economic aid to support the French against Communist revolutionaries in Vietnam.

Yet the power of the imperial presidency did not go unchecked. Congress deferred to Truman on key issues of military policy, but on one important occasion the Supreme Court stepped in to restrain him. The central issue grew out of a labor dispute in the steel industry. In 1952 the United Steel Workers of America threatened to go on strike for higher wages, which would have had a serious impact on war production as well as the economy in general. On May 2, after the steel companies refused the union's demands, Truman announced the government seizure and operation of the steel mills to keep them running. He argued that as president he had the "inherent right" to take over the steel plants.

The steel companies objected and brought the matter before the Supreme Court. On June 2, 1952, the Court ruled against Truman. It held that the president did not have the intrinsic authority to seize private property, even during wartime. For the time being, the Supreme Court affirmed some limitations on the unbridled use of presidential power even during periods of war.

REVIEW & RELATE

• What were the causes and consequences of the militarization of the containment strategy in the late 1940s and early 1950s?

• How did the Korean War contribute to the centralization of power in the executive branch?

Peacetime Challenges, 1945–1948

As the Cold War heated up overseas, at home Americans faced numerous challenges posed by the reconversion of the economy from a war footing to peacetime. Consumers experienced shortages and high prices; businesses complained about tight regulations; and labor unions sought higher wages and a greater voice in companies' decision making. African Americans attempted to build on the gains they had achieved during World War II and to secure new civil rights victories at home. The return to peace also occasioned debates about whether married women, especially those with children, should continue to work outside the home. Even as the Cold War created new anxieties, Americans tried to achieve the peace and prosperity that had eluded them for the past two decades.

Coming Home

In August 1945, 12 million troops, two-thirds of all men between the ages of eighteen and thirty-four, were in uniform. One year later, 9 million had returned to the United States. Some wanted to continue their education, most wanted jobs, and all sought to reunite with their families. They came home to a changed world. The Great Depression was over, but industries still needed to shift to peacetime production before consumers could enjoy the fruits of the new prosperity. In the meantime, consumers faced shortages and high prices. Indeed, there was no guarantee that, with the booming war industries dismantled, the depression would not return.

World War II had also exerted pressures on traditional family life. During the war, millions of women had left their homes and worked jobs that their husbands, sons, and boyfriends had vacated (see chapter 23). Most of the 150,000 women who served in the military received their discharge, and like their male counterparts they hoped to obtain employment. Many other women who had tasted the benefits of wartime employment also wanted to keep working and were reluctant to give up their positions to men.

The war disrupted other aspects of family life as well. During the war, husbands and wives had spent long periods of time apart, resulting in marital tensions and an increased divorce rate. The relaxation of parental authority during the war led to a rise in juvenile delinquency, which added to the anxieties of adults. In 1948 the noted psychiatrist William C. Menninger observed, "While we alarm ourselves with talk of . . . atom bombs, we are complacently watching the disintegration of our family life." Some observers worried that the very existence of the traditional American family was in jeopardy. These fears proved unfounded, as the baby boom of the postwar decades would dramatically demonstrate.

Veterans Return Home   After World War II, many veterans returned home, married, and started families. They went to school with funds provided by the GI Bill. This twenty-four-year-old former soldier, a student at the University of Iowa, tries to study while holding his baby daughter on his lap as his wife irons in their cramped house trailer.   Time & Life Pictures/Getty Images

Economic Conversion and Labor Discontent

Before the Cold War became the focus of U.S. foreign policy in 1947, Americans worried more about economic security than about fighting communism. In the absence of war-driven production and with the return of millions of veterans to the job market, Americans feared massive unemployment and another depression. Many families had managed to save money during the war with rationing in place, and they looked forward to spending it on consumer goods. Instead, they found shortages of manufactured items and foodstuffs as the economy moved slowly to peacetime production. Workers who had remained on the home front enjoyed rising incomes from overtime pay, but they worried about holding on to their increased earnings in peacetime.

Even before the war ended, the U.S. government took some steps to meet postwar economic challenges. In 1944, for example, Congress passed the **Servicemen's Readjustment Act**, commonly known as the GI Bill, which offered veterans educational opportunities and financial aid as they adjusted to civilian life. Overall, however, the Truman administration did not handle the economic problems of reconversion well. In the face of shortages and high prices for available commodities, the president wavered between retaining World War II price controls to benefit consumers and eliminating them to help corporate industrialists. He satisfied neither.

Nor did the Employment Act of 1946 improve matters. Contrary to its name, the legislation did not guarantee jobs but merely recommended using tax policies to make adjustments to the economy and created a three-member Council of Economic Advisors to make suggestions to the president.

The president also ran into serious difficulty with labor unions. In the years immediately following the war, real incomes fell, undermined by inflation and reduced overtime hours. As corporate profits rose, workers in the steel, automobile, and fuel industries struck for higher wages and a greater voice in company policies. Truman responded harshly. Labor had been one of Franklin Roosevelt's strongest allies, but his successor put that relationship in jeopardy. In 1946 the federal government took over railroads and threatened to draft workers into the military until they stopped striking. Truman took a tough stance, but in the end union workers received a boost in pay, though it did little to relieve inflation.

Political developments forced Truman to change course. In the 1946 midterm elections, Republicans won control of the Eightieth Congress (1947–1949). Stung by this defeat, Truman sought to repair the damage his anti-union policies had done to the Democratic Party coalition. In 1947 Congress passed the **Taft-Hartley Act**. The act hampered the ability of unions to organize and limited their power to go on strike if larger, national interests were seen to be at stake. Seeking to regain labor's support, Truman vetoed the measure. Congress, however, overrode the president's veto, and the Taft-Hartley Act became law.

The Postwar Civil Rights Struggle

With the war against Nazi racism and tyranny over, African Americans expected to win first-class citizenship in the United States. During World War II, A. Philip Randolph, a black activist and union leader, had led a successful effort to pressure the federal government to tackle discrimination. New organizations such as the **Congress of Racial Equality (CORE)** had emerged to attack racial exclusion in public accommodations, and older groups such as the National Association for the Advancement of Colored People (NAACP) had flourished by attracting new members and leading the legal battle against racial inequality. African American veterans returned home to the South determined to build on these victories, especially by extending the right to vote. "A Voteless citizen is a Voiceless citizen" became the slogan of campaigns throughout the South. Yet African Americans found that most whites resisted demands for racial equality.

Violence surfaced as the most visible evidence of many white people's determination to preserve the traditional racial order. In 1946 a race riot erupted in Columbia, Tennessee, in which blacks were killed and black businesses were burned down. In February 1946 in South Carolina, Isaac Woodard, a black veteran still in uniform and on his way home on a bus, got into an argument with the white bus driver. When the local sheriff arrived, he pounded Woodard's face with a club, permanently blinding the ex-GI. Five months later, the Ku Klux Klan in Monroe, Georgia, shot a black veteran and three members of his family to death for "acting uppity." In Mississippi, Senator Theodore Bilbo, running for reelection in the Democratic primary, told his white audiences that they could keep blacks from voting "by seeing them the night before" the election. Groups such as the NAACP and the National Association of Colored Women demanded that the president take action to combat this reign of terror.

In December 1946, after meeting with a delegation of concerned African Americans, Truman issued an executive order creating the President's Committee on Civil Rights to investigate the situation and report back to him. Truman's response reflected moral concerns and good politics: It provided the opportunity to increase Democratic Party support among African Americans, which Roosevelt had first succeeded in gaining in 1936. In April 1947, while the President's Committee on Civil Rights conducted its work, Jackie Robinson achieved a milestone by becoming the first black baseball player to enter the major leagues. This accomplishment proved to be a sign of changes to come.

After extensive deliberations, the committee, which consisted of blacks and whites, northerners and southerners, issued its report, *To Secure These Rights*, on October 29, 1947. The document placed the problem of what it called "civil rights shortcomings" within the context of the Cold War, arguing that racial inequality and unrest could only aid the Soviets in their global anti-American propaganda efforts. "The United States is not so strong," the committee asserted, "the final triumph of the democratic ideal not so inevitable that we can ignore what the world thinks of us or our record." A far-reaching document, the report called for racial desegregation in the military, interstate transportation, and education, as well as extension of the right to vote. The following year, in the midst of the presidential election and once again pressured by A. Philip Randolph, the president signed an executive order to desegregate the armed forces.

The Election of 1948

By supporting civil rights measures recommended by his presidential committee, Truman alienated white southern segregationists, a significant force in the Democratic Party. On the president's political right, Strom Thurmond, the governor of South Carolina, mounted a presidential challenge by heading up the States' Rights Party, known as the Dixiecrats, which threatened to take away traditional southern Democratic voters from Truman.

At the same time, Truman's conduct of foreign affairs brought criticism from the left wing of his party. Former vice president Henry Wallace ran on the Progressive Party ticket, backed by disgruntled liberals living mainly in the North who opposed Truman's hard-line Cold War policies. Besides these two independent candidates, Truman also faced the popular Republican governor of New York, Thomas E. Dewey. Under these circumstances, political pundits and public opinion polls predicted that Truman would lose the 1948 presidential election.

Truman confounded these voices of gloom by winning the election. His victory resulted from a number of factors, including his vigorous campaign style; the complacency of his Republican opponent, who placed too much faith in opinion polls; and his success in winning over many potential Thurmond and Wallace voters. Much of his victory, however, depended on the continuing power of the New Deal coalition. Truman succeeded in holding together the winning alliance that Franklin Roosevelt had first put together. He did this by stitching together a coalition of labor, minorities, farmers, and liberals and won enough votes in the South to come out ahead despite long odds. In the four-candidate race, Truman did very well in winning slightly less than 50 percent of the popular vote. Democrats also regained control of Congress.

Having won election as president in his own right and armed with a Democratic majority in Congress, Truman still faced tough opposition in his second term. A coalition of southern Democrats and conservative Republicans blocked passage of civil rights proposals and Truman's so-called Fair Deal programs, including national health insurance, federal aid to education, and agricultural reform. The president did manage to obtain budget increases for New Deal measures such as Social Security, minimum wages, and public housing.

By this time, many liberals, as a result of their experience during World War II, had made peace with cooperative corporate executives and relied on the federal government to produce prosperity by tinkering with the economy through tax and monetary adjustments; these liberals no longer supported the more radical approaches of income redistribution or reducing corporate concentration. They practiced what historian Arthur Schlesinger Jr. labeled **vital center liberalism**, avoiding what they considered the ideological dogmatism of the extreme political left and right. Militantly anti-Stalinist, centrist liberals supported civil rights, the prosecution of Communists through due process of law, and the expansion of New Deal social welfare programs. In the end, however, preoccupation with fighting the Cold War in Europe and the hot war in Korea diverted Truman's attention from aggressively pursuing a truly liberal political agenda in Congress.

> **REVIEW & RELATE**

- What social and economic challenges did America face as it made the transition from war to peace?
- Why did Truman have only limited success in implementing his domestic agenda?

The Anti-Communist Consensus, 1945–1954

For most of Truman's second administration, fear of Communist subversion within the United States consumed domestic politics. This focus on anticommunism did not emerge abruptly; rather it carried over from policies the president had employed in fighting the Cold War during his first term in office. There was a consensus within the Truman administration that Soviet-sponsored Communists were attempting to infiltrate American society and that such efforts constituted a grave threat to capitalist and democratic values and institutions. This consensus turned into an anti-Communist obsession, as evidence of Soviet espionage came to light. In an atmosphere of fear, lawmakers and judges blurred the distinction between actual Soviet spies and political radicals who were merely attracted to Communist beliefs. In the process, these officials trampled on individual constitutional freedoms.

Loyalty and Americanism

The postwar fear of communism echoed earlier anti-Communist sentiments. The government had initiated the repressive Palmer raids during the Red scare following World War I, which led to the deportation of immigrants sympathetic to the Communist doctrines of the Russian Revolution (see chapter 21). In 1938 conservative congressional opponents of the New Deal established the **House Committee on Un-American Activities (HUAC)** to investigate domestic communism, which they tied to the Roosevelt administration. Much of anticommunism, however, was bipartisan. In 1940 Roosevelt signed into law the **Smith Act**, which prohibited teaching or advocating the "duty, necessity, desirability, or propriety of overthrowing or destroying any government in the United States by force or violence" or belonging to any group with that aim. At the same time, President Roosevelt secretly authorized the FBI to monitor and wiretap individuals suspected of violating the act.

The Cold War produced the second Red scare. Just two weeks after his speech announcing the Truman Doctrine in March 1947, the president signed an executive order creating the **Federal Employee Loyalty Program**. Under this program, a board investigated federal employees to see if "reasonable grounds [existed] to suspect disloyalty." The attorney general compiled a list of suspect organizations to assist the board. Soviet espionage was, in fact, a cause for legitimate concern. Spies operated in both Canada and the United States during and after World II, and they had infiltrated the Manhattan Project. The Venona papers, declassified intercepts of Soviet intelligence communications first released in 1995, suggest that a cadre of government officials and federal employees worked for Soviet intelligence during the 1930s and 1940s.

The loyalty board, however, did not focus on espionage. Rather, it concentrated its attention on individuals who espoused dissenting views on a variety of political, social, and economic issues. It failed to uncover a single verifiable case of espionage or find even one actual Communist in public service. This lack of evidence did not stop the board from dismissing 378 government employees for their political beliefs and personal behavior. People lost jobs because they did not satisfactorily answer such questions as "Do you believe in racial integration?" or "Do you listen to the records of Paul Robeson?" (Robeson was an African American singer and actor who had close ties to Communists and the Soviet Union.) Some employees were dismissed because they were homosexuals and considered susceptible to blackmail by foreign agents. (Heterosexual men and women who were having extramarital affairs were not treated in the same manner.) The accused rarely faced their accusers and at times did not learn the nature of the charges against them. This disregard for due process of law spread as loyalty boards at state and municipal levels questioned and fired government employees, including public school teachers and state university professors.

 Online Document Project   McCarthyism in Higher Education
bedfordstmartins.com/hewittlawsonvalue

Congress also investigated communism in the private sector, especially in industries that shaped public opinion. In 1947 HUAC broadened the anti-Red probe from Washington to Hollywood. Convinced that the film industry had come under Communist influence and threatened to poison the minds of millions of moviegoers, HUAC conducted hearings that attracted much publicity. HUAC cited for contempt ten witnesses, among them directors and screenwriters, for refusing to answer questions about their political beliefs and associations. These and subsequent hearings assumed the form of a ritual. The committee already had information from the FBI about the witnesses; HUAC really wanted the accused to confess their Communist heresy publicly and to show contrition by naming their associates. Those who did not comply were considered "unfriendly" witnesses and were put on an industry **blacklist** that deprived them of employment.

Online Document Project   McCarthyism and the Hollywood Ten
bedfordstmartins.com/hewittlawsonvalue

HUAC grabbed even bigger headlines in 1948. With Republicans in charge of the committee, they launched a probe of Alger Hiss, a former State Department official in the Roosevelt administration who had accompanied the president to the Yalta Conference. The hearings resulted from charges brought by former Soviet spy Whittaker Chambers that Hiss had passed him classified documents. Hiss denied the allegations, and President Truman dismissed them as a distraction. In fact, Democrats viewed the charges as a politically motivated attempt by Republicans to characterize the Roosevelt and Truman administrations as having been riddled with Communists.

The Democrats' concerns proved well founded. Following Truman's victory in the 1948 presidential election, first-term Republican congressman Richard M. Nixon kept the Hiss affair alive. A member of HUAC, Nixon went to Chambers's farm and discovered a cache of documents that Chambers had stored for safekeeping in a hollowed-out pumpkin. Armed with these "Pumpkin Papers," Nixon reopened the case. Hiss never wavered in maintaining his innocence, and the statute of limitations for espionage from the 1930s had expired. Nonetheless, the federal government had enough evidence to prosecute him for perjury. One trial produced a hung jury, but a second convicted Hiss; he was sentenced to five years in prison.

Hiss's downfall tarnished the Democrats, as Republicans charged them with being "soft on communism." It did not matter that Truman was a cold warrior who had advanced the doctrine of containment to stop Soviet expansionism or that he had instituted the federal loyalty program to purge Communists from government. In fact, in 1949 Truman tried to demonstrate his cold warrior credentials by authorizing the Justice Department to prosecute twelve high-ranking officials of the Communist Party for violating the Smith Act. In 1951 the Supreme Court upheld the conviction of the Communist leaders on the grounds that they posed a "clear and present danger" to the United States by advocating the violent overthrow of the government. Despite the presence of some 43,000 Communists, nearly all of them known to the FBI, out of a total population of 150 million and with no evidence of immediate danger, in *Dennis v. United States* the justices decided that "the gravity of the [Communist] evil" was enough to warrant conviction under the Smith Act.

In 1950 the Truman administration also prosecuted Julius and Ethel Rosenberg. Unlike the *Dennis* case, which involved political beliefs, the Rosenbergs were charged with espionage. When the Russians successfully tested an atomic bomb in 1949, anyone accused of helping them obtain this weapon became "Public Enemy Number One." The outbreak of the Korean War the following year, in which tens of thousands of soldiers died, made the Rosenbergs appear as conspirators to murder. After a lengthy trial in 1951, the couple received the death penalty, rather than a possible thirty-year sentence, undoubtedly because they refused to confess and because the trial took place during the war. The presiding judge, Irving Kaufman, admitted as much. In sentencing them to death, he told the Rosenbergs that their actions "caused . . . the Communist aggression in Korea, with the resultant casualties exceeding 50,000 and who knows what millions more innocent people may pay the price of your treason. Indeed, by your betrayal, you undoubtedly have altered the course of history to the disadvantage of our country."

By 1950 the anti-Communist crusade included Democrats and Republicans, liberals and conservatives. Liberals had the most to lose because conservatives could easily brand them as ideologically tainted. In his successful campaign to become a U.S. senator from California in 1950, Richard Nixon had accused his opponent, the liberal Democrat Helen Gahagan Douglas, of being "pink down to her underwear," not quite a Red but close enough. Liberal civil rights and civil liberties groups as well as labor unions were particularly vulnerable to such charges and rushed to rid their organizations of suspected Communists. Such efforts did nothing, however, to slow down conservative attacks. The conservative Republican chairman of HUAC, Harold Velde, linked the anti-Communist issue to traditional Republican fiscal policy in the slogan "Get the Reds out of Washington and Washington out of the red." In 1950 Republicans supported legislation proposed by Senator Pat McCarran, a conservative Democrat from Nevada, which required Communist organizations to register with the federal government, established detention camps to incarcerate radicals during national emergencies, and denied passports to American citizens suspected of Communist affiliations. (As a result, singer Paul Robeson lost his right to travel abroad.) The severity of the entire measure proved too much for President Truman, and he vetoed it. Reflecting the bipartisan consensus on the issue, the Democratic-controlled Congress overrode the veto.

McCarthyism

Joseph Raymond McCarthy, a Republican senator from Wisconsin, did not create the phenomenon of postwar anticommunism, which was already in full swing from 1947 to 1950, but he served as its most public and feared voice from 1950 until 1954. Senator McCarthy used his position as the head of the Permanent Investigation Subcommittee of the Committee on Government Operations to harass current and former government officials and employees who, he claimed, collaborated with the Communist conspiracy. He had plenty of assistance from members of his own party who considered McCarthy a potent weapon in their battle to reclaim the White House. Robert A. Taft, the respected conservative Republican senator from Ohio, told McCarthy "to keep talking and if one case doesn't work [you] should proceed with another." The press also courted the young senator by giving his charges substantial coverage on the front pages of daily newspapers and then shifting the story to the back pages when McCarthy's claims turned out to be false. McCarthy bullied people, exaggerated his military service, drank too much, and did not pull his punches in making speeches—but he was not a maverick. He did seek publicity, but his anti-Communist tirades fit into mainstream Cold War politics.

Aware of the power of the Communists-in-government issue, McCarthy gave a speech in February 1950 at a Republican women's club in Wheeling, West Virginia. Waving sheets of paper in his hand, the senator announced that he had "the names of 205 men known to the Secretary of State as being members of the Communist Party and who nevertheless are still working and shaping the policy of the State Department," a claim that was based on old information. McCarthy cared more about the message than about the truth. As he continued campaigning for Republican congressional candidates across the country, he kept changing the number of alleged Communists in the government. When Senator Millard Tydings of Maryland, a Democrat who headed the Senate Foreign Relations Committee, launched an investigation of McCarthy's charges, he concluded that they were irresponsible and unfounded.

This finding did not stop McCarthy; if anything, it emboldened him to go further. He accused Tydings of being "soft on communism" and campaigned against his reelection in 1952. Tydings's defeat in the election helped give McCarthy a reputation of political invincibility and scared off many critics from openly confronting him. McCarthy won reelection to the Senate, and when Republicans once again captured a majority in Congress, he became chair of the Permanent Investigations Subcommittee. Not only did he make false accusations and smear witnesses with anti-Communist allegations, but he also dispatched two aides to travel to Europe and purge what they considered disreputable books from the shelves of overseas libraries sponsored by the State Department.

McCarthy stood out among anti-Communists not for his beliefs but for his tactics. His name became synonymous with anticommunism as well as with manipulating the truth. At once jovial and sneering, McCarthy publicly hurled charges so astounding, especially coming from a U.S. senator, that people thought there must be something to them. He specialized in the "multiple untruth," a concoction of allegations so complex and convoluted that it was impossible to refute them simply or quickly. By the time the accusations could be discredited, the damage was already done. The senator bullied and

Fighting Communism in the Movies As part of a series of movies alerting audiences to the insidious dangers of communism, Hollywood produced *I Married a Communist* (1949). Although the story revolved around a shipping executive with a Communist past, the poster features a woman who uses her beauty to serve "a mob of terror" intent on destroying America.   Courtesy Everett Collection

badgered witnesses, called them names, and if necessary furnished phony documents and doctored photographs linking them to known Communists.

In 1954 McCarthy finally went too far. After one of his aides got drafted and the army refused to give him a special commission, McCarthy accused the army of harboring Communists at Camp Kilmer and Fort Monmouth in New Jersey. To sort out these charges and to see whether the army had acted appropriately, McCarthy's own Senate subcommittee conducted an investigation, with the Wisconsin senator stepping down as chair. For two months, the relatively new medium of television broadcast live the army-McCarthy hearings, during which the cameras showed many viewers for the first time how reckless McCarthy had become. As his public approval declined, the Senate decided that it could no longer tolerate McCarthy's outrageous behavior and that he was making anticommunism look ridiculous at home and abroad. The famous television journalist Edward R. Murrow ran an unflattering documentary on McCarthy on his evening program on CBS, which further cast doubt on the senator's character and veracity. In December 1954, the Senate voted to censure McCarthy for conduct unbecoming a senator, having violated senatorial decorum by insulting colleagues who criticized him. McCarthy retained his seat on the subcommittee and all his Senate prerogatives, but he never again wielded substantial power. In 1957 he died from acute hepatitis, a disease related to alcoholism.

The anti-Communist consensus did not end with the execution of the Rosenbergs in 1953 or the censure of Joseph McCarthy in 1954 and his death three years later. Even J. Robert Oppenheimer, "the father of the atomic bomb" (see chapter 23), came under scrutiny. In 1954 the Atomic Energy Commission revoked Oppenheimer's security clearance for suspected, though unproven, Communist affiliations. That same year, Congress passed the Communist Control Act, which required "Communist infiltrated" groups to register with the federal government. Federal, state, and municipal governments required employees to take a loyalty oath affirming their allegiance to the United States and disavowing support for any organization that advocated the overthrow of the government. In addition, the blacklist continued in Hollywood throughout the rest of the decade. In the South, anticommunism actually flourished following the Senate's punishment of McCarthy. After the Supreme Court declared racial segregation in public schools unconstitutional in 1954, a number of southern states, including Florida and Louisiana, set up committees to investigate Communist influence in the civil rights movement. In a case concerning civil liberties, the Supreme Court still upheld HUAC's authority to investigate communism and to require witnesses who came before it to answer questions about their affiliations. Yet the Court did put a stop to the anti-Communist momentum. In 1957 the high court dealt a severe blow to enforcement of the Smith Act by ruling in *Yates v. United States* that the Justice Department could not prosecute someone for merely advocating an abstract doctrine favoring the violent overthrow of the government. In response, Congress tried, but failed, to limit the Supreme Court's jurisdiction in cases of this sort.

Even without the presence of Senator Joseph McCarthy, many Americans would have fallen victim to anti-Communist hysteria. J. Edgar Hoover and the FBI did more to fuel the second Red scare than did the Wisconsin senator. Hoover and his bureau did greater damage than McCarthy because they provided the information that Communist-hunters used throughout the government. The FBI was involved in criminal prosecutions in the *Dennis* and *Rosenberg* cases, supplied evidence to congressional committees and loyalty boards, and wiretapped suspected targets and used undercover agents to monitor and harass them. Historian Ellen Schrecker has suggested that because of the FBI's prominent role in the anti-Communist crusade we should call the attacks on suspected radicals during this period not **McCarthyism** but Hooverism.

(**REVIEW & RELATE**)

• Why did fear of Communists in positions of influence escalate in the late 1940s and early 1950s?

• Why was McCarthyism much more powerful than Joseph McCarthy?

Conclusion: The Cold War and Anticommunism

Anticommunism remained a potent weapon in political affairs as long as the Cold War operated in full force. When George Kennan designed the doctrine of containment in 1946 and 1947, he had no idea that it would lead to permanent military alliances such as NATO or to a war in Korea. He viewed the Soviet Union as an unflinching ideological enemy, but he believed that it should be contained through economic rather than military means, along the lines of the Marshall Plan. When the Korean War ended in 1953, the Truman administration had already put into operation around the world the heightened military plans called for by NSC-68. Hard-line Cold War rhetoric portrayed the struggle as a battle between good and evil, summed up in the phrase "I'd rather be dead than Red." Casting the conflict in apocalyptic terms did little justice to the nature of its origins. Born out of different perceptions of national interests and mutual misunderstandings of the other side's actions, the Cold War became frozen in the language of competing moralistic assumptions and self-righteousness. Within this context, though some Americans rallied to obtain clemency for the Rosenbergs, most considered that they got just what they deserved.

The Cold War remained the backdrop for life during the 1950s. Americans accepted it and took it for granted as part of the hazard of modern everyday life. Occasionally, overseas crises riveted their attention on the perilous possibilities of atomic brinksmanship with the Soviets, but for the most part Americans focused their attention on pursuing their economic dreams and raising their families. They could not avoid the Cold War, but they would try to work around it.

Chapter Review

MAKE IT STICK

LearningCurve **bedfordstmartins.com/hewittlawsonvalue**
After reading the chapter, use LearningCurve to retain what you've read.

IDENTIFY KEY TERMS

Identify and explain the significance of each term below.

Truman Doctrine (p. 624)

Marshall Plan (p. 624)

imperial presidency (p. 625)

National Security Council (NSC) (p. 625)

Berlin airlift (p. 627)

North Atlantic Treaty Organization (NATO) (p. 627)

NSC-68 (p. 627)

Servicemen's Readjustment Act (p. 632)

Taft-Hartley Act (p. 633)

Congress of Racial Equality (CORE) (p. 633)

To Secure These Rights (p. 634)

vital center liberalism (p. 635)

House Committee on Un-American Activities (HUAC) (p. 635)

Smith Act (p. 636)

Federal Employee Loyalty Program (p. 636)

blacklist (p. 636)

McCarthyism (p. 641)

REVIEW & RELATE

Answer the focus questions from each section of the chapter.

1. Why did American policymakers believe that containing Communist expansion should be the foundation of American foreign policy?

2. What role did mutual misunderstandings and mistrust play in the emergence of the Cold War?

3. What were the causes and consequences of the militarization of the containment strategy in the late 1940s and early 1950s?

4. How did the Korean War contribute to the centralization of power in the executive branch?

5. What social and economic challenges did America face as it made the transition from war to peace?

6. Why did Truman have only limited success in implementing his domestic agenda?

7. Why did fear of Communists in positions of influence escalate in the late 1940s and early 1950s?

8. Why was McCarthyism much more powerful than Joseph McCarthy?

ONLINE DOCUMENT PROJECTS

◆ **McCarthyism and the Hollywood Ten**
◆ **McCarthyism in Higher Education**

After reading the primary sources in these document sets, answer the **Interpret the Evidence** questions to help you analyze each of the documents, and then answer the **Put It in Context** question(s) to help you relate the documents to the topics and themes you read about in the chapter.

bedfordstmartins.com/hewittlawsonvalue

TIMELINE OF EVENTS

1938	• House Committee on Un-American Activities (HUAC) established
1944	• Servicemen's Readjustment Act (GI Bill) passed
1945	• Potsdam Conference
1946	• George Kennan sends telegram outlining containment strategy
	• Winston Churchill delivers "iron curtain" speech
1947	• Truman Doctrine articulated
	• Taft-Hartley Act passed
	• National Security Act passed; Central Intelligence Agency (CIA) established
	• Truman creates Federal Employee Loyalty Program
	• President's Committee on Civil Rights issues *To Secure These Rights*
	• Jackie Robinson becomes the first black baseball player to enter the major leagues

1948–1949	• Berlin blockade and airlift
	• Alger Hiss affair
1948	• Truman orders desegregation of the military
	• Congress approves Marshall Plan
1949	• National Security Agency established
	• Communists win Chinese civil war
	• North Atlantic Treaty Organization (NATO) formed
	• Soviet Union successfully tests atomic weapon
1950–1953	• Korean War
1950–1954	• Senator Joseph McCarthy carries out anti-Communist crusade
1950	• NSC-68 issued
1952	• Truman administration seizes steel mills; Supreme Court reverses the action
1953	• Julius and Ethel Rosenberg executed for espionage

25

LearningCurve
bedfordstmartins.com/hewittlawsonvalue
After reading the chapter, use LearningCurve
to retain what you've read.

Troubled Innocence

1950–1961

AMERICAN HISTORIES

Alan Freed shook up American youth culture in the 1950s by rebranding existing black music and making it popular with white teenagers. *Rock 'n' roll* was a slang term among African Americans for sexual intercourse, but Freed turned it into an expression of musical rebellion. In 1951, at the age of twenty-nine, Aldon (Alan) James Freed was spinning records as a disc jockey, or "deejay," at a Cleveland, Ohio, radio station. He started out playing classical music but switched to rhythm and blues, an African American music style considered "race music." Freed began calling himself Moondog, howling like a dog, and using sound effects to rattle his radio listeners. Although he initially appealed mainly to a black audience, Freed's radio show and live concerts of music he dubbed rock 'n' roll soon attracted white teenagers.

In 1954 Freed moved to New York City radio station WINS, where his evening rock 'n' roll broadcast became a number one hit. Three years later at the height of his popularity, he hosted a nationally televised rock 'n' roll program, but only briefly. The American Broadcasting Company canceled Freed's show after four telecasts because of outrage from affiliate stations in the South after the black singer Frankie Lymon was shown dancing with a white girl.

The television incident was only the start of Freed's professional problems. In 1960 Freed was brought before a congressional committee investigating "payola," a common practice among deejays of receiving gifts from record companies in exchange for playing their records. His career sank further when Freed was indicted in 1962 for commercial bribery by New York State. He was found guilty, was fined $300, and received a six-month suspended jail sentence. Freed never regained his earlier stature. Impoverished and struggling with alcoholism, Freed died in 1965 at the age of forty-three.

Like Alan Freed, Grace Metalious sent shock waves through American popular culture in the 1950s. Metalious grew up in poverty in a small mill town in southern New Hampshire. In 1943, while still a teenager, she married George Metalious and became a mother and housewife. In 1956 Metalious published her first novel, *Peyton Place*. Based on her hometown, the book sold more than three million copies the first year and unsettled the literary world. Considered provocative and racy because of its discussion of sex, rape, and incest, the novel punctured myths about the straitlaced life of small-town America. It criticized small-minded conformity that enforced a double standard of sexual behavior on women.

Despite the book's popularity, which inspired a toned-down Hollywood film and a television series, Metalious was never seen as a serious writer. Detractors described her as an untalented author who disseminated filth. In response to such allegations, she countered, "If I'm a lousy writer, then an awful lot of people have lousy taste." Metalious could not reconcile her success with the criticism she received and, like Alan Freed, increasingly turned to alcohol for comfort. She wrote other novels, but they never achieved the success that *Peyton Place* had. In 1964, a year before Freed's death and just eight years after publication of *Peyton Place*, she died at age thirty-nine of cirrhosis of the liver. Both Metalious and Freed challenged notions of conventional taste, and both found their lives upended by the conservative backlash their work inspired.

IRONICALLY, THE AMERICAN HISTORIES of Alan Freed and Grace Metalious, both of whom attacked conformity, were made possible by the emergence of a mass-consumption economy fueled by technological innovation. The production of inexpensive paperback books enabled *Peyton Place* to reach a broad market. The development of low-cost records made rock 'n' roll

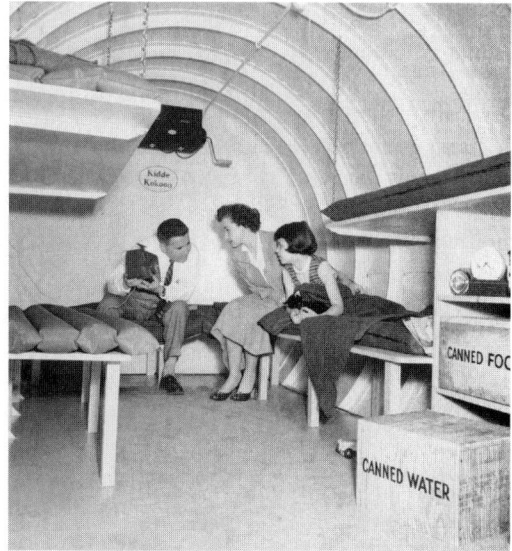

Backyard bomb shelter, Garden City, New York, 1955. © Bettmann/Corbis

songs widely available, and the creation of handheld transistor radios allowed teenagers to listen to music—played by deejays like Alan Freed—away from their parents' supervision. Young people were not the only ones to challenge their parents' culture. Writers and musicians experimented with freer forms of artistic expression and attacked the conformity they associated with mainstream America. African Americans challenged racial segregation directly in the Supreme Court and through powerful community protests. The Cold War remained the chief feature of foreign affairs and, despite wide-ranging prosperity, continued to generate fears for the safety and security of all Americans.

The Boom Years

The notoriety of Grace Metalious and Alan Freed came at a time of renewed economic growth and prosperity in the United States. With more disposable income than they had enjoyed in decades, American consumers responded enthusiastically to the wide range of products that advertisers promised would make their lives easier and more enjoyable. The search for the good life propelled middle-class families from cities to the suburbs. At the same time, a postwar baby boom added millions of children to the population and created a market to supply them with goods from their infancy and childhood to their teenage years.

Economic Boom

The United States emerged from World War II in strong financial shape. The gross national product (GNP) soared 250 percent between 1945 and 1960, and per capita income (total income divided by the population) grew 35 percent. During this fifteen-year period, the average real income (actual purchasing power) for American workers increased by as much as it had during the fifty years preceding World War II. Equally striking, 60 percent of Americans achieved middle-class status, and the number of salaried office workers rose 61 percent. Factory workers also experienced gains. Union membership leaped to the highest level in U.S. history, reaching nearly 17 million. In the mid-1950s, the American Federation of Labor (AFL) and the Congress of Industrial Organizations (CIO) merged to increase labor union bargaining power, and the new AFL-CIO concentrated on improving its members' income.

The affluence of the 1950s was much more equally distributed than the prosperity of the 1920s had been. As the middle class grew, the top 5 percent of wealthy families dropped in the percentage of total income they earned from 21.3 percent to 19 percent. Though poverty remained a persistent problem, the rate of poverty decreased, falling from 34 percent in 1947 to 22.1 percent in 1960 (Figure 25.1). A college education served as a critical marker of entry into the middle class. Traditionally, colleges and universities had been accessible only to the upper class. That began to change in the postwar era. Between 1940 and 1960, the number of high school students who went on to college more than doubled, with the percentage of Americans who went to college vastly exceeding that of the British and the French.

In addition to purchasing paperbacks, transistor radios, and rock 'n' roll records, consumers bought televisions. TV sets became a household staple in the 1950s, and by 1960, 87 percent of Americans owned a television. Americans also continued to purchase automobiles—75 percent owned a car, most likely one produced by General

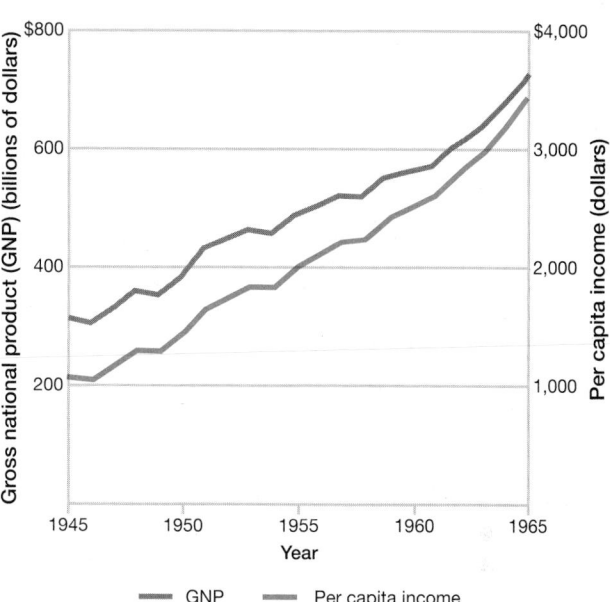

FIGURE 25.1
Economic Growth, 1945–1965 As industries shifted from war equipment to consumer goods, productivity remained high. More Americans entered the middle class in the two decades following World War II, while rising union membership ensured higher incomes for the working class. As a result, the purchasing power of most Americans increased in the immediate postwar period.

Motors, Ford, or Chrysler. With gas supplies plentiful and the price per gallon less than 30 cents, automakers concentrated on size, power, and style to compete for buyers. With more cars on the road, motels built by chains such as Holiday Inn sprang up along the highways. Fast-food establishments proliferated to feed motorists and their families. McDonald's hamburger restaurants, which first appeared in 1940 in San Bernardino, California, became the prototypical franchise chain for roadside fast food.

Baby Boom

In 1955 Illinois governor Adlai Stevenson told the graduating class of women at Smith College that they could do their part to maintain a free society as wives and mothers. Educated women had an important role to play in maintaining a household that boosted their husband's morale. "It is home work," Stevenson declared. "You can do it in the living-room with a baby in your lap or in the kitchen with a can opener in your hand . . . while you're watching television!" The mothers of these college graduates had suffered through the Great Depression, a time when the birthrate was 40 percent lower than in the 1950s. This was soon about to change.

In the 1950s, the average age at marriage was younger than it had been in the 1930s. On average, men married for the first time at the age of just under twenty-three, and 49 percent of women married at nineteen. Couples also produced children at an astonishing rate. In the 1950s, the growth rate in the U.S. population approached that of India, a country with one of the highest birthrates in the world (Figure 25.2).

Marriage and parenthood reflected a culture that increasingly emphasized early marriages and large families. The Cold War spurred this development. In the Atomic Age, public officials and the media urged young American men and women to build

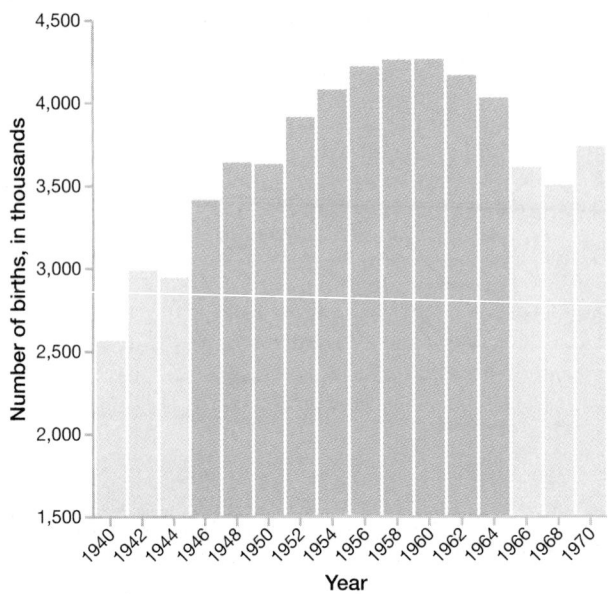

FIGURE 25.2
The Baby Boom, 1946–1964   The U.S. population increased dramatically in the postwar decades. Economic prosperity made it easier to support large families, women's early age at marriage contributed to high fertility, and improved health care led to the survival of more children.

nuclear families in which the father held a paying job and the mother stayed at home and raised her growing family. Doing so would strengthen the moral fiber of the United States in its battle to contain Soviet communism. Religious leaders echoed this message. "The family that prays together stays together" became a popular refrain and served as an inducement to encourage marital fertility alongside spiritual fidelity.

Parents could also look forward to their children surviving childhood diseases that had resulted in many childhood deaths in the past. In the 1950s, children received vaccinations against diphtheria, whooping cough, and tuberculosis before they entered school. The most serious illness affecting young children remained the crippling disease of polio, or infantile paralysis. Each year, usually around summertime, parents and children feared a renewed outbreak of the polio virus, which they believed was spread through contact at crowded swimming pools and beaches. An outbreak of polio in 1952 and 1953 infected 93,000 people nationwide. In 1955 Dr. Jonas Salk developed a successful injectable vaccine against the disease. On April 12, 1955, news bulletins interrupted scheduled television programs to announce Salk's breakthrough, and, as one writer recalled, "citizens rushed to ring church bells and fire sirens, shouted, clapped, sang, and made every kind of joyous noise they could." Dr. Albert Sabin later developed a more convenient oral vaccine, and by the mid-1960s polio was no longer a public health menace in the United States.

Suburban Boom

In 1948 real estate developer William Levitt remarked: "No man who owns his own house and lot can be a Communist. He has too much to do." Levitt did not invent the suburbs, but he promoted them as no one before him had. The economic and demographic booms encouraged migration out of the cities so that growing families could have their own homes, greater space, and a healthier environment. By 1960 nearly 60 million people, one-third of the nation's population, lived in suburbs.

Residential communities outside New York City drew some 1.5 million people, and around Los Angeles the population tripled in size.

No section of the nation expanded faster than the West and the South. Attracted by the mild climate and jobs in the defense, petroleum, and chemical industries, transplanted Americans swelled the populations of California and Texas. The proliferation of air-conditioning in residences and businesses made the hot summer temperatures of these and other southern states more livable. California's population increased the most, adding nearly six million new residents between 1940 and 1960. In 1957, in a sign of the times, New York City lost two of its baseball teams, the New York Giants and the Brooklyn Dodgers, to San Francisco and Los Angeles. Retirees also flocked to California, and many others headed to Florida and Arizona. In Miami alone, the population jumped around 80 percent in the three decades after World War II. This migration to the **Sun Belt**, as the southern and western states would be called, transformed the political and social landscapes of the nation.

The extraordinary housing demand following World War II drove the suburban boom. The available housing stock could not accommodate returning veterans who married and started families. Many sought escape from crowded cities and a chance to achieve a piece of the American dream: a home with a front lawn, a backyard, and plenty of fresh air. To meet this demand, private enterprise and the federal government provided veterans and civilians opportunities to purchase their own homes.

William Levitt, a thirty-eight-year-old veteran from Long Island, New York, devised the formula for attracting home buyers to the suburbs. After World War II, Levitt, his father, and his brother saw their opportunity in the housing crunch and pioneered the idea of adapting Henry Ford's mass-production principles to the housing industry. To build his subdivision of **Levittown** in Hempstead, Long Island, twenty miles from Manhattan, he bulldozed 4,000 acres of potato fields and brought in trucks that dumped piles of building materials at exact intervals of sixty feet. Specialized crews then moved from pile to pile, each performing their assigned job. In July 1948, Levitt's workers constructed 180 houses a week, or 36 a day, in two shifts. These simple houses, placed on 60-by-100-foot lots, contained a living room, a kitchen, two bedrooms, and one bathroom. Levitt originally sold the homes for an affordable $7,990 and threw in a free television and washing machine. Mass-production methods kept prices low, and Levitt quickly sold his initial 17,000 houses and soon built other subdivisions in Pennsylvania and New Jersey. With Levitt leading the way, the production of new single-family homes nearly doubled from 937,000 in 1946 to 1.7 million in 1950.

Levitt and his fellow builders received a good deal of public help in making suburbia possible. The Federal Housing Administration, created in the 1930s, provided long-term mortgages to qualified buyers at low interest rates. After the war, the Veterans Administration offered even lower mortgage rates and did not require substantial down payments for ex-GIs to purchase a home. The federal government also cooperated by building roads that allowed drivers to commute to and from the suburbs. In 1956 the **National Interstate and Defense Highway Act** provided funds for the construction of 42,500 miles of roads throughout the country. In fashioning this policy of highway construction, Congress gave a tremendous boost not only to the development of the suburbs but also to the automobile industry. Between 1945 and 1960, the number of cars in the United States more than doubled. For many families living in suburban housing tracts, purchasing a second car became a necessity as husbands traveled by automobile to nearby cities and wives drove cars to go on errands and chauffeur their children to after-school activities.

Although millions of Americans took advantage of opportunities to move to the suburbs, millions of others could not. Levitt closed his subdivisions to African Americans. Many whites moved out of the cities because they did not want to live near the growing number of southern blacks who migrated north during World War II and the influx of Puerto Ricans who came to the United States after the war, and they did not welcome these minorities to their new communities. Levitt defended his racist exclusionary policy on business rather than on racial grounds. "I have come to know," he declared, "that if we sell one house to a Negro family, then 90 or 95 percent of our white customers will not buy into the community." Levitt was not alone in his discriminatory practices. Residents of many communities in the North purchased homes with restrictive covenants, which prohibited resale to blacks and members of other minority groups, including Hispanics, Jews, and Asian Americans. Although the Supreme Court outlawed restrictive covenants in *Shelley v. Kraemer* (1948), housing discrimination remained prevalent in urban and suburban neighborhoods. Real estate brokers steered minority buyers away from white communities, and banks refused to lend money to black purchasers who sought to move into white locales, an illegal policy called redlining.

 Online Document Project   **The Postwar Suburbs**
bedfordstmartins.com/hewittlawsonvalue

REVIEW & RELATE

• What factors contributed to the economic and population growth of the 1950s?

• How did economic and demographic trends in the 1950s contribute to the growth of suburbs?

The Culture of the 1950s

In the 1950s, popular culture developed as the United States confronted difficult political, diplomatic, and social issues. Amid this turmoil, television played a large role in shaping people's lives, reflecting their desire for success, and depicting the era as a time of innocence. The rise of teenage culture as a powerful economic force also influenced this portrayal of the 1950s. Teenage tastes, including rock 'n' roll, and consumption patterns reinforced the impression of a simpler and more carefree time. Religion painted a similar picture, as attendance at houses of worship rose. Still, the decade held a more complex social reality. Cultural rebels—writers, actors, and musicians—emerged to challenge mainstream values. Even women did not always act the suburban parts that television and society assigned them, and religion seemed to serve more of a communal, social function than an individual, spiritual one.

The Rise of Television

Few postwar developments had a greater impact on American society and politics than the advent of television. The first commercial TV broadcast occurred in 1939, but television sets did not become widely available until after World War II. The three major television networks—the Columbia Broadcasting System (CBS), the National Broadcasting Company (NBC), and the American Broadcasting Company (ABC)—offered programs nationwide that appealed to mainstream tastes while occasionally challenging the public with serious drama, music, and documentaries. During the 1950s, congressional investigations became a staple of television, and none provided a better morality tale than coverage of the army-McCarthy hearings in 1954 (see chapter 24). In the same manner, television networks began to feature intense presidential campaign coverage, from the national nominating conventions to election day vote tallies, and political advertisements began to fill the airwaves.

If many Americans recall the 1950s as a time of innocence, they have in mind television shows aimed at children, such as *Howdy Doody, Superman, Hopalong Cassidy, The Cisco Kid,* and *The Lone Ranger.* In the course of a half hour, the casts performed in shows that pitted good versus evil and in which honesty and decency triumphed. These youth-oriented television programs showcased a simple world of moral absolutes.

In similar fashion, adults enjoyed evening television shows that depicted old-fashioned families entertaining themselves, mediating quarrels sensibly and peacefully, and relying on the wisdom of parents. In *The Adventures of Ozzie and Harriet,* the Nelsons raised two clean-cut sons. In *Father Knows Best,* the Andersons—a father and mother and their three children—lived a tranquil life in the suburbs, and the father solved whatever dilemmas arose. The same held true for the Cleaver family on *Leave It to Beaver.* In *I Love Lucy,* the show's namesake, played by Lucille Ball, and her female sidekick tried to outwit their husbands on a weekly basis. Despite the focus on the women and the sympathy they engendered, men usually won this battle of the sexes. Television portrayed working-class families in grittier fashion on shows such as *The Life of Riley,* whose lead character worked at a factory, and *The Honeymooners,* whose male protagonists were a bus driver and a sewer worker. Nevertheless, like their middle-class counterparts, these families stayed together and worked out their problems despite their more challenging financial circumstances.

By contrast, African American families received little attention on television. Black female actors usually appeared as maids, and the one show that featured an all-black cast, *The Amos 'n' Andy Show,* generally portrayed African Americans according to the racial stereotypes of the period. American Indians faced similar difficulties. Few appeared on television, and those who did served mainly as targets for "heroic" cowboys defending the West from "savage" Indians. When Indians did appear, white actors often played them. There were exceptions. Tonto, the Lone Ranger's sidekick, was played by Jay Silverheels, a Canadian Mohawk; he offered a sympathetic character, mainly because he grunted his approval and showed his loyalty to his *kimosabe* (trusty scout). With the notable exception of Cuban American musician Desi Arnaz (Lucille Ball's husband and her costar in *I Love Lucy*), minorities such as Latinos, Native Americans, and Asians rarely appeared in television series.

Wild Ones on the Big Screen

If young people in the 1950s were expected to behave like Ozzie and Harriet Nelson's sons, Ricky and David, or the Cleaver boys, the popular culture industry also provided teenagers with alternative role models. Hollywood films offered several. In *Rebel without a Cause* (1955), actor James Dean portrayed Jim Stark, a seventeen-year-old filled with anguish about his role in life. A sensitive but misunderstood young man, Stark muses that he wants "just one day when I wasn't all confused . . . [when] I wasn't ashamed of everything . . . [when] I felt I belonged some place." After making only three films, Dean died in a car crash, further enhancing his mystique among young people. *The Wild One* (1954), which starred Marlon Brando as Johnny Strabler, also popularized youthful angst. Strabler, the leather-outfitted leader of a motorcycle gang, rides into a small town, hoping to shake it up. When asked by a local resident, "What are you rebelling against?" Strabler coolly replies, "Whaddya got?" Real gangs did exist on the streets of New York and other major cities. Composed of working-class members from various ethnic and racial backgrounds, these gangs were highly organized, controlled their neighborhood turfs, and engaged in "rumbles" (fights) with intruders. These battles came to Broadway with the production of *West Side Story* (1957), which pitted a white gang against a Puerto Rican gang in a musical version of *Romeo and Juliet*; its popularity later spawned a Hollywood film.

Hollywood generally did not portray women as rebels; rather they appeared as mothers, understanding girlfriends, and dutiful wives. If they sought a career, like many of the women played by actor Doris Day, they pursued it only as long as necessary to meet the right man. Yet the film industry did offer a more tantalizing woman, a sexual being who displayed her attributes, albeit in decorous fashion, to seduce and outwit men. Marilyn Monroe played such a woman in *The Seven Year Itch* (1955), as did Elizabeth Taylor in *Cat on a Hot Tin Roof* (1958), revealing that women also had a powerful libido, though in the end they became domesticated or paid a terrible price.

The Influence of Teenage Culture

In 1941 *Popular Science* magazine coined the term *teenager*, and by the middle of the next decade members of this age group viewed themselves not as prospective adults but as a distinct group with its own identity, patterns of behavior, and tastes in music and fashion. Postwar prosperity provided teenagers with money to support their own choices and styles. In 1956 teenage boys were estimated to have a weekly income from family allowances or part-time jobs of $8.96 a week, up from $2.41 in 1944. Four years later, *Seventeen* magazine surveyed teenage girls and reported that they earned $9.53 a week. In 1959 *Life* magazine found that teenagers had $10 billion at their disposal, "a billion more than the total sales of GM [General Motors]."

 Online Document Project **Teenagers in Postwar America**
bedfordstmartins.com/hewittlawsonvalue

Teenagers owned 10 million record players, more than 1 million TV sets, 13 million cameras, and what *Life* called "a fantastic array of garish and often expensive baubles and amusements." They spent 16 percent of their disposable income on entertainment, particularly the purchase of rock 'n' roll records. The comic book industry also attracted a huge audience among teenagers by selling inexpensive, illustrated, brief, and easy-to-read pulp fiction geared toward romance and action adventure.

Public high schools reinforced teenage identity. Following World War II, high school attendance grew. In 1930, 50 percent of working-class children attended high school; thirty years later, the figure had jumped to 90 percent. Also, from 1940 to 1960, the percentage of black youths attending high school doubled. For the first time, white middle-class teenagers saw the fashions and heard the language of working-class youths close-up and both emulated and feared what they encountered. Their parents told them to avoid young people who smoked cigarettes, dressed in blue jeans, wore leather jackets, and used expressions like "man" and "cat" to address each other, and to keep away from young women who wore tight skirts and sweaters. Nobody wanted to run afoul of such students in school bathrooms or on the playgrounds, but their clothes, hairdos, and swagger appealed to high school teenagers, many of whom incorporated them into their own behavior.

More than anything else, rock 'n' roll music set teenagers apart from their elders. The pop singers of the 1940s and early 1950s—such as Frank Sinatra, Perry Como, Rosemary Clooney, and Patti Page, who had appealed to both adolescents and parents—lost much of their teenage audience after 1954 to rock 'n' roll, with its heavy downbeat and lyrics evoking teenage passion and sexuality. Black artists such as Chuck Berry, Little Richard, and Antoine "Fats" Domino and groups such as the Platters, the Channels, the Chords, the Chantels, and the Teenagers popularized the sound of classic, up-tempo rock and its soaring, harmonic variation known as doo-wop.

Although blacks pioneered the sound, the music entered the mainstream largely through white artists who added rural flavor to rhythm and blues. Elvis Presley was not the first white man to sing rock 'n' roll, but he became the most famous. Born in Tupelo, Mississippi, and living in Memphis, Tennessee, Elvis adapted the fashion and sensuality of the black performers he encountered to his own style. Elvis's snarling singing and wild pelvic gyrations excited young people, both black and white, while upsetting their parents. In an era when matters of sex remained private or were not discussed at all and when African Americans were still treated as second-class citizens, a white man singing "black" music and shaking his body to the frenetic tempo of the music caused alarm. When Elvis sang on the popular *Ed Sullivan Show* in 1956, cameras were allowed to show him only from the waist up to uphold standards of decency. Four years later while Elvis was in the army, Congress targeted rock 'n' roll through its investigation of payola and the notorious deejay Alan Freed.

The Lives of Women

Throughout the 1950s, movies, women's magazines, mainstream newspapers, and medical and psychological experts informed women that only by embracing domesticity could they achieve personal fulfillment. Dr. Benjamin Spock's best-selling *Common Sense Book of Baby and Child Care* (1946) advised mothers that their children would reach their full potential only if wives stayed at home and watched over their offspring. In another best seller, *Modern Women: The Lost Sex* (1947), Ferdinand Lundberg and Marynia Farnham called the independent woman "a contradiction in terms." A 1951 study of corporate executives found that most businessmen viewed the ideal wife as one who devoted herself to her husband's career. College newspapers described female undergraduates as distraught if they did not become engaged by their senior year. Certainly many women professed to find such lives fulfilling, but not all women were so content. Many experienced anxiety and depression, and, in their despair, some turned to alcohol and tranquilizers. Far from satisfied, these women suffered from what the social critic Betty Friedan would later call "a problem that has no name," a malady that derived not from any personal failing but from the unrewarding roles women were expected to play.

Not all women fit the stereotype, however. Although most married women with families did not work during the 1950s, the proportion of working wives doubled from 15 percent in 1940 to 30 percent in 1960, with the greatest increase coming in women over the age of thirty-five. Married women were more likely to work if they were African American or came from working-class immigrant families. Moreover, women's magazines did not offer readers a unified message of domesticity. Alongside articles about and advertisements directed at stay-at-home mothers, these periodicals profiled career women who served in politics, such as Maine senator Margaret Chase Smith, the African American educator Mary McLeod Bethune, and sports figures such as the golf and tennis great Babe (Mildred) Didrikson Zaharias. At the same time, working women played significant roles in labor unions, where they formulated plans to reduce disparities between men's and women's income and to provide a wage for housewives, recognizing the unpaid work they did at home in maintaining the family. Many other women joined women's clubs and organizations like the Young Women's Christian Association (YWCA), where they engaged in charitable and public service activities. Some participated in political organizations, such as Henry Wallace's Progressive Party, and peace groups, such as the Women's International League for Peace and Freedom, to campaign against the violence caused by racial discrimination at home and Cold War rivalries abroad.

Religious Revival

Along with marriage and the family, religion experienced a revival in the postwar United States. The arms race between the United States and the Soviet Union heightened the dangers of international conflict for ordinary citizens, and the social and economic changes that accompanied the Cold War intensified personal anxiety. Churchgoing underscored the contrast between the United States, a nation of religious worship, and the "godless" communism of the Soviet Union. The link between religion and Americanism prompted Congress in 1954 to add "under God" to the pledge of allegiance and to make "In God We Trust" the national motto. Even President Dwight D. Eisenhower joined a church for the first time in his life.

Americans turned in great numbers to religious worship. Between 1940 and 1950, church and synagogue membership rose by 78 percent, and more than 95 percent of the population professed a belief in God. Yet religious affiliation appeared to reflect a greater emphasis on togetherness than on specific doctrinal beliefs. Theologian Will Herberg wrote that this religious revival constituted "religiousness without religion." It offered a way to overcome isolation and embrace community in an increasingly alienating world. "The people in the suburbs want to feel psychologically secure, adjusted, at home in their environment," Herberg explained. "Being religious and joining a church is . . . a fundamental way of 'adjusting' and 'belonging.'"

Television also helped spread religiosity into millions of homes. The Catholic bishop Fulton J. Sheen spoke to a weekly television audience of ten million and alternated his message of "a life worth living" with attacks on atheistic Communists. The Methodist minister Norman Vincent Peale, also a popular TV figure, combined traditional religious faith with self-help remedies prescribed in his best-selling book *The Power of Positive Thinking* (1952). The Reverend Billy Graham, a preacher from Charlotte, North Carolina, who became the greatest evangelist of his era, was a traveling minister who blended his call for Americans to accept Jesus Christ into their hearts with fervent anticommunism.

Graham used his considerable oratorical powers to preach at huge outdoor crusades in baseball parks and large arenas, which were broadcast on television. Religious Americans derived a variety of meanings from their religious experiences, but they embraced Americanism as their national religion. A good American, one magazine proclaimed, could not be "un-religious."

Beats and Other Nonconformists

As many Americans migrated to the suburbs, spent money on leisure and entertainment, and cultivated religion, a small group of young poets, writers, intellectuals, musicians, and artists attacked mainstream politics and culture. Known as **beats** (derived from "beaten down"), they attacked white middle-class society with stinging critiques of what they considered the sterility and conformity of American life. In 1956 Allen Ginsberg began his epic poem *Howl* with the line "I saw the best minds of my generation destroyed by madness, starving hysterical naked." In his novel *On the Road* (1957), Jack Kerouac, a friend of Ginsberg's, praised the individual who pursued authentic experiences and mind-expanding consciousness through drugs, sexual experimentation, and living in the moment. At a time when whiteness was not just a skin color but a standard of beauty and virtue, the beats and authors such as Norman Mailer looked to African Americans as cultural icons, embracing jazz music and the spontaneity and coolness they attributed to inner-city blacks. The beats formed their own artistic enclaves in New York City's Greenwich Village and San Francisco's North Beach and Haight-Ashbury districts. Wherever they lived, they provided a lifestyle that a younger generation of political and cultural rebels would adopt in the 1960s.

The beat writers frequently read their poems and prose to the rhythms of jazz, reflecting both their affinity with African American culture and the innovative explorations taking place in music. From the big bands of the 1930s and 1940s, postwar jazz musicians formed smaller trios, quartets, and quintets and experimented with sounds more suitable for serious listening than for dancing. The bebop rhythms of trumpeter Dizzy Gillespie and alto saxophonist Charlie Parker revolutionized jazz and reflected the accompanying black rebellion against white supremacy. Trumpeter Miles Davis and tenor saxophonist John Coltrane experimented with more complex and textured forms of this music and took it to new heights. Like rock 'n' roll musicians, these black artists broke down racial barriers as their music crossed over to white audiences.

Homosexuals also attempted to live nonconformist sexual lifestyles, albeit clandestinely. According to studies by researcher Dr. Alfred Kinsey of Indiana University, homosexuals made up approximately 10 percent of the adult population. During World War II, gay men and lesbians had the opportunity to meet other homosexuals in the military and in venues that attracted gay soldiers. Though homosexuality remained taboo and public displays of it were a crime, politically radical gay men organized against homophobia after the war. In 1951 they formed the Mattachine Society in Los Angeles, which then spread to the East Coast. In 1954 a group of lesbians founded the Daughters of Bilitis in San Francisco. Because of police harassment, most homosexuals refused to reveal their sexual orientation, which made sense practically but reduced their ability to counter antihomosexual discrimination.

Alfred Kinsey also shattered myths about conformity in the private conduct of heterosexuals. In *Sexual Behavior in the Human Female* (1953), Kinsey revealed that

Recording *1958 Miles*   Jazz underwent great changes in the 1950s and became a soundtrack to the literary rebels of the beat generation. This 1958 recording session features four of the greatest jazz musicians of their era. From left to right, John Coltrane plays the tenor saxophone, Nat "Cannonball" Adderley the alto saxophone, Miles Davis (the leader) the trumpet, and Bill Evans the piano.   Rue des Archives/The Granger Collection, New York

many women rejected the double standard that allowed men, but not women, to lose their virginity before marriage. Fifty percent of the women he interviewed had had sexual intercourse before marriage, and 25 percent had had extramarital affairs. Kinsey's findings were supported by other data. Between 1940 and 1960, the frequency of out-of-wedlock births among all women rose from 7.1 newborns to 21.6 newborns per thousand women of childbearing age. The tawdry relations that Grace Metalious depicted in *Peyton Place* merely reflected what many Americans practiced but did not talk about. The brewing sexual revolution further went public in 1953 with the publication of *Playboy* magazine, founded by Hugh Hefner. Through a combination of serious articles and photographs of nude women, the magazine provided its chiefly male readers with a guide to pursuing sexual pleasure and a sophisticated lifestyle.

Like Metalious, many writers denounced the conformity and shallowness they found in suburban America. Novelist Sloan Wilson wrote about the alienating experience of suburban life in *The Man in the Gray Flannel Suit* (1955). "Without talking about it much," Wilson wrote of his fictional suburban couple, "they both began to think of the house as a trap, and they no more enjoyed refurbishing it than a prisoner would delight in shining up the bars of his cell." In J. D. Salinger's novel *Catcher in the Rye* (1951), the young protagonist, Holden Caulfield, mocks the phoniness of the adult world while ending up in a mental institution. Journalists and scholars joined in the criticism. Such critics often overstated the conformity that characterized the suburbs by minimizing the ethnic, religious, and political diversity of their residents. Yet they tapped into a growing feeling, especially among a new generation of young people, of the dangers of a mass culture based on standardization, compliance, and bureaucratization.

REVIEW & RELATE

• What trends in American popular culture did the television shows and popular music of the 1950s reflect?

• How did artists, writers, and social critics challenge the mainstream politics and culture of the 1950s?

The Civil Rights Movement

African Americans wanted what most other Americans desired after World War II—the opportunity to make a decent living, buy a nice home, raise a healthy family, and get the best education for their children. Yet blacks faced much greater obstacles than did whites in obtaining these dreams, particularly in the South, where African Americans attended separate and unequal schools, faced discrimination if not outright exclusion from public accommodations, were not permitted to vote, and encountered vigilante violence. Determined to eliminate these injustices, black Americans mounted a campaign against white supremacy in the decades after World War II. African Americans increasingly viewed their struggle as part of an international freedom movement of black people in Africa and other nonwhites in the Middle East and Asia to obtain their freedom from Western colonial rulers.

School Segregation and the Supreme Court

Led by the National Association for the Advancement of Colored People (NAACP), African Americans launched a prolonged assault on school segregation. Pursuing a strategy designed in the 1930s by its chief lawyer, Charles Hamilton Houston, the association filed lawsuits against states that excluded blacks from publicly funded law schools and universities. After victories in Missouri and Maryland, Houston's successor, Thurgood Marshall, convinced the Supreme Court in 1950 to disband the separate law school that Texas had set up for blacks and to allow them to attend the University of Texas Law School. At the same time, the Court also eliminated separate facilities for black students at the University of Oklahoma graduate school and ruled against segregation in interstate rail transportation.

Before African Americans could attend college, they had to obtain a first-class education in public schools. All-black schools typically lacked the resources provided to white schools. The NAACP understood that without federal intervention southern officials would never live up to the "separate but equal doctrine" asserted in *Plessy v. Ferguson* (1896). African Americans sought to integrate schools not because they wanted their children to sit next to white students in classrooms and adopt their ways, but because they believed that integration offered the best and quickest way to secure quality education.

In fighting segregated education, the NAACP drew on grassroots organizing techniques in southern communities. In the late 1940s, black families in towns throughout the South joined together to pressure white officials to provide buses to transport children to school, to raise the salaries of black teachers, and to furnish classrooms with critical supplies. Led by black activists in South Carolina and Virginia, the NAACP filed lawsuits seeking to overturn *Plessy*. The association added cases from Delaware and Kansas, where a measure of segregation persisted, as well as from Washington, D.C., where the federal government was responsible for maintaining segregated schools in the nation's capital.

On May 17, 1954, in **Brown v. Board of Education of Topeka, Kansas**, the Supreme Court overturned *Plessy*. In a unanimous decision read by Chief Justice Earl Warren, the Court concluded that "in the field of public education the doctrine of 'separate but equal' has no place. Separate educational facilities are inherently unequal." This ruling undercut the legal foundation for segregation and officially placed the law on the side of those who sought racial equality. Nevertheless, the ruling did not end the controversy; in fact, it led to more battles over segregation. In 1955 the Court issued a follow-up opinion calling for implementation with "all deliberate speed." But it left enforcement of *Brown* to federal district courts in the South, which consisted mainly of white southerners who espoused segregationist views. As a result, southern officials emphasized "deliberate" rather than "speed" and slowed the implementation of the *Brown* decision.

The Montgomery Bus Boycott

The *Brown* decision encouraged African Americans to protest against other forms of racial discrimination. In 1955 in Montgomery, Alabama, the Women's Political Council, a group of middle-class and professional black women, petitioned the city commission to improve bus service for black passengers. Among other things, they wanted blacks not to have to give up their seats to white passengers who boarded the bus after black passengers did. Their requests went unheeded until December 1, 1955, when Rosa Parks, a black seamstress and an NAACP activist, refused to give up her seat to a white man. Parks's arrest rallied civic, labor, and religious groups around her and sparked a bus boycott that involved nearly the entire black community. Instead of riding buses, black commuters walked to work or joined car pools. One elderly woman reportedly declined a ride and insisted on walking, explaining, "My feet are tired, but my soul is rested." White officials refused to capitulate and fought back by arresting leaders of the Montgomery Improvement Association, the organization that coordinated the protest. Other whites hurled insults at blacks and engaged in violence. After more than a year of conflict, the Supreme Court ruled in favor of the complete desegregation of Montgomery's buses.

Out of this landmark struggle, Martin Luther King Jr. emerged as the civil rights movement's most charismatic leader. The son of a prominent Atlanta minister, King had graduated from the historically black Morehouse College and received a doctorate in theology from Boston University. Twenty-six years old at the time of Parks's arrest, King was a recent arrival in Montgomery and the pastor of the prestigious Dexter Avenue Baptist Church. He did not seek to lead the boycott, but instead he had it thrust upon him. In Dr. King, Montgomery's blacks had found a man whose personal courage and power of oratory could inspire nearly all segments of the African American community. Though King was familiar with the nonviolent methods of the Indian revolutionary Mohandas Gandhi and the civil disobedience of the nineteenth-century writer Henry David Thoreau, he drew his inspiration and commitment to these principles mainly from the black church and secular leaders such as A. Philip Randolph and Bayard Rustin. King understood how to convey the goals of the civil rights movement to sympathetic white Americans, but his vision and passion grew out of black communities. At the outset of the Montgomery bus boycott, King noted proudly the achievement of African Americans: "When the history books are written in future generations, the historians will have to pause and say 'There lived a great people—a Black people—who injected new meaning and dignity into the veins of civilization.'"

The Montgomery bus boycott made King a national civil rights leader, but it did not guarantee him further success. In 1957 King and a like-minded group of southern black ministers formed the **Southern Christian Leadership Conference (SCLC)** to spread nonviolent protest throughout the region, but except in a few cities, such as Tallahassee, Florida, bus boycott spinoffs did not take hold.

White Resistance to Desegregation

Segregationists responded forcefully to halt black efforts to eliminate Jim Crow. In 1956, 101 southern congressmen issued a manifesto declaring the 1954 *Brown* opinion "a clear abuse of judicial power" and pledging to resist its implementation through "lawful means." Other southerners went beyond the law, as events in Little Rock, Arkansas, showed. In 1957 a federal court approved a plan submitted by the Little Rock School Board to integrate Central High School. However, the governor of Arkansas, Orval Faubus, obstructed the court ruling by sending the state National Guard to keep out nine black students chosen to attend Central High. Faced with blatant state resistance to federal authority, President Eisenhower, a lukewarm supporter of school desegregation, placed the National Guard under federal control and sent in the 101st Airborne Division to restore order after a mob blocked the students from entering the school. The black students, who became known as the **Little Rock Nine**, attended classes for the year under the protection of the National Guard but still encountered considerable harassment from white pupils inside the school. In June 1958, one of the black students, Ernest Green, graduated, but Governor Faubus and the state legislature shut down the school for a year until the Supreme Court in 1959 ordered its reopening. In defiance of the high court, other school districts, such as Prince Edward County, Virginia, chose to close their public schools rather than desegregate. By the end of the decade, public schools in the South remained mostly segregated, and only a token number of black students in a handful of states attended school with whites.

The white South used other forms of violence and intimidation to preserve segregation. The third incarnation of the Ku Klux Klan (KKK) appeared after World War II to strike back at growing African American challenges to white supremacy. This terrorist group threatened, injured, and killed those blacks they considered "uppity." Following the *Brown* decision, segregationists also formed the White Citizens' Council (WCC). The WCC drew members largely from businessmen and professionals. Rather than condoning murder and violent confrontation, the WCC generally relied on intimidating blacks by threatening to fire them from jobs or denying them credit from banks. In

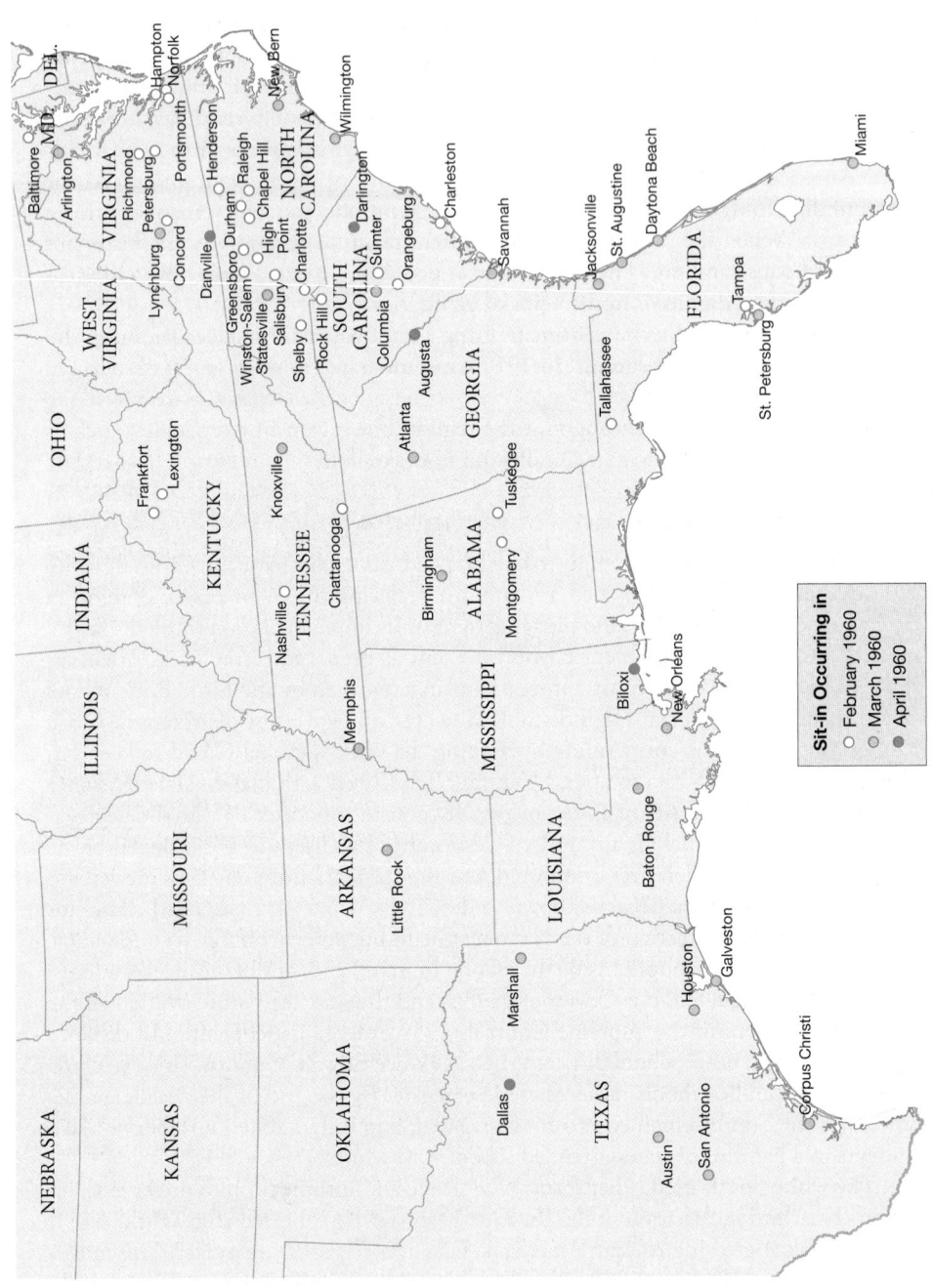

Sit-in Occurring in
○ February 1960
◔ March 1960
● April 1960

< MAP 25.1
Lunch Counter Sit-Ins, February–April 1960   After starting slowly in the late 1950s, lunch
counter sit-ins exploded in 1960 following a sit-in by college students in Greensboro, North
Carolina. Within three months, sit-ins erupted in fifty-eight cities across the South. The
participation of high school and college students revitalized the civil rights movement and led to
the formation of the Student Nonviolent Coordinating Committee in April 1960.

Alabama, WCC members launched a campaign against radio stations playing the kind
of rock 'n' roll music that Alan Freed popularized in New York City because they believed
that it fostered close interracial contact. Reflecting much of the sentiment in the region,
an Alabama segregationist called rock 'n' roll "the basic, heavy beat music of Negroes,"
which, if left unchecked, would result in the downfall of "the entire moral structure . . .
the white man has built."

The WCC and the KKK created a racial climate in the deep South that encouraged
whites to believe they could get away with murder to defend white supremacy. In the
summer of 1955, Emmett Till, a fourteen-year-old from Chicago who was visiting his
great-uncle in Mississippi, was killed because he allegedly flirted with a white woman
in a country store. Although the two accused killers were brought to trial, an all-white
jury quickly acquitted them. Elsewhere in Mississippi that same year, an NAACP official,
George Lee, was killed for organizing voter registration drives; the crime was never
prosecuted.

The Sit-Ins

With boycotts petering out and white violence rising, African Americans, especially high
school and college students, developed new techniques to confront discrimination,
including sit-ins, in which protesters seat themselves in a strategic spot and refuse to
move until their demands are met or they are forcibly evicted. In 1958 the NAACP
organized a sit-in against segregated lunch counters in Oklahoma City, and in 1959 the
Congress of Racial Equality (CORE) did the same in Miami. However, mass demonstrations did not really get off the ground until February 1960, when four students at
North Carolina A&T University in Greensboro waged sit-ins at the whites-only lunch
counters in Woolworth and Kress department stores. Their protests sparked similar
efforts throughout the Southeast, expanding to more than two hundred cities within a
year (Map 25.1).

A few months after the sit-ins began, a number of their participants formed the
Student Nonviolent Coordinating Committee (SNCC). The organization's young
members sought not only to challenge racial segregation in the South but also to create interracial communities based on economic equality and political democracy. This
generation of black and white sit-in veterans came of age in the 1950s at a time when
the democratic rhetoric of America's role in the Cold War and the Supreme Court's
decision in the *Brown* case raised their expectations for racial equality. Yet these young
activists often saw their hopes dashed by numerous examples of southern segregationist resistance, including the 1955 murder of Emmett Till, an incident that both horrified and helped mobilize them to fight for black equality. "Emmett Till was only
three years older than me and I identified with him," recalled Cleveland Sellers, a

SNCC staff member from South Carolina. "I tried to put myself in his place and imagine what he was thinking when those white men took him from his home that night. . . . I couldn't get over the fact that the men who were accused of killing him had not been punished at all."

REVIEW & RELATE

• What strategies did African Americans adopt in the 1950s to fight segregation and discrimination?

• How and why did white southerners resist efforts to end segregation?

The Eisenhower Era

Despite the existence of civil rights protesters, rock 'n' roll upstarts, intellectual dissenters, and sexual revolutionaries, the 1950s seemed to many a tranquil, even dull period—one commentator referred to it as "the bland leading the bland." This impression owes a great deal to the leadership of President Dwight D. Eisenhower. Serving two terms from 1953 to 1961, Eisenhower, or "Ike" as he was affectionately called, convinced the majority of Americans that their country was in good hands regardless of political turbulence at home and heated international conflicts abroad.

Modern Republicanism

President Eisenhower, a World War II hero, radiated strength and trust, qualities the American people found very attractive as they rebuilt their lives and established families in the 1950s. Nominated by the Republican Party in 1952, the sixty-two-year-old Eisenhower shrewdly balanced his ticket by choosing as his running mate California senator Richard M. Nixon, a man twenty-three years his junior who had risen in politics by attacking Democrats as soft on communism. On election day, Eisenhower coasted to victory, winning 55 percent of the popular vote and 83 percent of the electoral vote. Despite Eisenhower's personal popularity, the Republicans managed to win only slim majorities in the Senate and the House. Within two years, they had lost even this slight edge in both houses, and the Democrats regained control of Congress.

With a limited electoral mandate, the president adopted what one of his speechwriters called **Modern Republicanism**, which tried to fit the traditional Republican Party ideals of individualism and fiscal restraint within the broad framework of Franklin Roosevelt's New Deal. With Democrats in control of Congress after 1954, Republicans agreed to raise Social Security benefits and to include coverage for some ten million additional workers. Congress and the president retained another New Deal mainstay, the minimum wage, and increased it from 75 cents to $1 an hour. Departing from traditional Republican criticism of big government, the Eisenhower administration added the Department of Health, Education, and Welfare to the cabinet in 1953. The president justified expanding the federal government in domestic matters as part of fighting the Cold War. In 1958 Eisenhower signed into law the National Defense Education Act, which provided aid for instruction in science, math, and foreign languages and graduate fellowships and loans for college students. He portrayed the new law as a way to catch up with the Soviets, who the previous year had successfully launched the first artificial satellite, called *Sputnik*, into outer space.

Eisenhower and the Cold War

In foreign affairs, Eisenhower perpetuated Truman's containment doctrine while at the same time espousing the contradictory principle of "rolling back" communism in Eastern Europe. However, when Hungarians rose up against their Soviet-backed regime in 1956, the U.S. government did little more than offering encouragement and allowing approximately eighty thousand Hungarian refugees to enter the country. Rather than pushing back communism, the Eisenhower administration expanded the doctrine of containment around the world by entering into treaties to establish regional defense pacts. In 1954 the Southeast Asia Treaty Organization was formed to protect Australia, France, Great Britain, New Zealand, Pakistan, the Philippines, and Thailand from Communist assault. In 1959 the Central Treaty Organization brought Iraq, Iran, Turkey, and once again Pakistan within the U.S. defense perimeter.

Eisenhower's commitment to fiscal discipline had a profound effect on his foreign policy. The president worried that the alliance among government, defense contractors, and research universities—which he dubbed "the military-industrial complex"—would bankrupt the economy and undermine individual freedom. With this in mind, he implemented the **New Look** strategy, which placed a higher priority on building a nuclear arsenal and delivery system than on the more expensive task of maintaining and deploying armed forces on the ground throughout the world. Nuclear missiles launched from the air by U.S. air force bombers or fired from submarines would give the United States, as Secretary of Defense Charles Wilson asserted, "a bigger bang for the buck." With the nation now armed with nuclear weapons, the Eisenhower administration threatened "massive retaliation" in the event of Communist aggression.

The New Look may have saved money and slowed the rate of defense spending, but it had serious flaws. First, it placed a premium on "brinksmanship," taking Communist enemies to the precipice of nuclear destruction, risking the death of millions, and hoping the other side would back down. Second, massive retaliation did not work for small-scale conflicts. For instance, in the event of a confrontation in Berlin, would the United States launch nuclear missiles toward Germany and expose its European allies in West Germany and France to nuclear contamination? Third, the buildup of nuclear warheads provoked an arms race by encouraging the Soviet Union to do the same. Peace depended on the superpowers terrifying each other with the threat of nuclear annihilation—that is, if one country attacked the other, retaliation was guaranteed to result in shared obliteration. This strategy was known as **mutually assured destruction**, and its acronym—**MAD**—summed up its nightmarish qualities. As each nuclear power increased its capacity to destroy the other many times over, the potential for mistakes and errors in judgment increased, threatening a nuclear holocaust that would leave little to rebuild. Fortunately, Eisenhower used the threat of massive retaliation judiciously, mainly against the Chinese rather than the Soviets. In 1953, after the United States threatened to deploy nuclear weapons against China, China agreed to an armistice that ended the fighting in Korea; two years later, similar American threats kept the Chinese from attacking Taiwan, where Jiang Jieshi's Nationalist government ruled in exile.

National security concerns occupied a good deal of the president's time. Fearing that a Soviet nuclear attack could wipe out nearly a third of the population before the United States could retaliate, the Eisenhower administration stepped up civil defense efforts. Schoolchildren took part in "duck and cover" drills, in which teachers shouted

"Take cover" and students hid under their desks. In the meantime, both the United States and the Soviet Union began producing intercontinental ballistic missiles armed with nuclear warheads. They also stepped up aboveground tests of nuclear weapons, which contaminated the atmosphere with dangerous radioactive particles.

Despite doomsday rhetoric of massive retaliation, Eisenhower generally relied more on diplomacy than on military action. Stalin's death in 1953 and his eventual replacement by Nikita Khrushchev in 1955 permitted détente, or a relaxation of tensions, between the two superpowers. In July 1955, Eisenhower and Khrushchev, together with British and French leaders, gathered in Geneva to discuss arms control. It was the first meeting of an American president and a Soviet head of state since the end of World War II. Nothing concrete came out of this summit, but Eisenhower and Khrushchev did ease tensions between the two nations. In a speech to Communist officials two years later, Khrushchev denounced the excesses of Stalin's totalitarian rule and reinforced hopes for a new era of peaceful coexistence between the Cold War antagonists. Khrushchev also visited the United States in 1959, yet peaceful coexistence remained precarious. Just as President Eisenhower was about to begin his own tour of the Soviet Union in 1960, the Soviets shot down an American U-2 spy plane flying over their country. Eisenhower canceled his trip, and tensions resumed.

Cold War Interventions

While relations between the Soviet Union and the United States thawed and then cooled during the Eisenhower era, the Cold War advanced into new regions. In a manner first

The Kitchen Debate   Soviet premier Nikita Khrushchev, second on the left, talks with Vice President Richard Nixon, second on the right, at a U.S. exhibit in Moscow on July 24, 1959. The two leaders argued about the relative merits of capitalism and communism, while looking at an American kitchen that displayed the latest washing machine. Khrushchev, pointing his finger at Nixon, appears unimpressed. Time & Life Pictures/Getty Images

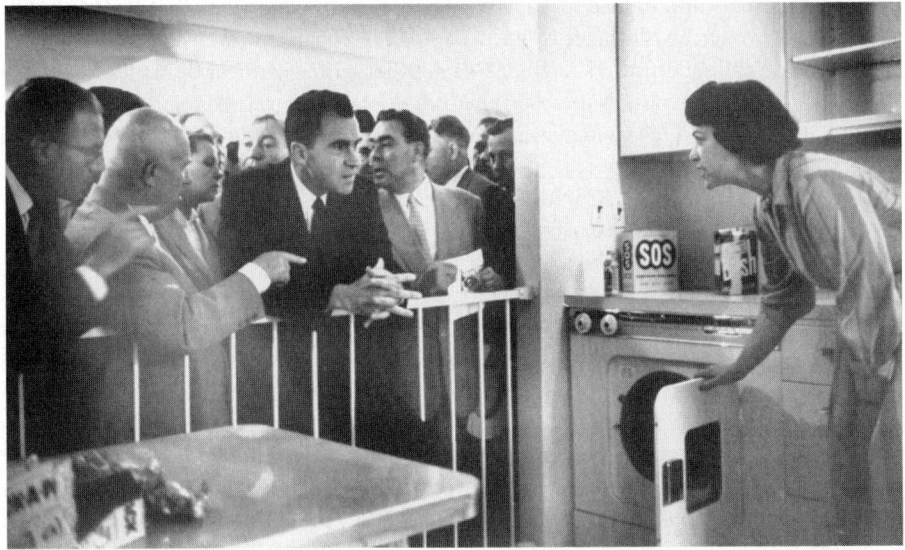

suggested in NSC-68 (see chapter 24), the Eisenhower administration deployed the CIA to help topple governments considered pro-Communist as well as to promote U.S. economic interests. For example, after Iranian prime minister Mohammed Mossadegh nationalized foreign oil corporations in 1953, the CIA engineered a successful coup that ousted his government and installed the pro-American Shah Mohammad Reza Pahlavi in his place. Mossadegh was not a Communist, but by overthrowing him American oil companies obtained 40 percent of Iran's oil revenue.

In 1954 fruit and sugar replaced oil as the catalyst for U.S. intervention. The elected socialist regime of Jacobo Arbenz Guzmán in Guatemala had seized 225,000 acres of land held by the United Fruit Company, a powerful American company in which Secretary of State John Foster Dulles and his brother, CIA Director Allen Dulles, held stock. According to the Dulles brothers, the land's seizure by the Guatemalan government posed a threat to the nearby Panama Canal. Eisenhower was unwilling to send in troops, but he allowed the CIA to hatch a plot that resulted in a coup d'état, or government overthrow, that installed a right-wing military regime in Guatemala, which safeguarded both the Panama Canal and the United Fruit Company.

The success of the CIA's covert efforts in Guatemala prompted the Eisenhower administration to plan a similar action in Cuba, ninety miles off the coast of Florida. In 1959 the Cold War inched closer to the United States as Fidel Castro led an uprising and came to power in Cuba after overthrowing the American-backed dictator Fulgencio Batista. A Cuban nationalist in the tradition of José Martí, Castro sought to regain full control over his country's economic resources, including those owned by U.S. corporations. He appropriated $1 billion worth of American property and signed a trade agreement with the Soviet Union. To consolidate his political rule, Castro jailed opponents and installed a Communist regime, forcing a large number of his adversaries to immigrate to Miami. In 1960 President Eisenhower authorized the CIA to design a clandestine operation to overthrow the Castro government, but he left office before the invasion could occur.

The efforts of Iranian, Guatemalan, and Cuban leaders to seize control of their countries' resources were but a few examples of the surge of nationalism that swept through former European colonies in the 1950s. Following World War II, revolutionary nationalists in the Middle East, Africa, and Southeast Asia toppled colonial governments and wielded the power of their newly liberated regimes to take charge of their own development. The United States and the Soviet Union each tried to gain influence over these emerging nations. Many newly independent countries tried to practice neutrality in foreign affairs, accepting aid from both of the Cold War protagonists. Nonetheless, they were often drawn into East-West conflicts.

Such was the case in Egypt, which achieved independence from Great Britain in 1952. Two years later under General Gamal Abdel Nasser, the country sought to modernize its economy by building the hydroelectric Aswan Dam on the Nile River. Nasser welcomed financial backing from the United States and the Soviet Union, but the Eisenhower administration refused to contribute so long as the Egyptians accepted Soviet assistance. In 1956 Nasser, falling short of funds, sent troops to take over the Suez Canal, the waterway run by Great Britain and through which the bulk of Western Europe's oil was shipped. He intended to pay for the dam by collecting tolls from canal users. In retaliation, Britain and France, the two European powers most affected by the seizure, invaded Egypt on October 29, 1956. Locked in a struggle with Egypt and other Arab nations since its creation in 1948, Israel joined in the attack. The invading forces—all

U.S. allies—had not warned the Eisenhower administration of their plans. Coming at the same time as the Soviet crackdown against the Hungarian revolution, the British-French-Israeli assault placed the United States in the difficult position of condemning the Soviets for intervening in Hungary while its anti-Communist partners waged war in Suez. Instead, Eisenhower cooperated with the United Nations to negotiate a cease-fire and engineer a pullout of the invading forces in Egypt. Ultimately, the Soviets proved the winners in this Cold War skirmish. The Suez invasion revived memories of European imperialism and fueled anti-Western sentiments and pan-Arab nationalism (a sense of unity among Arabs across national boundaries), which worked to the Soviets' advantage. Nasser obtained financial assistance from the Soviets and built the Aswan Dam.

The Eisenhower administration soon moved to counter growing Soviet power in the region. In 1957, fearing increasing Communist influence in the oil-rich Middle East, Congress approved the **Eisenhower Doctrine**, which gave the president a free hand to use U.S. military forces in the Middle East "against overt armed aggression from any nation controlled by International Communism," as he remarked to Congress. In effect, the Eisenhower administration was more concerned with protecting access to oil fields from hostile Arab nationalist leaders than with any Communist incursion. In 1958, when an anti-American, non-Communist regime came to power in Iraq, the president sent fourteen thousand marines to neighboring Lebanon to prevent a similar outcome there. A military realist, Eisenhower made his choice for intervention carefully—the invasion required limited force and allowed a speedy exit without any fatalities.

Just before Eisenhower left office in January 1961, his administration intervened in a civil war in the newly independent Congo. This former colony of Belgium held valuable mineral resources, which Belgium and the United States still coveted. After the Congo's first prime minister, Patrice Lumumba, stated his intentions to remain neutral in the Cold War, President Eisenhower and CIA Director Allen Dulles declared him unreliable in the conflict with the Soviet Union. With the support of Belgian military troops and encouragement from the United States, the resource-rich province of Katanga seceded from the Congo in 1960. After the Congolese military, under the leadership of Joseph Mobuto, overthrew Lumumba's government, the CIA launched an operation that culminated in the execution of Lumumba on January 17, 1961. Several years later, Mobuto became president of the country, changed its name to Zaire, and allied with the West. The Eisenhower administration had extended the Cold War to central Africa in a covert, but nonetheless bloody, manner.

Early U.S. Intervention in Vietnam

Eisenhower's intervention in Vietnam would have profound, long-term consequences for the United States. By the 1950s, Vietnamese revolutionaries (the Vietminh) had been fighting for independence from the French for decades. They were led by Ho Chi Minh, a revolutionary who had studied Communist doctrine in the Soviet Union but was not controlled by the Soviets. In fact, he modeled his 1945 Vietnamese Declaration of Independence on that of the United States. Ho's overriding objective was the liberation of Vietnam along socialist principles. In 1954 the Vietminh defeated the French at the Battle of Dien Bien Phu. With the backing of the United States, the Soviet Union, and China, both sides agreed to divide Vietnam at the seventeenth parallel and hold free elections to unite the country in 1956.

President Eisenhower believed that if Vietnam fell to the Communists, the rest of Southeast Asia and Japan would "go over very quickly" like "a row of dominoes," threatening American strategic power in the Far East as well as free access to Asian markets. Convinced that Ho Chi Minh and his followers would win free elections, the Eisenhower administration installed the anti-French, anti-Communist Ngo Dinh Diem to lead South Vietnam and then supported his regime's refusal to hold national elections in 1956. The anti-Communist interests of the United States had trumped its democratic promises. With the country now permanently divided, Eisenhower funneled economic aid to Diem to undertake needed land reforms that would strengthen his government and weaken the appeal of Ho Chi Minh. The president also dispatched CIA agents and military advisers to help the South Vietnamese government set up security forces, train military units, and extend educational opportunities. However, Diem used most of the money to consolidate his power rather than implement reforms, which only widened opposition to his regime from Communists and non-Communists alike. This prompted Ho Chi Minh in 1959 to support the creation in the South of the National Liberation Front, or **Vietcong**, to wage a military insurgency against Diem. By the end of the decade, the Eisenhower administration had created a major diplomatic problem with no clear plan for its resolution.

The Election of 1960

Even after experiencing eight years of dramatic challenges in both foreign and domestic affairs, Eisenhower remained popular. In 1956 voters had returned Eisenhower to the White House with greater support than in 1952. Once again, Eisenhower's personal popularity did not carry over to the Republican Party, as Democrats increased their control over Congress. Eisenhower, however, could not run for a third term, barred by the Twenty-second Amendment (1951), and Vice President Richard M. Nixon ran as the Republican candidate for president in 1960. Unlike Eisenhower, Nixon was not universally liked or respected. His manipulation of the anti-Communist issue and his reputation for unsavory political combat drew the scorn of Democrats, especially liberals. Moreover, Nixon had to fend off charges that Republicans, as embodied in the seventy-year-old Eisenhower, were out-of-date and out of new ideas.

Running as the Democratic candidate for president in 1960, Senator John F. Kennedy of Massachusetts promised to instill renewed "vigor" in the White House and get the country moving again. Yet Kennedy did not differ much from his Republican rival on domestic and foreign policy issues. Kennedy's willingness to employ a rhetoric of high-minded change did not seem to be dampened by the fact that he had not compiled a distinguished or courageous record in the Senate, that his family's fortune had paved the way for his political career, and that he had earned a well-justified reputation in Washington as a playboy and womanizer.

The outcome of the 1960 election turned on several factors. The country was experiencing a slight economic recession, reviving memories in older voters of the Great Depression, which had begun with the Republican Hoover in power. In addition, presidential candidates faced off on television for the first time, participating in four televised debates. As the leading medium for information, TV emphasized visual style and presentation. With Nixon having just recovered from a stay in the hospital and looking haggard, Kennedy in the first debate convinced a majority of television viewers

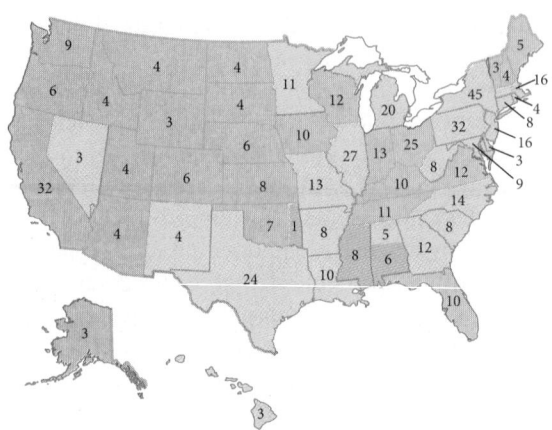

MAP 25.2
The Election of 1960 The 1960 presidential candidates differed little on major policy issues. John F. Kennedy gained the White House by winning back black voters who had supported Eisenhower, gaining crucial support from Catholic voters across the country, and appearing more presidential in the first televised debate in history. Still, his margin of victory was razor thin.

Candidate	Electoral Vote	Popular Vote	Percentage of Popular Vote
John F. Kennedy (Democrat)	303	34,227,096	49.7
Richard M. Nixon (Republican)	219	34,108,546	49.5
Harry F. Byrd (Independent)	15	501,643	0.7

that he possessed the presidential bearing for the job. Nixon performed better in the next three debates, but the damage had been done. Still, Kennedy had to overcome considerable religious prejudice to win the election. No Catholic had ever won the presidency, and the prejudices of Protestants, especially in the South, threatened to divert critical votes from Kennedy's Democratic base. While many southern Democrats did support Nixon, Kennedy balanced out these defections by gaining votes from the nation's Catholics, especially in northern states rich in electoral votes (Map 25.2).

Race also exerted a critical influence. Nixon and Kennedy had similar records on civil rights, and if anything, Nixon's was slightly stronger. However, on October 19, 1960, when Atlanta police arrested Martin Luther King Jr. for participating in a restaurant sit-in, Kennedy sprang to his defense, whereas Nixon kept his distance. Kennedy telephoned the civil rights leader's wife to offer his sympathy and used his influence to get King released from jail. As a result, King's father, a Protestant minister who had intended to vote against the Catholic Kennedy, switched his position and endorsed the Democrat. In addition to the elder King, Kennedy won back for Democrats 7 percent of black voters who had supported Eisenhower in 1956. Kennedy won by a margin of less than 1 percent of the popular vote, underscoring the importance of the African American electorate.

REVIEW & RELATE

• Why did Eisenhower adopt a moderate domestic agenda? What were his most notable accomplishments?

• How did Eisenhower use the CIA and covert actions to protect and expand American influence around the world?

Conclusion: Cold War Politics and Culture

Following the end of World War II, the return of peace and prosperity fostered a baby boom that sent families scrambling for new housing and increasingly away from the cities. Suburbs grew as housing developers such as William Levitt built affordable, mass-produced homes in the suburbs and as the federal government provided new highways that allowed suburban residents to commute to their jobs in the cities. With increased income, consumers purchased the latest models in automobiles as well as newly introduced televisions, reshaping how they spent their leisure time. As the baby boom generation entered their teenage years, their sheer numbers and general affluence helped make them a significant economic and cultural force. They poured their dollars into clothes, music, and other forms of entertainment, which reinforced their identity as teenagers and set them apart from adults.

The increasingly distinct teenage culture owed a great deal to African Americans, who contributed to the development of rock 'n' roll and revolutionized jazz, thereby providing a standard for teenage rebellion and attacks on mainstream values by the beats. Yet African Americans remained most focused on tearing down the legal and institutional foundations of white supremacy. First in the courts and then in the streets, they confronted segregation and disfranchisement in the South. By the end of the 1950s, African Americans had persuaded the Supreme Court to reverse the doctrine of "separate but equal" that buttressed Jim Crow; they also won significant victories in desegregating buses in Montgomery, schools in Little Rock, and lunch counters in Greensboro. Black teenagers reinvigorated the civil rights movement through their boldness and energy, opening the path for even greater racial changes in the coming decade.

In addition to struggles over racial equality, the 1950s witnessed serious tensions at home and overseas. Teenage cultural rebellion; sexual revolution; McCarthyite witch-hunts; a bloody war in Korea; foreign crises in the Middle East, Eastern Europe, and Southeast Asia; clandestine operations in Iran, Guatemala, and the Congo—all of these confronted the citizens of Alan Freed's and Grace Metalious's America. Nevertheless, the popular image of the 1950s as a tranquil and innocent period persists, mainly because of the presence of President Dwight Eisenhower as a symbol for the age. A cheerful, grandfatherly patriarch, Eisenhower in this version of historical memory reflects a kinder and gentler time. The Republican Eisenhower provided moderate leadership that helped the country adjust to the changes it was undergoing. His critics complained that the nation had lost its spirit of adventure, had misplaced its ability to distinguish between community and conformity, had failed to live up to ideals of racial and economic justice, and had relinquished its primary place in the world. Nevertheless, most Americans emerging from decades of depression and war felt satisfied with the new lives they were building. Despite upheavals at home and abroad, they still liked Ike.

When Eisenhower left office in 1961, a new decade began with a Democratic president in charge. Yet the challenges that Eisenhower had faced and the diplomatic, social, and cultural forces that propelled them continued to confront his successors. During the following years, many of the teenagers and young people who had benefited from the peace and prosperity of the 1950s would lead the way in questioning the role of the United States in world affairs and its commitment to democracy, freedom, and equality at home.

Chapter Review

MAKE IT STICK

LearningCurve bedfordstmartins.com/hewittlawsonvalue
After reading the chapter, use LearningCurve to retain what you've read.

IDENTIFY KEY TERMS

Identify and explain the significance of each term below.

Sun Belt (p. 649)

Levittown (p. 649)

National Interstate and Defense Highway
    Act (p. 649)

beats (p. 655)

*Brown v. Board of Education of Topeka,
    Kansas* (p. 658)

Montgomery Improvement Association
    (p. 658)

Southern Christian Leadership Conference
    (SCLC) (p. 659)

Little Rock Nine (p. 659)

Student Nonviolent Coordinating
    Committee (SNCC) (p. 661)

Modern Republicanism (p. 662)

New Look (p. 663)

mutually assured destruction (MAD)
    (p. 664)

Eisenhower Doctrine (p. 666)

Vietcong (p. 667)

REVIEW & RELATE

Answer the focus questions from each section of the chapter.

1. What factors contributed to the economic and population growth of the 1950s?

2. How did economic and demographic trends in the 1950s contribute to the growth of suburbs?

3. What trends in American popular culture did the television shows and popular music of the 1950s reflect?

4. How did artists, writers, and social critics challenge the mainstream politics and culture of the 1950s?

5. What strategies did African Americans adopt in the 1950s to fight segregation and discrimination?

6. How and why did white southerners resist efforts to end segregation?

7. Why did Eisenhower adopt a moderate domestic agenda? What were his most notable accomplishments?

8. How did Eisenhower use the CIA and covert actions to protect and expand American influence around the world?

ONLINE DOCUMENT PROJECTS

◆ **Teenagers in Postwar America**
◆ **The Postwar Suburbs**

After reading the primary sources in these document sets, answer the **Interpret the Evidence** questions to help you analyze each of the documents, and then answer the **Put It in Context** question(s) to help you relate the documents to the topics and themes you read about in the chapter.

bedfordstmartins.com/hewittlawsonvalue

TIMELINE OF EVENTS

1940–1960
- Migration to Sun Belt swells region's population

1945–1960
- U.S. gross national product soars 250 percent; 60 percent of Americans achieve middle-class status; union membership reaches new high

1951–1954
- Alan Freed promotes rock 'n' roll with radio show and concerts

1953
- CIA coup puts Shah Mohammad Reza Pahlavi in power in Iran

1954–1958
- Eisenhower adopts Modern Republicanism and expands domestic programs

1954
- CIA plot results in a military takeover of Guatemala
- *Brown v. Board of Education of Topeka, Kansas* Supreme Court ruling

1955–1956
- Montgomery bus boycott

1955
- Jonas Salk develops polio vaccine
- Emmett Till murdered

1956
- Grace Metalious publishes *Peyton Place*

- National Interstate and Defense Highway Act passed

- U.S. begins supporting anti-Communist government of South Vietnam

1957
- Martin Luther King Jr. and other black ministers form Southern Christian Leadership Council (SCLC)
- Eisenhower uses federal troops to enforce school desegregation in Little Rock, Arkansas
- Soviet Union launches *Sputnik*
- Congress approves Eisenhower Doctrine

1958
- Eisenhower sends U.S. marines into Lebanon

1959
- Fidel Castro takes power in Cuba

1960
- U-2 spy plane shot down over Soviet Union
- Student Nonviolent Coordinating Committee (SNCC) formed

1960–1961
- U.S. intervenes in civil war in Congo

26

☑ LearningCurve
bedfordstmartins.com/hewittlawsonvalue
After reading the chapter, use LearningCurve
to retain what you've read.

The Liberal Consensus and Its Challengers

1960–1973

AMERICAN HISTORIES

How did a Republican politician who advocated the internment of Japanese Americans during World War II end up presiding over the most liberal Supreme Court in U.S. history? As attorney general of California at the outset of World War II, Earl Warren helped convince President Franklin D. Roosevelt to order the relocation of 110,000 Japanese Americans. After the war, as governor, he continued to fight against perceived threats to national security by joining the anti-Communist crusade. In 1953 President Dwight D. Eisenhower appointed Warren to be chief justice of the Supreme Court, a choice that many observers saw as a safe conservative pick by a safe conservative president.

As chief justice, however, Warren defied expectations and instead led the Court in a liberal direction. In 1954 Warren wrote the landmark opinion ordering school desegregation in *Brown v. Board of Education of Topeka, Kansas.* Departing from his own strong anti-Communist record, Warren upheld the rights of political dissenters and extended the boundaries of free speech. The Warren Court did not shrink from controversy, and its rulings expanding the rights of accused criminals, banning prayer in public school classrooms, and upholding birth control as a right of privacy evoked harsh criticism from the police, religious fundamentalists, and conservative politicians.

Unlike Earl Warren, Bayard Rustin worked outside of regular political and social channels to achieve change. Raised by his Quaker grandparents in Pennsylvania, Rustin began his career as an activist for social justice in 1937 when he moved to New York City to work as a youth organizer. He joined the Young Communist League because of its commitment to economic justice, racial equality, and international peace, but the pacifist Rustin quit the organization in 1941 when the party supported U.S. intervention in World War II and retreated on its fight against racial discrimination during the war.

In 1942 Rustin helped found the Congress of Racial Equality (CORE), an interracial organization that pioneered nonviolent, direct-action protests against racial bias. A committed pacifist, Rustin was imprisoned from 1943 to 1946 for declining to perform alternative service after he refused to register for the military draft. Prison strengthened his determination to challenge racial injustice through unconventional means. After his release, he continued to push for racial equality, and in 1947 Rustin helped plan and lead the Journey of Reconciliation, which challenged segregation on interstate buses in the South (see chapter 24). In the 1950s and 1960s, he became an adviser to Martin Luther King Jr. and a major strategist in the civil rights movement in his own right.

Rustin remained active in various causes throughout his life. One of his last efforts was perhaps his most personal: the struggle against antigay prejudice. As a homosexual, Rustin had to conceal his sexual identity at a time when the public and his political allies rejected homosexuals. Rustin often had to work behind the scenes to avoid unfavorable publicity, and even Dr. King on occasion kept his distance from him. In the 1980s, as the gay liberation movement grew more vocal, Rustin spoke out for tolerance and equality until his death in 1987.

THE AMERICAN HISTORIES of Earl Warren and Bayard Rustin demonstrate the complexity of social change. The federal government had the power to encourage social movements by interpreting the Constitution, enacting legislation, and enforcing the

Demonstrators carry American flags on the march from Selma to Montgomery to support voters' rights, 1965.   Robert Abbott Sengstacke/Getty Images

law in a manner that eliminated barriers to racial, sexual, and political equality. Yet federal action likely would not have happened without the pressure applied by activists like Rustin. At the same time, efforts to promote equality and social justice produced a strong reaction from conservatives who feared that their political and social values were under assault. By the end of the 1960s, liberal reformers had achieved many of their objectives, but they had also triggered a stiff challenge from conservative opponents who sought to roll back those gains and pursue their own policies of small government, low taxes, and self-help.

The Politics of Liberalism

In 1960 the liberal agendas of Presidents Franklin Roosevelt and Harry Truman remained unfinished. Hoping to build on the legacy of the New Deal, liberals sought to increase the role of the federal government in the economy, education, and health care. Most liberals supported a staunchly anti-Communist foreign policy, differing with Republicans more over means than over ends. Indeed, when Democrats recaptured the White House in 1960, they seized opportunities in Cuba and Southeast Asia to vigorously challenge the expansion of Soviet influence.

Kennedy's New Frontier

With victory in World War II and the revival of economic prosperity, liberal thinkers regained confidence in capitalism. Many saw the postwar American free-enterprise system as different from the old-style capitalism that had existed before Franklin Roosevelt's New Deal. In their view, this new "reform capitalism," or democratic capitalism, created abundance for all and not just for a few elites. Rather than pushing for the redistribution of wealth, liberals now called on the government to help create conditions conducive to economic growth and increased productivity. In this context, the liberal economist John Kenneth Galbraith argued in *The Affluent Society* (1958) that increased public investments in education, research, and development were the key to American prosperity and progress.

These ideas guided the thinking of Democratic politicians such as Senator John F. Kennedy of Massachusetts. Elected president in 1960, the forty-three-year-old Kennedy brought good looks, charm, a beautiful wife, and young children to the White House— presenting a public image that matched the kind of nuclear family that Americans tuned in to watch on their television sets during the 1950s. Yet this was no ordinary family. The Kennedy family had numerous estates, and the president's father had used his fortune to bankroll his son John's political ambitions, first as a Massachusetts congressman, then as a U.S. senator, and finally as president. As president, John Kennedy pledged a **New Frontier** to battle "tyranny, poverty, disease, and war," but lacking strong majorities in Congress, he contented himself with making small gains on the New Deal foundation established by Franklin Roosevelt. Congress expanded unemployment benefits, increased the minimum wage, extended Social Security benefits, and raised appropriations for public housing, but Kennedy's caution disappointed many liberals.

The Kennedy administration showed greater zeal in fighting the Cold War abroad. The president believed that the same reform capitalism that had worked well in the United States should become a global model, especially in newly developing nations in

Asia, Africa, and the Middle East. Communism, like fascism before it, posed a fundamental threat to American interests and to other countries' ability to emulate the economic miracle of the United States. The faith of liberals in American ingenuity, willpower, technological superiority, and moral righteousness encouraged them to reshape the "free world" in America's image.

President Kennedy's first Cold War battle took place in Cuba. During the 1960 campaign, Kennedy criticized the Eisenhower administration for allowing Fidel Castro to establish a Communist dictatorship in Cuba—despite Kennedy's knowledge of a secret CIA plan, devised by the Eisenhower administration, to topple Castro from power. After becoming president, Kennedy approved the scheme that Eisenhower had already set in motion.

The operation ended disastrously. On April 17, 1961, the invasion force of between 1,400 and 1,500 Cuban exiles, trained by the CIA, landed by boat at the Bay of Pigs on Cuba's southwest coast. Kennedy refused to provide backup military forces for fear of revealing America's role in the attack. After three days of fighting, Castro's troops defeated the insurgents. CIA planners had underestimated Cuban popular support for Castro, falsely believing that the invasion would inspire a national uprising against the Communist regime. The Kennedy administration had blundered its way into a bitter foreign policy defeat.

Two months later, Kennedy met Soviet leader Nikita Khrushchev at a summit meeting in Vienna. At the conference, Khrushchev took advantage of the president's embarrassing defeat in Cuba to press his own demands. The confrontational summit meeting increased tensions between the superpowers. Returning from Vienna, Kennedy persuaded Congress to increase the defense budget, dispatch additional troops to Europe, and bolster civil defense. In August, the Soviets responded by constructing a wall through Berlin, making it more difficult for refugees to flee from East Berlin to West Berlin, but they did not close off U.S. access to West Berlin. After the building of the Berlin Wall, tensions seemed to subside for a time, only to spike again the following year in a confrontation over Cuba that brought the world to the brink of nuclear disaster.

Following the Bay of Pigs disaster, the United States continued its efforts to topple the Castro regime. Such attempts were uniformly unsuccessful, but a wary Castro decided to invite the Soviet Union to install short- and intermediate-range missiles in his country to protect against further U.S. incursion. On October 22, 1962, Kennedy went on national television to inform the American people that Soviet missile sites were under construction in Cuba. The Kennedy administration decided to blockade Cuba to prevent Soviet ships from supplying the deadly missile warheads that would make the missiles fully operational. If this effort failed and Soviet ships defied the blockade, the president would order air strikes on Cuba. Ordinary Americans, particularly those within striking distance of Cuban-based Soviet missiles, nervously contemplated the very real possibility of nuclear destruction.

On the brink of nuclear war, both sides decided to compromise. Khrushchev agreed to remove the missiles, and Kennedy pledged not to invade Cuba and secretly promised to dismantle U.S. missile sites in Turkey that were aimed at the Soviet Union. The outcome did not please everyone. Castro, who still feared U.S. intervention, remained disappointed, as did Soviet hard-line leaders who believed that Khrushchev had displayed weakness. (Two years later, they deposed him.) The rest of the world breathed a sigh of relief, and Kennedy and Khrushchev, having stepped back from the edge of nuclear holocaust, worked to ease tensions further. In 1963 they signed a Partial Nuclear Test Ban Treaty—which prohibited atmospheric but not underground testing—and installed an electronic "hot line" to ensure swift communications between Washington and Moscow.

Containment in Southeast Asia

In addition to Cuba, Kennedy inherited the policy of containing communism in Southeast Asia. He shared his predecessors' belief that the Soviet Union was behind wars of national liberation throughout the third world. Like Eisenhower, Kennedy believed that if Communists toppled one regime in Asia it would produce a "domino effect," with one country after another falling to the Communists. Kennedy, a World War II veteran, also believed that aggressive nations that attacked weaker ones threatened world peace unless they were challenged.

Kennedy's containment efforts ran into difficulty in Vietnam because the United States did not control the situation on the ground. After supporting Ngo Dinh Diem as president of South Vietnam in 1955, the United States poured more than $1 billion into the country to implement land reform and create a stable government capable of withstanding Communist opposition from the Vietcong and North Vietnamese leader Ho Chi Minh's Communist forces in North Vietnam. However, Diem spent the money on building up military and personal security forces to suppress all political opposition. In 1961 Kennedy sent military advisers to help the South Vietnamese fight the Communists, but the situation deteriorated in 1963 when the Catholic Diem prohibited the country's Buddhist majority from holding religious celebrations. In protest, Buddhist monks committed suicide by setting themselves on fire, a grisly display captured on television news programs in the United States. With political opposition mounting against Diem's oppressive regime and the war going poorly, the Kennedy administration endorsed a military coup to replace the Diem government with one more capable of fighting Communists. On November 1, 1963, the coup leaders removed Diem from office, assassinated the deposed president and key members of his regime, and installed a military government.

Diem's death, however, did little to improve the worsening war against the Communists. The Vietcong had more support in the rural countryside than did the South Vietnamese government because the rebels promised land reform and recruited local peasants disturbed by the corruption and ruthlessness of the Diem regime. The Kennedy administration committed itself to supporting Diem's successor, but by late November 1963 Kennedy seemed ambivalent about what to do next. He was torn between sending more American troops and finding a way to negotiate a peace.

This ambivalence was reflected in Kennedy's more general effort to balance his hard-line anti-Communist policies with new outreach efforts to inspire developing nations to follow a democratic path. The Peace Corps program sent thousands of volunteers to teach and advise developing nations, and Kennedy's Alliance for Progress supplied economic aid to emerging democracies in Latin America. In June 1963, Kennedy announced his departure from his earlier militant Cold War stance in a commencement address at American University. Instead of describing a bipolar world of good and evil, Kennedy envisioned a "world safe for diversity. For in the final analysis, our most basic common link is that we all inhabit this small planet. We all breathe the same air. We all cherish our children's future and we are all mortal."

On November 22, 1963, three weeks after the assassination of Diem, Lee Harvey Oswald murdered Kennedy as he rode in an open motorcade in Dallas, Texas. The fatal shots from the assassin's rifle brought the nation to a standstill and prompted an outpouring of public grief not seen since President Roosevelt died in office in 1945. In death, Kennedy achieved immense popularity, and many Americans viewed him as a martyr. Yet Kennedy had left many problems unresolved. His legislative agenda, including civil rights, remained unfulfilled, and at the time of his death there were 16,000 American military advisers in Vietnam.

Johnson Escalates the War in Vietnam

Kennedy's successor, Lyndon B. Johnson, faced a difficult decision about Vietnam. Privately, the new president harbored reservations about fighting in Vietnam, but he was fearful of being considered soft on communism and was concerned that a demonstration of weakness would jeopardize congressional support for his domestic plans. Although President Johnson eventually concluded that more U.S. forces had to be sent to Vietnam, he hesitated to act immediately. Instead, he waited for the right moment to rally Congress and the American public behind an escalation of the war.

That moment came in August 1964. On August 2, North Vietnamese gunboats sixty miles off the North Vietnamese coast in the Gulf of Tonkin attacked an American spy ship. Two days later, another U.S. destroyer reported coming under torpedo attack, but because of stormy weather this second ship was not certain that it had actually been fired on. Neither ship suffered any damage. In fact, when informed of the assaults, the president responded: "For all I know, our navy might have been shooting at whales out there." Despite the considerable uncertainty about what actually happened, Johnson seized the opportunity to prompt Congress to authorize military action. On August 7, with only two dissenting votes, Congress passed the Gulf of Tonkin Resolution, which empowered the president to "repel any armed attacks against the forces of the United States and to prevent further aggression." In effect, Congress provided Johnson with unlimited power to make military decisions regarding Vietnam.

After winning election in 1964, President Johnson stepped up U.S. military action. In March 1965, with North Vietnamese forces flooding into the South, the president initiated Operation Rolling Thunder, a massive bombing campaign over North Vietnam and infiltration routes into the South along the Vietnamese borders with Cambodia and Laos, known as the Ho Chi Minh Trail. For more than three years, American planes dropped a million tons of bombs on North Vietnam, more than the total amount the United States used in World War II. Despite this massive firepower, the operation proved ineffective. A largely agricultural country, North Vietnam did not have the type of industrial targets best suited for air attacks. It stored its vital military resources underground, and the North Vietnamese were able to reconstruct rudimentary bridges and roads to maintain the flow of troops into the South within hours after U.S. bombers had pounded them.

Responding to the need to protect American air bases and the persistent ineffectiveness of the South Vietnamese government and military, Johnson deployed ever-increasing numbers of ground troops to Vietnam. In 1963, when Johnson became president, 16,000 American troops were serving in Vietnam; this number grew to 380,000 in 1966, to 485,000 in 1967, and to 536,000 in 1968, with Johnson hoping that each new infusion would be the last. An estimated 200,000 North Vietnamese reached draft age annually, and Hanoi replenished its troops to counter the U.S. escalation. The U.S. military also deployed napalm bombs, which spewed burning jellied gasoline, and Agent Orange, a chemical defoliant that denuded the Vietnamese countryside and produced long-term adverse health effects for those who came in contact with it, including American soldiers. These attacks added to the resentment of the South Vietnamese peasants living in the countryside and helped the Vietcong gain new recruits.

The United States confronted a challenging guerrilla war in Vietnam. The Vietcong fought at night and blended in during the day as ordinary residents of cities and villages. They did not provide a visible target, and they recruited women and men of all ages, making it difficult for U.S. ground forces to distinguish friend from foe. To meet this challenge, the military, under the direction of General William C. Westmoreland, established "strategic hamlets" to separate the Vietcong from noncombatants. Troops moved residents out of their villages to a new location, set up a defense perimeter around it, and assumed that anyone found outside this zone must be the enemy. Westmoreland then instituted "search and destroy" missions throughout the countryside to defeat the Vietcong. In the end, these policies did little to advance the U.S. military effort and alienated the population they were designed to safeguard.

On the ground, frustration also bred racism, as many American soldiers could not relate to the Vietnamese way of life and dismissed the enemy as "gooks." Lieutenant Philip Caputo later admitted that he could order his men to burn the thatch and bamboo shacks the Vietnamese lived in because to him a "home had brick or frame walls, a window, a lawn, a TV antenna on the roof." This attitude pushed some of the troops over the line between legitimate wartime practices and murder. Frustrated by rising casualties from an enemy they could not see, some American soldiers indiscriminately burned down villages and killed noncombatant civilians. Such disreputable behavior peaked in March 1968 with the My Lai massacre, when an American platoon murdered between 347 and 504 unarmed Vietnamese civilians in the village of My Lai.

On January 31, 1968, the Buddhist New Year of Tet, some 67,000 Communist forces mounted a surprise offensive throughout South Vietnam that targeted major population centers (Map 26.1). For six hours, a suicide squadron of Vietcong surrounded the U.S. Embassy in Saigon. U.S. forces finally repelled the **Tet Offensive**, but the battle proved psychologically costly to the United States. Following the Tet Offensive, the most revered television news anchor of the era, Walter Cronkite of CBS, turned against the war and expressed the doubts of a growing number of viewers when he announced: "To say that we are mired in stalemate seems the only reasonable, yet unsatisfactory conclusion."

Tet marked the beginning of the end of the war's escalation. On March 31, 1968, President Johnson ordered a halt to the bombing campaign and called for peace negotiations. He also stunned the nation by announcing that he would not seek reelection. By the time he left the White House in 1969, peace negotiations had stalled and some 36,000 Americans had died in combat, along with 52,000 South Vietnamese troops.

REVIEW & RELATE

• How did President Kennedy's domestic agenda reflect the liberal political ideology of the early 1960s?

• How and why did the United States escalate its role in the Vietnam War?

Civil Rights

Back home, the most critical issue facing the nation in the early 1960s was the intensification of the civil rights movement. As a candidate, Kennedy had promised vigorous action on civil rights, but as president he did little to follow through on his promises. With southern Democrats occupying key positions in Congress and threatening to block any civil rights proposals, Kennedy hesitated to upset this critical component of his political base. Following Kennedy's death in 1963, President Johnson succeeded in breaking the legislative logjam and signed into law three major pieces of civil rights legislation. He did so under considerable pressure from the civil rights movement.

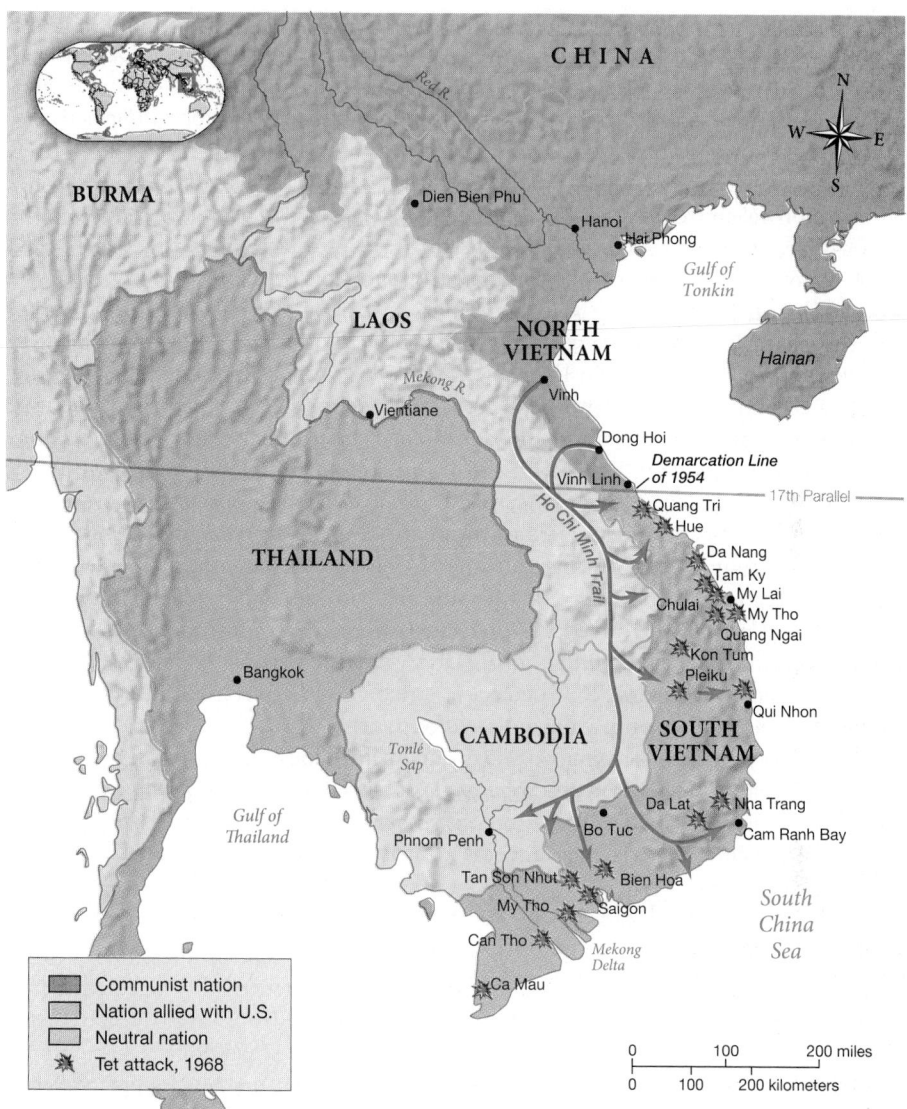

MAP 26.1

The Vietnam War, 1968   The United States wielded vastly more military personnel and weaponry than the Vietcong and North Vietnamese but faced a formidable challenge in fighting a guerrilla war in a foreign country. Massive American bombing failed to defeat the North Vietnamese or stop their troop movements and supply lines along the Ho Chi Minh Trail. The 1968 Tet Offensive demonstrated the shortcomings in the U.S. strategy.

Freedom Rides

The Congress of Racial Equality took the offensive on May 4, 1961. Similar to Bayard Rustin's efforts in the 1940s, CORE mounted racially integrated **Freedom Rides** to test whether facilities in the South, from Virginia to Louisiana, were complying with the 1960 Supreme Court ruling that outlawed segregated bus and train stations serving passengers who were traveling interstate. CORE had alerted the Justice Department and the FBI of its plans, but the riders received no protection when Klan-dominated mobs in Anniston and Birmingham, Alabama, attacked two buses containing activists, seriously wounding several passengers.

After safety concerns forced CORE to forgo the rest of the trip, members of the Student Nonviolent Coordinating Committee (SNCC) rushed to Birmingham to continue the bus rides. The Kennedy administration urged them to reconsider, but Diane Nash, a SNCC founder, explained that although the group realized the peril of resuming the journey, "we can't let them stop us with violence. If we do, the movement is dead." When the replenished busload of riders reached Montgomery on May 20, they were brutally assaulted by a mob. Dr. Martin Luther King Jr., who supported the rides but had not participated in them, subsequently held a rally in a Montgomery church, which became the target of renewed white attacks that threatened the lives of King and the Freedom Riders inside the building. Faced with the prospect of serious bloodshed, the Kennedy administration dispatched federal marshals to the scene and persuaded the governor to call out the Alabama National Guard to ensure the safety of everyone in the church.

The president and his brother, Attorney General Robert Kennedy, worked out a compromise to let the rides continue with minimal violence and publicity; at the same time, Robert Kennedy petitioned the Interstate Commerce Commission (ICC) to issue an order prohibiting segregated transportation facilities, which went into effect in November 1961. Despite the ICC declaration, many southern communities refused to comply. When Freedom Riders encountered opposition in Albany, Georgia, in the fall of 1961, SNCC workers remained in Albany and helped local leaders organize residents of the town against segregation and other forms of racial discrimination. Even with the assistance of Dr. King and the Southern Christian Leadership Conference (SCLC), the Albany movement stalled, as the Kennedy administration refused to provide support.

The Government Responds on Civil Rights

Despite the setback in Albany, the civil rights movement kept up pressure on other fronts. In September 1962, Mississippi governor Ross Barnett tried to thwart the registration of James Meredith as an undergraduate at the University of Mississippi. Barnett's obstruction precipitated a riot on campus, and as Eisenhower had done at Little Rock, President Kennedy dispatched army troops and federalized the Mississippi National Guard to restore order, but not before two bystanders were killed.

The following year, King and the SCLC joined the Reverend Fred Shuttlesworth's freedom movement in Birmingham, Alabama, in its battle against employment discrimination, segregation in public accommodations, and police brutality. With the white supremacist Eugene "Bull" Connor in charge of law enforcement, civil rights protesters, including children ranging in age from six to sixteen, encountered violent resistance, the use of vicious police dogs, and high-powered water hoses. Connor ordered mass arrests, including Dr. King's, prompting the minister to write his famous "Letter from Birmingham Jail," in which he justified the use of nonviolent direct action. Seeking to defuse the crisis and concerned about America's image abroad, President Kennedy sent an emissary in early May 1963 to negotiate a peaceful solution that granted concessions to Birmingham blacks and ended the demonstrations. On Sunday, September 15, 1963, however, a few months after the successful end of the conflict, the Ku Klux Klan dynamited Birmingham's Sixteenth Street Baptist Church, a freedom movement staging ground. The blast killed four young girls attending services.

Meanwhile, after several years of caution, the president finally decided to speak out about the nation's duty to guarantee equal rights regardless of race. On June 11, 1963, shortly after negotiating the Birmingham agreement, Kennedy delivered a nationally televised address. He acknowledged that the country faced a "moral crisis" heightened by the events in Birmingham, and he noted the difficulty of preaching "freedom around the world" while "this is a land of the free except for Negroes." He proposed congressional legislation to end segregation in public accommodations, increase federal power to promote school desegregation, and broaden the right to vote.

Events on the day Kennedy delivered his powerful speech reinforced the need for swift action. Earlier that morning, Alabama governor George C. Wallace, a segregationist, had stood in front of the administration building at the University of Alabama to block the entrance of two black undergraduates. To uphold the federal court decree ordering their admission, Kennedy deployed federal marshals and the Alabama National Guard, and Wallace, having dramatized his point, stepped aside. Victory soon turned into tragedy. Later that evening, the president learned of the killing of Medgar Evers, the head of the NAACP in Mississippi, who was shot in the driveway of his Jackson home by the white supremacist Byron de la Beckwith. (Following two trials, de la Beckwith remained free until 1994, when he was retried and convicted for Evers's murder.)

Nonetheless, Congress was still unwilling to act. To increase pressure on lawmakers, civil rights organizations held a **March on Washington for Jobs and Freedom** on August 28, 1963, carrying out an idea first proposed by A. Philip Randolph in 1941 (see chapter 23). With Randolph as honorary chair, his associate Bayard Rustin directed the proceedings, delivering 250,000 black and white peaceful protesters to a rally in front of the Lincoln Memorial. Two speakers in particular caught the attention of the crowd. John Lewis, the chairman of SNCC, expressed the frustration of militant blacks with both the Kennedy administration and Congress. "The revolution is at hand. . . . We will not wait for the President, nor the Justice Department, nor Congress," Lewis asserted. "But we will take matters into our own hands." In a more conciliatory tone, King delivered a speech expressing his dream for racial and religious brotherhood. Still, King issued a stern warning to "those who hope that the Negro needed to blow off steam and will now be content. . . . There will be neither rest nor tranquility in America until the Negro is granted his citizenship rights. The whirlwinds of revolt will continue to shake the foundations of our nation until the bright day of justice emerges."

Freedom Summer and Voting Rights

Following Kennedy's death and three months after the March on Washington, President Johnson took charge of the pending civil rights legislation. Under Johnson's leadership, a bipartisan coalition turned back a southern filibuster (a tactic that delays or prevents action in Congress) in the Senate and passed the **Civil Rights Act of 1964**. The law prohibited discrimination in public accommodations, increased federal enforcement of school desegregation and the right to vote, and created the Community Relations Service, a federal agency authorized to help resolve racial conflicts. The act also contained a final measure to combat employment discrimination on the basis of race and sex.

Yet even as President Johnson signed the 1964 Civil Rights Act into law on July 2, black freedom forces launched a new offensive to secure the right to vote in the South.

The 1964 act contained a voting rights provision but did little to address the main problems of the discriminatory use of literacy tests and poll taxes and the biased administration of voter registration procedures that kept the majority of southern blacks from voting. Three years earlier, the Kennedy administration had brokered a deal to secure private funding for voter registration drives in the South directed by the Atlanta-based Voter Education Project. Civil rights workers believed that the Justice Department would provide federal protection for voter drives, but the Kennedy and Johnson administrations let them down. Beatings, killings, arson, and arrests became a routine response to voting rights efforts. Although the Justice Department filed lawsuits against recalcitrant voter registrars and police officers, the government refused to send in federal personnel or instruct the FBI to safeguard vulnerable civil rights workers.

To focus national attention on this problem, SNCC, CORE, the NAACP, and the SCLC launched the **Freedom Summer** project in Mississippi. They assigned eight hundred volunteers from around the nation, mainly white college students, to work on voter registration drives and in "freedom schools" to improve education for rural black youngsters stuck in inferior, segregated schools. White supremacists fought back against what they perceived as an enemy invasion. In late June 1964, the Ku Klux Klan, in collusion with local law enforcement officials, killed three civil rights workers. This tragedy brought national attention, and President Johnson pressed the usually uncooperative FBI to find the culprits, which it did. However, civil rights workers continued to encounter white violence and harassment throughout Freedom Summer.

 **Online Document Project   Freedom Summer**
bedfordstmartins.com/hewittlawsonvalue

One outcome of the Freedom Summer project was the creation of the **Mississippi Freedom Democratic Party (MFDP)**. Because the regular all-white state Democratic Party excluded blacks, the civil rights coalition formed an alternative Democratic Party open to everyone. In August 1964, the mostly black MFDP sent a delegation to the Democratic National Convention meeting in Atlantic City, New Jersey, to challenge the seating of the all-white delegation from Mississippi. One of the MFDP delegates, Fannie Lou Hamer, who had lost her job on a Mississippi plantation for her voter registration activities, offered passionate testimony broadcast on television. To avoid a bruising political fight, Johnson hammered out a compromise that gave the MFDP two general at-large seats, imposed a loyalty oath on members of the regular delegation to support the Democratic presidential ticket, and prohibited racial discrimination in the future by any state Democratic Party. Although both sides rejected the compromise, four years later an integrated delegation, which included Hamer, represented Mississippi at the Democratic National Convention in Chicago.

Freedom Summer highlighted the problem of disfranchisement, but it took further demonstrations in Selma, Alabama, to resolve it. After state troopers shot and killed a black voting rights demonstrator in February 1965, Dr. King called for a march from Selma to the capital of Montgomery to petition Governor George Wallace to end the violence and allow blacks to vote. Local law enforcement officials answered their peaceful protests with arrests and beatings. On Sunday, March 7, as black and white marchers left Selma, the sheriff's forces sprayed them with tear gas, beat them, and sent them running for their lives back to town. A few days later, a white clergyman who had joined the protesters was killed on the streets of Selma by a group of white thugs. On March 21, following another failed attempt to march to Montgomery, King led protesters on the fifty-mile hike to the state capital, where they arrived safely four days later. Tragically, after the march, the Ku Klux Klan murdered a white female marcher from Michigan.

Events in Selma prompted President Johnson to take action. On March 15, he addressed a joint session of Congress and told lawmakers and a nationally televised audience that the black "cause must be our cause too. Because it is not just Negroes, but really it is all of us, who must overcome the crippling legacy of bigotry and injustice." In the words of the civil rights movement anthem, Johnson added, "And we shall over-come." On August 6, 1965, the president signed the **Voting Rights Act**, which banned the use of literacy tests for voter registration, authorized a federal lawsuit against the poll tax (which succeeded in 1966), empowered federal officials to register disfranchised voters, and required seven southern states to submit any voting changes to Washington before they went into effect. With strong federal enforcement of the law, by 1968 a majority of African Americans and nearly two-thirds of black Mississippians could vote in the South (Figure 26.1).

FIGURE 26.1

Black Voter Registration in the South, 1947–1976 After World War II, the percentage of black adults registered to vote in the South slowly but steadily increased, largely as a result of grassroots voting drives. Despite the Kennedy administration's support for voter registration drives, a majority of southern blacks remained prohibited from voting in 1964. The passage of the 1965 Voting Rights Act removed barriers such as literacy tests and poll taxes, strengthened the federal government's enforcement powers, and enabled more than 60 percent of southern blacks to vote by the late 1960s.   Source: Data from David Garrow, *Protest at Selma* (New Haven: Yale University Press, 1978), and U.S. Department of Commerce, Bureau of the Census, *Statistical Abstract of the United States*, 1976.

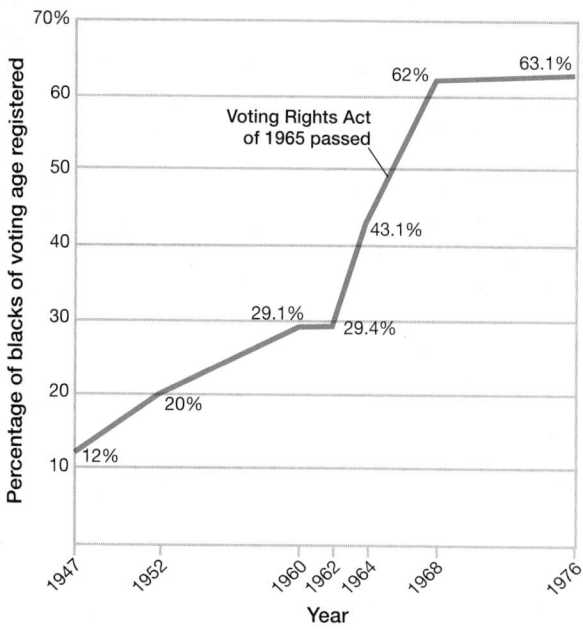

REVIEW & RELATE

• What role did the federal government play in advancing the cause of racial equality in the early 1960s?

• How did civil rights activists pressure state and federal government officials to enact their agenda?

Reforming the Social Order

President Johnson carried liberal reform to its greatest heights, drawing on Kennedy's legacy and his own considerable political skills to win passage of the most important items on the liberal agenda. While Johnson pressed ahead in the legislative arena, Chief Justice Earl Warren's Supreme Court issued rulings that extended social justice to minorities and the economically oppressed and favored those who believed in a firm separation of church and state, in free speech, and in a right to privacy.

The Great Society

In an address at the University of Michigan on May 22, 1964, President Johnson sketched out his dream for the **Great Society**, one that "rests on abundance and liberty for all. It demands an end to poverty and racial justice, to which we are totally committed in our time. But that is just the beginning." According to Johnson, increasing the power and wealth of America was not enough. He saw the Great Society as "a place where the city of man serves not only the needs of the body and the demands of commerce but the desire for beauty and the hunger for community." Besides poverty and race, he outlined three broad areas in need of reform: education, the environment, and cities.

Johnson did not hesitate to approve plans to develop Kennedy's unfinished fight against poverty. Kennedy had persuaded lawmakers to provide federal aid to poor regions such as Appalachia. In designing the Economic Opportunity Act of 1964, Johnson wanted to offer the poor "a hand up, not a handout." His program provided job training, remedial education (later to include the preschool program Head Start), a domestic Peace Corps called Volunteers in Service to America (VISTA), and a Community Action Program that empowered the poor to shape policies affecting their own communities. The antipoverty program helped reduce the proportion of poor people from 20 percent in 1963 to 13 percent five years later, and it helped reduce the rate of black poverty from 40 percent to 20 percent during this same period.

Johnson intended to fight the War on Poverty through the engine of economic growth. In 1962 Congress had passed the Revenue Act, which gave more than $1 billion in tax breaks to businesses. Kennedy had agreed to the targeted tax reduction because he believed it would encourage businesses to plow added savings into new investments and to expand production, thereby creating new jobs. Johnson's tax cut, which applied across the board, stimulated the economy and sent the gross national product soaring from $591 billion in 1963 to $977 billion by the end of the decade. Thus the logic of economic expansion rather than redistribution guided Johnson's War on Poverty.

Despite considerable success, Johnson's program failed to meet liberal expectations. It would have taken an annual appropriation of about $11 billion to lift every needy person above the poverty line. To reduce opposition from cost-minded legislators who wanted to starve his programs if they could not stop them, Johnson asked Congress for just under $1 billion a year. Because the president refused to press lawmakers harder for money, his ability to fight the War on Poverty was severely limited.

Whatever the limitations, Johnson campaigned on his antipoverty and civil rights record in his bid to recapture the White House in 1964. His Republican opponent, Senator Barry M. Goldwater of Arizona, personified the conservative right wing of the Republican Party and rejected the Modern Republicanism identified with President Eisenhower (see chapter 25). The Arizona senator condemned big government, supported states' rights, and accused liberals of not waging the Cold War forcefully enough. His aggressive conservatism appealed to his grassroots base in small-town America, especially in southern California, the Southwest, and the South. His tough rhetoric, however, scared off moderate Republicans, resulting in a landslide for Johnson on election day, as well as considerable Democratic majorities in Congress.

Flush with victory, Johnson moved quickly and achieved impressive results. To cite only a few examples, the Eighty-ninth Congress (1965–1967) provided federal aid to public schools; subsidized health care for the elderly and the poor by creating Medicare and Medicaid; expanded voting rights for African Americans in the South; authorized funds to cities for housing, jobs, education, mass transportation, crime prevention, and recreation; raised the minimum wage; created national endowments for the fine arts and humanities; and adopted regulations to preserve clean air and water supplies. The 1965 Immigration Act repealed discriminatory national origins quotas established in 1924, resulting in a shift of immigration from Europe to Asia and Central and South America (Table 26.1).

The Warren Court

The Warren Court reflected this high tide of liberalism. The Court affirmed the constitutionality of the Voting Rights Act and struck down the poll tax as a voting requirement in 1966. A year later, the justices overturned state laws prohibiting interracial marriages. And in 1968, fourteen years after the *Brown* school desegregation decision, they ruled that school districts in the South could no longer maintain racially exclusive schools and must desegregate immediately. In a series of cases, the Warren Court ensured fairer legislative representation for blacks and whites by removing the disproportionate power that rural districts had held over urban districts.

The Supreme Court's most controversial rulings dealt with the criminal justice system, religion, and private sexual practices, all of which involved liberal interpretations of the individual freedoms guaranteed by the Bill of Rights. Strengthening the rights of criminal defendants, the justices ruled in *Gideon v. Wainwright* (1963) that states had to provide indigents accused of felonies with an attorney, and in *Miranda v. Arizona* (1966) they ordered the police to advise suspects of their constitutional rights.

The Court also moved into new, controversial territory concerning school prayer, contraception, and pornography. In 1962 the Court outlawed a nondenominational Christian prayer recited in New York State schools as a violation of the separation of church and state guaranteed by the First Amendment. Three years later, in *Griswold v. Connecticut*, the justices struck down a state law that banned the sale of contraceptives

TABLE 26.1 • **Major Great Society Measures, 1964–1968**

Year	Legislation or Order	Purpose
1964	Civil Rights Act	Prohibited discrimination in public accommodations, education, and employment
	Economic Opportunity Act	Established War on Poverty agencies: Head Start, VISTA, Job Corps, and Community Action Program
1965	Elementary and Secondary Education Act	Federal funding for elementary and secondary schools
	Medical Care Act	Provided Medicare health insurance for citizens 65 years and older and Medicaid health benefits for the poor
	Voting Rights Act	Banned literacy tests for voting, authorized federal registrars to be sent into seven southern states, and monitored voting changes in these states
	Executive Order 11246	Required employers to take affirmative action to promote equal opportunity and remedy the effects of past discrimination
	Immigration and Nationality Act	Abolished quotas on immigration that reduced immigration from non-Western and southern and eastern European nations
	Water Quality Act	Established and enforced federal water quality standards
	Air Quality Act	Established air pollution standards for motor vehicles
	National Arts and Humanities Act	Established National Endowment of the Humanities and National Endowment of the Arts to support the work of scholars, writers, artists, and musicians
1966	Model Cities Act	Approved funding for the rehabilitation of inner cities
1967	Executive Order 11375	Expanded affirmative action regulations to include women
1968	Civil Rights Act	Outlawed discrimination in housing

because such laws, they contended, infringed on an individual's right to privacy. In a 1966 case reversing Massachusetts's ban of an erotic novel, the Supreme Court ruled that states could not prohibit what they deemed pornographic material unless it was "utterly without redeeming social value," a standard that opened the door for the dissemination of sexually explicit books, magazines, and films. These verdicts unleashed a firestorm of criticism, especially from religious groups that accused the Warren Court of undermining traditional values of faith and decency.

REVIEW & RELATE

• What problems and challenges did Johnson's Great Society legislation target?

• In what ways did the Warren Court's rulings advance the liberal agenda?

Challenges to the Liberal Center

Even at its peak in the 1960s, liberalism faced major challenges from both the left and the right. A generation of young activists, mainly in colleges and universities, became impatient with what they saw as the slow pace of social progress and were increasingly disturbed by the escalation of the Vietnam War. At the same time, the right contended that liberals had instituted reforms that diminished individual initiative and benefited racial minorities at the expense of the white middle class. They disparaged liberals for not winning the Vietnam War and depicted the left as unpatriotic and out of step with mainstream American values. By 1969 liberalism and the left were in retreat, and Richard M. Nixon, a political conservative, had captured the White House.

Movements on the Left

The civil rights movement had inspired many young people to activism. Combining ideals of freedom, equality, and community with direct-action protest, civil rights activists offered a model for those seeking to address a variety of problems, including the Cold War threat of nuclear devastation, the loss of individual autonomy in a corporate society, racism, poverty, sexism, and the poisoning of the environment. The formation of SNCC in 1960 illuminated the possibilities for personal and social transformation and offered a movement culture founded on democracy.

Tom Hayden helped apply the ideals of SNCC to predominantly white college campuses. After spending the summer of 1961 registering voters in Mississippi and Georgia, the University of Michigan graduate student returned to campus eager to recruit like-minded students who questioned America's commitment to democracy. "Beyond lunch counter demonstrations," Hayden wrote, "there are more serious evils which must be ripped out by any means: exploitation, socially destructive capital, evil political and legal structure, and myopic liberalism which is anti-revolutionary."

Hayden became an influential leader of the **Students for a Democratic Society (SDS)**, which advocated the formation of a "New Left." They considered the "Old Left," which revolved around the Communist Party, as autocratic and no longer relevant. In its **Port Huron Statement** (1962), SDS condemned mainstream liberal politics, Cold War foreign policy, racism, and research-oriented universities that cared little for their undergraduates. It called for the adoption of "participatory democracy," which would return power to the people. SDS argued that the age of the military-industrial complex, with its mega-universities and giant corporations, had created a new educated class of alienated white-collar workers and college students perfectly suited to lead the revolution.

The New Left never consisted of one central organization such as SDS; after all, many protesters challenged the very idea of centralized authority. In fact, SDS did not initiate the New Left's most dramatic, early protest. In 1964 the University of California at Berkeley banned political activities just outside the main campus entrance in response to CORE protests against racial bias in local hiring. When CORE defied the prohibition, campus police arrested its leader, prompting a massive student uprising. The university's prohibition also spurred students to form the **Free Speech Movement (FSM)**, which held rallies in front of the administration building, culminating in a nonviolent, civil rights–style sit-in to assert their right to participate in such activities. When California governor Edmund "Pat" Brown dispatched a large force of state and county police to evict the demonstrators, students and faculty joined together in protest and forced the university administration to yield to FSM's demands for amnesty and reform. By the end of the decade, hundreds of demonstrations had erupted on campuses throughout the nation, culminating in 1968 in a bloody confrontation at Columbia University between students and New York City police. Unlike protests in the South aimed at reactionary white supremacists, campus revolts targeted liberals, dismissing them as obstacles to genuine social change.

The Vietnam War accelerated student radicalism, and college campuses provided a strategic setting for antiwar activities. Like most Americans in the mid-1960s, undergraduates had only a dim awareness of U.S. activity in Vietnam. Yet all college men were eligible for the draft once they graduated and lost their student deferment. As more troops were sent to Vietnam, student concern intensified.

Protests escalated in 1966 as President Johnson authorized an additional 250,000-troop buildup in Vietnam. This mobilization required higher draft calls, which began to affect more college men. With induction into the military a looming possibility, student protesters engaged in a variety of activities. Some burned draft cards; disrupted attempts by outside firms, such as the CIA and Dow Chemical Company (which made napalm), to recruit on campus; or campaigned against the presence on campus of Reserve Officers' Training Corps (ROTC), which prepared future military leaders. Others resisted the draft by fleeing to Canada, and still others engaged in various forms of civil disobedience.

Draft Card   In 1963 Steven F. Lawson reached the age of eighteen and registered with his draft board, but as a college undergraduate he received a student deferment (II-S). With draft calls climbing due to the escalation of the Vietnam War, Lawson like many others was reclassified to I-A status—"available for military service." When a draft lottery was introduced in 1969, he drew a high number and was not drafted.   Courtesy of Steven F. Lawson

Most college students, however, were not activists—between 1965 and 1968, only 20 percent of college students attended demonstrations. Nevertheless, the activist minority received wide media attention and helped raise awareness about the difficulty of waging the Vietnam War abroad and maintaining domestic tranquillity at home.

By the end of 1967, as the number of troops in Vietnam approached half a million, protests increased. Antiwar sentiment had spread to faculty, artists, writers, business people, and elected officials. Earlier that year in April, Martin Luther King Jr. delivered a powerful antiwar address at Riverside Church in New York City. "The world now demands," King declared, ". . . that we admit that we have been wrong from the beginning of our adventure in Vietnam, that we have been detrimental to the life of the Vietnamese people." In 1968 SDS split into factions, with the most prominent of them, the **Weathermen**, going underground and adopting violent tactics.

The New Left's challenge to liberal politics attracted many students, and the **counterculture**'s rejection of conventional middle-class values of work, sexual restraint, and faith in reason captivated even more. Cultural rebels emphasized living in the present, immediate gratification, authenticity of feelings, and reaching a higher consciousness through mind-altering drugs like marijuana and LSD. These youth rebels, popularly called "hippies," mocked their elders in the slogan "Don't trust anyone over thirty." Despite differences in approach, both the New Left and the counterculture expressed concerns about modern technology, bureaucratization, and the possibility of nuclear annihilation and sought new means of creating political, social, and personal liberation.

Rock 'n' roll became the soundtrack of the counterculture. In 1964 Bob Dylan's song "The Times They Are A-Changin'" became an anthem for youth rebellion, just as his "Blowin' in the Wind" did for the civil rights movement. In 1964 the Beatles, a British quartet influenced by 1950s black and white rock 'n' rollers, came to the United States and revolutionized popular music. Originally singing tuneful compositions of teenage love and angst, the Beatles embraced the counterculture and began writing songs about alienation and politics, flavoring them with the drug-inspired sounds of psychedelic music. The Beatles launched a "British invasion," which also brought the Rolling Stones, who offered a harder-edged and raunchier sound than did the Beatles. Although most of the songs that reached the top ten on the record charts did not undermine traditional values, the music of groups like the Beatles, the Rolling Stones, the Who, the Grateful Dead, Jefferson Airplane, and the Doors spread counterculture messages of youth rebellion. At the same time, young black and white rebels embraced "soul music," black dance music popularized through the African American–owned Motown Records in Detroit and the white-owned Stax Records in Memphis.

The counterculture viewed the elimination of sexual restrictions as essential for transforming personal and social behavior. The 1960s generation did not invent sexual freedom, but it did a great deal to shatter time-honored moral codes of monogamy, fidelity, and moderation. Promiscuity—casual sex, group sex, extramarital affairs, public nudity—and open-throated vulgarity tested public tolerance. Yet within limits, the popular culture reflected these changes. The Broadway production of the musical *Hair* showed frontal nudity, the movie industry adopted ratings of "X" and "R" that made films with nudity and profane language available to a wider audience, and new television comedy shows featured sketches including risqué content and double entendres. With a nod from the Warren Court's easing definitions of pornography, counterculture writers assaulted the boundaries of "good taste."

With sexual conduct in flux, society had difficulty maintaining the double standard of behavior that privileged men over women. The counterculture gave many women a chance to pursue and enjoy sexual pleasure that had long been denied to them. The availability of birth control pills for women, introduced in 1960, made much of this sexual freedom possible. Although sexual liberation still carried more risks for women than for men, increased openness in discussing sexuality allowed many women to gain greater control over their bodies and their relationships.

Women's Liberation

Struggles in the 1960s for racial equality, peace, economic justice, and cultural and sexual freedom helped revive the fight for women's emancipation. Despite passage of the Nineteenth Amendment in 1920, which gave women the right to vote (see chapter 19), women did not have equal access to employment and education or control over reproduction. Nor did they have sufficient political power to remove the remaining obstacles to full equality. By 1960 nearly 40 percent of all women held jobs—representing one-third of the labor force—and women made up 35 percent of college enrollments. Subsequently, the social movements of the 1960s—civil rights, the New Left, and the counterculture—included large numbers of women and provided them with experience, connections, principles, and grievances that would lead women to create their own movement for liberation.

The federal government played a significant role in addressing gender discrimination. In 1961 President Kennedy appointed the **Commission on the Status of Women**. The commission's report, *American Women*, issued in 1963, reaffirmed the primary role of women in raising the family but cataloged the inequities women faced in the workplace. In 1963 Congress passed the Equal Pay Act, which required employers to give men and women equal pay for equal work. The following year, the 1964 Civil Rights Act opened up further opportunities when it prohibited sexual bias in employment and created the Equal Employment Opportunity Commission (EEOC). However, women remained divided over the need for the Equal Rights Amendment (ERA), first proposed in 1923 by suffragist Alice Paul. The Commission on the Status of Women refused to endorse it largely because labor union women believed that adopting the ERA would eliminate laws that specifically protected women workers with respect to hours, wages, and safety conditions.

In 1963 Betty Friedan published a landmark work in the history of the women's rights movement, *The Feminine Mystique*, a book that questioned society's prescribed gender roles. In *The Feminine Mystique*, she described the isolation and alienation experienced by her female friends and associates, raising the consciousness of many women, particularly college graduates and professionals. However, not all women saw themselves reflected in Friedan's book. Many working-class women from African American and other minority families had not had the opportunity to attend college and had to work to help support their families, and younger women had not yet experienced the burdens of domestic isolation.

Nevertheless, in October 1966, Betty Friedan and like-minded women formed the **National Organization for Women (NOW)**. With Friedan as president, NOW dedicated itself to moving society toward "true equality for all women in America, and toward a fully equal partnership of the sexes." NOW also called on the EEOC to enforce women's employment rights more vigorously and favored passage of the ERA, maternity leave rights in employment, the establishment of child care centers, and reproductive rights. Although NOW advocated job training programs and assistance for impoverished women, it attracted a mainly middle-class white membership. Some blacks were among its charter members, but most African American women chose to concentrate on first eliminating racial barriers that affected black women and men alike. Some union women also continued to oppose the ERA, and antiabortion advocates wanted to steer clear of NOW's support for reproductive rights. Despite these concerns, between 1966 and 1971 NOW's membership increased dramatically from 1,000 to 15,000.

Supporters of women's equality drew lessons from the black freedom struggle. SNCC empowered women staff through community-organizing projects, but even within the civil rights movement women had not always been treated equally, often being assigned clerical duties. Women came up against even greater discrimination in the antiwar movement. Men held a higher status in such groups because women were not eligible for the draft. Ironically, men's claims of moral advantage justified many of them in seeking sexual favors. "Girls say yes to guys who say no," quipped draft-resisting men who sought to put women in their traditional sexual place.

As a result of these experiences, radical women formed their own, mainly local organizations. They created "consciousness-raising" groups that allowed them to share their experiences of oppression in the household, the workplace, the university, and movement organizations. These women's liberationists went beyond NOW's emphasis on legal equality and attacked male domination, or patriarchy, as the primary source of women's subordination. They criticized the nuclear family and cultural values that glorified women as the object of male sexual desires, and they protested creatively against discrimination. In 1968 radical feminists picketed the popular Miss America contest in Atlantic City, New Jersey, the epitome of male conceptions of female beauty, and set up a "Freedom Trash Can" into which they threw undergarments and cosmetics. Radical groups such as the Redstockings condemned all men as oppressors and formed separate female collectives to affirm their identities as women.

Online Document Project   **Women's Liberation**
bedfordstmartins.com/hewittlawsonvalue

In 1973 feminists won a major battle in the Supreme Court over a woman's right to control reproduction. In *Roe v. Wade*, the high court ruled that states could not prevent a woman from obtaining an abortion in the first three months of pregnancy but could impose some limits in the next two trimesters. In furthering the constitutional right of privacy for women, the justices classified abortion as a private medical issue between a patient and her doctor. This decision marked a victory for a woman's right to choose to terminate her pregnancy, but it also stirred up a fierce reaction from women and men who considered abortion to be the murder of an unborn child. Although the basic principle of the right to an abortion has remained intact, legal and cultural battles have raged to the present day.

Power to the People

In addition to stimulating feminist consciousness, the civil rights movement emboldened other oppressed groups to emancipate themselves. African Americans led the way in influencing the liberationist struggles of Latinos, Indians, and gay men and women.

Malcolm X shaped the direction that many African Americans would take in seeking independence and power. Born Malcolm Little, he had engaged in a life of crime, which landed him in prison. Inside jail, he converted to the Nation of Islam, a religious sect based partly on Muslim teachings and partly on the belief that white people were devils (not a doctrine associated with orthodox Islam). After his release from jail, Malcolm rejected his "slave name" and substituted the letter *X* to symbolize his unknown African forebears. A charismatic leader, Minister Malcolm helped convert thousands of disciples in black ghettos by denouncing whites and encouraging blacks to embrace their African cultural heritage and beauty as a people. Favoring self-defense over nonviolence, he criticized civil rights leaders for failing to protect their women, their children, and themselves. After 1963, Malcolm X broke away from the Nation of Islam, visited the Middle East and Africa and accepted the teachings of traditional Islam, moderated his rhetoric against all whites as devils, but remained committed to black self-determination. He had already influenced the growing number of disillusioned young black activists when, in 1965, members of the Nation of Islam murdered him, apparently in revenge for challenging the organization.

Black militants, echoing Malcolm X's ideas, further challenged the liberal consensus on race. They renounced King's and Rustin's ideas, rejecting their principles of integration and nonviolence in favor of black power and self-defense. Instead of welcoming whites within their organizations, black radicals believed that African Americans had to assert their independence from white America. In 1966 SNCC decided to expel whites and create an all-black organization. That same year, Stokely Carmichael, SNCC's chairman, proclaimed the rallying cry of "black power" as the central goal of the freedom struggle, linking the cause of African American freedom to revolutionary conflicts in Cuba, Africa, and Vietnam.

Black power seemed menacing to most whites. Its emergence in the midst of riots in black ghettos, which erupted across the nation starting in the mid-1960s, underscored the concern. Few white Americans understood the horrific conditions that led to riots in Harlem and Rochester, New York, in 1964; in Los Angeles in 1965; and in Cleveland, Chicago, Detroit, Newark, and Tampa in the following two years. Black northerners still faced problems of high unemployment, dilapidated housing, and police mistreatment, which civil rights legislation had done nothing to correct. While whites perceived the ghetto uprisings solely as an exercise in criminal behavior, many blacks viewed the violence as an expression of political discontent—as rebellions, not riots. The Kerner Commission, appointed by President Johnson to assess urban disorders and chaired by Governor Otto Kerner of Illinois, concluded in 1968 that white racism remained at the heart of the problem: "Our nation is moving toward two societies, one black, one white—separate and unequal."

New groups emerged to take up the cause of black power. In 1966 Huey P. Newton and Bobby Seale, two black college students in Oakland, California, formed the **Black Panther Party**. Like Malcolm X and Stokely Carmichael, the Panthers linked their cause to revolutionary movements around the world. Dressed in black leather, sporting black berets, and carrying guns, the Panthers appealed mainly to black men. They did not, however, rely on armed confrontation and bravado alone. The Panthers established day care centers and health facilities, which gained the admiration of many in their communities. Much of this good work was overshadowed by violent confrontations with the police, which led to the deaths of Panthers in shootouts and the imprisonment of key party officials. By the early 1970s, local and federal government crackdowns on the Black Panthers had destabilized the organization and reduced its influence.

Black militants were not the only African Americans to clash with the government. After 1965, King increasingly criticized the Johnson administration for waging war in Vietnam and failing to fight the War on Poverty more vigorously at home. In 1968 he prepared to mount a massive Poor People's March on Washington when he was shot and killed by James Earl Ray in Memphis, where he was supporting demonstrations for striking sanitation workers. The death of King furthered black disillusionment. In the wake of his murder, riots again erupted in hundreds of cities throughout the country. Little noticed amid the fiery turbulence, President Johnson signed into law the 1968 Fair Housing Act, the final piece of civil rights legislation of his term.

The African American freedom movement inspired Latinos struggling for equality and advancement. During the 1960s, the size of the Spanish-speaking population in the United States tripled from three million to nine million. Hispanic Americans were a diverse group who hailed from many countries and backgrounds. In the 1950s, Cesar Chavez had emerged as the leader of oppressed Mexican farmworkers in California. In seeking the right to organize a union and gain higher wages and better working conditions, Chavez shared King's nonviolent principles. In 1962 Chavez formed the National Farm Workers Association, and in 1965 the union called a strike against California grape growers, one that attracted national support and lasted five years before reaching a successful settlement.

Younger Mexican Americans, especially those in cities such as Los Angeles and other western *barrios* (ghettos), supported Chavez's economic goals but challenged older political leaders who sought cultural assimilation. Borrowing from the Black Panthers, Mexican Americans formed the Brown Berets, a self-defense organization. As a sign of their increasing militancy and independence, in 1969 some 1,500 activists gathered in Denver and declared themselves *Chicanos*, a term that expressed their cultural pride and identity, instead of Mexican Americans. Chicanos created a new political party, La Raza Unida (The United Race), to promote their interests, and the party and its allies sponsored demonstrations to fight for jobs, bilingual education, and the creation of Chicano studies programs in colleges. Chicano and other Spanish-language communities also took advantage of the protections of the Voting Rights Act, which, in 1975, was amended to include sections of the country—from New York to California to Florida and Texas—where Hispanic literacy in English and voter registration were low.

American Indians also joined the upsurge of activism and ethnic nationalism. By 1970 some 800,000 people identified themselves as American Indians, many of whom lived in poverty on reservations. They suffered from inadequate housing, high alcoholism rates, low life expectancy, staggering unemployment, and lack of education. Conscious of their heritage before the arrival of white people, determined to halt their continued deterioration, and seeking to assert "red" pride, they established the American Indian Movement (AIM) in 1968. The following year, AIM protesters occupied the abandoned prison island of Alcatraz in San Francisco Bay, where they remained until 1971. In 1972 AIM occupied the headquarters of the Federal Bureau of Indian Affairs in Washington, D.C., where protesters presented twenty demands, ranging from reparations for treaty violations to abolition of the bureau. AIM demonstrators also seized the village of Wounded Knee, South Dakota, the scene of the 1890 massacre of the Sioux residents by the U.S. army (see chapter 15), to dramatize the impoverished

Native American Power   Drawing on the civil rights movement, this group of Native Americans occupied the former prison at Alcatraz Island on November 25, 1969. Among their demands, they offered to buy the island for $24 in beads and cloth—a reference to the purchase of Manhattan Island in 1626—and turn it into an Indian educational and cultural center.   AP Photo

living conditions on the reservation. They held on for more than seventy days with eleven hostages until a shootout with the FBI ended the confrontation, killing one protester and wounding another.

The results of the red power movement proved mixed. Demonstrations focused media attention on the plight of American Indians but did little to halt their downward spiral. Nevertheless, courts became more sensitive to Indian claims and protected mineral and fishing rights on reservations. Still, in the early 1970s the average annual income of American Indian families hovered around $1,500.

Unlike African Americans, Chicanos, and American Indians, homosexuals were not distinguished by the color of their skin. Estimated at 10 percent of the population, gays and lesbians remained invisible to the rest of society. Homosexuals were a target of repression during the Cold War, and the government treated them harshly and considered their sexual identity a threat to the American way of life. In the 1950s, gay men and women created their own political and cultural organizations and frequented bars and taverns outside mainstream commercial culture, but most lesbians and gay men like Bayard Rustin hid their identities. It was not until 1969 that they took a giant step toward asserting their collective grievances in a very visible fashion. Police regularly cracked down on the Stonewall Tavern in New York City's Greenwich Village, but gay patrons battled back on June 27 in a riot that the *Village Voice* called "a kind of liberation, as the gay brigade emerged from the bars, back rooms, and bedrooms of the

Village and became street people." In the manner of black power and the New Left, homosexuals organized the Gay Liberation Front, voiced pride in being gay, and demanded equality of opportunity regardless of sexual orientation.

As with other oppressed groups, gays achieved victories slowly and unevenly. In the decades following the 1960s, homosexuals faced discrimination in employment, could not marry or receive domestic benefits, and were subject to violence for public displays of affection.

The Revival of Conservatism

These diverse social movements did a great deal to change the political and cultural landscapes of the United States, but they did not go unchallenged. Many mainstream Americans worried about black militancy, opposed liberalism, and were even more dismayed by the radical offshoots they spawned. Generally overshadowed by more colorful protests for progressive causes, conservatives soon attracted support from many Americans who did not see change as progress. Many believed that the political leadership of the nation did not speak for them about what constituted a great society.

Conservatism had suffered a severe political blow with the ascendancy of Franklin Roosevelt's New Deal liberalism. Yet as conservatives lost political influence, they joined together to keep alive and publicize their beliefs. The brand of conservatism that emerged in the 1960s united libertarian support for a laissez-faire political economy and opposition to social welfare policies with moralistic concerns for defeating communism and defending religious devotion, moral decency, and family values. Unlike earlier conservatives, the new generation believed that the United States had to escalate the struggle against the evil of godless communism anywhere it posed a threat in the world, but they opposed internationalism as represented in the United Nations.

Conservative religious activists who built grassroots organizations to combat liberalism joined forces with political and intellectual conservatives such as William F. Buckley, the founder of the *National Review*, an influential journal of conservative ideas. The Reverend Billy Joe Hargis's Christian Crusade and Dr. Frederick Charles Schwartz's Christian Anti-Communist Crusade, both formed in the early 1950s, spun conspiracy theories about how the eastern liberal establishment intended to sell the country out to the Communists by supporting the United Nations, foreign aid, Social Security, and civil rights. The John Birch Society, named after a Baptist missionary and U.S. military intelligence officer killed during World War II by Communists in China, packaged these ideas in periodicals and radio broadcasts throughout the country and urged readers and listeners to remain vigilant to attacks against their freedom.

In the late 1950s and early 1960s, the conservative revival grew, mostly unnoticed, at the grassroots level in the suburbs of southern California and the Southwest. Bolstered by the postwar economic boom that centered around the military research and development of the Cold War, these towns in the Sun Belt attracted college-educated engineers, technicians, managers, and other professionals from the Midwest (or Rust Belt) seeking new economic opportunities. These migrants brought with them Republican loyalties as well as traditional conservative political and moral values. Women played a large part in conservative causes, especially in protesting against public school curricula that they believed encouraged secularism over religion, sex education over abstinence, and anti-Americanism over patriotism. Young housewives built an extensive network of conservative study groups.

In addition, the conservative revival, like the New Left, found fertile recruiting ground on college campuses. In October 1960, some ninety young conservatives met at William Buckley's estate in Sharon, Connecticut, to draw up a manifesto of their beliefs. The Sharon Statement affirmed the conservative doctrines of states' rights, the free market, and anticommunism. Participants at the conference formed the **Young Americans for Freedom (YAF)**, which six months later boasted 27,000 members on one hundred college campuses, far more than were in SDS in 1960. The *National Review* became its bible as subscriptions to Buckley's journal tripled to more than 90,000 by 1964. In 1962 the YAF filled Madison Square Garden to listen to a speech by the one politician who excited them: Republican senator Barry M. Goldwater of Arizona.

Goldwater's book *The Conscience of a Conservative* (1960) attacked New Deal liberalism and advocated abolishing Social Security; dismantling the Tennessee Valley Authority, the government-owned public power utility; and eliminating the progressive income tax. His firm belief in states' rights put him on record against the ruling in *Brown v. Board of Education of Topeka, Kansas* and prompted him to vote against the Civil Rights Act of 1964, positions that won him increasing support from conservative white southerners. However, Goldwater's advocacy of small government did not prevent him from supporting increased military spending to halt the spread of communism abroad. The senator may have anticipated growing concerns of government excess, but he was ahead of his time. His defeat to Lyndon Johnson by a landslide in the 1964 presidential election indicated that most voters perceived Goldwater's brand of conservatism as too extreme and were not yet ready to support it.

The election of 1964 also brought George C. Wallace onto the national stage as a leading architect of the conservative revival. As Democratic governor of Alabama, the segregationist Wallace had supported states' rights and opposed federal intervention to reshape social and political affairs. Wallace began to attract white northerners fed up with rising black militancy, forced busing to promote school integration, and open housing laws to desegregate their neighborhoods. Running in the Democratic presidential primaries in 1964, the Alabama governor had no chance to win, but he garnered 34 percent of the votes in Wisconsin, 30 percent in Indiana, and 43 percent in Maryland.

More so than Goldwater, Wallace united a populist message against the political establishment with concern for working-class Americans. Wallace voters identified with the governor as an "outsider," despised by liberal elites as uncouth, uncultured, and unrespectable. Many of them also backed Wallace for attacking privileged college students who, he claimed, mocked patriotism, violated sexual taboos, and looked down on hardworking, churchgoing, law-abiding Americans. How could "all those rich kids—from the fancy suburbs," one father wondered, "[avoid the draft] when my son has to go over there and maybe get his head shot off?" Each in his own way, George Wallace and Barry Goldwater waged political campaigns against liberals for undermining the economic freedom of middle- and working-class whites and coddling what they considered "racial extremists" and "countercultural barbarians."

REVIEW & RELATE

• How did organizations on the left challenge social, cultural, and economic norms in the 1960s?

• What groups were attracted to the 1960s conservative movement? Why?

Conclusion: Liberalism and Its Discontents

The presidencies of John Kennedy and Lyndon Johnson marked the high point of liberal reform. Kennedy's New Frontier and Johnson's Great Society expanded the power of the national state to provide both compassionate government and bureaucratic regulation. Liberalism permitted greater freedom for racial, ethnic, and sexual minorities; expanded educational opportunities for the disadvantaged; reduced poverty; extended health care; and began to clean up the environment. However, liberalism imposed a degree of federal oversight that seemed too restrictive and expensive to many Americans. Johnson's escalation of the Vietnam War weakened many of these accomplishments and fractured the liberal consensus of the 1960s.

Kennedy and Johnson did not achieve liberal triumphs by themselves. The civil rights movement, with unsung heroes like Bayard Rustin, forced the federal government into action by creating crises and raising the stakes for preserving domestic tranquillity. In addition, Earl Warren's Supreme Court affirmed the constitutionality of major pieces of reform legislation and charted a new course for expanding the guarantees of the Bill of Rights.

Although the Vietnam War tarnished liberalism, the struggles of African Americans, women, Chicanos, Indians, and gays continued. Indeed, the civil rights movement spurred other exploited groups to seek greater freedom, and they flourished in the late 1960s and early 1970s despite the waning of the liberal consensus. Even the counterculture, which lost its most extreme elements to drugs and overindulgence, saw its styles, music, and attitudes toward pleasure blended into mainstream consumer culture.

Liberalism produced unparalleled accomplishments but planted the seeds for its own unraveling. During the 1960s, liberal policies and programs generated powerful counterattacks from radicals and conservatives alike. Indeed, over the next twenty-five years conservatives mobilized the American electorate and gained power by attacking liberal political, economic, and cultural values. The liberal ascendancy proved short-lived, but its impact on the United States has had a lasting effect.

Rather than encompassing any one political and social philosophy, the decade of the 1960s was a time when reform, revolution, and reaction intermingled. Although the era remains known for radicalism and excess, it also saw the revival of conservatism as a force that would dominate politics for the rest of the twentieth century and into the beginning of the next millennium.

Chapter Review

MAKE IT STICK

 LearningCurve **bedfordstmartins.com/hewittlawsonvalue**
After reading the chapter, use LearningCurve to retain what you've read.

IDENTIFY KEY TERMS

Identify and explain the significance of each term below.

New Frontier (p. 674)
Gulf of Tonkin Resolution (p. 677)
Tet Offensive (p. 678)
Freedom Rides (p. 679)
March on Washington for Jobs and
    Freedom (p. 681)
Civil Rights Act of 1964 (p. 681)
Freedom Summer (p. 682)
Mississippi Freedom Democratic Party
    (MFDP) (p. 682)
Voting Rights Act (p. 683)
Great Society (p. 684)
Students for a Democratic Society
    (SDS) (p. 687)
Port Huron Statement (p. 687)

Free Speech Movement (FSM) (p. 687)
Weathermen (p. 689)
counterculture (p. 689)
Commission on the Status of Women
    (p. 690)
National Organization for Women
    (NOW) (p. 690)
Roe v. Wade (p. 691)
Black Panther Party (p. 692)
La Raza Unida (The United Race) (p. 693)
American Indian Movement (AIM) (p. 693)
Stonewall Tavern (p. 694)
Young Americans for Freedom (YAF)
    (p. 696)

REVIEW & RELATE

Answer the focus questions from each section of the chapter.

1. How did President Kennedy's domestic agenda reflect the liberal political ideology of the early 1960s?

2. How and why did the United States escalate its role in the Vietnam War?

3. What role did the federal government play in advancing the cause of racial equality in the early 1960s?

4. How did civil rights activists pressure state and federal government officials to enact their agenda?

5. What problems and challenges did Johnson's Great Society legislation target?

6. In what ways did the Warren Court's rulings advance the liberal agenda?

7. How did organizations on the left challenge social, cultural, and economic norms in the 1960s?

8. What groups were attracted to the 1960s conservative movement? Why?

ONLINE DOCUMENT PROJECTS

◆ **Freedom Summer**
◆ **Women's Liberation**

After reading the primary sources in these document sets, answer the **Interpret the Evidence** questions to help you analyze each of the documents, and then answer the **Put It in Context** question(s) to help you relate the documents to the topics and themes you read about in the chapter.

bedfordstmartins.com/hewittlawsonvalue

TIMELINE OF EVENTS

1960
- Young Americans for Freedom founded; Sharon Statement issued

1961
- Kennedy sends military advisers to South Vietnam
- Cuban exile invasion force lands at Bay of Pigs
- CORE mounts Freedom Rides
- Soviets build Berlin Wall

1962
- Students for a Democratic Society (SDS) issues Port Huron Statement
- Cuban missile crisis

1963–1968
- U.S. troop levels in Vietnam rise from 16,000 to 536,000

1963
- Betty Friedan publishes *The Feminine Mystique*
- U.S. and Soviet Union agree to Partial Nuclear Test Ban Treaty
- March on Washington for Jobs and Freedom
- John F. Kennedy assassinated by Lee Harvey Oswald; Lyndon B. Johnson becomes president

1964–1966
- Great Society domestic programs enacted

1964
- Civil Rights Act of 1964 passed
- Freedom Summer project in Mississippi
- Congress passes Gulf of Tonkin Resolution

1965
- Operation Rolling Thunder begins
- Voting Rights Act passed
- *Griswold v. Connecticut* Supreme Court decision

1966
- Black Panther Party formed
- National Organization for Women (NOW) formed

1968
- American Indian Movement (AIM) founded
- Martin Luther King Jr. assassinated
- Tet Offensive begins in Vietnam

1969
- Gays fight police at Stonewall Tavern

1973
- *Roe v. Wade* Supreme Court decision

27

✓ LearningCurve
bedfordstmartins.com/hewittlawsonvalue
After reading the chapter, use LearningCurve
to retain what you've read.

The Conservative Ascendancy

1968–1992

AMERICAN HISTORIES

Allan Bakke was not a political ideologue or an activist. He had always played by the rules. Born in Minnesota in 1940, Bakke grew up in a white middle-class family, earned a degree in mechanical engineering, and served in Vietnam. When his tour of duty was over, Bakke returned home, found an engineering job in Sunnyvale, California, and received a master's degree from Stanford University. However, he had not satisfied his great ambition—to become a physician.

In 1972 Bakke applied to two California medical schools and was turned down, probably because at age thirty-two he was considered too old. The next year, he applied to twelve schools but was rejected by all of them, including the University of California at Davis. Bakke learned that of the one hundred available spaces in the incoming class, the university awarded sixteen spots to minority group members, consisting mainly of African Americans, Chicanos, and Asian Americans. Contending that the policy amounted to reverse discrimination, he sued the University of California at Davis for violating his constitutional rights. In his challenge to the university's admission policy, Bakke complained: "I realize that the rationale for these quotas is that they attempt to atone for past racial discrimination, but insisting on a new racial bias in favor of minorities is not a just situation." In 1978 the U.S. Supreme Court ruled in his favor, and Bakke successfully completed his studies and graduated with a medical degree.

Like Allan Bakke, Anita Faye Hill did not seek celebrity, yet like Bakke she, too, would gain notoriety in a cause not of her own making. Born in Oklahoma in 1956, Hill grew up in a large family whose ancestors included Creek Indians and former slaves. Like other African Americans in the state, she encountered racial segregation when she attended school, but her parents encouraged her to work hard and abide by strong religious and moral values.

A bookish and determined young woman, Hill graduated from Yale Law School in 1980. The following year, she went to work in the Office of Civil Rights at the Department of Education. Her boss, Clarence Thomas, was an African American supporter of President Ronald Reagan. When Thomas moved to the Equal Employment Opportunity Commission in May 1982, Hill transferred as well. Although a pragmatic moderate who privately favored affirmative action, she tried not to make waves and defended the positions that the conservative Thomas implemented to further reduce the scope of affirmative action in the aftermath of the *Bakke* case.

Anita Hill would have remained an obscure public servant had President George H. W. Bush not nominated Thomas to the Supreme Court in 1991. During the course of Thomas's Senate confirmation hearing, Hill testified before the Senate Judiciary Committee and a nationally televised audience that Thomas had made unwanted sexual advances to her on and off the job. Disturbed by Thomas's harassment and sexual impropriety, Hill had quit her job in 1983 and returned to Oklahoma to teach at a law school. It was difficult for this usually shy black woman to publicly describe these embarrassing moments concerning a high-ranking black man, but her courage was not rewarded. Black and white conservatives defended Thomas and attacked Hill's credibility, and Thomas won confirmation by a 52–48 vote. Nevertheless, she became a hero for many working women who faced similar incidents of sexual bias and harassment.

ALLAN BAKKE and Anita Hill were not engaged in politics in the usual sense of the word. Nonetheless, their American histories took on profound political importance in the

Political activist Phyllis Schlafly and other women at a government hearing on the Equal Rights Amendment in Kansas City, Missouri, 1976.   Time & Life Pictures/Getty Images

larger context of the rise and ascendancy of conservatism in the late twentieth century. Scoring their first national victory with the election of Richard Nixon in 1968, conservatives became the dominant force on the political landscape with the election of Ronald Reagan in 1980. Reagan led a New Right coalition that meshed the traditional economic conservatism of lower taxes, deregulation, and anti-unionism with the concerns of religious conservatives over abortion and family values. By 1992 conservatives had built upon the judicial victory of Allan Bakke and brushed back the complaint of Anita Hill in reshaping the nation's political priorities. Still, they had neither silenced their progressive critics nor eliminated the impact of liberal achievements from the 1960s.

Richard M. Nixon, War, and Politics, 1969–1974

Richard Nixon won the presidency in 1968 by forging a conservative coalition behind him, blaming liberals for the radical excesses of the 1960s. While continuing to fight Communists in Vietnam, Nixon improved relations with the Soviet Union and China, creating a thaw in the Cold War. At home, Nixon mixed conservatism with pragmatic politics, supporting some liberal measures while defending the virtues of limited government and traditional values. Nixon won reelection in 1972 by a landslide, but his victory was short-lived. In an effort to ensure electoral success, the Nixon administration engaged in illegal activities that subsequently came to light in the Watergate scandal. Nixon was forced to resign, and the conservative movement suffered a temporary setback.

The Election of President Nixon

The year 1968 was a turbulent one. In February, police shot indiscriminately into a crowd gathered for civil rights protests at South Carolina State University in Orangeburg, killing three students in the so-called Orangeburg massacre. The following month, student protests at Columbia University led to a violent confrontation with the New York City police. On April 4, the murder of Martin Luther King Jr. sparked an outburst of rioting by blacks in more than one hundred cities throughout the country (see chapter 26). The assassination of Democratic presidential aspirant Robert Kennedy in June further heightened the mood of despair. Adding to the unrest, demonstrators gathered in Chicago in August at the Democratic National Convention to press for an antiwar plank in the party platform. Thousands of protesters were beaten and arrested by Chicago police officers, who violently released their frustrations on the crowds. Many Americans watched in horror as television networks broadcast the bloody clashes, but a majority of viewers sided with the police rather than the protesters.

Similar protests occurred around the world. In early 1968, university students outside of Paris protested educational policies and what they perceived as their second-class status. When students at the Sorbonne in Paris joined them in the streets, police attacked them viciously. In June, French president Charles de Gaulle sent in tanks to break up the strikes but also instituted political and economic reforms. Protests erupted during the spring in Prague, Czechoslovakia, as well. President Alexander Dubček, vowing to reform the Communist regime by initiating "socialism with a human face," lifted press censorship, guaranteed free elections, and encouraged artists and writers to express themselves freely. Unaccustomed to such dissent and fearful it would spread to other nations within its imperial orbit, the Soviet Union sent its military into Prague in August 1968 to crush the reforms. Czechoslovakian protesters were no match for Soviet forces, and the brief experiment in freedom remembered as the "Prague Spring" came to a violent end. During the same year, student-led demonstrations erupted in Yugoslavia, Poland, West Germany, Italy, Spain, Japan, and Mexico.

It was against this backdrop of protest, violence, and civil unrest that Richard Nixon ran for president against the Democratic nominee Hubert H. Humphrey, who was Johnson's vice president, and the independent candidate, George C. Wallace, the segregationist governor of Alabama and a popular archconservative. To outflank Wallace on the right, Nixon appealed to disaffected Democrats as well as traditional Republicans. He declared himself the "law and order" candidate, a phrase that became a code for reining in black militancy. To win southern supporters, he pledged to ease up on enforcing federal civil rights legislation and opposed forced busing to achieve racial integration in schools. He criticized antiwar protesters and promised to end the Vietnam War with honor (without disclosing exactly how he would achieve this goal). Seeking to portray the Democrats as the party of social and cultural radicalism, Nixon geared his campaign message to the "silent majority" of voters—what one political analyst characterized as "the unyoung, the unpoor, and unblack."

Although Nixon won 301 electoral votes, 110 more than Humphrey, none of the three candidates received a majority of the popular vote (Map 27.1). Yet Nixon and Wallace together received about 57 percent of the popular vote, a dramatic shift to the

MAP 27.1

The Election of 1968
Democratic presidential candidate Hubert Humphrey lost across the South as white voters turned to Republican Richard Nixon or segregationist George Wallace. Many working-class whites in the North and West also shifted their allegiance to these "law and order" candidates, rejecting the civil rights and antipoverty agendas promoted by President Johnson and blaming Democrats for the turmoil over the Vietnam War.

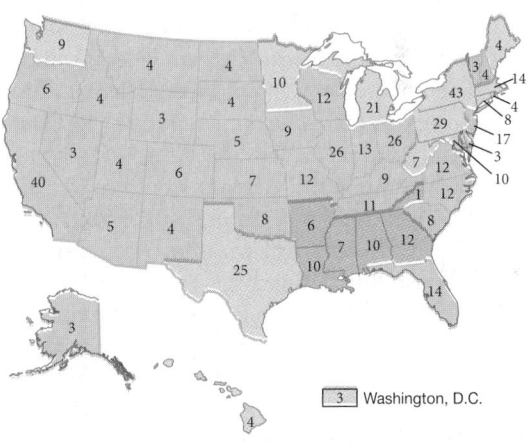

Candidate	Electoral Vote	Popular Vote	Percentage of Popular Vote
Richard M. Nixon (Republican)	301	31,770,237	43.4
Hubert H. Humphrey (Democrat)	191	31,270,533	42.7
George C. Wallace (American Independent)	46	9,906,141	13.5

right compared with Johnson's landslide victory just four years earlier. Nixon's election ushered in more than two decades of Republican presidential rule, interrupted only by scandal. The New Left, which had captured the imagination of many of America's young people, would give way to the **New Right**, an assortment of old and new conservatives, overwhelmingly white, who were determined to contain, if not roll back, the Great Society.

The Failure of Vietnamization

Vietnam plagued Nixon as it had his Democratic predecessor. Despite intimations during the campaign that he had a secret plan to end the war, Nixon's approach to Vietnam turned out to look much the same as Johnson's. Henry Kissinger, who served first as national security adviser and then as secretary of state, continued peace talks with the North Vietnamese, which had been initiated by Johnson. Over the next four years, Nixon and Kissinger devised a strategy that removed U.S. ground forces and turned over greater responsibility for the fighting to the South Vietnamese army, a process called **Vietnamization**.

Vietnamization did not, however, mean an end to U.S. belligerence in the region. In 1969, at the same time that American troop levels were being drawn down, the president ordered secret bombing raids in Cambodia, a neutral country adjacent to South Vietnam that contained enemy forces and parts of the Ho Chi Minh Trail. Meant to pressure the North Vietnamese into accepting U.S. peace terms, the bombing accomplished little in the mountainous jungle. In April 1970, Nixon ordered the invasion of Cambodia, which destabilized the country and eventually brought to power the Communist Khmer Rouge, who later slaughtered two million Cambodians. In 1971 the United States sponsored the South Vietnamese invasion of Laos, another neutral neighbor that harbored North Vietnamese troops and supply lines, which again yielded no battlefield gains. Finally, in December 1972, shortly before Christmas, the United States carried out a massive eleven-day bombing campaign of targets in North Vietnam meant to force the North Vietnamese government to come to a peace accord.

The intense bombing of North Vietnam did end formal U.S. involvement in the war. An agreement signed on January 27, 1973, stipulated that the United States would remove all American troops, the North Vietnamese would return captured U.S. soldiers, and North and South Vietnam would strive for peaceful national unification. Nixon and Kissinger could now claim that they had achieved "peace with honor," ending U.S. involvement in Vietnam without compromising America's credibility with its anti-Communist allies around the world. In fact, peace had not been achieved, and the United States had failed in its stated goal of preventing a Communist takeover of South Vietnam. The war in Vietnam continued, and in 1975 North Vietnamese and Vietcong forces captured Saigon, resulting in a Communist victory. This outcome came at a terrible cost. Some 58,000 American soldiers, 215,000 South Vietnamese soldiers, 1 million North Vietnamese and Vietcong soldiers, and an estimated 4 million South and North Vietnamese civilians were killed in the conflict.

The Nixon administration's war efforts generated great controversy at home. In 1969 the president eliminated most draft deferments and introduced an impartial lottery system. This procedure was more equitable, but it exposed a wider range of young men to the draft. More important, the invasion of Cambodia touched off widespread campus demonstrations in May 1970. At Kent State University in Ohio, four student protesters were shot and killed by the National Guard. Large crowds of antiwar demonstrators descended on Washington in 1969 and 1971, though the president refused to heed their message. Nevertheless, the American public, and not just radicals, had turned against the war. By 1972 more than 70 percent of those polled believed that the Vietnam War was a mistake, and 31 percent disapproved of Nixon's handling of it. Growing numbers of Vietnam veterans also spoke out against the war. Contributing to this disillusionment, in 1971 the *New York Times* and the *Washington Post* published a classified report known as the **Pentagon Papers**. This document, leaked by former Defense Department analyst Daniel Ellsberg, confirmed that the Kennedy and Johnson administrations had misled the public about the origins and nature of the Vietnam War. The Nixon administration tried, unsuccessfully, to block its publication. Congress reflected growing disapproval for the war by repealing the Gulf of Tonkin Resolution in 1970 after the Cambodian invasion. In 1973 Congress passed the **War Powers Act**, which required the president to consult with Congress within forty-eight hours of deploying military forces and to obtain a declaration of war from Congress if troops remained on foreign soil beyond sixty days. That same year, as the U.S. combat mission in Vietnam drew to a close, President Nixon disbanded the draft and created an all-volunteer military.

 Online Document Project   **Debating the Vietnam War**
bedfordstmartins.com/hewittlawsonvalue

Cold War Realism and Détente

As Nixon maneuvered to end the Vietnam War, he embarked on a parallel effort to improve relations with his Cold War Communist enemies. Nixon had begun his political career as a fierce anti-Communist, but he also considered himself a realist in foreign affairs. He was concerned less about promoting abstract ideals of democracy than about fashioning a stable world order based on a balance of power. With this in mind, Nixon and Secretary of State Kissinger worked to establish closer relations with both the People's Republic of China and the Soviet Union, hoping each power could be persuaded to pressure the North Vietnamese to accept an American peace settlement and end the war quickly. In addition, with the Soviet Union and China competing for influence in Asia, Nixon sought to exploit this conflict to keep these nuclear powers divided.

Nixon and Kissinger's plans succeeded in many ways. Their efforts to use great-power diplomacy to pressure the North Vietnamese into concessions failed, but their greatest triumph came in easing tensions with the country's Cold War adversaries. Through secret maneuvering, Kissinger prepared the way for Nixon to make the bold move of visiting mainland China in 1972, the first president to do so since the Cold War began. The meeting set in motion a new relationship between the capitalist and Communist nations. After blocking the People's Republic of China's admission to the United Nations for twenty-two years, the United States announced that it would no longer oppose China's entry to the world organization. This cautious renewal of relations between the two countries benefited both. It opened up possibilities of American access to the huge China market, and for the Chinese it promised trade with the United States.

Shaken by the movement toward closer relations between China and the United States, Soviet premier Leonid Brezhnev invited President Nixon to Moscow in May 1972, the first time an American president had visited the Soviet Union since 1945. The main topic of discussion concerned arms control, and with the Soviet Union eager to make a deal in the aftermath of Nixon's trip to China, the two sides worked out the historic **Strategic Arms Limitation Treaty (SALT I)**, the first to curtail nuclear arms production during the Cold War. The pact restricted the number of antiballistic missiles that each nation could deploy and froze the number of intercontinental ballistic missiles and submarine-based missiles for five years, with each side agreeing to pursue nuclear "sufficiency" rather than "superiority."

Nixon's diplomatic initiatives, however, failed to resolve festering problems in the Middle East, an area of strategic concern to both the United States and the Soviet Union. Since its victory in the Six-Day War of 1967, Israel had occupied territory once controlled by Egypt and Syria as well as the former Palestinian capital of East Jerusalem. On October 6, 1973, during the start of the Jewish High Holidays of Yom Kippur, Egyptian and Syrian troops, fortified with Soviet arms, caught the Israelis off guard and quickly managed to recapture territory lost in 1967. An Israeli counterattack, reinforced by a shipment of $2 billion of American weapons, repelled Arab forces, and the Israeli military stood ready to destroy the Egyptian army. To avoid a complete breakdown in the balance of power, the United States and the Soviet Union agreed to broker a cease-fire that left the situation the same as before the war.

U.S. involvement in the struggle between Israel and its Arab enemies exacerbated economic troubles at home. On October 17, 1973, in the midst of the Yom Kippur War, the Arab-dominated **Organization of Petroleum Exporting Countries (OPEC)** imposed an oil embargo on the United States as punishment for its support of Israel. As a result of the embargo, the price of oil skyrocketed, and reduced oil supplies produced long lines at the gas pumps. The effect of high oil prices rippled through the economy, leading to increased inflation and unemployment, which rose from 5 to 7 percent. The embargo also affected America's allies in Western Europe, which imported 80 percent of its oil supply from Arab states, compared with 12 percent for the United States. The crisis lasted until May 1974, when OPEC lifted its embargo following six months of diplomacy by Kissinger.

The United States preferred to support stability over democracy when its strategic or economic interests were at stake. Under Nixon's leadership, the United States supported repressive regimes in Nicaragua, South Africa, the Philippines, and Iran. In Chile, the United States overthrew the democratically elected socialist president Salvador Allende, who was murdered in a CIA-backed operation in 1973. The coup brought nearly two decades of dictatorial rule to that country.

Pragmatic Conservatism at Home

On the domestic front, Nixon had pledged during his 1968 campaign to "reverse the flow of power and resources from the states and communities to Washington" and redirect "power and resources" back to the American people, a key objective of conservatism. He kept his promise by dismantling Great Society social programs, cutting funds for the War on Poverty, and eliminating the Office of Economic Opportunity. In 1972 the president adopted a program of revenue sharing, which transferred federal tax revenues to the states to use as they wished. Hoping to rein in the liberal Warren Court, Nixon nominated conservative justices, such as William Rehnquist and Lewis Powell, to the Supreme Court.

However, in several areas Nixon departed from conservatives who favored limited government. In 1970 he persuaded Congress to pass the Environmental Protection Act, which strengthened federal oversight of environmental programs throughout the country. In 1972 the federal government increased its responsibility for protecting the health and safety of American workers through the creation of the Occupational Safety and Health Administration (OSHA). The Consumer Products Safety Commission was established to provide added safety for the buying public. The president also signed a law banning cigarette advertising on radio and television because of the link between smoking and cancer.

Nixon applied this pragmatic conservatism to racial issues. The president proposed legislation that prevented the use of busing to promote school desegregation, which the Democratic Congress rejected. In general, he supported "benign neglect" concerning the issue of race and therefore rejected new legislative attempts to remove the vestiges of racial discrimination. In this way, Nixon courted southern conservatives in an attempt to deter George Wallace from mounting another third-party challenge in 1972. Still, Nixon moved back to the political center with efforts that furthered civil rights. Expanding **affirmative action** programs begun under the Johnson administration, he adopted plans that required construction companies and unions to recruit minority workers according to their percentage in the local labor force. His support of affirmative action was part of a broader approach to encourage "black capitalism," a concept designed to convince African Americans to seek opportunity within the free-enterprise system. Moreover, in 1970 Nixon signed the extension of the 1965 Voting Rights Act, thereby renewing the law that had provided suffrage to the majority of African Americans in the South. The law also lowered the voting age from twenty-one to eighteen for national elections. In 1971 the Twenty-sixth Amendment was ratified to lower the voting age for state and local elections as well.

The Nixon administration also veered away from the traditional Republican free market philosophy by resorting to wage and price controls to curb rising inflation brought on, for the most part, by increased military spending during the Vietnam War. In 1971 the president declared a ninety-day freeze on wages and prices, placed a temporary 10 percent surtax on imports, and let the value of the dollar drop on the international market, leading to increased U.S. exports. Taken together, these measures stabilized consumer prices, reduced unemployment, and boosted the gross national product. Although these proved to be only short-term gains, they improved Nixon's prospects for reelection.

The Nixon Landslide and Disgrace, 1972–1974

By appealing to voters across the political spectrum, Nixon won a monumental victory in 1972. The president invigorated the "silent majority" by demonizing his opponents and encouraging Vice President Spiro Agnew to aggressively pursue Nixon's strategy of polarization. Agnew called protesters "kooks" and "social misfits" and attacked the media and Nixon critics with heated rhetoric. As Nixon had hoped, George Wallace rejected a third-party bid and ran in the Democratic primaries. Wallace won impressive victories in North Carolina, Florida, Tennessee, Maryland, and Michigan, but his campaign ended after an assassination attempt left him paralyzed. With Wallace out of the race, the Democrats helped Nixon look more centrist by nominating George McGovern, a liberal antiwar senator from South Dakota, who ran a generally inept campaign.

The election marked the personal triumph of Richard Nixon. Winning in a landslide, he captured more than 60 percent of the popular vote and nearly all of the electoral votes. Democrats retained control of Congress but were trounced in their bid for the White House. However, Nixon would have little time to savor his victory, for within the next two years his conduct in the campaign would come back to destroy his presidency.

In the early hours of June 17, 1972, five men broke into Democratic Party headquarters in the Watergate apartment complex in Washington, D.C. What appeared initially as a routine robbery turned into the most infamous political scandal of the twentieth century. It was eventually revealed that the break-in had been authorized by the Committee for the Re-Election of the President in an attempt to steal documents from the Democrats.

Whether President Nixon knew about the break-in in advance and approved it remains in dispute, but he did authorize a cover-up of his administration's involvement. Nixon ordered his chief of staff, H. R. Haldeman, to get the CIA and FBI to back off from a thorough investigation of the incident by claiming that it would breach national security. To silence the burglars at their trials, the president promised them $400,000 and hinted at a presidential pardon after their conviction.

Nixon embarked on the cover-up to protect himself from revelations of his administration's other illegal activities. Several of the Watergate burglars belonged to a secret band of operatives known as "the plumbers," which had been formed in 1971 and authorized by the president. Their mission was to find and plug up unwelcome information leaks from government officials. On their first secret operation, the plumbers broke into the office of Daniel Ellsberg's psychiatrist to look for embarrassing personal information with which to discredit Ellsberg, who had leaked the *Pentagon Papers*. The president had other unsavory matters to hide. In an effort to contain leaks about the administration's secret bombing of Cambodia in 1969, the White House had illegally wiretapped its own officials and members of the press.

Watergate did not become a major scandal until after the election. The trial judge forced one of the burglars to reveal their backers. This revelation led two *Washington Post* reporters, Bob Woodward and Carl Bernstein, to doggedly investigate the link between the administration and the plumbers. With the help of Mark Felt, a top FBI official whose identity long remained secret and whom the reporters called "Deep Throat," Woodward and Bernstein succeeded in exposing the true nature of the crime. With the president still denying any knowledge of the offense, the Senate created a special committee in February 1973 to investigate the scandal. Televised hearings absorbed the public. White House counsel John Dean, whom Nixon had fired, testified about discussing the cover-up with the president and his closest advisers. His testimony proved accurate after the committee learned that Nixon had secretly taped all Oval Office conversations. When the president refused to release the tapes to a special prosecutor, the Supreme Court ruled against him. In the meantime, the hearings and investigations produced a number of political casualties. Nixon's attorney general, John Mitchell, and his closest advisers, H. R. Haldeman and John Ehrlichman, resigned, and twenty-five administration members went to jail.

Nixon Resigns, 1974   On August 8, 1974, President Richard M. Nixon announced his resignation on national television. His decision came after the House Judiciary Committee voted to impeach Nixon and as he was rapidly losing support in both houses of Congress. Before leaving the White House the next day, Nixon bid farewell to his cabinet members and White House staff. Nixon chokes up as his wife Pat (partially visible) and his daughter Tricia look on.   AP Photo

The eventual release of the tapes finally revealed the truth about Nixon's cover-up, and the House Judiciary Committee voted to bring articles of impeachment to the House of Representatives. After concluding that the House would vote to impeach him and the Senate would very likely convict him, Nixon resigned on August 9, 1974. After receiving overwhelming support from the American electorate less than two years earlier, Richard Nixon left the White House in disgrace.

Vice President Gerald Ford served out Nixon's remaining term. The Republican representative from Michigan had replaced Vice President Spiro Agnew after Agnew resigned in 1973 following charges that he had taken illegal kickbacks while governor of Maryland. Ford chose Nelson A. Rockefeller, the moderate Republican governor of New York, as his vice president. In the wake of the Watergate scandal, the nation now had both a president and a vice president who had never been elected to those offices.

President Ford's most controversial and defining act took place shortly after he entered the White House. Explaining to the country that he wanted to quickly end the "national nightmare" stemming from Watergate, Ford pardoned Nixon for any criminal offenses he might have committed as president. Rather than healing the nation's wounds, this preemptive pardon polarized Americans and cost Ford considerable political capital.

Ford also wrestled with a troubled economy as Americans once again experienced rising prices and high unemployment.

REVIEW & RELATE

• Who made up the New Right coalition that brought Nixon to power? How did Nixon appeal to the New Right?

• How did Nixon's pragmatism shape both his foreign and domestic policies?

The Challenges of the 1970s

Though deeply disillusioned by Vietnam and the Watergate scandal, most Americans hoped that, with these disasters behind them, better times lay ahead. Nixon's resignation did not, however, mark the beginning of a new era of peace and prosperity. Under the leadership of the Democratic president Jimmy Carter, the economy worsened as oil-producing nations in the Persian Gulf and Latin America raised the price of petroleum. Carter's efforts to revive the economy and rally the country behind energy conservation were ineffective, sharpening Republicans' attack on his policies and presidency. Activists on both the left and the right continued to fight over the role of the federal government in economic affairs as well as over the racial and cultural issues that divided the nation.

Jimmy Carter and the Limits of Affluence

Despite his political shortcomings, Gerald Ford received the Republican presidential nomination in 1976 and ran against James Earl (Jimmy) Carter, a little-known former governor of Georgia, who used his "outsider" status to his advantage. Shaping his campaign with Watergate in mind, Carter stressed character over economic issues and promised voters that he would run the government honestly, truthfully, and morally. As a postsegregationist governor of Georgia, Carter won the support of the family of Martin Luther King Jr. and other black leaders. Carter needed all the help he could get and eked out a narrow victory.

The greatest challenge Carter faced once in office was a faltering economy. America's consumer-oriented economy depended on cheap energy, a substantial portion of which came from sources outside the United States. By the 1970s, four-fifths of the world's oil supply came from Saudi Arabia, Iran, Iraq, and Kuwait, all members of OPEC. The organization had been formed in 1960 by these Persian Gulf countries together with Venezuela, and it used its control of petroleum supplies to set world prices. By the time Carter became president, the cost of a barrel of oil had jumped to around $30. American drivers who had paid 30 cents a gallon for gas in 1970 paid more than four times that amount ten years later.

Energy concerns helped reshape American industry. With energy prices rising, American manufacturers sought ways to reduce costs by moving their factories to Mexico, Central and South America, and several Asian nations that offered cheaper labor and lower energy costs. This outmigration of American manufacturing had two significant consequences. First, it weakened the American labor movement, particularly in heavy industry. In the 1970s, union membership dropped from 28 to 23 percent of the workforce and continued to decline over the next decade. Second, this process of deindustrialization accelerated a significant population shift that had begun during World War II from the old industrial areas of the Northeast and the Midwest (the Rust Belt) to the South and the Southwest (the Sun Belt), where cheaper costs and lower wages were enormously attractive to businesses (Map 27.2). Only 14 percent of southern workers were unionized in a region with a long history of opposition to labor organizing. The North's loss was the South's gain, and cities such as Houston, Texas; Atlanta, Georgia; Phoenix, Arizona; and San Diego, California, flourished, while the steel and auto towns of Youngstown, Ohio; Flint, Michigan; and Johnstown, Pennsylvania, decayed.

These monumental shifts in the American economy produced widespread pain. Higher gasoline prices affected all businesses that relied on energy, leading to serious inflation. Between 1974 and 1980, housing prices more than doubled, and the average cost of a new car jumped from $3,900 to $5,770. To maintain their standard of living in the face of rising inflation and stagnant wages, many Americans went into debt, using a new innovation, the credit card, to borrow more than $300 billion. The American economy had gone through inflationary spirals before, but they were usually accompanied by high employment, with wages helping to drive up prices. In the 1970s, however, rising prices were accompanied by growing unemployment, a situation that economists

MAP 27.2

The Sun and Rust Belts   Dramatic economic and demographic shifts during the 1970s led to industrial development and population growth in the "Sun Belt" in the South and Southwest at the expense of the "Rust Belt" in the Northeast and Midwest. As manufacturers sought cheap, non-unionized labor, they moved factories to the South or overseas while defense industries and agribusiness fueled growth from Texas to California.

called "stagflation." Joblessness had risen to 9 percent on the eve of Carter's election and stood at 7 percent when he ran for reelection in 1980. Traditionally, remedies to control inflation increased unemployment, yet most unemployment cures also spurred inflation. With both occurring at the same time, economists were confounded, and many Americans felt they had lost control over their economy. In 1978, 55 percent of survey respondents declared, "Next year will be worse than this year."

President Carter had no better solutions than did his predecessor. To reduce dependency on foreign oil, in 1977 Carter devised a plan for energy self-sufficiency, which he called the "moral equivalent of war." Critics poked fun at the proposal by reducing the president's words to the acronym MEOW, suggesting that it had all the bite of a pussycat. A more substantial accomplishment came on August 4, 1977, when Carter signed into law the creation of the Department of Energy, with responsibilities covering research, development, and conservation of energy.

The Persistence of Liberalism

Despite the elections of Richard Nixon and the economic hard times that many encountered in the 1970s, political activism did not die out with the end of the militant 1960s. Many of the changes sought by liberals and radicals during the 1960s had entered the political and cultural mainstreams. Nor did the influence of the counterculture disappear. During the 1970s, long hairstyles and colorful clothes also entered the mainstream, and rock continued to dominate popular music. American youth and many of their elders experimented with recreational drugs, and the remaining sexual taboos of the 1960s fell. Many parents became resigned to seeing their daughters and sons living with boyfriends or girlfriends before getting married. And many of those same parents sought to expand their own sexual horizons by engaging in extramarital affairs or divorcing their spouses. The divorce rate increased 116 percent in the decade after 1965; in 1979 the rate peaked at 23 divorces per 1,000 married couples.

Rock music, long linked to sexual experimentation, continued to dominate the era. The popularity of disco music, glamorized by John Travolta in the blockbuster motion picture *Saturday Night Fever* (1977), emphasized dance beats over social messages, much like early rock 'n' roll. However, listeners could still get deeper meaning and engaging melodies from the works of singer-songwriters, who crafted and recorded their own songs. The decade inspired artists such as Bruce Springsteen, Jackson Browne, and Billy Joel, whose performing energy and songs of loss, loneliness, urban decay, and adventure carried folk-rock music in new directions.

The antiwar movement and counterculture influenced popular culture in other ways. The film *M*A*S*H* (1970), though dealing with the Korean War, was a thinly veiled satire of the horrors of the Vietnam War, and in the late 1970s filmmakers began producing movies specifically about Vietnam and the toll the war took on ordinary Americans who served there. The television sitcom *All in the Family* gave American viewers the character of Archie Bunker, an opinionated blue-collar worker, in a comedy that dramatized the contemporary political and cultural war pitting conservatives against liberals. The show recounted the battle of the generations as Archie taunted his hippie-looking son-in-law with politically incorrect remarks about religious, racial, and ethnic minorities, feminists, and liberals.

The battles fought in the fictional Bunker household played out in real life. In the 1970s, the women's movement gained strength, but it also attracted powerful opponents.

The 1973 Supreme Court victory for abortion rights in *Roe v. Wade* (see chapter 26) mobilized women on all sides of the issue. Pro-choice advocates pointed out that previous laws criminalizing abortion exposed pregnant women who sought the procedure to unsanitary and dangerous methods of ending pregnancies. However, *Roe v. Wade* produced an equally strong reaction from abortion opponents. Pro-life advocates believed that a fetus was a human being and must be granted full protection from what they considered to be murder. In 1976 Congress responded to abortion opponents by passing legislation prohibiting the use of federal funds for impoverished women seeking to terminate their pregnancies.

Feminists engaged in other debates in this decade, often clashing with more conservative women. The National Organization for Women (NOW) and its allies succeeded in getting thirty-five states out of a necessary thirty-eight to ratify the Equal Rights Amendment (ERA), which prevented the abridgment of "equality of rights under law . . . by the United States or any State on the basis of sex." In response, other women activists formed their own movement to block ratification. Phyllis Schlafly, a conservative activist, founded the Stop ERA organization. She argued that the ERA would create a "unisex society" and deprive "women of the rights they already have, such as the right of a wife to be supported by her husband," attend a single-sex college, use women's-only bathrooms, and avoid military combat. Despite the inroads made by feminists, traditional notions of femininity appealed to many women and to male-dominated legislatures. The remaining states refused to ratify the ERA, thus killing the amendment in 1982, when the ratification period expired.

Despite the failure to obtain ratification of the ERA, feminists achieved significant victories. In 1972 Congress passed the Educational Amendments Act. Title IX of this law prohibited colleges and universities that received federal funds from discriminating on the basis of sex, leading to substantial advances in women's athletics. Many more women sought relief against job discrimination through the Equal Employment Opportunity Commission, resulting in major victories against such firms as the American Telephone and Telegraph Company. NOW membership continued to grow, and the number of battered women's shelters and rape crisis centers multiplied in towns and cities across the country. Women saw their ranks increase on college campuses, in both undergraduate and professional schools. Women also began entering politics in large enough numbers, especially at the local and state levels, to justify the formation of the National Women's Political Caucus in 1971. At the national level, women such as Shirley Chisholm and Geraldine Ferraro of New York, Barbara Jordan of Texas, and Patricia Schroeder of Colorado won seats in Congress. Women's political associations—such as Emily's List, founded in 1984, and the Fund for a Feminist Majority, founded in 1987—saw their memberships and donations soar, especially after Anita Hill testified against the nomination of Clarence Thomas to the Supreme Court.

At the same time, women of color sought to broaden the definition of feminism to include struggles against race and class oppression as well as sex discrimination. In 1974 a group of black feminists, led by author Barbara Smith, organized the Combahee River Collective and proclaimed: "We . . . often find it difficult to separate race from class from sex oppression because in our lives they are most often experienced simultaneously." Chicana and other Latina feminists drew strength from African American women in extending women's liberation beyond the confines of the white middle class. In 1987 feminist poet and writer Gloria Anzaldúa wrote: "Though I'll defend my race and culture when they are attacked by non-mexicanos . . . I abhor some of my culture's ways, how it cripples its women . . . our strengths used against us, lowly [women] bearing humility with dignity."

Another outgrowth of 1960s liberal activism that flourished in the 1970s was the effort to clean up and preserve the environment. The publication of Rachel Carson's *Silent Spring* in 1962 had renewed awareness of what Progressive Era reformers called conservation (see chapter 19). Carson expanded the concept of conservation to include ecology, which addressed the relationships of human beings and other organisms to their environments. By exploring these connections, she offered a revealing look at the devastating effects of powerful pesticides, especially DDT, on birds and fish, as well as on the human food chain and water supply.

This new environmental movement not only focused on open spaces and national parks but also sought to publicize urban environmental problems. By 1970, 53 percent of Americans considered air and water pollution to be one of the top issues facing the country, up from only 17 percent five years earlier. Responding to this shift in public opinion, in 1971 President Nixon established the **Environmental Protection Agency (EPA)** and signed the Clean Air Act, which regulated auto emissions. Two years later, Congress banned the sale of DDT.

Not everyone embraced environmentalism. As the EPA toughened emission standards, automobile manufacturers complained that the regulations forced them to raise prices and hurt an industry that was already feeling the threat of foreign competition, especially from Japan. Workers were also affected, as declining sales forced companies to lay off employees. Similarly, passage of the Endangered Species Act of 1973 pitted timber companies in the Northwest against environmentalists. The new law prevented the federal government from funding any projects that threatened the habitat of animals at risk of extinction.

Several disasters heightened public demands for stronger government oversight of the environment. In 1978 women living near Love Canal outside of Niagara Falls, New York, complained about unusually high rates of illnesses and birth defects in their community. Investigations revealed that their housing development had been constructed on top of a toxic waste dump. This discovery spawned grassroots efforts to clean up this area as well as other contaminated communities. In 1980 Congress responded by passing the Comprehensive Environmental Response, Compensation, and Liability Act (known as Superfund) to clean up sites contaminated with hazardous substances. Further inquiries showed that the presence of such poisonous waste dumps disproportionately affected minorities and the poor. Critics called the placement of these waste locations near African American and other minority communities "environmental racism" and launched a movement for environmental justice.

The most dangerous threat came in March 1979 at the Three Mile Island nuclear plant near Harrisburg, Pennsylvania. A broken valve at the plant leaked coolant and threatened the meltdown of the reactor's nuclear core. As officials quickly evacuated residents from the surrounding area, employees at the plant narrowly averted catastrophe by fixing the problem before an explosion occurred. Grassroots activists, such as the Clamshell Alliance in New Hampshire, protested and raised public awareness against the construction of additional power facilities. They also convinced existing utility companies to slow down their plans for expanding the output of nuclear power.

Racial Struggles Continue

The civil rights struggle did not end with the last great interracial march in Selma, Alabama, in 1965 or the death of Martin Luther King Jr. in 1968. The civil rights coalition of organizations that banded together in the 1960s had disintegrated, but the National Association for the Advancement of Colored People remained active, as did local organizations in communities nationwide. The 1965 Voting Rights Act, through the election of black officials, provided a significant path for the continuation of the civil rights movement. A black candidate in South Carolina summed up electoral politics as the new form of activism. "There's an inherent value in office holding," he declared. "A race of people excluded from public office will always be second class." By 1992 there were more than 7,500 black elected officials in the United States. Many of them had participated in the civil rights movement and subsequently worked to gain for their constituents the economic benefits that integration and affirmative action had not yet achieved. Black mayors were elected in Atlanta and New Orleans as well as in smaller municipal and county governments in the South where African Americans could scarcely vote a decade earlier. These mayors appointed black officials, improved public health, and filled government jobs and contracts through affirmative action programs. At the same time, the number of Latino American and Asian American elected officials increased, and as with African Americans, most held office at the state and local levels.

The issue of school busing highlighted the persistence of racial discrimination. In the fifteen years following the landmark decision in *Brown v. Board of Education of Topeka, Kansas* in 1954 (see chapter 25), few schools had been integrated. Starting in 1969, the U.S. Supreme Court ruled that genuine racial integration of the public schools

Shirley Chisholm, 1968 On November 6, 1968, Shirley Chisholm won election to the House of Representatives from a predominantly black district in Brooklyn, New York, becoming the first African American woman in Congress. This photo shows Chisholm (center) surrounded by campaign workers flashing the victory sign. AP Photo

must no longer be delayed. In 1971 the Court went even further in *Swann v. Charlotte-Mecklenburg Board of Education* by requiring school districts to bus pupils to achieve integration. Cities such as Charlotte, North Carolina; Lexington, Kentucky; and Tampa, Florida, embraced the ruling and carefully planned for it to succeed.

However, the decision was more controversial in other municipalities around the nation. The civil rights movement had primarily addressed injustices in the South, but it also exposed racism as a national problem. There were no Jim Crow laws in the North, but in many northern communities racially discriminatory housing policies created segregated neighborhoods and, thus, segregated schools. When white parents in the Detroit suburbs objected to busing their children to inner-city, predominantly black schools, the Supreme Court in 1974 departed from the *Swann* case and prohibited busing across distinct school district boundaries. This ruling created a serious problem for integration efforts because many whites were fleeing the cities and moving to the suburbs where few blacks lived.

As the conflict over school integration intensified, violence broke out in communities throughout the country. In Boston, Massachusetts, busing opponents tapped into the racial and class resentments of the largely white working-class population of South Boston, which was paired with the black community of Roxbury for busing, leaving mainly middle- and upper-class white communities unaffected. In the fall of 1974, battles broke out inside and outside the schools. Antibusing protesters gathered in front of the Federal Building in downtown Boston, threw eggs and tomatoes, and cursed Senator Edward Kennedy, a busing supporter who sent his children to private school. "You're a disgrace to the Irish," one protester shouted. "Let your daughter get bussed [to Roxbury] so she can get raped." Despite the violence, schools stayed open, and for the next three decades Boston remained under court order to continue busing.

Along with busing, affirmative action generated fierce controversy, as the case of Allan Bakke showed. From 1970 to 1977, with the acceleration of affirmative action programs, the number of African Americans attending college doubled, constituting nearly 10 percent of the student body, a few percentage points lower than the proportion of blacks in the national population. Though blacks still earned lower incomes than the average white family, black family income as a percent of white family income had grown from 55.1 percent in 1965 to 61.5 percent ten years later. African Americans, however, still had a long way to go to catch up with whites. The situation was even worse for those who did not reach middle-class status: About 30 percent of African Americans slid deeper into poverty during the decade.

Despite the persistence of economic inequality, many whites believed that affirmative action placed them at a disadvantage with blacks in the educational and economic marketplaces. In particular, many white men condemned policies that they thought recruited blacks at their expense. "Talk about rights; we've got no rights," a white Detroit policeman stated in voicing his disapproval over an affirmative action decision in favor of blacks. Polls showed that although most whites favored equal treatment of blacks, they disapproved of affirmative action as a form of "reverse discrimination."

Online Document Project **The Affirmative Action Debate**
bedfordstmartins.com/hewittlawsonvalue

The furor over affirmative action did not end with the *Bakke* case, and over the next three decades affirmative action opponents succeeded in narrowing the use of racial considerations in employment and education. However, they did so without Bakke, who chose to live a very private life with his family and refused to take up the larger cause against affirmative action with which his name became identified.

REVIEW & RELATE

• What issues and trends shaped the presidency of Jimmy Carter?

• How and why did the social and cultural developments of the 1960s continue to create conflict and controversy in the 1970s?

The Conservative Political Ascendancy

The backlash against affirmative action and the ERA confirmed that liberal reformers were losing ground to conservatives. By the early 1990s, liberalism had become identified with special interests and elitism, and conservatives could boast of numerous successes. The election of former California governor Ronald Reagan as president in 1980 reflected the spectacular growth in political power of the New Right, finishing what Barry Goldwater had started in his unsuccessful bid for the presidency in 1964 (see chapter 26). Reagan pushed the conservative economic agenda of lower taxes and business deregulation alongside the New Right's concern for traditional religious and family values. His presidency installed conservatism as the dominant political ideology for the remainder of the twentieth century.

The New Right Revival

The New Right emerged from a mixture of forces: the revolt against high taxes, the backlash against the growth of the federal government, the disillusionment of former liberal intellectuals known as neoconservatives, and the growth of the Christian Right. In the 1970s, working- and middle-class white resentment against antiwar protesters, hippies, black power militants, and feminist agitators found a new target in big government spending and high taxes. During the 1970s, taxation claimed 30 percent of the gross national product, up 6 percent from 1960. Although Americans still paid far less in taxes than their counterparts in Western Europe, and even though tax rates had fallen since World War II, Americans objected to rising state and federal taxes. Leading the tax revolt was the Sun Belt state of California. In a 1978 referendum, California voters passed Proposition 13, a measure that reduced property taxes and placed strict limits on the ability of local governments to raise them in the future. In the wake of Proposition 13, a dozen states enacted similar measures.

Economic conservatives also set their sights on reducing the federal income tax. They supported cutting personal and corporate taxes by a third in the belief that reducing taxes would encourage new investment and job creation. "Supply-side" economists, such as Arthur Laffer, argued that lowering tax rates would actually boost tax receipts: With lower taxes, companies and investors would have more capital to invest, leading to expanded job growth; with increased employment, more people would be paying taxes. At the same time, supply-side conservatives called for reduced government spending, especially in the social service sector, to ensure balanced budgets and to eliminate what they saw as unnecessary spending on domestic programs.

The New Right also benefited by the defection of disillusioned liberals. Labeled neoconservatives, intellectuals such as Irving Kristol, Norman Podhoretz, and Nathan Glazer reversed course and condemned the Great Society programs that they had originally supported. They believed that federal policies had aggravated rather than improved the problems government planners intended to solve. Of particular concern to many neoconservatives were affirmative action programs, the domination of campus debate and discourse by New Left radicals, and left-wing criticism of the use of American military and economic might to advance U.S. interests overseas.

Perhaps the greatest spark igniting the New Right came from socially conservative religious believers, mainly evangelical Christians and Catholics. Phyllis Schlafly—a Catholic, a former Goldwater supporter, and an ERA opponent—played a major role in connecting the political conservatism of the 1960s with the social conservatism of the following decade. Yet evangelical Christians most often provided the leadership and core support for this political movement. Evangelicals considered themselves to have been "born again"—literally experiencing Jesus Christ's saving presence inside of them. By the end of the 1970s, evangelical Christians numbered around 50 million, about a quarter of the population. The Christian Right opposed abortion, gay rights, and sex education; attacked Supreme Court rulings banning prayer in the public schools; denounced Darwin's theory of evolution in favor of divine creationism; and supported the traditional role of women as mothers and homemakers. Certainly not all evangelical Christians held all of these beliefs; for example, President Jimmy Carter, a born-again Christian, did not. Still, conservative Christians believed that the liberals and radicals of the 1960s had spread the secular creed of individual rights and personal fulfillment at the expense of traditional Christian values.

Social conservatives worried that the traditional nuclear family was in danger, as households consisting of married couples with children declined from 30 percent in the 1970s to 23 percent thirty years later, and the divorce rate soared. The number of unmarried couples living together doubled over the last quarter of the twentieth century, and the percentage of children born to single mothers jumped from 18 in 1980 to 40 in 2007. This increase was part of a trend in developed countries worldwide, and among these nations the United States ranked in the middle between Iceland at the top and Japan at the bottom.

Since the 1950s, Billy Graham, a charismatic Southern Baptist evangelist from North Carolina, had used television to conduct nationwide crusades that attracted millions of followers. Television became an even greater instrument in the hands of New Right Christian preachers in the 1970s and 1980s. The Reverend Pat Robertson of Virginia founded the Christian Broadcasting Network, and ministers such as Jerry Falwell used the airwaves to great effect. What distinguished Falwell and Robertson from earlier evangelists like Graham was their fusion of religion and electoral politics. In 1979 Falwell founded the Moral Majority, an organization that backed political candidates who supported a "family values" social agenda. Within two years of its creation, the Moral Majority counted four million members who were eager to organize in support of New Right politicians. The alliance of economic, intellectual, and religious conservatives offered a formidable challenge to liberalism.

The Triumph of Ronald Reagan

Ronald Reagan's presidential victory in 1980 consolidated the growing New Right coalition and reshaped American politics for a generation to come. The former movie actor had transformed himself from a New Deal Democrat into a conservative Republican politician when he ran for governor of California in 1966. As governor, he implemented conservative ideas of free enterprise and small government and denounced Johnson's Great Society for threatening private property and individual liberty. "Government," Reagan observed, "is like a baby, an alimentary canal with a big appetite at one end and no sense of responsibility at the other." His winning combination of support for conservative economic and social issues carried him to the presidency.

Reagan triumphed over Jimmy Carter and John Anderson, a moderate Republican who ran as an independent candidate (Map 27.3). The high unemployment and inflation of the late 1970s worked in Reagan's favor. Reagan appealed to a coalition of conservative Republicans and disaffected Democrats, promising to cut taxes and reduce spending, to relax federal supervision over civil rights programs, and to end what was left of expensive Great Society measures and affirmative action. Finally, he energized members of the religious right, who flocked to the polls to support Reagan's demands for voluntary prayer in the public schools, defeat of the Equal Rights Amendment, and a constitutional amendment to outlaw abortion.

Reagan's first priority, however, was stimulating the stagnant economy. The president's strategy, known as Reaganomics, reflected the ideas of supply-side economists and conservative Republicans. Stating that "government is not the solution to our problem; government is the problem," Reagan asked Congress for a huge income tax

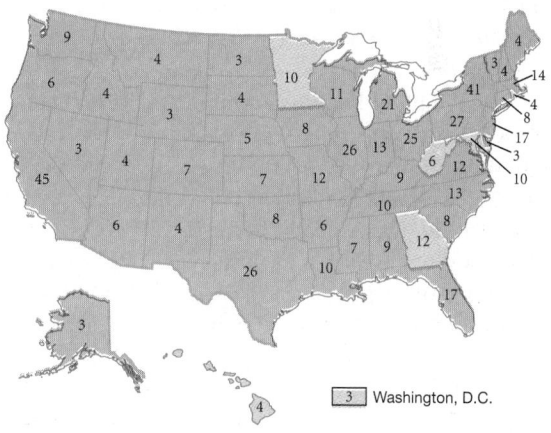

MAP 27.3
The Election of 1980 Ronald Reagan won 50.7 percent of the popular vote in the 1980 election, but his margin of victory over Jimmy Carter was much greater in the electoral vote. Reagan won the votes of the South and many disaffected Democrats in the urban North. A third-party candidate, John Anderson of Illinois, won 6.6 percent of the popular vote, demonstrating significant disapproval with both major parties.

Candidate	Electoral Vote	Popular Vote	Percentage of Popular Vote
Ronald Reagan (Republican)	489	43,899,248	50.7
Jimmy Carter (Democrat)	49	35,481,435	41.0
John B. Anderson (Independent)	—	5,719,437	6.6

cut of 30 percent over three years, a reduction in spending for domestic programs of more than $40 billion, and new monetary policies to lower rising rates for loans.

The president did not operate in isolation from the rest of the world. He learned a great deal from Margaret Thatcher, the British prime minister who took office two years before Reagan. Thatcher combated inflation by slashing welfare programs, selling off publicly owned companies, and cutting back health and education programs. An advocate of supply-side economics, Thatcher reduced income taxes on the wealthy by more than 50 percent to encourage new investment. West Germany also moved toward the right under Chancellor Helmut Kohl, who reined in welfare spending. In the 1980s, Reaganomics and Thatcherism dominated the United States and the two most powerful nations of Western Europe.

In March 1981, Reagan survived a nearly fatal assassin's bullet. More popular than ever after his recovery, the president persuaded the Democratic House and the Republican Senate to pass his economic measures in slightly modified form. The initial results were disastrous—unemployment rose to 9.5 percent in the wake of government cutbacks in spending. However, the government's tight money policies, as engineered by the Federal Reserve Board, reduced inflation from 14 percent in 1980 to 4 percent in 1984. By 1983 the unemployment rate had also fallen, while the gross national product grew by a healthy 4.3 percent, an indication that the recession of the previous two years had ended.

The success of Reaganomics came at the expense of the poor and the lower middle class. The Reagan administration slashed federal spending by cutting benefits that affected mainly the poor and marginal workers dependent on government supplements. The president reduced spending for food stamps, school lunches, Aid to Families with Dependent Children (welfare), and Medicaid, while maintaining programs that middle-class voters relied on, such as Medicare and Social Security. However, rather than diminishing the government, the savings that came from reduced social spending went into increased military appropriations. Together with lower taxes, these expenditures benefited large corporations that received government military contracts and favorable tax write-offs.

As a result of Reagan's economic policies, financial institutions and the stock market earned huge profits. The Reagan administration relaxed antitrust regulations, encouraging corporate mergers to a degree unseen since the Great Depression. Fueled by falling interest rates, the stock market created wealth for many investors. The number of millionaires doubled during the 1980s, as the top 1 percent of families gained control of 42 percent of the nation's wealth and 60 percent of corporate stock. Reflecting this phenomenal accumulation of riches, television produced melodramas depicting the lives of oil barons (such as *Dallas* and *Dynasty*), whose characters lived glamorous lives filled with intrigue and extravagance. In *Wall Street* (1987), a film that captured the money ethic of the period, Gordon Gekko, the main character, utters the memorable line summing up the moment: "Greed, for lack of a better word, is good. Greed is right. Greed works."

In reality, however, greed did not work for most people. The gap between the rich and the poor widened. During the 1980s, the nation's share of poor people rose from 11.7 percent to 13.5 percent, representing 33 million Americans. Severe cutbacks in government social programs that had alleviated suffering in the past worsened the plight of the poor. Poverty disproportionately affected women and minorities. The number of homeless people grew to as many as 400,000 during the 1980s, as chronically unemployed workers, the mentally ill, and single mothers sought shelter in subways, under bridges, and in parks. While the rich got richer and the poor got poorer, the middle class diminished in size. From a high of 53 percent of families in the early 1970s, the middle class shrank to 49 percent in 1985.

The Reagan administration's relaxed regulation of the corporate sector also contributed to the unbalanced economy. Federal agencies concerned with environmental protection, consumer product reliability, and occupational safety saw their key functions shifted to the states, which made them less effective. The president also aided big business by challenging labor unions. In 1981 air traffic controllers went on strike to gain higher wages and improved safety conditions. In response, the president fired the strikers who refused to return to work, and in their place he hired new controllers. Reagan's anti-union actions both reflected and encouraged a decline in union membership throughout the 1980s, with union membership falling to its lowest level since the New Deal (16 percent). Without union protection, wages failed to keep up with inflation, further increasing the gap between rich and poor.

Reagan's landslide victory over Democratic candidate Walter Mondale in 1984 sealed the national political transition from liberalism to conservatism. Voters responded overwhelmingly to the improving economy, Reagan's defense of traditional social values, and his boundless optimism about America's future. Despite the landslide, the election was notable for the nomination of Representative Geraldine Ferraro of New York as Mondale's Democratic running mate, the first woman to run on a major party ticket for national office.

Reagan's second term did not produce changes as significant as did his first term. Democrats still controlled the House and in 1986 recaptured the Senate. The Reagan administration focused on foreign affairs and the continued Cold War with the Soviet Union, thus escalating defense spending. Most of the Reagan economic revolution continued as before, but with serious consequences: The federal deficit mushroomed, and by 1989 the nation was saddled with a $2.8 trillion debt, a situation that jeopardized the country's financial independence and the economic well-being of succeeding generations.

The president also reshaped the future through his nominations to the U.S. Supreme Court. Starting with the choice of Sandra Day O'Connor, the Court's first female justice, in 1981, Reagan's appointments moved the Court in a more conservative direction. The elevation of Associate Justice William Rehnquist to chief justice in 1986 reinforced this trend, which would have significant consequences for decades to come.

The Implementation of Social Conservatism

Throughout his two terms, President Reagan pushed the New Right's social agenda with mixed success. Conservatives blamed political liberalism and an increasingly secular society for what they saw as a decline in family values. Their solution was a renewed focus on conservative Christian principles. In addition to trying to remove evolution and sex education from the classroom and bring in prayer and patriotism, the New Right stepped up its opposition to abortion. The Reagan administration required family planning agencies seeking federal funding to notify parents of children under age eighteen before dispensing birth control, cut off financial aid to international organizations supporting abortion, and provided funds for "chastity clinics" that preached sexual abstinence. Despite these efforts, conservatives could not convince the Supreme Court to overturn *Roe v. Wade*.

Social conservatives also felt threatened by more tolerant views of homosexuality. The gay rights movement, which began in the 1960s, strengthened during the 1970s as thousands of gay men and lesbians made known their sexual orientation, fought discrimination, and expressed pride in their sexual identity. However, the gay rights movement also inspired personal and political attacks. Then, in the early 1980s, physicians traced an outbreak of a deadly illness among gay men to a virus that attacked the immune system (human immunodeficiency virus, or HIV), making it vulnerable to infections that were usually fatal. This disease, called **acquired immune deficiency syndrome (AIDS)**, was transmitted through bodily fluids during sexual intercourse, through blood transfusions, and by intravenous drug use. Scientists could not explain why the disease initially showed up among gay men in the United States; however, New Right critics insisted that AIDS was a plague visited on sexual deviants by an angry God. "The poor homosexuals," mocked Pat Buchanan, a Reagan adviser. "They have declared war on nature and now nature is exacting an awful retribution." As the epidemic spread beyond the gay community, mainly through blood transfusions and illegal intravenous drug use, gay rights organizers and their heterosexual allies raised research money and public awareness. By the early 1990s, medical advances had begun to extend the lives of AIDS patients and manage the disease.

Increased immigration also troubled social conservatives as another reflection of the general societal breakdown. The number of immigrants to the United States rose dramatically in the 1970s and 1980s following the relaxation of foreign quota restrictions after 1965 (Figure 27.1). During these decades, immigrants came mainly from Mexico, Central America, the Caribbean, and eastern and southern Asia and tended to settle in California, Florida, Texas, New York, and New Jersey. Like those who came nearly a century before, most sought economic opportunity, political freedom, and

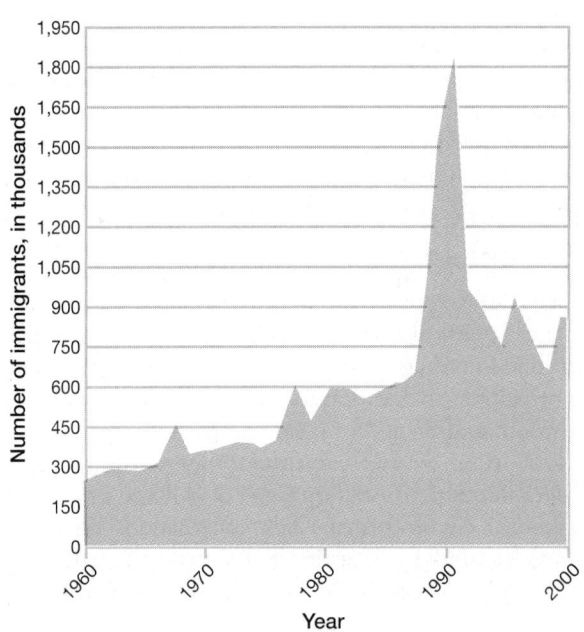

FIGURE 27.1

Immigrant Arrivals to the United States, 1960–2000

Following the relaxation of foreign quota restrictions after 1965, immigration to the United States rose dramatically in the 1970s and 1980s, peaking in the early 1990s. Between 1970 and 2000, nearly 21 million immigrants arrived in the United States, mainly from Mexico, Central America, the Caribbean, and eastern and southern Asia.

Source: Data from *2000 Statistical Yearbook of the Immigration and Naturalization Service.*

escape from wars; and like their predecessors, they brought with them foreign languages, their native cultural practices, and poverty. By 1990 one-third of Los Angeles's and New York City's populations were foreign-born, figures similar to the high numbers of European immigrants at the turn of the twentieth century.

As happened during previous immigration waves, many Americans whose ancestors had immigrated to the United States generations earlier expressed hostility toward the new immigrants. The New Right provoked traditional fears that immigrants took away jobs and depressed wages, and questioned whether these culturally diverse people could assimilate into American society. Cities and states, led by California, enacted laws making English their official language. The migration of illegal immigrants intensified the controversy. In 1985 the Reagan administration, with bipartisan congressional support, fashioned a compromise that extended amnesty to undocumented aliens residing in the United States for a specified period and allowed them to acquire legal status. At the same time, the act penalized employers who hired new illegal workers. The measure allowed Reagan and the Republicans to appeal to Latino voters in the Sun Belt states while convincing the New Right that the administration intended to halt further undocumented immigration.

The Presidency of George H. W. Bush

After Reagan left office, his two-term vice president, George H. W. Bush, carried on his legacy. The son of a former senator from Connecticut, Bush made a fortune in the Texas oil business and began his political career as a member of Congress in the mid-1960s. After losing the Republican nomination to Reagan in 1980, Bush joined the ticket as vice president. In doing so, he abandoned his moderate Republican political views and became a loyal follower of Reaganomics. In his 1988 presidential campaign against Michael Dukakis, the Democratic governor of Massachusetts, Bush defended conservative principles when he promised: "Read my lips: No new taxes." The Republican candidate attacked Dukakis for his liberal positions and accused him of being soft on crime. Bush also affirmed his own opposition to abortion and support for gun rights and the death penalty. At the same time, however, he also called for a "kinder, gentler nation" in dealing with social justice and the environment.

Once in office, George Bush had to deal with problems that he inherited from his predecessor. Reagan's economic programs and military spending had left the nation with a mounting federal budget deficit, which reached nearly $300 billion in 1992 and slowed economic growth, resulting in another recession in 1990. Unemployment reached 7 percent, and state and local governments had difficulty paying for the educational, health, and social services that the Reagan and Bush administrations had transferred to them. To reverse the downward spiral, Bush abandoned his "no new taxes" pledge. In 1990 he supported a deficit reduction package that included more than $130 billion in new taxes, which failed to solve the economic problems and angered Reagan conservatives who had never fully trusted Bush. He also departed from anti-Washington conservatives when he signed the Americans with Disabilities Act (1990), extending an assortment of protections to some 40 million Americans with physical and mental handicaps.

Bush had a mixed record on the environment. In 1989 he continued supporting oil drilling after the oil tanker *Exxon Valdez* struck a reef off the coast of Alaska, dumping nearly 11 million gallons of oil into Prince William Sound. By contrast, in 1990 the president signed the Clean Air Act, which reduced emissions from automobiles and power plants. Two years later, however, the president opposed international efforts to limit carbon dioxide emissions, greenhouse gases that contribute to climate change.

Bush also courted conservatives in his nomination of Clarence Thomas to fill the Supreme Court vacancy left by Justice Thurgood Marshall, the first African American justice. Thomas belonged to a rising group of conservative blacks who shared Republican views supporting private enterprise and the free market system and opposing affirmative action. As chief of the Equal Employment Opportunity Commission under Reagan, Thomas had generally weakened the agency's enforcement of racial and gender equality in the workplace. He also opposed abortion and denounced welfare. Anita Hill's charges of sexual harassment did not stop his advancement. Following his confirmation battle in 1991, Thomas became one of the most conservative members of the Court.

Despite Bush's overtures to conservatives, his popularity plummeted to 34 percent in 1992 based largely on his inability to revive the sagging economy. He ran for reelection against Governor William Jefferson (Bill) Clinton of Arkansas, a candidate skilled in the art of political maneuvering. Learning from the mistakes of Michael Dukakis, Clinton ran as a centrist Democrat who promised to reduce the federal deficit by raising taxes on the wealthy and who supported conservative social policies such as the death penalty, tough measures against crime, and welfare reform. Though he did pledge to extend health care and opposed discrimination against homosexuals, Clinton relied on his mainstream southern Democratic credentials to deflect any claims that he was a liberal. Bush also faced a challenge from the independent candidate Ross Perot, a wealthy self-made businessman from Texas, whose campaign against rising government deficits won 19 percent of the popular vote, mostly at Bush's expense. In turn, Clinton defeated the incumbent by a two-to-one electoral margin.

(REVIEW & RELATE)

• What was Reaganomics, and what were its most important long-term consequences?

• How did conservative ideas shape the social, cultural, and political landscape of the 1980s and 1990s?

Conclusion: The Conservative Legacy

The defeat of George Bush in 1992 did not signal the end of the conservative political consensus of the previous twenty years. The Nixon-Reagan-Bush era had succeeded in dismantling most of Lyndon Johnson's Great Society, and what it did not disassemble these Republican administrations starved by underfunding. President Reagan managed to reorient the political discourse in the country by turning liberalism into an outmoded idea and a pejorative label. The conservatism that Reagan had rallied behind in the unsuccessful Goldwater campaign of 1964 now provided the political instrument with which Republicans defeated Democrats. The Democratic presidential administration of Jimmy Carter acknowledged the conservative notions of limited government and a deregulated market economy while embracing key conservative social values, such as faith in God and prayer. Both Carter and Bill Clinton, who won in 1992, departed from conservatives on some key issues concerning the economy, race, and gender, but neither of them portrayed himself as the heir of the liberal ideals promoted by Franklin Roosevelt, Harry Truman, and Lyndon Johnson.

The movement toward conservatism had been slow and sporadic. Nixon's pragmatic course and his downfall following the Watergate scandal stalled the march toward greater conservatism, and indeed his expediency angered many conservatives to his political right. Reagan represented the triumph of the New Right and transformed the politics of resentment toward the excesses of the 1960s into the politics of revivalism, convincing many that traditional values once again might guide the nation. In constructing this winning coalition, Reagan tapped into the political awakening of the Christian Right, led by evangelicals and Catholics.

The conservative political ascendancy, however, did not stifle dissent. For much of the 1970s and 1980s, Democrats controlled Congress and tried to restrain conservative presidents. The Supreme Court shifted in a more conservative direction, but the Court did not reject the precedents established by the Warren Court. Conservative justices limited controversial decisions on affirmative action and abortion but did not overturn their constitutional foundations. Civil rights reformers, feminists, environmentalists, and antinuclear activists continued to press their concerns and achieve victories.

The New Right bestowed a mixed legacy. Although the Reagan administration reduced inflation and revived economic growth, it burdened the country with unsupportable budget deficits that damaged economic growth and international trade. Tax and spending cuts further enriched the wealthy but hurt the poor and the middle class. Fiscal and monetary policies encouraged widespread speculation on Wall Street and increased the power of giant corporations over political and economic life. Americans learned about the dangers to the environment, took some measures to correct them, but generally refused to alter their lifestyles. African Americans and women broke through barriers that denied them equal access to education and politics, but they confronted white male opposition to further progress.

Yet ordinary people of all backgrounds still made a difference. Allan Bakke was not a conservative ideologue, but his desire to go to medical school helped reshape affirmative action and stimulate a controversy that lasted far beyond his graduation from medical school. Anita Hill rode the conservative wave that brought Reagan to power. However, when she was subjected to sexual harassment, she broke ranks with conservatives and testified against the nomination of Clarence Thomas. Her assertions failed to derail his appointment to the Supreme Court, but her testimony encouraged more women to challenge sexual harassment.

Conservative successes on the home front did not take place in a vacuum. The rise of conservatism coincided with political shifts taking place in the United Kingdom and West Germany. Moreover, conservatives came to power amid major changes occurring in foreign affairs, most notably the proliferation and then the cessation of the Cold War.

Chapter Review

MAKE IT STICK

 LearningCurve **bedfordstmartins.com/hewittlawsonvalue**
After reading the chapter, use LearningCurve to retain what you've read.

IDENTIFY KEY TERMS

Identify and explain the significance of each term below.

New Right (p. 704)

Vietnamization (p. 704)

Pentagon Papers (p. 705)

War Powers Act (p. 705)

Strategic Arms Limitation Treaty
(SALT I) (p. 706)

Organization of Petroleum Exporting
Countries (OPEC) (p. 706)

affirmative action (p. 707)

Watergate (p. 708)

Equal Rights Amendment (ERA) (p. 713)

Environmental Protection Agency (EPA)
(p. 714)

neoconservatives (p. 718)

Reaganomics (p. 719)

acquired immune deficiency syndrome
(AIDS) (p. 722)

REVIEW & RELATE

Answer the focus questions from each section of the chapter.

1. Who made up the New Right coalition that brought Nixon to power? How did Nixon appeal to the New Right?

2. How did Nixon's pragmatism shape both his foreign and domestic policies?

3. What issues and trends shaped the presidency of Jimmy Carter?

4. How and why did the social and cultural developments of the 1960s continue to create conflict and controversy in the 1970s?

5. What was Reaganomics, and what were its most important long-term consequences?

6. How did conservative ideas shape the social, cultural, and political landscape of the 1980s and 1990s?

ONLINE DOCUMENT PROJECTS

- **The Affirmative Action Debate**
- **Debating the Vietnam War**

After reading the primary sources in these document sets, answer the **Interpret the Evidence** questions to help you analyze each of the documents, and then answer the **Put It in Context** question(s) to help you relate the documents to the topics and themes you read about in the chapter.

bedfordstmartins.com/hewittlawsonvalue

TIMELINE OF EVENTS

1970
- Nixon orders invasion of Cambodia
- Four students shot by National Guardsmen at Kent State University
- Congress repeals Gulf of Tonkin Resolution

1971
- Environmental Protection Agency (EPA) created
- *New York Times* and *Washington Post* publish the *Pentagon Papers*

1972
- Nixon visits China
- U.S. and Soviet Union sign the Strategic Arms Limitation Treaty (SALT I)
- Watergate break-in

1973
- Endangered Species Act passed
- Congress passes the War Powers Act
- U.S. supports Israel in Yom Kippur War
- U.S. agrees to withdraw from Vietnam

1973–1974
- OPEC oil embargo against the United States creates gas shortages

1974
- Nixon resigns

1975
- North Vietnam defeats South Vietnam

1977
- Department of Energy created

1978
- Proposition 13 passed in California
- Allan Bakke wins his affirmative action case

1979
- Divorce rate peaks at 23 divorces per 1,000 married couples
- Moral Majority founded
- Three Mile Island nuclear accident

1981
- Reagan fires striking air traffic controllers
- Reagan survives assassination attempt

1982
- Ratification period expires for Equal Rights Amendment

1991
- Senate confirmation hearing for Clarence Thomas

28

☑ LearningCurve
bedfordstmartins.com/hewittlawsonvalue
After reading the chapter, use LearningCurve
to retain what you've read.

Ending the Cold War

1977–1991

AMERICAN HISTORIES

As secretary of state, George Pratt Shultz presided over the end of the Cold
War. A skilled mediator, Shultz believed in the brand of hard-nosed diplomacy
practiced by Henry Kissinger during the Nixon administration, asserting that
"negotiations are a euphemism for capitulation if the shadow of power is not
cast across the bargaining table." After graduating from Princeton with an
economics degree in 1942, the twenty-two-year-old Shultz joined the Marine
Corps and served in the Pacific during World War II. Three years later, Captain
Shultz returned home, got married, and earned a Ph.D. in industrial
economics. Shultz taught at the Massachusetts Institute of Technology and the
University of Chicago and published several books on labor and wage issues.
In 1955 he joined President Eisenhower's Council of Economic Advisors, the
first of many government posts he would fill.

Known for his judicious temperament and bipartisanship, Shultz, a
Republican, served under Democratic presidents John F. Kennedy and Lyndon
B. Johnson, as well as Republican president Richard Nixon, who appointed him
secretary of labor. With Nixon's resignation in 1974, Shultz left government for
the corporate world.

In 1982 Shultz returned to Washington to serve as President Ronald
Reagan's secretary of state. Like Reagan, Shultz believed that the United
States needed to reassert itself as a global power and rebound from the
insecurity and self-doubt that followed the Vietnam War. The president
believed that a tough approach would bring peace, and he revived the fiery
rhetoric and military preparedness of the darkest days of the Cold War. As a
seasoned economist, Shultz doubted that the Soviet Union was financially

able to sustain its military strength, and his predictions proved correct. Faced with an escalating arms race, a fresh group of Soviet leaders decided to pursue peaceful relations, a decision that had great repercussions for the internal structure of the Soviet Union and the nations subject to its control.

While President Reagan and Secretary of State Shultz advocated confrontation with the Soviet Union, Barbara Deming challenged their efforts and devoted her life to promoting peace in a far different manner. She was born in 1917, three years earlier than Shultz, to a middle-class family living in New York City. Deming attended Quaker schools before graduating from Bennington College with a degree in theater and literature. She became an outspoken proponent of nuclear disarmament, feminism, civil rights, and pacifism. Her radical political beliefs and her recognition that she was a lesbian at the age of sixteen placed her outside the social and cultural mainstream. She lived in a women's commune and mobilized heterosexual and gay women to demonstrate for peaceful coexistence with the Soviet Union.

In the 1980s, Deming applied her nonviolent, pacifist beliefs against Reagan and Shultz's muscular approach to fighting the Cold War. "We can put *more* pressure on the antagonist for whom we show human concern," Deming argued. As part of a worldwide campaign against the deployment of nuclear weapons, she joined the Women's Encampment for a Future of Peace and Justice, which opened in western New York in 1983 next to an army depot that stored nuclear missiles. On July 30, 1983, Deming led a march of seventy-five women from the camp into the small town of Waterloo. "Four miles into our walk," she recalled, "our way was blocked by several hundred townspeople brandishing American flags and chanting, 'Commies, go home!'" The marchers then sat down in the style of nonviolent protest and engaged their opponents in dialogue to no avail, as the police arrested Deming and fifty-three other protesters. Demonstrations continued throughout the rest of the summer, inspiring protests in other American communities and throughout Europe.

THE AMERICAN HISTORIES of George Shultz and Barbara Deming were shaped in profound ways by decades of conflict between the United States and the Soviet Union. Both Shultz and Deming believed that the conflict was one of the defining issues of their times, and both were convinced that their approach was the best way to achieve lasting global peace.

The Cold War that Shultz and Deming were dedicated to ending underwent significant changes in the decades following the Nixon administration's reduction of tensions with the Soviet Union. In the late 1970s, President Jimmy Carter emphasized

President Ronald Reagan greets a baby held by Soviet leader Mikhail Gorbachev during a visit to Moscow, 1988.   AP Photo/Ira Schwartz

the moralistic diplomacy of human rights, but by the end of his term he had increased the size of the U.S. military in response to Soviet aggression in Afghanistan. His successor, Ronald Reagan, employed harsher rhetoric and accelerated the military buildup begun under Carter. However, Reagan would have been far less successful had it not been for the willingness of Soviet leader Mikhail Gorbachev to join him in ending the Cold War. With the ultimate collapse of the Soviet Union and its empire, the United States became the world's sole superpower. At the same time, the United States had to operate in an increasingly globalized world. Embracing new challenges, the United States tested its strength in Central America, the Middle East, and the Persian Gulf.

Carter's Diplomacy, 1977–1980

Drawing on the foreign policies of Gerald Ford and Richard Nixon, President Jimmy Carter sought to negotiate with the Soviets over arms reduction while at the same time challenging them to do more to protect human rights. In practice, Carter found this balancing act difficult to sustain, and despite his desire to find ways to cooperate with the Soviets, relations between the superpowers deteriorated over the course of his term in office. Trouble in the Persian Gulf also added to the Carter administration's woes.

The Perils of Détente

Carter made human rights a cornerstone of his foreign policy, and he was vocal in his criticism of the Soviet Union for violating the human rights requirements of the Helsinki accords that President Ford and Soviet leader Leonid Brezhnev had signed in 1975. His emphasis on human rights extended to other regimes as well. Unlike previous presidents who had supported dictatorial governments as long as they were anti-Communist, Carter intended to hold such regimes to a higher moral standard. Thus the Carter administration cut off military and economic aid to repressive regimes in Argentina, Uruguay, and Ethiopia. Still, Carter was not entirely consistent in his application of moral standards to diplomacy. Important U.S. allies around the world such as the Philippines, South Korea, and South Africa were hardly models of democracy, but national security concerns kept the president from severing ties with them.

One way that Carter tried to set an example of responsible moral leadership was by signing an agreement to return control of the Panama Canal Zone to Panama at the end of 1999. The treaty that President Theodore Roosevelt negotiated in 1903 gave the United States control over this ten-mile piece of Panamanian land forever (see chapter 20). Panamanians resented this affront to their sovereignty, and Carter considered the occupation as a vestige of colonialism. Conservative critics viewed the transfer of land as a sign of weakness, but after extended debate the Senate ratified the treaty to relinquish the canal.

The president's pursuit of **détente**, or the easing of tensions, with the Soviet Union was less successful. In 1978 the Carter administration extended full diplomatic recognition to the People's Republic of China. Abandoning the United States' traditional ally of Taiwan, Carter sought to drive a greater wedge between China and the Soviet Union. Nevertheless, Carter did not give up on cooperation with the Soviets. In June 1979, Carter and Brezhnev signed **SALT II**, a new strategic arms limitation treaty. Six months later, however, the Soviet Union invaded Afghanistan to bolster its pro-Communist Afghan regime. President Carter viewed this action as a violation of international law and a threat to Middle East oil supplies and persuaded the Senate to drop consideration of SALT II. To counter Soviet aggression in Afghanistan, Carter obtained from Congress a 5 percent increase in military spending. The Carter administration also reduced grain sales to the USSR and led a boycott of the 1980 Olympic Games in Moscow to punish the Soviet Union for its invasion of Afghanistan.

Of perhaps the greatest long-term importance was President Carter's decision to authorize the CIA to provide covert military and economic assistance to Afghan rebels resisting the Soviet invasion. Chief among these groups were the **mujahideen**, or warriors who wage jihad. Although portrayed as freedom fighters, these Islamic fundamentalists (including a group known as the Taliban) did not support democracy in the Western sense, and many of them were dedicated to creating a theocratic Islamic nation in Afghanistan. Among the mujahideen who received assistance from the United States was Osama bin Laden, a Saudi Arabian Islamic fundamentalist.

In ordering these CIA operations, Carter ignored recent revelations about questionable intelligence practices. Responding to presidential excesses stemming from the Vietnam War and the Watergate scandal, the Senate had held hearings in 1975 into clandestine CIA and FBI activities at home and abroad. Led by Frank Church of Idaho, the Senate Select Committee to Study Governmental Operations with Respect to Intelligence Activities (known as the Church Committee) issued reports revealing that both intelligence agencies had illegally spied on Americans and that the CIA had fomented revolution abroad, contrary to the provisions of its charter. Despite the Church Committee's findings, Carter revived some of these murky practices to combat the Soviets in Afghanistan.

Challenges in the Middle East

Before President Carter attempted to restrain the Soviet Union in Afghanistan, he did have some notable diplomatic successes. Five years after the 1973 Yom Kippur War (see chapter 27), with relations between Israel and its Arab neighbors in a deadlock, Carter invited the leaders of Israel and Egypt to the United States. Following two weeks of discussions in September 1978 at the presidential retreat at Camp David, Maryland, Israeli prime minister Menachem Begin and Egyptian president Anwar Sadat reached an agreement on a "framework for peace." For the first time in its history, Egypt would extend diplomatic recognition to Israel in exchange for Israel's agreement to return the Sinai peninsula to Egypt, which Israel had captured and occupied since 1967. Carter facilitated Sadat's acceptance of the **Camp David accords** by promising to extend foreign aid to Egypt. The treaty, however, left unresolved controversial issues between Israelis and Arabs concerning the establishment of a Palestinian state and control of Jerusalem.

Whatever success Carter had in promoting peace in the Middle East suffered a serious setback in the Persian Gulf nation of Iran. In 1953 the CIA helped overthrow Iran's democratically elected president, replacing him with a monarch and staunch ally, Mohammad Reza Pahlavi, the shah of Iran. For more than two decades, the shah ruled Iran with U.S. support, seeking to construct a modern, secular state allied with the United States. In doing so, he used repressive measures against Islamic fundamentalists, deploying his secret police to imprison, torture, and exile dissenters. The shah's lavish lifestyle stood in contrast to the poverty of most Iranians, and in 1979 revolutionary forces headed by Ayatollah Ruholla Khomeini, an Islamic fundamentalist exiled by the shah, overthrew his government. Khomeini intended to end the growing secularism in Iran and reshape the nation according to strict Islamic law.

When the deposed shah needed treatment for terminal cancer, President Carter invited him to the United States for medical assistance as a humanitarian gesture, despite warnings from the Khomeini government that it would consider this invitation a hostile action. On November 4, 1979, the ayatollah ordered fundamentalist Muslim students to seize the U.S. Embassy in Tehran and hold its fifty-two occupants hostage until the United States returned the shah to Iran to stand trial. Rather than submit to this violation of international law, President Carter retaliated by freezing all Iranian assets in American banks, breaking off diplomatic relations, and imposing a trade embargo. Carter's response did nothing to free the hostages, and the cutoff of Iranian oil shipments contributed to a 130 percent increase in the price of gasoline in the United States. For most Americans, the oil embargo meant shortages and high gas prices. In response, Khomeini incited Iranian nationalism by denouncing the United States as "the Great Satan." As the impasse dragged on and with the presidential election of 1980 fast approaching, Carter became desperate. After a failed U.S. rescue attempt, Khomeini's guards separated the hostages, making any more rescue efforts impossible. Further humiliating the president, Khomeini released the hostages on January 20, 1981, the inauguration day of Carter's successor, Ronald Reagan.

Despite good intentions and some notable achievements, Jimmy Carter left office with many of his foreign policy objectives unfulfilled. His administration was inconsistent in its approach to the Soviet Union, with attempts at improving relations, as evidenced in the SALT II talks, undermined by moral outrage at the Soviets for invading Afghanistan. The Camp David accords marked a high point of Carter's diplomatic efforts; however, his policies satisfied neither liberals nor conservatives in the United States, and the Iran fiasco helped ensure Carter's defeat in 1980 (see chapter 27).

REVIEW & RELATE

- How did Carter's foreign policy differ from that of Ford and Nixon?
- How did events in Afghanistan and Iran undermine the Carter administration?

Reagan's Cold War Policy, 1981–1988

Ronald Reagan entered the White House determined to offer a direct challenge to the Soviets. Reagan and Secretary of State George Shultz believed that détente would become feasible only after the United States achieved military supremacy over the Soviet Union. Reagan also took strong measures to fight communism around the globe, from Central America to the Middle East. Yet military superiority alone would not defeat the Soviet Union. A shift of leadership within the USSR, as well as a worldwide protest movement for nuclear disarmament, involving people like Barbara Deming, helped bring an end to the Cold War and prepare the way for the dissolution of the Soviet empire.

"The Evil Empire"

In running for president in 1980, Reagan wrapped his hard-line anti-Communist message in the rhetoric of peace. "I've called for whatever it takes to be so strong that no other nation will dare violate the peace," he told the Veterans of Foreign Wars Convention on August 18, 1980. Still, he made it clear that he did not intend to pursue peace at any price; it "must not be a peace of humiliation and gradual surrender." Once in the White House, Reagan left no doubt about his anti-Communist stance. He called the Soviet Union "the evil empire," regarding it as "the focus of evil in the modern world." The president planned to confront that evil with both words and deeds, backing up his rhetoric with a massive military buildup.

In a show of moral and economic might, Reagan proposed the largest military budget in American history. Under the Reagan administration, the defense budget grew about 7 percent per year, increasing from $157 billion in 1981 to around $282 billion in 1988. Reagan clearly intended to win the Cold War by outspending the Soviets, even if it meant running up huge deficits that greatly burdened the U.S. economy (see chapter 27).

The president sought to expand the Cold War by developing new weapons to be deployed in outer space. He proposed a Strategic Defense Initiative (SDI), or "Star Wars," as it was dubbed, to create an orbiting shield of antiballistic missiles, which even Secretary of State Shultz privately called "lunacy." Seeming more like a page out of science fiction, the SDI was never carried out, though the government spent $17 billion on research.

Reagan was unyielding in his initial dealings with the Soviet Union, and negotiations between the superpowers moved slowly and unevenly. The Reagan administration's initial "zero option" proposal called for the Soviets to dismantle all of their intermediate-range missiles in exchange for the United States agreeing to refrain from deploying any new medium-range missiles. The administration presented this option merely for show, expecting the Soviets to reject it. However, in 1982, after the Soviets accepted the principle of "zero option," Reagan sent negotiators to begin Strategic Arms Reduction Talks (START). Influenced by antinuclear protests in Europe, which had a great impact on European governments, the Americans proposed shelving the deployment of 572 Pershing II and cruise missiles in Europe in return for the Soviets' dismantling of Eastern European–based intermediate-range ballistic missiles that were targeted at Western Europe. The Soviets viewed this offer as perpetuating American nuclear superiority and rejected it.

Relations between the two superpowers deteriorated in September 1983 when a Soviet fighter jet shot down a South Korean passenger airliner, killing 269 people.

The Soviets charged that the plane had veered off course and violated their airspace on a trip from Anchorage, Alaska, to Seoul, South Korea. Although the disaster resulted mainly from Soviet mistakes, Reagan chose to condemn this attack as further proof of the malign intentions of the USSR, and country singer Lee Greenwood wrote the patriotic song "God Bless the USA" in support of the country and of Reagan. The United States sent additional missiles to bases in West Germany, Great Britain, and Italy; in response, the Soviets abandoned the disarmament talks and replenished their nuclear arsenal in Czechoslovakia and East Germany. More symbolically, the Soviets boycotted the 1984 Olympic Games in Los Angeles, in retaliation for the U.S. boycott of the Olympics in Moscow four years earlier. As the two adversaries swung from peace talks to threats of nuclear confrontation, one European journalist observed: "The second Cold War has begun."

Human Rights and the Fight against Communism

The Reagan administration extended its firm Cold War position throughout the world, emphasizing anticommunism often at the expense of human rights. The president saw threats of Soviet intervention in Central America and the Middle East, and he aimed to contain them. As had former presidents John Kennedy, Lyndon Johnson, and Richard Nixon, Reagan exploited the fear of communism in Central America and the Caribbean, where for nearly a century the United States had guarded its sphere of influence. During the 1980s, the United States continued its economic isolation of Cuba via the trade embargo, and it sought to prevent other Communist or leftist governments from emerging in Central America and the Caribbean. In doing so, the Reagan administration interfered in the internal affairs of small nations struggling to lift themselves from the poverty caused by decades of oppressive rule that had benefited private companies and commercial interests in the United States.

In the late 1970s, Nicaraguan revolutionaries, known as the National Liberation Front or Sandinistas, had overthrown the tyrannical government of General Anastasio Somoza, a brutal dictator who had suppressed dissent and tortured opponents. President Jimmy Carter, who had originally supported Somoza's overthrow, halted all aid to Nicaragua in 1980 after the Sandinistas began nationalizing foreign companies and drawing closer to Cuba. In the early years of the Reagan administration, Secretary of State Shultz suggested a U.S. invasion of Nicaragua, reflecting the administration's belief that the Sandinistas were "Soviet proxies" and that the revolution in Nicaragua had been sponsored by Moscow. Rather than invade, Reagan adopted a more indirect but no less violent approach. In 1982 he authorized the CIA to train approximately two thousand guerrilla forces outside the country, known as Contras (Counterrevolutionaries), to overthrow the Sandinista government. Although Reagan praised the Contras as "the moral equivalent of our Founding Fathers," the group consisted of pro-Somoza reactionaries as well as anti-Marxist democrats who blew up bridges and oil dumps, burned crops, and killed civilians. In 1982 Congress, unwilling to support such actions, passed the **Boland Amendment**, which prohibited direct aid to the Contras, thereby limiting the president's ability to aid the anti-Sandinista forces.

Proponents of the Boland Amendment drew on the lessons of the Vietnam War. Recalling that President Johnson had manipulated Congress and the public to support intervention in a civil war conducted by guerrillas, supporters of the amendment sought to prevent Reagan from producing another disaster of this kind. Members of the Reagan administration viewed Vietnam differently. They believed that the United States had to restore its honor and credibility following the defeat in Vietnam, especially in fighting Communists in its own backyard. In the face of congressional opposition, Reagan and his advisers came up with a plan that would secretly fund the efforts of their military surrogates in Nicaragua.

Elsewhere in Central America, the Reagan administration supported a corrupt right-wing government in El Salvador that, in an effort to put down an insurgency, sanctioned military death squads and killed forty thousand people during the 1980s. Despite the failings and abuses of the El Salvadoran government, Reagan insisted that Communist regimes in Nicaragua and Cuba were behind the Salvadoran insurgents. The United States sent more than $5 billion in aid to El Salvador and trained its military leaders to combat guerrilla forces.

While many Americans supported Reagan's strong anti-Communist stance, others opposed to the president's policy mobilized protests. Marches, rallies, and teach-ins were organized in cities and college campuses nationwide. U.S.-sponsored wars also drove many people to flee their dangerous, poverty-stricken countries and seek asylum in the United States. Between 1984 and 1990, 45,000 Salvadorans and 9,500 Guatemalans applied for asylum in the United States, but because the United States supported the established governments in those two nations, nearly all requests for refugee status were denied. Approximately five hundred American churches and synagogues established a sanctuary movement to provide safe haven for those fleeing Central American civil wars. Other Americans, especially in California and Texas, began to view the influx of refugees from Central America with alarm. This immigration, both legal and illegal, meant an increase in medical and educational costs for state and local communities, which taxpayers considered a burden.

In addition to financing secret wars in Central America, on October 25, 1983, Reagan sent 7,000 marines to invade the tiny 133-square-mile Caribbean island of Grenada. After a coup toppled the leftist government of Maurice Bishop, who had received Cuban and Soviet aid, the United States stepped in, ostensibly to protect American medical school students in Grenada from political instability following the coup. A swift victory in Grenada boosted Reagan's popularity and installed a pro-American government.

In Reagan's worldview, securing human rights was less important than fighting communism. Thus Reagan supported repressive governments in the Middle East, Asia, Latin America, and Africa without reservations. Reagan embraced the distinction made by his ambassador to the United Nations, Jeane Kirkpatrick, between non-Communist "authoritarian" nations, which were acceptable, and Communist "totalitarian" regimes, which were not. The difference remained fuzzy in practice, particularly in South Africa, where a white totalitarian government ruled over the black majority. Reagan considered the South African government an example of an acceptable authoritarianism, even though it practiced apartheid (white supremacy and racial separation) and torture. The fact that the South African Communist Party had joined the fight against apartheid reinforced Reagan's desire to support the white-minority, anti-Communist government. Interested in the country's vast mineral wealth, Reagan opted for what he called "constructive engagement" with South Africa, meaning that the United States would maintain and expand trade with a nation whose government had been condemned by the United Nations for its racist practices. The Reagan administration did so even as protesters across the United States and the world spoke out against South Africa's repressive white-minority government and campaigned for divestment of public and corporate funds from South African companies.

As early as 1977, the Reverend Louis Sullivan, an African American clergyman from Philadelphia and a board member of General Motors, convinced the company, the largest employer of blacks in South Africa, to treat its employees equally and in a nonsegregated manner. Supporters of this approach campaigned to persuade other companies doing business in South Africa to adopt what became known as the Sullivan Principles and to get investment funds to withdraw their portfolios from the apartheid nation. In the mid-1980s, students on U.S. college campuses nationwide joined the **divestment movement** by building "shantytowns" to protest the squalid, segregated living conditions of black South Africans. They also conducted demonstrations to demand that universities remove investments in South Africa from their endowment funds. Antiapartheid forces staged similar protests against municipal and state governments. At the same time, numerous African American officials and their allies conducted sit-ins at the South African Embassy in Washington, D.C. These efforts were largely successful. Between 1984 and 1988, the number of colleges and universities divesting either partially or fully from South Africa tripled from 53 to 155. In 1986 Congress passed the Comprehensive Anti-Apartheid Act, which prohibited new trade and investment in South Africa. President Reagan vetoed it, but in testimony to the strength of this popular grassroots movement, Congress overrode the president's veto.

Fighting International Terrorism

Two days before the Grenada invasion in 1983, the U.S. military suffered a grievous blow halfway around the world. In the tiny country of Lebanon, wedged between Syrian occupation on its northern border and the Palestine Liberation Organization's (PLO) fight against Israel to the south, a civil war raged between Christians and Muslims. Reagan believed that stability in the region was in America's national interest. With this in mind, in 1982 the Reagan administration sent 800 marines, as part of a multilateral force that included French and Italian troops, to keep the peace, but fighting continued in Beirut between Christian and Muslim militias. On October 23, 1983, a suicide bomber drove a truck into a marine barracks, killing 241 soldiers. Reagan withdrew the remaining troops.

The removal of troops did not end threats to Americans in the Middle East. Terrorism had become an ever-present danger, especially since the Iranian hostage crisis in 1979–1980. In 1985, 17 American citizens were killed in terrorist assaults, and 154 were injured. In June 1985, Shi'ite Muslim extremists hijacked a TWA airliner in Athens with 39 Americans on board and flew it to Beirut. The Israeli government acceded to the hijackers' demands to release Shi'ite prisoners in its jails, and the crisis ended safely for the hostages. That same year, PLO members hijacked an Italian cruise ship in the Mediterranean. Before the dangerous situation was resolved, an elderly American man in a wheelchair was killed and his body dumped in the sea.

In response, the Reagan administration targeted the North African country of Libya for retaliation. Its military leader, Muammar al-Qaddafi, supported the Palestinian cause and provided sanctuary for terrorists. In 1981 a squadron of Libyan planes attacked a U.S. naval flotilla conducting maneuvers off Libyan shores, and American pilots shot down two enemy planes. The Reagan administration placed a trade embargo on Libya,

Bombing of Marine Barracks, Lebanon, 1983   On October 23, 1983, an Islamic terrorist group ignited two truck bombs that blasted U.S. marine barracks in Beirut, killing 241. Here rescuers search for survivors in the wreckage of the U.S. marine command. The troops were part of a multilateral peacekeeping force during the Lebanese civil war. President Reagan removed American forces after the bombings.   AP Photo/Zouki

and Secretary of State Shultz remarked: "We have to put Qaddafi in a box and close the lid." In 1986, after the bombing of a nightclub in West Berlin killed 2 American service-men and injured 230, Reagan charged that Qaddafi was responsible. In late April, the United States retaliated by sending planes to bomb the Libyan capital of Tripoli. The military strongman survived, but one of his daughters perished in the attack. Following the bombing, Qaddafi took a much lower profile against the United States. Reagan had demonstrated his nation's military might despite the retreat in Lebanon (Map 28.1).

The Reagan administration's efforts to fight communism in Central America and terrorism in the Middle East continued unabated. Despite passage of the Boland Amendment in 1982 and its extension in 1984, the president continued to support the Nicaraguan Contras. By 1985 the Contras numbered somewhere between 10,000 and 20,000 troops and relied almost entirely on U.S. assistance. Barred from providing direct military or economic aid to the Contras, Reagan ordered the CIA and the National Security Council (NSC) to raise money from anti-Communist leaders abroad and wealthy conservatives at home. This effort, called "Project Democracy," raised millions of dollars. In violation of federal law, CIA director William Casey also authorized his agency to continue train-ing the Contras in assassination techniques and other methods of subversion.

In the meantime, the situation in Lebanon remained critical as the strife caused by civil war led to the seizing of American hostages. By mid-1984, seven Americans,

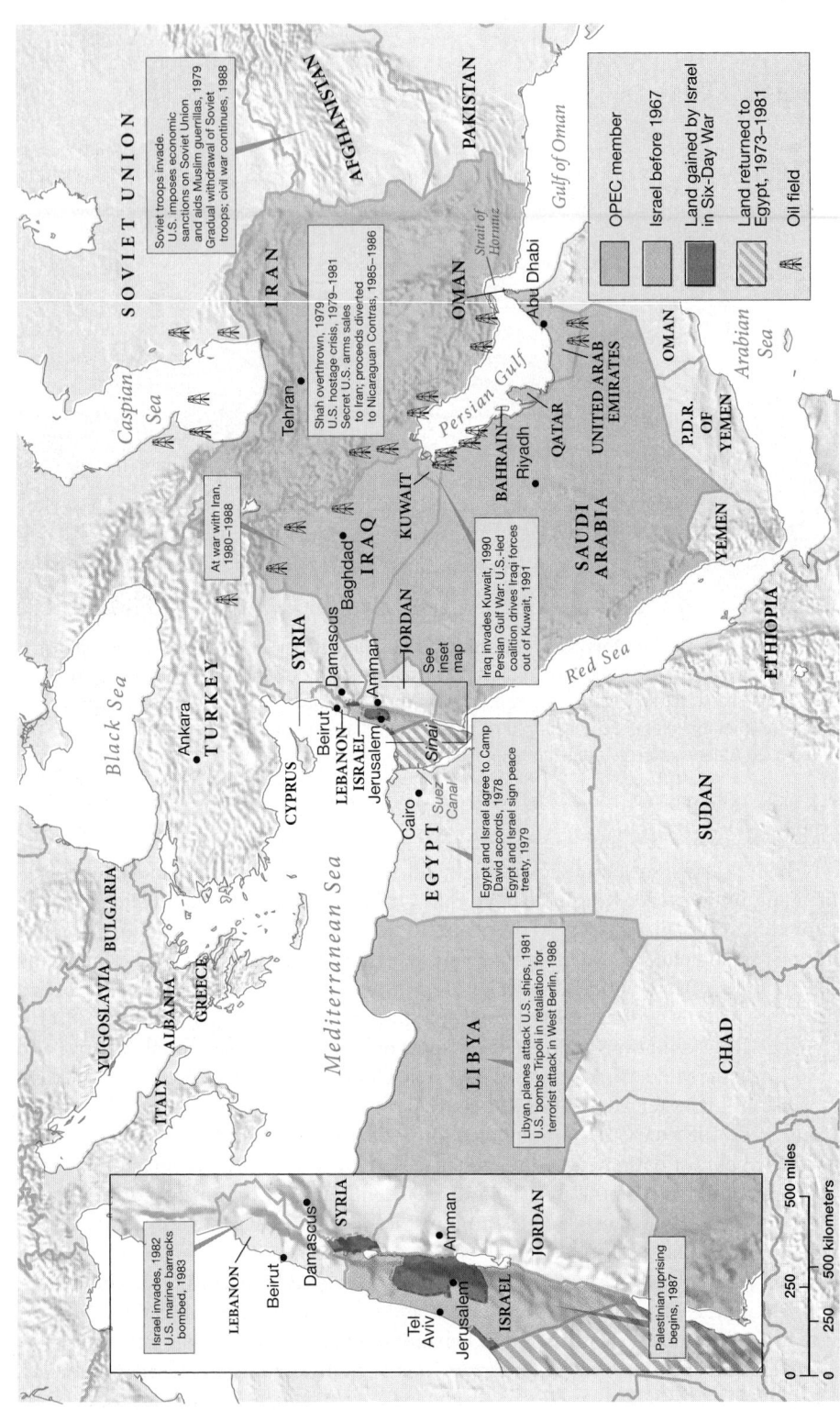

Soviet troops invade. U.S. imposes economic sanctions on Soviet Union and aids Muslim guerrillas, 1979 Gradual withdrawal of Soviet troops; civil war continues, 1988

Shah overthrown, 1979 U.S. hostage crisis, 1979–1981 Secret U.S. arms sales to Iran; proceeds diverted to Nicaraguan Contras, 1985–1986

At war with Iran, 1980–1988

Iraq invades Kuwait, 1990 Persian Gulf War: U.S.-led coalition drives Iraqi forces out of Kuwait, 1991

Egypt and Israel agree to Camp David accords, 1978 Egypt and Israel sign peace treaty, 1979

Libyan planes attack U.S. ships, 1981 U.S. bombs Tripoli in retaliation for terrorist attack in West Berlin, 1986

Israel invades, 1982 U.S. marine barracks bombed, 1983

Palestinian uprising begins, 1987

Legend:
- OPEC member
- Israel before 1967
- Land gained by Israel in Six-Day War
- Land returned to Egypt, 1973–1981
- Oil field

SOVIET UNION
AFGHANISTAN
PAKISTAN
IRAN
Gulf of Oman
Strait of Hormuz
OMAN
Abu Dhabi
UNITED ARAB EMIRATES
OMAN
Arabian Sea
P.D.R. OF YEMEN
Caspian Sea
Tehran
Persian Gulf
QATAR
BAHRAIN
Riyadh
SAUDI ARABIA
YEMEN
Baghdad
IRAQ
KUWAIT
Black Sea
Ankara
TURKEY
SYRIA
Damascus
JORDAN
Amman
See inset map
Red Sea
ETHIOPIA
CYPRUS
Beirut
LEBANON
ISRAEL
Jerusalem
Sinai
Suez Canal
Cairo
EGYPT
SUDAN
YUGOSLAVIA
BULGARIA
ALBANIA
GREECE
ITALY
Mediterranean Sea
LIBYA
CHAD

SYRIA
Damascus
Amman
JORDAN
LEBANON
Beirut
Tel Aviv
Jerusalem
ISRAEL

500 miles
500 kilometers
250
250
0
0

< MAP 28.1
The United States in the Middle East, 1978–1991　The United States has historically needed access to the rich oil reserves of the Middle East. From the 1970s to the 1990s, both Democratic and Republican administrations were committed to the security of Israel, supportive of Afghan rebels fighting Soviet invaders, and opposed to the rising power of Islamic regimes. These principles often led to contradictory policies that further embroiled the United States in Middle East affairs.

including the CIA bureau chief in Beirut, had been kidnapped by Shi'ite Muslims financed by Iran. Since 1980, Iran, a Shi'ite nation, had been engaged in a protracted war with Iraq, which was ruled by military leader Saddam Hussein and his Sunni Muslim party, the chief rival to the Shi'ites. With relations between the United States and Iran having deteriorated in the aftermath of the 1979 coup, the Reagan administration backed Iraq in this war. The fate of the hostages, however, motivated Reagan to make a deal with Iran. In late 1985, Reagan's national security adviser Robert McFarlane negotiated secretly with an Iranian intermediary for the United States to sell antitank missiles to Iran in exchange for the Shi'ite government using its influence to induce the Muslim kidnappers to release the hostages. This covert bargain produced mixed success. Two Americans were freed by the end of 1986, but by then another three had been captured.

Had the matter ended there, the secret deal might never have come to light. However, NSC aide Lieutenant Colonel Oliver North developed a plan to transfer the proceeds from the arms-for-hostages deal to fund the Contras and circumvent the Boland Amendment. Despite opposition from Secretary of State Shultz, Reagan liked North's plan, although the president seemed vague about the details, and some $10 million to $20 million of Iranian money flowed into the hands of the Contras.

In 1986 information about the Iran-Contra connection came to light. Not since the Watergate scandal had a presidential administration received such intense media scrutiny. In the summer of 1987, televised Senate hearings exposed much of the tangled, covert dealings with Iran. In 1988 a special federal prosecutor indicted NSC adviser Vice Admiral John Poindexter (who had replaced McFarlane), North, and several others on charges ranging from perjury to conspiracy to obstruct justice. However, Reagan did not suffer the same fate or disgrace as had Nixon. Certainly the president knew what had been going on and had even approved it, but what he said publicly about his responsibility was circumscribed: "A few months ago, I told the American people I did not trade arms for hostages. My heart and best intentions still tell me that is true, but the facts and the evidence tell me it is not."

 Online Document Project　**The Iran-Contra Scandal**
bedfordstmartins.com/hewittlawsonvalue

The Nuclear Freeze Movement

Despite his tough talk and military buildup, Reagan was not immune to public pressure. Rising protests against nuclear weapons in the United States and Europe in the early 1980s revealed a public increasingly anxious about the possibility of nuclear confrontation with the Soviet Union. At the end of the Carter administration, the United States had promised NATO that it would station new missiles in England, Italy, West Germany, and Belgium. Coupled with his confrontational stance against the Soviet Union, Reagan's decision to implement this policy sparked enormous protest. The campaign for nuclear disarmament included men and women, but women played a particularly strong leadership role in opposing nuclear proliferation. In 1981 peace activists set up camp at Greenham Common in England outside of one of the military bases prepared to house the arriving missiles. With twenty such camps in England, the disarmament forces organized nonviolent protests, including marches and sit-ins. The peace camp at Greenham Common became the model for the Women's Encampment for a Future of Peace and Justice at Seneca Falls, where Barbara Deming and other activists staged demonstrations. Protesters engaged in various forms of nonviolent expression, including singing, dancing, and performing skits to affirm women's solidarity for peace. As the participation of Deming as well as those at Greenham Common showed, women came together not only to promote disarmament but also to empower themselves and create communities based on mutual respect, trust, equality, and nonviolence.

These activities were part of a larger **nuclear freeze movement** that began in 1980. Its proponents called for a "mutual freeze on the testing, production, and deployment of nuclear weapons and of missiles and aircraft designed primarily to deliver nuclear weapons." Grassroots activists also held town meetings throughout the United States to mobilize ordinary citizens to speak out against nuclear proliferation. In 1982 some 750,000 people rallied in New York City's Central Park, the largest demonstration of its kind, to support a nuclear freeze resolution presented at the United Nations. Despite opposition from the United States and its NATO allies, measures favoring the freeze easily passed in the UN General Assembly. In the 1982 elections, peace groups placed nonbinding, nuclear freeze referenda on local ballots, which passed with wide majorities. The nuclear freeze movement's momentum carried over to Congress, where the House of Representatives narrowly rejected an "immediate freeze" by only two votes. Catholic bishops in the United States sent a pastoral letter to their parishioners condemning the spread of nuclear armaments. Even hard-line anti-Communists like Republican senator and former presidential candidate Barry Goldwater of Arizona joined the critics. "I'm not one of those freeze-the-nukes nuts," he explained in opposing new missile production, "but I think we have enough."

Demonstrations in the United States and in Europe influenced Reagan. According to a 1982 public opinion poll, 57 percent of Americans favored an immediate nuclear freeze. Reflecting this sentiment, a 1983 television drama, *The Day After*, graphically portrayed the devastating horror of a nuclear attack on America. Reagan acknowledged that he was more inclined to reconsider deploying missiles abroad because European leaders felt pressure from protesters in their home countries. Ironically, the president credited Europeans' sentiments on the matter while claiming to ignore widespread efforts of domestic opponents such as Barbara Deming. However, the freeze movement inside and outside the United States created a favorable climate in which the president and Soviet leaders could negotiate a genuine plan for nuclear disarmament by the end of the decade.

The Road to Nuclear De-escalation

As frightening as this massive arms buildup was and despite the continuation of peace protests, Ronald Reagan won reelection in 1984 by a landslide (see chapter 27). Following his enormous victory, the popular Reagan softened his militant stance and became more amenable to negotiating with the USSR. Like Nixon, Reagan came to office with a well-deserved reputation as a fervent anti-Communist and left the White House having eased tensions between the United States and the Soviet Union. It took a president with impeccable credentials in fighting communism to reduce Cold War conflicts. Had a liberal or even a moderate Democratic president copied Reagan's actions, he would have been seen as a traitor for succumbing to what many considered the godless Soviet villains. Reagan, even more than Nixon, espoused conservative principles during his presidency, but he refused to let rigid dogma interfere with more pragmatic considerations to foster peace. Notwithstanding his aggressive, moralistic rhetoric, he perceived the limits of America's power in the post-Vietnam era, as evidenced by his decision to invade a very weak Grenada rather than Cuba, Nicaragua, or El Salvador, and he quickly withdrew U.S. marines from Lebanon rather than risk a wider war. By the time President Reagan left office, little remained of the Cold War.

In the mid-1980s, powerful changes were sweeping through the Soviet Union, which helped bring the Cold War to a close. In September 1985, Mikhail Gorbachev became general secretary of the Communist Party and head of the Soviet Union. The first Soviet chief of state born after the 1917 Bolshevik Revolution, Gorbachev introduced a program of economic and political reform. Through *glasnost* (openness) and *perestroika* (restructuring), the Soviet leader hoped to reduce massive state control over the declining economy and to extend democratic elections and freedom of speech and freedom of the press. Gorbachev understood that the success of his reforms depended on reducing Cold War tensions with the United States and slowing the arms escalation that was bankrupting the Soviet economy. Gorbachev's *glasnost* brought the popular American musical performer Billy Joel to the Soviet Union in August 1987, staging the first rock concert in the country.

The changes that Gorbachev brought to the internal affairs of the Soviet Union carried over to the international arena. From 1986 to 1988, the Soviet leader negotiated in person with the American president, something that had not happened during Reagan's first term. In 1986 at a summit in Reykjavik, Iceland, the two leaders agreed to cut the number of strategic nuclear missiles in half. Gorbachev even proposed to eliminate his nation's entire nuclear stockpile of weapons if Reagan terminated the SDI program, an offer Reagan declined. Despite widespread skepticism in the scientific community about the practicality of the SDI, Reagan sincerely believed that it offered the best hope of preventing nuclear warfare. In 1987 the two sides negotiated an Intermediate Nuclear Forces Treaty, which provided for the destruction of existing intermediate-range missiles and on-site inspections to ensure compliance. The height of détente came in December 1987, when Gorbachev traveled to the United States to take part in the treaty-signing ceremony. Reagan no longer referred to the USSR as "the evil empire," and Gorbachev impressed Americans with his personal charm and by demonstrating the media savvy associated with American politicians. The following year, Reagan flew to the Soviet Union and hugged his new friend Mikhail at Lenin's Tomb and told reporters, "They've changed," referring to the once and not-so-distant "evil empire." Citizens of the two adversarial nations breathed a collective sigh of relief; at long last, the Cold War appeared to be winding down.

Online Document Project **Ronald Reagan and the End of the Cold War**
bedfordstmartins.com/hewittlawsonvalue

REVIEW & RELATE

- How did anticommunism shape Ronald Reagan's foreign policy?
- What role did ordinary citizens play in prompting the superpowers to move toward nuclear de-escalation?

The Fall of the Iron Curtain

When George H. W. Bush, Reagan's vice president and successor, took office in January 1989, he encountered a very different Soviet Union from the one Ronald Reagan had faced a decade earlier. The USSR was undergoing an internal revolution, one that allowed Bush and the United States to take on a new role in a world that was no longer divided between capitalist and Communist nations and their allies. The United States led the formation of new global partnerships that included the former Soviet Union. Globalization became the hallmark of the post–Cold War era, replacing previously dualistic economic and political systems, with mixed consequences. Following the collapse of the old world order, local and regional conflicts long held in check by the Cold War broke out along religious, racial, and ethnic lines.

The Breakup of the Soviet Union

Bush's first year in office coincided with upheavals in the Soviet-controlled Communist bloc, with Poland leading the way. In 1980 Polish dockworker Lech Walesa organized Solidarity, a trade union movement that conducted a series of popular strikes that forced the Communist government to recognize the group. Solidarity had ten million members and attracted various opponents of the Communist regime, including working-class democrats, Catholics, and nationalists who favored breaking ties with the Soviet Union. In 1981 Soviet leaders, disturbed by Solidarity's growing strength, forced the Polish government to crack down on the organization, arrest Walesa, and ban Solidarity. However, in 1989 Walesa and Solidarity were still alive and seized on the changes ushered in by Mikhail Gorbachev's *glasnost* in the USSR to press their demands for democracy in Poland. This time, with Gorbachev in command, the Soviets refused to intervene, and Poland conducted its first free elections since the beginning of the Cold War, electing Lech Walesa as president of the country. In July 1989, Gorbachev further broke from the past and announced that the Soviet Union would respect the national sovereignty of all the nations in the Warsaw Pact, which the Soviet Union had controlled since the late 1940s. "There is no universal road toward socialism," the Soviet chief declared.

Gorbachev's proclamation spurred the end of communism throughout Eastern Europe. Within the next year, Soviet-sponsored regimes fell peacefully in Hungary and Czechoslovakia, and elected governments replaced them. In Bulgaria, government officials dropped the word *Communist* from their party's name and held free elections, which brought reformers to power. Only in Romania did Communist rulers put up a fight. There, it took a violent popular uprising to topple the brutal dictator Nicolae Ceausescu. The pent-up animosity was so great that Romanian revolutionaries executed Ceausescu and his wife in 1989. The Baltic states of Latvia, Lithuania, and Estonia, which the Soviets had incorporated into the USSR at the outset of World War II, also regained their independence, signaling the geographical breakup of the Soviet Union itself.

Perhaps the most striking symbolism in the dismantling of the Soviet empire came in Germany, a country that had been divided between East and West states since 1945 and had been the scene of confrontations between the two superpowers throughout the Cold War (see chapters 24 and 26). With Communist governments collapsing around them, East Germans demonstrated against the regime of Erich Honecker. With no Soviet help forthcoming, Honecker decided to open the border between East and West Germany. On November 9, 1989, East and West Germans flocked to the Berlin Wall and jubilantly joined workers in knocking down the concrete barricade that divided the city. A year later, East and West Germany merged under the democratic, capitalist Federal Republic of Germany, the nation that the United States and its anti-Communist allies had set up after World War II.

Gorbachev also brought an end to the costly nine-year Soviet-Afghan War. More than 14,000 Soviet troops had died in the war, and more than 450,000 suffered from wounds and diseases. The war cost the Soviets more than $20 billion, which severely strained their already ailing economy. When the Soviets withdrew their last troops on February 15, 1989, they left Afghanistan in shambles. One million Afghans had perished, and another 5 million fled the country for Pakistan and Iran, resulting in the political destabilization of Afghanistan. Following a civil war, the Taliban, a group of Sunni Muslim fundamentalists, came to power in the mid-1990s and established a theocratic regime that, among other things, strictly regulated what women could wear in public and denied them educational and professional opportunities. The Taliban also provided sanctuary for many of the mujahideen rebels who had fought against the Soviets, including Osama bin Laden, who would use the country as a base for his al-Qaeda organization to promote terrorism against the United States.

Meanwhile, the Soviet Union disintegrated. Free elections were held in 1990, which ironically threatened Gorbachev's own power by bringing non-Communists to local and national political offices. Although an advocate of economic reform and political openness, Gorbachev remained a Communist and was committed to preserving the USSR. Challenges to Gorbachev came from both ends of the political spectrum. Boris Yeltsin, his former protégé, led the non-Communist forces that wanted Gorbachev to move more quickly in adopting capitalism; on the other side, hard-line generals in the Soviet army disapproved of Gorbachev's reforms and his cooperation with the United States. On August 18, 1991, a group of conspirators from the army, the Communist Party, and the KGB (the Soviet intelligence agency) staged a coup against Gorbachev, placed him under house arrest, and surrounded the parliament building with troops. Yeltsin, the president of the Russian Republic, rallied fellow legislators and Muscovites against the plotters and brought the uprising to a peaceful end. After Gorbachev was set free, he resigned in December 1991. Following the official dissolution of the Soviet Union, Yeltsin engineered the formation of the Commonwealth of Independent States (CIS), consisting of the Russian Federation and eleven of fifteen former Soviet republics (the Baltic states of Latvia, Lithuania, and Estonia did not join). Later that month, the CIS removed the hammer and sickle, the symbol of

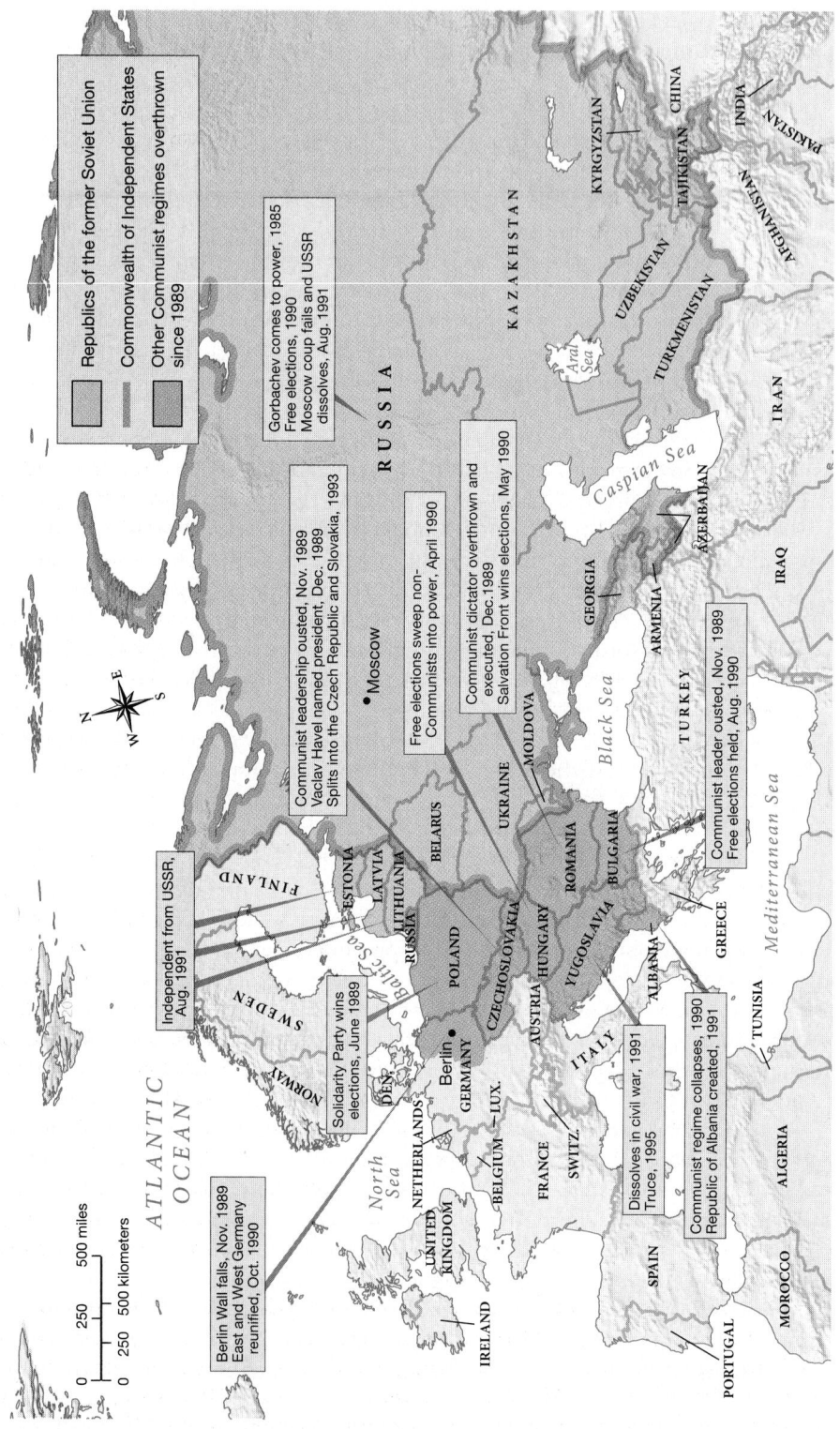

Republics of the former Soviet Union

Commonwealth of Independent States

Other Communist regimes overthrown since 1989

Gorbachev comes to power, 1985
Free elections, 1990
Moscow coup fails and USSR dissolves, Aug. 1991

Communist leadership ousted, Nov. 1989
Vaclav Havel named president, Dec. 1989
Splits into the Czech Republic and Slovakia, 1993

Free elections sweep non-Communists into power, April 1990

Communist dictator overthrown and executed, Dec.1989
Salvation Front wins elections, May 1990

Communist leader ousted, Nov. 1989
Free elections held, Aug. 1990

Independent from USSR, Aug. 1991

Solidarity Party wins elections, June 1989

Dissolves in civil war, 1991
Truce, 1995

Communist regime collapses, 1990
Republic of Albania created, 1991

Berlin Wall falls, Nov. 1989
East and West Germany reunified, Oct. 1990

The Fall of Communism in Eastern Europe and the Soviet Union, 1989–1991 The collapse of Communist regimes in Eastern Europe was due in part to political and economic reforms initiated by Soviet premier Mikhail Gorbachev, including agreements with the United States to reduce nuclear arms. These changes inspired demands for free elections that were supported by popular uprisings, first in Poland and then in other former Soviet satellites.

communism, from its flag. With the Soviet Union dismantled, Yeltsin, as head of the Russian Federation and the CIS, expanded the democratic and free market reforms initiated by Gorbachev (Map 28.2).

Despite his fall from power, Gorbachev deserves a great deal of credit for ending the Cold War. In bringing economic and political reforms to the Soviet Union, he opened the way for greater dialogue with the United States on arms control. His refusal to intervene when communism collapsed in Eastern Europe ensured that the nations in the region would follow their own course toward independence and democracy. He paid a high price for his efforts to restructure his country, as the reforms he set in motion ultimately led to his overthrow and the breakup of the Soviet Union. Yet he must be recognized as one of the prime movers in bringing the Cold War to an end.

Before Gorbachev left office, he completed one last agreement with the United States to curb nuclear arms. In mid-1991, just before conspirators staged their abortive coup, Gorbachev met with President Bush, who had traveled to Moscow to sign a strategic arms reduction treaty. Under this pact, each side agreed to reduce its bombers and missiles by one-third and to trim its conventional military forces. This accord led to a second strategic arms reduction treaty, signed in 1993. Gorbachev's successor, Boris Yeltsin, met with Bush in January 1993, and the two agreed to destroy their countries' stockpile of multiple-warhead intercontinental missiles within a decade.

Globalization and the New World Order

With the end of the Cold War, cooperation replaced economic and political rivalry between capitalist and Communist nations in a new era of **globalization**—the extension of economic, political, and cultural relationships among nations, through commerce, migration, and communication. In 1976 the major industrialized democracies had formed the Group of Seven (G7). Consisting of the United States, the United Kingdom, France, West Germany, Italy, Japan, and Canada, the G7 nations met annually to discuss common problems related to issues of global concern, such as trade, health, energy, the environment, and economic and social development. After the fall of communism, Russia joined the organization, which became known as G8. This group of countries represented only 14 percent of the globe's population but produced 60 percent of the world's economic output. Four of the G8 members—the United States, the United Kingdom, Russia, and France—controlled more than 95 percent of the nuclear weapons in the world.

The United States took an active lead in promoting the World Trade Organization (WTO). The WTO emerged from the General Agreement on Tariffs and Trade, a multilateral agreement fashioned after World War II to encourage tariff reductions and free trade. Created in 1995, the WTO consists of more than 150 nations and seeks "to ensure that trade flows as smoothly, predictably and freely as possible." The policies of the WTO generally benefit wealthier nations, such as the United States. From 1978 to 2000, the value of U.S. exports and imports jumped from 17 percent to 25 percent of the gross national product.

Globalization was accompanied by the extraordinary growth of **multinational (or transnational) corporations**—companies that operate production facilities or deliver services in more than one country. Between 1970 and 2000, the number of such firms soared from 7,000 to well over 60,000. By 2000 the 500 largest corporations in the world generated more than $11 trillion in revenues, owned more than $33 trillion in assets, and employed 35.5 million people. American companies left their cultural and social imprint on the rest of the world. Walmart greeted shoppers in more than 1,200 stores outside the United States, and McDonald's changed global eating habits with its more than 1,000 fast-food restaurants worldwide. Traveling abroad, American tourists marveled at local inhabitants in Europe, Asia, and Africa wearing T-shirts and baseball caps with the logos of American companies. As American firms penetrated other countries with their products, foreign companies changed the economic landscape of the United States. For instance, by the twenty-first century Japanese automobiles, led by Toyota and Honda, captured a major share of the American market, surpassing Ford and General Motors, once the hallmark of the country's superior manufacturing and salesmanship.

Globalization also affected popular culture. In the 1990s, reality shows, many of which originated in Europe, became a staple of American television. British imports included the hugely popular *American Idol*. At the same time, American programs were shown as reruns all over the world. As cable channels proliferated, American viewers of Hispanic or Asian origin could watch programs in their native languages. The Cable News Network (CNN), the British Broadcasting Corporation (BBC), and Al Jazeera, an Arabic-language television channel, competed for viewers with specially designed international broadcasts.

Globalization also had some negative consequences. Organized labor in particular suffered a severe blow. By 2004 union membership in the United States had dropped to 12.5 percent of the industrial workforce. Fewer and fewer consumer goods bore the label "Made in America," as multinational companies shifted manufacturing jobs to low-wage workers in third world countries in Central America, East Asia, and Southeast Asia. Many of these foreign workers earned more than the prevailing wages in their countries, but by Western standards their pay was extremely low. There were few or no regulations governing working conditions or the use of child labor, and many foreign factories resembled the sweatshops of early-twentieth-century America. Not surprisingly, workers in the United States could not compete in this market. Furthermore, China, which by 2007 had become a prime source for American manufacturing, failed to regulate the quality of its products closely. Chinese-made toys, including the popular Thomas the Train, showed up in U.S. stores with excessive lead paint and had to be returned before endangering millions of children.

Globalization also posed a danger to the world's environment. As poorer nations sought to take advantage of the West's appetite for low-cost consumer goods, they industrialized rapidly and chaotically, with little concern for the excessive pollution that accompanied their efforts. The landscapes of some countries were transformed beyond recognition. The desire for wood products and the expansion of large-scale farming eliminated one-third of Brazil's rain forests. The health of indigenous people suffered wherever globalization-related manufacturing appeared. In Taiwan and China, chemical by-products of factories and farms turned rivers into polluted sources of drinking water and killed the rivers' fish and plants.

The older, industrialized nations added their share to the environmental damage. Besides using nuclear power, Americans consumed electricity and gas produced overwhelmingly from coal and petroleum. Gas-guzzling automobiles, and particularly sport-utility vehicles (SUVs) beginning in the 1990s, further harmed the environment. The burning of fossil fuels by cars and factories released greenhouse gases, which has raised the temperature of the atmosphere and the oceans and contributed to the phenomenon known as global warming. Most scientists believe that global warming has led to the melting of the polar ice caps and threatens the existence of human and animal survival on the planet. However, after the industrialized nations of the world signed the Kyoto Protocol in 1998 to curtail greenhouse-gas emissions, the U.S. Senate refused to ratify it. Critics of the agreement maintained that it did not address the newly emerging industrial countries that polluted heavily and thus was unfair to the United States.

Globalization also highlighted health problems such as the AIDS epidemic. By the outset of the twenty-first century, approximately 33.2 million people worldwide suffered from the disease, though the number of new cases diagnosed annually had dropped to 2.5 million from more than 5 million a few years earlier. Africa remained the continent with the largest number of AIDS patients and the center of the epidemic. Initially concentrated in gay men, intravenous drug users, and sex workers, AIDS constituted a continual though diminished threat. Increased education and the development of more effective pharmaceuticals to treat the illness reduced cases and prolonged the lives of those affected by the disease. Though treatments were more widely available in prosperous countries like the United States, agencies such as the United Nations and the World Health Organization, together with nongovernmental groups such as Partners in Health, were instrumental in offering relief in developing countries.

Globalization did not mean the end of regional cooperation. To boost their economic might, western European nations formed the European Union (EU) in 1993, and by 2007 twenty-seven countries had joined the EU. The EU allowed people to move freely by abolishing passport control and customs checks for residents traveling from one member state to another. The organization encouraged free trade and investment. In 1999 the EU introduced a common currency, the euro, which has been adopted by thirteen nations. In 2007 the EU had representation in the G8, contained a population of 500 million, and accounted for approximately 31 percent of the world's output of goods and services.

To strengthen its trading position, the United States formed its own regional economic partnership in North America. In 1993, together with the governments of Mexico and Canada, the U.S. Congress ratified the North American Free Trade Agreement (NAFTA), and it went into effect the following year. The agreement removed tariffs and other obstacles to commerce and investment among the three countries to encourage trade. NAFTA produced noteworthy gains: Between 1994 and 2004, trade among NAFTA nations increased nearly 130 percent. Although income disparity remains large between Mexico and the United States, Mexico has seen a significant drop in poverty rates and a rise in real income. At the same time, NAFTA has harmed workers in the United States. From 1994 to 2007, net manufacturing jobs dropped by 3,654,000, as

U.S. companies outsourced their production to plants in Mexico, taking advantage of the low wage and benefits structure.

Managing Conflict after the Cold War

The end of the Cold War left the United States as the only remaining superpower. Though Reagan's Cold War defense spending had created huge deficits (see chapter 27), the United States emerged from the Cold War with its economic and military strength intact. With the power vacuum created by the breakup of the Soviet Union, the question remained how the United States would use its strength to preserve world order and maintain peace.

In several areas of the globe, the move toward democracy that had begun in the late 1980s proceeded peacefully into the 1990s. The oppressive, racist system of apartheid fell in South Africa, and antiapartheid activist Nelson Mandela was released after twenty-seven years in prison to become president of the country in 1994. In 1990 Chilean dictator Augusto Pinochet stepped down as president of Chile and ceded control to a democratically elected candidate. That same year, the pro-Communist Sandinista government lost at the polls in Nicaragua, and in 1992 the ruling regime in El Salvador signed a peace accord with the rebels.

The end of the Cold War allowed President Bush to turn his attention to explosive issues in the Middle East. The president brought the Israelis and Palestinians together to sign an agreement providing for eventual Palestinian self-government in the Gaza Strip and the West Bank. In doing so, the United States for the first time officially recognized Yasser Arafat, the head of the PLO, whom both the Israelis and the Americans had considered a terrorist.

Before Bush left the White House in 1993, he had deployed military forces in both the Caribbean and the Persian Gulf, confident that the United States could exert its influence without a challenge from the former Soviet Union. During the 1980s, the United States had developed a precarious relationship with Panamanian general Manuel Noriega. Noriega played the United States against the Soviet Union in this region that was vital to American security. Although he channeled aid to the Contras with the approval and support of the CIA, he angered the Reagan administration by maintaining close ties with Cuba. Noriega cooperated with the U.S. Drug Enforcement Agency in halting shipments of cocaine from Latin America headed for the United States at the same time that he collaborated with Latin American drug kingpins to elude U.S. agents and launder the drug lords' profits. In 1988 two Florida grand juries indicted the Panamanian leader on charges of drug smuggling and bribery, pressuring President Reagan to cut off aid to Panama and to ask Noriega to resign. Not only did Noriega refuse to step down, but he also nullified the results of the 1989 presidential election in Panama and declared himself the nation's "maximum leader."

After the United States tried unsuccessfully to foment an internal coup against Noriega, in 1989 the Panamanian leader proclaimed a "state of war" between the United States and his country. The situation worsened in mid-December when a U.S. marine was killed on his way home from a restaurant, allegedly by Panamanian defense forces. On December 28, 1989, President Bush launched Operation Just Cause, sending some 27,000 marines to invade Panama. Bush justified the invasion as necessary to protect the Panama Canal and the lives of American citizens, as well as to halt the drug traffic promoted by Noriega. In reality, the main purpose of the mission was to overthrow and capture the Panamanian dictator. In Operation Just Cause, the United States easily defeated a much weaker enemy. The U.S. government installed a new regime, and the marines captured Noriega and sent him back to Florida to stand trial on the drug charges. In 1992 he was found guilty and sent to prison.

Flexing military muscle in Panama was more feasible than doing so in China. President Bush believed that the acceleration of trade relations that followed full U.S. diplomatic recognition of Communist China in 1978 would prompt the kind of democratic reforms that swept through the Soviet Union in the 1980s. His expectation proved far too optimistic. In May 1989, university students in Beijing and other major cities in China held large-scale protests to demand political and economic reforms in the country. Some 200,000 demonstrators consisting of students, intellectuals, and workers gathered in the capital city's huge Tiananmen Square, where they constructed a papier-mâché figure resembling the Statue of Liberty and sang songs borrowed from the African American civil rights movement. Deng Xiaoping, Mao Zedong's successor, cracked down on the demonstrations by declaring martial law and dispatching the army to disperse the protesters. Peaceful activists were mowed down by machine guns and stampeded by tanks. Rather than displaying the toughness he showed in Panama, Bush merely issued a temporary ban on sales of weapons and nonmilitary items to China. When outrage over the Tiananmen Square massacre subsided, the president restored normal trade relations.

By contrast, the Bush administration's most forceful military intervention came in Iraq. Maintaining a steady flow of oil from the Persian Gulf was vital to U.S. strategic interests. During the prolonged Iraq-Iran War in the 1980s, the Reagan administration had switched allegiance from one belligerent to the other to ensure that neither side emerged too powerful. Though the administration had orchestrated the arms-for-hostages deal with Iran, it had also courted the Iraqi dictator Saddam Hussein. U.S. support for Hussein ended in 1990, after Iraq sent 100,000 troops to invade the small oil-producing nation of Kuwait, on the southern border of Iraq.

President Bush responded aggressively. He compared Saddam Hussein to Adolf Hitler and warned the Iraqis that their invasion "will not stand." Oil was at the heart of the matter. Hussein needed to revitalize the Iraqi economy, which was devastated after a decade of war with Iran. In conquering Kuwait, which held huge oil reserves, Hussein would control one-quarter of the world output of the "black gold." Bush feared that the Iraqi dictator would also attempt to overrun Kuwait's neighbor Saudi Arabia, an American ally, thereby giving Iraq control of half of the world's oil supply. Bush was also concerned that an emboldened Saddam Hussein would then upset the delicate balance of power in the Middle East and pose a threat to Israel by supporting the Palestinians. The Iraqis were rumored to be quickly developing nuclear weapons, which Hussein could use against Israel.

Rather than act unilaterally, President Bush organized a multilateral coalition against Iraqi aggression. Secretary of State James Baker persuaded the United Nations—including the Soviet Union and China, the United States' former Cold War adversaries—to adopt a resolution calling for Iraqi withdrawal from Kuwait and imposing economic sanctions. Thirty-eight nations, including the Arab countries of Egypt, Saudi Arabia, Syria, and Kuwait, contributed 160,000 troops, roughly 24 percent of the 700,000 allied forces that were deployed in Saudi Arabia in preparation for an invasion if Iraq did not comply. Hussein's bellicosity against an Islamic nation won him few allies in the Middle East.

With military forces stationed in Saudi Arabia, Bush gave Hussein a deadline of January 15, 1991, to withdraw from Kuwait or else risk attack. However, the president faced serious opposition at home against waging a war for oil. Demonstrations occurred throughout the nation, and most Americans supported the continued implementation of economic sanctions, which were already causing serious hardships for the Iraqi people. In the face of widespread opposition, the president requested congressional authorization for military operations against Iraq. Lawmakers were also divided, but after long debate they narrowly approved Bush's request.

Saddam Hussein let the deadline pass. On January 16, **Operation Desert Storm** began when the United States launched air attacks on Baghdad and other key targets in Iraq. After a month of bombing, Hussein still refused to capitulate, so a ground offensive was launched on February 24, 1991. Under the command of General Norman H. Schwarzkopf, more than 500,000 allied troops moved into Kuwait and easily drove Iraqi forces out of that nation; they then moved into southern Iraq. Although Hussein had confidently promised that the U.S.-led military assault would encounter the "mother of all battles," the vastly outmatched Iraqi army, worn out from its ten-year war with Iran, was quickly defeated. Desperate for help, Hussein ordered the firing of Scud missiles on Israel to provoke it into war, which he hoped would drive a wedge between the United States and its Arab allies. Despite sustaining some casualties, Israel refrained from retaliation. The ground war ended within one hundred hours, and

Gulf War Protests, 1991   The United States gave Iraq a January 15, 1991, deadline to withdraw from Kuwait or face military force. Protesters at the University of South Florida in Tampa favored continued diplomatic efforts. They carry signs that refer to the January 15 deadline, which also was the birthday of Martin Luther King Jr., a critic of U.S. militarism.
Courtesy of Steven Lawson and Nancy Hewitt

Iraq surrendered. An estimated 100,000 Iraqis died; by contrast, 136 Americans perished (see Map 28.1 on page 738).

With the war over quickly, President Bush resisted pressure to march to Baghdad and overthrow Saddam Hussein. Bush's stated goal had been to liberate Kuwait; he did not wish to fight a war in the heart of Iraq. The administration believed that such an expedition would involve house-to-house, urban guerrilla warfare. Marching on Baghdad would also entail battling against Hussein's elite Republican Guard, not the weaker conscripts who had put up little resistance in Kuwait. Bush's Arab allies opposed expanding the war, and the president did not want to risk losing their support. Finally, getting rid of Hussein might make matters worse by leaving Iran and its Muslim fundamentalist rulers the dominant power in the region. For these reasons, President Bush held Schwarzkopf's troops in place.

The Gulf War preserved the U.S. lifeline to oil in the Persian Gulf. President Bush and his supporters concluded that the United States had the determination to make its military presence felt throughout the world. Bush and the chairman of the Joint Chiefs of Staff, General Colin Powell, understood that the United States had succeeded because it had pieced together a genuine coalition of nations, including Arab ones, to coordinate diplomatic and military action. Military leaders had a clear and defined mission—the liberation of Kuwait—as well as adequate troops and supplies. When they carried out their purpose, the war was over. However, American withdrawal later allowed Saddam Hussein to slaughter thousands of Iraqi rebels, including Kurds and Shi'ites, to whom Bush had promised support. In effect, the Bush administration had applied the Cold War policy of limited containment in dealing with Hussein. The end of the Cold War and peaceful relations with former adversaries in Moscow and Beijing made possible the largest and most successful U.S. military intervention since the war in Vietnam.

REVIEW & RELATE

• What led to the end of Communist rule in Eastern Europe and the breakup of the Soviet Union?

• How did the end of the Cold War contribute to the growth of globalization?

Conclusion: Farewell to the Cold War

The Cold War between the United States and the Soviet and Chinese Communists occupied the attention of two generations of Americans from 1945 to 1991. Citizens in these nations faced the nightmare of nuclear holocaust caused by even small missteps between the adversaries. But some unlikely people were responsible for ending the Cold War. Ronald Reagan, a militant anti-Communist crusader, together with his pragmatic and steady secretary of state, George Shultz, guided the United States through a policy of heightened military preparedness in order to push the Soviet Union toward peace. It was a dangerous gambit, but it worked; diplomacy rather than armed conflict prevailed. Reagan's Cold War strategy succeeded largely because during the 1980s an enlightened leader, Mikhail Gorbachev, governed the Soviet Union. He envisioned the end of the Cold War as a means of bringing political and economic reform to his beleaguered and bankrupt nation. What Gorbachev began, his successor, Boris Yeltsin, finished: the dismantling of the Soviet Union and its empire, and the infusion of democracy and capitalism into Russia.

The activism of ordinary people around the world also helped transform the relationship between the superpowers. Antinuclear protesters in Western Europe and the United States, including Barbara Deming and her feminist cadre at the Seneca Falls Women's Encampment, kept up pressure on Western leaders to make continued nuclear expansion unacceptable. In Eastern Europe, Polish dockworker Lech Walesa and other fighters for democracy broke from the Soviet orbit and tore down the bricks and barbed-wire fences of the iron curtain. Who won the Cold War? Clearly, the United States did, thereby gaining dominance as the world's sole superpower. Yet this did not necessarily guarantee peace. In assuming this preeminent role, the United States faced new threats to international security from governments and insurgents seeking to rebuild nations along ethnic and religious lines in the Balkans, the Middle East, the Persian Gulf, and Africa. Ironically, the bipolar Cold War in some ways had meant a more stable and manageable world presided over by the two superpowers. The collapse of the Soviet empire created a power vacuum that would be filled by a variety of unchecked and combustible local and regional forces intent on challenging the political and economic dominance of the United States and, even more sweeping, the values of Western civilization. At the same time, as globalization and digital technology shrank the world economically and culturally, the United States became the chief target of those who wanted to contain the spread of Western values. Terrorism, which transcended national borders, replaced communism as the leading enemy of the United States and its allies.

Chapter Review

MAKE IT STICK

 LearningCurve **bedfordstmartins.com/hewittlawsonvalue**
After reading the chapter, use LearningCurve to retain what you've read.

IDENTIFY KEY TERMS

Identify and explain the significance of each term below.

détente (p. 731)
SALT II (p. 731)
mujahideen (p. 731)
Camp David accords (p. 732)
Boland Amendment (p. 734)
divestment movement (p. 736)
Iran-Contra (p. 739)
nuclear freeze movement (p. 740)
glasnost (p. 741)

perestroika (p. 741)
Solidarity (p. 742)
globalization (p. 745)
**multinational (or transnational)
   corporations** (p. 746)
European Union (EU) (p. 747)
**North American Free Trade Agreement
   (NAFTA)** (p. 747)
Operation Desert Storm (p. 750)

REVIEW & RELATE

Answer the focus questions from each section of the chapter.

1. How did Carter's foreign policy differ from that of Ford and Nixon?

2. How did events in Afghanistan and Iran undermine the Carter administration?

3. How did anticommunism shape Ronald Reagan's foreign policy?

4. What role did ordinary citizens play in prompting the superpowers to move toward nuclear de-escalation?

5. What led to the end of Communist rule in Eastern Europe and the breakup of the Soviet Union?

6. How did the end of the Cold War contribute to the growth of globalization?

ONLINE DOCUMENT PROJECTS

◆ **The Iran-Contra Scandal**
◆ **Ronald Reagan and the End of the Cold War**

After reading the primary sources in these document sets, answer the **Interpret the Evidence** questions to help you analyze each of the documents, and then answer the **Put It in Context** question(s) to help you relate the documents to the topics and themes you read about in the chapter.

bedfordstmartins.com/hewittlawsonvalue

TIMELINE OF EVENTS

1975 • U.S. and USSR sign Helsinki accords

1978 • Camp David accords between Israel and Egypt

1979 • U.S. Embassy staff in Tehran taken hostage

• U.S. and USSR sign SALT II; Congress does not ratify

• Soviet Union invades Afghanistan

1980 • Solidarity founded in Poland

1982 • Boland Amendment passed

• 750,000 attend nuclear freeze rally in New York City's Central Park

1983 • Suicide bomb attack in Lebanon kills 241 U.S. soldiers

• U.S. invasion of Grenada

1985 • Reagan administration sells arms to Iran for release of hostages and to fund Nicaraguan Contras

• Mikhail Gorbachev assumes leadership of the Soviet Union

1987 • Senate hearings on Iran-Contra affair

• U.S. and Soviet Union sign Intermediate Nuclear Forces Treaty

1989 • Tiananmen Square protests and crackdown in China

• Fall of the Berlin Wall

1990–1991 • Soviet Union dismantled

1991 • U.S. pushes Iraq out of Kuwait

1993 • European Union (EU) formed

1994 • North Atlantic Free Trade Agreement (NAFTA) goes into effect

The Challenges of a New Century

1993 to the present

AMERICAN HISTORIES

William Henry Gates III started tinkering with computers at age thirteen. At that time in the late 1960s, computers were big, bulky machines that filled entire rooms. As a teenager in 1969, the enterprising Gates and some of his friends set up a business to make computerized traffic counters to gauge the speed of automobiles and other vehicles, for which they earned $20,000.

His brilliant mathematical mind and entrepreneurial inclinations led Gates to enroll at Harvard, where those same qualities soon led him to drop out. He spent more time at the university's computer center than he did in class, and in 1974 he became interested in microcomputers as an alternative to large conventional computers. A year later, Gates went to Albuquerque, New Mexico, and formed a computer software company called Microsoft (an amalgam of *microcomputer* and *software*). He envisioned the microcomputer on every office desktop and in homes throughout America. Gates actively pursued the lucrative financial rewards that microcomputers would bring, in contrast to other microcomputer pioneers who did not seek commercial gain and shared information and software with one another freely and unconditionally.

Bill Gates succeeded beyond all expectations. In 1980 Microsoft, now headquartered in Bellevue, Washington, collaborated with International Business Machines (IBM) to create a software package for IBM's new line of personal computers. Additional technological breakthroughs came rapidly. Microsoft joined the financial boom of the 1980s and in 1986 became a publicly traded company on the New York Stock Exchange. Within a decade, Gates became the richest man in America, and like other industrial titans a century earlier, he has donated generously to fund philanthropic activities worldwide.

Despite the enormous benefits of computer technology, the digital revolution has had unforeseen consequences. The terrorists who attacked the World Trade Center and the Pentagon on September 11, 2001, communicated through e-mail and cell phones and trained on computerized flight simulators. They belonged to al-Qaeda, an international terror network that spread its ideology and raised and transferred money over the Internet.

Kristen Breitweiser was a young housewife and mother living in suburban New Jersey on September 11, 2001 (9/11). Her husband, Ron, a senior vice president at an investment management service, worked in Tower Two of the World Trade Center. When one of the planes commandeered by terrorists crashed into the building, her husband died in the fiery collapse of the building, leaving her a widow with a two-year-old daughter. Breitweiser's loss transformed her from a grieving victim and a stay-at-home mother into a political activist.

She started attending meetings of the Victim Compensation Fund established by the federal government following 9/11. She met Mindy Kleinberg, Lorie Van Auken, and Patty Casazza, widows like herself living in New Jersey. The "Jersey Girls," as they became known, addressed concerns over victims' compensation but soon confronted larger political issues. Seeking more than financial compensation for their losses, they demanded to know how the 9/11 attacks could have happened and what the federal government might have done to prevent them. Breitweiser and her colleagues favored an investigation by an independent commission to gather information about what had occurred and to make recommendations to prevent other attacks. However, they found themselves in opposition to President George W. Bush, who initially resisted the creation of such a commission.

Undeterred, the four women mounted a vigorous campaign to pressure the White House and Congress to form a national commission. Breitweiser testified before the Joint Congressional Intelligence Committee to garner support. The women's perseverance paid off: In November 2002, Congress established a bipartisan commission that President Bush signed into law.

However, the commission's final report in 2004 disappointed Breitweiser. She called the report "hollow" and criticized President Bush for not fully and openly cooperating with the investigation. Although Breitweiser had voted for Bush in the 2000 election and considered herself a conservative, her rapid political education since 9/11 turned her against his candidacy in 2004. She also spoke out against the Iraq War, which the administration had initiated in 2003 in response to the 9/11 attacks. Breitweiser continued her political activism as a blog writer for *The Huffington Post*. In this way, this housewife from New Jersey shared her views with millions of people through technology that Bill Gates's generation had developed.

A girl sits on her father's shoulders at an Occupy Miami protest in Miami, Florida, 2011. Joe Raedle/ Getty Images

THE AMERICAN HIS-TORIES of Bill Gates and Kristen Breitweiser were deeply affected by the twin forces of digital technology and terror that dominated life in the United States and throughout the world at the start of the twenty-first century. Computers, the Internet, and cell phone technology reformulated commerce and social relations, fostering the globalization that emerged after the Cold War (see chapter 28). Google, the Web, Facebook, and Twitter became household words and broke down domestic and global barriers that twentieth-century technology had not yet demolished. Computer technology revolutionized political communication and organization, mobilized ordinary citizens into action, and expanded opportunities for disgruntled and oppressed citizens of foreign countries to overthrow despotic rulers. Driven by new computer models for trading in financial securities, the stock market grew highly volatile, and downturns in the economy became greater in intensity and scope. At the same time, the threat of terrorism continued to preoccupy the United States and its allies around the world, and their governments used the latest technologies to monitor suspected terrorists. Ordinary people paid for this increased surveillance each time they boarded an airplane and were subjected to intimate security searches.

Transforming American Society

The decade of the 1990s was a period of great economic growth and technological advancement in the United States. Computers stood at the center of the technological revolution of the late twentieth and early twenty-first centuries, allowing both small and large businesses to reach new markets and transform the workplace. Digital technology also altered the personal habits of individuals in the way they worked, purchased goods and services, communicated, and spent their leisure time. As the Internet and World Wide Web connected Americans to the rest of the world, corporate leaders embraced globalization as the key to economic prosperity. They put together business mergers so that their companies could operate more powerfully in the international market. Government officials generally supported their efforts by reducing regulations on business and financial practices, thus encouraging greater risk taking and easing the way for freer trade overseas. Globalization not only thrust American business enterprises outward but also brought a new population of immigrants to the United States.

The Computer Revolution

The first working computers were developed for military purposes during World War II and the Cold War and were enormous in size and cost. Engineers began to resolve the size issue with the creation of transistors. Invented by Bell Laboratories in the late 1940s, these silicon pieces of equipment came into widespread use in running computers during the 1960s. As companies manufactured smaller and smaller silicon chips, computers became faster, cheaper, and more reliable. The design of integrated circuits in the 1970s led to the production of microcomputers in which a silicon chip the size of a nail head did the work once performed by huge computers. Bill Gates was not the only one to recognize the potential market of microcomputers for home and business use. Steve Jobs, like Gates a college dropout, founded Apple Computer Company in 1976. By 1980 the company had become a publicly traded corporation, turning its founder into a multimillionaire.

Microchips and digital technology found a market beyond home and office computers. Beginning in the 1980s, computers replaced the mechanical devices that ran household appliances such as washing machines, dishwashers, and refrigerators. Over the next twenty years, computers operated everything from standard appliances such as televisions and telephones, to new electronic gadgets such as VCR and CD players, fax machines, cell phones, and iPods. Computers controlled traffic lights on the streets and air traffic in the skies. They changed the leisure patterns of youth: Many young people preferred to play video games at home, rather than engage in outside activities. Consumers purchased goods online, and companies such as Amazon sold merchandise through cyberspace without any actual retail stores. Computers became the stars of movies such as *The Matrix* (1999), *A.I. Artificial Intelligence* (2001), and *Iron Man* (2008). In 2010 *The Social Network* became a hit in portraying the life of Mark Zuckerberg, the primary developer of the social media Web site Facebook, which in 2012 had 900 million users worldwide.

The Internet—an open, global series of interconnected computer networks that transmit data, information, electronic mail, and other services—made social networking possible. The Internet grew out of military research in the 1970s, when the Department of Defense constructed a system of computer servers connected to one another throughout the United States. The main objective of this network was to preserve military communications in the event of a Soviet nuclear attack. At the end of the Cold War, the Internet was repurposed for nonmilitary use, and it now links government, academic, business, and organizational systems. In 1991 the World Wide Web came into existence as a way to access the Internet and share documents and images. Search engines like Google and Yahoo were developed to allow computer users to "surf the Net" and gain access to Web pages. Consumers could shop online as they once had in stores, and researchers could find information previously available only in libraries. Politicians learned how to use the Internet to raise campaign funds and spread their messages to voters more widely and more quickly than they had been able to do in person or on television. Terrorist groups, such as al-Qaeda, also went online. In 2010 around 75 percent of people in the United States used the Internet, as did nearly 2 billion people worldwide, about a quarter of the globe's population.

Digital communication revolutionized globalization. Bill Gates's computer software programs, along with the Internet and World Wide Web, dramatically reduced the time it took for trading partners around the world to converse and make business decisions. Consumers in the United States called customer service operators stationed in India and other remote sites. E-mail largely replaced postal mail, allowing Americans to instantly contact relatives, friends, or professional and business associates around the country or the world.

Business Consolidation

The incredible growth of the computer industry led to increased business consolidation, making it possible for large firms to communicate instantly within the United States and throughout the world and to keep control over their far-flung operations. In addition, the federal government aided the merger process by relaxing financial regulation. Media companies took the greatest advantage of this situation. In 1990 the giant Warner Communications merged with Time Life to create an entertainment empire that included a film studio (Warner Brothers), a television cable network (Home Box Office), a music company (Atlantic Records), a baseball team (the Atlanta Braves), and several magazines (*Time*, *Sports Illustrated*, and *People*). Before Warner Communications combined with the Internet service provider America Online (AOL) in 2001, it had topped $21 billion annually in sales. Several other media conglomerates formed during this period as well. The Australian-born Rupert Murdoch, who already owned considerable holdings in his home country and in Great Britain, moved his operations to the United States. Murdoch soon purchased the Fox Broadcasting Company to go along with a satellite dish company; a movie studio; a variety of newspapers, including the *New York Post* and the *Wall Street Journal*; and thirty television stations. Media mergers mirrored the trend in the rest of the economy. The estimated number of business mergers rose dramatically from 1,529 in 1991 to 4,500 in 1998. The market value of these transactions in 1998 was approximately $2 trillion, compared with $600 billion for 1989, the previous peak year for consolidation.

Corporate consolidation brought corporate malfeasance, as some chief executives of major companies abused their power by expanding their companies too quickly and making risky financial deals, which put workers and stockholders in jeopardy. Such practices led to a number of scandals, including one involving Enron. Enron was the product of a merger in 1985 between Houston Natural Gas and InterNorth, a gas company headquartered in Omaha, Nebraska. Operating out of Houston, Texas, Enron benefited from the deregulation of the gas and electric industry in the 1990s, which brought exorbitant profits and encouraged corporate greed. As Enron thrived, its prices shot up and its stock soared, earning the company more than $50 billion in 2001. In October of that year, information began to trickle out about insider trading, faulty business deals, and questionable accounting practices. As these revelations mounted, Enron's stock and its credit rating plunged, jeopardizing the solvency of the company. In December 2001, the once mighty Enron filed for bankruptcy and fired four thousand employees; its top two executives were subsequently convicted on charges of criminal fraud. This scandal affected companies beyond Enron, leading to the conviction of executives from Enron's accounting firm, Arthur Andersen, and another Andersen client, WorldCom.

The Changing American Population

At the same time as the technological revolution helped transform the U.S. economy and society, an influx of immigrants began to greatly alter the composition of the American population. Since passage of the Immigration Act of 1965 (see chapter 26), the country had experienced a wave of immigration comparable to that at the turn of the twentieth century. As the population of the United States grew from 202 million to 300 million between 1970 and 2006, immigrants accounted for some 28 million of the increase. They came to live in the United States for much the same reasons as those who had journeyed before: to seek economic opportunity and to find political and religious freedom.

Most newcomers who came in the 1980s and 1990s arrived from Latin America and South and East Asia; relatively few Europeans (approximately 2 million) moved to the United States, though their numbers increased after the collapse of the Soviet empire in the early 1990s. Poverty and political unrest pushed migrants out of Mexico, Central America, and the Caribbean. The prizewinning film *El Norte* (1983) dramatized the plight of undocumented Guatemalan Indians who traveled through Mexico to settle in California. Yet most others took advantage of a provision in the 1965 act that permitted them to join family members already settled in the United States. At the beginning of the twenty-first century, Latinos (35 million) had surpassed African Americans (34 million) as the nation's largest minority group. However, with the arrival of Caribbean and African immigrants, black America was also becoming more diverse in this period.

In addition to the 16 million immigrants who came from south of the U.S. border, another 9 million headed eastward from Asian nations, including China, South Korea, and the Philippines, together with refugees from the Vietnam War and Cambodia. By 2007 an estimated 1.6 million Indians from South Asia had immigrated to the United States, most arriving after the 1960s. Indian Americans became the third-largest Asian American group behind Chinese and Filipinos. Another 1 to 2 million people came from predominantly Islamic nations such as Pakistan, Lebanon, Iraq, and Iran (Figure 29.1).

Like their predecessors, new immigrants formed ethnic and religious enclaves. California displayed this fresh face of immigration most vividly. Latinos and Asians had long settled there, and by 2001, 27 percent of the state's population was foreign-born. The majority of Californians consisted of Latinos, Asian Americans, and African Americans, with whites in the minority. In addition to California and the Southwest, immigrants flocked to northeastern and midwestern cities—New York City, Jersey City, Chicago, and Detroit—as they had in the past. However, they now fanned out through the Southeast, adding to the growing populations of Atlanta, Raleigh-Durham, Charlotte, Columbia, and Memphis and providing these cities with an unprecedented ethnic mixture. Like immigrants before them, they created their own businesses, spoke their own languages, and retained their own religious and cultural practices.

They also encountered hostility from many native-born Americans. Some workers felt threatened by immigrants who took jobs, both commercial and agricultural, at lower

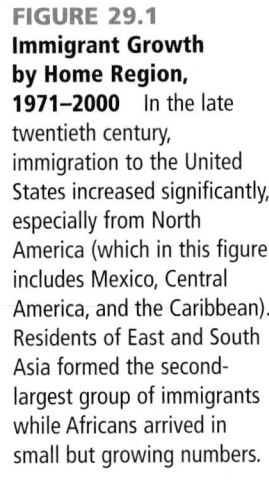

FIGURE 29.1

Immigrant Growth by Home Region, 1971–2000   In the late twentieth century, immigration to the United States increased significantly, especially from North America (which in this figure includes Mexico, Central America, and the Caribbean). Residents of East and South Asia formed the second-largest group of immigrants while Africans arrived in small but growing numbers.

Source: Data from *2000 Statistical Yearbook of the Immigration and Naturalization Service.*

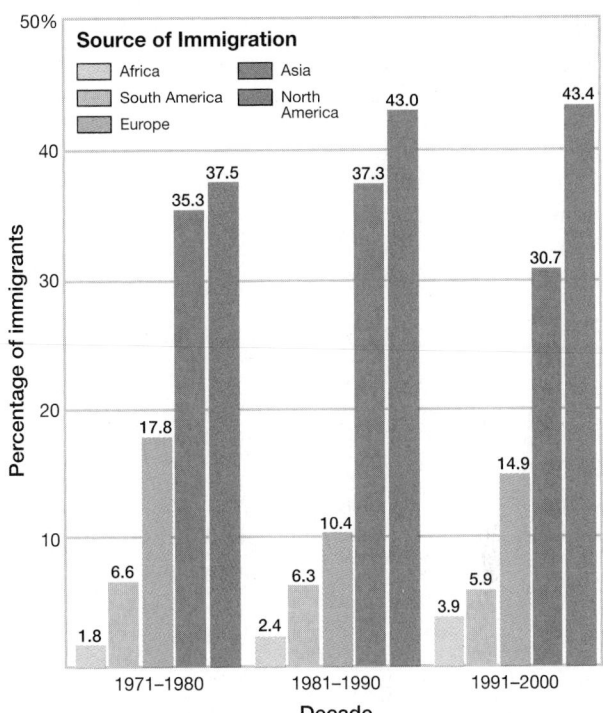

wages. Middle-class taxpayers complained that the flood of impoverished immigrants placed the burden on them to fund the social services—schools, welfare, public health—that the newcomers required. Some of the children and grandchildren of immigrants who had assimilated into American culture resented foreigners who pushed for bilingual education and public signs and instructions in their native languages. Immigration critics also complained about the influx of illegal foreign residents among the immigrant population. Besides breaking the law, these critics argued, undocumented immigrants further depressed wages and taxed public resources.

California led the way in rolling back the effects of immigration. In 1986 Californians approved Proposition 63, which declared English to be the state's official language. Thirty states passed similar laws. In 1994 California voters approved Proposition 187, which prohibited illegal residents from attending public schools and using any social services except emergency health facilities. This proposal never went into effect because federal courts ruled it unconstitutional. Also, some conservative Republicans like President Ronald Reagan, former governor of California, along with agribusiness and other corporate interests that relied on cheap immigrant labor to keep their operating costs low, opposed such severe measures.

REVIEW & RELATE

• How have computers changed life in the United States?

• How has globalization affected business consolidation and immigration?

Politics at the End of the Twentieth Century

The baby boom generation that produced Bill Gates and Kristen Breitweiser also brought President Bill Clinton (and his successors George W. Bush and Barack Obama). The first president born after 1945, Clinton had to deal with the challenges facing the post–Cold War world. He embraced globalization as the key to economic prosperity and showed his readiness to promote and defend U.S. national security. Despite achieving general prosperity and peace, Clinton could not escape the political polarization that divided the American electorate, and his tenure in office only made this schism worse.

The Clinton Presidency

Born in Arkansas in 1946, William Jefferson (Bill) Clinton served five terms as Democratic governor of his home state. As governor, Clinton spoke out for equal opportunity and improved education and economic development. After defeating President George H. W. Bush in 1992 (see chapter 27), Clinton entered the White House brimming with energy and enthusiasm. An admirer of President John F. Kennedy, Clinton echoed Kennedy's sentiments in his inaugural address: "Today a new generation raised in the shadow of the Cold War assumes new responsibilities in a world warmed by the sunshine of freedom but threatened still by ancient hatreds and new plagues."

President Clinton failed in his first attempt to achieve his goals. Against powerful congressional opposition, he backed away from ordering the admission of gays and lesbians into the military, though many already served secretly. Under pressure, the president instead devised the policy of **"don't ask, don't tell,"** which permitted homosexuals to serve in the armed forces so long as they kept their sexual orientation a secret. Gay service members did not benefit from this compromise and continued to encounter discrimination in the military.

Clinton had even less success in reforming health care. Since President Harry Truman had first proposed a system of universal health care coverage in the late 1940s (see chapter 24), the American Medical Association and private insurance companies had succeeded in blocking passage of this and all subsequent plans, despite the general approval of the American public. The Clinton administration recommended a system of universal medical coverage based on "managed competition"—the establishment of regional health care cooperatives to purchase low-cost, private insurance paid for largely by employers. Although Clinton's plan did not advocate "socialized medicine" (government-run medical care) as many critics charged, the plan nonetheless went down to defeat.

President Clinton was more successful in achieving his goals in other areas, some of which were no less controversial. In 1993, reversing Reagan-Bush policies, President Clinton signed executive orders allowing physicians in federally funded clinics to advise patients about abortion; authorizing military hospitals to perform abortions; and funding UN programs that included abortions. Clinton also demonstrated that women's rights were not incompatible with family values. He approved the 1993 Family and Medical Leave Act, which allowed parents to take up to twelve weeks of unpaid leave to care for newborn children without risk of losing their jobs.

Clinton tried to appeal to voters across the political spectrum on other issues. He signed a tough anticrime law that funded the recruitment of an additional 100,000 police officers to patrol city streets, while supporting gun control legislation. Managing to overcome the powerful lobby of the National Rifle Association, in 1993 Clinton signed the Brady Bill (named after Ronald Reagan's aide who was shot in the attempted assassination of the president in 1981), which imposed a five-day waiting period to check the background of gun buyers.

The president achieved even greater success in promoting racial diversity. He appointed African Americans to high-level positions in his cabinet—his selection of four African Americans at one time was unprecedented. His "rainbow administration" welcomed women and minorities to other important posts. Born in the segregated South, Clinton had become a strong advocate of affirmative action and did what he could to protect it from conservative challenges in the states and the courts.

Clinton's fiscal policies ushered in a period of economic growth and prosperity, which ended the recession of the early 1990s. With congressional support, the president reduced domestic and defense spending by $500 billion, while raising taxes on wealthy individuals and corporations. By the end of the 1990s, the Clinton administration had eliminated the deficit, the gross domestic product was rising 3 percent annually, unemployment dropped from 6 percent to 4 percent, and the stock market reached record highs.

President Clinton's accomplishments aroused fierce opposition from conservatives. Right-wing talk radio hosts criticized the president and his wife, Hillary Rodham Clinton, a lawyer and leader in the effort to reform health care. Conservatives blamed Clinton for all they considered wrong in society—feminism, abortion, affirmative action, and secularism. Rush Limbaugh, a popular conservative talk-show host, donned the self-proclaimed mantle of the "angry white male." His rhetoric respected few boundaries, even on publicly owned airwaves, where he uttered comments such as "Feminism was established to allow unattractive women access to mainstream society." Clinton's personal life also provided ammunition for his opponents. Rumors of marital infidelity hounded him, and questions about his and his wife's pre-presidential dealings in a controversial real estate development project known as Whitewater prompted the appointment in 1994 of a special prosecutor to investigate allegations of impropriety.

Facing conservative opposition, the president and the Democratic Party fared poorly in the 1994 congressional elections. Republicans, led by House Minority Leader Newt Gingrich of Georgia, championed the **Contract with America**. This document embraced conservative principles of a constitutional amendment for a balanced budget, reduced welfare spending, lower taxes, and term limits for lawmakers. Democrats lost fifty-four seats in the House, and for the first time since 1952 Republicans captured a majority of both houses of Congress. This election also underscored the increasing electoral influence of white evangelical Christians, who turned out to vote in large numbers for Republican candidates.

Stung by this defeat, Clinton tried to outmaneuver congressional Republicans by shifting rightward politically and championing welfare reform. In 1996 he signed the **Personal Responsibility and Work Opportunity Reconciliation Act**, which abolished the Aid to Families with Dependent Children provision of the Social Security law, the basis for welfare in the United States since the New Deal. The measure required adults on the welfare rolls to find work within two years or lose the benefits provided to families earning less than $7,700. Welfare had provided Republicans with a wedge issue to divide the Democratic electorate, and Clinton diminished its effect by supporting reform. Also in 1996, the president approved the Defense of Marriage Act, which denied married same-sex couples the federal benefits granted to heterosexual married couples, including Social Security survivor's benefits.

In adopting such positions as deficit reduction, welfare reform, and antigay legisla-tion, Clinton ensured his reelection in 1996. Running against Republican senator Robert Dole of Kansas, a military veteran of World War II, and the independent candidate Ross Perot, Clinton captured 49 percent of the popular vote and 379 electoral votes. Dole received 41 percent of the vote, and Perot came in a distant third with 8 percent, a sharp decline from the 19 percent he had received four years earlier (see chapter 27).

Global Challenges and Economic Renewal

Clinton faced numerous foreign policy challenges during his two terms in office. As the first president elected to office in the post–Cold War era, Clinton could approach trouble spots without the rigid anti-Communist views of his predecessors. Increasingly, the problems facing the United States did not result from customary military aggression by one nation against another; rather, the greatest threats came from the implosion of national governments into factionalism and genocide, as well as the dangers posed by Islamic extremists.

At first, the Clinton administration acted cautiously. During a civil war in the African nation of Rwanda, Hutu extremists dispatched armed militias to exterminate the ethnic Tutsi population. The United States watched from the sidelines, along with most of the rest of the world. The slaughter of more than 800,000 Tutsis and moderate Hutus brought condemnation but little action other than the United Nations' attempt to evacuate refugees from the massacre. Following this tragedy, Hollywood told the story of this genocide in the movie *Hotel Rwanda* (2004), which occasioned sympathy for the plight of the Rwandan victims, if not shame for the inaction of the United States.

By contrast, Clinton responded boldly to violence in the Balkans, an area considered more vital to U.S. national security than Rwanda. Along with the collapse of Eastern European regimes in 1989, Yugoslavia splintered into religious and ethnic pieces after the crumbling of the ruling Communist regime. The predominantly Roman Catholic states of Slovenia and Croatia declared their independence from the largely Russian Orthodox Serbian population in Yugoslavia. In 1992 the mainly Muslim territory of Bosnia-Herzegovina also broke away, much to the chagrin of its substantial Serbian population (Map 29.1). This unleashed a civil war between Serb and Croatian minori-ties and the Muslim-dominated Bosnian government. Supported by Slobodan Milošević, the leader of the neighboring province of Serbia, Bosnian Serbs wrested control of large parts of the region and slaughtered tens of thousands of Muslims through what they euphemistically called **ethnic cleansing**. In 1995, following three years of violence, Clinton sponsored NATO bombing raids against the Serbs and dispatched 20,000 American troops as part of a multilateral peacekeeping force. At the same time, the president brokered a peace agreement, known as the **Dayton Peace Accords**, among Serbia, Croatia, and Bosnia at a conference in Dayton, Ohio. In 1999 renewed conflict erupted when Milošević's Serbian government attacked the province of Kosovo to eliminate its Albanian Muslim residents. Clinton and NATO responded by initiating air strikes against the Serbs and placing troops on the ground, actions that preserved Kosovo's independence. (Milošević was later brought before the World Court to face trial for war crimes but died before the court reached a verdict.)

The United States faced an even graver danger from Islamic extremists intent on wag-ing a religious struggle (jihad) of terror against their perceived enemies and establishing a

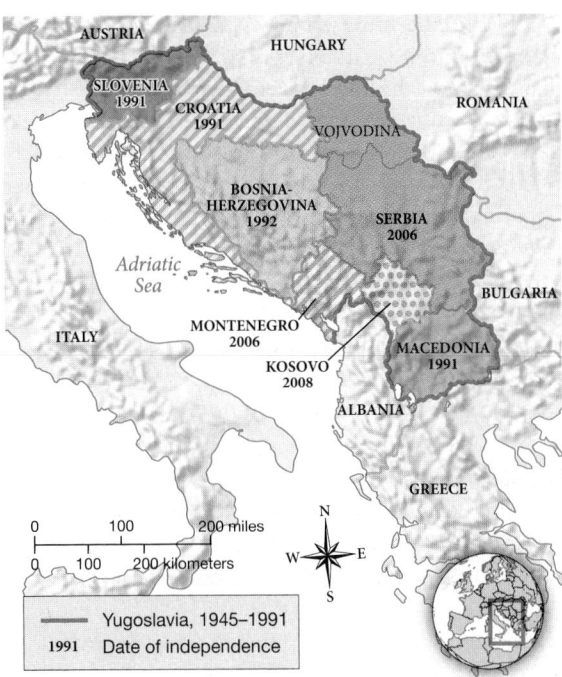

MAP 29.1

The Breakup of Yugoslavia, 1991–2008 With the collapse of Communist control of Yugoslavia in 1989, the country splintered along ethnic and religious lines, eventually forming seven separate nations. A civil war between Serbia and Croatia ended in 1995, but Serbs then attacked Muslims in Bosnia and Kosovo.

transnational Muslim government, or caliphate. Former presidents Jimmy Carter in Iran and Ronald Reagan in Lebanon had experienced the wrath of radical Muslims (see chapter 28). The United States' close relationship with Israel placed it high on the list of terrorist targets, along with pro-American Muslim governments in Egypt, Pakistan, and Indonesia. In 1993 Islamic militants orchestrated the bombing of the World Trade Center's underground garage, which killed six people and injured more than one thousand. Five years later, terrorists blew up American embassies in the African nations of Kenya and Tanzania, killing hundreds and injuring thousands of local workers and residents. In retaliation, Clinton ordered air strikes against terrorist bases in Sudan and Afghanistan. However, the danger persisted. In 2000 al-Qaeda terrorists blew a gaping hole in the side of the USS *Cole*, a U.S. destroyer anchored in Yemen, killing seventeen American sailors.

International terrorism did not lead to the undoing of President Clinton, but more mundane, sexual indiscretions nearly brought him down. Starting in 1995, Clinton had engaged in consensual sexual relations with Monica Lewinsky, a twenty-two-year-old White House intern. Clinton denied these charges under oath and before a national television audience, but when Lewinsky testified about the details of their sexual encounters, the president recanted his earlier statements that he had never had "sexual relations with *that* woman." After an independent prosecutor concluded that Clinton had committed perjury and obstructed justice, the Republican-controlled House voted to impeach the president on December 19, 1998, the first time it had done so in 130 years (see chapter 14). However, on February 12, 1999, Republicans in the Senate failed to muster the necessary two-thirds vote to convict Clinton on the impeachment charges.

Despite his impeachment, Clinton left the country in more prosperous shape than he had found it. At the height of the sex scandal in 1998, the unemployment rate fell to 4.3 percent, the lowest level since the early 1970s. The rate of home ownership reached a record-setting nearly 67 percent. As the "misery index"—a compilation of unemployment and inflation—fell, the gross domestic product grew by more than $250 billion. By 1999 the stock market's Dow Jones average reached a historic 10,000 points, up 2,000 points from just two years before. The Clinton administration boasted that its economic policies had succeeded in canceling the Reagan-Bush budget deficit, yielding a surplus of $230 billion for the fiscal year 2000. This boom, however, did not affect everyone equally. African Americans and Latinos lagged behind whites economically. The gap between rich and poor widened, as the wealthiest 13,000 American families earned as much income as the poorest 20 million. Despite these shortcomings, most Americans seemed pleased with the economic renaissance of the Clinton years.

REVIEW & RELATE

- How did conflicts between Democrats and Republicans affect President Clinton's accomplishments?
- How did the end of the Cold War shape President Clinton's foreign policies?

The New Millennium

Following the prosperous but turbulent Clinton years, Americans looked forward to celebrating the new millennium with hope for the future. Yet this did not happen. Within two years, the country endured a bruising presidential election, experienced unprecedented terrorism at home, and engaged in two wars abroad. The second baby boomer president, George W. Bush, left the country as politically divided as had his predecessor.

George W. Bush and Compassionate Conservatism

In the first presidential election of the new century, the Democratic candidate, Vice President Al Gore, ran against George W. Bush, the Republican governor of Texas and son of the forty-first president. This election marked the first contest between members of the baby boom generation, but in many ways politics remained the same. Candidates began to use the latest technology—the Internet and sophisticated phone banks to mobilize voters—but they rehashed issues stemming from the Clinton years. Gore ran on the coattails of the Clinton prosperity, endorsed affirmative action, was pro-choice on women's reproductive rights, and warned of the need to protect the environment. Presenting himself as a "compassionate conservative," Bush opposed abortion, gay rights, and affirmative action while at the same time supporting faith-based reform initiatives in education and social welfare. Also in the race was Ralph Nader, an anticorporate activist who ran under the banner of the Green Party, a party formed in 1991 in support of grassroots democracy, environmentalism, social justice, and gender equality. According to Nader, Gore and Bush were "Tweedledee and Tweedledum—they look and act the same, so it doesn't matter who you get." Despite this claim, Nader appealed to much the same constituency as did Gore.

Nader's candidacy drew votes away from Gore, but fraud and partisanship hurt the Democrats even more. Gore won a narrow plurality of the popular vote (48.4 percent) compared with 47.8 percent for Bush and 2.7 percent for Nader. However, Bush won a slim majority of the electoral votes: 271 to 267. The key state in this Republican victory was Florida, where Bush outpolled Gore by fewer than 500 popular votes. Counties with high proportions of African Americans and the poor encountered the greatest difficulty and outright discrimination in voting, and in these areas voters were more likely to support Gore. A subsequent recount of the vote might have benefited Bush because Republicans controlled the state government. (Jeb Bush, the Republican candidate's younger brother, was Florida's governor, and Republicans held a majority in the legislature.) Eventually, litigation over the recount reached the U.S. Supreme Court, and on December 12, 2000, more than a month after the election, the Court proclaimed Bush the winner in a decision that clearly reflected the preferences of the conservative justices appointed by Ronald Reagan and George H. W. Bush.

George W. Bush did not view his slim, contested victory cautiously. Rather, he intended to appeal mainly to his conservative political base and govern as boldly as if he had received a resounding electoral mandate. Republicans still controlled the House, whereas a Republican defection in the Senate gave the Democrats a one-vote majority. According to the veteran political reporter Ronald Brownstein, Bush and his congressional leaders "would rather pass legislation as close as possible to his preferences on a virtual party-line basis than make concessions to reduce political tensions or broaden his support among Democrats."

The president promoted the agenda of the evangelical Christian wing of the Republican Party. He spoke out against gay marriage, abortion, and federal support for stem cell research, a scientific procedure that used discarded embryos to find cures for diseases. The president created a special office in the White House to coordinate faith-based initiatives, programs that provided religious institutions with federal funds for social service activities without violating the First Amendment's separation of church and state.

At the turn of the twenty-first century, a growing number of churchgoers were attending **megachurches**. These congregations, mainly Protestant, each contained 2,000 or more worshippers and reflected the American impulse for building large-scale organizations, the same passion for size as could be seen in corporate consolidations. Between 1970 and 2005, the number of megachurches jumped from 50 to more than 1,300, with California, Texas, and Florida taking the lead. The establishment of massive churches was part of a worldwide movement, with South Korea home to the largest congregation. Joel Osteen—the evangelical pastor of Lakewood Church in Houston, Texas, the largest megachurch in the United States—drew average weekly audiences of 43,000 people, with sermons available in English and Spanish. Preaching in a former professional basketball arena and using the latest technology, Osteen stood under giant video screens that projected his image. He and other pastors of megachurches have earned enormous wealth from preaching and writing, which their followers consider justified. "Many preachers tell us that God loves us, but Osteen makes us believe that God loves us. And this is why he is so successful," one observer reflected.

While courting such people of faith, Bush did not neglect economic conservatives. The Republican Congress gave the president tax-cut proposals to sign in 2001 and 2003, measures that favored the wealthiest Americans. Yet to maintain a balanced budget, the cardinal principle of fiscal conservatism, these tax cuts would have required a substantial reduction in spending, which Bush and Congress chose not to do. Furthermore, continued deregulation of business encouraged unsavory and harmful activities that resulted in corporate scandals and risky financial practices.

At the same time, Bush showed the compassionate side of his conservatism. Like Clinton's cabinet appointments, Bush's appointments reflected racial, ethnic, and sexual diversity. They included African Americans as secretary of state (Colin Powell), national security adviser (Condoleezza Rice, who later succeeded Powell as secretary of state), and secretary of education (Rod Paige). In addition, the president chose women to head the Departments of Agriculture, Interior, and Labor and also appointed one Latino and two Asian Americans to his cabinet.

In 2002 the president signed the No Child Left Behind Act, which raised federal appropriations for the education of students in primary and secondary schools, especially in underprivileged areas. The law imposed federal criteria for evaluating teachers and school programs, relying on standardized testing to do so. Another display of compassionate conservatism came in the 2003 passage of the Medicare Prescription Drug, Improvement, and Modernization Act. The law was projected to cost more than $400 billion over a ten-year period to lower the cost of prescription drugs to some 40 million senior citizens under the 1965 Medicare Act and received support from the American Association of Retired Persons (AARP).

The United States at War

President Bush ultimately spent little of his presidency focusing on domestic issues because events originating from abroad vaulted him into the role of wartime president. To make up for his lack of experience in foreign affairs, Bush relied heavily on Vice President Richard (Dick) Cheney, Secretary of Defense Donald Rumsfeld, and Condoleezza Rice. In running for election in 2000, Bush had pledged: "I would be very careful about using our troops as nation builders. I believe the role of the military is to fight and win war and therefore prevent war from happening in the first place." However, Bush's closest advisers had other ideas and sought to reshape critical parts of the post–Cold War world through preemptive force, most notably in the Persian Gulf.

After the attacks on the World Trade Center and the Pentagon on September 11, 2001, the president abandoned his campaign promise to use U.S. troops cautiously and followed the counsel of his advisers. The violence that killed Kristen Breitweiser's husband and thousands of others on that day changed the direction of U.S. foreign and domestic policies. The country undertook a war on terror, one that led to protracted and costly conflicts in Afghanistan and Iraq and the erosion of civil liberties at home. As part of that effort, in 2002 Congress created a cabinet-level superagency, the Department of Homeland Security, responsible for developing a national strategy against further terrorist threats. Congress also enacted into law a key recommendation of the national commission that Breitweiser and the Jersey Girls pressured the government to establish. In 2004 Congress created the Office of the Director of National Intelligence to coordinate the work of security agencies more effectively.

In the immediate aftermath of the September 11 terrorist attacks, Bush acted decisively. The president dispatched U.S. troops to Afghanistan, whose Taliban leaders refused to turn over Osama bin Laden and other terrorists operating training centers in the country. A combination of anti-Taliban warlords and U.S. military special forces,

President Bush at Ground Zero   On September 14, 2001, President George W. Bush toured the wreckage of the destroyed World Trade Center. Standing on a pile of rubble, he heard firefighters, police officers, and other rescuers shout, "USA, USA." He responded: "I can hear you. The rest of the world hears you. And the people who knocked these buildings down will hear all of us soon."   Reuters/Win McNamee/Landov

backed up by American aircraft, toppled the Taliban regime and installed a pro-American government; however, the United States did not immediately capture the elusive bin Laden, who escaped somewhere in the remote territory of Pakistan.

On the home front, the war on terror prompted passage of the **Patriot Act** in October 2001. The measure eased restrictions on domestic and foreign intelligence gathering and expanded the authority of law enforcement and immigration officials in detaining and deporting immigrants suspected of terrorism-related acts. The act gave law enforcement agencies nearly unlimited authority to wiretap telephones, retrieve e-mail messages, and search the medical, financial, and library borrowing records of individuals, including U.S. citizens, suspected of involvement in terrorism overseas or at home. The computer age had provided terrorist networks like al-Qaeda with the means to communicate quickly through electronic mail and cell phones across national boundaries and to raise money and launder it into safe bank accounts online. Computer technology also gave U.S. intelligence agencies ways to monitor these communications and transactions.

Amid rising anti-Muslim sentiments, the overwhelming majority of Americans supported the Patriot Act. In the weeks and months following September 11, some people committed acts of violence against mosques, Arab American community centers and businesses, and individual Muslims and people thought to be Muslims (such as Sikhs). Near Chicago, a crowd of about three hundred anti-Arab youths waved flags, shouted "USA, USA," and attempted to march on a mosque. In this atmosphere, some critics complained about the harsh provisions of the Patriot Act, comparing them to the measures restricting civil liberties during the Red scare following World War I (see chapter 21). Nevertheless, in 2006 Congress renewed the act with only minor changes.

President Bush and his advisers, particularly Vice President Cheney and Secretary of Defense Rumsfeld, did not believe that the defeat of the Taliban in Afghanistan had ended the war on terror. Rather, they saw it as part of a larger plan to reshape the politics of the Middle East and Persian Gulf regions along pro-American lines. In doing so, the United States and its European allies would ensure the flow of cheap oil in order to satisfy the energy demands of consumers in these countries. Furthermore, by replacing authoritarian regimes with democratic governments in places like Iraq and Afghanistan, the Bush administration envisioned a domino effect that would lead to the toppling of reactionary leaders throughout the region. The establishment of pro-American, democratic nations, according to this strategy, would defeat extremist Islamic powers, thereby paving the way for resolving deep-seated, ongoing conflicts between Arabs and Israelis. In crafting this strategy, the Bush administration departed from the well-established, post–World War II policy of containing enemies short of going to war. Instead, the **Bush Doctrine** proposed undertaking preemptive war against despotic governments deemed a threat to U.S. national security, even if that danger was not imminent.

Following this doctrine, President Bush declared in January 2002 that Iraq was part of an "axis of evil," along with Iran and North Korea. Although the United States had supported Saddam Hussein in Iraq's war against Iran in the 1980s, Bush considered the Iraqi dictator to be in the same terrorist camp with Osama bin Laden. Little had changed in Iraq since the 1980s, but President Bush sought to complete the job that his father had started and then retreated from in the 1991 Gulf War—removing Hussein from power. The Iraqi leader was considered too undependable to protect U.S. oil interests in the region. Removing him would also open a path to overthrowing the radical Islamic government of neighboring Iran, which had embarrassed the United States in 1979 and remained its sworn enemy (see chapter 28).

Over the next two years, Bush convinced Congress and a majority of the American people that Iraq presented an immediate danger to the security of the United States in its effort to fight global terrorism. He did so by falsely connecting Saddam Hussein to the 9/11 al-Qaeda terrorists. The president also accused Iraq of being well along the way to building and stockpiling "weapons of mass destruction." Even after UN inspectors examined alleged nuclear and chemical weapons facilities in Iraq and found nothing harmful, the Bush administration remained adamant. Further, the government manipulated questionable intelligence information to defend its claims. In a speech to the United Nations based on dubious and inaccurate information, Secretary of State Powell charged that intelligence services had gathered direct evidence that Iraq was working on a nuclear device.

Online Document Project   **The Uses of September 11**
bedfordstmartins.com/hewittlawsonvalue

Challenging the Bush administration's assumptions and allegations about Iraq, antiwar critics staged mass demonstrations in major cities throughout the country, but with little success. Most Americans gave the president the benefit of the doubt. At the very least, they agreed with Bush that Saddam Hussein was "evil" and that his removal was justified. Thus in March 2003, after a congressional vote of approval, U.S. military aircraft unleashed massive bombing attacks on Baghdad as part of the Bush-Rumsfeld strategy of "shock and awe." Unlike the 1991 Gulf War, in which the first President Bush had responded to the Iraqi invasion of Kuwait and led a broad coalition of nations, including Arab countries (see chapter 28), the United States did not wait for any overt act of aggression and created merely a nominal alliance of nations, with only Great Britain supplying significant combat troops. Nevertheless, within weeks Hussein went into hiding, prompting Bush to declare that "major combat operations" had ended in Iraq.

This triumphant declaration proved premature, although Hussein was captured several months later. Despite the presence of 130,000 U.S. and 30,000 British troops, the war dragged on. More American soldiers (more than 4,000) died after the president proclaimed victory than had died during the invasion. The perception of the United States as an occupying power destabilized Iraq, leading to a civil war between the country's Shi'ite Muslim majority, which had been persecuted under Saddam Hussein, and its Sunni minority, which Hussein represented. In the northern part of the nation, the Kurdish majority, another group brutalized by Hussein, also battled Sunnis. Moreover, al-Qaeda forces, which previously had been absent from the country, joined the fray.

The U.S. occupation and attempts at nation building, something that Bush during the 2000 campaign vowed he would not support, caused serious problems. American soldiers staffing jails containing Iraqi war prisoners, such as Abu Ghraib, were caught in photographs abusing their captives. The reconstituted Iraqi army and police lacked experience and harbored rebels within their ranks. Absent a military draft, Bush could not put sufficient active-duty troops into Iraq without exhausting them through extended tours of duty. In 2004 the military began relying on National Guard units to meet troop requirements, and they eventually constituted about 40 percent of the U.S. armed forces in Iraq. To make up for staffing shortages, the Pentagon outsourced to private companies jobs that would normally be performed by military personnel. American companies profited immensely from construction projects; from supplying troops with housing, meals, and uniforms; and from providing security for high-ranking military and diplomatic personnel. The Defense Department awarded contracts without competitive bidding to companies such as Halliburton, which had close ties to Vice President Cheney.

Amid a protracted war in Iraq, President Bush won reelection in 2004 by promising to finish the course of action he had started in Iraq. Bush argued that to do less would encourage terrorists, subvert burgeoning democracy in Iraq and Afghanistan, and dishonor the troops who had been killed and wounded. Although the Democratic presidential candidate, Senator John Kerry of Massachusetts, criticized Bush's handling of Iraq, Bush eked out a victory; however, this time, unlike four years before, the president won a majority of the popular vote (50.7 percent).

Bush's Second Term

Bush won reelection, but over the next four years his credibility suffered. Several issues—the continued presence of sectarian violence in Iraq, the lack of progress in training Iraqi troops and police to safeguard civilians, the mounting death tolls, and the failure of the U.S.-supported Iraqi government to work out a political solution to the country's problems—turned the majority of Americans against the war. Even when in 2007 the president ordered an increase of 30,000 troops, known as "the surge," which succeeded in reducing mayhem in Baghdad and its vicinity, many Americans had had enough. In 2008 polls showed that 54 percent of Americans considered the invasion of Iraq a mistake, and 49 percent wanted U.S. troops to return home (compared with 47 percent who opposed withdrawal).

However, the president seemed impervious to criticism. The Bush administration continued to enforce the Patriot Act with little concern for the protection of privacy and civil liberties, and it justified its actions on the belief that in a time of war the president had few limits on his power. Bush also refused to back down from the policy of incarcerating suspected al-Qaeda rebels in the U.S. military base in Guantánamo, Cuba. The facility housed more than six hundred men classified as "enemy combatants," who were subject to extreme interrogation and were deprived of legal counsel. This policy changed somewhat when the Supreme Court, in *Hamdan v. Rumsfeld* (2006), ruled that the military tribunals established by the president to prosecute Guantánamo prisoners were unconstitutional. Shortly after, Congress passed legislation providing a small measure of protection for the four hundred prisoners who remained in Guantánamo.

As Bush's handling of the Iraq War generated rising disapproval, his management of a major natural disaster further diminished his popularity. On August 29, 2005, **Hurricane Katrina** slammed into the Gulf coast states of Louisiana and Mississippi. This powerful storm devastated New Orleans, a city with a population of nearly 500,000, a majority of whom were African American. A thirty-foot flood surge caused poorly maintained levees to break, placing large areas of the city underwater. Despite the evacuation of hundreds of thousands of people from New Orleans before the hurricane struck, approximately 50,000 residents remained trapped by the flood. Not only did local and state officials respond slowly and ineptly, but so, too, did the federal government in providing assistance to those trapped in the city.

In the days after the storm hit, chaos reigned in New Orleans. Evacuees were housed in the Superdome football stadium and a municipal auditorium without adequate food, water, and sanitary conditions, and the scenes of despair were broadcast on national television. The flooding killed at least 1,800 residents of the Gulf coast, New Orleans's population dropped by around 130,000 residents, and critics blamed the president for his lack of leadership and slow response to the disaster. Some argued that just as Bush had failed to manage the war in Iraq, he also lacked the ability to handle the Katrina catastrophe. Overall, Hurricane Katrina was just as much a human-made disaster as a natural one.

Displeased with the Bush administration, voters elected a Democratic majority to the House and Senate in 2006, yet little changed. American troops remained in Iraq and Afghanistan. Mobilization for the war on terror had become a permanent part of life in the United States, much like the growth of the national security state during the Cold War (see chapter 24). However, not all Americans experienced the war equally. With military enlistments at low levels, the men and women who served in Iraq and Afghanistan were disproportionately poor and from minority communities. At the same time, Osama bin Laden remained alive and in hiding, and al-Qaeda had regrouped in Pakistan and Yemen. The Bush administration did little to address the perennial problem of Israeli-Palestinian relations, one of the chief elements that fueled terrorism and Islamic radicalism. Making the situation even more combustible, in 2006 Hamas (the Islamic Resistance Movement), which the United States considered an anti-Semitic, terrorist organization, won Palestinian parliamentary elections and posed a new threat to peace in the Middle East.

With turmoil continuing in the Middle East and the Persian Gulf, the threat of nuclear proliferation grew. Iraq did not have nuclear weapons, but Iran sought to develop nuclear capabilities. Iranian leaders claimed that they wanted nuclear technology for peaceful purposes, but the Bush administration believed that Iran's real purpose was to build nuclear devices to attack Israel and establish its supremacy in the region. The election in 2005 of Mahmoud Ahmadinejad, an avowed enemy of Israel, as president of Iran reinforced Bush's fears. Pakistan, a country that already had nuclear weapons, also proved troublesome. Although an ally of the United States, Pakistan was largely ineffective in removing al-Qaeda and Taliban forces from their bases along the country's border with Afghanistan. Equally disturbing, a high-ranking nuclear scientist in Pakistan had previously sold information to North Korea, one of the states in Bush's "axis of evil." North Korea, a totalitarian nation and one of the few remaining Communist dictatorships left from the Cold War era, conducted underground nuclear tests in 2006.

REVIEW & RELATE

• How did President Bush put compassionate conservatism into action?

• How did the war on terror prompt U.S. leaders to rethink America's position in the world?

Challenges Ahead

The changes brought by the digital technology of Bill Gates and the war on terror following September 11 had become firmly embedded in the United States and throughout an interconnected, globalized world. In 2008 a new concern emerged with the arrival of the worldwide Great Recession. At the same time, many Americans rallied behind the presidential candidacy of Barack Obama with renewed hope. Obama's election reflected sweeping demographic changes in the United States and brought reform, but Obama's victory did not eliminate the deep political and cultural divisions in the nation or eradicate pervasive economic and social inequality.

The Great Recession

In 2008 the boom times of the early years of the twenty-first century came to a sudden halt. The stock market's Dow Jones average, which had hit a high of 14,000, fell 6,000 points, the steepest percentage drop since 1931. Americans who had invested their money in the stock market lost trillions of dollars. The stock market crash plunged investment firms into crisis. Lehman Brothers, a financial services firm founded in 1850, lost more than $2 billion and went bankrupt. The gross domestic product fell by about 6 percent, a loss too great for the economy to absorb quickly. Americans lost their jobs as consumer spending decreased, and many forfeited their homes when they could no longer afford to pay their mortgages. Unemployment jumped from 4.9 percent in January 2008 to 7.6 percent a year later. Confronted by this spiraling disaster, President Bush approved a $700 billion bailout plan to rescue the nation's largest banks and brokerage houses.

The causes of the **Great Recession** were many and had developed over a long period. Since the Reagan presidency, the federal government had relaxed regulation of the financial industry. The Clinton administration supported repeal of the Glass-Steagall Act (see chapter 22). This measure, enacted during the New Deal, had separated commercial and investment banking to protect small business people and American families and to avoid the intense financial speculation that preceded the stock market crash of 1929 and the Great Depression. The Federal Reserve Bank encouraged excessive borrowing through keeping interest rates very low and relaxed its oversight of Wall Street practices that placed ordinary investors' money at risk. Investment houses developed elaborate computer models that produced new and risky kinds of financial instruments, which went unregulated and whose complex nature few people understood. Insurance companies such as American International Group marketed so-called credit default swaps as protection for risky securities, exacerbating the financial crisis. In addition, some financial managers engaged in corrupt practices. One of the most notorious, securities broker Bernard Madoff, swindled investors out of billions of dollars through phony securities dealings.

Consumers also shared some of the blame. Many took advantage of the easy mortgage policies that had been devised to allow buyers to purchase homes beyond their means. Known as **subprime mortgages**, these loans appealed to borrowers with low incomes or poor credit ratings, especially minorities, who historically had had difficulty obtaining mortgages and personal loans. On the surface, subprime mortgages appeared to make possible the American dream of home ownership. However, when the housing market collapsed, they turned into the nightmare of home foreclosure as many homeowners ended up owing banks and mortgage companies much more than their homes were worth. Investment banks, which had bundled risky mortgages together for speculative purposes, made the situation even worse. Enticed by the easy availability of credit, consumers also went heavily into personal debt to finance purchases of new technology-driven goods, such as personal computers, smartphones, and larger and larger digital televisions.

The economy might have experienced a less severe downturn if there had been stricter regulation of the securities industry and greater economic equality to bolster consumer spending. But this was not the case. Wealth remained concentrated in relatively few hands. In 2007 the top 1 percent of households owned 34.6 percent of all privately held wealth, and the next 19 percent held 50.5 percent. Thus 80 percent of Americans owned only 15 percent of the wealth, and the gap between rich and poor widened further. The poverty rate stood at around 13 percent (and as high as 20 percent for those under eighteen years of age). This maldistribution of wealth made it extremely difficult to support an economy that required ever-expanding purchasing power and produced steadily rising personal debt (Figure 29.2).

In the age of globalization, the Great Recession spread rapidly throughout the world. Great Britain's banking system teetered on the edge of collapse. Some of the other nations in the European Union (EU)—most notably Greece and Spain, which were the most heavily in debt—verged on bankruptcy and had to be rescued by stronger EU nations. Ireland, whose economy had leaped in the early years of the twenty-first century, abruptly fell on hard times. In providing financial assistance to its member states, the EU required countries such as Greece to slash spending for government services and to lower minimum wages. Even in China, where the economy had boomed as a result of globalization, businesses shut down and unemployment rose as consumer demand for its products declined in the wake of worldwide recession.

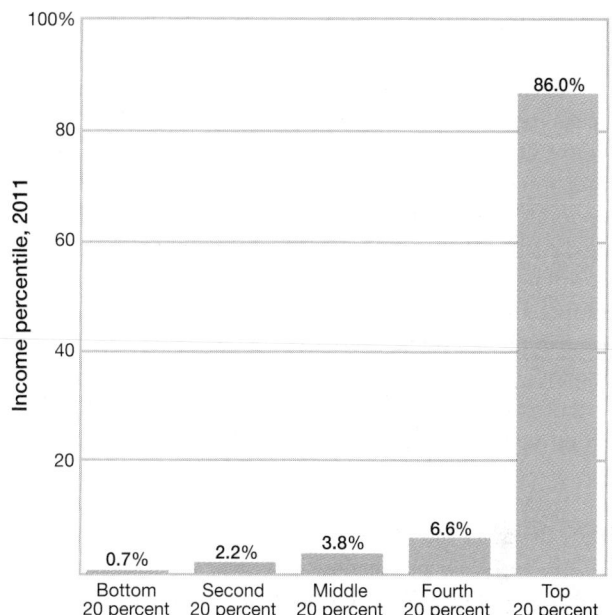

FIGURE 29.2
Wealth Inequality (Capital Income), 2011
The decline of American manufacturing and the expansion of the low-wage service sector, combined with the rise of high-tech industries and unregulated investment banking, led to growing disparities of wealth in the early twenty-first century. Disparities exist even within the top 20 percentile, as the top 1 percent controlled more than half of all capital income in 2011.

Note: Capital income includes taxable and nontaxable interest income, as well as income from dividends, capital gains, and corporate tax liability. Capital income does not include earned income in the form of salaries and wages.

The Rise of Barack Obama

In the midst of the Great Recession, the United States held the 2008 presidential election. The Republican candidate, John McCain, was a Vietnam War hero and a longtime senator from Arizona. His Democratic opponent was Barack Obama, who was a young boy during the Vietnam War and had served a mere four years in the Senate from Illinois. For their vice presidential running mates, McCain chose Sarah Palin, the first-term governor of Alaska, and Obama selected Joseph Biden, the senior senator from Delaware. Whoever won would represent a break with tradition. If McCain triumphed, for the first time a woman would serve as vice president. An Obama victory would place an African American in the White House for the first time in history.

In the end, Obama overcame lingering racial prejudices in the country by speaking eloquently about his background as an interracial child, the son of an immigrant from Kenya and the grandson of a World War II veteran from Kansas. He also refuted charges that he was a Muslim (he is a Christian), that he was not born in the United States (he was born in Hawaii), and that he associated with terrorists (in the 1990s, he had participated in a few Chicago civic engagements with a past 1960s radical). The former community organizer succeeded in building a nationwide, grassroots political movement through digital technology. He raised an enormous amount of campaign money from ordinary donors through the Internet and used Web sites and text messaging to mobilize his supporters. Obama won the presidential election most of all because the public blamed the Bush administration for the recession, and Obama offered hope—"Yes we can" was his campaign slogan—for economic recovery. Obama captured 53 percent of the popular vote, obtaining a majority of votes from African Americans, Latinos, women, and the young, who turned out in record numbers, and a comfortable 365 electoral votes. The Democrats also scored big victories in the House and Senate.

Yet the election of President Obama did not erase the impact of generations of racism from the United States or usher in what some have called a "postracial" America. From 1975 to 2002, the number of black elected officials in the United States increased from around 3,500 to more than 9,000. African Americans had also made significant economic progress as a result of antidiscrimination laws and affirmative action, expanding the size of the black middle class. However, the racial gap in wealth, education, and rates of incarceration remained wide. In 2006 the median income for blacks was $32,132, compared with $50,673 for whites. About 75 percent of whites owned their home, compared with slightly less than 50 percent for blacks, a reflection of the continued disparity in wealth between the races. By 2008 approximately 24 percent of African Americans (compared with 8 percent of whites) lived in poverty, nearly double the national poverty rate of 12.7 percent. The percentage of whites who received a bachelor's degree was almost double that for blacks. More than 28 percent of black men were expected to be imprisoned during their lifetime, compared with 4 percent for whites. More than half the prison population in the United States is black and another quarter Latino, far out of proportion with their percentages among the total U.S. population.

Despite the persistence of racism, President Obama achieved notable victories during his first term in office. He continued the Bush administration's bailout of collapsing banks and investment firms and expanded it to include American automobile companies,

The Election of Barack Obama   On the evening of November 4, 2008, after Barack Obama won the 2008 presidential election, he gave his victory speech at Grant Park in his home city of Chicago, Illinois, before a crowd of approximately 240,000 people. The first African American to be elected president, Obama echoed the words in speeches by Martin Luther King Jr. and Abraham Lincoln.   AP Photo/ David Guttenfelder

which within three years bounced back, became profitable again, and began paying back the government for the bailout. The president supported passage of an economic stimulus plan that provided federal funds to state and local governments to create jobs and keep their employees, including teachers, on the public payroll. Congress also extended the period of unemployment insurance benefits. More controversially, President Obama pushed Congress to pass a health care reform measure, which mandated that all Americans had to obtain health insurance and that no one could be denied coverage for a preexisting condition. He also signed into law repeal of the "don't ask, don't tell" policy, which discriminated against gays in the military. Although the Supreme Court in 2003 had declared unconstitutional a Texas law making homosexual acts a crime, the issue of same-sex marriage remained unresolved. Initially Obama supported civil unions rather than gay marriage, but in 2012 he declared his support for same-sex marriage.

In foreign affairs, the president appointed Hillary Clinton, the former First Lady and a senator from New York, as secretary of state. The U.S. military increased combat troop withdrawals from Iraq and turned over security for the country to the newly elected Iraqi government. At the same time, the Obama administration stepped up the war in Afghanistan by increasing U.S. troop levels, which led to a rise in casualties. Still, the president pledged withdrawal of combat soldiers by 2014. His most dramatic success came in 2011, when U.S. special forces killed Osama bin Laden in his hideout in Pakistan. The Obama administration also persuaded the Senate to approve the renewal of a nuclear disarmament treaty with Russia.

President Obama continued to encounter vigorous political opposition. Most Republican lawmakers refused to support his economic stimulus and health care reform bills. A group of Republican conservatives formed the **Tea Party movement**, which they named after colonial Americans who sought to topple British rule. Its followers attacked the president as a "socialist" for what they perceived as an effort to expand federal control over the economy and diminish individual liberty with passage of the health care act. The Fox News media empire, owned by Rupert Murdoch, backed this movement and its leaders, such as Sarah Palin and talk-show host Glenn Beck.

Obama encountered growing political difficulties because the economy remained stagnant. The president did save the financial system from collapse, and the stock market had rebounded by 2012, but unemployment remained over 8 percent (a drop from its high of 10.2 percent). As millions of people remained out of work, a resurgent Wall Street rewarded its managers and employees with big financial bonuses. Large corporations earned millions of dollars in profits but did not create new jobs. The 2010 midterm elections illustrated the growing dissatisfaction of American voters, as Republicans regained control of the House and the Democratic majority in the Senate narrowed. The Tea Party flexed its electoral muscle in successfully campaigning for Republican congressional and gubernatorial candidates who supported its positions. Exit polls showed that 41 percent of the voters endorsed the Tea Party movement. Governor Scott Walker of Wisconsin, backed by the Tea Party, took aim at public employee unions in his state and signed into law a measure limiting collective bargaining. (In 2012 his opponents failed to win a recall election to remove him from office.)

Dissent also came from the left. In 2011 protesters in cities around the nation launched the **Occupy Wall Street** movement, which attacked corporate greed, economic inequality, and the inability of the federal government to relieve the widespread suffering. Many in the movement were inspired to act by massive cuts in education spending,

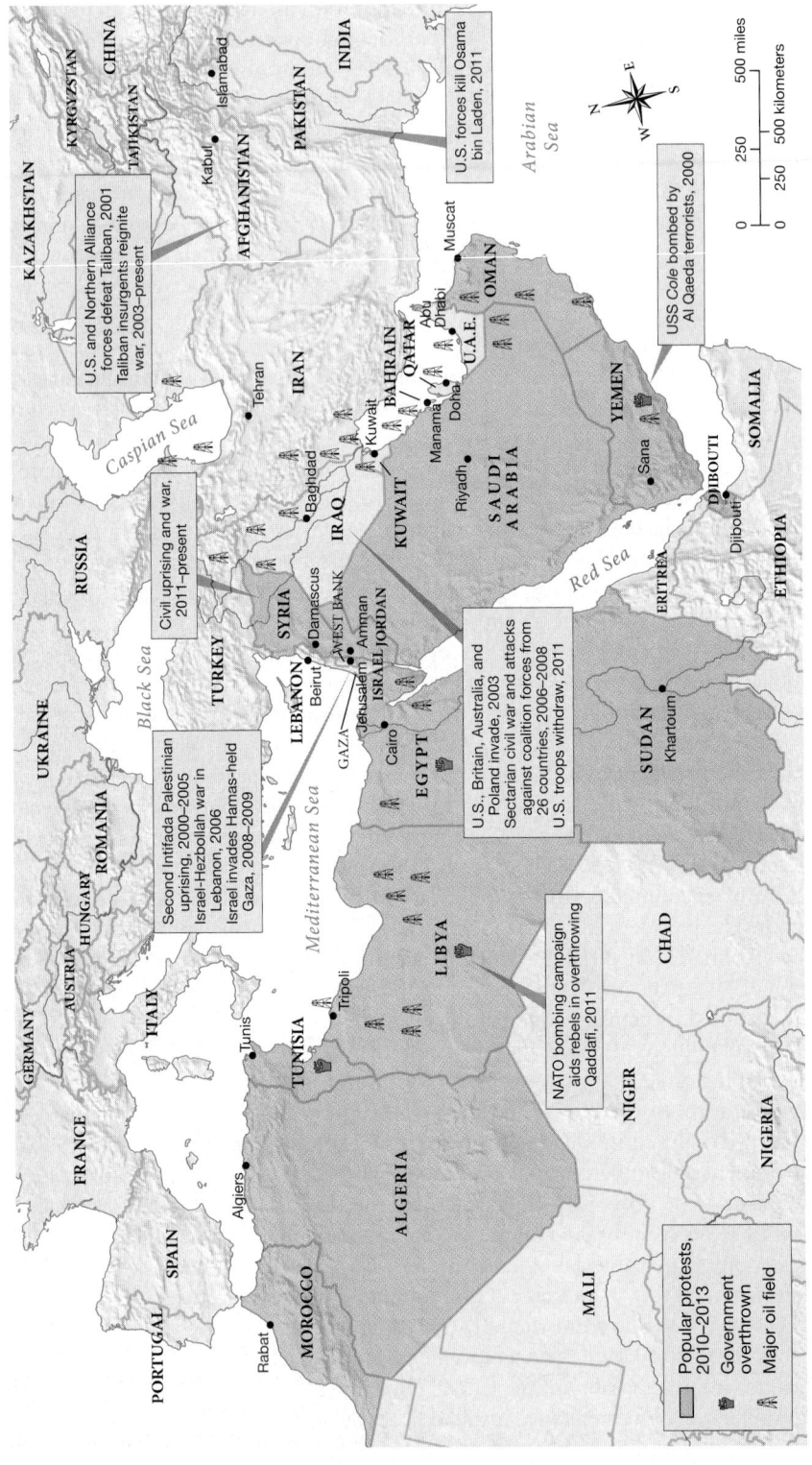

U.S. and Northern Alliance forces defeat Taliban, 2001
Taliban insurgents reignite war, 2003–present

U.S. forces kill Osama bin Laden, 2011

USS Cole bombed by Al Qaeda terrorists, 2000

Civil uprising and war, 2011–present

Second Intifada Palestinian uprising, 2000–2005
Israel-Hezbollah war in Lebanon, 2006
Israel invades Hamas-held Gaza, 2008–2009

U.S., Britain, Australia, and Poland invade, 2003
Sectarian civil war and attacks against coalition forces from 26 countries, 2006–2008
U.S. troops withdraw, 2011

NATO bombing campaign aids rebels in overthrowing Qaddafi, 2011

Popular protests, 2010–2013

Government overthrown

Major oil field

KAZAKHSTAN

KYRGYZSTAN

CHINA

TAJIKISTAN

Islamabad •

PAKISTAN

INDIA

Kabul •

AFGHANISTAN

RUSSIA

Tehran •

IRAN

Caspian Sea

Arabian Sea

Muscat •

OMAN

Abu Dhabi •

U.A.E.

QATAR

Doha •

BAHRAIN

Manama •

Kuwait •

Baghdad •

IRAQ

KUWAIT

Riyadh •

SAUDI ARABIA

YEMEN

Sana •

Red Sea

DJIBOUTI

Djibouti •

SOMALIA

ETHIOPIA

ERITREA

UKRAINE

Black Sea

TURKEY

Damascus •

SYRIA

Beirut •

LEBANON

WEST BANK

Amman •

JORDAN

Jerusalem •

ISRAEL

GAZA

Cairo •

EGYPT

SUDAN

Khartoum •

ROMANIA

HUNGARY

AUSTRIA

GERMANY

ITALY

Mediterranean Sea

Tripoli •

LIBYA

CHAD

Tunis •

TUNISIA

FRANCE

NIGER

SPAIN

Algiers •

ALGERIA

NIGERIA

PORTUGAL

Rabat •

MOROCCO

MALI

0   250   500 miles

0   250   500 kilometers

< MAP 29.2
The Middle East, 2000–2013   Since 2000, the Middle East has been marked by both terrorism and democratic uprisings. After 9/11 the United States tried to transform Iraq and Afghanistan by military might, which led to prolonged wars. Yet popular rebellions in 2011, led by young people and fueled by new technology, created hope that change was possible. However, as of 2013 the most brutal government repression of the uprisings continued in Syria, including the alleged use of chemical weapons against rebel forces.

crippling state budget deficits and declining tax revenues that slashed social services, decaying infrastructure, and crushing student loan debts. These and other Americans continued to be concerned about environmental issues, including dependence on foreign oil, global warming, and air and water pollution.

With unemployment remaining high, economic growth moving at a slow pace, and a number of European economies still in recession and unable to pay mounting debts, the economy loomed as the top issue in the 2012 presidential election. The Republican nominee, Mitt Romney, the former governor of Massachusetts, appealed to conservative voters by opposing Obama's economic programs, including health care reform, and by embracing the social agenda of the Christian Right. Although admitting that much remained to be done, Obama defended his record on creating new jobs, reducing unemployment, and rescuing the automobile industry. He also criticized economic inequality in the country and promised to raise taxes on the rich. Despite the slower-than-expected economic recovery, Barack Obama won reelection by holding together his coalition of African American, Latino, female, young, and lower-income voters.

An Unfinished Agenda

The United States will continue to face serious tests to its international leadership in the twenty-first century. Terrorism remains a potent threat. Iraq has yet to prove that it can survive as a stable nation in the absence of a strong American military presence, and the outcome of the war against al-Qaeda and the Taliban in Afghanistan remains questionable. Despite Osama bin Laden's death, al-Qaeda in Yemen still poses a serious danger, and U.S.-trained Afghan forces must demonstrate that they can maintain control once the U.S. military withdraws. If Iran succeeds in developing nuclear weapons, it will present an even greater threat, as will the continuing stalemate between the Israeli government and the Palestinians in reaching agreement over issues of peace and land that have been unresolved since 1967.

In 2011 great changes swept across the Middle East, as young people, armed mainly with cell phones and connected through social media networks, peacefully toppled pro-Western but despotic governments in Egypt and Tunisia. In Libya, armed rebels succeeded in overthrowing the government of the dictator Muammar al-Qaddafi. Elsewhere, a hostile North Korea has developed nuclear weapons. Prolonged instability in the Middle East, the Persian Gulf, and Asia is harmful to U.S. security interests and to achieving lasting peace in these regions (Map 29.2).

Whatever happens in the war on terror, the United States still faces challenges of globalization. China, a nation of 1.3 billion people, is contesting American economic supremacy. As China flourishes economically, American workers have lost jobs, and the Chinese have amassed a nearly $200 billion trade surplus with the United States. China also owns a substantial portion of America's national debt, a situation that further alters the balance of economic power between the two nations. In addition, the growth of manufacturing and the market economy in China has resulted in the rising consumption of oil and gasoline, thereby adding to soaring fuel prices in the United States.

Along with the United States and China, the rest of the world faces the problem of climate change and ultimately the survival of the planet. Global warming during the twentieth century resulted mainly from emissions of greenhouse gases into the atmosphere and the erosion of the ozone layer. As temperatures climb, they cause a rise in the sea level, the melting of glaciers, extreme fluctuations of weather, and famines. Powerful hurricanes such as Katrina have been attributed to rising temperatures in the Atlantic Ocean and Caribbean. Disruptions in industrial production caused by storms and the subsequent expense of rebuilding have a negative impact on the U.S. and world economies.

 Online Document Project
The Environment and Federal Policy in the Twenty-First Century
bedfordstmartins.com/hewittlawsonvalue

As the twenty-first century unfolds, immigration will continue to arouse considerable political controversy. Immigration restrictionists, particularly in Arizona and California, support such policies as building a fence along the U.S.-Mexican border and strengthening the administration of immigration laws. Supporters of immigration reform favor amnesty for illegal residents who have lived in this country for a designated period and have jobs, opening up a path to citizenship. At the heart of this issue is the question that has always existed during periods of intense foreign immigration, especially from non-English-speaking nations: Do the nation's vitality and character still depend on welcoming a new generation of foreigners to make their living and their home in the United States? Whatever the answer, by the end of the twenty-first century the population of the United States will look much different. The percentage of Latinos and Asian Americans will increase, while that of whites and blacks will decline. In 2012 the U.S. Census Bureau reported that nonwhite babies made up the majority of births for the first time. If present trends continue, the country's racial and ethnic composition will become much more mixed through intermarriage. In 2010 the Census Bureau reported that one of seven new marriages, or 14.6 percent, was interracial or interethnic. In 1961, when Barack Obama was born, the figure for interracial marriages was less than one in a thousand.

And, as for the institution of marriage, there have been both setbacks and advances for proponents of same-sex marriage. In 2012 voters approved state referenda that rejected same-sex marriage, but in 2013 the U.S. Supreme Court ruled in *Windsor v. United States* that the Defense of Marriage Act (see page 763) is unconstitutional. This landmark ruling allows same-sex married couples to receive the same federal benefits as heterosexual married couples, regardless of whether the state in which they live recognizes same-sex marriage.

REVIEW & RELATE

• What were the causes and consequences of the Great Recession?

• What effects did the election and presidency of Barack Obama have on American politics and society?

Conclusion: Technology and Terror in a Global Society

Since 1993, Americans have faced new forms of globalization, new technologies, and new modes of warfare. The computer revolution that Bill Gates helped initiate changed the way Americans gather information, communicate ideas, purchase goods, and conduct business. It has also shaped national and international conflicts. The September 11, 2001, attacks on the World Trade Center and the Pentagon demonstrated that terrorists could use computers and digital equipment to wreak havoc on the most powerful nation in the world. At the same time, Kristen Breitweiser used the Internet to mobilize public support for the families of 9/11 victims. And Barack Obama's 2008 presidential campaign, protesters demonstrating against various Middle East dictatorships, and the leaders of the Tea Party and Occupy Wall Street movements also used technology to inspire men and women to join their causes.

Along with the computer revolution, globalization has encouraged vast economic transformation throughout the world. Presidents as politically different as Bill Clinton and George W. Bush supported deregulation, free trade, and other policies that fostered corporate mergers that allowed businesses to reach beyond U.S. borders for cheap labor, raw materials, and markets in new and more profitable ways. While the 1990s witnessed the fruits of the new global economy, by 2008 the dangers of financial speculation and intertwined national economies became striking in the onset of the Great Recession. This economic collapse has underscored the inequalities of wealth that continue to exist and grow larger, aggravated by racial, ethnic, and gender disparities. Gripped by ongoing partisan deadlock, U.S. lawmakers have been unable to address the troublesome problems of unemployment, budget deficits, health care, global warming, immigration reform, energy consumption, and the protection of civil liberties.

Throughout its history, the United States has shown great strength in developing and adapting to new technology, with the computers of Bill Gates and other digital pioneers only the latest. At the same time, the nation has incorporated diverse populations into its midst, redefined old cultural identities and created new ones, expanded civil rights and civil liberties, extended economic opportunities, and joined other nations to fight military aggression and address common international concerns. The election of Barack Obama in 2008 shows that the nation has progressed significantly from the Reconstruction era to the present. Still, many problems remain before the United States achieves the "more perfect union" that the Founders and their successors envisioned. Ordinary Americans such as Kristen Breitweiser and many others who came before her have tried to make this country live up to its principles. The United States will have to draw on the many histories of its diverse peoples if it expects to continue to exert leadership in the world and maintain its greatness into the twenty-first century.

Chapter Review

MAKE IT STICK

LearningCurve **bedfordstmartins.com/hewittlawsonvalue**
After reading the chapter, use LearningCurve to retain what you've read.

IDENTIFY KEY TERMS

Identify and explain the significance of each term below.

"don't ask, don't tell" (p. 762)

Contract with America (p. 763)

Personal Responsibility and Work
   Opportunity Reconciliation Act (p. 763)

ethnic cleansing (p. 764)

Dayton Peace Accords (p. 764)

megachurches (p. 767)

Patriot Act (p. 769)

Bush Doctrine (p. 770)

Hurricane Katrina (p. 772)

Great Recession (p. 774)

subprime mortgages (p. 774)

Tea Party movement (p. 777)

Occupy Wall Street (p. 777)

REVIEW & RELATE

Answer the focus questions from each section of the chapter.

1. How have computers changed life in the United States?

2. How has globalization affected business consolidation and immigration?

3. How did conflicts between Democrats and Republicans affect President Clinton's accomplishments?

4. How did the end of the Cold War shape President Clinton's foreign policies?

5. How did President Bush put compassionate conservatism into action?

6. How did the war on terror prompt U.S. leaders to rethink America's position in the world?

7. What were the causes and consequences of the Great Recession?

8. What effects did the election and presidency of Barack Obama have on American politics and society?

ONLINE DOCUMENT PROJECTS

◆ **The Uses of September 11**
◆ **The Environment and Federal Policy in the Twenty-First Century**

After reading the primary sources in these document sets, answer the **Interpret the Evidence** questions to help you analyze each of the documents, and then answer the **Put It in Context** question(s) to help you relate the documents to the topics and themes you read about in the chapter.

bedfordstmartins.com/hewittlawsonvalue

TIMELINE OF EVENTS

1975	• Microsoft formed
1976	• Apple Computer Company formed
1980–1990s	• Immigration surges from Mexico, Central America, the Caribbean, and South and East Asia
1991	• World Wide Web comes into existence
1993–2011	• "Don't ask, don't tell" policy enacted
1994	• Contract with America announced; Republicans win control of Congress
1995	• Dayton Peace Accords
1996	• Personal Responsibility and Work Reconciliation Act reforms welfare
	• Defense of Marriage Act
1998	• President Clinton impeached
2000	• Al-Qaeda bombs USS *Cole* in Yemen
	• Supreme Court rules in favor of George W. Bush in contested presidential election

2001	• September 11 al-Qaeda attacks on World Trade Center and Pentagon
	• U.S. troops invade Afghanistan; Patriot Act passed
2002	• No Child Left Behind Act passed
2003–2011	• War in Iraq
2005	• Hurricane Katrina hits Gulf coast
2008	• Great Recession begins
	• Barack Obama elected president
	• Tea Party movement formed
2009	• Congress passes health care reform act
2011	• Osama bin Laden killed by U.S. special forces
	• Occupy Wall Street movement formed
2012	• U.S. Census Bureau reports majority of nonwhite births for first time in U.S. history

Appendix

THE DECLARATION OF INDEPENDENCE

In Congress, July 4, 1776.
The unanimous Declaration of the thirteen united States of America,

When in the course of human events, it becomes necessary for one people to dissolve the political bands which have connected them with another, and to assume, among the powers of the earth, the separate and equal station to which the laws of nature and of nature's God entitle them, a decent respect to the opinions of mankind requires that they should declare the causes which impel them to the separation.

We hold these truths to be self-evident, that all men are created equal; that they are endowed by their Creator with certain unalienable rights; that among these, are life, liberty, and the pursuit of happiness. That, to secure these rights, governments are instituted among men, deriving their just powers from the consent of the governed; that, whenever any form of government becomes destructive of these ends, it is the right of the people to alter or to abolish it, and to institute a new government, laying its foundation on such principles, and organizing its powers in such form, as to them shall seem most likely to effect their safety and happiness. Prudence, indeed, will dictate that governments long established, should not be changed for light and transient causes; and, accordingly, all experience hath shown, that mankind are more disposed to suffer, while evils are sufferable, than to right themselves by abolishing the forms to which they are accustomed. But, when a long train of abuses and usurpations, pursuing invariably the same object, evinces a design to reduce them under absolute despotism, it is their right, it is their duty, to throw off such government and to provide new guards for their future security. Such has been the patient sufferance of these colonies, and such is now the necessity which constrains them to alter their former systems of government. The history of the present King of Great Britain is a history of repeated injuries and usurpations, all having, in direct object, the establishment of an absolute tyranny over these States. To prove this, let facts be submitted to a candid world: He has refused his assent to laws the most wholesome and necessary for the public good.

He has forbidden his governors to pass laws of immediate and pressing importance, unless suspended in their operation till his assent should be obtained; and, when so suspended, he has utterly neglected to attend to them.

He has refused to pass other laws for the accommodation of large districts of people, unless those people would relinquish the right of representation in the legislature; a right inestimable to them, and formidable to tyrants only.

He has called together legislative bodies at places unusual, uncomfortable, and distant from the depository of their public records, for the sole purpose of fatiguing them into compliance with his measures.

He has dissolved representative houses repeatedly for opposing, with manly firmness, his invasions on the rights of the people.

He has refused, for a long time after such dissolutions, to cause others to be elected; whereby the legislative powers, incapable of annihilation, have returned to the people at large for their exercise; the state remaining in the mean-time exposed to all the danger of invasion from without, and convulsions within.

He has endeavoured to prevent the population of these States; for that purpose, obstructing the laws for naturalization of foreigners, refusing to pass others to encourage their migration hither, and raising the conditions of new appropriations of lands.

He has obstructed the administration of justice, by refusing his assent to laws for establishing judiciary powers.

He has made judges dependent on his will alone, for the tenure of their offices, and the amount and payment of their salaries.

He has erected a multitude of new offices, and sent hither swarms of officers to harass our people, and eat out their substance.

He has kept among us, in times of peace, standing armies, without the consent of our legislature.

He has affected to render the military independent of, and superior to, the civil power.

He has combined, with others, to subject us to a jurisdiction foreign to our Constitution, and unacknowledged by our laws; giving his assent to their acts of pretended legislation:

For quartering large bodies of armed troops among us:

For protecting them by a mock trial, from punishment, for any murders which they should commit on the inhabitants of these States:

For cutting off our trade with all parts of the world:

For imposing taxes on us without our consent:

For depriving us, in many cases, of the benefit of trial by jury:

For transporting us beyond seas to be tried for pretended offences:

For abolishing the free system of English laws in a neighboring province, establishing therein an arbitrary government, and enlarging its boundaries, so as to render it at once an example and fit instrument for introducing the same absolute rule into these colonies:

For taking away our charters, abolishing our most valuable laws, and altering, fundamentally, the powers of our governments:

For suspending our own legislatures, and declaring themselves invested with power to legislate for us in all cases whatsoever.

He has abdicated government here, by declaring us out of his protection, and waging war against us.

He has plundered our seas, ravaged our coasts, burnt our towns, and destroyed the lives of our people.

He is, at this time, transporting large armies of foreign mercenaries to complete the works of death, desolation, and tyranny, already begun, with circumstances of cruelty and perfidy scarcely paralleled in the most barbarous ages, and totally unworthy the head of a civilized nation.

He has constrained our fellow citizens, taken captive on the high seas, to bear arms against their country, to become the executioners of their friends, and brethren, or to fall themselves by their hands.

He has excited domestic insurrections amongst us, and has endeavored to bring on the inhabitants of our frontiers, the merciless Indian savages, whose known rule of warfare is an undistinguished destruction of all ages, sexes, and conditions.

In every stage of these oppressions, we have petitioned for redress; in the most humble terms; our repeated petitions have been answered only by repeated injury. A prince, whose character is thus marked by every act which may define a tyrant, is unfit to be the ruler of a free people.

Nor have we been wanting in attention to our British brethren. We have warned them, from time to time, of attempts made by their legislature to extend an unwarrantable jurisdiction over us. We have reminded them of the circumstances of our emigration and settlement here. We have appealed to their native justice and magnanimity, and we have conjured them, by the ties of our common kindred, to disavow these usurpations, which would inevitably interrupt our connections and correspondence. They, too, have been deaf to the voice of justice and consanguinity. We must, therefore, acquiesce in the necessity which denounces our separation, and hold them as we hold the rest of mankind, enemies in war, in peace, friends.

We, therefore, the representatives of the United States of America, in general Congress assembled, appealing to the Supreme Judge of the world for the rectitude of our intentions, do, in the name, and by authority of the good people of these colonies, solemnly publish and declare, that these united colonies are, and of right ought to be, free and independent states: that they are absolved from all allegiance to the British Crown, and that all political connection between them and the state of Great Britain is, and ought to be, totally dissolved; and that, as free and independent states, they have full power to levy war, conclude peace, contract alliances, establish commerce, and to do all other acts and things which independent states may of right do. And, for the support of this declaration, with a firm reliance on the protection of Divine Providence, we mutually pledge to each other our lives, our fortunes, and our sacred honor.

The foregoing Declaration was, by order of Congress, engrossed, and signed by the following members:

JOHN HANCOCK

New Hampshire
Josiah Bartlett
William Whipple
Matthew Thornton

Massachusetts Bay
Samuel Adams
John Adams
Robert Treat Paine
Elbridge Gerry

Rhode Island
Stephen Hopkins
William Ellery

Connecticut
Roger Sherman
Samuel Huntington
William Williams
Oliver Wolcott

New York
William Floyd
Phillip Livingston
Francis Lewis
Lewis Morris

New Jersey
Richard Stockton
John Witherspoon
Francis Hopkinson
John Hart
Abraham Clark

Pennsylvania
Robert Morris
Benjamin Rush
Benjamin Franklin
John Morton
George Clymer
James Smith
George Taylor
James Wilson
George Ross
Caesar Rodney
George Read
Thomas M'Kean

Maryland
Samuel Chase
William Paca
Thomas Stone
Charles Carroll, of Carrollton

North Carolina
William Hooper
Joseph Hewes
John Penn

South Carolina
Edward Rutledge
Thomas Heyward, Jr.
Thomas Lynch, Jr.
Arthur Middleton

Virginia
George Wythe
Richard Henry Lee
Thomas Jefferson
Benjamin Harrison
Thomas Nelson, Jr.
Francis Lightfoot Lee
Carter Braxton

Georgia
Button Gwinnett
Lyman Hall
George Walton

Resolved, That copies of the Declaration be sent to the several assemblies, conventions, and committees, or councils of safety, and to the several commanding officers of the continental troops; that it be proclaimed in each of the United States, at the head of the army.

THE ARTICLES OF CONFEDERATION AND PERPETUAL UNION

Agreed to in Congress, November 15, 1777.
Ratified March 1781.

Between the states of New Hampshire, Massachusetts Bay, Rhode Island and Providence Plantations, Connecticut, New York, New Jersey, Pennsylvania, Delaware, Maryland, Virginia, North Carolina, South Carolina, Georgia.*

Article 1

The stile of this confederacy shall be "The United States of America."

Article 2

Each State retains its sovereignty, freedom and independence, and every power, jurisdiction, and right, which is not by this confederation expressly delegated to the United States, in Congress assembled.

Article 3

The said states hereby severally enter into a firm league of friendship with each other for their common defence, the security of their liberties and their mutual and general welfare; binding themselves to assist each other against all force offered to, or attacks made upon them, or any of them, on account of religion, sovereignty, trade, or any other pretence whatever.

Article 4

The better to secure and perpetuate mutual friendship and intercourse among the people of the different states in this union, the free inhabitants of each of these states, paupers, vagabonds, and fugitives from justice excepted, shall be entitled to all privileges and immunities of free citizens in the several states; and the people of each State shall have free ingress and regress to and from any other State, and shall enjoy therein all the privileges of trade and commerce, subject to the same duties, impositions, and restrictions, as the inhabitants thereof respectively; provided, that such restrictions shall not extend so far as to prevent the removal of property, imported into any State, to any other State of which the owner is an inhabitant; provided also, that no imposition, duties, or restriction, shall be laid by any State on the property of the United States, or either of them. If any person guilty of, or charged with treason, felony, or other high misdemeanor in any State, shall flee from justice and be found in any of the United States, he shall, upon demand of the governor or executive power of the State from which he fled, be delivered up and removed to the State having jurisdiction of his offence. Full faith and credit shall be given in each of these states to the records, acts, and judicial proceedings of the courts and magistrates of every other State.

Article 5

For the more convenient management of the general interests of the United States, delegates shall be annually appointed, in such manner as the legislature of each State shall direct, to meet in Congress, on the 1st Monday in November in every year, with a power reserved to each State to recall its delegates, or any of them, at any time within the year, and to send others in their stead for the remainder of the year.

---

*This copy of the final draft of the Articles of Confederation is taken from the Journals, 9:907–925, November 15, 1777.

No State shall be represented in Congress by less than two, nor by more than seven members; and no person shall be capable of being a delegate for more than three years in any term of six years; nor shall any person, being a delegate, be capable of holding any office under the United States, for which he, or any other for his benefit, receives any salary, fees, or emolument of any kind.

Each State shall maintain its own delegates in a meeting of the states, and while they act as members of the committee of the states.

In determining questions in the United States, in Congress assembled, each State shall have one vote.

Freedom of speech and debate in Congress shall not be impeached or questioned in any court or place out of Congress: and the members of Congress shall be protected in their persons from arrests and imprisonments, during the time of their going to and from, and attendance on Congress, except for treason, felony, or breach of the peace.

Article 6

No State, without the consent of the United States, in Congress assembled, shall send any embassy to, or receive any embassy from, or enter into any conference, agreement, alliance, or treaty with any king, prince, or state; nor shall any person, holding any office of profit or trust under the United States, or any of them, accept of any present, emolument, office or title, of any kind whatever, from any king, prince, or foreign state; nor shall the United States, in Congress assembled, or any of them, grant any title of nobility.

No two or more states shall enter into any treaty, confederation, or alliance, whatever, between them, without the consent of the United States, in Congress assembled, specifying accurately the purposes for which the same is to be entered into, and how long it shall continue.

No state shall lay any imposts or duties which may interfere with any stipulations in treaties entered into by the United States, in Congress assembled, with any king, prince, or state, in pursuance of any treaties already proposed by Congress to the courts of France and Spain.

No vessels of war shall be kept up in time of peace by any State, except such number only as shall be deemed necessary by the United States, in Congress assembled, for the defence of such State or its trade; nor shall any body of forces be kept up by any State, in time of peace, except such number only as, in the judgment of the United States, in Congress assembled, shall be deemed requisite to garrison the forts necessary for the defence of such State; but every State shall always keep up a well regulated and disciplined militia, sufficiently armed and accoutred, and shall provide, and constantly have ready for use, in public stores, a due number of field pieces and tents, and a proper quantity of arms, ammunition and camp equipage.

No State shall engage in any war without the consent of the United States, in Congress assembled, unless such State be actually invaded by enemies, or shall have received certain advice of a resolution being formed by some nation of Indians to invade such State, and the danger is so imminent as not to admit of a delay till the United States, in Congress assembled, can be consulted; nor shall any State grant commissions to any ships or vessels of war, nor letters of marque or reprisal, except it be after a declaration of war by the United States, in Congress assembled, and then only against the kingdom or state, and the subjects thereof, against which war has been so declared, and under such regulations as shall be established by the United States, in Congress assembled, unless such State be infested by pirates, in which case vessels of war may be fitted out for that occasion, and kept so long as the danger shall continue, or until the United States, in Congress assembled, shall determine otherwise.

Article 7

When land forces are raised by any State for the common defence, all officers of or under the rank of colonel, shall be appointed by the legislature of each State respectively, by whom such forces shall be raised, or in such manner as such State shall direct; and all vacancies shall be filled up by the State which first made the appointment.

Article 8

All charges of war and all other expences, that shall be incurred for the common defence or general welfare, and allowed by the United States, in Congress assembled, shall be defrayed out of a common treasury, which shall be supplied by the several states, in proportion to the value of all land within each State, granted to or surveyed for any person, as such land and the buildings and improvements thereon shall be estimated according to such mode as the United States, in Congress assembled, shall, from time to time, direct and appoint.

The taxes for paying that proportion shall be laid and levied by the authority and direction of the legislatures of the several states, within the time agreed upon by the United States, in Congress assembled.

Article 9

The United States, in Congress assembled, shall have the sole and exclusive right and power of determining on peace and war, except in the cases mentioned in the 6th article; of sending and receiving ambassadors; entering into treaties and alliances, provided that no treaty of commerce shall be made, whereby the legislative power of the respective states shall be restrained from imposing such imposts and duties on foreigners as their own people are subjected to, or from prohibiting the exportation or importation of any species of goods or commodities whatsoever; of establishing rules for deciding, in all cases, what captures on land or water shall be legal, and in what manner prizes, taken by land or naval forces in the service of the United States, shall be divided or appropriated; of granting letters of marque and reprisal in times of peace; appointing courts for the trial of piracies and felonies committed on the high seas, and establishing courts for receiving and determining, finally, appeals in all cases of captures; provided, that no member of Congress shall be appointed a judge of any of the said courts.

The United States, in Congress assembled, shall also be the last resort on appeal in all disputes and differences now subsisting, or that hereafter may arise between two or more states concerning boundary, jurisdiction or any other cause whatever; which authority shall always be exercised in the manner following: whenever the legislative or executive authority, or lawful agent of any State, in controversy with another, shall present a petition to Congress, stating the matter in question, and praying for a hearing, notice thereof shall be given, by order of Congress, to the legislative or executive authority of the other State in controversy, and a day assigned for the appearance of the parties by their lawful agents, who shall then be directed to appoint, by joint consent, commissioners or judges to constitute a court for hearing and determining the matter in question; but, if they cannot agree, Congress shall name three persons out of each of the United States, and from the list of such persons each party shall alternately strike out one, the petitioners beginning, until the number shall be reduced to thirteen; and from that number not less than seven, nor more than nine names, as Congress shall direct, shall, in the presence of Congress, be drawn out by lot; and the persons whose names shall be so drawn, or any five of them, shall be commissioners or judges to hear and finally determine the controversy, so always as a major part of the judges who shall hear the cause shall agree in the determination; and if either party shall neglect to attend at the day appointed, without shewing reasons which Congress shall judge sufficient, or, being present, shall refuse to strike, the Congress shall proceed to nominate three persons out of each State, and the secretary of Congress shall strike in behalf of such party absent or refusing; and the judgment and sentence of the court to be appointed, in the manner before prescribed, shall be final and conclusive; and if any of the parties shall refuse to submit to the authority of such court, or to appear or defend their claim or cause, the court shall nevertheless proceed to pronounce sentence or judgment, which shall, in like manner, be final and decisive, the judgment or sentence and other proceedings begin, in either case, transmitted to Congress, and lodged among the acts of Congress for the security of the parties concerned: provided, that every commissioner, before he sits in judgment, shall take an oath, to be administered by one of the judges of the supreme or superior court of the State where the cause shall be tried, "well and truly to hear and determine the matter in question, according to the best of his judgment, without favour, affection, or hope of reward:" provided, also, that no State shall be deprived of territory for the benefit of the United States.

All controversies concerning the private right of soil, claimed under different grants of two or more states, whose jurisdictions, as they may respect such lands and the states which passed such grants, are adjusted, the said grants, or either of them, being at the same time claimed to have originated antecedent to such settlement of jurisdiction, shall, on the petition of either party to the Congress of the United States, be finally determined, as near as may be, in the same manner as is before prescribed for deciding disputes respecting territorial jurisdiction between different states.

The United States, in Congress assembled, shall also have the sole and exclusive right and power of regulating the alloy and value of coin struck by their own authority, or by that of the respective states; fixing the standard of weights and measures throughout the United States; regulating the trade and managing all affairs with the Indians not members of any of the states; provided that the legislative right of any State within its own limits be not infringed or violated; establishing and regulating post offices from one State to another throughout all the United States, and exacting such postage on the papers passing through the same as may be requisite to defray the expences of the said office; appointing all officers of the land forces in the service of the United States, excepting regimental officers; appointing all the officers of the naval forces, and commissioning all officers whatever in the service of the United States; making rules for the government and regulation of the said land and naval forces, and directing their operations.

The United States, in Congress assembled, shall have authority to appoint a committee to sit in the recess of Congress, to be denominated "a Committee of the States," and to consist of one delegate from each State, and to appoint such other committees and civil officers as may be necessary for managing the general affairs of the United States, under their direction; to appoint one of their number to preside; provided that no person be allowed to serve in the office of president more than one year in any term of three years; to ascertain the necessary sums of money to be raised for the service of the United States, and to appropriate and apply the same for defraying the public expences; to borrow money or emit bills on the credit of the United States, transmitting, every half year, to the respective states, an account of the sums of money so borrowed or emitted; to build and equip a navy; to agree upon the number of land forces, and to make requisitions from each State for its quota, in proportion to the number of white inhabitants in such State; which requisitions shall be binding; and thereupon, the legislature of each State shall appoint the regimental officers, raise the men, and cloathe, arm, and equip them in a soldier-like manner, at the expence of the United States; and the officers and men so cloathed, armed, and equipped, shall march to the place appointed and within the time agreed on by the United States, in Congress assembled; but if the United States, in Congress assembled, shall, on consideration of circumstances, judge proper that any State should not raise men, or should raise a smaller number than its quota, and that any other State should raise a greater number of men than the quota thereof, such extra number shall be raised, officered, cloathed, armed, and equipped in the same manner as the quota of such State, unless the legislature of such State shall judge that such extra number cannot be safely spared out of the same, in which case they shall raise, officer, cloathe, arm, and equip as many of such extra number as they judge can be safely spared. And the officers and men so cloathed, armed, and equipped, shall march to the place appointed and within the time agreed on by the United States, in Congress assembled.

The United States, in Congress assembled, shall never engage in a war, nor grant letters of marque and reprisal in time of peace, nor enter into any treaties or alliances, nor coin money, nor regulate the value thereof, nor ascertain the sums and expences necessary for the defence and welfare of the United States, or any of them: nor emit bills, nor borrow money on the credit of the United States, nor appropriate money, nor agree upon the number of vessels of war to be built or purchased, or the number of land or sea forces to be raised, nor appoint a commander in chief of the army or navy, unless nine states assent to the same; nor shall a question on any other point, except for adjourning from day to day, be determined, unless by the votes of a majority of the United States, in Congress assembled.

The Congress of the United States shall have power to adjourn to any time within the year, and to any place within the United States, so that no period of adjournment be for a longer duration than the space of six months, and shall publish the journal of their proceedings monthly, except such parts thereof, relating to treaties, alliances or military operations, as, in their judgment, require secrecy; and the yeas and nays of the delegates of each State on any question shall be entered on the journal, when it is desired by any delegate; and the delegates of a State, or any of them, at his, or their request, shall be furnished with a transcript of the said journal, except such parts as are above excepted, to lay before the legislatures of the several states.

Article 10

The committee of the states, or any nine of them, shall be authorized to execute, in the recess of Congress, such of the powers of Congress as the United States, in Congress assembled, by the consent of nine states, shall, from time to time, think expedient to vest them with; provided, that no power be delegated to the said committee, for the exercise of which, by the articles of confederation, the voice of nine states, in the Congress of the United States assembled, is requisite.

Article 11

Canada acceding to this confederation, and joining in the measures of the United States, shall be admitted into and entitled to all the advantages of this union; but no other colony shall be admitted into the same, unless such admission be agreed to by nine states.

Article 12

All bills of credit emitted, monies borrowed and debts contracted by, or under the authority of Congress before the assembling of the United States, in pursuance of the present confederation, shall be deemed and considered as a charge against the United States, for payment and satisfaction whereof the said United States and the public faith are hereby solemnly pledged.

Article 13

Every State shall abide by the determinations of the United States, in Congress assembled, on all questions which, by this confederation, are submitted to them. And the articles of this confederation shall be inviolably observed by every State, and the union shall be perpetual; nor shall any alteration at any time hereafter be made in any of them, unless such alteration be agreed to in a Congress of the United States, and be afterwards confirmed by the legislatures of every State.

These articles shall be proposed to the legislatures of all the United States, to be considered, and if approved of by them, they are advised to authorize their delegates to ratify the same in the Congress of the United States; which being done, the same shall become conclusive.

THE CONSTITUTION OF THE UNITED STATES*

Agreed to by Philadelphia Convention, September 17, 1787. Implemented March 4, 1789.

Preamble

We the people of the United States, in order to form a more perfect union, establish justice, insure domestic tranquility, provide for the common defense, promote the general welfare, and secure the blessings of liberty to ourselves and our posterity, do ordain and establish this Constitution for the United States of America.

Article I

Section 1. All legislative powers herein granted shall be vested in a Congress of the United States, which shall consist of a Senate and a House of Representatives.

Section 2. The House of Representatives shall be composed of members chosen every second year by the people of the several States, and the electors in each State shall have the qualifications requisite for electors of the most numerous branch of the State Legislature.

No person shall be a Representative who shall not have attained to the age of twenty-five years, and been seven years a citizen of the United States, and who shall not, when elected, be an inhabitant of that State in which he shall be chosen.

Representatives and direct taxes shall be apportioned among the several States which may be included within this Union, according to their respective numbers, which shall be determined by adding to the whole number of free persons, including those bound to service for a term of years and excluding Indians not taxed, three-fifths of all other persons. The actual enumeration shall be made within three years after the first meeting of the Congress of the United States, and within every subsequent term of ten years, in such manner as they shall by law direct. *The number of Representatives shall not exceed one for every thirty thousand, but each State shall have at least one Representative; and until such enumeration shall be made,* the State of New Hampshire shall be entitled to choose three, Massachusetts eight, Rhode Island and Providence Plantations one, Connecticut five, New York six, New Jersey four, Pennsylvania eight, Delaware one, Maryland six, Virginia ten, North Carolina five, South Carolina five, and Georgia three.

When vacancies happen in the representation from any State, the Executive authority thereof shall issue writs of election to fill such vacancies.

The House of Representatives shall choose their Speaker and other officers; and shall have the sole power of impeachment.

Section 3. The Senate of the United States shall be composed of two Senators from each State, *chosen by the legislature thereof,* for six years; and each Senator shall have one vote.

Immediately after they shall be assembled in consequence of the first election, they shall be divided as equally as may be into three classes. The seats of the Senators of the first class shall be vacated at the expiration of the second year, of the second class at the expiration of the fourth year, and of the third class at the expiration of the sixth year, so that one-third may be chosen every second year; *and if vacancies happen by resignation or otherwise, during the recess of the legislature of any State, the Executive thereof may make temporary appointments until the next meeting of the legislature, which shall then fill such vacancies.*

No person shall be a Senator who shall not have attained to the age of thirty years, and been nine years a citizen of the United States, and who shall not, when elected, be an inhabitant of that State for which he shall be chosen.

*Passages no longer in effect are in italic type.

The Vice-President of the United States shall be President of the Senate, but shall have no vote, unless they be equally divided.

The Senate shall choose their other officers, and also a President pro tempore, in the absence of the Vice-President, or when he shall exercise the office of President of the United States.

The Senate shall have the sole power to try all impeachments. When sitting for that purpose, they shall be on oath or affirmation. When the President of the United States is tried, the Chief Justice shall preside: and no person shall be convicted without the concurrence of two-thirds of the members present.

Judgment in cases of impeachment shall not extend further than to removal from the office, and disqualification to hold and enjoy any office of honor, trust or profit under the United States: but the party convicted shall nevertheless be liable and subject to indictment, trial, judgment and punishment, according to law.

Section 4. The times, places and manner of holding elections for Senators and Representatives shall be prescribed in each State by the legislature thereof; but the Congress may at any time by law make or alter such regulations, except as to the places of choosing Senators.

The Congress shall assemble at least once in every year, and such meeting *shall be on the first Monday in December,* unless they shall by law appoint a different day.

Section 5. Each house shall be the judge of the elections, returns and qualifications of its own members, and a majority of each shall constitute a quorum to do business; but a smaller number may adjourn from day to day, and may be authorized to compel the attendance of absent members, in such manner, and under such penalties, as each house may provide.

Each house may determine the rules of its proceedings, punish its members for disorderly behavior, and with the concurrence of two-thirds, expel a member.

Each house shall keep a journal of its proceedings, and from time to time publish the same, excepting such parts as may in their judgment require secrecy; and the yeas and nays of the members of either house on any question shall, at the desire of one fifth of those present, be entered on the journal.

Neither house, during the session of Congress, shall, without the consent of the other, adjourn for more than three days, nor to any other place than that in which the two houses shall be sitting.

Section 6. The Senators and Representatives shall receive a compensation for their services, to be ascertained by law and paid out of the treasury of the United States. They shall in all cases except treason, felony and breach of the peace, be privileged from arrest during their attendance at the session of their respective houses, and in going to and returning from the same; and for any speech or debate in either house, they shall not be questioned in any other place.

No Senator or Representative shall, during the time for which he was elected, be appointed to any civil office under the authority of the United States, which shall have been created, or the emoluments whereof shall have been increased, during such time; and no person holding any office under the United States shall be a member of either house during his continuance in office.

Section 7. All bills for raising revenue shall originate in the House of Representatives; but the Senate may propose or concur with amendments as on other bills.

Every bill which shall have passed the House of Representatives and the Senate, shall, before it become a law, be presented to the President of the United States; if he approve he shall sign it, but if not he shall return it with objections to that house in which it shall have originated, who shall enter the objections at large on their journal, and proceed to reconsider it. If after such reconsideration two-thirds of that house shall agree to pass the bill, it shall be sent, together with the objections, to the other house, by which it shall likewise be reconsidered, and, if approved by two-thirds of that house, it shall become a law. But in all such cases the votes of both houses shall be determined by yeas and nays, and the names of the persons voting for and against the bill shall be entered on the journal of each house respectively. If any bill shall not be returned by the President within ten days (Sundays excepted) after it shall have been presented to him, the same shall be a law, in like manner as if he had signed it, unless the Congress by their adjournment prevent its return, in which case it shall not be a law.

Every order, resolution, or vote to which the concurrence of the Senate and House of Representatives may be necessary (except on a question of adjournment) shall be presented to the President of the United States; and before the same shall take effect, shall be approved by him, or being disapproved by him, shall be repassed by two-thirds of the Senate and House of Representatives, according to the rules and limitations prescribed in the case of a bill.

Section 8. The Congress shall have power

To lay and collect taxes, duties, imposts, and excises, to pay the debts and provide for the common defense and general welfare of the United States; but all duties, imposts and excises shall be uniform throughout the United States;

To borrow money on the credit of the United States;

To regulate commerce with foreign nations, and among the several States, and with the Indian tribes;

To establish an uniform rule of naturalization, and uniform laws on the subject of bankruptcies throughout the United States;

To coin money, regulate the value thereof, and of foreign coin, and fix the standard of weights and measures;

To provide for the punishment of counterfeiting the securities and current coin of the United States;

To establish post offices and post roads;

To promote the progress of science and useful arts by securing for limited times to authors and inventors the exclusive right to their respective writings and discoveries;

To constitute tribunals inferior to the Supreme Court;

To define and punish piracies and felonies committed on the high seas and offences against the law of nations;

To declare war, grant letters of marque and reprisal, and make rules concerning captures on land and water;

To raise and support armies, but no appropriation of money to that use shall be for a longer term than two years;

To provide and maintain a navy;

To make rules for the government and regulation of the land and naval forces;

To provide for calling forth the militia to execute the laws of the Union, suppress insurrections and repel invasions;

To provide for organizing, arming, and disciplining the militia, and for governing such part of them as may be employed in the service of the United States, reserving to the States respectively the appointment of the officers, and the authority of training the militia according to the discipline prescribed by Congress;

To exercise exclusive legislation in all cases whatsoever, over such district (not exceeding ten miles square) as may, by cession of particular States, and the acceptance of Congress, become the seat of the government of the United States, and to exercise like authority over all places purchased by the consent of the legislature of the State, in which the same shall be, for erection of forts, magazines, arsenals, dock-yards, and other needful buildings;—and

To make all laws which shall be necessary and proper for carrying into execution the foregoing powers, and all other powers vested by this Constitution in the government of the United States, or in any department or officer thereof.

Section 9. The migration or importation of such persons as any of the States now existing shall think proper to admit shall not be prohibited by the Congress prior to the year one thousand eight hundred and eight; but a tax or duty may be imposed on such importation, not exceeding ten dollars for each person.

The privilege of the writ of habeas corpus shall not be suspended, unless when in cases of rebellion or invasion the public safety may require it.

No bill of attainder or ex post facto law shall be passed.

No capitation, or other direct, tax shall be laid, *unless in proportion to the census or enumeration herein before directed to be taken.*

No tax or duty shall be laid on articles exported from any State.

No preference shall be given by any regulation of commerce or revenue to the ports of one State over those of another; nor shall vessels bound to, or from, one State be obliged to enter, clear, or pay duties in another.

No money shall be drawn from the treasury, but in consequence of appropriations made by law; and a regular statement and account of the receipts and expenditures of all public money shall be published from time to time.

No title of nobility shall be granted by the United States: and no person holding any office of profit or trust under them, shall, without the consent of the Congress, accept of any present, emolument, office, or title, of any kind whatever, from any king, prince, or foreign state.

Section 10. No State shall enter into any treaty, alliance, or confederation; grant letters of marque and reprisal; coin money; emit bills of credit; make anything but gold and silver coin a tender in payment of debts; pass any bill of attainder, ex post facto law, or law impairing the obligation of contracts, or grant any title of nobility.

No State shall, without the consent of Congress, lay any imposts or duties on imports or exports, except what may be absolutely necessary for executing its inspection laws: and the net produce of all duties and imposts, laid by any State on imports or exports, shall be for the use of the treasury of the United States; and all such laws shall be subject to the revision and control of the Congress.

No State shall, without the consent of Congress, lay any duty of tonnage, keep troops, or ships of war in time of peace, enter into any agreement or compact with another State, or with a foreign power, or engage in war, unless actually invaded, or in such imminent danger as will not admit of delay.

Article II

Section 1. The executive power shall be vested in a President of the United States of America. He shall hold his office during the term of four years, and, together with the Vice-President, chosen for the same term, be elected as follows:

Each State shall appoint, in such manner as the legislature thereof may direct, a number of electors, equal to the whole number of Senators and Representatives to which the State may be entitled in the Congress; but no Senator or Representative, or person holding an office of trust or profit under the United States, shall be appointed an elector.

The electors shall meet in their respective States, and vote by ballot for two persons, of whom one at least shall not be an inhabitant of the same State with themselves. And they shall make a list of all the persons voted for, and of the number of votes for each; which list they shall sign and certify, and transmit sealed to the seat of government of the United States, directed to the President of the Senate. The President of the Senate shall, in the presence of the Senate and House of Representatives, open all the certificates, and the votes shall then be counted. The person having the greatest number of votes shall be the President, if such number be a majority of the whole number of electors appointed; and if there be more than one who have such majority, and have an equal number of votes, then the House of Representatives shall immediately choose by ballot one of them for President; and if no person have a majority, then from the five highest on the list said house shall in like manner choose the President. But in choosing the President the votes shall be taken by States, the representation from each State having one vote; a quorum for this purpose shall consist of a member or members from two-thirds of the States, and a majority of all the States shall be necessary to a choice. In every case, after the choice of the President, the person having the greatest number of votes of the electors shall be the Vice-President. But if there should remain two or more who have equal votes, the Senate shall choose from them by ballot the Vice-President.

The Congress may determine the time of choosing the electors, and the day on which they shall give their votes; which day shall be the same throughout the United States.

No person except a natural-born citizen, or a citizen of the United States at the time of the adoption of this Constitution, shall be eligible to the office of President; neither shall any person be eligible to that office who shall not have attained to the age of thirty-five years, and been fourteen years a resident within the United States.

In cases of the removal of the President from office or of his death, resignation, or inability to discharge the powers and duties of the said office, the same shall devolve on the Vice-President, and the Congress may by law provide for the case of removal, death, resignation, or inability, both of the President and Vice-President, declaring what officer shall then act as President, and such officer shall act accordingly, until the disability be removed, or a President shall be elected.

The President shall, at stated times, receive for his services a compensation, which shall neither be increased nor diminished during the period for which he shall have been elected, and he shall not receive within that period any other emolument from the United States, or any of them.

Before he enter on the execution of his office, he shall take the following oath or affirmation:—"I do solemnly swear (or affirm) that I will faithfully execute the office of the President of the United States, and will to the best of my ability preserve, protect and defend the Constitution of the United States."

Section 2. The President shall be commander in chief of the army and navy of the United States, and of the militia of the several States, when called into the actual service of the United States; he may require the opinion, in writing, of the principal officer in each of the executive departments, upon any subject relating to the duties of their respective offices, and he shall have power to grant reprieves and pardons for offenses against the United States, except in cases of impeachment.

He shall have power, by and with the advice and consent of the Senate, to make treaties, provided two-thirds of the Senators present concur; and he shall nominate, and by and with the advice and consent of the Senate, shall appoint ambassadors, other public ministers and consuls, judges of the Supreme Court, and all other officers of the United States, whose appointments are not herein otherwise provided for, and which shall be established by law: but Congress may by law vest the appointment of such inferior officers, as they think proper, in the President alone, in the courts of law, or in the heads of departments.

The President shall have power to fill up all vacancies that may happen during the recess of the Senate, by granting commissions which shall expire at the end of their next session.

Section 3. He shall from time to time give to the Congress information of the state of the Union, and recommend to their consideration such measures as he shall judge necessary and expedient; he may, on extraordinary occasions, convene both houses, or either of them, and in case of disagreement between them, with respect to the time of adjournment, he may adjourn them to such time as he shall think proper; he shall receive ambassadors and other public ministers; he shall take care that the laws be faithfully executed, and shall commission all the officers of the United States.

Section 4. The President, Vice-President and all civil officers of the United States shall be removed from office on impeachment for, and on conviction of, treason, bribery, or other high crimes and misdemeanors.

Article III

Section 1. The judicial power of the United States shall be vested in one Supreme Court, and in such inferior courts as the Congress may from time to time ordain and establish. The judges, both of the Supreme and inferior courts, shall hold their offices during good behavior, and shall, at stated times, receive for their services a compensation which shall not be diminished during their continuance in office.

Section 2. The judicial power shall extend to all cases, in law and equity, arising under this Constitution, the laws of the United States, and treaties made, or which shall be made, under their authority;—to all cases affecting ambassadors, other public ministers and consuls;—*to all cases of admiralty and maritime jurisdiction;—to controversies to which the United States shall be a party;*—to controversies between two or more States;—between a State and citizens of another State;—between citizens of different States;—between citizens of the same State claiming lands under grants of different States, and between a State, or the citizens thereof, and foreign states, citizens or subjects.

In all cases affecting ambassadors, other public ministers and consuls, and those in which a State shall be party, the Supreme Court shall have original jurisdiction. In all the other cases before mentioned, the Supreme Court shall have appellate jurisdiction, both as to law and fact, with such exceptions, and under such regulations, as the Congress shall make.

The trial of all crimes, except in cases of impeachment, shall be by jury; and such trial shall be held in the State where said crimes shall have been committed; but when not committed within any State, the trial shall be at such place or places as the Congress may by Law have directed.

Section 3. Treason against the United States shall consist only in levying war against them, or in adhering to their enemies, giving them aid and comfort. No person shall be convicted of treason unless on the testimony of two witnesses to the same overt act, or on confession in open court.

The Congress shall have power to declare the punishment of treason, but no attainder of treason shall work corruption of blood, or forfeiture except during the life of the person attainted.

Article IV

Section 1. Full faith and credit shall be given in each State to the public acts, records, and judicial proceedings of every other State. And the Congress may by general laws prescribe the manner in which such acts, records, and proceedings shall be proved, and the effect thereof.

Section 2. The citizens of each State shall be entitled to all privileges and immunities of citizens in the several States.

A person charged in any State with treason, felony, or other crime, who shall flee from justice, and be found in another State, shall on demand of the executive authority of the State from which he fled, be delivered up, to be removed to the State having jurisdiction of the crime.

No Person held to service or labor in one State, under the laws thereof, escaping into another, shall, in consequence of any law or regulation therein, be discharged from such service or labor, but shall be delivered up on claim of the party to whom such service or labor may be due.

Section 3. New States may be admitted by the Congress into this Union; but no new State shall be formed or erected within the jurisdiction of any other State; nor any State be formed by the junction of two or more States, or parts of States, without the consent of the legislatures of the States concerned as well as of the Congress.

The Congress shall have power to dispose of and make all needful rules and regulations respecting the territory or other property belonging to the United States; and nothing in this Constitution shall be so construed as to prejudice any claims of the United States, or of any particular State.

Section 4. The United States shall guarantee to every State in this Union a republican form of government, and shall protect each of them against invasion; and on application of the legislature, or of the executive (when the legislature cannot be convened), against domestic violence.

Article V

The Congress, whenever two-thirds of both houses shall deem it necessary, shall propose amendments to this Constitution, or, on the application of the legislatures of two-thirds of the several States, shall call a convention for proposing amendments, which, in either case, shall be valid to all intents and purposes, as part of this Constitution, when ratified by the legislatures of three-fourths of the several States, or by conventions in three-fourths thereof, as the one or the other mode of ratification may be proposed by the Congress; provided that no amendments which may be made prior to the year one thousand eight hundred and eight shall in any manner affect the first and fourth clauses in the ninth section of the first article; and that no State, without its consent, shall be deprived of its equal suffrage in the Senate.

Article VI

All debts contracted and engagements entered into, before the adoption of this Constitution, shall be as valid against the United States under this Constitution, as under the Confederation.

This Constitution, and the laws of the United States which shall be made in pursuance thereof; and all treaties made, or which shall be made, under the authority of the United States, shall be the supreme law of the land; and the judges in every State shall be bound thereby, anything in the Constitution or laws of any State to the contrary notwithstanding.

The Senators and Representatives before mentioned, and the members of the several State legislatures, and all executive and judicial officers, both of the United States and of the several States, shall be bound by oath or affirmation to support this Constitution; but no religious test shall ever be required as a qualification to any office or public trust under the United States.

Article VII

The ratification of the conventions of nine States shall be sufficient for the establishment of this Constitution between the States so ratifying the same.

Done in convention by the unanimous consent of the States present, the seventeenth day of September in the year of our Lord one thousand seven hundred and eighty-seven and of the Independence of the United States of America the twelfth. In witness whereof we have hereunto subscribed our names.

GEORGE WASHINGTON, President and Deputy from Virginia

New Hampshire
John Langdon
Nicholas Gilman

Massachusetts
Nathaniel Gorham
Rufus King

Connecticut
William Samuel
 Johnson
Roger Sherman

New York
Alexander Hamilton

New Jersey
William Livingston
David Brearley
William Paterson
Jonathan Dayton

Pennsylvania
Benjamin Franklin
Thomas Mifflin
Robert Morris
George Clymer
Thomas FitzSimons
Jared Ingersoll
James Wilson
Gouverneur Morris

Delaware
George Read
Gunning Bedford, Jr.
John Dickinson
Richard Bassett
Jacob Broom

Maryland
James McHenry
Daniel of St. Thomas
 Jenifer
Daniel Carroll

Virginia
John Blair
James Madison, Jr.

North Carolina
William Blount
Richard Dobbs Spaight
Hugh Williamson

South Carolina
John Rutledge
Charles Cotesworth
  Pinckney
Charles Pinckney
Pierce Butler

Georgia
William Few
Abraham Baldwin

AMENDMENTS TO THE CONSTITUTION
(including six unratified amendments)

Amendment I
[RATIFIED 1791]

Congress shall make no law respecting an establishment of religion, or prohibiting the free exercise thereof; or abridging the freedom of speech, or of the press; or the right of the people peaceably to assemble, and to petition the government for a redress of grievances.

Amendment II
[RATIFIED 1791]

A well-regulated militia being necessary to the security of a free State, the right of the people to keep and bear arms shall not be infringed.

Amendment III
[RATIFIED 1791]

No soldier shall, in time of peace, be quartered in any house without the consent of the owner, nor in time of war, but in a manner to be prescribed by law.

Amendment IV
[RATIFIED 1791]

The right of the people to be secure in their persons, houses, papers, and effects, against unreasonable searches and seizures, shall not be violated, and no warrants shall issue but upon probable cause, supported by oath or affirmation, and particularly describing the place to be searched, and the persons or things to be seized.

Amendment V
[RATIFIED 1791]

No person shall be held to answer for a capital, or otherwise infamous crime, unless on a presentment or indictment of a grand jury, except in cases arising in the land or naval forces, or in the militia, when in actual service in time of war or public danger; nor shall any person be subject for the same offence to be twice put in jeopardy of life or limb; nor shall be compelled in any criminal case to be a witness against himself, nor be deprived of life, liberty, or property, without due process of law; nor shall private property be taken for public use without just compensation.

Amendment VI

[RATIFIED 1791]

In all criminal prosecutions, the accused shall enjoy the right to a speedy and public trial, by an impartial jury of the State and district wherein the crime shall have been committed, which district shall have been previously ascertained by law, and to be informed of the nature and cause of the accusation; to be confronted with the witnesses against him; to have compulsory process for obtaining witnesses in his favor, and to have the assistance of counsel for his defence.

Amendment VII

[RATIFIED 1791]

In suits at common law, where the value in controversy shall exceed twenty dollars, the right of trial by jury shall be preserved, and no fact tried by a jury shall be otherwise reexamined in any court of the United States, than according to the rules of the common law.

Amendment VIII

[RATIFIED 1791]

Excessive bail shall not be required, nor excessive fines imposed, nor cruel and unusual punishments inflicted.

Amendment IX

[RATIFIED 1791]

The enumeration in the Constitution, of certain rights, shall not be construed to deny or disparage others retained by the people.

Amendment X

[RATIFIED 1791]

The powers not delegated to the United States by the Constitution, nor prohibited by it to the States, are reserved to the States respectively, or to the people.

Unratified Amendment

[REAPPORTIONMENT AMENDMENT (PROPOSED BY CONGRESS SEPTEMBER 25, 1789, ALONG WITH THE BILL OF RIGHTS)]

After the first enumeration required by the first article of the Constitution, there shall be one Representative for every thirty thousand, until the number shall amount to one hundred, after which the proportion shall be so regulated by Congress, that there shall be not less than one hundred Representatives, nor less than one Representative for every forty thousand persons, until the number of Representatives shall amount to two hundred; after which the proportion shall be so regulated by Congress, that there shall not be less than two hundred Representatives, nor more than one Representative for every fifty thousand persons.

Amendment XI

[RATIFIED 1798]

The judicial power of the United States shall not be construed to extend to any suit in law or equity, commenced or prosecuted against one of the United States by citizens of another State, or by citizens or subjects of any foreign state.

Amendment XII

[RATIFIED 1804]

The electors shall meet in their respective States, and vote by ballot for President and Vice-President, one of whom, at least, shall not be an inhabitant of the same State with themselves; they shall name in their ballots the person voted for as President, and in distinct ballots the person voted for as Vice-President, and they shall make distinct lists of all persons voted for as President, and of all persons voted for as Vice-President, and of the number of votes for each, which lists they shall sign and certify, and transmit sealed to the seat of government of the United States, directed to the President of the Senate;—the President of the Senate shall, in the presence of the Senate and House of Representatives, open all the certificates and the votes shall then be counted;—the person having the greatest number of votes for President shall be the President, if such number be a majority of the whole number of electors appointed; and if no person have such majority, then from the persons having the highest numbers not exceeding three on the list of those voted for as President, the House of Representatives shall choose immediately, by ballot, the President. But in choosing the President, the votes shall be taken by States, the representation from each State having one vote; a quorum for this purpose shall consist of a member or members from two-thirds of the States, and a majority of all the States shall be necessary to a choice. And if the House of Representatives shall not choose a President whenever the right of choice shall devolve upon them, before *the fourth day of March* next following, then the Vice-President shall act as President, as in the case of the death or other constitutional disability of the President.

The person having the greatest number of votes as Vice-President shall be the Vice-President, if such number be a majority of the whole number of electors appointed; and if no person have a majority, then from the two highest numbers on the list the Senate shall choose the Vice-President; a quorum for the purpose shall consist of two-thirds of the whole number of Senators, and a majority of the whole number shall be necessary to a choice. But no person constitutionally ineligible to the office of President shall be eligible to that of Vice-President of the United States.

Unratified Amendment

[TITLES OF NOBILITY AMENDMENT (PROPOSED BY CONGRESS MAY 1, 1810)]

If any citizen of the United States shall accept, claim, receive or retain any title of nobility or honor or shall, without the consent of Congress, accept and retain any present, pension, office or emolument of any kind whatever, from any emperor, king, prince or foreign power, such person shall cease to be a citizen of the United States, and shall be incapable of holding any office of trust or profit under them or either of them.

Unratified Amendment

[CORWIN AMENDMENT (PROPOSED BY CONGRESS MARCH 2, 1861)]

No amendment shall be made to the Constitution which will authorize or give to Congress the power to abolish or interfere, within any State, with the domestic institutions thereof, including that of persons held to labor or service by the laws of said State.

Amendment XIII

[RATIFIED 1865]

Section 1. Neither slavery nor involuntary servitude, except as a punishment for crime whereof the party shall have been duly convicted, shall exist within the United States, or any place subject to their jurisdiction.

Section 2. Congress shall have power to enforce this article by appropriate legislation.

Amendment XIV

[RATIFIED 1868]

Section 1. All persons born or naturalized in the United States, and subject to the jurisdiction thereof, are citizens of the United States and of the State wherein they reside. No State shall make or enforce any law which shall abridge the privileges or immunities of citizens of the United States; nor shall any State deprive any person of life, liberty, or property, without due process of law; nor deny to any person within its jurisdiction the equal protection of the laws.

Section 2. Representatives shall be appointed among the several States according to their respective numbers, counting the whole number of persons in each State, excluding Indians not taxed. But when the right to vote at any election for the choice of Electors for President and Vice-President of the United States, Representatives in Congress, the executive and judicial officers of a State, or the members of the legislature thereof, is denied to any of the *male* inhabitants of such State, being *twenty-one* years of age and citizens of the United States, or in any way abridged, except for participation in rebellion, or other crime, the basis of representation therein shall be reduced in the proportion which the number of such *male* citizens shall bear to the whole number of *male* citizens *twenty-one* years of age in such State.

Section 3. No person shall be a Senator or Representative in Congress, or Elector of President and Vice-President, or hold any office, civil or military, under the United States, or under any State, who, having previously taken an oath, as a member of Congress, or as an officer of the United States, or as a member of any State legislature, or as an executive or judicial officer of any State, to support the Constitution of the United States, shall have engaged in insurrection or rebellion against the same, or given aid or comfort to the enemies thereof. Congress may, by a vote of two-thirds of each house, remove such disability.

Section 4. The validity of the public debt of the United States, authorized by law, including debts incurred for payment of pensions and bounties for services in suppressing insurrection or rebellion, shall not be questioned. But neither the United States nor any State shall assume or pay any debt or obligation incurred in aid of insurrection or rebellion against the United States, or any claim for the loss or emancipation of any slave; but all such debts, obligations, and claims shall be held illegal and void.

Section 5. The Congress shall have power to enforce, by appropriate legislation, the provisions of this article.

Amendment XV

[RATIFIED 1870]

Section 1. The right of citizens of the United States to vote shall not be denied or abridged by the United States or by any State on account of race, color, or previous condition of servitude.

Section 2. The Congress shall have power to enforce this article by appropriate legislation.

Amendment XVI

[RATIFIED 1913]

The Congress shall have power to lay and collect taxes on incomes, from whatever source derived, without apportionment among the several States, and without regard to any census or enumeration.

Amendment XVII

[RATIFIED 1913]

Section 1. The Senate of the United States shall be composed of two Senators from each State, elected by the people thereof, for six years; and each Senator shall have one vote. The electors in each State shall have the qualifications requisite for electors of [voters for] the most numerous branch of the State legislatures.

Section 2. When vacancies happen in the representation of any State in the Senate, the executive authority of such State shall issue writs of election to fill such vacancies: Provided, that the Legislature of any State may empower the executive thereof to make temporary appointments until the people fill the vacancies by election as the Legislature may direct.

Section 3. *This amendment shall not be so construed as to affect the election or term of any Senator chosen before it becomes valid as part of the Constitution.*

Amendment XVIII

[RATIFIED 1919; REPEALED 1933 BY AMENDMENT XXI]

Section 1. *After one year from the ratification of this article the manufacture, sale, or transportation of intoxicating liquors within, the importation thereof into, or the exportation thereof from the United States and all territory subject to the jurisdiction thereof, for beverage purposes, is hereby prohibited.*

Section 2. *The Congress and the several States shall have concurrent power to enforce this article by appropriate legislation.*

Section 3. *This article shall be inoperative unless it shall have been ratified as an amendment to the Constitution by the legislatures of the several States, as provided by the Constitution, within seven years from the date of the submission thereof to the States by the Congress.*

Amendment XIX

[RATIFIED 1920]

Section 1. The right of citizens of the United States to vote shall not be denied or abridged by the United States or by any State on account of sex.

Section 2. Congress shall have the power to enforce this article by appropriate legislation.

Unratified Amendment

[CHILD LABOR AMENDMENT (PROPOSED BY CONGRESS JUNE 2, 1924)]

Section 1. *The Congress shall have power to limit, regulate, and prohibit the labor of persons under eighteen years of age.*

Section 2. *The power of the several States is unimpaired by this article except that the operation of State laws shall be suspended to the extent necessary to give effect to legislation enacted by Congress.*

Amendment XX

[RATIFIED 1933]

Section 1. The terms of the President and Vice-President shall end at noon on the 20th day of January, and the terms of Senators and Representatives at noon on the 3rd day of January, of the years in which such terms would have ended if this article had not been ratified; and the terms of their successors shall then begin.

Section 2. The Congress shall assemble at least once in every year, and such meeting shall begin at noon on the 3rd day of January, unless they shall by law appoint a different day.

Section 3. If, at the time fixed for the beginning of the term of the President, the President-elect shall have died, the Vice-President-elect shall become President. If a President shall not have been chosen before the time fixed for the beginning of his term, or if the President-elect shall have failed to qualify, then the Vice-President-elect shall act as President until a President shall have qualified; and the Congress may by law provide for the case wherein neither a President-elect nor a Vice-President-elect shall have qualified, declaring who shall then act as President, or the manner in which one who is to act shall be selected, and such person shall act accordingly until a President or Vice-President shall have qualified.

Section 4. The Congress may by law provide for the case of the death of any of the persons from whom the House of Representatives may choose a President whenever the right of choice shall have devolved upon them, and for the case of the death of any of the persons from whom the Senate may choose a Vice-President whenever the right of choice shall have devolved upon them.

Section 5. Sections 1 and 2 shall take effect on the 15th day of October following the ratification of this article.

Section 6. This article shall be inoperative unless it shall have been ratified as an amendment to the Constitution by the Legislatures of three-fourths of the several States within seven years from the date of its submission.

Amendment XXI

[RATIFIED 1933]

Section 1. The eighteenth article of amendment to the Constitution of the United States is hereby repealed.

Section 2. The transportation or importation into any State, Territory, or Possession of the United States for delivery or use therein of intoxicating liquors, in violation of the laws thereof, is hereby prohibited.

Section 3. This article shall be inoperative unless it shall have been ratified as an amendment to the Constitution by conventions in the several States, as provided in the Constitution, within seven years from the date of the submission thereof to the States by the Congress.

Amendment XXII

[RATIFIED 1951]

Section 1. No person shall be elected to the office of the President more than twice, and no person who has held the office of President, or acted as President, for more than two years of a term to which some other person was elected President shall be elected to the office of President more than once. But this article shall not apply to any person holding the office of President when this Article was proposed by the Congress, and shall not prevent any person who may be holding the office of President, or acting as President, during the term within which this Article becomes operative from holding the office of President or acting as President during the remainder of such term.

Section 2. This article shall be inoperative unless it shall have been ratified as an amendment to the Constitution by the legislatures of three-fourths of the several States within seven years from the date of its submission to the States by the Congress.

Amendment XXIII

[RATIFIED 1961]

Section 1. The District constituting the seat of Government of the United States shall appoint in such manner as the Congress may direct: A number of electors of President and Vice-President equal to the whole number of Senators and Representatives in Congress to which the District would be entitled if it were a State, but in no event more than the least populous State; they shall be in addition to those appointed by the States, but they shall be considered for the purposes of the election of President and Vice-President, to be electors appointed by a State; and they shall meet in the District and perform such duties as provided by the twelfth article of amendment.

Section 2. The Congress shall have the power to enforce this article by appropriate legislation.

Amendment XXIV

[RATIFIED 1964]

Section 1. The right of citizens of the United States to vote in any primary or other election for President or Vice-President, for electors for President or Vice-President, or for Senator or Representative in Congress, shall not be denied or abridged by the United States or any State by reason of failure to pay any poll tax or other tax.

Section 2. The Congress shall have the power to enforce this article by appropriate legislation.

Amendment XXV

[RATIFIED 1967]

Section 1. In case of the removal of the President from office or of his death or resignation, the Vice-President shall become President.

Section 2. Whenever there is a vacancy in the office of the Vice-President, the President shall nominate a Vice-President who shall take office upon confirmation by a majority vote of both Houses of Congress.

Section 3. Whenever the President transmits to the President pro tempore of the Senate and the Speaker of the House of Representatives his written declaration that he is unable to discharge the powers and duties of his office, and until he transmits to them a written declaration to the contrary, such powers and duties shall be discharged by the Vice-President as Acting President.

Section 4. Whenever the Vice-President and a majority of either the principal officers of the executive departments or of such other body as Congress may by law provide, transmit to the President pro tempore of the Senate and the Speaker of the House of Representatives their written declaration that the President is unable to discharge the powers and duties of his office, the Vice-President shall immediately assume the powers and duties of the office as Acting President.

Thereafter, when the President transmits to the President pro tempore of the Senate and the Speaker of the House of Representatives his written declaration that no inability exists, he shall resume the powers and duties of his office unless the Vice-President and a majority of either the principal officers of the executive department[s] or of such other body as Congress may by law provide, transmit within four days to the President pro tempore of the Senate and the Speaker of the House of Representatives their written declaration that the President is unable to discharge the powers and duties of his office. Thereupon Congress shall decide the issue, assembling within forty-eight hours for that purpose if not in session. If the Congress, within twenty-one days after receipt of the latter written declaration, or, if Congress is not in session, within twenty-one days after Congress is required to assemble, determines by two-thirds vote of both Houses that the President is unable to discharge the powers and duties of his office, the Vice-President shall continue to discharge the same as Acting President; otherwise, the President shall resume the powers and duties of his office.

Amendment XXVI

[RATIFIED 1971]

Section 1. The right of citizens of the United States, who are eighteen years of age or older, to vote shall not be denied or abridged by the United States or by any State on account of age.

Section 2. The Congress shall have power to enforce this article by appropriate legislation.

Unratified Amendment

[EQUAL RIGHTS AMENDMENT (PROPOSED BY CONGRESS MARCH 22, 1972; SEVEN-YEAR DEADLINE FOR RATIFICATION EXTENDED TO JUNE 30, 1982)]

Section 1. *Equality of rights under the law shall not be denied or abridged by the United States or by any State on account of sex.*

Section 2. *The Congress shall have the power to enforce, by appropriate legislation, the provisions of this article.*

Section 3. *This amendment shall take effect two years after the date of ratification.*

Unratified Amendment

[D.C. STATEHOOD AMENDMENT (PROPOSED BY CONGRESS AUGUST 22, 1978)]

Section 1. *For purposes of representation in the Congress, election of the President and Vice-President, and article V of this Constitution, the District constituting the seat of government of the United States shall be treated as though it were a State.*

Section 2. *The exercise of the rights and powers conferred under this article shall be by the people of the District constituting the seat of government, and as shall be provided by Congress.*

Section 3. *The twenty-third article of amendment to the Constitution of the United States is hereby repealed.*

Section 4. *This article shall be inoperative, unless it shall have been ratified as an amendment to the Constitution by the legislatures of three-fourths of the several states within seven years from the date of its submission.*

Amendment XXVII

[RATIFIED 1992]

No law, varying the compensation for the services of the Senators and Representatives, shall take effect, until an election of Representatives shall have intervened.

Admission of States to the Union

State	Year of Admission	State	Year of Admission
Delaware	1787	Michigan	1837
Pennsylvania	1787	Florida	1845
New Jersey	1787	Texas	1845
Georgia	1788	Iowa	1846
Connecticut	1788	Wisconsin	1848
Massachusetts	1788	California	1850
Maryland	1788	Minnesota	1858
South Carolina	1788	Oregon	1859
New Hampshire	1788	Kansas	1861
Virginia	1788	West Virginia	1863
New York	1788	Nevada	1864
North Carolina	1789	Nebraska	1867
Rhode Island	1790	Colorado	1876
Vermont	1791	North Dakota	1889
Kentucky	1792	South Dakota	1889
Tennessee	1796	Montana	1889
Ohio	1803	Washington	1889
Louisiana	1812	Idaho	1890
Indiana	1816	Wyoming	1890
Mississippi	1817	Utah	1896
Illinois	1818	Oklahoma	1907
Alabama	1819	New Mexico	1912
Maine	1820	Arizona	1912
Missouri	1821	Alaska	1959
Arkansas	1836	Hawaii	1959

Presidents of the United States

President	Term	President	Term
George Washington	1789–1797	Benjamin Harrison	1889–1893
John Adams	1797–1801	Grover Cleveland	1893–1897
Thomas Jefferson	1801–1809	William McKinley	1897–1901
James Madison	1809–1817	Theodore Roosevelt	1901–1909
James Monroe	1817–1825	William H. Taft	1909–1913
John Quincy Adams	1825–1829	Woodrow Wilson	1913–1921
Andrew Jackson	1829–1837	Warren G. Harding	1921–1923
Martin Van Buren	1837–1841	Calvin Coolidge	1923–1929
William H. Harrison	1841	Herbert Hoover	1929–1933
John Tyler	1841–1845	Franklin D. Roosevelt	1933–1945
James K. Polk	1845–1849	Harry S. Truman	1945–1953
Zachary Taylor	1849–1850	Dwight D. Eisenhower	1953–1961
Millard Fillmore	1850–1853	John F. Kennedy	1961–1963
Franklin Pierce	1853–1857	Lyndon B. Johnson	1963–1969
James Buchanan	1857–1861	Richard M. Nixon	1969–1974
Abraham Lincoln	1861–1865	Gerald R. Ford	1974–1977
Andrew Johnson	1865–1869	Jimmy Carter	1977–1981
Ulysses S. Grant	1869–1877	Ronald Reagan	1981–1989
Rutherford B. Hayes	1877–1881	George H. W. Bush	1989–1993
James A. Garfield	1881	Bill Clinton	1993–2001
Chester A. Arthur	1881–1885	George W. Bush	2001–2009
Grover Cleveland	1885–1889	Barack Obama	2009–

Glossary of Key Terms

acquired immune deficiency syndrome (AIDS) Immune disorder that reached epidemic proportions in the United States in the 1980s.

affirmative action Programs meant to overcome historical patterns of discrimination against minorities and women in education and employment. By establishing guidelines for hiring and college admissions, the government sought to advance equal opportunities for minorities and women.

Agricultural Adjustment Act New Deal legislation that raised prices for farm produce by paying farmers subsidies to reduce production. Large farmers reaped most of the benefits from the act. The Supreme Court declared it unconstitutional in 1936.

Alamo Texas fort captured by General Santa Anna on March 6, 1836, from rebel defenders. Sensationalist accounts of the siege of the Alamo increased popular support in the United States for Texas independence.

Albany Congress June 1754 meeting in Albany, New York, of Iroquois and colonial representatives meant to facilitate better relations between Britain and the Iroquois Confederacy. Benjamin Franklin also put forward a plan for colonial union that was never implemented.

Alien and Sedition Acts 1798 security acts passed by the Federalist-controlled Congress. The Alien Act allowed the president to imprison or deport noncitizens; the Sedition Act placed significant restrictions on political speech.

America First Committee Isolationist organization founded by Senator Gerald Nye in 1940 to keep the United States out of World War II.

American Anti-Slavery Society (AASS) Abolitionist society founded by William Lloyd Garrison in 1833 that became the most important northern abolitionist organization of the period.

American Colonization Society (ACS) Organization formed in 1817 to establish colonies of freed slaves and freeborn blacks in Africa. The ACS was led by a group of white elites whose primary goal was to rid the nation of African Americans.

American Equal Rights Association Group of black and white women and men formed in 1866 to promote gender and racial equality. The organization split in 1869 over support for the Fifteenth Amendment.

American Federation of Labor (AFL) Trade union federation founded in 1886. Led by its first president, Samuel Gompers, the AFL sought to organize skilled workers into trade-specific unions.

American Indian Movement (AIM) An American Indian group, formed in 1968, that promoted "red power" and condemned the United States for its continued mistreatment of Native Americans.

American Plan Voluntary program initiated by businesses in the early twentieth century to protect worker welfare. The American Plan was meant to undermine the appeal of labor unions.

American Protective League (APL) An organization of private citizens that cooperated with the Justice Department and the Bureau of Investigation during World War I to spy on German residents suspected of disloyal behavior.

American System Plan proposed by Henry Clay to promote the U.S. economy by combining federally funded internal improvements to aid farmers with federal tariffs to protect U.S. manufacturing and a national bank to oversee economic development.

American system of manufacturing Production system focused on water-powered machinery, division of labor, and the use of interchangeable parts. The introduction of the American system in the early nineteenth century greatly increased the productivity of American manufacturing.

American Woman Suffrage Association Organization founded in 1869 to support ratification of the Fifteenth Amendment and campaign for women's suffrage.

Anti-Imperialist League An organization founded in 1898 to oppose annexation of the Philippines. Some feared that annexation would bring competition from cheap labor; others considered Filipinos racially inferior and the Philippines unsuitable as an American territory.

Antifederalists Opponents of ratification of the Constitution. Antifederalists were generally more rural and less wealthy than the Federalists.

Appeal . . . to the Colored Citizens Radical abolitionist pamphlet published by David Walker in 1829. Walker's work inspired some white abolitionists to take a more radical stance on slavery.

Articles of Confederation Plan for national government proposed by the Continental Congress in 1777 and ratified in March 1781. The Articles of Confederation gave the national government limited powers, reflecting widespread fear of centralized authority.

Atlantic Charter August 1941 agreement between Franklin Roosevelt and Winston Churchill that outlined potential war aims and cemented the relationship between the United States and Britain.

Aztecs Spanish term for the Mexica, an indigenous people who built an empire in present-day Mexico in the centuries before the arrival of the Spaniards. The Aztecs built their empire through conquest.

Bacon's Rebellion 1676 uprising in Virginia led by Nathaniel Bacon. Bacon and his followers, many of whom were former servants, were upset by the Virginia governor's unwillingness to send troops to intervene in conflicts between settlers and Indians and by the lack of representation of western settlers in the House of Burgesses.

Battle of Saratoga Site of key Revolutionary War battle. The patriot victory at Saratoga in October 1777 provided hope that the colonists could prevail and increased the chances that the French would formally join the patriot side.

Battle of Shiloh April 1862 battle in Tennessee that provided the Union entrance to the Mississippi valley. Shiloh was the bloodiest battle in American history to that point.

Battle of the Little Big Horn 1876 battle in the Montana Territory in which Lieutenant Colonel George Armstrong Custer and his troops were massacred by Lakota Sioux.

beats A small group of young poets, writers, intellectuals, musicians, and artists who attacked mainstream American politics and culture in the 1950s.

benign neglect British colonial policy from about 1700 to 1760 that relaxed supervision of internal colonial affairs as long as the North American colonies produced sufficient raw materials and revenue; also known as *salutary neglect*.

Beringia Land bridge that linked Siberia and Alaska during the Wisconsin period. Migrants from northeast Asia used this bridge to travel to North America.

Berlin airlift During the Berlin blockade by the Soviets from 1948 to 1949, the U.S. and British governments dispatched their air forces to transport food and supplies to West Berlin.

Bill of Rights The first ten amendments to the Constitution. These ten amendments helped reassure Americans who feared that the federal government established under the Constitution would infringe on the rights of individuals and states.

black codes Racial laws passed in the immediate aftermath of the Civil War by southern legislatures. The black codes were intended to reduce free African Americans to a condition as close to slavery as possible.

Black Death The epidemic of bubonic plague that swept through Europe beginning in the mid-fourteenth century and wiped out roughly half of Europe's population.

Black Panther Party Organization founded in 1966 by Huey P. Newton and Bobby Seale to advance the black power movement in black communities.

Black Tuesday October 29, 1929, crash of the American stock market. The 1929 stock market crash marked the beginning of the Great Depression.

blacklist Informal list of individuals barred from employment in the entertainment industry in the late 1940s and early 1950s as a result of their suspected Communist connections.

Bleeding Kansas The Kansas Territory during a period of violent conflicts over the fate of slavery in the mid-1850s. The violence in Kansas intensified the sectional division over slavery.

Boland Amendment 1982 act of Congress prohibiting direct aid to the Nicaraguan Contra forces.

Bonus Army World War I veterans who marched on Washington, D.C., in 1932 to demand immediate payment of their service bonuses. President Hoover refused to negotiate and instructed the U.S. army to clear the capital of protesters, leading to a violent clash.

boss Leader of a political machine. Men like "Boss" George Washington Plunkitt of New York's Tammany Hall wielded enormous power over city life.

Boston Massacre 1770 clash between colonial protesters and British soldiers in Boston that led to the death of five colonists. The bloody conflict was used to promote the patriot cause.

Brown v. Board of Education of Topeka, Kansas Landmark 1954 Supreme Court case that overturned the "separate but equal" principle established by *Plessy v. Ferguson* and applied to public schools. Few schools in the South were racially desegregated for more than a decade.

buffalo soldiers African American cavalrymen who fought in the West against the Indians in the 1870s and 1880s and served with distinction.

bully pulpit Term used by Theodore Roosevelt to describe the office of the presidency. Roosevelt believed that the president should use his office as a platform to promote his programs and rally public opinion.

Bush Doctrine President George W. Bush's proposal to engage in preemptive war against despotic governments, such as Iraq, deemed to threaten U.S. national security, even if the danger was not imminent.

Californios Spanish and Mexican residents of California. Before the nineteenth century, Californios made up California's economic and political elite. Their position, however, deteriorated after the conclusion of the Mexican-American War in 1848.

Camp David accords 1978 peace accord between Israel and Egypt facilitated by the mediation of President Jimmy Carter.

carpetbaggers Derogatory term for white Northerners who moved to the South in the years following the Civil War. Many white Southerners believed that such migrants were intent on exploiting their suffering.

Chinese Exclusion Act 1882 act that banned Chinese immigration into the United States and prohibited those Chinese already in the country from becoming naturalized American citizens.

Church of England National church established by Henry VIII after he split with the Catholic Church.

civic housekeeping Idea promoted by Jane Addams for urban reform by using women's traditional skills as domestic managers; caregivers for children, the elderly, and the needy; and community builders.

Civil Rights Act of 1964 Wide-ranging civil rights act that, among other things, prohibited discrimination in public accommodations and employment and increased federal enforcement of school desegregation.

Civilian Conservation Corps (CCC) New Deal work program that hired young, unmarried men to work on conservation projects. The CCC employed about 2.5 million men and lasted until 1942.

Coercive Acts (Intolerable Acts) 1774 act of Parliament passed in response to the Boston Tea Party. The Coercive Acts were meant to force the colonists into submission, but they only resulted in increased resistance. Colonial patriots called them the Intolerable Acts.

collective bargaining The process of negotiation between labor unions and employers.

Columbian exchange The biological exchange between the Americas and the rest of the world. Although the initial impact of the Columbian exchange was strongest in the Americas and Europe, it was soon felt all over the world.

Commission on the Status of Women Commission appointed by President Kennedy in 1961. The commission's 1963 report, *American Women,* highlighted employment discrimination against women and recommended legislation requiring equal pay for equal work regardless of sex.

committee of correspondence Type of committee first established in Massachusetts to circulate concerns and reports of protests and other events to leaders in other colonies in the aftermath of the Sugar Act.

Committee on Public Information (CPI) Committee established in 1917 to create propaganda and promote censorship in order to generate enthusiasm for World War I and stifle antiwar dissent.

Common Sense Pamphlet arguing in favor of independence written by Thomas Paine and published in 1776. *Common Sense* was widely read and had an important impact on the debate over declaring independence from Britain.

Compromise of 1850 Series of acts following California's application for admission as a free state. Meant to quell sectional tensions over slavery, the act was intended to provide something for all sides but ended up fueling more conflicts.

Compromise of 1877 Compromise between Republicans and southern Democrats that resulted in the election of Rutherford B. Hayes. Southern Democrats agreed to support Hayes in the disputed presidential election in exchange for his promise to end Reconstruction.

Comstock Lode Massive silver deposit discovered in the Sierra Nevada in the late 1850s.

Confederate States of America Nation established in 1861 by the eleven slave states that seceded between December 1860 and April 1861.

Congress of Racial Equality (CORE) Civil rights organization, founded in 1942, that fought against racial exclusion in public accommodations. The emergence of organizations like CORE signaled a new phase in the civil rights struggle.

conquistadors Spanish soldiers who were central to the conquest of the civilizations of the Americas. Once conquest was complete, conquistadors often extracted wealth from the people and lands they now ruled.

conservative coalition Alliance of southern Democrats and conservative northern Republicans in Congress that thwarted passage of New Deal legislation after 1938.

Continental Congress Congress convened in Philadelphia in 1774 in response to the Coercive Acts. The delegates hoped to reestablish the freedoms colonists had enjoyed in earlier times.

contraband Designation assigned to escaped slaves by Union general Benjamin Butler in May 1861. By designating slaves as property forfeited by the act of rebellion, the Union was able to strike at slavery without proclaiming a general emancipation.

Contract with America A document that called for reduced welfare spending, lower taxes, term limits for lawmakers, and a constitutional amendment for a balanced budget. In preparation for the 1994 midterm congressional elections, Republicans, led by Representative Newt Gingrich, drew up this proposal.

convict lease The system used by southern governments to furnish mainly African American prison labor to plantation owners and industrialists and to raise revenue for the states. In practice, convict labor replaced slavery as the means of providing a forced labor supply.

Copperheads Northern Democrats who did not support the Union war effort. Such Democrats enjoyed considerable support in eastern cities and parts of the Midwest.

corporation A form of business ownership in which the liability of shareholders in a company is limited to their individual investments. The formation of corporations in the late nineteenth century greatly stimulated investment in industry.

Corps of Discovery Expedition organized by the U.S. government to explore the Louisiana Territory. Led by Meriwether Lewis and William Clark, the expedition set out in May 1804 and journeyed to the Pacific coast and back by 1806 with the aid of interpreters like Sacagawea.

cotton gin Machine invented by Eli Whitney in 1793 to deseed short-staple cotton. The cotton gin dramatically reduced the time and labor involved in deseeding, facilitating the expansion of cotton production in the South and West.

counterculture Young cultural rebels of the 1960s who rejected conventional moral and sexual values and used drugs to reach a higher consciousness. These so-called hippies bonded together in their style of clothes and taste in rock 'n' roll music.

court-packing plan Proposal by President Franklin Roosevelt in 1937 to increase the size of the Supreme Court and reduce its opposition to New Deal legislation. Congress failed to pass the measure, and the scheme increased resentment toward Roosevelt.

Coxey's army 1894 protest movement led by Jacob Coxey. Coxey and five hundred supporters marched from Ohio to Washington, D.C., to protest the lack of government response to the depression of 1893.

Crusades Eleventh- and twelfth-century campaigns to reclaim the Holy Land for the Roman Catholic Church. The Crusades were, on the whole, a military failure, but they did stimulate trade and inspire Europeans to seek better connections with the larger world.

Cuba Libre Vision of Cuban independence developed by José Martí, who hoped that Cuban independence would bring with it greater social and racial equality.

D Day June 6, 1944, invasion of German-occupied France by Allied forces. The D Day landings opened up a second front in Europe and marked a major turning point in World War II.

Dawes Act 1887 act that ended federal recognition of tribal sovereignty and divided Indian land into 160-acre parcels to be distributed to Indian heads of household. The act dramatically reduced the amount of Indian-controlled land and undermined Indian social and cultural institutions.

Dayton Peace Accords 1995 peace agreement ending the war in Bosnia that emerged from a conference hosted by President Bill Clinton in Dayton, Ohio.

Declaration of Independence Document declaring the independence of the colonies from Great Britain. Drafted by Thomas Jefferson and then debated and revised by the Continental Congress, the Declaration was made public on July 4, 1776.

Declaration of Sentiments Call for women's rights in marriage, family, religion, politics, and law issued at the 1848 Seneca Falls convention. It was signed by 100 of the 300 participants.

Democratic-Republican Party Political party that emerged out of opposition to Federalist policies in the 1790s. The Democratic-Republicans chose Thomas Jefferson as their presidential candidate in 1796, 1800, and 1804.

Democrats and National Republicans Two parties that resulted from the split of the Democratic-Republicans in the early 1820s. Andrew Jackson emerged as the leader of the Democrats.

depression of 1893 Severe economic downturn triggered by railroad and bank failures. The severity of the depression, combined with the failure of the federal government to offer an adequate response, led to the realignment of American politics.

deskilling The replacement of skilled labor with unskilled labor and machines.

détente An easing of tense relations with the Soviet Union during the Cold War. This process moved unevenly through the 1970s and early 1980s but accelerated when Soviet leader Mikhail Gorbachev came to power in the mid-1980s.

divestment movement 1980s campaign against apartheid by ending investments by U.S. corporations, universities, and municipalities in South Africa.

dollar diplomacy Term used by President Taft to describe the economic focus of his foreign policy. Taft hoped to use economic policies and the control of foreign assets by American companies to influence Latin American nations.

"don't ask, don't tell" The official policy toward gays in the U.S. military established by President Bill Clinton in 1993. The policy prohibited discrimination against homosexuals as long as they did not reveal their sexual identity, but it banned openly gay men and women from serving in the armed forces. It was repealed by President Barack Obama in 2011.

***Dred Scott* decision** 1857 Supreme Court case centered on the status of Dred Scott and his family. In its ruling, the Court denied the claim that black men had any rights and blocked Congress from excluding slavery from any territory.

Dunmore's Proclamation 1775 proclamation issued by the British commander Lord Dunmore that offered freedom to all enslaved African Americans who joined the British army. The proclamation heightened concerns among some patriots about the consequences of independence.

Eisenhower Doctrine A doctrine guiding intervention in the Middle East. In 1957 Congress granted President Dwight Eisenhower the power to send military forces into the Middle East to combat Communist aggression. Eisenhower sent U.S. marines into Lebanon in 1958 under this doctrine.

Emancipation Proclamation January 1, 1863, proclamation that declared all slaves in areas still in rebellion "forever free." While stopping short of abolishing slavery, the Emancipation Proclamation was, nonetheless, seen by blacks and abolitionists as a great victory.

Embargo Act 1807 act that prohibited American ships from leaving their home ports until Britain and France repealed restrictions on U.S. trade. The act had a devastating impact on American commerce.

encomiendas System first established by Columbus by which Spanish leaders in the Americas received land and the labor of all Indians residing on it. From the Indian point of view, the encomienda system amounted to little more than enslavement.

Enlightenment European cultural movement that emphasized rational and scientific thinking over traditional religion and superstition. Enlightenment thought appealed to many colonial elites.

Enola Gay American B-29 bomber that dropped an atomic bomb on Hiroshima on August 6, 1945. The dropping of a second bomb on Nagasaki three days later led to Japan's surrender.

Enrollment Act March 1863 Union draft law that provided for draftees to be selected by an impartial lottery. A loophole in the law that allowed wealthy Americans to escape service by paying $300 or hiring a substitute created widespread resentment.

Enterprise of the Indies Columbus's proposal to sail west across the Atlantic to Japan and China. In 1492 Columbus gained support for the venture from Ferdinand and Isabella of Spain.

Environmental Protection Agency (EPA) Federal agency established by Richard Nixon in 1971 to regulate activities that resulted in pollution or other environmental degradation.

Equal Rights Amendment (ERA) A proposed amendment that prevented the abridgment of "equality of rights under law . . . by the United States or any State on the basis of sex." Not enough states had ratified the amendment by 1982, when the ratification period expired, so it was not adopted.

Erie Canal Canal built in the early 1820s that made water transport from the Great Lakes to New York City possible. The success of the Erie Canal inspired many similar projects and ensured New York City's place as the premier international port in the United States.

Espionage Act 1917 act that prohibited antiwar activities, including opposing the military draft. It punished speech critical of the war as well as deliberate actions of sabotage and spying.

ethnic cleansing Ridding an area of a particular ethnic minority in order to achieve ethnic homogeneity. In the civil war between Serbs and Croatians in Bosnia from 1992 to 1995, the Serbian military attempted to eliminate the Croatian population through murder, rape, and expulsion.

eugenics The pseudo-science of producing genetic improvement in the human population through selective breeding. Proponents of eugenics often saw ethnic and racial minorities as genetically "undesirable" and inferior.

European Union (EU) Organization formed by European nations in 1993 to boost their economic and political power. Member nations took steps to facilitate free trade, investment, and migration among EU states.

Exodusters Blacks who migrated from the South to Kansas in 1879 seeking land and a better way of life.

Fair Employment Practice Committee (FEPC) Committee established in 1941 to help African Americans gain a greater share of wartime industrial jobs.

Fair Labor Standards Act 1938 law that provided a minimum wage of 40 cents an hour and a forty-hour workweek for employees in businesses engaged in interstate commerce.

Farmers' Alliances Regional organizations formed in the late nineteenth century to advance the interests of farmers. The most prominent of these organizations were the Northwestern Farmers' Alliance, the Southern Farmers' Alliance, and the Colored Farmers' Alliance.

Federal Employee Loyalty Program Program established by President Truman in 1947 to investigate federal employees suspected of disloyalty.

Federalists Supporters of ratification of the Constitution, many of whom came from urban and commercial backgrounds.

Field Order Number 15 Order issued by General Sherman in January 1865 setting aside more than 400,000 acres of Confederate land to be divided into plots for former slaves. Sherman's order came in response to pressure from African American leaders.

Fifteenth Amendment Amendment to the Constitution prohibiting the abridgment of a citizen's right to vote on the basis of "race, color, or previous condition of servitude." From the 1870s on, southern states devised numerous strategies for circumventing the Fifteenth Amendment.

fireside chats Radio addresses by Franklin Roosevelt during the depression. Roosevelt's addresses boosted morale and informed the public about government efforts to help ease their difficulties.

Fort Sumter Union fort that guarded the harbor in Charleston, South Carolina. The Confederacy's decision to fire on the fort and block resupply in April 1861 marked the beginning of the Civil War.

Fourteen Points The core principles President Wilson saw as the basis for lasting peace, including freedom of the seas, open diplomacy, and self-determination for colonial peoples.

Fourteenth Amendment Amendment to the Constitution defining citizenship and protecting individual civil and political rights from abridgment by the states. Adopted during Reconstruction, the Fourteenth Amendment overturned the *Dred Scott* decision.

Free Speech Movement (FSM) Movement protesting policies instituted by the University of California at Berkeley that restricted free speech. In 1964 students at Berkeley conducted sit-ins and held rallies against these policies.

Freedmen's Bureau Federal agency created in 1865 to provide ex-slaves with economic and legal resources. The Freedmen's Bureau played an active role in shaping black life in the postwar South.

Freedom Rides Integrated bus rides through the South organized by CORE in 1961 to test compliance with Supreme Court rulings on segregation.

Freedom Summer 1964 civil rights project in Mississippi launched by SNCC, CORE, the SCLC, and the NAACP. Some eight hundred volunteers, mainly white college students, worked on voter registration drives and in freedom schools to improve education for rural black youngsters.

Fugitive Slave Act of 1850 Act strengthening earlier fugitive slave laws, passed as part of the Compromise of 1850. The Fugitive Slave Act provoked widespread anger in the North and intensified sectional tensions.

gag rule Rule passed by the House of Representatives in 1836 to table, or postpone action on, all antislavery petitions without hearing them read in order to stifle debate over slavery. It was renewed annually until it was rescinded in 1844.

Gettysburg Key July 1863 battle that helped turn the tide for the Union. Union victory at Gettysburg, combined with a victory at Vicksburg that same month, positioned the Union to push farther into the South.

ghettos Neighborhoods dominated by a single ethnic, racial, or class group.

Ghost Dance Religious ritual performed by the Paiute Indians in the late nineteenth century. Following a vision he received in 1888, the prophet Wovoka believed that performing the Ghost Dance would cause whites to disappear and allow Indians to regain control of their lands.

Gilded Age Term coined by Mark Twain and Charles Dudley Warner to describe the late nineteenth century. The term referred to the opulent and often ostentatious lifestyles of the era's superrich.

glasnost Policy of political "openness" initiated by Soviet leader Mikhail Gorbachev in the 1980s. Under *glasnost,* the Soviet Union extended democratic elections, freedom of speech, and freedom of the press.

globalization The extension of economic, political, and cultural relationships among nations, through commerce, migration, and communication. Globalization expanded in the late twentieth century because of free trade agreements and the relaxation of immigration restrictions.

Glorious Revolution 1688 rebellion that forced James II from the English throne and replaced him with William and Mary. The Glorious Revolution led to greater political and commercial autonomy for the British colonies.

gold rush The rapid influx of migrants into California after the discovery of gold in 1848. Migrants came from all over the world seeking riches.

"The Gospel of Wealth" 1889 essay by Andrew Carnegie in which he argued that the rich should act as stewards of the wealth they earned, using their surplus income for the benefit of the community.

Grangers Members of an organization founded in 1867 to meet the social and cultural needs of farmers. Grangers took an active role in the promotion of the economic and political interests of farmers.

Great Awakening Series of religious revivals in colonial America that began in 1720 and lasted to about 1750.

great migration Population shift of more than 400,000 African Americans who left the South beginning in 1917–1918 and headed north and west hoping to escape poverty and racial discrimination. During the 1920s another 800,000 blacks left the South.

Great Plains Semiarid territory in central North America.

Great Recession The severe economic decline in the United States and throughout the world that began in 2008, leading to bank failures, high unemployment, home foreclosures, and large federal deficits.

Great Society President Lyndon Johnson's vision of social, economic, and cultural progress in the United States.

greenbacks U.S. treasury notes issued by the federal government during the Civil War. Using its new control over the currency and banking systems, the federal government issued large quantities of greenbacks during the war, contributing to inflation.

Gulf of Tonkin Resolution 1964 congressional resolution giving President Lyndon Johnson wide discretion in the use of U.S. forces in Vietnam. The resolution followed reported attacks by North Vietnamese gunboats on two American destroyers.

Haitian Revolution Revolt against French rule by free and enslaved blacks in the 1790s on the island of Saint Domingue. The revolution led in 1803 to the establishment of Haiti, the first independent black-led nation in the Americas.

Harpers Ferry, Virginia Site of the federal arsenal that was the target of John Brown's 1859 raid. Brown hoped to rouse the region's slave population to a violent uprising.

Hartford Convention 1814 convention of Federalists opposed to the War of 1812. Delegates to the convention considered a number of constitutional amendments, as well as the possibility of secession.

Haymarket Square Site of 1886 rally and violence. In the aftermath of the events in Haymarket Square, the union movement in the United States went into temporary decline.

Hetch Hetchy valley Site of a controversial dam built to supply San Francisco with water and power in the aftermath of the 1906 earthquake. The dam was built over the objections of preservationists such as John Muir.

Homestead Act 1862 act that established procedures for distributing 160-acre lots to western settlers, on condition that they develop and farm their land, as an incentive for western migration.

Homestead strike 1892 strike by steelworkers at Andrew Carnegie's Homestead steel factory. The strike collapsed after a failed assassination attempt on Carnegie's plant manager, Henry Clay Frick.

Hoovervilles Shantytowns that sprang up in the years following the 1929 stock market crash. Many Americans believed that President Hoover did not do enough to relieve the suffering that accompanied the Great Depression.

Hopewell people Indian people who established a thriving culture near the Mississippi River in the early centuries C.E.

horizontal integration The ownership of as many firms as possible in a given industry by a single owner. John D. Rockefeller pursued a strategy of horizontal integration when he bought up rival oil refineries.

horticulture A form of agriculture in which people work small plots of land with simple tools.

House Committee on Un-American Activities (HUAC) House committee established in 1938 to investigate domestic communism. After World War II, HUAC conducted highly publicized investigations of Communist influence in government and the entertainment industry.

House of Burgesses Local governing body in Virginia established by the English crown in 1619.

Hull House Settlement house established in 1889 by Jane Addams and Ellen Starr. Hull House inspired a generation of young women to work directly in immigrant communities.

Hurricane Katrina 2005 storm that hit the Gulf coast states of Louisiana, Mississippi, and Alabama. The hurricane caused massive flooding in New Orleans after levees broke. Federal, state, and local government responses to the storm were inadequate and highlighted racial and class inequities.

imperial presidency Term used to describe the growth of presidential powers during the Cold War, particularly with respect to war-making powers and the conduct of national security.

import duty Tax imposed on goods imported into the colonies, paid by the importer rather than directly by the consumer; also known as a *tariff*.

impressment The forced enlistment of civilians into the army or navy. The impressment of residents of colonial seaports into the British navy was a major source of complaint in the eighteenth century.

Incas Andean people who built an empire in the centuries before the arrival of the Spaniards. At the height of their power in the fifteenth century, the Incas controlled some sixteen million people.

indentured servants Servants contracted to work for a set period of time without pay. Many early migrants to the English colonies indentured themselves in exchange for the price of passage to North America.

Indian Removal Act 1830 act by which Indian peoples in the East were forced to exchange their lands for territory west of the Mississippi River. Andrew Jackson was an ardent supporter of Indian removal.

Indian Reorganization Act (IRA) 1934 act that ended the Dawes Act, authorized self-government for those living on reservations, extended tribal landholdings, and pledged to uphold native customs and language.

Industrial Workers of the World (IWW) Organization that grew out of the activities of the Western Federation of Miners in the 1890s and formed by Eugene V. Debs. The IWW attempted to unite all skilled and unskilled workers in an effort to overthrow capitalism.

internment The relocation of persons seen as a threat to national security to isolated camps during World War II. Nearly all people of Japanese descent living on the West Coast were forced to sell or abandon their possessions and relocate to internment camps during the war.

Interstate Commerce Commission (ICC) Regulatory commission established by Congress in 1887. The commission investigated interstate shipping, required railroads to make their rates public, and could bring lawsuits to force shippers to reduce "unreasonable" fares.

Intolerable Acts *See* Coercive Acts.

Iran-Contra Reagan administration scandal involving the funneling of funds from an illegal arms-for-hostages deal with Iran to the Nicaraguan Contras in the mid-1980s.

Jamestown The first successful English colony in North America. Settled in 1607, Jamestown was founded by soldiers and adventurers under the leadership of Captain John Smith.

Jay Treaty 1796 treaty that required British forces to withdraw from U.S. soil, required American repayment of debts to British firms, and limited U.S. trade with the British West Indies.

Jim Crow Late-nineteenth-century statutes that established legally defined racial segregation in the South. Jim Crow legislation helped ensure the social and economic inferiority of southern blacks.

jingoists Superpatriotic supporters of the expansion and use of military power. Jingoists such as Theodore Roosevelt longed for a war in which they could demonstrate America's strength and prove their own masculinity.

Joint Electoral Commission Commission created by Congress to resolve the disputed presidential election of 1876. The commission consisted of five senators, five House members, and five Supreme Court justices—seven Republicans, seven Democrats, and one independent. The commission sided with the Republican presidential candidate, Rutherford B. Hayes.

Judiciary Act of 1801 Act passed by the Federalist-controlled Congress to expand the federal court system by creating sixteen circuit (regional) courts, with new judges appointed for each, just before Democratic-Republicans took control of the presidency and Congress.

Kansas-Nebraska Act 1854 act creating the territories of Kansas and Nebraska out of what was then Indian land. The act stipulated that the issue of slavery would be settled by a popular referendum in each territory.

King Philip's War 1675–1676 conflict between New England settlers and the region's Indians. The settlers were the eventual victors, but fighting was fierce and casualties on both sides were high.

King William's War 1689–1697 war that began as a conflict over competing French and English interests on the European continent but soon spread to the American frontier. Both sides pulled Indian allies into the war.

Knights of the Ku Klux Klan (KKK) Organization formed in 1865 by General Nathan Bedford Forrest to enforce prewar racial norms. Members of the KKK used threats and violence to intimidate blacks and white Republicans.

La Raza Unida (The United Race) A Chicano political party, formed in 1969, that advocated job opportunities for Chicanos, bilingual education, and Chicano cultural studies programs in universities.

laissez-faire French for "let things alone." Advocates of laissez-faire believed that the marketplace should be left to regulate itself, allowing individuals to pursue their own self-interest without any government restraint or interference.

League of Nations The international organization proposed by Woodrow Wilson after the end of World War I to ensure world peace and security in the future through mutual agreement. The United States failed to join the league because Wilson and his opponents in Congress could not work out a compromise.

Lend-Lease Act March 1941 law permitting the United States to lend or lease military equipment and other commodities to Great Britain and its allies. Its passage marked the end of American neutrality before the United States entered World War II.

Levittown Suburban subdivision built in Long Island, New York, in the 1950s in response to the postwar housing shortage. Subsequent Levittowns were built in Pennsylvania and New Jersey.

Liberal Republicans Political group organized to challenge the reelection of President Grant in 1872. The Liberal Republicans called for an end to federal efforts at Reconstruction in the South.

Liberator Radical abolitionist newspaper launched by William Lloyd Garrison in 1831. Through the *Liberator,* Garrison called for immediate, uncompensated emancipation of slaves.

Liberty Party Antislavery political party formed in 1840. The Liberty Party, along with the Free-Soil Party, helped place slavery at the center of national political debates.

Little Rock Nine Nine African American students who, in 1957, became the first black students to attend Central High School in Little Rock, Arkansas. Federal troops were required to overcome the resistance of white officials and to protect the students.

Long Drive Cattle drive from the grazing lands of Texas to rail depots in Kansas. Once in Kansas, the cattle were shipped eastward to slaughterhouses in Chicago.

Lost Generation A term used by the writer Gertrude Stein to describe the writers and artists disillusioned with the consumer culture of the 1920s.

Louisiana Territory Vast territory stretching from the Mississippi River to the Rocky Mountains and from New Orleans to present-day Montana that the United States purchased from France in 1803, doubling the size of the nation.

loyalist A colonial supporter of the British during the Revolutionary War. Loyalists came from all economic backgrounds and had a variety of motives for siding with the British.

Manhattan Project Code name for the secret program to develop an atomic bomb. The project was launched in 1942 and directed by the United States with the assistance of Great Britain and Canada.

manifest destiny Term coined by John L. O'Sullivan in 1845 to describe what he saw as the nation's God-given right to expand its borders. Throughout the nineteenth century, the concept of manifest destiny was used to justify U.S. expansion.

Marbury v. Madison 1803 Supreme Court decision that established the authority of the Supreme Court to rule on the constitutionality of federal laws.

March on Washington for Jobs and Freedom August 28, 1963, rally by civil rights organizations in Washington, D.C., that brought increased national attention to the movement.

Marshall Plan Post–World War II European economic aid package developed by Secretary of State George Marshall. The plan helped rebuild Western Europe and served American political and economic interests in the process.

Maya People who established large cities in the Yucatán peninsula. Mayan civilization was strongest between 300 and 800 C.E.

Mayflower Compact Written constitution created by the Pilgrims upon their arrival in Plymouth. The Mayflower Compact was the first written constitution adopted in North America.

McCarthyism Term used to describe the harassment and persecution of suspected political radicals. Senator Joseph McCarthy was one of many prominent government figures who helped incite anti-Communist hysteria in the early 1950s.

McCulloch v. Maryland 1819 Supreme Court decision that reinforced the federal government's ability to employ an expansive understanding of the implied powers clause of the Constitution.

megachurches Mainly Protestant congregations containing at least two thousand members. The number of megachurches in the United States increased dramatically during the 1980s and 1990s.

melting pot Popular metaphor for immigrant assimilation into American society. According to this ideal, all immigrants underwent a process of Americanization that produced a homogeneous society.

mercantilism Economic system centered on the maintenance of a favorable balance of trade for the home country, with more gold and silver flowing into that country than flowed out. Seventeenth- and eighteenth-century British colonial policy was heavily shaped by mercantilism.

Mexican revolution 1911 revolution in Mexico, which led to nearly a decade of bloodshed and civil war.

Middle Passage The brutal voyage of slave ships laden with human cargo from Africa to the Americas. The voyage was the middle segment in a triangular journey that began in Europe, went first to Africa, then to the Americas, and finally back to Europe.

military-industrial complex The government-business alliance related to the military and national defense that developed out of World War II and that greatly influenced future development of the U.S. economy.

Mississippi Freedom Democratic Party (MFDP) Political party formed in 1964 to challenge the all-white state Democratic Party for seats at the 1964 Democratic presidential convention and run candidates for public office. Although unsuccessful in 1964, MFDP efforts led to subsequent reform of the Democratic Party and the seating of an interracial, convention delegation from Mississippi in 1968.

Missouri Compromise 1820 act that allowed Missouri to enter the Union as a slave state and Maine to enter as a free state and established the southern border of Missouri as the boundary between slave and free states throughout the Louisiana Territory.

Modern Republicanism The political approach of President Dwight Eisenhower that tried to fit traditional Republican Party ideals of individualism and fiscal restraint within the broad framework of the New Deal.

Monroe Doctrine Assertion by President James Monroe in 1823 that the Western Hemisphere was part of the U.S. sphere of influence. Although the United States lacked the power to back up this claim, it signaled an intention to challenge Europeans for authority in the Atlantic world.

Montgomery Improvement Association Organization founded in Montgomery, Alabama, in 1955 to coordinate the boycott of city buses by African Americans.

Mormons Religious sect that migrated to Utah to escape religious persecution; also known as the Church of Jesus Christ of Latter-Day Saints.

muckrakers Investigative journalists who specialized in exposing corruption, scandal, and vice. Muckrakers helped build public support for progressive causes.

mujahideen Religiously inspired Afghan rebels who resisted the Soviet invasion of Afghanistan in 1979.

multinational (or transnational) corporations Companies that operate production facilities or deliver services in more than one country. Between 1970 and 2000, the number of such firms increased ninefold.

multiplier effect The diverse changes spurred by a single invention, including other inventions it spawns and the broader economic, social, and political transformations it fuels.

mutual aid societies Voluntary associations that provide a variety of economic and social benefits to their members.

mutually assured destruction (MAD) Defense strategy built around the threat of a massive nuclear retaliatory strike. Adoption of the doctrine of mutually assured destruction contributed to the escalation of the nuclear arms race during the Cold War.

Nat Turner's rebellion 1831 slave uprising in Virginia led by Nat Turner. Turner's rebellion instilled panic among white Southerners, leading to tighter control of African Americans and reconsideration of the institution of slavery.

National Association for the Advancement of Colored People (NAACP) Organization founded by W. E. B. Du Bois, Ida B. Wells, Jane Addams, and others in 1909 to fight for racial equality. The NAACP strategy focused on fighting discrimination through the courts.

National Interstate and Defense Highway Act 1956 act that provided funds for construction of 42,500 miles of roads throughout the United States.

National Labor Relations Act 1935 act (also known as the Wagner Act) that created the National Labor Relations Board (NLRB). The NLRB protected workers' right to organize labor unions without owner interference.

National Organization for Women (NOW) Feminist organization formed in 1966 by Betty Friedan and like-minded activists.

National Origins Act 1924 act establishing immigration quotas by national origin. The act was intended to severely limit immigration from southern and eastern Europe as well as prohibit all immigration from East Asia.

National Recovery Administration (NRA) New Deal agency established in 1933 to create codes to regulate production, prices, wages, hours, and collective bargaining. The NRA failed to produce the intended results and was eventually ruled unconstitutional.

National Republicans *See* Democrats and National Republicans.

National Road Road constructed using federal funds that ran from western Maryland through southwestern Pennsylvania to Wheeling, West Virginia; also called the Cumberland Road. Completed in 1818, the road was part of a larger push to improve the nation's infrastructure.

National Security Council (NSC) Council created by the 1947 National Security Act to advise the president on military and foreign affairs. The NSC consists of the national security adviser and the secretaries of state, defense, the army, the navy, and the air force.

National War Labor Board (NWLB) Government agency created in 1918 to settle labor disputes. The NWLB consisted of representatives from unions, corporations, and the public.

National War Labor Board Board established in 1942 to oversee labor-management relations during World War II. The board regulated wages, hours, and working conditions and authorized the government to take over plants that refused to abide by its decisions.

National Woman Suffrage Association Organization founded in 1869 to support women's voting rights. Founders Susan B. Anthony and Elizabeth Cady Stanton objected to the Fifteenth Amendment because it did not provide suffrage for women.

nativism The belief that foreigners pose a serious danger to a nation's society and culture. Nativist sentiment rose in the United States as the size and diversity of the immigrant population grew.

nativists Anti-immigrant Americans who launched public campaigns against foreigners in the 1840s. Nativism emerged as a response to increased immigration to the United States in the 1830s and 1840s, particularly the large influx of Catholic immigrants.

Navigation Acts Acts passed by Parliament in the 1650s and 1660s that prohibited smuggling, established guidelines for legal commerce, and set duties on trade items. In the 1760s, British authorities sought to fully enforce these laws, leading to resistance by colonists.

neoconservatives Disillusioned liberals who condemned the Great Society programs they had originally supported. Neoconservatives were particularly concerned about affirmative action programs, the domination of campus discourse by New Left radicals, and left-wing criticism of the use of American military and economic might to advance U.S. interests overseas.

Neutrality Act 1793 act prohibiting ships of belligerent nations—including France and Great Britain—from using American ports. The act was meant to help keep America out of the conflict between France and Great Britain and to enhance U.S. commerce.

Neutrality Acts Legislation passed between 1935 and 1937 to make it more difficult for the United States to become entangled in overseas conflicts. The Neutrality Acts reflected the strength of isolationist sentiment in 1930s America.

New Deal The policies and programs that Franklin Roosevelt initiated to combat the Great Depression. The New Deal represented a dramatic expansion of the role of government in American society.

New Freedom Term used by Woodrow Wilson to describe his limited-government, progressive agenda. Wilson's New Freedom was offered as an alternative to Theodore Roosevelt's New Nationalism.

New Frontier President Kennedy's domestic agenda. Kennedy promised to battle "tyranny, poverty, disease, and war," but, lacking strong majorities in Congress, he achieved relatively modest results.

New Light clergy Colonial clergy who called for religious revivals and emphasized the emotional aspects of spiritual commitment. The New Lights were leaders in the Great Awakening.

New Look The foreign policy strategy implemented by President Dwight Eisenhower that emphasized the development and deployment of nuclear weapons in an effort to cut military spending.

New Nationalism Agenda articulated by Theodore Roosevelt in his 1912 presidential campaign. Roosevelt called for increased regulation of large corporations, a more active role for the president, and the extension of social justice using the power of the federal government.

New Negro 1920s term for the second generation of African Americans born after emancipation and who stood up for their rights.

New Right The conservative coalition of old and new conservatives, as well as disaffected Democrats. The New Right came to power with the election of Ronald Reagan in 1980.

New South Term popularized by newspaper editor Henry Grady in the 1880s, a proponent of the modernization of the southern economy. Grady believed that industrial development would lead to the emergence of a "New South."

new woman 1920s term for the modern, sexually liberated woman. The new woman, popularized in movies and magazines, flouted traditional morality.

Noble Order of the Knights of Labor Labor organization founded in 1869 by Uriah Stephens. The Knights sought to include all workers in one giant union.

Non-Intercourse Act Act passed by Congress in 1809 allowing Americans to trade with every nation except France and Britain. The act failed to stop the seizure of American ships or improve the economy.

North American Free Trade Agreement (NAFTA) Free trade agreement approved in 1993 by the United States, Canada, and Mexico.

North Atlantic Treaty Organization (NATO) Cold War military alliance intended to enhance the collective security of the United States and Western Europe.

Northwest Land Ordinance (1785 and 1787) Act of the confederation congress that provided for the survey, sale, and eventual division into states of the Northwest Territory. The 1787 act clarified the process by which territories could become states.

NSC-68 April 1950 National Security Council document that advocated the intensification of the policy of containment both at home and abroad.

nuclear freeze movement 1980s protests calling for a mutual freeze on the testing, production, and deployment of nuclear weapons and of missiles and aircraft designed primarily to deliver nuclear weapons.

nullification The doctrine that individual states have the right to declare federal laws unconstitutional and, therefore, void within their borders. South Carolina attempted to invoke the doctrine of nullification in response to the tariff of 1832.

Occupy Wall Street A loose coalition of progressive and radical forces that emerged in 2011 in New York City and around the country to protest corporate greed and federal policies that benefit the very wealthy.

Old Light clergy Colonial clergy from established churches who supported the religious status quo in the early eighteenth century.

Open Door 1899 policy in which Secretary of State John Hay informed the nations occupying China that the United States had the right of equal trade in China.

Operation Desert Storm Code name of the 1991 allied air and ground military offensive that pushed Iraqi forces out of Kuwait.

Oregon Trail The route west from the Missouri River to the Oregon Territory. By 1860, some 350,000 Americans had made the three- to six-month journey along the trail.

Organization of Petroleum Exporting Countries (OPEC) Organization formed by oil-producing countries to control the price and supply of oil on the global market.

Palmer raids Government roundup of some 6,000 suspected alien radicals in 1919–1920, ordered by Attorney General A. Mitchell Palmer and his assistant J. Edgar Hoover. The raids resulted in the deportation of 556 immigrants.

panic of 1819 The nation's first severe recession. The panic of 1819 lasted four years and resulted from irresponsible banking practices and the declining demand for American goods, including cotton, abroad.

panic of 1837 Severe economic recession that began shortly after Martin Van Buren's presidential inauguration. The panic of 1837 started in the South and was rooted in the changing fortunes of American cotton in Great Britain.

patriarchal family Model of the family in which fathers have absolute authority over wives, children, and servants. Most colonial Americans accepted the patriarchal model of the family, at least as an ideal.

Patriot Act 2001 law passed in response to the September 11 terror attacks. It eased restrictions on domestic and foreign intelligence gathering and expanded governmental power to deport immigrants.

Peace of Paris 1763 peace treaty that brought the Seven Years' War to a close. Under the terms of the treaty, Britain gained control of North America east of the Mississippi River and of present-day Canada.

Pendleton Civil Service Reform Act 1883 act that required federal jobs to be awarded on the basis of merit through competitive exams rather than through political connections.

Pentagon Papers Classified report on U.S. involvement in Vietnam leaked to the press in 1971. The report confirmed that the Kennedy and Johnson administrations had misled the public about the origins and nature of the Vietnam War.

Pequot War 1636–1637 conflict between New England settlers, their Narragansett allies, and the Pequots. The English saw the Pequots as both a threat and an obstacle to further English expansion.

perestroika Policy of economic "restructuring" initiated by Soviet leader Mikhail Gorbachev. Gorbachev hoped that by reducing state control he could revive the Soviet economy.

Personal Responsibility and Work Opportunity Reconciliation Act 1996 act reforming the welfare system in the United States. The law required adults on the welfare rolls to find work within two years or lose their welfare benefits.

Petticoat Affair 1829 political conflict over Jackson's appointment of John Eaton as secretary of war. Eaton was married to a woman of allegedly questionable character, and the wives of many prominent Washington politicians organized a campaign to snub her.

Pietists German Protestants who decried the power of established churches and urged individuals to follow their heart rather than their head in spiritual matters. Pietism had a profound influence on the leaders of the Great Awakening.

Pilgrims Group of English religious dissenters who established a settlement at Plymouth, Massachusetts, in 1620. Unlike more mainstream Protestants, the Pilgrims were Separatists who aimed to sever all connections with the Church of England.

Pinckney Treaty 1796 treaty that defined the boundary between U.S. and Spanish territory in the South and opened the Mississippi River and New Orleans to U.S. shipping.

Platt Amendment 1901 act of Congress limiting Cuban sovereignty. American officials pressured Cuban leaders to incorporate the amendment into the Cuban constitution.

Plessy v. Ferguson 1896 Supreme Court ruling that upheld the legality of Jim Crow legislation. The Court ruled that as long as states provided "equal but separate" facilities for whites and blacks, Jim Crow laws did not violate the equal protection clause of the Fourteenth Amendment.

political machine Urban political organizations that dominated many late-nineteenth-century cities. Machines provided needed services to the urban poor, but they also fostered corruption, crime, and inefficiency.

Populists The People's Party of America, formed in 1892. The Populists sought to appeal to both farmers and industrial workers.

Port Huron Statement Students for a Democratic Society manifesto written in 1962 that condemned liberal politics, Cold War foreign policy, racism, and research-oriented universities. It called for the adoption of "participatory democracy."

Powhatan Confederacy Large and powerful Indian confederation in Virginia. The Jamestown settlers had a complicated and contentious relationship with the leaders of the Powhatan Confederacy.

pragmatism Philosophy that holds that truth can be discovered only through experience and that the value of ideas should be measured by their practical consequences. Pragmatism had a significant influence on the progressives.

Proclamation Line of 1763 Act of Parliament that restricted colonial settlement west of the Appalachian Mountains. The Proclamation Line sparked protests from rich and poor colonists alike.

Proclamation of Amnesty and Reconstruction 1863 proclamation that established the basic parameters of President Lincoln's approach to Reconstruction. Lincoln's plan would have readmitted the South to the Union on relatively lenient terms.

Progressive Party Third party formed by Theodore Roosevelt in 1912 to facilitate his candidacy for president. Nicknamed the "Bull Moose Party," the Progressive Party split the Republican vote, allowing Democrat Woodrow Wilson to win the election.

proprietary colonies Colonies granted to individuals, rather than held directly by the crown or given to chartered companies. Proprietors of such colonies, such as William Penn of Pennsylvania, had considerable leeway to distribute land and govern as they pleased.

Protestantism Religious movement initiated in the early sixteenth century that resulted in a permanent division within European Christianity. Protestants differed with Catholics over the nature of salvation, the role of priests, and the organization of the church.

Pueblo revolt 1680 uprising of Pueblo Indians against Spanish forces in New Mexico that led to the Spaniards' temporary retreat from the area. The uprising was sparked by mistreatment and the suppression of Indian culture and religion.

Pullman strike 1894 strike by workers against the Pullman railcar company. When the strike disrupted rail service nationwide, threatening the delivery of the mail, President Cleveland ordered federal troops to get the railroads moving again.

Puritans Radical English Protestants who hoped to reform the Church of England. The first Puritan settlers in the Americas arrived in Massachusetts in 1630.

Reaganomics Ronald Reagan's economic policies based on the theories of supply-side economists and centered on tax cuts and cuts to domestic programs.

Red scare The fear of Communist-inspired radicalism in the wake of the Russian Revolution. The Red scare following World War I culminated in the Palmer raids on suspected radicals.

Redeemers White, conservative Democrats who challenged and overthrew Republican rule in the South during Reconstruction.

redemptioners Immigrants who borrowed money from shipping agents to cover the costs of transport to America, loans that were repaid, or "redeemed," by colonial employers. Redemptioners worked for their "redeemers" for a set number of years.

Regulators Local organizations formed in North and South Carolina to protest and resist unpopular policies. After first seeking redress through official institutions, Regulators went on to establish militias and other institutions of self-governance.

Renaissance The cultural and intellectual flowering that began in Italy in the fifteenth century and then spread north. The Renaissance occurred at the same time that European rulers were pushing for greater political unification of their states.

Republican Party Party formed in 1854 that was committed to stopping the expansion of slavery and advocated economic development and internal improvements. Although their appeal was limited to the North, the Republicans quickly became a major political force.

Roe v. Wade The 1973 Supreme Court opinion that affirmed a woman's constitutional right to abortion.

Roosevelt Corollary 1904 addition to the Monroe Doctrine that affirmed the right of the United States to intervene in the internal affairs of Caribbean and Latin American countries to preserve order and protect American interests.

Sacco and Vanzetti case 1920 case in which Nicola Sacco and Bartolomeo Vanzetti were convicted of robbery and murder. The trial centered on the defendants' foreign birth and political views, rather than the facts pertaining to their guilt or innocence.

SALT II 1979 strategic arms limitation treaty agreed on by President Jimmy Carter and Soviet leader Leonid Brezhnev. After the Soviet Union invaded Afghanistan, Carter persuaded the Senate not to ratify the treaty.

scalawags Derisive term for white Southerners who supported Reconstruction.

Scottsboro Nine Nine African American youths convicted of raping two white women in Scottsboro, Alabama, in 1931. The Communist Party played a key role in defending the Scottsboro Nine and in bringing national and international attention to their case.

seasoning The period of time in which newly arrived slaves regained their strength, adapted to their new environments, and were absorbed into American slave culture.

Second Continental Congress Assembly of colonial representatives that served as a national government during the Revolutionary War. Despite limited formal powers, the Continental Congress coordinated the war effort and conducted negotiations with outside powers.

second front Beginning in 1942, Stalin wanted an immediate invasion by U.S., British, and Canadian forces into German-occupied France to take pressure off the Soviet forces fighting the Germans on the eastern front. The attack in western Europe did not begin until 1944, fostering resentment in Stalin.

Second Great Awakening Evangelical revival movement that began in the South in the early nineteenth century and then spread to the North. The social and economic changes of the first half of the nineteenth century were a major spur to religious revivals, which in turn spurred social reform movements.

second industrial revolution Revolution in technology and productivity that reshaped the American economy in the early twentieth century.

Second Seminole War 1835–1842 war between the Seminoles, including fugitive slaves who had joined the tribe, and the U.S. government over whether the Seminoles would be forced to leave Florida and settle west of the Mississippi River. Despite substantial investments of men, money, and resources, it took seven years for the United States to achieve victory.

Sedition Act 1918 act appended to the Espionage Act. It punished individuals for expressing opinions deemed hostile to the U.S. government, flag, or military.

separate spheres The notion that men and women should occupy separate social, economic, and political spheres. According to this middle-class ideal, men were best suited for the public world of business and politics, while women were meant to manage the home.

Servicemen's Readjustment Act 1944 act that offered educational opportunities and financial aid to veterans as they readjusted to civilian life. Known as the GI Bill, the law helped millions of veterans build new lives after the war.

settlement houses Community centers established by urban reformers in the late nineteenth century. Settlement house organizers resided in the institutions they created and were often female, middle-class, and college educated.

Share Our Wealth Plan devised by Senator Huey Long of Louisiana to provide families with a $5,000 homestead and a guaranteed annual income of $2,000. These results would be achieved by taxing the wealthy.

sharecropping A system that emerged as the dominant mode of agricultural production in the South in the years after the Civil War. Under the sharecropping system, sharecroppers received tools and supplies from landowners in exchange for a share of the eventual harvest.

Shays's Rebellion 1786 rebellion by western Massachusetts farmers caused primarily by economic turmoil in the aftermath of the Revolutionary War.

Sherman Antitrust Act 1890 act that outlawed monopolies that prevented free competition in interstate commerce.

sit-down strike A strike in which workers occupy their place of employment. In 1937 the United Auto Workers conducted sit-down strikes in Flint, Michigan, against General Motors to gain union recognition, higher wages, and better working conditions. The union won its demands.

skilled workers Workers with particular training and skills. Skilled workers were paid more and were more difficult for owners to replace than unskilled workers.

skyscrapers Buildings more than ten stories high that first appeared in U.S. cities in the late nineteenth century. Urban crowding and high prices for land stimulated the drive to construct taller buildings.

Smith Act 1940 act that prohibited teaching or advocating the violent overthrow of the U.S. government or belonging to any group with that aim.

social gospel Religious movement that advocated the application of Christian teachings to social and economic problems. The ideals of the social gospel inspired many progressive reformers.

Social Security Act Landmark 1935 act that created retirement pensions for most Americans, as well as unemployment insurance.

Solidarity Polish trade union movement led by Lech Walesa. During the 1980s, Solidarity played a central role in ending Communist rule in Poland.

Sons of Liberty Boston organization first formed to protest the Stamp Act. The Sons of Liberty spread to other colonies and played an important role in the unrest leading to the American Revolution.

Southern Christian Leadership Conference (SCLC) Organization founded in 1957 by Martin Luther King Jr. and other black ministers to encourage nonviolent protests against racial segregation and disfranchisement in the South.

spectral evidence Evidence given by spirits acting through possessed individuals. A number of the accused in the 1692 Salem witch trials were convicted on the basis of spectral evidence.

spoils system Patronage system introduced by Andrew Jackson in which federal offices were awarded on the basis of political loyalty. The system remained in place until the late nineteenth century.

Stamp Act 1765 act of Parliament that imposed a duty on all transactions involving paper items. The Stamp Act prompted widespread, coordinated protests and was eventually repealed.

Stonewall Tavern The gay bar in Greenwich Village in New York City where, in 1969, its patrons fought the police in response to harassment. This encounter helped launch the gay liberation movement.

Stono rebellion 1739 uprising by African American slaves in South Carolina. In the aftermath of the uprising, white fear of slave revolts intensified.

Strategic Arms Limitation Treaty (SALT I) 1972 agreement between the United States and Soviet Union to curtail nuclear arms production during the Cold War. The pact froze for five years the number of antiballistic missiles (ABMs), intercontinental ballistic missiles (ICBMs), and submarine-based missiles that each nation could deploy.

Student Nonviolent Coordinating Committee (SNCC) Civil rights organization that grew out of the sit-ins of 1960. The organization focused on taking direct action and political organizing to achieve its goals.

Students for a Democratic Society (SDS) Student activist organization formed in the early 1960s that advocated the formation of a "New Left" that would overturn the social and political status quo.

subprime mortgages Mortgages that are normally made out to borrowers with lower credit ratings. During the early twenty-first century, banks and mortgage companies devised lenient lending policies to allow buyers to purchase homes beyond their means.

subtreasury system A proposal by the Farmers' Alliances in the 1880s for the federal government to extend loans to farmers and store their crops in warehouses until prices rose and they could buy back and sell their crops to repay their debts.

suffragists Supporters of voting rights for women. Campaigns for women's suffrage gained strength in the late nineteenth and early twentieth centuries and culminated in ratification of the Nineteenth Amendment in 1920.

Sugar Act 1764 act of Parliament that imposed an import tax on sugar, coffee, wines, and other luxury items. The Sugar Act sparked colonial protests that would escalate over time as new revenue measures were enacted.

Sun Belt The southern and western part of the United States. After World War II, millions of Americans moved to the Sun Belt, drawn by the region's climate and jobs in the defense, petroleum, and chemical industries.

sweatshops Small factories or shops in which workers toiled under adverse conditions. Business owners, particularly in the garment industry, turned tenement apartments into sweatshops.

syncretic culture A hybrid culture that combines elements of previously distinct cultures. Enslaved African Americans created a syncretic culture by combining elements of African, West Indian, and European cultures.

Taft-Hartley Act 1947 law that curtailed unions' ability to organize. It prevented unions from barring employment to non-union members and authorized the federal government to halt a strike for eighty days if it interfered with the national interest.

Tea Party movement A loose coalition of conservative and libertarian forces that arose around 2008. Generally working within the Republican Party, the Tea Party advocates small government, low taxes, and reduced federal deficits.

Teapot Dome scandal Oil and land scandal during the Harding administration that highlighted the close ties between big business and the federal government in the early 1920s.

Tejanos Mexican residents of Texas. Although some Tejano elites allied themselves with American settlers, most American settlers resisted the adoption of Tejano culture.

Teller Amendment Amendment to the 1898 declaration of war against Spain stipulating that Cuba should be free and independent. The amendment was largely ignored in the aftermath of America's victory.

temperance The movement to moderate and then ban the sale and consumption of alcohol. The American temperance movement emerged in the early nineteenth century as part of the larger push for improving society from the 1820s to the 1850s.

tenements Multifamily apartment buildings that housed many poor urban dwellers at the turn of the twentieth century. Tenements were crowded, uncomfortable, and dangerous.

Tennessee Valley Authority (TVA) New Deal agency that brought low-cost electricity to rural Americans and redeveloped the Tennessee River valley through flood-control projects. The agency built, owned, and supervised a number of power plants and dams.

Tenure of Office Act Law passed by Congress in 1867 to prevent President Andrew Johnson from removing cabinet members sympathetic to the Republican Party's approach to congressional Reconstruction without Senate approval. Johnson was impeached, but not convicted, for violating the act.

Tet Offensive January 31, 1968, offensive mounted by Vietcong and North Vietnamese forces against population centers in South Vietnam. The offensive was turned back, but it shocked many Americans and increased public opposition to the war.

Thirteenth Amendment Amendment to the Constitution abolishing slavery. The Thirteenth Amendment was passed in January 1865 and sent to the states for ratification.

three-fifths compromise Compromise between northern and southern delegates to the 1787 Constitutional Convention to count enslaved persons as three-fifths of a free person in apportioning representation in the House of Representatives and taxation by the federal government.

To Secure These Rights Report issued by President Truman's Committee on Civil Rights in 1947 that advocated extending racial equality. Among its recommendations was the desegregation of the military, which Truman instituted by executive order in 1948.

total war The strategy of attacking civilian as well as military targets. Engaging in a war of attrition to wear down the Confederacy, General Grant and his commanders used this strategy in 1864 and 1865.

Townshend Act 1767 act of Parliament that instituted an import tax on a range of items including glass, lead, paint, paper, and tea. The Townshend Act prompted a boycott of British goods and contributed to violence between British soldiers and colonists.

Trail of Tears The forced march of some 15,000 Cherokees from Georgia to Indian Territory. Inadequate planning, food, water, sanitation, and medicine led to the deaths of thousands of Cherokees.

transcendentalism A movement founded by Ralph Waldo Emerson in the 1830s that proposed that individuals look inside themselves and to nature for spiritual and moral guidance rather than to the dogmas of formal religion. Transcendentalism attracted a number of important American writers and artists to its vision.

transcontinental railroad A railroad linking the East and West Coasts of North America. Completed in 1869, the transcontinental railroad facilitated the flow of migrants and the development of economic connections between the West and the East.

Treaty of Fort Laramie 1851 treaty that sought to confine tribes on the northern plains to designated areas in an attempt to keep white settlers from encroaching on their land. In 1868, the second Treaty of Fort Laramie gave northern tribes control over the "Great Reservation" in parts of present-day Montana, Wyoming, North Dakota, and South Dakota.

Treaty of Guadalupe Hidalgo 1848 treaty ending the Mexican-American War. By the terms of the treaty, the United States acquired control over Texas north and east of the Rio Grande plus the New Mexico territory, which included present-day Arizona and New Mexico and parts of Utah, Nevada, and Colorado. The treaty also ceded Alta California, which had declared itself an independent republic during the war, to the United States.

Treaty of New Echota 1836 treaty in which a group of Cherokee men agreed to exchange their land in the Southeast for money and land in Indian Territory. Despite the fact that the treaty was obtained without tribal sanction, it was approved by the U.S. Congress.

Treaty of Paris 1783 treaty that formally ended the conflict between Britain and its North American colonies. The newly established United States gained benefits from the treaty.

Triangle Shirtwaist Company Site of an infamous industrial fire in New York City in 1911. Inadequate fire safety provisions in the factory led to the deaths of 146 workers.

Truman Doctrine U.S. pledge to contain the expansion of communism around the world. Based on the idea of containment, the Truman Doctrine was the cornerstone of American foreign policy throughout the Cold War.

Tuskegee Institute African American educational institute founded in 1881 by Booker T. Washington. Following Washington's philosophy, the Tuskegee Institute focused on teaching industrious habits and practical job skills.

Uncle Tom's Cabin Novel published in 1852 by Harriet Beecher Stowe. Meant to publicize the evils of slavery, the novel struck an emotional chord in the North and was an international best seller.

underground railroad A series of routes from southern plantation areas to northern free states and Canada along which abolitionist supporters, known as conductors, provided hiding places and transportation for runaway slaves seeking freedom.

unions Groups of workers seeking rights and benefits from their employers through their collective efforts.

Universal Negro Improvement Association (UNIA) Organization founded by Marcus Garvey in 1914 to promote black self-help, pan-Africanism, and racial separatism.

unskilled workers Workers with little or no specific expertise. Unskilled workers, many of whom were immigrants, made up the vast majority of the late-nineteenth-century industrial workforce.

U.S. Sanitary Commission Federal organization established in June 1861 to improve and coordinate the medical care of Union soldiers. Northern women played a key role in the commission.

utopian societies Communities formed in the first half of the nineteenth century to embody alternative social and economic visions and to create models for society at large to follow.

Valley Forge Site of Continental Army winter encampment in 1777–1778. Despite the harsh conditions, the Continental Army emerged from its encampment at Valley Forge as a more effective fighting force.

vertical integration The control of all elements in a supply chain by a single firm. For example, Andrew Carnegie, a vertically integrated steel producer, sought to own suppliers of all the raw materials used in steel production.

Vietcong The popular name for the National Liberation Front (NLF) in South Vietnam, which was formed in 1959. The Vietcong waged a military insurgency against the U.S.-backed president, Ngo Dinh Diem, and received support from Ho Chi Minh, the leader of North Vietnam.

Vietnamization President Richard Nixon's strategy of turning over greater responsibility for the fighting of the Vietnam War to the South Vietnamese army.

Virginia Plan Plan put forth at the beginning of the 1787 Constitutional Convention that introduced the ideas of a strong central government, a bicameral legislature, and a system of representation based on population.

vital center liberalism Political ideology of Harry Truman supporters who took a middle political ground between the extreme right and left. Vital center liberals supported the Cold War, favored civil rights measures and federal government support for public housing and medical care, and opposed McCarthyism while supporting domestic anticommunism efforts.

Voting Rights Act 1965 act that eliminated many of the obstacles to African American voting in the South and resulted in dramatic increases in black participation in the electoral process.

Walking Purchase 1737 treaty that allowed Pennsylvania to expand its boundaries at the expense of the Delaware Indians. The treaty, quite possibly a forgery, allowed the British to add territory that could be walked off in a day and a half.

War Industries Board (WIB) Government commission created in 1917 to supervise the purchase of military supplies and oversee the conversion of the economy to meet wartime demands. The WIB embodied a government-business partnership that lasted beyond World War I.

War of the Spanish Succession 1702–1713 war over control of Spain and its colonies; also called Queen Anne's War. Although the Treaty of Utrecht that ended the war in 1713 was intended to bring peace through the establishment of a balance of power, imperial conflict continued to escalate.

War Powers Act 1973 act that required the president to consult with Congress within forty-eight hours of deploying military forces and to obtain a declaration of war from Congress if troops remained on foreign soil beyond sixty days.

War Production Board Board established in 1942 to oversee the economy during World War II. The War Production Board was part of a larger effort to convert American industry to the production of war materials.

Watergate Scandal and cover-up that forced the resignation of Richard Nixon in 1974. The scandal revolved around a break-in at Democratic Party headquarters in 1972 and subsequent efforts to conceal the administration's involvement in the break-in.

Weathermen A group advocating the use of revolutionary violence, formed in 1968 by dissident members of Students for a Democratic Society (SDS). The Weathermen went underground to avoid criminal prosecution.

Whig Party Political party formed in the 1830s to challenge the power of the Democratic Party. The Whigs attempted to forge a diverse coalition from around the country by promoting commercial interests and moral reforms.

Whiskey Rebellion Uprising by western Pennsylvania farmers who led protests against the excise tax on whiskey in the early 1790s.

white-collar workers Managerial, clerical, and technical workers. The creation of large numbers of white-collar jobs in the late nineteenth century was the key factor in the expansion of the American middle class.

Wilmot Proviso 1846 proposal by Democratic congressman David Wilmot of Pennsylvania to outlaw slavery in all territory acquired from Mexico. The proposal was defeated, but the fight over its adoption foreshadowed the sectional conflicts of the 1850s.

Woman's Christian Temperance Union (WCTU) Organization founded in 1874 to campaign for a ban on the sale and consumption of alcohol. In the late nineteenth century, under Frances Willard's leadership, the WCTU supported a broad social reform agenda.

Women's National Loyal League Organization founded by abolitionist women during the Civil War to press Lincoln and Congress to enact universal emancipation.

Works Progress Administration (WPA) New Deal agency established in 1935 to put unemployed Americans to work on public projects ranging from construction to the arts.

XYZ affair 1798 incident in which French agents demanded bribes before meeting with American diplomatic representatives.

Yalta Agreement Agreement negotiated at the 1945 Yalta Conference by Roosevelt, Churchill, and Stalin about the fate of postwar eastern Europe. The Yalta Agreement did little to ease growing tensions between the Soviet Union and its Western allies.

yellow journalism Sensationalist news accounts meant to provoke an emotional response in readers. Yellow journalism contributed to the growth of public support for American intervention in Cuba in 1898.

yeomen farmers Southern independent landowners who did not own slaves. Although yeomen farmers had connections to the South's plantation economy, many realized that their interests were not always identical to those of the planter elite.

Yorktown Site of decisive patriot victory. The surrender of British forces on October 19, 1781, at Yorktown, Virginia, effectively sealed the patriot victory in the Revolutionary War.

Young Americans for Freedom (YAF) A group of young conservatives from college campuses formed in 1960 in Sharon, Connecticut. It favored free market principles, states' rights, and anticommunism.

Zimmermann telegram 1917 telegram in which Germany offered Mexico an alliance in the event that the United States entered World War I. The telegram's publication in American newspapers helped build public support for war.

zoot suit riots Series of riots in 1943 in Los Angeles, California, sparked by white hostility toward Mexican Americans. White sailors attacked Mexican American teenagers who dressed in zoot suits—suits with long jackets with padded shoulders and baggy pants tapered at the bottom.

Index

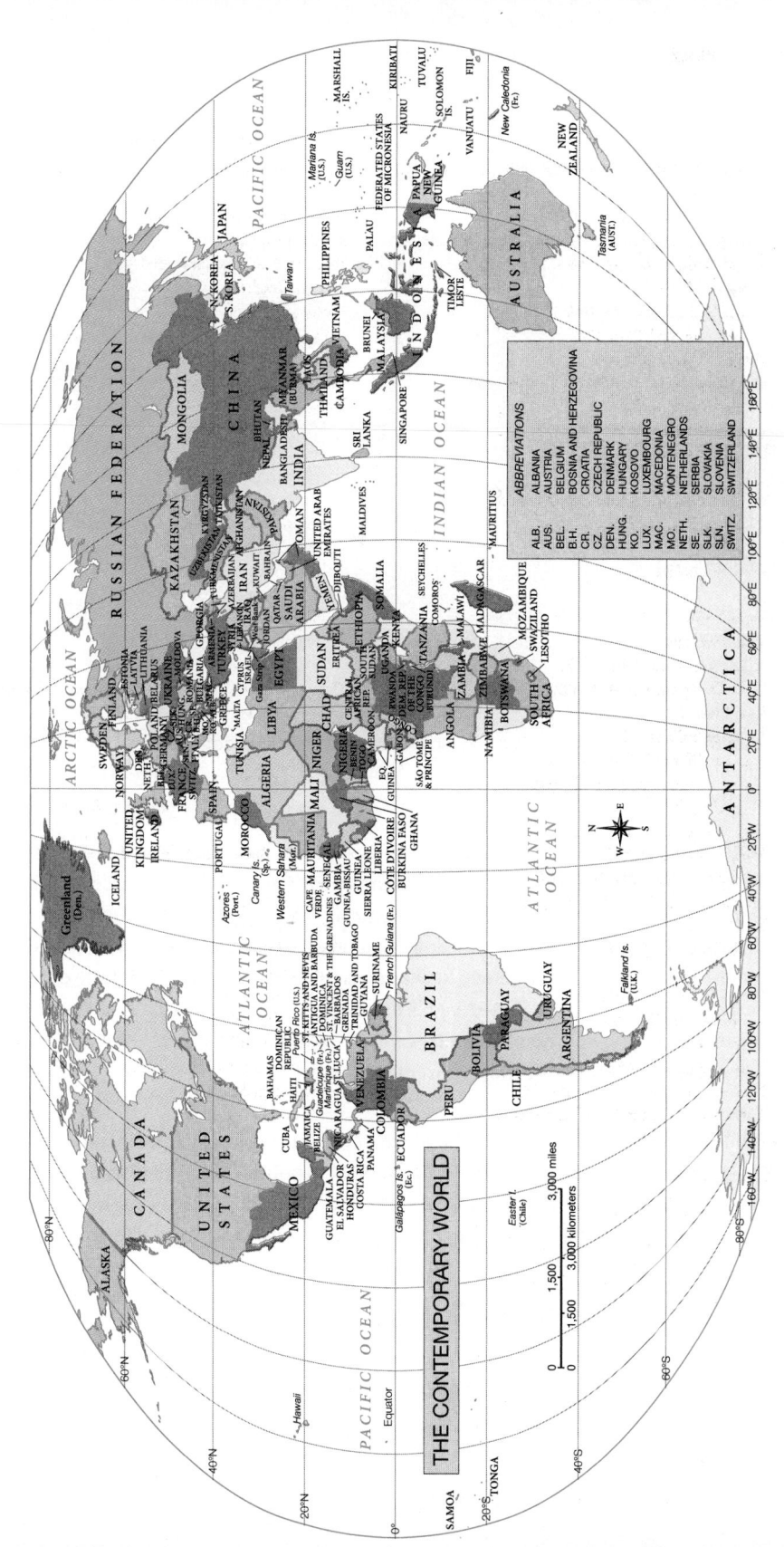

THE CONTEMPORARY WORLD

About the authors

Authors Steven F. Lawson and Nancy A. Hewitt outside the couple's home with their trusty consultant, Scooter.

Nancy A. Hewitt (Ph.D., University of Pennsylvania) is professor of history and of Women's and Gender Studies at Rutgers University. Her publications include *Southern Discomfort: Women's Activism in Tampa, Florida, 1880s–1920s*, for which she received the Julia Cherry Spruill Prize from the Southern Association of Women Historians; *Women's Activism and Social Change: Rochester, New York, 1822–1872*; and the edited volume *No Permanent Waves: Recasting Histories of U.S. Feminism*. She is currently working on a biography of the nineteenth-century radical activist Amy Post and a book that recasts the U.S. woman suffrage movement.

Steven F. Lawson (Ph.D., Columbia University) is professor emeritus of history at Rutgers University. His research interests include U.S. politics since 1945 and the history of the civil rights movement, with a particular focus on black politics and the interplay between civil rights and political culture in the mid-twentieth century. He is the author of many works, including *Running for Freedom: Civil Rights and Black Politics in America since 1941*; *Black Ballots: Voting Rights in the South, 1944–1969*; and *In Pursuit of Power: Southern Blacks and Electoral Politics, 1965–1982*.